PLATE I

1. Black Duck
2. Baldpate
3. Green-winged Teal
4. Canvasback
5. Redhead

6. Bufflehead
7. Golden-eye
8. Surf Scoter
9. Old Squaw
10. Red-breasted Merganser

HANDBOOK OF BIRDS OF EASTERN NORTH AMERICA

WITH INTRODUCTORY CHAPTERS ON THE STUDY OF BIRDS IN NATURE

By FRANK M. CHAPMAN

With Illustrations By
LOUIS AGASSIZ FUERTES, TAPPAN ADNEY,
ERNEST THOMPSON SETON,
and FRANCIS L. JAQUES

DOVER PUBLICATIONS, INC., NEW YORK

Published in Canada by General Publishing Company, Ltd., 30 Lesmill Road, Don Mills, Toronto, Ontario.
Published in the United Kingdom by Constable and Company Ltd., 10 Orange Street, London W. C. 2.

This Dover edition, first published in 1966, is an unabridged republication of the second revised edition, as published by D. Appleton-Century Company in 1939. This edition is published by special arrangement with Appleton-Century-Crofts Trade Books, an affiliate of Meredith Press.

This Dover edition differs from the 1939 printing in the following ways:

The text, halftone illustrations and all line drawings not drawn to size or specific scale have been enlarged by 10 percent in order to increase legibility.

A new Color Chart prepared especially for this edition replaces the 1939 chart. The publisher is grateful to Miss Helen Hays of The American Museum of Natural History for her assistance in the preparation of this chart.

The Zone Map of North America which appeared on the inside front cover of the 1939 edition is here reproduced considerably larger on a separate sheet attached to the inside back cover.

Plates IV, V, VII, XXI, XXII, XXIII, XXV, XXVI were reproduced in color in the earlier edition, but are here reproduced as black-and-white halftones.

Information concerning American ornithological societies and current ornithological magazines (pp. 26-27) has been brought up-to-date.

Library of Congress Catalog Card Number 66-14553

Manufactured in the United States of America
Dover Publications, Inc.
180 Varick Street
New York, N. Y. 10014

TO THE MEMORY OF
MY MOTHER

WHO EVER ENCOURAGED HER SON IN HIS
NATURAL HISTORY STUDIES
THIS BOOK IS AFFECTIONATELY DEDICATED

PREFACE TO THE FIRST REVISED EDITION

In preparing a revised edition of the 'Handbook,' it was decided that any increase in size which would remove it from the ranks of true handbooks was not to be considered for a moment. The question, then, with which I have been confronted, was, how, within given limits, to meet the wants of the bird student of today, who demands, primarily, information concerning the bird in nature. To add materially to the space given to each of the species contained in the first edition would result in widely overstepping the bounds set by necessity. But, if it were not possible to present a complete biography of every bird, at least a suggestive biography of *the* bird could be given, and the expansion in size permitted has been largely used for this purpose.

This added material will be found in the introductory pages, which number 116, as compared with 31 in the original edition.

Here I have dealt with those phases of bird-life which, to a greater or less extent, enter into the existence of every species. These chapters on migration, song, nesting habits, color, structure and function, food, etc., may be read not only alone, but they are intended to be a guide to the study in life of any bird to which we may devote our attention. In short, they are designed to arouse an interest in the bird in relation to its environment, and to stimulate and direct original observations.

Aside from this Introduction, which constitutes both the largest and most important addition to the new 'Handbook,' the remainder of the book has been thoroughly revised, much of it has been rewritten, and not a little of it is wholly new. The nomenclature is that of the last (1910) edition of the A. O. U. 'Check-List'. The Ranges have also been taken from this same authoritative source, and are a vast improvement over those of the first edition of the 'Handbook.' In addition to the migration notes given in preceding editions, data are now also included for northern Ohio, Glen Ellyn, Illinois, and southeastern Minnesota. A new feature, which we believe will prove helpful, is the series of nesting dates from localities often covering the breeding range of the species.

If space has prohibited giving all that is known about a bird, at least one may say where recent information concerning it may be found, and to this end I have added many references not contained in earlier editions. This bibliographical feature of the new 'Handbook' is best shown in the Appendix giving references to the more important faunal lists of birds in eastern North America, a knowledge of which is believed to be of the utmost importance to the local student.

In the preparation of the first edition of this book, the author gratefully acknowledged assistance which he had received from Florence Merriam Bailey, J. A. Allen, and Ernest Thompson Seton, and he now desires to express his indebtedness to Waldron DeWitt Miller for aid in reading the proof of the present edition, and to Henry W. Henshaw, Chief of the Biological Survey, for permission to reproduce the faunal map.

It is proper, in closing this preface, for the author to express the pleasure and gratification which the reception of the first edition of the 'Handbook' has given him. So far as circumstances permit, he has endeavored to make this new 'Handbook' worthy of the praise which has so generously been accorded its predecessor.

FRANK M. CHAPMAN

AMERICAN MUSEUM OF NATURAL HISTORY
New York City, October 1, 1911.

PREFACE TO THE
SECOND REVISED EDITION

For forty-five years American ornithologists have used the classification of birds contained in the 'Check-List' of the American Ornithologists' Union. This classification remained unchanged through three editions (1886, 1895, 1910) of this work, but in the fourth edition (October, 1931) it was replaced by a very different one presenting current beliefs regarding the relationships of birds. The 'Check-List' is authoritative and it is, therefore, followed in this, just as it was in preceding editions of the 'Handbook.'

In other fields of ornithological research, also, an effort has been made to bring the 'Handbook' up to date, both by the inclusion of new material and the deletion of old; while the references selected from the literature of the past twenty years should acquaint the student with the titles of the more important works on birds that have been published during that period. In spite, therefore, of the limitations of space imposed by the size of a true handbook, there have been added over fifty pages of text and numerous illustrations to the present edition of this manual.

The defects of a work which, for thirty-six years, bird students have honored by their use, are pretty certain to be discovered; and I have to thank many readers of the second (as well as of the first) edition of the 'Handbook' for their response to my published request for a list of the errors of commission and omission that they have detected. If their replies have been somewhat overwhelming, at least their generous assistance has made it possible to increase the accuracy, clarity, and, I trust, usefulness of this revised edition. In this connection I am especially indebted to Mr. Francis Harper, while for assistance in reading proof I express my thanks to Mr. William Vogt.

More particularly, and in unstinted measure, my gratitude is due Mrs. Alice K. Fraser who, for twenty-three years, has made my chirography legible to printers, and whose experience in reading proofs and making indexes has been of inestimable value in the preparation of this volume.

Acknowledgment is also made to the staff of the Mt. Pleasant Press who, as printers of *Bird-Lore* for a third of a century, have had an experience with ornithological manuscripts which was of rare value in the making of this book.

Above all, my thanks go out to those thousands of friends, seen and unseen, whose continued use of this volume is cherished evidence that, at least in a measure, I have succeeded in sharing with them my lifelong and ever-growing love of birds.

FRANK M. CHAPMAN

AMERICAN MUSEUM OF NATURAL HISTORY
New York City, November 24, 1931.

(ix)

LIST OF ABBREVIATIONS

Ad.	Adult; a fully matured bird.
A. V.	Accidental visitant (see pages xxvii and 36).
B.	Bill.
B. from N.	Bill from nostril.
♀	The sign employed to designate female sex (see page 21).
♂	The sign employed to designate male sex (see page 21).
Im.	Immature; the term is generally applied to birds less than a year old, or to those in first winter plumage.
Juv.	Juvenal; the plumage succeeding natal down.
Mig.; pl.	Migration data, plate and notes on plumage in Bird-Lore.
L.	Total length.
P. R.	Permanent resident (see page 36).
S. R.	Summer resident (see page 36).
T.	Tail.
Tar.	Tarsus = Metatarsus.
T. V.	Transient visitant (see page 36).
W.	Wing.
W. V.	Winter visitant (see page 36).

CONTENTS

CONTENTS

LIST OF ILLUSTRATIONS

FULL-PAGE PLATES

(xv)

FIGURES IN THE TEXT

PLAN OF THE WORK

Extent of Area.—The area covered by this work is North America east of the ninetieth meridian. There have also been included certain western species which, while not constant inhabitants of this territory, may be expected to occur within its boundaries with more or less frequency.

The Introduction.—The Introduction to the present edition of the 'Handbook' is designed to meet the wants of a class of bird-students that was almost unknown when the first (1895) edition was written. Field-work in eastern North America then meant chiefly collecting birds; now it means chiefly observing them. The observation blind, the camera, the bird-band, the notebook to record prolonged, consecutive, definitely directed studies, were then rarely used or wholly unknown. Now they form part of the equipment of all serious students of birds in nature. It is to them that this Introduction is addressed.

Nomenclature.—The names used, both popular and scientific, are those of the American Ornithologists' Union's 'Check-List of North American Birds' (fourth edition, 1931). The fact that the former name is more frequently used and more stable than the latter has induced me to give it first, rather than second place, as in preceding editions. In the current edition of the 'Check-List' the birds are not numbered. I have, however, retained their former numbers, placing them in brackets and after, instead of before, the name as in preceding editions of the 'Handbook.' The serial number preceding each species, and used in the Keys, is for purposes of reference.

With the object of encouraging uniformity in the use of the common or vernacular names of our birds, I have given in the body of the book only those names employed by the American Ornithologists' Union. These may be called official, as opposed to local titles. The latter are given in the index with a cross reference to the names with which they are synonymous.

Definition of Terms.—The accompanying figure (1), with its named parts, will explain the meaning of the terms used in describing birds. The words 'upperparts' and 'underparts' mentioned so frequently, refer respectively to the whole upper or under surfaces of the *body* from the base of the bill to the root of the tail, but not to the wings or tail or their coverts.

There are infinite variations in the markings of feathers, and those figured present only the patterns occurring most frequently. The shaft of the feather is the midrib to each side of which the vanes or webs are attached. (Fig. 3.)

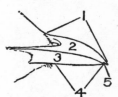

FIG. 2. Parts of the Bill.
1. Culmen. 2. Maxilla.
3. Mandible. 4. Gonys.
5. Maxillary notch.

(xxi)

The Synopses of Orders and Families.—The scheme here presented is, with some modifications and expansions, based on one contributed by Ernest Thompson Seton at a time when he was expected to become

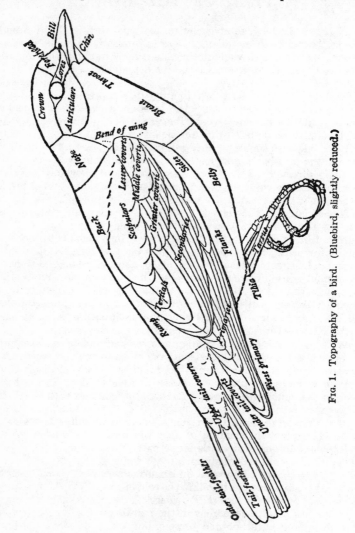

Fig. 1. Topography of a bird. (Bluebird, slightly reduced.)

a joint author of this work. Every earnest bird-student should know the names of the Orders and Families of North American birds, their most obvious characters, and their interrelations as they are expressed by the sequence of their arrangement. This knowledge is fundamental; once it is acquired a bird may be referred to its proper family almost at a glance. It cannot be gained by the use of an artificial 'Key,' which gives only the characters necessary for identification and violates the order of arrangement. In order to lay a sound foundation on which to build, the Synopsis is employed rather than the 'Key.' It should be understood that the characters here presented relate primarily to the members of the Orders and Families found in eastern North America and not necessarily to groups occurring beyond our geographical limits.

The Keys to Species.—The keys to species are wholly artificial and their one aim is identification. It is of the utmost importance thoroughly to understand the system upon which they are constructed. Once it is mastered you will be surprised at the ease and rapidity with which even in large families you can "run a bird down."

If a bird always wore the same plumage, it would be a comparatively easy matter to place it in a certain section of a key and keep it there. But, unfortunately, not only are the males and females of the same species frequently quite unlike, and the young different from either, but their plumages may vary with the season. Furthermore, an individual of a given species may not only wear two very different costumes, but, in doffing one for another, he does it gradually, and, in the meantime, appears in changing or transition plumage.

For this reason it has been customary to base keys on only adult males. Such keys do very well in the nesting season, when birds are in song, and when males constitute probably nine-tenths of the birds one sees. But at other times of the year young birds outnumber the old ones, and the adults themselves may lose their breeding plumage and wear quite a different one. I have, therefore, attempted to make keys which will identify a bird in any plumage. To do this, it was necessary to use many more specimens than there were species. For example, the key to our some 40 species of Warblers is based on 110 specimens, representing as many phases of plumage.

With identification as the sole end in view, I have, in the keys, abandoned all attempts to follow the current system of classification, and, taking color as the most tangible character, have to a great extent arranged the species on this character alone. The result, from the systematist's standpoint, is most unnatural. Species of different genera are brought into the same subsections, and the more variable species may be placed in several widely separated sections.

The maker of keys, however, should not try to serve two masters. If the keys will identify, they will have accomplished their purpose. The classification of our birds is shown in the Synopses and the body of the book, where the species are arranged according to the system adopted by the American Ornithologists' Union. The keys proper are usually dichotomous, but I have not hesitated to divide the larger families into three, or even four, primary sections, the characters of which are placed together at the head of the keys to permit of direct comparison. The

heading of a group or section applies to all the species included in it.
Thus, if I does not apply to the bird you are identifying, you must pass
at once to II, or III, or IV, as the case may be. Even should the first
section describe your bird, it is well to read the sections which are
contrasted with it.

As a lesson in the use of the keys let us identify a Song Sparrow. The
figure on Plate VII will present its more obvious characters. If we have
given due attention to the Synopsis of Orders and Suborders, we will
know at a glance that our bird belongs in the Suborder Oscines. Here,
also, if we have familiarized ourselves with the characters given in the
Synopsis, the conical bill, with its angled cutting edge (commissure)
and the apparent absence of a rudimentary outer primary (the one
visible being nearly as long as the longest), will at once show us that our
bird is a member of the family Fringillidæ. The absence of red and presence of streaks on the underparts obviously place it in the third of the
three preliminary sections into which these birds are divided before we
reach the true key. Turning to this section we read:

"1. Tail-feathers without white or yellow spots or patches." The
dichotomous system on which the keys are made leaves us only the contrasted division. "2. Tail with white patches or base of tail yellow."
Our bird, therefore, belongs in "1." Proceeding we read: "A. Outer
tail-feathers little if any shorter than the middle pair." The contrasted
division reads: "B. Tail-feathers narrow and generally sharply pointed,
the outer ones always much shorter than the middle pair." Of the two
"A" evidently fits our bird better than "B" and we go thence to "a.
Head of the same general color as the back." The opposing statement
reads: "b. Head not the same color as the back." In our specimen head
and back are much alike and we therefore select "a," but if there should
be any doubt here, further examination of "b" shows that it contains
only birds with the head red or black and our choice of "a" is thus
confirmed. Now we read: "a^1. No yellow over the eye or on the bend of
the wing or under wing-coverts." In "b^1," as usual the opposite is
stated and since our specimen lacks yellow marks it falls in "a^1." We
have now to choose between the two following: "a^2. Rump yellowish or
yellowish green; mandibles crossed." "b^2. Rump brownish or sandy or
rufous, mandibles not crossed."

Our bird belongs in "b^2" in which without further subdivision I have
placed seven species. Comparison of our specimen with their diagnoses
shows that "b^4" applies to it. We conclude, therefore, that it is a Song
Sparrow and turn to the description of this species to test our identification. In doubtful cases a species may be entered in both sections of a
key. For example, in the present instance, since the outer tail-feathers
in the Song Sparrow are not as long as the middle pair it might be
difficult to decide whether to place it in "A" or "B," and I have therefore
included it in both.

Descriptions of Plumage.—The descriptions of plumage, with quoted
exceptions, are from specimens in the American Museum of Natural

History. They have been made as concise and simple but, at the same time, as detailed as seems necessary to identify a species, its age and plumage. In only a few instances have I attempted to describe minutely all the plumages acquired by species that vary widely in color with sex, season, and age, and the manner by which these changes are accomplished. (See, especially, the Orchard Oriole, Bobolink, and Scarlet Tanager.) It should be explained that, where the sexes are alike, they are described under the subheading *"Ads.,"* meaning adult specimens in breeding dress. The subheading *"Im.,"* in the light of our present

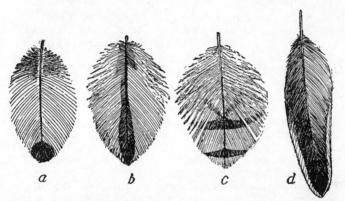

Fig. 3. Spotted (a), streaked (b), barred (c) and margined (d) feathers.

more exact knowledge, is somewhat indefinite; but, as has just been said, absolute exactness in this connection is not possible in a book of this size, where descriptions are intended primarily for the purpose of identification. It may be explained, however, that, with but few exceptions, *"Im."* signifies a bird in first winter plumage, or the one following that (the juvenal) in which the bird leaves the nest. Where, however, the juvenal plumage is worn for some time, as with the Snipe, in which it largely takes the place of a first winter plumage, then it is described under the term *"Juv."*

Measurements.—The measurements given are in English inches and hundredths. They represent the average of a number of specimens from which a variation of about 10 per cent may occur. They were taken mainly from specimens in the American Museum of Natural History. I have, also, with the author's permission, made use of the series of measurements in Dr. E. A. Mearns' 'Birds of the Hudson Highlands.'

The total length (= L.) of a specimen is found by gently stretching it, laying it on its back, and measuring the distance from the end of its bill to the tip of its longest tail-feather. Since in life the bird does not assume this position, the living bird appears to be somewhat shorter than the size here given. The length of the wing (= W.) is the distance from the "bend of the wing" to the end of the longest primary. The length of the tail (= T.) is the distance from the base, or insertion of the middle feathers, to the end of the longest feather. The length of the tarsus (= Tar.) is the distance from the base, or insertion of the toes, to the end of the tibia, or what in reality is the heel. The "tarsus" is therefore the true foot of the bird, while the part to which this name is generally applied consists only of the toes. The length of the bill (= B.), or "culmen," is the distance from the base of the feathers on the forehead to the tip of the upper mandible in a straight line. With the exception of total length, these measurements are generally taken with a pair of dividers.

Range.—The paragraphs under this heading are taken from the American Ornithologists' Union's 'Check-List of North American Birds' (fourth edition, 1931). In some instances I have abridged the original. Based primarily on the unequaled series of records in the files of the Biological Survey of the United States Department of Agriculture, and revised by regional authorities, these outlines accurately and fully represent our existing knowledge of the distribution of North American birds.

Following the paragraphs on range are exact, concise statements of the birds' status, manner, and times of occurrence at various localities from the District of Columbia northward to Boston, and westward to southeastern Minnesota. The data from these localities contained in the preceding editions of the 'Handbook' have been revised and those here given represent existing conditions. A comparison of the statements of 1912 with those that follow will reveal the changes of the intervening nineteen years. The dates given represent the usual times of migration, followed in some cases by exceptional dates in parentheses.

The records from Washington, D. C., were supplied by Dr. C. W. Richmond of the United States National Museum, who has had prolonged personal experience in this field as well as access to the notes of many other local ornithologists who have worked in this region.

The notes on the water-birds of Long Island, which appeared in the first edition of the 'Handbook,' were supplied by William Dutcher, then the authority on the birds of this area. They have been expanded and brought up to date by John T. Nichols, who, as a resident of Long Island, has, for the past twenty years, made a special study of its bird-life. The dates here given in parentheses are 'casual' dates, the remaining ones show average times of occurrence.

Dr. A. K. Fisher has long since moved from Ossining, and in the absence of a successor to continue his intensive observations there, I have been fortunate in securing from J. F. Kuerzi a list of the species known from the area from approximately Peekskill, N. Y., and Greenwich, Conn., to the southern boundary of Bronx County in New York City. Embodying the notes of Dr. Fisher, as an historical background, and adding thereto his own extended observations and those of over thirty fellow members of the Linnæan Society, Mr. Kuerzi's records accurately and thoroughly reflect existing knowledge of what is called the New York region.

I have to thank Francis H. Allen for the data from the Boston region. They constitute a revision of Mr. William Brewster's observations contained in earlier editions of the 'Handbook,' and include many additional species as a result of extending the area covered from Cambridge to Boston and a distance of ten or a dozen miles in every direction from that city.

The migration dates of land-birds are in the main those of the Brewster list, but have been revised in the light of recent information. For the water-birds, Mr. Allen has depended on Forbush's 'Birds of Massachusetts' and Townsend's 'Birds of Essex County' in addition to his own notes, in most cases giving only the months in which the species may be expected, with no attempt to present exact average dates. In view of the constantly increasing number of records of accidental occurrences of birds outside their normal range, Mr. Allen has not cited the number of Boston records, but has let the statement stand simply as "A. V."

The records from Ohio were contributed by Prof. Lynds Jones, of Oberlin, long an authority on the birds of that state. They cover Lorain and Erie counties. The dates given are median dates of arrival.

B. T. Gault, who sends the notes from Glen Ellyn, near Chicago, writes: "The dates given are extreme [thus contrary to the plan followed by other contributors], excepting in isolated cases of extra-limital species. My observations really cover the township of Milton, but every bird listed, except *Gallinula galeata*, *Strix varia*, and *Aquila chrysaëtos*, has been noted within the corporate limits of the village of Glen Ellyn."

The records from southeastern Minnesota were supplied by Dr. Thomas S. Roberts, for many years the leading authority on the birds of Minnesota and author of the forthcoming monumental work on the birds of that state. They are based, in the main, on observations made in the vicinity of Minneapolis.

Nests and Eggs.—The brief descriptions of nests and eggs are based on the collections of the American Museum of Natural History, supplemented by the use of Baird, Brewer, and Ridgway's 'History of North American Birds,' Davies' 'Nests and Eggs of North American Birds,' Ridgway's 'Manual,' and Bendire's 'Life Histories of North American Birds.' In describing the eggs, the color chart was used when possible; but it was designed with particular reference to the plumages of our birds, and is of less assistance in describing their eggs. The measurements of eggs are mostly from series of measurements made by H. B. Bailey, accompanying the Bailey collection in the American Museum, supplemented by reference to the works mentioned above.

Nesting-Dates.—The dates following the descriptions of nest and eggs are designed to indicate when the nesting season of the species in question begins at various localities. They are the earliest dates I have found for the taking of full sets of (presumably) fresh eggs of the first laying. These records were compiled chiefly from the data accompanying the collections of the United States National Museum (to which I have kindly been given access by Dr. C. W. Richmond), those of the American Museum of Natural History, and the collection of J. P. Norris, Jr., to whom I gratefully express my indebtedness. The "Cambridge" records are all extracted, by permission, from Brewster's 'Birds of the Cambridge Region,' while for those from "SE. Minn." I have to thank my friend Dr. Thomas S. Roberts. The Charleston and South Carolina coast records are from Wayne's excellent work on 'The Birds of South Carolina.'

Biographies.—After devoting separate paragraphs to the bird's general range, its manner of occurrence, comparative numbers, times of migration at several specific points, and its nest and eggs, the space remaining is given to a brief sketch of its haunts, notes, and disposition, with the particular object of aiding in its identification in the field.

In preparing these biographical sketches, I have aimed to secure the best material possible, using my own notes only when I felt they were based on adequate observations. Not only have I carefully examined the literature relating to the habits of our birds, selecting what seemed to be the most trustworthy accounts of their appearance in life, but, through the generous coöperation of fellow-students of living birds, I am able to present character sketches of some of our birds, written by observers known for their sympathy with birds out-of-doors. Thus, I have to thank Mrs. Miller, Mrs. Bailey, Mrs. Wright, Mr. Bicknell, Mr. Brewster, Dr. Dwight, Mr. Seton, and Mr. Torrey, for pen pictures of birds, each sketch being signed by its author.

Illustrations.—To the illustrations by Louis Agassiz Fuertes, Tappan Adney, and Ernest Thompson Seton, there have been added a number of line-cuts and full-page drawings by Francis L. Jaques, designed still further to portray the structure and plumage of birds and their appearance in life.

The Color Chart.—It must not be supposed for a moment that the colors on this chart represent the colors of all the birds of eastern North America. It does not do so any more than an artist's palette shows all the colors of his picture; in fact, I have called this plate my mental palette, and have frequently used two, and even three, terms to describe a given shade or tint.

It should be clearly understood, therefore, that when grayish brown, for example, is mentioned, it does not follow that the feathers to which the term is applied are of exactly the same color as the plate, but that they are nearer to this color than to any other in the plate. Used even in this general way, the plate will prove a far more definite basis for description than if everyone were left to form his own idea of the colors named.

HISTORICAL REVIEW

I. 1895–1911

A review of the progress which has been made in the study of North American birds during the sixteen years since the first edition of the 'Handbook' was published must impress one with the fact that it is our knowledge of living rather than of dead birds which has increased.

A more exact discrimination, larger and better collections, and gradually changed standards as to the degree of differentiation which deserves recognition by name, have added many forms to our 'Check-List,' and rendered more definite our knowledge of the relationships of others. Particularly is this true of the birds of the Pacific coast region. This systematic work has appeared in various special papers and monographs, the most thorough of which, not only for the period under consideration, but for any preceding period in the history of North American ornithology, is Ridgway's 'Birds of North and Middle America,' of which five volumes have thus far been issued.

Thanks to the American Ornithologists' Union, our nomenclature has been revised with the utmost care and, while the numerous resulting changes in names may be annoying to present-day students, those who follow us will enjoy, in greater measure, that stability which is the ideal of the biologist. The third (1910) edition of the Union's 'Check-List' contains this modern nomenclature; but it is worthy of note that the classification employed in this work is the same as that used in the first (1886) edition of the 'Check-List.' So little advance has been made in this branch of ornithology that no system of classification proposed since 1886 was considered sufficiently satisfactory to warrant adoption by the Committee of the Union having in charge the preparation of the 1910 edition.

The studies of Dwight and others have made far more definite our knowledge of the molt of birds, the times and manner of feather-loss and renewal having been determined for many species, with an exactness made possible only by the collecting of specimens for this special purpose. At the same time, Beebe, by experiments on captive birds, has attacked the problem of the causes of molt, while Strong's histological work on the feather has increased our understanding of its growth and development.

In laboratory experiment on living birds, Beebe has shown certain effects of humidity upon the colors of feathers; Davenport has used Canaries and domestic fowls in working on the laws of heredity; Porter and others have conducted psychological investigations upon certain species; and Watson has pursued similar studies upon the Noddy and the Sooty Tern in nature. The highly original researches of Thayer have greatly stimulated interest in the study of the colors of birds in relation to their environment.

Dealing still with the more technical branches of ornithology, the investigations of Fisher, Beal, and other members of the Biological Survey of the United States Department of Agriculture, of Forbush in Massachusetts, and of other state ornithologists, have supplied by far the larger part of our exact knowledge of the food-habits of our birds and determined for the first time the economic status of many species. This work constitutes one of the most pronounced and important phases of research during the period under consideration. While based, primarily, on field work in observing as well as in collecting, special training in laboratory methods is required to make the analyses of stomach contents, from which, in the main, the nature of a bird's food is ascertained.

Field, as well as laboratory work, has also been required to produce the faunal papers and books which, in volume, form the greatest addition to the ornithological literature of the past decade and a half. From the pioneer explorations of Merriam, Fisher, Nelson, Bailey, Preble, Osgood, and other members of the Biological Survey, in new or but little-known regions, to the almost final reports of Brewster and others on the bird-life of localities which have been studied for years by many observers, these publications have added enormously to our knowledge of the distribution of North American birds. This is particularly true of western North America, especially of the Pacific coast region, where Grinnell, W. K. Fisher, Swarth, and other members of the Cooper Ornithological Club, have placed on record a vast amount of data concerning the birds of this area.

Besides furnishing material for the more philosophic phases of faunal work, these monographs and local lists often treat also of the migration of the birds with which they deal. Most important contributions of this subject have been made by the large and widely distributed corps of observers acting under the direction of the Biological Survey, which, under the authorship of Cooke, has published several important bulletins on migration. Here also should be mentioned the significant experiments of Watson upon the homing instincts of Terns, which are referred to beyond (p. 59).

Possibly, in no other branch of definitely directed ornithological research has greater advance been made than in the study of the nesting habits of birds. For the first time in the history of ornithology, trained biologists have devoted an entire nesting season to the continuous study of certain species, and the results obtained by Watson, Herrick, Finley, and others, have, in a high degree, both scientific value and popular interest.

No small part of the educational value of work of this kind is due to the photographic illustrations by which it is usually accompanied, and bird-study with a camera may be said to be the most novel and, in many respects, the most important development in ornithological field work during the past fifteen years. Not only has the fascination of camera hunting itself stimulated the bird photographer, but the results he has obtained have at times had a commercial value, which has enabled him to pursue his labors in before unexplored fields. In consequence, in the books of Job, Finley, Dugmore, and others, and in numerous magazine articles, we now have thousands of graphic records, not one of which existed fifteen years ago, depicting the home-life of some of our rarest as well as commonest birds, and possessed of a power for conveying and diffusing information with which the written word cannot compare.

Here, too, should be mentioned the work of the ornithological artists who, led by Fuertes, have given us an unsurpassed series of faithful and beautiful portraits of our birds, to the educational value of which, in no small measure, is to be attributed the existing widespread interest in bird-study.

It is the growth of this interest which has chiefly distinguished the past two decades; for, much as they have been marked by activity in various branches of ornithology, it is less as an exponent of natural laws than as a most attractive form of wild life that the bird has made its appeal. In the history of North American ornithology, therefore, this period may well stand as the Epoch of Popular Bird-Study. Where, in 1895, there was one person who could claim acquaintance with our commoner birds, today there are hundreds; and the plea for the development of our inherent love of birds, which was made in the first edition of the 'Handbook,' has been answered with an effectiveness few would have predicted.

Opportunity alone was needed to bring to its fulfilment this inborn interest in creatures which have such manifold claims to our attention, and with which we may become so intimately associated. This opportunity has come in popular manuals of bird-study, which, in the aggregate, have been sold by hundreds of thousands; in the introduction of nature study in the schools, in the formation of bird clubs and classes, through the far-reaching and important work of the National and State Audubon Societies, through popular lectures, through magazines devoted to bird-study, and the greater attention of the press in general to bird-studies—particularly such as are illustrated by photographs,—through increased museum facilities, and through the closer relation everywhere existing between the professional or advanced student and the amateur, a relation which must be attributed primarily to the influence exerted by the American Ornithologists' Union.

It is the diffusion of this widespread knowledge of the economic, as well as the esthetic importance of birds, which has made it possible to secure the passage and enforcement of effective laws for their protection; and it is in this continued and increasing interest in birds, not alone as our efficient co-workers in garden, field, orchard and forest, but as the most eloquent expression of nature's beauty, joy and freedom, that we shall doubtless find a true measure of their greatest value to man.

II. 1912–1931

To understand the forces that have been most active in making the history of North American ornithology during the past twenty years, one should read the outline of the history of the preceding sixteen years to which what follows is a supplement.

On the whole, the second period has been more productive than the first. From about 1880 to the first decade of the twentieth century American ornithology was finding itself. With the formation of the American Ornithologists' Union, in 1883, bird-study in this country first became an organized science. With the appearance of the Union's 'Check-List of North American Birds,' in 1886, we had an orderly statement of our assets in bird-life. With the publication in October, 1931, of the fourth edition of this work, this statement became more accurate and more detailed. In works of this nature are contained the results of those objective studies which *must* precede more intensive, subjective researches.

The publication of the fourth edition of the A. O. U. 'Check-List'[1] is, therefore, the outstanding practical event not only in the thirty-six years that have elapsed since the 'Handbook' appeared, but in the forty-five years that have elapsed since its first edition was issued. In this new work our list of North American birds has been appreciably increased, their ranges and nomenclature have been brought up-to-date, and their classification has been revised to conform to generally accepted beliefs concerning the relationships of birds.

If change means progress, one has only to compare the 'Check-List' of 1931 with that of 1886, to be impressed by the advances that have accompanied an intensive study of specimens and the annals of ornithology. While we may resent the inconveniences caused by the abandonment of a classification we had come to regard as fixed, we may be assured that the new system expresses a more truthful view of the relationships of our birds, and that the current nomenclature has been brought nearer that stability in names which has seemed ever to retreat before us.

The sources of the new 'Check-List' are to be found in the labor of hundreds of workers in study and field, but more specifically we are indebted to the Union's Committee on Classification and Nomenclature as follows: Witmer Stone, Chairman; Jonathan Dwight, Waldron DeWitt Miller, Harry C. Oberholser, T. S. Palmer, James Lee Peters, Charles W. Richmond, Alexander Wetmore, and John T. Zimmer.

Dr. Wetmore, whom we have to thank for the recent notable increase in a knowledge of our fossil avifauna, supplies the list of fossil birds occupying 70 pages of the present 'Check-List.'

[1]Publication data relating to the works mentioned in this 'Review' will be found in their appropriate place in the references given beyond. Students who would gain some conception of the extent and nature of the recorded knowledge concerning birds are referred to John T. Zimmer's guide to the literature of ornithology contained in his two-volume 'Catalogue of the Edward E. Ayer Ornithological Library' (Publications 239 and 240, of the Field Museum).

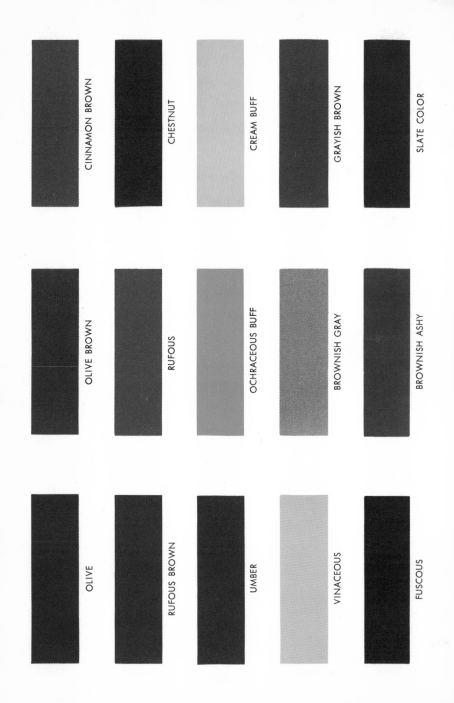

CINNAMON BROWN

CHESTNUT

CREAM BUFF

GRAYISH BROWN

SLATE COLOR

OLIVE BROWN

RUFOUS

OCHRACEOUS BUFF

BROWNISH GRAY

BROWNISH ASHY

OLIVE

RUFOUS BROWN

UMBER

VINACEOUS

FUSCOUS

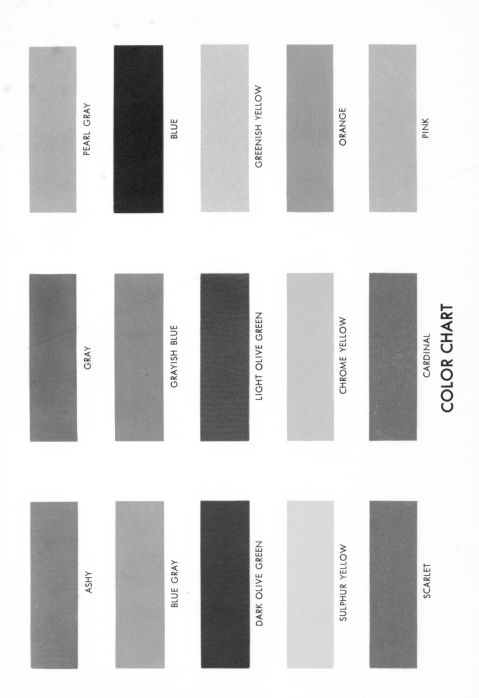

PEARL GRAY

BLUE

GREENISH YELLOW

ORANGE

PINK

GRAY

GRAYISH BLUE

LIGHT OLIVE GREEN

CHROME YELLOW

CARDINAL

COLOR CHART

ASHY

BLUE GRAY

DARK OLIVE GREEN

SULPHUR YELLOW

SCARLET

Other important systematic works include three additional volumes, making eight in all, of Robert Ridgway's great work on the 'Birds of North and Middle America,' which, unfortunately, the author did not live to complete. Death also brought to a close the labors of Charles B. Cory, on his 'Birds of the Americas,' but this undertaking has been continued by Dr. C. E. Hellmayr, and in all six volumes have been issued.

Dr. Ernst Hartert's 'Die Vögel der Palaarktischen Fauna' and Dr. J. Dwight's 'Gulls of the World' include the North American species and should be mentioned here. Systematic works of this nature prepare the way for those biological, biographical, faunal, ecologic, and economic treatises through which ornithologists make their most important contributions to our knowledge of the bird's place in nature.

Among the more notable additions to the literature of bird biology are J. Arthur Thomson's 'Biology of Birds'; Glover M. Allen's 'Birds and Their Attributes'; Gerhard Heilmann's 'Origin of Birds,' and Arthur A. Allen's 'Book of Bird-Life.'

A significant and welcome feature of the period under review is the number of exhaustive monographs treating either of a group, a species, or a problem. Representing the first is John C. Phillips' 'Ducks of the World,' with its colored illustrations by Fuertes and Brooks; while in the second are the intensive life-histories of the Red-winged Blackbird and the Screech Owl by Arthur A. Allen; the Herring Gull, by Reuben M. Strong, the Dickcissel, Heath Hen and other species by Alfred O. Gross, and the Bald Eagle by Francis H. Herrick.

Notable, both in methods and results, are the intensive studies of the House Wren conducted at the Baldwin Ornithological Laboratory by S. Prentiss Baldwin and his assistants. Mr. Baldwin is also primarily responsible for the support which made possible H. L. Stoddard's unique studies of Bob-white in relation to its environment, forming ornithology's most important contribution to ecology. The section on food-habits in this work, in connection with numerous special papers also originating in the Biological Survey, forms a notable contribution to the literature of economic ornithology. More general works in this field are a new edition of Forbush's 'Useful Birds and Their Protection' and Junius Henderson's 'The Practical Value of Birds.' The subject will be found fully covered by W. L. McAtee's reviews in 'The Auk' for the past twenty years.

Mr. H. Eliot Howard's 'Territory in Bird-Life' opens new fields in the study of the home-life of birds, a fact amply demonstrated by Herbert Friedmann's exhaustive study of parasitism in 'The Cowbirds.' In their comprehensiveness and breadth of treatment these investigations by trained biologists show the trend of modern ornithological research.

Since the day of Audubon no period in the history of American ornithology has seen the appearance of more elaborate regional biographic works than the one under review. Elon Howard Eaton's two quartos on the 'Birds of New York,' with colored plates by Fuertes, held first place among state monographs until it was replaced by Edward Howe Forbush's three volumes on the 'Birds of Massachusetts and Other New England States,' with colored plates by Fuertes and Brooks. In the completeness and authenticity of its text and the beauty and accuracy of its illustrations, this work must be accorded first place among those relating to the habits of North American birds.

Covering the entire country, and based in large part on the field-work of a lifetime, is Arthur Cleveland Bent's standard 'Life Histories' of North American birds, of which eight volumes, covering all the 'Water-Birds,' have appeared.

Other members of the first rank in this group are Leon Dawson's 'Birds of California,' Florence Merriam Bailey's 'Birds of New Mexico,' Thomas S. Roberts' 'Birds of Minnesota' (in press), Arthur H. Howell's 'Florida Bird Life,' and P. A. Taverner's 'Birds of Eastern Canada' and 'Birds of Western Canada,' two volumes which effectively fill a before unoccupied field.

Attracted by problems originating in their diversified environment, the ornithologists of the Pacific coast, led by Joseph Grinnell and H. S. Swarth, have continued those studies of the relations between birds and their habitats in a search for the causes that govern the distribution of life. Their papers will be found chiefly in *The Condor*, and in the publications of the University of California and of the California Academy of Sciences.

The contributions to that peculiarly distinctive field of bird-study, bird migration, have been of exceptional importance. Three general works on the subject have appeared: Landsborough Thomson's 'Problems of Migration,' Alexander Wetmore's 'The Migration of Birds,' and William Rowan's 'The Riddle of Migration.'[1] The last-named contains much original material including an account of its author's highly original experiments with captive birds, showing the relation between increased activity incident to longer days, development of the gonads, and time of migration.

Among the important special papers in this field are those by Watson and Lashley on the homing instinct in the Terns of the Dry Tortugas, and the numerous contributions resulting from the banding of birds.

It is, indeed, to the bird-banders that we must give first place in any review of the activities of ornithologists during the past two decades. Inspired by S. Prentiss Baldwin, and led by Frederick C. Lincoln and others, they have developed methods of study of the living birds to which we owe the greater part of our increased knowledge concerning the movements of birds. The post-breeding northward wanderings of Herons, the surprising differences in direction of the routes pursued by water-fowl banded at the same station, the west to east and return migrations of Evening Grosbeaks, the transoceanic journeys of the Common Tern, the return of winter visitants to the same locality, the

[1]Williams and Wilkins, Baltimore, Md.

apparent failure of migrants to return to the place of their birth, these, and many other observations have proved theory or revealed before unsuspected facts concerning the travels of birds. Nor does the value of the bird-band end here; it is an aid to every study of the living bird in which it is important to identify the individual. Some conception of the extent to which this method of bird-study has stimulated the activities of the field-student, and supplied definite data concerning certain phases of bird-life, may be gained from Frederick C. Lincoln's statement (*The Auk*, October, 1931, p. 539) that since 1920, when the Biological Survey assumed direction of this work, more than 900,000 birds have been banded and 52,000 returns recorded.

The possibilities of bird-photography, that other comparatively new method in bird-study, have been greatly enlarged by the addition of the motion-picture camera. Birds and bird-colonies that had been pictured by the pioneers in bird-photography have now become subjects for this more adequate means of portraying the habits of birds. Here, as in the period of 'still' photography, William L. Finley and Norman McClintock have been among the leaders. Great as is the educational power of the film, it is in organized instruction in both the sentiment and science of bird-study that we find one of the important developments of the preceding twenty years. Junior Audubon classes, with their annual enrollment of over 300,000 children, make it possible to arouse an inherent love of birds which may lead through preparatory school and college courses to post-graduate work with its thesis on an ornithological subject.

The natural result of this widely increased knowledge of birds has been a corresponding growth in our desire to protect them. With non-game birds this has led, not alone to their conservation, but, in many instances, to their increase. Thanks chiefly to the Audubon Societies, the continued existence of species after species that were threatened with extermination by millinery interests is apparently now assured. Again our beaches and coastal islands abound with Gulls and Terns. The white Egrets, that in the early part of this century seemed doomed to destruction, have now so multiplied that their post-breeding northward journeys have become a regular feature of midsummer bird-life in the northern states. Our gardens are now bird sanctuaries where, with friendly hospitality, we provide food and drink for bird-guests the year around and offer them homes in the nesting season. In short, Citizen Bird has won his rightful place as a community asset.

Would it were possible to tell an equally encouraging story of our game-birds. For them, civilization has meant decrease in habitable areas and increase in foes. This is particularly true of water-fowl which, for obvious reasons, are usually denied that close association with man so advantageous to the birds of our lawns and gardens. Their case is convincingly stated in Phillips' and Lincoln's 'American Waterfowl,' and if under the leadership of the Federal Government the lessons of this volume could be heeded and the birds' haunts, as well as the birds themselves, conserved, we might hope for marked improvement in the conditions that have so seriously threatened both.

There has also been a sad thinning in the ranks of our Hawks and Owls. This, too, must be charged to sportsmen. To them these birds, without exception, are 'vermin' to be destroyed by fair means or foul. The fact that most of the species of this group have beneficial food-habits they refuse to admit, and as long as their fate remains in the hands of sportsmen I see faint hope for the preservation of our raptorial birds.

On the other hand, as the need for providing our water-fowl with nesting and resting areas becomes increasingly apparent, I believe that the demands of the situation will be met, with a resulting possible increase in their numbers. The birds that live about us have now so firmly established themselves in our hearts that we may look forward to an ever-growing intimacy with them.

In the science of ornithology we shall doubtless witness marked developments during the immediate future. The fully equipped bird-student of today has a training not available to his predecessors. His education reflects the marked advance which recent years have seen in our knowledge of biology and in laboratory technique, and he is prepared to attack problems unknown to the ornithologist of an earlier day. It follows, therefore, that the study of birds will become increasingly technical. But it is essential that this study should be made by men who are primarily ornithologists and not by laboratory workers with a 'problem.'

We want anatomists who, in studying structure, are also acquainted with habits. We want geneticists who are also systematists familiar with the variations shown by birds and the conditions in nature with which they are associated. We want faunalists who, in addition to a knowledge of geology, climatology, and botany, also know birds and will deal with specimens, not merely with names. We want students of behavior who are not alone trained in the methods of the animal psychologist but are experienced in the ways of birds.

While these developments will widen the differences, they will strengthen the ties between the professional and amateur student of birds. Ornithology is, and will remain, primarily a field-study. Its problems may be solved in the laboratory but they will originate with the living bird in its haunts. However technical may become the methods of the professional, there will always be a place for the amateur. As more intensive studies require increased observations, he will be called upon to make them, and his joy and satisfaction in his work will grow as he acquires a wider understanding of its significance.

And in addition to these "born ornithologists," to whom the "birds are all in all," there is, and ever will be, that infinitely greater number of nature-lovers to whom the bird is neither a specimen nor a problem, but "the most eloquent expression of Nature's beauty, joy, and freedom."

A HANDBOOK OF THE
BIRDS OF EASTERN NORTH AMERICA

INTRODUCTION

WHY WE SHOULD STUDY BIRDS
A WORD TO THE BEGINNER
THE STUDY OF BIRDS IN NATURE

CHAPTER I

WHY WE SHOULD STUDY BIRDS

Birds occupy a fourfold relation to man: an economic, esthetic, what may be termed a mythological or symbolic, and a scientific relation.

Birds are Nature's most potent checks upon the undue increase of noxious insects and harmful rodents; they devour the seeds of weeds and act as scavengers. The more we learn of their food-habits, the greater becomes the realization of our indebtedness to them, and of the importance of protecting them.

Birds, however, not only make life upon the globe possible, but they may add immeasurably to our enjoyment of it. Where in all animate nature shall we find so marvelous a combination of beauty of form and color, of grace and power of motion, of musical ability and intelligence, to delight our eyes, charm our ears and appeal to our imagination?

To the birds' mastery of the air, to their mysterious appearances and disappearances occasioned by migration, to the weird or peculiar character of their notes, as well as to their human-like characteristics, we may doubtless attribute the influence they have exerted on the mind of primitive man. This is shown in a thousand myths and legends investing the bird with supernatural powers, in savage art and symbolism, and in the folk-lore of a later day. The Stork brings us into the world, and at the call of the Owl we leave it. The Dove is our messenger of peace, and we make war beneath the ægis of the Eagle; while at all times it is 'a little bird' that tells us things we are not supposed to know. Thus, from birth to death, in peace and at war, as well as in our daily relations with our fellow man, the bird is an omen and a symbol.

It is not surprising, therefore, that civilized man should devote especial attention to creatures possessed of such unusual interest, studying their origin and relationships, their distribution in time and space, their migrations, their nesting habits, their form and color, and all the details of their structure and life which go to make up the science of ornithology. The claims of birds to our attention may then be formally summarized as follows:

First, because, as the natural enemies of harmful insects and rodents, as destroyers of weed seeds and as scavengers, birds are of inestimable value in the economics of nature.

Second, because birds are sensitively organized creatures, and respond so readily to the influences of their surroundings that in their structure, distribution, migration and habits they convincingly demonstrate the creative and controlling forces of Nature.

Third, because birds, more effectively than any other forms of life, arouse our inborn interest in animals, not only through their abundance and familiarity, but because their form, color, and power of flight stimulate our love of beauty and of grace; because their songs appeal to us as the most eloquent of Nature's voices; because their migrations excite our wonder and continually renew our interest in the bird-life of the same locality, and because their human-like traits emphasize our kinship with them. Hence it follows that birds, more than any other animals, may serve as bonds between man and Nature.

CHAPTER II

A WORD TO THE BEGINNER

FINDING AND NAMING BIRDS
THE EQUIPMENT OF THE FIELD STUDENT
COLLECTING BIRDS, THEIR NESTS AND EGGS
BIRD-BANDING
AMERICAN ORNITHOLOGICAL SOCIETIES
CURRENT ORNITHOLOGICAL MAGAZINES

FINDING AND NAMING BIRDS

How to Find Birds
How to Identify Birds
How Birds Are Named

How to Find Birds.—The best times of the day in which to look for birds are early morning and late afternoon. After a night of fasting and resting, birds are active and hungry. When their appetites are satisfied, they may rest quietly until hunger again sends them forth in search of food.

Experience will soon show you where birds are most abundant. The more varied the nature of the country, the greater number of species you may expect to find inhabiting it. An ideal locality would be a bit of tree-dotted meadow with a reed-bordered pond or stream, surrounded by woods, rolling uplands and orchards.

Common sense will tell you how to act in the field. Birds are generally shy creatures and must be approached with caution. You must not, therefore, go observing or collecting dressed in flaming red, but in some inconspicuous garb and as quietly as a cat. Furthermore, unless your companion is another self, go alone and keep the sun at your back—two apparently unrelated but equally important bits of advice.

The naturalist generally has the instincts of the hunter, and practice will develop them. The 'squeak' is one of his most valuable aids. It is made by placing the lips to the back of the hand or finger and kissing vigorously. The sound produced bears some resemblance to the cries of a wounded or young bird. In the nesting season its utterance frequently creates much excitement in the bird-world, and at all times it is useful as a means of drawing bush- or reed-haunting species from their retreats. One may enter an apparently deserted thicket, and, after a few minutes' 'squeaking,' find himself surrounded by an anxious or curious group of its feathered inhabitants.

The observer of birds will find that by far the best way to study their habits is to take a sheltered seat in some favored locality and become a part of the background. Your passage through the woods is generally attended by sufficient noise to warn birds of your coming long before you see them. They are then suspicious and ill at ease, but secrete yourself near some spot loved by birds, and it may be your privilege to learn the secrets of the forest. In this connection I cannot too highly recommend the observation blind described beyond. Adequate natural cover cannot always be found and, at best, rarely permits of much freedom of movement. In it, therefore, one becomes so cramped and tired that what should be a pleasure becomes hard labor. Whereas, I have passed as much as eight consecutive hours in a blind without undue fatigue; and, it may be added that, although I was in an open field only 20 feet from a Meadowlark's nest, the birds had not the slightest suspicion of my proximity.[1]

How to Identify Birds.—Whether your object be to study birds as a scientist or simply as a lover of nature, the first step is the same—you must learn to know them. This problem of identification has been given up in despair by many would-be ornithologists. We can neither pick, press, net, nor impale birds; and here the botanist and the entomologist have a distinct advantage. Even if we have the desire to resort to a gun, its use is not always possible. But with patience and practice the identification of birds is comparatively an easy matter, and in the end you will name them with surprising ease and certainty. There is generally more character in the flight of a bird than there is in the gait of a man. Both are frequently indescribable but perfectly diagnostic, and you learn to recognize bird friends as you do human ones—by experience.

If you confine your studies to one locality, probably not more than one-third of the species described in this volume will come within the field of your observation. To aid you in learning which species should be included in this third, the paragraphs on *Range* are followed by a statement of the bird's standing at several localities distributed throughout the eastern United States. Take the list of birds from the point nearest your home as an index of those you may expect to find. This may be abridged for a given season by considering the times of the year at which a bird is present. Often you can secure a published list of the birds of your state, county, or immediate vicinity, and publications of this nature are of such exceptional value and interest to the local student that a list of the more important ones has been prepared as an appendix to this edition of the 'Handbook.'

After this slight preparation, you may take to the field with a much clearer understanding of the situation. Two quite different ways of identifying birds are open to you. Either you may shoot them, or study them through a field- or opera-glass. (See beyond, under Collecting.) A bird in the hand is a definite object whose structure and color can be studied to such advantage that in most cases you will afterward recognize it at sight. After learning the names of its parts, its identity is simply a question of keys and descriptions.

If you would "name the birds without a gun," by all means first

[1]See 'Camps and Cruises.' pp. 15–19.

visit a museum, and, with text-book in hand, study those species which you have previously found are to be looked for near your home. This preliminary introduction will serve to ripen your acquaintance in the field. A good field- or opera-glass is absolutely indispensable. (See beyond, under Equipment.) Study your bird as closely as circumstances will permit, and write, *on the spot*, a comparative description of its size, the shape of its bill, tail, etc., and a detailed description of its colors. In describing form, take a Robin, Chipping Sparrow, or any bird you know, which best serves the purpose, as a basis for comparison. A bird's bill is generally its most diagnostic external character. A sketch of it in your note-book will frequently give you a good clue to its owner's family. It is of the utmost importance that descriptions and sketches should be made *in the field*. Not only do our memories sometime deceive us, but we really see nothing with exactness until we attempt to describe it. Haunts, actions, and notes should also be carefully recorded.

Even better than a description is a figure colored with crayons or water-colors. It may be the crudest outline and in ridiculous pose, but at least it is definite. There is no possibility of error through the wrong use of terms; the observer draws or charts what he sees. Neither art nor skill is required. Anyone can learn to make the outline of the normal bird figure as readily as he can learn to make the letters of the alphabet, and a little practice will enable one to give the shape of bill, wings and tail, and even a hint of characteristic form and position. Typical, passerine outline figures may be made in advance in one's field note-book, and the shape of the bill and color may be added while the bird is under observation. A collection of diagrams or sketches of this kind will be found to possess far greater individuality and value than mere written descriptions. If the sketch cannot be completed, if essential details are lacking, it is obvious that the subject has not been seen with that definiteness upon which satisfactory field identification should rest. With this description or sketch you may now proceed to use the 'Keys' as explained on an earlier page.

How Birds Are Named.—It is extremely doubtful if from our Mexican boundary to the Arctic Ocean there remains a single unknown *species* of bird. Of geographical races, climatic varieties or subspecies, a gradually decreasing number will be described from at least western North America for years to come, but in eastern North America we have practically reached, if indeed we have not passed, the point where such forms may be profitably named.

The bird student in this area may be reasonably certain, therefore, that every bird he sees has a name, and in the preceding section having suggested ways in which this name may be learned, the somewhat obscure details of nomenclature may be made clearer by explaining how the bird got it. In doing so I draw freely from a similar effort in the 'Color Key to North American Birds.'

Birds have two kinds of names. One is a common, vernacular, or popular name; the other is a technical or scientific name. The first is usually given to the living bird by the people of the country it inhabits. The second is applied to specimens of birds by ornithologists who classify them. Common names in their origin and use know no law. Technical names are bestowed under the system of binomial nomenclature established by Linnæus in 1758, and their formation and adoption are governed by certain definite, generally accepted rules. The Linnæan system, as it is now employed by most ornithologists, provides that a bird, in addition to being grouped in a certain Order, Family, etc., shall have a generic, a specific, and, often, a subspecific name which, together, shall not be applied to any other animal.

Generally speaking, Orders and Families are based on skeletal, muscular, and visceral, or what may be termed internal characters; while genera are based on the form of bill, wings, feet and tail, and sometimes on pattern of markings, and species and subspecies on color and size, or external characters. Thus, all the members of an Order agree in major internal characters; those of a Family further agree in minor internal characters; those of a Genus, in addition, resemble one another in external characters, while species and subspecies differ only in color and in size.

Frequently it happens that a bird may possess some of the characters of one group in connection with some of the characters of another group, and such birds, collectively, create intergrading groups known as Suborders, Subfamilies, Subgenera, or Subspecies. With the last, the student is especially concerned since they figure in the name by which a bird is known.

In pre-Darwinian days it was generally believed that a species was a distinct creation whose characters did not vary from a certain type. But in later years comparison of many specimens of a species from throughout the region it inhabits shows that specimens from one part of a bird's range may differ in size and color, or both, from those taken in another part of its range. At intervening localities, however, intermediate specimens will be found connecting the extremes. (See beyond, under Color and Climate.) Variations of this kind are termed geographic, racial, or subspecific, and the birds exhibiting them are known as subspecies. In naming them, a third name, or trinomial, is employed, and the possession of such a name indicates at once that the bird is a geographic or racial representative of a species with one or more representatives of which it is believed to intergrade.

The fact that the criteria for the determination of subspecies are numerous and their value not standardized is the cause for wide difference of opinion among ornithologists concerning the distinction between species and subspecies. The German school favors ranking all representative forms, whether or not their ranges adjoin, and without relation, therefore, to whether or not they intergrade, as subspecifically related, the whole group, combined, forming what they term a *Formenkreis*. The American school favors the use of the trinomial to express the subspecific relationship only when the forms concerned are known to, or believed to, intergrade, and this usually implies that their ranges adjoin. In my opinion this question of a bird's relationships should be decided in the light of our knowledge concerning it and not prejudged by the application of a hard and fast rule. (See Chapman, 'The Criteria for the Determination of Subspecies.' *Auk*, XLI, 1924, pp. 17–29.)

Let us now trace the history of a trinomial name, taking, for example, that of our Eastern Robin, *Turdus migratorius migratorius* Linnæus. The first account of this bird appears in Catesby (1731), and it was later classified by Linnæus in the twelfth edition (1766) of his epoch-making 'Systema Naturæ' as *Turdus migratorius*. By this name the Robin or 'Migratory Thrush' was known for over one hundred years, when that finer discrimination, which has increasingly characterized systematic ornithology, showed that the genus *Turdus* of Linnæus contained species which, in the light of this more modern view, were generically separable. The type of the genus having been determined to be *Turdus viscivorus* Linnæus, the Mistle Thrush of Europe, the name *Turdus* was restricted to that bird and its congeneric allies, and the genus *Merula* of Leach was accepted for our Robin and the species with which it is generically related. The bird's name then became *Merula migratoria* (Linnæus), the termination of the specific name being changed from *us* to *a* in order that it might conform to the gender of the generic name with which it was associated. The parentheses now enclosing the name of Linnæus indicate that while Linnæus described the species *migratorius*, he did not place it in the genus *Merula*.

Now, by one of those unfortunate coincidences which have done so much to create confusion in zoölogical nomenclature, it was discovered, in 1907, that the generic name *Merula* of Leach was 'preoccupied' by the *Merula* of Koch, proposed by the latter for a genus of Starlings, and, under the ruling of the 'Law of Priority,' the name *Merula* could therefore no longer be applied to the Robin and its congeners, and the next available name proved to be *Planesticus* of Bonaparte. Thus the case stood for years. But the so-called generic differences between *Turdus* and *Planesticus* are so slight and so fully bridged by species other than those to which these names were first applied, that their value as a base for generic distinction is a matter of opinion. With the passage of time, standards, and the 'opinions' based on them, are subject to change. Hence, influenced by a more conservative view of what constitutes generic characters, systematists today believe that the creation of a distinct genus for the bird originally described as *Turdus migratorius* was unwarranted, and that the proposed genus *Planesticus* should therefore be treated as a synonym of *Turdus*, and its species, including *migratorius*, be placed in that genus. So our Robin is now known as *Turdus migratorius* Linnæus, the name that was first applied to it.

So far as nomenclature is concerned, such cases are the inevitable result of the rigid enforcement of the now universally accepted laws of nomenclature, which, if they had been in existence and observed from the time of Linnæus, would have prevented these seemingly unnecessary changes in the technical names of animals. Each change, however, is designed to bring us nearer to that stability which is the dream of those who believe that "nomenclature is the means, not the end, of zoölogical science." But when a bird's name is based on relationships, the value of which is a matter of opinion, it cannot be fixed by law, and it will ever be as subject to change as the opinion on which it is based.

So much for the Robin's generic designation. Passing now to its specific name, *migratorius*, which being again associated with a masculine generic name resumes its original termination of *us*, this name was applied to the bird throughout its entire North American range until 1877, when Ridgway proposed the name *propinquus* for the Robin of western North America on the ground that in this race the outer tail-feather had little or no white, and on other characters, and this western bird, after sharing the various generic experiences of our eastern form, is now known as *Turdus migratorius propinquus* Ridgway.

After the recognition of a western race of the Robin under a trinomial name, it would be obviously inconsistent to apply a binomial to our eastern bird, the former being no more a subspecies of the latter than the latter is of the former. In other words, to continue to apply only generic and specific names to the Eastern Robin would imply that it was a species, while the use of a trinomial for the Western Robin would imply that it was a subspecies. As a matter of fact, we know that there is but one species of true Robin in North America, consequently, in accordance with the logical and now generally accepted method, we apply to that species the name *Turdus migratorius*, and this is equally applicable to Robins from the West and from the East. The eastern subspecies is, therefore, known by the trinomial *Turdus migratorius migratorius*, the western subspecies by the exact nomenclatural equivalent, *Turdus migratorius propinquus*, and the more recently described small, pale Southern Robin, as *Turdus migratorius achrusterus*. Thus we have one Robin which is represented by three subspecies. It may be asked, why give names to these geographical races? Why not call Eastern, Western, and Southern Robins by one name without regard to their climatic variations? To which it may be replied, that subspecies often differ more from each other than do species. For example, it would clearly be inadvisable to apply the same name to the small, pale Song Sparrow of Arizona, and the large, dark Song Sparrow of Alaska. (See figures, Pl. VII.) Seen without the connecting forms from the intervening regions, and they apparently are specifically distinct, but the application to each of a subspecific name, or trinomial, not only indicates that they are different, but it shows also that they are representative forms which are joined by a series of intergrades; a contribution of the first importance to the study of evolution.

For much the same reason we should recognize by name those birds which, like the Robin, show less pronounced climatic variations. Here we have species in the earliest stages of development from a common ancestor, and in naming them we are, in effect, giving 'a handle to the fact' of their evolution by environment. The study of the distribution and migration of birds and the mapping of natural life-areas are also intimately connected with this recognition by name of geographical variations.

Since it is evident that a species may vary much or little according to the extent of its range, the governing conditions, and its tendency to respond to them, no fixed rule can be drawn which shall state just what degrees of difference are deserving a name. It follows, therefore, that in some cases ornithologists do not agree upon the validity of a bird's claims to subspecific rank.[1] In North America, however, questions of this kind are referred to a Committee of the American Ornithologists' Union, and its decisions establish a nomenclature which is accepted as the standard by other American ornithologists and which is adopted in this volume.

Finally, the student should be warned not to permit this matter of names to have an undue significance. A species is not an entity or distinct creation, but merely one link in the chain of bird-life, which, because of the loss of the adjoining link or links, appears to stand by itself. Nor should he think of a subspecies as materially different from the species which it represents, simply because it has received a distinctive name. Nomenclature gives undue emphasis to differences, whereas, it is equally important to emphasize resemblances.

REFERENCES

1912. NICHOLS, J. T., Recognition Marks in Certain Species of Birds. Auk, p. 44 (see also, McAtee, W. L., pp. 226–232).—**1922.** GRISCOM, L., Problems of Field Identification. Auk, pp. 31–41.

THE EQUIPMENT OF THE FIELD STUDENT

The Glass	*Photographic Outfit*
Note-books and Journals	*The Collector's Outfit*
The Observation Blind	*The Bird-bander's Outfit*

The Glass.—A good field-glass is necessary, not alone as an aid in identifying birds, but in observing their actions. When one is working in fields and woods where the birds are comparatively near, a low-power glass with good illumination can be used more quickly and to better advantage than the higher-power glasses which require more frequent adjustment of focus, with consequent loss of time. But on the shore, or over the water, where birds are seen at great distances and where there is an abundance of light, the high-power glasses are much more serviceable. There is, however, a limit to the magnification which can be used effectively; the 8-power prism binocular of any one of half-a-dozen makes proving, in practice, to be best adapted to the bird student's needs. Beyond this power, the increased precision required in focusing, and the need for greater steadiness when in use do not compensate one for the larger image it is possible to obtain.

[1]See Allen, *The Auk*, 1890, pp. 1–9

Note-books and Journals.—The necessity for a well-kept journal and full field-notes cannot be too strongly urged. Specimens may be duplicated, but no one can ever see with your eyes. Do not trust your memory—a willing servant too frequently imposed on. It may receive and retain one impression clearly, but as others are added the earlier ones lose their distinctness or become entirely effaced.

The system adopted for recording notes should be simple to keep and easy of reference. In the field, I use a pocket note-book arranged to hold perforated leaves. In such a book one enters descriptions of birds' appearance and of their calls and song, and other memoranda which it is desired to commit at once to writing. No leaf should contain notes relating to more than one species, and the leaves, properly headed,

Date.					
Locality.					
Weather.					
Temperature					
Wind.					
Start					
Return					
Remarks					
Bluebird					

may then be filed for reference, either alphabetically or according to the classification of the American Ornithologists' Union.

For a journal I use a college lecture note-book, also arranged to hold perforated loose leaves which measure 6½ by 8½ inches. The first half-dozen leaves (others can be inserted when needed) should be ruled in small squares, leaving a space wide enough to enter birds' names at the left-hand page, with only horizontal lines. A portion of such a page is appended.

After returning from the field, I enter on these roll-call sheets a record of weather, temperature, direction and force of the wind, route, time of starting and returning, and incidental observations on the blooming of flowers, appearance of certain insects, calling of frogs, etc.

After filling in these preliminary data, I write after the name of each bird either the exact or approximate number of individuals seen, or else the letters 'A.,' 'C.,' or 'T.C.,' meaning abundant, common, or tolerably common. This is accompanied by an 's' if the bird is in song, or 'calls' if it is simply heard calling. The possibilities of abbreviation are unlimited, but use no abbreviation which is not fully explained. If you wish to make a record of some length concerning a certain species, place a cross or asterisk in its square. This refers to your journal of the same date which is entered on the horizontally ruled sheets following those used for the roll-call.

Read from left to right, such a roll-call gives in a graphic, condensed form the standing of a species during the period of observation. Read from the top to the bottom of the page, it gives, in an easily comparable way, the complete record of each day, and, at the same time, it becomes an index to the bird-notes in the journal, which follows.

To prevent needlessly multiplying these roll-call sheets, the series of birds' names should be made to last at least during an entire season. To this end do not completely fill the *right-hand* page, but when you have used all of it but a space equal in width to the space occupied by the column of birds' names on the left side of the left page, cut this part of the page—the extreme right—off; the part remaining will, when turned over to the left, just meet the column of names, and the lines of this column and of the new page will thus run continuously. As before remarked, the roll-book should be attended to immediately on returning from the field, while your impressions are fresh. The journal may, if necessary, wait, when a reference to the roll-call will aid in recalling the day's experiences. Only one cover, with clasps for the retention of the perforated sheets, will be needed, and at the end of a trip or season the sheets may be removed and bound. This is essentially the method of note-keeping described in the first edition of the 'Handbook' and which, after thirty-six years' additional use, I still unreservedly recommend.

The Observation Blind.—The observation blind which, during the past thirty years, has met the demands of many and varied situations, is, in brief, an umbrella opened within a bag long enough to conceal one. It is described in my 'Camps and Cruises of an Ornithologist' (p. xiii) as follows:

"The umbrella employed in making an observation blind is known to the trade as a 'sign' umbrella. It agrees with the normal variety in size but differs from it in having a large hole in the center. This permits a current of air to pass through the blind—a matter of the first importance when one spends hours in the little structure on beach or marsh, where it is fully exposed to the sun. The 'stick' of this umbrella is a

Fig. 4. The umbrella and supporting
rods of the umbrella blind.

metal tube without the usual wooden handle.

"The umbrella is supported by two brass tubes, each of the same length as the umbrella, or 32 inches. The larger is shod with a steel point, by the insertion of a small cold chisel or nail-punch, which is brazed in position. The rod can then be readily driven into the ground. At the upper end a thumb-screw is placed. The smaller tube should enter the larger snugly, and should in turn be just large enough to receive the umbrella-rod which will enter it as far as the spring 'catch.' The height of the umbrella may, therefore, be governed by the play of the smaller tube in the larger, while the thumb-screw will permit one to maintain any desired adjustment, as one would fix the height of a music-rack.

"If the blind is to be used about home, a light denim may be employed; if it is to see the harder service of travel and camp-life, a heavier grade of the same material will be found more serviceable. In the former case the denim may be sewed to the edge of the umbrella, which then has only to be opened and placed in the brass tube, the latter having been thrust into the ground when the blind is erected, an operation requiring less than a minute. [Of later years I have employed gunny sacking for the blind. Its coarse weave enables one to see from within in any direction without sacrifice of concealment. The numerous peep-holes which, sooner or later, are cut in a denim blind thus become unnecessary.]

"When traveling, it seems more desirable not to attach the walls of the blind to the umbrella. The covering then consists of several strips of material sewed together to make a piece measuring 10½ feet wide by 6½ feet high. The two ends of this piece are sewed together at what then becomes the top of the blind, for about 2 feet. The unjoined portion below becomes the door of the blind. Openings should be cut in the opposite side for the lens and for observation. A strong draw-cord is then run about the top edge of the cloth, so that, before inserting and opening the umbrella, one can draw it up as one would the neck of a bag, until the opening corresponds in size to that of the umbrella. The draw-cord should be long enough to serve as a guy or stay. This covering places less strain on the umbrella and may be packed in smaller space than one which is sewed to the umbrella, and, when in camp, it may be used to sleep on, as a covering, as a shelter tent or in a variety of ways.

"The color of the umbrella should be leaf-green. The covering should be sand- or earth-colored and should be dyed leaf-green on its upper third whence it should gradually fade to the original cloth color at about the center. Such a color scheme conforms to Abbott Thayer's law that animals are darkest where they receive the most light, and palest where they are most in shadow; and renders the blind much less conspicuous than if it were uniformly green or gray. It is not amiss to run belts of braid about the covering, sewing them to it at intervals and thus forming loops in which, when desired, reeds or branches may be thrust.

"In erecting the blind, if circumstances permit, it is desirable to place the 'door' toward the wind to insure better ventilation. When the situation is exposed, an additional stay or two may be required. If the camera box is not strong enough to sit on, a collapsible, artist's camp-stool should be added to the outfit. One cannot spend half a day in such close quarters and observe and record to advantage unless one is comfortably seated."

Photographic Outfit.—The camera has, unquestionably, won its place as the most important item in the field student's outfit; not merely because it enables one to record facts in a graphic, communicable form, but also because it supplies an incentive for definitely directed study by satisfying the hunting instinct and gratifying the desire for some tangible return for effort expended. Photographs can be made not alone of birds, their nests and eggs, but of haunts, and of vegetation showing its condition at certain dates as it develops in the spring or dies in the autumn.

The naturalist-photographer should seek the advice and instruction of someone with experience, or, when this is not possible, the books on the subject should be consulted. Much may be done in the study of nest-life with a camera and lens costing between $30 and $40. Select a strong, not too light, 4 x 5 camera, having a bellows-length of not less than 16 inches and fitted with a trade shutter; and a lens of about 7-inch focus, convertible in type, in order that either the front or rear half of the lens can be used alone, giving an image about double the size of that produced by both combined.

Such a camera should be used from a tripod, and, under favorable conditions of light and time, it will do excellent work. It cannot be employed to photograph flying birds or to do many other things which require the most rapid lenses and special apparatus; but, from a blind, with the nest, food, or decoys to act as a lure, bringing birds within range, one may secure an endless number of valuable and interesting photographic records of bird-life.

By using one of the modern, very rapid multi-speed lens-shutters, and guessing at the focus, such a camera may be used in photographing birds in flight; but the best results are attained in this somewhat difficult field with a reflecting camera of the Graflex type, equipped with a focal-plane shutter. Satisfactory flight photographs, at close range, require an exposure of not more than $\frac{1}{800}$ part of a second. This necessitates the use of a high-class, rapid lens, and the outfit becomes too costly to be within the reach of many. However, except under the conditions which sometimes prevail in large bird rookeries, one can do far more and better work from a blind with inexpensive apparatus than with a high-priced hand-camera in the open, while the notes on birds' habits obtained from the blind are incomparably more valuable.

Modified telephoto lenses with a focal length of about twice that of the bellows employed are serviceable when the subject cannot be closely approached. But for technical and ornithological reasons, I commend the shorter focus lens. We are not out merely to get birds' pictures, but to record their habits with a camera, and the nearer we can get to the bird without disturbing it, the better we can accomplish our object.

In motion-picture photography it is desirable to use standard size film. While excellent enlargements suitable for separate reproduction may be made from motion-picture negatives, motion pictures, as a rule, are used only for projection with consequent magnification. The original image, therefore, may be very small, and still, when thrown on a screen, be large enough to show all desirable details. For this reason, satisfactory motion pictures may be made with a much shorter focus lens than will give satisfactory results in 'still' photography. A 6-inch lens will, therefore, generally give sufficient enlargement.

The Collector's Outfit.—Individual preference will always play a part in the selection of a gun. My own choice for general collecting is a 16-bore equipped with 0.32 and 410 auxiliary barrels. In general collecting in a more or less wooded region, fully 90 per cent of your shots will be fired from the auxiliaries—or 'auxes,' as they are commonly termed—and the smaller barrel will be used far more often than the larger.

Crude but effective auxiliary barrels may be made with a 16-gauge brass shell and a brass tube about 6 inches long having a diameter of the gauge desired. Enlarge the cap opening of the 16-gauge shell until it will exactly receive the brass tube; stand the shell on a level surface squarely on its base, place the tube upright in it with its end in the enlarged cap-hole and flush with the base of the shell; now, using extreme care to have the tube exactly in the center of the shell, fill the shell about the sides of the tube with molten lead. When it has cooled, counter-sink a shoulder in the base of the tube of sufficient size and depth to receive the rim of the shell for which it is designed, file a narrow slot to enable one to remove with an awl or properly sharpened nail the exploded shell, and your 'aux' is made.

A gunsmith could do a better job and give you a barrel with an extractor which will work automatically with that of your gun, and such barrels may sometimes be purchased from natural history dealers; but the one I have described can be made by anyone and will answer every purpose. In any event, test your 'aux' thoroughly until you have learned its range and what load will give the best pattern and penetration. In the .32 shell I use about three-fifths fine smokeless powder with a cardboard and felt or leather wad, and two-fifths shot with a cardboard wad. In loading a large number of shells for a prolonged collecting trip, the wad over the shot may be dipped lightly in liquid paraffine, which, in hardening, will tend to keep the wad from slipping. Since the .32 'aux' is used almost exclusively for birds no larger than a Blue Jay, the shells for it should be loaded with No. 12 shot. For the .410 and 16-bore, one should carry variously loaded shells, as the nature of the collecting directs.

A hunting-coat with large pockets, a fisherman's creel, or a game-bag, for carrying specimens, a bottle of cornmeal for cleaning them, non-absorbent cotton for 'plugging' them, stiff paper for wrapping them, and a mixture of equal parts powdered alum and arsenic for preserving them, are all part of the collector's outfit.

The bird-skinner's outfit, in its simplest form, consists of one or more scalpels having blades with well-rounded ends, and one, at least, with a handle small enough to be used as a spoon in removing brains; three pairs of scissors, one with short, heavy blades for bone-crushing, one with sharp points and long handles, and one of medium size with blunt ends; one medium size, flat-end 'eye-forceps'; thread, pins and needles. This outfit, which can be purchased of a dealer in naturalists' supplies or surgical instruments, can be enlarged as circumstances require or taste directs.

Any cotton will do for filling skins, but for use in wrapping them, procure the *best* cotton batting that money will buy. Usually it will be found that absorbent cotton, such as may be purchased at drug stores, will be as good if not better than any which is available. Large birds may be filled with excelsior or a body made of crumpled newspaper, possibly covered with a thin sheet of cotton.

The Bird-bander's Outfit.—The most essential item in the bird-bander's outfit is a permit from the Biological Survey of the United States Department of Agriculture (and, when required, from the proper authorities in his own state) authorizing him to band birds. Application for permits should be made on blanks which will be supplied on request. At the same time, a copy of Lincoln and Baldwin's 'Manual for Bird Banders' (Misc. Pub. No. 58, U. S. Dept. of Agric.) should be purchased from the Superintendent of Documents, Government Printing Office, Washington, D. C. (Price, 30 cents).

This publication contains detailed descriptions of the traps, bands, tools for their attachment, recording cards, etc., and instructions for their use, and is itself so indispensable a part of the bird-bander's equipment that it is not necessary to go further into this subject here.

REFERENCES

1900. PYNCHON, W. H. C., A Method of Recording Observations, **Bird-Lore**, II, pp. 19–22.—**1900.** CHAPMAN, F. M., Bird Studies with a Camera, 12mo., 218 pp., illus. (Appleton).—**1901.** HERRICK, F. H., The Home Life of Wild Birds, rev. ed., 1905, 8vo, 255 pp. (Putnam's).—**1902.** BAILEY, F. M., Handbook of Birds of Western United States, introduction (Houghton, Mifflin & Co.).—**1902.** DUGMORE, A. R., Nature and the Camera, 8vo, 126 pp. (Doubleday).—**1902.** FELGER, A. H., A Plan for Recording in a Condensed Form the Life History Notes of Birds, Auk, XIX, pp. 189–195.—**1904.** BROWNELL, Photography for the Sportsman-Naturalist (Macmillan).—**1910.** JOB, H. K., How to Study Birds (Outing Co.).—**1911.** BEETHAM, B., Photography for Bird Lovers, 12mo, 126 pp., illus. (Witherby, London).—**1925.** NESBIT, W., How to Hunt with a Camera, 4to, 337 pp., illus. (Dutton & Co.).—**1927.** ALLEN, FUERTES, and PIRNIE, General Ornithology Laboratory Notebook (Comstock Pub. Co., Ithaca, N. Y.).

COLLECTING BIRDS, THEIR NESTS AND EGGS

> *Collecting Birds*
> *Care of the Bird in the Field*
> *Making Birdskins*
> *Sexing*
> *Cataloguing and Labeling*
> *Care of a Collection*
> *Collecting and Preserving Nests and Eggs*

Collecting Birds.—When one goes to a country whose birds are unknown or but little known, the first thing to do is to collect and preserve them in order that they may be properly named and classified, and that our records of their distribution may rest on the tangible ground of specimens. This is the essential procedure in beginning the study of bird-life the world over, but once thoroughly done, it is neither necessary nor desirable to repeat it indefinitely.

To say that one cannot become an ornithologist without first having been a collector of birds' skins, is to confess ignorance of the advance which has been made in the methods and possibilities of bird-study. The non-collector will possibly never have that intimate, personal, first-hand knowledge of specific differences which has been gained by the man who has handled many birds of his own killing, nor will he have added as many definite 'records' of the occurrence of species beyond the normal limits of their range; but in regions whose birds have been adequately collected, he will unquestionably render ornithology a far higher service by devoting himself to a study of biographic problems than by collecting specimens which, however much they may gratify his desire for acquisition and increase his personal acquaintance with birds, will add but little or nothing to the fund of ornithological knowledge.

The student with some definite problem in view is always justified in taking the specimens which are required to aid in prosecuting his researches, nor can there be any reasonable objection to collecting for purposes of identification; but there can be no doubt that throughout the greater part of eastern North America there is no longer need for general, indiscriminate collecting. No better proof of the truth of this statement can be required than the fact that, as our introductory 'Historical Review' shows, some of the most important additions to our knowledge of birds in this area, during the past thirty years, have been made by men who are not collectors.

There is no question of the destruction of life involved here. In only two or three instances has the collecting of birds for specimens appreciably affected the numbers of a species; and, as everyone familiar with the facts involved knows, the results of general amateur collecting are absolutely inappreciable. Therefore, it is the student, rather than the bird, I have in mind, when I discourage further collecting in regions whose bird-life is already well known. In most cases the time which he can give to bird-study is limited, and the question is, shall he devote it to doing exactly what ornithologists for generations before him have done, or shall he, by concentrating on a definite problem, do what no one has done? Can he not well afford to forego a general superficial knowledge of a large number of birds, such as many have had, for a special knowledge of some few birds such as no one has had? For the real student, imbued with the true spirit of research, there can be only one answer to this question.

After this protest against unnecessary collecting, and the waste of opportunity it occasions, I add a description of the technique of birdskin making, for the use of those who may properly employ it.

Care of the Bird in the Field.—On killing a bird, pick it up by the bill or feet, and at once sprinkle meal or dry earth on any blood which may be visible. When this is saturated, scrape it off with a knife-blade and repeat the operation until all the blood is absorbed. Sprinkle some meal at the base of the feathers about the shot-holes from which the blood appears, or, if necessary, plug these holes with bits of cotton. Place a large plug of cotton in the mouth and force it well down the throat to prevent bleeding at the mouth from an internal wound. In some cases it is also necessary to plug the nostrils. Now make a cornucopia of stiff paper, drop the bird in it, head foremost, taking care that the bill is not turned forward on to the throat, and, if the bird is not too large, fold in the edges of the cornucopia and place the specimen in your bag or basket. In the case of very large specimens—Hawks, Owls, etc.—it is advisable to skin out the body in the field, when they can be packed in much smaller space.

Making Birdskins.—With proper instruction it is not difficult to learn to skin birds. I have known beginners, who had closely watched experts at work, make fair skins at their first attempt—better skins, indeed, than the person who learns only from written directions may ever make. I am speaking from experience. Only too clearly do I remember my own first attempts at skinning birds and their hopelessly wretched results. In despair I at last sought the assistance of a distant ornithological friend. In one lesson he made the process so clear to me that I was at once enabled to make skins twice as quickly and twice as well. However, we unfortunately are not all blessed with ornithological friends to whom we can turn for advice, and I therefore append the following directions for making birdskins:

Let us begin with a bird, say, the size of a Robin: 1. Plug the bird's throat and nostrils tightly with fresh cotton. If the eyeball is ruptured, pull it out with the forceps and fill the cavity with meal. 2. Lay the bird before you on its back, its bill pointing to the left; place your open left hand lengthwise on it, so that the base of your first and second fingers rests on the middle of the breastbone; use these fingers and the handle of the scalpel to separate the feathers from near the end of the breastbone to the vent, and when the parting is made use the same fingers to hold the feathers aside. 3. With the scalpel make an incision in the skin from just in *front* of the end of the breastbone, or at the base of the V formed by the spread fingers, to the vent, being careful not to cut through into the abdomen. 4. Sprinkle a pinch of meal along the cut. 5. Lift the skin at the front end of the cut and insert the end of the scalpel handle between it and the breastbone. If you try to do this lower down on the cut, over the belly, you will find it difficult to separate the skin on which the feathers grow from the immediately underlying skin which covers the abdomen. Separate the skin from the body the whole length of the cut and as far down toward the backbone as possible, thus exposing the bare knee. 6. Take hold of the foot and push the knee farther up into view, then take the blunt-ended scissors and, on the inside of the skin, clip the leg entirely in two. 7. Repeat operations 5 and 6 on the other side of the body. 8. Press away the skin as much as possible on either side of the rump, and place the thumb at the left side (left, seen from above) of the base of the tail or 'pope's nose,' with the first finger on the other side (both inside the skin) and the second finger behind (above) on the rump; now with the blunt scissors cut through the flesh between the thumb and first finger toward the second finger, which serves the purpose of a guard to prevent you from cutting through the skin. 9. Stand the bird on its breastbone, the belly toward you, and with both thumbs press the tail and skin of the rump over and down off the stump from which you have just cut it. 10. When the stump is free from the skin, take hold of it with the right hand and with the fingers of the left gently press the skin from the body, keeping it constantly turned inside out and using an abundance of meal. 11. Soon the wing-bones (humeri) will appear. Clip them off at each side close to the body, and resume skinning as before. 12. The skin will slip easily over the neck, and you will then meet with an obstruction in the head. 13. Work the skin carefully over the head, using the tips of the first two fingers of either hand, placing the thumbs as a brace farther forward over the eyes.[1] 14. Pull the ears

[1]In large-headed birds, like Ducks and Woodpeckers, this is impossible, and it is necessary to slit the skin down the back of the neck and push the skull through the opening.

carefully from their sockets. 15. The eyes will now appear; carefully cut the membrane joining the skin and eyeball, making the incision as far back as possible, in order to avoid cutting the skin, which should be pulled forward until it is entirely free of the eyeball. 16. Remove the eyes with the forceps. 17. With the sharp-pointed scissors make an incision directly across the roof of the mouth, inside the branches of the lower mandible, just back of the skin, and below the eye-sockets. 18. With the sharp-pointed scissors make incisions from each end of this cut back along the branches of the lower mandible through the base of the skull on each side of the neck at its junction with the skull. 19. Connect these cuts by a fourth, which passes through the base of the skull just above the neck, and pull the body and neck from the skull. 20. Scoop out what brains remain with the handle of the scalpel. 21. Pull the end of the wingbone (humerus) inward, skinning the feathers off the bones of the forearm (radius and ulna), and remove the flesh. 22. Do the same thing for the legs, but, after cleaning, do not in either case pull the bones back. 23. Remove as much flesh as possible from the base of the tail, including the oil-gland at the base of the tail above. 24. Hold the skin over the arsenic and alum box, and with a bit of fluffy cotton at the end of a stick, or held in the forceps, dust it thoroughly with the poison, giving an extra allowance to the base of the tail and bones of the skull, wings, and legs. 25. Pull the legs back into place. 26. Place a fluff of cotton on the end of a wire and roll it into a firm, smooth ball, placing one in each eye-socket. 27. Coax the skin back over the head, using the first two fingers of each hand and placing the thumbs at the base of the skull. When the tip of the bill appears through the feathers, use the fingers outside, on the feathers, pressing the skin back over the head, and keeping the thumbs in the same position. When the bill is free, take it with the right hand, and use the fingers of the left to urge the skin over the skull, being careful to get it in its former place so that the feathers of the head will lie smoothly. 28. Dress the feathers of the head, particularly those about the eye. 29. Take hold of the tip of the bill and shake the skin gently but vigorously to aid in settling the plumage. 30. Lay the skin on its back, the bill pointing from you, and turn back the feathers about the opening on the belly. 31. See that the wing-bones lie flat on the back of the skin, with their ends touching each other.[1] 32. Take a stick nearly as long as the bird's body and neck, its size depending on that of the bird (a toothpick does very well for birds as small as Warblers), twirl it in loose cotton held between the thumb and

---

[1]The most difficult part in making a birdskin is to induce the wings to assume anything like their natural position when closed. This is because the artificial cotton body is apt to force them outward on to the *sides* rather than on the *back*, where they belong.

In the bird in the flesh the wings are held in place by being attached to the body; in the skin they are loose and hanging. To remedy this, after drawing the wing-bones in to remove the flesh from them, they should be pushed back only far enough to enable one to see plainly the elbow or bend of the wing outside of the skin. This prevents the wings from hanging, and, to further keep them in place, it will be well at first to tie the ends of the bones (humeri) together.

first two fingers until enough cotton is firmly wrapped about it to make a 'neck'; increase the amount of cotton used to form a body, continuing the twirling process until the cotton is firm and smooth. 33. Insert the end of the cotton neck, which should be thin and pointed, gently into the neck of the skin, working the skin down on to it in order to avoid stretching, until the end of the cotton appears in the mouth. 34. Carefully fit the cotton body to the skin, seeing that it lies on, not between, the ends of the humeri. 35. Put one or two stitches in the incision on the belly. 36. Ascertain the sex of the bird (see beyond). 37. Cross the legs, and at the point of intersection attach a label (see beyond). 38. Squeeze the wing-bones together until you feel the tips of your fingers meet over the bird's back. 39. Prepare a sheet of cotton about 5 inches square and as thin as you can make it; lay the bird on this on its right side, the bill pointing to your right hand. 40. Put the left wing in place and dress the feathers about it. 41. Take hold of the sheet of cotton, and turn the bird over in it in order that you may dress the right wing. 42. Roll the bird on to its belly, holding the wings in position with the thumb and first finger

FIG. 5. A completed birdskin (reduced).

of the left hand, and with the right hand bring the tips of the wing-feathers into their proper place over the back. 43. Roll the bird back on to its back, the bill pointing to your right hand; take the end of the sheet of cotton farthest from you and draw it *lightly* over the bird to the side nearest you. 44. Draw the end nearest you in the opposite direction. 45. See that the feet, tail, and tips of the wings are in their proper position, and place your specimen out of harm's way to dry.

It will doubtless take you from half an hour to an hour to make your first birdskin. It will probably be a sorry-looking object, perhaps minus a head or tail or half its feathers; but do not let this discourage you. An expert can make ten birdskins an hour, and you need only practice to approach this.

Sexing.—A specimen without a sex-mark on its label is of comparatively little value. The sexes in many birds can, of course, be distinguished by their color, but the young male frequently resembles the female, while in some instances the female has been known to assume the plumage of the male. Dissection, therefore, is the only safe way to determine sex. Upon reaching stage 36, in the operation of making a birdskin, cut through the left side of the body from the vent to the neck, taking care not to disturb the internal organs. Force the edges of the opening apart, and, pressing the intestines gently to one side, look for the sexual organs, which will be found on the walls of the small of the back very near to the backbone. The male organs (testes), two in number, are usually dull-white, elongate bodies lying side by side. The female organs (ovary) are composed of numerous round bodies lying in a mass or cluster at the left (the observer's right) of the median line. In the breeding season the sexual organs of birds become much enlarged, and at this season the testes of a male Chipping Sparrow are about the size of a pea, while the ovary of the female has been likened to a bunch of grapes, the largest being the size of the yolk of the egg of this species. After the breeding season the sexual organs decrease in size, and in adults in the winter and in young birds are sometimes difficult to find. The testes of a male Chipping Sparrow at that season are about as large as a small pinhead, while a hand-lens is required to distinguish plainly the ovary of the female. The arrow of Mars ($\male$) is used to indicate the male sex; the mirror of Venus ($\female$) the female sex.

Cataloguing and Labeling.—Before skinning your birds you should catalogue them. The catalogue should have columns giving (1) the date, (2) your serial collection number, (3) name of the bird, (4) sex and condition of the sexual organs, (5) place of capture, (6) name of collector, and (7) remarks. In the last column enter any notes on the color of the eyes, or parts which will change color when drying, contents of the stomach, and other notes. In addition to this 'day-book' or 'blotter' some ornithologists open a ledger account with their collection and devote a folio to each species, on which are posted the entries made in the collection register.

Labels should be of strong bond paper, 2½ inches long and ½ inch wide. They are attached to the crossed legs of the bird by linen thread strung through their left end. The face of the label bears the name and sex of the bird, place and date of capture, name of collector, and serial collection number. The label shown in Fig. 5 is small, but will illustrate the appearance and manner of attachment. The name of the owner of the collection is printed on the back of the label, preceded by the words 'Collection of.' Many collectors prefer to use as a field-label a small jeweler's tag upon which the collection number, sex, and date are written. The large label is added after the specimen is dry.

Care of a Collection.—So many types of cabinets are now in use for storing collections that I hesitate to recommend any particular one. A wooden cabinet with tight-fitting drawers and door, with ordinary care, will preserve specimens for a practically indefinite period. The drawers should be 30 inches long by 16 inches in width. For birds the size of a Robin, a depth of 1¾ inches is sufficient, while drawers 4 inches deep will take the largest Hawks or Owls. These drawers will hold about thirty birds the size of a Robin, eighty the size of a Chickadee, and eight to ten Hawks and Owls.

Well cleaned and thoroughly poisoned specimens of small birds are not likely to be attacked by the moth (*Tinea*) or beetles (*Dermestes* and *Anthrenus*) which so often infest poorly prepared or nonpoisoned skins. Naphthaline crystals or camphor gum should be placed in each drawer of the cabinet, the door of which should not be left open needlessly. If a specimen falls a victim to insects, the better plan is to discard it at once. If, however, it is rare, it may be taken *out-of-doors* and placed in an air-tight box with a few tablespoonfuls of bisulphuret of carbon.

Collecting and Preserving Nests and Eggs.—The following quotation, from the late Major Bendire's 'Instructions for Collecting, Preparing, and Preserving Birds' Eggs and Nests'[1] may be taken as authoritative: "Unless the would-be collector intends to make an especial study of oölogy and has a higher aim than the mere desire to take and accumulate as large a number of eggs as possible regardless of their proper identification, he had better not begin at all, but leave the nests and eggs of our birds alone and undisturbed. They have too many enemies to contend with, without adding the average egg collector to the number. The mere accumulation of specimens is the least important object of the true oölogist. His principal aim should be to make careful observations on the habits, call notes, song, the character of the food, mode and length of incubation, and the actions of the species generally, from the beginning of the mating season to the time the young are able to leave the nest. This period comprises the most interesting and instructive part of the life-history of our birds." Very heartily do I endorse every word of this, and to the concluding sentence I would add: and there can be no better way to avoid increasing our knowledge of a bird's domestic life than to rob it of its eggs, and destroy its home and our own opportunities at the same time. Studied from a local standpoint, I confess I can see only two points of interest in a bird's egg—one is what the egg is in, the other is what is in the egg.

Nevertheless, I can understand the pleasure attending the legitimate formation of what Major Bendire has called "a small, thoroughly identified, well-prepared, and neatly cared for collection," which, as the same author adds, "is worth far more scientifically and in every other way than a more extensive one gained by exchange or purchase."

An egg-collector's outfit consists of several drills, an embryo-hook, a blowpipe, forceps, and scissors. A fresh egg should be blown through a hole slightly larger than the tip of the blowpipe. Drill the hole in the side of the egg, and, after inserting the blowpipe about one-sixteenth of an inch, blow gently and steadily until the contents have been removed. Then rinse the egg thoroughly with water and lay it, hole downward, on cornmeal to drain. In eggs containing embryos it is necessary to make a hole large enough to permit of the use of the embryo-hook, scissors, or forceps, as the case may be.

There are many ways of displaying collections of eggs. Some collectors place their eggs in little boxes or partitions filled with sawdust

[1]Part D, Bull. U. S. Nat. Mus., No. 39, 1891, pp. 3–10.

or cotton; Major Bendire used small pasteboard trays lined, bottom and sides, with cotton wadding, and divided into partitions for each egg by strips of cotton wadding set on edge. It is, however, very largely a matter of taste, and collectors generally have their own ideas on these matters.

A collection of birds' nests is a telling object lesson in the study of ornithology. Familiar as I am with them, I never see the nests of some birds without feeling the most intense admiration for the marvelous skill which has aided them in forming a structure man would find it difficult, if not impossible, to duplicate. A bird's nest in its original site is a concrete expression of the intelligence of its maker; for the foresight displayed in the choice of a situation, and the ingenuity shown in the construction of the nest, even if largely instinctive now, originated in the intelligence of a line of ancestors.

Nests may be collected before they have been used, when the birds will generally build again; or you may wait and take them after the birds have left them, labeling each nest with what you have learned of the history of its owners. For example: Time required for its construction; whether made by one or both sexes; notes on the laying of the eggs; period of incubation; whether both sexes assisted in incubation; care of the young; number of days they were in the nest, etc.

Some nests, for example the pendent 'baskets' of Vireos or such as are placed in crotches, should be taken with the crotch or branch to which they are attached. With others it is obviously impossible to do this. They should, therefore, be placed in a frame of wire and wrapped about with fine wire thread. To make this frame, twist two pieces of annealed wire, painted brown, into the shape of a letter X. About midway from the point of intersection and the end of the arm, bend the wires upward at right angles. Now take the fine hair or thread wire and wind it about the four horizontal arms of the frame until its bottom looks like a spider's web; place the nest in this half-formed basket, bend the upright wires inward or outward as the case requires, and continue winding until the nest is bound firmly. The size of the frame and the wire used in its construction may be varied to suit the nest.

REFERENCES

1891. HORNADAY, W. T., Taxidermy and Zoölogical Collecting, 8vo, 362 pp., illus. (Scribner's).—1923. CHAPIN, J. P., The Preparation of Birds for Study, Guide Leaflet No. 58, Amer. Mus. Nat. Hist., 45 pp., illus.— 1925. ROWLEY, J., Taxidermy and Museum Exhibition, 8vo, 331 pp., illus. (Appleton).

BIRD-BANDING

What collecting was to the ornithologist of the preceding generation, bird-banding is to the ornithologist of today. It supplies a definite and highly important outlet for his desire 'to do' something, brings him into intimate contact with the individual bird, stimulates an interest in the activities of his fellow banders as well as in the

problems their labors are helping to solve. These problems, as stated
by Lincoln and Baldwin (1929), are in part as follows:

"*Migration.*—What are the arriving and leaving times? How long
will individuals of different species remain at the station? Is departure
before or after a storm? What is the effect of weather on daily movements? Is the same route followed in successive seasons? Is the same
route followed in spring and fall flights? Is travel continued daily or
only when weather conditions are favorable? Do males, females, and
young travel together, or if separately, which comes or goes first? Is
there much return to the same nest or nesting locality? Is there much
return to the same winter quarters? What proportion of adults and
young return, regardless of seasons? Are the same stop-overs made in
succeeding seasons? Do some individuals of a species remain sedentary
while others of the same species pass over them in migration? Do
adults or young make any postnuptial migrations to the north before
starting south?

"*Territory.*—What is the range-limit during breeding, winter, or
other seasons? What are the territorial limits about nests? Do both
birds defend the territory?

"*Dispersal.*—What are the facts in connection with dispersal of
young that do not return to area where they were hatched? (This
may have to do with extension of range locally or on a large scale.)
What proportion of males and females return to the same nesting-sites?
When leaving the nest do the parents keep the young in the nesting
locality or lead them into adjacent territory? How strong is the homing
instinct of different species? (Tests by experiment.)

"*Ecological Preferences.*—What are the reasons for preference of
different types of environment, and can different species be attracted
away from the preferred type? Is the preferred habitat valley, upland,
mountain, marsh, shore, etc.? What appears to be the effect of changes
in temperature, moisture, vegetative covering, etc.? What species are
adaptable to changes in environment, that is, are plastic?

"*Family Groups.*—What is the length of time that the unity of the
family is preserved? Are these groups the family parties from a neighborhood? If not, are they grouped by age or sex?

"*Permanent Residents.*—Are so-called 'permanent residents' the
same individuals or is there a movement of greater or lesser extent
in such species?

"*Mating Activities.*—What are the facts relative to permanence of
matings? Does polygamy, polyandry, or inbreeding take place? In
case of death of one of a mated pair, will the other obtain a new mate?
What is the number of broods per season? What part is taken by both
sexes in nest-building and care of the young? Is the first nest used
for a second brood? What species breed their first year, i. e., when one
year old? Are eggs laid at the rate of one a day; and if so, at about
what hour? When is incubation begun, and do eggs hatch in the order
in which they were laid? Do both sexes participate in incubation; and

if so, what is the regular period of duty for each? During incubation (when by one bird only), how much time is taken and when for feeding, or is food supplied by the mate?

"Plumage.—What is the sequence of plumage changes by fading, wear, and molt? How does the development of feather tracts, feather colors, and patterns from fledgling to adult take place? Are there detectable differences in sex in species where male and female are similarly colored and marked? Is there any variation in the color of the iris, bill, and feet among individuals of a single species? How does the plumage develop on young birds from the first down to the fully formed feather? Are there any differences in the development within one brood?

"Longevity.—What is the normal length of life of different species as shown by yearly return records?

"Personality.—Do individual birds have peculiarities in appearance, habits, and manners? (Banded birds are individuals and should be studied as such. Some will be wild, others tame and gentle; some will always fight, others will scold or squeal; some will exhibit courage or daring, others will show fear; some will give characteristic notes or even sing under stress of excitement. All of these and many other items have a bearing upon bird psychology, and should be watched for and carefully investigated.)"

Several times during the first two decades of this century attempts were made to promote bird-banding in this country but it was not until 1920 when, inspired by S. Prentiss Baldwin, it became a part of the work of the Biological Survey, that this important branch of field ornithology received adequate and continuous support. In 1928, Frederick C. Lincoln, of the Biological Survey, states that bands had been supplied to 1200 persons most of whom operate stations where birds are systematically trapped and banded throughout the year, and, he adds that at the end of that year more than 400,000 birds had been banded, from which more than 19,000 usable returns had been received. While the results to be obtained are of wide scientific value, they are of especial importance to the Survey in the administration of the Federal Migratory Bird Law.

Under the impetus of thorough organization supplied by the Survey, bird-banding has become the most important field activity of American ornithologists. Several societies and publications are devoted to its special interests, and its results appear in many other mediums.

Before the Biological Survey issues the permit required legally to band birds it must be convinced that the applicant's knowledge of ornithology is sufficiently advanced to enable him to identify correctly the bird banded. Given this knowledge—and the permit—there is no activity in which the student with limited time and opportunity can engage with greater profit to himself and his science. His 'field' may be no larger than his window-sill and still yield data of value. Certain of the discoveries of the bird-bander are referred to elsewhere and will not be recounted here. The literature of bird-banding has already assumed surprising proportions. The more comprehensive of these publications have been issued by the Government, and those still in print may be secured from the Superintendent of Documents, at Washington, D. C., at a nominal price. To these publications the interested student is referred.

REFERENCES

Mr. F. C. Lincoln's 'Bibliography of Bird Banding in America,' published in *The Auk* for 1928 (Suppl. pp. 1–73) fully covers the subject up to that year. From it I select the more important titles relating chiefly to the general subject and add references to several of more recent date.

1910. COLE, L. J., The Tagging of Wild Birds, Auk, pp. 153–168.—1913. CLEAVES, H. H., What the American Bird Banding Assoc. Has Accomplished During 1912, Auk, pp. 248–261, illus.—1919. BALDWIN, S. P., Bird Banding by Means of Systematic Trapping. Abst. Proc. Linn. Soc., N. Y., No. 31, pp. 23–56, illus. Reprinted by the Cleveland Mus. Nat. Hist., 1931, Sci. Pub. I, No. 5.—1921. LINCOLN, F. C., History and Purposes of Bird Banding, Auk, pp. 217–228.—1923. OBERHOLSER, H. C., Bird Banding as an Aid to the Study of Migration, Auk, pp. 436–441.—1924a. LINCOLN, F. C., Instructions for Banding Birds, Misc. Circ. No. 18, U. S. Dept. Agric., pp. 1–28, illus.—1924b. LINCOLN, F. C., Returns from Banded Birds, 1920 to 1923. Bull. 1268, U. S. Dept. Agric., pp. 1–56, illus.—1924. LLOYD, H., Official Canadian Record of Bird-banding Returns. Can. Field Nat. See also Ibid., following years.—1925. GROSS, A. O., Work for Bird Banders, Auk, pp. 95–104.—1927. FORBUSH, E. H., Some Problems for the Bird Bander. Bull. Northeastern Bird Banding Assoc., pp. 33–35.—1927. LINCOLN, F. C., Returns from Banded Birds, 1923–1926. Tech. Bull. 32, U. S. Dept. Agric., pp. 1–96.—1928. NELSON, E. W., Bird Banding: The Telltale of Migratory Flight. Nat. Geog. Mag., Jan., pp. 91–132.—1928. ROWAN, W., Scientific Aspects of Bird-Banding. Bull. Northeastern Bird-banding Assoc., pp. 31–42.—1929. LINCOLN, F. C., and BALDWIN, S. P., Manual for Bird Banders. Misc. Circ. 58, U. S. Dept. Agric., pp. 1–112, illus.—1931. FRIEDMANN, H., Distribution and Bird-banding. Bird-Banding, pp. 45–51.—1931. LINCOLN, F. C., Bird-banding: Its First Decade under the Biological Survey. Bird-Banding, pp. 27–32.

AMERICAN ORNITHOLOGICAL SOCIETIES

The bird student, particularly if, as so often happens, he be isolated from others of kindred tastes, should, if possible, affiliate himself with one or more of the ornithological societies in this country. In any event, he should aim to secure election to Associate Membership in the American Ornithologists' Union, not alone because this is the first step toward becoming a Fellow of this organization, "the highest honor to which an American ornithologist can attain," but also because he will be brought into communication with the leading bird students of this country, who, he may be assured, will never fail to respond to his requests for information or advice. A list of the principal ornithological societies, together with one of their official organs, is therefore appended.

The American Ornithologists' Union.—Founded 1883. This is

the leading as well as the largest ornithological organization in the country. Membership, which totals more than 3000, is divided into the following classes: Fellows (limited to 50 of 60 years of age or less; unlimited for persons of more than 60 years of age), Honorary Fellows (limited to 25), Corresponding Fellows (limited to 75), Elective Members (limited to 200, unlimited for persons of more than 60 years of age), Members (unlimited in number). All bird students are eligible as candidates for election to membership. Annual Congresses are held in late summer or fall at various places in the United States and Canada. Dues $5 per year.

Official organ, *The Auk*, free to all members. Address, American Ornithologists' Union, c/o L. Richard Mewaldt, Department of Biological Sciences, San Jose State College, San Jose, California 95114. (For a history of the Union, see J. A. Allen in *Bird-Lore*, 1899, pp. 143–148.)

Cooper Ornithological Society, Inc.—Founded 1893. Organ, *The Condor*. Address, c/o Alden H. Miller, Museum of Vertebrate Zoology, Berkeley 4, California.

Delaware Valley Ornithological Club.—Founded 1890. Organ, *Cassinia*. Address, c/o the Academy of Natural Sciences, Philadelphia, Pennsylvania. (For a history of the Club, see S. N. Rhoads in *Bird-Lore*, 1902, pp. 57–61.)

Linnæan Society of New York.—Founded 1878. While devoted to Natural History in general, the active membership of the Linnæan Society is composed chiefly of bird students. Organ, *Newsletter, Proceedings and Transactions*. Address, c/o the American Museum of Natural History, Central Park West at 79th Street, New York, New York 10024.

National Audubon Society.—Founded 1905. Organ, *Audubon Magazine*. Issues educational leaflets for teachers and literature relating to bird conservation. Address, 1130 Fifth Avenue, New York, New York 10028.

Ottawa Field-Naturalists' Club.—Founded 1879. Organ, *The Canadian Field-Naturalist*. Address, F. R. Cook, Editor, National Museum, Ottawa, Canada. The objects of the club are to foster an acquaintance with and love of nature, to encourage investigation and the publication of the results of original research and observations in all branches of natural history.

Wilson Ornithological Society.—Founded 1888. Organ, *Wilson Bulletin*. Address, c/o C. Chandler Ross, Treasurer, Academy of Natural Sciences, 19th and Parkway, Philadelphia 3, Pennsylvania.

CURRENT ORNITHOLOGICAL MAGAZINES

Audubon Magazine.—Organ of the National Audubon Society. Bi-monthly. Formerly *Bird-Lore*, established 1899. Annual subscription $7 (free to members of N. A. S.). Address, 1130 Fifth Avenue, New York, New York 10028.

The Auk.—Organ of the American Ornithologists' Union. Quarterly. Established as the Bulletin of the Nuttall Ornithological Club in 1876, taking its present name in 1884 after the organization of the A. O. U. in 1883. Each recent volume contains about 600 pages, a number of half-tones and, occasionally, colored plates. Subscription, $6 per annum (free to members of the A. O. U.). Address, c/o L. Richard Mewaldt, Department of Biological Sciences, San Jose State College, San Jose, California 95114.

Bird-Banding.—Organ of the Northeastern, Eastern, and Inland Bird-Banding Associations. Quarterly. Address, Mrs. J. R. Downs, Treasurer, South Londonderry, Vermont 05155.

The Condor.—Organ of the Cooper Ornithological Society. Bi-monthly. Established in 1899. Each volume contains about 500 pages and numerous half-tones. Annual subscription $5 (free to members of the C. O. S.). Address, c/o Alden H. Miller, Museum of Vertebrate Zoology, Berkeley 4, California.

Wilson Bulletin.—Quarterly. Organ of the Wilson Ornithological Society. Established in 1889. Each volume contains about 300 pages, a number of half-tones, and occasional colored plates. Annual subscription, $5 (free to members of the W. O. S.). Address, c/o C. Chandler Ross, Treasurer, Academy of Natural Sciences, 19th and Parkway, Philadelphia 3, Pennsylvania.

CHAPTER III

THE STUDY OF BIRDS IN NATURE

THE DISTRIBUTION OF BIRDS
THE MIGRATION OF BIRDS
THE VOICE OF BIRDS
THE NESTING SEASON
THE PLUMAGE OF BIRDS
THE FOOD OF BIRDS
GENERAL ACTIVITIES OF THE ADULT BIRD

For one person with the time and equipment essential to research in systematic ornithology, there are hundreds, equally ambitious, but handicapped by limited opportunity and inadequate material. To what problems can these amateur students turn their attention? How can they gratify their ambition to make some noteworthy contribution to the science of birds?

Large collections and museum facilities are within reach of comparatively few, but living birds are everywhere; even the Sparrow of our streets is worthy of our attention, and anyone who can get out-of-doors has the opportunity to add to our knowledge of birds. Indeed, observations of real value have been made from a window or from an invalid's chair.

It is proposed, therefore, to present here at least an outline of those branches of ornithology which relate to the habits of birds, with the object of suggesting some field to which the student may devote his attention. To do this at great length, however, would require a volume alone, and I have therefore dwelt fully on only those two branches of bird-study which especially interest the field student—migration and nesting—treating other phases of the subject in less detail.

The importance of specialization, with a definite end in view, cannot be too strongly emphasized. Select a subject for investigation, or a species, preferably the most common one in your vicinity, for continued observation, and your studies will acquire a character, importance, and interest which they lacked before. Not only will you pursue your field-work with renewed pleasure and enthusiasm, but your researches will lead to the reading of publications which before seemed unattractive, and your search for information will develop a correspondence with fellow students throughout the country, widening your horizon and leading to those delightful associations born of kindred tastes.

It must not, however, be supposed that one cannot enjoy an acquaintance with birds without a formal attempt to add to our knowledge of them. Bird study may not necessarily be anything so serious as a study; it may be merely a recreation, a pastime, even a 'fad,' if you like; but so long as our interest in birds is sufficient to take us to their haunts, or so long as the voice of a bird expresses for us that joy in nature which is the rightful heritage of every human being, just so long will it repay us to add to our sources of pleasure that knowledge of birds which will permit us to "come at these enchantments." But, however specialized or localized one's studies may be, they should rest on a broad general survey of the whole field of ornithology. To this end we especially commend a careful reading of the works mentioned below.

REFERENCES

1910. PYCRAFT, W. P., A History of Birds, 8vo, 458 pp., illus. (Methuen & Co., London).—1916. HUXLEY, J. S., Bird Watching and Biological Science, Auk, XXXIII, pp. 142–161; 256–270.—1923. THOMPSON, J. A., Biology of Birds, 436 pp., illus. (Macmillan).—1926. ALLEN, G. M., Birds and Their Attributes, 335 pp., (Marshall Jones Co., Boston).—1927. HEILMANN, G., The Origin of Birds, 210 pp., illus. (Appleton).—1931. WELLS, HUXLEY, and WELLS, The Science of Life, 2 vols. (Doubleday, Doran & Co.); especially chapters on Variation and Distribution, Genetics, Habitats, Ecology, and Behavior.

(See also beyond references to Monographs under Bob-white, Red-winged Blackbird, and Cowbird.)

THE DISTRIBUTION OF BIRDS

Factors Influencing Distribution
Faunal Areas
Zones of the Boreal Region
Zones of the Austral Region
Floridian Fauna

Factors Influencing Distribution.—Possessed of a space-defying means of locomotion, birds are more widely distributed than any other vertebrates; but in spite of their unexcelled mobility their sensitive organizations respond quickly to those influences which determine the distribution of life. Consequently we find that while some species have an almost world-wide range, others are confined to surprisingly restricted areas. The factors determining the boundaries of the region inhabited by any given bird may be classed primarily under the heads of Past and Present. Past factors include those great earth-forming forces which, through a series of profoundly important changes, have brought about the now long-standing inter-relation of land areas—in other words, the world as we know it. The land bridges which connected Great Britain with the Continent, or Alaska with Siberia, and the strait which separated the American continents at Panama are factors of this kind. In their time they obviously exercised a powerful influence on the distribution of life. Were we equally sure of all the land connections and water separations which have existed since life appeared on the earth, we might hope to solve many at present inexplicable problems in distribution.

Of far-reaching importance also has been the evolution of climates which this globe has witnessed, and which, through tJ e last Glacial Period, has introduced the climate under which we now live. Reference to page 63 will explain how the distribution of White Pelicans, for example, is believed to have been affected by such past climatic changes.

Climate, of course, has never ceased to exert its influence on the distribution of life, and we find it the most active present-day factor. It is expressed mainly through temperature, and, to a lesser extent, through rainfall. Thus the boundaries of the three transcontinental zones forming the Austral Region (see map) conform more or less closely to certain isotherms, or lines of equal temperature, but their eastern and western faunal subdivisions are determined by the annual precipitation of rain. Any factors such as altitude, exposure in relation to the sun, or proximity to water, which affect temperature exert a marked influence on the boundaries of faunas and must of course be considered in mapping faunal areas.

Outside of purely tropical regions, as Merriam ('94) has shown, temperature is not active throughout the year, but only at certain seasons. Merriam has therefore formulated the following Laws of Temperature Control: First, "Animals and plants are restricted in northward distribution by the total quantity of heat during the season of growth and reproduction." Second, "Animals and plants are restricted in southward distribution by the mean temperature of a brief period covering the hottest part of the year." With birds, of course, it should be understood that the southern as well as northern limits of the *breeding*-range are here referred to.

Faunal Areas.—It is not possible for us to treat, even in outline, this absorbing and important subject, but for practical purposes, if for no other reasons, the student should become familiar with the boundaries of the faunal areas of North America, as well as the names of the birds which characterize them. This is the study of faunal geography, or zoögeography, as compared with that of political geography.

Examination of maps showing (1) the ranges of the families, (2) the genera, and (3) the species of birds, reveals the fact that many families, genera and species are distributed, respectively, over essentially the same parts of the earth's surface. It will also be found that these areas are occupied by other families, genera and species of animals as well as of plants. Such areas are therefore called natural life areas, and their rank conforms more or less closely to the systematic standing of the groups of animals inhabiting them. While the faunal terms employed are not always used in the same sense (see Merriam '92, and Allen '93), it may be said that families are distributed through regions, genera through zones, and species in faunas.

North America, it will be observed on the map, here reproduced by courtesy of the Biological Survey, is divided primarily into three Regions,[1] the Boreal, the Austral and the Tropical. The last, occupying only the southern extremities of Florida and Lower California, has in these limits no zonal subdivisions.

Zones of the Boreal Region.—The Boreal Region includes three transcontinental zones—the Arctic, the Hudsonian, and the Canadian. The first-named extends southward to the northern limit of forests, and not only crosses this continent but is circumpolar; the uniform climatic conditions of the Arctic portions of both hemispheres, in connection with their comparative proximity, being responsible for essentially similar faunas. Consequently, Ptarmigan, Gyrfalcons, Snowy Owls, Snow Buntings, and numerous species of water-birds are found in northern Eurasia as well as in northern North America. In fact, as Allen ('93) has shown, 60 of the 65 genera of birds occurring in the American Arctic are circumpolar. The parts of the Rocky Mountains and Sierras reaching above timberline, where, at the border of perpetual snow, Leucostictes, the Pipit and White-tailed Ptarmigan nest, should, it seems, also be included in the Arctic Zone, altitude rather than latitude here giving the required low temperature.

The Hudsonian Zone marks the northern limit of forest-growth of firs and spruces. It will be observed that on both the Atlantic and Pacific coasts, as well as along the Mackenzie River, its northern limits are considerably extended, while southward it pushes a spur down the crest of the Rocky Mountains with outlying 'islands' as far south as Colorado and New Mexico. The Rough-legged Hawk, Great Gray Owl, Northern Shrike, Alice's Thrush and Pine Grosbeak are characteristic birds of this zone.

The Canadian Zone is distinguished by the high development of its coniferous forests. Its extension southward along the Alleghanies will be noted, its altitude increasing as the latitude decreases. Thus, where primeval coniferous forests have not been destroyed, the Canadian Zone appears in Massachusetts at an elevation of 1,800 feet (Howe and Allen), in Pennsylvania at 2,000 feet (Dwight), and in North Carolina at 4,500 feet (Brewster).

Reference to the Biological Survey map will show how numerous are the Canadian Zone 'islands' on the higher portions of our western mountain systems. Evidences of this zone should also be shown at least as far south as the southern end of the Mexican tableland, where at an elevation of from 8,000 to 13,000 feet in heavy forests of pine and spruce, such characteristic Canadian species as the Red Crossbill, Evening Grosbeak, Junco, Siskin, and Brown Creeper are represented by closely allied forms which breed there in abundance.

In addition to the species just named, the Canadian Zone is characterized by the presence, in the nesting season, of the Goshawk, Hawk Owl, Spruce Partridge, Three-toed Woodpeckers, Yellow-bellied Flycatcher, Canada Jay, Red-breasted Nuthatch, Winter Wren, Hermit, Olive-backed and Bicknell's Thrushes, Golden-crowned and Ruby-

[1]For detailed consideration of the characteristics of these Regions, consult Merriam '98.

crowned Kinglets, Tennessee, Bay-breasted, Blackpoll, Magnolia, Myrtle, Blackburnian and Canadian Warblers, White-throated Sparrow.

Zones of the Austral Region.—The Transition, Upper Austral, and Lower Austral Zones, as has been before remarked, are transcontinental, but differences in rainfall separate them into eastern humid, western arid, and Pacific coast humid divisions.

The eastern humid and western arid divisions merge into one another at about the one-hundredth meridian, or, approximately, where, in going westward, the prairies pass into the plains. To the eastward of this meridian the annual rainfall exceeds 25 inches; to the westward, except on the Pacific coast, it is below this amount.

In the present connection we may restrict our statements concerning the three zones of the Austral Region to their eastern or humid portions, which have long been known as the Alleghanian, Carolinian, and Austroriparian or Louisianian faunas (see Allen '71).

The Alleghanian, as will be observed on the map, extends at sealevel only as far south as Long Island, where, in response to conditions which produce scrub oak and pitch pines, it occupies the southern portion of the island, while the Carolinian element is restricted to the more fertile northern shore.

Crossing northern New Jersey and northeastern Pennsylvania, the Alleghanian fauna extends southwestward along the Alleghanies to northern Georgia, appearing at an ever-increasing altitude. Thus in western Maryland its lower limit is 1,200–1,300 feet (Preble), in North Carolina 2,500 feet (Brewster), and in Georgia 3,500 feet (Howell).

The following species are characteristic of the Alleghanian fauna: Sora, Virginia Rail, Bob-white, Mourning Dove, Yellow-billed Cuckoo, Black-billed Cuckoo, Kingbird, Crested Flycatcher, White-breasted Nuthatch, House Wren, Long-billed Marsh Wren, Brown Thrasher, Catbird, Wood Thrush, Veery, Yellow-throated and Blue-headed Vireos, Golden-winged and Pine Warblers, Meadowlark, Baltimore Oriole, Bobolink, Cowbird, Indigo Bunting, Towhee, and Chipping and Field Sparrows.

The Carolinian fauna, or humid division of the Upper Austral Zone, reaches the Atlantic seaboard only between Virginia and southeastern New York. Westward it ascends the Alleghanies to an altitude of 1,200 feet in Maryland (Preble), 2,500 feet in North Carolina (Brewster), and 3,500 feet in extreme northeastern Georgia (Howell). At this point it sweeps around the extreme southern extension of the Alleghanian fauna and expands toward the north and west as indicated by the map. In the Atlantic States a tinge of the Carolinian fauna is present at least as far east as Saybrook, Conn., and as far north as Portland in the Connecticut Valley, and Fishkill in the Hudson Valley.

Characteristic Carolinian birds are Acadian Flycatcher, Fish Crow, Tufted Titmouse, Carolina Wren, Blue-winged, Worm-eating, Hooded and Kentucky Warblers, Louisiana Water-Thrush, Chat, Cardinal.

The Austroriparian fauna, or humid division of the Lower Austral Zone, as its name implies, occupies the South Atlantic States from the vicinity of Cape Charles, Virginia, to the sub-tropical portions of southern Florida, thence westward through the Gulf States and northward in the Mississippi Valley to southern Illinois and southern Kansas. Among its characteristic birds are the Water-Turkey, Louisiana Heron, Black Vulture, Ground Dove, Carolina Paroquet (now extinct), Chuckwill's-widow, Ivory-billed Woodpecker, Brown-headed Nuthatch, Yellow-throated Warbler, Boat-tailed Grackle, Bachman's Sparrow, Nonpareil.

Floridian Fauna.—To the three faunas above named may be added the Floridian fauna, a name applied to that part of the Subtropical Region which occupies southern Florida as far north as Lake Worth on the Atlantic Coast and the mouth of the Caloosahatchie River on the Gulf Coast, which is approximately the northern limit of cocoanut palms. The species which characterize this fauna are mainly West Indian, and a number of them are confined to the Florida Keys. They are the Great White Heron, Reddish Egret, Noddy and Sooty Terns, Everglade Kite, Caracara, White-crowned Pigeon, Mangrove Cuckoo, Black-whiskered Vireo.

SUGGESTIONS FOR THE STUDENT

What group of animals is most widely distributed? Mention several wide-ranging species of birds and outline their distribution. Mention several having a restricted range on continental areas. Mention several which are confined to islands. What factors have exerted an influence on the distribution of birds? Illustrate with definite instances. Mention several islands which were formerly connected with continents. Compare their bird-life with that of the adjoining part of the continent from which they have been separated. Describe the probable influence of the Glacial Period on the distribution of the White Pelicans (see beyond, under Migration). Mention other groups of birds which have probably been similarly affected. What are the factors now controlling the distribution of birds? Compare the effect of temperature with that produced by humidity. What is Merriam's Law of Temperature Control? How may altitude and slope exposure influence distribution? Compare political with zoölogical geography. How are the boundaries of natural life areas determined? What are the primary life areas of North America? Name and outline the three zones of the Boreal Region and mention several species characteristic of each. Describe the general characters of each zone: topography, climate, forest-growth, etc. Treat in a similar manner the humid portions of the Austral Region, and the Floridian fauna of the Tropical Region, tracing their extent in the map, mentioning some characteristic trees, plants and crops as well as birds, and discussing their general topographic and climatic features in relation to their effect on the distribution of life.

REFERENCES

1871. ALLEN, J. A., A Sketch of the Bird Faunæ of Eastern North America, Bull. Mus. Comp. Zoöl., II, pp. 375–425.—**1892.** ALLEN, J. A., The Geographical Distribution of North American Mammals, Bull. Am. Mus. Nat. Hist., IV, pp. 199–244; maps.—**1892.** MERRIAM, C. H., The

Geographic Distribution of Life in North America with Special Reference to the Mammalia, Proc. Biol. Soc. Wash., VII, pp. 1–64, 1 map.—1893. ALLEN, J. A., The Geographical Origin and Distribution of North American Birds Considered in Relation to the Faunal Areas of North America, Auk, X, pp. 97–150, 2 maps.—1894. MERRIAM, C. H., Laws of Temperature Control of the Geographical Distribution of Terrestrial Animals and Plants, Nat. Geog. Mag., VI, pp. 229–238, 3 maps.—1895. MERRIAM, C. H., The Geographic Distribution of Animals and Plants in North America, Yearbook U. S. Dept. Agric., 1894, pp. 203–214.—1898. MERRIAM, C. H., Life Zones and Crop Zones of the United States, Bull. 10, Biol. Surv., pp. 1–79, 1 map.—1904. RUSSELL, I. C., North America, Chap. III, Climate, pp. 184–203 (Appleton).—1917. GRINNELL, J., Field Notes of Theories Concerning Distributional Control, Am. Nat., LI, pp. 115–128.—1919. HALL, H. M. and GRINNELL, J., Life Zone Indicators in California, Proc. Calif. Acad. Sci., IX, pp. 37–67.

NOTE.—Discussion of the faunal affinities of the region in question will frequently be found as introductory matter in 'local' or state bird lists; see especially (in the Bibliographical Appendix) under Georgia, 1909, Howell; Illinois, 1890, Ridgway; Iowa, 1907, Anderson; Kentucky, 1910, Howell; Maine, 1908, Knight; Maryland, 1900, Merriam and Preble; Massachusetts, 1901, Howe and Allen; Nebraska, 1909, Wolcott; New Hampshire, 1904, Allen; New Jersey, 1894, 1909, Stone; New York, 1910, Eaton; North Carolina, 1886, Brewster; Ohio, 1903, Jones; Pennsylvania, Stone, 1891, 1894; Dwight, 1892; Todd, 1893, 1904. South Carolina, 1890, 1891, Loomis; Tennessee, 1910, Howell; Virginia, 1890, Rives; West Virginia, 1890, 1898, Rives.

THE MIGRATION OF BIRDS

Times of Migration
Extent of Migration
Routes of Migration
How Birds Migrate
Why Do Birds Migrate?

Migration is the most distinctive phase of bird-life. Certain mammals, fishes, and even insects migrate, but no animals approach birds in the extent of their migrations. Wholly aside from the interest which is attached to a study of bird-migration in the broader aspects, as we attempt to determine its origin and extent and the various factors which govern the times and manner of a bird's journeys, there is a fascination and excitement for the student in observing the arrival and passage of the great army of feathered travelers which ever renews itself when birds

> Part loosely wing the region; part more wise,
> In common, ranged in figure, wedge their way
> Intelligent of seasons, and set forth
> Their aëry caravan, high over seas.

To the nature-lover, birds are a living calendar. "What was that sound that came on the softened air? It was the warble of the Bluebird from the scraggy orchard yonder. When this is heard, then has spring arrived."

Times of Migration.—According to the nature of their occurrence the birds of temperate regions may be grouped seasonally as follows:

1. *Permanent Residents.*—Includes species that are represented in the same locality throughout the year. In temperate and boreal eastern North America few species are permanently resident as individuals. Banding shows that Bob-whites and Screech Owls pass their lives in a comparatively restricted area, but that Crows, Jays, and Song Sparrows as individuals are migrants.

2. *Summer Residents.*—Includes species that come to us from farther south in the spring, rear their young, and return to the south in the fall. As a rule, the first species to come in the spring are the last to leave in the fall, while the later arrivals are among the first departures. With this group should also be placed a small number of what may be called 'summer visitants,' composed of birds which, like the Little Blue Heron and White Egrets, after breeding in more southern latitudes may wander as far as several hundred miles northward. The term 'summer visitant' may also be applied to Shearwaters and Petrels, which, having bred in the Southern Hemisphere during our winter, pass the summer off our coasts.

3. *Transient Visitants.*—Includes species which, nesting north of a given locality and wintering south of it, consequently pass through it when migrating. Most transient visitants may be found at a certain locality on both their spring and fall migrations, but a small number occur at only one season. In the Mississippi Valley, for example, the Golden Plover is found in the spring but much less frequently in the fall; while on the Atlantic Coast the Black Tern appears during the fall migration but is rare or unknown in the spring. The earlier transient visitants, for example the Fox Sparrow and Hermit Thrush, may remain in the latitude of New York City for a month or more, but the later arrivals pass by in a week or ten days.

4. *Winter Residents.*—Includes species which come to us in the fall and remain until the spring. Some, like the Junco, are of regular occurrence. Others, like the Pine Grosbeak, may be abundant some winters and rare or wanting other winters. To these four groups may be added a fifth of birds of accidental occurrence.

Let us now review the bird-life of the vicinity of New York City for the year as it is affected by migration. I here abridge from 'Bird-Life.'

January.—Probably during no other month is there less movement among our birds than in January. The regular winter residents have come; the fall migrants, which may have lingered until December, have gone, and the earliest spring migrants will not arrive before the latter part of February or early March. January, in fact, is the only month in the year in which as a rule some birds do not arrive or depart. This rule, however, may be broken by such irregular birds as the Snowy Owl, Pine Grosbeak, or Redpoll, which wander southward in search of food, or by the Evening Grosbeak that comes from the Northwest. Food, indeed, is now the one concern of birds and their movements are largely governed by its supply. Snow may fall and blizzards rage, but so long as birds find sufficient to eat they apparently are not affected by the weather. Where seed-bearing weeds are accessible there we may look for Juncos and Tree Sparrows; cedar trees bearing berries often tempt Waxwings, Robins and Bluebirds to winter near them. When bayberries are abundant we may expect Myrtle Warblers to remain through the winter. I recall a sheltered pile of buckwheat chaff at Englewood, N. J., which furnished food for a small flock of Mourning Doves all one winter. In Central Park, New York City, a Mockingbird, which had evidently escaped from a cage, was under daily observation from October to January, and thrived during the exceptionally severe winter while nourished by the berries of a privet tree. Food, therefore, rather than temperature is the all-important factor in a bird's life at this season.

February.—The conditions prevailing during January will be practically unchanged until the latter half of February. Then, should there be a period of mild weather, we may expect to hear the Meadowlark, Song Sparrow, and Bluebird inaugurate the season of song, and note the appearance of Robins, Purple Grackles, and Red-winged Blackbirds, which pass the winter such a short distance south that they appear at the first sign of returning spring. It is probable that in most cases the first individuals of our summer resident species to arrive remain to nest. (See beyond, under Nesting.)

March.—While March is certain to witness a general northward movement among the birds, the date of their arrival is as uncertain as the weather of the month itself. Continued severe weather prevents the advance which a higher temperature as surely occasions. When ice leaves the bays, ponds, and rivers, we may look for Ducks and Geese. When successive thaws have made the ground soft enough to probe, we may expect the Woodcock. With the advent of insects, their enemy, the Phœbe will appear.

The weather which hastens the arrival of birds from the south also prompts certain of our winter residents to begin their northward journey.

April.—The developments in the plant-world, in early April, which are apparent to the least observant, are accompanied by corresponding but less-noticed activities in the world of birds. The migratory movement now gains strength rapidly, and during the latter part of the month one may expect new arrivals daily.

It will be noted that the earlier migrants of the month are largely seed-eaters, while those which come later are insectivorous, particularly those insect-eaters, which like the Swallow, Swift, and Nighthawk feed upon the wing.

May.—As the season advances, marked changes in temperature are less likely to occur, and the migration becomes more regular and continuous. In February and March there may be two weeks or more variation in the times of arrival of the same species in different years; in May, birds usually arrive within a day or two of a certain date.

Nevertheless, the force of the migratory current is still closely dependent on meteorologic conditions, and under the encouragement of high temperature may reach the proportions of a 'wave,' which when dammed by a sudden return of cold weather, floods the woods with migrants. Birds are then doubtless more abundant than at any other season. The arrival of ten or a dozen species may be noted on the same date, and more than half the birds regularly occurring in a given area may be found in it on a single day Thus, on May 13, 1907, Lynds Jones and two associates observed 144 species of birds on the south shore of Lake Erie, particularly on the sand-spit reaching out to Cedar Point, opposite Sandusky, Ohio.[1] Ten censuses taken yearly in mid-May in Dutchess County, New York, by Maunsell S. Crosby and from two to four associates yielded from 102 to 129 species.[2] The record appears to be held by a group of 50 observers who, on May 17, 1931, found 166 species in and within 10 miles of Potter Swamp, western New York. They worked, however, in detached groups, and the greatest number of species seen by an individual was 102. On the same day, Charles Urner and 10 associates, working as one party, recorded 163 species between Morristown and Atlantic City, N. J.[3]

After the middle of the month, birds begin to decrease in numbers as the transient visitants pass northward, and by the first week in June our bird-life is composed of permanent residents and summer residents.

It will be noticed that with but few exceptions the birds arriving in May are insectivorous, particularly those insect-eating birds which obtain their food from vegetation. Thus, no sooner are the unfolding leaves and opening blossoms exposed to the attack of insects than the Vireos and Warblers appear to protect them, and the abundance of these small birds is the distinctive feature of the bird-life of the month.

June.—June is the home month of the year. Nest-building, egg-laying, incubating, and the care of the young now make constant and exceptional demands on the birds, which, in response, exhibit traits shown only during the nesting season.

A feature of the month is the formation of roots which are nightly frequented by the now fully grown young of such early-breeding birds as European Starlings, Grackles and Robins. When a second brood is reared, as with the Robin, the young may be accompanied to the roost by only the male parent, but in the one-brooded Grackle the roost is used by both adults and young.

July.—The full development of the bird's year is reached in June, and as early as the first week in July there are evidences of a preparation for the journey southward. The young of certain species which rear but one brood, accompanied by their parents, now wander about the country, and may be found in new localities. In some cases these families join others of their kind, forming small flocks, the nucleus of the great gatherings seen later. Examples are Grackles, Starlings, Red-winged Black-birds, Bobolinks, and Tree Swallows. The latter increase rapidly in

[1]*Wilson Bull.*, 1907, p. 104.   [2]*Wilson Bull.*, 1925, p. 150.   [3]*Bird-Lore*, 1931, p. 246.

number, and by July 10 we may see them, late each afternoon, flying to their roosts in the marshes.

It is during this and the following month that the post-breeding northward wanderings of certain more southern birds, notably Herons, occur.

August.—August is the month of molt, and when molting, birds are less in evidence than at any other time. What becomes of many of our birds in August it is difficult to say. Baltimore Orioles, for instance, are rare from the 1st to the 20th, but after that date are seen commonly. Possibly their apparent increase in numbers may in part be due to the fact that they have now in a measure regained their voices and often utter nearly their full song. However this may be, whether the seeming scarcity of birds in August is due to their silence and inactivity or to their actual departure, certain it is that before the fall migration brings arrivals daily from the north, one may spend hours in the woods and see little besides Wood Pewees and Red-eyed Vireos, whose presence is betrayed by the fact that they are still in song.

After the middle of the month, migrants from the north will be found in increasing numbers, but the characteristic bird-life of August will be found in the marshes. There the Swallows, Red-winged Blackbirds and Bobolinks, known now as Reed-birds, come in increasing numbers to roost in the reeds, the last two with the Sora Rail, attracted also by the ripening wild rice.

September.—The first marked fall in the temperature will be followed by a flight of migrants which, because of the denser vegetation and absence of song, are much more difficult of observation than in May. Birds of the year, that is those born the preceding season, will outnumber the adults, and in most cases their plumage will be quite unlike that worn by their parents in May, while, in many instances, even the adults themselves will appear in a changed costume. Often this new dress will resemble that of the immature bird, a fact which in part accounts for the apparent scarcity of old birds in the fall migration.

In September more migrating birds are killed by striking lighthouses or illuminated towers than in any other month of the year. This is doubtless owing to the facts that stormy or foggy weather is more apt to prevail in September than during any other period of active migration; that the majority of migrants are young and inexperienced, and that probably more migrants pass in September than in any other month. It does not follow from this statement, however, that birds may be so abundant on any one day as they are under certain conditions in May, when, as before described, low temperature checks the northward movement and causes an overflow.

About September 25 the first winter residents arrive, and after that date birds rapidly decrease in numbers.

October.—Early October generally brings the first killing frost, causing the leaves to fall in fluttering showers and depriving many insectivorous birds of their food and shelter. Flycatchers, Warblers, Vireos, as well as

Swallows, now take their departure, and after the 15th of the month few insect-eating birds remain, except those which, like Woodpeckers, feed on insects' eggs or larvæ.

This is the season of Sparrows. In countless numbers they throng old stubble, potato- and corn-fields, doing untold good by destroying the seeds of noxious weeds. Song, Field, Chipping and Vesper Sparrows may be found in flocks, and with them will be the lately arrived Juncos, Tree and Fox Sparrows.

The diurnal migration of Crows and of Hawks, which in scattered companies string across the sky, the foraging flocks of Grackles, and the gatherings of European Starlings, are features of the bird-life of the month.

November.—It is an interesting fact that the first migrants to come in the spring are the last to leave in the fall. The bird-life of November, therefore, closely resembles that of March. Doubtless this is because both months furnish essentially the same kind of food. Thus Loons, Grebes, Ducks, Geese and Kingfishers remain until November or early December, when the forming of ice deprives them of food and forces them to seek open water. Woodcock and Snipe linger until they can no longer probe the frost-hardened earth; but the thaws of March will bring all these birds back to us by restoring their food.

December.—The character of the bird-life of December depends largely upon the mildness or severity of the season. Should the ponds and streams remain open, the ground be unfrozen, and little or no snow fall, many of the migrant species of November will linger into December. They rarely are found, however, after the middle of the month, when our bird-life is again reduced to its simplest terms of permanent residents and winter visitants.

Similarity of feeding habits now brings certain species into loose bands whose movements are governed largely by the presence or absence of food and bird-banding has shown that the individuals composing these groups may remain associated throughout the season and even rejoin one another for several successive seasons. Their wanderings may lead them over large areas, and our orchards and dooryards may now be visited by species which will eagerly partake of our bounty. Crumbs and seeds will bring Juncos, Tree Sparrows, and Purple Finches; an old seed-filled sunflower head may prove a feast for Goldfinches, while bits of meat, suet, or ham-bone will be welcomed by Chickadees, Nuthatches, and Downy Woodpeckers. (On this subject of winter feeding, consult the publications of the National Association of Audubon Societies.)

The flight of Crows to and from their roosts is one of the characteristic sights of the bird-life of this season, though in the northeastern states, at least, this movement is less pronounced than in was in former years.

During the winter, 30 species is a good day's record for an area not more than 15 miles in diameter in an inland locality in the eastern United States, but when both upland and coast are explored, this number may be greatly increased. The following records appear in *Bird-Lore's* thirty-first Christmas Census (*Bird-Lore*, Jan.–Feb. 1931, pp. 25–78): Bronx Region, N. Y., 12 observers, 85 species; Cape May County, N. J., 17 observers, 78 species; Jacksonville, Fla., 2 observers, 103 species; Columbus, Ohio, 11 observers, 48 species. On the Pacific Coast, the record is held by Santa Barbara, 22 observers, 129 species.

This outline of changes in the bird-life of the year occasioned by migration, may be summarized by presenting a list of the commoner permanent residents of the vicinity of New York City and adding chronological tables of migration.

PERMANENT RESIDENTS

Sharp-shinned Hawk, Cooper's Hawk, Red-tailed Hawk, Red-shouldered Hawk, Broad-winged Hawk,[1] Marsh Hawk,[1] Bald Eagle,[1] Duck Hawk,[1] Sparrow Hawk, Ruffed Grouse, Bob-white, Screech Owl, Barred Owl, Short-eared Owl, Great Horned Owl, Long-eared Owl, Hairy Woodpecker, Downy Woodpecker, Red-headed Woodpecker,[1] Flicker, Blue Jay, American Crow, Fish Crow, Tufted Titmouse, Chickadee, White-breasted Nuthatch, Carolina Wren,[1] Robin,[1] Bluebird, Cedar Waxwing,[1] Starling, House Sparrow, Meadowlark, Cardinal, American Goldfinch, Purple Finch, Song Sparrow.

To complete the possible winter avifauna, a list of winter resident land birds and of the commoner winter water-birds is added.

WINTER RESIDENTS

Surf Scoter, Old Squaw, White-winged Scoter, Herring Gull, Black-backed Gull, Bonaparte's Gull, Kittiwake, Saw-whet Owl,[1] Horned Lark, Prairie Horned Lark, Red-breasted Nuthatch,[1] Brown Creeper, Winter Wren, Golden-crowned Kinglet, Northern Shrike,[1] Pine Grosbeak,[1] Evening Grosbeak,[1] Red Crossbill,[1] White-winged Crossbill,[1] Redpoll,[1] Pine Siskin,[1] Tree Sparrow, Junco, Lapland Longspur,[1] Snowflake.

SPRING MIGRATION

Arrival of Summer Residents and Transients[2] from the South.

February 15–March 10.—Canada Goose (April 20–30), Mallard (May), Baldpate (April 15), Pintail (April), Greater Scaup Duck (April 20–30), Canvasback (April 15), Robin, Bluebird, Red-winged Blackbird, Purple Grackle, Rusty Blackbird (May 1–10).

March 10–20.—Great Blue Heron, Killdeer, Piping Plover, Woodcock, Phœbe, Meadowlark, Cowbird, Fox Sparrow (April 1–15).

March 20–31.—Gannet (May 30), Black-crowned Night Heron, Blue-winged Teal (May), Wood Duck, Red-breasted Merganser

---

[1] Rare or irregular in winter.
[2] The date of departure for the North of Transient Visitants is enclosed in parentheses. The omission of this date indicates a Summer Resident.

(May 1–10), Hooded Merganser (May), Wilson's Snipe (May 1–10), Greater Yellowlegs (June 10), Mourning Dove, Kingfisher, Field Sparrow, White-throated Sparrow (May 15–30), Swamp Sparrow.

April 1–10.—Pied-billed Grebe, Double-crested Cormorant (June 20), Little Blue Heron, Bonaparte's Gull (May 20), Osprey, Tree Swallow (May 15–31), Hermit Thrush (April 25–May 5), Pipit (April 15–25), Myrtle Warbler (May 10–20), Purple Finch, Vesper Sparrow, Savannah Sparrow (May 1–15), Chipping Sparrow.

April 10–20.—Green Heron, Bittern, Clapper Rail, Least Sandpiper (June 1), Red-backed Sandpiper (June 10), Sanderling (June 1), Common Tern, Yellow-bellied Sapsucker (April 20–30), Barn Swallow, Ruby-crowned Kinglet (May 1–15), Pine Warbler, Yellow Palm Warbler (April 25–May 10), Louisiana Water-Thrush.

April 20–30.—Sora, Virginia Rail, Semipalmated Plover (June 10), Spotted Sandpiper, Northern Phalarope (June 1), Whip-poor-will, Chimney Swift, Least Flycatcher, Rough-winged Swallow, Bank Swallow, Cliff Swallow, Purple Martin, House Wren, Brown Thrasher, Catbird, Wood Thrush, Blue-headed Vireo (May 10–15), Black and White Warbler, Black-throated Green Warbler (May 15–25), Ovenbird, Towhee, Seaside Sparrow, Sharp-tailed Sparrow.

May 1–10.—Least Bittern, Black-bellied Plover (June 10), Ruddy Turnstone (June 10), Semipalmated Sandpiper (June 1–10), Solitary Sandpiper (June 1), Parasitic Jaeger, Laughing Gull, Yellow-billed Cuckoo, Black-billed Cuckoo, Nighthawk, Ruby-throated Humming-bird, Kingbird, Crested Flycatcher, Veery, Red-eyed Vireo, White-eyed Vireo, Warbling Vireo, Yellow-throated Vireo, Worm-eating Warbler, Blue-winged Warbler, Nashville Warbler (May 15–25), Parula Warbler, Yellow Warbler, Black-throated Blue Warbler (May 15–30), Magnolia Warbler (May 15–30), Chestnut-sided Warbler, Prairie Warbler, Maryland Yellow-throat, Hooded Warbler, Northern Water-Thrush (May 10–30), Chat, Redstart, Scarlet Tanager, Bobolink, Orchard Oriole, Baltimore Oriole, Rose-breasted Grosbeak, Indigo Bunting, Grasshopper Sparrow, Lincoln's Sparrow (May 15–25).

May 10–20.—Knot (June 10), Wood Pewee, Yellow-bellied Fly-catcher (May 20–30), Alder Flycatcher, Acadian Flycatcher, Long-billed Marsh Wren, Short-billed Marsh Wren, Olive-backed Thrush (May 20–30), Gray-cheeked Thrush (May 25–June 5), Bicknell's Thrush (May 25–June 5), Golden-winged Warbler (May 15–30), Tennessee Warbler (May 15–30), Cape May Warbler (May 15–30), Blackburnian Warbler (May 15–30), Bay-breasted Warbler (May 15–30), Blackpoll Warbler (May 25–June 5), Mourning Warbler (May 20–30), Wilson's Warbler (May 20–30), Canadian Warbler (May 25–June 5), White-crowned Sparrow (May 20–30).

May 20–31.—Greater Shearwater, Sooty Shearwater, Wilson's Petrel.

FALL MIGRATION

I. Departure of Summer Residents for the South.

September 1–10.—Acadian Flycatcher, Rough-winged Swallow, Worm-eating Warbler, Blue-winged Warbler, Orchard Oriole.

September 10–20.—Least Tern, Wilson's Petrel, Purple Martin, Yellow Warbler, Chat, Baltimore Oriole.

September 20–30.—Least Bittern, Spotted Sandpiper, Hummingbird, Kingbird, Crested Flycatcher, Wood Pewee, Veery, Warbling Vireo, Yellow-throated Vireo, Louisiana Water-Thrush, Hooded Warbler, Rose-breasted Grosbeak, Seaside Sparrow.

October 1–10.—Clapper Rail, Yellow-billed Cuckoo, Black-billed Cuckoo, Chimney Swift, Least Flycatcher, Cliff Swallow, Barn Swallow, Wood Thrush, White-eyed Vireo, Chestnut-sided Warbler, Redstart, Ovenbird, Scarlet Tanager, Bobolink, Indigo Bunting, Grasshopper Sparrow.

October 10–20.—Sooty Shearwater, Green Heron, Piping Plover, Whip-poor-will, Nighthawk, House Wren, Long-billed Marsh Wren, Short-billed Marsh Wren, Catbird, Brown Thrasher, Red-eyed Vireo, Black and White Warbler, Maryland Yellow-throat, Sharp-tailed Sparrow.

October 20–31.—Phœbe, Tree Swallow, Towhee.

November 1–30.[1]—Greater Shearwater, Black-crowned Night Heron, Wood Duck, Virginia Rail, Clapper Rail, Killdeer, Woodcock, Laughing Gull, Common Tern, Mourning Dove, Kingfisher, Red-winged Blackbird, Purple Grackle, Cowbird, Vesper Sparrow, Field Sparrow, Chipping Sparrow, Swamp Sparrow.

II. Arrival of Transients and Winter Visitants from the North.[2]

July 1–10.—Little Blue Heron (September 20), Dowitcher (October 1), Pectoral Sandpiper (November 1), Least Sandpiper (October 15), Greater Yellowlegs (November 20), Lesser Yellowlegs (October 15), Hudsonian Curlew (October 10).

July 10–20.—Parasitic Jaeger (November 15), Great Blue Heron (January 1), American Egret (September 20), Semipalmated Plover (October 31), Semipalmated Sandpiper (October 31), Solitary Sandpiper (October 10), Sanderling (December).

July 20–31.—Blue-winged Teal (November 20), Black-bellied Plover (November 20), White-rumped Sandpiper (November 10), Knot (November).

August 1–15.—Cory's Shearwater (November), Double-crested Cormorant (December 15), Mallard (December 15), Baldpate (December 20), Pintail (December 20), Sora (October 15–31), Ruddy Turnstone (October 10), Wilson's Snipe (December 1), Northern Phalarope (October 20), Ring-billed Gull (May), Forster's Tern (October 15),

[1]Should the weather be mild some of these birds may remain until late December.
[2]Figures in parentheses show date of departure.

Black Tern (October 15), Yellow bellied Flycatcher (September 20–30), Golden-winged Warbler (September 1–10), Canadian Warbler (September 20–30), Northern Water-Thrush (September 25–October 5).

August 15–31.—Common Loon (June), Golden Plover (November), Herring Gull (May), Olive-sided Flycatcher (September 10–20), Redbreasted Nuthatch (November 1–30), Migrant Shrike (September), Tennessee Warbler (September 25–October 5), Nashville Warbler (September 25–October 5), Cape May Warbler (September 25–October 5), Black-throated Green Warbler (October 15–31), Magnolia Warbler (October 10–20), Blackburnian Warbler (September 20–30), Wilson's Warbler (September 20–30).

September 1–10.—Greater Scaup Duck (May), American Coot (December 25), Black-backed Gull (May), Bonaparte's Gull (January 20), Blackpoll Warbler (October 15–25), Connecticut Warbler (September 20–30), Lincoln's Sparrow (November 15–30).

September 10–20.—Red-throated Loon (May), White-winged Scoter (May 31), Red-backed Sandpiper (December), Wilson's Snipe (October 15–30), Olive-backed Thrush (October 20–30), Bicknell's Thrush (October 20–30), Blue-headed Vireo (October 15–25), Philadelphia Vireo (October 15–25).

September 20–30.—Red-breasted Merganser, Yellow-bellied Sapsucker (October 20–30), Brown Creeper (April), Winter Wren (April), Gray-cheeked Thrush (October 15–25), Ruby-crowned Kinglet (October 20–30), Golden-crowned Kinglet (April), Myrtle Warbler (May 5–20), Yellow Palm Warbler (October 15–30), Junco (May 1–10), White-throated Sparrow (May 1–20), White-crowned Sparrow (October 15–30).

October 1–10.—Horned Grebe (May), Gannet (January 1), Canada Goose (May 30), Canvasback (January 1), Lesser Scaup (May 20), Bufflehead (April 20), Hermit Thrush (November), Pipit (October 25–November 5), Bronzed Grackle (December), Rusty Blackbird (December).

October 10–31.—Holbœll's Grebe (May), Brant (May 30), Old Squaw (May), Hooded Merganser (December 10), Horned Lark (April), Northern Shrike (April), Pine Finch (April), Redpoll (April), Fox Sparrow (November 25–December 10), Tree Sparrow (April), Snow Bunting (March).

November.—Golden-eye (April 20), American Merganser (April 20), Purple Sandpiper (March 15), Iceland Gull (May), Glaucous Gull (May), Kittiwake (March 20), Pine Grosbeak, White-winged Crossbill, Red Crossbill.

Extent of Migration.—After this glimpse of the swing of the pendulum of migration, from a local point of view, we may extend our inquiry by following the birds to their winter quarters, with the object of learning where they go and the routes they travel.

Generally speaking, the extent of a bird's migration is related to the character of its food; insect-eating birds journey much farther than seed-eaters, many of which travel but a short distance south of their birthplace. There are, however, some marked exceptions to this statement. The Bobolink, for instance, is in part granivorous, but it winters south of the Amazon, while the Golden-crowned Kinglet is insectivorous and winters as far north as New England. Again, of two insectivorous birds, one, the Short-billed Marsh Wren, does not winter north of the Gulf or South Atlantic States, while the other, the Winter Wren, is found northward to New England in winter. Numerous similar instances might be cited, all indicating that some cause other than food has determined the extent of the journeys made by many migratory birds. It will be observed that of the species just mentioned, the Bobolink and Short-billed Marsh Wren are American types of austral origin, while the Golden-crowned Kinglet and Winter Wren are European types and of boreal origin. Further inquiry will show that among land-birds the migrants which go farthest south belong in the first class, while those which winter farthest north belong in the second class. It is not improbable, therefore, that the extent of a bird's migrations may give some indication of its place of origin as a migrant.

In the western states the migration of birds is not so pronounced as it is east of the Rocky Mountains, and the latitudinal movement is complicated by an altitudinal one. The migrants of this region, which winter south of the United States, pass this season largely in Mexico. Comparatively few land-birds go beyond Guatemala and practically none crosses the Isthmus of Panama.

In eastern North America, not only are migrants proportionally more abundant, but their movements are more clearly defined, and the journeys of those birds that leave the United States are far more extended than those performed by the birds of the western portion of the continent.

Of our 39 species of Warblers, 27 winter entirely south of the United States, 20 of them reaching South America, the Yellow Warbler and Blackpoll having been recorded from as far south as Peru. The shortest journey of any Blackpoll, as Cooke points out, is 3,500 miles, "while those that nest in Alaska have 7,000 miles to travel to their probable winter home in Brazil." ('Warblers of North America,' p. 15; see also his admirable 'Distribution and Migration of Warblers,' Bull. No. 18, Biological Survey.)

Of our ten species of Flycatchers, 9 leave the United States for the winter (the Crested Flycatcher is of rare occurrence in southern Florida at this season), and all of them reach South America, the Kingbird (*Tyrannus tyrannus*) going as far south as Bolivia.

Two of our 8 Vireos remain in Florida during the winter, 5 winter in Central America, and 1, the Red-eye, extends its winter journey to Bolivia and southwestern Brazil.

Even more extended migrations are performed by certain Sandpipers and Plovers which nest within the Arctic Circle and winter as far south as the southern extremity of South America.

Routes of Migration.—Lying within those regions climatically most favorable for the human race, the boundaries of the summer ranges of most of our migrating birds are known with more or less definiteness; but when they leave the temperate zone to enter tropical wilds, our knowledge of their distribution is far less satisfactory. The data now available show, however, that a field of exceptional interest awaits the investigator who, with adequate information, traces the routes of migration followed by birds in journeying between their summer and winter homes.

For exact information of this character we must look to the bird-bander. Already he has shown us that Common Terns born on the coast of Massachusetts winter near the mouth of the Orinoco, while one banded on the coast of Maine was found, four years later, soon after its death, at the mouth of the Niger River, British West Africa; that a Blue-winged Teal banded in Ontario was killed seventy-five days later on the Island of Trinidad, B. W. I., while a Great Blue Heron, banded at Waseca, Minn., was taken near Gatun Lake in the Canal Zone. But it is less the length than the direction of migration on which banding has thrown light. Ducks follow a regular traveled route from Utah to California, and individuals banded as far east as Illinois have also been taken in California. Young Herring Gulls banded in northern Lake Michigan have been reported, according to Lincoln, the same season from the region of the Gulf of St. Lawrence. Evening Grosbeaks banded at Sault Sainte Marie, Mich., have been taken in Connecticut.

In eastern North America some migrant land-birds leave the United States by passing through Texas into Mexico and are unknown in the southeastern Atlantic States (*e. g.* the Mourning Warbler); others leave through Florida and are unknown in Texas and Mexico (*e. g.* the Bobolink and Blackpoll Warbler). Others still (*e. g.* the Redstart), travel through both Texas and Florida into Mexico as well as to the West Indies. There is also a route which appears to cross the Gulf of Mexico from the region at the mouth of the Mississippi, though no species is confined to it.

It was at one time supposed that the birds which left the United States by way of Florida all crossed directly to Cuba, but, according to Cooke ('03), "The main traveled highway is that which stretches from northwestern Florida across the Gulf, continuing the southwest direction which most of the birds of the Atlantic Coast follow in passing to Florida. A larger or smaller proportion of nearly all the species bound for South America take this roundabout course, quite regardless of the 700-mile flight over the Gulf of Mexico."

The observations of Scott[1] and Bennett[2] in the Tortugas show that these islets evidently lie in a migratory highway, and we know as yet too little about the birds of western Cuba to be sure that many of the birds which pass over them do not pause on that island. But, in any

[1]See *Auk*, VII, 1890, pp. 301–314.
[2]See *Bird-Lore*, XI, 1909, pp. 110–113.

event, it is evident that, whether to or from western Cuba and Yucatan, there is a direct flight across the Gulf to or from western Florida, and, as Cooke ('05) remarks, it is this route which is followed by most of our

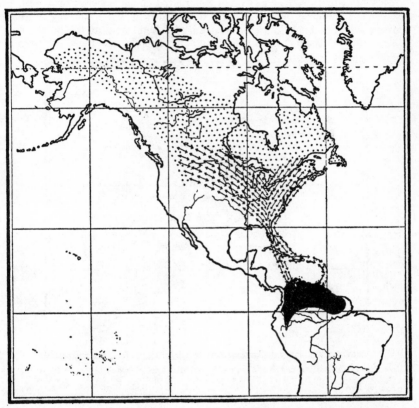

FIG. 6. Migration of the Blackpoll Warbler. A species which breeds as far northwest as Alaska, but leaves North America through Florida, and reaches South America through the West Indies, avoiding Mexico and Central America.

Dotted area—Breeding range. Black area—Winter range. Arrows—Migration route.

migrant land-birds which winter in South America. He sums the matter up as follows:

Species that reach South America or Panama:

By way of the West Indies 10
By an unknown route 7
By way of the Gulf of Mexico 49

There is apparently, also, a small off-shore or southeastward flight to the eastward of Florida leading into and through the Bahamas, and possibly even farther east.

According to Reid, the migrant land-birds which visit the Bermudas with more or less regularity are the Belted Kingfisher, Yellow-billed Cuckoo, Bobolink, and Northern Water-Thrush. The last two were recorded by Julien[1] during a short stay on Sombrero, at the northern extremity of the Lesser Antilles; and in Granada, the most southern

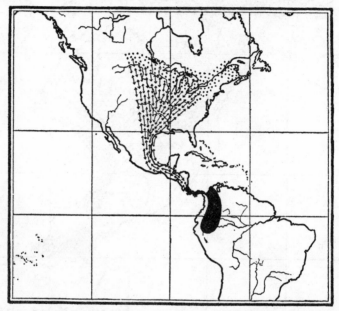

FIG. 7. Migration of the Mourning Warbler. A species which breeds as far northeast as Nova Scotia, but migrates southwestward, reaching South America through Mexico and Central America, and avoiding the South Atlantic States and West Indies. Dotted area—Breeding range. Black area—Winter range. Arrows—Migration route.

island of this chain, Wells[2] has found the Kingfisher, Bobolink, and Water-Thrush.

Possibly these birds may have reached the Lesser Antilles through Porto Rico from the westward. This route, however, is followed by only a small portion of the birds which migrate southward, through Florida and the Bahamas, into the Greater Antilles. If they continue their journey to South America, most of them do so through Jamaica, the 400 miles of water separating this island from northern South America being evidently no barrier to such great travelers as the Bobolink and Blackpoll Warbler.

[1] *Ann. Lyc. Nat. Hist.*, New York, VIII, 1864, p. 93.
[2] *Proc. U. S. Nat. Mus.*, IX, 1886, p. 609.

Within the limits of the United States, coast-lines, mountain chains, and the larger river valleys, appear to be followed by birds in their migrations; nevertheless, there is a more or less pronounced highway of migration which crosses the southern Alleghanies from northwest to southeast. This is evidently followed by Kirtland's Warbler, which

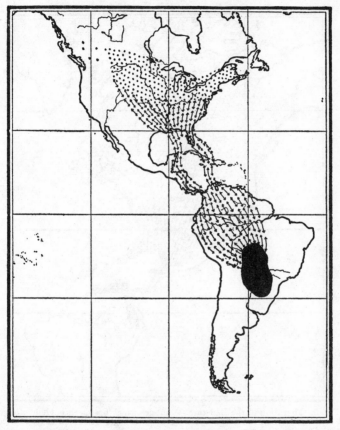

FIG. 8. Migration of the Bobolink. A species which breeds west of the Rocky Mountains, but migrates through the southeastern United States, reaching South America through the Greater Antilles and Central America.
  Dotted area—Breeding range. Black area—Winter range. Arrows—Migration route.

nests in northern Michigan and winters in the Bahamas, and it brings to our southeast Atlantic Coast, with more or less regularity, birds which are practically unknown in our North Atlantic States. There are also minor routes or paths of migration formed, generally, by favorable local conditions, but in some instances difficult to explain. I have seen Tree

Swallows, in the spring, on the Gulf Coast of Florida, migrating northward low over the great expanse of unbroken marshes, but evidently
following a definite track. The scattered flocks were often separated
by several miles, but each one followed in the wake of its invisible
predecessor as though guided by the marks of wing-beats in the air.

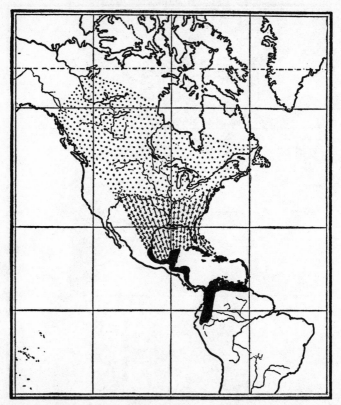

FIG. 9. Migration of the Redstart. A species which breeds throughout the greater
part of temperate North America, and migrates through the West Indies, Mexico and
Central America.
Dotted area—Breeding range. Black area—Winter range. Arrows—Migration routes.

Most birds appear to return to their summer homes over much the
same route by which they left them. There are, however, a few marked
exceptions to this rule. Among our land-birds, the Connecticut Warbler enters the United States through Florida and journeys thence
northwestward along the Alleghanies, and west to Missouri, to the
Upper Mississippi Valley and Manitoba. At this season it is unknown
on the Atlantic Coast north of Florida; but during its return migration,

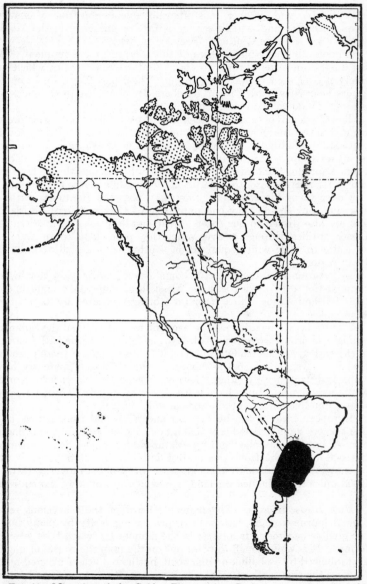

Fig. 10. Migration of the Golden Plover (after Cooke). A species which has seasonal migration routes, going south from Labrador and Nova Scotia, over the ocean, to the Lesser Antilles and South America, and north up the Mississippi Valley. Dotted area—Breeding range. Black area—Winter range. Arrows—Migration routes.

in September and October, it is often not uncommon from Massachusetts southward and, at this season, is rare or unknown in the Mississippi Valley south of Chicago. (See Cooke, '04.)

Among our water-birds, cases of this kind are more frequent. The fall migration often brings to the Atlantic Coast species which are rarely if ever seen there in the spring. The Black Tern, for example, occurs near New York City in numbers, from August to October, but is rarely found there in the spring.

The Golden Plover, as has been shown by Cooke ('93), after breeding in June on the shores of the Arctic Ocean, in August migrates southeastward to Labrador, where it feeds on the crowberry (*Empetrum*), laying on a supply of fat as fuel for the remarkable voyage which follows. From Labrador the birds fly south to Nova Scotia and thence lay their course for northern South America in a direct line across the Atlantic.

Under favorable conditions they may pass the Bermudas without stopping, but should they encounter storms they rest in these islands and are also driven to our coast. Their first stop may be made in the Lesser Antilles, through or over which they proceed to South America, en route to their winter quarters in southwestern Brazil and the La Plata region.

In returning to their Arctic home these Plover pass northward through Central America and the Mississippi Valley, the main line of their fall and spring routes, therefore, being separated by as much as 1,500 miles.

The explanations advanced to account for the gradual development of migration routes, over which birds in the fall retrace the path followed in the spring, are inadequate to account for the origin of these phenomenal journeys, on which the pioneer voyagers must apparently have embarked unguided by either inherited or acquired experience. Nor do we understand how birds have learned to cross regularly over bodies of water, hundreds or even thousands of miles in width.

European birds cross the Mediterranean, to and from Africa, at a point where soundings indicate that a much closer land relation formerly existed; but the 400-mile flight from Jamaica to northern South America, the 600-mile flight from the nearest land to the Bermudas, or the journey regularly made by the Turnstone and Golden Plover to Hawaii, 2,000 miles from the nearest land, are evidently not to be explained in this way.

How Birds Migrate.—The more we learn of the marvelous semi-annual journeys made with such surprising regularity by many birds, the greater becomes our interest in the manner by which they are performed. It is well enough to point out on the map the routes of migration followed by Bobolink or Blackpoll, but how do the feathered mites traverse the thousands of miles which separate their summer and winter homes?

It is evidently essential that the bird be prepared for the journey. Fall migration usually follows the annual post-breeding molt, and the birds, in fresh plumage, proceed slowly, often lingering in favorable feeding-grounds, as does the Golden Plover among the crowberries of Labrador, or the Bobolink in the wild-rice marshes of our Atlantic Coast, until they are in physical condition to endure the strain of prolonged flight.

In the spring they have had months' exemption from family cares, with no other duty than to wander where food was most abundant; excellent preparation for the return journey to the nesting-ground. We know less, however, about birds' movements at this season than when, after breeding, they prepare to leave us.

Some species begin to flock immediately after the nesting season and, as a preliminary to actual migration, develop regular and definitely directed movements in their daily returns to and departure from a certain roosting-place. Such roosting-places form stations on the migratory journey and are focal points for small bodies of birds which later take flight in one great company. Red-winged Blackbirds, Grackles, and the various species of Swallows inaugurate their southward migrations in this way.

Less gregarious birds, at the conclusion of their post-breeding molt or even before it is completed, simply disappear without our knowing when they go.

The adult birds, either alone or accompanied by birds of the year, migrate first. Later, the adults decrease in number and the last flights may be composed entirely of young birds. In the fall the sexes appear to travel together, but in the spring the males usually precede the females.

Some birds migrate only by day, others only during the night, while a smaller number travel both by day and night. In his now classic Memoir on 'Bird Migration,' Brewster ('86) puts the matter clearly as follows:

"1. Species which migrate exclusively by night habitually feed in or near the shelter of trees, bushes, rank herbage or grass, and when not migrating are birds of limited powers of flight and sedentary habits, restricting their daily excursions to the immediate vicinity of their chosen haunts. As a rule they are of timid, or at least retiring disposition, and when alarmed or pursued seek safety in concealment rather than by extended flights.

"2. Species which migrate chiefly or very freely by day, habitually feed in open, exposed situations, and in their daily excursions for food often cover considerable distances. As a rule they are of bold, restless disposition, and when alarmed or pursued seek safety in long flights rather than by concealment.

"3. Species which migrate exclusively by day habitually feed either on the wing or over very extensive areas. In disposition they are either trustful and unsuspecting or wary and self-reliant. Without exception they are birds of strong, easy flight, and rely solely on their wings for escape from danger."

A wedge of honking Geese, a close-massed flock of chattering Grackles or Redwings, a straggling train of Crows or Hawks, are familiar evidences of diurnal migration; while the passage, by day, of the Wild Pigeon was one of the most pronounced and impressive of daylight travels by migrating birds of which we have any record.

Other of our land-birds "which migrate freely, chiefly or exclusively by day" (Brewster, *l. c.*) are the Hummingbird, Chimney Swift, Horned Lark, Blue Jay, Waxwing, Shrike, Swallow, Pipit, Robin, and Bluebird. To this list may be added certain gregarious Finches, like Crossbills, Siskins, Redpolls, Pine and Evening Grosbeaks, Purple Finches and Snow Buntings. I have also seen Dickcissels, high in the air, traveling in compact bodies by day, though they apparently also migrate by night.

Ducks, shore-birds (Limicolæ) and sea-birds (Alcidæ, Laridæ, and Tubinares) migrate both by day and by night. The sportsman is first made aware of the passage of Plover or Yellow-legs by their mellow calls, as they journey through the air beyond the reach of unaided vision.

An interesting note on the diurnal migration of birds at an apparently high altitude, is supplied by R. A. Bray ('95) who records a flight of birds observed through a telescope, directed toward the sun, at 3 P.M. on September 30, 1894, at Shere, England. Every few seconds a bird was seen to pass slowly across the sun, and there was no decrease in their numbers during the ten minutes of observation. The birds were flying in a southerly direction and were invisible to the naked eye.

The daily flight of vast numbers of sea-birds along the Pacific Coast is recorded in detail by L. M. Loomis ('00, p. 280) who states that on one occasion (September 23, 1896) "not less than a quarter of a million" Dark-bodied Shearwaters "passed in review during two hours and a half." "There were several divisions—each a solid phalanx about an eighth of a mile deep—following closely one upon the other," low, over the water.

Loons may be seen migrating by day, but the weaker-winged Grebes, relying on their diving powers for safety, evidently travel by night. Other water-birds, like the Bitterns, Woodcock, Wilson's Snipe, Rails, Coot, and Gallinules, whose habits do not lead them over the sea or its shores, migrate, as Brewster has said, by night.

Our knowledge of the nocturnal migration of birds is based on evidence supplied by the call-notes of passing birds, on data from lighthouses, on observations through telescopes, and on field-work on days succeeding flights.

It is a common experience, during the season of migration, to hear the notes of birds which are passing overhead. From an elevation in a line of flight, or where the city lights may attract birds, such notes, when birds are moving in numbers, are almost continuous. O. G. Libby ('99) states that on the night of September 14, 1896, on "a small elevation west of the city of Madison, Wis.," a total of 3,800 bird-calls were recorded. The average was twelve per minute, but the rate "varied greatly, sometimes running as high as two or three per second, and again falling to about the same number per minute. . . . The great space of air above swarmed with life. Singly, or in groups, large and small, or more seldom in a great throng, the hurrying myriads passed southward."

Lighthouses, because of their location on the coast, on promontories or outlying islets, are often situated in the path of migrating birds. This fact, in connection with the fatal attraction which the rays of the light possess for migrating birds during stormy weather, has supplied an extended and definite series of records, which also emphasize the high mortality often prevailing in the ranks of night-migrating birds. Shortly after its erection, 1,400 dead birds are said to have been picked up at the base of the Bartholdi statue, in New York harbor, which had been killed by striking the statue the preceding night.

For years, light-keepers have reported to the Biological Survey at Washington on the birds seen about or striking the lights in their care, and, in not a few instances, our knowledge of the migration of a species rests largely on this class of data. (Allen, '80, p. 131.)

We have also the testimony of ornithologists who have visited light-houses especially for the purpose of observing the nocturnal journeys of birds. Brewster (l. c. p. 7), who visited Point LePreaux lighthouse, in the Bay of Fundy, for this purpose, gives an impressive picture of observations made there on the night of September 4.

Observations through telescopes, though limited in number, when one considers how easily they are made and how interesting and valuable are the results to be obtained, supply probably our most satisfactory data on nocturnal migration. They can be made only on clear, moonlight nights, when the current of migration, flowing smoothly through the air above, is viewed under wholly normal conditions.

A low-power telescope is focused on the moon, the glowing surface of which forms a background against which the birds, in passing, are clearly silhouetted. On September 3, 1886, at Tenafly, N. J., with the aid of a 6½-inch equatorial glass, 262 birds were seen to cross the narrow angle subtended by the limits of the moon between the hours of eight and eleven (Chapman, '88). Subsequent observations from the observatory of Columbia University and at Englewood, N. J., have revealed the vast numbers of birds which throng the upper air during nights of active migration.

At Madison, Wisc, on the nights of September 11 to 13, 1897, Libby (l. c.) saw 583 birds through a 6-inch glass, the largest number counted during a fifteen-minute period being forty-five. Additional data of this nature are included in a paper by H. A. Winkenwerder ('02), while Stone's ('06) observations on birds seen migrating at night by the light of a great conflagration in Philadelphia have exceptional interest.

The height at which migrating birds fly has been variously estimated. Many diurnal migrants may be seen traveling from a few yards (e. g. Shearwaters) to several hundred yards (e. g. Geese) above the earth, but shore-birds evidently seek a greater altitude, and the experience of Bray, referred to above, hints at a diurnal flight of which we know practically nothing.

Our knowledge of the height at which nocturnal migrants journey is based on the telescopic observations already mentioned. As intimated in the article itself (l. c.), the conclusions presented in my paper on birds seen flying over Tenafly were not satisfactory. More recently the problem has been attacked by F. W. Carpenter ('06) and Stebbins,[1] with results which seem far more worthy of acceptance. Their calculations show that while an altitude of 4,000 to 5,000 feet may occasionally be reached, the greater number of birds observed were not over 1,600 feet above the earth, while many passed considerably below this elevation. The ease with which the calls of night-flying birds may be heard also argues for a lower altitude than has been commonly accredited to them. This view is supported by R. Meinertzhagen who, in a paper[2] based on all the available data, concludes that "birds met with above 5,000 feet are the exception and not the rule" and that "the bulk of migratory flight is conducted below 3,000 feet whether by day or by night."

The speed at which migrating birds fly has also been greatly overrated. Two observations with theodolites give to migrating Ducks a speed of 47.8, and to migrating Geese a speed of 44.3 miles an hour.[3] Homing Pigeons do not often exceed 40 to 45 miles an hour. It is a common experience, when traveling in a train at a rate of 35 to 45 miles an hour, to pass birds which are flying parallel to the track. I have had this occur repeatedly with such comparatively large and swift birds as the Mourning Dove. It seems probable, therefore, that our smaller birds do not average more than 30 to 40 miles an hour when migrating.

The rate at which a bird migrates, however, is of course not to be considered its limit of speed. The migrating bird, like the long-distance runner, must adopt a pace which will enable it to reach the goal without danger of exhaustion by the way. Should necessity arise, it doubtless, for a time, could more than double the speed at which it normally travels. The preceding statements are fully confirmed by R. Meinertzhagen's detailed observations[4] in which he states that "the normal and migratory rate of flight in miles per hour" for Corvidæ is 31 to 45; smaller Passeres, 20 to 37; Starlings, 38 to 49; Geese, 42 to 55; Ducks, 44 to 59; domestic Pigeons, 30 to 36.

Alex. Wetmore's observations[5] in southern California from an automobile, timed to keep pace with the birds, produced the following results in miles per hour: Great Blue Heron, 28; Sparrow Hawk, 22 to 25; Red-shafted Flicker, 25; Raven, 24; Horned Lark, 23 to 28; Loggerhead Shrike, 28. In a similar manner, R. J. Longstreet,[6] on the Daytona, Fla., beach, secured the following records: Gannet, 25; Brown Pelican,

[1]Popular Astronomy, XIV, 1906, pp. 65–70.　　[4]The Ibis, 1921, pp. 228–238.
[2]The Ibis, 1920, pp. 920–936.　　　　　　　　[5]The Condor, 1916, p. 112.
[3]Clayton, Science, 1897, pp. 26, 585.　　　　　[6]The Auk, 1930, p. 429.

26; Knot, 38; Semipalmated Sandpiper, 32; Hudsonian Curlew, 34; Semipalmated Plover, 32; Ruddy Turnstone, 27.

The rate of progress of the individual must not be confused with that at which the species advances. Nocturnal migrants probably cover 200 to 400 miles in a single night's journey; but, as Cooke ('03) has shown, "The average speed of migration from New Orleans to southern Minnesota for all species is close to 23 miles per day." From this latitude northward, however, in response to the more rapid development of the season, the speed is constantly accelerated until the breeding-place is reached. Thus, the same author remarks, "Sixteen species maintain a daily average of 40 miles from southern Minnesota to southern Manitoba, and from this point twelve species travel to Lake Athabasca at an average speed of 72 miles a day, five others to Great Slave Lake at 116 miles a day, and five more to Alaska at 150 miles a day."

The slow rate at which a species moves, when compared with that at which the individuals composing it travel, is evidence that its migration is not performed continuously, night after night, until the haven is reached, but that after a flight birds pause to rest, to await favorable weather conditions, and the further seasonal change which such conditions hasten. The observations of Wright ('09) in the Boston Public Garden, where, as in other city parks, local conditions are exceptionally favorable for the correct interpretation of migration phenomena, also confirm this view, if indeed further confirmation be required.

The impelling motive being more powerful, the object more definite, and the seasonal influences more pronounced, the spring migration of birds is a more orderly and regular movement than the return in the fall. Clear nights and a rising thermometer are most likely to induce birds to travel, a 'wave' of migrants coming often on the crest of a 'wave' of warmer temperature. When such a movement is checked by cold or stormy weather, the result is an overflow of migrants which flood the woods. Ordinarily rare species may then become comparatively common, and the impression is produced of an actual increase in bird-life. In the fall, when physiological factors incident to reproduction are not potent and seasonal changes are less marked, birds travel more leisurely. Clear nights and a falling thermometer are then most favorable for a general movement.

The high mortality in the ranks of migrating birds occasioned by the storms they encounter is evidence of their inability to anticipate changes in the weather. On the coast of Texas I have known birds to migrate northward in great numbers directly into the face of a 'norther,' with evidently no warning of the unfavorable conditions toward which they were hastening. Again, under the influence of exceptionally warm weather, Tree Swallows have been induced to travel northward and appear near New York City in numbers late in December.

And now we ask the question to which any consideration of the phenomena of migration inevitably leads, "How do birds find their way?" What faculty directs them over thousands of miles of land and water through the darkness of the night with a regularity and accuracy that brings them to the same locality, even the same nest-site, on essentially the same date year after year?

Granted that in birds, sight, hearing, and the power of association are exceptionally developed; that the chirping and calling of night migrants is an effective means of holding them to the main traveled way; that diurnal migrants are guided by prominent topographical features; still something far more potent than eye, ear, and memory is evidently required to lead birds over journeys where landmarks are wanting.

While at sea, on May 24, 1905, a Curlew boarded the steamer when we were 140 miles south of Fastnet Light. While photographing the bird, I alarmed it, when it took wing and headed for Ireland with as much confidence as though land had been visible, and was soon far beyond us. There was here no established line of flight in which to join, no evident external guiding influence; nevertheless the bird set its course without hesitation.

Terns, Murres, and other sea-birds go out to feed and return to their breeding-grounds through dense fog and with unfailing precision. Tropic-birds reach Bermuda, 600 miles from the nearest land, regularly each spring; Turnstones and Pacific Golden Plover travel twice each year over at least 2,000 miles of water in their journey to and from Hawaii. The Eastern Golden Plover strikes boldly out over the Atlantic bound from Nova Scotia to the Lesser Antilles; vast numbers of birds of many species cross the Gulf of Mexico, others fly from Jamaica to South America.

This power of 'distant orientation' is apparently only to be explained through the birds' possession of a 'homing instinct' or 'sense of direction' which, when the impulse to migrate is active, automatically induces them to follow a certain route.

The experiments of Reynaud ('00) and others with Homing Pigeons appear to have definitely established the existence of the sense of direction in this species, and more recently Watson ('09) has demonstrated in a most noteworthy manner its evident possession by Sooty and Noddy Terns. Among other tests, Reynaud transported five Pigeons, under the influence of chloroform, from Orleans to Evreux, France, a locality which they had not visited before. Two days later, having evidently recovered from the effects of the drug, they were released and all returned to Orleans. While the senses of sight, smell, taste, touch, and hearing were not functional during the time when the birds were under the influence of chloroform, Reynaud expresses his belief that "the sense of direction, on the contrary, whose action is based on the automatic and mechanical registration of the road followed, continued to work, in spite of the chloroform, absolutely like other mechanical functions—the circulation of the blood, the digestive organs, and respiration—in some way, without the knowledge of the animal."

Watson's experiments were made with Sooty and Noddy Terns, among which he passed the breeding season of 1907 on their nesting-ground on Bird Key, Dry Tortugas. He first captured and marked six Noddies, and had them released at distances varying from 19.5 to 65.8 miles from the Key. All returned within from one and three-quarters to about three and a half hours after being released.

July 8, two Noddies and two Sooties were captured and marked and sent to Havana (108 miles) where they were released early on the morning of the 11th; all returned to the Key on the 12th.

None of these birds, however, was sent beyond the normal range of their species, and it may be claimed that they were simply traveling over a route with which they were familiar. In any event, the journey was made unassisted by any trend of migration or established migratory movement which they had simply to join. When breeding, these birds are closely confined to the vicinity of their homes. Watson found that they rarely went farther than 15 knots from Bird Key. Some of the birds returned alone, evidently dependent only on themselves for guidance.

A third test, in which the surrounding conditions were ideal, was made with three Noddies and two Sooties which were captured and marked on June 13, and sent from Bird Key to Key West. Here they were transferred to the hold of the steamship *Denver* where they were both watered and fed while en route. On June 16, the birds were released about 12 miles east of Cape Hatteras, approximately 1,081 miles by water from Bird Key. Both the Sooties were found on their respective nests on the morning of June 21, and one of the Noddies was observed several days later.

Neither the Noddy nor Sooty Tern ranges, as a rule, north of the Florida Keys. There is small probability, therefore, that the individuals released off Hatteras had ever been over the route before and, for the same reason, they could not have availed themselves of the experience or example of migratory individuals of their own species; nor, since the birds were released at the height of the nesting season, was there any marked southward movement of birds in the line of which they might follow.

Even had there been such a movement, it is not probable that it would have taken the birds southwest to the Florida Keys and thence west to the Tortugas. This marked change in direction, due to the fact that the birds' maritime habits would force them to take a course over the water, removes the direction of the wind as a possible guiding agency, while the birds' unfamiliarity with the coast-line makes it improbable that sight was of service to them in finding their way. In short, we cannot but feel that this experiment constitutes the strongest argument for the existence of a sense of direction as yet derived from the study of wild birds; with this established, the so-called 'mystery of migration' becomes no more a mystery than any other instinctive, functional activity.

Why Do Birds Migrate?—Any attempt to reply to this question should be prefaced by the statement that birds have been migrating for an incalculable period. The existing phenomena are not therefore to be explained solely by observable causes, but they may often have their origin in influences which have long ceased to be potent. In other words, the migration of birds, as well as the birds themselves, is an outcome of those gradual adjustments between an organism and its environment which has led, on the one hand, to activities which existing causes only in part explain, and on the other to the evolution of certain types of form and color the reasons for which we cannot now wholly determine. To attack the problem with any hope of success we should know where birds originated, what was their distribution, when they acquired the power of flight, and what climatic conditions prevailed at this period of their evolution. Possessed of this information, we might hope to discover the origin of the migratory movement and trace its growth.

Particularly do we lack definite information concerning those climatic factors which we may assume were the prime cause in increasing the length of birds' migrations. If prior to the establishment of seasonal conditions resembling those now existing, the climate of northern latitudes was favorable for the production and maintenance of a food-supply throughout the year, the necessity for prolonged migration, as Dr. J. A. Allen long ago remarked (see beyond), did not exist, and major migratory movements originated with the development of those climatic changes (whether glacial or seasonal) which drove a bird from its home with the coming of winter and did not permit it to return until the following spring or, if glaciation were the cause of its southward journey, until the ice retreated.

On the other hand, if seasonal climates have always prevailed it may be suggested that birds originated in the warmer parts of the earth whence, as they acquired the power of flight, they visited those regions that were habitable only during a part of the year and left them as the returning cold season reduced or cut off the food-supply.

Purely for purposes of illustration we may imagine that migrants of northern origin may have had somewhat the distribution of most of our Gulls, the Scoters, Snow Bunting, Crossbills, Brown Creeper, Northern Shrike, Golden-crowned Kinglet, and other boreal species that come to us in the winter. On the other hand, those migrants which have, apparently, acquired the migratory habit through seasonal range-extension under the impulse of the breeding period are represented by the members of such distinctively tropical American families as Hummingbirds, Flycatchers, Wood Warblers, and Tanagers. Indeed, so numerous are the birds illustrating both the theories of northern and southern origin of existing migration phenomena that one is tempted to believe there is truth in each of them.

We observe that bird migration is most highly developed in those parts of the world which are subjected to marked seasonal changes. In endeavoring, therefore, to ascertain the factors governing migration either north or south of subtropical regions, we find our problem greatly complicated by questions of climate, past and present, and of food which seem to exert a powerful influence on the movements of birds.

Fortunately we are not obliged to begin our examination of the subject in this, its most complex form, but in the tropics may find perfectly well-defined instances of bird migration in which the matters of food and climate seem to play no part. Nevertheless, the individuals of species whose habits have been closely studied nest at the same time and place annually. A colony of Oropendolas (*Zarhynchus wagleri*) which I observed for three consecutive nesting seasons on Barro Colorado Island in the Canal Zone, came each year to the same tree and began nesting the first two years, January 8, and third year, January 2. When not nesting the birds of this species were seen only at intervals about our laboratory where the nest-tree was situated and during this part of the year they were presumably local wanderers, but with the return of the breeding season they came back to their nesting-place. Their journey may have been a mile or even less in length but, functionally, it was as much a migration as that of a bird that winters in the tropical, and nests in the temperate zone.

From a study of tropical sea-birds, we learn the same lesson. They are often great wanderers and during the year many cover vast distances within the tropic zone in their search for food. They cannot, however, nest on the water, and when the season of reproduction approaches, they are, of necessity, forced to go to the land. Now it is of the highest importance for us to know that their visits to their breeding resorts are made with the same regularity that marks the journey of Oriole, Bobolink or Warbler. They return each year to the same place and they all reach it, almost to the day, at the same time. The Brown Pelicans of eastern Florida came in thousands to Pelican Island the first week in November; Boobies and Man-o'-war-birds return to certain Bahama keys in January; the Noddy and Sooty Terns appear on Bird Key in the Tortugas the last week in April.

Temperature, obviously, has nothing to do with these journeys, since with the Pelicans the average daily temperature is decreasing, with the Terns increasing, while the Boobies and Man-o'-war-birds have probably experienced no change of temperature. Nor are the birds induced to travel by a more abundant supply of food. Indeed, the focusing of so large a number of individuals in a comparatively limited area doubtless increases the severity of the competition for subsistence.

In discussing the periodicity of the migratory impulse in a paper presented before the American Ornithologists' Union in November, 1893, I said: "It is evident, therefore, that external conditions have not created this impulse, though it is possible that in many instances they may have governed its periodicity. On the contrary, its causes are internal. In the case of the sea-birds, for example, dissection will show an enlargement of the sexual organs, and it is this physiological change which warns the birds that the season of reproduction is at hand. The organs of male birds apparently begin to enlarge before those of the females, and it is not improbable that this may account for the earlier migration of the males of many species. Furthermore, individuals found south of the breeding-range of the species during the nesting season are generally barren birds, and their presence may be due to an absence of conditions which would impel them to migrate to the nesting-grounds." (*The Auk*, 1894, p. 14.)

Nearly forty years' additional experience have convinced me of the fundamental truth of this explanation which has since been removed from the field of theory by the experiments of William Rowan ('26, '29) who has shown a definite relation between increase in size of the gonads and the impulse to migrate.

Migration, then, is only one phenomenon in a cycle of events which includes, in regular order, migration, courtship, nest-building, egg-laying, incubation, the care of the young, the molt, and the retreat to winter quarters—or, as might be better said of tropical and subtropical birds, the desertion of the nesting-ground.

The yearly life-cycle in the vegetable world parallels, in a sense, that which exists in the world of birds. In orderly succession the plant develops leaf, blossom, and fruit, sheds its foliage, and, after a period of rest, the phenomena are repeated. With birds it is the return of the season of physical fruition which arouses not only the sexual but also the homing instinct under the guidance of which these mobile creatures repair to the place of their birth.

Thus, migration in its simplest form is merely a journey to the nesting-ground made without apparent relation to food or temperature. Whether the bird migrates only a few miles or several thousand miles, the initial impulse is supplied by the annual recurrence of the period of reproduction with its attendant physiological phenomena. The migration of fish to their spawning-ground and of seals to their 'rookeries' are further examples of periodic journeys made solely to reach definite breeding-grounds.

It is not difficult for us to understand why Pelicans, Boobies, Terns, and other birds return to certain islets within the area of their winter wanderings, but when we attempt to discover why birds perform apparently unnecessary journeys, thousands of miles in length, we are confronted by the cumulative results of habits which may have had their beginnings with the birds themselves. Without attempting to discuss the origin of seasons and zonal climates, and the profound influence they have undoubtedly exercised on the extent of birds' migrations, it seems evident, as Dr. W. R. Eckardt has pointed out,[1] that the annual recurrence of a polar night has always supplied a cause for more or less extended migration. Without regard, therefore, to the character of arctic climates, it is apparent that this part of the globe was far better adapted to support life when the sun was present than when it was absent. How long after their acquisition of the power of flight the mobility of birds enabled them to take advantage of the fact

[1] *Journ. für Orn.*, 1921, pp. 469–504.

that the habitable earth was larger at one part of the year than at another, we shall doubtless never know. But, if we may judge of the the past by the present, we may assume that the periodically sunlit area was entered just as soon as the pressure of life in the adjoining regions to the south created a need for new breeding-areas.

Dr. J. A. Allen found the origin of bird-migration in the 'Glacial Period.' He wrote ('80, p. 151): "Nothing is doubtless more thoroughly established than that a warm temperate or subtropical climate prevailed down to the close of the Tertiary Epoch nearly to the Northern Pole, and that climate was previously everywhere so far equable that the necessity for migration can hardly be supposed to have existed. With the later refrigeration of the northern regions, bird-life must have been crowded thence toward the tropics; and the struggle for life thereby greatly intensified. The less-yielding forms may have become extinct; those less sensitive to climatic changes would seek to extend the boundaries of their range by slight removal northward during the milder intervals of summer, only, however, to be forced back again by the recurrence of winter. Such migration must have been at first 'incipient and gradual,' extending and strengthening as the cold-wave Ice Age receded and opened up a wider area within which existence in summer became possible. What was at first a forced migration would become habitual, and through the heredity of habit give rise to the wonderful faculty which we call migration."

To the influence of the more recent periods of glaciation, perhaps the most recent, we may attribute the presence in the warmer parts of the globe today of such physically closely related but geographically widely separated birds as Ibises, Spoonbills, Pelicans, Anhingas, and Flamingoes.

It is out of the question to believe that birds, so like each other and so unlike other birds, can have originated independently in the Old World and in the New; whence it follows, of course, that they have descended from a common ancestor, or, in other words, that their ranges were at one time continuous. This time we may well believe to have been that portion of the Tertiary Period preceding the Glacial Epoch, when the warm climate of the polar regions was adapted to their wants. With the climatic change which culminated in the Ice Age, their boreal representatives either became extinct or were forced southward, some in the Old World, some in the New, and the territory thus deserted has never been reacquired. The White Pelicans, and many other species closely related to Old-World forms, and now breeding north of the most southern limit of the great Ice-Field (for instance, the Eared Grebe, Gannet, Great Blue Heron, Gallinule, Oyster-catcher, Crossbill, and Brown Creeper), have, however, evidently extended their summer ranges to the northward of the area which they occupied during the maximum development of the Ice Age. To speak of only the White Pelican, the reasons have just been stated for believing this species to have formerly inhabited the shores of the Arctic Ocean, whence it was

forced southward, below possibly the fortieth degree of latitude, by the
rigors of the climate of the Ice Age. Nevertheless, it now breeds regularly as far north as latitude 61°, and has therefore regained at least a
thousand miles in latitude, of the region from which it has been forced;
but each year the individual repeats the history of the species, by retreating before what may be termed a seasonal Ice Age, as winter seals
the lakes and rivers on which it has passed the summer.

Beyond question, therefore, the distribution and migration of birds
have been profoundly affected by the most recent period of glaciation.
But we know now that even before the appearance of birds there were
Glacial Periods, and that, unnumbered, they have followed one another,
producing faunal changes, the extent and nature of which will doubtless
be forever unknown.

SUGGESTIONS FOR THE STUDENT

Returning now to the more practical and personal side of bird-migration, I append here a few hints to the local student for observing and recording it.

Too much time cannot be spent in the field during the migration season. If possible, one should go out both in the early morning and late
afternoon, visiting as great a variety of ground as opportunity permits.
It is desirable also to follow the same route daily, in order that changes in
bird-life, other than the first arrival of certain species (for example, increase
or decrease, flocking, roosting, pairing, etc., of species which have already
been noted), may be more readily and definitely ascertained.

Weather conditions should be observed as closely as the migration
itself and the charts issued by the Weather Bureau at Washington should
be studied. Examine also published tables of migration. One's chances of
finding a given species are greatly increased if one knows where to look for it.

The blooming of plants, shrubs, and trees, and the advance of vegetation
in general, together with the appearance of various forms of insect life,
calling of hylas, etc., should all be recorded.

The record of each species of bird should show its date of arrival, with
the number and, if possible, sex of the individuals observed, if migrating
singly, in scattered companies or in flocks. Succeeding records of the same
species should be entered with as much detail as the first one, in order that
the whole record may show the rise and fall of its migration.

Try to observe closely the movements of the same birds—a certain
flock of Robins, for example, which is found day after day near the same
place, or an isolated Red-winged Blackbird or two, which appear to remain
in some small marsh—with the object of learning whether the first individuals
to come, among summer resident species, are the birds which nest with us,
or those which continue their journey northward.

Note the movements of winter birds—Juncos, Tree Sparrows, and
others—indicating that their migration is under way. Do the winter resident individuals of these species start before their ranks receive additions
from the South?

Observe the connection between the time of a bird's arrival and the
character of its food; for example, water-fowl appearing when the ice breaks;
Woodcock when frost leaves the ground and worms can be secured; Phœbes
when aërial insects appear.

At night listen for the calls of birds passing overhead as evidence of a
general movement, or use a low-power telescope in the manner before
described.

By day note the extended migratory flights of such birds as Hawks, Crows, and other diurnal migrants. Are they dependent on the direction of the wind? Do they follow certain routes regularly?

Observe also the more restricted movements of such night-fliers as Warblers and Vireos, which as they feed still move toward their goal.

During the summer note the gathering of birds in flocks and the formation of regularly frequented roosts, as a first step in their southward migration. Be on the lookout also for certain more southern species, which may wander northward after their breeding season has closed.

Close observation is required to detect the arrival of the first Warblers, Vireos, and Flycatchers from the North, as well as to determine when our earlier departing summer residents leave us.

When possible, the age of first comers from the North should be recorded; but the plumage of adult and young are now often alike, and a bird's age can be ascertained with exactness only by dissection, the condition of the bones of the cranium furnishing one of the most dependable clues.

REFERENCES

1836. BACHMAN, J., On the Migration of the Birds of North America, Sillim. Am. Journ. Sci., XXX, pp. 81–100. Reprinted in The Warbler, II, 1907, p. 24.—**1866.** BAIRD, S. F., The Distribution and Migration of North American Birds, Am. Journ. Sci., XLI, pp. 78–90; 184–192; 339–347.—**1880.** ALLEN, J. A., Destruction of Birds by Lighthouses, Bull. Nutt. Orn. Club, V, pp. 131–138.—**1880.** ALLEN, J. A., Origin of the Instinct of Migration in Birds, Ibid, 151–154.—**1881.** ALLEN, J. A., The Migration of Birds, Scribner's Mag., XXII, pp. 932–938.—**1881.** SCOTT, W. E. D., Some Observations on the Nocturnal Migration of Birds, Bull. Nutt. Orn. Club, VI, pp. 97–100.—**1884.** DUTCHER, W., Migration at L. I. Lighthouses, Auk, I, pp. 174–179.—**1885.** MERRIAM, C. H., Preliminary Rep. of the A. O. U. Comm. on Bird Migration, Auk, II, pp. 53–64.—**1886.** BREWSTER, W., Bird Migration, Mem. Nutt. Orn. Club, I, 22 pp.—**1888.** CHAPMAN, F. M., The Nocturnal Migration of Birds, Auk, V, pp. 37–39.—**1888.** COOKE, W. W., Bird Migration in the Mississippi Valley, Bull. 2, Biol. Surv., 313 pp.—**1889.** STONE, W., Graphic Representation of Bird Migration, Auk, VI, pp. 139–144; VIII, 1891, pp. 194–198.—**1892-1894.** LOOMIS, L. M., Observations on Migration in South Carolina, Auk, IX, pp. 28–39; XI, 1894, 26–39, 94–117.—**1893.** MACKAY, G. H., Fly Lines, Auk, X, pp. 245–249.—**1894.** CHAPMAN, F. M., Remarks on the Origin of Bird Migration, Auk, XI, pp. 12–17.—**1894.** STONE, W., Bird Migration in the Vicinity of Philadelphia, Birds E. Pa. and N. J., pp. 15–28.—**1895.** BRAY, R. S., A Remarkable Flight of Birds, Nature, LII, p. 45.—**1895.** JONES, L., Bird Migration at Grinnell, Ia., Auk, XII, pp. 117–134; 231–244.—**1895-1900.** LOOMIS, L. M., California Water Birds, Proc. Acad. Sci., 2d ser., V, pp. 177–224; VI, 1896, 1–30, 353–366; 3d ser., 1900; 277–322, 349–363.—**1896.** ALLEN, J. A., The Migration of Birds, Papers Presented to the World's Congress of Ornithology, pp. 31–38.—**1898.** STONE, W., Methods of Recording and Using Bird Migration Data, Proc. Acad. Nat. Sci., Phila., pp. 128–156.—**1899.** LIBBY, O. G., The Nocturnal Flight of Migratory Birds, Auk, XVI, pp. 140–146.—**1900.** REYNAULD, G., The Orientation of Birds, Bird-Lore, II, pp. 101–108, 141–147.—**1901.** COLE, L. J., Suggestions for a Method of Studying the Migration of Birds, 3d. Rep. Mich. Acad. Sci., pp. 67–70.—**1902.** WINKENWERDER, H. A., The Migration of Birds with Special Reference to Nocturnal Flight, Bull. Wisc. Nat. Hist. Soc., II, pp. 177–263.—**1903.** BONHOTE, J. L., Bird Migration at Some of the Bahama Lighthouses, Auk, XX, pp. 169–179.—**1903.** COOKE, W. W., Some New Facts about the Migration of Birds, Yearbook, U. S. Dept. Agric., pp. 371–386.—**1904.** COOKE, W. W., Distribution and Migration of N. A. Warblers, Bull. 18, Biol. Surv., 142 pp.; see also pp. 14–20, Warblers of N. A.—**1904.** COOKE, W. W., The Effect of Altitude on Bird Migration, Auk, XXI, pp. 338–341.—**1904.** TAVERNER, P. A., A Discussion of the Origin of Migration, Auk, XXI, pp. 322–333.—**1905.** ALLEN, J. A. (Review), Auk, XXII, pp. 325–328.—**1905.** BISHOP, L. B., The Direction of Flight in the Fall Migration at New Haven, Conn., Auk, XXII, pp. 372–377.—**1905.** COOKE, W. W., Routes of Bird Migration, Auk, XXII, pp. 1–11.—**1906.** CARPENTER, F. W., An Astronomical Determination of the Heights of Birds During Nocturnal Migration, Auk, XXIII, pp. 210–217.—**1906.** COOKE, W. W., Distribution and Migration of N. A. Ducks, Geese, and Swans, Bull. 26, Biol. Surv., 90 pp.—**1906.** STEBBINS, J., A Method of Determining the Heights of Migrating Birds, Pop. Astronomy, XIV, pp. 65–70.—**1906.** STONE, W., Some Light on Night Migration, Auk, XXIII, pp. 249–252. Exceptionally interesting.—**1908.** COOKE, W. W., Bird Migration in the District of Columbia, Proc. Biol. Soc., XXI, pp. 107–118.—**1909.** WATSON, J. B., Some Experiments on Distant Orientation. Papers from the Tortugas Lab. of the Carnegie Inst., II, pp. 227–230.—**1909.** WRIGHT, H. W., Birds of the Boston Public Garden. A Study in Migration, 229 pp. (Houghton, Mifflin & Co.).—**1910.** HENSHAW, H. W., Migration of the Pacific Plover to and from the Hawaiian Islands, Auk, XXVII, pp. 246–262.—**1910.** COOKE, W. W., The Migratory Movements of Birds in Relation to the Weather, Yearbook, U. S. Dept. Agric., pp. 379–390.—**1911.** COOKE, W. W., Our Greatest Travelers, Nat. Geog. Mag., XXII, pp. 346–365, 12 maps.—**1912.** CLARKE, W. E., Studies in Bird Migration, 2 vols., 8vo., 669 pp. (Gurney & Jackson, London).—**1913.** COOKE, W. W., The Relation of Bird Migration to the Weather, Auk, XXX, pp. 205–221.—**1915.** COOKE, W. W., Bird Migration, Bull. 185, U. S. Dept. Agric., 47 pp.—**1915.** WATSON, J. B., and LASHLEY, K. S., Homing and Related Activities of Birds, Pub. No. 211, Carnegie Inst., p. 104.—**1916.** CHAPMAN, F. M., Travels of Birds, 12mo., 160 pp. (Appleton).—**1916.** COOKE, W. W., Second Annual Report of Bird Counts in the U. S., Bull. 396, U. S. Dept. Agric., 20 pp.—**1916.** TYLER, W. M., Call-Notes of Some Nocturnal Migrating Birds, Auk, XXXIII, pp. 132–141.—**1920.** ANDRUS, C. G., Observation of a Remarkable Night Migration, Auk, XXXVII, pp. 603–605.—**1920.** AVERILL, C. K., Migration and Physical Proportions, Auk, XXXVII, pp. 572–579.—**1926.** ROWAN, W., Photoperiodism, Reproductive Periodicity and the Annual Migrations of Birds, Proc. Boston Soc. Nat. Hist., pp. 38, 147–189.—**1926.** THOMSON, A. L., Problems of Bird Migration, 8vo., 350 pp. (Houghton, Mifflin & Co.),—**1926.** BERGTOLD, W. H., Avian Gonads and Migration, Condor, pp. 114–120.—**1927.** WETMORE, A., The Migration of Birds, 12mo., 217 pp. (Harvard Univ. Press, Cambridge).—**1928.** MILLER, L., The Antiquity of the Migratory Instinct, Condor, pp. 119–120.—**1929.** ROWAN, W., Experiments in Bird Migration, Proc. Boston Soc. Nat. Hist., pp. 39, 151–208, illus.—**1929.** ROWAN, W., Migration in Relation to Barometric and Temperature Changes, Bull. Northeastern Bird-banding Assoc., pp. 85–92.—**1930.** ROWAN, W., Reversed Migration, Proc. Nat. Acad. Sci., pp. 16, 520–525.—**1931.** GRINNELL, J., Some Angles in the Problem of Bird Migration, Auk, pp. 22–32.

THE VOICE OF BIRDS

Call-Notes
Song

The gift of song is the bird's most appealing and charming attribute; but, wholly aside from their esthetic importance, the notes of birds have an especial interest for every one who would attempt to interpret and ascertain their significance. The weird cries and enraptured warbles which are often so strangely expressive of nature itself and which so strongly appeal to the wild and primitive within us constitute, in truth, the language of birds, to understand which is to bring one to a new and intimate knowledge of bird-life. It is out of the question to present here anything like an adequate essay on the calls and songs of birds, but the subject is so attractive, and its investigation is so well within reach of the local or isolated student, that it must at least be treated in sufficient detail to suggest lines of study.

Call-Notes.—The term call-notes is somewhat loosely applied to a great variety of bird utterances, including true *call* notes as well as notes or 'calls' of alarm, anger, etc.

The student may first consider the origin of voice in birds, beginning with silent species, like the Man-o'-war-bird and Brown Pelican (though the young of both are noisy enough), through others, like the Cormorant, Water-Turkey, or Black Vulture, which utter only the most rudimentary sounds, to those which have acquired an extended vocabulary, like the Crow or Jay. Then may follow a study of the calls of young birds. With altricial birds, which are reared in the nest, the hunger or food-call with which the returning parent is greeted is the most characteristic, and is common to such unlike birds as Thrushes and other Oscines, Swifts, Pelicans and Herons, in fact, doubtless, to all birds which are fed in the nest.

On the other hand, with præcocial birds which follow the parent shortly after birth, what may be termed the 'lost' or 'location' call is the most important. Here the chick is quickly taught to feed itself, and its life depends chiefly on its ability to keep up with the flock and receive parental care and guidance. The peep of a chick or duckling will be readily recalled as a note of this kind.

When threatened by danger, both altricial and præcocial young, as a rule, try to avoid observation by squatting and remaining motionless, but young Vultures hiss in the most curious manner; young Pelicans and young Boobies scream; young Man-o'-war-birds squeal and rattle their bills; and all three species strike at one most viciously. Possibly the size and snowy plumage of these young birds renders them so conspicuous that they cannot expect to escape observation by remaining motionless, and therefore adopt a more direct and aggressive means of self-preservation.

As the young bird develops, its range of calls increases until finally we have the full vocabulary of maturity. This varies widely with different species, and it may, I think, be truly said that no exhaustive study has as yet been made of the calls of a single species of wild bird.

When the young bird is old enough to care for itself, the language of the nursery is forgotten, and the recognition call, by which individuals of the same species are brought together in flocks or companies, is doubtless its most valuable and most frequently employed vocal asset. This is particularly true with migratory species, whose oft-repeated notes, while winging their way through the night, serve to mark the line of flight and keep stragglers in line. The *pink* of the Bobolink, the liquid *purt* of the Olive-backed Thrush, and the fine but far-carrying *cheep* of Warblers, are familiar illustrations.

Calls of this nature, by which a bird simply announces its presence, together with those of alarm, are uttered by most birds, and it is probable that they constitute a common language, the significance of which is generally understood. That is, a migrating bird may be guided by the notes of other species, without necessarily knowing to what species the call it follows belongs, just as it will recognize as an alarm-call the warning-note of a bird of a different species, which has been the first to see and give notice of the presence of a Hawk or Owl or other form of danger.

Crows, however, immediately recognize the hoot of a Barred Owl as such, and on hearing it at once utter a certain *caw-caw* which may be termed their 'rally-call,' and which is so quickly responded to by other Crows that within a few minutes a throng of them has surrounded the cause of the disturbance. This example serves well to illustrate the difference between the common or characteristic call of a certain species, its simple "I am here" or "This is I," and others possessing a special significance. That the rally-call of the Crow is clearly understood by all the Crows that hear it, no one will doubt who has observed its effect; while further attention to Crow *caws* will reveal a surprising variation in their character and the manner in which they are uttered; all of which doubtless possesses an exact significance to Crows and may some day be intelligible to man.

The Robin also supplies a familiar illustration of a bird possessing a wide variety of calls, each one of which has its own meaning, and indeed one need go no further than the hen-yard to find opportunities for the study of bird-language and to be convinced of the possibilities which may arise from close, sympathetic observation of this phase of the bird's life.

Each species will offer its own problem, but in every instance the greatest interest will center about the life of the nest, where the complex relations of parent with parent and of both with offspring, supply occasions for the utterance of notes heard under no other conditions. Not the least interesting of these will be the warning calls by which the adult conveys to her inexperienced, or even blind, young, knowledge of a threatening danger, in the presence of which they must betray no sign of life. Perhaps no one case more strongly illustrates the importance of a means of exact communication among birds, for failure to understand and obey may here be followed by death.

Song.—As a rule, the songs of birds are uttered by the male alone and mainly or only during the nesting season. It is true that in rare cases the female sings; the female Cardinal and Rose-breasted Grosbeak, for example, sometimes sing to a limited extent, and the females of certain tropical American Wrens sing a delightful duet with their mates. It is also true that some birds sing more or less throughout the year, while many have a short, second song-season after the postnuptial molt. But song in its full development, and with its real significance, is restricted to the nesting season. It is, therefore, a secondary sexual character, an irrepressible manifestation of the greatly increased vitality of the bird during the period of reproduction.

Attention is often called to the fact that the best songsters are dull in color, while brightly plumaged birds are poor singers, but the musical standard here adopted is wholly human, and so far as we know harsh tones may be just as effective in winning a mate as sweet ones. (See also, under Color.)

The systematist classifies as Oscines, or true singing birds, those species which have the "syrinx with four or five distinct pairs of intrinsic muscles, inserted at ends of three upper bronchial half-rings and thus constituting a highly complex and effective musical apparatus" (Coues); but while this group contains the most gifted singers, it does not by any means contain all our song-birds, many species having a less highly developed syrinx with fewer muscles, which are inserted into the middle, not the ends, of the bronchial half-rings, still being able to produce both pleasing and complex vocal sounds. Note, for example, the songs of certain Snipe and Plover or of Goatsuckers. On the other hand, some true Oscines, like Crows, Magpies, and Jays, with a highly developed vocal apparatus, are practically songless, while the Cactus Wren, a member of a family of noted songsters, utters only harsh squawks.

Song, therefore, is not restricted solely to the Oscines, but in a broad sense is the attribute of every species of birds which gives expression to the emotions inspired by the nesting period. The whistling of Grebes, the 'bleating' of Snipe, the 'booming' of Bitterns, the 'trumpeting' of Cranes, the 'whinny' of Soras or 'cooing' of Doves, the hooting of the Owls, are, therefore, types of songs, and we may even include here such mechanical forms of bird music as the 'drumming' of Grouse, tapping of Woodpeckers or 'booming' of Nighthawks.

Through the exercise of these vocal and instrumental gifts, which so delightfully voice the joys and hopes of spring, the male bird announces his territorial rights, replies to the challenge in kind of a rival, and, in due time, informs the female of his presence. Seasonally, therefore, the first object of song is to 'stake a claim' to a nesting area and this is usually done before the female arrives. Recall a flock of male Redwings chanting their gurgling chorus with no streaked female to hear them. Later, when the flock has broken and its individuals have taken possession of their own special bit of marsh- or swamp-land, they sing to warn possible trespassers, as well as to attract the attention of the later-migrating females.

While the chief functions of song are to secure a nesting-ground and a mate, song itself is evidently an expression of the physiological condition incident to the breeding season at which time birds sing with no other incentive than that which comes from within. So the solitary captive sings day after day, spring after spring, with no possibility of securing either home or mate.

The first evidence of the near approach of the nesting season among birds is usually given by the notes of the male. Even before he addresses the female, and, among migratory species, often before the female has arrived, he selects his nesting ground or 'territory,' as Elliot Howard has termed it, and, from a more or less regularly frequented perch, gives notice to rival claimants of his intent to occupy a definite area, and at the same time proclaims his eligibility to any passing female.

While the main object of song is now accomplished, fortunately for the nature-lover the singer continues to voice his passion during the period of nest-building, while his mate is incubating, and rarely (e. g. the Warbling Vireo and Rose-breasted Grosbeak) while he himself sits upon the nest.

With the appearance of the young the song wanes, and with one-brooded species it now soon ceases, but the excess vitality possessed by those birds which rear a second brood is manifested also in their renewed vocal efforts, and their song season is prolonged to midsummer or early August.

As has been said, many species have a second song-period, at the conclusion of the annual post-breeding molt, but it lasts only for a few days and the song rarely reaches the fullness of springtime. As diminishing vigor of the later nesting season ceases to demand full expression, the song may decrease in volume and, at times, is uttered *sotto voce* with closed bill, when, though perfect in form, it may be heard only at close range.

The time of the day, as well as the time of the year in which a species sings, is also to be noted. Early morning and late afternoon are the periods of greatest activity in the bird's day, and it is then that most species are heard singing, but each species will be found to be more or less regular in regard to the time of its singing. Some begin earlier and sing later, some sing more or less throughout the day, others only before sunrise and after sunset, others still by night as well as by day.

In recording a bird's biography one should also learn the duration of the song itself, noting whether it is a short, definite effort, like, for example, that of the Meadowlark or House Wren, or a more or less continuous performance like that of the Red-eyed Vireo, Mockingbird, or Robin. Nothing so stimulates song as song, and the frequency of song in its relation to the abundance of the species should be observed. The partial or complete cessation of song during periods of cold or inclement weather will further illustrate the connection between song and the bird's physical condition.

Singing usually claims all a bird's attention. Some birds, it is true, like the Red-eyed Vireo or Black and White Warbler, sing as they work, but in most instances the bird seeks a point of vantage from which to deliver his message. The Brown Thrasher mounts to the topmost twig of the tallest tree, the Mocker often takes his stand on a chimney, Bob-white mounts to a fence-post, while most of the song-birds of prairie and plain, like the Horned Larks, Pipits, Longspurs, and Lark Buntings, for lack of other perch, deliver their songs from the air.

Other birds, like the Bobolink and Rose-breasted Grosbeak, sing while flying as well as while perching, and observation will show that each species of bird has a more or less well-defined taste in the selection of its song-perch.

The flight-song of birds inhabiting treeless regions must not be confused with the exceptional and infrequent flight—or ecstasy—song of certain birds, like the Ovenbird, Water-Thrushes, and Maryland Yellow-throat, which usually sing from a perch, but which, on occasion, bound into the air, rising only a few feet in the case of the Yellow-throat, but a hundred or more with the *Seiuri*, and on trembling wing utter a hurried, ecstatic outburst of twittering notes wholly unlike their normal song. The Meadowlark has such a flight-song, but in my experience the bird of the plains (*Sturnella neglecta*) utters it far more frequently than does our eastern *Sturnella magna*, a variation possibly due to the difference in the nature of their haunts.

A further study of Meadowlark songs opens the subject of geographical variation in the songs of the same species. Its widely different song is one of the Western Meadowlark's best claims to specific distinctness from the eastern bird, but even among the slightly differentiated forms of *Sturnella magna* there are striking variations in voice. The songs of some Florida Meadowlarks are scarcely recognizable to one familiar only with the Meadowlark in the North, while the Meadowlark of Cuba would not be known to him by its notes.

The 'musical' ear will detect more or less pronounced variations in the voices of other widely distributed species as they are heard in the various parts of their range, and, in addition to this geographical variation, a variation with age may be detected. This is obvious enough with species like the Song Sparrow, the young of which, while still wearing in whole or part their nestling plumage, sing an evidently immature song; and is still apparent with birds like the Orchard Oriole or Indigo Bunting, whose first spring plumage betrays their age and explains why their songs are less finished, less developed than those of the adults of their kind.

Birds inherit at least the calls they utter when in the nest, just as a child cries instinctively, but they apparently do not inherit their songs any more than the child inherits the language of its parents, and in many recorded instances they have learned the notes of the birds within sound of whose voices they have been reared. There are, for example, a number of cases in which young House or English Sparrows when reared with Canaries have learned the Canary's song. Two Baltimore Orioles, reared by W. E. D. Scott ('04) apart from all other birds, developed a song of their own which was wholly unlike that of their species, and this song was learned by four other Baltimore Orioles which were subsequently reared in the companionship of the first two.

It is this strong tendency to imitate which has given rise to the theory of the mimetic origin of bird-song, and which is no doubt largely responsible for much of the individual variation so prevalent in birds' songs. There is, for example, a Maryland Yellow-throat living near my home, the first half of whose song is that of the Yellow Warbler, while the remainder resembles that of its own species, evidence that the inherent predisposition toward the acquisition of the song of its ancestors was not sufficiently strong to prevent its song from being modified by the notes of another species.

It would be interesting to determine just when this presumably inherent tendency is active. Is the nestling unconsciously influenced by the song of its parent during the period of its infancy? Single-brooded birds may not hear the song of their species from the time they leave the nest until the following spring song again announces the opening of the nesting season. It seems probable, therefore, that their song is acquired during the formative period of immaturity and before they come into contact with other species whose notes their strong mimetic gifts might lead them to adopt as their own, as doubtless did the Maryland Yellow-throat mentioned above.

With some species the tendency to imitate is functional long after it has served its universal purpose of giving them the notes characteristic of their species. Among our birds the Mockingbird takes first rank as a mimic, and L. M. Loomis tells me of one with a repertoire containing no less than thirty-two songs of other species of birds; but on the other hand some Mockingbirds sing only their own song. The Catbird, White-eyed Vireo, Blue Jay, and introduced Starling are also to be numbered among the mimics.

SUGGESTIONS FOR THE STUDENT

What North American birds are voiceless? Which possess rudimentary voices? Trace the development of voice. Define the difference between call-notes and song. Note the development of call-notes in the young of præcocial birds; of altricial birds. Interpret, as far as possible, the call-notes of certain species. Give illustrations of different types of anger calls (*e. g.* spitting of brooding Chickadee, snapping of bill by Screech Owl, hiss of Duck, etc.); of alarm-notes; of scolding notes. How are call-notes used by migrating birds? Do birds understand the call-notes of other than their own species? Do the young understand the notes of their parents? What relation exists between voice and character (*e. g.* scream of Hawk, coo of Dove)? Define Oscines. Give instances of song in non-Oscines; in the female. Define the song season. What species have been heard singing in the fall or winter? What is the relation between song and the advance of the nesting season? Among single-brooded species? Among double-brooded species? Mention types of mechanical and other forms of bird-music. What is the function of song? What are the earliest and latest dates on which certain species have been heard singing? What species arrive in song? What is the relation between song and the color of a bird's plumage? What birds sing *sotto voce?* Note the hours at which certain birds sing. What relation exists between the song-perch, haunt, and habit (terrestrial or arboreal)? What birds sing at night? What birds sing on the wing or have a true flight-song? Give instances of individual variation in song; of variation with age; of geographical variation. Do young birds sing their first fall? Do birds inherit the call-notes and songs? When does the young bird acquire its song? Give instances of mimicry in birds.

REFERENCES

1871. DARWIN, C., The Descent of Man.—**1884-5.** BICKNELL, E. P., A Study of the Singing of Our Birds, Auk, I, pp. 60–71, 126–140, 209–218, 322–332; II, pp. 144–154, 249–262.—**1889.** RHOADS, S. N., The Mimetic Origin and Development of Bird Language, Am. Nat., XXIII, pp. 91–102.—**1895.** SHALER, N. S., Domesticated Animals, 155 pp., 8vo. (Scribner's).—**1896.** WITCHELL, C. A., The Evolution of Bird-Song, 10mo., 253 pp., (Black, London).—**1901.** SCOTT, W. E. D., Data on Song in Birds, Science, N. S., XIV, p. 522.—**1904.** MATHEWS, F. S., Field Book of Wild Birds and Their Music, 16mo., 262 pp., illus. (Putnam's).—**1904.** SCOTT, W. E. D., Inheritance of Song in Passerine Birds, Science, N. S., XIX, p.154; XX, p. 282.—**1908.** CRAIG, W., The Voices of Pigeons Regarded as a Means of Social Control, Am. Journ. Sociology, XIV, pp. 86–100.—**1915.** SAUNDERS, A. A., Methods of Recording and Studying Bird-Songs, Auk, XXXII, pp. 173–183; see also, MOORE, R. T., pp. 535–538.—**1916.** SAUNDERS, A. A., Bird-Song, Auk, XXXIII, pp. 103–107, 228–230.—**1918.** HAWKINS, C. J., Sexual Selection and Bird-Song, Auk, XXXV, pp. 421–437.—**1919.** ALLEN, F. H., Evolution of Bird-Song, Auk, XXXVI, pp. 528–536.—**1919.** MOUSLEY, H., How Near to Nest Do Male Birds Sing?, Auk, pp. 339–348.—**1920.** GRINNELL, J., Sequestration Notes, Auk, XXXVII, pp. 84–88.—**1924.** TOWNSEND, C. W., Mimicry of Voice in Birds, Auk, XLI, pp. 541–552.—**1929.** SAUNDERS, A. A., Bird Song, Handbook No. 7, N. Y. State Mus., 202 pp. (a monograph).—**1930.** SHAVER, J. M., and WALKER, G., Effects of Temperature on Singing, 385–397.—**1931.** LUTZ, F. E., Light as a Factor in Controlling the Start of Daily Activity in a Wren and Stingless Bees, Amer. Mus. Novit. No. 468, pp. 1–4.

THE NESTING SEASON

Date	*The Egg, continued*
Number of Broods	*Colors*
Courtship	*Shape*
The Nest	*Variations*
Enemies of Nesting Birds	*Incubation*
Nesting-site	*The Young Bird*
Material	*Condition at Birth*
Construction	*Food*
Character of the Nest	*Nest-sanitation*
Inheritance	*Defence of the Young*
Parasitism	*Voice*
The Egg	*Nest-exercises*
Number Laid	*Fear*
Size	*Flight*

Date.—Why should a bird build its nest at a certain time of the year? Some variation in nesting dates, it is true, is shown by all birds, but this does not affect the truth of the statement that most species have a definite nesting season.

In a general way it may be answered that the nesting period, as a whole, is determined by those climatic changes which, independent of latitude, divide the year into seasons. In the extreme North, where it is possible for birds to nest only during a small portion of the year, the relation between nesting-time and season is obvious enough. But in the South, so far as climate is concerned, birds might rear their young any month in the year; nevertheless, even in the tropics most species, or at least the individuals of a species, appear to have a more or less well-defined nesting season.

So we look for a deeper reason why there should be this regular, annual, nesting period, and we apparently find it, as remarked under Migration, in the bird itself. In the bird-world as in the plant-world there exist cycles of physiological development. The tree buds, leaves, blossoms, fruits, loses its foliage, and rests; then, all in due time, the same events are repeated in proper order. Thus the bird migrates (if it be migratory), mates, builds its nest, lays its eggs, incubates, rears its young, molts, and retreats to winter quarters. There are exceptions to this program, as where a bird raises more than one brood, or has more than one molt, but they are only the results of variations in the under-lying physiological processes which, through a regular series of events, prepare the bird for the nesting season.

Confining our attention to our own birds, we observe that some species nest early and some late in the nesting season. Why is this? The character of the food of the young is the most obvious cause deter-mining the exact date of a bird's nesting. Hence those birds of prey which feed their offspring on mammals or birds are the first birds to nest, while those birds that rear their brood on insects or fruit nest later.

But is not a bird's nesting-time also dependent on whether it be migratory or resident? This is a difficult question to answer, since it is by no means easy to determine whether or not a species is resident, in the strict sense of the word. Among resident species of not dissimilar feeding habits, there is often much difference in nesting dates. The White-breasted Nuthatch near New York City, for instance, nests in the middle of April, while the Downy Woodpecker waits until a month later. The Bluebird nests in the first half of April, the Cedar Waxwing the latter half of June. Possibly a study of the food of their young may ex-plain this difference in dates.

Some migratory birds which arrive at about the same time also nest on widely different dates. Robins and Red-winged Blackbirds, for instance, reach New York City in late February or early March, but the Robin nests nearly a month earlier than the Redwing. Haunts may here exert some influence. The early nesting Robins find favorable sites in evergreens long before the vegetation in the marshes the Redwings frequent affords concealment for their nests. The Woodcock, on the other hand, nests shortly after its arrival, possibly because a site is at once available.

Consequently, in addition to those physiological factors which induce an annual nesting season as one of the phenomena in the cycle of the bird's year, the exact date of a bird's nesting appears to be governed by (1) the nature of the food of its young; (2) whether it is resident or migratory, though this remains to be determined; and (3) the condition of its nesting haunts. To these will doubtless be added other causes, as we become more intimate with the facts involved.

Number of Broods.—Why do some birds raise only one brood and others two or even three? We should look for a partial answer to this question in the length of time required by a species to rear a brood. If the period from the beginning of the nest-building to the date when the resulting young are able to care for themselves is so short that the parents are still in the physiological condition incident to reproduction, a second family may be expected, and under similar circumstances a third may follow. The eggs of the English Sparrow hatch in about twelve days, the young remain in the nest only about a week, and the species is reported to have reared six broods in a season near New York City, but this number is doubtless exceptional. Robins' eggs hatch in thirteen days; the young leave the nest when about two weeks old, and the species raises two or even three broods. But the eggs of Fish Hawks, for example, require four weeks' incubation; the young do not fly until about six weeks old, and the species is one-brooded. These facts, however, fail to explain why many birds in which the periods of incubation and rearing of the young are quite as short as those of the Robin, should have only one brood. The time of a bird's arrival on the nesting-ground doubtless has some bearing on the question, and we should also take into account the time of return to its winter haunts, without in the least being able to say why it should come and go at a certain time. Still, among permanent residents and migrants, which arrive and depart at about the same season, some are single-brooded while others raise two or even three broods. For instance, of the former, the Song Sparrow rears two and on occasions, three broods, while the Chickadee has but one. Here size of the brood may be a factor. Among migrants, the Robin is two- or rarely three-brooded, while the Purple Grackle, which comes just as early and remains nearly as long, is one-brooded. Possibly there are here temperamental differences not to be explained by observable influences.

The question, not infrequently asked, whether any of our migrant birds nest in their winter homes, makes it necessary to add that a bird has only one nesting season, and with those species which rear more than one brood there is no appreciable interval of rest between the first and succeeding broods.

A table of dates showing when one may expect to find full sets of birds' eggs of the first laying near New York City is appended:

Feb.	28.	Great Horned Owl.	Apr. 9.	Long-eared Owl.
Mch.	12.	Barred Owl.	9.	American Crow.
	28.	Carolina Wren.	10.	Bluebird.
	30.	Duck Hawk.	17.	White-breasted Nuthatch.
Apr.	1.	Woodcock.	18.	Broad-winged Hawk.
	3.	Red-shouldered Hawk.	20.	Robin.
	3.	Screech Owl.	25.	Mourning Dove.
	6.	Red-tailed Hawk.	25.	Purple Grackle.

Apr. 28. Phœbe.
29. Song Sparrow.
May 1. Black-crowned Night Heron.
1. Cooper's Hawk.
1. Kingfisher.
2. Osprey.
3. Cardinal.
5. Cowbird.
6. Green Heron.
6. Wood Duck.
7. Flicker.
8. Barn Swallow.
10. Sparrow Hawk.
10. Ruffed Grouse.
10. Clapper Rail.
10. Vesper Sparrow.
11. Louisiana Water-Thrush.
12. Ruby-throated Humming-bird.
13. Red-headed Woodpecker.
14. Acadian Flycatcher.
14. Blue Jay.
14. Chipping Sparrow.
14. Towhee.
15. Virginia Rail.
15. Hooded Warbler.
15. Meadowlark.
15. Field Sparrow.
15. Swamp Sparrow.
16. Brown Thrasher.
16. Blue-winged Warbler.
17. Fish Crow.
17. Catbird.
17. Wood Thrush.
17. Redstart.
18. House Wren.
18. Black and White Warbler.
18. Red-winged Blackbird.
19. Tree Swallow.
19. Bank Swallow.
19. Chickadee.
20. Veery.

May 20. Worm-eating Warbler.
20. Ovenbird.
20. Rose-breasted Grosbeak.
21. Sharp-shinned Hawk.
21. Downy Woodpecker.
21. Least Flycatcher.
22. Northern Parula Warbler.
23. Hairy Woodpecker.
23. Chat.
24. Spotted Sandpiper.
25. Chimney Swift.
25. Purple Martin.
25. White-eyed Vireo.
25. Maryland Yellow-throat.
25. Baltimore Oriole.
26. Bob-white.
26. Marsh Hawk.
28. Red-eyed Vireo.
28. Yellow-throated Vireo.
28. Grasshopper Sparrow.
29. Black-billed Cuckoo.
29. Kingbird.
29. Chestnut-sided Warbler.
29. Bobolink.
29. Indigo Bunting.
30. Yellow-billed Cuckoo.
30. Rough-winged Swallow.
30. Cliff Swallow.
30. Warbling Vireo.
30. Orchard Oriole.
30. Seaside Sparrow.
30. Sharp-tailed Sparrow.
31. Least Bittern.
31. Long-billed Marsh Wren.
June 1. Nighthawk.
1. Kentucky Warbler.
3. Whip-poor-will.
3. Crested Flycatcher.
3. Scarlet Tanager.
5. Wood Pewee.
7. Short-billed Marsh Wren.
19. Cedar Waxwing.
20. American Goldfinch.

Courtship.—Song, as we have seen, has a double function, but display of plumage, fighting, dancing, and other often remarkable activities through which birds give vent to their emotions at this period of maximum vitality are designed sexually to stimulate the female and thus aid the performer to win a mate. The function of song has been discussed, but combat so closely associates action and cause that the development of spurs, for instance, is generally considered a result of that form of natural selection which awards success to the strongest, best-armed fighter and enables it to transmit its own desirable characters to its off-spring. This matter is, however, primarily to be settled by the males. Two or more males meet, battle, and the victor gets the prize of a mate; but has this mate any voice in the matter? In those more peaceful contests where rival males attempt to outdo one another through display of plumage or violent actions, it is even more difficult to decide to what extent the female is influenced, but it seems probable that there is less actual selection than passive acceptance on her part of the male which is most active in battle or display.

It is much easier to make observations in this field than to interpret them. What, for example, is the significance of the squabbles, struttings, and irrepressible vociferousness of the English Sparrow when courting?

Most of our birds are monogamous and doubtless take a new mate for each nesting season, but some of the larger birds, notably among the Hawks and Owls, are known to be more constant and are believed to be mated for life. In either case, however, the mate, if lost, is usually soon replaced, at least in the earlier stages of the nesting season.

Exceptions to the rule of monogamy are shown by the Anis (*Croto-phaga*) which are communistic, and by certain species which are polyg-amous. The Anis live in small flocks throughout the year. The females lay in a common nest and all share the family duties.

Among our North American birds, the Wild Turkey is polygamous, though all association with the female ceases after incubation begins, while the male of the Prairie Hen and of some other members of the Grouse family are said to have more than one mate. The Great-tailed Grackle in Mexico has, at least, as many as five or six wives, and our Red-winged Blackbird has been suspected of Mormonism.

Cowbird males, according to Friedmann, outnumber the females about three to two, and while this author states that the species may occasionally be polyandrous, he believes that it shows a strong ten-dency toward monogamy.

The Nest

Enemies of Nesting Birds.—It will add to our appreciation of a bird's resources, and most assuredly to our sympathy with birds, if before discussing their nesting habits we merely mention some of the enemies and dangers which threaten birds at this season. These are of two kinds: first, the elements; second, predatory animals, including parasites. High winds, heavy rains, prolonged wet or cool periods, and hailstorms are among the weather phenomena often fatal to the life of the nest; while chief among the animals that prey upon the eggs or young of our birds are Crows, Jays, Grackles, cats, squirrels, opossums, minks, weasels, skunks, snakes, and man, who either directly, as an egg-collector for the table or cabinet, or indirectly in mowing fields, clearing hedge-rows, and in other ways has won a prominent place among the enemies of nest-life.

With such an array of adverse conditions and relentless foes, the bird which reaches maturity may be said to have escaped nine-tenths of the dangers to which bird-flesh is heir. One realizes, therefore, how important it is for birds to select a site, build a nest, and care for their young in a way which has proved to be most desirable for their species; and how readily imperfect inheritance of the proper activities or inability to conform to new conditions may mean failure to rear a brood, and in the end extinction of the species.

Nesting-site.—The nature of a bird's nesting-site appears to be determined by (1) the necessity for protection; (2) condition of the young at birth; (3) temperament, as shown by extent of 'territory' (Elliot, '20); (4) habit, whether arboreal, terrestrial, or aquatic; (5) haunt, whether in woodland, field, marsh, etc.

Protection may be secured by hiding the nest, by placing it in more or less inaccessible situations in trees or on cliffs, or by frequenting some isolated islet uninhabited by predatory animals. As I have elsewhere said ('Camps and Cruises of an Ornithologist,' pp. 35–37), "So far as my experience goes, *all* colonial ground-nesting birds breed only on islands." Auks, Murres, Skimmers, Petrels, Tropic Birds, Gannets, Cormorants, Pelicans, and Flamingoes are examples among North American birds, with which Bank Swallows appear to be the only exception. It is less to their terrestrial habit than to their gregariousness that we must attribute the necessity of an island home for these birds. When nesting, all the individuals of a given species, which at other seasons are scattered over a wide area, are focused in a small space. To find one nest is to find all, and to a large degree the fortune of one nest is also the fate of its neighbor.

Even when arboreal, colonial birds like Herons, Spoonbills, Anhingas, and Cormorants usually breed in trees growing in water and which are thus insulated. The birds just mentioned are all exceptions to the rule that terrestrial feeding birds usually nest on the ground, while arboreal feeders nest in trees. But here the condition of the young at birth exerts an influence. The young of Herons, Spoonbills, Anhingas, Cormorants, and Ibises are altricial, hence require the protection of a more or less inaccessible nest during the comparatively long period they are confined to it. On the other hand, the Whip-poor-will is, in feeding habit, a bird of the air, but the eggs are laid on the ground, the præcocial young apparently not requiring the shelter of a nest.

Exceptions to the rule that exclusively terrestrial feeding birds usually nest upon the ground have already been referred to under Herons, Ibises, Spoonbills, etc., whose gregariousness in connection with the condition of the young at birth evidently demands an arboreal site; but the reasons why such terrestrial birds as the Quail and Grouse, Snipe and Plover, or the Loons and Grebes nest on the ground are obvious. It is equally to be expected that birds, like the Catbird, which live among bushes should nest among them, and that arboreal species, like Tanagers, should nest in trees, though we shall always find interesting variations or departures from the normal; as, for example, the nesting of the

Solitary Sandpiper in the old homes of such arboreal species as the Robin, or of the Wood Duck and Golden-eye in trees, while such purely individual variations as a Wild Goose occupying a Fish Hawk's nest or a Mallard laying in a Rough-leg's nest, occur without number.

It is to be expected, too, that the character of a bird's haunts should be reflected in its nesting-site, and as a result we have some most interesting variations in site among birds of the same family but which live in unlike haunts. Many Hawks, for example, are wood-dwellers, and the ideal Hawk's nest is placed in a tree, but the Marsh Hawk lives in treeless areas and nests upon the ground. So the Burrowing Owl of the prairies nests in holes in the ground, while the forest-haunting members of its family usually select hollow trees. Consequently it follows that when there is a marked difference in the range of the same species there is apt to be a corresponding variation in the nature of its nesting-site. The Red-winged Blackbirds living in reedy marshes weave their nests to the reed-stems, while those Redwings of the adjoining alder growths place their nests in alder bushes. Mourning Doves nest in trees in the East and on the ground in treeless areas of the West. Night Herons, which in the East may build 70 to 80 feet from the ground, in the West build near water-level among reeds. Even more surprising is it to find the Great Blue Heron in treeless areas nesting on the bare ground or on rocks, rarely, or never, however, using a terrestrial site except upon islands. While many birds show little or no variation in the character of their nesting-sites, others place their nests in many and widely different situations, even under the same conditions. Robins, for example, aside from nesting in trees at varying heights, place their nests on window-sills, in arbors, summer-houses or barns, on fence-rails, etc., and in cases of this kind it is interesting to learn the fate of those nests which in site depart from the prevailing type.

Civilization, which while it has added the cat to the Robin's enemies, has also decreased the number of its natural foes, is no doubt responsible for much of this variation; few of our native birds have so prospered through the change from forest to farm, though even more marked departure from feral nesting habit has been shown by the Chimney Swift, Barn and Cliff Swallows, Martin, House Wren, and Bluebird, not to mention the irrepressible English Sparrow. Herring Gulls on the same islet build in trees as well as on the ground, and, as Dutcher and Baily have shown, the tree-nests have a solid foundation of sticks and twigs which is lacking in ground-nests. (*The Auk*, XX, 1903, p. 419.)

On Gardiner's Island, where there are no predatory mammals, and, with the exception of Crows, practically no enemies of nesting birds, Robins build their nests in almost any situation, even on the ground, with apparently equal chances of rearing their young. Here, too, Fish Hawks nest, not only in trees, but also in the most exposed situations on the beach; and because of the protection afforded by an insular home, their eggs and young are as safe as those of the tree-nesting individuals of their kind.

As I have elsewhere said ('Camps and Cruises,' p. 37, also pp. 38–61; and *Bird-Lore*, V. 1903, p. 59), it is not probable that in instances of this kind certain birds have with deliberate intent abandoned the customs of their species, but the tendency to vary, being unchecked, finds tangible expression under conditions where new habits may be successfully formed. Doubtless the same tendency exists in the Fish Hawks nesting on the mainland, but there the struggle for existence is so much more intense that any wide departure from the standard may be attended by disastrous results. Environment is thus the mold in which habit is cast.

Through these generalizations we come to the more practical, definite side of the question of nesting-site, and ask which sex selects it. With some species it is known to be the female; with others the male; and with still others the situation must evidently be satisfactory to both sexes; but exact observations on this subject are few.

More difficult it will be to learn whether the same individual occupies the same site and even the same nest season after season. Fish Hawks and birds which return to the same islet year after year are known to do this, and the habit is probably common to many species. Doubtless the practice of banding birds will yield much valuable information in this field.

With birds which have more than one brood in a season, a new nest is usually built. It is then of interest to compare its site with that chosen for the earlier nest, to ascertain how much variation in site-selection the same individuals may exhibit.

Material.—The material of which a bird builds its nest depends in most cases upon the nature of the bird's haunts. The nests of marsh-haunting birds are usually made of reeds or woven of wet marsh grasses; woodland birds generally employ twigs, rootlets, bark, leaves, mosses, etc.; while field-inhabiting species, as a rule, use chiefly dried grasses. It follows, therefore, that a change in the nature of a bird's haunts often causes more or less variation in the character of its nesting material. In the North, for example, the Acadian Flycatcher builds its nest of plant-stems, grasses, and dried blossoms, but in Florida it uses the Spanish or *Tillandsia* 'moss,' a material, by the way, which enters into the nests of many birds. In the East, Night Herons, building in trees, use sticks; in the West, where they nest in marshes, the nest is composed of reeds. There are many similar instances.

A familiar case of local variation, due to change in environment, is furnished by the Baltimore Oriole, which gathers string, worsteds, etc., in place of plant fibers; and experimenters have tried to determine the bird's choice of colors by supplying it with worsteds of varied hues, without, however, other result than a demonstration of range in choice among different individuals, since some selected gay and others dull colors.

The use by birds of rags, paper, horse-hair, etc., also clearly illustrates the influence of civilization on the bird's selection of material with which to build a nest.

PLATE II

WELL-FORMED NEST OF RED-WINGED BLACKBIRD—AN ALTRICIAL SPECIES
Englewood, N. J.

SIMPLE NEST OF PHEASANT (*Phasianus*)—A PRÆCOCIAL SPECIES
Gardiner's Island, L. I.

The necessity for concealment is, in some cases, a potent influence in the choice of nesting material. What is generally spoken of as 'nest decoration,' if it have any significance, is assuredly not designed to make the nest conspicuous through display, but inconspicuous by matching it with its surroundings. The lichen-covered nests of the Wood Pewee, Blue-gray Gnatcatcher, and Hummingbird are examples of this class.

The Great-crested Flycatcher introduces a bit of cast-off snake-skin into its nest, it has been said, to serve the purpose of a scare-crow. The explanation is important if true but lacks evidence to support it.

The student should try to observe the methods employed by birds in gathering and carrying the material for their nests, noting for example, Robins, Barn and Eave Swallows picking up billfuls of mud, a Chimney Swift breaking off dead twigs with bill or feet, a Hummingbird collecting lichens from a tree-trunk, an Oriole tugging at a plant-fiber, etc.

Construction.—Then follows a study of nest-construction, from the simple method of the Skimmer which, by squatting low and turning around again and again, hollows a nest in the sand, to the more complex activities of Swallows, Swifts, and Orioles which respectively exhibit the arts of the mason, joiner, and weaver. Herrick's detailed study of a pair of Robins while nest-building should be read in this connection. The work may be performed by one or both sexes. In the former case the female is usually the builder when the male may assist by bringing material. The nest may be completed in a day and occupied at once, or a longer time may be required, and it may apparently be deserted for days after its completion. The weather, particularly if the temperature is much below the average, is a factor here. In some species, notably the Long-billed Marsh Wren, the nest-building instinct does not seem to be satisfied by the making of a single structure, and the male continues his work after the female is sitting, building one or more additional homes in which possibly he may sleep, and which are sometimes called 'cock-nests.'

Character of the Nest.—From an architectural point of view, nests may differ greatly even when the material of which they are composed is the same. The tools (bill and feet) with which a bird is provided do not often bear any relation to the character of the home their owner builds. A Swallow, it is true, could not construct a Woodpecker's dwelling, but a momentary comparison of the widely different kinds of nests built by various species of Swallows and Swifts (which so far as nesting tools are concerned may be classed with Swallows) readily shows how little the structure of the bird has to do with nest architecture.

Most of the causes determining the nature of site and material are also more or less active in shaping the nest itself, but of them all by far the most important is the condition of the young bird at birth. Indeed in considering this question we are brought very near to an inquiry concerning the origin of birds' nests.

As regards their condition when leaving the egg, birds may be roughly classified in two groups: First, those which leave the nest shortly after hatching; second, those which are reared in the nest. Birds of the first class are termed præcocial; those of the second, altricial. Compare the newly hatched young of a Grouse and a Robin and we have two excellent examples of præcocialism and altricialism; while a further comparison of the Grouse's simple bed of leaves with the Robin's firm, deep cup of mud and grasses equally well illustrates the difference in the nests of præcocial and altricial birds. The former serve only to hold the eggs; the latter perform not only this function but must also house the young during their period of helplessness.

The significance of the condition of the young at birth is doubtless far-reaching, but, unfortunately, it is not as yet understood. It appears that most of the older or lower forms of birds—that is, those which most closely approach the reptilian types, whence it is believed birds have descended—are præcocial. On the other hand, all the higher birds, that is those farthest removed from reptilian ancestors, are altricial. For example, among North American birds the Grebes, Loons, Gulls, Terns, Ducks, Rails, Coots, Snipe, Plovers, Quail, and Grouse, are præcocial, and build, as a rule, nests of the most rudimentary kind, while the great group of Perching Birds (Passeres), containing half the known birds, are altricial, and all build more or less complex nests.

It is possible, therefore, that as altricialism has been evolved from præcocialism, so the type of nest has changed, keeping pace with the demands which the young birds make upon it. There are, however, some exceptional cases of birds, like Pelicans, Water-Turkeys, and Cormorants, which, while low in the evolutionary scale, have altricial young, and in consequence build well-formed, complex nests. The Noddy Tern, sole tree nest-builder of its group, usually constructs in bushes a nest of sufficient strength to harbor the young for two months. (Thompson, *Bird-Lore*, V, 1903, p. 81.)

Other low types of altricial birds secure shelter for their helpless young without actually building a nest, but by using a natural cavity in tree or cliff, or by making a burrow, and we doubtless have here a primitive type of bird home.

It is impracticable to go into further detail here, but the study of birds' nests may be indefinitely extended by taking up certain species of birds and considering their nesting-habits in the light of what appears in this chapter.

Inheritance.—There is no reason to doubt that nest-building is as much an instinctive activity with birds as it is with bees or wasps. Some writers would have us believe that the young bird in the nest makes mental notes of its surroundings for use the following spring; but even man himself could not tell how certain birds' nests were built merely by looking at them. The young bird, therefore, builds its first nest without ever having seen one made and with no other experience with nests than is implied by having lived in one.

There can be no question that the impulse to build is as much the result of a physiological prompting as the impulse to mate which precedes it, or the impulse to lay which follows it. Inherited habit directs the impulse in normal channels and, allowing for the range of individuality present in a greater or less degree in all birds, the bird, in its proper environment, selects a site and constructs a home after the manner of its species. When, however, the environment is changed and new conditions of site or material are introduced, the nest-building impulse, unchecked, and inevitably demanding an outlet, finds expression through new media. Possibly it is governed to some extent by intelligence, but any departure from type is usually an experiment, and the progressive individual pays the price or gains the reward of the pioneer by dire failure on the one hand or exceptional success on the other.

It is not unusual to observe evidences of sexual activity among birds in the fall—a mere reflection of the instincts of the nesting season—and among them is what might be called 'play' at site-hunting and material gathering. So I have seen Tree Swallows, in August, investigate the openings in piles and pick up bits of dried grass only to drop them after a flight of 50 yards or more; and in this connection it is of significance to learn that they were all birds of the year ('Bird Studies with a Camera,' p. 103; see also Brewster, *The Auk*, 1898, p. 194).

Parasitism.—In a comparatively few cases, the instinct to build a nest is wanting, when the bird entrusts its egg to the care of another species. The European Cuckoo and our own Cowbird are examples of this kind of parasitism.

Of the 113 species of birds in whose nests the egg of the Eastern Cowbird (*Molothrus ater ater*) has been found, thirty-nine or about one-third, are Warblers and Vireos, showing how often the Cowbird selects a host materially smaller than herself. The Warbler may nest upon the ground, or 80 feet above it and still be victimized by the Cowbird which, never having had a nest of its own, has formed no attachment for any particular site. In his notable monograph, of 'The Cowbirds' ('29), Friedmann finds the origin of the Cowbirds' parasitism in the partial loss of its territorial instincts and hence of a desire to protect its eggs: but his work should be read in this connection.

The Egg

Number Laid.—The number of eggs comprising a full 'set' or 'clutch' ranges from one to as many as twenty. No law governing this number is known, though birds of temperate zones usually lay more eggs than their representatives in the tropics. Our northern Terns (Common, Roseate, Arctic), for example, usually lay three eggs, while southern Terns (Noddy, Sooty, Bridled) lay but one. Our Thrushes lay normally four eggs, but tropical Thrushes lay only two or three.

Generally speaking, birds of the same family lay approximately the same number of eggs, but there is much variation between birds of closely related families (*e. g.* Loons and Grebes, Thrushes and Wrens), while birds of similar nesting-sites may not lay the same number of eggs (*e. g.* Bob-white and Meadowlark).

The young of præcocial birds require less care than do those which are wholly dependent on their parents, and among Grouse, Quail, and Ducks we find the largest families. But, on the other hand, the eminently præcocial Snipe and Plover have but four young. These birds, however, are too small to cover more than four of their disproportionately large eggs, while the gallinaceous birds can readily cover a dozen or more. Therefore, size of the parent, as well as condition of the young at birth, is here a governing factor.

The number of eggs laid is no indication of the fecundity of the bird. At the time of laying, the ovary contains a large number of partly formed eggs, of which, normally, only the required number will become fully developed. But if the nest be robbed, the stolen eggs will frequently be replaced. The oft-cited case of the Flicker which laid seventy-one eggs in seventy-three days is in point, while the long-continued laying of our domestic fowls is a familiar illustration of the results following unnatural stimulation of the ovaries caused by persistent robbing.

Size of the Eggs.—Primarily, the size of the egg depends upon the size of the bird that lays it. Hummingbirds, the smallest birds, lay the smallest eggs, while Ostriches, the largest birds, lay the largest eggs. This scale, however, is not always maintained, the eggs of præcocial birds being relatively larger than those of altricial birds of the same size, obviously because of the more advanced, larger young they hold. Compare, for example, the eggs of a Meadowlark with those of an Upland Plover, or a Robin's eggs with those of a Spotted Sandpiper.

The Colors of Eggs.—The colors of eggs are due to pigments deposited by ducts while the egg is receiving its shell in the lower or uterine dilation of the oviduct. One or all the layers of the shell may be pigmented, and variation in color may be caused by a superimposed stratum of carbonate of lime, producing lilac tints and 'clouded' or 'shell' markings. In the earlier stages of their descent from reptilian ancestors all birds doubtless laid white eggs, as do all reptiles, and color is believed to have been acquired for purposes of protection, as the bird has departed from the reptilian habit of covering its eggs or laying them in covered situations and has adopted a more or less open nest. Hence, where the eggs are still placed in holes or hollowed trees, they as a rule are white, and where they are laid in exposed situations they are usually protectively marked. Compare, for example, the eggs of Kingfishers, Woodpeckers, and Owls, with those of Terns, Snipe, or Plover. There are, however, numerous exceptions to this rule; for instance, Doves lay white eggs in frail, open nests. But here both sexes incubate and the eggs are rarely exposed. Again, Grebes lay white or whitish eggs in flat, open nests, but they generally cover them with nest material before leaving the nest.

PLATE III

EGGS OF MEADOWLARK AND UPLAND PLOVER

Size of eggs in relation to condition of young birds when hatched. Note that, while the birds are of about the same size, the eggs of the Meadowlark, an altricial bird, are much smaller than those of the Upland Plover, a præcocial bird.

EGGS OF COMMON TERN

Collected in a small colony on an island in Shoal Lake, Man., to show variation in color and pattern.

While we cannot so readily explain why Chickadees or Cliff Swallows lay pigmented eggs, it is obvious that the significance of the colors of eggs can be ascertained only by a study of them where they were laid.

Shape of Eggs.—Birds' eggs are usually ovate, but may be elliptical, spherical, pyriform, or conical. The pyriform egg of the Murre, when moved slowly, describes a circle about its own point, and is therefore less apt to roll over the narrow, rocky ledges on which Murres usually lay, than an oval egg. The conical eggs of Snipe and Plover are placed in the nest point downward or inward, thus fitting together so closely that they can be easily covered by the comparatively small-bodied parent. Thus with form, as with color, it is clear that the egg should be studied where the bird placed it.

Variations.—Although, generally speaking, the eggs of the same species resemble one another, there is a wide range of variation in color, size and shape, and to a lesser degree in number. Doubtless these variations are in the main an index of the physical condition of the bird concerned. Fully adult, vigorous birds probably lay larger and more heavily pigmented eggs and more of them than their younger or weaker fellows. Again, the first eggs of a set, as well as those of first sets, where more than one is laid, may be more strongly pigmented or larger than those laid later. But whatever their cause, the cataloguing of these variations constitutes no small part of the labors of the oölogist, whose delight in finding an unusually large set, or one containing 'runt' eggs, or colored eggs which should be plain, or plain eggs which should be colored, is somewhat out of proportion to the scientific value of the 'discovery.'

Incubation.—The period of incubation is more or less closely related to the size of the egg. With the Chipping Sparrow it is twelve days, but with the Ruby-throated Hummingbird fourteen; the English Sparrow requires twelve or thirteen, the Robin thirteen or fourteen, the Fish Hawk about twenty-eight.

Incubation is usually performed by the female and is sometimes equally shared by the male; or the male may merely cover the eggs during the female's absence; or again, as with the Ruby-throated Hummingbird, he may not be seen near the nest after the eggs are laid. With the Phalaropes the male alone incubates.

The treatment of their eggs by sitting birds is a subject concerning which we have not much information, though some birds are known to turn them with their feet and others with their bills. I have seen a Least Bittern calmly eat two of her five eggs which had been punctured by a Marsh Wren, and then settle herself on the remaining three. ('Bird Studies with a Camera,' p. 75.)

The disposal of the eggshell is also a matter of interest. Most birds carry it some distance from the nest before dropping it, but young Flamingoes eat it!

The Young Bird

Condition at Birth.—The treatment of the young bird during its period of dependence on parental care is determined primarily by its state on leaving the egg. If it be præcocial and hence runs or swims with the parent the day it is born, its early life will differ greatly from that of the altricial bird, which hatched naked, blind, and helpless, is reared in the nest.

In either case, the act which in natural succession follows incubating is brooding. Præcocial birds are usually hatched within a few hours of each other, and are as a rule brooded in the nest only until the water-proof sheath, in which their natal down is enclosed, is dry and slits, transforming the nestling from an apparently scantily haired little creature to one thickly covered with down. After that they are brooded only at night or when, tired, they are permitted to 'snuggle' beneath the parental breast.

But altricial birds, which may be hatched at longer intervals, are brooded more or less constantly for days or until their own feathers are sufficiently grown to protect them. Even then, when exposed to rain or sun, the parent may stand above them with half-spread wings.

Food.—The young of præcocial birds feed themselves, but either learn by experience or are taught by their parents what they shall eat. Recall a hen clucking to her chicks and picking up and dropping bits of food she desires them to have. Even the act of drinking is not instinc-tive. (See especially Lloyd Morgan's 'Habit and Instincts.')

The young of altricial birds, not only when they are in the nest, but as long as a month after leaving it, are fed by the parents. The nature of the food and the manner in which it is given are subjects of far too great import to be adequately treated here. The food, at first, is usually more or less digested in the crop or stomach of the parent whence it is regurgitated into the mouth of the young. With Passerine birds, this method, when employed, is soon abandoned, and food in a more or less natural state is captured and given directly to the open-mouthed offspring; but the Flicker, Hummingbirds, and Doves, for example, feed only by regurgitation, inserting their bill far into the mouth of their young.

Young Pelicans, Cormorants, Water-Turkeys, Spoonbills, and Ibises thrust their bill down the throat of their parents. Flamingoes introduce the tip of their great bill into that of their single chick, giving it, by regurgitation, a few drops of predigested liquid food, an exceptional method of feeding among præcocial birds; young Herons grasp the bill of their parent at the base with their own, as one would with a pair of scissors, when the old bird either disgorges food into the nest or skill-fully into the mouth of the young. Hawks tear the food into bits and give it to their young, and larger insects are beaten or pulled apart by Passerine birds, both parents sometimes working together at the task.

The young of Passerine birds are fed every few minutes throughout a greater part of the day, but the young of larger birds are waited on less frequently, hours often elapsing between meals, at which, however, they receive large portions.

The rate of growth of young birds, particularly of young perching birds, is little short of marvelous. Herrick ('08, p. 187) writes of a young Cedar Waxwing the weight of which "doubled on the first day, more than trebled on the second, and nearly quadrupled on the third. On the twelfth day, when it weighed approximately one and one-fifth ounces, and had increased in weight thirteen-fold, it left the nest." "At a corresponding rate of growth," he adds, "a ten-pound baby when one day old would weigh twenty-one pounds, and at the age of twelve days one hundred and thirty-four pounds." A young Song Sparrow, studied by Owen, weighed, on hatching, 2.9 grams, and when at the age of seven days it left the nest, 16 grams. (*The Auk*, 1899, p. 222.)

Herrick ('05, p. 181), whose continued, systematic studies have added so greatly to our knowledge of the life of the nest, was among the first to discover that admirable adjustment of the young bird's nervous system which prevents it from being overfed. He writes: "The food is placed not simply in the mouth of the young bird but well down the sensitive throat, and if the bird does not immediately respond, it is withdrawn and passed to another, and often to a third, until a throat is found which has the proper reaction time. If the gullet is already full, the swallowing reflex is inhibited, and the bird must wait."

Nest-sanitation.—Second only in importance to the subject of food is that of nest-sanitation. The young of altricial birds as unlike as Hawks and Hummingbirds, void their excreta far over the edge of the nest, but with probably all our Passerine birds, and with some others, it is enclosed in a membranous sac which is removed and, in some cases, devoured by the parent.

Defence of the Young.—Just how birds defend their young from their natural enemies we cannot always say, but before man as a possible nest-robber, some species (*e. g.* Pelicans, Flamingoes, Cormorants, Ibises, Spoonbills, Herons, and most Raptores) desert the nest without protest; others (Gulls, Terns, some Raptores) protest loudly and dart at the enemy, sometimes actually hitting him; the Passeres, with some exceptions (*e. g.* Crows and Jays), utter loud alarm or call-notes, which more often betray their secret than conceal it, and the Thrasher will occasionally strike the intruder; while many ground-nesting birds (*e. g.* Ducks, Snipe, Grouse, Nighthawks, Doves) seek to draw attention from their nest or young, by feigning partial helplessness and fluttering painfully before the marauder, always, however, keeping just beyond his reach, a wonderful exhibition of parental devotion the origin and development of which it is difficult to explain.

Voice.—Some suggestions for a study of the notes of young birds are made in the chapter on the 'Voice of Birds.' Their instinctive obedience to parental command is also mentioned. Observe, for example, how young Gulls, Terns, or Grouse squat and remain perfectly

motionless in response to a certain alarm-note; and how, under the
same stimulus, a brood of young Ducks scatters.

Certain birds have a feeding-note which induces the young bird to
open its mouth in preparation for the coming morsel. On leaving the
nest some young birds (*e. g.* Baltimore Oriole, Yellow-headed Blackbird) develop a food-call which is lost when they have learned to care
for themselves.

Nest-exercises.—While in the nest, young birds devote much attention
to their newly grown feathers, preening them carefully and repeatedly.
The parasites which infest some birds, notable Phœbes, while in the nest
also give the young bird much occupation. The frequent stretching of
the wing is a characteristic nest-activity, and, according to Scott, the
grasping of the nest-lining with the toes is an important nest-exercise.

Fear.—Herrick (*l. c.* p. 227) considers the instinct of fear to be inherited, but it apparently is often wanting in birds which have never
known parental care. I have seen young Wild Geese, which were hatched
from eggs taken from a wild bird's nest and placed under a hen, so
devoid of the sense of fear that when two weeks old they would attempt
to crowd into a hand-basin when it was being used; while innumerable
instances of birds raised from the nest, which have never developed a
sense of fear, could be mentioned. In a state of nature, the young bird
does not evince fear until it has acquired sufficient strength to respond
to the impulses born of fear; in other words, until it can run, swim, or
flutter in the first attempts at flight.

Flight.—Some young birds remain in the nest only a week (*e. g.* Song
Sparrow, House Sparrow), while the Wandering Albatross is said not to
leave its nest until forced to by the parents at the beginning of the
nesting season succeeding its birth.

It is of interest to note the stimulus which finally induces flight,
whether supplied by the parent, for example, through a refusal to bring
further food to the nest, or through increasing strength which prompts
the bird to make its initial venture in the world. The first flight may be
a mere flutter to an adjoining limb, or so well directed that the young
bird (*e. g.* Swallows) directs its movements with the ease, grace, and
precision of the adult.

The nest may now be used as a roosting-place, and the young remain
under the care of the parents for as much as a month. With the Robin,
the male is said to frequent the summer roosts formed by these birds,
with the young, while the female incubates the second set of eggs.

Suggestions for the Student

Necessity for Concealment.—If one would study the habits of birds
under natural conditions, it is of the first importance that they be unalarmed
by one's presence. With birds, as with man, the consciousness of being
under observation induces more or less artificiality of behavior, and if one
would gain true insight into either bird-life or human life one's subject
should be unaware that it is an object of scrutiny.

Some nests may be built within range of already existing hiding-places, but in the end it will be found desirable to employ a portable blind such as has been described. During thirty years' experience this blind has met many and widely different demands, and whether one uses a camera or only a note-book it will enable one to reach a point of vantage from which either photographs or observations can be satisfactorily made. It is unnecessary to speak of the value of the camera as a means of securing graphic, communicable records of the life of the nest, but in any event I cannot too strongly urge the use of a blind. When one wishes to have several nests under observation, a blind may be placed and left near each one, and with extremely wary species it may be erected at night. It is then not associated with any cause of alarm, and is more quickly accepted than if the birds were disturbed when it was being set up. It will usually save much time to have a companion accompany you to the blind and depart as you enter it. The impression of fear caused by your approach will be largely dispelled by his withdrawal, since birds do not distinguish between two and one.

Professor Herrick's plan of cutting off the limb containing the nest and removing it to the blind may be employed by careful, conscientious students, who are in a position to assume the responsibilities involved and who desire not merely to photograph but to see at close range the details of the later phases of nest-life, but it is not a method to be recommended to the general public. In the beginning, at any rate, one will find abundant opportunity afforded by nests which can be studied without moving them or unduly disturbing their surroundings.

Do not imagine that the most thorough history of the life of one nest completes your studies of that species. It may serve for the individuals concerned, but the behavior of many individuals must be learned before one can assert what are the habits of the species. Again I emphasize the need for specialization. Better a mass of data which permit one to judge of the significance of the facts involved, than an accumulation of isolated, unrelated observations.

The preceding annotated outline of the principal phases of bird-study in the nesting season will be of greater value to the student if read with the nesting habits of some particular species in mind, and as a further guide to the study of nest-life there is appended a summary of the more important problems confronting the local student.

Date.—What species are among the first to nest? Why? How long after its arrival does a migratory species nest? Are there any relations between the development of foliage and nesting-date? Between food and nesting-date? What appear to be the local factors governing the nesting-date? What species raise more than one brood? Do you know of any definite cases of third broods? Why are some birds single- and others double-brooded?

Courtship.—Does the male arrive in advance of the female? Do the birds ever arrive mated? What evidences of courtship are noted? Does the male display before the female? Does the female appear to be interested? Does she select or accept a mate? Does the sexual display continue after mating? Does display precede a second brood?

Nest Enemies.—To what forms of danger are nesting birds subjected in your vicinity?

Nesting-site.—What factors influence the choice of nesting-site? Which of them are potent in your vicinity? Why do gregarious ground-builders nest on islands? What variations in site have been noted? How are they to be accounted for? With what species has civilization affected the nature of the nesting-site? Which sex selects the site? Is the same site used for the nests of second broods? or in succeeding years?

Material.—What factors govern the bird in the choice of material? What variations have been noted? What birds use artificial material, string, etc.? How is it gathered? How far from the nest? By one or both sexes? How is so-called 'nest decoration' to be explained?

Nest-building.—Is the nest made by one or both sexes? If the male does not build, does he bring material? How is the nest constructed? How much time is required for its completion? Is it delayed by inclement weather? Is more than one nest built? If the nest is abandoned, state why.

The Nest.—What relation exists between the nest and the structure of its builder? What causes determine the appearance of the nest? What variations in form have been noted? How are they to be explained? Which nests are of the most primitive kind? Which nests are most advanced? How do new conditions change the character of the nest? Do birds inherit their nest-building abilities? Do second nests resemble those built for the first brood?

The Egg.—How long after the completion of the nest is the first egg laid? Are the eggs laid at regular intervals? At certain hours? How many are laid? What factors appear to govern the number? the size? the shape? the color? What variations have been noted? If an egg should be removed will the bird replace it? Will a Cowbird's egg be rejected? How?

Incubation.—When does incubation begin? How long does it continue? Is it performed by one or both sexes? Is there any regularity in the daily periods of sitting? Does one sex ever feed the other while on the nest? Will the sitting bird permit a near approach? Does the bird return to the nest directly or with much caution? Are the eggs turned in the nest? Are they covered when left? How is the eggshell disposed of after hatching?

The Young Bird.—What is the condition of the young bird at birth? If blind, when do the eyes open? What notes does it utter? How long is it in the nest? How is it fed? on what? how often? Is the food prepared? What prevents the young bird from being overfed? At what rate does it increase in weight? How is it brooded? How is the nest cleaned? Do the young obey the parent? When is fear first shown? Is it instinctive? What nest-exercises are manifested? How long after leaving the nest is the young bird dependent on the parents? What induces it to leave the nest? Does it fly at once? Does it return to the nest? Does it frequent roosts? Does it flock with other young or with adults or both? How do the parents protect the young?

REFERENCES

(Restricted largely to the more recent studies of the nesting habits of birds.)

1844. RENNIE, J., Bird Architecture (London).—**1878.** ALLEN, J. A., An Inadequate Theory of Birds' Nests, Bull. Nutt. Orn. Club, III, pp. 22–32.—**1900.** CHAPMAN, F. M., Bird Studies with a Camera, 12mo, 218 pp., illus., (Appleton).—**1900.** DUGMORE, A. R., Bird Homes, 4to, 183 pp., illus., (Doubleday).—**1902.** JOB, H. K., Among the Water-Fowl, 12mo, 224 pp., illus., (Doubleday).—**1905.** JOB, H. K., Wild Wings, 8vo, 341 pp., illus., (Houghton, Mifflin & Co.).—**1905.** HERRICK, F. H., Home Life of Wild Birds, rev. ed., 255 pp., illus., (Putnam's). (Important.)—**1907.** FINLEY, W. L., American Birds, 12mo, 256 pp., illus., (Scribner's).—**1907.** CHAPMAN, F. M., Camps and Cruises of an Ornithologist, 8vo, 432 pp., illus., (Appleton).—**1908.** WATSON, J. B., The Behavior of the Noddy and Sooty Terns, Papers from Tortugas Lab. of Carn. Inst., II, pp. 189–255. (Important.) —**1910.** HERRICK, F. H., Instinct and Intelligence in Birds, Pop. Sci. Monthly, June, July, and August.—**1911.** HERRICK, F. H., Nests and Nest-building in Birds, Journ. of Animal Behavior, Vol. I, (Holt).—**1914.** SAUNDERS, A. A., Ecological Study of Breeding Birds, Auk, XXXI, pp. 200–210.—**1915.** BURNS, F. L., Periods of Incubation, Wilson Bull., No. 90, pp. 275–286.—**1917.** BERGTOLD, W. H., A Study of the Incubation Periods of Birds, Denver, Colo., 8vo, 109 pp.—**1917.** MOUSLEY, H. A., A Study of Subsequent Nestings after the Loss of the First, Auk, XXXIV, pp. 381–393, illus. —**1920.** HOWARD, H. E., Territory in Bird-Life, 308 pp., illus., (Dutton & Co.).—**1921.** BURNS, F. L., Comparative Periods of Nestling-Life of Some North American Nidicolæ, Wilson Bull., pp. 4–15, 90–99, 177–182.—**1922.**

PLATE IV

PLUMAGES OF THE SCARLET TANAGER

1. Adult male, summer. 2. Adult male in post-nuptial (fall) molt, by which it passes into (3) winter plumage. 4. Young male, first winter. 5. Female, which, after the post-juvenal molt, undergoes no changes in color. 6. Juvenal, or nestling plumage, which, in the male, is followed by plumage No. 4, and, in the female, by plumage No. 5.

ALLEN, A. A., Home-Life of Birds, Bird-Lore, pp. 232–241, illus.—**1924.**
HANNA, W. C., Weights of About 3,000 Eggs, Condor, pp. 146–153.—**1929.**
FRIEDMANN, H., The Cowbirds, A Study in the Biology of Social Parasitism,
421 pp. (C. C. Thomas, Springfield, Ills.).

THE PLUMAGE OF BIRDS

The Molt
Plumage Wear
The Colors of Plumage
Color and Age
Color and Season
Color and Sex
Color and Climate
Mutation
Color and Concealment
Banner-marks
Albinisn and Dichromatism

Feathers are the only character which birds do not share with other forms of life. No other animals are feathered and no birds are featherless.

It is apart from our object to describe here the development and structure of feathers, but rather to discuss their function, as in their form they fit the bird for locomotion (see beyond, under Uses of the Wing and Tail) or in color adapt it to the special needs of its haunts and habits. In the first place, however, the field student should have some knowledge of the laws of feather-change included under the general term of molt.

The Molt.—When hatched, a Passerine bird is naked except for a scanty growth of filmy down on the feather-tracts of the upper half of the body. This is the 'natal down' of Dwight ('00) whose terminology I adopt. The natal down is quickly succeeded by the 'juvenal' or nestling plumage, which is sufficiently grown in from eight to fourteen days to enable the bird to leave the nest. The tail is still only about half-grown and the wings, as a rule, barely large enough to permit of short, uncertain flight.

Some birds (*e. g.* Sharp-tailed and Seaside Sparrows) wear this juvenal or nestling plumage between two and three months, but most species lose it shortly after leaving the nest. In either case it is followed by the first winter plumage, which is acquired by molt (postjuvenal) of all the body-feathers, most of those of the wings and tail usually being retained. If the young bird now resembles its parent, their plumage changes are thenceforth the same.

In the fall all birds molt but in the spring there is no regularity as to feather-renewal, even among closely related species. The Bobolink and the Sharp-tailed Sparrow have a complete spring molt (prenuptial), even to the wings and tail; the Scarlet Tanager and Goldfinch molt only the body-feathers; other species acquire some new feathers about the head and chin; and with many there is no feather growth at this season, the differences between the winter and breeding plumages being due to wear or fading.

After the breeding season all adult birds pass through a complete molt (postnuptial), and the bird is again in winter plumage.

In its simplest form, and ignoring the comparatively few cases in which an essentially adult plumage is not acquired at or before the first prenuptial (spring) molt, the molt among the Passeres may be summarized as follows: (1) Natal down, lost by postnatal molt which brings the (2) juvenal or nestling plumage; lost by postjuvenal molt which brings the (3) first winter plumage; lost to a greater or less extent in some species by prenuptial molt which brings the (4) nuptial plumage; lost by postnuptial molt which brings the (5) second and subsequent winter plumages.

With some minor variations this is also the general order of molt among other than Passerine birds. Except the Ducks and Ptarmigan all birds have a complete postnuptial molt, and with many Snipe the spring or prenuptial molt is complete. Some Snipe wear the juvenal plumage until winter or even until the prenuptial molt, the postjuvenal molt being omitted.

Among the præcocial Gulls, Terns, Ducks, shore-birds and gallinaceous birds the natal down thickly covers the body and the chick swims or runs about in it shortly after hatching. In the Gallinæ the wing-quills are large enough to permit of short flights while the body of the chick is still in the downy plumage. They are lost at the succeeding postnatal molt, which is entire, new wing- and tail-feathers, as well as body-feathers, being acquired.

Ptarmigan unmistakably demonstrate the need of a protective coloration by undergoing only a limited instead of complete molt at the close of the nesting season. It affects solely the upperparts and breast, or exposed surfaces, and is obviously a transition plumage, of neutral browns and grays, designed to prevent the acquisition of the wholly white winter dress until the coming of snow, at which time a complete molt follows and the bird becomes as white as its surroundings.

The males of northern Ducks, which differ in color from the female, have a not dissimilar partial postnuptial molt by which they acquire what is known as the 'eclipse' plumage which more or less resembles that of the female. It is assumed soon after the female begins to incubate and, according to Phillips, "remains in its full development for only about three or four weeks." During this period the bird loses its primaries and tail-feathers and becomes flightless. The characteristic male plumage is regained usually by October or November. Whatever be the fundamental cause for this exception to the general law of molt, the fact remains that it renders the bird less conspicuous during a period of comparative helplessness.

The simultaneous loss of the flight-feathers is common to swimming birds which have a secondary means of locomotion in their natatorial powers, but with other birds the wing-quills are molted slowly and

PLATE V

ADULT MALE WOOD DUCK IN 'ECLIPSE' PLUMAGE

Note the absence of primaries, indicating inability to fly. From a specimen collected by E. A. Mearns, at Fort Snelling, Minn., July 24, 1888.

symmetrically from the middle of the wing both inwardly and outwardly. As the old feathers are lost, new ones grow, and the bird can therefore fly during the whole period of feather-renewal.

In other feather-tracts, also, normal molt follows an orderly sequence, feather succeeding feather and plumage plumage throughout the life of the individual. The minor variations of molt within the limits above outlined for the Passeres are endless, but they can be considered adequately only by treating of each species separately. For further details the student is therefore referred to the succeeding descriptions of plumage, and particularly to the papers of Dwight ('00) cited beyond.

Plumage Wear.—Molt, wear, and fading are the only processes by which the color of a bird's plumage is changed. The claim that a feather may be repigmented, and that consequently a bird's plumage may undergo radical changes in color without the growth of new feathers and without the aid of wear and fading, has never been substantiated, and by students of the development of the feather from germ to maturity such a change is declared to be impossible. (See, especially, Strong.)

Striking changes are, however, effected by wear, chiefly of the tips or margins. These differ in color from that of the base of the feather which is wholly or in part concealed. The loss of these margins may completely alter the bird's appearance, as where the brown Snow Bunting of October is transformed to the black-and-white bird of June, and this without the acquisition of a feather. (Fig. 11.) The Bobolink, Red-winged and Rusty Blackbirds also illustrate color-change by wear.

With the Purple Finch and Indigo Bunting, as Dwight ('00) has shown, wear increases the brightness of the bird's colors.

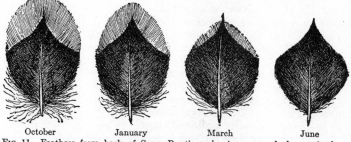

| October | January | March | June |

FIG. 11. Feathers from back of Snow Bunting, showing seasonal changes in form and color due to wearing off of tips. (Natural size.)

The Colors of Plumage.—Color is Nature's last touch in adapting a bird to the needs of its own special environment. In many instances it apparently has been given during the prevalence of existing conditions of haunt and habit; consequently, in studying color, there is a greater possibility of associating cause and effect than exists when we attempt to determine the origin of the older, more stable characters of form. One, therefore, may reasonably ask what is the significance of the manifold shades and tints, marks and patterns, not to mention various appendages found in the plumage of birds? But before a reply is justified, the bird must be studied in nature, its food, its foes, its general habits and special actions learned; and at all times the student should avoid the human viewpoint, but imagine himself in the position of food or foe, an individual of the same species or one of a species with which the bird under consideration may come in contact.

It is not to be expected that any color character should invariably achieve its end; if it does so more than half the time, it will in the aggregate prove beneficial to the species. (See A. H. Thayer, 'Concealing Coloration,' p. 8.)

In the study of color there is a wide field for laboratory experiment on captive birds to determine the laws of molt, the effects of food, humidity, hybridizing, artificial selection, etc., into which it is not possible to enter here. (See Beebe, '08.)

Color and Age.—Most Passerine birds acquire an essentially adult plumage not later than their first prenuptial (spring) molt. Prominent exceptions are the Orchard Oriole, Crossbill, and Redstart which breed in a plumage more like that of the female than of the adult male and acquire their mature plumages at the first postnuptial (fall) molt.

Less striking instances of failure to acquire a fully adult plumage at the first spring molt are shown by birds like the Scarlet Tanager, which at its first prenuptial molt retains most if not all the brownish wing-quills and some of their coverts of its first winter plumage, the black wing-quills of maturity not appearing until the first postnuptial molt; or the American Goldfinch, which does not gain the yellow shoulder-patch until after the first breeding season.

When the adults of both sexes are alike in color, the young in juvenal plumage more or less closely resembles them (*e. g.* Flycatchers, Jays, Crows, most Sparrows, Chickadees, Thrushes); when the male differs from the female, the young in juvenal plumage more nearly resembles the mother (*e. g.* Red-winged Blackbirds, Orioles, Purple Finches, Goldfinches, Hooded Warblers, Redstarts). (Pl. VI.)

The juvenal plumage often gives interesting clues to relationships and ancestry. The nestlings of the Blackpoll and Bay-breasted Warblers, for instance, are almost indistinguishable, as are indeed the first winter costumes of these species; while the spotted breasts of nestling Robins and Bluebirds betray their relationship with the Thrushes.

Color and Season.—Dull or inconspicuously colored birds, having once acquired the plumage of maturity, exchange it only for another of the same kind at their respective molts; but birds of striking colors frequently change their bright breeding costume for one less likely to expose them to danger while migrating. The male Scarlet Tanager, for instance, at the postnuptial molt takes the olive-green body plumage

PLATE VI

RED-WINGED BLACKBIRDS IN JUVENAL PLUMAGE
Illustrating the law that when the adults differ in color the young of both sexes
usually resemble the female.

CHICKADEES IN JUVENAL PLUMAGE
Illustrating the law that when the adults are alike the young resemble them.

of his mate, only the black wings and tail coming in the same color as before. At the same molt, the male Bobolink assumes a plumage practically indistinguishable from that of his mate. With both birds this dull plumage is worn until the prenuptial molt the following spring. Other examples are the American Goldfinch, Bay-breasted, Blackpoll, and Myrtle Warblers. (Pls. IV, XXV.)

Among gallinaceous birds the Ptarmigan alone have marked seasonal changes in plumage, but in the shore-birds, Gulls, Terns, and Grebes, they are more or less pronounced.

Here should be mentioned the various appendages like the plumes of the Night Heron and Egrets, and crests or other head decorations in the White Pelican and Grebe, which are usually acquired at the prenuptial molt and are worn only during the nesting season.

Color and Sex.—When there is a sexual difference in color among birds, with few exceptions the male is the brighter. In North America the exceptions are the three species of Phalaropes. No conclusive reason why the male should be brighter than the female has been advanced. Darwin's theory of sexual selection endows the female with an esthetic sense, making the most brightly plumed male more acceptable in her eyes than his less effectively attired rivals. No one who has watched a bird display its charms before the female (and this is done more commonly than is generally supposed, and by species which do not possess pronounced sexual characters of color or plume), will doubt the ardor or objects of the suitor; but it seems probable that the effect of such display is to stimulate the female to the point of accepting rather than of selecting a mate. It should not be forgotten, however, that if this theory be true the male which breeds in immature plumage (*e. g.* Orchard Oriole, Redstart) is placed at a distinct disadvantage.

Wallace ('91) attributes gay colors and showy plumes to the action of the surplus vital energy which, because of a bird's perfect adaptation to its environment, can expend itself in the production of brilliant colors and ornamental appendages without endangering their owner; but in this connection we should recall that when, as with the Phalaropes, the male plays the part of the female, incubating unaided by her, then it is the female that wears the brighter colors.

Thayer, without positively committing himself on the subject of sexual coloration, contends that, whatever be the minor uses of the distinctively male costumes, their main function is for the purposes of concealment; but it is difficult to believe that the male of the Redwinged Blackbird, Bobolink, Scarlet Tanager or Lark Bunting, for example, is as protectively colored as his dull-plumaged mate, which lives in the same environment. If, however, his brighter colors increase his chances of death, there must be born a greater number of males than females, to offset the higher mortality.

Again, it has been suggested that it is only the female's plumage which has an especial significance, the task of incubation requiring in her a concealing coloration which will protect the contents of the nest as well as herself. The whole subject is as attractive as it is difficult. It should be studied in connection with other secondary sexual characters of which a synopsis from 'Bird-Life' is appended:

Synopsis of the Secondary Sexual Characters of Birds

I. Structural

Size . . . .
{ Male larger than female (usual).
{ Female larger than male (rare).

Plumage . .
{ Color { Male brighter than female.
{ { Female brighter than male (rare).
{
{ Form { Assumption of plumes, ruffs, crests, trains, etc.;
{ { special modification of wing- and tail-feathers.
{ { a. Worn by male alone.
{ { b. Worn by both sexes.

Of the body .
{ Sole or greater development in male of brightly colored
{ bare tracts of skin, combs, wattles, caruncles, and other
{ fleshy or horny appendages.

Of the feet . Sole or greater development in male of spurs.

Of the bill . . Male with more highly colored or larger bill than female.

II. Functional

Pursuit . . .
{ By male when similar to or brighter than female.
{ By female when brighter than male.

Display . . . By male of accessory plumes and other appendages.

Battle . . . By male using spurs, wings, bill, etc.

Music . . .
{ Vocal, by male and rarely female.
{ Mechanical, by male and sometimes female.

Special
habits . .
{ Dances, mock fights, aërial evolutions, construction of
{ bowers, decoration of playgrounds, attitudinizing, strut-
{ ting, etc.
{
{ a. By male before the female.
{ b. Among the males alone.

Color and Climate.—The immediate effect of climate on a bird's plumage is to increase or decrease its general tone of color; thus, those representatives of a species living in arid regions are paler than representatives of the same species living in humid regions. The degree of difference is closely related to the annual rainfall, as it indicates relative humidity; and where there are no abrupt changes in climate, these climatic variations change as gradually as the conditions which cause them. At first so slight that only the expert systematic ornithologist, with access to large series of specimens, can detect them, they become, in some instances, so pronounced that not only the general tone of color but pattern itself is affected. It is on such variations that most subspecies or geographical races of birds are based. (See Allen, '77.)

Among North American birds, they are best illustrated by the oft-cited case of the Song Sparrow. (Pls. VII, VIII.) Twenty-nine races

PLATE VII

SONG SPARROWS

1. Aleutian Song Sparrow.
2. Sooty Song Sparrow.
3. Samuels's Song Sparrow.
4. Desert Song Sparrow.
5. Eastern Song Sparrow.

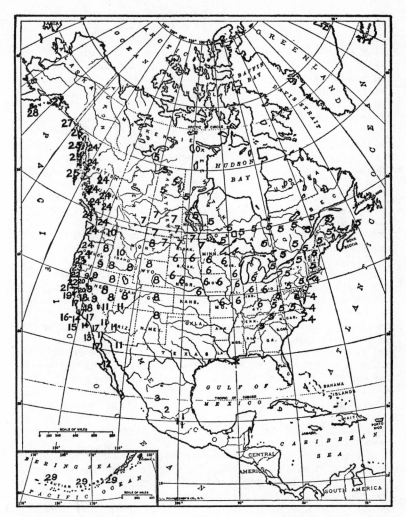

PLATE VIII. SEMI-DIAGRAMMATIC REPRESENTATION OF THE BREEDING RANGES OF SONG SPARROWS (*Melospiza melodia*).

1. Mexican Song Sparrow.
2. Michoacan Song Sparrow.
3. Durango Song Sparrow.
4. Atlantic Song Sparrow.
5. Eastern Song Sparrow.
6. Mississippi Song Sparrow.
7. Dakota Song Sparrow.
8. Mountain Song Sparrow.
9. Modoc Song Sparrow.
10. Merrill's Song Sparrow.
11. Desert Song Sparrow.
12. Brown's Song Sparrow.
13. Coronados Song Sparrow.
14. San Miguel Song Sparrow.
15. San Clemente Song Sparrow.
16. Santa Barbara Song Sparrow.
17. San Diego Song Sparrow.
18. Heermann's Song Sparrow.
19. Alameda Song Sparrow.
20. Modesto Song Sparrow.
21. Suisun Song Sparrow.
22. Samuel's Song Sparrow.
23. Mendocino Song Sparrow.
24. Rusty Song Sparrow.
25. Sooty Song Sparrow.
26. Yakutat Song Sparrow.
27. Kenai Song Sparrow.
28. Bischoff's Song Sparrow.
29. Aleutian Song Sparrow.

of this exceedingly plastic species are recognized. They are distributed from the Valley of Mexico northward throughout the United States and a large part of Canada to the Aleutian Islands. Note, however, that only four of them are found east of the Rocky Mountains, where climatic conditions are comparatively uniform; while California alone has eleven resident races, an indication of its great diversity of climate.

The Desert Song Sparrow (Pl. VII, Pl. VIII, No. 11), the palest race, inhabits the Colorado desert region where the average rainfall is about six inches; the Sooty Song Sparrow (Pl. VIII, No. 25; Pl. VII), the darkest race, is found on the northwest Pacific Coast where the annual rainfall averages over 90 inches.

Again, observe that the Mexican Song Sparrow (Pl. VIII, No. 1) at the southern extremity of the range of the species is one of the smallest races, measuring some 6 inches in length, and that there is a gradual increase in size northward until the maximum is reached at the northern extremity of the range of the species, where the Aleutian Song Sparrow (Pl. VIII, No. 29) attains a length of nearly 9 inches.

If we compared only the palest Song Sparrow with the darkest, we might well believe, so unlike are they, that each form represents a distinct species; but when we include in our comparison representatives of all the twenty-nine races of Song Sparrows we find complete intergradation in color and in size. Nowhere can one draw the line. As the climatic conditions under which the birds live change, the birds keep pace. Cause and effect go hand in hand. Here we have a species in flower, as it were, a single Song Sparrow stalk with its twenty-nine blossoms, any one of which might make an independent growth as a species if it were separated from the parent stem. Doubtless some day the separation will come, when we shall have several species of Song Sparrow, each with its group of races, but at present we have only one species, divided into some twenty-nine subspecies, or species in process of formation.

A variety of reasons may be advanced to account for the pronounced geographical variations shown by the Song Sparrow. Its wide range indicates physical adaptability and ready adjustment to differences in food and habitat. Its variations in size, while they conform to the general law of increase in size northward, are exceptionally marked, and are not equalled by those of any other North American bird—a further indication of an inherent plasticity.

The species is comparatively non-migratory. Several races, notably in California, are permanently resident in contiguous and restricted areas. Such strictly non-migratory species are continuously subjected to the influences of their environment, which are heightened by permanent isolation. But even the most migratory forms come early and stay late, and are thus in the breeding area for a much greater part of the year than, for example, many Warblers which come in May and leave in August.

But, suggest as we may the various factors which appear to be active in producing such geographic variations as the Song Sparrows exhibit, they are not potent with all birds, even when other things are equal, and it seems probable that some species are in an active state of development and readily respond to the influences of their surroundings, while others are fixed and make no such response. The latter represent older types of birds, which are, so to speak, near to or a part of the trunk of the bird's family tree, while the former class includes the birds at the terminal branches of this tree.

Mutation.—Variations in size and color similar in character to those presented by Song Sparrows are so frequently found among birds and other animals, we have learned to expect that variable species will increase in size with decrease in temperature and become darker with increased humidity.

But birds also exhibit racial characters which cannot so readily be correlated with climatic or other environmental conditions. These usually affect their markings rather than their general tone of color. The Eastern Robin (*Turdus migratorius migratorius*), for example, has the outer tail-feathers tipped with white, whereas in the Western Robin (*Turdus migratorius propinquus*) these marks are wholly wanting or much smaller. Other representative geographic races may be distinguished by the presence in one and absence in the other of superciliary lines, breast-bands, or wing-bars. Differences of this kind are considered mutational and the races distinguished by them are known as mutants. They are due to an inherent tendency to vary independent of environment and have long been recognized by systematists as 'individual variations.' But given the isolation where a variation of this kind may become dominant and in time it may characterize a new race. In the case of these mutants the variation arises from within and there is consequently no question of its inheritance. But with climatic races the originating cause is found in the environment, not in the organism. Nevertheless it is the organism that supplies the media through which the environment expresses itself. (See especially Morgan, Scientific Monthly, 1923, pp. 237–246; Chapman, Bull. Amer. Mus. Nat. Hist., XLVIII, 1923, pp. 243–278; Amer. Mus. Novit., No. 261, 1927, pp. 1–19.)

Color and Concealment.—It is clear that the life of the individual bird, and hence the continued existence of its species, depends primarily on its success in securing food and in escaping from its foes. The colors of predaceous species must, therefore, tend to conceal them from their prey (aggressive or deceptive colors), while the colors of those that are preyed on are designed to conceal them from their enemies (protective colors).

When, however, a bird's food may be secured without the exercise of caution, when it apparently is not preyed upon, or when it is protected by the character of its haunts, its colors, unchecked by any need for concealment, may make it conspicuous.[1]

[1] In this connection see Reighard on the colors of coral-reef fishes. Papers from Tortugas Lab. of Carnegie Inst., Wash., 1908, pp. 261–325.

Inconspicuousness is achieved primarily, not alone in birds but also in most other animals, by that disposition of color which makes them darkest where they receive the most light, and palest where they are most in shadow. This is the far-reaching principle of counter-shading discovered by Abbott H. Thayer and announced by him in 1896 (*The Auk*, 1896, pp. 124, 318). Of it Poulton remarks: "For ages the artist has known how to produce the appearance of solid objects standing out on his canvas, by painting in the likeness of the shadows. It has remained for this great artist-naturalist to realize the logical antithesis, and show how solid objects may be made to fade away and become ghost-like, or even invisible, by painting out the shadows."

Thayer's experiments in conclusive demonstration of this law may be repeated, even if crudely, by taking, say, four bits of wood shaped to resemble a bird's body, or, failing these, several symmetrical potatoes of about the same size. Run a stout wire rod through these objects, leaving intervals of about 8 to 10 inches and, selecting a spot not in direct sunlight, support the rod at both ends, on uprights which will raise it 6 to 8 inches from the ground. The models should be uniformly colored to resemble the earth against which they are seen, and the resemblance may be heightened by sprinkling some of the earth upon them.

If the secret of protective coloration is an exact likeness in color between an animal and its background, these models should be essentially invisible, whereas they are exceedingly conspicuous. Now, in imitation of nature, paint out the shadow on the lower half of two of the models by grading through earth color laterally, to pure white on the lower median line, when it will be seen that at a distance of 30 feet or more these white-bottomed models have, in a magical manner, become nearly if not quite invisible, although they are still the same color on the upper half as the untouched models, which are plainly visible at a distance of at least 40 to 50 yards.

To prove that this result is due to the disposition of color as regards light and shade, rather than to color alone, turn the models so that the white is uppermost, thus reversing Nature's law, and thereby rendering the two models which before were indistinguishable even more prominent than those which are uniformly colored.

Such, in briefest outline, is an explanation of Thayer's law of counter-shading, for a fuller description of which, as well as of its various modifications, the student is referred to Thayer's work on 'Concealing Coloration.' Thayer's law of obliterative markings is also presented in this book. This explains the pattern of coloration or markings of counter-shaded birds which bear on their plumage a picture of the background against which they are most commonly seen by their prey or by their enemies. Or, as Gerald Thayer puts it: the object's "obliteratively shaded surface must bear *a picture of such background as would be seen through it, if it were transparent.*" (*l. c.* p. 31.) Thus our Woodcock is said to bear a picture of "dead leaves, twigs and grasses, variously disposed over shadow-holes," while the plumage of Wilson's Snipe

PLATE IX

WOODCOCK ON NEST

A protectively colored bird which, relying on its color to escape detection, may sometimes be touched before it takes wing.

BLACK SKIMMER ON NEST

A conspicuously colored bird which is so shy that it leaves its nest at the first indication
of danger.

represents "sticks, grasses, etc., with their shadows at various distances." The plumage of the Upland Plover shows a "grass" pattern, a type common to many field or upland species. Certain of the Plovers and Sandpipers wear this plumage during the summer, when they live among weeds and grasses, but lose it for one of pure and simple counter-shading when they winter along the shores and beaches.

From these more obvious instances of obliterative picture patterns, Thayer leads us to an interpretation of the brilliantly colored and intricately marked plumage of birds like the male Wood Duck, Peacock, and Paradise Bird (*Paradisea*), or of such special markings and appendages as the speculum in Ducks, gorget in Hummingbirds, tail-coverts in the Resplendent Trogon, etc., all of which, under certain vital conditions, are considered by him to make or to aid in making their wearers inconspicuous. The use of no pattern, mark or appendage is left unexplained by the proposer of this law, and while naturalists recognize the importance of his studies, Thayer's contention "that patterns and utmost contrasts of color (not to speak of *appendages*) of animals make *wholly* for their 'obliteration,' " finds few supporters.

Flamingoes, Crows, Ravens, and Turkey Vultures, for example, are seemingly from any point of view conspicuous. The nature of their food or their excessive wariness or absence of foes apparently remove them from the action of the laws producing a true concealing coloration.

Protected primarily by the character of their haunts, it is not improbable that the striking and endlessly varied colors of Tanagers, Honey Creepers, Cotingas, Toucans, Trogons, Parrots and other brilliantly marked arboreal birds may be explained in a similar manner. It is important to remember in this connection that many birds of such habits are dull while others are brightly colored, and we may suggest that among tree-haunting, and to a less extent thicket-haunting birds, the actual physical causes of color, uncontrolled by natural selection, have run riot. When, however, the nature of a bird's haunts affords it less adequate means of concealment, then color plays a more important part in protecting it, and there is consequently less variation from the type of color which presumably has proved to have the highest concealing value.

Thrushes, Ovenbirds and Doves, for example, which feed on the ground, may frequent the tree-tops without unduly exposing themselves to danger, but let a male Scarlet Tanager or other brightly colored arboreal bird alight upon the ground and, even when motionless, it is conspicuous.

This illustration may serve also to remind us that the protective value of any color-scheme or pattern of marking is active only when the animal bearing it is at rest. Without regard to color, movement at once reveals, and bearing this in mind, the action of a bird in the presence of danger is a supreme test of the protective or non-protective value of its colors.

If the bird is wary and can be approached only with difficulty, we may feel assured that it realizes its conspicuousness and consequently it relies for safety on its watchfulness and its wings. But if the bird attempts to hide and flies only when convinced that it has been discovered, then we may believe that it relies primarily on the nature of its coloring to escape observation, when we are evidently justified in assuming that its colors are truly protective. Compare the colors and actions of such 'wild' birds as Gulls, Terns, Skimmers, Ducks, Geese, Cormorants, Cranes, Herons, Flamingoes, Stilts, Avocets, and Crows, with those of birds which take wing only to avoid being stepped on (*e. g.* Bitterns, Rails, Woodcock, Wilson's Snipe, Quails, Grouse, Whip-poor-wills) to appreciate how closely color is here correlated with habit.

Compare further the colors and habits of the flightless young of Gulls, Terns, Skimmers, Stilts, or Avocets with those of their parents to observe how there may be both a protective and a conspicuous plumage in the same species. Enter the breeding resorts of any of these birds and the conspicuously colored adults at once take wing while the protectively colored young, squatting motionless, make no attempt to escape, even by running, until they are actually touched.

Obviously, then, the significance of the colors of birds is to be learned only by the study of the problem in nature. The whole subject is preëminently within the domain of the field naturalist. Only when our knowledge of a bird's haunts and habits, its food and foes, and its actions in the presence of danger is reasonably complete are we in a position to determine to what factors we may attribute its particular colors and markings. This is the ground taken by Theodore Roosevelt in his extended criticism ('11) of Abbott Thayer's theories, and while one may argue that Mr. Roosevelt underrates the necessity of concealing coloration in animals, one must commend his admirable plea for the accumulation of further evidence from nature before giving a verdict.

Banner-marks.—The plumage of many birds contains marks which are usually conspicuous only when the bird is in motion. White outer tail-feathers (*e. g.* Junco, Vesper Sparrow, Meadowlark), or wing-patches (*e. g.* Mockingbird), or a white rump (*e. g.* Flicker), are markings of this type and are termed 'banner', 'recognition' or 'directive' marks.

Some authors would have us believe that such flight-revealed markings have a directive value which assists birds of the same species in keeping together (see Tracy, '10) but the ease with which dull-eyed man learns to recognize birds, even at a great distance, makes it difficult to believe that birds require some conspicuous mark to distinguish others of their own kind, as Abbott Thayer has well shown (*The Auk*, 1900, p. 108). On the other hand, there seems better ground for belief in the theory, advanced by Dr. C. Hart Merriam, that these so-called banner-marks protect their possessors by being so strikingly evident when their wearers are in flight that their sudden and complete effacement when the creature takes to cover, tends to puzzle the pursuer, which, looking in vain for a victim conspicuously marked with white, soon abandons the chase.

The subject is a fascinating one and is to be especially commended to field students, who alone can supply the data on which a solution of the problems involved can be based.

Albinism.—Albinism is not infrequent among birds and may occur in any species. I have seen a white Crow and a white Turkey Vulture. It is, however, rarely complete but more frequently affects a part of the plumage, when it is usually symmetrical; that is, if a feather in one wing be white the corresponding feather in the other wing will also be white.

The presence of an albino bird always excites interest. When, because of its markings, the history of the individual may be learned, and possibly its return to a certain locality noted year after year, albinism permits of the making of observations of real value. But albinism in itself is a matter calling for no special record or comment. It is due to an absence of pigment in the part affected and may indicate a more or less degenerate condition in the individual exhibiting it. Albinistic English Sparrows are not uncommon, a fact which may be due to the abundance of the species and ease with which it is observed, or to excessive inbreeding among a comparatively limited number of very local individuals.

Melanism, or undue blackness, implies an excess of pigment, while xanthochroism and erythrism are terms applied respectively to abnormally yellow or red birds. These three phases of color are, as a rule, shown only in caged birds and are then evidently due to unnatural diet or other conditions. (See Beebe, '07.)

Dichromatism.—Dichromatism implies the existence of two phases of color in the same species. It is well illustrated by our Screech Owl, some individuals of which are gray and others rufous.

This difference in color is not dependent upon age, sex, or season; indeed, gray and rufous birds may be found in the same family. It appears, however, to be connected with locality, since a species may be dichromatic in one part of its range and less so or not at all in another part of its range. The rufous phase of the Screech Owl, for example, is rare in Florida, just as the black phase of the gray squirrel is rare in Florida. Beyond this relation between dichromatism and locality its causes are not understood.

SUGGESTIONS FOR THE STUDENT

The processes of molt and feather-growth may be studied in captive birds provided they be kept under proper conditions. Change in conditions may advance or retard molt. (See Beebe, '08.)

Describe condition of a Passerine bird at birth and its subsequent plumages and molts. About how long is it in the nest? How long does it wear the juvenal plumage? What plumage follows? What feathers are usually retained at the postjuvenal molt? When does the prenuptial molt occur? Is it usually complete? What molt is complete? How does the natal down of præcocial birds differ from that of altricial birds? How long do some Snipe wear the postjuvenal plumage? What variation in the law of molt is shown by Ptarmigan and most swimming birds? Describe changes in color due to wear or fading. Give illustrations of the acquisition by molt of nuptial plumes. Describe differences in color due to age. When do most birds acquire their mature plumage? Mention several species which do not reach full plumage until at least their second year. Describe the plumage changes of the Scarlet Tanager, American Goldfinch, and Bobolink. When the adults are unlike in color, which is usually the brighter? Which parent does the nestling usually resemble? What may be inferred from the spotted juvenal plumage of the Bluebird? What is Darwin's theory of sexual selection? What is Wallace's theory? Describe what is meant by secondary sexual characters and give cases in illustration. What relations exist between the degree of intensity of a bird's color and the climatic conditions under which it lives? Describe the case of the Song Sparrows. Is it believed that their changes in color are due to the direct influence of environment rather than to the influence of natural selection in establishing protective colors? Why are concealing colors necessary? To what factors other than color may a bird owe its comparative immunity from its foes? Are they required by all species? How may we account for the wide range of color in arboreal birds? What is Thayer's principle of counter-shading? Demonstrate this theory with the aid of decoys. What are 'obliterative' markings? What are 'banner' or 'directive' marks? What theories have been advanced to account for their significance? Mention all the birds you know which reveal white marks in flight. What is albinism? melanism? xanthochroism? erythrism? Describe an albino which you have seen. Did it act like normally colored birds of its own species? What may be learned from observing albinos or other birds so marked that they may be recognized? Have you ever known a caged bird to change in color?

References

1871. DARWIN, C., The Descent of Man, Chaps. XIII–XVI.—**1877.** ALLEN, J. A., The Influence of Physical Conditions on the Genesis of Species, Radical Review, I, pp. 108–140. (Reprinted in Smithsonian Rep. 1905, pp. 375–402.)—**1891.** WALLACE, A. R., Darwinism, Chaps. VIII–XI, (Macmillan).—**1890.** POULTON, E. B., The Colours of Animals, (Appleton).—**1893.** NEWTON and GADOW, Colors of Birds, in Dictionary of Birds, (Macmillan). —**1896.** STONE, W., The Molting of Birds, Proc. Acad. Nat. Sci., Phila., pp. 108–167.—**1900.** DWIGHT, J., JR., Sequence of Plumages and Moults of the Passerine Birds of New York, Annals Acad. Sci., XIII, pp. 73–360; see also Auk, XVII, pp. 34, 143, 368.—**1907.** BEEBE, C. W., Geographic Variation in Birds with Especial Reference to the Effects of Humidity, Zoölogica, I, pp. 1–41.—**1908.** BEEBE, C. W., Seasonal Changes of Color in Birds, Am. Nat., XLII, pp. 34–38.—**1909.** THAYER, G. H., Concealing Coloration in the Animal Kingdom, 4to, 260 pp., illus., (Macmillan).—**1910.** TRACY, H. C., Significance of White Markings in Birds of the Order Passeriformes, Univ. Cal. Pub. in Zoöl., VI, pp. 285–312.—**1910.** PYCRAFT, W. P., A History of Birds, (Methuen & Co., London).—**1911.** BARBOUR, T., and PHILLIPS, J. C., Concealing Coloration Again, Auk, XXVIII, pp. 179–188.—**1911.** THAYER, A. H., Concealing Coloration, Pop. Sci. Monthly, July, pp. 20–35. —**1911.** ROOSEVELT, THEODORE, Revealing and Concealing Coloration in Birds and Mammals, Bull. Am. Mus. Nat. Hist., XXX, pp. 119–231.— **1911.** ALLEN, J. A., Roosevelt's Revealing and Concealing Coloration in Birds and Mammals, Auk, XXVIII, pp. 472–480.—**1912.** MCATEE, W. L., Testing the Efficiency of Warning and Cryptic Coloration in Protecting Animals from Their Enemies, Proc. Acad. Nat. Sci., pp. 281–364.—**1920.** ALLEN, G. M., Pattern Development in Teal, Auk, XXXVII, pp. 558–564.— **1921.** ALLEN, A. A., Coloration of Birds, Bird-Lore, pp. 260–267, 320–326, illus.—**1929.** CHAPMAN, F. M., The Colors of Tropical Birds, My Tropical Air Castle, pp. 356–373 (Appleton).

THE FOOD OF BIRDS

Food and Distribution
Food and Habit
Economic Value of Birds
Birds and Insects
Birds and Weeds
Birds and Rodents
Birds as Scavengers

Food and Distribution.—Birds consume a large amount of food and they rarely store it. No one factor, therefore, exercises a greater or more constant influence on their activities than the ever-present necessity of securing a sufficient amount of the proper kind of nourishment.

Not only are a bird's daily movements more or less governed by the search for food, with pronounced local variations in numbers, due to the ripening of fruits, unusual abundance of insects, supply of carrion, etc., but the presence or absence of the species during certain seasons may depend directly on the abundance or scarcity of a certain kind of food. Given bayberries, and one may expect Myrtle Warblers to winter in numbers near New York City; buckwheat in a pile of chaff induced a flock of Mourning Doves to pass the winter at Englewood, N. J.; the failure of the coniferous seed-crop is evidently the reason for the irregular occurrence of great numbers of Crossbills south of their usual winter range, to cite only a few of the innumerable instances showing how both the local and general movements of birds are influenced by the food-supply.

Food and Habit.—From the Swifts, coursing the sky almost beyond the reach of vision, to the Diver beneath the waters, birds neglect no spot containing food. The result is not only great diversity of fare, but a correspondingly wide range in the methods, or feeding habits, by which it is secured. (See under Uses of the Bill and Feet.)

Economic Value of Birds.—Interesting as we shall find the study of a bird's food in relation to its distribution and habits, it is of even greater importance for us to learn in what way or ways the nature of its food determines its economic relations to man.

In no branch of American ornithology has greater advance been made, during the past forty years, than in the study of the value of birds to man based on a knowledge of their food. This is due chiefly to the investigations of the Biological Survey of the United States Department of Agriculture, and also to the researches conducted by certain states, notably Massachusetts, New Hampshire, and Pennsylvania. The subject is too wide and too important to be treated adequately here and the student is referred to the many valuable papers listed beyond, particularly to those issued by the Department of Agriculture (many of which can be secured from the Superintendent of Documents at Washington) and to Forbush's 'Useful Birds.'

The nature of a bird's food can be determined by observing what it eats and by an examination of what it has eaten. It is, of course, often impossible to see just what a bird is eating or, even having seen, one still may not recognize the particular kind of insect, fruit or seed which has been swallowed. Expert analysis of the contents of the digestive tract is therefore essential to an accurate knowledge of the character of a bird's food. The conclusions drawn from laboratory work should, however, be checked by studies in nature, to which the field ornithologist may make valuable contributions.

Looking from my window as I write, I see five Starlings (*Sturnus*) running actively about the lawn beneath a cherry tree, picking up fallen fruit. An examination of the contents of their stomachs would unquestionably reveal the presence of cherries, but I see this ground-feeder gather fallen cherries far more frequently than growing ones, and stomach analysis alone might, therefore, in a case of this kind, lead to a false estimate of a bird's destructiveness. (On the study of food habits in the field, see especially Forbush's 'Useful Birds.')

Equally true is it that verdicts based only on casual observations of the bird in nature are far from the truth; and it is this kind of hasty conclusion that the economic ornithologist finds the greatest difficulty in combating. A Cooper's Hawk may be seen to catch a chicken or scatter a flock of Bob-whites; Robins may be noted in the cherry trees or Catbirds in the strawberry bed, and without further evidence all Hawks are declared to be destroyers of poultry and game, and small birds generally devourers of fruit. But thanks to the investigations made by Federal and State governments, as already mentioned, we are now in possession of accurate, incontrovertible data, and there is no excuse for signing a bird's death-warrant on false or insufficient observation. It has thus been determined that birds are of inestimable value to man (1) by eating harmful insects, their eggs and larvæ; (2) by destroying the seeds of noxious weeds; (3) by devouring field-mice and other small mammals which injure crops; and (4) by acting as scavengers.

Birds and Insects.—Dr. C. L. Marlatt, of the United States Department of Agriculture, estimates that in the year 1904 the loss to our agricultural interests occasioned by insects amounted to $795,000-000 (Yearbook, U. S. Dept. Agr., 1904, p. 464). Dr. A. D. Hopkins, also of the Department of Agriculture, estimates that insects cause an annual loss to our forestry and timber interests of $100,000,000, and in his 'The Menace of Insects' ('31) Dr. L. O. Howard states that insects cause an annual economic loss to the world of $2,000,000,000. It is difficult for us to comprehend fully the significance of these figures, but at least they may serve to impress us with the value of any form of life which in turn preys upon insects, and in the front rank of insect enemies stand the birds.

It is possible here only to give references (see beyond) to the now extensive literature containing exact statistics of this battle of the birds and the bugs. In these papers, for example, it will be found stated that the stomach of a single Cedar Waxwing contained 100 canker-worms, that one Cuckoo had eaten 250 caterpillars, that 454 plant-lice were found in the stomach of one Chickadee, that a Nighthawk had made a meal on 60 grasshoppers, that a Flicker had devoured 1,000 chinch bugs, that a Scarlet Tanager was seen to eat 630 gypsy moth caterpillars in eighteen minutes, or at the rate of 2,100 an hour; while a Maryland Yellow-throat ate 3,500 plant-lice in forty minutes, or at the rate of 5,270 an hour!

As the destroyers of insects that breed disease, birds stand in an even closer economic relation to man. Five hundred mosquitoes, for example, were found in the stomach of a single Nighthawk; Swallows and other wing-feeding birds also feed upon this pest, which, in the larval form, is eaten by various marsh-inhabiting birds. It is probable, therefore, that as our knowledge of the history of various diseases to which man is subject through insect attack increases, birds will here be found to be correspondingly valuable.

In spite of the immense amount of authoritative data of which we are now in possession, we are far from beginning to realize the profoundly important part played by insectivorous birds in holding in check the insects injurious to vegetation and to man. We may, however, accept without question the opinion of Henry W. Henshaw, former Chief of the Biological Survey, who states as his conviction that without the services of insect-eating birds "it is more than likely—nay, it is almost certain— that within a limited time not only would successful agriculture become impossible, but the destruction of the greater part of vegetation would follow." (*Nat. Geog. Mag.*, 1908, p. 89.)

Birds and Weeds.—It is not, however, only as a scourge to insects that the bird is of value to the farmer, but also as a destroyer of the seeds of weeds it performs a service of incalculable importance. Again we must turn to the researches of the economic ornithologist for those definite data (see especially papers by Judd) without which satisfactory conclusions cannot be reached. In passing we may merely state that 700 seeds of the pigeon grass were taken from the stomach of a Tree Sparrow by Professor Beal, who estimates that this species destroys no less than 875 *tons* of weed-seed annually in the single state of Iowa; that 1,000 pigweed seeds were found in the stomach of a Snow Bunting; that a Bob-white contained 5,000 seeds of pigeon grass, while a Mourning Dove had eaten the enormous number of 7,500 seeds of the yellow wood sorrel.

Birds and Rodents.—Still we have not given the birds all the credit due them as powerful allies of the agriculturist. Every farmer knows all too well how seriously small rodents, particularly field-mice, can damage his crops in the field as well as in the storehouse or granary; but few farmers know that Hawks and Owls, birds they have always believed should be killed on sight, are among Nature's most potent checks on the undue increase of these destructive little creatures.

The loss which may follow ignorance of the economic value of Hawks and Owls has never been more clearly shown than by Dr. Merriam, who as early as 1886 made the following comments on the then recently passed 'Scalp Act' of the State of Pennsylvania, and subsequent investigations have confirmed his views:

"On the 23d of June, 1885, the Legislature of Pennsylvania passed an act known as the 'scalp act,' ostensibly 'for the benefit of agriculture,' which provides a bounty of fifty cents each on Hawks, Owls, weasels and minks killed within the limits of the State, and a fee of twenty cents to the notary or justice taking affidavit.

"By virtue of this act about $90,000 has been paid in bounties during the year and a half that has elapsed since the law went into effect. This represents the destruction of at least 128,571 of the above-mentioned animals, most of which were Hawks and Owls.

"Granting that 5,000 chickens are killed annually in Pennsylvania by Hawks and Owls, and that they are worth twenty-five cents each (a liberal estimate in view of the fact that a large portion of them are killed when very young), the total loss would be $1,250, and the poultry killed in a year and a half would be worth $1,875. Hence it appears that during the past eighteen months the State of Pennsylvania has expended $90,000 to save its farmers a loss of $1,875. But this estimate by no means represents the actual loss to the farmer and the taxpayer of the State. It is within bounds to say that in the course of a year every Hawk and Owl destroys at least a thousand mice or their equivalent in insects, and that each mouse or its equivalent so destroyed would cause the loss of two cents per annum. Therefore, omitting all reference to the enormous increase in the numbers of these noxious animals when Nature's means of holding them in check has been removed, the lowest possible estimate of the value to the farmer of each Hawk, Owl, and weasel would be $20 a year, or $30 in a year and a half.

"Hence, in addition to the $90,000 actually expended by the State in destroying 128,571 of its benefactors, it has incurred a loss to its agricultural interests of at least $3,857,130, or a total loss of $3,947,130 in a year and a half, which is at the rate of $2,631,420 per annum. In other words, the State has thrown away $2,105 for every dollar saved! And even this does not represent fairly the full loss, for the slaughter of such a vast number of predaceous birds and mammals is almost certain to be followed by a correspondingly enormous increase in the numbers of mice and insects formerly held in check by them, and it will take many years to restore the balance thus blindly destroyed through ignorance of the economic relations of our common birds and mammals."

Birds as Scavengers.—Besides destroying various species of insects inimical to the health of the human race, birds further increase the healthfulness of the world by acting as scavengers. It would be difficult to overestimate the value of Buzzards, Vultures, and other offal-eating birds to the countries in which they live. In most instances the economic importance of these birds is too obvious to be overlooked, and they are, therefore, protected by law, and by what is far more powerful than law, public sentiment.

In our southern states the Turkey 'Buzzard' and Black Vulture, or 'Carrion Crow,' have become so numerous and tame as a result of the protection there given them that they walk around the streets of the towns and cities in great numbers, and with no more evidence of fear than is shown by poultry. Everyone realizes that a living Buzzard is of infinitely more value than a dead one, and in many years' experience in the South I have never seen a Buzzard molested.

The value of Gulls as scavengers was forcibly impressed on my mind when, some years ago, I visited the lower harbor of New York Bay to see the Gulls which were attracted by the scows of the Street-cleaning Department of New York City. The number of Gulls present on this occasion was beyond calculation, but certainly exceeded 300,000. Before the scows began to discharge their cargo most of the birds were resting on the water, but at the sound of the whistle giving the signal to dump, they arose in clouds and clustered thickly over the wake of each of the eleven scows to feed on the vegetable and animal matter thrown overboard. It was a most impressive object lesson in the economic value of these birds, which only a few years before had been destroyed in enormous numbers for millinery purposes.

Suggestions for the Student

How may a bird's local or seasonal distribution be governed by the food-supply? Give instances. Group our land-birds under general headings according to the nature of their food. How is the nature of a bird's food determined? Give instances illustrating the importance of field observation; of laboratory examination. To what extent are insects believed to injure our agricultural and forestry interests annually? Give definite instances based on personal observation in which insectivorous birds were seen to destroy injurious insects. How may birds aid in preventing disease? What birds are known to feed on mosquitoes? Is it probable that agriculture would be possible without the service rendered by birds? Describe the feeding habits of aërial, arboreal, scansorial, and terrestrial insectivorous birds. Is the food of young birds like that of their parents? Why are insectivorous birds particularly valuable in the winter? Describe the value of birds as weed-seed eaters and give statistics of their destructive powers. What birds are the natural enemies of small rodents? Give the results of stomach analyses of various species of Hawks and Owls (see body of book). Which are considered beneficial? Which injurious? What birds are known to act as scavengers?

References

1880. FORBES, S. A., The Food of Birds, Bull. 3, Ills. State Lab. Nat. Hist., pp. 80–149; see also Bull. 6, pp. 3–32.—1883. KING, F. H., Economic Relations of Wisconsin Birds, Geol. Wisc., I, pp. 441–610.—1886–1909. MERRIAM, C. HART, Chief and others, reports on investigations of the Biological Survey of the U. S. Dept. of Agriculture; some of these papers are cited here, others under the species to which they refer.—1888. WARREN,

B. H., Birds of Pennsylvania with Special Reference to their Food Habits, 266 pp.—1889. BARROWS, W. B., The English Sparrow in North America, Bull. 1, Biol. Surv., 405 pp.—1893. FISHER, A. K., Hawks and Owls of the U. S. in their Relation to Agriculture, 209 pp.—1895. BARROWS, W. B., and SCHWARZ, E. A., The Common Crow, 98 pp.—1895. FORBUSH, E. H., Birds as Protectors of Orchards, Bull. 3, Mass. Board Agric., pp. 20–32.— 1895. BEAL, F. E. L., The Food of Woodpeckers, Bull. 7, Orn. and Mam., 39 pp.—1896. PALMER, T. S., Extermination of Noxious Animals by Bounties, Yearbook, U. S. Dept. Agric., pp. 55–68.—1897. BEAL, F. E. L., Some Common Birds in Their Relation to Agriculture, Farmer's Bull., U. S. Dept. of Agric., 54, 40 pp.—1898. FORBUSH. E. H., Nature's Foresters, Bull. 1, Mass. Board Agric., pp. 27–40.—1898. PALMER, T. S., The Danger of Introducing Noxious Animals and Birds, Yearbook, U. S. Dept. of Agric., pp. 87–110.—1898. NASH, C. W., Birds of Ontario in Relation to Agriculture, Rep. Farmer's Inst., Ont. Dept. Agric., pp. 1–32.—1898. JUDD, S. D., Birds as Weed Destroyers, Yearbook, U. S. Dept. of Agric., pp. 221–232. —1899. PALMER, T. S., Review of Economic Ornithology in U. S., Yearbook, U. S. Dept. of Agric., pp. 259–292.—1900. BEAL, F. E. L., How Birds Affect the Orchard, Yearbook, U. S. Dept. of Agric., pp. 291–304.—1900. CHAPMAN, F. M., The Value of Birds to the Commonwealth, Rep. Conn. Board Agric., 41 pp.—1901. BRUNER, L., Birds in Their Relation to Agriculture, Proc. Nebr. Orn. Union, pp. 18–29.—1901. JUDD, S. D., Relation of Sparrows to Agriculture, Bull. 15, Biol. Surv., 98 pp.—1902. JUDD, SYLVESTER D., Birds of a Maryland Farm, Bull. 17, Biol. Surv., 116 pp.—1902. FORBUSH, E. H., Two Years with the Birds on a Farm, Mass. State Board Agric., 2nd. ed.—1903. CHAPMAN, F. M., The Economic Value of Birds to the State, Seventh Rep. N. Y. Forest, Fish and Game Comm., 66 pp.; with bibliography.—1903. WEED, C. M., and DEARBORN, NED, Birds in Their Relations to Man—A Manual of Economic Ornithology for the U. S. and Canada, 380 pp.; with bibliography.—1905. HENSHAW, H. W., Does It Pay the Farmer to Protect Birds? Yearbook, U. S. Dept. of Agric., pp. 165–178.—1906. HOWELL, A. H., Birds That Eat the Cotton Boll Weevil, Bull. 25, Biol. Surv., 22 pp.; Bull. 29, 30 pp.; Circ. 64, 5 pp.—1906. MCATEE, W. L., Birds That Eat Scale Insects, Yearbook, U. S. Dept. of Agric., pp. 189–198.—1906. BEAL, F. E. L., Birds as Conservators of the Forests, Rep. N. Y. Forest, Fish and Game Comm., 1902, pp. 235–274. —1907. FORBUSH, E. H., Useful Birds and Their Protection, Mass. Board Agric., 437 pp. (Comprehensive).—1907. HENSHAW, H. W., Value of Swallows as Insect Destroyers, Circ. 56, Biol. Surv., 4 pp.—1907. HENSHAW, H. W., Birds Useful in the War Against the Cotton Boll Weevil, Circ. 57, Biol. Surv., 4 pp.—1908. HENSHAW, H. W., The Policemen of the Air, Nat. Geog. Mag., pp. 79–118.—1911. BEAL, F. E. L., Food of the Woodpeckers of the United States, Bull. 37, Biol. Surv., 64 pp.—1911–1931. W. L. M., Students of economic entomology are referred to W. L. McAtee's reviews of papers on this subject which for the past twenty years have appeared in The Auk.—1913. MCATEE, W. L., Index to papers relating to the food of birds, by members of the Biological Survey in Publications of the U. S. Dept. Agric., Bull. 4, Biol. Surv., 69 pp., 131 titles.—1926. MCATEE, W. L., Relation of Birds to Woodlots, Roosevelt Wild Life Bull. IV, pp. 1–154, illus. (University of Syracuse, N. Y.).—1927. BUTTS, W. K., The Feeding Range of Certain Birds, Auk, pp. 44, 329–350.—1927. HENDERSON, J., The Practical Value of Birds, 342 pp. (Macmillan).—1929. SAUNDERS, A. A., Interrelations of Birds and Forests, Roosevelt Wild Life Bull., Vol. V, No. 3, pp. 477–489.—1931. HOWARD, L. O., The Insect Menace (Century Co.).

GENERAL ACTIVITIES OF THE ADULT BIRD

Habitat
Habit and Structure
Uses of the Bill
Uses of the Wing
The Tail
The Feet
The Senses
Intelligence
Status of the Species

Having devoted the larger part of the space allotted to this Introduction to those features of bird-study in nature which seem most important from the field student's point of view, our outline of a bird's life may be completed by briefly calling attention to certain other subjects, each of which must be considered if we would approach anything like a complete local biography of a given species.

Habitat.—The range or geographical distribution of a species is ascertained only by compiling the data of many workers, but its local distribution, habitat, or ecologic range, can be determined by a single observer. Wonderful as it is that the range of so mobile a creature as a bird should have more or less well-defined boundaries beyond which it rarely advances, even more remarkable is it that within the limits of this range the bird often should have still more sharply marked haunts. Thus, shore, salt and fresh marshes, meadow, upland, bush, deciduous or coniferous forests, all have birds which, when nesting, are restricted to them, and the mapping of the habitats of the birds in one's locality is one of the interesting duties of the local ornithologist. The rarer birds will often be found confined to certain areas where perhaps a small colony may be established, and one should note whether it increases or decreases and attempt to learn the reasons for its success or failure.

Vegetation as it influences the food-supply or offers suitable nesting-sites, will be found to be the chief factor in controlling the distribution of birds locally; and it is important to record, during the course of years, those fluctuations in the numbers of a species due to changes in the character of the country incident to man's presence as he fells forests, drains marshes, permits the growth of scrub on fallow land, introduces new types or sources of food, furnishes new nesting-sites, etc. (See, especially, the Introduction to Brewster's 'Birds of the Cambridge Region, and to Forbush's 'Birds of Massachusetts,' Vol II.)

It is interesting, too, to observe the distribution of a bird during the day: where does it feed? where does it sleep? does it have regular flyways between feeding-ground and roost?

Habit and Structure.—The relation between form and function is in most cases so obvious that even the casual observer is impressed by the admirable adjustment existing between a bird's habits and its structure. The subject has been dealt with at length by Headley, Beebe, and others, and offers far less opportunity for original investigation by the local student than is found, for example, in a study of

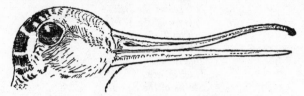

Fig. 12. Probelike bill of Woodcock, showing extent to which upper mandible can be moved. (One-half natural size.)

nesting habits. Nevertheless he should learn from personal observation, when possible, the part that bill, wings, feet, and tail play in a bird's life.

Uses of the Bill.—Birds' bills usually take the form of forceps or probes, rivaling in variety of shape the combined outfits of the surgeon and dentist, but spears, awls, chisels, picks, hooks, crackers, trowels, needles, scoops, and strainers are also represented in the bird's equipment. Primarily these instruments or weapons are designed to secure food

for the adult and to feed its young, but the bill is also of service in preening, in gathering and placing nesting material or excavating nesting-sites, and as

Fig. 13. Recurved bill of Avocet. (Two-thirds natural size.)

a weapon of attack or defence in the usually harmless struggles of birds. Woodpeckers use it as a drumstick. Owls rattle their mandibles threateningly, and Pelicans snap theirs in loud defiance.

With some birds the bill is the seat of some special growth or color during the breeding season. The White Pelican then wears a keel-like knob on the upper mandible, and the bills of Auks, Puffins, and some Ducks are brightly colored or modified in form.

Uses of the Wing.—The student should observe the relation between the shape of a bird's wing and the character of its flight and the

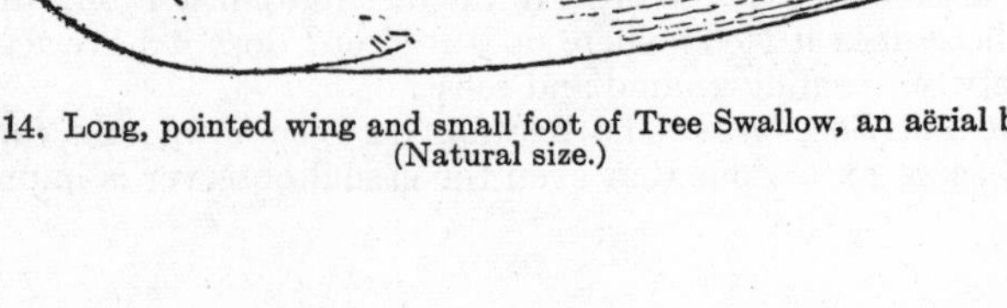

Fig. 14. Long, pointed wing and small foot of Tree Swallow, an aërial bird. (Natural size.)

further relation between the manner of its flight and its general habits. Compare, for example, the wing of a Turkey Vulture with that of a Quail or Partridge—one aerial, the other terrestrial in habit. Note the length-ened flight-feathers and broad ex-panse of the Vulture's wing, its comparative slowness in getting under way, its ability to soar in-definitely, in short, to remain in the air with the least possible expenditure of effort; while the rounded wing of the Quail, although incapable of prolonged flight and

FIG. 15. Short, rounded wing and large foot of Little Black Rail, a terrestrial bird. (Natural size.)

requiring great exertion for effective use, can nevertheless be employed at highest speed so quickly that the bird is in full flight almost the moment it leaves the ground. Continue the comparison through your list of birds, noting not only the power but the rhythm of the wing-stroke, whether it be regular or varied, whether the flight be direct or undulating, etc.

Auks and other members of their family fly under water and some

FIG. 16. Man-o'-war-bird, a species in which the wings have been developed at the expense of the feet.

Ducks also use their wings when diving, while the true Divers use both feet and wings. (See Townsend, *The Auk*, and 'A Labrador Spring,' pp. 180–205.) The loss by molting, depriving birds of all their flight-feathers at the same time, has already been mentioned (see Molt), and it will be interesting to learn whether at this time the Auks use their feet when progressing under water or whether a wing devoid of its quills supplies sufficient power. Young birds rest upon their wings as they would upon fore-feet, and in some instances (*e. g.* Grebes and Galli-nules) they are employed in climbing about among reeds, etc., or with young Herons, among branches. Adult Grebes and Loons, like the flightless Penguins, rely on their wings to aid them when on land.

The whistling or humming of wings may be the accom-paniment of regular flight, as

FIG. 17. The wing as a musical organ. Wing of Woodcock, showing outer attenuate feathers which produce the 'whistling' sound in flight.

with the Mourning Dove, certain Ducks, or the Hummingbirds; it may
be the result of an especial evolution, as with the swooping Nighthawk, or
it may proceed from some special structure, as with the narrowed outer
primaries of the Woodcock. The drumming of Grouse and the 'clapping'

a   b

Fig. 18. Tip of tail of (a) Downy Woodpecker and of (b) Brown Creeper, to show the
pointed shape in tails of climbing birds of different families. (Natural size.)

of roosters, before crowing, are further illustrations of the use of the wing
as a musical organ.

Sitting hens threaten with their wings; Swans and Pigeons strike
with them; Herons use the wing as a shield; altricial birds protect their
young from sun or rain by standing over them with spread wings, and they
shelter præcocial birds; fledg-
lings flutter the wings tremu-
lously when begging for food.

Fig. 19. Flamingo, showing relative length
of legs and neck in a wading bird.

The Tail.—A bird's tail is
primarily a rudder. Compare
the direct line of flight of a short-
tailed bird, for example, a Duck
or Quail, with the darting, erratic movements of a Tern or
Barn Swallow. Soaring birds
spread the tail as an additional
means of support and balance,
and, when spread and thrown
downward and forward, it serves
as a brake for the bird when
alighting.

With Woodpeckers, Creepers,
and Chimney Swifts, the tail is
modified for use as a prop.

The tail is exceedingly variable in form and is the seat of
many interesting marks and
colors which are displayed intentionally or when the bird is in
motion. Turkeys, Sage Cocks,
and Woodcocks spread the tail
when strutting; with a host of

birds, white on the outer tail-feathers is conspicuously shown in flight or when the tail is nervously 'jetted' or twitched by the hopping bird (see Color). Some birds not closely related wag the tail (*e. g.* Spotted Sandpiper, Water-Thrush, Palm Warbler, Pipit), though why they should do so does not appear to be known.

The Feet.—Birds' feet serve a greater variety of uses than any of the four organs whose uses we are considering. Primarily they are of

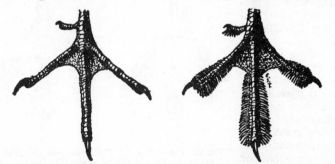

Fig. 20. Toes of Ruffed Grouse—naked in summer, fringed in winter to serve as snowshoes—illustrating seasonal adaptation in structure.

value as aids to locomotion, and the student should first note their length in wading birds like Flamingoes, Herons, and Stilts, and the relation between length of foot and length of neck. Aside from its length, the foot is variously modified by the development of webs and lobes and lengthening of the toes and nails, for swimming, running, hopping, climbing, and perching. The growth in the fall of horn-like marginal fringes on the toes of the Ruffed Grouse and of feathers on the toes of Ptarmigan, presents an unusual case of seasonal adaptation in structure.

In short-tailed birds, like Murres, the feet, when extended backward, act as rudders in flight. It may be added that all the water-birds, the Gallinæ, Columbæ, and Raptores, carry the feet extended backward in flight, while all the Passeres, or Perching Birds, carry them drawn up forward. In the intermediate groups (Cuckoos, Trogons, Woodpeckers, Swifts, Hummingbirds, and Parrots) the manner in which the feet are held in flight does not appear to be definitely known, though it seems probable that they are drawn up as in the Passeres. (See Townsend, 'A Labrador Spring,' pp. 180–205.)

Fig. 21. Foot of Osprey, to show large, apposed claws and spicules on under surface of toes.

The longer-winged diving birds, like Cormorants and Water-Turkeys, use only the feet to propel them when under water; Grebes and

Loons also use the feet for a similar purpose, and to a lesser extent the wings.

The relation between the two organs of locomotion, wings and feet, should be observed, when it will be found that when the former are greatly developed the feet are correspondingly small (*e. g.* Man-o'-war-bird, Swallows), while when the feet are large the wings are proportionately short and weak (*e. g.* the Rails and Gallinules).

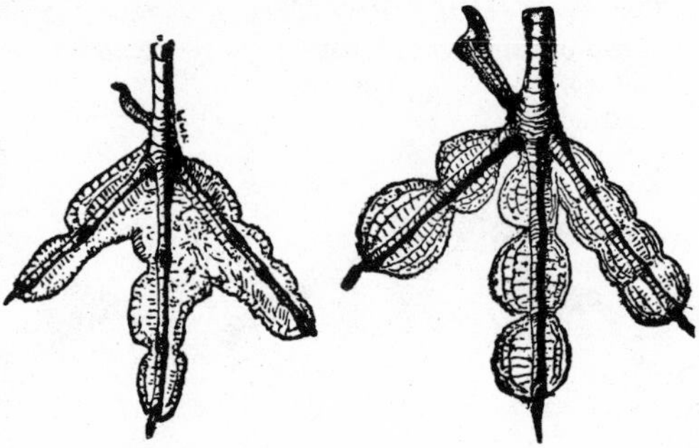

In securing food, feet are of service in scratching (*e. g.* Gallinæ, Fox Sparrows), while in predacious birds long, recurved talons and grasping power reach their maximum among birds.

Parrots use the foot as a hand, and many

Fig. 22. Lobed feet (*a*) Phalarope and (*b*) Coot, swimming birds of the Snipe and Rail families.

birds employ it to gather and place nesting material. With gallinaceous birds, particularly those that have spurs, the foot is a weapon. In Herons and Goatsuckers, the middle toe has a lateral terminal comb or pectination the function of which is unknown.

It should be repeated, as we close this short section on structure and habit, that the species mentioned in connection with the functions of bill, wings, tail, and feet have been restricted mainly to North American birds, in order that the student may verify, by personal observation, the close relation existing between the form of an organ and the manner in which it is employed.

The Senses.—In order that we may more nearly take the birds' point of view and appreciate the significance of their actions, it is essential that we should have some knowledge of the development of their senses. Briefly, it is believed that in birds the senses of smell, taste, and touch are inferior to our own, but that in sight and hearing they are immeasurably our superiors.

We have very little exact information concerning the sense of smell in birds, but my observations[1] on Barro Colorado Island have shown conclusively that Turkey Buzzards, aided only by their sense of smell, can readily find food which has been carefully concealed.

To what extent birds taste their food it is difficult for us to determine. That certain things are pleasant and others disagreeable will be obvious to anyone who has seen a bird vigorously wipe its bill after attempting to eat an ill-tasting bug; but it is also clear that the bird's standard of gustation is not to be measured by our own. The experi-

[1] 1929, 'My Tropical Air Castle', pp. 147-166.

ments of Judd (*Am. Nat.*, 1899, p. 474) showed that many insects, which to man are both nauseating and foul-smelling, are relished by birds while others are refused. It is, however, certain that the bird's restricted sense of smell in a large degree limits its ability to detect finer differences in taste.

The bird's sense of touch is evidently more highly developed than either the sense of smell or that of taste. It is seated mainly in the tip of the bill, and the precision and delicacy with which this organ is used in picking up the smallest seeds, dislodging insects, their eggs and larvæ from the crevices in bark, grasping worms or grubs out of sight in the ground, or catching minute forms of life in muddy water, demonstrates the degree of ability with which it is employed.

When we reach the sense of hearing, we must at once concede that the bird is so far beyond us that we probably do not fully realize the extent of its powers. A Barred Owl, which alighted with his back toward me at a distance of about 50 yards, turned his head instantly in response to the slightest 'squeak' made to test its hearing. The same sound will often turn a passing Hawk when he might be thought to be beyond its reach. The snapping of the smallest twig throws a whole Heron colony into wildest commotion. Woodpeckers locate the grubs of boring beetles, and Robins apparently listen for crawling worms.

That birds not only have incredibly acute hearing, but can also distinguish minor differences in sound, is implied by the wide range of sounds which birds themselves produce and which, in the economy of their lives, are obviously not intended to fall on deaf or inappreciative ears, as other writers have before remarked.

A colony of Roseate Spoonbills, studied from a blind, were not alarmed by various noises made in manipulating a camera, but at a single word, spoken in a low voice, every bird sprang into the air.

White Egrets, in Florida, have acquired so great a fear of a gun that the birds of a rookery in which my blind was placed left their nests with a rush at the faint report of a gun fired by a guide a mile and a half away.

Crows immediately respond to an imitation of the call of the Barred Owl, and though this may be uttered but once, they come from some distance directly to the spot whence the 'hoot' proceeded.

In default of definite experiments, it is on casual observations of this nature that our knowledge of the comparative power of a bird's hearing is based. There is much need for further data here.

With eyes, the relation between cause and action is more apparent, and without knowing exactly how well a bird can see, we have at least seen enough to be impressed by its marvelous power of vision. Recall a quietly observant Loggerhead Shrike leaving its lookout and flying so directly to a grasshopper in the grass a hundred feet away that it is clear the insect was seen before starting; or, again, Gulls and Petrels picking up small bits of food from waves so boisterous that a man would be lost to sight in them. "Observe," says Coues ('Key,' 5th ed., p. 185), "an Eagle soaring aloft until he seems to us but a speck in the blue expanse.

He is far-sighted; and scanning the earth below, descries an object much smaller than himself, which would be invisible to us at that distance. He prepares to pounce upon his quarry; in the moment required for the deadly plunge, he becomes near-sighted, seizes his victim with unerring aim, and sees well how to complete the bloody work begun. A Humming-bird darts so quickly that our eyes cannot follow him, yet instantaneously settles as light as a feather upon a tiny twig. How far off it was when first perceived we do not know, but in the intervening fraction of a second the twig has rushed into the focus of distinct vision from many yards away. A Woodcock tears through the thickest cover as if it were clear space, avoiding every obstacle. The only things to the accurate perception of which birds' eyes appear not to have accommodated themselves are telegraph wires and lighthouses; thousands of birds are annually hurled against these objects to their destruction."

A probable sense of direction has already been considered in the chapter on Migration.

Intelligence.—It is the human side of bird-life which in recent years has most attracted bird students and has been most emphasized by popular writers. With the bird's already pronounced human-like traits to build on, it has required only imagination, unrestrained by scientific method or analysis, to make of the bird a creature of marvelous mental endowment, whose reasoning powers, within the limits of its normal activities, are equal if not superior to those of man.

Such treatment finds favor with those whose love of birds exceeds their knowledge of ornithology, but it is strongly resented by others who, yielding nothing in their appreciation of the birds' claims to our attention, would still have them regarded as birds rather than as feathered human beings. But in attempting to administer a corrective, the critics of the ultra-human point of view have given an overdose. They not only deny the bird ability to reason, but assert that all its mental activities are wholly instinctive; in short, that the bird is a feathered automaton.

It is not possible here to discuss this question in the light of all the available evidence, but only to record my own views as they are based mainly on personal observations. These lead me to believe that neither point of view is wholly right nor wholly wrong; in other words, that there is a measure of truth in both contentions. In each case, however, it would appear that a fundamental error is made in speaking of the 'mind of birds' collectively, or as a unit. We would not attempt thus to consider the mind of mammals, and while there is not, it is true, so wide a range of mental development in birds as there is in mammals, the difference between the least intelligent and the most intelligent is far too great for us to discuss the mind of the Class Aves without distinction as to species and even individuals.

For example, a prolonged, intimate study of Pelicans seems to emphasize the low order of their intelligence. Perfectly as they are adapted to their own environment, they exhibit, when confronted by new conditions, what, judged by human standards, can only be called stupidity.

On the other hand, the Blue Jays, Crows, Jackdaws, and others of their near kin often exhibit so high a degree of intelligence that the bird-lover, unmindful of exact definitions, is tempted to assert that they show ability to reason.

The Herons of Cuthbert Rookery were alarmed into hurried flight by the firing of a gun a mile and a half away, but the Crows which were with them paid no attention to the report. The Herons' experience with firearms has developed an unreasoning fear, while Crows show the nicest judgment in estimating the range of a gun.

The Herons of this rookery permitted the Crows to rob them of their eggs by the hundred without the slightest indication of protest or resentment, but Kingbirds attack every Crow which ventures near their nest, often pursuing them for several hundred yards.

Similar instances, illustrating the wide range of intelligence among birds of different species, might be multiplied endlessly, but any consideration of the subject renders this variation so evident that it is assuredly unnecessary to present further proof.

Variation in intelligence is not confined to these differences between species, but within narrower limits is shown by the individual. To those who study birds as individuals rather than as species, this statement will seem superfluous, but advocates of automatic bird-life would have us believe that, in the same species, one bird is essentially the duplicate of another. Birds which nest closely associated in colonies, where a certain standard of behavior is developed by similarity of environment and imitation, show less individuality than those species of more solitary habits; but it requires only intimate experience with representatives of either class to convince one that pronounced characteristics are often shown by certain individuals, and indeed one rarely finds in the latter group two birds which act exactly alike. It is the range of intelligence among the individuals which, in the end, determines the degree of success of the species. It is among the Passerine birds that we shall find species possessing the highest intelligence, and the Passeres are the birds of the day, the dominant group in the Class Aves, outnumbering the members of all other orders combined.

Admitting then that some species of birds exhibit barely a glimmer of intelligence, and are indeed very near to being feathered automata, are there not at the other end of the scale birds which possess the power to reason?

By reason, accepting Lloyd Morgan's definition, is meant the "process of drawing a logical inference," the ability "to think the *therefore*." We can of course determine the bird's mental status only on the basis of its actions. Birds' notes, so far as we understand them, express only primary emotions. If birds then can draw an inference, we can be aware of it only through its effect on their behavior. Those direct responses to conditions which lead to change of action, or of habit, as where a bird becomes shy through persecution or tame through protection, are not to be attributed to reason, as the term is here used, but are unreasoning exhibitions prompted by sense associations. They occasion no sequence of thought on the part of the bird, no drawing of conclusions or performance of acts made with such indubitable reference to other following, dependent acts, that it is evident the latter were conceived of as the logical consequence of the former. The bird, with truly wonderful quickness, learns to associate a certain thing with danger, another thing with safety. The Pelicans of Pelican Island, Florida, for the first time in their known history, failed to return to their island because a sign had been erected on it. This illustrates the keenness of the birds' perception, but it also demonstrates their inability to infer that a piece of board was harmless.

A pair of Blue Jays, after an absence of nearly two hours, immediately returned to their nest and fed their young, their suspicions completely allayed by the presence of a mounted Jay in the nest tree. Here was a response so quick and satisfactory that it might be considered evidence of the bird's ability to draw an inference, but the bird's failure to distinguish a poorly mounted, discarded museum specimen of its own kind, and later, of an Owl, from the living bird, indicates its inability to reason. (See 'Camps and Cruises,' pp. 5–14.)

Using the word reason, therefore, as psychologists commonly define it, I may say at once that I have seen no conclusive evidence of reasoning power in my study of birds. But in place of this characteristic of the human mind, one finds in birds certain other senses and faculties so much more highly developed than they are in man that we doubtless have but a faint conception of their value. Birds exhibit a truly surprising power of memory—implying also association of experiences—while in their hearing, sight, and probable sense of direction, they are incomparably our superiors. In my judgment, then, it is to the keenness of these powers rather than to an alleged gift of reason that the bird owes its success in life. Before their manifestation, reason, following the slower channels of logical inference, may often well stand aghast. What form of reason would lead a bird night after night on a journey of thousands of miles with such nice precision of movement that the goal is reached on a certain day? For men, with only the bird's physical equipment, the feat would be impossible.

In thus denying the bird's power to reason, we add rather than detract from the interest with which we study the evidences of its own peculiar and remarkable gifts; and our interest is intensified by the wide range of variation in the mental development among individuals as well as groups, which often renders it uncertain just what response will follow a certain stimulus.

Nor, in denying the birds close association with us on the higher planes of intelligence, should we lose our feeling of kinship with them. We have distanced them in the race of mental development, but that should not render us any the less eager to discover in some of their traits those which characterized the childhood of our race.

Status of the Species.—The measure of a bird's success in life is determined not alone by its powers as a migrant (if it be migratory); its attractiveness when wooing a mate; its skill as a nest-builder; its devotion and courage as a parent; the nature of its physical and mental endowment, or the degree of its intelligence, but also by the extent of its adaptability and the character of its temperament. When, therefore, we ask why some birds are abundant and others rare, all these factors are to be considered in connection with all the conditions under which the bird lives; and to do this with due attention to the many influences involved, is one of the ultimate objects of the study of ornithology; for, to determine the causes of the success and failure of life is second only to determining the origin of life itself.

Species which are the direct object of man's unbridled greed *must* succumb to an enemy before whom neither swiftness of flight nor excessive wariness avail. Thus, the Wild Pigeon and white Egrets, however well they were fitted to contend with nature, could not escape man.

But when man enters the bird's life only indirectly, altering its environment without actually killing the bird itself, the species in undiminished numbers is left to face the problem; and its ability to adjust itself to new conditions is now put to a vital and immediate test.

The Pileated and Ivory-billed Woodpeckers have decreased with the forests, but the Crow and the Robin, both naturally forest-inhabiting species, have more than held their own. Both, in different ways, have adapted themselves to the new order of things: the Crow meets the distinctly hostile if not actively aggressive attitude of man by wariness and more than average intelligence; the Robin, through its fearlessness, has won man's friendship and protection. Near his dwellings its natural enemies have been reduced in number and the normal food-supply greatly augmented by fruits of various kinds, a more accessible supply of worms on close-cropped lawns, and various insects which also thrive on man's bounty.

The introduction into this country of the House or English Sparrow has, from a biological point of view, been an overwhelming success. Not only did the bird fill an unoccupied place in our cities, but when brought into competition with native species, its hardiness, general adaptability, pugnacity, and continuous presence have all been in its favor. When the migratory Bluebirds or Purple Martins returned, they often found the Sparrows in possession of their nesting-boxes, and the decrease in the numbers of both these species is unquestionably to be attributed to their inability to compete with the Sparrow.

In the changes wrought by man, directly or indirectly, we may find many similar illustrations of sudden alterations in the bird's environment, and the manner in which they are met demonstrates what is meant by adaptability. In nature, equally great changes may occur, but they take place more slowly, and the adjustment between them and the bird, while not the less essential, is not so severe and sudden a tax on the bird's resources.

But aside from these external influences, which may remain unchanged and hence inactive for long periods of time, there are certain internal influences which are constantly potent. Chief among these is temperament as it is expressed in sociability or desire for solitude. It is obvious that only birds of social, or at least peaceable, disposition could live in such close juxtaposition as do colonial birds, like Gannets, Murres, Flamingoes, Cliff Swallows, and many others, where nests or nesting birds almost or actually touch one another. Such social species are usually represented by numerous individuals, while, on the other hand, the relative abundance of solitary species is related to the extent of the area over which they claim guardianship while nesting, to the exclusion only of other birds of their own kind. Hence, Hawks and Owls, for example, which resent the intrusion of other individuals of the species into their nesting area, are comparatively rare, while Robins and Chipping Sparrows, which, though not colonial, often nest near others of their kind, are comparatively abundant. The abundance of a species is, therefore, doubtless more dependent upon the number of nests which, under favorable conditions of environment, constitute the normal number for a given area, than upon the supply of food in that area.

On this subject, Brewster ('Birds of the Cambridge Region,' pp. 62, 63) remarks, "In my opinion the desire for exclusive possession so conspicuously shown by the male, and often by him alone, is usually the direct result of *sexual jealousy*. This, as is natural, makes him intolerant, during the breeding season, of the near presence of rival males. If his concern were chiefly in respect to the food supply, it would be equally manifested at every season and towards all birds who subsist on the same food that he and his mate require, which is certainly not the case." It is this question of area occupied when nesting that is developed in Howard's 'Territory in Bird Life' (London, 1920).

When in possession of all the essential facts, we may, therefore, in many instances present more or less conclusive reasons for the success or failure of a species, but there will remain many others which are apparently inexplicable. Species will be observed, practically alike in structure and habits, some of which in incalculable numbers flood the land, while others are represented by but a few individuals scattered here and there in small colonies or concentrated in a narrow area.

All other explanations failing, such cases tempt the belief that species as well as individuals have a life, that some full of the vigor of youth are advancing, while others past their prime are declining; that some in short are dominant, and others decadent. Dominant species are possessed of the vitality which admits of adaptiveness and power to overcome unfavorable conditions to which decadent species would succumb.

Thus we may think of a dominant species as an expansive force which is preëminently fitted to fill, with the utmost precision of adjustment, its own place in nature, and is also constantly pressing against all the governing influences which go to make up its environment, to increase its number and extend its range. Up to a certain point it meets a degree of success in proportion to its mental and physical endowment; beyond that it advances or retreats only after a struggle.

In February, 1895, the South Atlantic States were visited by a blizzard which practically annihilated the Bluebirds wintering or resident in them, and the following spring the species was absent from large areas where the preceding year it had been common. The loss of a beautiful bird, so intimately associated with man, was deplored as irreparable, but within three years the species was as abundant as ever, so quickly did the expansive force of the species bring it to the limit where contact with environment checks further advance.

Less evident, but in the end of greater significance, is the Bluebird's struggles with the English Sparrow and the European Starling, both growing, expansive species. The conflict is not over food, for all the species are of different feeding habits, but over the nesting-site. We cannot imagine that the Bluebird will, even through force of circumstances, exhibit the Sparrow's adaptability, and, in default of a normal site, build in branches, vines, electric-light hoods—in short, any place which will hold nest-material—nor has it strength to compete successfully with the Starling.

Let us, therefore, join forces with this gentle-voiced messenger of sky and earth by providing it with suitable homes in which these enemies, for whose presence we are responsible, shall not be permitted to abide.

SUGGESTIONS FOR THE STUDENT

Habitat.—Define the difference between 'Range' and 'Habitat.' Describe the habitat of a given species. What are the more important factors in determining the nature of a bird's habitat? Can you mention an instance where a change in the character of the habitat has been followed by a change in the character of the bird-life? Give instances of daily change in habitat.

Habit and Structure.—Name the principal functions of the bill, and give illustrations of each. Describe the feeding habits of Woodpeckers, of Hawks, of the Woodcock, of Flycatchers, of Sparrows in relation to the character of their bill. What birds use the bill when climbing? In what birds is the bill adorned by bright colors or appendages in the breeding season? Name the functions of the wing. Describe the flight of Ducks, Quail, Hawks, Vultures, Woodpeckers, Purple Finches, Swallows, etc. Describe the relation between the shape of their wings and their manner of flight. What relation exists between the size of the wing and foot? What North American bird was flightless? What North American birds use their wings as musical instruments? Which use them under water? How are they used in defence? Describe their use in sheltering the young.

Name the functions of the tail. Which of our birds use it in display? Which as a prop? Describe its relation to manner of flight.

What are the functions of the feet? Describe the various means of locomotion employed by birds. What birds use only the feet under water? In what way is a Coot's (*Fulica*) adapted to its wants? Why is a Phalarope's foot webbed? In what birds does the structure of the foot change with season? How is the foot held in flight by various birds? What is the relation of length of foot to length of neck? (There is almost no limit to the questions which may be asked in regard to the form and function of birds, and the student is urged to draw largely on local material to stimulate his powers of observation in this direction.)

The Senses.—How do the senses of birds compare with those of man? Is the sense of smell well developed in birds? Can you mention any instances illustrating the bird's power of taste? Its powers of touch? Is the power of hearing well developed in birds? Mention several instances. Do birds learn quickly the significance of certain sounds? Mention several instances illustrating the bird's power of sight. Define what is meant by intelligence in birds. Are some species more intelligent than others? What is the difference between intelligence and reason? What is Lloyd Morgan's definition of 'reason'? Have you found any evidence illustrating the bird's ability to reason? Why is it desirable to base stories of bird-life presented as 'true' on known facts in their habits?

Status of the Species.—What are the most important factors in determining whether a bird is rare or common? How may man directly or indirectly affect the members of a species? Give illustrations. Why does the English Sparrow present an interesting biological problem? How may a bird's temperament affect its numbers? Give illustrations. When were Bluebirds destroyed by a blizzard? How long before their numbers reached normal? What is the probable reason of their sudden increase?

REFERENCES

1883. MARTIN and MOALE, How to Dissect a Bird (Macmillan).—1884. COUES, E., Key to North American Birds (Dana Estes), rev. ed. 1902, Vol. I, pp. 59–233. (Important.)—1893-1896. NEWTON, A., and others, A Dictionary of Birds, 1 vol., 1088 pp. (Macmillan).—1894. MORGAN, C. L., An Introduction to Comparative Psychology, 12mo, 382 pp. (Scribner's).— 1895. HEADLEY, F. W., The Structure and Life of Birds, 12mo, 412 pp., illus. (Macmillan).—1898. BEDDARD, F. E., Structure and Classification of Birds, 8vo, 548 pp., illus. (Longmans).—1897. BASKET, J. N., The Story of the Birds, 12mo, 263 pp., illus. (Appleton).—1906. BEEBE, C. W., The Bird: Its Form and Function, 8vo, 496 pp., illus. (Holt).—1910. PYCRAFT, W. P., A History of Birds, 8vo, 458 pp., illus. (Methuen & Co., London).— 1910. HERRICK, F. H., Instinct and Intelligence in Birds, Pop. Sci. Monthly, June, July, and August.—1911. Various Authors, Journ. of Animal Behavior (Holt).—1929. HOWARD, H. E., An Introduction to the Study of Bird Behavior, 4to, xii+136 pp., illus. (Cambridge Univ. Press).

SYNOPSIS OF ORDERS AND SUBORDERS OF THE BIRDS OF NORTH AMERICA EAST OF THE NINETIETH MERIDIAN

Both as an aid to memory and as an expression of relationships, it is deemed more desirable to follow here the arrangement of the American Ornithologists' Union through the medium of a Synopsis than to destroy this natural grouping by the use of an artificial Key. If the student will memorize the names of the orders and suborders, their sequence and distinctive characters, he will have laid a broad foundation for his subsequent studies.

It should be understood that the characters presented in this Synopsis relate primarily to those members of the Orders included which are found in eastern North America and not necessarily to groups occurring beyond our geographical limits.

ORDER I. GAVIIFORMES.—Loons (no suborders).

Large swimmers, comparatively helpless on land; length over 2 feet; tail-feathers short, but stiff and well formed; legs set far back; tarsi flattened; toes four, front ones fully webbed, with nails rather than claws; bill higher than wide, sharply pointed, without flutings, 'gutters,' or serrations; wings without a colored patch or speculum, well developed, but when closed not reaching beyond the tail, pointed, the primaries much longer than tertials, p. 139.

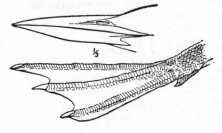 

Fig. 23. Loon.	Fig. 24. *a.* Pied-billed Grebe. *b.* Horned Grebe.

ORDER II. COLYMBIFORMES.—Grebes (no suborders).

Smaller swimmers, when pursued usually dive, comparatively helpless on land; length usually under 2 feet; tail rudimentary, its feathers downy, not evident; legs set far back; tarsi flattened; toes four-lobed, their nails broad and flattened; bill higher than wide, slender, sharply pointed (except Pied-billed Grebe which has the culmen curved, the maxilla hooked), without flutings, 'gutters,' or serrations; wings when closed, not reaching beyond tail, no speculum, tertials nearly as long or longer than primaries, p. 142.

(125)

ORDER III. PROCELLARIIFORMES.

—TUBE-NOSED SWIMMERS: ALBA-TROSSES, SHEARWATERS, PETRELS, etc. (no suborders).

Strictly marine birds which glide or course low over the water, often skimming the waves. They are gray or black (rarely white), more often a combination of these colors. The hind toe is small or absent; the front toes are fully webbed; the wings (except in the diving Petrels) are long and narrow; the bill hooked, the nostrils tubular, p. 147.

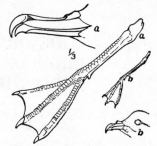

FIG. 25. *a.* Cory's Shearwater.
b. Leach's Petrel.

ORDER IV. PELECANIFORMES.—TOTI-PALMATE SWIMMERS: TROPIC-BIRDS, PELICANS, GANNETS, CORMORANTS, etc. (three suborders).

1. Suborder Phaëthontes.—Tropic-birds.

Largely white, tern-like sea-birds, with two central tail-feathers narrow, projecting far beyond others; toes fully webbed; bill sharply pointed; gular sac not evident, p. 154.

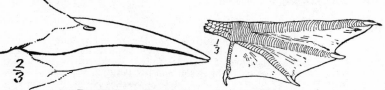

FIG. 26. Tropic-bird.   FIG. 27. Cormorant.

2. Suborder Pelecani.—Pelicans, Gannets, Cormorants, Darters.

All four toes fully webbed; gular sac bare; neither outer nor central pair of tail-feathers notably longer than others, p. 155.

3. Suborder Fregatæ. — Man-o'-war-birds.

Large, fork-tailed sea-birds, the outer pair of rectrices about 17 inches long; front toes not fully webbed; bill long, strongly hooked; gular sac bare, p. 162.

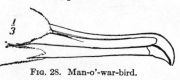

FIG. 28. Man-o'-war-bird.

ORDER V. CICONIIFORMES.—LONG-LEGGED WADING BIRDS: HERONS, STORKS, IBISES, SPOONBILLS, AND FLAMINGOES (four suborders, three North American).

1. Suborder Ardeæ.—Herons and Bitterns.

Bill straight, sharply pointed, lores bare; toes four, all on same level; webs small or absent; middle toe-nail with a comblike margin; neck curved in flight, p. 163.

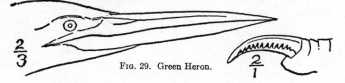

FIG. 29. Green Heron.

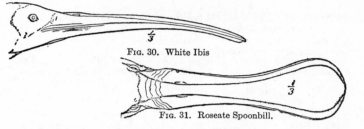

FIG. 30. White Ibis

FIG. 31. Roseate Spoonbill.

2. Suborder Ciconiæ.—Storks, Ibises, Spoonbills.
Bill cylindrical or flattened and spatulate; lores bare; toes four on same level, webs small or absent; no comb on middle toe-nail; neck straight in flight, p. 172.

3. Suborder Phœnicopteri.—Flamingoes.
End half of bill bent downward, its sides with strainers, lores bare; toes four, hind toe elevated above level of front ones, latter fully webbed; neck extended in flight, p. 175.

FIG. 32. Flamingo.

ORDER VI. ANSERIFORMES.—DUCKS, GEESE, AND SCREAMERS (two suborders, one North American).

1. Suborder Anseres.—Ducks, Geese, and Swans.
Swimming birds, at home on land; tail well formed; legs short, not set far back; tarsi rounded; toes four, front ones fully webbed; bill broad and flattened, its sides fluted or guttered with strainers, or rounded and with tooth-like projections; the tip of the maxilla with a 'nail' or hook; wing pointed; primaries stiff, p. 176.

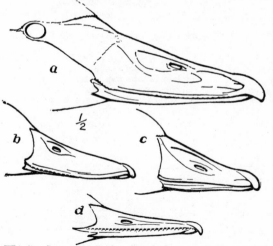

FIG. 33. *a.* Whistling Swan. *b.* Mallard. *c.* Canada Goose. *d.* Red-breasted Merganser.

ORDER VII. FALCONIFORMES.—Vultures and diurnal birds of prey (two suborders).

1. **Suborder Cathartæ.**—American Vultures.
   Head and upper neck bare or nearly so; nostrils large, completely piercing the maxilla; bill less hooked; claws duller than in Falcones; hind toe less than half as long as middle toe; its claw small, p. 210.

FIG. 34. Turkey Vulture.

FIG. 35. *a*. Duck Hawk.
b. Cooper's Hawk.

2. **Suborder Falcones.**—Falcons, Hawks, Eagles, Kites, etc.
   Head feathered; nostrils opening in a cere, not completely piercing maxilla; bill strongly hooked; claws long, sharp, curved; hind toe usually as long or longer than shortest front toe; its claw as large or larger than longest front claw, p. 212.

ORDER VIII. GALLIFORMES.—Gallinaceous birds (two suborders, one North American).

1. **Suborder Galli.** — Grouse, Quails, Pheasants, Turkeys.
   Our species, terrestrial, scratching birds; bill short, stout; culmen decurved; wings short, rounded; primaries stiff and curved, producing a whirring sound as the bird takes flight; feet strong, hind toe short, slightly elevated, p. 235.

FIG. 36. *a*. Ruffed Grouse. *b*. Bob-white.

ORDER IX. GRUIFORMES.—Cranes, Rails, etc. (eight suborders, one North American).

1. **Suborder Grues.**—Cranes, Rails, Limpkin, Coots, and Gallinules.
   Marsh inhabitants with toes unwebbed (except in the Coot, which is more aquatic and has lobate toes) and without 'comb' on claw; lores feathered or (Cranes) with hair-like 'bristles'; neck extended in flight; wings rounded; tertials often as long as primaries, p. 249.

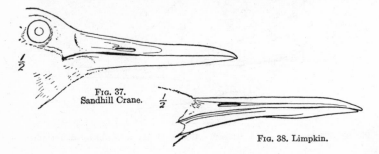

FIG. 37.
Sandhill Crane.

FIG. 38. Limpkin.

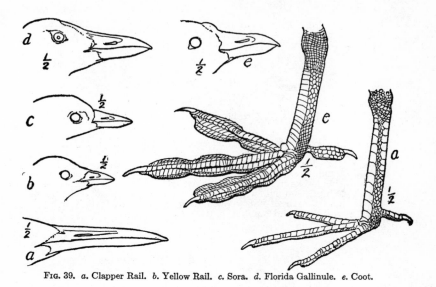

Fig. 39. *a.* Clapper Rail. *b.* Yellow Rail. *c.* Sora. *d.* Florida Gallinule. *e.* Coot.

ORDER X. CHARADRIIFORMES.—SHORE-BIRDS, GULLS, AUKS, etc. (three suborders).

1. **Suborder Charadrii.**—Plovers, Sandpipers, Snipe, Avocets, Stilts, Phalaropes, etc.

Long-legged, shore—sometimes plains-inhabiting—birds; usually less than a foot in length; toes four or three (Plovers), the hind toe, when present, elevated and less than half the length of inner (except in Jacanas); toes never fully webbed (except Avocets); bill usually soft, slender, elongate, rounded; nostrils opening through slits or grooves; wings long, 'flat,' pointed; tertials long, p. 259.

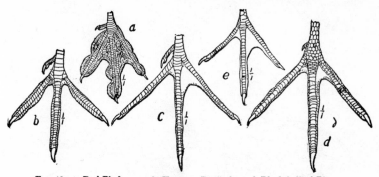

Fig. 40. *a.* Red Phalarope. *b.* Knot. *c.* Dowitcher. *d.* Black-bellied Plover. *e.* Semipalmated Sandpiper.

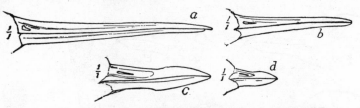

Fig. 41. *a.* Dowitcher. *b.* Knot. *c.* Black-bellied Plover. *d.* Semipalmated Plover.

2. Suborder Lari.—Gulls, Terns, Jaegers, Skuas, and Skimmers.
Long-winged water-birds, largely marine; usually seen in flight; light-colored (most Terns and adult Gulls) or dark (Jaegers and young Gulls); bill strong, thick, hooked in Gulls and Jaegers, pointed in Terns, blade-like in Skimmers, in part yellow or red; nostrils opening in a slit and completely perforating the maxilla; no gular sac; toes four, hind toe small not webbed to front ones, front toes webbed; wings very long and pointed, p. 294.

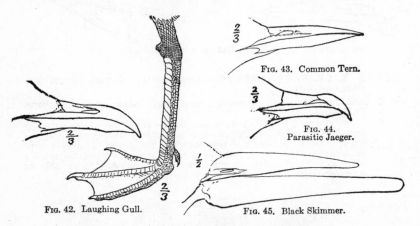

Fig. 43. Common Tern.

Fig. 44.
Parasitic Jaeger.

Fig. 42. Laughing Gull.

Fig. 45. Black Skimmer.

3. Suborder Alcæ.—Auks, Murres, Puffins.
Marine birds of North Atlantic and North Pacific; toes three, fully webbed, their nails sharp and pointed; bill variable, but never with 'gutters' or 'strainers'; tail evident; wings short but pointed and rather duck-like, p. 318.

Fig. 46. *a.* Puffin. *b.* Murre. *c.* Guillemot. *d.* Razor-billed Auk.

ORDER XI. COLUMBIFORMES.—Pigeons, Sand Grouse, etc. (two suborders, one North American).

1. Suborder Columbæ.—Pigeons and Doves.

Bill rather slender, its basal half or more grooved, the nostrils opening in a soft fleshy membrane; toes four, all on same level, the hind toe about as long as shortest front one, p. 324.

Fig. 47. Passenger Pigeon.

ORDER XII. PSITTACIFORMES.—Parrots, Macaws, etc. (no suborders).

Toes four, two in front, two behind (zygodactyl); bill strong with a cere; maxilla decurved, hooked; mandible scoop-shaped, p. 330.

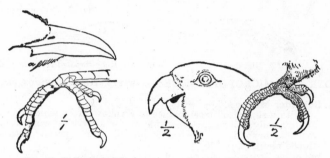

Fig. 48. Yellow-billed Cuckoo.   Fig. 49. Carolina Paroquet.

ORDER XIII. CUCULIFORMES.—Cuckoos and their Allies, etc. (two suborders, one North American).

1. Suborder Cuculi.—Cuckoos, Anis, etc.

Toes four, two in front, two behind (zygodactyl); bill without a cere; tail long, feathers not stiffened or pointed, outer pair shortest; central pair longest (graduated), p. 331.

Fig. 50. Barn Owl.   Fig. 51. Barred Owl.

ORDER XIV. STRIGIFORMES.—Owls (no suborders).

Eyes large, set in a feathered disc or face; bill strongly hooked, with a cere, its base concealed by feathers; tarsi usually feathered; toes with large, sharply pointed claws, p. 334.

ORDER XV. CAPRIMULGIFORMES.—GOATSUCKERS AND OIL-BIRDS (two suborders, one North American).

1. Suborder Caprimulgi.—Whip-poor-wills, Nighthawks, etc.

Head large; bill small; mouth-opening reaching to below the eyes, usually bordered by long bristles; tarsus more or less feathered; feet small, middle toe much the longest, its claw with a comb (pectinate); plumage soft, mixed brown, buff, and black, p. 344.

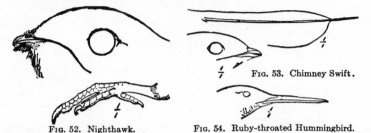

FIG. 53. Chimney Swift.

FIG. 52. Nighthawk.   FIG. 54. Ruby-throated Hummingbird.

ORDER XVI. MICROPODIFORMES.—SWIFTS, HUMMINGBIRDS, etc. (two suborders).

1. Suborder Micropodii.—Swifts.

With a superficial resemblance to Swallows from which they differ anatomically; bill small; gape wide; no rictal bristles; wings very long reaching beyond tail, the latter (in our single species) with spine-tipped rectrices, p. 348.

2. Suborder Trochili.—Hummingbirds.

Size small; bill longer than head, extremely slender, rounded, almost needle-like; upperparts in our one species (and most others) shining green; feet small, weak, fit only for perching, p. 349.

ORDER XVII. CORACIIFORMES.—KINGFISHERS, ROLLERS, HORNBILLS, etc. (four suborders, one North American).

1. Suborder Alcedines. — King-fishers.

Feet very small, unfitted for walking; toes four, the middle and outer ones joined for half their length; bill long, strong, pointed. p. 351.

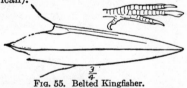

FIG. 55. Belted Kingfisher.

ORDER XVIII. PICIFORMES.—WOODPECKERS, JACAMARS, TOUCANS, etc. (two suborders, one North American).

1. Suborder Pici.—Woodpeckers, Piculets, and Wrynecks.

Climbing birds with strong feet and nails; toes four, two in front and two behind, or three, two in front and one behind; bill stout, pointed or wedge-tipped; nostril bristly; tail-feathers with pointed, stiffened tips, p. 352.

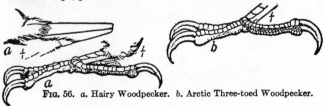

FIG. 56. a. Hairy Woodpecker. b. Arctic Three-toed Woodpecker.

ORDER XIX. PASSERIFORMES. — Perching birds (four suborders, two North American).

Toes four, without webs, all on the same level; hind toe as long as middle one, its claw usually longer than that of middle one, a grasping, perching foot; tail of twelve feathers.

1. **Suborder Tyranni.**—Flycatchers and 12 other families. The following characters relate to the former —Family Tyrannidæ.

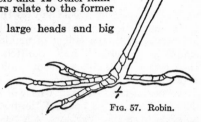

Rather stocky birds with large heads and big mouths, fringed at the base (rictus) with long, stiff rictal bristles; bill rather flattened, wider than high at the base, from above triangular in outline; tip of the maxilla decurved and slightly hooked; nostrils rounded,

FIG. 57. Robin.

more or less covered by bristly feathers; primaries ten, the first (outer) never less than two-thirds length of second; the tail (except in Kingbird) without conspicuous white markings; feet comparatively small; the tarsus short, its back rounded rather than edged or ridged, p. 363.

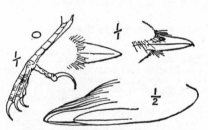

FIG. 58. Phœbe. Showing bill, wing and tarsus (also cross-section) of Tyrannine bird.

FIG. 59. Bluebird, tarsus (and cross-section) of Oscinine bird

2. **Suborder Oscines.**—Larks, Swallows, Crows and Jays, Titmice, Nuthatches, Wrens, Thrashers, Thrushes, Waxwings, Vireos, Warblers, Tanagers, Sparrows, etc.

Obvious primaries[1] nine, or if ten, the first (outer) rudimentary; back of tarsus edged or ridged, not rounded (except Alaudidæ in which hind claw is longer than middle toe); bill not flattened and wider than high at base (except in *Setophaga* and *Wilsonia*), p. 373.

---

[1]All the Oscines have ten primaries but in the Fringillidæ, Tanagridæ, Icteridæ, Compsothlypidæ, Hirundinidæ, and some of the Vireos the first primary (from without) "lies upon the *outer* side of the wing next to the outermost primary covert" (Ridgway), and is not evident. In our remaining Oscines the outer primary, though rudimentary, lies upon the inner side of the wing and is obvious.

A FIELD KEY TO OUR
COMMONER EASTERN LAND BIRDS

The following is a field key to those birds which, either because of their abundance or conspicuous colors, most frequently attract our attention. With the object of making it as brief, and consequently as simple, as possible, I have omitted species which can be referred to their respective families without difficulty—for example, Hawks, Owls, Woodpeckers, and Swallows. It is designed simply as an aid to the first steps of the beginner, who will soon graduate from it to the more detailed keys in the body of the book. Like the field keys to Finches and Sparrows and Warblers, it is based largely upon adult males.

First Group.—With yellow or orange in the plumage.
Second Group.—With red in the plumage.
Third Group.—With blue in the plumage.
Fourth Group.—Plumage conspicuously black, or black and white.
Fifth Group.—Without either yellow, orange, red, or blue in the plumage; not conspicuously black, or black and white.

First Group.—With yellow or orange in the plumage

I. Throat yellow.
  1. Throat and breast pure yellow, *without* streaks or spots.
    A. Length 5·00; cap, wings, and tail black; back yellow; song canary-like, sometimes uttered on the wing; flight undulating, frequently accompanied by the notes *chic-o-ree, per-chic-o-ree.*
                                492. GOLDFINCH.
    B. Length 5·50; lower belly and wing-bars white; back olive-green; frequents the upper branches, generally in woodland; actions deliberate; song loud and musical, uttered slowly, often with pauses: "See me? I'm here; where are you?"
                            406. YELLOW-THROATED VIREO.
    C. Length 5·25; cheeks and forehead black bordered by ashy; upper parts olive-green; no wing-bars; haunts thickets and undergrowth; movements nervous and active; call-note, *pit* or *chack;* song, a vigorous, rapid *witch-e-wèe-o, witch-e-wèe-o, witch-e-wèe-o.*
                         451a. MARYLAND YELLOW-THROAT.
    D. Length 7·25; upperparts olive-green; no wing-bars; a white line before the eye; haunts thickets and undergrowth; song, a striking mixture of whistles, *chucks,* and *caws,* sometimes uttered on the wing . . . . 452. YELLOW-BREASTED CHAT.
  2. Underparts streaked or spotted.
    A. Underparts streaked with rufous-brown; length 5·00; general appearance of a yellow bird; haunts shrubbery of lawns, orchards, second growths, and particularly willows near water; song, rather loud, *wēē, chēē-chēē-chēē, chĕr-wēē,* or *chēē-chēē-chēē-chēē, wȧy-o.*
                                425. YELLOW WARBLER.
    B. Breast yellow, with a conspicuous black crescent; length 10·00; fields and meadows, largely terrestrial; flight quail-like, outer white tail-feathers showing when on the wing; song, a loud, musical whistle . . . : . . . . 460. MEADOWLARK.

II. Throat not yellow.
   1. Throat white.
     A. With yellow on the sides.
       a. Length 5·50; rump yellow; breast streaked or spotted with black; tail-feathers marked with white; note, a characteristic *tchip;* Sept. to May, usually rare or local in winter.
                     429. MYRTLE WARBLER.
       b. Length 5·00; no streaks on underparts or white in the tail; yellow extending along the whole sides; back olive-green, iris white; haunts thickets; call, an emphatic "Who are you, eh?"
                     404. WHITE-EYED VIREO.
       c. Length 5·25; tail and wings banded with yellow, showing conspicuously in flight; haunts woodland; movements active, much in the air, tail frequently spread . . . . 456. REDSTART.
     B. No yellow on sides.
       a. Length 6·75; a yellow line from the bill to the eye; crown black, with a white stripe through its center; haunts in and about thickets and bushy woodlands; song, a high, clear, musical whistle; call-note, *chink* . . . 523. WHITE-THROATED SPARROW.
       b. Length 4·00; a yellow or yellow and orange crown-patch, bordered by black; flits restlessly about outer limbs of trees and bushes; note, a fine *ti-ti;* Oct. to Apr.. 393. GOLDEN-CROWNED KINGLET.
   2. Throat not white.
     A. Throat vinaceous; length 12·00; a black breast-patch; belly white, spotted with black; rump white, showing conspicuously in flight; linings of wings yellow; call-note, a loud *kèe-yer.* . 312. FLICKER.
     B. Throat and head black; length 7·50; breast, belly, and lower back deep orange; an active inhabitant of fruit and shade trees; song, a loud, ringing whistle . . . . . . 465. BALTIMORE ORIOLE.
     C. Throat and upper breast ashy; length 9·00; crested; belly yellow; tail-feathers largely pale rufous; haunts upper branches in woodland; note, a loud questioning, or grating whistle.
                  330. CRESTED FLYCATCHER.
     D. Grayish brown; length 7·00; crested; tip of tail yellow.
                  400. CEDAR WAXWING.

Second Group.—With red in the plumage

I. With red on the underparts.
   A. Throat red.
     a. Length 7·00; wings and tail black; rest of plumage bright scarlet; call-note, *chip-chirr* . . . . 473. SCARLET TANAGER.
     b. Length 6·00; dull, pinkish red, wings and tail brownish; frequently seen feeding on buds or blossoms; call-note, a sharp *chink*, often uttered during flight; song, a sweet, flowing warble.
                  485. PURPLE FINCH.
     c. Length 6·00; dull red or green tinged with red; mandibles crossed; generally seen in flocks feeding on pine-cones. 493. Red CROSSBILL.
     d. Length 5·00; a red crown-cap; back streaked black and brown; breast rosy; feeds on seeds or catkins; Nov. to Mch. 490. REDPOLL.
   B. Throat black.
     a. Length 8·00; breast rose-red, rest of plumage black and white; song loud and musical; call-note, *peek.* 476. ROSE-BREASTED GROSBEAK.
     b. Length 8·00; a conspicuous crest; region about the base of the bill black; rest of the plumage and bill red; song, a clear whistle.
                  475. CARDINAL.
     c. Length 5·50; wings and tail banded with orange-red, showing conspicuously in flight; movements active; much in the air; tail frequently spread; haunts woodland . . . . . . 456. REDSTART.

II. No red on the underparts.
  A. Length 9·00; black; shoulders red; haunts marshes; migrates in flocks.
    463. RED-WINGED BLACKBIRD.
  B. Length 5·25; crown-cap red; chin black; rest of underparts streaked with blackish; feeds on seeds and catkins; Nov. to Mch.
    490. REDPOLL, im.
  C. Length 4·00; underparts whitish; back olive-green; a ruby crown-patch; eye-ring white; movements restless, wings flitted nervously; call-note, *cack;* song remarkably loud and musical; Sept. and Oct. Apr. and May . . . . 394. RUBY-CROWNED KINGLET.

Third Group.—With blue in the plumage

  A. Length 11·50; a conspicuous crest; upperparts dull blue; underparts whitish; a black patch on the breast . . . . . 354. BLUE JAY.
  B. Length 7·00; upperparts bright blue; breast cinnamon-rufous.
    389. BLUEBIRD.
  C. Length 5·50; entire plumage indigo-blue . . 478. INDIGO BUNTING.

Fourth Group.—Plumage conspicuously black, or black and white

I. Black and white birds.
  A. Throat black.
    a. Length over 6·00.
      a¹. Entire underparts black; nape buffy; rump white; a musical dweller of fields and meadows; frequently sings on the wing.
        459. BOBOLINK.
      a². Breast rose-red; rest of the plumage black and white; song rapid, loud, and musical; call-note, *peek;* a tree dweller in rather open woodland . . . . 476. ROSE-BREASTED GROSBEAK.
      a³. Sides rufous; rest of the plumage black and white; call-note, *chewink* or *towhee;* inhabits the undergrowth . 496. TOWHEE.
    b. Length under 6·00.
      b¹. Crown black; cheeks white; back ashy; unstreaked; call, *chick-a-dee,* or a musical, double-noted whistle . . 363. CHICKADEE.
      b². Conspicuously streaked with black and white; a tree creeper.
        414. BLACK AND WHITE WARBLER.
  B. Underparts white or whitish.
    a. Length 8·00; upperparts grayish slate-color; tail tipped with white; a bird of the air, catching its insect food on the wing, and occasionally sallying forth from its exposed perch in pursuit of a passing Crow; note, an unmusical, steely chatter . . . 324. KINGBIRD.
    b. Length 5·75; crown black; back bluish gray; a tree creeper; call-note, *yank, yank* . . . . 367. WHITE-BREASTED NUTHATCH.
    c. Length 6·50; upperparts washed with rusty; generally seen in flocks; terrestrial; Nov.–Mch. . . . . 532. SNOW BUNTING.

II. No white in the plumage.
  A. Length 19·00; jet-black . . . . 358. CROW.
  B. Length 12·00; black with metallic reflections; iris yellowish; migrates in flocks; nests usually in colonies in coniferous trees; voice cracked and reedy; tail 'keeled' in short flights; a walker.
    470. PURPLE GRACKLE. 470b. BRONZED GRACKLE.
  C. Length 9·50; shoulders red; haunts marshes; call, *kong-quĕr-rēē.*
    463. RED-WINGED BLACKBIRD.
  D. Length 7·50; head and neck coffee-brown; frequently seen on the ground near cattle . . . . 471. COWBIRD.

Fifth Group.—Without either yellow, orange, red, or blue in the plumage; not conspicuously black, or black and white

I. Underparts all *one* color, *without* streaks or spots.
  1. Back *without* streaks or spots.
    A. Underparts white or whitish.
      a. Length under 7·50.
        a^1. Back olive, olive-green, or slaty fuscous.
          a^2. No white line over the eye; fly-catchers, capturing their prey on the wing and returning to their perch, where they sit quietly until making a fresh sally.
            a^3. Crown blackish; frequently found nesting under bridges or about buildings; tail wagged nervously; note, *pewit-phœbe.*
                331. Phœbe.
            a^4. Wing-bars whitish; haunts orchards, lawns, and open woodland; note, *chebèc, chebèc* . . 336. Least Flycatcher.
            a^5. Haunts woodlands; generally frequents the upper branches; note, a plaintive *pee-a-wee* . . . . 337. Wood Pewee.
          b^2. A white line over the eye, or wing-bars white; gleaners; patiently exploring the foliage for food or flitting about the outer branches.
            b^3. White line over the eye bordered by a narrow black one; cap gray; iris red; song, a rambling recitative: "You see it —you know it—do you hear me?" etc.
                410. Red-eyed Vireo.
            b^4. White line over the eye not bordered by black; prefers the upper branches of rows of elms and other shade trees; song a rich, unbroken warble with an alto undertone.
                412. Warbling Vireo.
            b^5. No white line over the eye; eye-ring and wing-bars white; length 4·00; a tiny, unsuspicious bird; flits about the outer branches of trees and shrubs; wings twitched nervously; note, *cack;* song, a remarkably loud, musical whistle.
                394. Ruby-crowned Kinglet.
        b^1. Back not olive-green, or slaty fuscous.
          b^2. Back gray or bluish gray.
            b^3. Crown black; cheeks white; a tree creeper; note, *yank, yank.*
                367. White-breasted Nuthatch.
            b^4. A gray, crested bird; forehead black; no white in the tail; note, a whistled *peto, peto,* or hoarse *de-de-de-de.*
                366. Tufted Tit.
        c^2. Back cinnamon-brown; length 4·75; a nervous, restless, excitable bird; tail carried erect; song, sweet, rapid and rippling, delivered with *abandon* . . . . . . 371. House Wren.
      b. Length over 7·50.
        b^1. Upperparts grayish slate-color; a white band at the end of the tail; a concealed orange-red crest; a bird of the air, catching its insect food on the wing, and occasionally sallying forth from its exposed perch in pursuit of a passing Crow; note, an unmusical, steely chatter . . . . 324. Kingbird.
        b^2. Length 12·00; slim, brownish birds with long tails; flight short and noiseless; perch *in* a tree, not in an exposed position; note *tut-tut, cluck-cluck,* and *cow-cow.*
        290. Yellow-billed Cuckoo. 291. Black-billed Cuckoo.
    B. Underparts *not* white.
      a. Slate-color; cap and tail black; inhabits the lower growth; call-note, nasal; song highly musical and varied; length 8·50.
                378. Catbird.

    b. Grayish brown; conspicuously crested; a black line through the eye; tail tipped with yellow; generally seen in small flocks; note thin and weak; length 7·00 . . . . . 400. CEDAR WAXWING.

    c. Underparts cream-buff; a conspicuous whitish line over the eye; upperparts rufous-brown; movements active; tail carried erect; haunts lower growth; notes loud and striking; length 5·50.

                                     374. CAROLINA WREN.

2. Back streaked.

   A. Crown rufous or chestnut without streaks.

     a. Length 5·25; bill black; a whitish line over the eye; a familiar bird of lawns and dooryards; song, a monotonous *chippy-chippy-chippy* . . . . 516. CHIPPING SPARROW.

     b. Length 5·50; bill *reddish brown*, back rufous, or rufous-brown; wing-bars and eye-ring whitish; haunts dry, bushy fields and pastures; song, a musical, plaintive *cher-wee, cher-wee, cher-wee, cheeo, dee-dee-dee-dee* . . . . 519. FIELD SPARROW.

     c. Length 5·50; forehead black; crown and wings chestnut-rufous; flanks pale grayish brown; haunts marshes; song, a rapidly repeated *weet-weet-weet*, etc. . . . . . 526. SWAMP SPARROW.

   B. Crown not rufous or chestnut.

     a. Length 6·75; crown, blackish with a central whitish stripe; throat white; breast gray; a yellow spot before the eye; haunts in and about thickets and bushy woodlands; song, a high, clear, musical whistle; call-note, *chink* . . 523. WHITE-THROATED SPARROW.

     b. Length 5·50; crown finely streaked; a tree-climber, winding patiently up tree-trunks in search of food; tail-feathers pointed.

                                     370. BROWN CREEPER.

     c. Length 5·50; bill slender; a white line over the eye; tail carried erect; haunts reedy marshes; call-note, scolding; song, rippling.

                      375. LONG-BILLED MARSH WREN.

II. Underparts not all one color.

  1. Underparts white or whitish, *streaked* or *spotted*.

   A. Back streaked.

     a. Crown streaked; underparts conspicuously streaked.

       a^1. Outer tail-feathers white, showing conspicuously when the bird flies; length 6·00; haunts dry fields and roadsides; song loud and musical . . . . 509. VESPER SPARROW.

       b^1. Outer tail-feathers not white.

       b^2. Length 6·00; plumage with a rufous-brown cast; spots on the breast tending to form one large spot in its center; haunts on or near the ground, generally in the vicinity of bushes; call-note, a characteristic *chimp;* song musical.

                                527. SONG SPARROW.

       b^3. Length 6·00; no rufous in the plumage; streaks on the underparts evenly distributed; frequently seen feeding on buds or blossoms; call-note, a sharp *chink*, often uttered during flight; song, a sweet, flowing warble.

                           485. PURPLE FINCH, im.

     b. Crown not streaked, rufous-brown; underparts whitish with an indistinct blackish spot in the center of the breast; Oct. to Apr. . . . . 515. TREE SPARROW.

   B. Back *not* streaked.

     a. Upperparts rufous, olive-brown, or cinnamon-brown.

       a^1. Bill slender and thrush-like; breast spotted with blackish.

       a^2. Length 11·00; tail 5·00; wing-bars white; upperparts, wings, and tail uniform rufous; haunts undergrowth; sings from an exposed and generally elevated position; song loud, striking and continuous . . . . 379. BROWN THRASHER.

b^2. Length under 9·00; tail under 3·00; no wing-bars.

b^3. Breast and *sides* heavily marked with large, *round*, black spots; head and upper back *brighter* than lower back and tail; call-note, a sharp *pit* or liquid *quirt*.

                                384. WOOD THRUSH.

b^4. Breast with wedge-shaped black spots; sides *unspotted*, washed with *brownish ashy;* tail rufous, *brighter* than back; call-note, a low *chuck* . . . . . 385. HERMIT THRUSH.

b^5. Upper breast lightly spotted with small, wedge-shaped, blackish spots; tail the same color as the back; sides *white;* call-note, a clearly whistled *whèeu* . . . . . . 388. VEERY.

b^1. Bill short and stout; breast and sides heavily spotted with rufous; length 7·00; haunts on or near the ground, generally in or about shrubbery; call-note, *tseep;* song loud, ringing, and musical.

                                524. FOX SPARROW.

b. Back olive-green; center of crown *pale rufous*, bordered by black; length 6·00; haunts on or near the ground in woodland; a *walker;* song, a ringing teacher, *teacher*, TEACHER, TEACHER, *TEACHER*.

                                444. OVENBIRD.

2. Underparts not white or whitish.

A. Throat and upper breast black or slate-color, very different from the white or chestnut belly.

a. Throat black.

a^1. Belly and rump chestnut; head, wings and tail black; haunts orchards, shade trees, etc.; song highly musical.

                                464. ORCHARD ORIOLE.

a^2. Belly white; sides rufous; tail black and white; haunts undergrowths; call-note, *chewink* or *towhee* . . . 496. TOWHEE.

b. Throat slate-color.

b^1. Back and wings slate-color; outer tail-feathers and belly white; haunts generally on or near the ground about shrubbery; Oct. to Apr. . . . . 513. JUNCO.

B. Throat streaked with black and white; rest of underparts rufous; upperparts grayish slate-color; length 10·00 . . . 381. ROBIN.

1. ORDER GAVIIFORMES. LOONS
(1 family)

FAMILY GAVIIDÆ. LOONS.

A family containing only four species, inhabiting the northern half of the Northern Hemisphere. The Loons are scarcely less aquatic than the Grebes, and are their equals as divers and swimmers. When nesting, they inhabit fresh-water lakes and ponds, but during the winter many live at sea, often 50 miles or more from land. They migrate by day (and doubtless also by night) and are strong fliers. Being larger than Ducks and smaller or with shorter necks than Geese, they should not be mistaken for either. They visit the land rarely, when their clumsy progress is assisted by the use of bill and wings. The nest is usually a mere depression on a mud-lump, or so near the shore that the bird can slide quickly into and under the water, to come to the surface some distance away. Two eggs are laid and the young are præcocial. Loons feed chiefly on fish, which they procure by diving, progressing when under water by aid of either feet or wings alone, or both combined.

1924. TOWNSEND, C. W. See under Grebes.

1. Throat black or gray (Ads. in summer).
   A. Throat black.
      a. Head black . . . . **1, 1***a.* **LOONS.**
      b. Head ashy . . . . **2. PACIFIC LOON.**
   B. Throat gray, foreneck chestnut . . . . . . 3. **RED-THROATED LOON.**
2. Throat white or whitish (Im. and ads. in winter).
   A. Back fuscous, margined with grayish.
      a. Wing over 13·00; culmen over 2·50 . . . . **1, 1***a.* **LOONS.**
      b. Wing under 13·00; culmen under 2·50 . . . . . 2. **PACIFIC LOON.**
   B. Back fuscous, spotted with white . . . . 3. **RED-THROATED LOON.**

1. COMMON LOON. GAVIA IMMER IMMER (*Brünnich*). [7.] (Fig. 23.)
Ads. in summer.—Upperparts, wings, tail, and neck black with bluish or greenish reflections; spaces on the throat and sides of neck streaked with white; back and wings spotted and barred with white; breast and belly white; sides and a band at base of under tail-coverts black spotted with white. *Ads. in winter and Im.*—Upperparts, wings and tail blackish *margined* with grayish, not *spotted* with white; underparts white; throat sometimes washed with grayish. L., 32·00; W., 14·00; Tar., 3·40; B., 3·60.
Range.—Breeds from Lab., N. F., N. S., and Me. s. to n. Ills. (formerly), n. Ind., n. O. (formerly), n. N. Y., n. Pa. (formerly), N. H., Conn. (casually), Mass. (rarely), and in Iceland; recorded in summer (not breeding), s. to N. J., N. C., S. C., and Miss. Winters from the Great Lakes, Me., and N. S. (casually), to Fla., the Gulf Coast, and L. Calif.; also from the British Isles south to the Azores, Madeira, and the Mediterranean and Black Seas.
Washington, uncommon W. V., Sept.–June. Long Island, abundant T. V., common W. V., rare S. V., Aug. 10–June 20. Bronx region, common T. V., uncommon W. V., July 31–June 1 (June 10); one possible breeding record. Boston, common W. V., Sept.–June. N. Ohio, not common T. V., Mch. 17–Apr. 30; Oct. 15–30. Glen Ellyn, irregular, uncommon T. V., Mch. 22–June 17. SE. Minn., formerly common, now uncommon S. R., common T. V., Mch. 30–Nov. 13.
Nest, a slight depression in the ground within a few feet of the water, sometimes on a mud-lump or muskrat-house. *Eggs*, 2, grayish olive-brown, thinly spotted with blackish, 3·50 × 2·20. *Date*, Upton, Me., June 15; Mitchell's Bay, Ont., May 31; Pewaukee, Wisc., May 7; se. Minn., May 12.

This wild inhabitant of our northern lakes and ponds possesses all the characteristic traits of the divers. Its remarkable notes are thus described by J. H. Langille:

"Beginning on the fifth note of the scale, the voice slides through the eighth to the third of the scale above in loud, clear, sonorous tones, which on a dismal evening before a thunderstorm, the lightning already playing along the inky sky, are anything but musical. He has also another rather soft and pleasing utterance, sounding like *who-who-who-who*, the syllables being so rapidly pronounced as to sound almost like a shake of the voice—a sort of weird laughter."

Loons may be seen migrating by day, singly or in small companies, generally at a considerable height. Their flight is strong, rapid, and direct. They winter in large numbers some distance off the coast. I have seen several thousand in a day (March 9, 1907) east of Hatteras when sailing from New York to Florida.

1899. MEAD, J. C., Journ. Me. Orn. Soc., I, 21–24 (habits).—1923. SIM, R. J., Bird-Lore, 167–175, illus. (nesting).—1928. WILSON, F. N., Habits and Portraits, Bird-Lore, 171–177; 1929, 95–103.

1a. LESSER LOON. GAVIA IMMER ELASSON *Bishop* [7 part.] Similar to *G. i. immer* but smaller. L., 29·20; W., 13·70; Tar., 3·30; B., 3·20 (Bishop).

Range.—Breeds from n. Calif , N. Dak., and n. Wisc. n. to B. C. and probably Man. Winters chiefly on coast of Calif., casually to s. Alaska, rarely farther east.

Nesting-date, Fish Lake, N. Dak., June 15 (Bishop).

Bishop (*The Auk*, 1921, p. 369) records specimens of this race from Massachusetts (Apr. 9) and Florida (Aug.), but since identification can be based only on examination of specimens, its exact status in the East is unknown.

2. PACIFIC LOON. GAVIA ARCTICA PACIFICA (*Lawrence*). [10.] *Ads. in summer.*—Throat, foreneck, back, wings, and tail black, with purplish and bluish reflections; a band of white streaks on throat; sides of neck, back, and wings streaked, barred, or spotted with white; top of head and nape gray; breast and belly white; a blackish band at the base of the under tail-coverts. *Ads. in winter and Im.*—Similar in color to *G. immer*, not spotted above with white. L., 27·00; W., 11·00; Tar., 2·60; B., 2·00.

Remarks.—Immature and winter birds may be distinguished from the corresponding stage of *immer* by their small size; from *stellata* by *grayish* margins instead of *white* spots, bars, or margins on the upperparts.

Range.—Breeds on the Arctic coasts and isls. from Pt. Barrow, Alaska, to Melville Peninsula and Southampton Isl., s. Baffin Island, and casually farther s. to York Factory, Great Slave Lake, Athabaska Lake and the Alaska Peninsula; casual in summer (not breeding) at Monterey, Calif. Winters mainly on the Pacific Coast of N. A. from se. Alaska and B. C. to L. Calif. Accidental in Ariz., N. Mex., N. H., and L. I.

Nest, a slight depression in the ground within a few feet of the water. *Eggs*, 2, grayish olive-brown, spotted or scrawled with blackish, 3·20 × 2·10.

This species is a very rare winter visitant to the northern border of the United States. The most southern record of its occurrence is Apr. 29, 1893, Sands Point lighthouse, Long Island Sound. (Dutcher, *The Auk*, X, p. 265.)

3. RED-THROATED LOON. GAVIA STELLATA (*Pontoppidan*). [11.] *Ads. in summer.*—Back, wings, and tail fuscous, more or less spotted with white; head and neck ashy gray; *foreneck chestnut;* back of the neck black, streaked with white; breast and belly white; longer under tail-coverts and band at the base of shorter ones fuscous. *Ads. in winter and Im.*—Similar in color to *G. immer*, but back *spotted* with white. L., 25·00; W., 11·00; Tar., 2·60; B., 2·00.

Range.—Breeds from n. Alaska and the Arctic coasts and isls. of Can. and Greenland, s. to n. B. C. isls., n. Man., se. Que., and N. F.; also throughout Arctic Europe and Asia. Winters from the Aleutian Isls. and the coast of B. C. to n. L. Calif., and from the Gulf of St. Lawrence and the Great Lakes to Fla. Casual in Mont., Mo., Nebr., Ariz., Ia., and Idaho.

Washington, rare W. V., Oct. 20 to spring. Long Island, tolerably common T. V., uncommon W. V. (Aug. 24) Sept. 14–May 29 (June 30). Bronx region, uncommon but regular T. V. on the Sound; Sept. 16–Feb. 22 (May 15). Boston, T. V. and W. V., common fall, less so winter and spring; Sept.–May. N. Ohio, casual on Lake Erie, in winter. Glen Ellyn, very rare T. V. spring only, Apr. 14–17.

Nest, a slight depression in the ground within a few feet of the water. *Eggs,* 2, grayish olive-brown, sometimes tinged with green and spotted with blackish, 2·80 × 1·75. *Date,* Resolution Isl., H. B., June 9; Iceland, May 23.

In the United States we know this bird only as a winter visitant when it occurs along our coasts, and, less commonly, on the larger bodies of water inland. At this season it resembles the Loon in habits. Nelson describes its notes as a harsh *gr-r-ga, gr-r, gr-r-ga, gr-r.*

II. ORDER COLYMBIFORMES. GREBES

(1 family)

FAMILY COLYMBIDÆ. GREBES.

The Grebes, or lobe-footed divers, are of world-wide distribution. Of the twenty-odd known species, six are North American. When nesting, Grebes usually frequent reed-grown ponds or sloughs, but during their migrations they are found in more open water and some species pass the winter well off the coast.

When on the water, Grebes bear a general resemblance to Ducks, but where the Duck would fly the Grebe usually dives. A few surface foot-strokes are the usual prelude to flight and, when in the air, the Grebe's smaller wings and shorter tail are evident, while when one is near enough to see their pointed bill no doubt is left of their family relationship.

Grebes are eminently aquatic birds, and rarely venture far on land, where their slow and awkward progress is more or less assisted by their wings, used as forefeet, though they can go a short distance aided by feet alone. When on shore, Grebes either lie flat on their breasts or sit erect on their tails and entire foot or tarsus.

The surprising rapidity with which Grebes dive, and the ease with which, formerly at least, they escaped the shot of the fowler, won for them such descriptive names as 'Hell-diver,' 'Water-witch,' etc.; but the cartridge of the modern breech-loader does not give the warning of the discarded flint-lock or percussion cap, and to 'dive at the flash' is now an obsolete expression. In diving, Grebes spring partly from the water and plunge downward, head first, or sink quietly backward, leaving scarce a ripple behind. Returning, they may pop suddenly from beneath the surface, or rise slowly and expose only the bill above the water, a habit which accounts for many apparently mysterious disappearances. When under water, Grebes progress usually by aid of the feet alone, but the wings are sometimes used. With other diving birds, they control their specific gravity by inhaling or exhaling air, and it has lately been suggested (Townsend, 'Labrador Spring,' p. 191) that, by compressing their feathers and expelling the air between them, the birds become less buoyant when diving.

Grebes' nests are usually rafts or islands of water-soaked vegetation. They lay from three to nine dull white eggs, which they generally cover with the nest-material before leaving. The young are born covered with down, which, in most species, has a boldly striped pattern. They swim soon after hatching, often using the back of the parent as a resting-place.

Grebes feed on fish, and also various small forms of aquatic life and some vegetable matter. Their stomachs usually contain feathers, often in astonishing numbers. I have found 331 body feathers of the adult Western Grebe in the stomach of a young bird of this species not more than three days old. It has been suggested by Dr. Alex. Wetmore ('24) that these "feathers act as a strainer to prevent the passage of fish-bones or large fragments of chetin into the intestine until they have been reduced to a proper size and condition by the process of digestion." The close-plumed, satiny breasts of Grebes were long used for turbans, muffs, capes, etc., and their slaughter for commercial purposes, added to the shrinkage in the area of their haunts, due to draining and land-reclamation, has greatly reduced their numbers.

1924. TOWNSEND, C. W., Diving of Grebes and Loons, Auk, 29–41.— 1924. WETMORE, A., Food and Economic Relations, Bull. 1196, U. S. Dept. Agric.—1930. ALLEN, A. A., Bird-Lore, 373–381, illus. (autobiography).

KEY TO THE SPECIES

I. Length over 18·00.
    a. Front and sides of neck rufous or grayish .   4. HOLBŒLL'S GREBE.
    b. Front and sides of neck white . . . .   7. WESTERN GREBE.
II. Length under 16·00.
    A. Throat black (summer).
        a. Neck gray . . . .   8. PIED-BILLED GREBE.
        b. Neck rufous . . . .   5. HORNED GREBE.
        c. Neck black . . . .   6. EARED GREBE.
    B. Throat white (winter).
        a. Bill at base higher than wide.
            a[1]. Secondaries largely white . . . .   5. HORNED GREBE.
            a[2]. Secondaries largely fuscous . . . . .   8. PIED-BILLED GREBE.
        b. Bill at base wider than high.
            b[1]. Secondaries largely white; foreneck usually dusky.
                        6. EARED GREBE.

4. HOLBŒLL'S GREBE. COLYMBUS GRISEGENA HOLBŒLLI (*Rein-hardt*). [2.] *Ads. in summer.*—Top of head, small crest, and back of neck, glossy black; back blackish; throat and sides of head silvery white; front and sides of neck rufous, changing gradually over breast into the silvery white belly; sides tinged with rufous. *Ads. in winter.*—Upperparts blackish brown; throat and underparts whitish; front and sides of neck pale rufous. *Im.*—Upperparts blackish; throat and underparts silvery white; neck and sides grayish. L., 19·00; W., 7·50; Tar., 2·20; B., 1·90.

Range.—Breeds from ne. Siberia, nw. Alaska, and n. Can. s. to n. Wash., N. Dak., and sw. Minn. Winters mainly on the Atlantic and Pacific coasts, from Me. to N. C. and from the Pribilof and Aleutian Isls., s. B. C., casually to Ga., Fla. and Tenn.; in Asia s. to Japan.

Washington, rare W. V., Sept. 30–Mch. or Apr. Long Island, irregular W. V., Oct. 7–May 25; tolerably common Feb.–Apr. Bronx region, irregular and uncommon T. V. and W. V., Oct. 15–May 15. Boston, common W. V., Oct.–May. N. Ohio, occasional in winter. SE. Minn., uncommon T. V., Apr. 26; Oct. 14.

Nest, of water-soaked, decaying vegetation, an island or floating among rushes in a slough, generally attached to its surroundings. *Eggs*, 3–8, dull white, more or less soiled, 2·25 × 1·35. *Date*, Grant Co., Minn., May 28.

Although this large Grebe breeds in reed-grown lake-borders, at other seasons it frequents large bodies of open water, and in winter resorts to the sea, where I have seen it 50 miles from land. So far as my experience goes, it thoroughly covers its eggs, even when frightened from the nest, and although making every effort to avoid being seen, remains near its home, uttering a sharp explosive *cluck* of protest. Brewster describes its call as deliberately uttered and exceedingly loud and harsh, not unlike the voice of an angry Crow, but with much greater volume.

1903. SIM, R. J., Wilson Bull., 67–74 (habits in captivity).

5. HORNED GREBE. COLYMBUS AURITUS *Linnæus*. [3.] (Fig. 24*b*.) *Ads. in summer.*—Top of head, hindneck, and throat, glossy blackish; lores pale chestnut; stripe, and plumes behind eye, buffy ochraceous, deeper posteriorly; back and wings blackish; secondaries white; foreneck, upper breast and sides chestnut; lower breast and belly white. *Ads. in winter and Im.*—Upperparts grayish black; underparts silvery white, sometimes washed with grayish on the throat and breast; white of cheeks nearly meeting on hindneck. L., 13·50; W., 5·40; Tar., 1·75; B., ·90.
Remarks.—Differs from *P. podiceps*, in more pointed bill, more white in wing, and, in winter, has no brown below.
Range.—Breeds from near the Arctic Coast to Me. and Lake Seul, Ont., Minn., s. Wisc., n. Nebr., and s. B. C.; also in Iceland, n. continental Europe and Siberia; recorded in summer in Mass., Conn., Mich., and Ind. Winters from Me. to Fla. and La. and from s. Alaska to s. Calif., interior winter records being mainly from the region of the Great Lakes. Casual in Greenland and Bermuda.
Washington, common W. V., July 15–May 28. Long Island, abundant T. V., common W. R., casual S. V., Sept. 14–May 30. Bronx region, common T. V. and W. V., Oct. 6–May 23. Boston, common W. V., Oct.–May. N. Ohio, not common T. V., Apr. 4–May 6; Oct. 1–Nov. 25; occasional in winter. Glen Ellyn, regular T. V., Mch. 31–Apr. 26; Sept. 6–Oct. 14. SE. Minn., common T. V., Apr. 13–May 18; Sept. 27–Nov. 11.
Nest, of water-soaked, decaying vegetation, an island or raft floating among rushes in a slough, generally attached to its surroundings. *Eggs*, 2–7, all white, more or less soiled, 1·74 × 1·15. *Date*, Grant Co., Minn., May 28.

This species and the next are probably frequently mistaken for each other in life, and the same common names are in some instances applicable to both. In breeding costume it is easily identifiable, but in the winter it is a grayish bird. In flight the white margin to its secondaries is clearly displayed. It then suggests a Gallinule, but is smaller and paler. Ernest Seton writes of a captive individual: "When ordinarily swimming, the feet strike out alternately, and the progression is steady; but sometimes both feet struck together, and then the movement was by great bounds, and was evidently calculated to force the bird over an expanse of very weedy water, or through any tangle of weeds or rushes in which it might have found itself. When lifted out of the water, the feet worked so fast as to be lost to the eye in a mere haze of many shadowy feet with one attachment. When placed on the ground, it

was perfectly helpless." ('Birds of Manitoba,' p. 466.) H. K. Job writes
of a pair of Horned Grebes which alighted in a brook and could not
fly out "because with their small wings they require a lot of room to
flutter and patter over the water in getting started." ('Sport of Bird
Study,' p. 272.) The same author writes of the notes of this species as
"a quick chatter ending with several prolonged notes I can only describe
as yells." ('Among the Water-Fowl,' p. 33.)

1919. DuBois, A. D., Auk, 170–180, illus. (habits).

6. EARED GREBE. Colymbus nigricollis californicus (*Heermann*).
[4.] *Ads. in summer.*—No chestnut on throat; broad postocular tufts ochraceous-buff, rest of head, throat and neck with back blackish; sides chestnut; belly white. *Ads. in winter and Im.*—Resembling same plumage of
auritus but smaller, bill wider than high at base. L., 12·50; W., 5·20; T.,
1·70; B., ·80.
Range.—Breeds from s. interior B. C. and s. Man. s. to n. L. Calif.,
cent. Ariz., s. Tex., and n. Ia.; casual in summer n. to Great Slave Lake.
Winters from Wash. to Cape San Lucas and Guat.; e. to Kans. in migration.
Casual in Mo. and Ind.
Nest, in colonies, of water-soaked vegetation, an island or floating raft,
when usually attached. *Eggs,* 3–9, dull white more, or less soiled, 1·73 ×
1·19. *Date,* Meckling, N. Dak., May 27.

The Eared Grebe barely comes within our limits. It nests in colonies
often containing hundreds of birds. They cover their eggs, even when
frightened from the nest, and Job observed some slipping back to complete the work. Eggs from which Job removed the covering placed on
them by the bird were soon eaten by a Franklin's Gull, evidence that
the birds cover their eggs to prevent their being seen. Experience on
Crane Lake, Saskatchewan, suggests that the call of this bird resembles
that of the Pied-billed Grebe.

7. WESTERN GREBE. Æchmophorus occidentalis (*Lawrence*)
[1.] Neck long and slender; no pronounced seasonal difference in plumage.
Ads.—Crown and hindneck black, browner in winter; back brownish gray;
underparts satiny white; inner web of wing-quills more or less white. L.,
22–28·00; W., 7·50; B., 2·60.
Range.—Breeds from Wash. and s. Man. s. to s. Calif., Utah, and n. N.
Dak. Winters from s. B. C. s. through Calif. to L. Calif. and cent. Mex.
Casual e. to Nebr., Kans., Wisc., Minn., Ia., O., and Ont. (?) n. to Craig,
Alaska.
Long Island, A. V.; one record, May. SE. Minn., two records, Apr., May.
Nest, in colonies of the stems and leaves of aquatic plants; an attached
but floating raft, or an island. *Eggs,* 3–5, pale bluish overlaid with chalky
white, 2·39 × 1·55. *Date,* Devil's Lake, N. Dak., June 1.

The long, slender neck gives to this species a singularly stately and
swanlike appearance. It is an exquisitely graceful creature, and there
is to me more beauty in the satiny white and shining black of its neck
and head than in the ornate breeding costumes of some other Grebes.
While preening their plumage they often lie on one side in the water,
when the light flashes from their glistening breasts as it would from a
mirror. Their call is a loud, double-toned, grating, whistle *c-r-r-ee,*

c-r-r-ee—which can be clearly heard when the bird is out of sight on the open waters of the lake. They nest in colonies often containing hundreds of pairs, and I have known them voluntarily to spend much time away from their nests, leaving the eggs uncovered. I have also seen the bird, while standing nearly erect in the nest, place some covering over the eggs before sliding into the water at my approach. Thousands of these birds have been killed for their breasts by millinery collectors.

1902. JOB, H. K., Among the Water-Fowl, 15–28.—1908. CHAPMAN, F. M., Camps and Cruises, 302, 330, 348.

8. PIED-BILLED GREBE. PODILYMBUS PODICEPS PODICEPS (*Linnæus*). [6.] (Fig. 24*a*.) *Ads. in summer.*—Upperparts glossy, brownish black; throat black; upper breast, front and sides of neck, and sides of body, *washed with brownish* and indistinctly mottled with blackish; lower breast and belly, centrally, white; a black band across bill. *Ads. in winter and Im.*—Much like the above, but throat white and no black band on bill. L., 13·50; W., 5·10; Tar., 1·45; B., ·85.

Range.—N. A. generally. Breeds locally from cent. B. C., Great Slave Lake, Sask., cent. Man., s. Ont., Que., N. B., and N. S., s. to Fla., Tex. and parts of Mex. Winters from N. Y. and N. J. (occasionally), and s. B. C., southward. Casual in Bermuda. [Closely allied races occur in the W. I. and in S. A.]

Washington, common T. V., Mch. 9–June 21; Aug. 22–Dec. 29. Long Island, locally common T. V., rare P. R., Apr. 1–May 1; July 19–Dec. 15. Bronx region, fairly common T. V., rare S. R., Mch. 18–May 5; Aug. 18– Nov. 28; casual in winter. Boston, T. V., common in fall, uncommon in spring; Apr.–May; July–Nov. N. Ohio, often common T. V., rare S. R., Apr. 1–May 10; Sept. 1–Oct. 25. Glen Ellyn, not common S. R., Mch. 20– Nov. 5. SE. Minn., common S. R., Apr. 2–Nov. 18.

Nest, of water-soaked, decaying vegetation, sometimes built up from the bottom in shallow water, sometimes floating among rushes in a slough, when it is generally attached to its surroundings. *Eggs,* 4–8, dull white, more or less soiled or stained, 1·74 × 1·19. *Date,* Cambridge, Apr. 23; Seneca River Marshes, N. Y., June 3; Winnebago, Ills., May 13; se. Minn., May 15.

Any Grebe found breeding in the eastern United States will probably prove to be this species which, generally speaking, is the best known of our Grebes. From the Eared Grebe, with which it shares various names indicative of its natatorial powers, it may be known by its brown breast and the absence of a white wing-patch. Its notes, as I have heard them in the Montezuma marshes, are very loud and sonorous with a cuckoolike quality, and may be written *cow-cow-cow-cow-cow- cow-cow-cow-cow-uh, cow-uh, cow-uh-cow-uh.* These notes vary in number and are sometimes followed by prolonged wailing *cows* or *uhs,* almost human in their expressiveness of pain and fear. This is appar- ently the love-song of the male in which his mate sometimes joins with a *cuk-cuk-cuk*—followed by a slower *ugh, ugh, ugh.* ('Bird Studies with a Camera,' p. 70.)

On Heron Lake, Minnesota, in early October, I have seen Pied- billed Grebes in close-massed flocks, containing a hundred or more birds, cruising about in open water.

1914. ALLEN, A. A., Bird-Lore, 243–253, illus. (home-life).—1929. WIL- SON, F. N., Bird-Lore, 243–248, illus. (home-life).

III. ORDER PROCELLARIIFORMES. TUBE-NOSED SWIMMERS
(4 families, 3 North American)

SYNOPSIS OF FAMILIES. (Fig. 25 *a.*, *b.*)

Nostril-tubes two, wholly separated by the culmen; size very large, length 28–48 in . . . . *Family Diomedeidæ.* ALBATROSSES. P. 147.
Nostril-tubes two, lying on the culmen, definitely separated by a distinct septum. Size variable.
Family Procellariidæ. SHEARWATERS, FULMARS, etc. P. 147.
Nostril-tube one, lying on the culmen. Size small; length 5·50–8·00.
Family Hydrobatidæ. STORM PETRELS. P. 151.

1907–1910. GODMAN, F. D., Monograph of the Petrels, 4to., lv +38 pp., 104 col. pls. (Witherby & Co., London).—1918. LOOMIS, L. M., A Review of the Albatrosses, Petrels, and Diving Petrels, Proc. Calif. Acad. Sci., 187 pp. —1928. Alexander, W. B., Birds of the Ocean, 16 mo., 428 pp. illus. (Putnam's.)

FAMILY DIOMEDEIDÆ. ALBATROSSES.

The Albatrosses, numbering about seventeen species, are confined chiefly to the seas of the Southern Hemisphere. Three species visit our Pacific Coast after nesting farther south, but on the Atlantic Coast of North America, Albatrosses are almost unknown, and there are but few records of their occurrence. Albatrosses are among the most tireless and wide-ranging of ocean wanderers. The flight of the Wandering Albatross (*Diomedea exulans*), which Coleridge's 'Rime of the Ancient Mariner' has made more widely known than all that naturalists have ever written about it, is thus described by Professor Hutton: "With outstretched, motionless wings, he sails over the surface of the sea, now rising high in the air, now with a bold sweep, and wings inclined at an angle with the horizon, descending until the tip of the lower one all but touches the crests of the waves as he skims over them." On the water "he is at home, breasting the waves like a cork. Presently he stretches out his neck, and with great exertion of his wings runs along the top of the water for seventy or eighty yards, until, at last, having got sufficient impetus, he tucks up his legs, and is once more fairly launched in the air."

Lucas writes, "The Albatross has that type of wing which best fulfils the conditions necessary for an aëroplane, being long and narrow, so that, while a full-grown Wandering Albatross may spread from 10 to 12 feet from tip to tip, this wing is not more than 9 inches wide."

9. The YELLOW-NOSED ALBATROSS, or MOLLYMAWK, *Thalassogeron chlororhynchos* (Gmelin), [83.1], of southern seas, is of accidental occurrence near Sea! Isl., Me. (Aug. 1, 1913), and in the Gulf of St. Lawrence (Sept., 1884).

FAMILY PROCELLARIIDÆ. SHEARWATERS, FULMARS, AND PETRELS.

This family formerly also included the Storm Petrels, now placed in the family Hydrobatidæ. So far as the species of regular occurrence in eastern North America are concerned, the Procellariidæ are large, gull-

like, light-colored birds (except *Puffinus griseus*), while the Hydrobatidæ
are small, swallowlike, and dark-colored. The former number about
80 species; the latter, 20-odd. The strong, swift, scaling, coursing,
flight of Shearwaters, and the graceful, dainty, flitting movements of
the Storm Petrels, or Mother Carey's Chickens, are familiar sights to
the observant who go "down to the sea in ships." Living where storms
attain their greatest power, where there is no shelter from the gale,
other than the troubled sea itself, these birds are sometimes carried far
out of their course by the wind, no less than 14 of the 38 species and
subspecies recorded from North America being of casual or accidental
occurrence. Only 2 of the 15 Shearwaters recorded from North
America nest in North Temperate latitudes, while about one-half breed
on islands in or near Subantarctica. After nesting during our winter,
they migrate northward to spend their winter (our summer) in northern
seas where the waters give them food by day and a resting-place at
night.

KEY TO THE SPECIES

I. Length over 17·00.
  A. Underparts wholly sooty or gray.
    a. Underparts grayish sooty . . . . . .   10. SOOTY SHEARWATER.
    b. Underparts slaty gray . . . .   20. FULMAR.
  B. Underparts wholly or largely white.
    a. A sooty patch in the center of the abdomen.
                                          14. GREATER SHEARWATER.
    b. No sooty patch on abdomen.
      b¹. Head white; back gray . . . .   20. FULMAR.
      b². Upperparts fuscous . . . .   15a. CORY'S SHEARWATER.
II. Length under 16·00.
  A. Length over 13·00.
    a. Forehead fuscous, like crown . . . . .   11. MANX SHEARWATER.
    b. Forehead white.
      b¹. Longer upper tail-coverts wholly white.
                                          16. BLACK-CAPPED PETREL.
      b². Longer upper tail-coverts terminally grayish . . .   17. CAHOW.
  B. Length under 13·00.
    a. Underparts wholly white.
      a¹. Wing over 7·50 . . . .   12. AUDUBON'S SHEARWATER.
      a². Wing under 7·50 . . . .   13. ALLIED SHEARWATER.

10. SOOTY SHEARWATER. PUFFINUS GRISEUS (*Gmelin*). [95.] *Ads.*—
Upper parts, wings and tail dark, sooty, brownish black; underparts some-
what grayer; bill blackish. L., 17·00; W., 12·00; Tar. 2·10; B., 1·65.
  Range.—Widely distributed over the great oceans; n. to Lab., Greenland,
Faroe and Orkney Isls. on the Atlantic coasts, and to the Aleutian and
Kurile Isls. on the Pacific. Breeds on N. Z. and adjacent isls. and isls. near
Cape Horn.
  Washington, an early record formerly associated with Audubon's Shear-
water now thought to be this species. Long Island, irregular S. V., May 22–
Oct. 24. Boston, uncommon S. V., off-shore, June–Nov.
  Nest, in burrows. *Egg*, 1, white, 2·60 × 1·60. *Date*, Feb. and Mch. (Buller).

"Its flight and habits seem to be identical with those of *major*
[= *gravis*], but its uniform dark coloring gives it a very different appearance. At a distance it looks as black as a Crow" (Brewster).

11. The MANX SHEARWATER, *Puffinus puffinus puffinus* (Brünnich), [90], of the eastern Atlantic is accidental in Greenland and on Long Island (Aug. 30, 1917). It resembles Audubon's Shearwater but is larger, except the tail, which is shorter. W., 9·00; T., 3·00; B., 1·40.

12. AUDUBON'S SHEARWATER. PUFFINUS LHERMINIERI LHERMINIERI
Lesson. [92.] *Ads*.—Upperparts, wings, and tail sooty black; underparts white; sides of the breast grayish; a patch on the flanks and under tail-coverts sooty brownish black; inner side of tarsi yellowish, outer brownish; bill blackish. L., 12·00; W., 8·00; T., 3·20; B., 1·20.

Range.—Warmer parts of the w. n. Atlantic, more or less regularly to Cuba, Gulf of Mex., and casually to the coast of Fla., S. C., Va., and N. J.; accidental at Bellport, N. Y. Breeds on Bermuda, the Bahamas, Little Saba Isl. (near St. Thomas), and the Lesser Antilles.

Long Island, one record, Aug. 1.

Nest, in a hole, in the rocks. *Egg*, 1, chalky white, 2·05 × 1·40. *Date*, Ragged Isl., Bahamas, Apr. 13.

This small Shearwater is an abundant West Indian species which breeds in Bermuda, the Bahamas and Antilles, and is doubtless not uncommon off our southern coasts. Its flight, low over the water, is strong and swift, five or six rapid wing-beats being followed by a short sail.

It is active about its nesting-ground only at night when the constant repetition of its uncanny *see-saw* notes is an indication of its before-un-suspected abundance. I have found either the male or female on the nest, and when exposed by the removal of protecting rock, they made no attempt to fly but scuttled away into another hole or under the vegetation.

1931. PALMER, T. S., Auk, 198–206 (in the United States).

13. The ALLIED SHEARWATER, *Puffinus assimilis baroli* Bonaparte, [92.1], of the eastern Atlantic is accidental on Sable Isl., N. S. (Sept. 1, 1896) and Sullivan's Isl., S. C. (Aug., 1883). It resembles *P. puffinus* but is smaller. W., 6·75; T., 2·50; B., 1·00.

14. GREATER SHEARWATER. PUFFINUS GRAVIS (*O'Reilly*). [89.]
Ads.—Upperparts fuscous, wings and tail slightly darker; longer upper tail-coverts tipped with whitish; underparts white; belly more or less ashy gray; *under tail-coverts ashy gray;* bill blackish. L., 20·00; W., 12·25; Tar., 2·20; B., 1·85.

Range.—Entire Atlantic Ocean from n. Europe and Greenland to S. Africa and s. S. A. Breeds on Inaccessible Isl. in the Tristan da Cunha group.

Long Island, irregular S. V., in varying numbers, May 31–Oct. 31. Boston, common S. V. off-shore, June–Nov.

"The long, narrow wings are set stiffly at right angles with the body, and the bird frequently glides half a mile at a time without moving them perceptibly. It usually follows a direct course, and invariably skims close over the waves. I know of no other sea-bird whose movements are as easy and graceful. Indeed, at times, especially during a gale, its evolutions will compare in grace and spirit with those of the Mississippi or Swallow-tailed Kites" (Brewster).

1905. JOB, H.K., Wild Wings, 198 (off Mass.).

15. The MEDITERRANEAN SHEARWATER, *Puffinus diomedea 'diomedea* (Scopoli), [88*a*], the eastern representative of Cory's Shearwater, has been recorded from Long Island (Aug. 15, 1907; Oct. 4, 1902).

15a. CORY'S SHEARWATER. PUFFINUS DIOMEDEA BOREALIS *Cory.*
[88.] (Fig. 25a.) *Ad.*—Upperparts ashy fuscous, wings and tail darker; sides
of head and neck slightly lighter; underparts white, sometimes washed with
grayish on the breast; under wing-coverts and *under tail-coverts white*, the
latter more or less mottled with grayish; bill yellowish. L., 21·00; W.,
14·00; Tar., 2·20; B., 2·10.
Range.—Atlantic Ocean, s. to at least 36° S., w. to coast of Brazil (Bahia)
and N. A. (N. F. to N. C.). Breeds in the Azores, Madeira, Salvage, and
Canary Isls.
Long Island, T. V., not uncommon, Aug. 3–Nov. 29.

Comparing the appearance in life of the Greater and Cory's Shearwaters, Griscom and Janvrin write (*The Auk*, 1922, p. 103): "In the
Greater Shearwater the dark fuscous cap extends down to a line just
below the eye, where it gives way abruptly to the white of the underparts, this white forming an incomplete collar on the neck. In the field
the cap appears black, and the bird has, consequently, a strongly
bicolored appearance on the side of the head, while the invasion of the
white half-collar in the darkly colored upperparts is equally noticeable.
The head and neck of Cory's Shearwater is a lighter ashy fuscous above.
This color extends much farther below the eye on the side of the head
than does the dark cap of the Greater Shearwater, and then fades *very
gradually* into the white of the throat and breast. There is no trace of
a half-collar. In the field, therefore, Cory's Shearwater appears as a
grey-headed bird with a white throat, without any contrast of color."

16. BLACK-CAPPED PETREL. PTERODROMA HASITATA (*Kuhl*). [98.]
Ads.—Region at the base of the bill white, the center of the forehead fuscous
margined with white; nape white, usually margined with fuscous; crown to
below the eye black, back and wings blackish, the former sometimes margined with gray; upper tail-coverts white; tail cuneate, fuscous, rectrices
white basally on both vanes, outer pair of feathers three-fourths white;
underparts white. W., 11·50; T., 5·00; B., length 1·20, depth at base ·60.
Remarks.—The whitish forehead and nape, setting off the black cap, and
the white upper tail-coverts will readily distinguish this species from any
other Petrel of regular occurrence in our district.
Range.—Warmer parts of the n. Atlantic Ocean, accidental in Fla.,
Va., Ky., O., Ont., N. H., etc., and in France and England. Bred formerly
on Guadeloupe and Dominica in the Lesser Antilles (not extinct in 1920).
Long Island, A. V., one record, July.

17. BERMUDA PETREL. PTERODROMA CAHOW (*Nichols and Mowbray*).
[98.1.] *Ads.*—Resembling *P. hasitata;* the region about base of bill white,
but nape fuscous, like the crown, the upper tail-coverts fuscous terminally;
inner vane of outer pair of tail-feathers almost wholly white, outer vane
fuscous. W., 10·25; T., 4·75; B., length, 1·15, depth at base, ·50.
Range.—Formerly Bermuda, probably now extinct.

18. The SCALED PETREL, *Pterodroma inexpectata* (Forster), [99, 100],
of southern seas is of accidental occurrence in Livingston Co., New York.

19. BULWER'S PETREL, *Bulweria bulweri* (Jardine and Selby), [101],
of the eastern Atlantic and western Pacific is accidental in Greenland (or
Labrador). Adults are sooty, the underparts somewhat browner, the greater
wing-coverts grayer. L., 10·50; W., 7·25; T., 9·75; B., ·80.

20. ATLANTIC FULMAR. FULMARUS GLACIALIS GLACIALIS (*Linnæus*).
[86.] *Light phase.*—Head, neck, and underparts white or whitish; back,

wings, and tail slaty gray. *Dark phase.*—Entire plumage nearly uniform dark, slaty gray. L., 19·00; W., 13·04; B., 1·50; depth of B. at base, ·75.

Range.—N. Atlantic, breeding from n. Greenland to Cumberland Sound and e. at least to Franz Josef Land; ranges n. to lat. 85° and w. to Melville Isl. and s. to Scotland, Ireland, and Iceland; winters s. of the Arctic Circle to the fishing-banks off N. F. and to Georges Bank off Mass.; casual in Conn., N. J., and Ont.

Long Island, A. V., one record, Oct.

Nest, on the ledges of rocky cliffs. *Egg*, 1, dull white, 2·85 × 2·01. *Date*, Iceland, May 10.

"The Fulmar is a constant attendant on whalers, sealers, etc.; who know it as the 'Mollimoke'—in order to obtain fatty substances and animal offal; but I never saw it take any while on the wing, and it always settles on the water to feed, like an Albatross. The pinions are often flapped slowly in an owl-like manner, but in scudding they are held very straight—a peculiarity by which it may easily be distinguished from a Gull at a distance" (Saunders).

21. The PINTADO PETREL, *Daption capense* (Linnæus), [102], of the Southern Hemisphere has been once recorded from Maine (Casco Bay, June, 1873).

FAMILY HYDROBATIDÆ. STORM PETRELS.

The Storm Petrels, or 'Mother Carey's Chickens', numbering twenty-odd species, are small, swallowlike sea-birds, most of which are largely sooty black or sooty brown in color. Except when nesting, they live chiefly at sea, but sometimes enter our harbors, and I have seen Wilson's Petrel in numbers 10 miles up the Hudson River. This species, with others, feeds commonly over the wake of vessels; others, with the dashing, erratic flight of Nighthawks, course to and fro over the water in their apparently ceaseless search for food.

Storm Petrels nest in burrows or similar situations, and lay but one, usually white, egg. So far as known, both sexes incubate. They are active about the nest only at night. The young are born covered with thick grayish or brownish down. Only two species of Storm Petrels regularly frequent our Atlantic Coast. Both occur during the summer: one, Leach's, comes to nest; the other, Wilson's, to spend its winter, after nesting in the south Atlantic.

KEY TO THE SPECIES

I. Underparts sooty brown or black.
  A. Longer upper tail-coverts tipped or mixed with blackish or gray.
    a. Wing under 5·00 . . . . 24. STORM PETREL.
    b. Wing over 5·00.
      b[1]. Tail forked for over ·50 . . . . 22. LEACH'S PETREL.
      b[2]. Tail nearly square . . . . 23. MADEIRA PETREL (accidental).
  B. Longer upper tail-coverts without black markings.
    a. No white in throat . . . . 25. WILSON'S PETREL.
    b. Throat-feathers white basally.
      26. WHITE-BELLIED PETREL (accidental).
II. Underparts wholly white . . 27. WHITE-FACED PETREL (accidental).

22. LEACH'S PETREL. OCEANODROMA LEUCORHOA LEUCORHOA (*Vieillot*). [106.] (Fig. 25*b*.) *Ads.*—Upperparts, wings, and tail sooty brown; underparts slightly browner; wing-coverts grayish brown; longer upper tail-coverts white, shorter ones mixed with sooty brownish; *tail forked*, outer feathers more than ˙50 longer than middle pair; bill and feet *wholly black.* L., 8˙00; W., 6˙20; T., 3˙50; B., ˙62.

Range.—N. Atlantic from s. Greenland to the Equator, casually to s. Africa; and n. Pacific from s. Alaska to Japan and Midway Isl. Breeds from s. Greenland and Iceland to Me. and Ireland, and from the Aleutian Isls. to the Commander and Kurile Isls.

Washington, A. V., several records, most frequent in Aug. Long Island, rare T. V., May 4–June 15; July 27 and Oct. 21, 22. Boston, rather common T. V., May–June; Sept.–Oct.

Nest, of a few bits of grasses and feathers in a burrow in the ground, or beneath a rock. *Egg*, 1, creamy white, sometimes with a wreath of minute or obscure markings at the larger end, 1˙34 × 1˙00. *Date*, Bird Rock, Que., May 29.

This is the only Petrel nesting on our Atlantic Coast, where, from about May 1, it is locally abundant on islets or isolated headlands from Maine northward. It digs its own nesting-holes or uses, sometimes in common, those made by Puffins. During the day it apparently never leaves its nest, on which, prior to laying, both birds may be found, but later, only one, either the male or female, incubates or remains with the young. The absent one of the pair is presumably then at sea, from which it returns after nightfall.

On Bird Rock in the Magdalens, where not a Petrel was seen during the day, I was given the most surprising evidence of their activity during the night. From the ground at my feet and from every side there issued the uncanny little song of birds, doubtless sitting at the mouths of their burrows. It was a distinctly enunciated call of eight notes with a certain crowing quality—such a call as might be uttered by elves or brownies. Occasionally I saw a blur of wings as a bird passed between me and the lighthouse.

1909. CHAPMAN, F. M., Bird Studies with a Camera, 180.

23. The MADEIRA PETREL, *Oceanodroma castro castro* Harcourt, [106.2], of the eastern Atlantic is accidental in Pennsylvania (Chambersburg, Apr. 15, 1912), Indiana (Martinsville, June 15, 1902), and District of Columbia (Aug. 29, 1893). It is nearly uniform brownish sooty; the median wing-coverts grayer; upper tail-coverts white, tipped with black; lower more or less white basally. L., 7˙75; W., 6˙00; T., 2˙70; only slightly forked; B., ˙60.

24. STORM PETREL. HYDROBATES PELAGICUS (*Linnæus*). [104.] *Ads.* —Upperparts, wings, their coverts, and tail sooty black; underparts slightly browner; upper tail-coverts white, the longer ones broadly *tipped with black;* under tail-coverts mixed with whitish; bill and feet black. L., 5˙50; W., 4˙80; T., 2˙50; B., ˙45.

Range.—Coasts of n. Europe, Greenland, Lab., N. F., N. S. and Me., s. along the coast of Africa to Zanzibar. Breeds mainly on isls. in the ne. Atlantic; including Iceland, Lofoten Isl. (Norway), Shetland, Faroe, Orkney Isls. and others; in the Mediterranean to Malta and s. to Madeira. Accidental in Ungava, Quebec, and the interior of Europe.

Nest, of a few bits of grasses and feathers in a burrow in the ground or beneath a rock. *Egg*, 1, dull white, sometimes with a wreath of minute or obscure markings at the larger end, 1·10 × ·80. *Date*, Hebrides, Great Britain, May 29.

This is the common Petrel of the east side of the Atlantic. It nests in numbers on the small islands along the coast of Great Britain, but is only a transient visitant in our waters.

25. WILSON'S PETREL. Oceanites oceanicus (*Kuhl*). [109.] (Pl. XVI.) *Ads.*—Upperparts, wings, and tail sooty black; underparts somewhat lighter; under tail-coverts mixed with whitish, longer upper tail-coverts white, shorter ones marked with sooty black; wing-coverts grayish brown, margined with whitish; bill and feet black, toe-webs mostly *yellow;* feet in flight projecting beyond the tail. L., 7·00; W., 5·90; T., 2·80; B., ·50.

Range.—All oceans except the Pacific n. of the Equator (once taken at Monterey, Calif.), n. to Lab. and Great Britain; Gulf of Mex., Mediterranean Sea and s. to the Antarctic Continent. Breeds on Mauritius and Kerguelen Isls., Adelie Land, and Victoria Land, S. Shetland, S. Orkney and S. Georgia Isls. Accidental in Ont.

Washington, A. V., three records. Long Island, irregularly common S. V., May 29–Sept. 14. Bronx region, A. V., one record, Aug. Boston, common S. V., May–Sept.

Nest, in burrows or the crevices of rocks. *Egg*, 1, white. *Date*, Feb.

It is generally known that some birds which nest in the northern parts of our continent migrate as far south as Patagonia to spend the winter, but comparatively few are aware that during the summer we receive several visitors from the southern parts of the Southern Hemisphere. They are all included in the order *Procellariiformes*, and Wilson's Petrel is doubtless the most common. It breeds in the islands of the south Atlantic in February, and after the cares of the breeding season are over migrates northward to pass its winter off our coasts. At this season its home is the sea, and its occurrence on land is generally due to storms. For this reason, and because of its long migration, it is the Petrel most frequently observed in western Atlantic waters during the summer.

Under the name of 'Stormy Petrels,' or 'Mother Carey's Chickens,' these birds are familiar to most people who have made sea voyages. On tireless wing they follow in the track of a ship, coursing ceaselessly back and forth, now beneath the stern, now hovering over the foam-flecked wake, reminding one of white-rumped Martins in their easy, graceful flight. If food be thrown overboard, they are at once attracted to it, and soon are left far behind, a little group of black, fluttering forms on the surface of the ocean. The meal disposed of, a few rapid wing-beats bring them to us, and again they resume their patient beating to and fro.

1905. Job, H. K., Wild Wings, 191 (off Mass.).

26. The White-bellied Petrel, *Fregetta tropica tropica* (Gould), [110,] of southern seas is accidental at St. Marks, Fla. It is sooty blackish; upper tail-coverts white; flanks white, spreading to the belly; lower tail-

coverts and throat-feathers basally white. L., 8·00; W., 6·20; T., 2·75; square; B., ·50.

27. The WHITE-FACED PETREL, *Pelagodroma marina hypoleuca* (Moquin-Tandon) of the north Atlantic has been recorded from 400 miles off the coast of New Jersey and is admitted to our 'Check-List' on the basis of this record. The upperparts are gray, crown darker, upper tail-coverts lighter; underparts, forehead, and a line over the eye white. L., 8·00; W., 9·00; B., ·75.

IV. ORDER PELECANIFORMES. TOTIPALMATE SWIMMERS

SUBORDER PHAËTHONTES. TROPIC-BIRDS.

(1 family)

FAMILY PHAËTHONTIDÆ. TROPIC-BIRDS.

The six species comprising this small but distinct family are distributed through the tropical and subtropical seas of both hemispheres, but none regularly reaches the United States. Tropic-birds frequent the high seas. They fly with quick, strong beats of the wing, quite unlike the more leisurely stroke of Gulls; and from Terns they may be known by the long, willowy tail-feathers which add greatly to their appearance when in the air. They hunt for food by beating back and forth over the water and plunging abruptly down upon it.

Tropic-birds lay their single brownish purplish egg on the bare ground or rock, in a burrow or crevice often some height above the water. Incubation is said to be performed by both parents. When on the nest, they vigorously resent being disturbed, by screaming, biting and scratching.

28. The RED-BILLED TROPIC-BIRD, *Phaëthon æthereus* Linnæus, [113], (Fig. 26), resembles *P. lepturus catesbyi*, but has the bill red and the upperparts finely barred with black. Its range in the Atlantic is more southern than that of the Yellow-billed Tropic-bird. The only records of its occurrence in eastern North America are off the Newfoundland Banks and in Bermuda.

29. YELLOW-BILLED TROPIC-BIRD. PHAËTHON LEPTURUS CATESBYI *Brandt.* [112.] (Fig. 26.) *Ads.*—White; a mark before and through eye; outer web of primaries, lesser wing-coverts, and tertials black; flanks streaked with slate; bill yellow; tail tinged with salmon, shafts of feathers black. W., 10·75; T., 19·00; B., 2·00.

Range.—Breeds in Bermuda and various isls. of the W. I. and Bahamas, ranging n. to 40° N. Lat. in the w. Atlantic Ocean. Winters from the Bahamas and W. I. s. at least to Brazil and Ascension Isl. Accidental in Fla., S. C., N. Y., and N. S.

Nest, in holes in rocks or cliffs. *Egg,* 1, white, heavily dotted or marked with chestnut, 2·10 × 1·45. *Date,* Bermuda, May 5.

This species breeds abundantly in the Bermudas, but is of rare occurrence on our coasts.

1912. GROSS, A. O., Auk, 49–71 (in Bermuda).—1913. PLATH, K., Bird-Lore, 345–349, illus. (in Bermuda).

SUBORDER PELECANI. PELICANS, GANNETS, CORMORANTS, DARTERS.

(4 families)

SYNOPSIS OF FAMILIES

Bill hooked, over 10·00 long; pouch large, extending entire length of mandible; grayish or white birds; neck curved in flight.
Family Pelecanidæ. PELICANS. P. 155.

Bill hooked, less than 4·00 long; pouch inconspicuous; black or blackish birds; neck straight in flight . . *Family Phalacrocoracidæ.* CORMORANTS. P. 159.

Bill unhooked, bluntly pointed, heavy; tail pointed; under 9·00 long, its feathers without transverse flutings . *Family Sulidæ.* GANNETS. P. 157.

Bill unhooked, sharply pointed, slender; tail rounded; over 9·00 long; with transverse flutings . . . . *Family Anhingidæ.* DARTERS. P. 161.

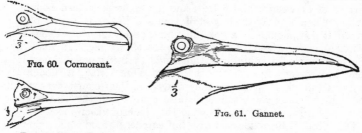

FIG. 60. Cormorant.

FIG. 61. Gannet.

FIG. 62. Water-Turkey.

FAMILY PELECANIDÆ. PELICANS.

The nearly ten known species of Pelicans are distributed throughout the warmer parts of the world. Two species are North American, of which one is exclusively maritime and is found on our southern coasts, while the second nests chiefly to the north, in the interior, and winters on the seacoasts and lakes southward. Pelicans are gregarious and nest in colonies. Their flight is strong but leisurely, six or seven wing-strokes being followed by a short sail, all the members of a flock flapping and sailing in unison. They often mount to great heights, there to soar majestically in broad circles, evidently for mere pleasure in the evolution. They feed on fish, for which some species plunge from the air, while others capture small fry with their scooplike pouches while swimming. The young are born naked, but are shortly covered with white down which is followed by the plumage of flight. They procure their food of fish by plunging their heads far down the parental pouch.

30. WHITE PELICAN. PELECANUS ERYTHRORHYNCHOS *Gmelin.* [125.]
Ads. in nuptial plumage.—White, more or less straw-color on breast and wing-coverts; wing-quills chiefly black; occipital crest white or straw-color; a horny prominence on the culmen. *Postnuptial plumage.*—Similar, but occiput of short gray feathers, no horny ridge on bill. *Ads. in winter.*—Similar,

but occiput white. *Im.*—Similar, but lesser wing-coverts and top of the head brownish gray. L., 60·00; W., 22·00; Tar., 4·50; B., 14·00.

Range.—Breeds from cent. B. C. and Great Slave Lake to cent. Man. (formerly to cent. Minn., n.-cent. Wisc., S. Dak. and Colo.), n. Utah, s. Tex., w. Nev. and s. Calif. Winters from n. Calif., the Gulf States, Fla., along both coasts of Mex. and in the interior, as far as Panama. Casual in W. I., occasional n. to Ont. and N. B.

Washington, casual, four records. Long Island, two records, May. N. Ohio, casual T. V. SE. Minn., T. V., Apr. 7–May 28; Sept. 7–Oct.

Nest, in colonies, on the ground, a depression in a mound of pebbles, or of grasses, sticks, or reeds. *Eggs*, 2–4, creamy or bluish white with a chalky deposit, more or less stained, 3·45 × 2·30. *Date*, Big Stick Lake, Sask., June 10, eggs hatching.

During the summer the White Pelican frequents largely fresh water; in winter it lives chiefly on salt water. At this season it is not uncommon locally on the Gulf Coast of Florida, and a few are usually seen each winter on the Mosquito Lagoon of the East Coast. With a wing-expanse of between 8 and 9 feet, and a weight of sixteen pounds the White Pelican is one of the largest of American birds. Its snowy plumage renders it conspicuous at a great distance, and a far-away Pelican may be mistaken for a sail. This species migrates by day. In mid-March I have seen flocks containing thousands of birds passing northward along the eastern face of the Sierras of Vera Cruz. Although they progressed in wheeling circles, they moved on their course very rapidly. The habit of soaring, or sailing, is also common in the nesting season when the birds go up almost beyond the reach of vision.

The White Pelican does not dive but catches its food while swimming.

1908. CHAPMAN, F. M., Camps and Cruises, 368–388 (biographical).— 1925. HALL, E. R., Condor, 147–160 (food-habits).

31. EASTERN BROWN PELICAN. PELECANUS OCCIDENTALIS OCCIDENTALIS *Linnæus.* [126.] *Ads. in breeding plumage.*—Top of head white, sometimes straw-yellow like a spot on upper breast; line down either side of breast white; hindhead, neck, and a spot on foreneck seal-brown; sides and back silvery gray bordered by brownish black; scapulars, wing-coverts, secondaries, and tail silvery gray; primaries black; underparts dark blackish brown narrowly streaked with white. *Ads. after the breeding season.*— Similar, but with hindhead and whole neck white, more or less tinged with straw-yellow. *Im.*—Above grayish brown margined with paler; chest brownish, belly white. L., 50·00; W., 19·50; Tar., 2·65; B., 11·00.

Range.—Breeds on the s. Atlantic and Gulf Coasts of the U. S. and the Atlantic Coast of Cent. and S. A. from S. C., La., and Tex. s. to Brazil; found also in the Bahamas, the W. I., coasts of Colombia and Ecuador, and the Galapagos Isls. Winters from Fla. and the Gulf Coast southward. Casual in N. C. and Va.; accidental in Bermuda, Kans., Wyo., Nebr., Colo., Ia., Mich., Ills., Ind., N. Y., N. J., Mass., R. I., and N. S.

Long Island, three records, May and Aug.

Nest, in colonies, of sticks or weed-stalks, etc., in mangrove bushes or on the ground. *Eggs*, 3, similar in color to those of the preceding species, 3·00 × 1·95. *Date*, Pelican Isl., Fla., usually Dec. 1; Gulf Coast, Fla., Apr. 4; S. C., May 23.

At all seasons the Brown Pelican is maritime. It is a permanent resident in Florida, but nevertheless migrates regularly to its ancestral nesting-grounds, those of the East Coast reaching their island home about November 1. Eggs are laid by December. They hatch in about four weeks, and their young fly when about ten weeks old. They are exceedingly noisy but the adults are virtually silent.

Pelicans go fishing possibly 50 miles or more from their breeding-ground. With a favorable wind they travel high before it; with a head wind they skim low over the waves usually just outside the breakers. The usual flock-formation is a diagonal single file, and the birds progress by alternate flapping and sailing in unison. The first wing-stroke after a sail is generally given by the leader, not because he is in command, but because, being in advance, he encounters greater air-resistance and is the first to lose momentum when sailing.

Unlike the White Pelican, this species secures its prey by diving. Singly, in pairs, or in small flocks, they beat back and forth, generally about 20 feet above the water, and when opportunity offers, plunge downward with such force that the spray dashes high about them, and the resulting *splash* may be heard half a mile. They usually fish at sea and feed chiefly on menhaden.

1900. CHAPMAN, F. M., Bird Studies with a Camera, 191–214. 1908. Camps and Cruises, 83–112 (biographical).—1905. JOB, H. K., Wild Wings, 1–18. 1918. Bird-Lore, 194–198 (food of).

FAMILY SULIDÆ. GANNETS.

The Gannets or Boobies number about ten species, of which one is northern while the remainder are distributed throughout the tropical and subtropical coasts of the world, five of them having been recorded from our southern borders. They are strictly maritime, but are more abundant near the coast than on the high seas. Their flight is strong and rapid, the vigorous strokes of the wing being interrupted at intervals by a short sail. They obtain their food of fish by plunging for it from the air. The northern species is migratory; the others are roving, but all return with regularity to their nesting-places, generally on some islet, where, during the breeding season, they may be found in large numbers. The young are born naked, but are soon covered with white down. In common with other members of the Order *Pelecaniformes* (except *Phaëthon*) they feed by thrusting their head down the parent's throat. They are wholly dependent on parental care until they acquire the power of flight.

KEY TO THE SPECIES

I. Length over 32·00; center of upper foreneck naked.
    A. White, primaries black . . . . 35. GANNET, ad.
    B. Brown above with wedge-shaped white markings . 35. GANNET, im.
II. Length under 32·00; neck wholly feathered.
    A. Entire upperparts white . . . . 34. RED-FOOTED BOOBY, ad.
    B. Entire upperparts brown.
       a. Belly white . . . . 33. WHITE-BELLIED BOOBY, ad.
       b. Belly brown.
          b^1. Throat and upper breast darker than belly.
                                 33. WHITE-BELLIED BOOBY, im.
          b^2. Underparts uniform or throat and breast lighter than belly.
                               34. RED-FOOTED BOOBY, im.

32. The ATLANTIC BLUE-FACED BOOBY, *Sula dactylatra dactylatra* Lesson, [114], of the Caribbean region, is accidental in southern Florida and Louisiana. The bare skin about the bill is slate or bluish; the feet are grayish or yellowish, *not* red; the adult is white with wing-quills and *tail* black. Young birds have the "head, neck and upperparts plain dark grayish brown, part of the back and rump streaked with white; lowerparts white, the flanks streaked with grayish" (Ridgway). L., 27·00; W., 17·00.

33. WHITE-BELLIED BOOBY. SULA LEUCOGASTER LEUCOGASTER (*Boddaert*). [115.] *Ads.*—Lower breast and belly white, sometimes washed with grayish; rest of plumage brownish fuscous; head and neck sometimes streaked with grayish brown and white; bill and feet yellowish. *Im.*—Entire plumage brownish fuscous, lighter below throat and upper breast darker than belly; bill blackish, feet yellow. L., 30·00; W., 15·50; T., 8·00; B., 3·80.

Range.—Breeds on the Bahamas, some of the W. I., and isls. off the coasts of Venezuela, Cent. A., and Brazil, and Ascension Isl. Winters throughout its breeding-range and perhaps farther south. Casual in Fla. and La. and accidental on L. I., in Mass., S. C., and Bermuda.

Nest, on the ground of a barren islet. *Eggs*, 2, chalky white, 2·30 × 1·55. *Date*, Cay Verde, Bahamas, Feb.

This Booby breeds abundantly on Cay Verde, southeast of Ragged Island in the Bahamas, and on other Bahaman Keys, but is known on our coasts only as an irregular visitant, though off eastern Florida it is probably of more frequent occurrence than the actual records would indicate. Bangs observed it in numbers off the coast east of Micco on February 16, 1895 (*The Auk*, 1902, p. 395), and on March 11, 1907, I saw twelve at the mouth of the St. John's River.

On its nesting-grounds the bird is exceedingly tame and will often strike at one viciously rather than take wing. It feeds on squids and fish, which, like other birds of its genus, it catches by diving.

1908. CHAPMAN, F. M., Papers from Tortugas Lab. of Carnegie Inst., II, 141–149; Camps and Cruises, 208–217 (nesting).

34. RED-FOOTED BOOBY. SULA PISCATOR (*Linnæus*). [116.] Wing-quills more or less frosty. *Ads.*—White, more or less tinged with straw; wings hoary fuscous, their coverts and inner tertials like back; face blue, pouch slate, feet red. *Young birds* are nearly uniform brown, and in a later plumage the head, neck and underparts are white, but at all times the wing-quills are frosty. L., 29·00; W., 15·00; B., 3·30.

Range.—Breeds on some of the W. I. and on isls. off the coasts of Venezuela and British Honduras, and on Ascension Isl. Accidental in Fla.

Bangs records the occurrence of great numbers of white, black-winged Boobies, doubtless this species, off the east Florida coast, opposite Micco, on February 16, 1895 during a storm (*The Auk*, 1902, p. 395). The species is not known to nest nearer Florida than the Cayman islands south of Cuba, but I have elsewhere given reasons for believing that the Booby recorded by Audubon as nesting in the Tortugas was this species and not *Sula leucogastra* (see Papers from Tortugas Lab. of Carnegie Inst., 1908, II, p. 144).

35. GANNET. MORIS BASSANA (*Linnæus*). [117.] (Figs. 61, Pl. XVIII.) *Ads.*—White, head and neck tinged with pale straw-yellow; primaries fuscous. *Im.*—Throat and upperparts, including wing-coverts, dark grayish brown, each feather with a small white wedge-shaped spot; breast and belly white, margined with grayish brown. L., 35·00; W., 19·00; T., 9·50; B., 4·00.

Range.—Breeds on Bird Rock, Bonaventure, and Anticosti Isls. in the Gulf of St. Lawrence, and on islets off se. N. F. (formerly in N. S., N. B., and at Mingan, Que.); also on islets off the British Isles and Iceland. Winters from the coast of Va. (rarely to Mass.) s. to the Gulf of Mexico, Cuba, and Vera Cruz, and on coasts of n. Africa, the Canaries and the Azores. Accidental in Greenland, Lab., Ind., Mich., and Ont.

Long Island, common T. V., casual W. V.; Mch. 23–June 2 (Aug.); Sept. 23–Jan. 25. Bronx region, rare T. V.; no spring records; Oct 16–Jan. 18. Boston, common T. V., Mch.–June; Sept.–Dec.

Nest, of seaweed on rocky cliffs. *Egg*, 1, pale bluish white, overlaid by a chalky deposit, more or less soiled and stained, 3·20×1·90. *Date*, Bird Rock, Que., May 5.

The distribution of this, the only boreal member of its family, indicates that at one time it was found even farther north than it is at present, and that through a climatic change the more northern birds were either exterminated or forced southward, leaving only the widely separated colonies on opposite sides of the north Atlantic.

They reach their American nesting-grounds early in April, and a month later are massed in snowy banks on the broader ledges of the precipitous cliffs, laying or incubating. Where they are not frequently disturbed, they are so tame that they can be touched as they sit on their nests. Their call is a harsh *gor-r-r-r-rok*.

During their migrations they are found usually well off the coast, though I have seen them fishing in the surf at Virginia Beach. They are splendid birds and when on the wing exhibit a striking combination of power and grace. They are most impressive when diving, as with half-closed wings, like great spearheads they strike the water with a force which takes them wholly out of sight and splashes the spray ten feet or more into the air.

1900. CHAPMAN, F. M., Bird Studies with a Camera, 139–145, 181, 189.—1908. Camps and Cruises, 408.—1913. GURNEY, J. H., The Gannet, 8vo., 567 pp., illus. (Witherby & Co., London).

FAMILY PHALACROCORACIDÆ. CORMORANTS.

Cormorants are found in all parts of the world. Ten of the fifty-odd known forms inhabit North America. As a rule they are maritime, but they also frequent bodies of fresh water far from the seacoast. They are more or less gregarious at all seasons, and breed in colonies. Their flight is strong and ducklike, and they often fly in diagonal lines with a somewhat gooselike formation. They secure their food of fish by pursuing it under water, using both feet and wings or either alone, their hooked bill assisting them in its capture. Unlike the Gannets, they do not dive from the air, but from the water or a low perch. They nest on the ground on islands, or on trees growing in water, building well-formed structures. The young are born naked, but are soon covered with a thick, short, black down, which is succeeded by the plumage of flight. They feed, as do the young of most Pelecaniformes, by thrusting their head and neck well down the parent's throat.

KEY TO THE SPECIES

A. Tail of 14 feathers, length over 33˙00 . . 36. EUROPEAN CORMORANT.
B. Tail of 12 feathers, length under 31˙00.
 a. Feathers of back and scapulars rounded.
   37, 37*a.* DOUBLE-CRESTED CORMORANTS.
 b. Feathers of back and scapulars pointed . 38. MEXICAN CORMORANT.

36. EUROPEAN CORMORANT. PHALACROCORAX CARBO CARBO (*Linnæus*). [119.] *Ads. in breeding plumage.*—Region about base of lower mandible white or whitish; head, upper neck, and throat glossy black, thickly sprinkled with white; rest of neck, underparts, and rump glossy black; a white patch on flank; upper back, scapulars, and wing-coverts light olive-brown, each feather bordered by glossy black; tail black, composed of *fourteen feathers.* *Ads. in winter.*—Similar, but without white on the head. *Im.*—Top of the head and hindneck brownish black; upper back, scapulars, and wing-coverts grayish brown, the feathers bordered by blackish; rump glossy black; throat and breast grayish brown, changing to white on belly; sides and under tail-coverts glossy black. L., 36˙00; W., 14˙00; T., 7˙00; B., 3˙00.

Range.—Breeds from the coasts of cent. Greenland and Cumberland Sound to N. F., N. S., and the Bay of Fundy; also breeds in Iceland, the British Isles and on the coasts of Scandinavia and n. Russia to the Kola Peninsula. Winters from Greenland to L. I., N. Y., and casually to Md., S. C., Ont. and cent. N. Y.

Long Island, rare, occurring at any season. Boston, rather common, W. V., Nov.–Apr.

Nest, of sticks and seaweed, in colonies, generally on the ledges of rocky cliffs. *Eggs,* 4–6, pale bluish white, more or less overlaid with a chalky deposit, 2˙50 ✕ 1˙50. *Date,* s. Lab., June 19.

37. DOUBLE-CRESTED CORMORANT. PHALACROCORAX AURITUS AURITUS (*Lesson*). [120.] (Figs. 27, 60.) *Ads. in breeding plumage.*—Head, neck, rump and underparts glossy black; upper back, scapulars, and wing-coverts light grayish brown, each feather margined with glossy black; tail black, composed of *twelve feathers;* a tuft of black feathers on either side of the head; a few white ones over the eye. *Ads. in winter.*—Similar, but without tufts on the head. *Im.*—Top of the head and back of the neck blackish brown; upper back, scapulars, and wing-coverts brownish gray, each feather margined with black; rump glossy black; sides of the head and foreneck grayish white, whiter on the breast and changing gradually to black on the lower belly. L., 30˙00; W., 12˙50; T., 6˙20; B., 2˙30.

Range.—Breeds from cent. Sask., n. Ont., Gulf of St. Lawrence, and N. F. s. to cent. Ills., ne. Ark., S. Dak., s. Minn., and Penobscot Bay, Me. Winters from Va. (casually Mich. and Me.) s. to the Gulf Coast. Casual in Bermuda, and n. to Great Slave Lake.

Washington, casual, several records; Apr.–July; Oct., Nov. Long Island, common T. V., rare S. V., casual W. V., (Feb. 23), Mch. 31–June 29; Aug. 10–Dec. 14. Bronx region, uncommon T. V., Apr. 13–June 23; July 12–Nov. 17. Boston, common T. V., Apr.–June; Aug.–Nov. N. Ohio, irregular T. V., seldom common. SE. Minn., common S. R., Mch. 25–Nov. 1.

Nest, of sticks, seaweed, etc., on the ledges of cliffs, in trees or bushes, or on the ground. *Eggs,* 2–4, similar in color to those of the preceding, 2˙40 ✕ 1˙40. *Date,* s. Lab., June 19; se. Minn., May 7.

This is the common Cormorant of the middle eastern states. We see it chiefly as a migrant when in flocks of varying size it passes far overhead, or pauses to rest on our bays. In migrating the flock is formed in a long line, comparatively few birds deep. On the wing they bear a general resemblance to large Ducks or to Geese.

1894. MACKAY, G. H., Auk, 18–25 (habits in R. I.).—1911. SMITH, F., Auk, 16–19 (breeding in Ills.).—1929. LEWIS, H. F., Natural History of the Double-crested Cormorant, 8vo., 94 pp., illus. (monograph); see also Auk, 1931, 207–214.—1931. ALLEN, A. A., Bird-Lore, 82–91, illus. (autobiography).

37a. FLORIDA CORMORANT. PHALACROCORAX AURITUS FLORIDANUS (*Audubon*). [120*a*.] Resembles the preceding species in color, but is smaller. W., 12·00; T., 5·50; B., 2·10.
Range.—Breeds in Fla., La., N. C., the Bahamas and the Isle of Pines. Winters n. to Tex. and through its breeding-range (except the Carolinas). Casual in the Lesser Antilles.
Nest, in bushes or trees, preferably mangroves or cypresses. *Eggs*, like those of preceding. *Date*, Wakulla, Fla., Mch. 20.

This is an abundant bird on the Florida coast and westward along the shores of the Gulf. Almost every buoy in the harbors of Florida is capped by a Cormorant.

38. MEXICAN CORMORANT. PHALACROCORAX OLIVACEUS MEXICANUS (*Brandt*). [121.] Scapulars and wing-coverts *pointed*. Resembling *P. auritus* but smaller, and feathers above more *pointed*. *Ads.* in breeding plumage with pouch and face bordered posteriorly by white. L., 25·00; W., 10·25; B., 1·80.
Range.—Breeds from nw. Mex., se. Tex., s. La., Cuba, the Isle of Pines, and the Bahamas s. to Nicaragua. Winter range the same. Accidental in Ills. and Colo.

FAMILY ANHINGIDÆ. DARTERS.

There are four species of Darters, Snakebirds or Water-Turkeys, one each in Africa, southern Asia, Australia, and tropical and subtropical America. They are silent birds, generally living in pairs or colonies on bodies of fresh water with wooded shores. They select a perch over the water, and when alarmed sometimes drop into the element below and disappear beneath its surface, or fly upward to a considerable height and circle about like sailing Hawks. They swim well, and when approached too closely, sink quietly backward, frequently leaving the long, thin neck and narrow, pointed head above the surface, when one at once observes the origin of the name 'Snakebird.' They obtain their food by pursuing it under water, and their finely serrated bill assists them in retaining their hold upon it. The young are born naked, but are soon covered with close, short, buff down. They obtain their food from the throat of the parent, and remain in or near the nest until they are able to fly.

39. WATER-TURKEY. ANHINGA ANHINGA (*Linnæus*). [118.] (Fig. 62.)
Ad. ♂ in summer.—General plumage glossy black with greenish reflections;

back of head and neck with scattered grayish plumes; upper back with numerous elongated silvery white spots, which on the scapulars become streaks; lesser wing-coverts spotted like back; exposed portion of median and greater coverts silvery gray; tail tipped with whitish, outer webs of middle pair of feathers with transverse flutings. *Ad. ♂ in winter.*—Similar, but without grayish plumes on head and neck. *Ad. ♀.*—Similar to ♂, but with whole head, neck, and breast brownish, darker above. *Im.*—Similar to ♀, but with black parts of plumage brownish. L., 34·00; W., 13·50; T., 10·50; B., 3·25.

Range.—Breeds through tropical America n. to Bexar Co., Tex., Helena, Ark., and Wilmington, N. C., s. to Paraguay. Winters in nearly the same area. Casual in O.

Nest, well formed, of sticks lined with moss, rootlets, etc., over the water in a low bush or high tree. *Eggs*, 2–5, bluish white with a chalky deposit, 2·15 × 1·35. *Date*, Tampa, Fla., Mch. 21.

This singular bird is a permanent resident in Florida but migratory farther north. They nest in isolated pairs, or in colonies of as many as two hundred birds. Although they soar with great ease they alight clumsily, tumbling onto their perches, with much flapping of wings before gaining their balance. When not alarmed, they seem to take flight with much hesitation, opening and closing their wings repeatedly before they trust themselves to their support. When alighting near the nest, they utter harsh, grating calls, which, if another bird chances to be near, are replied to with threatening motions of the sharply pointed bill.

1908. CHAPMAN, F. M., Camps and Cruises, 116–118 (nesting).

SUBORDER FREGATÆ. MAN-O'-WAR-BIRDS
(1 family)

FAMILY FREGATIDÆ. MAN-O'-WAR-BIRDS.

Man-o'-war-birds, or Frigate-birds, are found throughout intertropical seas. One of the two known species occurs in America. They are strictly maritime, and, while sometimes observed at great distances from the land, are met with in numbers only near the coasts. They have a greater expanse of wing in proportion to the weight of their body than any other bird, and in power of flight are unsurpassed. Facing the wind, they pass hours resting motionless on outstretched wings, sometimes ascending to great heights and calmly soaring far above storms. It is when feeding that their marvelous aërial powers are displayed to the best advantage. By swift, indescribably graceful darts they secure fish which are near the surface, or capture those which have leaped from the water to escape some enemy below. They also pursue Gulls and Terns, and, forcing them to disgorge their prey, catch it in midair. As a rule they are gregarious at all seasons, and nest and roost on bushes near the shore. The feet are exceedingly small and of little use except in perching. The single young is born naked but is quickly clothed in long white down. The black scapulars appear at a very early age.

40. MAN-O'-WAR-BIRD. FREGATA MAGNIFICENS *Mathews.* **[128.]**
(Figs. 16, 28.) *Ad.* ♂.—Entire plumage black, more glossy above; dilatable gular pouch in breeding season orange-red or carmine. ♀.—Similar, but browner; lesser wing-coverts grayish brown; breast and upper belly white. *Im.*—Similar to the ♀ but whole head and neck white. L., 40·00; W., 25·00; T., 17·00; B., 4·50.

Range.—Breeds in the W. I., Bahamas, and on isls. off the coast of Venezuela in the Caribbean Sea, isls. along the w. coast of Mex. and in the Galapagos Isls. Winters in the breeding area and adjacent seas, ranging n. more or less regularly to Fla., La., and the coast of Calif. as far as Humboldt Bay. Casual in Bermuda, N. J., N. Y., Conn., N. S., Que., Wisc., Kans., Ind., Ills., Ia., and O.

Long Island, two records, Aug.

Nest, of sticks, in colonies, on bushes or rocks. *Egg,* **1,** chalky white, 2·65 × 1·75. *Date,* Atwood Key, Bahamas, Feb. 9.

This species is found at all seasons in Florida, but I know of no authentic record of its nesting there. It becomes more common in late spring after its breeding season in the Bahamas.

1908. CHAPMAN, F. M., Camps and Cruises, 217–221 (nesting).

V. ORDER CICONIIFORMES. HERONS, BITTERNS, STORKS, IBISES, SPOONBILLS, FLAMINGOES

SUBORDER ARDEÆ. HERONS AND BITTERNS
(2 families, 1 North American)

FAMILY ARDEIDÆ. HERONS AND BITTERNS.

This family contains about one hundred species distributed in most parts of the globe, but more numerously in the intertropical regions. About one-fourth this number occur in the New World and of these twelve are North American. Generally speaking, Herons are gregarious, nesting and roosting in flocks. While feeding they are more solitary, but each night they regularly return to roost with their kind in a 'rookery.' Bitterns do not associate in flocks, and are generally found singly or in pairs. As a rule, they feed in grassy marshes, while Herons more commonly resort to the shores of lakes, rivers, bays, or salt-water lagoons. Herons perch, and usually nest in trees; Bitterns rarely or never do. Some species secure their food of frogs, fish, small reptiles, etc., by standing rigidly motionless and waiting for it to come within striking distance, or by wading for it with the utmost caution. Others run rapidly and noisily through the water, trusting to their agility and the rapidity of their spearlike thrusts to supply their wants. Herons, unlike our Ibises and Cranes, fly with their folded neck drawn in between their shoulders. Their voice is a hoarse squawk. Many species wear elongated plumes, the Egrets particularly, and all have tracts of concealed powder-down feathers, the function of which is unknown. The young are born with a scanty covering of long, filamentous down and are reared in the nest. In feeding, young Herons, and possibly also young Bitterns, take a scissorlike grasp of the base of the parent's bill with their own, when the parent disgorges food into the nest or skillfully into the mouth of the young.

1913. COOKE, W. W., Distribution and Migration of North American Herons and Their Allies, Bull. 45, Biol. Surv., 70 pp., illus.

KEY TO THE SPECIES

I. Wing over 13·00.
  A. Plumage pure white.
    a. Wing 17·00 or over; feathers on the lower neck long, narrow.
                              41. GREAT WHITE HERON.
    b. Wing under 17·00; neck-feathers not lengthened.
                              44. AMERICAN EGRET.
  B. Upperparts generally slaty or grayish blue.
             42*a.* WARD'S HERON. 42. GREAT BLUE HERON.
II. Wing under 13·00.
  1. Crown without streaks.
    A. Crown white or whitish.
      a. Wing over 11·00.
        a^1. Plumage entirely or mostly white . . . 46. REDDISH EGRET.
        a^2. Plumage gray streaked with black; throat and sides of neck
          black . . . . . . 51. YELLOW-CROWNED NIGHT HERON.
      b. Wing under 11·00.
        b^1. Plumage pure white; legs and bill black; feet yellow.
                          45. SNOWY EGRET.
        b^2. Tips of primaries slate-color; plumage white, sometimes irregularly marked with slaty blue. 48. LITTLE BLUE HERON, im.
    B. Crown not white or whitish.
      a. Crown umber or reddish brown.
        a^1. Head and neck reddish brown; body slate-color.
                        46. REDDISH EGRET.
        a^2. Neck conspicuously streaked; body variegated.
                       52. AMERICAN BITTERN.
      b. Crown not umber or reddish brown.
        b^1. Crown slaty or slate-blue with sometimes a purplish cast.
        b^2. Wing-coverts more or less margined with rufous.
                    47. LOUISIANA HERON.
        b^3. Wing-coverts without rufous . . 48. LITTLE BLUE HERON.
      c^1. Crown not slaty, but greenish or bluish black.
        c^2. Wing over 10·00; entire underparts pure white.
                50. BLACK-CROWNED NIGHT HERON.
      d^2. Wing under 10·00.
        d^3. Wing-coverts green . . . 49. EASTERN GREEN HERON.
        e^3. Wing-coverts rufous-chestnut and buff.
          e^4. Underparts buffy, more or less streaked.
                       53. LEAST BITTERN.
  2. Crown streaked.
    A. Wing under 10·00; upperparts greenish.49. EASTERN GREEN HERON.
    B. Wing over 10·00; upperparts brownish or blackish brown streaked with white.
      a. Upperparts light brown; outer edge of primaries reddish.
                50. BLACK-CROWNED NIGHT HERON, im.
      b. Back dark brown; crown nearly black with white streaks; primaries dark slate-color . 51. YELLOW-CROWNED NIGHT HERON, im.

41. GREAT WHITE HERON. ARDEA OCCIDENTALIS *Audubon.* [192.]
Ads.—Entirely white; in breeding plumage, with long, narrow, stiffened feathers on the back and lower foreneck, and two narrow plumes on the

back of the crown, "L., 45·00–54·00; W., 17·00–21·00; B., 6·00–7·00; Tar., 8·00–8·75" (Ridgway).

Range.—S. Fla. and Fla. Keys; casual n. to Anclote River, and Daytona Beach.

Nest, in small colonies, a platform of sticks usually in mangrove bushes. *Eggs*, 3–4, pale, dull blue, 2·50 × 1·80. *Date*, Florida Keys, Jan. and Feb.

This is a common species on the coasts of southern Florida, particularly in the vicinity of Cape Sable. Rarely it is found as far north as the Anclote River on the west coast and Micco on the east coast. This bird is as large as the Great Blue Heron, and must not be confused with the American Egret, to which the name Great White Heron is frequently misapplied.

"*Ardea wuerdemanni*" Baird may be described as a Ward's Heron with a whitish head and neck. It is thus intermediate between *occidentalis* and *wardi* and, as Holt ('28) has shown, is doubtless a hybrid between them. On March 27, 1908, on Clive Key, southeast of Cape Sable, I found two young Ward's Herons and one pure white bird in the same nest. One of the parents was *Ardea occidentalis;* the identity of the other was not ascertained.

1905. JOB, H. K., Wild Wings, 27.—1928. HOLT, E. G., Cleveland Mus. Sci. Pub. I, 1–35 (status).

42. GREAT BLUE HERON. ARDEA HERODIAS HERODIAS *Linnæus.*
[194.] *Ads. in breeding plumage.*—Center of crown and throat white, sides of crown black, this color meeting on back of head, where the feathers are lengthened to form an occipital crest; neck pale grayish brown, a narrow black, white, and ochraceous line down the middle of the foreneck; feathers of lower foreneck narrow and much lengthened, whitish with sometimes black streaks; back, wing-coverts, and tail slaty gray, the scapulars paler, narrow and much lengthened; bend of wing chestnut-rufous; a patch of black and white feathers on side of breast; breast and belly streaked with black and white and sometimes pale rufous; feathers on legs dull rufous, legs and feet black, upper mandible olive-yellow, the culmen blackish; lower mandible yellow; lores blue. *Im.*—Similar, but entire crown black, throat white, neck brownish gray washed with buffy ochraceous; no black at sides of the breast or plumes on the lower neck; underparts streaked with black, slaty, white and ochraceous; bend of wings and feathers on legs paler; back slaty grayish brown without lengthened plumes. "L., 42·00–50·00; W., 17·90–19·85; B., 4·30–6·25; Tar., 6·00–8·00" (Ridgway).

Range.—Breeds from N. S., cent. Que., n. Ont., s. Man., cent. Alberta, and se. B. C. to Tenn. and S. C., w. to Ia. and Nebr., and in Bermuda. Winters from N. Y. (rarely Mass.) and the Ohio Valley to Fla., Tex., and Panama, casually to Col. and Ven.

Washington, rather common P. R., not commonly present in midwinter. Long Island, common T. V., rare W. V. and S. V., Mch.–June 14, July 3–Jan. 1. Bronx region, fairly common T. V., occasional in winter; Mch. 24–June 9; July 3–Dec. 30. Boston, rather common T. V., Apr.–May; July–Nov. N. Ohio, tolerably common S. R., Mch. 20–Oct. 10. Glen Ellyn, not common T. V., Apr. 3–26; Aug. 3–Oct. 24. SE. Minn., common S. R., Mch. 18–Nov. 20.

Nest, a platform of sticks, generally in colonies, usually in tall trees, sometimes on the ground on islets. *Eggs*, 3–4, pale, dull blue, 2·50 × 1·50. *Date*, coast S. C., Mch. 20; Oneida Co., N. Y., May 1; SE. Minn., Apr. 28.

Is it due to the influence of the artists of the Orient that these long-legged, long-necked birds are so frequently miscalled 'Cranes'? With head drawn in and legs trailing on behind, they flap slowly over the water, resembling, no doubt, the 'Cranes' of fans, screens, and bronzes; nevertheless, they are Herons. With all a Heron's immovable alertness they watch patiently for passing fish, sometimes wading with extreme caution, placing one foot slowly before the other. They feed both by day and night. Fishes, frogs, reptiles, even small mice, all are welcome; and all are powerless to escape the lightning thrust of the spearlike bill. Their voice is harsh and rasping. When alarmed they utter a croak which is sometimes prolonged into a series of *squawks*. They nest and roost in colonies, but at other times are solitary birds.

42a. WARD'S HERON. ARDEA HERODIAS WARDI *Ridgway*. [194*b*.]
The Florida representative of *A. h. herodias*. The average differences in color between it and *A. h. herodias* consist in its whiter lowerparts, darker neck, and olive instead of black legs. These differences, however, cannot always be relied upon, and size is the character by which the two birds can best be distinguished, *wardi* being the larger, as the following measurements show: L., 52·00; W., 19·75–20·50; B., 6·40–6·80; Tar., 8·00–8·50.
Range.—Breeds from se. S. C., s. Ga., s. Ala., sw. Ind., se. Ills., se. Ia., and Kans., to Okla., se. Tex., the Gulf Coast, and the Fla. Keys. Winters in Fla., s. Ala., Tex. and s. in Mex. to Jalisco.
Nest, in colonies, a platform of sticks, usually in trees, sometimes bushes, generally over water. *Eggs*, 3–4, pale, dull blue, 2·65 × 1·85. *Date*, Tarpon Springs, Fla., Jan. 20.

This is the Florida form of the Great Blue Heron, which it resembles in habits.

1908. CHAPMAN, F. M., Camps and Cruises, 119–122 (nesting).

43. The EUROPEAN HERON, *Ardea cinerea cinerea* Linnæus [195] is accidental in southern Greenland. It may be distinguished from the Great Blue Heron by the white instead of rufous feathers on the legs.

44. AMERICAN EGRET. CASMERODIUS ALBUS EGRETTA (*Gmelin*).
[196.] *Ads. in breeding plumage.*—Entire plumage pure white; about fifty *straight* 'aigrette' plumes grow from the interscapular region and reach beyond the tail; legs and feet black; bill yellow; lores orange, bordered below by greenish. *Ads. after the breeding season and Im.*—Without the interscapular plumes. L., 41·00; W., 15·00; Tar., 5·60; B., 4·50.
Range.—Breeds in Ore. and Calif., and from Ark., Tenn., N. C., Fla., the Gulf Coast and Mex. s. to Patagonia; formerly bred n. to Cape May Co., N. J., and Wisc.; now greatly reduced in numbers. Winters from Ore., Calif., Tex., the Gulf of Mex. and S. C. s. In late summer migrates n., regularly to N. J. and s. N. E., and casually to Man., Ont., Que., N. B., N. S., and N. H.
Washington, not common and irregular S. R., May–Oct. Long Island, rare S. V. from July 1–Sept. 27. Bronx region, rare S. V., July 6–Oct. 9. Boston, rare S. V., July–Oct. N. Ohio, not common fall wanderer.
Nest, a platform of sticks, in colonies, in trees or bushes over water. *Eggs*, 3–5, dull blue, of a rather deeper shade than those of the preceding, 2·25 × 1·60. *Date*, s. Fla., Feb.; Santee, S. C., Apr. 5.

Thanks to the enforcement of laws protecting the Egrets and prohibiting the sale of their plumes, as well as to the activity of Audubon

Society wardens, these beautiful birds have been saved from the annihilation which at the opening of this century threatened them in this country. They now seem to be holding their own and even to be increasing slightly in numbers. Doubtless, for this reason we see them regularly in summer as post-breeding wanderers northward to Massachusetts and Wisconsin.

1887. Scott, W. E. D., Auk, 135 (destruction in Fla.).—1905. Job, H. K., Wild Wings, 134–149 (habits, destruction).—1908. Chapman, F. M., Camps and Cruises, 122–134 (nesting).

45. SNOWY EGRET. Egretta thula thula (*Molina*). [197.] *Ads. in breeding plumage.*—Entire plumage pure white; about fifty *recurved* 'aigrette' plumes grow from the interscapular region and reach to or just beyond the end of the tail; legs *black*, feet *yellow*, bill *black*, yellow at the base; lores orange-yellow. *Ads. after the breeding season and Im.*—Without the interscapular plumes. L., 24·00; W., 9·75; Tar., 3·80; B., 3·20.

Range.—Formerly bred from Cape May Co., N. J., Nebr., Ind., and Ills., s. to Chile and Argentina; now breeds in the U. S. locally along the coast from N. C. to La. and Tex. Winters from Fla. and Mex. s. In late summer migrates n. to Kans. and Md. and casually farther (recorded from Alberta, N. S., N. B., Wisc., Mich., O., Vt., Mass., R. I., N. Y. and N. J., and in Bermuda but some of the records are doubtless based on the young of *Florida cœrulea*).

Washington, casual; irregular in fall. Long Island, casual S. V., Aug. 3–20. Bronx region, A. V.; one record at Ossining many years ago. Boston, A. V. N. Ohio, casual, in autumn.

Nest, a platform of sticks, in colonies, in bushes over water. *Eggs,* 3–5, pale, dull blue, 1·80 × 1·20. *Date,* s. Fla., Mch.; coast S. C., May 5.

The forces which have saved the Egret have also preserved this species. Never as common as the larger bird, it is now comparatively rare. Nevertheless, a few individuals are seen each summer in the northern states during its post-breeding travels. Its resemblance to the abundant Little Blue Heron in the white, first-year plumage calls for extreme care in field identification. Note particularly the black legs and yellow toes of this species. In the Little Blue these parts are greenish yellow.

46. REDDISH EGRET. Dichromanassa rufescens rufescens (*Gmelin*). [198.] *Ads. dark phase.*—Head and neck rufous-chestnut, glossed with vinaceous; rest of plumage dark bluish slate-color; about thirty 'aigrette' plumes grow from interscapular region and reach beyond tail; legs and feet bluish plumbeous; front of tarsi and toes black. *Im.*—Similar, but without 'aigrette' plumes; legs and feet fuscous. *White phase.*—Similar in size and form, but entire plumage white, except tips of primaries, which are sometimes very finely speckled with grayish. *Im.*—Similar, but without 'aigrette' plumes. L., 29·00; W., 12·50; Tar., 5·40; B., 3·60.

Remarks.—The two color phases of this bird were supposed to represent two species, the white phase being called *Ardea pealei* Bonaparte. They have, however, been found mated together, and intermediates or parti-colored specimens are known.

Range.—Breeds from the Gulf Coast to Haiti, Jamaica, and Guatemala. Winters from s. Fla. s. Casual in Colo. and s. Ills.

Nest, a platform of sticks, singly or in colonies, in bushes generally over salt-water. *Eggs,* 2–4, pale, dull blue, 1·95 × 1·45. *Date,* Tampa Bay, Apr.

This is now a rare bird on the coasts of southern Florida and it is occasionally seen in the interior, the reddish phase prevailing. It is a graceful, active fisher and instead of waiting for its prey to come within spearing distance, pursues it rapidly through the shallow water.

1922. PEMBERTON, J. R., Condor, 3–12, illus. (habits).

47. LOUISIANA HERON. HYDRANASSA TRICOLOR RUFICOLLIS (*Gosse*). [199.] *Ads.*—Upperparts dark bluish slate-color; back of head and upper neck with elongated chestnut-rufous and white feathers; back with pale brownish gray 'aigrette' plumes reaching to tail; lower back, rump and belly white; neck bluish slate-color; throat white, an indistinct rufous line down the middle of foreneck; legs blackish; base of bill and lores bluish. *Im.*— Throat, and an indistinct line down the foreneck, white; rest of head and neck brownish rufous; upper back and wings bluish slate-color, more or less washed with brownish rufous; no plumes; lower back, rump and belly white; breast with more or less slaty streaks; legs yellow behind, blackish before; lower mandible and lores orange; upper mandible black. L., 26·00; W., 10·00; Tar., 3·70; B., 3·90.

Range.—Breeds from N. C. and the Gulf States to the W. I. and Cent. A., and on the Pacific Coast of Mex. n. to cent. L. Calif. Winters from L. Calif. and S. C. s. Migrates casually n. in late summer (recorded from Calif., Ariz., Mo., Ind., N. J., and L. I.).

Washington, several records; July–Sept. Long Island, casual S. V., June–Aug. 20.

Nest, a platform of sticks, in colonies, in bushes or small trees over water. *Eggs*, 3–4, pale, dull blue, 1·75 × 1·35. *Date*, s. Fla., Apr. 1; Santee, S. C., Apr. 20.

The Louisiana Heron has, fortunately, never found favor with the milliners and consequently is doubtless as abundant today as it ever was, rookeries containing thousands of birds being not uncommon in Florida. It flies with its neck less drawn in than do our other Herons, and its sharply defined white abdomen is a further excellent field-mark. It is very noisy and excitable when mating and nesting, and when challenging a rival the neck-feathers are so erected and ruffled that the bird seems to be wearing a feather boa. It is sometimes a slow, stealthy feeder, and at others dashes for its prey.

1908. CHAPMAN, F. M., Camps and Cruises, 143.

48. LITTLE BLUE HERON. FLORIDA CÆRULEA CÆRULEA (*Linnæus*). [200.] *Ads.*—Head and neck maroon-chestnut; rest of plumage dark bluish slate-color; interscapulars and lower neck-feathers lengthened and narrowly pointed; lores blue; legs and feet black. *Im.*—White, plumage sometimes more or less washed with slaty; *tips of the primaries always bluish slate-color*; legs, feet and lores *greenish yellow*. L., 22·00; W., 10·25; Tar., 3·70; B., 3·00.

Remarks.—Between the young and adult there is every stage of inter-gradation of color, some specimens being irregularly marked with blue and white in about equal proportions. Young birds are sometimes mistaken for Snowy Herons, but can always be distinguished by the greenish yellow legs and slaty tips of the primaries. They breed sometimes in the white plumage.

Range.—Formerly bred from Mo., Ills., Ind. and N. J. to w. Mex.; now breeds from Del. s. to Fla. and the Gulf Coast and in Ark. and cent. Tex., Mex. and Cent. A. Winters from N. C. and Tex. s. Migrates in late sum-mer regularly to N. J., s. N. Y. and N. E., and casually farther (recorded from N. S., Que., Ont., N. E., Nebr., Man., Mich., Wisc., Ia., Nebr., Colo., and s. L. Calif.).

Washington, casual May–Oct.; sometimes quite common. Long Island,
T. V. and S. V., rare in spring; tolerably common in late summer; Apr. 3–
May 27, July 3–Sept. 25. Bronx region, rare S. V., Apr. 26; June 24–Sept.
15. Boston, rare S. V. N. Ohio, casual in fall.

Nest, a platform of sticks, in colonies, in bushes or small trees over water.
Eggs, 3–4, pale, dull blue, 1·70 × 1·30. *Date*, San Mateo, Fla., Apr. 1; coast
S. C., Apr. 23.

Thanks to their lack of 'aigrette' plumes Little Blue Herons are
one of the most common Herons in Florida today. They are generally
found in flocks, sometimes composed entirely of blue adults, sometimes
of white, immature birds, and at others both young and old are associated. I have seen a few white-plumaged birds nesting in colonies
composed of blue adults. The white birds resemble *E. thula*, but the
color of their legs and feet serves as a distinguishing character at some
distance. They are silent when feeding, but when undisturbed in their
rookeries, each bird seems to have something to say, and the result is
a strange chorus of croaking voices. They feed by day, and generally
wait for their prey to come within striking distance.

49. EASTERN GREEN HERON. Butorides virescens virescens
(*Linnæus*). [201.] (Fig. 29.) *Ads.*—Crown and a short line below eye glossy
greenish black; throat buffy white, this color extending down foreneck as a
narrow line mixed with blackish, widening on breast; rest of head and neck
rufous-chestnut glossed with vinaceous; back, with lengthened interscapulars, green, more or less washed with bluish gray; wing-coverts green,
margined with white or buffy; belly ashy gray, more or less washed with
buffy. *Im.*—Similar, but with neck and underparts streaked with blackish;
back without lengthened feathers or wash of blue-gray; wing-coverts widely
margined with buffy ochraceous. L., 17·00; W., 7·25; Tar., 1·90; B., 2·50.

Range.—Breeds from N. Dak., cent. Minn., n. Wisc., s. Ont., s. Que.,
and N. S., s. to the Dry Tortugas, and n. Honduras, and w. to cent. Colo.
and N. Mex. Winters from Fla. (casually S. C.) and se. Tex. to Col. Casual
in Bermuda, Porto Rico, and Haiti.

Washington, common S. R., Apr. 9–Oct. 2. Long Island, common S. R.,
Apr. 7–Oct. 13 (Nov. 1). Bronx region, common S. R., Apr. 5–Oct. 12.
Boston, common S. R., May 1–Sept. 30. N. Ohio, common S. R., Apr. 14–
Nov. 15. Glen Ellyn, fairly common S. R., Apr. 18–Oct. 12. SE. Minn.,
common S. R., Apr. 18–Oct. 10.

Nest, a platform of sticks in a bush or low branch of a tree. *Eggs*, 3–6,
pale, dull blue, 1·50 × 1·14. *Date*, San Mateo, Fla., Mch. 25; Chester Co.,
Pa., Apr. 30; Boston, May 10.

The shores of wooded streams or ponds are frequented by this small
Heron in preference to more exposed situations. It is most active in
the early morning or at nightfall; during the day it rests quietly in some
sheltered situation. When startled, it springs into the air with a frightened *skeow* or explosive whistle, and, alighting at a safe distance on a
tree or on some elevated perch, with upstretched neck watches the
intruder, betraying its apprehension by nervous twitchings of the tail.
It is a solitary bird, and, unlike most Herons, is not found in flocks,
and usually nests alone, though as many as a dozen pairs may sometimes
be found associated. In the mating season it utters a surprising variety
of hen-like notes and a hoarse, choking gulp.

1929. Allen, A. A., Bird-Lore, 289–297, illus. (autobiography).

50. BLACK-CROWNED NIGHT HERON. NYCTICORAX NYCTICORAX HOACTLI (*Gmelin*). [202.] *Ads.*—Forehead, neck, and underparts white or whitish; crown, upper back and scapulars glossy, greenish black; lower back, wings and tail ashy gray; legs and feet yellow; lores greenish; two or three white rounded occipital plumes about 8·00 in length; eye ruby. *Im.*— Upperparts grayish brown, the feathers streaked or with wedge-shaped spots of white or buffy; outer web of primaries pale rufous; underparts white, streaked with blackish; eyes yellow. L., 24·00; W., 12·00; Tar., 3·20; B., 3·00.

Range.—Breeds from n. Ore., s. Wyo., s. Man., s. Que., s. to Patagonia. Winters from Ore. and N. Y. s. Casual in winter n. to N. E., s. Ills., Mich., Colo., Utah, Nev., N. B., and in Bermuda.

Washington, not uncommon S. R., less so in winter. Long Island, common S. R., rare in winter, Mch. 15–Nov. 21. Bronx region, common P. R. Boston, common T. V. and S. R., Apr.–Oct. N. Ohio, not common in summer. Glen Ellyn, not common S. R., Mch. 5–Oct. 20. SE. Minn., uncommon S. R., Apr. 8–Nov. 26.

Nest, of sticks, in colonies, in the upper parts of tall trees, sometimes in bushes or on the ground. *Eggs,* 3–6, pale, dull blue, 2·00 × 1·40. *Date,* San Mateo, Fla., Mch. 29; Chester Co., Pa., May 3; Ossining, N. Y., May 7.

These birds live in colonies composed sometimes of thousands of pairs. Their day begins after sunset, when they leave their roosts and start for their feeding-grounds. Occasionally they utter a loud, hoarse *quawk*, the origin of their common name; and looking up we may catch a glimpse of them hurrying through the gloom. During the nesting-season the demands of the young force them to feed both by day and night.

1900. CHAPMAN, F. M., Bird Studies with a Camera, 76–85 (nesting on L. I.).—1915. BAILEY, S. W., The Plum Island Night Herons, Auk, 424–441.—1923. GROSS, A. O., Auk, 1–30, 191–214, illus. (monograph).—1926. MAY, J. B., Bull. Northeastern Bird-Banding Assoc., 25–28, map; also, 1929, 7–16 (banding).

51. YELLOW-CROWNED NIGHT HERON. NYCTANASSA VIOLACEA VIOLACEA (*Linnæus*). [203.] *Ads.*—Crown white, generally washed with buffy; ear-coverts white; rest of head and throat black; neck, breast and belly blue-gray; back the same; the lengthened interscapulars, scapulars and wing-coverts streaked with black; two or three black and white rounded occipital plumes; lores greenish yellow; legs greenish; eyes orange. *Im.*— Crown *black*, the feathers streaked with white or buffy; rest of upperparts, including wing-coverts, fuscous-brown with wedge-shaped buffy or white spots; primaries *dark bluish slate-color without rufous;* underparts white or buffy streaked with blackish. L., 23·00; W., 12·00; Tar., 3·75; B., 3·00.

Remarks.—Young birds bear a general resemblance to those of the preceding species, but differ in being darker, in having the head darker than the back, and the primaries without rufous.

Range.—Breeds from s. Tex., Okla., Kans., s. Ills., s. Ind., N. J. (rarely Mass.) and S. C., s. to Brazil and Peru. Winters from s. Fla. s. Occurs casually n. to Colo., Ia., Nebr., Ont., Mass., N. H., Me., and N. S.

Washington, A. V., several records, May–Aug. Long Island, rare T. V., Mch. 26–May 7, July 7–Nov. 1. Bronx region, A. V., one record, July 10. Boston, A. V.

Nest, a platform of sticks, in pairs or small colonies, generally on a branch over water. *Eggs,* 4–5, pale, dull blue, 1·95 × 1·45. *Date,* San Mateo, Fla., Apr. 2; coast, S. C., Apr. 20.

This is a less common species than the preceding. It nests in pairs along the borders of wooded streams and is also found nesting in association with other Herons.

52. AMERICAN BITTERN. Botaurus lentiginosus (*Montagu*). [190.]
Ads.—A glossy black streak on each side of upper neck; top of head and back of neck bluish slate, more or less washed with buffy; back brown, bordered and irregularly mottled with buffy, and buffy ochraceous, wing-coverts similarly marked, but ground color grayer; underparts creamy buff, the feathers all widely streaked with buffy brown, which is finely speckled with buffy and narrowly margined by brownish gray. *Im.*—Similar, but buffy everywhere deeper and more ochraceous. L., 28·00; W., 10·50; Tar., 3·50; B., 3·00.

Range.—Breeds from cent. B. C., and s. Ungava, s. to s. Calif., and s. N. J.; less frequently in the s. U. S. Winters from B. C., D. of C., and Va. s. to Panama, and casually to the Bahamas, Porto Rico, Jamaica, and Bermuda. Accidental in Iceland, Greenland, Great Britain, and the Azores.

Washington, rather uncommon S. R., Mch. 22–Nov. 7. Long Island, common T. V., rare S. R., (Apr. 3), Apr. 16–Dec. 6 (Jan.). Bronx region, fairly common T. V., uncommon S. R., Mch. 31–Nov. 23 (Dec.·26). Boston, common S. R., Apr.–Nov. N. Ohio, tolerably common S. R., Apr. 1–Oct. 1. Glen Ellyn, fairly common S. R., Apr. 9–Nov. 17. SE. Minn., common S. R., Apr. 2–Nov. 16.

Nest, of grasses, etc., on the ground in marshes. *Eggs*, 3–5, pale olive-buff, 1·90 × 1·45. *Date*, Cambridge, May 5; Pewaukee, Wisc., May 23.

The Bittern makes its home in extensive grassy meadows with plenty of water, but in the season of migration may be found and heard 'booming' in smaller and more accessible swampy places. Like the other members of its family, it excels in standing still, and will hold its head erect and motionless amid the tall grass till the watcher tires of looking and pronounces the suspicious object nothing but a stick after all. The Bittern's fame rests upon its vocal performance, or 'boom.' This is sometimes exactly like the working of an old-fashioned wooden pump, and sometimes—even with the same bird—like the driving of a stake in a bog. It can be heard for a long distance. The performance is best witnessed in spring, while the grass is still low. That it is not so very difficult at that season to steal a march upon the bird may perhaps be considered as established on the testimony of a man who has never lived near a Bittern meadow, and yet has watched the performance at much length and at near range on several occasions. His first experience of this kind is described somewhat fully in *The Auk*, Vol. VI, page 1. The strange notes are delivered with equally strange contortions, as if the bird were horribly nauseated, and are preceded by a succession of quick snapping or gulping sounds—'hiccoughs,' one observer has called them. No water is employed in the operation, in spite of the circumstantial assertions of several persons who profess to have seen the bird swallowing and then ejecting it.

BRADFORD TORREY.

Brewster, Wm., Auk, 1911, 90–100 (display of plumes).—1922. Chapin, J. P., Auk, 196–202, illus. (function of the esophagus in 'booming').

53. EASTERN LEAST BITTERN. Ixobrychus exilis exilis (*Gmelin*). [191,191.1.] *Ad.* ♂.—Top of head, back and tail shining black; back of neck chestnut-rufous; most of the greater wing-coverts and outer vanes of the secondaries darker; lesser wing-coverts and part of greater ones buffy; underparts, *including under tail-coverts*, washed with buffy; a blackish patch at each side of the breast. *Ad.* ♀.—Similar, but the head browner and back light, glossy umber; underparts darker and more or less streaked with brownish. *Im.* ♂.—Similar to ad. ♂, but the back washed and tipped with chestnut; underparts darker and lightly streaked with black. *Im.* ♀.— Similar to ad. ♀, but the back rufous, margined with buffy ochraceous. L., 13·00; W., 4·60; Tar., 1·60; B., 1·80.

Range.—Breeds from s. Que., Ont., s. Me., s. Vt., Wisc., cent. Minn., and N. Dak., s. to the W. I. and s. Mex. Winters from Ga. and s. Tex., s. to the W. I. and Brazil. Casual or accidental in Man., Sask., N. B., and N. S. Washington, not very numerous S. R., May 5–Sept. 26. Long Island, local S. R., rare T. V., (Apr. 27) May 14–Sept. 29 (Dec. 12). Bronx region, rather rare S. R., Apr. 28–Sept. 26 (Oct. 2). Boston, local S. R., May– Sept. N. Ohio, common S. R., Apr. 20–Sept. 20. Glen Ellyn, local S. R., becoming rare late spring and summer records only. SE. Minn., common S. R., May 6–Sept. 20.

Nest, a platform of grasses, reeds, etc., in marshes among rushes, some- times in a small bush, usually over water. *Eggs*, 3–6, pale bluish white, 1·20 × ·92. *Date*, Ft. Thompson, Fla., Mch. 25; Mt. Pleasant, S. C., May 1; Boston, June 1; Pewaukee, Wisc., May 27.

Wet, grassy marshes such as Rail love, or reed-grown ponds that Gallinules frequent, are the resorts of these retiring, secretive little birds. With outstretched necks and lowered heads they make their way without difficulty through the jungle of roots and stalks. Some- times they climb up a slender reed, and, hanging on like Marsh Wrens, survey their surroundings. They take wing almost from beneath one's feet, and, with a low, frightened *qua*, fly slowly for a short distance and then drop back into the grass. During the breeding season one may hear what presumably is the voice of only the male—a soft, slowly repeated, dovelike *coo, coo, coo, coo, coo*. It floats over the marsh like the voice of a spirit bird.

Cory's Least Bittern (191.1) is now considered to be a color-phase of the Least Bittern.

1900. CHAPMAN, F. M., Bird Studies with a Camera, 62–75 (nesting).

SUBORDER CICONIÆ.   STORKS, IBISES, SPOONBILLS
(3 families, 2 North American)
SYNOPSIS OF FAMILIES

Bill 7·00, heavy, at base the size of head; decurved at end; no grooves in sides of maxilla. Wing over 16·00.
        Family Ciconiidæ. STORKS AND WOOD IBISES. P. 172.
Bill under 7·00; maxilla with lateral grooves from nostril to end; slender and decurved for at least end half, or broadly flattened (spatulate).
        Family Threskiornithidæ. IRISES AND SPOONBILLS. P. 173.

FAMILY CICONIIDÆ. STORKS AND WOOD IBISES.

About twenty known species of this family are distributed through- out the world, but only three are found in the Western Hemisphere,.

and of these but one occurs north of Mexico. The Common Stork (*Ciconia ciconia*) of Europe, the Adjutant (*Leptoptilus dubius*) of India, and Marabou (*L. crumeniferus*) of Africa are the best known of the Old-World species. The Marabou feathers of commerce are from the last-named species.

While terrestrial in feeding habit, Storks usually nest some distance above the ground. They perch readily in trees and in this respect differ from Cranes, with which, however, they agree in flying with the neck fully extended. The young are hatched with but a scanty covering of down and are reared in the nest, Storks, in this respect, resembling Herons rather than Cranes. They are essentially voiceless.

54. WOOD IBIS. MYCTERIA AMERICANA *Linnæus*. [188.] *Ads.*—Head and neck bare; primaries, secondaries and tail glossy greenish black, rest of plumage white. *Im.*—Head more or less feathered; head and neck grayish brown, blacker on the nape; rest of plumage as in the adult, but more or less marked with grayish; wings and tail less greenish. L., 40·00; W., 18·00; Tar., 7·60; B. from N., 8·00.

Range.—Breeds and usually winters along the Gulf Coast from Tex. to Fla. and n. to S. C., also in the W. I., Mex., Cent. and S. A. to Argentina and Peru. Migrates irregularly and casually after the breeding season to cent. Calif., Ariz., Mont., Wyo., Mo., s. Ills., s. Ind., Ky., Colo., Wisc., Mich., Ont., N. Y., Pa., N. J., Mass. and Vt.

Washington, casual in July; three records. Long Island, one record, June.

Nest, in colonies, a platform of sticks in trees. *Eggs*, 2–3, dull white with a soft calcareous deposit, 2·75 × 1·75. *Date*, Brevard Co., Fla., Mch. 14.

This is a locally common species in Florida.

1929. HOLT, E. G., Wilson Bull., 3–18, illus. (haunts and habits).

FAMILY THRESKIORNITHIDÆ. IBISES AND SPOONBILLS.

Ibises are distributed throughout the warmer parts of the globe; they number about thirty species, of which four occur in North America. They are usually silent birds, and live in flocks during the entire year. They feed along the shores of lakes, bays, and salt-water lagoons, and on mud-flats over which the tide rises and falls. Their food consists principally of crustaceans, frogs, and small fish. They fly with the neck extended and their wing-strokes are often followed by a short sail.

The Spoonbills inhabit the warmer parts of the world. Only one of the six species is found in America. They frequent the shores both on the seacoast and in the interior. They are generally found in flocks and they nest in colonies. Spoonbills have the general habits of Ibises, but feed by immersing the bill and swinging it from side to side in their search for food. They fly with the neck fully extended, and with steady, uninterrupted wing-strokes.

55. EASTERN GLOSSY IBIS. PLEGADIS FALCINELLUS FALCINELLUS (*Linnæus*). [186.] *Ads.*—Rich chestnut, upper and under tail-coverts, back, wings and *front of the head* with greenish and purplish reflections; lores (in skins) blackish; in winter, head and neck more or less streaked with whitish. *Im.*—Head and neck fuscous-brown, the feathers laterally margined with white; rest of underparts dull fuscous-brown; back with greenish reflections. L., 24·00; W., 11·50; Tar., 3·10; B., 5·00.

Range.—Tropical and subtropical regions, mainly of the Eastern Hemisphere. Breeds rarely and locally at Micanopy and Orange Lake, Fla., and probably in La. and Mex., also in Haiti and Cuba, ranging casually n. (Recorded from Ont., N. S., Que., Colo., Mo., Wisc., Mich., O., N. H., Conn., Mass., N. Y., N. J., Del., D. of C. and S. C.)

Washington, two records. Long Island, two records, Sept., Oct. Boston, A. V.

Nest, of rushes, plant-stems, etc., in reedy swamps or low bushes. *Eggs*, 3, rather deep, dull blue, 2·01 × 1·47. *Date*, Orange Lake, Fla., Apr.

Of this once doubtless widely distributed species comparatively few individuals remain, and in the New World it is of rare and irregular occurrence.

1913. BAYNARD, O. E., Wilson Bull., 103–117, illus. (home-life).

56. The WHITE-FACED GLOSSY IBIS, *Plegadis guarauna* (Linnæus), [187], a locally common species from Texas westward, has been recorded but once from east of the Mississippi, viz., at or near Lake Washington, Florida, where a female was shot on a nest containing three eggs (Brewster, *The Auk*, III, 1886, 482). Occasional in fall in Minnesota; bred once at Heron Lake. This species resembles the Glossy Ibis, but adults have the feathers about the base of the bill white. Rarely this white marking may be absent or barely evident, when the species may be distinguished by its reddish instead of blackish bare lores. In young birds the head and neck average paler brown than in the Glossy Ibis, but the two are not certainly distinguishable.

57. WHITE IBIS. GUARA ALBA (*Linnæus*). [184.] (Fig. 30.) *Ads.*—White, the tips of the four outer primaries black; face red; in winter head and neck lightly streaked, face dull. *Im.*—Head and neck white, streaked with grayish brown; upper back and wings grayish brown; rump, breast and belly white. L., 25·00; W., 11·00; Tar., 3·40; B. from N., 4·60.

Range.—Breeds from L. Calif. and S. C. s. to Venezuela and Peru.

Winters from cent. Mex., the coast of La. and Fla. s. Casual in Colo., S. Dak., Ills., N. C., Vt., Conn., and L. I.
Long Island, two records, Mch. and summer.
Nest, in colonies, of reeds and weed-stalks, in trees, bushes and reedy marshes. *Eggs*, 3–5, pale greenish white, with chocolate markings generally most numerous at the larger end, 2·25 × 1·50. *Date*, s. Fla., Apr. 2.

This locally abundant species is generally found in flocks of five or six to as many hundred birds which frequent mud-flats, marshes, or the borders of lagoons. They fly in close rank, and when in large flocks, with their snowy plumage glistening in the sunlight and their wing-strokes accented by the black-tipped primaries, form a strikingly beautiful picture. They progress by alternate flapping and sailing, tne neck being fully extended. Birds in the brown immature plumage may be seen in large flocks in the spring, indicating that the birds do not breed until at least their second spring.

58. The SCARLET IBIS, *Guara rubra* (Linnæus), [185], a South American species, has been recorded from Florida, Louisiana, Texas, and New Mexico.

59. ROSEATE SPOONBILL. AJAIA AJAJA (*Linnæus*). [183.] (Fig. 31.)
Ads.—Head and throat bare, neck and upper back white, sometimes tinged with pink; sides of breast in front of the wings and end half of tail ochraceous-buff; rest of plumage pink; lengthened feathers at the base of the neck darker; lesser wing-coverts, upper and under tail-coverts carmine. *Im.*—Similar, but head and throat feathered, ochraceous-buff and carmine of the adult replaced by pink. L., 32·00; W., 14·50; Tar., 4·00; B., 6·25.
Range.—Breeds locally in s. Tex., La., Ga., Fla., the Bahamas., s. to Argentina and Chile. Formerly casual n. to Pa., Ind., Ills., and S. C. Accidental in Calif., Utah, Kans., Colo., Wisc., and the Falkland Isls.
Nest, in colonies, a platform of sticks in small trees, usually about 10 feet up. *Eggs*, 3–5, white, spotted and speckled with shades of olive-brown, 2·57 × 1·73. *Date*, Marquesas Key, Fla., Jan. 11, 1883; s. Fla., Mch. 11; Tamiahua Lagoon, Vera Cruz, Apr. 17, second plumage well grown.

In eastern North America, Spoonbills are largely confined to the southern part of Florida where they are said to be increasing in number. The Spoonbill's flight is rather ibislike, the neck being fully extended, but the wing-strokes are not interrupted by short sails. The pink color is very evident at a great distance, against either sky or foliage.

1908. CHAPMAN, F. M., Camps and Cruises, 141, 146 (Fla.).

SUBORDER PHŒNICOPTERI. FLAMINGOES
(1 family)

FAMILY PHŒNICOPTERIDÆ. FLAMINGOES.

Four of the six species contained in this family inhabit the Western Hemisphere where they range from the Bahamas to southern Chile. Flamingoes are gregarious at all seasons. Their favorite resorts are shallow bays and lakes or vast mud-flats which are flooded at high water. In feeding, the bill is pressed downward into the mud, its peculiar shape making the point then turn upward. The ridges along its sides, as in the bills of Ducks, serve as strainers through which are forced the sand and mud taken in with the food. The wing-quills are molted simultaneously, as with the *Anatidæ*, indicating relationship with that family.

60. FLAMINGO. PHŒNICOPTERUS RUBER *Linnæus.* [182.] (Figs. 19, 32.) *Ads.*—Beautiful rosy vermilion, scapulars and underparts somewhat paler; flanks carmine; primaries and secondaries black; bill red-tinged at base, black at the tip. *Im.*—Above brownish gray, back with black shaft-streaks, scapulars basally pink-tinged; wing-quills black, primary and under wing-coverts pinkish; below paler than above fading to whitish, pink-tinged on the belly. L., 45'00; W., 16'25; Tar., 12'50; B., 5'50.
Range.—Breeds locally in the Bahamas, Cuba, Haiti, Yucatan, Galapagos and Guiana; winters mainly in the same region; formerly a regular visitor at the southern tip of the Fla. Peninsula; now of casual occurrence on the Fla. coast. Said by Audubon to have been found on the coast of S. C.
Nest, in colonies on mud-flats, a truncate cone of mud 8–14 inches in height, hollowed on top. *Egg*, 1, whitish with a chalky deposit, 3'55 × 2'20. *Date*, Andros Isl., Bahamas, May 5.

The Flamingo was formerly a regular winter visitant to the vast shoals at the extremity of Florida, but it is now of rare occurrence there. (Scott, *The Auk*, VII, pp. 221–226; Ingraham, World's Congress in Orn., pp. 59–69.) There is no record of its ever having nested in Florida but it still nests on Andros Island, Bahamas. The nests are placed within a few feet of each other, 2,000 being counted in a space 130 yards long. Both sexes incubate. The period of incubation is about four weeks. The young are hatched covered with down and leave the nest when two or three days old. They are fed by regurgitation on the partially digested juices of a small mollusk of the genus *Cerithium*, which forms apparently the only food of the adult. The note of the young is a shrill whistling, that of the adult a gooselike honking. In flight the neck is fully extended.

1902. CHAPMAN, F. M., Bird-Lore, 177–181.—1908. Camps and Cruises, 155–191 (nesting habits).

VI. ORDER ANSERIFORMES. LAMELLIROSTRAL SWIMMERS

SUBORDER ANSERES. DUCKS, GEESE, SWANS, AND ALLIES

FAMILY ANATIDÆ. DUCKS, GEESE AND SWANS.

The about two hundred species of this family are distributed throughout the world, one-fourth occurring in North America. The *Anatidæ* in common with other diving birds whose natatorial powers give them a secondary means of locomotion, lose all their wing-quills simultaneously during the annual postnuptial molt, and at this time cannot fly. With our northern Ducks, in which the male differs from the female (and this includes every species but the Black Duck and its near allies), this period of flightlessness occurs when the bird is in 'eclipse' plumage,

PLATE X

DUCKS AND GEESE

Shoveller.	Canada Geese.
Mallard.	Pintail.
Canvasback.	Scaup Duck.
Ruddy Duck.	Blue-winged Teal.

which, as before remarked (see p. 92 and Pl. V), whatever its origin, certainly makes the bird less conspicuous at a time when it needs concealment. The molts of Ducks, and particularly the significance of the eclipse plumage, are treated at length by J. C. Phillips in his exhaustive monograph of this group ('22), and to this work the student is referred. Ducks are notable for their highly developed courtship evolutions, in which the males woo the females with vigorously executed and surprisingly varied performances.

Most of these birds breed north of the United States; in eastern North America, only five of our forty species nesting south of latitude 41°. We know them, therefore, as migrants and as winter visitants and to those who are so fortunate as to live near their haunts, their goings and comings are among the most important events in the birds' calendar. Strong of wing, hardy of body, many species pass the winter on the open sea, while the river and bay Ducks remain until ice forms, and return the first day of open water. How the eye is held by the sight of their swiftly moving forms silhouetted against the sky! Through them, bird-life makes its strongest appeal to our love of the wild and elemental in nature.

As the ancestors of our domesticated water-fowl and as game, the *Anatidæ* are doubtless better known to man than any other birds. Of late years their numbers have been greatly reduced by excessive shooting, and by the reclamation for the agriculturist of vast areas in which formerly they bred. We have, consequently, only to examine the history of the past few decades to be assured that, unless we conserve both breeding and feeding areas and reduce our annual toll upon their numbers, few Ducks will remain to draw brain-weary toilers to marsh, bay, and headland.

1896. Job, H. K., Ducks of Plymouth Co., Mass., Auk, 197–204.— 1897. Cory, C. B., How to Know the Ducks, Geese and Swans, 8vo., 94 pp., many illus.—1898. Elliot, D. G., Wild-Fowl of United States and British Possessions, 8vo., 316 pp., 63 pls. (Francis Harper).—1901–2. Bent, A. C., Nesting Habits of Anatidæ in N. Dak., Auk, 328–336; 1902, 1–12, 165–174. —1902. Job, H. K., Among the Water-Fowl (Doubleday).—1903. Huntington, D. W., Our Feathered Game, 8vo., 396 pp., 37 pls.—1903. Sanford, L. C., Bishop, L. B., Van Dyke, T. S., The Water-Fowl Family, 12mo. ix+598 pp., 20 pls. (Macmillan).—1906. Cooke, W. W., Dist. and Migr. of N. A. Ducks, Geese, and Swans, Bull. 26, Biol. Surv.—1907. Rich, W. H., Feathered Game of the Northeast, 8vo., 432 pp., 87 pls.— 1909. DeHaven, I. N., Duck Shooting on N. J. Coast, Cassinia, 11–18.— 1910. Grinnell, G. B., American Game Bird Shooting, 8vo., xviii+558 pp. (Forest and Stream).—1910. Huntington, D. W., Our Wild Fowl and Waders, 207 pp. (New York City).—1911. Phillips, J. C., Ten Years' Migration of Anatidæ at Wenham, Mass., Auk, 188–200; see also, 319– 323.—1912. Forbush, E. H., Game Birds, Wild Fowl and Shore Birds of Massachusetts, 8vo., 622 pp., illus.—1920. Brooks, Allan, Notes on Some American Ducks, Auk, 353–367, illus.—1920. Oberholser, H. C., and McAtee, W. L., Food of Wild Ducks in Nebraska, Bull. 794, U. S. Dept. Agric., 77 pp., illus.—1922. Griscom, L., Field Studies of the Anatidæ of the Atlantic Coast, Auk, 517–530; 1923, 69–80.—1922–6. Phillips, J. C., A Natural History of the Ducks of the World, 4to, 4 vols., 1545 pp., illus. (Houghton, Mifflin & Co.).—1926. Nelson, E. W., Migratory Wild

Fowl: Present Conditions, Special Report Biol. Surv.—1930. PHILLIPS, J. C. and LINCOLN, F. C., American Waterfowl, Their Present Situation and the Outlook for the Future, 8vo., 312 pp., illus.

SYNOPSIS OF SUBFAMILIES
(1 family, 12 subfamilies, 7 North American)

Bill, more or less flattened; much wider than high at the tip; its sides with interlocking gutters and ridges.

Tarsus usually longer than middle toe without nail, scales on its front rounded; lores bare. . . . . *Subfamily Cygninæ.* SWANS. P. 179.

Tarsus usually longer than middle toe without nail, scales on its front rounded; lores feathered. . . . . *Subfamily Anserinæ.* GEESE. P. 181.

Tarsus shorter than middle toe without nail, scales on its front transverse, more or less square; hind toe *without* a well-developed lobe; wing usually with an iridescent patch (speculum).
Subfamily Anatinæ. SURFACE-FEEDING DUCKS. P. 185.

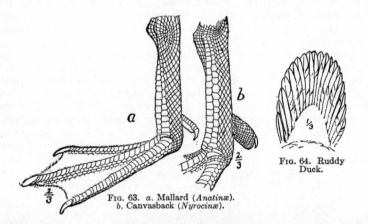

FIG. 63. *a.* Mallard (*Anatinæ*).
b. Canvasback (*Nyrocinæ*).

FIG. 64. Ruddy Duck.

Tarsus shorter than middle toe without nail, scales on its front transverse, more or less square; hind toe *with* a well-developed lobe; wing usually without an iridescent patch (or speculum).

Tail-feathers and upper tail-coverts normal; wing over 6·00.
Subfamily Nyrocinæ. DIVING DUCKS. P. 195.

Tail-feathers stiff and narrow; upper tail-coverts very short; wing under 6·00. . *Subfamily Erismaturinæ.* RUDDY AND MASKED DUCKS. P. 207.

Bill long, narrow and rounded, with tooth-like projections (serrate).
Subfamily Merginæ. MERGANSERS. P. 208.

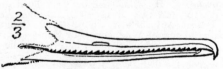

FIG. 65. Merganser.

In a detailed study of the field characters of the Ducks of the Atlantic Coast, Griscom ('22) presents the following Field Key to the Sub-families:

A. Plumage pure white; head and neck ½ total length; wings very long and broad; size very large, length 55 inches . . . . . CYGNINÆ
AA. Plumage never entirely white, neck ⅓ of total length or less; length under 43 inches.
   a. Wing-beats slow; wings very broad; neck ⅓ of total length; size comparatively large . . . . ANSERINÆ.
   b. Wing-beats more rapid; wings not broad; neck not of striking length (except in Pintail); size comparatively small.
     1. Bill, head, neck, and body held in a straight line in flight; bill long, narrow and slender; head, neck, and body very slender. MERGINÆ.
     2. Bill, head, neck, and body not held in a straight line in flight; bill short and comparatively stout; shape not so slender as the last.
       a. Neck long; head narrow; body slender; wings narrow and taper-ing gradually to a point . . . . ANATINÆ.
       b. Neck usually short and always stout; head stout and round; body stout; wings broad and suddenly pointed or else rounded; wing-beats much more rapid than in last.
          NYROCINÆ [including ERISMATURINÆ].

Subfamily Cygninæ. Swans.

A group containing eight species distributed throughout the world. Swans feed from the surface, either by 'tipping' or by simply immersing the long neck and head. Their food consists largely of vegetable matter, but they eat also small mollusks. They migrate in V-shaped flocks. When on the wing, and also when feeding, they utter at times loud, trumpeting notes. When pursued, they do not at once take flight, but swim rapidly away, and in this manner easily distance a strong rower. The sexes are alike in color and both share in the task of incubation and care of the young.

KEY TO THE SPECIES

A. With yellow on the lores; distance from the eye to the nostril greater than the distance from the nostril to the tip of the bill.
                   63. WHISTLING SWAN.
B. No yellow on the lores; distance from the eye to the nostril not greater than from the nostril to the end of the bill . 64. TRUMPETER SWAN.
C. Bill largely orange with a knob at its base . . . . . 61. MUTE SWAN.

61. MUTE SWAN. STHENELIDES OLOR (*Gmelin*). [178.1.] White; base of bill with an overhanging black knob or tubercle; maxilla orange; nail, nostrils, mandible, bare region in front of the eye and feet black. *Im.*—Sooty brownish gray; bill black; tubercle noticeable. L., 58·00; W., 27·00; T., 10·00; B., 4·20.
   Range.—Breeds from n. and s. Europe to Turkestan, Mongolia, Persia, and e. Siberia. Winters s. to n. Africa, the Black Sea, and ne. India. Introduced and naturalized in the British Isles, and in the lower Hudson Valley, N. Y., and L. I., straying casually to the coast of N. J.
   Long Island, uncommon (feral), reported in summer and fall (to Dec. 27). Bronx region, occasional at any season.
   1922. CROSBY, M. S., Mute Swans on the Hudson, Auk, p. 100.

62. The WHOOPER SWAN, *Cygnus cygnus* (Linnæus), [179], of northern Europe is of casual occurrence in Greenland where it formerly bred.

63. WHISTLING SWAN. CYGNUS COLUMBIANUS (*Ord*). [180.] (Fig. 33a.) *Ads.*—White; bill and feet black; *a small yellow spot on the lores;* tail usually with but 20 feathers. *Im.*—Head and neck brownish and rest of plumage more or less washed with grayish; bill and feet light. L., 55·00; W., 22·00; Tar., 4·00; Eye to N., 2·40; N. to tip of B., 2·25.

Remarks.—Few unquestionably distinct species of birds resemble each other more closely, superficially, than do the Whistling and Trumpeter Swans. In freshly killed specimens, at least in the spring, the yellow on the bill of the former and red on the bill of the latter is wholly and sufficiently diagnostic. Lacking these characters, which are always wanting in old, dried skins, the birds can be distinguished by the larger size of *buccinator* in connection with the fact that its nostrils are nearer the center of the bill than in *columbianus* (which has them nearer the tip) while *buccinator* usually has 24, instead of the 20 tail-feathers of *columbianus*.

Range.—Breeds mainly n. of the Arctic Circle from n. Alaska to Baffin Land, s. to the barren grounds of Can., the Alaska Peninsula and St. Lawrence Isl. Winters on Chesapeake Bay and its estuaries, on Currituck Sound and vicinity, N. C., and less numerously elsewhere on the Atlantic Coast, from Mass. to Fla., and formerly, at least, on the coast of La. and Tex.; on the Pacific Coast from s. Alaska to n. L. Calif.; in migration through Pa., N. Y., Ont., Mich., Wisc., Minn., N. Dak. and occasionally Utah. Casual in Bermuda, Commander Isls., and Mex.

Washington, rare W. V., Oct. 15–Apr. 10. Long Island, rare T. V., Oct.–Feb. Bronx region, one record, late Nov. Boston, casual T. V. N. Ohio, occasional T. V., Mch., early Apr. SE. Minn., T. V., Mch. 23–Apr. 17; Oct. 13–Nov 18.

Nest, of grasses, moss, etc., lined with down, on the ground near water *Eggs*, 2–5, soiled whitish, 4·25 × 2·70. *Date*, St. Michael's, Alaska, May 29.

This is a rare bird on the Atlantic Coast north of Virginia. In the Currituck region, it is common in winter. "When feeding, or dressing their plumage, this Swan is usually very noisy, and at night their clamors may be heard to the distance of several miles. Their notes are varied, some resembling the lower ones made by the common tin horn, others running through the various modulations of the notes of the clarionet. These differences are presumed to be dependent upon age." (B., B., and R.)

64. TRUMPETER SWAN. CYGNUS BUCCINATOR *Richardson*. [181.] *Ads.*—White, bill and feet black, no yellow on the lores; cutting edge of the lower mandible, at least in spring, reddish; tail usually with 24 feathers. *Im.*—Head and neck brownish, rest of plumage more or less washed with grayish. L., 65·00; W., 23·00; Tar., 4·25; Eye to N., 2·70; N. to tip of B., 2·20.

Range.—Bred formerly from Alaska (Ft. Yukon), n. Mackenzie, and James Bay s. to B. C., Alberta, w. Mont., Man., Wyo., Nebr., Ia., Mo., and Ind. Wintered formerly from w. cent. B. C. and the cent. Miss. Valley to the Gulf of Mex. and s. Calif. Now so greatly reduced in numbers that only a few are living in captivity and a small number in a wild state in B. C. and the Yellowstone Park region.

Nest, of grasses and down, on the ground. *Eggs*, 2–6, soiled whitish, 4·40 × 2·80. *Date*, Mackenzie Bay, June 17, 1900 (Thayer Coll.).

The Trumpeter Swan is now one of the rarest of American birds. I know of no recent records of its capture in eastern North America.

Heard in captivity, its call has more of a clarion tone than that of the Whistling Swan.

1914. COALE, H. K., Auk, 82-90, illus. (present status).

Subfamily *Anserinæ*. *Geese*.

Excluding the members of the subfamilies *Anseranatinæ* and *Plectropterinæ*, we have left the true Geese, numbering about thirty species. With Geese the sexes are alike in color. The male is the larger and he takes part in incubation and in the care of the young.

Geese are vegetarians. When on the water they feed largely by tipping, as, with head and neck immersed and tail pointing skyward, they search for the roots or seeds of aquatic plants. They are far more terrestrial than Ducks, and visit the land to nip the herbage, young corn, or cereals. When wounded, they dive readily and, with their body just below the surface of the water and only the bill exposed, head for the shore, where they attempt to hide in the vegetation. On migrating, the flock is formed in a V-shaped wedge, the lead, it is said, being taken by an old gander.

KEY TO THE SPECIES

I. Whole head or forehead white.
  A. Bill yellowish.
    a. Forehead and feathers at the base of bill white.
                       69. WHITE-FRONTED GOOSE, ad.
    b. Head and neck white or grayish, sometimes tinged with rusty.
      b^1. Primaries black, rest of plumage white.
          72. LESSER SNOW GOOSE. 72a. GREATER SNOW GOOSE.
      b^2. Back grayish brown, rump and belly whitish, wing-coverts and tertials widely margined with white.
        72. LESSER SNOW GOOSE, im. 72a. GREATER SNOW GOOSE, im.
      b^3. Back grayish brown, rump, belly and wing-coverts gray, the latter not conspicuously margined with white.
                        73. BLUE GOOSE, ad.
  B. Bill black, throat and sides of the head white, lores black.
                       68. BARNACLE GOOSE.
II. Head or forehead not white.
  1. Head and neck brown, bill yellow or yellowish.
    A. Nail of bill black, rump fuscous.. 69. WHITE-FRONTED GOOSE, im.
    B. Nail of bill yellow, rump gray . . . . . . 73. BLUE GOOSE, im.
  2. Head black or brownish black, bill black.
    A. Throat white . . . 65. CANADA GOOSE. 65a. HUTCHINS'S GOOSE.
    B. Throat black or brownish black, neck speckled with white.
      a. Belly white . . . . 66. AMERICAN BRANT.
      b. Belly brownish gray . . . . 67. BLACK BRANT.

65. CANADA GOOSE. BRANTA CANADENSIS CANADENSIS (*Linnæus*). [172.] (Fig. 33c, Pl. X.) *Ads.*—Throat and a large patch on side of head behind eye white or whitish; chin and rest of head and neck black; back and wings grayish brown, more or less edged with lighter; tail and shorter upper tail-coverts black, longer and lateral ones white; breast and belly grayish, fading to white on lower belly; sides like back. *Im.*—Similar, but throat and cheeks sometimes mixed with blackish. "L., 35·00–43·00; W., 15·60–21·00; Tar., 2·45–3·70; B., 1·55–2·70" (Ridgway).

Range.—Breeds from Mack. and n. Que. to Lab., s. to the Gulf of St. Lawrence, n. Utah, w. to cent. B. C., occasionally, at least formerly, to Reelfoot Lake, Tenn., and Walker Lake, Ark. Winters from s. B. C., s. Ont., and N. S., s. to Fla., La., and Tex., Mex., and s. Calif.; w. nearly or quite to the Pacific Coast. Casual in Bermuda and Jamaica.

Washington, W. V. and rather common T. V., Oct. 5–May 14. Long Island, common T. V., uncommon W. V., casual (perhaps feral birds) in summer (Sept. 8), Oct. 1–May 30. Bronx region, fairly common T. V., a few winter; Feb. 27–May 21; Oct. 5–Jan. 2. Boston, common T. V., Mch.–May; Oct.–Dec. N. Ohio, not common T. V., Mch. 1–30. Glen Ellyn, W. V., quite common in spring, Oct. 17–May 5. SE. Minn., T. V., Mch. 6–Apr. 24; Sept. 30–Nov. 18.

Nest, on the ground, often on an island, of twigs, grasses, or reeds and large quantity of down. *Eggs*, 4–10, white. *Date*, Kossuth Co., Ia., May 7, 1883; Grant Co., Minn., Apr. 29, 1876.

Probably the migration of no bird attracts more universal interest than that of the Wild Goose. Ornithologists talk of 'waves' and 'flights' of migrants passing in the night, but the semi-annual pilgrimage of the Canada Goose appeals to us all with the directness of a personal experience. We see the living wedge of long-necked birds passing high overhead; the unbroken sound-waves bring the sonorous 'honks' with unexpected distinctness to our ears; and we receive an impressive lesson in the migration of birds. They are embarked on a journey of several thousand miles, but they come and go as surely as though they carried chart and compass.

1910. PHILLIPS, J. C., Auk, 263–271; 1911, 319–323 (migration in Mass.).—1925. MINER, J., Attracting Wild Geese, 176 pp. (Kingsville, Ont.).

65a. HUTCHINS'S GOOSE. BRANTA CANADENSIS HUTCHINSII (*Richardson*). [172a.] Resembles the preceding in color, but averages smaller. "L., 25·00–34·00; W., 14·75–17·75; Tar., 2·25–3·20; B., 1·20–1·90" (Ridgway).

Range.—Breeds on Melville Peninsula, Southampton and Baffin Isls., and probably in other parts of e. Arctic America. Migrates through Hudson Bay, s. Man., and the Miss. Valley and winters on the Gulf Coast of Mex. Casual on the Atlantic Coast (Md. and N. C.).

Long Island, A. V.

66. AMERICAN BRANT. BRANTA BERNICLA HROTA *Muller*. [173.] *Ads.* —Head, neck, throat and upper breast black; *sides* of the neck speckled with white; back brownish gray, margined with grayish brown; longer and lateral upper tail-coverts white; lower breast ashy gray fading to white on lower belly; sides darker. *Im.*—Similar, but with less white on sides of neck and wing-coverts, and secondaries tipped with white. L., 26·00; W., 13·20; Tar., 2·20; B., 1·35.

Range.—Breeds in Arctic regions of e. N. A., n. to Parry Isls., Axel Heiberg Land, and on both coasts of Greenland and apparently the Spitzbergen archipelago. Winters on the Atlantic Coast of America, from N. J. to N. C., rarely to Mass. and Fla.; also less frequently on the coasts of the British Isles. Less regularly on the Pacific Coast of the U. S. and B. C. Casual in Lab., N. S., Ont., Man., N. Dak., Mich., Wisc , Nebr., La., and Tex., and in Barbados.

Washington, rare W. V. Long Island, common T. V., uncommon W. V. (Sept. 29), Oct. 15–May 30. Bronx region, rather rare T. V., Nov. 4–Jan. 2; Feb. 2–Apr. 17. Boston, uncommon T. V., Oct.–Dec.; Mch.–May.

Nest, of grasses, moss, etc., lined with down, on the ground. *Eggs*, 3–5, smooth and creamy white in color, 2·70 × 1·80 (Saunders). *Date*, Buchanan Bay, Ellesmere Land, June 17 (Thayer Coll.).

"Its manner of flying is different from that of the Canada Goose—moving in more compact bodies, less rapidly, and without seeming to have a chosen leader—that marked characteristic in the flight of the latter.

"While in our bays it appears inactive, seldom taking to wing unless disturbed by a passing boat or the near report of a gun.

"The Brant rises slowly, and when on the wing moves sluggishly for a short distance, and, if not attracted by a distant flock, frequently returns to the place it had left. Its food consists of a marine plant (*Zostera marina*), commonly called 'eel grass.' At low water it is seen industriously at work tearing up its favorite plant. After the tide has risen to such a height as to compel it to relinquish its vocation, it is seen drifting with the current, feeding sumptuously on the fruits of its labor." (Giraud.)

67. BLACK BRANT. BRANTA NIGRICANS (*Lawrence*). [174.] Bears a general resemblance to the preceding species, but may be readily distinguished by its much darker lower breast and upper belly, which are nearly as dark as the back, and by having white markings on the front as well as on the sides of the neck.

Range.—Breeds on Arctic coasts and islands from the Taimyr Peninsula, Siberia; on islands to about 100° W. and on the mainland to Coronation Gulf. Winters mainly on the Pacific Coast from Vancouver to L. Calif., and on the Asiatic Coast to n. China and Japan; casually in the interior; accidental on the Atlantic Coast (Mass., N. Y., and N. J.). Long Island, A. V., 3 records.

Nest, of grasses, moss, etc., lined with down, on the ground. *Eggs*, 5–7, dull ivory-white or grayish white, 2·85 × 1·82 (B., B., and R.). *Date*, Admiralty Bay, Alaska, June 19.

This is the western representative of the preceding species. It is of casual occurrence on the Atlantic Coast.

1910. FAY, S. P., Auk, 336.

68. The BARNACLE GOOSE, *Branta leucopsis* (Bechstein), [175], an Old-World species, casual in Labrador, Baffin Island, James Bay, Quebec, Ontario, Massachusetts, Long Island, North Carolina, and Vermont. It differs from any of the preceding in having the forehead, sides of the head, throat and chin white, the lores being black.

69. WHITE-FRONTED GOOSE. ANSER ALBIFRONS ALBIFRONS (*Scopoli*). [171a.] *Ads.*—Forehead and region bordering base of bill white; upperparts and foreneck grayish brown, more or less margined on back with lighter; longer and lateral upper tail-coverts white; breast somewhat lighter than throat, more or less irregularly marked with black, and fading gradually into pure white on lower belly; sides like back. *Im.*—Similar, but no white at base of bill or black marks on breast; nail of the bill black. "L., 27·00–30·00; W., 14·25–17·50; B., 1·80–2·35; depth of mandible at base, ·90–1·20; width, ·85–1·05; Tar., 2·60–3·20" (Ridgway).

Range.—Breeds in Arctic America from the Yukon Valley e. to Anderson River and Mack., and also on the w. coast of Greenland, Iceland, Lapland, and on the Arctic Coast of Siberia to Bering Strait. Winters in w. U. S. e.

to the Miss. Valley, from s. B. C. and s. Ills., s. to La. and Tex. and to cent. w. Mex. Casual on the Atlantic Coast (Lab., Mass., Va., S. C. and N. C.), and Cuba.

Washington, one record, Mch. Long Island, casual, Oct. and Nov., Mch.–Apr. 5. Boston, casual T. V. N. Ohio, not common T. V. Glen Ellyn, rare T. V., Nov. 5. SE. Minn., rare T. V., Apr. 1–Apr. 30; no fall records.

Nest, on the ground, of grasses lined with down. *Eggs*, 6–7, dull greenish yellow with obscure darker tints, 3·10 × 2·07 (Davie). *Date*, Pt. Barrow, Alaska, June 19.

"These birds are rarely met with on the Atlantic Coast, but are quite common in the Mississippi Valley and abundant on the Pacific slope. They prefer low, wet grounds in the vicinity of timber, or where the prairie is dotted here and there with bushes; and, while they occasionally forage off the wheat-fields and other grains on the bottom-lands, they seldom visit the high, dry prairies, like the Snow and Canada Geese." (Goss.)

70. The BEAN GOOSE, *Anser fabalis* (Latham), [171.1], of northern Europe is accidental in Greenland.

71. The PINK-FOOTED GOOSE, *Anser brachyrhynchus* Baillon, [171.2], of northern Europe is casual in Greenland and accidental in Massachusetts.

72. LESSER SNOW GOOSE. CHEN HYPERBOREA HYPERBOREA (*Pallas*). [169.] *Ads.*—Entire plumage, except primaries with their coverts, white; primaries black, their bases and coverts ashy. *Im.*—"Head, neck and upperparts pale grayish, the feathers of the latter with whitish edges and (especially wing-coverts and tertials) striped medially with darker; rump, upper tail-coverts, tail and lower parts plain white. L., 23·00–28·00; W., 14·50–17·00; B., 1·95–2·30; Tar., 2·80–3·25" (Ridgway).

Range.—Breeds along the Arctic Coast from P. Barrow, Alaska, to Hudson Bay and Baffin Land, and on Arctic isls. to the n. Winters over the w. U. S., especially in Calif., e. to the Miss. Valley and from s. B. C., and s. Ills. s. to the Gulf Coast from Fla. to Tex. and cent. Mex. and rarely on the Atlantic Coast (lower St. Lawrence River, R. I., Va., and N. C.). Casual in the W. I.

Long Island, A. V., two records, Oct. SE. Minn., T. V., Mch. 18–Apr. 18; Oct. 20–Nov. 24.

Eggs, uniform dirty, chalky white, 3·40 × 2·20 (B., B., and R.). *Date*, Pt. Barrow, Alaska, June 18.

1931. SUTTON, G. M., Auk, 335–364 (nesting on Southampton Isl.).

72a. GREATER SNOW GOOSE. CHEN HYPERBOREA ATLANTICA *Kennard.* [169a.] Resembles the preceding in color, but is larger. "L., 30·00–38·00; W., 17·35–17·50; B., 2·55–2·70; Tar., 3·15–3·50" (Ridgway).

Range.—Breeds at McCormick Bay, Greenland, and probably in Ellesmere Land, Grinnell Land, and Grant Land. Winters on the Atlantic Coast of Md., Va., and N. C., from Chesapeake Bay (sometimes Delaware Bay) to Core Sound; n. along the Atlantic Coast in migration.

Long Island, rare T. V. and W. V., Sept. 28–Apr. 17. Bronx region, very rare T. V., Apr. 8, 1882 (several hundred); also Apr. 11, 1926; Mch. 9, 1929. Boston, one spring record. N. Ohio, a Snow Goose is pretty regular T. V.

Nesting date, Admiralty Bay, Alaska, June 17, 1898 (Norris); Mackenzie Bay, June 15 (Thayer Coll.).

This Snow Goose does not appear to be a common bird on any part of the Atlantic Coast. It migrates both by night and day, and when on the wing its white plumage and black-tipped primaries render it easily identifiable. It is a noisier bird than the Canada Goose and its voice is higher and more cackling.

1927. KENNARD, F. H., Proc. N. E. Zoöl. Club, 85–93; see also Auk, 1927, 276–278, 471, 472 (status).

73. BLUE GOOSE. CHEN CÆRULESCENS (*Linnæus*). [169.1.] *Ads.*— Head and upper neck white; middle of hindneck sometimes blackish, lower neck all around fuscous, rest of underparts brownish gray edged with buffy; lower belly generally paler, sometimes white; upper back and scapulars like breast; lower back, rump and upper tail-coverts gray; tail fuscous-gray edged with whitish; wing-coverts like the rump or slightly darker, with little or no whitish margins; wing-quills and tertials fuscous, the latter more or less margined with whitish. *Im.*—"Similar to adult, but head and neck uniform deep grayish brown, only the chin being white. L., 26·50–30·00; W., 15·00–17·00; B., 2·10–2·30; Tar., 3·00–3·30" (Ridgway).

Range.—Breeds in Baffin Land and on Southampton Isl. Winters on the coast of La. from the Miss. to Vermilion Bay and in lesser numbers to Brownsville, Tex., casually to Fla., the Bahamas, and Cuba, also occasionally n. to O., and in Calif. Recorded in migration e. to the Atlantic Coast (Me., Mass., Md., Va., N. C., S. C.).

Long Island, casual T. V., Mch. 21–Apr. 28; Nov. N. Ohio, not common T. V. SE. Minn., rare T. V., Apr. 12; Oct. 16.

Nest, on a slight grassy swell, bulky, of finely plucked and shredded tundra moss, or of grass and a kind of chickweed, lined with a mixture of fine dead grasses and light-colored down. *Eggs*, 1–4, white. *Date*, Baffin Island, June 26, 1929 (Soper '30).

The winter home of the Blue Goose was not discovered until 1910; its summer home remained unknown until 1929. Prior to the first-named date it was considered to be a rare species. It proves to be abundant, an illustration of how little we may see of birds that occur only as migrants and pass rapidly. Why a species which makes a semi-annual journey over the 2,500 miles between Louisiana and Baffin Land should be restricted to so small an area in winter is a mystery.

1930. SOPER, J. D., Can. Field-Nat., 1–11, illus. (discovery of breeding-grounds).—1931. SUTTON, G. M., Auk, 335–364 (nesting on Southampton Isl.).

74. ROSS'S GOOSE, *Chen rossi* (Cassin), of western North America, has been recorded from Louisiana.

75. The FULVOUS TREE-DUCK, *Dendrocygna bicolor helva* Wetmore and Peters [178], subfamily *Dendrocygninæ*, of southwestern United States and southward, is accidental in North Carolina and Missouri.

76. The WHITE-FACED TREE-DUCK, *Dendrocygna viduata* (Linnæus), of South America and Africa, has been recorded from Hackensack, N. J. (Oct., 1912).

Subfamily Anatinæ. Surface-feeding Ducks.

The Ducks of this subfamily are distinguished by lacking a large lobe on the hind toe. They are, for the most part, northern breeding birds, and appear on our waters chiefly as migrants. At this time, they differ but little in habits, and, as a rule, frequent sluggish streams, shallow ponds, arms of bays, and marshes. In comparison with the deep-water *Nyrocinæ*, they might be called 'dabblers' or 'tip-ups,' and any one who has seen them dabbling along the shore, or with upturned tail and head immersed, probing the bottom in shallow water, like a flock of animated tenpins, will recognize the appropriateness of these terms. They dive but little and when under water are said to use both feet and wings. They feed upon mollusks, crustaceans, insects and their larvæ, the seeds and roots of aquatic plants. The 'gutters' on the sides of the bill act as strainers, and, after probing the bottom, the mere act of closing the bill forces out the mud and water taken in with the food. As a rule, they feed more commonly by night than by day. They do not gather in such large flocks as the Sea Ducks, and in our waters are generally found in groups of less than fifty. They spring from the water at a bound, and on whistling wing are soon beyond the fowler's reach.

All our *Anatinæ*, but the Wood Duck, nest on the ground, lining a slight hollow with grasses, leaves, moss or rootlets, and with more or less down from the breast of the incubating bird, which is used to cover the eggs, doubtless for purposes of warmth, as well as concealment, during the absence of the sitter. The nesting-site is usually near water, but may be half a mile or more from the shore, and is sometimes in grass so scanty that the sitting bird may be plainly seen, but as a rule it is in denser vegetation or under bushes.

The generally greenish, cream, or buff eggs, number from six to fourteen or rarely more, and hatch within a surprisingly short time of one another. Incubation is performed by the female alone. She sits close and springs from the nest at one's feet in a most disconcerting manner, to flutter off through the grass or, with halting flight, make for the water, there to alight with much show of anxiety. The young are in the highest degree præcocial, leaving the nest almost as soon as they leave the egg, and under the guidance of their mother, at once taking to water. Few birds show more concern for the safety of their offspring than do Wild Ducks. When danger threatens, the young, evidently acting under direction, scatter and seek cover in every direction, while the female gives a remarkable and courageous exhibition of partial helplessness.

KEY TO THE SPECIES

I. Wing under 8·50.
  a. Lesser wing-coverts gray.
                88. GREEN-WINGED TEAL.   87. EUROPEAN TEAL.
  b. Lesser wing-coverts blue.
    b¹. Cheeks gray, a broad white band on face.
                89. BLUE-WINGED TEAL, ♂ ad.
    b². Cheeks and underparts chestnut-rufous.
                90. CINNAMON TEAL, ♂ ad.
    b³. Cheeks buffy finely streaked with black.
      89. BLUE-WINGED TEAL, ♀.   90. CINNAMON TEAL, ♀.
II. Wing over 8·50.
  A. Belly white or grayish white, not conspicuously streaked or spotted.
    a. Whole head shining dark green . . . . . . 79. MALLARD, ♂ ad.

PLATE XI

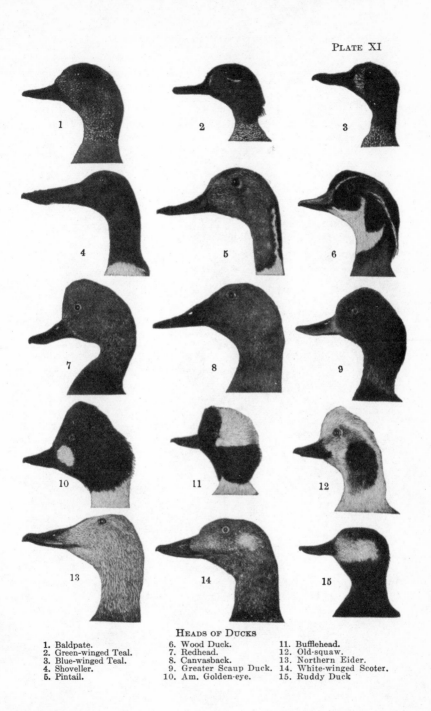

HEADS OF DUCKS

1. Baldpate.
2. Green-winged Teal.
3. Blue-winged Teal.
4. Shoveller.
5. Pintail.
6. Wood Duck.
7. Redhead.
8. Canvasback.
9. Greater Scaup Duck.
10. Am. Golden-eye.
11. Bufflehead.
12. Old-squaw.
13. Northern Eider.
14. White-winged Scoter.
15. Ruddy Duck

b. Center of head white or whitish, a large streak behind the eye.

84. BALDPATE, ♂ ad.

c. Throat white, crown green or grayish green, tips of primaries greenish.

92. WOOD DUCK.

d. Throat blackish, center of crown buffy, rest of head rufous.

83. EUROPEAN WIDGEON, ♂ ad.

e. Throat and sides of head olive-brown, darker on the crown.

85. PINTAIL, ♀ ad.

f. Throat, crown and sides of head more or less finely streaked with blackish.

   *f*¹. Wing-coverts with more or less chestnut . . . . 82. GADWALL.

   *g*¹. No chestnut in wing-coverts.

      *g*². Axillars¹ and sides barred with black . . . 85. PINTAIL, ♀.

      *g*³. Axillars white or speckled with black, sides plain brownish.

84. BALDPATE, ♀.

      *g*⁴. Axillars white, sides thickly spotted or barred with black.

82. GADWALL, ♀.

B. Underparts conspicuously mottled, spotted, or streaked, or feathers margined with chestnut-rufous—or belly chestnut.

  a. With white conspicuous in wing-coverts.

   *a*¹. Lesser wing-coverts ashy blue . . . . 91. SHOVELLER.

   *b*¹. Lesser wing-coverts brownish gray, bordered with white or tipped with black.

      *b*². Speculum² purple . . . . 79. MALLARD, ♀.

      *b*³. Speculum gray and white . . . . . . 82. GADWALL, ♀.

  b. No conspicuous white in wing-coverts.

   *b*¹. Throat fulvous or buffy, without streaks . . 81. FLORIDA DUCK.

   *b*². Throat finely streaked with black . . . 80, 80a. BLACK DUCKS.

77. The SHELD-DUCK, *Tadorna tadorna* (Linnæus), [141.2], of Europe is accidental in Massachusetts (Ipswich Bay, Oct. 15, 1921).

78. The RUDDY SHELDRAKE, *Casarca ferruginea*, [141.1], of Europe and Asia is accidental in Greenland, New Jersey (Barnegat Bay, Nov. 14, 1916) and North Carolina.

79. COMMON MALLARD. ANAS PLATYRHYNCHOS PLATYRHYNCHOS *Linnæus.* [132.] (Figs. 33*b*, 63*a*, Pl. X.) *Ad.* ♂.—Whole head and throat glossy greenish or bluish black; a white ring around the neck; breast rich chestnut; belly grayish white, finely marked with wavy black lines; under tail-coverts black; upper back dark grayish brown; rump and upper tail-coverts black; four middle tail feathers recurved; speculum rich purple, bordered at the *base* and tip by narrow bands of *black and white. Ad.* ♀.— Top and sides of head streaked with fuscous and buffy; back fuscous, the feathers with internal rings or loops and sometimes borders of pale ochraceous buffy; speculum as in the preceding; breast and belly ochraceous buffy, mottled with dusky grayish brown. L., 23·00; W., 11·00; Tar., 1·75; B., 2·25.

Range.—Breeds from the Aleutian and Pribilof Isls., nw. Alaska, and N. B., s. to n. L. Calif., s. Tex., se. Ills., se. Ind., s. O., and n. Va.; breeds also in Iceland, through Europe to n. Africa; Siberia to China, Japan. Winters from Aleutian Isls., cent. Alaska, s. Sask. and N. S. s. to s. Mex., Lesser Antilles and Panama; casual in Bermuda, Hawaii, Cuba, Jamaica, Grenada, and Bahamas.

Washington, common W. V., Aug. 1–May 11. Long Island, uncommon T. V., rare P. R. (a few, probably feral, breed), Feb. 21–May 6; July 31– Dec. 23. Bronx region, fairly common T. V., Feb. 13–May 15; Sept. 1– Jan. 22. Boston, uncommon T. V.; semidomesticated birds are abundant P. R. on protected waters. N. Ohio, tolerably common T. V., Mch. 1– May 15; Oct. 1–Dec. 1. Glen Ellyn, regular but uncommon T. V., occasional

¹See Fig. 81.   ²A colored patch in the wing.

S. R., Mch. 10–Apr. 7; Sept. 13–Nov. 23. SE. Minn., S. R., casual W. R., Mch. 4–Nov. 22; rare W. V.

Nest, on the ground, usually near water and among high grass or reeds. *Eggs*, 6–13, light greenish buff to light grayish buff, with very little luster, 2·27 × 1·61. (Bent.) *Date*, Heron Lake, Minn., May 11.

The loud, resonant *quacking* of the female Mallard and much lower, less clearly enunciated *quack* of the drake are familiar sounds, though the loud notes are usually attributed to the male. When flying, the white under wing-coverts are sometimes conspicuous when the birds are too far away to distinguish the green head of the male. In Minnesota the Mallard is considered the wildest of wild Ducks.

79a. GREENLAND MALLARD. ANAS PLATYRHYNCHOS CONBOSCHAS *Brehm*. [132a.] Resembling *A. p. platyrhynchos* but male with wing-coverts grayer; markings on sides coarser and grayer; margin of breastshield with black markings. W., 11·00–12·00. Female grayer above than *platyrhynchos*, markings grayish brown, rather than reddish brown.

Range.—W. coast of Greenland as far n. as Upernavik and on the e., at least to Angmagsalik. Apparently resident, but may migrate locally.

80. RED-LEGGED BLACK DUCK. ANAS RUBRIPES RUBRIPES *Brewster*. [133 part.] *Ads.*—Top of head fuscous slightly streaked with buffy; sides of head and *throat* pale buffy *thickly* streaked with blackish; rest of underparts fuscous-brown bordered with ochraceous-buff; back slightly darker and narrowly margined with buffy; speculum rich purple tipped with black which is narrowly margined with white; no white in greater wing-coverts; in life, legs and feet bright red, bill yellow or greenish yellow. ♂, W., 11·00; Tar., 1·68; B., 2·5. ♀, W., 10·47; Tar., 1·60; B., 2·05.

Range.—Breeds n. of the range of *A. r. tristis*, in n. Que. (Ungava), n. Man., and n. Ont. Winters s. to Ark., s. Tex., La., and Ala., and from the Great Lakes and N. E. down the Atlantic Coast to n. Fla. Casual in Colo.

Washington, abundant W. V. Long Island, abundant W. V. Bronx region, common W. V. Boston, abundant W. V., Sept.–May. N. Ohio, common T. V., occasional W. V. SE. Minn., uncommon T. V., Mch. 30 - May 23; Sept. 28–Nov. 10.

80a. COMMON BLACK DUCK. ANAS RUBRIPES TRISTIS *Brewster*. [133a.] Similar to *A. r. rubripes* but smaller; in life, legs and toes brownish; bill olivaceous; throat and neck less heavily streaked, the former sometimes unstreaked. ♂, W., 10·50; Tar., 1·65; B., 2·05. ♀, W., 10·15; Tar., 1·60; B., 1·95.

Range.—Breeds in the Atlantic Coast region from Me. to Del. (sparingly to N. C.), and w. to n. Ind., Wisc., and s. Ont. Winters from N. E. to N. C., Ga., and La.

Washington, abundant W. V., Sept. 17–May 3; probably rare S. R. (Cooke). Long Island, common P. R. (not typical). Bronx region, chiefly abundant T. V., a few breed. Boston, common P. R., more common T. V.

Nest, on the ground in grass or brush, often far from water. *Eggs*, 6–12, pale greenish or bluish white, or creamy buff, 2·43 × 1·75. *Date*, Montauk Point, L. I., Apr. 5; Boston, Apr. 19; St. Croix River, Me., Apr. 30.

Though not literally a *black* Duck, this bird appears so much darker in life than the female of its near relative the Mallard, that it is sometimes known as Black Mallard. Its loud, resonant *quack* resembles that of the Mallard. It is more common in the Atlantic Coast States than inland, and when molested will sometimes pass the day at sea, returning at night to feed in the ponds and marshes. It has won a deserved reputation for wariness.

The gullet and gizzard of a Black Duck shot by E. H. Eaton were found by him to contain 23,704 weed seeds. ('Birds of New York.')

Of the two races of the Black Duck as observed in New England, Dr. John C. Phillips writes that *tristis* feeds in both ponds and salt meadows, but if in the latter they resort to fresh water once or twice a day. It is much less nocturnal in feeding habits than *rubripes*, less shy and less inclined to spend the day on the open ocean. It comes readily to decoys and is more loquacious than *rubripes*. Of *rubripes* he writes that it is a late migrant, very seldom resorts to small ponds, but likes open sheets of fresh water near the ocean to which it makes daily trips to drink and rest, but not to feed. It is much more wary and more silent than *tristis* and comes less easily to live decoys.

1893. ALLEN, C. S., Auk, 53–59 (nesting).

81. FLORIDA DUCK. ANAS FULVIGULA FULVIGULA *Ridgway.* [134.]
Ads.—Top of head streaked with black and buffy; sides of head and entire throat buffy, *without streaks;* rest of underparts rich buffy ochraceous, widely streaked with black; back black, the feathers broadly margined and sometimes internally striped with ochraceous-buff; speculum rich purple bordered by black; bill olive-yellow, its nail black. L., 20·00; W., 10·50; Tar., 1·65; B., 2·05.
Remarks.—Easily distinguished from *A. rubripes* by the absence of streaks on the throat.
Range.—S. and cent. Fla. n. at least to Alachua Co. and along the nw. coast.
Eggs, 8–10, pale dull buff or pale grayish buff, 2·15 × 1·61 (Ridgway).
Date, Caloosahatchie River, Fla., Apr. 16.

This southern representative of the Black Duck is permanently resident in Florida, where it has apparently decreased in numbers in recent years. It resembles the Black Duck in voice and feeding habits, but I have never known it to go out to sea.

81a. MOTTLED DUCK. ANAS FULVIGULA MACULOSA *Sennett.*—Closely resembling *A. f. fulvigula* but averaging darker and with the head and neck "coarser and more consistently striped" (Phillips, Auk, 1916, 433).
Range.—Coasts of La. and Tex., less commonly inland, along the Miss. in La. and to cent. Tex. Casual in Colo. and Kans.

82. GADWALL. CHAULELASMUS STREPERUS (*Linnæus*). [135.] *Ad.*
♂.—Top of head streaked with rufous-brown and black; sides of head and neck pale buffy, thickly streaked or spotted with black; breast and neck all around black, each feather with a border and an internal ring of white, giving the plumage a beautifully scaled appearance; belly white or grayish; rump, upper and under tail-coverts black; lesser wing-coverts *chestnut.*
Ad. ♀.—Head and throat as in male; back fuscous margined with buffy; breast and *sides* ochraceous buffy, thickly spotted with blackish; belly and under tail-coverts white, more or less thickly spotted with blackish; little or no chestnut on wing-coverts; speculum ashy gray and white; axillars and under wing-coverts *pure white.* L., 19·50; W., 10·40; Tar., 1·55; B., 1·70.
Range.—Breeds from Little Slave Lake, Lake Athabasca, and Hudson Bay (n. Man.), to interior Wash., and Calif., Utah, sw. Kans., n. Ia. and

cent. Minn.; and formerly in O.; also in the British Isles, and temperate Europe and Asia. Winters from Chesapeake Bay and s. B. C. to s. Fla., Jamaica, s. cent. Mex., and s. L. Calif. Accidental in Bermuda.

Washington, uncommon to rare W. V., Aug. 24–Apr. Long Island, rare T. V., Feb. 21–May 9; Aug. 26–Dec. 13. Bronx region, very rare T. V.; Aug.–Jan. 9. Boston, rare T. V. N. Ohio, not common T. V. Glen Ellyn, one record, Oct. 18, 1927. SE. Minn., common T. V., uncommon S. R., Mch. 18–Oct. 16.

Nest, on the ground, near water, in short prairie grass or concealed beneath rose bushes. *Eggs*, 8–12, pale buff or buffy white, 2·09 × 1·57 (Ridgway.). *Date*, N. Dak., June 7.

The Gadwall is common in the interior but rare on the Atlantic Coast, except in Florida. Its voice is a *quack* higher and with less volume than that of the Mallard. It is a surprising sight to see these birds in courtship flight, when the male pursues the female often high in the air and for some time, on a course as erratic as that of a Barn Swallow.

83. EUROPEAN WIDGEON. MARECA PENELOPE (*Linnæus*). [136.] *Ad.* ♂.—Crown creamy buff; throat blackish, rest of head and neck rufous-brown; upper breast vinaceous, lower breast and belly white; *sides* and back finely marked with wavy black and white lines. *Ad.* ♀.— Head and throat deep ochraceous-buff, finely streaked and barred with black, darker above; upper breast and sides much the same color, but without black markings; lower breast and belly white; back grayish brown, the feathers with small ochraceous buffy bars; tertials fuscous, bordered by deep *ochraceous buffy;* greater wing-coverts *brownish gray,* usually whiter on the outer webs and tipped with black. W., 10·50; B., 1·40.

Remarks.—The females of the European and American Widgeons bear a general resemblance to one another. Their distinguishing characters are mainly in the color of the head and throat, which are browner in the European species, and in the color of the greater wing-coverts, which are whiter in the American bird.

Range.—Breeds in Iceland, Scotland, and outlying isls., e. to Kamchatka. Winters in the British Isles, n. Africa to Japan; also frequent in B. C., Calif., and less so, but apparently regular, in the upper Miss. Valley and on the Atlantic Coast (Gulf of St. Lawrence to Fla.).

Washington, A. V., two records. Long Island, rare W. V., Sept. 12– Apr. 27. Bronx region, several records; Jan. 3–Apr. 16. Boston, rare T. V., sometimes W. V.

Eggs, 5–8, buffy white, 2·23 × 1·53. *Date*, Iceland, June 2.

The European Widgeon is of rare but regular occurrence in eastern North America. "The call-note of the male is a shrill, whistling *whée-yŏŭ*, whence the local names 'Whew Duck' and 'Whewer'; but the female utters a low *purr*-ing growl. Both sexes, however, rise in silence" (Saunders).

84. BALDPATE. MARECA AMERICANA (*Gmelin*). [137.] (Pls. I, XI.) *Ad.* ♂.—Middle of crown white or buffy; sides of crown, from eye to nape, glossy green, more or less sprinkled with black; lores, cheeks and throat buffy, finely barred with black; upper breast and *sides* vinaceous, the latter more or less finely barred with wavy black lines; lower breast and belly white; back grayish brown, more or less tinged with vinaceous and finely barred with black; greater and median wing-coverts largely white, forming a large white patch in the wing; speculum green and black. *Ad.* ♀.—Head and throat white or pale, creamy buff, finely streaked and barred with black, darker above; upper breast and sides pale vinaceous washed with grayish; lower breast and belly white; back grayish brown, the feathers with small creamy buff bars; tertials fuscous, bordered with *whitish* or creamy buff; greater wing-coverts brownish gray, their outer webs mostly or entirely *white*, their ends black, sometimes tipped with white. L., 19˙00; W., 10˙50; Tar., 1˙50; B., 1˙40.

Range.—Breeds from nw. Alaska, n. B. C., and Hudson Bay, s. to n. Ind. and ne. Calif. Winters from Chesapeake Bay (rarely Mass.), the O. Valley, and Vancouver Isl., to Panama, and on the Pacific Coast of Cent. A. Casual or accidental in Bermuda, the W. I., N. B., Aleutian, Commander, and Hawaiian Isls., the Azores, British Isles, France, and Japan.

Washington, common W. R., Sept. 4–Apr. 17. Long Island, tolerably common T. V., occasional W. V., Feb. 16–Apr. 16 (May 11); Aug. 2–Dec. 27. Bronx region, uncommon T. V., Feb. 2–Apr. 21; July 30–Nov. 30. Boston, not uncommon T. V., more uncommon in spring; Mch.–Apr.; Sept.–Nov.; occasional in winter. N. Ohio, common T. V., Mch. 10–Apr. 25. Glen Ellyn, not common, Mch. 4–Apr. 12; Oct. 24. SE. Minn., common T. V., Mch. 17–May 6; Sept. 21–Nov. 26.

Nest, on the ground near water, sometimes exposed, usually concealed in grass, weeds or bushes. *Eggs,* 7–12, buffy white, 2˙05 × 1˙50. *Date,* N. Dak., May 31.

N. S. Goss writes that, as a rule, Widgeons are "not shy, and their note, a sort of *whew, whew, whew,* uttered while feeding and swimming, enables the hunter to locate them in the thickest growth of water-plants; and when in the air the whistling noise made by their wings heralds their approach." They are fond of wild celery, which they procure by robbing the Canvasback and other diving Ducks, "snatching their catch from their bills the moment their heads appear above the water." "The female utters a loud cry like the syllables *kaow, kaow*" (Eaton).

85. AMERICAN PINTAIL. DAFILA ACUTA TZITZIHOA (*Vieillot*). [143.] (Pls. X, XI.) *Ad.* ♂.—Head and throat olive-brown; back of neck blackish, bordered by white stripes, which pass to breast; breast and belly white; the abdomen faintly and sides strongly marked with wavy lines of black and white; back somewhat darker than sides; scapulars black, bordered or streaked with buffy white; wing-coverts brownish gray, greater ones tipped with rufous; speculum green; central tail-feathers glossed with green, and much elongated. *Ad.* ♀.—Throat white or whitish, crown and sides of head streaked with blackish and buffy ochraceous, darker above; breast washed with buffy ochraceous and spotted with blackish; belly white; abdomen more or less indistinctly mottled with blackish; sides with bars and lengthened black and white crescents; under wing-coverts *fuscous, bordered with whitish;* axillars *barred or mottled with black;* back fuscous, the feathers with borders, bars, or crescents of white or buffy; speculum grayish brown bordered with white. *Im.*—The im. ♂ is variously intermediate between the ad. ♂ and ♀; the im. ♀ resembles the ad. ♀, but the underparts are more heavily streaked or spotted. L., ♂, 28˙00, ♀, 22˙00; W., 10˙00; T., ♂, 7˙50, ♀, 3˙60; B., 2˙00.

Remarks.—The female of this species is a rather obscure-looking bird, but may always be known by its broad, sharply pointed central tail-feathers and dusky under wing-coverts.

Range.—Breeds from nw. Alaska, e. to Hudson Bay, s. to cent. Ia., and s. Calif., formerly or rarely to n. Ills., s. Mich. and Wisc. Winters from s. B. C. down the Pacific Coast to Cent. A. and from ne. Colo. and Chesapeake Bay (casually from Nebr., Wisc., and Me.) to the W. I. and Panama, also in the Hawaiian Isls. Casual or accidental in Bermuda, Greenland, and Lab.

Washington, W. V., Sept. 13–June 27. Long Island, common T. V., rare W. V., Feb. 1–May 3 (23); (July 19) Aug. 2–Dec. 24. Bronx region, fairly common T. V., Feb. 22–Apr. 25; Sept. 24–Dec. 30. Boston, uncommon T. V., Mch.; Sept.–Nov.; rare W. V. N. Ohio, common T. V., Mch. 1–Apr. 7; Sept. 20–Dec. 1. Glen Ellyn, irregular T. V., Mch. 19–Apr. 17, Oct. 18. SE. Minn., common T. V., Mch. 1–June 1; July 26–Nov. 20.

Nest, on the ground, often but little concealed, sometimes near to, at others far from water. *Eggs,* 6–12, pale olive-green or olive-buff, 2·20 × 1·50. *Date,* Minor Co., S. Dak., May 7.

"Its note is seldom heard by day, but while coming into the feeding-grounds at night with the Widgeons, Black Ducks and Mallards, the hoarse, muffled quack of the duck and the mellow whistle of the drake are heard mingled with the whistling of the Widgeon and the loud calls of the Black Duck. In the springtime the drake often gives utterance to low, soft notes which seem to flow from deep down in the throat, especially while performing curious courting antics in the presence of the ducks" (Eaton). The Pintail's long, slender neck, and, in the male, the long tail-feathers, are good field-marks.

86. The BAHAMA PINTAIL, *Dafila bahamensis bahamensis* (Linnæus), of the Bahamas and southward has been once recorded from Cape Canaveral, Florida (Mch., 1912).

87. The EUROPEAN TEAL, *Nettion crecca* (Linnæus), [138], is casual or accidental in Greenland, Labrador, Nova Scotia, Maine, Massachusetts, Connecticut, New York, New Jersey, Virginia, North Carolina, and Ohio. The adult male resembles that of *N. carolinense,* but the white bar in front of the wing is lacking, and the inner scapulars are creamy buff, with a sharply defined black mark on their outer webs. The female cannot be distinguished from that of *N. carolinense.*

88. **GREEN-WINGED TEAL.** NETTION CAROLINENSE (*Gmelin*). [139.] (Pls. I, II.) *Ad.* ♂.—Chin black, sides of head from eye to nape shining green, rest of head and neck rufous-chestnut; breast washed with vinaceous and spotted with black; belly white; sides finely marked with wavy black and white lines; middle under tail-coverts black, lateral ones creamy buff; upper back like sides, lower back grayish fuscous; a *white bar* in front of the bend of the wing; wing-coverts brownish gray, tipped with ochraceous buffy; speculum green and black tipped with white. *Ad.* ♀.—Top of head brownish fuscous, margined with cinnamon; throat and sides of neck white, finely spotted with black; breast and sides washed with cinnamon and spotted or barred with black; belly and under tail-coverts white, sometimes spotted with black; back fuscous, the feathers with crescent-shaped marks of ochraceous buffy, and bordered with grayish; wings as in the male. L., 14·50; W., 7·00; Tar., 1·10; B., 1·35.

Range.—Breeds from n. Alaska and James Bay, s. to cent. Calif., s. Minn., n. Mich., s. Ont., w. N. Y., Gulf of St. Lawrence and Que., formerly to Wisc., Ia., and Ills. Winters from s. B. C., n. Nebr. and Chesapeake Bay to the Bahamas, W. I., British Honduras, and s. Mex.; occasionally to Sitka, the Great Lakes, N. Y., Mass., and N. S. Casual in Bermuda, Greenland, Great Britain, the Hawaiian Isls., and Japan.

Washington, common W. V., Sept.–Apr. Long Island, uncommon T. V., casual W. V., Mch. 8–May 3; Sept. 4–Dec. 25. Bronx region, uncommon T. V., Mch. 20–Apr. 29; Sept. 15–Dec. 12 (21). Boston, uncommon T. V., Mch.–Apr.; Sept.–Nov.; rare W. V. N. Ohio, not common T. V. Glen

Ellyn, quite regular T. V., Mch. 10–Apr. 14; Sept. 22–Oct. 18. SE. Minn., common T. V., rare S. R.; Mch. 11–Nov. 16.

Nest, on the ground near water. *Eggs*, 6–18, buffy white or creamy buff, 1·80 × 1·25. *Date*, N. Dak., May 20.

"The Green-wing is a noisier bird than the Blue-winged Teal, the male uttering a short, mellow whistle and the duck a quack after the fashion of a Black Duck, but small, high-pitched and often repeated" (Eaton).

89. BLUE-WINGED TEAL. Querquedula discors (*Linnæus*). [140.] (Pls. X, XI.) *Ad.* ♂.—Crown fuscous, chin and sides of base of bill black; a broad white band across front of head, its hinder margin bordered by black; rest of head and throat dark ashy with purplish reflections; breast and belly cinnamon-rufous, thickly spotted with black; back fuscous, the feathers with crescents of ochraceous-buff; *lesser and median wing-coverts grayish blue*, end half of greater ones white; speculum green. *Ad.* ♀.—Crown fuscous, lightly margined with grayish; sides of the head and the neck whitish, finely spotted with blackish, except on the throat; breast and belly with less cinnamon wash than in the preceding; back and wings quite similar to the preceding, but ochraceous bars sometimes wanting, speculum darker and greater coverts with less white. L., 16·00; W., 7·25; Tar., 1·20; B., 1·60.

Range.—Breeds from cent. B. C., Great Slave Lake, cent. Man., N. B., s. to w. N. Y. (rarely L. I. and e. Pa.), O., cent. Kans., and n. Nev. (has bred in Fla., La., Tex., and Okla.). Winters from S. C., La., Tex., and Mex. (casually Chesapeake Bay and the O. Valley) and s. Calif. to Brazil and cent. Chile. Accidental in Bermuda, the British Isles, and Denmark.

Washington, uncommon W. V., Aug. 18–June 2. Long Island, uncommon in spring; common in fall, casual S. R. (Mch. 9); Mch. 24–May 30; July 24– Nov. 24 (Dec. 13). Bronx region, rather rare T. V., Mch. 18–Apr. 26 (May 6); Aug. 29–Nov. 14. Boston, T. V., uncommon in spring, rather common in fall; Apr.–May; Aug.–Nov. N. Ohio, not common T. V., Apr. 20–May 4; less common S. R. Glen Ellyn, regular not common S. R., Apr. 2–Oct. 24. SE. Minn., common S. R., Mch. 18–Oct. 26.

Nest, on ground, well concealed in grass, near water. *Eggs*, 6–12, buffy white or creamy buff, 1·85 × 1·30. *Date*, SE. Minn., May 10.

The Blue-winged Teal is one of the swiftest of our Ducks. The white face-mark of the male can be discerned at some distance, and, in connection with the bird's small size, is a good field-mark. "The Blue-wing's note is a whistling '*peep*' repeated five or six times, but is seldom heard. The duck quacks less plainly and in a hoarser voice than the Green-wing" (Eaton).

90. CINNAMON TEAL. Querquedula cyanoptera (*Vieillot*). [141.] *Ad.* ♂.—Head, neck, and underparts cinnamon-rufous, crown and often middle of belly blackish; upperparts fuscous margined brownish; wings as in *discors*. *Ad.* ♀.—Resembles female of *discors* but generally darker and more heavily marked below with streaks encroaching more on throat; bill larger. W., 7·40; B., 1·70.

Range.—Breeds from s. B. C. and w. Sask., to cent. w. Tex., n. Mex., and n. L. Calif., and from the cent. valleys of Calif., cent. Ore. and nw. Wash., e. to w. Mont., e. Wyo. and sw. Kans.; also in S. A. from Buenos Aires and the Andes of Peru, to the Falkland Isls., and Straits of Magellan. Winters from cent. Calif. (sparingly), s. Ariz. and cent. N. Mex. to s. Mex. Casual in Alberta, Wisc., O., N. Y., S. C., Fla. and La.

91. SHOVELLER. SPATULA CLYPEATA (*Linnæus*). [142.] (Pls. X, XI.)
Ad. ♂.—Head and neck fuscous, glossed with bluish green; back and a broken line down back of lower neck fuscous; rest of lower neck and breast white; lower breast and belly rufous-chestnut; upper and under tail-coverts dark greenish; lesser wing-coverts grayish blue, greater ones brownish gray tipped with white; speculum green. *Ad.* ♀.—Throat buffy white; head and neck streaked with buffy and black; rest of underparts more or less washed with buffy ochraceous, everywhere indistinctly spotted with fuscous except on middle of belly; back fuscous, the feathers with margins and internal crescents of whitish and buffy; wing-coverts and speculum much as in ♂. *Im.*—The im. ♂ is intermediate between the ad. ♂ and ♀; the im. ♀ resembles the ad. ♀, but the wing-coverts are slaty gray, the speculum with little or no green. L., 20·00; W., 9·50; B., 2·50; greatest width of B., 1·20.

Range.—Breeds from the Bering Sea coast of Alaska irregularly e. to the valley of the Sask., s. to w. Ia. and s. Calif., formerly or occasionally to w. N. Y., Ind., Ills., and Tex.; also from the Arctic Circle to s. Europe and cent. Asia, and from Great Britain to Kamchatka and the Commander Isls. Winters from s. B. C., and Atlantic Coast from S. C., s. to the W. I., Pacific Coast of Mex. and Cent. A., Col., and the Hawaiian Isls.; rarely n. to Minn., Ills., N. J., and Va.; casual along the Atlantic Coast to Me. and Lab. Accidental in Bermuda.

Washington, uncommon W V., Sept.–Apr. Long Island, rare T. V., Feb. 12–Mch. 30; Sept. 15–Nov. 29. Bronx region, rare T. V., Mch. 6–Apr. 25; several fall records at Ossining. Boston, rare T. V. N. Ohio, common T. V., Mch. 12–Apr. 6; Sept. 20–Nov. 1. Glen Ellyn, not common T. V., Mch. 26–Apr. 12; Oct. 11–Nov. 8. SE. Minn., common T. V., uncommon S. R., Mch. 18–Nov. 9.

Nest, on the ground, well concealed in grass, sometimes near to, sometimes far from water. *Eggs*, 6–11, pale olive-buff or pale greenish gray similar to a Mallard's or Pintail's but smaller, 2·03 × 1·42 (Bent). *Date*, Heron Lake, Minn., May 9.

The Shoveller is generally a silent bird, but its note in the breeding season is said to be *took, took*. It feeds largely by *tipping* in shallow water.

1922. McATEE, W. L., Auk, 380–386 (food-habits).

92. WOOD DUCK. AIX SPONSA (*Linnæus*). [144.] (Pls. V, XI.) *Ad.* ♂.—A line from bill over eye, a similar line at base of side of crest, and some of elongated crest-feathers white; throat, a band from it up side of head, and a wider one to nape, white; rest of cheeks and crown green with purplish reflections; a white band in front of wings; breast and a spot at either side of the base of the tail purplish chestnut, the former spotted with white; belly white; sides buffy ochraceous, finely barred with black, longer flank-feathers tipped with wider bars of black and white; back greenish brown; scapulars blacker; speculum steel-blue; primaries tipped with greenish blue. *Ad.* ♀.—Throat and a stripe from the eye backward white; crown purplish brown; sides of the head ashy brown; breast and sides grayish brown streaked with buffy; belly white; back olive-brown glossed with greenish; inner primaries tipped with greenish blue. *Im.*—The im. ♂ resembles the ♀. L., 18·50; W., 9·00; Tar., 1·35; B., 1·30.

Range.—Breeds locally in almost every one of the U. S., and s. Can. Provinces, from s. B. C., nw. Mont., s. Man., se. Ont.; rarely n. to Great Slave Lake. Winters from s. B. C., cent. Mo., s. Ills., and s. Va., to Jamaica and cent. Mex., rarely n. to Mich. and Mass. Casual in Bermuda.

Washington, uncommon P. R. Long Island, uncommon T. V., local S. R., Mch. 17–Dec. 21 (Jan. 1). Bronx region, common T. V., decreasing as S. R., Feb. 13–Dec. 23; Jan. 4; 28. Boston, uncommon T. V., perhaps rare S. R., Mch.–Nov.; rare W. V. N. Ohio, rare S. R., Mch. 20–Oct. 15.

Glen Ellyn, rather rare, T. V., possibly S. R., May; Aug. 3–Oct. 24. SE. Minn., uncommon S. R., Mch. 17–Oct. 30.

Nest, of grasses, leaves, twigs, down, etc., in a hole in a tree or stump, which the downy young leave unaided. *Eggs*, 8–14, pale buffy white, 2·05 × 1·50. *Date*, Chester Co., S. C., Mch. 10; Black Hawk Co., Ia., May 4.

Woodland ponds and forest-bordered streams make a proper setting for the grace and beauty of these richly attired birds. I know of no sight in the bird-world which more fully satisfies the eye than to see them in the unconscious enjoyment of their secluded homes. Alarm them, and with a frightened, plaintive whistle, *oo-eek*, they spring from the water and make off through the woods. At other times they will swim ahead of one's canoe, and, rounding a bend in the stream, go ashore and walk rapidly away.

1924. Dixon, J., Condor, 41–66, illus. (nesting).

Subfamily Nyrocinæ. Diving Ducks.

The members of this subfamily are to be distinguished from those of the preceding by the presence of a large lobe on the hind toe. They are open-water Ducks, frequenting our large lakes, bays and seacoasts. Their food consists chiefly of mollusks, crustaceans, and the seeds and roots of aquatic plants. They obtain it principally by diving, sometimes descending one hundred and fifty feet or more. According to Townsend ('Labrador Spring,' p. 92), the Old Squaw, Scoters, and Eiders use their wings when diving, while the Redhead, Canvasback, Bufflehead, Scaups and Golden-eyes use only their feet. The bill, as in the *Anatinæ*, acts as a sieve or strainer. As a rule they feed by day and pass the night at a distance from the shore or at sea. Some of the species occur in our waters in large flocks—indeed, our most abundant Ducks are members of this subfamily. With one exception, they are northern breeding birds, seldom nesting south of our northern tier of states. Their nests are composed of leaves, grasses, stems of aquatic plants, seaweed, etc., lined with down from the breast of the incubating bird, and are variously located.

KEY TO THE SPECIES

I. Feathers at the base of the bill not reaching ·50 forward along its sides.
  1. Wing over 7·00.
    A. Axillars and most, if not all, the linings of the wings white.
      a. Head and neck black, with greenish or purplish reflections.
        a¹. Back black; bill with a bluish band near its tip.
            94. RING-NECKED DUCK, ♂.
       b¹. Back finely barred with black and white.
        b². Back of head generally with purplish reflections; wing generally under 8·25; nail of bill generally under ·25 in width.
            97. LESSER SCAUP DUCK, ♂.
        b³. Back of head generally with greenish reflections; wing generally over 8·25; nail of bill over ·25 in width.
            96. GREATER SCAUP DUCK, ♂.

  b. Head and neck not black.

    b^1. Head and neck rufous or rufous-brown, sharply defined from the black breast.

      b^2. Head and upper neck rich rufous; bill 2·00 or under; flanks finely barred, like the back . . . . . . 93. REDHEAD, ♂.

      b^3. Head and neck rufous-brown; crown blackish; bill over 2·00; flanks very slightly if at all barred. 95. CANVASBACK, ♂.

    c^1. Head and neck brownish or grayish.

      c^2. A white patch in the wing.

        c^3. Feathers at base of bill white; wing generally under 8·25; nail of bill generally under ·25 in width.
                  97. LESSER SCAUP DUCK, ♀.

        c^4. Feathers at base of bill white; wing generally over 8·25; nail of bill generally over ·25 in width.
                96. GREATER SCAUP DUCK, ♀.

      d^2. No white in wing.

        d^3. An indistinct bluish band near the tip of bill; bill under 2·00.

          d^4. Wing under 8·00 . . . . 94. RING-NECKED DUCK, ♀.

          d^5. Wing over 8·00 . . . . 93. REDHEAD, ♀.

        e^3. No band on bill; bill over 2·00 . . 95. CANVASBACK, ♀.

B. Axillars and most, if not all, the under wing-coverts blackish.

  a. Head and throat dark steel-blue or steel-green.

    a^1. Head and throat steel-blue; white patch at base of bill 1·00 or more in height . . . . 100. BARROW'S GOLDEN-EYE, ♂.

    a^2. Head and throat steel-green; white patch at base of bill less than 1·00 in height . . . 99. AMERICAN GOLDEN-EYE, ♂.

  b. Head and throat not steel-blue.

    b^1. Whole head and throat brown, sharply defined from the gray or white neck; a white patch (speculum) in the wing.

    b^2. Nostril nearer the tip than the base of the bill.
                99. AMERICAN GOLDEN-EYE, ♀.

    b^3. Nostril in the middle of the bill.
                100. BARROW'S GOLDEN-EYE, ♀.

    c^1. Head and throat not brown but with more or less black.

      c^2. Whole head and neck black.

        c^3. Plumage black . . . . . . 108. AMERICAN SCOTER, ♂.

      d^2. Whole head and neck not black.

        d^3. Crown-patch or cheeks white.

          d^4. A white patch on the top of the head and another on the nape . . . . 111. SURF SCOTER, ♂.

          d^5. Middle of crown black, bordered by chestnut; front half of face white . . . 103. HARLEQUIN DUCK, ♂.

        e^3. Head and neck whitish, grayish, or brownish, no white in wing.

          e^4. Bill over 1·25.

            e^5. Feathers on culmen reaching much farther forward than those at sides of the bill. 111. SURF SCOTER, ♀.

            e^6. Feathers on culmen reaching little if any beyond those at sides of bill . . 108. AMERICAN SCOTER, ♀.

          f^4. Bill under 1·25.

            f^5. Central tail-feathers longest, sharply pointed, under tail-coverts white . . . . . 102. OLD SQUAW.

            f^6. Central tail-feathers not sharply pointed; under tail-coverts grayish brown . . 103. HARLEQUIN DUCK.

  2. Wing under 7·00 . . . . 101. BUFFLEHEAD.

II. Feathers at sides or top of bill extending forward generally as far as nostril.

  A. Feathers on sides of bill not reaching nostril.

    a. Nostril narrow, elongate; feathers on culmen extending forward in a narrow line, a V-shaped mark on throat. 107. KING EIDER, ♂.

   b. Nostril large, rounded; feathers on culmen not extending forward
in a narrow line . . . . . .   110. WHITE-WINGED SCOTER.
  B. Feathers on sides of bill extending as far as nostril.
    a. Bare base of bill on top narrow, ending posteriorly in a sharp
point . . . . 106. NORTHERN EIDER.
    b. Bare base of bill on top broad, the posterior end rounded.
                  106*a.* AMERICAN EIDER.

   93. REDHEAD. NYROCA AMERICANA (*Eyton*). [146.] (Pls. I, XI.) *Ad.*
♂.—Head and throat bright rufous; lower neck, breast, back of neck and
upper back black; rest of back and scapulars finely barred with wavy black
and white lines of *equal width;* wing-coverts brownish gray; upper tail-
coverts black; belly white, lower belly more or less finely barred with black;
under tail-coverts black; sides *like back. Ad.* ♀.—Upperparts dark grayish
brown, darker on rump, the feathers more or less margined with buffy or
ashy; sides of head lighter; upper throat white; neck buffy ochraceous;
breast and sides grayish brown, more or less washed or margined with buffy
or buffy ochraceous; belly white; lower belly and under tail-coverts tinged
with ochraceous; an indistinct bluish gray band across end of bill. L.,
19·00; W., 8·90; Tar., 1·55; B., 1·85.
   Remarks.—This species is frequently confused with the Canvasback,
from which it may be distinguished by the characters given under that
species. The female Redhead suggests the female Ringneck in coloration,
but the latter is browner, and they can also be distinguished with certainty
by the difference in their size.
   Range.—Breeds from s. B. C. and s. cent. Man. to se. Mich., s. Wisc.,
s. Minn., cent. Nebr., s. Colo., and s. Calif. Winters from s. B. C. to the coast
of Mex. and from ne. Colo. and Chesapeake Bay to the W. I. and w. Mex.,
rarely n. to Lake Erie and s. N. E.
   Washington, uncommon W. V., Oct. 5–Apr. 21. Long Island, irregular
T. V., uncommon W. V., Sept. 24–Apr. 15. Bronx region, rather rare T. V.
and W. V., Oct. 12–Jan. 18; Feb. 2–Apr. 4. Boston, uncommon T. V.,
especially spring, Mch.; Oct.–Dec.; rare W. V. N. Ohio, tolerably common
T. V., Mch. 1–Apr. 25. SE. Minn., uncommon T. V., Mch. 18–May 5;
Oct. 14–Nov. 10.
   Nest, of reeds, with more or less white down, in reeds, usually over
water. *Eggs,* 6–18; light olive-buff to light cream-buff, 2·40 × 1·70. *Date,*
Dodge Co., Wisc., May 22, 1888; Heron Lake, Minn., May 19, 1887.

   The Ducks of the genus *Nyroca* possess to some extent the habits
of both the River Ducks and true Sea Ducks. They are divers in deep
water, but along the shores or in shallow water they are also 'dabblers.'
On the Atlantic Coast the Redhead is a Bay Duck, and feeds in salt
and brackish water; but in the West it inhabits prairie sloughs and
lakes. When feeding on wild celery its flesh is equal to that of the Canvasback, indeed, by the discriminating it is considered slightly superior,
being as much finer as the bird is smaller than its more famous cousin.

   94. RING-NECKED DUCK. NYROCA COLLARIS (*Donovan*). [150.] *Ad.*
♂.—Chin *white;* head, neck, breast and upper back black, head with bluish
reflections, neck with a not sharply defined *chestnut collar;* back and scapulars *black,* speculum *gray;* upper and under tail-coverts black, belly white,
lower belly and sides finely barred with wavy black lines; bill black, base and
a band across end *bluish gray. Ad.* ♀.—Upperparts fuscous-brown, more or
less margined with ochraceous; speculum *gray;* sides of head and neck mixed
grayish brown and white; breast, sides and lower belly grayish brown, more
or less margined with ochraceous; upper belly white or whitish; bill blackish,
an indistinct band of bluish gray across its end. L., 16·50; W., 7·50; Tar.,
1·25; B., 1·80.

Remarks.—The male Ringneck may be known from any of its allies by its chestnut collar and other excellent characters; the female resembles the female Redhead, but is smaller and generally browner.

Range.—Breeds from cent. B. C. and w. Ont., s. to s. Wisc., n. Ia., n. Nebr., n. Utah, and cent. Ariz.; formerly, at least, to n. Ills. Winters from s. B. C. down the Pacific Coast to Mex. and from n. Ark., the O. Valley and Chesapeake Bay to the Bahamas, Mex., and Guat.; rarely in Porto Rico and Cuba, and n. to Mass. Casual in Bermuda and N. S.

Washington, not rare W. V., Oct. 6–Apr. 13. Long Island, rare, irregular T. V. or W. V., Oct. 4–Mch. 19. Bronx region, rare but rather regular T. V., Oct. 22–Jan. 11; Jan. 31–Feb. 11–May 15. Boston, rare T. V. and W. V. N. Ohio, not common T. V., Mch. 20–Apr. 15. Glen Ellyn, fairly common T. V., Mch. 16–May 24; Oct. 12–Nov. 29. SE. Minn., common T. V., uncommon S. R., Mch. 3–Nov. 30.

Nest, on the ground, near grassy sloughs or marshy lakesides. *Eggs,* 6–12, similar in color to those of the Scaups, 2·28 × 1·63. *Date,* SE. Minn., May 27.

This is more of a fresh-water bird than the Scaups, frequenting lakes and marshes rather than open bays. It is not common on the Atlantic Coast north of Maryland but winters commonly in Florida and westward along the Gulf.

95. CANVASBACK. NYROCA VALISINERIA (*Wilson*). [147.] (Fig. 63*b;* Pls. I, X, XI.) *Ad.* ♂.—Head and neck rufous-brown, chin and crown generally *blackish;* breast and upper back black; rest of back and generally *wing-coverts* finely barred with wavy lines of black and white, *white* lines wider; belly white; lower belly more or less finely barred with black; upper and under tail-coverts black; sides *white, much more lightly* barred with wavy black lines than back, or even entirely without bars. *Ad.* ♀.—Head, neck, upper breast, and upper back cinnamon, throat lighter, and, with front parts of head, more or less washed with rufous; back grayish brown, feathers more or less barred with *wavy white lines;* belly white or grayish white; sides the same or grayish brown, generally marked like back. L., 21·00; W., 9·00; Tar., 1·60; B., 2·40.

Remarks.—This species is sometimes mistaken for the Redhead, to which it bears a general resemblance. The males of the two species may be distinguished (1) by the color of the head and neck, which is rufous in the Redhead and rufous-brown in the Canvasback; (2) by the generally blackish chin and crown of the Canvasback, these parts in the Redhead being colored like the rest of the head; (3) by the difference in the markings of the back, wing-coverts, and sides; and (4) by the difference in the size and shape of the bill, as shown by the accompanying measurements. The females of the two species may be at once distinguished by the color of the back, which in the Canvasback is finely barred with wavy white lines, markings which do not appear on the back of the female Redhead.

Range.—Breeds from Ft. Yukon to cent. Man., cent. w. Nebr., n. N. Mex., n. Utah, and w. Nev., occasionally e. to s. Minn., and s. Wisc. Winters from s. B. C., along the Pacific Coast to Mex. and from nw. Mont. and Chesapeake Bay, s. to Fla., coast of La., Tex., cent. Mex., and rarely Guat. Casual in Bermuda, N. B., and N. S.

Washington, common W. V., Oct. 15–Mch. 25, rarely to June and July. Long Island, irregular T. V. in varying numbers, occasionally winters, Feb. 11–Apr. 16 (May 1), (Aug. 2) Sept. 24–Jan 1. Bronx region, fairly common (occasionally abundant) T. V., Oct. 23–Apr. 11. Boston, uncommon T. V., Oct.–Dec.; Mch.; rare W. V. N. Ohio, tolerably common T. V., Mch. 20–Apr. 10, Oct. 1–Nov. 25. SE. Minn., uncommon T. V., Mch. 18–June 2; Oct. 21–Nov. 2.

Nest, of reeds, lined with gray down, in reeds, or tules over water. *Eggs,*

6–10, (often with eggs of the Ruddy Duck or Redhead added) "rich grayish olive or greenish drab of a darker shade than is usually seen in the eggs of other species" of Ducks, 2·48 × 1·75 (Bent). *Date*, Heron Lake, Minn., May 9, 1886, adv.

While the fame of the Canvasback has no doubt been unduly sung by the epicure, there can be no question that from the sportsman's viewpoint it is king among the Ducks.

In October, 1910, ten thousand Canvasbacks were estimated to be on Heron Lake, Minnesota. They were feeding on the wild celery which nearly covers the bottom of this shallow body of water, and, as a rule, kept near the center of the lake (where shooting is prohibited) massed in one great body. On still mornings, the shining white backs of the males could be clearly seen, while at a distance of half a mile, one could hear distinctly a dabbling sound as they ate the celery brought to the surface.

"The female Canvasback can quack almost as well as a Black Duck, and also gives voice to a screaming *curr-row* when startled. The males, when together, frequently utter a peeping or growling note" (Eaton).

96. GREATER SCAUP DUCK. NYROCA MARILA (*Linnæus*). [148.] *Ad.* ♂.—Head, neck, breast and upper back black, top and sides of head with generally *greenish* reflections; back and scapulars with wavy black and white bars; speculum white; upper and under tail-coverts black; belly white; lower belly strongly and sides *faintly* marked with wavy black bars. *Ad.* ♀.— Region around base of bill *white;* head, neck, breast and upper back umber, margined with ochraceous on breast; back and scapulars fuscous-brown; sides dark grayish brown, both generally marked with fine, wavy bars of white; *speculum* and belly *white*. ♂ L., 18·50; W., 8·75; Tar., 1·40; B., 1·65; greatest width of B., 1·00. ♀ L., 17·50; W., 8·25; Tar. 1·36; B., 1·65; greatest width of B., 1·00.

Range.—Breeds from the Aleutian Isls. and the Arctic Coast of Alaska to w. Ungava, cent. Man., cent. Sask., and cent. Alberta, occasional or formerly to the Gulf of St. Lawrence, se. Mich., Minn., and N. Dak., and n. Ia. Winters on the Pacific Coast from the Aleutian Isls. to L. Calif., and on the Atlantic Coast from s. N. E. to N. C., also on the Gulf Coast of Fla., La., and Tex.; occasionally n. to Me. and the Great Lakes and from Colo. to Nev., N. Mex. and Ariz. Casual in Greenland, e. Lab. and N. F.

Washington, common W. V., Sept. 26–May 27. Long Island, abundant T. V., common W. V., rare in summer, Sept. 12–May 19. Bronx region, abundant T. V. and W. V., Oct. 4–Apr. 24 (May 30). Boston, abundant W. V., Sept.–May. N. Ohio, common T. V., Mch. 10–May 1; Oct. 1–Dec. 10, breeds occasionally. Glen Ellyn, April records only.

Nest, on the ground, near grassy sloughs or marshy lake sides. *Eggs,* 6–10, olive-buff, 2·54 × 1·71. *Date*, Bering Isls., June 6.

This is one of our most common Bay Ducks. While with us it seems to prefer salt and brackish water. It feeds largely on mollusks, which it obtains by diving. "Ducks of this species utter a soft, purring whistle when excited or calling to their mates, and rarely the discordant note described by Seebohm as resembling the word *scaup*, screamed out in an exceptionally harsh voice. On two or three occasions I have heard a flock of Scaups give utterance to these notes, and the effect was the loudest and most discordant chorus of bird-notes to which I ever listened, coming as it did from scores of voices over silent water" (Eaton).

97. LESSER SCAUP DUCK. NYROCA AFFINIS (*Eyton*). [149.] *Ad.* ♂.— Similar to preceding species but smaller, head, as a rule, glossed with purplish instead of greenish, and flanks strongly instead of faintly marked with wavy black bars. *Ad.* ♀.—Similar to ♀ of the preceding species, but smaller. ♂ L., 16·50; W., 8·00; Tar., 1·35; B., 1·60; greatest width of B., ·95. ♀ L., 16·50; W., 7·60; Tar., 1·30; B., 1·55; greatest width of B., ·90.

Remarks.—The Scaup Ducks resemble each other so closely that it is sometimes impossible to tell them apart, but they may generally be distinguished by the characters given above.

Range.—Breeds from s. Alaska, the Mack. and Anderson River regions, w. coast of Hudson Bay and se. Ont. to s. B. C., formerly bred or recorded in summer in Mich., n. O., s. Wisc., and se. Colo. Winters from s. B. C. s. along the Pacific Coast of Mex. and both coasts of Cent. A. to Panama, and from ne. Colo., ne. Ark., s. Ills., N. J., and Chesapeake Bay to the Bahamas and Lesser Antilles, and occasionally n. to Mass. Casual in Bermuda, N. F., N. S., and Greenland.

Washington, common W. R., Sept. 25–May 30. Long Island, common T. V., uncommon W. V., Oct. 1–May 20; rarely to June and July. Bronx region, fairly common T. V., Mch. 18 (July 14); Aug. 31–Jan 11. Boston, T. V., common fall, rare spring, Mch.–Apr.; Oct.–Nov., rare W. V. N. Ohio, common T. V., Mch. 15–May 10; Oct. 1–Dec. 1; less common S. R. Glen Ellyn, regular T. V., Mch. 10–May 30; Sept. 5–Nov. 4. SE. Minn., common T. V., Mch. 9–May 30; Oct. 12–Nov. 26.

Nest, on the ground near grassy sloughs and marshy lake sides. *Eggs,* 6–15, "rich olive-buff," 2·25 × 1·58. *Date,* N. Dak., May 31.

This species has much the same habits as the preceding, but is more southern in its distribution during the winter. It is by far the most abundant Duck in Florida waters at that season, where it occurs in large flocks in the rivers and bays along the coasts. When protected it soon becomes as tame as a domesticated Duck, frequenting the vicinity of piers and water-fronts. But beyond the limits of protection it exhibits its normal shyness. I have heard it utter a soft, purring note.

98. The RUFOUS-CRESTED DUCK, *Netta rufina* (Pallas), [145], is an Old-World species which has been taken once in America. The record is based on an immature male found in Fulton Market, New York City, which was supposed to have been shot on Long Island. (Ridgway, Bull. U. S. Nat. Mus., 1881, 25.)

99. AMERICAN GOLDEN-EYE. GLAUCIONETTA CLANGULA AMERICANA (*Bonaparte*). [151.] (Pls. I, XI.) *Ad.* ♂.—Head and throat dark, glossy *green,* a circular white patch at base of bill measuring, along bill, less than *half an inch* in height; neck all around, breast, belly, exposed part of wing-coverts, speculum, and most of the scapulars white; rest of plumage black. *Ad.* ♀.—Head and throat cinnamon-brown, foreneck white; upper breast, back, and sides ashy gray bordered with grayish; wing-coverts tipped with white, speculum, lower breast and belly white. L., 20·00; W., 9·00; B. from anterior margin of white patch to anterior margin of nostril, 1·00; from anterior margin of nostril to tip, ·75.

Range.—Breeds from the Yukon Valley, Alaska, ne. Lab., to N. B., n. Vt., the Adirondacks, n. Mich., n. Minn., and interior B. C. Winters on the Atlantic Coast from Me. to S. C.; on the Pacific from the Commander and Aleutian isls. to L. Calif. and on lakes Mich., Erie, and Ont.; irregularly in the interior from s. B. C. and n. Mont. to Colo., and Ark., and in the Miss. and Mo. valleys, to Ia. and Nebr.; more rarely to the Gulf of St. Lawrence, Fla., Gulf Coast, Tex. and Mex. Casual in Bermuda, Cuba, Barbados, and the Pribilof Isls.

Washington, not rare, W. V., Oct. 8–Apr. 27. Long Island, common W. V., (Oct. 5), Nov. 3–Apr. 27 (June 12). Bronx region, common W. V., Oct. 25–May 19 (June 3). Boston, abundant W. V., Sept.–Apr. N. Ohio, not common T. V., Mch. 10–30; Oct. 5–Nov. 20. SE. Minn., common T. V., Mch. 1–Apr. 4; Oct. 12–Dec. 12; regular W. V.

Nest, in a stump or hollow tree. *Eggs*, 6–12, pale greenish, 2·35 × 1·75. *Date*, Upton, Me., May 10; Sweetwater Lake, N. Dak., May 14.

The rapidly moving wings of most Ducks make a whistling sound, but this species excels in wing music. As a diver it can also claim high rank. Brewster records a brood of young birds which, in response to the calls of their mother at the base of the nest-tree, jumped from the nest-opening to the water 12 feet below. (See his important paper, *The Auk*, XVII, 1900, pp. 207–216.) "The note of the male Whistler is a single *peep*, accompanied by a kicking up of the feet, while the head is thrown far back toward the tail. The Duck, when startled or lost, calls out a sharp *cur-r-rew*" (Eaton).

1910. TOWNSEND, C. W., Auk, 177–181 (courtship).—1911. BREWSTER, W., Condor, 22–30, illus. (courtship).

100. BARROW'S GOLDEN-EYE. GLAUCIONETTA ISLANDICA (*Gmelin*). [152.] *Ad.* ♂.—Head and throat dark, glossy, *purplish blue*, an irregular, somewhat *spread-wing*-shaped white patch at the base of the bill measuring, along the bill, about *one inch* in height; neck all around, breast, belly, speculum, lesser wing-coverts, ends of greater ones, and the shaft part of the scapulars white; rest of plumage black. *Ad.* ♀.—Resembles the ♀ of the preceding species but has the bill shorter and more tapering, with more or less yellow instead of brown; brown of head and neck darker; ashy on chest broader and more pronounced; greater wing-coverts usually tipped with black. (W. Brewster, Auk, 1909, 158). W., 9·25; B., from anterior margin of white patch to anterior margin of nostril, ·80; from anterior margin of nostril to tip, ·66.

Range.—Breeds in Greenland and Iceland and on the Lab. coast; also from s. cent. Alaska, B. C., sw. Ore. and the Sierra Nevada of Calif. e. to nw. Mont. and s. Colo., more rarely n. to n. Mack. and Great Slave Lake. Winters on the Atlantic Coast from the Gulf of St. Lawrence to Mass., rarely farther; on the Pacific Coast from s. Alaska to cent. Calif., and in the interior irregularly from s. B. C. and n. Mont., to s. Colo. Casual in N. C., Mich. and Wisc.

Long Island, A. V. or casual W. V. Boston, uncommon but regular W. V., Nov.–Apr. N. Ohio, casual T. V.

Nest, in a stump or hollow tree. *Eggs*, 6–10, pale greenish, 2·40 × 1·70. *Date*, Iceland, May 30; Flathead Valley, Mont., May 14.

A much rarer species than the preceding, which it is said to resemble in habits.

101. BUFFLEHEAD. CHARITONETTA ALBEOLA (*Linnæus*). [153.] (Pls. I, XI.) *Ad.* ♂.—A broad white band passes around back of head from eye to eye; rest of head, upper neck, and throat beautifully glossed with purple, greenish and bluish; lower neck all around, breast, belly, wing-coverts, speculum and outer scapulars white; back black; upper tail-coverts and tail ashy grayish. *Ad.* ♀.—A white patch on either side of head, throat and entire upperparts fuscous-brown; speculum, breast and belly white. L., 14·75; W., 6·50; Tar., 1·25; B., 1·05.

Range.—Breeds from the interior of B. C., w. cent. Alaska, coasts of Hudson and James bays, to n. Mont.; reported as breeding formerly in Me., N. B., Wisc., Ia. and Wyo., and recently at Eagle Lake, Calif. Winters from the Aleutian and Commander isls. and the Alaska Peninsula, s. to cent. Mex., and L. Calif., and from nw. Mont., Great Lakes, and the coast of Me. to S. C., n. Fla., the Gulf Coasts of La. and Tex. Casual in Bermuda, Cuba, Porto Rico, and Hawaiian Isls.

Washington, uncommon W. V., Nov.–Apr. Long Island, tolerably common local W. V., (Sept. 16) Oct. 1–Apr. 20 (May 13). Bronx region, uncommon but regular W. V., Oct. 12–Apr. 15 (May 3). Boston, common W. V., Oct.–Apr. N. Ohio, common T. V., Mch. 25–May 1; Oct. 15–Nov. 30. Glen Ellyn, rather rare T. V. Apr. 5–27, Nov. 20. SE. Minn., common T. V., Mch. 31–Apr. 29; Nov. 2–Dec. 12.

Nest, in a stump or hollow tree. *Eggs,* 6–12, dull light buff, 1·98 × 1·46 (Ridgway). *Date,* Ft. Simpson, Mack., May 25.

"The flight of the Bufflehead is exceedingly swift and direct, generally at no very great elevation above the water, and it is performed with steady and very rapid beats of its strong little wings. It is one of the best divers, disappearing with the suddenness of a Grebe. Under water it can swim with closed wings swiftly enough to catch the small fish on which it so largely feeds" (Bent).

102. OLD SQUAW. Clangula hyemalis (*Linnæus*). [154.] (Pls. I, XI.) *Ad. ♂ in winter.*—Sides of front of head washed with grayish brown; sides of back of head and sides of upper neck black, more or less margined with ochraceous; rest of head, neck all around, upper back, scapulars, and lower belly white; back black, breast and upper belly brownish black; tail pointed, middle feathers very long and narrow; band across end of bill yellowish orange. *Ad. ♂ in summer.*—Sides of the front of head white; rest of head, neck, throat, breast and upper belly black; back and scapulars black, the latter margined with dark buffy ochraceous; lower belly white; tail and bill as in preceding. *♀ in winter.*—Upperparts black or fuscous; scapulars and upper back more or less margined with grayish or grayish brown; sides of head and neck and sometimes back of neck white or whitish; breast grayish; belly white; tail pointed, but without long feathers of male; under wing-coverts dark. *Ad. ♀ in summer.*—Generally similar to above, but sides of head and throat mostly blackish, and feathers of upperparts more or less margined with ochraceous. L., ♂, 21·00, ♀, 16·00; W., 8·60; T., ♂, 8·00, ♀, 2·50; B., 1·05.

Remarks.—The male Old Squaw is too distinct to be confused with any other species, its long tail-feathers being its most striking character; the female bears some resemblance to the female of the Harlequin Duck, but has the belly pure white instead of grayish dusky.

Range.—Breeds on the Arctic Coasts of both hemispheres, s. to n. Lab., Ungava Bay, and Fort Chimo, down the e. and w. shores of Hudson Bay, to Cape Jones and Churchill w. over the Barren Grounds of Can. and Alaska, down the coasts of Bering Sea to the Aleutian and Commander Isls., and B. C., also over the Barren Grounds of Asia and Europe, the Faroes, Iceland, and both coasts of Greenland. Winters on the Atlantic Coast s. to Chesapeake Bay and N. C. (rarely Fla.), on the Pacific from the Aleutian Isls. to Wash., less frequently to s. Calif., and in the interior on the Great Lakes and irregularly elsewhere to Wisc., Nebr., Colo., and Tex.

Washington, rare W. V., Oct. 20–Apr. 21. Long Island, abundant W. V., casual in summer, Sept. 27–May 27. Bronx region, common W. V. (mostly on the Sound), Oct. 12–May 15 (July 9). Boston, common W. V., Oct.–May. N. Ohio, irregular W. V., Nov. 1–Apr. 16. SE. Minn., rare fall visitant.

Nest, on the ground near water, under low bushes or tall grasses. *Eggs*, 6–12, pale bluish tinged with olive, 2·05 × 1·49. *Date*, Disco Bay, Greenland, June 15.

In *The Auk* for 1892, pp. 330–337, George H. Mackay gives a capital account of the habits of this species in our waters. He speaks of them as the swiftest flying as well as the noisiest (in the spring) of all the sea-fowl which tarry with us, and gives their curious scolding or talking notes as *o-onc-o-onc-ough, egh-ough-egh.* Their flight is generally near the water, and when shot at while flying they sometimes dive from the wing. He also mentions their habit of towering, "usually in the afternoon, collecting in mild weather in large flocks if undisturbed, and going up in circles so high as to be scarcely discernible, often coming down with a rush and great velocity, a portion of the flock scattering and coming down in a zigzag course similar to the Scoters when whistled down."

103. EASTERN HARLEQUIN DUCK. HISTRIONICUS HISTRIONICUS HISTRIONICUS (*Linnæus*). [155.] *Ad.* ♂.—Center of the crown black, margined by white and rufous; front of sides of head, a spot on ear, a stripe back of it, and a collar around back and sides of neck white; rest of head and throat rich slaty blue; a band in front of the wing white, margined with black; inner scapulars white; back and breast bluish slate; belly fuscous; sides rufous-chestnut. *Ad.* ♀.—Front of head whitish, a white spot on ears; upperparts brownish fuscous; throat, breast and sides lighter; belly grayish brown, margined with whitish. L., 17·00; W., 7·80; Tar., 1·50; B., 1·05.

Range.—Breeds in Iceland, s. Greenland, to n. Lab. Winters on the Atlantic Coast of N. A. s. to the coast of Me., more rarely to L. I.; resident in Iceland. Casual on Lake Ontario, and in S. C., and Fla.; also in Great Britain and Europe.

Long Island, rare W. V., Nov. 10–Feb. 27.

Nest, near water, on the ground, "under rocks or driftwood," or in a hollow stump. *Eggs*, 5–10, yellowish buff or greenish yellow, 2·30 × 1·62 (Davie). *Date*, Holsteinborg, Greenland, June 24. Labrador, June 3 (Bent).

Bent writes that in winter "on the Atlantic they are not common south of Maine and not abundant even there. They are often seen about the rocky bays of the eastern Provinces in winter but more often they frequent the outlying rocky islands and ledges. In spite of the brilliant coloring of the males they are surprisingly inconspicuous among the kelp-covered rocks and the wet, shining seaweeds of varied hues."

1896. NORTON, A. H., Auk, 229–234 (habits in Maine).—1922. MICHAEL, C. W. and E., Auk, 14–23, illus. (adventure with).

104. LABRADOR DUCK. CAMPTORHYNCHUS LABRADORIUS (*Gmelin*). [156.] *Ad.* ♂.—Center of crown black; rest of head, throat and upper neck white; a black band around lower neck connected behind with the black back; primaries fuscous, rest of wing white; front and sides of upper breast white, lower breast and belly black. *Ad.* ♀.—Brownish gray, speculum white. *Im.* ♂.—Like ♀, but with throat and ends of greater wing-coverts white. L., 20·00; W., 8·40; Tar., 1·50; B., 1·58.

Range.—Bred probably on the s. coast of the Ungava Peninsula. Wintered on the Atlantic Coast from N. S. to N. J. and probably to Chesa-

peake Bay. Casual at Elmira, N. Y. and on the St. Lawrence above Montreal. Now extinct.
Nesting, unknown.

William Dutcher (1891) quotes the late George N. Lawrence, as follows: "I recollect that about forty or more years ago it was not unusual to see them in Fulton Market, and without doubt killed on Long Island; at one time I remember seeing six fine males, which hung in the market until spoiled for want of a purchaser; they were not considered desirable for the table, and collectors had a sufficient number, at that time a pair being considered enough to represent a species in a collection."

The cause of this Duck's extinction is unknown. Bent records the last three specimens to be taken as follows: Grand Manan, April, 1871; Long Island, fall, 1875; Elmira, N. Y., December 12, 1878. Of these three birds only the Long Island specimen (in the National Museum) is preserved. In all, forty-four specimens are known to exist.

1891. DUTCHER, W., Auk, 201–216; 1894. XI, 4–12 (history).

105. STELLER'S EIDER, *Polysticta stelleri* (Pallas), [157], a North Pacific species, is of accidental occurrence in Greenland and Quebec.

106. NORTHERN EIDER. SOMATERIA MOLLISSIMA BOREALIS (*Brehm*).
[159.] *Ad. ♂.*—Top of head black, a greenish white line on the crown; rest of head, throat, neck, upper breast, back, scapulars and lesser wing-coverts white, tinged with greenish on sides and back of head, and with vinaceous on breast; middle of rump, upper and under tail-coverts, lower breast and belly black. *Ad. ♀.*—Head, throat and neck buffy ochraceous, darker above and streaked with black; back black, feathers all widely margined, and sometimes partly barred with buffy ochraceous; breast buffy ochraceous, barred with black; belly grayish brown or olive-brown, indistinctly margined or barred with buffy. *Im.*—Similar, but distinctly marked with buffy. L., 23·00; W., 11·00; Tar., 1·80; B., 2·10.
Range.—Breeds on the coastal isls. of Greenland and ne. A., s. on the Atlantic Coast to Lab. (Hamilton Inlet) and Que. Winters from s. Greenland to the coast of Me., rarely to Mass.
Nest, on the ground, amid coarse herbage and rocks. *Eggs*, 4–6, pale bluish or greenish, tinged with olive, 2·95 × 2·00. *Date*, Shertook Isl., Greenland, June 20.

This is the American representative of the Eider Duck of northern Europe, from which it differs only slightly. The highly prized Eider down is taken from the nest of this bird and its allies. As incubation progresses the sitting bird plucks the down from her breast to serve as a nest lining. In Iceland, according to Saunders, the average yield from each nest is about one-sixth of a pound. When the females begin to sit the males leave them, and, gathering in small flocks, live at sea.

106a. AMERICAN EIDER. SOMATERIA MOLLISSIMA DRESSERI *Sharpe*.
[160.] Resembles the preceding in color, but differs in the feathering of the base of the culmen. In both species the culmen is divided by a wedge of feathers reaching forward from the forehead. Looked at from the tip of the bill, the base of the culmen is thus V-shaped. In *dresseri* the arms of the V are very broad and *rounded* at the ends, while in *borealis* they are much

narrower and generally pointed at the ends. L., 23·00; W., 11·30; Tar., 1·70; B., 2·10.

Range.—Breeds on coastal isls. of Lab. s. of Hamilton Inlet, N. F., e. Que., N. S., and Me.; also on Hudson Bay and James Bay, as far n. as Southampton Isl. and Cape Fullerton. Winters on the seacoast from N. F. and the Gulf of St. Lawrence to Mass., and rarely to Va. Reported in Wisc., Ia., and Colo., but these records may be based on *S. spectabilis.*
Washington, one record. Long Island, casual W. V., Nov. 8–Mch. 25. Bronx region, A. V., Dec. 14. Boston, uncommon W. V., Nov.–Apr.

Nest, on the ground, generally sheltered by rocks. *Eggs,* 4–6, pale bluish or greenish, tinged with olive, 3·00 × 2·00. *Date,* Labrador, June 5.

This species nests from the coast of Maine northward, and is therefore a species of more southern distribution than the preceding, which it resembles in habits. Eiders are true Sea Ducks, living some distance offshore, generally over a bed of mussels, which they secure by diving, and which constitute their chief food.

1890. MACKAY, G. H., Auk, 315–319 (habits in Mass.).—1910. TOWN-SEND, C. W., Auk, 177–181 (courtship).—1914. TOWNSEND, C. W., Auk, 14–21 (conservation of).—1927. LEWIS, H. F., Report Can. Nat. Parks, Ottawa; also Can. Field-Nat., XLI, 31–38 (producing down).

107. KING EIDER. SOMATERIA SPECTABILIS (*Linnæus*). [162.] *Ad.* ♂.—Region about base of upper mandible and a large *V-shaped* mark on throat black; top of head bluish gray; cheeks greenish; neck all around white; front and sides of breast creamy buff; upper back, sides of rump, and wing-coverts white; rest of plumage black. *Ad.* ♀.—Head and throat buffy ochraceous, the former streaked with black; back black, the feathers widely margined with ochraceous or rufous; underparts varying from brownish gray to fuscous, more or less washed, especially on breast, with ochraceous or rufous. *Im.*—Paler and with less ochraceous. L., 23·00; W., 10·80; Tar., 1·80; B., 1·30.

Remarks.—The adult male of this species may at once be known by its bluish gray head and the V-shaped mark on its throat. Females and young birds resemble those of the two preceding species, but are to be distinguished by the generally unstreaked throat and the feathering of the side of the base of the bill, which in this species does not, as in the two preceding, reach to the nostril.

Range.—Breeds on both coasts of Greenland and the entire Arctic Coast of Can. and Alaska, s. to n. Lab., Hudson Strait, n. Hudson Bay, St. Lawrence, and St. Mathew Isls., Bering Sea, also on the Arctic Coast of Siberia, Novaya Zemlya, and Spitzbergen. Winters from s. Greenland to Mass. and N. Y., more rarely to Va., the Great Lakes, and occasionally farther in the interior, and from Bering Sea to the Aleutian, Kodiak, and Shumagin isls., also Iceland, Great Britain, Norway, Holland, and the Baltic Sea. Casual in Alberta, Ga., Ia., Calif., and also France and Italy.
Long Island, rare W. V. (Oct.), Nov. 1–Apr. 27 (June 8). Boston, casual in early winter.

Nest, on the ground, among rocks or herbage. *Eggs,* 4–7, light olive-gray to grayish green, 3·12 × 1·92 (Davie). *Date,* Pt. Barrow, Alaska, June 25.

While in our waters this species does not differ from the preceding in habits.

108. AMERICAN SCOTER. OIDEMIA AMERICANA *Swainson.* [163.]
Ad. ♂.—Entire plumage black, feathers on side of bill extending little if any forward beyond corner of mouth; bill black; upper mandible orange or

yellowish at the base. *Ad.* ♀ *and Im.*—Above chest and sides grayish brown; cheeks whitish, sharply defined from crown; belly whitish faintly barred with dusky. L., 19·00; W., 9·00; Tar., 1·70; B. along culmen, 1·75; B. along side, 1·85.

Range.—Breeds from ne. Siberia, Mack. Bay, and n. Lab., to the Bering Sea coast of Alaska, the Aleutian and Kurile isls., James Bay, and N. F. Winters on the Atlantic Coast from Me. and more rarely N. F. to N. J., and irregularly to S. C. and Fla. and on the Pacific from the Pribilof and Aleutian isls. to s. Calif.; in the interior to the Great Lakes and irregularly to Wyo., Colo., and La.

Washington, casual W. V. Long Island, uncommon W. V., rare in summer, Sept. 5–May 30. Bronx region, irregular W. V. (chiefly along the Sound), Sept. 2–May 18. Boston, common W. V., Sept.–May.

Nest, on the ground, near water. *Eggs*, "6–10, pale dull buff or pale brownish buff, 2·55 × 1·80" (Ridgway). *Date*, Cape Lisburne, Alaska, June 15.

All three species of Surf Scoters, or 'Coots,' are winter residents off the coasts of the New England and Middle States. At this time their habits are practically alike—indeed, they are often found associated. As a rule, they frequent only the sea and its estuaries, where they live over beds of mussels, clams, or scallops, which they obtain by diving; but they are sometimes found in ponds near the coast where food of this nature is abundant.

The flight of the Surf Scoter "is marked by a shrill whistling, and when the birds are in large numbers this sound is heard a long distance off." (Sanford.)

1891. MACKAY, G. H., Auk, 279–290; 1892, 292–294 (habits in Mass.).— 1914. DWIGHT, J., Auk, 293–308, illus. (molts and plumages).

109. The VELVET SCOTER, *Melanitta fusca* (Linnæus), [164], an Old-World species, has been recorded from Greenland.

110. WHITE-WINGED SCOTER. MELANITTA DEGLANDI (*Bonaparte*). [165.] (Pl. XI.) *Ad.* ♂.—A spot below eye and *speculum white*, rest of plumage black; bill orange, black at base, the feathers on it reaching *forward far beyond corners of mouth. Ad.* ♀ *and Im.* ♂.—Grayish or fuscous-brown, lighter below; *speculum white*, feathers at base of upper bill and a spot on the ears whitish. L., 22·00; W., 11·00; Tar., 2·00; B. along culmen, 1·50; B. along side, 1·55.

Remarks.—The white speculum and feathering of the bill will always serve to distinguish this species from its allies.

Range.—Breeds from ne. Alaska, and cent. B. C. to Lab., the Gulf of St. Lawrence, s. Man., cent. N. Dak., and ne. Wash. Winters on the Atlantic Coast from the Gulf of St. Lawrence to S. C., and on the Pacific from the Commander, Pribilof, and Aleutian isls. to L. Calif., also to the Great Lakes, and irregularly to B. C., Colo., La., and Fla.

Washington, uncommon W. V., Oct.–May. Long Island, abundant W. V., rare in summer, Sept. 14–June 10. Bronx region, common (occasionally abundant), W. V. on the Sound, Sept. 6–June 5 and later. Boston, abundant W. V., Aug.–May. SE. Minn., casual T. V. and W. V.

Nest, on the ground, beneath bushes, or in high growth. *Eggs*, "6–14, pale dull buff, varying to cream-color, 2·68 × 1·83" (Ridgway). *Date*, N. Dak., June 20.

"The flight of the White-winged Scoter is heavy and apparently labored; it seems to experience considerable difficulty in lifting its heavy body from the surface of the water; except when facing a strong wind, it has to patter along the surface, using its feet to gain momentum" (Bent).

111. SURF SCOTER. MELANITTA PERSPICILLATA (*Linnæus*). [166.] (Pl. I.) *Ad.* ♂.—A square mark on crown and a triangular one on nape white, rest of plumage black; bill with white, red and yellow, a black spot on its side at base; feathers on culmen extending nearly to a level with nostril, feathers on *side* of bill *not* extending forward. *Ad.* ♀ *and Im.*—A whitish spot at base of the bill and on ears; upperparts fuscous-brown; throat, breast, sides and lower belly grayer, belly white. L., 20·00; W., 9·30; Tar., 1·60; B. along culmen, 1·55; B. along side 2·30.

Remarks.—The forward extension of the feathers on the *culmen* will always distinguish this species from *O. americana*, while it may be known from *deglandi* by the absence of white in the wings.

Range.—Breeds from nw. Alaska and, casually, Greenland, s. to the Gulf of St. Lawrence, and probably Alberta. Winters on the Atlantic Coast from the Bay of Fundy to Fla., and on the Pacific from the Aleutian Isls. to L. Calif., also on the Great Lakes and sparingly in the interior to s. B. C., and La. Casual in Bermuda.

Washington, casual W. V., Nov. until Apr. Long Island, abundant W. V., rare in summer, Sept. 1–June 4. Bronx region, irregular W. V., Nov. 1–May 2. Boston, abundant W. V., Sept.–May.

Nest, in tall grasses near water. *Eggs*, "5–8, pale buff or pale creamy buff, 2·47 × 1·70" (Ridgway). *Date*, Ft. Anderson, Mack., June 25.

"The flight of the Surf Scoter is not quite so heavy as that of the White-winged Scoter; it is a smaller, lighter, and livelier bird on the wing, but it so closely resembles the American Scoter in flight that the two cannot be distinguished at any great distance" (Bent).

Subfamily Erismaturinæ. Ruddy and Masked Ducks.

112. RUDDY DUCK. ERISMATURA JAMAICENSIS RUBIDA *Wilson*. [167.] (Fig. 64, Pl. XI.) *Ad.* ♂.—Top of head black, cheeks and chin white, throat and back rufous-chestnut, lower back blackish; breast and belly silvery white; upper tail-coverts *very* short, tail-feathers *stiff and pointed;* bill blue. *Ad.* ♀ *and Im.*—Upperparts dark grayish brown, the feathers marked with fine wavy bars of buffy; sides of head and upper throat whitish, lower throat grayish, rest of underparts silvery white. L., 15·00; W., 5·90; Tar., 1·15; B., 1·55.

Remarks.—The short upper tail-coverts and stiff, pointed tail-feathers will always serve to identify this species.

Range.—Breeds from cent. B. C., Alberta, and n. Man. to w. Minn., se. Wisc., se. Mich., n. Ills., n. Ia., cent. Tex., n. N. Mex., cent. Ariz., and n. L. Calif., w. to cent. Calif., cent. Ore., and nw. Wash.; has also bred sporadically in Ungava, Me., Mass., (Cape Cod), R. I., and cent. N. Y., and breeding colonies, have been found in s. L. Calif., the Valley of Mex., and Guat. Winters on the Atlantic Coast from Chesapeake Bay (more rarely from Mass.) to the W. I.; on the Pacific Coast from s. B. C., to Costa Rica, and in the interior from cent. Ariz., and w. Pa. Casual or accidental in Bermuda, N. S., N. B. and Alaska. [A closely allied race occurs in P. R., Haiti, and Jamaica.]

Washington, common W. V., Aug. 20–June 28. Long Island, T. V. and W. V., irregular and local in fall, rare in winter and spring, may breed (July 27), Oct. 5–June 10. Bronx region, irregular and uncommon T. V., Oct. 2–

Jan. 27; Feb. 21–May 15. Boston, uncommon, T. V., rare in spring, Mch.–May; Sept.–Dec. N. Ohio, common T. V., Apr. 1–May 15; Oct. 10–Nov. 20. Glen Ellyn, rare T. V., Mch. 21–May 21. SE. Minn., T. V., Apr. 4–May 17; Oct. 22–Nov. 17.

Nest, of reeds, in reeds over water. *Eggs,* 6–10, white, 2·50 × 1·80. *Date,* N. Dak., June 10.

This plump little Duck swims jauntily with upturned tail. When pursued it dives, unless too hard pressed, and then, after pattering over the water, it takes to the air, with rapidly whirring wings and low, straight flight which suggests that of a great bumblebee. The male, in breeding plumage, is unmistakable and its bright, sky-blue bill is distinguishable from a distance.

113. The MASKED DUCK, *Nomonyx dominicus* (Linnæus), [168], is a tropical American species rare north of the Rio Grande. Single specimens have been taken in Wisconsin, Massachusetts, Vermont, and Maryland.

Subfamily *Merginæ. Mergansers.*

The five subfamilies into which our Anatidæ fall are so well defined, it seems advisable to treat of each one separately. The first of these, the Sheldrakes or Sawbills, are fish-eating Ducks. They pursue and capture their prey under water, progressing chiefly by aid of the feet, and their serrate bills seem especially adapted to this mode of feeding. Three of the nine known species are found in North America, and all may be recognized in life by their cylindrical bill. Their notes are variously described as 'croaks.'

KEY TO THE SPECIES

1. Bill under 1·75, wing 8·00 or under . . . . 114. HOODED MERGANSER
2. Bill over 1·75, wing over 8·00.
   A. Head and throat black.
      a. Breast and belly white, tinged with salmon.
                  115. AMERICAN MERGANSER, ♂ ad.
      b. Breast brownish, thickly streaked and spotted with black.¹
              116. RED-BREASTED MERGANSER, ♂ ad.
   B. Head and throat not black.
      a. Head and sides of the neck rich rufous-brown; distance from nostril to end of bill less than 1·50.
             115. AMERICAN MERGANSER, ♀ and im.
      b. Crown grayish brown, more or less washed with cinnamon-rufous; sides of the neck cinnamon-rufous; distance from nostril to end of bill over 1·50 . . 116. RED-BREASTED MERGANSER, ♀ and im.

114. HOODED MERGANSER. LOPHODYTES CUCULLATUS (*Linnæus*). [131.] *Ad.* ♂.—Front part of large circular crest black; remaining part white, bordered by black; rest of head, the neck and back black; breast and belly white; sides of breast with a black band; sides cinnamon-rufous, finely barred with black. *Ad.* ♀.—Upper throat white; head, neck and upper breast grayish brown, more or less tinged with cinnamon, especially on the small crest; lower breast and belly white; sides grayish brown; back fuscous. *Im.* ♂.—Similar, but throat blackish. L., 17·50; W., 7·50; Tar., 1·10; B., 1·45.

Range.—Breeds locally in temp. N. A., from n. B. C., Great Slave Lake, and N. B. to N. Y., cent. Pa., e. S. C., cent. Fla., s. Tenn., and Wash. Winters mainly in the southern states n. to Mass., Lake Mich., and B. C.; s. to Cuba and cent. e. Mex. Accidental in Bermuda.

Washington, uncommon W. V., Sept. 17–May 11. Long Island, tolerably common, rather local T. V., rare W. V., casual S. V., Mch. 11–May; Oct. 23–Dec. 14. Bronx region, uncommon but regular T. V., Oct. 22–Jan. 16; Feb. 20–Apr. 29. Boston, uncommon T. V., Mch. and Apr.; Sept.–Dec.; rare W. V. N. Ohio, not common T. V., Apr. 1–15; Nov. 1–30. Glen Ellyn, rare T. V.; Apr. 8–June 5; July 17–Nov. 2. SE. Minn., common T. V., uncommon S. R., Mch. 24–Nov. 16; a few winter.

Nest, of grasses, leaves, moss, etc., lined with down, in a hollow tree or stump near water. *Eggs*, 8–10, buffy white, 2·10 × 1·75. *Date*, Saranac, Mich., Apr. 22.

This bird prefers 'dead' waters, or quiet ponds and lakes. In Florida it lives in small ponds in the 'hammocks,' where one expects to find Wood Ducks, and feeds on roots, seeds, etc. It visits also the lakes frequented by Black Ducks, Mallards, and other Anatinæ. The male is a striking bird in life, and cannot be mistaken for any other species.

115. AMERICAN MERGANSER. MERGUS MERGANSER AMERICANUS

Cassin. [129.] *Ad.* ♂.—Whole head and upper neck glossy greenish black; hindneck, secondaries, lesser wing-coverts, and ends of greater ones white; back black, rump and tail ashy gray; breast and belly white, delicately tinged with salmon. *Ad.* ♀ *and Im.*—Chin and upper throat white; lower throat and entire top of the head (crested in ♀) rufous-brown; rest of upperparts and tail ashy gray; speculum, or colored patch in the wing, white; breast and belly white. L., 25·00; W., 10·50; Tar., 1·85; B., from N. 1·50.

Range.—Breeds in Can. and the n. U. S., from the base of the Alaskan Peninsula, to Lab. and N. F., s. to s. Me., cent. N. H., cent. Vt., cent. N. Y., s. Ont., cent. Mich., ne. Wisc., sw. Minn., sw. S. Dak., n. N. Mex., n. cent. Ariz., and cent. Calif.; formerly to the mountains of w. Mass., cent. Pa. and O. Winters mainly within the U. S. from the Aleutian Isls. (rarely Pribilof Isls.), s. B. C., Great Lakes, St. Lawrence Valley, and Prince Edward Isl., to Fla., the Gulf States and n. Mex.

Washington, uncommon W. V., Oct. 13–May 28. Long Island, tolerably common, local W. V. (Oct. 12), Nov. 4–Apr. 29 (May 22). Bronx region, common W. V., Oct. 30–Apr. 12, and (May 13). Boston, common W. V., Oct.–Apr. N. Ohio, W. V., Nov. 1–May. Glen Ellyn, T. V., spring only, May 7–12. SE. Minn., formerly S. R. now T. V., Mch. 9–Apr. 26; Nov. 8–Dec. 1; casual W. R.

Nest, of leaves, grasses, and moss lined with down in a hole in a tree (which the downy young leave unaided), beneath bushes or boulders. *Eggs*, 6–7, creamy buff, 2·65 × 1·75. *Date*, Saginaw Isl., Mich., May 26.

"This bird is fond of plunging beneath rushing currents for its food and should it encounter a raft of floating rubbish, or an ice-cake, it will readily pass underneath it. It swims so deeply as to afford the gunner but a small mark, and dives so quickly at the snap or flash of his gun that he stands but a small chance of killing it.

"On being surprised, the Goosander may rise directly out of the water, but more commonly pats the surface with his feet for some yards and then rises to windward. A whole flock thus rising from some foaming current affords a spirited scene. Once on the wing, the flight is straight, strong, and rapid" (Langille).

116. RED-BREASTED MERGANSER. Mergus serrator *Linnæus.*
[130.] (Pl. I, Figs. 33d, 65.) *Ad.* ♂.—Head, crest, and throat black, more greenish above; a white ring around neck; back black, *a broad cinnamon-rufous
band with black streaks* on upper breast and sides of lower neck; lesser wing-
coverts, tips of greater ones, secondaries, breast and belly white; rump and
sides finely barred with black and white. *Ad.* ♀ *and Im.*—Top and back
of crested head, sides of head and throat cinnamon-rufous, paler or white
on chin; rest of underparts white; back and tail ashy gray; speculum white.
L., 22·00; W., 9·00; Tar., 1·70; B. from N., 1·80.

Remarks.—Adults of this and the preceding species may always be distinguished by the color of the breast; females and young, by the differently
colored heads, while the position of the nostril is always diagnostic.

Range.—Breeds from the Arctic Coast of Alaska, and cent. Greenland s.
to coast of Me., n. N. Y., cent. Ont., cent. Mich., and Wisc., cent. Minn.,
s. Man., n. B. C., se. Alaska, and the Aleutian Isls. Winters on the Atlantic
and Gulf coasts from Me. to Fla. and Tex.; on the Pacific Coast from B. C.
to s. L. Calif., and in the interior from the Great Lakes southward.

Washington, uncommon W. V., Oct. 23–May 30. Long Island, common
W. V., abundant T. V., occasional S. V., Sept. 15–June 18. Bronx region,
common to abundant T. V. and W. V., occasional in summer; Aug. 8, Sept.
15–May 23 (June 7). Boston, common to abundant W. V., Sept.–May.
N. Ohio, tolerably common T. V., Mch. 10–May 10; Dec. 1–29. SE. Minn.,
formerly S. R., now common T. V., Mch. 30–May 14; Oct.–Nov.; casual
W. R.

Nest, of leaves, grasses, mosses, etc., lined with down, on the ground near
water, among rocks or scrubby bushes. *Eggs,* 6–12, creamy buff, 2·55 ×
1·75. *Date,* Seal Isl., Magdalen Isls., June 17.

"These Mergansers are often observed to hunt in company, a large
flock sometimes advancing with wide extended front, driving the fish
before them and diving simultaneously, so that whichever way their
prey may dart there is a serrated beak and capacious gullet ready to
receive them" (Eaton).

1911. Townsend, C. W., Auk, 341–345 (courtship and migration).—
1912. Strong, R. M., Auk, 479–488 (life-history).

VII. ORDER FALCONIFORMES. VULTURES AND DIURNAL BIRDS OF PREY.

SUBORDER CATHARTÆ. AMERICAN VULTURES
(1 family)

Family Cathartidæ. American Vultures.

A New-World family of six species, of which three are North American. Within their range Vultures are found wherever there is food.
Far above the earth on firm wing they sail in broad circles, and from
this outlook in the sky descend to feast upon the stricken deer in the
forest or the cur lying in the gutters of a thoroughfare. Both eye and
nose assist them in finding food. Except during the nesting season,
they are generally found in flocks, which each night return to a regularly
frequented roost. When alarmed or excited, they utter low, grunting
sounds, but at other times are silent. They build no nest, but lay their

one to three eggs under logs or stumps, on the ground, in caves, or similar places. The young are born naked, but are soon thickly covered with white or buff down.

117. TURKEY VULTURE. Cathartes aura septentrionalis *Wied.* [325.] (Fig. 34.) *Ads.*—Head and neck naked, the skin and base of the bill *bright red;* plumage glossy black, edged with grayish brown; longer lower wing-coverts gray, under surface of wings silvery, except at tips of primaries. *Im.*—Similar, but the head covered with grayish brown, furlike feathers. L., about 30·00; W., 22·00; T., 11·00; B., 2·30.

Range.—Austral Zones (chiefly) from s. B. C., cent. Alberta, Sask., s. Man., Wisc., Mich., n. Minn., s. Ont., cent. N. Y., w. Conn , and N. J. s. to s. L. Calif., the Gulf Coast of the U. S. and Mex., breeding n. at least to s. Mich. and s. Minn., se. N. Y., and w. Conn. Winters throughout most of its regular range on the Atlantic slope, but not n. of the Ohio valley, Nebr. and Calif. casual in n. Ont., N. E. n. to N. H. and Me., N. B., and N. F.

Washington, common P. R. Bronx region, rare T. V. and S. R., Mch. 29–Nov. 22. Boston, casual T. V. N. Ohio, tolerably common, S. R., Mch. 5–Oct. 30. Glen Ellyn, rare, Mch. 31, 1912, 3 seen. SE. Minn., common S. R., Mch. 24–Oct. 31.

Nest, in hollow stumps or logs, or on the ground beneath rocks, bushes or palmettos. *Eggs,* 1–3, dull white, generally spotted and blotched with distinct and obscure chocolate markings, but sometimes plain or but slightly spotted, 2·80 × 2·00. *Date,* Florida Keys, Mch. 1; Buckingham Co., Va., Apr. 3; Deer Creek, Md., Apr. 16; se. Minn., May 2, July.

One of the first birds to attract the attention of the bird student in our southern states is the Turkey 'Buzzard.' Indeed, there are few moments between sunrise and sunset when these birds are not in sight. On outstretched wings they soar overhead in graceful circles, perfect pictures of 'repose in motion.' Without once flapping their broad pinions, they sail in spirals up the sky until they are hidden by the storm-clouds they have purposely avoided. Again, one sees them winging their way low over fields or through the streets of a town in search of food which my experiments show they find by scent as well as sight. At times they may be seen high in the air hurrying to a distant repast, to which they are guided by the food-flight of other Buzzards. Their services as scavengers are invaluable. Experiments disprove the belief that Buzzards are distributors of disease.

After a rain it is a common sight to see Buzzards perching with wings held in spread-eagle fashion as they dry their water-soaked plumage. Frequently they stand on the top of a chimney to take advantage of the heat arising with the smoke. Their only note is a low, grunting sound uttered when they are disturbed. Just after sunset Buzzards may be seen sailing to their roosting-place, generally in the upper branches of a dead tree.

1913. M [cATEE]. W. L., Auk, 295–298 (relation to diseases of live-stock). —1928. Leighton, A. H., Auk, 352–355 (eye-sight).—1928. Lewis, J. B., Auk, 467–470; Wilson Bull., 154–156 (sight and scent).—1929. Chapman, F. M., My Tropical Air Castle (scent).

118. BLACK VULTURE. Coragyps atratus atratus *(Meyer).* [326.] *Ads.*—Head and neck bare, the skin and base of the bill *blackish;* plumage glossy black; longer lower wing-coverts black, under surface of the wings silvery; light-colored area near ends showing in life from above or below (Forbush); shafts of primaries white both above and below. L., about 24·00; W., 17·00; T., 8·00; B., 2·20.

Range.—Tropical and L. Austral Zones from w. Tex., Kans., Mo., s. Ills., s. Ind., and s. Md., s. through the southern states to Mex. and Cent. A.; casual or accidental in Ariz., in O., Que., Ind., s. Mich., N. Y., Me , N. B., N. S. and Jamaica. (An allied race occurs in S. A.)

Washington, irregular; Dec.–Mch.; May, July, Aug. Boston, A. V.

Nest, on the ground, under logs, bushes, palmettos, etc. *Eggs,* 1–3, pale bluish white, generally more or less spotted with distinct and obscure chocolate markings, 2·95 X 2·00. *Date,* Warrior River Swamp, Ala., Apr. 1; St. Simon's, Ga., Mch. 26.

This species is more abundant near the seacoast and less common in the interior than the preceding. It is also more often found living in towns or cities.

Black Vultures are heavier birds than Turkey Buzzards, and whenever the ownership of food is in question the dispute is invariably settled in the Vulture's favor. Their stretch of wing, however, is not so great, and for this reason their flight is far less easy and graceful than that of the Buzzard. They flap their wings oftener, and this habit, in connection with their black heads, grayish wing linings, and comparatively short tails, serves to identify them in the field. The only note I have ever heard from them is a low grunt uttered when they are disturbed.

SUBORDER FALCONES. FALCONS, HAWKS, EAGLES, KITES
(3 families, 2 North American)

SYNOPSIS OF FAMILIES

Front of tarsus scutellate, with more or less square, transverse scales (except Osprey, in which rounded); nostrils not circular, without a central, bony tubercle . . . *Family Accipitridæ.* HAWKS, EAGLES, KITES, etc. P. 213.

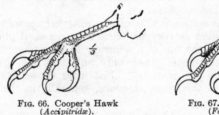

FIG. 66. Cooper's Hawk   FIG. 67. Duck Hawk
 (*Accipitridæ*).   (*Falconidæ*).

Front of tarsus reticulate, with rounded scales, nostrils small, circular with a central bony tubercle (except Caracara, in which oblique)
Family Falconidæ. FALCONS, CARACARAS. P. 230.

Consult FISHER, A. K., The Hawks and Owls of the United States in Their Relation to Agriculture, Bull. No. 3, 1893. Div. Orn. and Mam. (Biol.

PLATE XII

FLYING HAWKS

Red-tailed Hawk.	Broad-winged Hawk.
Cooper's Hawk.	Sparrow Hawk.
	Sharp-shinned Hawk.
Marsh Hawk.	

Surv.), Washington. 8vo. 210 pp.; 26 col. pls.—1922. SWANN, H. K., A Synopsis of the Accipitres, 2nd ed., London, viii + 233 pp.

FAMILY ACCIPITRIDÆ. HAWKS, EAGLES, KITES, ETC.

The Accipitridæ, numbering about two hundred and sixty species, are distributed throughout the world; of this number, thirty-two are North American. These present much diversity of form and habit, but our eastern species of the genera *Buteo* and *Accipiter* may, in the northern states, at least, be seen during the migratory seasons, traveling in scattered flocks, which may take hours to pass a given point. At this season large numbers are killed by so-called sportsmen whose defense for shooting these inedible birds is their alleged destructiveness to game. At other times of the year, with few exceptions, they are solitary birds, having no intercourse with their kind. During the breeding season many species have definitely bounded haunts, upon which intrusion by individuals of the same species is not permitted. With much regularity they return to the same locality and even the same nest year after year, and some species are known to mate for life. Their days are an unceasing vigil. At all times they are on the alert for food. With the *Buteos* this consists to a large extent of small mammals and insects, birds and poultry forming a comparatively insignificant part of the diet of most species. Most Hawks are thus of great value to the agriculturist as the natural check upon the increase of the myriads of small rodents so destructive to crops. This fact has been proved by many independent investigators, but the influence of sportsmen, who class all Hawks as 'vermin' has thus far denied these birds the protection that most of them deserve.

The cries of Hawks are generally loud, startling, and characteristic of their fierce natures. They strike their prey with their feet, and use the bill to tear it into fragments.

Hawks' nests are generally bulky affairs, composed of coarse twigs and sticks. The presence of downy feathers gives evidence that they are or have been recently occupied. The young are hatched with a scanty growth of white down which soon covers the body.

To facilitate identification in the field, the Hawks of this and the following family (Falconidæ) have been placed in one key as below.

KEY TO THE SPECIES OF ACCIPITRIDÆ AND FALCONIDÆ

I. Wing over 19·00.
    A. Upper half of tarsus feathered.
        a. Whole head and neck white . . . . 137, 137*a.* BALD EAGLES, ad.
        b. Head or neck brown or brownish.
            b¹. Bill mostly yellow (Greenland) . . . 136. GRAY SEA EAGLE, ad.
            b². Bill black or blackish . . . . . . 137, 137*a.* BALD EAGLES, im.
    B. Whole tarsus feathered . . . . 135. GOLDEN EAGLE.
II. Wing under 19·00. Placed in three sections as follows:
    1. Underparts more or less streaked and spotted, *without* cross-bars.
    2. Underparts *with* more or less numerous cross-bars.
    3. Underparts without streaks or bars.

1. Underparts more or less streaked and spotted, without cross-bars.
A. Outer primary with numerous black or blackish bars.
  a. Wing under 10·00.
    a^1. Back bright rufous, with or without black bars.
                 147, 147a. SPARROW HAWKS.
    a^2. Back bluish slate-color . . . . 144. PIGEON HAWK, ad.
    a^3. Back fuscous, second primary longest. . 144. PIGEON HAWK, im.
    a^4. Back fuscous, fourth primary longest, tail-feathers of nearly equal length; wing under 9·00 . . 124. SHARP-SHINNED HAWK, im.
    a^5. Back fuscous, fourth primary longest, outer tail-feathers half an inch or more shorter than the middle ones; wing over 9·00.
                 125. COOPER'S HAWK, im.
  b. Wing over 10·00.
    b^1. Second primary longest.
      b^2. Tail generally over 9·00.
        b^3. Lower tail-coverts immaculate white.
                 141. WHITE GYRFALCON.
        b^4. Lower tail-coverts always more or less marked with dusky.
                 141a. BLACK GYRFALCON.
      c^2. Tail under 9·00.
        c^3. Tarsus shorter than middle toe without nail, upperparts blackish . . . . 143a. DUCK HAWK.
        c^4. Tarsus longer than middle toe without nail, upperparts brownish . . . . 142. PRAIRIE FALCON.
    c^1. Third or fourth primary longest.
      c^2. Upper tail-coverts white . . . . 138. MARSH HAWK.
      c^3. Upper tail-coverts brownish . . . . . 123. GOSHAWK, im.
B. Outer primary generally one color, base sometimes whitish or with a few imperfect bars.
  a. Tarsus entirely bare, scales on its front large, rounded.
                 140. AUDUBON'S CARACARA.
  b. Tarsus not entirely bare.
    b^1. Tarsus entirely feathered . . 132. FERRUGINOUS ROUGH-LEG.
    c^1. Tarsus partly feathered.
      c^2. Scales on front of tarsus, small, rounded . . . 139. OSPREY.
      d^2. Scales on tarsus not rounded, square.
        d^3. Three outer primaries emarginate or 'notched.'[1]
          d^4. Wing under 12·00 . . . 128. BROAD-WINGED HAWK, im.
          d^5. Wing over 12·00 . . . . . 129. SWAINSON'S HAWK, im.
        e^3. Four outer primaries emarginate or 'notched.'[2]
          e^4. Upper tail-coverts pure white . . 138. MARSH HAWK.
          e^5. Upper tail-coverts not pure white; wing under 13·50; lesser wing-coverts conspicuously margined with rufous.
            127, 127a, 127b. RED-SHOULDERED HAWKS, im.
          e^6. Upper tail-coverts not pure white; wing over 13·50; lesser wing-coverts not conspicuously margined with rufous.
           126, 126a–c. RED-TAILED HAWK and races.

2. Underparts with more or less numerous cross-bars.
A. Front of tarsus with sharply defined scales.
  a. Scales on front of the tarsus numerous, rounded.
    a^1. Wing under 15·00 . . . . 143a. DUCK HAWK.
    a^2. Wing over 15·00 . . . . 140. AUDUBON'S CARACARA.
  b. Scales on front of the tarsus sharply defined, transverse, more or less square.
    b^1. Four or five outer primaries emarginate or 'notched.'[2]
      b^2. Tail white at the base and tipped with whitish.
                122. EVERGLADE KITE.
      b^3. Tail rufous, with sometimes a black band near the end.
        126, 126a–d. RED-TAILED HAWK, ad. and races.

[1]See Fig. 71.   [2]See Fig. 70.

b^4. Tail black or blackish, with four to six white or grayish cross-
bars . . . . 127. RED-SHOULDERED HAWK, ad.
127a. FLORIDA RED-SHOULDERED HAWK, ad.
  b^5. Tail 10·00 long, gray, with several indistinct blackish bands.
123. GOSHAWK.
  c^1. Three outer primaries emarginate or 'notched.'[1]
  c^2. Tail with two or three broad whitish bars.
128. BROAD-WINGED HAWK, ad.
  c^3. Tail with numerous narrow, indistinct blackish bars.
129. SWAINSON'S HAWK, ad.
B. Front of the tarsus smooth, or with the scales not sharply defined.
  a. Tarsus not entirely feathered.
    a^1. Wing under 9·00, tail-feathers of nearly equal length.
124. SHARP-SHINNED HAWK, ad.
    a^2. Wing over 9·00, outer tail-feathers half an inch shorter than the
    middle ones; upper tail-coverts not white.
125. COOPER'S HAWK, ad.
    a^3. Wing over 9·00; upper tail-coverts white.
138. MARSH HAWK, ad.
  b. Tarsus entirely feathered.
    b^1. Legs rich rufous, heavily barred. 132. FERRUGINOUS ROUGH-LEG.
    b^2. Legs ochraceous-buff, more or less barred.
131. ROUGH-LEGGED HAWK.

3. Underparts without streaks or bars.
  A. Underparts white.
    a. Scales on front of tarsus transverse, more or less square.
130. SHORT-TAILED HAWK.
    b. Scales on front of tarsus numerous, rounded.
      b^1. Tail barred.
        b^2. Upperparts not barred . . . . 139. OSPREY.
        b^3. Upperparts barred . . . . . . 141. WHITE GYRFALCON.
      c^1. Tail not barred.
        c^2. Tail square, white . . . . . . 119. WHITE-TAILED KITE.
        c^3. Tail forked, bluish black . . . . 120. SWALLOW-TAILED KITE.
  B. Underparts dark brown, slate, gray, or black.
    a. Tarsus entirely feathered . . . . . . 131. ROUGH-LEGGED HAWK.
    b. Tarsus partly feathered, scales transverse, more or less square.
      b^1. Wing over 13·00.
        b^2. Upper tail-coverts, base and tip of the tail white; two outer
        primaries slightly 'notched' . . . 122. EVERGLADE KITE.
        b^3. Three outer primaries 'notched'[1] . 129. SWAINSON'S HAWK.
        b^4. Four outer primaries 'notched' . . . 126c. HARLAN'S HAWK.
      c^1. Wing under 13·00.
        c^2. Primaries more or less distinctly barred; general plumage sooty
        black . . . . 130. SHORT-TAILED HAWK.
        c^3. Primaries not barred; general plumage slaty blue.
121. MISSISSIPPI KITE.

119. NORTHERN WHITE-TAILED KITE. ELANUS LEUCURUS MAJUS-
CULUS *Bangs and Penard.* [328.] *Ads.*—Upperparts ashy gray, whiter on
the head; wing-coverts black; tail and underparts white. *Im.*—Very different, head streaked black and whitish; back black narrowly tipped with
rusty, many of the feathers with more or less concealed white bars; tail
black, central feathers barred with gray, others with white; underparts
rufous with buff margins; throat white, region around eye velvety black.
A later plumage has the back grayish brown edged with whitish, tail gray
tipped with white; wings much as in the adult, underparts white breast
streaked with rufous. L., 15·50; W., 12·50; T., 7·00; B. from N., ·70.
[1]See Fig. 71.

Range.—Calif. w. of the desert divides; from the Upper Sacramento Valley and Humboldt Co. s. to the San Diegan district and n. L. Calif. (rarely); also in Tex., Okla. and Fla. s. rarely to Guat.; casual in La., Ills., Mich. and S. C.

Nest, in trees. *Eggs*, 3–5, "handsomely marbled or clouded with various shades of rich madder-brown on a paler (sometimes whitish) ground, 1·71 X 1·31" (Ridgway). *Date*, Brownsville, Tex., May 11.

This species is not often found east of the Mississippi. It frequents open, marshy situations. A pair which I observed in Texas hunted by hovering over the reeds, sustaining a position facing the wind, and about 40 feet from the ground, by a gentle movement of the wings.

120. SWALLOW-TAILED KITE. ELANOIDES FORFICATUS FORFICATUS (*Linnæus*). [327.] *Ads.*—Head, neck, linings of wings, part of tertials, and underparts white; foreback and lesser wing-coverts glossy purplish black; wings and tail glossy bluish black; tail deeply forked, outer feathers about 8·00 longer than middle ones. L., 24·00; W., 16·50; T., 13·50; B. from N., ·80. (In life the dark areas bear a powdery 'bloom.')

Range.—Breeds locally from n. Minn., s. Wisc., s. Ind. (formerly O.), N. C., S. C. to Fla., and through e. Mex. to Cent. A. Winters s. of the U. S. Accidental or casual in N. Mex., Colo., s. Sask., s. Man., Mich., n. Wisc., Ont., Pa., N. Y., Vt., Mass. and Conn.; England and the Greater Antilles.

Washington, three records, Aug.; Apr. Bronx region, A. V., two records, Oct. 2; Apr. 30. SE. Minn., formerly common S. R., now rare; May 4– Sept.

Nest, in the upper branches of tall trees. *Eggs*, 2–3, white or buffy white, boldly spotted or blotched, chiefly round the larger end, with hazel-brown, chestnut, or rich madder-brown, 1·87 X 1·49 (Ridgway). *Date*, San Mateo, Fla., Apr. 11; Black Hawk Co., Ia., June 2, 1878.

The Swallow-tailed Kite winters in Central and South America, and appears in the United States in March. Its home is the air, and it is far more frequently seen on the wing than at rest. It captures its prey of tree-snakes and lizards from the branches of trees and devours it while under way. Its flight possesses all the marvelous ease and grace of a Swallow's, made more evident, and consequently more impressive, by the bird's much greater size.

121. MISSISSIPPI KITE. ICTINIA MISISIPPIENSIS (*Wilson*). [329.] *Ads.* —Head, neck, exposed margins of the secondaries, and underparts gray; back bluish slate-color; primaries streaked or spotted with rufous-chestnut; tail black, without bars. *Im.*—Head streaked with black and white; back blackish, tipped with rufous or white, the concealed parts of the feathers white and with generally one blackish bar; primaries *without* rufous; tail with three or four broken white bars; below buffy, streaked with rufous and grayish brown. L., 14·00; W., 11·25; T., 6·50; B. from N., ·60.

Range.—L. Austral Zone (chiefly); breeds from ne. Kans., s. Ills., s. Ind., and S. C. s. to Tex. and Fla.; winters in Fla. and s. Tex. and s. rarely to Guat.; casual in Ia.; accidental in Colo., Nebr., Wisc., N. J. and Pa.

Nest, in tall trees. *Eggs*, 1–3, dull white, sometimes with a bluish tinge, 1·63 X 1·32. *Date*, Lee Co., Tex., May 22; coast S. C., May 27, large embryo.

This bird is chiefly a summer resident in the United States, arriving from the South in April. It is not common. It migrates in flocks, sometimes flying within gun-shot, and at others so far above the earth as to be almost beyond the bounds of vision.

122. EVERGLADE KITE. ROSTRHAMUS SOCIABILIS PLUMBEUS *Ridgway.*
[330.] *Ad.* ♂.—Dark slate-color; under, and longer upper tail-coverts, and base of the tail white, tip of the tail whitish; upper mandible much lengthened and hooked. ♀ and *Im,.*—Upperparts black, tipped with rufous; underparts barred and mottled with rufous, black and buffy; tail as in the *Ad.* ♂. L., 18·00; W., 14·00; T., 7·75; B., 1·20.

Range.—Peninsular Fla., Cuba, e. Mex. and Cent. A. Winters from cent. Fla. s.

Nest, in bushes, among reeds or tall grasses. *Eggs,* 2–3, pale bluish white, heavily spotted, blotched, or washed with cinnamon or chocolate, 1·85 × 1·47. *Date,* near Ft. Myers, Fla., Mch. 1.

This species is a resident in southern Florida. Mr. W. E. D. Scott writes of it as observed at Lake Panasofkee, Florida: "Their food at this point apparently consists of a kind of large, fresh-water snail, which is very abundant, and the local name of 'Snail-Hawk' is particularly applicable to this bird as I have met with it. They fish over the shallow water, reminding one of Gulls in their motions; and having secured a snail by diving, they immediately carry it to the nearest available perch, where the animal is dexterously taken from the shell without injury to the latter." (*Bull. Nutt. Orn. Club,* 1881, p. 16.)

1926. NICHOLSON, D. J., Auk, 62–67, illus. (nesting).

123. EASTERN GOSHAWK. ASTUR ATRICAPILLUS ATRICAPILLUS (*Wilson*). [334.] *Ads.*—Upperparts bluish slate-color; head blackish, a white line over and behind the eye; inner tail-feathers like the back, outer ones more fuscous, and slightly marked with blackish; tip whitish; entire underparts evenly marked with irregular, wavy bars of gray and white, the feathers of the throat and breast with darker shaft streaks. *Im.*—Upperparts fuscous, margined with rufous; primaries barred with black; tail brownish gray, barred with black; underparts white or buffy, streaked with black. ♂ L., 22·00; W., 13·00; T., 10·00; B. from N., ·65. ♀ L., 24·00; W., 13·40; T., 11·50.

Range.—Breeds in the Boreal zones from nw. Alaska, se. Ont. and n. Que. (Ungava), s. to interior B. C., Mich., n. N. Y., n. N. E., Mass. (casually) and in the mountains to Pa. and n. Md. Winters from Alaska and the s. Canadian Provinces to s. Calif., n. Mex., Tex., Okla., Mo., Ky., Ills., Ind., n. O., W. Va. and Va. Accidental in the British Isles.

Washington, irregular in winter. Bronx region, usually rare W. V., sometimes well-marked flights; Oct. 10–Apr. 29. Boston, irregular and uncommon W. V. N. Ohio, casual W. V. SE. Minn., W. R., Sept. 12–Apr. 13.

Nest, in trees. *Eggs,* 2–5, "white, or glaucous-white, sometimes very faintly marked with pale brownish, 2·31 × 1·74" (Ridgway). *Date,* Moorehouseville, N. Y., Apr. 20; Kentville, N. S., Apr. 8; St. Croix Co., Wisc., Apr. 17.

With the general habits of the two following species, this larger bird is much bolder than either. Usually a rare bird in the United States, at irregular intervals it appears in exceptional numbers and is then most destructive to Ruffed Grouse. Dr. Fisher remarks: "This species is one of the most daring of all the Hawks, and while in pursuit of its prey is apparently less concerned by the presence of man than any other. It will dart down unexpectedly at the very feet of the farmer and carry off a fowl.

"Of 28 stomachs examined, 9 contained poultry or game-birds; 2, other birds; 10, mammals; 3, insects; 1, centiped and 8 were empty."

1927. GROSS, A. O., Auk, 479–493 (invasion of in 1926–27); see also SUTTON, G. M., The Cardinal (Pittsburgh), July, 1927.

124. SHARP-SHINNED HAWK. ACCIPITER VELOX VELOX (*Wilson*). [332.] (Fig. 68, Pl. XII.) *Ads.*—Upperparts slaty gray; *primaries barred with blackish;* tail nearly *square*, ashy gray, with blackish cross-bars and a whitish tip; throat white, streaked with blackish; rest of underparts barred with white and ochraceous-buff or pale rufous. *Im.*—Upperparts fuscous, margined with rufous; primaries and tail much as in the ad.; underparts white or buffy white, streaked or spotted with blackish or pale rufous-brown. ♂ L., 11·25; W., 6·60; T., 5·50; B. from N., ·40. ♀ L., 13·50; W., 8·00; T., 7·00.

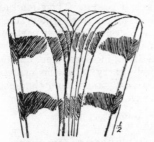

FIG. 68. Square tail of Sharp-shinned Hawk.

Remarks.—This species very closely resembles Cooper's Hawk. In adult plumage the black cap characterizes that species, but immature birds may be distinguished only by size, and the difference in the shape of the tail, which in *velox* is nearly square, and in *cooperi* decidedly rounded.

Range.—Breeds nearly throughout the U. S. and Can. from nw. Alaska to s. Lab. s. to n. Fla., and w. cent. Calif. Winters from se. Alaska, s. Minn. (casually), s. Ont., and N. B. (casually), to Panama (casually). Accidental in the Bahamas.

Washington, uncommon P. R. Bronx region, common T. V., uncommon P. R., Mch. 10–May 30; Aug. 3–Dec. 28. Boston, rather common T. V., uncommon S. R. and W. V., Mch.–May; Sept.–Nov. N. Ohio, common T. V., not common P. R. Glen Ellyn, rare S. R., Mch. 19–Dec. 9. SE. Minn., uncommon S. R., Mch. 18–Nov. 30; a few winter.

Nest, in trees, 15–40 feet up. *Eggs*, 3–6, bluish white to pale cream-buff, distinctly spotted, heavily blotched, or even washed with chocolate or cinnamon-rufous, 1·55 × 1·20. *Date*, Weaverville, N. C., May 1; Northampton Co., Pa., May 14; Boston, May 20; Knox Co., O., May 11; se. Minn., May 8.

The generally misapplied names 'Hen Hawk' and 'Chicken Hawk' should be restricted to the birds of the genera *Accipiter* and *Astur* for they deserve the reputation commonly attributed to the large Hawks of the genus *Buteo*.

The Sharp-shinned Hawk differs decidedly in habits from the mouse- or insect-eating species, which watch for their prey from a lookout and capture it on the ground. It is a fearless, daring, aggressive bird, and flying swiftly, rather low, either in the open or through woods, it makes sudden dashes at the frightened birds, which hurry to cover to escape its talons. One hears a commotion among the birds; calls of alarm, and a dark form darts through the foliage in close pursuit, or, missing its aim, alights in the center of some thickly leaved tree, there to await in silence a fresh opportunity. I have seen it follow its prey on foot through the undergrowth. Sometimes it may be seen soaring in narrow circles, when its disproportionately long tail forms a good field character.

It is usually a voiceless bird except during the nesting season, when a too close approach to its nest causes it to utter its peculiar notes.

"Of 159 stomachs examined, 6 contained poultry or game-birds; 99, other birds; 6, mice; 5, insects; and 52 were empty" (Fisher).

125. COOPER'S HAWK. ACCIPITER COOPERI (*Bonaparte*). [333.]
(Figs. 35*b*, 66, 69; Pl. XII.) *Ads.*—Similar to adults of the preceding, but larger and with the crown blackish. *Im.* —Similar in color to young of *A. velox*, but larger. ♂ L., 15·50; W., 9·50; T., 7·75; B. from N., ·55. ♀ L., 19·00; W., 10·50; T., 9·00.

Range.—Breeds from s. B. C. and s. Que. to the s. border of the U. S. and n. Mex. Winters from sw. B. C., s. Mich. (rarely), s. Ont. (rarely), and s. Me. to Costa Rica.

Washington, uncommon P. R. Bronx region, fairly common T. V., uncommon S. R. and in winter, Mch. 12–June 2; July 18–Jan. 12. Boston, rather common T. V., not uncommon S. R., rare W. V., Apr. 10–Oct. 20. N. Ohio, not common, Mch. 20–Nov. 1; a few winter. Glen Ellyn, local S. R., a few winter. SE. Minn., common S. R., Mch. 24–Oct. 26; two winter records.

Nest, in trees, 25–50 feet up. *Eggs*, 3–6, pale bluish white, sometimes lightly spotted with brownish, 1·90 × 1·55.

FIG. 69. Rounded tail of Cooper's Hawk.

Date, Montgomery Co., Pa., Apr. 30; New London, Conn., Apr. 27; Boston, May 5; Herkimer Co., N. Y., May 6.

This species resembles the preceding in habits, but because of its larger size is more destructive to poultry.

"Of 133 stomachs examined, 34 contained poultry or game-birds; 52, other birds; 11, mammals; 1, frog; 3, lizards; 2, insects; and 39 were empty" (Fisher).

126. EASTERN RED-TAILED HAWK. BUTEO BOREALIS BOREALIS
(*Gmelin*). [337.] (Pl. XII.) *Ads.*—Upperparts dark grayish brown or fuscous-brown, more or less edged with rufous, ochraceous-buff, and whitish; *four* outer primaries 'notched,' the outer one not regularly barred; wing-coverts *not* edged with rufous; tail *rich rufous*, with a narrow black band near its end and a white tip; upper breast heavily streaked with grayish brown and ochraceous-buff, lower breast lightly streaked and sometimes without streaks; upper belly streaked, spotted, or barred with black or blackish, forming a kind of broken band across the belly; lower belly generally white without streaks. *Im.*—Similar, but the tail of about the same color as the back, crossed by numerous more or less distinct blackish bands; no rufous in the markings of the underparts. ♂ L., 20·00; W., 15·50; T., 9·25; B. from N., ·95. ♀ L., 23·00; W., 16·50; T., 9·75.

Range.—Breeds from Mack., n. Man., n. Ont., s. Que. and N. F., cent. s. Tex., ne. Okla., Ark., Ala. and n. Fla. Winters from Kans., ne. Ia., cent. N. Y., and s. Me. to ne. Mex. and the Gulf Coast of the U. S.

Washington, formerly common, now rare P. R. Bronx region, uncommon S. R.; common T. V. and in winter; Aug. 22–May 23. Boston, uncommon T. V. and rare W. V., Oct. 10–Apr. 20. N. Ohio, common P. R. Glen Ellyn,

P. R., not common, chiefly T. V. SE. Minn., common S. R., Mch. 2–
Nov. 23; rare in winter.

Nest, in trees, 30–70 feet up. *Eggs*, 2–4, dull white, generally scantily
and irregularly marked with shades of cinnamon-brown, 2·40 × 1·85. *Date*,
San Mateo, Fla., Mch. 4; Litchfield Co., Conn., Apr. 8; Richland Co., Ills.,
Mch. 6; se. Minn., Apr. 23.

The Red-tailed Hawk resembles its near relative, the Red-shouldered
Hawk, in the selection of its haunts, and, to a large extent, in habits.
It is to be distinguished in life from that species by its larger size,
which, even in the field, is noticeable, and by its call. The usual note
of the Redtail is a long-drawn 'squealing' whistle, which to my ear
suggests the sound produced by escaping steam.

"Of 562 stomachs examined, 54 contained poultry or game-birds;
51, other birds; 278, mice; 131, other mammals; 37, batrachians or
reptiles; 47, insects; 8, crawfish; 1, centiped; 13, offal; and 89 were
empty" (Fisher).

1927. TAVERNER, P. A., Victoria Mem. Mus. Biol. Ser. 13, 1–21 (relationships).

126a. FLORIDA RED-TAILED HAWK. BUTEO BOREALIS UMBRINUS
Bangs. [337*f.*] Resembling *B. b. borealis* in size, but darker, throat and
middle of belly marked with broad conspicuous striping and banding of
deep chocolate-brown; tail-feathers with dark brown markings (the remains
of bands) near the shafts (Bangs).
Range.—S. Fla., Cuba, and the Isle of Pines.

126b. KRIDER'S HAWK. BUTEO BOREALIS KRIDERI *Hoopes.* [337*a.*]
Similar to *B. b. borealis*, but with much more white in the plumage; the head
sometimes almost entirely white; the underparts only lightly streaked, and
with the band on the belly sometimes obsolete; the tail in the ad. pale
rufous, generally without a terminal black band; in the im., pale rufous, or
white, washed with rufous, and with numerous blackish bars. ♂ W., 15·00;
T., 9·50.
Range.—Breeds from s. Alberta, s. Man., Wyo., N. Dak., and Minn.
s. to Nebr. and Mo. Winters s. to Wisc., Ills., La., and Miss.; accidental in
Fla. and Ga.
SE. Minn., uncommon S. R., Mch. 27–Nov. 23.
Nesting-date, se. Minn., Apr. 22.

126c. HARLAN'S HAWK. BUTEO BOREALIS HARLANI (*Audubon*).
[337*d.*] *Ads.*—Upperparts dark sooty fuscous, bases of the feathers more or
less barred with grayish or whitish and at times with some rusty; tail closely
mottled with black, fuscous, rufous, and whitish; underparts varying from
white more or less spotted across the belly to sooty fuscous. *Im.*—Similar,
but the tail barred with blackish, grayish, rufous, or whitish, tipped with
white. ♂ L., about 19·00; W., 15·50; T., 8·25. ♀ L., about 21·00; W.,
17·00; T., 9·25.
Remarks.—The status of this form has not been satisfactorily established.
Range.—Breeds in nw. B. C., sw. Yukon, and adjoining parts of Alaska
s. at least to s. Alberta. In winter down the Miss. Valley to the Gulf States.
Casual in Calif.

Dr. William L. Ralph, in Bendire's 'Life Histories of North American Birds' (p. 218), reports this species as not uncommon during the
winter in St. John's and Putnam counties, Florida. He writes: "They

are exactly like the Red-tailed Hawks except in color, and their call-note is the same, only being longer drawn out. The call of the latter bird, as already stated, sounds like the squealing of a pig, or *kee-ee-e*, and that of Harlan's Hawk like *kee-ee-ee-e-e-ee*."

126*d*. The WESTERN REDTAIL, *Buteo borealis calurus* Cassin, [337*b*], has been recorded from Illinois and Minnesota.

127. NORTHERN RED-SHOULDERED HAWK. BUTEO LINEATUS LINEATUS (*Gmelin*). [339.] (Fig. 70.) *Ads.*—Upperparts dark grayish fuscous-brown, more or less edged with rufous, ochraceous-buff, and whitish; four outer primaries 'notched,' all barred with black and white; lesser wing-coverts *rufous*, forming a conspicuous 'shoulder'-patch; tail black or fuscous, with four or five white cross-bars and a white tip; throat streaked with blackish; rest of underparts rufous or ochraceous-buff, everywhere barred with white or whitish. *Im.*—Upperparts much as in the adult; basal part of the primaries mostly *ochraceous-buff*, fading to whitish on the inner web, with broken bars of fuscous; lesser wing-coverts conspicuously margined with rufous or rufous-chestnut; tail dark grayish brown, indistinctly barred with fuscous, and on the basal half with more or less rufous, the inner webs of the feathers with sometimes white bars; underparts white or whitish, streaked or spotted with black or blackish, the legs sometimes barred with rufous. ♂ L., 18·30; W., 12·50; T., 8·00; B. from N., ·75. ♀ L., 20·35; W., 13·50; T., 9·00.

Remarks.—Adults of this species may always be known by the rich rufous lesser wing-coverts. Immature birds are sometimes confused with the young of the Red-tailed or Broad-winged Hawks. From the former they may be distinguished by their small size, rufous margins of the lesser wing-coverts,

FIG. 70. Four-notched primaries of Red-shouldered Hawk. (Reduced.)

ochraceous-buff markings on the primaries, and the continuously streaked underparts; from the latter they differ in having four instead of three outer primaries 'notched,' in being larger, and in having ochraceous-buff on the primaries.

Range.—Breeds from Man., and s. Que., s. to s. Kans., ne. Tenn., and N. C., w. to the edge of the Great Plains. Winters from cent. Ia., Ills., Ind., s. O., s. Ont., cent. N. Y. and s. Vt., s. to the Gulf Coast and Tex.

Washington, common P. R. Bronx region, common P. R. Boston, common S. R., Apr.–Nov.; uncommon in winter. N. Ohio, common P. R. Glen Ellyn, P. R., more common than the Redtail; chiefly T. V., Mch. 3–Dec. 20. SE. Minn., rare S. R., Mch. 24–Sept. 14.

Nest, in trees, 30–60 feet up. *Eggs*, 3–5, dull white, generally more or less sprinkled, spotted, or blotched with cinnamon-brown or chocolate, 2·15 × 1·65. *Date*, Iredell Co., N. C., Mch. 26; New London, Conn., Apr. 3; Boston, Apr. 10.

The present species and the Red-tailed Hawk are the birds to which the names 'Chicken Hawk' and 'Hen Hawk' are most frequently misapplied. Being both common species whose habits render them easily observed, they are often unjustly made to suffer for the sins of their bird-killing relatives of the genera *Accipiter* and *Astur*.

The farmer sees a Hawk sailing in wide circles above him, uttering its fierce, screaming cry of *keè-you, keè-you*. While he is watching it a sly, low-flying *Accipiter* slips by him and makes a sudden dash into the poultry-yard. The farmer does not discriminate—a Hawk is a Hawk—and shaking his fist at the bird in the air, he vows vengeance at the first opportunity.

The Red-shouldered Hawk is at most times of the year a bird of the woods. Particularly does it like low woods watered with small streams from which it can obtain its favorite food of frogs. Its note is one of the common sounds of summer, and can be heard when the bird is almost lost to sight far up in the sky. It is frequently imitated by the Blue Jay.

"Of 220 stomachs examined, 3 contained poultry; 12, other birds; 102, mice; 40, other mammals; 20, reptiles; 39, batrachians; 92, insects; 16, spiders; 7, crawfish; 1, earthworms; 2, offal; 3, fish; and 14 were empty" (Fisher).

1894. KENNARD, F. H., Auk, 197–210, 270 (biography).

127a. FLORIDA RED-SHOULDERED HAWK. BUTEO LINEATUS ALLENI *Ridgway*. [339a.] Adults of this species may easily be distinguished from those of *B. l. lineatus* by their smaller size, grayish white head, with black shaft-streaks and *no* rufous, the smaller fuscous tips on the scapulars and interscapulars, which do not conceal the ashy gray bases of the feathers, by the whitish or grayish cheeks and throat, and the ochraceous-buff, indistinctly barred underparts. Immature birds are very similar to those of *B. l. lineatus*, and can be distinguished only by their smaller size and darker color. ♂ W., 11·00; T., 7·50; B., 1·20.

Range.—L. Austral Zone of southern states from Okla., Ark., Ala., and S. C. to La. and se. Fla.

Nesting-date, San Mateo, Fla., Feb. 22.

1930. NICHOLSON, D. J., Wilson Bull., 32–35 (habits).

127b. INSULAR RED-SHOULDERED HAWK. BUTEO LINEATUS EXTIMUS *Bangs*. [339c.] Resembling *B. l. alleni* in color, perhaps slightly darker; size smaller. ♂ W., 11·85; T., 6·75; ♀ W., 11·75; T., 6·73 (Bangs).

Range.—Fla. Keys.

128. BROAD-WINGED HAWK. BUTEO PLATYPTERUS PLATYPTERUS (*Vieillot*). [343.] (Pl. XII.) *Ads.*—Upperparts dark grayish brown or fuscous, more or less margined with buffy and rufous; *three* outer primaries 'notched' and *without* ochraceous-buff markings; tail fuscous, with two bars and the tip grayish white; underparts *heavily* barred with brownish ochraceous-buff. *Im.*—Upperparts like the preceding; tail grayish brown, with three to five indistinct black bars and a narrow whitish tip; underparts white or buffy white, streaked and spotted with fuscous. ♂ L., 15·89; W., 10·68; T., 6·75; B. from N., ·70. ♀ L., 16·76; W., 11·41; T., 7·09.

Remarks.—Compared with the other members of this genus, the *three* 'notched' primaries and small size are the principal characters of this Hawk.

Range.—Breeds from cent. Alberta, cent. Que., N. B., and Cape Breton Isl. s. to the Gulf Coast and cent. Tex., mainly e. of the Miss. Winters from

s. Fla. and s. Mex. through Cent. A. to Peru; rarely farther n. (reported from Conn., N. J., W. Va., O., Ind., and Ills.). Recorded also from Cuba, Haiti, and Porto Rico.

Washington, rare P. R. Bronx region, common, occasionally abundant T. V., uncommon S. R., Mch 15–May 23; Aug. 22–Oct. 14. Boston, uncommon T. V., and rare S. R., Apr.–Nov. N. Ohio, not common T. V.; tolerably common S. R. Glen Ellyn, not common S. R., Apr. 10–Nov. 7. SE. Minn., common S. R, Mch. 15–Nov. 11.

Nest, in trees, 25–50 feet up. *Eggs*, 2–4, dull white or buffy white, spotted, blotched, or washed with ochraceous-buff or cinnamon-brown, 2·10 × 1·60. *Date*, D. C., Apr. 23; Monroe Co., Pa., May 10; Lancaster, N. H., May 11; se. Minn., May 29.

Fig. 71. Three-notched primaries of Broad-winged Hawk. (Reduced.)

"Of all our Hawks, this species seems to be the most unsuspicious, often allowing a person to approach within a few yards of it, and, when startled, flies but a short distance before it alights again. During the early summer the Broad-winged Hawk often may be seen sitting for hours on the dead top of some high tree. At other times it is found on the smaller trees in the deep woods, along streams, or on the ground, where its food is more often procured. Although sluggish and unusually heavy in its flight, it is capable of rapid motion, and sometimes soars high in the air. One of its notes resembles quite closely that of the Wood Pewee. . . .

"Of 65 stomachs examined, 2 contained small birds; 15, mice; 13, other mammals; 11, reptiles; 13, batrachians; 30, insects; 2, earthworms; 4, crawfish; and 7 were empty" (Fisher).

1911. BURNS, F. L., Wilson Bull., 141–320 (monograph).

129. SWAINSON'S HAWK. BUTEO SWAINSONI *Bonaparte.* [342.] *Ad.*

♂.—Upperparts fuscous-brown, more or less margined with rufous or buffy; primaries *unbarred, three* outer ones 'notched'; tail slightly grayer than the back, with numerous indistinct, blackish bars showing more plainly on the under surface; breast covered by a large, *cinnamon-rufous patch;* belly white or ochraceous-buff, streaked, spotted, or barred with blackish, rufous, or buff. *Ad.* ♀.—Similar, but larger, the breast patch of the same color as the back. ♂ *and* ♀ *in dark or melanistic plumage.*—Entire plumage fuscous, the under tail- and under wing-coverts and the tail sometimes spotted or barred. *Im.*—Upperparts fuscous-brown, widely margined with buffy and rufous; base of the primaries grayish, and sometimes with a few broken bars; tail much as in the ad.; underparts *ochraceous-buff,* spotted and streaked with blackish. ♂ L., 20·00; W., 15·00; T., 8·50; B. from N., ·75.

Remarks.—Between the light and dark phases of coloration there is every degree of intergradation, but in any plumage this Hawk may be distinguished from our other species by having only *three* outer primaries notched. In this respect it agrees with *B. platypterus,* from which, however, it differs decidedly both in size and color.

Range.—Breeds from interior B. C., Ft. Yukon, Great Slave Lake, and Man. s. to n. Mex. Winters in s. S. A., only occasionally n. of the Equator. Casual in Que., Ont., Mich., Vt., N. Y., Me., and Mass. SE. Minn., S. R., rare Apr. 12–Nov. 12.

Nest, in trees, 30–80 feet up. *Eggs*, 2–3, varying from dull bluish white to creamy white, sometimes unmarked, but generally more or less spotted or blotched with shades of cinnamon-brown, 2·30 × 1·72. *Date*, Tom Green Co., Tex., Apr. 7; Dry Lake, N. Dak., May 12.

Swainson's Hawk is of rare occurrence east of the Mississippi. Dr. Fisher writes: "By preference it frequents the timber in the vicinity of streams, though often it is found far out on the prairie, where its only perch is the earth-mound of some mammal, or some other slightly elevated knoll."

1913. CAMERON, E. S., Auk, 167–176, 381–394 (habits).

130. SHORT-TAILED HAWK. BUTEO BRACHYURUS *Vieillot.* [344.]
Ads.—Upperparts slaty gray or fuscous grayish brown; forehead whitish; tail barred with black and narrowly tipped with white, its under surface grayish; sides of the breast or neck with some rufous-brown markings; rest of the underparts *pure white*. *Im.*—Similar, but upperparts browner and margined with cream-buff; underparts washed with cream-buff; no rufous-brown on the breast. *Dark phase.*—Fuscous-black with a slight metallic luster with, in some specimens, more or less concealed white spots or bars more evident below; forehead whitish; tail lighter than back, barred with black, its under surface and the under surface of the primaries grayish. L., 17·00; W., 12·50; T., 7·00; Tar., 2·35; B. from N., ·70.
Range.—Fla., e. Mex., and Cent. A. s. to Peru, Bolivia, and Brazil.
Nest, in trees. *Eggs*, dull white, spotted at the larger end with small spots and blotches of reddish brown over about one-fourth the surface, 2·16 × 1·61 (Pennock). *Date*, San Mateo, Fla., Apr. 4 (Ralph).

A rare resident in Florida. According to Mr. C. J. Pennock, who found its nest at St. Marks on April 3, its call somewhat resembles the scream of the Red-shouldered Hawk, but is finer and more prolonged (*The Auk*, 1890, p. 56; see also Scott, *Ibid.*, 1889, p. 243).

1924. BRANDT, H. W., Auk, 59–64 (nesting).

131. AMERICAN ROUGH-LEGGED HAWK. BUTEO LAGOPUS S. JOHANNIS (*Gmelin*). [347a.] *Ad., light phase.*—Upperparts fuscous-brown, margined with whitish and ochraceous-buff; inner vanes of wing-quills white at the base, a black patch at base of primaries evident in flight; basal half of the tail *white* or *buffy*, end with two or three grayish or whitish bars; underparts varying from white to ochraceous-buff, streaked and spotted with black, these marks uniting to form a broken band across the belly; front of *tarsi entirely feathered*. *Im., normal phase.*—Similar to the ad., but the end half of the tail without bars except for the white tip, the underparts more heavily marked with black, the belly band being broad and continuous. *Black phase.*—Plumage more or less entirely black, the primaries and tail barred with whitish and grayish. L., 22·00; W., 16·00; T., 9·50.
Remarks.—Its feathered tarsi and heavily marked underparts characterize this species.
Range.—Breeds chiefly in the Hudsonian Zone from the Aleutian Isls., nw. Alaska, and n. Que. (Ungava), and ne. Lab. to n. Alberta, and N. F. Winters from s. B. C., Colo., Minn. and the n. boundary of the U. S. and s. Ont. s. to s. Calif., Tex., and N. C. Accidental at St. George, Pribilof Isls.
Washington, rare and irregular W. V. Bronx region, uncommon W. V., Oct. 11–Apr. 4. Boston, uncommon W. V., Nov.–Apr. N. Ohio, not common W. V., Nov. 20–Apr. 3. Glen Ellyn, quite common W. V., decreasing, Oct. 12–Apr. 30. SE. Minn., W. V., Sept. 10–Mch. 19.
Nest, on rocky ledges or in trees. *Eggs*, 2–5, dull white, sometimes un-

marked, but generally more or less spotted, blotched, or scrawled with cinnamon-brown or chocolate, 2·20 × 1·75. *Date,* Ft. Chimo, Lab., May 24.

"The Rough-leg is one of the most nocturnal of our Hawks, and may be seen in the fading twilight watching from some low perch or beating with measured, noiseless flight over its hunting-ground. It follows two different methods of securing its food—one by sitting on some stub or low tree and watching the ground for the appearance of its prey, as the Red-tail does; the other by beating back and forth just above the tops of the grass or bushes and dropping upon its victim, after the manner of the Marsh Hawk. . . .

"The flight of the Rough-leg is seldom rapid and often appears labored, and when on the wing this Hawk resembles the Osprey more than any other bird of prey. . . .

"Of 49 stomachs examined, 40 contained mice; 5, other mammals; 1, lizards; 1, insects; and 4 were empty" (Fisher).

132. FERRUGINOUS ROUGH-LEG. Buteo regalis (*Gray*). [348.]
Ad., light phase.—Upperparts mostly rufous, the centers of the feathers fuscous; tail grayish white, margined with rufous; legs rufous, barred with black; rest of underparts white, more or less barred with rufous on the sides and belly; tarsi fully feathered in front. *Im.*—Upperparts dark grayish brown, slightly varied with ochraceous-buff; tail silvery grayish brown, *without* bars, the base white; underparts white, lightly spotted and streaked with fuscous. *Dark phase.*—Dark fuscous-brown, more or less varied with rufous; primaries and tail as in the ad. L., 23·00; W., 17·00; T., 10·50.
Remarks.—This species is to be distinguished from the preceding principally by its much larger bill and differently colored tail and underparts.
Range.—Breeds from extreme s. Alberta and s. Man., to ne. Calif., e. Ore., Utah, N. Mex., and Kans. Winters from Calif. and Mont. to L. Calif. and n. Mex.; casual e. to Wisc. and Ills.
Nest, in trees or on the ground in rocky places. *Eggs,* 2–4, "white, or buffy white, usually more or less spotted, blotched, or clouded with brown or grayish purple (or both), 2·42 × 1·88" (Ridgway). *Date,* Ft. Totten, N. Dak., Apr. 12.

This bird is rarely found east of the Mississippi. Dr. Fisher remarks: "The Squirrel Hawk is preëminently a bird of the prairie, and, unlike the common Rough-leg, shows little partiality to the vicinity of water, though in other respects it closely resembles the latter bird in habits."

1914. Cameron, E S., Auk, 159–167, illus. (habits).

133. HARRIS'S HAWK. Parabuteo unicinctus harrisi (*Audubon*). [335.] Larger upper tail-coverts, and base of tail white; lesser and under wing-coverts rufous. *Ads.*—Above and below fuscous-brown more or less washed with rufous, especially on the rump; tail black, its base and tip white; thighs rufous, under tail-coverts white. *Im.*—Similar, but tail without white tip and, seen from below, with broken bars; underparts streaked or barred with white; thighs barred with white. ♀ L., 22·00; W., 14·50; T., 10·00. ♂ L., 19·00; W., 13·25; T., 9·50.
Range.—L. Austral Zone in se. Calif., s. Ariz., s. N. Mex., s. Tex., La., and Miss. s. to Cape San Lucas and Panama. Accidental in Ia.
Nest, of sticks, etc., often in 'chaparral' growth or small trees. *Eggs,* 2–4, white, sometimes with small cinnamon spots, 2·08 × 1·70. *Date,* Corpus Christi, Tex., Mch. 19.

I found this Hawk a common inhabitant of the chaparral about Corpus Christi, Texas, where it nested in the low mesquites and hui-saches. Dresser observed it feeding on carrion with Caracaras and Vultures, but specimens dissected by Sennett contained mice, lizards, birds, and spermophiles. The white upper tail-coverts, as in the Marsh Hawk, make a good field-mark, but Harris's Hawk lacks the light, graceful, bounding flight of that species.

134. The MEXICAN GOSHAWK, *Asturina plagiata plagiata* Schlegdel, [346], a tropical species which reaches the southwestern border of the United States, was seen by Robert Ridgway in southern Illinois, August 19, 1871.

135. AMERICAN GOLDEN EAGLE. AQUILA CHRYSAËTOS CANADENSIS

(*Linnæus*). [349.] Tarsi densely feathered to the toes; hind head and elon-gate feathers of nape deep to pale buffy ochraceous. *Ads.*—Tail blackish brown with obscure grayish bands or mottling basally; plumage generally blackish more or less washed or marked with brown or rufous. *Im.*—Similar,

FIG. 72. Foot of Golden Eagle.

but generally blacker, the basal two-thirds of tail largely white. ♂ L., 30·00–35·00; Ex., 78·00–84·00; W., 23·00–24·70; T., 14·00–15·00; Tar., 3·65–3·80. ♀ L., 35·00–40·00; Ex., 84·00–90·00; W., 25·00–27·00; T., 15·00–16·00; Tar., 4·15–4·25 (Ridgway).

Range.—Breeds in mountainous regions from n. Alaska, nw. Mack., and perhaps cas-ually in the Canadian Provinces e. of the Rocky Mts. s. to n. L. Calif., cent. Mex., w. Tex., and formerly to N. C. Probably no longer breeds in the U. S. e. of the Miss. ex-cept possibly in N. C. and e. Tenn. In winter s. casually to La., Ala., n. Fla., and s. Tex.

Washington, rare W. V. Bronx region, A. V. at Ossining many years ago. Boston, cas-ual T. V. N. Ohio, rare W. V. SE. Minn., rare W. V., Nov. 15–Mch. 14.

Nest, on cliffs, rocky ledges, or in trees. *Eggs*, dull white, obscurely or distinctly blotched or speckled with shades of cinnamon-brown, 2·93 × 2·34. *Date*, San Benito Co., Calif., Feb. 19; Gold Hill, Colo., Apr. 3.

"It seems to be nowhere a common species in the East, but it is much more numerous in the mountainous parts of the Far West. It is confined chiefly to the mountains and more northern latitudes, where it breeds. It is able to endure intense cold, and sometimes remains far north in winter. In fact, its movements at that season are more in the form of wandering for food than regular migration to the south.

"The food consists mainly of mammals and birds, of which sper-mophiles, rabbits, fawns, lambs, turkeys, grouse, waterfowl, and other large birds form the principal part, though offal and carrion are some-times taken. . . . Of 6 stomachs examined, 1 contained feathers; 2, mammals; 2, carrion; and 1 was empty" (Fisher).

In view of the ever-recurring story of Golden Eagles bearing away children, it is well to say that Cameron shows that six pounds is about the greatest weight a Golden Eagle can carry while on the wing.

1905. CAMERON, E. S., Auk, 158–167; 1908, 251–268 (biography).—
1909. MacPHERSON, H. B., 8vo., 1–45; pls. 1–32 (Witherby, London).—
1927. Goodson, S., Days with the Golden Eagle, 176 pp., illus. (Williams
and Norgate, London).—1929. SLEVIN, J. R., Nesting Habits of Golden
Eagle, Proc. Calif. Acad. Sci., 45–71.

136. GRAY SEA EAGLE. HALIÆETUS ALBICILLA (*Linnæus*). [351]
Ads.—Tail white, rest of plumage varying from grayish brown to fuscous.
Im.—"With plumage largely light cinnamon-brown or isabella-color. ♂ L.,
31·00–34·00; W., 23·00–26·00; T., 11·50–12·00" (Ridgway).
Range.—Breeds from Scotland, n. Europe, and n. Asia to Spitzbergen and
Novaya Zemlya; in migration s. to Japan, China, n. India, s. Europe, and n.
Africa; resident in Iceland and Greenland; recorded also from Cumberland
Sound. Casual on the Aleutian Isls. and accidental off the coast of Mass.
(Apr. 14, 1914).
Nest, on cliffs or in trees. *Eggs,* 2–3, dull white, "occasionally with small,
faint spots of light brown" (Davie), 3·00 × 2·35. *Date,* Crimea, S. Russia,
Apr. 12 (Thayer Coll.).

137. NORTHERN BALD EAGLE. HALIÆETUS LEUCOCEPHALUS
ALASCANUS *C. H. Townsend.* Resembling *H. l. leucocephalus* in color but
larger. ♂ W., 23·80. ♀ W., 24·60.
Range.—Boreal Zones of nw. Alaska, nw. Mack., n. Que. (Ungava) s. to
B. C. and the Great Lakes. Winters s. at least to Wash., Mont., and Conn.

137a. SOUTHERN BALD EAGLE.
HALIÆETUS LEUCOCEPHALUS LEUCOCE-
PHALUS (*Linnæus*). [352.] *Ads.*—Head,
neck, and tail white, rest of the plumage fuscous; bill yellow; tarsus not fully
feathered. *Im.*—Fuscous, more or less
varied with white; tail fuscous, more or
less mottled with white, particularly on the
inner vanes of the feathers; bill black. ♂
L., 32·85; Ex., 84·10; W., 22·00; T., 11·90;
B., 2·48. ♀ L., 35·50; Ex., 89.00; W.,
24·00; T., 12·25; Weight, 12 lbs.
Remarks.—At any age the Bald Eagle
may be distinguished from the Golden
Eagle by its partly feathered tarsi.
Range.—U. S. to s. L. Calif. and cent.
Mex., breeding in suitable locations
throughout its range; rare and local in
Calif. (common on the Santa Barbara Isls.)
and in the arid interior states. Accidental
in Sweden.
Washington, not common P. R. Bronx
region, fairly common W. V.; rare P. R.
Boston, rare T. V. N. Ohio, tolerably
common P. R. SE. Minn., T. V., becoming rare, Mch. 14–Sept. 9; rare W. V.

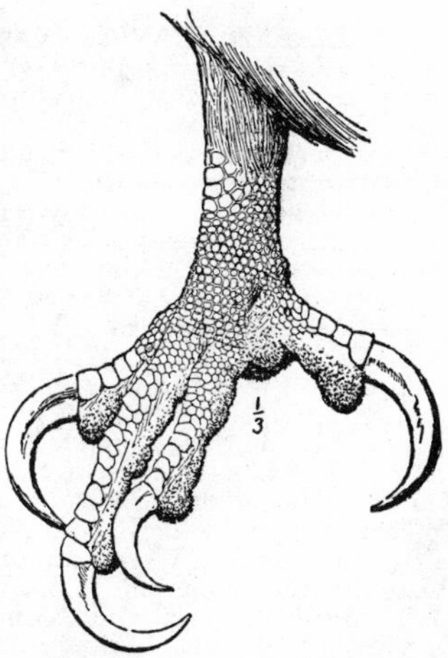

FIG. 73. Foot of Bald Eagle.

Nests, generally in tall trees, sometimes
on cliffs. *Eggs,* 2–3, dull white, 2·85 × 2·20. *Date,* Brevard Co., Fla., Nov. 25;
Tampa, Fla., Dec. 3; coast S. C., Nov. 27, large embryos; Lancaster Co.,
Pa., Feb. 11; Stone Isl., Me., Apr. 21.

Bald Eagles are seldom found far from the water. Here they may be
seen soaring overhead, winging their way to and from their feeding-
ground, or occupying some favorite perch, generally in an exposed

position. They subsist principally upon fish. As a last resort they sometimes capture these themselves, but dead fish cast up on the shore are eagerly taken, and their habit of robbing the Fish Hawk of his well-earned booty is too well known to be commented upon. In some localities, particularly in the South during the winter, they live largely upon waterfowl which they capture themselves.

The voice of the Bald Eagle has a weird, human quality. Dr. Fisher says: "At a distance the note of the Bald Eagle is not altogether unpleasant, resembling somewhat that of Sea Gulls, but nearby it is grating and suggests a maniacal laugh." Dr. William L. Ralph writes in Bendire's 'Life Histories': "The cry of the male is a loud and clear cac-cac-cac, quite different from that of the female—so much so that I could always recognize the sex of the bird by it; the call of the latter is more harsh and often broken."

The conspicuous white head and tail of adults of this species render it easy of identification even at a considerable distance. Young birds too closely resemble Golden Eagles to be distinguished with certainty, but the rarity of that species in the East makes it probable that any Eagle observed is a Bald Eagle.

1926. HERRICK, F. H. Auk, 89–105, 213–231, 389–422, 517–541, illus. (nesting).

138. MARSH HAWK. CIRCUS HUDSONIUS (*Linnæus*). [331.] (Pl. XII.) *Ad.* ♂.—Upperparts gray or ashy; upper tail-coverts *white;* tail silvery gray, irregularly barred or marked with blackish; upper breast pearl-gray; the lower breast and belly white, spotted or barred with rufous. *Ad.* ♀. —Upperparts fuscous, the head and neck streaked, and the wing-coverts spotted or margined with rufous; longer upper tail-coverts *white;* middle tail-feathers barred with ashy and black, others barred with ochraceous-buff and black; underparts ochraceous-buff, widely streaked on the breast and narrowly streaked on the belly with fuscous or light umber. *Im.*—Similar to the ♀, but somewhat darker above; the underparts darker, almost rufous; the belly without streaks. ♂ L., 19·00; W., 13·75; T., 9·00; B. from N., ·60. ♀ L., 22·00; W., 15·00; T., 10·00.

Range.—Breeds from nw. Alaska, nw. Mack., n. Man., n. Ont., cent. Que. and N. F. s. to n. L. Calif., s. Ariz., s. Tex., s. Ills., s. Ind., O., Md. and se. Va. Winters from s. B. C., w. Mont., w. S. Dak., s. Wisc., s. Mich., s. N. Y., s. Vt., s. N. H. s. to the Bahamas, Fla., Cuba, and Colombia. Accidental in Hawaii and Barbados.

Washington, formerly common, now rare W. V., July–Apr. Bronx region, fairly common T. V., uncommon S. R., Mch. 6–Jan. 12; rare in midwinter. Boston, rather common T. V., and uncommon S. R., occasional in winter, Mch. 20–Nov. 10. N. Ohio, common P. R. Glen Ellyn, S. R., several pairs, Apr. 4–Nov. 6. SE. Minn., common S. R., Mch. 4–Nov. 25; a few winter records.

Nest, on the ground, in marshes. *Eggs,* 4–6, dull white or pale bluish white, 1·75 × 1·40. *Date,* New London, Conn., May 18; Boston, June 5; Meridian, N. Y., May 12; Baxter, Ia., May 8.

This Hawk is essentially a bird of the unwooded country, and we might as well look for a Ruffed Grouse in the open marsh as for a Harrier in the thick woods. It flies low, and may be easily identified by the large white patch on its rump. Quartering the country with slow, vacillating flight, it usually captures its living prey by surprising it away from its retreats.

The Harrier is a low-perching Hawk, and most frequently will be seen alighting on a slight elevation or in the grass. During the nesting season the male may be seen performing a number of extraordinary aërial evolutions. Sometimes he soars to a great height, then falls straight downward nearly to the ground, turning several somersaults during the descent, and uttering at the same time a reiterated screeching. At other times he flies across the marsh in a course which would outline a gigantic saw, each of the descending parts being done in a somersault and accompanied by the screeching notes, which form the only love song within the range of his limited vocal powers.

ERNEST T. SETON.

"Of 124 stomachs examined, 7 contained poultry, or game-birds; 34, other birds; 57, mice; 22, other mammals; 7, reptiles; 2, frogs; 14, insects; 1, indeterminate matter, and 8 were empty" (Fisher). Stoddard states that of 1,098 pellets collected at a roosting-place near Thomasville, Ga., 4 contained the remains of Bob-white and 925 contained one or more cotton-rats.

1925. URNER, C. A., Auk, 37–41, illus. (nesting).—1927. WILSON, F. N , Bird-Lore, 397–402, illus. (nesting).—1929. ALLEN, A. A., Bird-Lore, 356–367, illus. (autobiography).

139. OSPREY. PANDION HALIAETUS CAROLINENSIS (*Gmelin*). [364.] (Fig. 21.) *Ad.* ♂.—Upperparts fuscous, the head and nape varied with white; tail with six to eight obscure bands, more distinct on the inner web; underparts white, breast sometimes slightly spotted with grayish brown. *Ad.* ♀.—Similar, but the breast always spotted with grayish brown. L., 23·10; W., 18·25; T., 8·40.

Range.—Breeds from nw. Alaska, and s. Lab. s. to L. Calif., w. Mex., the Gulf States, and the Fla. Keys. Winters from Fla. and the Gulf States, through L. Calif. and Mex. to the W. I. and Cent. A. Casual s. to Chile and Paraguay.

Washington, uncommon S. R., Mch. 19–Nov. 30. Bronx region, common T. V., occasional in summer but no longer breeds regularly; Mch. 19–June 12; Aug. 5–Oct. 28 (Nov. 14). Boston, rather common T. V., Apr.–May; Sept.–Oct. N. Ohio, rare S. R., Apr. 20–Oct. Glen Ellyn, three records, May and Sept. SE. Minn., S. R., Apr. 10–Oct. 21.

Nest, generally in a tree, 20–50 feet up, sometimes on rocks, rarely on the ground. *Eggs*, 2–4, extremely variable, sometimes dull white, unmarked, sometimes almost solid chocolate, but generally buffy white, heavily marked with chocolate, chiefly at the larger end, 2·45 × 1·80. *Date*, Bull's Mt., Md., Apr. 20; Shelter Isl., N. Y., May 3; Carver's Harbor, Me., May 8.

The Fish Hawk or Osprey has occasioned systematists no little difficulty, and it is variously placed in its own subfamily, family, or even suborder. There is virtually but a single species which ranges throughout the world, presenting in this wide area only sufficient variation on which to base the three or four currently recognized forms. Unlike most Raptorial birds, Ospreys sometimes nest in close proximity to one another, drawn together not by sociability of temperament, but by community of interests. On Gardiner's Island, L. I., there are about two hundred Osprey nests, the protection of an insular home and an abundant food-supply being the principal factors in the development of this 'colony.'

Its firm, dense plumage, large claws, the spicules which thickly beset the grasping surface of the toes, and the reversible outer toe are all distinctive characters and the evident outcome of the Osprey's specialized feeding habits.

The Osprey lives in colonies, and also in pairs, along our coasts, returning year after year to the same nesting-ground. Its food consists solely of fish, which, as a rule, it captures alive. Winging its way slowly over the water, it keeps a keen watch for fish which may appear near the surface. When one is observed, it pauses, hovers a moment, and then closing its wings descends with a speed and directness of aim that generally insure success. It strikes the water with great force, making a loud *splash*, and frequently disappears for a moment before rising with its prey grasped in its powerful talons. As a rule, it carries its food to some favorite perch, there to devour it.

The alarm-note of the Fish Hawk is a high, rapidly repeated, complaining whistle, which is sometimes varied and prolonged to the semblance of a song.

1892. ALLEN, C. S., Auk, 313–321 (on Plum Isl.).—1908. CHAPMAN, F. M., Camps and Cruises, 47–59 (Gardiner's Isl.).—1911. ABBOTT, C. G., The Home Life of the Osprey. 54 pp., illus. (Witherby & Co., London).

FAMILY FALCONIDÆ. THE FALCONS AND CARACARAS.

About fifty species are contained in this family. It is resemblance in structure rather than in habit that places the members of the genera *Falco* and *Polyborus* in the same family. In the former, predatory bird-life reaches its highest development; in the latter, we have birds not distantly removed from Vultures in the character of their food. From the great Arctic Gyrfalcons, nearly two feet in length, to the Indian Pygmy Falcon, no longer than a Song Sparrow, the Falcons are keen winged, dashing, fearless hunters among birds. They have not the soaring habits of the *Buteos*, from which they may be distinguished by their more pointed wings and more rapid wing-stroke. Their nests are less bulky than those of our buteonine Hawks, the eggs in some species being laid on the bare rock or in a hollow tree. (For Key, see *antea* under *Accipitridæ*.)

140. AUDUBON'S CARACARA. POLYBORUS CHERIWAY AUDUBONI *Cassin.* [362.] *Ads.*—Face bare; crown, lower back, wings, and belly black; throat buffy; nape, interscapulars, and breast barred with black and buffy; tail white, barred and tipped with black. *Im.*—Similar, but browner, and with few or no bars on the interscapulars and breast. L., 22·00; W., 16·00; B. from N., 1·25.

Range.—N. L. Calif., sw. Ariz., Tex., and Fla.; through Mex. and Cent. A.; s. to Guiana and Ecuador; accidental in Ont.

Nest, in a cabbage palmetto or on the tops of dense bushes. *Eggs*, 2–3, varying from cream-buff to rufous, heavily marked with shades of reddish brown and chocolate, 2·35 × 1·85. *Date*, Lake Kissimmee, Fla., Mch. 19.

Caracaras frequently associate with Vultures and feed on carrion, but they also capture their own food. This consists largely of frogs, lizards, and small snakes, which the birds find while walking about on the ground in search of them. Their flight is strong, rapid, and direct, and bears no resemblance to that of a Vulture.

141. WHITE GYRFALCON. Falco rusticolus candicans *Gmelin.* [353, 354.] Under tail-coverts usually white, *unmarked. Ads.*—Head white, finely streaked with black; scapulars, interscapulars, and wing-coverts white with broad bars or semi-lunes, rarely guttate spots of *slaty fuscous;* tail sometimes wholly white, usually broadly or narrowly barred with slaty fuscous; underparts white, with sometimes a few *small* grayish spots or streaks. *Im.*—Similar, but upperparts brownish gray with white margins and broken bars; tail barred with brownish gray; underparts more heavily, sometimes uniformly streaked. L., 22·00; W., 16·00; T., 10·00; B. from N., ·95.

Remarks.—The white, unmarked under tail-coverts and prevailing white color will distinguish this bird.

Range.—Resident in Greenland, e. Arctic A. (probably) and Spitzbergen and Franz Josef Land (probably). Casual in winter s. to B. C., Mont., Ont., Que., N. S., and Me.; and to the British Isles, France, and Germany.

Nest, on rocky cliffs. *Eggs*, 3–4, varying from creamy white, spotted or blotched with cinnamon-brown, to uniform pale reddish brown, spotted or blotched with shades of the same color, 2·30 × 1·85. *Date*, Umanak, Greenland, May 26 (Thayer Coll.).

"The food consists of water-fowl and other birds—largely of various arctic species of Grouse which are captured on the wing. All these northern Falcons were formerly esteemed for hawking, as they still are by the Mongol races; their style of flight is magnificent—much swifter than that of the Peregrine—and both are deadly 'footers' (i. e., tenacious of grip), but they lack spirit and dash" (Saunders).

141a. BLACK GYRFALCON. Falco rusticolus obsoletus *Gmelin.* [354b.] Under tail-coverts and legs streaked or barred. *Ads.*—General color above dark slaty gray; head unmarked or with some buffy, lateral margins or spots; back with distinct buffy or indistinct grayish *bars;* rump and upper tail-coverts grayer than back barred with whitish or gray; tail barred with the color of the back and mottled whitish or gray, the darker bars wider; underparts white more or less heavily streaked or spotted with fuscous, the sides, legs and under tail-coverts barred with slate. *Im.*—Upperparts dark grayish brown, head and nape streaked with buffy or whitish; back usually unmarked; rump and upper tail-coverts, usually more or less margined or laterally marked with buffy; tail like the back with incomplete, irregular buffy bars usually restricted to the inner webs of the inner feathers; underparts chiefly fuscous margined with buffy, the sides and under tail-coverts usually barred. L., 21·00; W., 15·50; T., 9·50; B. from N., ·95.

Remarks.—The relationships of the Gyrfalcons of Greenland are not definitely known, and the A. O. U. 'Check-List' includes, therefore, only the two forms above given. Schiöler ('Birds of Denmark') recognizes three Greenland forms: *Falco rusticolus candicans, F. r. obsoletus,* as here described, and *F. r. holbœlli.* Judging from adult specimens in the American Museum, which agree with Schiöler plates, this bird is intermediate between *candicans* and *obsoletus*, but nearer the latter. The upperparts and tail are evenly barred with slate and grayish white, the darker bars being slightly wider on the back and much narrower on the tail; the underparts are white sparingly marked with fuscous, the under tail-coverts are barred with fuscous.— See also Jourdain (Auk, 1931, Oct.).

Range.—N. N. A. from P. Barrow to Greenland and Lab. S. in winter to N. S., Que., and Me., casually to N. Y., N. H., Mass., R. I., and Conn., also probably S. Dak., Kans., Minn., O., and Pa.

Nesting-date, Ft. Chimo, Lab., May 22.

In view of the unsettled status of North American Gyrfalcons there is some question concerning the identity of specimens of this superb Hawk from south of the St. Lawrence, but most of them have, no doubt, been correctly referred to this race.

142. PRAIRIE FALCON. FALCO MEXICANUS *Schlegel*. [355.] *Ads.*— Above, grayish brown; primaries and inner webs of all but the middle tail-feathers with numerous buffy bars or spots; below, white, streaked and spotted with dark grayish brown. *Im.*—Similar, but with the upperparts margined with ochraceous-buff or buffy. ♂ L., 17·00; W., 12·20; T., 7·00.

Range.—Transition and Austral zones from the e. border of the Great Plains and from s. B. C. and se. Sask. to s. L. Calif. and s. Mex. Casual e. to Minn. and Ills.

Nest, on cliffs, sometimes in hollow trees. *Eggs*, 2–5, "creamy white, vinaceous-white, or pale vinaceous-buffy, sprinkled, speckled, or irregularly spotted with madder-brown, 2·06 × 1·60" (Ridgway). *Date*, Gilmer, Wyo., Mch. 25.

"The Prairie Falcon, as the name implies, is a typical plains bird, and inhabits the dry interior. . . .

"The flight of this Hawk is swift and graceful, though in most cases it is carried on at no great distance from the ground. It is not a shy bird, except in sections where it has been persecuted and has learned that man is its worst enemy" (Fisher).

143. The PEREGRINE FALCON, or OLD-WORLD DUCK HAWK, (*Falco peregrinus peregrinus* Tunstall, [356], occurs in Greenland.

143a. DUCK HAWK. FALCO PEREGRINUS ANATUM *Bonaparte*. [356a.] (Figs. 35a, 67.) *Ads.*—Upperparts dark bluish slate-color; back barred with black; cheeks black; primaries barred with ochraceous; tail indistinctly barred with blackish and tipped with white; underparts cream-buff, barred and spotted with black, except on the breast. *Im.*—Upperparts fuscous, more or less margined with ochraceous or rufous; region below the eye black; ear-coverts buffy; wings as in the ad.; upper surface of the tail barred with grayish, under surface barred with ochraceous-buff; underparts cream-buff or ochraceous-buff, streaked, spotted or barred with black. ♂ L., 16·00; W., 12·25; T., 6.50; B. from N., ·68. ♀ L., 19·00; W., 14·00; T., 7·50.

Range.—Breeds locally from Norton Sd., Alaska, and w. coast of cent. Greenland, s. to cent. L. Calif., cent. Mex., cent. w. Tex., Kans., Mo., Ind., Pa., and Conn. and in the mountains to Tenn. Winters from Vancouver Isl., Colo., se. Nebr., Pa., and Mass., to the W. I. and S. A.

Washington, rare and irregular W. V. Bronx region, uncommon P. R. Boston, uncommon T. V., and rare W. V., Aug.–Apr. N. Ohio, occasionally breeds. SE. Minn., uncommon S. R., Apr. 4–Sept. 30.

Nest, on rocky cliffs and in the hollow limbs of tall trees. *Eggs*, 3–4, creamy white, heavily marked with cinnamon-brown, to pale reddish brown, more or less marked with shades of the same color, 2·05 × 1·68. *Date,* Wyoming Co., Pa., Apr. 18, inc. adv.; Mt. Tom, Mass., Apr. 23.

This species is the 'Noble Peregrine' of falconry. It would be difficult to imagine a bird more highly endowed with qualities which make the ideal bird of prey. Its strength of wing and talon is equaled by its courage. Few birds fly more swiftly than the Duck Hawk. Even Teal—those winged bullets—cannot escape it. No bird is more daring. I have had Duck Hawks dart down to rob me of wounded Snipe lying almost at my feet, nor did my ineffective shots prevent them from returning. Duck Hawks are generally found near water, where they prey largely on water birds.

"Of 20 stomachs examined, 7 contained poultry or game-birds; 9, other birds; 1, mice; 2, insects; and 4 were empty" (Fisher).

1913. ALLEN A. A. and KNIGHT, H. K., The Duck Hawks of Taughannock Gorge, Bird-Lore, 1–8, illus.

144. PIGEON HAWK. FALCO COLUMBARIUS COLUMBARIUS *Linnæus.* [357.] *Ads.*—Upperparts slaty blue, a broken buffy or rusty color on the neck; primaries barred with white; tail with three or four distinct grayish white bars and a white tip; underparts varying from cream-buff to deep ochraceous, streaked with blackish, except on the throat. *Im.*—Upperparts fuscous or brownish fuscous, a broken buffy collar on the nape; primaries barred with ochraceous; tail with three or four incomplete buffy bars and a whitish tip; underparts much as in the ad. L., 10·00–13·00; W., 8·00; T., 5·50; B. from N., ·45.

Remarks.—This little Falcon bears some resemblance to a Duck Hawk, but is much smaller.

Range.—Breeds from the limit of trees in e. Can. s. to N. F., N. S., n. Me., Ont., n. Mich., and s. Man. w. to the e. border of the Great Plains. Winters from the Gulf States s. through e. Mex. to Ecuador and n. Venezuela and the W. I.

Washington, not uncommon T. V., Mch. 21–May 11; Sept. 4–Nov. 11. Bronx region, uncommon T. V., Apr. 6–May 17; Aug. 10–Nov. 16 (Jan. 3). Boston, rather uncommon T. V., Apr. 25–May 5; Sept. 25–Oct. 20; occasional W. V. N. Ohio, rare P. R. Glen Ellyn, regular but rare T. V., Apr. 26–May 5; Sept. 10–Oct. 16. SE. Minn., Apr. 13–Oct. 15.

Nest, in trees, in hollow limbs, or on cliffs. *Eggs,* 4–5, creamy white, more or less heavily marked with reddish brown or chocolate, to reddish brown marked with shades of the same color, 1·65 × 1·20. *Date,* Bingham Co., Idaho, May 13; Lab., June 2.

"This Falcon, with the exception possibly of the Broad-winged Hawk, is the least shy of all our diurnal birds of prey, and often may be approached within a few rods. It frequents the more open country and edges of woods, and is common along the shores of large bodies of water. . . . The flight is very rapid and resembles that of the Wild Pigeon quite closely; nor does the similarity end here, for while sitting on a tree the general poise is that of a Pigeon in repose, and specimens have been mistaken and shot for the latter bird. . . .

"Of 56 stomachs examined, 2 contained poultry; 41, small birds; 2, mice; 16, insects; and 5 were empty" (Fisher).

144a. The WESTERN PIGEON HAWK, *Falco columbarius bendirei* Swann, of northwestern North America is recorded as casual in Louisiana, Florida, North Carolina, and South Carolina.

145. The MERLIN, *Falco æsalon æsalon* Tunstall, [358.1], an Old-World species, is accidental in Greenland.

146. The KESTREL, *Falco tinnunculus tinnunculus* Linnæus, [359.1], an Old-World species, is accidental in Greenland and Massachusetts.

147. EASTERN SPARROW HAWK. FALCO SPARVERIUS SPARVERIUS *Linnæus.* [360.] *Ad.* ♂.—Back rufous, more or less barred with black; tail rufous, a black band near its end, the tip white; head slaty blue, with generally a rufous spot on the crown; wing-coverts slaty blue, primaries barred with white; a black mark before and behind the white ear-coverts; underparts varying from cream-buff to ochraceous-buff; belly and sides spotted with black. *Ad.* ♀.—Back, tail, and wing-coverts rufous, barred with black; head as in the male; underparts more or less heavily streaked with dark ochraceous-buff. *Im.*—Closely resemble the adults. L., 10·00; W., 7·30; T., 4·80; B. from N., ·45.

Range.—Breeds from the Upper Yukon, B. C., nw. Mack., and N. F. s. to nw. Calif., e. Tex., and the e. Gulf States (except the s. border and Fla.). Winters from s. B. C., Kans., Ind., cent. Ills., O., s. Ont., s. Mich., s. Vt., s. through e. Mex. to Panama.

Washington, uncommon P. R. Bronx region, common P. R. Boston, P. R., common in summer, less so in winter. N. Ohio, common P. R. Glen Ellyn, not common S. R., Mch. 10–Oct. 26; occasional W. V. SE. Minn., S. R., formerly abundant, now infrequent; Mch. 11–Oct. 15.

Nest, in a hole in a tree, frequently in a Woodpecker's deserted nest. *Eggs,* 3–7, creamy white to rufous, generally finely and evenly marked with shades of the ground color, 1·40 × 1·12. *Date,* Nazareth, Pa., Apr. 9; Boston, May 5; SE. Minn., Apr. 25.

An old stub or branchless trunk of a dead tree standing well out in a field is the kind of perch the Sparrow Hawk most frequently chooses. From this lookout, like a Loggerhead Shrike, he awaits the appearance of game below. Generally it is a grasshopper which falls his victim. When he detects one, he flies directly over it, and poises on hovering wings until the right opportunity offers, when he drops lightly downward, clutches his prey in his talons, and then returns to his perch to devour it at leisure.

The Sparrow Hawk's call is a rather high, quickly repeated *killy-killy-killy-killy*, which in some sections gives it the name of 'Killy Hawk.'

"Of 320 stomachs examined, 1 contained a game bird; 53, other birds; 89, mice; 12, other mammals; 12, reptiles or batrachians; 215, insects; 29, spiders; and 29 were empty" (Fisher).

147a. LITTLE SPARROW HAWK. FALCO SPARVERIUS PAULUS (*Howe & King*). [360c.] Similar to *F s. sparverius* but "rufous of upperparts very dark, particularly on the rectrices. Tail and wings short. Bill large and heavy." (Howe, Cont. to N. A. Orn., I, 1902, 28.)

Range.—Fla. peninsula and the s. border of the Gulf States n. to cent. Ala.

Nesting-date, Ft. Thompson, Fla., Apr. 1.

VIII. ORDER GALLIFORMES. GALLINACEOUS BIRDS

SUBORDER GALLI. GROUSE, QUAILS, PHEASANTS, TURKEYS

(7 families. 4 North American, 3 eastern North American.)

SYNOPSIS OF FAMILIES.

Tarsi without spurs. Tarsi, and often toes, more or less feathered; nostril opening feathered.
> *Family Tetraonidæ.* GROUSE AND PTARMIGAN. P. 235.

Tarsi and toes bare; nostrils not feathered.
> *Family Perdicidæ.* QUAILS. P. 243.

Tarsi spurred.
> Head bare, tail square . . . . . *Family Meleagridæ.* TURKEYS. P. 247.
> Head feathered, tail pointed. . *Family Phasianidæ.* PHEASANTS. P. 247.

1897. ELLIOT, D. G., Gallinaceous Game-Birds of North America, 8vo., 220 pp., 46 pls. (Francis Harper).—1900. DWIGHT, J., JR., The Moult of North American Tetraonidæ, Auk, 34–51, 143–166.—1902. SANDYS, E. and VANDYKE, T. S., Upland Game Birds, 8vo., 429 pp., 9 pls. (Macmillan). —1903. HUNTINGTON, D. W., Our Feathered Game, 8vo., 396 pp., 37 pls.— 1907. RICH, W. H., Feathered Game of the Northeast, 8vo., 430 pp., 87 pls. —1928. PHILLIPS, J. C., Wild Birds Introduced or Transplanted in North America, Tech. Bull. No. 61, U. S. Dept. Agric.

FAMILY TETRAONIDÆ. GROUSE.

The Grouse, numbering some thirty species, inhabit the northern parts of the Northern Hemisphere. Two species of Ptarmigan are found throughout the Arctic regions, while the remaining members of the family are about equally divided between the Old World and the New. After the nesting season they commonly gather in 'coveys' or bevies. In some species, these bevies unite or 'pack,' forming large flocks. As a rule, they are terrestrial, but may take to trees when flushed, while some species habitually call and feed in trees. They are game-birds *par excellence*, and, trusting to the concealment afforded by their protective coloration, attempt to avoid detection by hiding rather than by flying, or, in sportsman's phraseology, "lie well to a dog." Their flight is rapid and accompanied by a startling *whirr*, caused by the quick strokes of their concave, stiff-feathered wings. Though not, as a rule, migratory, or given to extended flights, their great weight as compared with their wing-expanse, and the necessity of getting under way at once, requires great strength, hence the exceptional development of the breast muscles which constitute most of the edible portion of these universally esteemed birds. Many species of this family are polygamous, and their strutting, dancing or actual fighting, tootings, hootings, boomings, or drummings make them among the most interesting of birds during their periods of courtship display.

The young, as with all Gallinaceous birds, are hatched thickly

covered with down, usually of a pronounced pattern, and leave the
nest soon after birth, generally under the care of the female alone.
Like the young of Terns, they instinctively squat at the warning note
of the parent, which then flutters painfully before one, using every
possible effort to draw one from the vicinity of her chicks.

KEY TO SPECIES

I. Wing-quills white.
   A. Bill stout, depth at nostril over ·40.
                150, 150a, 150b. WILLOW PTARMIGAN AND RACES.
   B. Bill smaller, depth at nostril under ·40.
                151, 151a–c. ROCK PTARMIGAN AND RACES.
II. Wing-quills brown.
   A. Neck with ruffs or tufts.
      a. Neck-tufts broad, black, tail over 6·00. 149, 149a. RUFFED GROUSE.
      b. Neck-tufts narrow, black and white, or buff, tail 4·00.
                152a. PRAIRIE CHICKEN.
       b^1. Neck-tufts of more than 10 feathers.
       b^2. Neck-tufts of less than 10 feathers. . . . . 152 HEATH HEN.
   B. Neck without ruffs or tufts.
      a. Central tail-feathers narrow, much elongated.
            153, 153a. SHARP-TAILED GROUSE AND RACES.
      b. Central tail-feathers broad, not elongated.
            148a. CANADA SPRUCE PARTRIDGE AND RACE.

148. HUDSONIAN SPRUCE GROUSE. CANACHITES CANADENSIS
CANADENSIS (*Linnæus*). [298.] Male indistinguishable from the male of *C.
c. canace;* female similar to female of *canace* but less rusty.
   Range.—Boreal forest region from the e. base of the Rocky Mts. w. of
Edmonton, Alberta, e. to Lab. Peninsula.

148a. CANADA SPRUCE GROUSE. CANACHITES CANADENSIS CANACE
(*Linnæus*). [298c.] *Ad.* ♂.—Upperparts barred with black, ashy, gray, and
grayish brown; tertials and wing-coverts irregularly marked with fuscous
and grayish brown; tail black, tipped with rufous; black throat separated
from black breast by a broken circular band of black and white and a band
of same color as back of neck; sides mottled with black and grayish brown,
ends of the feathers with white shaft streaks; rest of underparts black,
broadly tipped with white, except in middle of lower breast; bare skin above
eye bright red in life. *Ad.* ♀.—Upperparts barred with black and pale rufous
and tipped with ashy gray; tail black, mottled and tipped with rufous;
throat and upper breast barred with pale rufous and black; sides mottled
with black and pale rufous, ends of feathers with white shaft streaks; rest
of underparts black, broadly tipped with white and more or less washed with
pale rufous. L., 15·00; W., 6·50; T., 4·75; B. from N., ·40.
   Range.—S. Man., s. Ont., s. Que., N. B. and N. S., s. to the n. parts of
Minn., Wisc., Mich., N. Y., and N. E. Accidental in Mass. (one instance).
Now largely extinct in s. part of range.
   Boston, A. V.
   Nest, on the ground, sheltered by overhanging limbs. *Eggs,* 6–7, buffy
or pale brownish, more or less speckled or spotted with deep brown, 1·71 ×
1·22 (Ridgway). *Date,* Kentville, N. S., June 2.

The excessive tameness of this inhabitant of swampy, coniferous
forests is responsible for its decrease in numbers, and it is now a rare
bird in the United States. "In April and early May the males strut

and drum somewhat after the manner of the Ruffed Grouse, the sound resembling the distant roll of thunder. It is usually produced when the cock is fluttering up an inclined tree trunk or a stump, and from this elevation to the ground again, or sometimes by merely springing into the air for several feet and fluttering to the ground" (Eaton).

1911. HARDY, M., Journ. Me. Orn. Soc., 47–49 (habits in Maine).

149. EASTERN RUFFED GROUSE. BONASA UMBELLUS UMBELLUS (*Linnæus*). [300.] (Fig. 20, 36a.) *Ad.* ♂.—Prevailing color of the upperparts rufous, much variegated with black, ochraceous, buffy, gray, and whitish; sides of the neck with large tufts of broad, glossy black feathers; tail varying from gray to rufous, irregularly barred and mottled with black, a broad black or brownish band near the end; tip gray; throat and breast ochraceous-buff, a broken blackish band on the breast; rest of the underparts white, tinged with buffy and barred with blackish or dark grayish brown, the bars indistinct on the breast and belly, stronger on the sides. *Ad.* ♀.— Similar, but with the neck tufts very small. L., 17·00; W., 7·25; T., 6·25; B. from N., ·52.

Range.—S. Minn., s. Wisc., s. Mich., s. N. Y., and Mass. s. to e. Kans., n. Ark. (formerly), Mo. (rarely), Tenn. and Va. and in the mts. to n. Ga. and n. Ala.

Washington, P. R., rare, formerly more numerous. Bronx region, uncommon and rather local P. R. Boston, sometimes rather common. N. Ohio, rare P. R. Glen Ellyn, formerly rare and local P. R., now probably extinct here. SE. Minn., common P. R.

Nest, a depression lined with leaves, at the base of a stump or tree, or beneath brush. *Eggs,* 8–14, pale ochraceous-buff, 1·52 × 1·13. *Date,* Chester Co., Pa., May 5; Ossining, N. Y., May 5; Portland, Conn., May 7; Boston, May 15; se. Minn., May 3.

Of all the characteristics of this superb game bird, its habit of drumming is perhaps the most remarkable. This loud tattoo begins with the measured thump of the big drum, then gradually changes and dies away in the rumble of the kettle-drum. It may be briefly represented thus: *Thump——thump——thump—thump, thump; thump, thump-rup rup rup rup r-r-r-r-r-r-r-r.* The sound is produced by the male bird beating the air with his wings as he stands firmly braced on some favorite low perch, and it is now quite well known to be the call of the male to the female; an announcement that he is at the old rendezvous—a rendezvous that has perhaps served them for more than one season, and a place that in time becomes so fraught with delightful associations that even in autumn or winter the male, when he finds himself in the vicinity, cannot resist the temptation to mount his wonted perch and vent his feelings in the rolling drum-beat that was in springtime his song of love. But now, alas! there is no lady Grouse to come, shy but responsive, at the sound of his reverberating summons.

There is good reason for supposing that the Ruffed Grouse is polygamous, and that the male, if he drums in vain at one place, will fly to another retreat and there seek the society of some more compliant female. The young Grouse can run about as soon as they are hatched, and can fly well when about a week old. Their mother is celebrated for the variety of expedients she puts in practice to save her brood from threatened danger, and their father has frequently been known to divide the charge with her. The young usually continue with their parents till the following spring, though it is rare at this time to see more than three or four surviving out of the original twelve or fourteen.

The food of this Grouse is largely insects and berries during the summer; in the autumn it adds seeds to the list, and when the ground is covered with snow the staples are catkins, leaves, and buds. Its toes are provided during the winter with a curious fringe of strong, horny points which act as snowshoes. In the northern part of its range this bird commonly burrows into a snowdrift to pass the night during the season of intense cold; but in summer and in the warmer region of its range it roosts habitually among the thickets of evergreen.

ERNEST T. SETON.

1919. TUTTLE, H. E., Auk, 325–339, illus. (drumming).—1923. SAWYER, E. J., Roosevelt Wild Life Bull. (Univ. Syracuse, N. Y.), 1, illus. (drumming). —1925. GROSS, A. O., Auk, 423–431 (diseases).—1926. ALLEN, A. A. and GROSS, A. O., Bull. Am. Game Protec. Assoc., Oct. (diseases).—1927. ALLEN, A A., Bird-Lore, 443–453, illus. (autobiography).

149a. CANADA RUFFED GROUSE. BONASA UMBELLUS TOGATA (*Linnæus*). [300a.] To be distinguished from the preceding by the prevailing color of the upperparts, which are gray instead of rufous, and the more distinctly barred underparts, the bars on the breast and belly being nearly as well defined as those on the side; the tail is generally gray.
Range.—N. Ont. and n. Que. to e. N. Dak., cent. N. Y., n. Mass., Vt., N. H. and Me.

149b. NOVA SCOTIA RUFFED GROUSE. BONASA UMBELLUS THAYERI *Bangs*. Similar to *B. u. togata* "but general color of the upperparts darker, more dusky or sooty, less grayish; the whole underparts (except throat) heavily and regularly banded with dusky, the dark bands much blacker and more boldly contrasted against the ground-color—less blended" (Bangs).
Range.—N. S.

150. WILLOW PTARMIGAN. LAGOPUS LAGOPUS LAGOPUS (*Linnæus*). [301.] *Ad. ♂ breeding plumage.*—Throat and chest, breast and sides rich *rufous*, chest and sides more or less barred with black; upperparts, including tail-coverts, black thickly but irregularly barred with ochraceous or rusty; tail fuscous narrowly tipped with white (worn off in some July specimens); primaries and secondaries white; tertials like back; belly largely white. *Ad. ♂ in fall (preliminary winter) plumage.*—Similar to the preceding, but with a variable number of deep rufous feathers, vermiculated with black, on the breast, sides, and upperparts; more white in wings and belly. *Ad. ♂ in winter.*—The preliminary winter plumage is a transition dress worn chiefly in September and October, when it is gradually replaced by the full winter plumage of snowy white with a fuscous, white-tipped tail. *Ad. ♀ breeding plumage.*—Upperparts, tail and wings as in the male, but with less rufous, or none, on the head and neck; throat, breast and sides ochraceous *broadly barred with black;* center of belly paler with broken black bars. *Ad. ♀ in fall (preliminary winter) plumage.*—Barred feathers of underparts largely replaced by rufous, more or less vermiculated feathers, which also appear in varying numbers on the upperparts. Resembles male in corresponding plumage except for the remaining feathers of the breeding plumage. *Ad. ♀ in winter.*—Similar to winter male. L., 15·00; W., 7·50; T., 4·40; B. from N., ·42; depth of B. at N., ·44.

Remarks.—The seasonal plumages of the species are as confusing as they are interesting. It is not possible to treat them fully here, and the student who would pursue the matter further is referred to Dwight's paper in *The Auk*, 1900, 147–163. Summer males and all fall plumage specimens may be known from corresponding stages of *L. rupestris* by their rich rufous breasts and other characters. Summer females are usually deeper, but cannot always be distinguished from summer females of *rupestris* save by the larger bill which alone serves to separate winter specimens of the two species.

Range.—Breeds from n. Banks Isl., w. coast of cent. Greenland, and the e. Aleutian Isls. s. to cent. Mack. and n. Que. (Ungava) and in the mts. to cent. Alberta and the coast ranges of n. B. C. Winters s. to s. Sask., s. Alberta, cent. Ont., and s. Que. Accidental in N. Dak., Mont., Wisc., Mich., N. Y., Me., and Mass.

Nest, on the ground. *Eggs*, 7–11, varying from cream-buff to rufous, heavily spotted and blotched with blackish, 1·75 × 1·20. *Date*, Ft. Chimo, Lab., June 3; Ft. Anderson, Mack., June 7.

This abundant and characteristic Arctic bird does not nest south of central Labrador, but migrates southward in winter to the St. Lawrence, and has once been taken in northern New York and once in New Brunswick. An extended account of its habits will be found in 'Nelson's Report on Natural History Collections Made in Alaska' (p. 131). It is quoted by Captain Bendire in his 'Life Histories of American Birds' (p. 70), where will be found a detailed account of the habits of this and the following members of this genus.

150a. UNGAVA PTARMIGAN. LAGOPUS LAGOPUS UNGAVUS *Riley.* [301*c*.] Resembles *L. l. albus* "but with a heavier bill." W., 8·10; T., 5·05; B., ·85; depth of B., ·60 (Riley).

Range.—N. Que. (Ungava) probably to the e. shore of Hudson Bay.

150b. ALLEN'S PTARMIGAN. LAGOPUS LAGOPUS ALLENI *Stejneger.* [301*a*.] Similar to *L. l. lagopus* but, at all seasons, primaries usually more or less mottled with fuscous or with some fuscous along the shaft; shafts of secondaries sometimes black.

RANGE.—N. F.

"It frequents rocky barrens, feeding on seeds and berries of the stunted plants that thrive in these exposed situations" (Merriam, *Orn. and Oöl.*, 1883, p. 43).

151. ROCK PTARMIGAN. LAGOPUS RUPESTRIS RUPESTRIS *(Gmelin).* [302.] *Ad. ♂ breeding plumage.*—Breast and sides rusty ochraceous closely and narrowly barred with black and more or less tipped with white; belly white; crown barred with rusty and ochraceous; back and upper tail-coverts black narrowly and irregularly but thickly barred with ochraceous and buff, and tipped with white; black predominating in the feathers of the center of the back; tail fuscous tipped with white; primaries and secondaries white, tertials like back. *Ad. ♂ in fall (preliminary winter) plumage.*—Similar to the preceding, but with the feathers of the breast, sides, back, and upper tail-coverts finely vermiculated with black and ochraceous in about equal proportions. *Ad. ♂ winter.*—The preceding plumage is gradually replaced by the winter dress of snow-white, with a fuscous, white-tipped tail and *black lores. Ad. ♀ breeding plumage.*—Similar in color to the breeding female of *L. l. lagopus*, but rusty markings averaging paler, particularly on under-

parts; edgings to feathers whiter, less buffy. *Ad.* ♀ *fall (preliminary winter)*
plumage.—Resembling corresponding plumage of Ad. ♂, but with a varying
number of the feathers of the breeding plumage remaining. *Ad.* ♀ *and Im.*
winter.—Snowy white, tail-feathers fuscous, tipped with white; lores sometimes black. W., 7·25; B. from N., ·35; depth of B. at N., ·32.

   Remarks.—In any plumage *rupestris* and its allies may be distinguished
from *lagopus* by their smaller bill.

   Range.—N. B. C. and s. Yukon, cent. Mack. and Keewatin, s. Baffin Isl.
and the Ungava peninsula.

   Nest, usually placed among the dwarf brush or sedge-covered patches of
the tundras. *Eggs,* 6–10, pale cream or yellowish buff, sometimes with a
vinaceous-rufous suffusion, spotted and blotched with clove-brown or dark
claret-red, 1·65 × 1·18 (Bendire). *Date,* n. Lab., June 16.

   "In its general manners and mode of living it is said to resemble
albus [=L. *lagopus*], but does not retire so far into the wooded country
in the winter" (B., B., and R.).

   151a. REINHARDT'S PTARMIGAN. Lagopus rupestris reinhardi
(*Brehm*). [302a.] *Ad.* ♂ *summer.*—Similar to corresponding plumage of *L.
r. rupestris* but less heavily and regularly barred above, breast more finely
barred. *Ads. in fall (preliminary winter) plumage.*—Similar to corresponding
plumage of *L. r. rupestris* but much grayer. *Ads. in winter.*—Not distinguishable from *L. r. rupestris* in winter.

   Range.—Sw. Greenland, n. nearly to Disco.

   "They prefer more open ground, and rarely straggle even into the
skirts of the wooded tracts. The hilltops and barrens (hence often
called the Barren Ground Bird) are their favorite resorts" (Turner).

   151b. WELCH'S PTARMIGAN. Lagopus rupestris welchi *Brewster.*
[303.] *Ad.* ♂ *in breeding plumage.*—Upperparts black, the head and neck barred
with white and ochraceous-buff, the back and wing-coverts finely and irregularly marked with wavy lines of buffy and white; tail grayish fuscous, tipped
with white; throat white, foreneck like hindneck, breast and sides like back;
rest of underparts white. *Ads. in fall (preliminary winter) plumage.*—Not
seen, but back and breast doubtless with finely vermiculated black and white
feathers. *Ad.* ♀ *breeding plumage.*—Similar to corresponding plumage of
rupestris. *Ads. in winter.*—Similar to winter ads. of *rupestris.* W., 7·25; B.
from N., ·35; depth of B. at N., ·32.

   Remarks.—This is a much blacker and grayer bird than *L. r. rupestris,*
and in this respect it appears most nearly to approach Rock Ptarmigan
from Sitka (*L. r. dixoni?*). (For comparison with *rupestris* see Stejneger,
Auk, 1885, 193.)

   Range.—N. F.

   Nest, a slight hollow in the moss, lined with a few feathers. *Eggs,* 8,
similar to those of *Lagopus rupestris.* *Date,* N. F., June 3 (Thayer Coll.).

   "According to Mr. Welch, these Ptarmigan are numerous in Newfoundland, where they are strictly confined to the bleak sides and
summits of rocky hills and mountains of the interior" (Brewster).

   151c. KELLOGG'S PTARMIGAN. Lagopus rupestris kelloggæ *Grinnell.*—Similar to *L. r. rupestris* "but coloration darker; black markings more
extended; brownish shades deeper toned; white tippings reduced and suffused
with ochraceous; top of head nearly uniform black" (Grinnell).

   Range.—Interior of Alaska and n. Yukon, the w. Arctic Coast to Coronation Gulf, the Arctic isls. (except Baffin Isl.), and nw. Greenland.

The races of the Rock Ptarmigan are given above as they appear
in the A. O. U. 'Check-List' (1931), but according to P. A. Taverner
(Ann. Rep. Nat. Mus. Can., 1929, pp. 28–38) the Rock Ptarmigan of
eastern North America should stand as follows:

Lagopus rupestris rupestris (Gmelin). Southern Rock Ptarmigan. Generally
grayish. Northern British Columbia and southern Yukon, central Mackenzie and Keewatin, southern Baffin Island and the Ungava Peninsula
to Newfoundland.
Lagopus rupestris reinhardi (Brehm). Reinhardt's Ptarmigan. Generally
pale sand-colored. Southwestern Greenland north to near Disco Island.
Lagopus rupestris kelloggæ Grinnell. Northern Rock Ptarmigan. Generally
yellowish. The interior of Alaska and northern Yukon, the western
Arctic Coast to Coronation Gulf, the Arctic islands, except southern
Baffin Island; and west Greenland north of Disco Island.

152. HEATH HEN. TYMPANUCHUS CUPIDO CUPIDO (*Linnæus*). [306.]
Similar to the following, but the scapulars broadly tipped with buffy; the
neck-tufts of *less* than ten feathers; these feathers *pointed*, not *rounded*,
at the ends.
Range.—Formerly Mass. (Cape Ann and Martha's Vineyard), s. N. H.,
N. Y. (L. I.), Pa. (Pocono plateau), N. J. (Schooly Mt. and the pine-barrens)
and probably the shores of Chesapeake Bay in Del. and Md.; now restricted
to Martha's Vineyard where only one bird survives.
Nest, "in oak woods, among sprouts at the base of a large stump" (Brewster). *Eggs*, "creamy buff in color, with a slight greenish tinge," 1·73 ×
1·29. *Date*, Martha's Vineyard, June 10.

In the early part of the nineteenth century the Heath Hen was a
locally common bird from northeastern Massachusetts, and possibly
Maine, southward to Virginia, and possibly the Carolinas. Unlike its
western representative, the Prairie Hen, it did not live in open country
but in sandy plains grown with scrub oak or scrub pines.

Excessive, uncontrolled hunting so decreased its numbers that it
had disappeared from the mainland of Massachusetts, from Connecticut
and Long Island by 1840 and from New Jersey and eastern Pennsylvania by about 1870. After this date it was known only from the
Elizabeth Islands off the coast of Massachusetts, and subsequent to
1880 was restricted to Martha's Vineyard, one of this group, an excellent
illustration of the protection afforded by insulation.

The area occupied, however, was too small to afford diversity of
conditions. The birds were "all in one basket." By 1890 it is said that
their numbers did not exceed 200. Fires and the introduction of foxes
further decreased them and, in 1905, only about 100 were believed to
exist. In response to an appeal by William Dutcher (*Bird-Lore*, 1905,
p. 329) a campaign for the protection of these birds and creation of conditions conducive to their increase was inaugurated by the Massachusetts
Commission of Fisheries and Game which, supported by individuals
and organizations, particularly the Federation of New England Bird
Clubs, has spared no effort since 1907 to conserve this species. For a
time these efforts were successful, and by 1916 the number of birds had
risen to an estimated 2,000. But extensive fires and an invasion of

Goshawks reduced the number to an estimated less than 100 the following year. In 1920, there were 600 birds reported from the island, but since that date, as a result of unfavorable conditions, disease and excess of males, their number has steadily decreased. In 1928, only three birds were believed to be alive and in April, 1931 but one was left.

The above facts are taken in the main from Dr. Gross' admirable memoir. In general, the habits of the Heath Hen resemble those of the Prairie Hen, but G. W. Field describes its call as a *toot* which can be "imitated by blowing gently into the neck of a two-drachm homœopathic vial. Each call extends over a period of two seconds and is repeated at frequent intervals." This call is evidently very unlike the emphatic *boom-ah-boom* of the western Prairie Hen, and this pronounced difference in notes suggests that the eastern and western birds are not so closely allied as their resemblance in plumage would indicate.

1913. FIELD, G. W., Present Status of Heath Hen, Bird-Lore, 352–358, illus.—1928. GROSS, A. O., The Heath Hen, Memoir, Bost. Soc. Nat. Hist., VI, 4, 491–588.

152a. PRAIRIE CHICKEN. TYMPANUCHUS CUPIDO AMERICANUS (*Reichenbach*). [305.] *Ad.* ♂.—Upperparts barred with rufous and black and spotted with rufous; sides of neck with tufts generally composed of *ten* or more narrow, stiffened black feathers marked with buffy and rufous, their ends *rounded*, the skin beneath these tufts bare; tail *rounded*, fuscous, the inner feathers somewhat mottled with ochraceous-buff, tip white; throat buffy, breast and belly white, evenly *barred* with black. *Ad.* ♀.—Similar, but neck-tufts much smaller and tail barred with ochraceous-buff or rufous. L., 18·00; W., 9·00; T., 4·00; B. from N., ·52.

Range.—W. cent. Alberta, se. Sask. and s. Man. to e. Colo., Ark., sw. La., w. Ky., and w. Ind.; probably extinct e. of Ind. but formerly reached sw. Ont., Mich., and ne. O., and w. Pa.

Glen Ellyn, P. R., fairly plentiful locally. SE. Minn., P. R., much decreased in numbers.

Nest, on the ground. *Eggs*, 11–14, buffy olive, sometimes finely speckled with brownish, 1·70 × 1·25. *Date*, Jasper Co., Ia., May 2.

"This familiar game-bird inhabits our fertile prairies, seldom frequenting the timbered lands except during sleety storms or when the ground is covered with snow. Its flesh is dark, and it is not very highly esteemed as a table bird.

"During the early breeding season they feed largely upon grasshoppers, crickets, and other forms of insect life, but afterward chiefly upon our cultivated grains, gleaned from the stubble in autumn and the cornfields in winter; they are also fond of tender buds, berries, and fruits. They run about much like our domestic fowls; but with a more stately carriage. When flushed they rise from the ground with a less whirring sound than the Ruffed Grouse or Bob-white, and their flight is not so swift, but more protracted and with less apparent effort, flapping and sailing along, often to the distance of a mile or more. In the fall the birds collect together and remain in flocks until the warmth of spring quickens their blood and awakes the passions of love; then, as with a view to fairness and the survival of the fittest, they select a smooth open courtship ground (usually called a 'scratching-ground'), where the males assemble at the early dawn to vie with each other in courage and pompous display, uttering at the same time their love call, a loud booming noise; as soon as this is heard by the hen birds desirous of mating they quietly put in an appearance, squat upon the ground, apparently indifferent observers, until claimed by victorious rivals, which they gladly accept, and receive their caresses" (Goss).

1908. CHAPMAN, F. M., Camps and Cruises, 231–235 (display).— 1930. GROSS, A. O., Wisconsin Prairie Chicken Investigation, Wisc. Conserv. Comm., Madison, 8vo., 1–112, illus. (See also Bird-Lore, 1929, 383–393.)

153. NORTHERN SHARP-TAILED GROUSE. PEDIŒCETES PHASIAN-ELLUS PHASIANELLUS (*Linnæus*). [308.] Similar to *P. p. campestris* but much darker and the black areas larger and more prominent than the ochraceous ones, the latter deeper, more rusty.

Range.—Cent. Alaska; n. Man. and n. Que. (Ungava) to Lake Superior and the Parry Sound district, Ont.; casual e. to Saguenay River, Que.

153a. PRAIRIE SHARP-TAILED GROUSE. PEDIŒCETES PHASIANELLUS CAMPESTRIS *Ridgway*. [308b.] *Ad.* ♂.—Prevailing color of the upperparts ochraceous-buff, barred and irregularly marked with black; *no neck-tufts;* outer web of the primaries spotted with white; middle tail-feathers projecting about an inch beyond the others, ochraceous-buff and black; throat buffy; breast with V-shaped marks of black; sides irregularly barred or spotted with black or buffy; middle of the belly white. *Ad.* ♀.—Similar, but smaller; the middle tail-feathers shorter. L., 17·50; W., 8·50; T., 4·50; B. from N., ·50.

Range.—S. Alberta and s. Man. to Wyo., e. Colo., cent. Nebr., and e. S. Dak.; formerly to Kans., Minn., e. Wisc., w. Mich., and ne. Ills.

Nest, on the ground. *Eggs*, 11–14, creamy buff or pale olive-brown, generally slightly spotted with fine, reddish brown markings, 1·65 × 1·22 (Bendire). *Date*, Carberry, Man., June 3.

There is more or less confusion in regard to the names Prairie Hen and Prairie Chicken, but where the two species are found together I have found that the former is applied to *Pediœcetes* and the latter to *Tympanuchus*. In central Nebraska, I found this species inhabiting the sand-hills while the Prairie Chicken (*Tympanuchus*) was nesting in immediately adjoining bushy bottom-lands. In Saskatchewan it lived among the rose bushes near the borders of streams. When 'dancing' the male inflates a pink sac, utters a bubbling crow, rattles its tail-quills, etc. The whole performance is well described by Seton, as quoted by Bendire, and by Cameron (*The Auk*, 1907, p. 256).

FAMILY PERDICIDÆ. PARTRIDGES AND QUAILS

This family includes two subfamilies, the Perdicinæ or Old-World Partridges and Quails, numbering about 140 species, and the Odontophorinæ, or American Quails, numbering some 60 species. Heretofore the latter group has been commonly accorded family rank, largely on the basis of its distribution, the single character of a 'toothed' mandible separating the New-World from the Old-World species being, as Coues has said "very faintly indicated in some forms, and entirely wanting in others."

The names of no Old-World birds, when applied to New-World species, have created more confusion than those of Partridge and Quail. Accepting the members of the Old-World genera *Perdix* and *Coturnix* as respectively typical of true Partridges and Quail, it is evident that we have no species closely resembling either. It is apparent, however, that the western genera *Oreortyx*, *Lophortyx*, etc., are nearer *Perdix* and hence should be termed Partridges rather than Quail (though the latter name is applied to them in the A. O. U. 'Check-List'), while the members of the genera *Colinus*, *Odontophorus*, etc., more nearly approach *Coturnix* and hence should be known as Quail rather than as Partridges.

The center of abundance of the Odontophorinæ is in the tropics, only seven of the 60-odd species reaching the United States. In eastern North America we have but a single species, our familiar Bob-white, not, as we are apt to imagine it, a distinctively North American bird but the most northern representative of a group whose stronghold is in Mexico where a dozen forms of the genus *Colinus* are known. Some of these are unlike our Bob-white in color; but the extremes are more or less closely connected by intermediates. All, so far as I am aware, have the characteristic 'bob-white' call. I have even heard this note uttered by the Yucatan and Colombian members of the so-called genus *Eupsychortyx*, evidence that voice is more stable than color, and also, in my opinion, that *Eupsychortyx* is not generically separable from *Colinus* (Bull. Amer. Mus. Nat. Hist., 1917, 36, 173).

154. PARTRIDGE. PERDIX PERDIX PERDIX (*Linnæus*). *Ad.* ♂.—A rufous-brown patch at the junction of breast and belly; throat and sides of the head rich ochraceous-buff, upperparts finely marked with brown, black and gray; scapulars and tertials with distinct buff shaft-streaks; primaries barred with buff; breast gray finely penciled with black. *Ad.* ♀.—Similar, but rufous-brown patch below smaller; tertials and scapulars with black markings, etc. L., 12·50; W., 6·20; T., 3·50.

This European game-bird has been brought to this country in large numbers for stocking purposes. Between 1900 and 1909, nearly 50,000 of these birds were released, chiefly in the northeastern states, and there have been subsequent importations. Only small colonies of these birds have survived in northeastern New York, near the Ontario line, Lehigh County, Pa., and in Kansas, Wisconsin, Iowa, and Minnesota. In the northwestern states and adjoining parts of Canada, the introduction of this Partridge has been surprisingly successful; the species has become abundant and is spreading eastward.

1928. PHILLIPS, J. C., Tech. Bull. 61, U. S. Dept. Agric. (history).—
1929. SPIKER, C. J., Wilson Bull., 24–29 (in Iowa).

155. BOB-WHITE. COLINUS VIRGINIANUS VIRGINIANUS (*Linnæus*). [289.] (Fig. 36b.) *Ad.* ♂ *in winter.*—Upperparts varying from reddish brown to chestnut; interscapulars with broken and sometimes complete black bars; inner vane of tertials widely margined with cream-buff; rump grayish brown, finely mottled, and with a few streaks of blackish; tail ashy gray, the inner feathers finely mottled with buffy; front of crown, a band from bill to beneath eye, and a band on upper breast black; throat and a broad line from bill over eye white; sides rufous-chestnut, margined with black and white; lower breast and belly white barred with black. *Ad.* ♀ *in winter.*—Similar, but the throat and line over the eye, forehead, and lores pale ochraceous-buff; little or no black on the upper breast. *Summer* examples of both sexes have the crown blacker, the buffy markings generally paler. L., 10·00; W., 4·50; T., 2·50; B. from N., ·35.

Range.—Upper Austral and s. half of the Transition zones of e. N. A. from S. Dak., s. Minn., s. Ont., and sw. Me. s. to se. and n. Tex., the Gulf Coast, and n. Fla. w. to e. Colo. Introduced in cent. Colo., N. Mex., Utah, Idaho, Calif., Mont., Ore., Wash., and Bermuda. Now generally mixed with western and southern races which have been introduced in the East.

Washington, common P. R. Bronx region, fairly common P. R. Boston, uncommon P. R. N. Ohio, common P. R. Glen Ellyn, fairly common P. R. SE. Minn., common P. R.

Nest, of grasses, usually arched, on the ground in bushy field borders, etc. *Eggs*, 10–18, white, conical, 1·20 × ·95. *Date*, Charleston, S. C., May 22; Shelter Isl., N. Y., June 2; Boston, June 20; Licking Co., Ohio, May 22; Mitchell Bay, Ont., June 5; se. Minn., June 17.

As stated under the family heading, the members of the genus *Colinus*, while not closely resembling the Old-World Quail of the genus *Coturnix*, are nearer to that species than they are to the Partridges of the genus *Perdix*, and hence should be known as Quail rather than Partridges. A better course, however, is to give them their own distinctive title of Bob-white.

During the nesting season Bob-whites are distributed in pairs through clearings and cultivated fields. The members of a brood constitute a bevy or covey, though occasionally two families or broods are found in one bevy. In the fall they frequent grain fields, but as winter approaches draw in toward thickets and wooded bottom-lands, sometimes passing the coldest weather in boggy alder swamps. They roost on the ground, tail to tail, with heads pointing outward; a bunch of closely huddled forms—a living bomb whose explosion is scarcely less startling than that of dynamite manufacture.

Like most grass-inhabiting birds whose colors harmonize with their surroundings, Bob-whites rely on this protective resemblance to escape detection, and take wing only as a last resort. Sometimes they take refuge in trees, but usually they head for wooded cover, where they remain if the growth is dense, but if it is open they generally run the moment they touch the ground.

About May 1 they begin to pair, and rival males may then be seen battling for mates like diminutive gamecocks. The name 'Bob-white' originated in the spring call of the male. Mounting a fence or ascending to the lower branches of a tree, he whistles the two clear musical, ringing notes *Bob-white!* Sometimes they are preceded by a lower one which can be heard only when one is near the singer. After the breeding season, when the birds are in bevies, their notes are changed to what sportsmen term 'scatter calls.' Not long after a bevy has been flushed and perhaps widely scattered, the members of the disunited family may be heard signaling to one another in sweet minor calls of two and three notes, when one can easily imagine them saying *"Where are you? Where are you?"* When excited they also utter low, twittering notes.

In the more northern part of Bob-white's range, severe winters, combined with excessive shooting, have greatly reduced and locally exterminated the native birds. They have been replaced by birds chiefly from Texas and Mexico, and in such areas few pure-blooded native birds remain. (See Phillips, Tech. Bull. 61, U. S. Dept. Agric. 25.)

1931. STODDARD, H. L., The Bob-white Quail, its Habits, Preservation, and Increase, 4to., 559 pp., illus. (Scribner's).

155a. FLORIDA BOB-WHITE. COLINUS VIRGINIANUS FLORIDANUS (*Coues*). [289*a*.] Similar to the preceding, but smaller, the plumage throughout darker, the black of the back more extensive, the rump and upper tail-coverts grayer, the black throat-band wider and sometimes reaching down upon the breast, the rufous-chestnut of the sides more extensive, the black bars of the breast and belly much wider. L., 8·50; W., 4·40; T., 2·50.
Range.—Fla., except extreme n. part and the Keys.
Nesting-date, Manatee Co., Fla., Apr. 19.

A common bird throughout the pine-grown portions of the Florida peninsula. It is especially numerous on old plantations, where it frequents patches of cowpeas. It resembles the northern Bob-white in habits, but is, I think, more inclined to take to the trees when flushed. I have seen a whole covey fly up into the lofty pine trees, where, squatting close to the limbs, they became almost invisible.

155b. KEY WEST BOB-WHITE. COLINUS VIRGINIANUS INSULANUS *Howe.* [289 a part.] Similar to *C. v. floridanus* but crown uniform dark fuscous, forehead showing more white. Size decidedly smaller. W., 3·80; Tar., 1·38; T., 2·00 (Howe).
Range.—Key West, Fla. Now extinct.

Based on a male secured by J. W. Atkins, July 5, 1888 (Scott, *The Auk*, 1889, p. 245).

155c. TEXAS BOB-WHITE. COLINUS VIRGINIANUS TEXANUS (*Lawrence*). Similar to *C. v. virginianus* but generally paler, the foreback conspicuously marked with black and buff; rump grayer; tertials without definite black areas, their margins paler; black throat-band narrower.
Range.—Se. corner of N. Mex. to s. Tex., and s. through ne. Coahuila and Nuevo Leon to cent. Tamaulipas. Introduced into various e. states

Many thousands of these birds have been released in the eastern United States where they interbreed with the resident form.

The EUROPEAN or MIGRATORY QUAIL, *Coturnix coturnix*, has been introduced into this country on several occasions, but none appear to have survived the first migration season after their release.

FAMILY PHASIANIDÆ. PHEASANTS.

The true Pheasants, numbering about one hundred species, are found from the eastern borders of the Mediterranean through central and southern Asia to the Malayan region.

The Ringneck and English Ringneck have been introduced and become naturalized in various parts of the United States.

156. ENGLISH PHEASANT. PHASIANUS COLCHICUS COLCHICUS (*Linnæus*); **156a. RING-NECKED PHEASANT.** PHASIANUS COLCHICUS TORQUATUS (*Gmelin*).—Most Pheasants of eastern North America are the descendants of crosses between the English Pheasant and the Ring-necked Pheasant, in which the blood of the latter predominates. The male of the true English Pheasant has the head and neck green; *no* white neck-ring; rump rich *bronzy red;* breast bronze-red; the *ends* of the feathers with broad greenish black bands; flanks reddish brown tipped with blue-black. This species is a native of Asia Minor whence it was introduced into Europe by the Greeks and, it is believed, by the Romans into England. The English stock remained pure until about the end of the eighteenth century when it was crossed with the Ring-necked Pheasant (*Phasianus c. torquatus*). The progeny proved fertile, and continued hybridization, has left but few or no pure-blooded birds of the true *colchicus* type in England.

The male of the Ring-necked Pheasant has the head and neck green with strong purplish reflections; a more or less complete *white neck-ring;* rump *gray* or *yellowish gray;* breast bronze-red, the feathers *very narrowly* margined with purple-black; the end of the feathers notched and with a narrow purple black wedge; flanks buffy, tipped with blue-black. The females of both races are mixed black, brownish, and rusty above, below brownish yellow; the breast and sides with rusty and black. This species is a native of China whence it has been introduced into the Pacific Coast region; but, as said above, its hybrid with English stock has been more frequently introduced in the eastern United States. Chiefly through the efforts of state game commissions, which breed and release many thousands of Pheasants annually, the bird is now established from southwestern Maine to Minnesota south to Pennsylvania and Kansas. In the more eastern part of this region it has become a common game-bird and it is estimated that in New York, 100,000, and in Pennsylvania, 50,000 are killed annually during the open season.

Nest, on the ground beneath cover. *Eggs,* 12–20, unmarked olive-buff, 1·75 × 1·35 (Pl. II).

1910. OLDYS, H. W., Farmers Bull. 390, U. S. Dept. Agric. (pheasant raising).—1928. PHILLIPS, J. C., Tech. Bull. 61, U. S. Dept. Agric. (introduction; bibliography).

FAMILY MELEAGRIDÆ. TURKEYS

This distinctively American family contains only two species, the Yucatan Turkey (*Agriocharis ocellata*) and our Wild Turkey. The former is confined to Yucatan and the adjoining portions of Guatemala and Honduras, and, except in isolated instances, has defied all attempts at domestication. The latter ranges from southern Mexico northward, and is represented by five subspecies as follows: (1) *Meleagris gallopavo gallopavo* of southern Mexico; (2) *M. g. merriami* of northern Mexico, southwestern Texas, New Mexico, Arizona and southern Colorado;

(3) *M. g. intermedia* of northeastern Mexico north to middle northern Texas; (4) *M. g. osceola* of southern Florida, and (5) *M. g. silvestris*, our Wild Turkey, which formerly extended as far north as southern Maine, southern Ontario and South Dakota. It is the southern Mexico form, with white-tipped upper tail-coverts, which is the ancestor of our domesticated Turkey. It was introduced from Mexico into Europe where it had become established as early as 1530, and was later brought by colonists to eastern North America. It breeds freely with our Wild Turkey (*silvestris*) and where the birds of the woods come in contact with the inhabitants of the poultry-yard, evidences of such alliances are frequent.

157. EASTERN TURKEY. MELEAGRIS GALLOPAVO SILVESTRIS *Vieillot*. [310*a*.] The Wild Turkey may be distinguished from the common domestic race chiefly by the chestnut instead of white tips to the upper tail-coverts and tail. "♂ ad. L., about 48·00–50·00; W., 21·00; T., 18·50; weight 16–40 lbs." (Ridgway).

Range.—W. Okla., e. Tex., the Gulf Coast, and cent. Fla. to se. Mo., e. Ky., and cent. Pa.; formerly to Nebr., Kans., S. Dak., sw. Ont., and s. Me.; now somewhat mixed with domestic and western stock in the eastern portion of its range.

Washington, rare P. R.

Nest, on the ground, at the base of a bush or tree. *Eggs*, 10–14, pale cream-buff, finely and evenly speckled with grayish brown, 2·45 × 1·95. *Date*, Pipemaker Swamp, Ga., Apr. 25; Ft. Smith, Ark., Apr. 3.

This noblest of American birds is rapidly decreasing in numbers, and in comparatively few years will doubtless be found only in the parts of its range which are unfit for the habitation of man.

Except during the breeding season, Wild Turkeys are found in small flocks of six to twelve or fifteen individuals of both sexes. They roost preferably in the trees in wooded bottom-lands, returning each night to the same locality.

At the opening of the breeding season in March the male begins to gobble. As a rule, he calls only early in the morning, before leaving his roost. Later he sails to the ground and at once begins his search for breakfast, or, attracted by the plaintive piping of some female, he struts and displays his charms before her. It is at this time that battles between the males occur. They are polygamists, and the victor becomes sultan of the harem. During the period of incubation, and while the young require their mother's care, the females do not associate with the males, who then flock together.

The calls of both sexes so closely resemble those of the domestic birds that it requires a practiced ear to distinguish them. In localities where both birds might be expected to occur, I could never be sure whether I was listening to the challenge of some defiant gobbler perched in a cypress in the valley below, or to the vainglorious effort of the lord of the poultry-yard.

1909. GRINNELL, G. B., Forest and Stream, 852, 891, 892 (biography). —1914–15. WRIGHT, A. H., Auk, 334–358, 463–473; 1915, 61–81, 207–224, 348–366 (early records).

157a. FLORIDA TURKEY. MELEAGRIS GALLOPAVO OSCEOLA *Scott.* [310b.] Resembles *M. g. silvestris,* but is smaller, and the primaries, instead of being regularly and widely barred with white, as in that bird, have much smaller, broken white markings. Weight, ♂ 12–22 lbs.; ♀ 4·75–9 lbs. (Scott, Auk, 1892, 115.)

Range.—Peninsular Fla. n. at least to Gainesville.

Nesting-date, St. John's River, Fla., Apr. 23.

The Florida Wild Turkey is locally common in southern Florida.

IX. ORDER GRUIFORMES. CRANES, RAILS, AND ALLIES

SUBORDER GRUES. CRANES, LIMPKINS, RAILS, COOTS AND GALLINULES

(4 families, 3 North American)

SYNOPSIS OF FAMILIES. (Figs. 37, 38, 39.)

Length over 36·00; crown more or less bare; hind toe comparatively small, about length of claw of middle toe, inserted above level of front toes; outer primary normal; tail well developed.

Family Gruidæ. CRANES. P. 249.

Length, 28·00; head feathered; hind toe more than twice as long as claw of middle toe, inserted on a level with front toes; outer primary much narrowed and incurved; tail well developed.

Family Aramidæ. LIMPKINS. P. 251.

Length, 5·00–15·00; head feathered; hind toe longer than claw of middle toe, inserted on level of front toes; outer primary normal; tail poorly developed.

Family Rallidæ. RAILS, COOTS, GALLINULES. P 251.

FAMILY GRUIDÆ. CRANES.

The Cranes number eighteen species, of which two are North American, while the remaining sixteen inhabit the Old World. They frequent plains and marshes, and are omnivorous feeders, eating frogs, lizards, field-mice, snakes, etc., and various kinds of vegetable food. Our species migrate in flocks, but are solitary rather than gregarious at other times of the year. Their voice is loud and resonant. Unlike the Herons, they fly with the neck fully extended. The nest is placed in the ground, and the eggs number two or, rarely, three. The young, again unlike Herons, are born covered with down and leave the nest shortly after birth.

158. WHOOPING CRANE. GRUS AMERICANA (*Linnæus*). [204.] *Ad.*—Top of head, lores and sides of the throat dull red, with a thin growth of black 'hairs'; primaries black, rest of the plumage white. *Im.*—Similar, but whole head feathered, and plumage more or less washed with buffy ochraceous. L., 50·00; W., 25·00; Tar., 11·50; B., 5·00.

Range.—Bred, formerly, from Mack. and Hudson Bay s. to Nebr. and Ia. and in migration not uncommon on the Atlantic Coast from N. E. to S. C. and Ga.; casual w. to Colo., Wyo., and Idaho. Wintered from the Gulf States to cent. Mex. Now very rare and mainly restricted to s. Mack. and n. Sask.; wintering in Tex.

SE. Minn., T. V., last record 1898.

Nest, an islet of grasses and weed stalks, in marshy places. *Eggs*, 2, olive-gray, spotted and blotched with distinct and obscure cinnamon-brown markings, 4˙00 × 2˙50. *Date*, Dubuque, Ia., Apr. 25, 1868.

This is now one of the rarest of North American birds. There are no recent records of its nesting. "In flight their long necks and stiltlike legs are stretched out in a line with the body to the full extent, moving strongly with slowly beating wings, but not swiftly, . . . often circling spiral-like to a great height. They occasionally bunch up, and I have seen them in triangular form; but as a rule they travel in single file, following their leader in a wavy line, croaking as they go, like hounds upon a cold trail" (Goss).

[The LITTLE BROWN CRANE, *Grus canadensis canadensis* (Linnæus), [205], breeds in Arctic North America and winters in Texas and Mexico. It has been reported from Rhode Island and South Carolina, but these records may apply to *G. c. tabida*, from which *G. c. canadensis* differs only in being smaller. W., 18˙50; B., 4˙10.]

159. SANDHILL CRANE. GRUS CANADENSIS TABIDA *(Peters).* [206 part.] Similar to *G. c. pratensis* but paler throughout, especially on the occiput and back of neck, which are pallid mouse-gray instead of light mouse-gray to mouse-gray; the underparts, particularly the lower breast and abdomen, are appreciably grayer. W., 23˙00; Tar., 9˙25; B., 5˙40 (Peters).

Range.—Bred, formerly, from B. C., Sask., Man., and sw. Mich., s. to Calif., Colo., Nebr., Ills., and O. and in migration e. to N. E.; now rare e. of the Miss. and rare or extinct as a breeder in the s. half of its former range but still breeds locally from ne. Calif., Wisc., and Mich. northward. Winters from Calif., Tex., and La. s. to Mex.

Washington, A. V., one record. N. Ohio, occasional. SE. Minn., now rare T. V., Mch. 29; Oct. 26, 1919.

Nesting-date, Dubuque, Ia., May 11, 1865.

"During courtship and the early breeding season their actions and antics at times are ludicrous in the extreme, bowing and leaping high in the air, hopping, skipping, and circling about with drooping wings and croaking whoop, an almost indescribable dance and din, in which the females (an exception to the rule) join, all working themselves up into a fever of excitement only equaled by an Indian war-dance, and, like the same, it stops only when the last one is exhausted" (Goss).

159a. FLORIDA CRANE. GRUS CANADENSIS PRATENSIS *Meyer.* [206 part.] (Fig. 37.) *Ad.*—Whole top of the head to below the eyes covered with rough, minutely warty, dull reddish skin thinly grown with short, black 'hairs'; plumage brownish gray, with more or less silvery gray and buffy ochraceous. *Im.*—Similar, but whole head feathered, and with more buffy ochraceous in the plumage. L., about 44˙00; W., 19˙00; Tar., 8˙75; B., 5˙00.

Range.—Peninsular Fla. and s. Ga. (Okefinokee Swamp) and probably s. Ala. and La.

Nest, an islet of roots, rushes, weed-stalks, etc., in marshy places. *Eggs*, 2, olive-gray, spotted and blotched with distinct and obscure cinnamon-brown markings, 3˙90 × 2˙40. *Date*, Lantana, Fla., Mch. 2.

Thanks to the preserving influences of peninsulation, this splendid bird is still common in south-central Florida, where its loud, resonant

LIMPKINS

trumpeting is one of the characteristic bird-notes. It feeds about the borders of sloughs in the prairies and pines and particularly over burned areas, and is one of the most wary of birds.

1930. HOLT, E. G., Wilson Bull., 163–183 (nesting).

FAMILY ARAMIDÆ. LIMPKINS.

Limpkins might be called large Rails with some of the habits of Herons. Two species are known, one in South America, the other in Central America, Mexico, the West Indies, Georgia and Florida. They frequent the borders of wooded streams and swamps, and at times the uplands. Their flight is short, and when on the wing their legs dangle below them. Like the Herons, they perch in trees. Their prolonged, melancholy call has won for them the name 'Crying-bird.' Their usual note is a loud, rather high *wah-ree-ow;* the last syllable is drawn out into a wail, and the effect is most gruesome. Limpkins feed to a large extent on land shells (*Ampullaria*), and, as Barrows has shown, the tip of the Limpkin's bill is sometimes turned slightly to one side, an evident result of forcing it into the spiral opening of the shell to extract the animal.

160. LIMPKIN. ARAMUS PICTUS PICTUS (*Meyer*). [207.] (Fig. 38.) *Ads.* —Glossy olive-brown, the feathers of the head and neck narrowly, those of the body broadly, striped with white; wings and tail more bronzy. *Im.*— Similar, but paler and duller. L., 28·00; W., 13·00; Tar., 4·50; B., 4·25.

Range.—Okefinokee Swamp, Ga., and peninsular Fla.; casual n. to S. C.

Nest, of leaves, twigs, etc., in a bush or small tree. *Eggs*, 4–7, pale buffy white, blotched, stained and speckled with light cinnamon-brown, 2·30 × 1·70. *Date*, Ocklawhaha River, Fla., Mch. 6.

This is now a local and uncommon bird in Florida where the drainage of vast areas has reduced the extent of its range.

1928. NICHOLSON, D. J., Auk, 305–309 (habits).

FAMILY RALLIDÆ. RAILS, GALLINULES, AND COOTS.

The approximately two hundred and twenty-five forms contained in this family are distributed throughout the greater part of the world, ten species (eighteen species and subspecies) inhabiting North America. Rails and Gallinules are not strictly gregarious, but are generally associated through a community of interests; Coots, however, are usually found in flocks. Rails inhabit grassy marshes, in which they seek safety by running or hiding, taking to wing, when pursued, only as a last resort. Their large, strong legs, therefore, have been developed at the expense of their weak, rounded wings. In several island species, this degeneracy of wing has been carried to such an extreme that the birds have lost the power of flight. At the best, their flight, when flushed, is short and labored, and with dangling legs they soon drop back into cover. Nevertheless, they perform extended migrations, traveling hundreds of miles without resting.

Gallinules live near the marshy borders of bodies of water, while the more aquatic Coots resemble some Ducks in habits. They are at times noisy birds and are more often heard than seen. All the forms nest on the ground, laying generally large sets of eggs, and the young are born covered with (usually black) down and can run soon after hatching.

1914. COOKE, W. W., Distribution and Migration of North American Rails and Their Allies, Bull. 128, U. S. Dept. Agric., 50.

KEY TO THE SPECIES

I. Bill over 1·75.
  A. Cheeks below the eye cinnamon-rufous, like the breast; flanks black barred with white; upperparts rich olive-brown streaked with black.
  161. KING RAIL.
  B. Cheek below the eye gray; flanks generally gray or brownish, barred with white; upperparts generally grayish, streaked with black.
  162, 162a–d. CLAPPER RAIL and races.

II. Bill under 1·75.
  A. Wing over 6·00.
    a. General color blue, feet yellow . . . . 170. PURPLE GALLINULE.
    b. General color slaty, feet dark greenish.
      b^1. Toes with large scalloped webs or flaps at the side. . . 173. COOT.
      b^2. Toes without flaps or webs . . . . . 171. FLORIDA GALLINULE.
  B. Wing under 6·00.
    a. Wing under 3·50.
      a^1. Back blackish, with small round, white spots. 168. BLACK RAIL.
      a^2. Back blackish, barred with white and margined with buffy.
      167. YELLOW RAIL.

    b. Wing over 3·50.
      b^1. Bill over 1·00 . . . . 163. VIRGINIA RAIL.
      c^1. Bill under 1·00.
        c^2. Wing over 4·50, lesser wing-coverts rufous. 169. CORN CRAKE.
        c^3. Wing under 4·50, lesser wing-coverts olive . . . . 166. SORA.

161. KING RAIL. RALLUS ELEGANS ELEGANS *Audubon.* [208.] *Ads.*—Upperparts varying from olive-brown to black, the back and scapulars widely margined with olive-gray; wings and tail olive-brown; wing-coverts *rufous;* throat white; neck and breast *cinnamon-rufous;* belly and sides *fuscous,* sharply barred with white. *Downy young.*—Glossy black. L., 15·00; W., 6·50; Tar., 2·20; B., 2·40.

Range.—E. N. A. Breeds from Nebr., s. Minn., Ont., N. Y., and Mass. s. to Tex., La. and Fla. w. to Kans. Winters mainly in the s. part of its breeding-range; from N. J. s. Casual n. to N. Dak. and Me.

Washington, uncommon S. R., May 11–Dec. 21. Long Island, rare P. R. and local S. R. Bronx region, rare T. V. and S. R., Mch. 31–Apr. 15–Dec. 8 (Feb. 1). Boston, very rare; probably breeds locally. N. Ohio, not common S. R., May 1–Sept. 5. Glen Ellyn, not common S. R., Apr. 10–Sept. 16. SE. Minn., uncommon S. R., Apr. 29–Sept. 26.

Nest, of grasses, on the ground in fresh-water marshes. *Eggs,* 7–12, buffy white, more heavily spotted and speckled with rufous-brown than those of the next species, 1·68 × 1·20. *Date,* Mercer Co., Ills., May 5; Raleigh, N. C., May 31; se. Minn., June 6.

PLATE XIII

CLAPPER RAIL
From Group in the American Museum of Natural History.

The King Rail is the fresh-water representative of the Clapper Rail. It is, however, a much less common bird, and less is known of its habits. Like other Rails, it is a skulker, and never flies when it can escape by running or hiding in the dense grass of its home. On three occasions I have heard what I am quite sure was the King Rail's call, a loud, startling *bŭp, bŭp, bŭp, bŭp, bŭp,* uttered with increasing rapidity until the syllables were barely distinguishable, then ending somewhat as it began. The whole performance occupied about five seconds.

162. NORTHERN CLAPPER RAIL. RALLUS LONGIROSTRIS CREPITANS

Gmelin. [211.] (Fig. 39a.) *Ad.*—Upperparts very pale greenish olive, the feathers widely margined with gray; wings and tail grayish brown; wing-coverts pale cinnamon much washed with gray; throat white; neck and breast *pale*, between ochraceous and cream-buff, more or less washed with grayish; belly and sides gray or brownish gray, barred with white. *Downy young.*--Glossy black. L., 14·50; W., 5·00; Tar., 2·00; B., 2·50.

Remarks.—The Clapper Rail may always be known from the King Rail by its generally grayish instead of brownish or blackish upperparts, and its much paler breast and flanks and paler wing-coverts.

Range.—Salt-marshes of the Atlantic Coast. Breeds from Conn. to N. C.; winters mainly s. of N. J., casually to N. Y. Casual n. to Me.

Washington, A. V., one record. Long Island, common S. R., Apr. 3–Dec. 5., casual in winter. Bronx region, occasional T. V.; apparently no longer breeds; Apr. 10 (Jan. 28). Boston, casual.

Nest, of grasses, near or on the ground, in grass-grown, salt-water marshes. *Eggs*, 8–12, buffy white, spotted and speckled with rufous-brown, 1·72 × 1·20. *Date*, Cobb's Isl., Va., May 19; Oyster Bay, N. Y., May 24.

The Clapper Rail is an inhabitant of grassy, salt-water marshes. It is almost impossible to flush these birds unless their haunts are invaded by an unusually high tide, when a boat may be pushed through the meadows and the birds forced to take wing. I have heard birds calling in the tall grass within a few feet of me, and have made a wild rush in their direction, only to be mocked a moment later by apparently the same bird calling from a point almost within reach. They dodge about over well-traveled pathways like children in a game of blindman's buff.

While not strictly gregarious, they live in colonies, and the call of one bird is sometimes taken up and repeated by others until the marsh vibrates with their cries.

162a. WAYNE'S CLAPPER RAIL. RALLUS LONGIROSTRIS WAYNEI

Brewster. [211c.] "Similar to *R. crepitans*, but the general coloring much darker, the underparts with more ashy, the under tail-coverts with fewer markings" (Brewster, Proc. N. E. Zoöl. Club, I, 1899, 50).

Range.—Salt-marshes of the s. Atlantic Coast from se. N. C. to cent. Fla. *Nesting-date*, McIntosh, Ga.; Mch. 29; Ft. Macon, N. C., May 9.

1927. NICHOLSON, D. J., Auk, 368–370, illus. (photographing).

162b. FLORIDA CLAPPER RAIL. RALLUS LONGIROSTRIS SCOTTI

Sennett. [211b.] Differs from *crepitans* in being black, fuscous or olive-brown above, with olive-gray margins to the feathers; in having the neck and breast cinnamon-rufous washed with brownish, and in having the belly and flanks black instead of gray. In fact, the general color of *scotti* suggests a King Rail, but the latter may always be known by its *rufous* wing-coverts

and *clear* cinnamon-rufous neck and breast. W., 5·50; Tar., 1·90; B., 2·40.
Range.—Salt-marshes of the Gulf Coast of Fla. and Atlantic Coast at
Jupiter Inlet and Palm Beach.

162c. MANGROVE CLAPPER RAIL. RALLUS LONGIROSTRIS INSULARUM

Brooks. "In size this Rail agrees essentially with its nearest relatives,—
coryi, *cubanus* and *waynei*. Its breast is paler than in *cubanus* or *waynei*,
but a trifle more intense than in *coryi*. On the back the brown centers of the
feathers are lighter, more olive, and narrower, and the slate-colored margins
are wider and of a bluish cast, giving the back a lighter and more blue appearance than in other members of the genus" (Brooks).
Range.—Salt-marshes of the Fla. Keys, Fla.

162d. LOUISIANA CLAPPER RAIL. RALLUS LONGIROSTRIS SATURATUS

Ridgway. [211a.] A local race of the Clapper Rail found in the marshes of
Louisiana. It is much darker than *crepitans*, but not so dark as *scotti*.
"W., 5·65; Tar., 1·97; B., 2·27" (Ridgway).
Range.—Salt-marshes on the coasts of La., Miss., Ala. and Tex.

1914. SIMONS, G. F., Auk, 363–384 (habits).

163. VIRGINIA RAIL. RALLUS LIMICOLA LIMICOLA *Vieillot.* [212.] *Ad.*—

Upperparts fuscous or black, the feathers bordered by pale grayish brown;
wings and tail dark grayish brown; wing-coverts rufous, lores whitish, cheeks
gray, throat white, rest of the underparts cinnamon-rufous; flanks and under
tail-coverts barred or spotted with black and white. *Downy young.*—Glossy
black. L., 9·50; W., 4·30; Tar., 1·30; B., 1·50.
Range.—Breeds from B. C., s. Que., and N. B. s. to n. L. Calif., and e.
N. C., and in Toluca Valley, Mex.; winters from s. B. C. to Guat., also in
the lower Miss. States, and from N. C. (casually Mass.) to Fla.; occurs
casually n. to Hudson Bay, Lab. and N. F.; also Bermuda and Cuba.
Washington, probably P. R. Long Island, tolerably common local S. R.,
rare in winter, Apr. 4–Nov. 28. Bronx region, fairly common S. R., Apr.
3–Nov. 25 (Jan. 13). Boston, locally abundant S. R., Apr. 20–Sept. 25.
N. Ohio, common S. R., Apr. 25–Sept. 10. Glen Ellyn, rare S. R., Apr. 25–
Sept. 13. SE. Minn., common S. R., Apr. 15–Oct. 6.
Nest, of grasses, on the ground in marshes. *Eggs*, 6–12, pale buffy white,
spotted and speckled with rufous-brown, 1·26 × ·96. *Date*, Boston, May 15;
Pewaukee, Wisc., May 20; se. Minn., May 28.

In almost any extensive fresh or brackish marsh, especially if it
has beds of cat-tail flags or scattered thickets of low bushes and briers,
one may hear in May and June, particularly in the early morning, late
afternoon, or during cloudy weather, a succession of grunting sounds
not unlike those of a hungry pig. Although by no means loud, they
have a penetrating quality which makes them carry to a considerable
distance; and they are apt to attract attention even when, as is usually
the case, they mingle with the songs of innumerable Red-winged Blackbirds, Marsh Wrens, and other swamp-loving birds. It is no easy matter
to trace them to their author, but if you are persevering and at the
same time fortunate, you may at length discover him skulking under
a bush or behind a tuft of grass. He is the Virginia Rail, an odd-look-
ing bird about the size of a Snipe. If you remain motionless, he may
presently come out into fairer view and walk slowly around the edge
of some pool, lifting and putting down his large feet with curious
deliberation, cocking up his absurdly short tail at each step, and every

now and then stopping to thrust his bill deep into the ooze in search of food. As he pauses to look at you, you are struck by his half-quizzical, half-sinister expression, due, no doubt, to the fact that his eyes are blood-red and deeply sunk in their long, narrow head. Startle him by some sudden movement, and he will do one of three things—dart back into cover as swiftly as a frightened mouse, skip across the pool over the floating leaves of the water plants, using both wings and feet, or rise with feebly fluttering wings and hanging legs to fly only a few rods before dropping beyond some intervening screen of grass or bushes. In any case you are not likely to find him again on this occasion.

Besides the grunting sound, the Virginia Rail utters during the breeding season, especially at night and in lowering weather, a guttural *cùt, cùtta-cùtta-cùtta*, often repeated at brief intervals for hours in succession. This cry appears to be peculiar to the male, and is, no doubt, his love-song. When heard at a distance of only a few yards it has a vibrating, almost unearthly, quality, and seems to issue from the ground directly beneath one's feet. The female, when anxious about her eggs or young, calls *ki-ki-ki* in low tones, and *kiu* much like a Flicker. The young of both sexes in autumn give, when startled, a short, explosive *kep* or *kik*, closely similar to that of the Carolina Rail.

WILLIAM BREWSTER.

164. The WATER RAIL, *Rallus aquaticus aquaticus* Linnæus, [212.1], an Old-World species, is accidental in Greenland.

165. The SPOTTED CRAKE, *Porzana porzana* (Linnæus), [213], an Old-World representative of our Sora, is accidental in Greenland.

166. SORA. PORZANA CAROLINA (*Linnæus*). [214.] (Fig. 39c.) *Ad.*—Region about the base of the bill, center of crown, and a line down the middle of the neck black; rest of the breast and throat, sides of the head, and front part of the crown pale blue-gray; rest of the upperparts olive-brown, most of the feathers with black centers, the scapulars and back streaked on each side with white; wings fuscous-brown, their coverts grayish cinnamon, outer edge of first primary white; lower belly white, flanks barred with black and white. *Im.*—Similar, but without black at the base of the bill or on the throat; breast washed with cinnamon and upperparts darker. L., 8·50; W., 4·30; Tar., 1·30; B., ·80.

Range.—Breeds from cent. B. C., Gulf of St. Lawrence and N. B. s. to n. L. Calif., Kans., s. Ills., n. Mo., s. O., Pa., and Md. Winters from Calif. and Fla. through the W. I. and Cent. A. to Venezuela and Peru. Occasional in Lab. and N. F.; accidental in Bermuda, Greenland, England, Wales, and Scotland.

Washington, common T. V., Mch.–May; July–Nov. Long Island, tolerably common T. V., rare W. R. and local S. R., Apr. 10–May, Aug. 10–Oct. 24. Bronx region, common T. V., probably no longer breeds, Apr. 7–Dec. 26. Boston, locally abundant S. R., Apr. 15–Oct. 31. N. Ohio, common S. R., May 1–Oct. 23. Glen Ellyn, common S. R., Apr. 14–Oct. 17. SE. Minn., common S. R., Apr. 19–Oct. 10.

Nest, of grasses, on the ground in or near marshes. *Eggs*, 8–15, buffy white or ochraceous-buff, spotted and speckled with rufous-brown, 1·24 × ·90. *Date*, Boston, May 20; se. Minn., June 3; Pewaukee, Wisc., May 19.

The Soras' summer home is in fresh-water marshes, where, if it were not for their notes, the reeds and grasses would long keep the secret of their presence. But knowing their calls, you have only to pass a May or June evening near a marsh to learn whether they inhabit it. If there, they will greet you late in the afternoon with a clear whistled *ker-wee*, which soon comes from dozens of invisible birds about you, and long after night has fallen it continues like a springtime chorus of piping hylas. Now and again it is interrupted by a high-voiced, rolling *whinny* which, like a call of alarm, is taken up and repeated by different birds all over the marsh.

They seem so absorbed by their musical devotions that even when calling continuously it requires endless patience and keen eyes to see the dull-colored, motionless forms in places where one would not suppose there was sufficient growth to conceal them.

Floating silently near the shore on my back in a canoe, I have seen them venture out to feed. With tails erect they step gingerly along, evidently aware of their exposed position, for on the least alarm they dart back to cover. Sometimes they cross small streams by swimming, and they are expert divers.

In the fall they gather in the wild rice or wild oat (*Zizania aquatica*) marshes, and a well-directed stone or unusual noise may bring a series of protesting interrogative *kuks* or *peeps* from the apparently deserted reeds. At this season 'gunners' in small flat-bottomed boats are poled through the flooded meadows, and the Soras, waiting until the last moment, rise on feeble wing—a mark which few can miss.

167. YELLOW RAIL. Coturnicops noveboracensis (*Gmelin*). [215.] (Fig. 39b.) *Ads.*—Upperparts black, the feathers bordered with ochraceous-buff and with from one to three narrow white bars; breast ochraceous-buff; middle of the belly white; sides and lower belly black or brownish, barred with white. L., 7·00; W., 3·40; Tar., ·95; B., ·52.

Range.—Breeds in N. Dak. and e. cent. Calif. and occurs in the breeding season in Wisc., Minn., n. Ills., Me., Mass., s. Mack., n. Man., cent. Que. (Ungava), and N. S. Winters in the Gulf States n. to N. C. and in Calif. Casula in Ore., Nev., Colo., Utah, and Ariz., and in Bermuda.

Washington, rare T. V., Mch.–May 20; Oct. 4–Nov. 17. Long Island, T. V., rare in spring, uncommon in fall, casual in winter, Mch. 31–Apr. 29, Aug. 30–Nov. 11. Bronx region, rare T. V., Sept. 29–Oct. 2. Boston, rare T. V., in fall. N. Ohio, rare S. R. SE. Minn., rare, May 14–Sept. 24.

Nest, on the ground in grassy marshes. *Eggs*, 6–10, creamy buff, densely sprinkled and speckled on larger end with rusty brown, 1·12 × ·83 (Ridgway). *Date*, Winnebago, Ills., May 17.

This little Rail inhabits marshes with others of its family. It seems to know that it can escape its enemies much more easily by hiding in the tangled grasses of its home than by taking wing, and it flies only to avoid actual capture. It can be hunted successfully, therefore, only with dogs. Nuttall describes its notes as "an abrupt and cackling cry, *'krèk,' 'krèk,' 'krèk,' 'krèk,' 'kuk,' 'k'kh*," and compares them to the croaking of the tree-frog, while a captive bird in the possession of J. H. Ames uttered a scolding *kik-kik-kik-kik-queah*. (*The Auk*, 1902, p. 94.)

168. BLACK RAIL. Creciscus jamaicensis stoddardi *Coale*. [216.] (Fig. 15.) *Ads.*—Head, breast and upper belly slate-color; lower belly and wings brownish black, barred or spotted with white; nape dark reddish brown. L., 5·00; W., 2·80; Tar., ·80; B., ·60.

Range.—Breeds from Mass., Minn., Ia., and Kans. s. to N. J. and Fla. Winters probably mainly s. of the U. S. to Guat., and casually in s. Ga., Fla. and s. La. Casual in Bermuda.

Washington, rare, May, June, Sept. Long Island, rare T. V., may breed, May 22–31 and early Aug. Boston, casual or very rare S. R. N. Ohio, rare S. R.

Nest, of grasses, on the ground in marshes. *Eggs*, 8–10, white, thinly sprinkled with reddish brown dots, more numerous at the larger end, 1·00 × ·80 (Nelson, *Bull. Nutt. Orn. Club*, I, 1876, p. 43). *Date*, Saybrook, Conn., July 10; Garden City, Kans., June 6.

This bird is about as difficult to observe as a field-mouse. It is said to prefer grassy meadows, where it never flies when it can escape by running or hiding. Apparently it is not common. Wayne describes the call of the female as *croo-croo-croo-o*, like the beginning of the song of the Yellow-billed Cuckoo. To this the male responded *kik, kik, kik, kik,* or *kuk, kuk, kuk, kuk.*

1900. ALLEN, J. A., Auk, 1–8 (historical); STONE, W., *Ibid*, 171 (nesting). —1901. BREWSTER, W., *Ibid*, 321–328 (in Mass.).—1905. WAYNE, A. T., The Warbler, No. 2.—1910. Birds of South Carolina, 39 (nesting).

169. The CORN CRAKE, *Crex crex* (Linnæus), [217], a bird of Europe and northern Asia, is casual in Greenland, Bermudas and eastern North America (L. I., 3 records, Aug.–Nov.). It is about the size of a Clapper Rail, but has a bill no larger than that of the Sora. The general color of the upperparts is between ochraceous-buff and cream-buff, the feathers with black centers; the wing-coverts and most of the quills are pale rufous; the breast is pale ochraceous-buff; the sides are the same, barred with white; the middle of the belly is white.

170. PURPLE GALLINULE. IONORNIS MARTINICA (*Linnæus*). [218.]

Ad.—Front of crown with a bare, bluish plumbeous plate; rest of head and underparts rich dark purplish blue; under tail-coverts white; back shining olive-green; wings light blue tinged with greenish; bill carmine, tipped with pale greenish (in skins, reddish orange, tipped with yellowish); legs yellow. *Im.*—Upperparts more or less washed with brownish; underparts more or less mottled with white; plate on the head smaller; bill without orange-red. *Downy young.*—Glossy black, head with numerous white, hairlike feathers; base of the bill yellowish, end black. L., 13·00; W., 7.10; Tar., 2·40; B., from posterior margin to nostril, ·80.

Range.—Breeds from Ala. and S. C. s. through Mex. and the W. I. to Argentina. Winters from Tex., La., and Fla. s. Irregularly n. in summer to Ariz., Colo., Nebr., Wisc., Ills., Mich., N. J., Mass., Me., Ont., Que., N. S., and N. B.; accidental in Bermuda.

Long Island, two records. Boston, A. V. N. Ohio, one record.

Nest, a platform of reed stalks built in rushes over the water or in grassy marshes. *Eggs*, 4–10, buffy white, finely speckled with rufous-brown, 1·60 × 1·15. *Date*, Avery's Isl., La., Apr. 15; coast S. C., May 21.

This is a common species on ponds densely grown with yellow pond-lilies (in Florida known as 'bonnets') and other aquatic plants, where it may be seen walking daintily over the leaves or swimming when occasion requires. It may be easily identified by its bright colors and conspicuous white under tail-coverts. The latter are especially evident when the bird takes wing.

1929. GROSS, A. O., and VAN TYNE, J., Auk, 431–446, illus. (nesting).

171. FLORIDA GALLINULE. Gallinula chloropus cachinnans *Bangs.* [219.] (Fig. 39d.) *Ad.*—Dark bluish slate-color; back and scapulars washed with olive-brown; belly whitish; flanks with a few conspicuous *white streaks;* under tail-coverts white; crown with a bare, bright red plate; bill the same color tipped with yellowish; legs bright red at the tibiæ. *Im.*— Similar, but underparts grayish white; crown plate much smaller and with the bill brownish; no red on the legs. *Downy young.*—"Glossy black, the lowerparts sooty along the median line; throat and cheeks interspersed with silvery white hairs" (Ridgway). L., 13·50; W., 7·00; Tar., 2·15; B., from posterior margin of nostril, ·80.

Range.—Breeds from cent. Calif., Minn., Ont., and Vt., s. to the W. I., Mex., the Cape district of L. Calif. and Panama and in the Galapagos, and Bermuda. Winters from s. Calif. and S. C. southward. Casual in S. Dak., Colo., Que., N. S., N. B., and Me.

Washington, rare S. R., Apr.–Oct. Long Island, uncommon T. V. and local S. R. (Apr. 2), May 4—Nov. 3. Bronx region, uncommon S. R., de-creasing, Apr. 16–Nov. 5. Boston, rare local S. R., May 15–Oct. 25. N. Ohio, common S. R., Apr. 25–Sept. 20. Glen Ellyn, rare and local S. R., May 4. SE. Minn., common S. R., Apr. 25–Sept. 25.

Nest, of rushes on a bed of rushes or similar slight elevation in marshes, lagoons, or swampy lake-sides. *Eggs,* 8–13, buffy white or ochraceous-buff, spotted and speckled with rufous-brown, 1·80 × 1·25. *Date,* Coast S. C., May 21; Boston, June 5; Pewaukee, Wisc., May 20; se. Minn., June 1.

There is something about the appearance and habits of Gallinules which always suggests to me the thought that they are chickens which for unknown reasons have been forced to adopt the ways of both Coots and Rails. Indeed, the names Water-hen and Moor-hen are applied to near relatives of our bird.

They frequent marshy, reed- or bush-grown shores of ponds and lakes, walking gracefully through the tangled vegetation. Their flight is short, and, like a Rail, with dangling legs they drop awkwardly to the ground. They swim readily, and when on the water resemble a Coot, though they are by no means so aquatic. Their notes are loud and varied, and during the nesting season they are unusually noisy. Their common note is an explosive *chuck;* other calls are suggestive of the barnyard, and remind one of the protest of a disturbed brooding hen or even the squawking of a struggling fowl.

1891. Brewster, Wm., Auk, 1–7 (nesting in Mass.).—1910. Miller, R. F., Auk, 181–184 (nesting in Pa.).—1931. Allen, A. A., Bird-Lore, 284–293, illus. (autobiography).

172. The European Coot, *Fulica atra atra* Linnæus, [220], inhabits the northern parts of the Old World, and is accidental in Greenland, Labrador, and Newfoundland. It closely resembles the American Coot, but lacks the white markings on the edge of the wing and under tail-coverts.

173. AMERICAN COOT. Fulica americana americana *Gmelin.* [221.] (Figs. 22, 39e.) *Ads.*—Head and neck blackish; rest of plumage dark, bluish slate-color, paler below; edge of wing, *tips of secondaries,* and under tail-coverts white; bill whitish, two spots near its tip and crown plate brownish; legs and feet greenish; toes with *scalloped flaps. Im.*—Similar, but much whiter below, a slight brownish wash above; crown plate much smaller. *Downy young.*—Blackish, white below; throat and upperparts with numerous bright *orange* hairlike feathers; lores red; bill red, tipped with black. L., 15·00; W., 7·50; Tar., 2·25; B. from posterior margin of nostril, ·80.

PLATE XIV

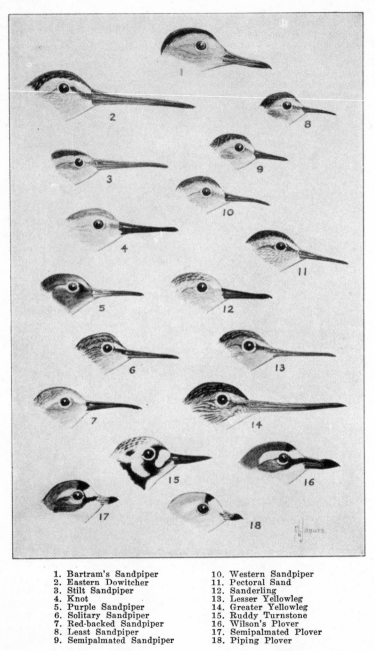

1. Bartram's Sandpiper
2. Eastern Dowitcher
3. Stilt Sandpiper
4. Knot
5. Purple Sandpiper
6. Solitary Sandpiper
7. Red-backed Sandpiper
8. Least Sandpiper
9. Semipalmated Sandpiper

10. Western Sandpiper
11. Pectoral Sand
12. Sanderling
13. Lesser Yellowleg
14. Greater Yellowleg
15. Ruddy Turnstone
16. Wilson's Plover
17. Semipalmated Plover
18. Piping Plover

Remarks.—The Coot bears a general resemblance to the Florida Gallinule, but, aside from the differences in color, the scalloped webbed feet of the Coot will always serve to distinguish it.

Range.—Breeds from cent. B. C., Que., and N. B., s. to s. L. Calif., Tamaulipas, Ark., Tenn. and N. J., and sporadically in Fla., also in s. Mex., W. I., and Guat. Winters from s. B. C., Colo. (casually), Ills., Ind., Mass. (casually) and Va. s. to Colombia. Casual at Ft. Yukon, Alaska, in Greenland, N. S., and Bermuda.

Washington, common T. V., Feb. 23–June 8; Sept. 1–Dec. 20. Long Island, T. V., tolerably common in fall, casual P. R., Feb. 28–May 4; Sept. 2–Dec. 27. Bronx region, uncommon T. V., Mch. 17–May 16; Sept. 22–Nov. 12 (Jan. 4). Boston, T. V., rare, Apr., May; not uncommon Sept.–Nov. N. Ohio, tolerably common T. V., Mch. 15–May 5; Sept. 1–Nov. 1, occasionally breeds. Glen Ellyn, not common S. R., Mch. 17–Nov. 2. SE. Minn., common S. R., Mch. 20–Nov. 20.

Nest, of reeds, grasses, etc., among reeds in fresh-water marshes. *Eggs*, 8–15, pale, buffy white, finely and uniformly speckled with chocolate or black, 1·85 × 1·25. *Date*, St. Clair Flats, Mich., May 17; se. Minn., May 27.

As one might imagine after seeing their lobed feet, Coots are more aquatic than either of the Gallinules. In the Middle States they are found in creeks and rivers with marshy and reed-grown shores, while in Florida they resort in enormous numbers to lakes covered with the yellow lilies locally known as 'bonnets' (*Nymphæa*); and in some of the large, shallow rivers, like Indian River, they may be found associated with Lesser Scaup Ducks.

In my experience they are as a rule quite shy, but near the long railway pier at Titusville, Fla., where shooting is prohibited, they are as tame as domestic Ducks. They evidently know the boundary line between safety and danger, however, and when beyond the protected limits show their usual caution.

Coots swim easily, with a peculiar bobbing motion of the head and neck. When alarmed they patter over the water, using their feet as much as their wings. Both the sound produced and the wake left are characteristic.

They are noisy birds, and when alarmed break out into a great chorus of high, cackling notes which I have heard at a distance of half a mile. Their ivory-white bill is an excellent field-mark, and readily serves to distinguish Coots from Gallinules.

1902. EVERMANN, B. W., The Osprey, 57 (feeding habits).

X. ORDER CHARADRIIFORMES. SHORE-BIRDS, GULLS, AUKS, ETC.

SUBORDER CHARADRII. OYSTER-CATCHERS, SANDPIPERS, SNIPE, AVOCETS, STILTS, PHALAROPES, ETC.

(11 families, 6 North American, 5 eastern North American)

Although placed in several well-defined family groups, the Charadrii have many traits in common. Their center of abundance when breeding is in the northern parts of the Northern Hemisphere, a large number of species nesting in the Arctic Zone. Many of these winter in the southern portions of the Southern Hemisphere, their migrations, therefore, being the most extended of those performed by any group of birds. With the exception of the European Green Sandpiper and its American representative, our Solitary Sandpiper, the Charadrii all nest on the ground, the nest being more or less simple in structure. The eggs, usually four in number, are large in proportion to the size of the bird, and are decidedly conical in shape, and some species, at least, arrange them in the nest, point down, in order that the exposed upper surface may be decreased in extent and thus be more easily and fully covered by the sitting bird. The young are born with a downy covering, usually of soft browns, grays and buffs, disposed in a more or less pronounced pattern, and can run about actively, shortly after hatching. This natal down is soon followed by the juvenal plumage, to the tips of which it may, in places, be seen adhering. But one brood is raised annually.

With some species (e. g., Spotted and Solitary Sandpipers) there is no postjuvenal molt, the postjuvenal plumage being also the first winter plumage. The larger number, however, acquire a winter plumage by postjuvenal molt during the fall migration. At the postnuptial molt, which often occurs during migration, the adults assume a plumage similar to the first winter plumage of the immature bird, when, as a rule, old and young birds, males and females, are alike in color. The spring or prenuptial molt often begins in January or February, which involves all the body feathers, and, in some cases, also the wings and tail (see Dwight).

1888. SEEBOHM, H., Distribution of the Family Charadriidæ, 4to., 524 pp., 21 pls.—1895. ELLIOT, D. G., North American Shore Birds, 8vo., 268 pp., 74 pls. (Francis Harper).—1897. CORY, C. B., How to Know the Shore Birds, 8vo., 89 pp., many illus.—1900. DWIGHT, J., JR., The Moult of the North American Shore Birds, Auk, 368–385.—1903. HUNTINGTON, D. W., Our Feathered Game, 8vo., 396 pp., 37 pls.—1903. SANFORD, L. C., BISHOP, L. B., VAN DYKE, T. S., The Water-Fowl Family, 12 mo., ix + 598 pp., 20 pls. (Macmillan).—1905. JOB, H. K., Wild Wings, 203–255 (Houghton, Mifflin & Co.).—1905. CLARK, A. H., Migrations of Certain Shore Birds, Auk, 134–140.—1907. RICH, W. H., Feathered Game of the Northeast, 8vo., 432 pp., 87 pls.—1910. COOKE, W. W., Distribution and Migration of North American Shore Birds, Bull. 35, Biol. Surv. U. S. Dept. Agric., 100 pp., 4 pls.—1920. NICHOLS, J. T., Limicoline Voices, Auk, 519–540.—1927. WETMORE, A., Our Migrant Shorebirds in Southern South America, Tech. Bull. 26, U. S. Dept. Agric., 1–24.—1929. BENT, A. C., Shore Birds (II), Bull. 146, U. S. Nat. Mus., 412 pp., 66 pls.—1930–31. URNER, C. A., Auk, 424–426; 1931, 418–422 (status of shore-birds on New Jersey coast).

SYNOPSIS OF FAMILIES

Bill over 3·00, straight, hard, vertically compressed, much higher than wide, its tip wedge-shaped; tarsi with rounded scales, toes three; a large black and white bird   . .   *Family Hæmatopodidæ.* OYSTER-CATCHERS. P. 261.

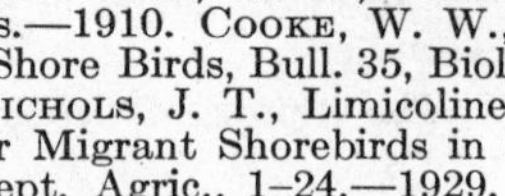

FIG. 74. Oyster-Catcher.

Bill usually under 1·00 (except Black-bellied Plover, 1·25), stiff, rather stout, higher than wide; tarsi with rounded scales (except Turnstone), toes three (except Black-bellied Plover and Turnstone).
Family Charadriidæ. PLOVERS, TURNSTONES, ETC. P. 262.

FIG. 75. Golden Plover.

Bill usually slender, pliable, a probe terminally rounded or slightly flattened, not obviously higher than wide; tarsi under 3·50, with transverse scales; toes four (except Sanderling), not lobate.
Family Scolopacidæ. SANDPIPERS, SNIPES, WOODCOCK. P. 268.

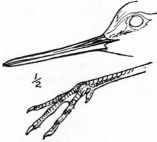

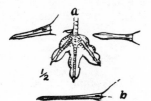

FIG. 76. Greater Yellow-legs.

FIG. 78. *a.* Red Phalarope.
b. Wilson's Phalarope.

Bill under 1·50, straight; toes lobate. *Family Phalaropodidæ.* PHALAROPES. P. 292.

FIG. 77. Black-necked Stilt.

Bill over 2·50, straight or recurved, very sharply pointed; tarsi over 3·50; large, noisy black and white or black and white and buff birds.
Family Recurvirostridæ. AVOCETS AND STILTS. P. 291.

174. The MEXICAN JACANA, *Jacana spinosa gymnostoma* (Wagler), [288], of the family Jacanidæ, inhabits the Rio Grande Valley and southward, and has been once recorded from Florida (Lake Okeechobee, Oct. 1889, Mearns, Auk, 1902, 79). The Florida record is doubtless based on the West Indian race. *J. s. violacea* Cory. (See A. O. U. 'Check-List,' 101).

FAMILY HÆMATOPODIDÆ. OYSTER-CATCHERS

The Oyster-catchers number about twelve species, represented in most of the warmer parts of the globe. But two species inhabit North America, and only one of these occurs in the eastern states. They are strictly maritime birds, and resort to bars and beaches in search of clams, mussels, etc., exposed by the tide.

175. The EUROPEAN OYSTER-CATCHER, *Hæmatopus ostralegus* Linnæus, [285], is occasional in Greenland.

176. AMERICAN OYSTER-CATCHER. HÆMATOPUS PALLIATUS PALLIATUS *Temminck.* [286.] (Fig. 74.) *Ad.*—Head, neck, and upper breast glossy black, back and wing-coverts olive-brown, secondaries white, primaries fuscous, upper tail-coverts white, base of tail white, end fuscous, lower breast and belly white. *Im•*—Similar, but head and neck blackish and upperparts more or less margined with buffy. L., 19·00; W., 10·50; Tar., 2·40; B., 3·40.

Range.—Atlantic and Gulf coasts from Va. (casually to N. J., Mass., and N. B.) to Tex. and Brazil, the W. I. (except the Bahama Isls.), and the Pacific Coast from Tehuantepec, Mex., to the Gulf of Panama and Colombia; breeds locally throughout its range; winters s. from Va.

Long Island, A. V., Mch.–Aug. Boston, A. V.

Nest, a depression in the sand. *Eggs*, 3, buffy white or creamy buff, rather evenly spotted and blotched with chocolate, 2·20 × 1·55. *Date*, Mouth St. John's River, Fla., Apr. 10; Coast S. C., Apr. 20; Cobb's Isl., Va., May 10.

Oyster-catchers are true beach birds. When nesting they are found in isolated pairs; after the breeding season they gather in small flocks. At all times they are excessively wary, but their large size and striking markings are diagnostic as far as the birds may be clearly seen. Their calls are loud, emphatic, and frequently uttered.

1905. Job, H. K., Wild Wings, 239 (nesting).—1925. Huxley, J., Ibis, 868–897 (courtship).

Family Charadriidæ. Plovers, Turnstones, and Surf-birds

The seventy-five-odd species contained in this family are, as a whole, of less boreal distribution than the Snipes, and during the nesting season are distributed throughout the world. Only twelve species are regularly found in North America. Their habits in a general way resemble those of other shore-birds, but their much shorter, stouter bills are not fitted for probing and they obtain their food from the surface. Probably for this reason several species are as frequently found on the uplands as near the shores.

KEY TO THE SPECIES

I. Toes three.
  A. Back marked with black and white, rufous, or golden yellow.
                                                       186. Golden Plover.
  B. Back ashy, brown, or brownish.
    a. Back brown rather than gray.
      a^1. Breast with a black or brown band.
        a^2. Rump rufous . . . . 184. Killdeer.
      a^3. Rump not rufous.
        a^4. Nuchal ring margined with black, toes webbed at base.
                              181. Semipalmated Plover.
        a^5. Nuchal ring with black, toes unwebbed 178. Ringed Plover.
        a^6. No black on nape . . . . 182. Wilson's Plover.
      b^1. Breast not banded . . . . 183. Mountain Plover.
    b. Back gray rather than brown.
      b^1. Feet and base of bill yellow . . . . . 179. Piping Plover.
      b^2. Feet and bill wholly black . . . . 180. Cuban Snowy Plover.
II. Toes four.
  A. Length over 10·00.
    a. Back black or fuscous and white . 187 Black-bellied Plover.
    b. Back greenish . . . . 177. Lapwing.
  B. Length under 10·00, lower back white . . . . . 188a. Turnstone.

177. The Lapwing, *Vanellus vanellus* Linnæus, [269], of Europe is casual in Greenland, Baffin Island, Newfoundland, Labrador, New Brunswick,

Nova Scotia, Maine, Long Island (two records, late fall, Dec.), New York, North Carolina, the Bahamas, and Barbados. Prior to 1927 there were records of the occurrence of only 8 individuals of this species in North America, but in December, 1927, high easterly winds in Great Britain drove large numbers of Lapwings westward and they occurred by hundreds in Newfoundland whence many wandered southward (Witherby, British Birds, XXI, 215, and Bird-Lore, 1928, 248) Its size (L. 13·00), slender, elongate crest-feathers, glossy greenish back, white tail broadly tipped with black and rusty under tail-coverts readily distinguish the Lapwing.

178. RINGED PLOVER. CHARADRIUS HIATICULA *Linnæus.* [275.] Resembles *C. semipalmatus* but is larger, has a broader breast-band, and there is no web between the inner and middle toes. W., 4·90; Tar. 1·00; B., ·60.

Range.—E. Arctic A. and the Old World. In N. A. breeds in Greenland, e. Baffin Land, and probably Ellesmere Land, migrating along European coasts.

Nest, "a hollow scratched in the sand." *Eggs,* 4–5, "stone-color to ochreous or clay-yellow, sometimes with a warm tinge, spotted, as a rule, rather sparingly with brownish black." *Date,* ne. Greenland, June 17–July 18 (Bent).

179. PIPING PLOVER. CHARADRIUS MELODUS Ord. [277.] (Pl. XIV.) Feet and base of bill yellowish or orange. *Ads. in summer.*—Upperparts pale whitish ashy; forehead, underparts and a ring around neck white; front of the crown and a band on each side of the breast, sometimes complete, black; inner tail-feathers largely fuscous, outer pair white, those between, white with a subterminal blackish bar. *Winter plumage.*—Similar, but black replaced by brownish gray. L., 7·00; W., 4·75; Tar., ·85; B., ·50.

Range.—Breeds locally from s. Sask., s. Que., Magdalen Isls., s. to cent. Nebr., ne. Ills., nw. Ind., n. O., nw. Pa., coasts of N. J. and Va. and Pea Isl., N. C. Winters on the Atlantic and Gulf coasts from Ga. to Tex. and n. Mex. Casual in the Bahamas, Greater Antilles, Bermuda, and N. F.

Washington, casual, two records, Mch. and May. Long Island, tolerably common S. R., Mch. 3–Oct. 17 (Nov. 7). Bronx region, A. V. (Ossining, Fisher); also Aug. 18. Boston, rare S. R., not uncommon T. V., Apr.–Oct. N. Ohio, breeds sparingly, May 5–Sept. 20. Glen Ellyn, two records, May and Sept. SE. Minn., rare T. V., May 19, 1926.

Nest, a depression in the beach. *Eggs,* 3–4, creamy white, finely spotted or speckled with chocolate, 1·24 × ·95. *Date,* Cape May, N. J., June 1, 1875; Shelter Isl., N. Y., June 3, 1881; Minor Co., S. Dak., June 5.

Because of their pale colors and absence of pronounced black breast-bands, Piping Plover are the most difficult to see of our small Plovers. They patter over the sand or pebbles like spirit birds and disappear the moment they stop. Their liquid *peep, peep,* or *peep-lo* has a true piping quality. As a breeding bird it is now rare, and man's increasing encroachment on its haunts threatens it with extinction as a summer resident in our Atlantic States.

180. CUBAN SNOWY PLOVER. CHARADRIUS NIVOSUS TENUIROSTRIS (*Lawrence*). [278 part.] Bill and feet black. *Ads. in summer.*—Forehead and underparts white; crown-band, ear-coverts, and patch on the sides of the breast black, duller in female; back pale ashy, the hindhead sometimes washed with buff; central tail-feathers brownish; outer ones white. *Winter plumage.*—The same, but crown-band, ear-coverts, sides of the breast-band ashy, upperparts finely margined with whitish. L., 6·00; W., 4·00; Tar., ·90; B., ·55.

Range.—Breeds on the Gulf Coast from Fla. to Tex. and apparently in

Haiti and Porto Rico; also on salt plains in Okla. and Kans. S. in winter to the Bahamas, Cuba, Haiti, Yucatan, and Venezuela (Margarita Isl.). Casual near Toronto, Ont.

Of this common southeastern representative of the Snowy Plover, F. M. Weston writes: "When on the ground the Cuban Snowy Plover gives a low-pitched, musical whistle roughly indicated by the words *pee-wee-ah* or *o-wee-ah*, the accent being on the second syllable with the first and third almost inaudible at a distance of 30 feet. The flight-note is a purring whistle, suggestive of the rolling note of the Carolina Wren, but pitched lower and not as strident."

181. SEMIPALMATED PLOVER. CHARADRIUS SEMIPALMATUS *Bonaparte.* [274.] (Fig. 41*d*, Pl. XIV.) *Ads. in summer.*—Feathers at base of

upper mandible, front of crown, sides of head below eye, and a band on breast, which generally encircles the neck all around, black; rest of underparts and a ring around the neck white; back of head and back brownish gray; inner tail-feathers brownish gray, outer ones becoming gradually white; *toes webbed at the base. Winter plumage.*—Similar, but black replaced by brownish gray. L., 6·75; W., 4·80; Tar., ·90; B., ·50.

Range.—Breeds on the Arctic Coast from Bering Sea to s. Baffin Isl. and Greenland s. to the valley of the Yukon, B. C. (Atlin Lake and the Queen Charlotte Isls.), s. James Bay, n. shore of the Gulf of St. Lawrence, N. B. and N. S. Winters from cent

FIG. 79. Semipalmated Plover. (Natural size.)

Calif., La., and S. C. to Patagonia, and the Galapagos. Casual in Siberia and Bermuda; accidental in England.

Washington, rare T. V., Apr.–June; Aug.–Oct. Long Island, common T. V. (Apr. 8) Apr. 19–June 13 (July 3); July 5–Nov. 8 (Dec. 9). Bronx region, common T. V., May 3–June 14; July 16–Oct. 27. Boston, abundant T. V., May–June; July–Oct. N. Ohio, common T. V., May 5–25; Aug. 25–Sept. 20. Glen Ellyn, irregular uncommon T. V., but few records, May 19; Aug. 12–Sept. 5. SE. Minn., common T. V., Apr. 30–June 7; July 17–Sept. 15.

Eggs, 3–4, buffy white or creamy buff, spotted with chocolate, 1·30 × ·90. *Date,* Ungava Bay, Lab., June 10.

This species frequents sandy beaches, mud-flats, and marshes. It is found generally in small flocks of five or ten individuals, which, unlike the Semipalmated Sandpipers, do not feed in a compact body, but run rapidly about, independently of one another. When they take wing, however, they close ranks at once and move as though governed by one desire. Their simple, sweet, plaintive call is one of the most characteristic notes heard on our shores. At noonday, when the heat waves are dancing over the marshes and even the twittering Oxeyes are silent, one may hear the *cool*, pure notes of this little Plover. They may be written. A third, shorter note is sometimes added. Even a whistled imitation of them takes me to the beaches.

182. WILSON'S PLOVER. Pagolla wilsonia wilsonia (*Ord*). [280.] (Pl. XIV.) *Ad.* ♂.—Lores, front of crown, and a band on the breast black; rest of underparts, forehead, and an indistinct ring on the nape white; sides of the head and nape sometimes with rufous markings; cheeks, crown, and back brownish gray; inner tail-feathers fuscous, outer ones becoming white. *Ad.* ♀.—Similar, but black replaced by brownish gray with rusty on breast. *Juv.*—Similar to ♀, but upperparts margined with grayish. L., 7·50; W., 4·50; Tar., 1·10; B., ·80.

Range.—Breeds from Va. (formerly N. J.) to the n. Bahama Isls. and Fla. and along the Gulf Coast to Tex. Winters from Fla. to Tex. and s. to Guat., Honduras, and the W. I. Casual n. to N. S. and N. E.

Long Island, A. V., May and July.

Nest, a depression in the sand. *Eggs*, 3, creamy white, evenly and rather finely spotted and speckled with chocolate, 1·42 × 1·03. *Date*, Sarasota, Fla., Apr. 12; Cobb's Isl., Va., May 15.

Fig. 80. Wilson's Plover. (Natural size.)

This is a strictly maritime species. Sandy beaches are its favorite resorts, but it is also found on mud-flats exposed by the falling tide. It is a gentle, unsuspicious bird, and when its nest is approached it runs about the intruder and begs as plainly as a bird can that he will not disturb its treasures. Its plaintive note is easily distinguishable from the calls of its near allies.

183. The Mountain Plover, *Eupoda montana* (J. K. Townsend), [281.] a western species, is of accidental occurrence in Florida and Massachusetts. The upperparts are grayish brown margined with rufous, the underparts are white tinged with buffy on the breast; in adults the front of the crown and lores are black. L., about 8·75; W., 5·75; Tar., 1·50; B., ·85.

184. KILLDEER. Oxyechus vociferus vociferus (*Linnæus*). [273.] *Ads.*—Forehead, a spot behind the eye, throat, and a ring around neck, a band on breast, lower breast, and belly white; front of crown, lores, a ring around neck, and a band on breast black; crown and back grayish brown tipped with rufous; rump and upper tail-coverts rufous; inner tail-feathers grayish brown, outer ones becoming rufous and white, all tipped with black and white. L., 10·50; W., 6·50; Tar., 1·35; B., ·75.

Range.—Breeds from n. B. C., s. Mack., n. Ont., s. Que., s. to the Bahamas and Fla., cent. Mex. and s. L. Calif. Winters from s. B. C., Colo., Mo., s. Ills., w. N. Y., N. J., s. to Bermuda, n. Venezuela and nw. Peru. Casual in N. S., N. B., N. F. and the British Isles.

Washington, P. R., most abundant in migrations. Long Island, uncommon S. R., more numerous T. V., casual P. R., Feb. 14–May 30, July 4–Dec. 26. Bronx region, common T. V., uncommon S. R., Jan. 31–Dec. 28

(Jan. 7). Boston, rare S. R., uncommon T. V., Mch.–Dec. N. Ohio, common
S. R., Feb. 27–Nov. 15. Glen Ellyn, fairly common S. R., Mch. 3–Nov. 17.
SE. Minn., common S. R., Mch. 7–Nov. 18.

Nest, often far from water, a slight depression in the ground, usually
scantily lined with bits of grass, etc., or stones. *Eggs*, 4, buffy white, spotted
and scrawled with chocolate chiefly at the larger end, 1·50 × 1·10. *Date*,
Chevy Chase, Md., Apr. 6; Pewaukee, Wisc., May 15.

In localities where this bird is common it is difficult to get beyond
the reach of its notes. Lakesides, meadows, pastures, and cultivated
fields all attract it, but it is more numerous in the vicinity of water.
It is a noisy, restless bird, running rapidly when on the ground, and
when on the wing flying swiftly and sometimes pursuing a most irregular course. When not nesting it is usually found in flocks, which
scatter when feeding but unite when taking wing. At the first sign of
danger it utters its half-plaintive, half-petulant *kill-dee, kill-dee,* and
when thoroughly alarmed its outcry increases until, beside itself with
fear, it reaches the limit of its vocal powers. Although by no means
shy, the Killdeer never seems to gain confidence in man, and at his
approach always gives voice to its fear. Even at night I have heard it
cry out at some real or fancied danger.

1889. CHADBOURNE, A. P., Auk, 255–263 (great flight of).—1925.
PICKWELL, G., Auk, 485–495, illus. (nesting).—1930. PICKWELL, G., Auk,
499–506 (only male incubates?).

185. The EUROPEAN GOLDEN PLOVER, *Pluvialis apricaria apricaria*
(Linnæus), [271], occurs in eastern Greenland. It resembles our species, but
has the under wing-coverts white instead of gray.

186. GOLDEN PLOVER. PLUVIALIS DOMINICA DOMINICA (*Müller*).
[272.] (Fig. 75.) *Ads. in summer.*—Upperparts black, spotted and margined
with golden yellow; tail brownish gray, indistinctly barred; forehead, sides
of head, neck, and breast white; rest of the underparts, including cheeks,
black; under wing-coverts and axillars (see Fig. 81) ashy. *Juv.*—Upperparts
and tail fuscous, spotted or barred with whitish or yellow; underparts whitish, more or less streaked or barred with brownish gray. *Ads. and Juv. in
winter.*—Similar, but less streaked below and less spotted above. L., 10·50;
W., 7·00; Tar., 1·60; B., ·90.

Remarks.—Immature birds are sometimes confused with those of the
Black-bellied Plover, but, aside from differences of size and color, the absence
of the fourth toe in the present species will always distinguish it.

Range.—Breeds from Pt. Barrow along the Arctic Coast to Melville
Peninsula and probably w. Baffin Isl. n. to Melville and N. Devon isls. and
s. to Ard Lake and Chesterfield Inlet. Winters on the pampas of Brazil,
Argentina, Paraguay, Bolivia, and Uruguay. Migrates s., mainly over the
Atlantic Ocean, from N. S. and N. E.; a few pass s. through the Miss.
Valley, and all migrate n. by this route; regular migrant on the Pacific
Coast in autumn. Formerly abundant, now much less common. Casual in
Greenland and Bermuda, accidental in Great Britain, Heligoland, and
Australia. (Fig. 10.)

Washington, rare and irregular T. V. Long Island, uncommon T. V.,
rare in spring, Apr. 7–May; Aug. 1–Nov. 13. Bronx region, rare T. V.,
Aug. 17–Nov. 13. Boston, T. V., rare spring, uncommon fall, Apr.–May;
Aug.–Nov. N. Ohio, not common T. V. Glen Ellyn, rare and irregular
T. V., Mch. 30–May 5; Sept. 6–Oct. 18. SE. Minn., now rare T. V., May 3;
Sept. 28–Nov. 2; no recent records.

Eggs, 3–4, ochraceous-buff or buffy white, heavily marked with chocolate, 1·85 × 1·28. *Date*, N. Alaska, May 23.

Golden Plovers frequent marshes, sandy hills, old fields, sand-flats exposed by the falling tide, plowed fields, and burned tracts which are free of trees and bushes. When on the ground they run rapidly and gracefully, and after alighting soon scatter. All their movements are quick, and after running a few yards they suddenly stop, hold their heads erect, and look about them. In feeding they seem to strike at an object with a motion that reminds one of a Loon or Grebe beginning to dive. When a flock is approaching decoys, every bird seems to be whistling, uttering a note like *coodle, coodle, coodle*. Unlike the Black-bellied Plover, the young birds are wary and more difficult to decoy than the old ones. When driven from a favorite resting- or feeding-ground they generally return in a short time. (Mackay, G. H., *The Auk*, 1891, 17–24; 1892, 199; 1893, 79–82; 1894, 75; 1895, 78; 1896, 80; 1897, 212; 1899, 180.)

187. BLACK-BELLIED PLOVER. Squatarola squatarola (*Linnæus*). [270.] (Figs. 40*d*, 41*c*.) *Ads. in summer.*—Upperparts black, bordered with white; tail white, barred with black; basal half of inner web of primaries white; sides of head and neck and entire underparts, except white lower belly and under tail-coverts, black; axillars (see Fig. 81) black. *Juv.*—Upperparts black, head and neck streaked, back spotted with whitish or buffy yellow; tail and wings as in adult; underparts white, breast and sides streaked with brownish gray. *Ads. and Juv. in winter.*—Similar to the preceding, but upperparts brownish gray, lightly margined with whitish. L., 11·00; W., 7·50; Tar., 1·90; B., 1·10.
Remarks.—The rounded scales on the front of the tarsus and the presence of a fourth, although very small, toe distinguish this bird.
Range.—Nearly cosmopolitan. Breeds on the Arctic Coast from Pt. Barrow to W. Baffin Land, and also on the Arctic Coast of Russia and Siberia. Winters from s. B. C., La., and N. C. to Brazil and Chile; in migration occurs throughout the U. S. and in Greenland and Bermuda. Accidental in Hawaii; casual all summer on the coast of Fla.
Washington, casual T. V., Sept., Oct. Long Island, common T. V., Apr. 30–July 14, July 11–Dec. 10 (Jan. 20). Bronx region, uncommon but regular T. V.; May 12–June 6; Aug. 9–Nov. 25. Boston, common T. V., May–June; July–Nov. N. Ohio, tolerably common T. V. Glen Ellyn, two records, May and Sept. SE. Minn., now uncommon T. V., May 16–June 3; Sept. 23–?.
Eggs, 3–4, light buffy olive, spotted and speckled with dark brown and brownish black or deep black, 2·04 × 1·43 (Ridgway). *Date*, Bering Sea coast of Alaska, May 27–June 4 (Bent).

Black-bellied Plovers are in a great degree *tide* birds, and seek a large part of their food on sand-flats left by the receding water. As the tide rises they resort to adjoining marshes or uplands, beaches, or the exposed crests of sandbars. In migrating they fly in lines and also in ranks, like Ducks and Geese. When on the ground they usually run very fast for four or five yards, then stop, elevate the head, and look around. They strike at the object they are going to pick up and eat with a very quick motion. They have two calls: one of several notes, with the accent on the second one, is mellow, clear, and far-reaching; the other is low, and is uttered when they are at ease and contented.

1892. Mackay, G. H., Auk, 143–152, 300.

188. EUROPEAN TURNSTONE. ARENARIA INTERPRES INTERPRES (*Linnæus*). [283.] Similar to No. 188a, *A. i. morinella*, but larger (W. 6·00) and, in the adult, the upperparts with black prevailing. *Im.*—Blacker than young of *morinella.*

Range.—Breeds from w. Greenland and Iceland through arctic Europe and Asia to Alaska (Yukon delta to Pt. Barrow). Winters on coasts of Europe and Asia to s. Africa. Accidental in Mass.

188a. RUDDY TURNSTONE. ARENARIA INTERPRES MORINELLA (*Linnæus*). [283a.] (Pl. XIV.) *Ads. in summer.*—Upperparts, including wings, strikingly variegated with rufous, black and white; tail white at base, a black band near its end, and tipped with white; throat and breast black and white; belly white. *Winter plumage.*—Upperparts blackish, bordered with brownish gray or ashy; *lower back white;* longer upper tail-coverts white, shorter ones black; tail as in adult; throat white, breast black margined with white, belly white. L., 9·50; W., 6·00; Tar., ·95; B., 1·00.

Range.—Breeds from w. and n. Alaska to w. Baffin Land. Winters from cent. Calif., Tex., La., Miss., and N. C. to s. Brazil and cent. Chile; occurs in migration over N. A. in general and individuals linger all summer on mainland beaches and on Laysan and other Pacific isls.

Washington, rare and irregular T. V., May; June; Sept. Long Island, common T. V., May 1–June 27 (July 3); (July 10) July 25–Oct. 18. Boston, fairly common T. V., May–June; July–Oct. N. Ohio, irregular T. V., May 5–25; Sept. 1–25. SE. Minn., uncommon T. V., May 20–June 4; no fall records.

Eggs, 3–4, clay-color, blotched and scrawled with grayish brown, 1·60 × 1·15. *Date*, Bering Sea coast of Alaska, May 29–June 7 (Bent).

This maritime species is found singly or in small flocks, generally on the outer beaches, where it obtains its food by turning over shells and pebbles in search of insects, crustaceans, etc.

"It is a stout, short-legged bird with a short neck and short, straight bill. The best field-marks, most conspicuous in the nuptial plumage, but present in all plumages, are the five white stripes on the upper surface, which show very plainly as the bird flies away; these are a broad central stripe on the back, separated by a black patch on the rump from the white area in the tail, a narrow stripe on the outer edge of the scapulars and a band across the wing on the secondaries and primaries" (Bent).

FAMILY SCOLOPACIDÆ. WOODCOCK, SNIPE, SANDPIPERS, ETC.

About ninety species are considered as belonging to this family. They are distributed throughout the world, but when nesting are mostly confined to the northern parts of the Northern Hemisphere. At this season, however, non-breeding individuals of many species occur in numbers far south of the nesting-range. I have seen hundreds of Black-bellied Plover, Hudsonian Curlew, and Long-billed Dowitchers on the coast of Ecuador, south of the Equator, in mid-July. Fifty-one species have been recorded from North America, but of these no less than eighteen, more than one-third, are of accidental occurrence. With the Plovers they constitute the great group known as shore-birds or bay-birds, and with few exceptions they are rarely found far from the vicinity of water. Generally speaking, they are more abundant on the coast than in the interior, but many species are quite as numerous inland as they are near the sea. As a rule, they migrate and pass the winter in flocks, but they are not gregarious during the nesting season.

Their long bills serve the purpose of both probes and forceps. Most of the species probe the soft mud for food, while some are known to have the power of moving the upper mandible independently of the lower one, curving it at the tip as one would a finger.

They are ardent wooers, and to courtship evolutions which rival those of Ducks in their abandon and elaborateness, add vocal performances sometimes weird and thrilling, sometimes equaling in beauty and musical quality those of our leading song-birds.

KEY TO THE SPECIES

I. Bill 2·00 or over.
  A. Axillars[1] barred with black.
    a. Bill curved downward.
        a^1. Bill over 3·00, under 4·50 . . . . . 198. HUDSONIAN CURLEW.
        a^2. Bill under 3·00 . . . . 199. ESKIMO CURLEW.
        a^3. Bill over 4·50 . . . . 195. LONG-BILLED CURLEW.
    b. Bill straight or curved slightly upward.
        b^1. Tail-feathers with numerous black bars.
        b^2. Wing over 7·00, primaries black or fuscous.
            205. GREATER YELLOW-LEGS.
        b^3. Wing over 7·00, inner web of primaries buff or rufous.
            221. MARBLED GODWIT.
        b^4. Wing under 7·00, bill widened and pitted at the tip.
          216. DOWITCHER. 216a. LONG-BILLED DOWITCHER.
        c^1. Tail black with a broad rufous tip or marked with rufous.
        c^2. Outer web of primaries with rufous bars.
            190. EUROPEAN WOODCOCK.
        c^3. Primaries not barred . . . . 192. WILSON'S SNIPE.
  B. Axillars not barred.
    a. Axillars rufous or ochraceous-buff.
        a^1. Bill over 5·00, much curved downward.
            195. LONG-BILLED CURLEW.
        a^2. Bill nearly straight, between 3·50 and 5·00.
            221. MARBLED GODWIT.
        a^3. Bill straight, under 3·50 . . . . . 189. AMERICAN WOODCOCK.
    b. Axillars black.
        b^1. Underparts chestnut-rufous, barred with black.
            223. HUDSONIAN GODWIT.
        b^2. Underparts white, with or without blackish bars.
          204. WILLET. 204a. WESTERN WILLET.
II. Bill under 2·00.
  1. Tail with cross-bars.
    A. Wing over 5·75.
        a. Outer tail-feathers white, more or less barred; outer primary without bars . . . . 206. LESSER YELLOW-LEGS.
        b. Outer primary with numerous black bars . 200. UPLAND PLOVER.

    B. Wing under 5·75.
        a. Underparts white, with numerous round blackish spots; upperparts brownish gray, barred with blackish.
          201. SPOTTED SANDPIPER.
[1] See Fig. 81.

    b. Underparts white, breast streaked with blackish; upperparts fuscous, spotted with white . . . . . 202. SOLITARY SANDPIPER.

    c. Underparts tinged with buffy, inner web of outer primary speckled with blackish . . . . 220. BUFF-BREASTED SANDPIPER.

    d. Underparts white, breast washed with grayish, inner primaries and secondaries with a concealed white patch.

                     201. SPOTTED SANDPIPER, im.

2. Tail without cross-bars.

  A. Toes 4.

    a. Bill over 1·10.

      a^1. Middle upper tail-coverts with cross-bars or streaks.

        a^2. Tarsus over 1·50 . . . . 217. STILT SANDPIPER.

        a^3. Tarsus under 1·50, wing under 6·00 214. CURLEW SANDPIPER.

        a^4. Tarsus under 1·50, wing over 6·00 . . . . . . 208. KNOT.

      b^1. Middle upper tail-coverts without cross-bars or streaks.

        b^2. Middle upper tail-coverts black or fuscous, without bars; bill straight.

          b^3. Tarsus under 1·50; upperparts blackish, more or less margined with gray . . . . 209. PURPLE SANDPIPER.

          b^4. Tarsus under 1·50; upperparts more or less margined with rufous . . . . 210. PECTORAL SANDPIPER.

          b^5. Tarsus over 1·50 . . . . 225. RUFF.

        c^2. Middle upper tail-coverts grayish, bill curved slightly downward . . . . 215a. RED-BACKED SANDPIPER.

    b. Bill under 1·10.

      b^1. Wing under 4·00.

        b^2. Toes partly webbed.

        218. SEMIPALMATED SANDPIPER. 219. WESTERN SANDPIPER.

        b^3. Toes not webbed . . . . 213. LEAST SANDPIPER.

      c^1. Wing over 4·00.

        c^2. Inner webs of primaries plain.

          c^3. Breast white or whitish, streaked or spotted with blackish; middle upper tail-coverts white.

                211. WHITE-RUMPED SANDPIPER.

          c^4. Breast buffy, heavily spotted or streaked with blackish; middle upper tail-coverts black, slightly margined with rufous . . . . 210. PECTORAL SANDPIPER.

          c^5. Breast buffy lightly spotted or streaked with black; middle upper tail-coverts fuscous, lightly margined with buffy.

                212. BAIRD'S SANDPIPER.

      d^2. Inner webs of primaries speckled.

          220. BUFF-BREASTED SANDPIPER.

  B. Toes 3 . . . . 226. SANDERLING.

---

189. WOODCOCK. PHILOHELA MINOR (*Gmelin*). [228.] (Pl. IX. Figs. 12, 17.) *Ads.*—Front of crown slaty, washed with buff, an indistinct blackish line in its center, and another from eye to bill; back of head black, with two or three bars of ochraceous-buff; rest of upperparts black, margined with slaty and barred and mottled with rufous or ochraceous-buff; tip of tail ashy gray above, silvery beneath; underparts between ochraceous-buff and rufous; outer three primaries very narrow and much stiffened. L., 11·00; W., 5·40; Tar., 1·25; B., 2·90.

    Range.—Breeds from ne. N. Dak., ne. Minn., Ont., n. Mich., s. Que., N. B. and N. S. s. to e. Colo., s. Kans. (formerly), s. La., and n. Fla. Winters from s. Mo., n. Man., Mont., the O. Valley, and s. N. J. (rarely, n. Ind. and Mass.) s. to Tex. and cent. Fla. Casual in Mont., Man., N. F., and Bermuda.

    Washington, uncommon from Feb. to Dec. Long Island, tolerably common S. R., casual W. V., Feb. 12–Dec. 8 (Dec. 26). Bronx region, fairly common S. R., Feb. 19–Dec. 2. Boston, uncommon S. R., common T. V., Mch.–Nov. N. Ohio, tolerably common S. R., Mch. 10–Oct. 20. Glen

Ellyn, not common S. R., Mch. 29–Sept. 18. SE. Minn., S. R., Apr. 5–Oct. 18.

Nest, of a few dry leaves, on the ground in the woods. *Eggs*, 4, buffy, distinctly and obscurely spotted with shades of rufous, 1·60 × 1·23. *Date*, Caper's Isl., S. C., Feb. 13; Lower Cedar Pt., Md., Feb. 25; Cambridge, Apr. 15; Wheatland, Ind., Mch. 4; Petersburg, Mich., Apr. 16.

During the spring and early summer this Owl among Snipe haunts low, wooded bottom-lands; in August, while molting, it resorts to corn-fields near woods, and in the fall migrating birds frequent wooded uplands. But at all times it requires soft, moist earth in which it may easily probe with its long bill for its fare of earthworms. The holes it makes are known as 'borings.' They are generally found in little groups, and are, of course, certain evidence of the presence of Wood-cock. Gurdon Trumbull discovered that the Woodcock can move the tip of its upper mandible independently of the lower one, and this organ is made to act as a finger to assist the bird in drawing its food from the ground. (*Forest and Stream*, 1890, p. 412.)

The flight of the Woodcock is sometimes accompanied by a high, whistling sound produced by its narrow, stiffened primaries in beating the air. When flushed near its nest or young, the parent bird generally feigns lameness or a broken wing, and leads the intruder some distance from its treasures before taking wing. The fact that the parents fly with their young held between their thighs or clasped between their toes is confirmed by numerous observations.

The cloak of night always lends a certain mystery to the doings of nocturnal birds, and more often than not their habits justify our unusual interest in them. Few of the mating evolutions of our birds are more remarkable than the sky dance of the Woodcock. He begins on the ground with a formal, periodic *peent, peent*, an incongruous preparation for the wild rush that follows. It is repeated several times before he springs from the ground, and on whistling wings sweeps out on the first loop of a spiral which may take him 300 feet from the ground. Faster and faster he goes, louder and shriller sounds his wing-song; then, after a moment's pause, with darting, headlong flight, he pitches in zigzags to the earth, uttering as he falls a clear, twittering whistle. He generally returns to near the place from which he arose, and the *peent* is at once resumed as a preliminary to another round in the sky. In the gray of early morning this strange performance is repeated.

1894. Brewster, W., Auk, 291–298 (song).—1922. Grinnell, G. B., Auk, 563, 564.—1929. Schorger, A. W., Auk, 232 (carrying young).

190. The European Woodcock, *Scolopax rusticola rusticola* Linnæus. [227], bears a general resemblance to our Woodcock, but is much larger; the underparts are barred with black, the wings are barred with rufous, and the outer primaries are not emarginate. It is of accidental occurrence in eastern North America.

191. The European Snipe, *Capella gallinago gallinago* (Linnæus), [229], inhabits the northern parts of the Old World, is casual in Greenland, and accidental in Labrador and Bermuda. It closely resembles Wilson's Snipe but usually has 14 instead of 16 tail-feathers, more white on the under wing-coverts, and broader outer tail-feathers.

192. WILSON'S SNIPE. Capella delicata (*Ord*). [230.] *Ads.*—Upperparts black, barred, bordered, and mottled with different shades of cream-buff; wings fuscous; outer edge of outer primary and tips of greater coverts white; throat white; neck and breast ochraceous-buff, indistinctly streaked with blackish; belly white, sides barred with black; under tail-coverts buffy, barred with black; outer tail-feathers barred with black and white, inner ones black, barred with rufous at their ends and tipped with whitish. L., 11·25; W., 5·00; Tar., 1·20; B., 2·50.

Range.—Breeds from nw. Alaska, n. Mack., n. Que. (Ungava), and N.:F., s. to s. Calif., n. Nev., s. Colo., e. S. Dak., n. Ia., n. Ills., n. Ind., and nw. Pa. Winters from s. B. C., s. Mont., and s. Va., through Cent. A. and W. I. to Colombia and s. Brazil; remains in winter casually and locally n. to Nebr., Minn., Ills., and N. S. Accidental in Greenland, Hawaii, Bermuda, and Great Britain.

Washington, common T. V., Feb. 17–May 14; Aug. 30–Dec. 22. Long Island, common T. V., rare W. V., (July 10) Aug. 6–Dec. 5; Mch. 12–May 31. Bronx region, fairly common T. V., casual in summer; occasional in winter; Mch. 8–May 22; Sept. 7–Dec. 28. Boston, common T. V., Apr. 6–May 6; Sept. 12–Nov. 15; occasionally winters. N. Ohio, common T. V., Mch. 19–May 15; Sept. 15–Oct. 30. Glen Ellyn, common T. V., Mch. 26–May 11; Sept. 1–Nov. 13. SE. Minn., common T. V., uncommon S. R., Mch. 1–Nov. 20; A. V. in winter.

Nest, of grasses, on the ground in marshy places. *Eggs*, 3–4, olive, clay-color, or brownish ashy, heavily marked with chocolate, principally at the larger end, 1·60 × 1·17. *Date*, Lake Co., Ills., Apr. 24; se. Minn., May 10.

Wilson's Snipe frequents fresh-water meadows and swamps, and in spring is often found in low-lying swales in meadows or mowing fields, but, excepting in very dry seasons, it seldom alights on salt-marshes. At times, especially in winter or early spring, when the meadows are covered with snow or ice, it resorts to springy runs wooded with alders, birches, and maples, but as a rule it prefers open places. Two things are essential to its requirements—ground so thoroughly water-soaked as to afford slight resistance to its long and highly sensitive bill when probing, and such concealment as tussocks, hillocks, or long grass afford, for, unlike the Sandpipers, the Snipe rarely ventures out on bare mud-flats, save under cover of darkness. Although less strictly nocturnal than the Woodcock, it feeds and migrates chiefly by night or in 'thick' weather. Its migratory movements are notoriously erratic, and meadows which one day are alive with birds may be quite deserted the next, or the reverse.

Dear to our sportsmen is Wilson's Snipe, partly because of the excellence of its flesh, but chiefly from the fact that it furnishes a mark which taxes their skill to the utmost, and which no mere novice need hope to hit, unless by accident; for the bird's flight is swift and tortuous, and it springs from the grass as if thrown by a catapult, uttering a succession of hoarse, rasping *scaipes* which have a peculiarly startling effect on inexperienced nerves.

In the springtime—and occasionally in autumn also—Wilson's Snipe mounts to a considerable height above his favorite meadows and darts downward with great velocity, making at each descent a low, yet penetrating, tremulous sound which suggests the winnowing of a domestic Pigeon's wings, or, if heard at a distance, the bleating of a goat, and which is thought to be produced by the rushing of the air through the outer tail-feathers of this Snipe. The performance may be sometimes witnessed in broad daylight when the weather is stormy, but ordinarily it is reserved for the morning and evening twilight and for moonlight nights, when it is often kept up for hours in succession.

Besides this 'drumming' or 'bleating,' as it is called, the Snipe, while mating, sometimes makes another peculiar sound, a *kŭk-kŭk-kŭk-kŭk-kŭp*, evidently vocal and occasionally accompanying a slow, labored, and perfectly direct flight, at the end of which the bird alights on a tree or fence-post for a few moments.   WILLIAM BREWSTER.

1902. GAULT, B. T., Wilson Bull., 7–10 (food habits).—1923. SUTTON, G. M., Wilson Bull., 191–202 (nesting).—1924. HOFFMANN, R., Condor, 175–176; also, Taylor, 1925, 224–226 (flight performance).

193. The GREAT SNIPE, *Capella media* (Latham), [230.1], an Old-World species, has been taken once on Hudson Bay (Coues, Auk, 1897, 209).

194. The EUROPEAN JACK SNIPE, *Limnocryptes minimus* (Brünnich), [230.2], an Old-World species, has been recorded from Labrador.

195. LONG-BILLED CURLEW. NUMENIUS AMERICANUS AMERICANUS *Bechstein.* [264.] *Ads.*—Head and neck streaked, and back barred with buffy and black; wing-coverts, inner webs of primaries, secondaries, and tail varying from buffy to pale rufous, barred or mottled with blackish; underparts ochraceous-buff, breast more or less streaked and sides sometimes barred with black; axillars rufous, generally unbarred. L., 24·00; W., 10·50; Tar., 3·10; B., 6·00.

Range.—Breeds in Utah, s. Idaho, and e. Nev.; formerly in s. Wisc., Ia., n. Ills., e. Nebr., and e. Kans. Winters from cent. Calif. and s. Ariz. s. to Guat., and formerly on the Atlantic Coast from S. C. to Fla., La., and Tex. Formerly a regular migrant n. to Mass., now a straggler e. of the Miss. Casual in the W. I.

Washington, one record, Apr., 1842. Long Island, rare T. V., Apr. 28; July 10–Sept. 12 (Oct. 15). Bronx region, A. V. at Ossining many years ago. N. Ohio, casual T. V.

Eggs, 3–4, olive clay-color or brownish ashy, spotted or blotched with chocolate, 2·58 × 1·85. *Date*, Utah, Apr. 1–May 22; Sask., May 3–June 4 (Bent).

"These birds, as a rule, inhabit the muddy shores and moist, grassy flats and plains, but often frequent and breed upon the uplands remote from water. Their food consists of worms, crickets, beetles, grasshoppers, small snails, crabs and crawfish; the latter they reach for with their long bills and pull them out of their holes; and I have seen them probe for and unearth the larvæ of the beetles and other forms of life that in the spring come to or near the surface preparatory to transformation. While feeding they move about with an easy carriage.

"Their flight is not rapid but well sustained, with regular strokes of the wings, and when going a distance usually high and in a triangular form, uttering now and then their loud, prolonged whistling note, so often heard during the breeding season; before alighting, suddenly drop nearly to the ground, then gather, and with a rising sweep gracefully alight" (Goss).

196. The EUROPEAN CURLEW, *Numenius arquatus arquatus* (Linnæus), [264.1], an Old-World species, is of casual occurrence in Greenland and on Long Island.

197. The WHIMBREL, *Phæopus phæopus phæopus* (Linnæus), [267], an Old-World species, is occasional in Greenland and is accidental in Nova Scotia and on Long Island, N. Y. (one record, Sept.).

198. HUDSONIAN CURLEW. PHÆOPUS HUDSONICUS *Latham*. [265.]

Ads.—Upperparts grayish brown, the sides of the feathers with buff or whitish spots; rump and tail barred with buffy and blackish; inner web of outer primaries and both webs of inner ones *barred with buffy or whitish and black;* underparts buffy or whitish, neck and breast streaked and sides and under wing-coverts barred with black. L., 17·00; W., 9·50; Tar., 2·20; B., 3·75.

Remarks.—Young birds often have the bill as short as in *P. borealis* from which, however, they may always be distinguished by their barred primaries.

Range.—Breeds on the coast of Alaska from mouth of Yukon to the coast of n. Mack. and n. Man. Winters from L. Calif. to s. Chile, and from British Guiana to mouth of the Amazon; migrates mainly along the Pacific and Atlantic Coasts; rare in the interior. Casual on the Pribilof Isls. and in Greenland and Bermuda; accidental in Iceland and Spain.

Long Island, T. V., rare spring, tolerably common fall T. V., (Apr. 17); Apr. 28–May 31; June 24–Oct. 12 (Dec. 24). Bronx region, rare T. V., May 15; July 23–Sept. 5. Boston, T. V., uncommon spring; rather common in fall, Apr.–May; July–Sept. N. Ohio, not common T. V.

Eggs, 3–4, pale olive, spotted with dull brown, 2·27 × 1·57 (Ridgway). *Date*, Alaska and Mackenzie, May 31–July 10 (Bent).

The Hudsonian Curlew appears to have more than held its own, and on the coasts of our South Atlantic States is an abundant migrant. They select isolated islets as roosting-places and, in V-shaped flocks, frequent them in thousands. "The flight-note of the Hudsonian Curlew in migration resembles somewhat that of the Greater Yellowlegs, but is easily distinguished therefrom, being less modulated and usually lower pitched" (Nichols).

1892. MACKAY, G. H., Auk, 345–352 (in Mass.).

199. ESKIMO CURLEW. PHÆOPUS BOREALIS (*J. R. Forster*). [266.]

Ads.—Upperparts black, margined and tipped with buffy or whitish; upper tail-coverts barred with buffy and black; tail brownish gray, edged with buffy and barred with black; primaries fuscous *without bars;* underparts buffy or whitish, the breast streaked, the sides and under wing-coverts barred with black. L., 13·50; W., 8·40; Tar., 1·75; B., 2·40.

Range.—Formerly bred on the Barren Grounds of n. Mack., nw. perhaps to Norton Sound, Alaska. Formerly a common autumn transient on the Atlantic Coast from Lab. s. to L. I. and n. N. J., thence over the ocean to S. A. Wintered on the plains of Argentina and Patagonia to Chile and casually the Falkland Isls. Accidental or casual in ne. Siberia, the Pribilof Isls., Greenland, Iceland, and the British Isles. Now nearly or quite extinct.

Long Island, formerly T. V., Aug. 3–Sept.

Eggs, 3–4, pale olive-greenish, olive, or olive-brownish, distinctly spotted, chiefly on the larger end, with deep or dark brown, 2·04 × 1·43 (Ridgway). *Date*, e. of Anderson River, Mack., June 20.

"Most of their habits closely resemble those of the Golden Plover. In migration they fly in much the same manner, with extended and broadside and triangular lines and clusters similar to those of Ducks and Geese at such times. They usually fly low after landing, sweeping slowly over the ground, apparently looking it over, generally standing motionless for quite a while after alighting, which, owing to their general color approximating so closely to the withered grass, renders it difficult at times to perceive them. . . . The only note I ever heard them make is a kind of squeak, very much like one of the cries of Wilson's Tern (*Sterna hirundo*), only finer in tone." (Mackay, *The Auk*, 1892, 16–21; 1893, 79; 1894, 75; 1897, 212; 1899, 180.) Apparently, as a result of excessive shooting, both during its migrations and in its winter quarters, the Eskimo Curlew, which sixty years ago was an exceedingly abundant bird, is now either extinct or on the verge of extinction. The last recorded instances of its occurrence are: Province of Buenos Aires, Argentina, Feb. 7, 1924, five or six seen, one captured (I saw this specimen the day after it was prepared), and Jan. 11, 1925, one captured (Dabbene). Hastings, Nebr., Apr. 8, 1926, eight birds (Swenk).

1915. Swenk, M. H., The Eskimo Curlew and Its Disappearance, Proc. Nebr. Orn. Union, VI, 2; also Smithsonian Report, 325–340.—1926. Swenk, M. H., Wilson Bull., 117 (seen at Hastings, Nebr., Apr. 8, 1926).

200. UPLAND PLOVER. Bartramia longicauda (*Bechstein*). [261.] (Pl. XIV.) *Ads.*—Head and neck streaked with black and ochraceous-buff; back and wing-coverts ochraceous-buff, barred with black; tertials olive, barred with black and margined with ochraceous-buff; primaries fuscous, the outer one *barred with white;* inner tail-feathers brownish gray, outer ones varying from ochraceous-buff to white, all more or less barred with black; breast and sides washed with buffy and streaked or barred with black; belly white or whitish. *Juv.*—Similar, but the ochraceous-buff is deeper. L., 11·50; W., 6·50; Tar., 1·90; B., 1·15.

Remarks.—The white bars on the outer primary will always serve to identify this species.

Range.—Breeds from nw. Alaska, n. Yukon, s. Mack., cent. Man., cent. Wisc., s. Mich., s. Ont., s. Que., and s. Me. to s. Ore., ne. Utah, Colo., s. Okla., s. Mo., s. Ills., s. Ind. and n. Va. (casually S. C.). Winters on the pampas of S. A. from s. Brazil to Argentina and Chile. Casual or accidental in ne. Calif., N. S., N. B., Bermuda and w. Europe. Rapidly becoming rare. Washington, common T. V., Mch. 21–May 11; June 29–Sept. 26. Long Island, uncommon T. V., rare S. R., Apr. 4–late May; June 30–Sept. 17 (Oct. 20). Bronx region, rare T. V., Aug. 8–Sept. 9 (Oct. 3). Boston, rare T. V., Apr.–May; July–Oct. N. Ohio, common S. R., Mch. 20–Sept. 20. Glen Ellyn, fairly common S. R., Apr. 10–Sept. 11. SE. Minn., S. R., formerly common, now rare, Apr. 7–Sept. 14.

Nest, concealed in the grass. *Eggs*, 4, creamy buff or white, spotted with reddish brown or chocolate, chiefly at the larger end, 1·80 X 1·30. *Date*, Haddonfield, N. J., May 6, 1887; Holland Patent, N. Y., May 21; Greenwood Co., Kans., May 11; se. Minn., June 17.

The Upland 'Plover' is at home on grassy plains and pastures. It is usually a shy bird, and can rarely be successfully approached on foot. It shows no fear, however, of a man who is riding or driving, and when on horseback I have passed within a few yards of birds which regarded me with some interest but no alarm. They so closely resemble dried grass in color that it is sometimes exceedingly difficult to distinguish them from their surroundings.

In alighting, the birds often stretch their wings to the utmost, high over their backs, before gently folding them. When flushed they utter a soft, bubbling whistle. During their migrations one may clearly hear these sweet notes from birds traveling beyond the limits of human vision. Langille describes their alarm note as a spirited and rapidly uttered *quip-ip-ip-ip*, *quip-ip-ip-ip*, and their song, given from the ground, a fence, or even a tree, as *chr-r-r-r-r-ee-e-e-e-e-oo-o-o-o-oo*. He remarks: "This prolonged, mournful, mellow whistle, more like the whistling of wind than a bird's voice, may be heard even in the night, and is one of the most weird and never-to-be-forgotten sounds in Nature."

Unable to contend with the many adverse factors brought by civilization, the Upland Plover has steadily decreased. It is no longer common in the West, and in the East is rare and local.

201. SPOTTED SANDPIPER. Actitis macularia (*Linnæus*). [263.] (Pl. XV.) *Ads. in summer.*—Upperparts brownish gray with a faint greenish luster, head and neck more or less streaked, and back barred or spotted with black; inner tail-feathers like back, outer ones white with blackish bars; underparts white; everywhere spotted with black. *Juv.*—Upperparts brownish gray, with a greenish tinge, back faintly and wing-coverts conspicuously barred with black and buffy; underparts pure white, unspotted, but slightly washed with grayish on breast. *Ads. and Juv. in winter.*—Similar, but back without bars. L., 7·50; W., 4·20; Tar., ·90; B., ·95.

Range.—Breeds from tree-limit in nw. Alaska, n. Man., and n. Que. (Ungava) s. to s. Calif., s. Tex., s. La., cent. Ala., and n. S. C. Winters from s. B. C., La., and S. C., to s. Brazil, and casually Argentina. Accidental in Great Britain, Helgoland, Belgium, and w. Germany.

Washington, common T. V., not common S. R., Apr. 2–Oct. 28. Long Island, common S. R., Apr. 20–Oct. 12 (Oct. 25). Bronx region, common S. R., Apr. 18–Oct. 23. Boston, common S. R., Apr. 26–Sept. 30. N. Ohio, common S. R., Apr. 9–Oct. 15. Glen Ellyn, fairly common S. R., Apr. 18–Oct. 30. SE. Minn., common S. R., Apr. 18–Oct. 22.

Nest, on dry ground, in the grasses or weeds, or beneath a bush near fresh or salt water. *Eggs,* 4, creamy buff or white, thickly spotted and speckled with chocolate, chiefly at the larger end, 1·25 × ·95. *Date,* Montgomery Co., Pa., May 16; Boston, May 25; se. Minn., May 30.

Few shore-birds are more generally known than this widely distributed little Sandpiper. It frequents the margins of bodies of both fresh and salt water, but is more common inland on the shores of our rivers, ponds and lakes. During the summer it is practically our only fresh-water Sandpiper, and is familiar to most of us under its common names. It runs rapidly along the beach, then pausing bobs, bows, and 'teeters' in a most energetic manner. When flushed it takes wing with a sharp *weet-weet weet-weet*, and after a few wing-strokes scales over the water to the beach beyond. It apparently dislikes to go beyond the limits of its 'territory' and after several flights makes a wide circle and returns to the starting-point.

1930. Nelson, T., Growth Rate of Spotted Sandpiper Chick, with Notes on Nesting Habits, Bird-Banding, 1–13, illus.

PLATE XV

SPOTTED SANDPIPER AND YOUNG

202. EASTERN SOLITARY SANDPIPER. TRINGA SOLITARIA SOLITARIA *Wilson.* [256.] (Pl. XIV.) *Ads. in summer.*—Upperparts olive-fuscous, with a slight greenish tinge, head and neck streaked and back spotted with white; upper tail-coverts fuscous, with fine whitish spots on their sides, lateral ones sometimes barred; central pair of tail-feathers fuscous, the others white, barred with black; breast streaked, and sides sometimes barred with black; belly white; axillars barred with black and white; legs greenish fuscous. *Ads. and Juv. in winter.*

—Similar, but upper-
parts grayish brown;
head and neck generally
unstreaked, and back
only lightly spotted
with buffy white; breast
streaked with brown-
ish gray. L., 8.40; W.,
5.25; Tar., 1.20; B.,
1.15.

FIG. 81. Inner view of wing of Solitary Sandpiper, showing barred axillars.

Range.—Summers from cent. Alberta and n. Que. (Ungava), s. to Nebr., Ills., n. Ia., Ind., n. O., and n. Pa.; breeds in Alberta and doubtless in the other portions of its summer range. Winters casually in Fla. and from the W. I. to Ecuador and probably Argentina. Accidental in n. Alaska, Galapagos Isls., Greenland, Bermuda and Great Britain, regular in migration in B. C., casual w. to N. Mex., Wyo. and Mont.

Washington, common T. V., Mch. 30–May 21; July 15–Oct. 28. Long Island, tolerably common T. V., Apr. 26–June 6; July 6–Oct. 18. Bronx region, common T. V., Apr. 7–June 6; July 6–Oct. 15 (Nov. 6; 11). Boston, common T. V., May 12–23; Aug. 10–Sept. 30. N. Ohio, common T. V., Apr. 20; Sept. 15. Glen Ellyn, fairly common T. V., Apr. 8–May 31; July 9–Oct. 6. SE. Minn., common T. V., Apr. 19–May 29; July 10–Oct. 26.

Nest, lays in the abandoned nests of such tree-building birds as the Robin, Bronzed Grackle or Cedar Waxwing. *Eggs,* 4, "pale greenish white, heavily blotched and spotted chiefly at the larger ends with vandyke-brown, chestnut-brown, and purplish gray," 1.36 × .98. (Raine, Ottawa Nat., 1904, 135–138; Auk, 1905, 100). *Date,* n. Alberta, June 9.

This is a wood Sandpiper. It is rarely found on the beaches or salt-marshes near the sea, but frequents fresh-water ponds, or lakes and woodland streams, both in the lowlands and mountains. It is a quieter, more dignified bird than the Spotted Sandpiper, and as a rule utters its *tweet-tweet* only when flushed. The nest of this species has long been sought for, but it was not until 1903 that, like its European representative, the Green Sandpiper, it was found laying in the nests of tree-building birds.

1923. STREET, J. F., Auk, 577–583, illus. (nesting).

203. The GREEN SANDPIPER, *Tringa ochrophus* (Linnæus), [257], an Old-World species, has been once recorded from Nova Scotia.

204. EASTERN WILLET. CATOPTROPHORUS SEMIPALMATUS SEMIPALMATUS *(Gmelin).* [258.] *Ads. in summer.*—Upperparts brownish gray, the head and neck streaked, and the back barred with black, and sometimes buffy, the centers of the feathers being occasionally wholly black; basal half of primaries and greater part of secondaries white showing in flight; upper tail-coverts white with a few blackish bars; central tail-feathers ashy, indistinctly *barred with blackish;* outer ones whitish, lightly mottled with grayish; foreneck heavily streaked; breast and sides heavily barred with dark brownish gray and more or less washed with buffy; belly generally white, with sometimes a few bars. *Ads. and Juv. in winter.*—Upperparts brownish gray, unmarked; tail gray without bars; rump and wings as in the adult; breast washed with grayish; belly white; *axillars black.* L., 15·00; W., 8·00; Tar., 2·30; B., 2·15.

Range.—Breeds in N. S. and from Va. and N. J. to Fla. and on the Gulf Coast to Tex.; also in the Bahamas and Greater Antilles. Winters from N. C. and the Bahamas to Brazil. Accidental in Kans., Bermuda, and Europe. Washington, rare T. V., May; June; Aug. Long Island, rare or casual T. V., Apr. 29–June 15; July–Sept. Bronx region, rare T. V., May 26; Aug. 4–Sept. 12. SE. Minn., now rare T. V., May 16.

Nest, in grassy marshes. *Eggs*, 3–4, clay-color or buffy, thickly spotted with chocolate, chiefly at the larger end, 2·10 × 1·55. *Date*, Sapelo Isl., Ga., Apr. 22; Cobb's Isl., Va., May 16.

Willets frequent both fresh- and salt-water marshes, shores, and beaches. If you visit their haunts during the nesting season, on fluttering wings they will hover above your head or fly low over the marsh to draw you away from their home, uttering, with scarce a moment's cessation, their loudly whistled call of *pilly-will-willet, pilly-will-willet.* All day long, and even at night, I have heard them repeat these notes until, wearied by their persistence, one is thankful to leave them in undisturbed possession of the ground.

1905. JOB, H. K., Wild Wings, 250 (nesting).

204a. WESTERN WILLET. CATOPTROPHORUS SEMIPALMATUS INORNA-TUS (*Brewster*). [258a.] Slightly larger than the preceding, and, in summer plumage, upperparts paler and less heavily marked with black; breast less heavily streaked and more suffused with buffy; middle tail-feathers without black bars. In winter plumage the two forms can be distinguished only by the slight and inconstant character of size. W., 8·50; Tar., 2·50; B., 2·40.

Range.—Breeds from cent. Ore. and s. Man., to ne. Calif., to w. Minn., and n. Ia. Winters from n. Calif. on the Pacific Coast, and from the coasts of La. and Fla. to Peru, and the Galapagos Isls.; in fall migration occurs on the Atlantic Coast from N. E. s. Accidental in sw. B. C. and se. Alaska.

Long Island, irregular, not uncommon T. V. in fall, July 10–Sept. 16 (perhaps confused with the preceding in spring). Boston, uncommon T. V., May; Aug.–Sept. N. Ohio, not common T. V.

205. GREATER YELLOW-LEGS. TOTANUS MELANOLEUCUS (*Gmelin.*) [254.] (Fig. 76, Pl. XIV.) *Ads. in summer.*—Upperparts black, head and neck streaked and back spotted or barred with white or ashy; upper tail-coverts white, more or less barred with black; tail white or ashy, barred with black; breast heavily spotted with black; sides barred with black; middle of the belly white. *Ads. and Juv. in winter.*—Similar, but upperparts brownish gray, edged with whitish; sides of scapulars, tertials, and wing-coverts with blackish and whitish spots; breast only lightly streaked with blackish, and sides slightly barred. L., 14·00; W., 7·70; Tar., 2·40; B., 2·20.

Range.—Breeds from Mt. Iliamna, Alaska, and Lab. to s. B. C., s. Man., N. F., Mingan and Anticosti Isls. Winters from cent. Calif. (casually Wash.), and S. C. (casually N. C.) s. to Patagonia; non-breeding birds are occasional at all times of year in the W. I., Bahamas, Fla., Tex. and Calif. Bermuda in migration. Accidental in the British Isles.

Washington, rather common T. V., Apr. 5; May 27; July 24–Nov. 2. Long Island, common T. V., (Mch. 9) Mch. 21–June 23; July 3–Dec. 7, casual late June to early July. Bronx region, common T. V., Mch. 26–June 18; July 4–Nov. 22. Boston, common T. V., Apr.–June; July–Nov. N. Ohio, common T. V., Apr. 10–May 15; Sept. 1–Oct. 30. Glen Ellyn, un-

common T. V., Apr. 27–May; Sept. 18–Oct. 24. SE. Minn., uncommon T.
V., Apr. 1–May 26; Sept. 7–Oct. 24.

Eggs, 3–4, brownish buffy, distinctly but very irregularly spotted with
rich vandyke- or madder-brown, 1·43 × 1·20 (Ridgway). *Date*, Ft. George,
B. C., May 20.

It needs only the musical notes of the Yellow-legs to recall memories
of many days passed along the shore and in the marshes. Half reclining
in my blind, I see in fancy the staring decoys, pointing like weather-
cocks with the wind, and hear the dull booming of surf behind the
brown sand-dunes.

Few birds are flying; lulled by the *lap, lap* of the water, I have
almost fallen asleep, when from far up in the gray sky comes a soft,
flutelike whistle, *wheu, wheu-wheu-wheu-wheu, wheu, wheu-wheu*. I
respond quickly, and, lying on my back, look eagerly upward. Not a
bird can be seen, but the questioning call grows stronger and is repeated
more frequently. Finally I distinguish five or six black points sailing
in narrow circles so high that I can scarcely believe they are the birds
I hear. But no bar or shoal breaks the sound waves. The birds grow
larger and on widening circles sweep earthward. Their soft whistle
has a plaintive tone; their long bills turn inquiringly from side to side.
The stolid decoys give no response, they repel rather than encourage,
but the whistling continues, and with murmured notes of interrogation
the deluded birds wheel over them and, if permitted, will alight before
discovering the deception.

206. LESSER YELLOW-LEGS. Totanus flavipes (*Gmelin*). [255.]
(Pl. XIV.) *Ads. in summer.*—Upperparts generally brownish gray, head and
neck streaked with black and white; back, scapulars, and wing-coverts with
sometimes black centers, spotted or tipped with whitish or brownish gray;
upper tail-coverts white, more or less barred with black, tail varying from
white to brownish gray, with numerous black or blackish cross-bars; breast
heavily spotted or streaked and sides barred with black; belly white, legs
yellow. *Ads. and Juv. in winter.*—Similar, but upperparts brownish gray,
the sides of the feathers with whitish spots; tail-bars grayish; breast lightly
streaked with ashy. L., 10·75; W., 6·40; Tar., 2·05; B., 1·40.

Remarks.— This bird closely resembles the Greater Yellow-legs in color,
but may always be distinguished by its smaller size.

Range.—Breeds from Kotzebue Sound and the upper Yukon Valley,
Alaska, n. Que. (Ungava) to n. B. C. and s. Man. Formerly reported to
breed casually s. to Ills., Ind., and N. Y. Winters in Argentina, Chile, and
Patagonia, and casually in Mex., La., Fla., and the Bahamas. Migrates
mainly e. of the Rocky Mts. but occurs in the Pribilof Isls., Calif., L. Calif.,
Bermuda, and Greenland; rare in spring on the Atlantic Coast; accidental
in Great Britain.

Washington, rather common T. V., Mch. 12–May 22; July 17–Nov. 1.
Long Island, T. V., rare in spring, common in fall, (Apr. 3) Apr. 23–June 1;
(June 17) June 24–Oct. 18 (Oct. 28). Bronx region, uncommon spring, com-
mon fall T. V., Apr. 22–June 7; June 27; Oct. 22. Boston, T. V., rare spring,
common fall, May; July–Sept. N. Ohio, common T. V., Apr. 20–May 15;
Sept. 1–Oct. 30. Glen Ellyn, quite regular T. V., Apr. 15–May 19; July 6–
Oct. 17. SE. Minn., common T. V., Apr. 7–June 1; July 15–Oct. 25.

Eggs, 3–4, buffy (variable as to shade), distinctly (sometimes broadly)
spotted or blotched with dark madder- or vandyke-brown and purplish
gray, 1·69 × 1·15 (Ridgway). *Date*, Ft. Anderson, Mack., June 5.

Comparing the Lesser with the Greater Yellow-legs, William Brewster writes (Bent, Bull. 142):
"The Summer Yellow-legs seems an exact counterpart of the Winter in respect to general appearance and behavior. It has the same firm, measured step when walking about in quest of food; the same perfection of form and outlines, and grace of position, when standing erect and watchful; the same habit of tilting its body and alternately lengthening and shortening its neck with a bobbing motion, when suspicious of danger and about to take wing. Its flight, also, is essentially similar to that of its big cousin, but somewhat slower and more buoyant, and hence not so suggestive of momentum as that of the larger, heavier-bodied bird."

1923. STREET, J. F., Auk, 577–583, illus. (nesting).

207. The ICELAND REDSHANK, *Totanus totanus robustus* Schiöler, an Old-World species, is casual in Greenland.

208. AMERICAN KNOT. CALIDRIS CANUTUS RUFUS (*Wilson*). [234.] (See Figs. 40*b*, 41*b*, Pl. XIV.) *Ads. in summer.*—Upperparts barred and streaked with black and white and rufous; tail ashy gray, narrowly margined with whitish; underparts dull rufous; lower belly white or whitish, sides sometimes with black bars. (See *The Auk*, 1893, p. 25.) *Ads. and Juv. in winter.*—Upperparts plain brownish gray; upper tail-coverts barred with black and white, tail brownish gray; breast and sides barred with black, belly white. *Juv.*—Upperparts pale brownish gray; head streaked with blackish; back, wing-coverts, and scapulars with distinct black and white borders; upper tail-coverts barred with blackish; tail ashy gray, narrowly margined with white; underparts white; breast finely streaked or spotted with blackish; flanks barred or streaked with blackish. L., 10·50; W., 6·75; Tar., 1·20; B., 1·30.
Range.—Breeds from n. Ellesmere Isl. e. to n. Greenland and w. possibly to Pt. Barrow, Alaska, where it has been found in summer; migrates along both coasts of N. A. Winters in S. A. s. to Patagonia and rarely on the coasts of S. C. and Fla., occasionally n. to N. E.; small numbers have been found throughout the summer on the coasts from Va. to Fla. [A closely allied race occurs in Europe and may breed in e. Greenland.]
Washington, casual T. V., May 26–June 3. Long Island, T. V., tolerably common in spring, uncommon in fall, (Apr. 29) May 15–June 10 (June 27); (July 6) July 15–Nov. 30 (Dec. 21). Bronx region, uncommon T. V., May 10–May 30; July 23–Sept. 27. Boston, fairly common T. V., May–June; July–Oct. N. Ohio, not common T. V. SE. Minn., rare T. V., Aug. 17–Sept. 7.
Eggs, ground-color olive-gray to olive-buff, heavily and somewhat evenly marked with dots and small blotches, chiefly of cinnamon-brown, its shades and tints, larger and more numerous at the larger end, 1·70 × 1·20. (Ekblaw, Museum Ridge, Greenland, June 30 "long incubated.") A breeding-place of thirty pairs was discovered in northeast Greenland by the Danish expedition of 1906–8. (See *Geog. Journ.*, XXXV, p. 541 and *Ibis*, 1910, p. 766.)

Knots feed along the beaches on the small crustaceans and mollusca brought in by the waves, and they also frequent muddy places where, like the true Snipe, they probe the ground for food. They decoy with ease, 'bunching' so closely as they wheel into the stools that the entire flock is sometimes killed by a single discharge. Mr. George H. Mackay, in one of his careful and detailed studies of our shore-birds, describes their notes as a soft *wah-quoit* and a little *honk*. The first is particularly noticeable when flocks are coming to the decoys (see *The Auk*, 1893, pp. 25–35).

209. PURPLE SANDPIPER. ARQUATELLA MARITIMA (*Brünnich*). [235.] (Pl. XIV.) *Ads. in summer.*—Upperparts black, margined with ochraceous-buff and cream-buff; wings fuscous-gray, greater coverts margined with white and some secondaries entirely white; upper tail-coverts *fuscous*, outer tail-feathers ashy gray, inner ones fuscous; throat and breast brownish gray, streaked with black; belly white, sides and under tail-coverts streaked with brownish gray. *Ads. and Juv. in winter.*—Head, neck, breast, and sides ashy, the two latter margined with white; back fuscous, margined with ashy; wings fuscous, the coverts, secondaries, and tertials distinctly bordered with white; upper tail-coverts and middle tail-feathers black or fuscous, outer tail-feathers ashy; belly and linings of the wings white. L., 9·00; W., 5·00; Tar., 9·00; B., 1·40.

Remarks.—The brownish gray or ashy breast of this species is a good distinguishing character.

Range.—Summers and probably breeds from Melville Isl., n. Ellesmere Isl., and n. Greenland s. to s. Baffin Isl. and s, Greenland; also in Spitzbergen, Franz Josef Land, Novaya Zemlya, Norway, Russia, Siberia, Iceland, and the Faroe Isls. Winters from s. Greenland to N. Y. (L. I.), and casually to s. N. J., and in the Old World to the Mediterranean. Casual in migration to the Great Lakes, Mo., Ga., Fla., and Bermuda.

Long Island, rare or local W. V., (July 28) Oct. 31–Mch. 25 (May 4). Bronx region, one record, Feb. 14. Boston, not uncommon W. V., Oct.–May.

Eggs, 3–4, olive-clay-color or brownish ashy, heavily marked with rufous-brown, 1·45 × 1·08. *Date*, Greenland Coast, May 16–June 30 (Bent).

The names 'Winter Snipe' and 'Rock Snipe' express both the season of occurrence and haunts of this species on our coast. Wave-washed, seaweed-grown rocks are its chosen feeding-places. "When about to take wing a flock of Purple Sandpipers is rather noisy, keeping up a swallow-like chatter" (J. T. Nichols).

210. PECTORAL SANDPIPER. PISOBIA MELANOTA (*Vieillot*). [239.] (Pl. XIV.) *Ads. in summer.*—Upperparts black, the feathers all heavily bordered with pale ochraceous-buff; rump and upper tail-coverts *black*, lightly tipped with ochraceous-buff; middle tail-feathers longest, pointed and margined with buffy; outer tail-feathers brownish gray, narrowly margined with white; throat white, neck and breast heavily streaked with black and buffy; rest of underparts white. *Ads. and Juv. in winter.*—Similar, but ochraceous-buff of upperparts replaced by rufous, and breast heavily washed with buffy. L. 9·00; W., 5·40; Tar., 1·10; B., 1·15.

Remarks.—This bird somewhat resembles both *P. fuscicollis* and *P. bairdi*, but it differs from them in its larger size, black instead of white or fuscous upper tail-coverts, and longer, more pointed middle tail-feathers.

Range.—Breeds on the Arctic Coast from n. Alaska to mouth of Yukon and ne. Mack., and in ne. Siberia. Winters in S. A. from Peru to cent. Patagonia; rare migrant on Pacific Coast, common in fall migration in Miss. Valley and on the Atlantic Coast, rare in spring. Casual or accidental in Hawaii, in Japan, Aleutian Isls., Greenland, and England.

Washington, common T. V., Mch. 26–June 11; Aug. 10–Nov. 1. Long Island, tolerably common T. V., Mch. 22–June 2; July 6–Nov. 10. Bronx region, fairly common T. V., May 2–May 26; July 14–Nov. 13. Boston, T. V., rare in spring, not uncommon in fall, May; July–Oct. N. Ohio, common T. V., Apr. 1–May 5. Glen Ellyn, common T. V., Mch. 31–May 20; July 29–Sept. 30. SE. Minn., common T. V., Apr. 14–May 27; July 18–Nov. 5.

Eggs, 4, drab, sometimes with a greenish tinge, blotched with clear umber-brown markings, more numerous at the larger end, 1·50 × 1·09 (Murdock). *Date*, Pt. Barrow, Alaska, June 18.

The names 'Grass Snipe' and 'Krieker' describe with equal truth and conciseness the haunts and notes of this Snipe. It frequents wet, grassy meadows rather than beaches, and, although it flies in flocks, the birds scatter while feeding and take wing one or more at a time. They thus remind one of Wilson's Snipe. Their note is a squeaky, grating whistle. They will respond to an imitation of it, but do not decoy so readily as the larger bay birds. Dr. E. W. Nelson writes that during the breeding season the male inflates its breast and throat until they are double their normal size, and utters a deep, hollow, resonant note. (Rep. on Nat. Hist. Coll. made in Alaska, p. 108.)

211. WHITE-RUMPED SANDPIPER. Pisobia fuscicollis (*Vieillot*).

[240.] *Ads. in summer.*—Upperparts black, edged with rufous; rump grayish fuscous, margined with ashy; longer upper tail-coverts *white*, with sometimes brownish gray markings; central tail-feathers fuscous, outer ones brownish gray, upper throat white; neck, breast, and *sides* distinctly streaked and spotted with black and more or less washed with ochraceous-buff. *Ads. and Juv. in winter.*—"Upperparts plain brownish gray, with indistinct, narrow mesial streaks of dusky; otherwise as in summer, but streaks on chest, etc., less distinct" (Ridgway). *Juv.*—Similar to summer examples, but the feathers of the upperparts with *rounded* whitish or ochraceous-buff *tips;* breast less distinctly streaked. L., 7·50; W., 4·90; Tar., ·90; B., ·95.

Remarks.—The white upper tail-coverts distinguish this species.

Range.—Breeds along the Arctic Coast from n. Alaska e.; occurs in summer e. to Greenland. Winters from Paraguay to s. Patagonia and the Falkland Isls.; in migration most abundant in the Miss. Valley, less so on the Atlantic Coast. Casual in Bermuda, the Azores, Great Britain, the W. I., Cent. A., and Franz Josef Land.

Washington, T. V., May, June; Sept., Oct. Long Island, tolerably common T. V., May 11–June 10 (June 20); (July 4) July 20–Nov. 13. Bronx region, uncommon T. V., May 5–June 5; July 9–Oct. 19. Boston, T. V., rare spring, not uncommon fall, May–June; July–Nov. N. Ohio, casual T. V. SE. Minn., rare T. V., May 16–30; no fall records.

Eggs, 3–4, light olive, or olive brownish, spotted (usually rather finely) with deep brown and dull, purplish gray, 1·37 × ·94 (Ridgway). *Date*, Herschel Isls., June 10 (Thayer Coll.).

"They frequent the sandy beach as well as the marshy shores upon the coast, but inland seem to prefer the edges of pools of water upon the uplands. They move in small flocks, are very social, often associating with other waders, are not as a rule shy or timid, and, when startled, usually fly but a short distance, drop back, and run about in an unconcerned and heedless manner, picking up the minute forms of life that usually abound in such places, occasionally uttering a rather sharp, piping *weet, weet*. Their flight is swift and well sustained" (Goss).

212. BAIRD'S SANDPIPER. Pisobia bairdi (*Coues*). [241.] *Ads. in summer.*—Upperparts fuscous; feathers of crown and nape margined laterally with pale buffy; back and scapulars tipped with pale buffy or brownish gray; middle upper tail-coverts *fuscous*, sometimes tipped with buffy; central tail-feathers fuscous, margined with whitish, outer ones pale brownish gray;

throat white; breast washed with buffy and *lightly* spotted or streaked with fuscous; *sides* and belly white. *Juv.*—Similar, but the back, scapulars, and wing-coverts with *rounded white* tips. (In the winter these tips are more or less worn off.) L., 7·40; W., 4·90; Tar., ·90; B., ·85.

Remarks.—This bird most closely resembles *P. fuscicollis*. In any plumage it may be known from that species by the fuscous instead of white middle upper tail-coverts. In summer it differs also in the absence of rufous above, the less heavily spotted throat, and the white instead of spotted sides. In winter the chief distinguishing marks of the two species, aside from the differently colored upper tail-coverts, are the buffy breast and generally paler, scaled upperparts of *bairdi*.

Range.—Breeds along the Arctic Coast from nw. Alaska to Baffin Isl. and probably Greenland. Winters in Chile, Argentina, and Patagonia; occurs regularly in migration from the Rocky Mts. to the Miss. River, and in Cent. A. and n. S. A., and irregularly in autumn on the Pacific Coast from Alaska to L. Calif. and on the Atlantic Coast from N. S. to w. Fla. Casual in summer in Guerrero, Mex.; accidental in England.

Washington, casual, two records, Sept. Long Island, rare T. V., May 2–30; Aug. 14–Oct. 31. Bronx region, probably rare T. V., May 26–30; Aug. 11–Sept. 17. Boston, rare T. V., Aug.–Sept. N. Ohio, not common T. V. SE. Minn., T. V., Aug. 11–Sept. 19; no spring specimens.

Eggs, 3–4, light, creamy buff, sometimes tinged with rusty, thickly speckled and spotted with deep reddish brown or chestnut, 1·30 × ·93 (Ridgway). *Date*, Pt. Barrow, Alaska, June 20.

"In habits they are similar to the White-rumped (which they so closely resemble), but are more inclined to wander from the water's edge. I have flushed the birds on high prairie lands, at least a mile from the water" (Goss).

"The *kreep* call they utter in flight is sufficiently unlike that of any other wader of similar size and general coloring to be of service when the birds are seen on the wing" (Brewster).

1917. Dixon, J., Condor, 77–84, illus. (home-life).—1923. Griscom, L., Auk, 529 (identification in life).

213. LEAST SANDPIPER. Pisobia minutilla (*Vieillot*). [242.] (Pl. XIV.) *Ads. in summer.*—Upperparts black or fuscous, edged and tipped with buffy or rufous; rump and middle upper tail-coverts plain black or fuscous; central tail-feathers black or fuscous, outer ones ashy gray; upper throat white; neck and breast white or buffy, streaked with fuscous; belly and sides white. *Juv.*—Similar, but feathers of the back with *rounded* rufous or buffy tips; breast not distinctly streaked. *Ads. and Juv. in winter.*—Upperparts brownish gray, sometimes with more or less black in the centers of the feathers; breast white or ashy, not distinctly streaked. L., 6·00; W., 3·50; Tar., ·70; B., ·75.

Remarks.—This is the smallest of our Sandpipers, and can be confused only with *Ereunetes pusillus*, from which, however, it may always be distinguished by the absence of webs between the bases of the toes, and by its yellowish instead of black or blackish tarsi.

FIG. 82. Least Sandpiper. (Natural size.)

Range.—Breeds from nw. Alaska, s. to N. F. and Sable Isl. Winters from s. Calif., Tex., and N. C. to Brazil, and the Galapagos, Bermuda, and cent. Patagonia; in migration occurs through-

out the U. S. and w. to ne. Siberia, N. to Greenland.   Accidental in
Europe.
  Washington, uncommon T. V., Apr. 19–June 14; July 17–Nov. 22.   Long
Island, abundant T. V., Apr. 20–June 12; June 19–Oct. 25.   Bronx region,
common T. V., Apr. 27–June 16; July 4–Nov. 3.   Boston, abundant T. V.,
May; July–Sept.   N. Ohio, common T. V., May 5–20; Sept. 1–30.   Glen
Ellyn, tolerably common T. V., May 4–15; July 29–Sept. 5.   SE. Minn.,
common T. V , Apr. 22–May 31; July 20–Sept. 19.
  Eggs, 3–4, pale, grayish buffy, varying to pale brownish, thickly spotted,
speckled, or sprinkled with deep chestnut and dull, purplish gray, 1·15 ×
·83 (Ridgway).   *Date*, Magdalen Isls., June 3–30 (Bent).

  This, the smallest of our Sandpipers, is frequently associated with
its larger cousin, the Semipalmated Sandpiper, on the shores and
beaches, but it also visits the grassy meadows, and for this reason is
known by baymen as the 'Meadow Oxeye.'
  1912. MOORE, R. T., Auk, 210–223 (nesting).

  214. CURLEW SANDPIPER.   EROLIA TESTACEA *(Pallas)*.   [244.]   Bill
slightly decurved.   *Ads. in summer.*—Below reddish brown, above rusty and
black.   *Juv.*—Above brownish gray, margined with whitish, back blacker;
below white.   *Ads. and Juv. in winter.*—Above plain brownish gray; below
white. L., 8·00; W., 5·00; B., 1·50; T., 1·10.
  Range.—Breeds in the Yenisei delta and on the Taimyr Peninsula,
Siberia.   Winters in Africa, India, Malay Archipelago, and Australia, casually
to Madagascar and N. Z.; in migration occurs from Great Britain to China
and the Philippines.   Occasional in N. A.: Alaska (Pt. Barrow), Ont., N. S.,
Me., Mass., N. Y., and N. J. and accidental in the W. I. (Grenada and Car-
iacou) and in Patagonia.
  Long Island, casual T. V., May 24–June 9; Sept. 3–Oct. 11.   Boston,
A. V.

  215. The DUNLIN, *Pelidna alpina alpina* Linnæus is the Old-World
representative of our Red-backed Sandpiper, from which it differs only in
being less brightly colored and somewhat smaller.   L., about 7·40; W.,
4·12–4·50; Tar., ·78–·90; B., 1·05–1·25.   It is of casual occurrence in eastern
North America.

  215a. RED-BACKED SANDPIPER.   PELIDNA   ALPINA   SAKHALINA
(Vieillot).   [243a.]   (Pl. XIV.)   *Ads. in summer.*—Upperparts broadly margined with rufous, centers of the feathers black, wings brownish gray; breast
whitish, lightly streaked with blackish; middle of the belly with a *large
black patch*, lower belly white.   *Juv.*— Upperparts blackish, the feathers with
rounded tips of rufous or buffy; breast washed with buffy and indistinctly
streaked with blackish; belly spotted with black.   *Ads. and Juv. in winter.*—
Upperparts brownish gray; middle upper tail-coverts fuscous; wing-coverts
brownish gray margined with buffy; throat white; breast ashy, indistinctly
streaked; belly white, the sides sometimes spotted with black.   L., 8·00;
W., 4·75; Tar., 1·00; B., 1·50.
  Remarks.—There is, of course, every degree of intergradation between
summer and winter plumage, but the species may always be known by its
slightly curved bill.
  Range.—Breeds on the n. coast of Siberia w. to mouth of the Yenisei,
and the mouth of the Yukon, to Boothia and Melville peninsulas, and n. Que.
(Ungava).   Winters on the Pacific Coast from s. B. C. to s. L. Calif. and
from N. J. (rarely Mass.) s. on the Atlantic and Gulf coasts to Fla., La.,
and s. Tex., and in Asia from China and Japan to the Malay Archipelago.
  Washington, rare T. V., Apr.; May; Sept.–Nov.   Long Island, tolerably
common T. V., Apr. 1–June 20, (Aug. 1) Aug. 31–Dec. 8 (Dec. 25).   Bronx

region, uncommon T. V., May 12–May 30; Sept. 20–Nov. 3. Boston, T. V., rare spring, fairly common fall, May; Sept.–Nov. N. Ohio, not common T. V. SE. Minn., T. V., May 18–June 4; Aug. 8–?.

Eggs, 3–4, varying from pale, bluish white to ochraceous-buff, heavily marked with chocolate, chiefly at the larger end, 1·43 × 1·01. *Date*, Pt. Barrow, Alaska, June 21.

Generally speaking, this is a shore- or beach-bird, though it also visits grassy marshes. It flies and feeds in flocks, and is an unsuspicious, rather stupid little Snipe, less active than most members of this family. The gray-plumaged fall birds are known as 'Leadbacks,' while in the spring they go by the names 'Blackbreast' or 'Redback.'

The "flushing note of a single bird is a fine *chit-l-it*. Its flight-note is an emphatic near-whistled *chu* or *chru* resembling some of the calls of the Pectoral and Semipalmated Sandpipers, but quite diagnostic when one is sufficiently familiar with it" (J. T. Nichols).

216. EASTERN DOWITCHER. LIMNODROMUS GRISEUS GRISEUS (*Gmelin*). [231.] (Figs. 40c, 41a.) *Ads. in summer.*—Upperparts, tertials, and wing-coverts black, the feathers edged or barred with ochraceous-buff or rufous; rump, upper tail-coverts, and tail barred with black and more or less ochraceous-buff; primaries fuscous; underparts dull, pale rufous, whitish on belly, more or less spotted and barred with black. *Ads. and Juv. in winter.*—Upperparts brownish gray; rump and tail barred with black and white; throat and breast washed with ashy, belly white, sides and under tail-coverts barred with black. *Juv.*—Upperparts black, the feathers edged with rufous; rump and tail barred with black and white, and sometimes washed with rufous; secondaries widely edged with white; underparts more or less washed with ochraceous-buff and obscurely spotted with blackish. L., 10·50; W., 5·75; Tar., 1·30; B., 2·05–2·50.

Remarks.—The barred tail and tail-coverts, with the peculiar flattened, pitted tip of the bill, are characteristic of this species.

Range.—Breeds from cent. Alberta (probably) to the w. side of Hudson Bay and n. Winters from Fla. (casually N. C.) to cent. Brazil and Peru; in migration regularly on the Atlantic Coast and less frequently in the interior and on the Pacific. Accidental in Greenland, Alaska, Prince Edward Isl., N. S., Idaho, Bermuda, the British Isles, and France.

Washington, casual, one specimen, Sept. Long Island, tolerably common T. V., Apr. 19–June 19; June 27–Oct. 1. Bronx region, fairly common T. V., chiefly fall, May 11–June 3; July 2–Sept. 30. Boston, common T. V., May; July–Sept. N. Ohio, not common T. V.

Eggs, 4, light buffy olive, distinctly spotted and speckled, especially about the larger end, with deep brown, 1·65 × 1·13 (Ridgway). Alberta, June 16 (Bent).

The Dowitchers are among our best-known bay-birds. They migrate in compact flocks which are easily attracted to decoys by an imitation of their call. Mud-flats and bars exposed by the falling tide are their chosen feeding-grounds. On the Gulf Coast of Florida I have seen several hundred gathered in such close rank that they entirely concealed the sandbar on which they were resting.

"The flight-note of the Dowitcher resembles that of the Lesser Yellow-legs but is recognizably different, less loud and more hurried, suggesting the bird's name" (J. T. Nichols).

216a. LONG-BILLED DOWITCHER. LIMNODROMUS GRISEUS SCOLO-PACEUS (*Say*). [232.] *Ads. in summer.*—Similar to the preceding, but averaging larger; the bill especially is longer, the underparts are more uniformly rufous, and the sides are more heavily barred with black. *Ads. in winter and Juv.*—To be distinguished from the corresponding stages of *griseus* only by their larger size. W., 6·00; Tar., 1·50; B., 2·10–2·90.

Range.—Breeds from Pt. Barrow to mouth of the Yukon, e. to nw. Mack. Winters from La., Fla., s. Calif., Cuba, Jamaica, and Mex. s. to Panama and Ecuador; in migration on the Pacific Coast and w. Miss. Valley. Casual on the Atlantic Coast from Sable Isl. s., and on the n. coast of e. Siberia, s. to Japan.

Washington, casual, seven shot in Apr. Long Island, rare T. V., Mch. 20; July 16–Nov. 2 (Nov. 30). Boston, T. V., fall. SE. Minn., uncommon T. V., May 14–24; July 7–Nov. 9.

Eggs, 4, not distinguishable from those of the preceding species. *Date*, St. Michael's, Alaska, May 23.

This bird resembles the preceding species in habits, but the baymen who 'gun' for Snipe say they can recognize it by its somewhat different notes. Like the Woodcock, Wilson's Snipe, and its near ally, *L. g. griseus*, the male utters a flight-song in the nesting season. It is well described by Dr. E. W. Nelson in his Report on Collections made in Alaska, p. 101.

217. STILT SANDPIPER. MICROPALAMA HIMANTOPUS (*Bonaparte*). [233.] (Pl. XIV.) *Ads. in summer.*—Upperparts black, bordered with grayish and buffy; ear-coverts and an indistinct line around back of head *rufous;* secondaries grayish, edged with white; primaries fuscous; rump ashy; upper tail-coverts barred with black and white; outer tail-feathers with broken dusky bars, inner ones with central streaks or margins of brownish gray or white; underparts white, heavily barred with fuscous. *Ads. and Juv. in winter.* —Upperparts brownish gray; upper tail-coverts *white;* tail white, margined with brownish gray; underparts white; throat, neck and sides indistinctly streaked or washed with grayish. *Juv.*—Similar, but upperparts blackish, margined with ochraceous-buff. L., 8·25; W., 5·00; Tar., 1·60; B., 1·55.

Remarks.—The distinguishing characters of this species are the flattened, pitted tip of the bill, in connection with the very long tarsi.

Range.—Breeds from near the mouth of the Mack. to Coronation Gulf and probably to Melville Peninsula. Winters in S. A. s. to Uruguay and Chile; casual in winter in s. Tex. and Mex.; in migration occurs in interior Canada, the w. Miss. Valley, the W. I., and Cent. A.; less common and irregular on the Atlantic Coast and the coast of B. C. Casual in N. F., N. B., N. S., and Bermuda.

Washington, casual, several records, June; Sept.; Oct. Long Island, T. V., in varying numbers, rare in spring, May 18; July 10–Oct. 19. Bronx region, irregular and uncommon fall T. V., July 14–Oct. 5. Boston, rare T. V., fall. N. Ohio, not common T. V. SE. Minn., uncommon T. V., Aug. 19–Sept. 17; no spring records.

Eggs, 3–4, pale grayish buff, or grayish buffy white, boldly spotted with rich vandyke-brown and purplish gray, 1·42 × 1·00 (Ridgway). *Date*, Anderson River, Mack., June 23.

"On the wing the Stilt Sandpiper resembles the Lesser Yellow-legs closely. . . . The somewhat shorter legs do not project so far beyond the tail, but the proportionately larger bill (with slight apparent drop at its tip) is the Stilt Sandpiper's best field-mark. . . . The color of its legs, dull olive-green, is usually diagnostic.

"The common flight-note of the Stilt Sandpiper is very like the single whistled *whu* of the Lesser Yellow-legs but recognizably lower pitched and hoarser. . ." (J. T. Nichols).

218. SEMIPALMATED SANDPIPER. EREUNETES PUSILLUS (*Linnæus*). [246.] (Fig. 40e, Pl. XIV.) *Ads. in summer.*—Upperparts black or fuscous, margined with brownish gray and a *small* amount of rufous; rump grayish brown; upper tail-coverts blackish; tail-feathers brownish gray, central ones darkest; breast streaked or spotted with blackish. *Juv.*—Similar, but upperparts and wing-coverts blackish, with rounded rufous or buffy tips to the feathers; breast unstreaked, tinted with buffy. *Ads. and Juv. in winter.*—Upperparts brownish gray, with darker shaft streaks; upper tail-coverts darker; underparts white, sometimes with faint streaks on the breast. L., 6·30; W., 3·75; Tar., ·75; B., ·65–·80.

Remarks.—The small size of this and the next species prevents their being confused with any other except *Pisobia minutilla*, from which they may always be known by their partially webbed toes and blackish tarsi.

Range.—Breeds from ne. Siberia and the Arctic Coast of N. A. s. to mouth of Yukon and e. to n. Lab.; winters from S. C. and the Gulf of Mex. through W. I. and Cent. A. to Patagonia; migrates mainly e. of the Rocky Mts.; occurs in migration in B. C. Casual in Pribilof Isls.; accidental in the British Isles.

Washington, uncommon T. V., May, June; July 27–Oct. 28. Long Island, abundant T. V., Apr. 26–June 27; July 4–Nov. 20 (Dec. 7), casual from late June to early July. Bronx region, abundant T. V., May 2–June 20; July 8–Oct. 22 (Nov. 2). Boston, very abundant T. V., May–June; July–Oct. N. Ohio, common T. V., May 5–May 25; Sept. 1–25. Glen Ellyn, T. V., May 31; Aug.–Sept. 13. SE. Minn., common T. V., May 14–June 19; July 6–Sept. 15.

Eggs, 3–4, pale, dull grayish buff, sprinkled, speckled, or spotted with dark brown and purplish gray, 1·21 × ·85 (Ridgway). *Date*, Lab., June 12.

The thought of these little Sandpipers always creates a mental picture of a long stretch of dazzling beach with its ever-changing surf-line. I hear the oft-repeated booming of the rolling, tumbling breakers, and in the distance see a group of tiny forms hurrying to and fro over the sand smoothed by the frothy waves. With what nimble gracefulness they follow the receding waves, searching for treasures cast up by the sea! What contentment and good-fellowship are expressed by their cheery, conversational twitterings! Up and down the beach they run, now advancing, now retreating, sometimes, in their eagerness, venturing too far, when the waters threaten to engulf them, and in momentary confusion they take wing and hover back to a place of safety. Suddenly, as though at a signal, they are off; a compact flock moving as one bird, twisting and turning to right and left, now gleaming white as the sun strikes their snowy bodies, now dark again like a wisp of sunless cloud flying before the wind.

219. WESTERN SANDPIPER. EREUNETES MAURI *Cabanis.* [247.] (Pl. XIV.) This bird closely resembles the preceding, from which, in summer plumage, it differs in having the upperparts *conspicuously* margined with rufous and the breast more heavily streaked. In fall and winter plumage the differences in coloration are not so apparent, but the birds are to be distinguished at any season by the size of the bill, which in the western species is always longer. W., 3·80; Tar., ·80; B., ·85–1·20.

Range.—Breeds along the Alaska coast from the Yukon delta to Pt. Barrow. Winters from N. C. and Wash. to Venezuela and Peru; in migration occurs mainly w. of the Rocky Mts., less commonly in the interior and on the Atlantic Coast as far n. as N. H. and in the W. I.

Washington, rare T. V., Aug.–Sept. Long Island, irregular T. V., sometimes common, May 12–June 2; July 4–Oct. 12. Bronx region, rare T. V., May 26; July 10, and Sept. 25. Boston, rare T. V., July–Sept. N. Ohio, casual T. V.

Eggs, 3–4, deep cinnamon buffy, sprinkled, speckled, or thickly spotted with bright rusty brown or chestnut, the general aspect decidedly rusty, 1·24 × ·87 (Ridgway). *Date*, St. Michael, Alaska, May 28.

This western representative of the preceding species is found on our coasts associated with its eastern relative. According to Wayne ('Birds of South Carolina') this is the most abundant winter wader on the South Carolina coast.

220. BUFF-BREASTED SANDPIPER. TRYNGITES SUBRUFICOLLIS (*Vieillot*). [262.] *Ads.*—Upperparts greenish black *widely* margined with pale grayish brown; primaries fuscous, inner half of their inner webs *speckled with black;* longer under wing-coverts conspicuously marked and tipped with black, then white; central tail-feathers fuscous, outer ones becoming buffy, irregularly marked and tipped with black and buffy; underparts pale ochraceous-buff, tipped with whitish, and with generally concealed black markings. *Juv.*—Similar, but back fuscous narrowly margined or ringed with whitish. L., 8·50; W., 5·25; B., ·80.

Remarks.—In any plumage this bird may be known by the peculiar *speckling* on the inner webs of *all* the primaries, and also the markings of the under wing-coverts.

Range.—Breeds along the Arctic Coast from n. Alaska to n. Mack. Winters in Argentina and Uruguay; most abundant in migration in the Miss. Valley; occasional on the Atlantic Coast in fall. Casual on the Pacific Coast n. to St. Michael, Alaska, and to ne. Siberia; casual or accidental in Bermuda, the W. I., w. Europe, and Japan.

Long Island, rare T. V., Aug. 22–Oct. 11. SE. Minn., very rare T. V., no record since 1892.

Eggs, 3–4, buffy grayish white, varying to pale olive-buff, boldly spotted longitudinally (and somewhat spirally) with dark vandyke- or madder-brown and purplish gray, 1·53 × 1·04 (Ridgway). *Date*, Pt. Barrow, Alaska, June 20.

This is a rare species on the Atlantic Coast. Dr. Hatch writes of it as observed by him in Minnesota: "They are an extremely active species when on the wing, and essentially ploverine in all respects, seeking sandy, barren prairies, where they live upon grasshoppers, crickets, and insects generally, and ants and their eggs specially. I have found them repasting upon minute mollusks on the sandy shores of small and shallow ponds, where they were apparently little more suspicious than the Solitary Sandpipers are notably. The flight is in rather compact form, dipping and rising alternately, and with a disposition to return again to the neighborhood of their former feeding-places."

221. MARBLED GODWIT. LIMOSA FEDOA (*Linnæus*). [249.] *Ads. in summer.*—Bill decurved; upperparts black, the head and neck streaked with buffy, back barred or the feathers spotted on the sides and sometimes tipped with buffy or ochraceous-buff; inner web of outer primaries and both webs of inner ones *ochraceous-buff* or pale buffy, speckled with black; tail ochraceous-buff barred with black; throat white, rest of underparts pale buffy, spotted or barred with black; bill curved slightly upward, yellowish at the base, black at the end. *Juv.*—Similar, but underparts with few or no bars except on flanks and under tail-coverts. L., 18·00; W., 8·75; Tar., 2·75; B., 4·00.

Range.—Breeds from s. Alberta and s. Man. s. to S. Dak. (formerly to Utah, Nebr., Ia., and Wisc.). Winters from cent. Calif., La., Fla., and Ga. s. to Ecuador and Peru (rarely Argentina); in migration occurs on the Pacific Coast n. to B. C. and formerly (but now very rare) on the Atlantic Coast s. to the Lesser Antilles. Casual in s. Ont., s. Que., Miss. Valley, and N. S.; accidental in Alaska.

Long Island, rare T. V., May, July 20–Sept. 15. Boston, A. V. SE. Minn., rare T. V., May 12–24; Aug. 20.

Eggs, 3–4, clay-color or brownish ashy, blotched, spotted, and scrawled with grayish brown, 2·15 × 1·60. *Date*, Minor Co., S. Dak., May 16.

This is a common bird about the sloughs of Alberta prairies where its loud, frequently uttered double-noted call makes it conspicuous. It is rare on the Atlantic Coast, and in the West is decreasing before the plow.

1907. BENT, A. C., Auk, 160–167 (nesting).

222. The BAR-TAILED GODWIT, *Limosa lapponica lapponica* (Linnæus), of Europe has been recorded from Cape Cod, Mass. (Sept. 16, 1907.)

223. HUDSONIAN GODWIT. LIMOSA HÆMASTICA *(Linnæus)*. [251.] *Ad. ♂ in summer.*—Bill slightly decurved; a broad white band across the middle of the upper tail-coverts; tail black, broadly white at the base and narrowly at the tip; upperparts black, the feathers with lateral ochraceous marks and narrow whitish tips; underparts rufous, narrowly barred with black and tipped with white. *Ad. ♀ in summer.*—Resembles the male but much less rufous below, the white markings wider. *Juv. and Ads. in winter.*—Upperparts largely brownish gray, throat and belly whitish, breast grayish. L., 15·00; W., 8·2; Tar., 2·2; B., 3·2.

Range.—Breeds on the lower Anderson River, e. to Hudson Bay, w. to Pt. Clarence, Alaska. Winters in Chile, Argentina, Patagonia, and the Falkland Isls.; in migration occurs principally e. of the Great Plains, more commonly on the Atlantic Coast in autumn and in the Miss. Valley in spring. Casual in Bermuda.

Long Island, rare T. V., May 23, Aug. 8–Oct. 16. Boston, rare T. V., in fall, July–Nov. SE. Minn., rare T. V., May 21.

Eggs, 3–4, deep olive, hair-brown or broccoli-brown (sometimes paler), usually more or less spotted with darker brown, but sometimes nearly uniform, 2·20 × 1·42 (Ridgway). *Date*, Ft. Anderson, Mack., June 9.

This species is now one of our rarest shore-birds.

224. The BLACK-TAILED GODWIT, *Limosa limosa limosa* (Linnæus), [252], of Europe and Asia is accidental in Greenland.

[The GREEN-SHANK, *Totanus nebularius* (Gunnerus), [253], is an Old-World species recorded by Audubon, May 28, 1832, from near Cape Sable, Fla., but the record is considered doubtful. It resembles our Greater Yellow-legs, but differs chiefly in having the lower back and rump white.]

225. RUFF; REEVE. PHILOMACHUS PUGNAX *(Linnæus)*. [260.] *Ad. ♂ in summer.*—Very variable; above and below black with purplish reflections; or rusty barred with purplish, etc.; feathers of breast much lengthened to form a shield of rusty, black, or black and white feathers; two variously colored tufts on the hindneck. ♂ *in winter.*—Above grayish brown; below white; throat and breast grayish; end of tail with remains of blackish bars; ruff absent. *Ad.* ♀.—Head, neck and underparts as in winter male; back black margined with grayish brown; inner wing-feathers *barred* with black and grayish brown. L., 12·50; W., 7·00; Tar., 1·70; B., 1·50.

Range.—Breeds from Russia and Siberia to Great Britain (rarely) and from Lapland to Holland, Belgium, n. France, Bavaria, and Hungary. Winters throughout Africa, and in India, Ceylon, Borneo, and Burma. Strays occasionally to the Western Hemisphere, on Bering and Pribilof isls. and in Greenland, Ont., N. S., L. I., Ind., D. C., N. C., Barbados, and n. S. A.

Washington, one record, Sept. 3. Long Island, A. V., 3 records, May, Sept. and Oct.

The twenty-odd records of the occurrence of this European species are about equally divided between spring and fall dates, and fourteen of them are from the Atlantic Coast.

1905. DEANE, R., Auk, 410.—1906. PALMER, T. S., *Ibid.*, 98 (Am. records).

226. SANDERLING. CROCETHIA ALBA (*Pallas*). [248.] (Pl. XIV.) *Ads. in summer.*—Feathers of upperparts with generally black centers, bordered and sometimes barred with pale rufous and tipped with ashy white; wings fuscous, basal half of outer web of inner primaries *white;* wing-coverts grayish fuscous, greater ones, broadly tipped with white; tail brownish gray, narrowly margined with white; throat and upper breast washed with *pale rufous* and spotted with blackish; rest of the underparts *pure* white. *Juv.*—Similar, but upperparts without rufous, glossy black, the feathers sometimes bordered with white, but generally with *two* white spots at their tips separated by the black of the central part of the feather; nape grayish white, lightly streaked with blackish; underparts *pure* white, with occasionally a few spots on the breast. *Ads. and Juv. in winter.*—Upperparts pale brownish gray, wings as in the preceding; underparts *pure* white. L., 8·00; W., 5·00; Tar., 1·00; B., 1·00.

Remarks.—The Sanderling is the only one of our Snipes or Sandpipers having *three* toes, and it may always be known by this character in combination with its transversely scaled tarsi.

Range.—Breeds on the w. Arctic isls. and in Greenland; also in Iceland, Spitzbergen and n. Siberia. Winters from cent. Calif., Tex., Va., and Bermuda to Patagonia. Casually in Mass. and Wash.; also from the Mediterranean, Burma, and Japan to S. Africa and various Pacific isls , including Hawaii; occurs casually all summer on the coast of Fla., etc.

Washington, rare T. V., May; Sept.–Oct. Long Island, common T. V., Apr. 10–June 24 (July 4); July 11–Jan. 7 (Jan. 25). Bronx region, uncommon T. V., Apr. 25–June 4; July 8–Nov. 18. Boston, abundant T. V , May– June; July–Nov. N. Ohio, common T. V., May 1–20; Sept. 1–Oct. 10. SE. Minn., uncommon T. V., May 20–June 14; Sept. 21–Oct. 6.

Eggs, 3–4, light olive-brown, finely spotted or speckled with darker, the markings larger and more blended on the larger end, 1·41 × ·91 (Ridgway). *Date*, Anderson River, Mack., June 27.

This is a true beach-bird, and is usually found on shores washed by the sea. It frequently associates with the Semipalmated Sandpiper, or Oxeye, but its larger size and lighter colors distinguish it from that species.

Its note is described by J. T. Nichols as "a soft *ket, ket, ket,* uttered singly or in a series of somewhat querulous tones."

FAMILY RECURVIROSTRIDÆ. AVOCETS AND STILTS.

The twelve species comprising this family are distributed throughout the warmer parts of the world. They are generally found in flocks, and may be called Wading Snipe. They feed in shallow water, wading to their heels, and, when necessary, swim with ease.

1925. WETMORE, A. (food of). See Phalaropes.

227. AVOCET. RECURVIROSTRA AMERICANA *Gmelin.* [225.] (Fig. 13.) Bill slender, recurved. *Ads. in summer.*—Head and neck cinnamon-rufous, back and tail white, scapulars and primaries black; middle coverts, tips of the greater ones, and part of secondaries white; belly white, bill turned upward. *Ads. in winter and Juv.*—Generally similar, but head and neck white or pearl-gray. L., 16·50; W., 9·00; Tar., 3·75; B., 3·75.

Range.—Breeds from e. Wash., s. Alberta, and s. Man. s. to s. Calif., s. N. Mex., s. Tex., and n. Ia. (formerly Wisc., s. to s. Calif. and s. Tex. to s. Guat.; casual in B. C., s. Mack., Ont. and N. B. to Fla. and the W. I., but rare e. of the Miss. River.

Long Island, A. V., summer (Aug.), formerly casual. Boston, A. V.

Nest, a slight depression in the ground, near water. *Eggs*, 3–4, pale olive or buffy clay-color, thickly spotted with chocolate, 1·95 × 1·35. *Date*, Loveland, Colo., June 3; Utah, Apr. 10–June 15 (Bent).

Avocets are common birds in parts of the interior, but are rare on the Atlantic Coast. They frequent shores and shallow pools, and in searching for shells, crustaceans, etc., their peculiar recurved bill is used in a most interesting manner. Dropping it beneath the surface of the water until its convexity touches the bottom, they move rapidly forward, and with every step swing their bill from side to side, as a mower does his scythe. In this way they secure food which the muddy water would prevent them from seeing. They are very noisy when nesting and with a loud, sharp *plee-eek* charge bravely toward one, swinging aside only when a few feet away.

228. BLACK-NECKED STILT. HIMANTOPUS MEXICANUS (*Müller*). [226.] (Fig. 77.) *Ad. ♂.*—A white spot above and another below eye; front of head, front of neck, lower back, rump, and underparts white; tail grayish; rest of plumage glossy, greenish black. *Ad. ♀.*—Similar, but with back fuscous-brown. *Juv.*—Similar, but whole upperparts margined with rusty. L., 15·00; W., 9·00; Tar., 4·15; B., 2·00.

Range.—Breeds from cent. Ore., n. Utah, s. Colo. and Nebr. to n. L. Calif., s. N. Mex., s. Tex., coast of La., and in Mex., and from cent. Fla. (formerly N. J.) and Bahamas through the W. I. to n. Brazil and Peru. Winters from L. Calif., s. Tex., s. La., and Fla. s. through Cent. A. and the W. I. to n. Brazil, Peru, and the Galapagos. Casual in migration to N. Dak., cent. Ia., Wisc., Mich., Ills. and N. B., and in Bermuda.

Long Island, two records, formerly casual. Boston, A. V.

Nest, near water, a slight depression in the ground lined with grasses. *Eggs*, 3–4, olive or buffy clay-color, thickly spotted with chocolate, 1·70 × 1·25. *Date*, Fla. Keys, Apr. 25; Brownsville, Tex., Apr. 26.

Stilts are fond of wading in shallow ponds in both fresh and salt-marshes, and are graceful and alert in their movements. During the nesting season they become very noisy, and express their solicitude for their eggs or young by the most surprising demonstrations. After nightfall I have heard Stilts utter their sharp *ip-ip-ip* as they darted erratically about over the marshes.

1908. CHAPMAN, F. M., Camps and Cruises, 288 (nesting).

FAMILY PHALAROPODIDÆ. PHALAROPES.

The Phalaropes, or Swimming Snipe, number three species, all distinguished by density and beauty of plumage, and unusual habits. When nesting, one is confined to the interior of North America; the two remaining inhabit the northern parts of both hemispheres. The former, Wilson's Phalarope, has but slightly webbed toes and is found during the winter, both at sea and on land. The two latter, the Northern and the Red Phalaropes, have well-lobed toes and winter at sea, but under stress of weather, or while migrating, they visit land to frequent bays, ponds and tidal pools. Contrary (p. 95) to the usual rule, the female in this family is the larger and more brightly colored—indeed, in the domestic economy of the Phalarope household, the female is male, except in the prime essentials of sex. She does the wooing, takes the lead in selecting the nesting-site, and, although she lays the eggs, the duties of incubation fall upon the male.

1908. CHAPMAN, F. M., Camps and Cruises, 268–271, 321, 322.—1925. WETMORE, A., Food of Phalaropes, Avocets and Stilts, Bull. 1359, U. S. Dept. Agric.

KEY TO THE SPECIES

A. Bill over 1ʻ10 . . . . 230. WILSON'S PHALAROPE.
B. Bill under 1ʻ10.
    a. Bill very slender; wing under 4ʻ75 . . 231. NORTHERN PHALAROPE.
    b. Bill stout; wing over 4ʻ75 . . . . 229. RED PHALAROPE.

229. RED PHALAROPE. PHALAROPUS FULICARIUS (*Linnæus*). [222.] (Figs. 40*a*, 78*a*.) Toes webbed at base and with scalloped lobes terminally; bill heavy, wider than deep. *Ad.* ♀ *in summer.*—Crown and chin fuscous; cheeks white; back black, the feathers bordered with cream-buff; wings gray; some of the secondaries and tips of greater coverts white; upper tail-coverts rufous; underparts dull, reddish brown, often with scattered white feathers. *Ad.* ♂ *in summer.*—Similar, but smaller, crown striped like back, little or no white in cheeks. *Juv.*—Similar to ads. in winter but upperparts margined with buff, chest washed with buff. *Ads. and Juv. in winter.*—Top of head and underparts white; region about eye and back of neck fuscous; back and scapulars dark pearl-gray; wings grayish fuscous, the coverts and secondaries tipped with white; rump and tail fuscous. L., 8ʻ12; W., 5ʻ37; B., ʻ87; Tar., ʻ82.

Remarks.—The juvenal plumage is worn until October or November. Molting spring birds are strikingly pied below.

Range.—Breeds from n. Alaska and Greenland s. to delta of the Yukon, n. Mack. (?), n. Man. (?), and Hudson Bay; also from Iceland (locally), Spitzbergen, and Novaya Zemlya to e. Siberia. Winters on the oceans off the coast of S. A., at least as far s. as Falkland and Juan Fernandez isls. and off the coasts of Arabia and W. Africa; reported in winter n. to s. Calif., Fla., and the Mediterranean Sea; migrates along both coasts of the U. S., mainly well off-shore. Casual in migration in s. Calif. (inland), Colo., Kans., Ala., Vt., Ont., N. Y., Pa., Ills., O., and Md.; rarely in Hawaii and N. Z.

Washington, casual, one record, Oct. Long Island, uncommon T. V., (Mch. 25), Apr. 30–June 5; Aug.–Nov. 28. Bronx region, one record, Oct. 14. Boston, rare T. V.

Nest, a slight hollow in the ground lined with a few bits of moss and grasses. *Eggs*, 3–4, similar to those of the following species, 1·25 × ·90. *Date*, Pt. Barrow, Alaska, June 14.

This pelagic species is found in numbers some distance off the coast; it occurs on our shores rarely, and generally only after storms.

230. WILSON'S PHALAROPE. STEGANOPUS TRICOLOR *Vieillot.* [224.] (Fig. 78*b*.) *Ad.* ♀ *in summer.*—Top of the head and middle of the back pearl-gray, nape white; a black streak passes through eye to side of neck, and, changing to rufous-chestnut, continues down the sides of the back and on scapulars; neck and upper breast washed with pale, brownish rufous; rest of underparts and upper tail-coverts white. *Ad.* ♂ *in summer.*—Upperparts fuscous-brown, bordered with grayish brown; upper tail-coverts, nape, and a line over the eye white or whitish; sides of the neck and breast washed with rufous; rest of the underparts white. *Ads. and Juv. in winter.*—Upperparts gray, margined with white; upper tail-coverts white; wings fuscous, their coverts margined with buffy; underparts white. *Juv.*—"Top of head, back, and scapulars dusky blackish, the feathers distinctly bordered with buff; wing-coverts also bordered with pale buff or whitish; upper tail-coverts, superciliary stripe, and lowerparts white, the neck tinged with buff" (Ridgway). ♂ L., 8·75; W., 4·75; Tar., 1·20; B., 1·20. ♀ L., 9·50; W., 5·25; Tar., 1·30; B., 1·30.

Range.—Breeds from s. B. C., cent. Wash., cent. Alberta, s. Sask., s. Man. s. to cent. Calif., Nev., Utah, Colo., Nebr., s. Kans. (formerly), cent. Ia., Mo. (formerly), n. Ills. and nw. Ind. Winters from cent. Chile and cent. Argentina s. to Falkland Isls.; occurs in migration on the Atlantic and Gulf coasts from Me. to Fla. and Ala., and on the Pacific Coast from s. B. C. to L. Calif.

Long Island, rare T. V. in fall, casual in spring, June 1–19; Aug. 15–Oct. 15. Bronx region, one record, Sept. 21. Boston, A. V. in fall. N. Ohio, casual T. V. SE. Minn., formerly common, now uncommon S. R., Apr. 25–Sept. 13.

Nest, a shallow depression in soft earth lined with a thin layer of fragments of grass. *Eggs*, 3–4, cream-buff or buffy white, heavily blotched with deep chocolate, 1·28 × ·94. (See Nelson, *Bull. Nutt. Orn. Club*, II, 1879, 38–43.) *Date*, Minor Co., S. Dak., May 25; s. Sask., June 15, downy young.

This beautiful bird is a common summer resident of our interior prairie sloughs, and ranges westward as far as the San Joaquin Valley of California. It feeds about the shores and often swims gracefully with a nodding motion of the head. Although the female does not incubate, she appears to be keenly interested in the welfare of the nest, and when I have flushed a sitting male, he has soon been joined by his mate who seemed to share his anxiety. Pairs of birds which evidently had young would utter a soft *qua* or *quok* and fly about me with a slow, jerky, halting flight and a peculiar sinuous stretching and shortening of the neck. Usually the female led.

231. NORTHERN PHALAROPE. LOBIPES LOBATUS (*Linnæus*). [223.] Toes webbed at base and with scalloped lobes terminally; bill very slender and sharply pointed. *Ad.* ♀ *in summer.*—Upperparts slaty gray; back and scapulars edged with ochraceous-buff; sides and front of the neck rufous, more or less mixed with slaty gray; rest of underparts white. *Ad.* ♂ *in summer.*—Similar, but upperparts black, and with more ochraceous; sides and front of the neck mixed with fuscous. *Ads. in winter and Juv.*—Upperparts grayish, more or less mixed with white; tips of greater wing-coverts and sometimes part of the secondaries white, occasionally (in ads.) with traces of rufous on the sides of the neck; underparts white, more or less mottled with grayish on the breast. *Juv.*—Upperparts black, edged with straw-color; forehead white; underparts white, chest sometimes lightly washed with buffy. L., 7·75; W., 4·50; Tar., ·80; B., ·85.

Range.—In N. A. breeds from Pribilof Isls., n. Alaska, Melville Isl., and cent. Greenland s. to Aleutian Isls. (including Near Isls.), valley of the Upper Yukon, n. Mack., n. Man., s. James Bay, and n. Que. (Ungava); also in n. Europe and Asia e. to the Commander Isls. Winters on the ocean off both coasts of N. A. and through interior Can. and U. S. s. to Patagonia. Winters off Peru and W. Africa. Casual in Bermuda.

Washington, casual, two records, Aug. Long Island, tolerably common T. V., (Apr. 2) Apr. 27–June 3; July 31–Oct. 22. Bronx region, rare T. V., Aug. 11–Oct. 26. Boston, rare T. V. SE. Minn., rare T. V., Aug. 13; no spring records.

Nest, a slight hollow in the ground lined with grass and mosses. *Eggs*, 3–4, pale olive-gray heavily blotched with deep chocolate, 1·18 × ·83. *Date*, Ft. Yukon, Alaska, June 7.

I have seen this species in great numbers about one hundred miles off Barnegat, N. J., in May. For several hours the steamer passed through flocks of these 'Sea Snipe,' which were swimming on the ocean. They arose in a body at our approach, and in close rank whirled away to the right or left in search of new feeding-grounds.

1908. CHAPMAN, F. M., Camps and Cruises, 223 (feeding habits).

SUBORDER LARI. LONG-WINGED SWIMMERS
(3 families)

SYNOPSIS OF FAMILIES (Figs. 42–45).

Bill with a terminal, nail-like hook; its base with a scaly shield or cere; plumage above dark; *central* tail-feathers (except in the Skua) longest.
       Family Stercorariidæ. JAEGERS AND SKUAS. P. 294.
Bill hooked but entire, no terminal nail or basal cere; adults white or pearl and white; tail-feathers usually of about equal length.
       Subfamily Larinæ. GULLS. P. 297.
Bill straight, usually sharply pointed; outer tail-feathers usually longest.
       Subfamily Sterninæ. TERNS. P. 308.
Bill thin, blade-like, vertically compressed, much higher than wide; lower mandible longer than upper. . *Family Rhynchopidæ.* SKIMMERS. P. 318.

FAMILY STERCORARIIDÆ. JAEGERS AND SKUAS.

Three of the seven known members of this family are birds of Antarctic seas; the remaining four nest in the northern parts of the Northern Hemisphere, but at other seasons are widely distributed. Except when nesting, they are maritime, but at times are found on large bodies of water inland.

The Jaegers are the pirates among birds of the high seas. With strong and dashing flight, they successfully pursue Gulls and Terns, forcing them to disgorge their prey. They carry their predacious habits to their nesting-grounds on the tundras, where they feed upon the eggs and young of other birds and even upon mice and lemmings. Their notes, uttered chiefly on the breeding-ground, are loud, harsh, and varied.

KEY TO THE SPECIES

A. Bill over 1·35; tarsus over 1·70; middle tail-feathers never pointed.
 a. Bill over 1·90 . . . . 235. NORTHERN SKUA.
 b. Bill under 1·90 . . . . 232. POMARINE JAEGER.
B. Bill under 1·35; tarsus under 1·70; middle tail-feathers generally pointed.
 a. Scaly shield on the bill longer than the distance from its end to the tip of the bill . . . . 233. PARASITIC JAEGER.
 b. Scaly shield on the bill shorter than the distance from its end to the tip of the bill . . . . 234. LONG-TAILED JAEGER.

232. POMARINE JAEGER. STERCORARIUS POMARINUS (*Temminck*). [36.] *Ads., light phase.*—Very similar in color to corresponding phase of *S. parasiticus* but with the upperparts darker, nearly black. *Ads., dark phase and Im.*—Similar in color to corresponding stages of *S. parasiticus.* L., 22·00; W., 13·50; T., Ad., 8·00; Im., 5·40; Tar., 2·00; B., 1·55.

 Remarks.—This species is to be distinguished from the two following by its larger size and the rounded ends of its central tail-feathers.

 Range.—Breeds from Banks, Somerset, and Melville Isls. and cent. Greenland s. to nw. Alaska, n. Mack., also on Arctic E. Hemisphere. Winters off Va. coast, s. to Gulf of Mex. and Peru and in the Old World to S. Africa and Australia. Common fall migrant on coast of Calif. Casual in interior U. S.

 Long Island, rare T. V., May 16–June 3; July 18–Nov. 8. Bronx region, A. V.; one record, Oct. 18. Boston, uncommon T. V., May; July–Oct.

 Nest, on the ground. *Eggs*, 2–3, deep olive-drab sparingly spotted with slate-color, and light and dark raw-umber markings and black dots, chiefly at the larger end, where confluent, 2·25 × 1·70 (Brewer). *Date*, Cape Lisburne, Alaska, June 10.

"Although this species is depicted as a coward in its relations to its smaller and more active congeners, it nevertheless does not hesitate to attack Gulls of all sizes, even the Great Glaucous Gull and the Black-backed Gull, in its attempt to rob them of their food" (Forbush).

233. PARASITIC JAEGER. STERCORARIUS PARASITICUS (*Linnæus*). [37.] (Fig. 44). *Ads., light phase.*—Back, wings and tail slaty fuscous; top of head and lores nearly black; sides of head and back of neck straw-yellow, this color sometimes spreading down sides of neck and on throat; breast and belly white; sides of breast, flanks, lower belly, and crissum slaty fuscous; tarsi and feet (in dried specimens) black; middle tail-feathers pointed and extending about 3.00 beyond the others. *Ads., dark phase.*—Entire plumage dark, slaty brown, darker on top of head; underparts slightly lighter; sometimes a trace of straw-yellow on sides and back of neck; tarsi, feet and tail as in preceding. *Im., light phase.*—Upperparts, wings and tail fuscous; feathers of back, neck and head more or less bordered, tipped or barred with buffy; hindneck and head sometimes buffy, streaked or barred with fuscous, and varying from this color to plain fuscous; longer, lateral upper tail-coverts barred with buffy; tail buffy, whitish at base; under wing-coverts barred with buffy; underparts white, washed with buffy, and irregularly barred with sooty fuscous; these bars sometimes very numerous when the under-parts look as if washed with sooty fuscous; again, they may be less numerous and confined to breast and sides, leaving the belly white; central tail-feathers pointed, projecting more or less beyond rest. *Im., dark phase.*—Sooty fus-cous feathers, particularly on underparts, more or less marked with ochra-ceous-buff. L., 17·00; W., 13·00; T., Ad., 8·60; Im., 6·40; B., 1·15.

Remarks.—This species closely resembles *S. longicaudus.* Adults of both species, whether in the dark or light phase of plumage, may always be dis-tinguished from each other by the difference in the length of their central tail-feathers, in addition to the characters given in the key. Young birds can not be distinguished by color, but may be identified by the differences in relative proportions of the bill. Eaton calls attention to the fact that in *parasiticus* the shafts of all the primaries are white, while in *longicaudus* only the outer two or three are white, the rest being abruptly brownish.

Range.—Breeds from nw. Alaska, Melville Isl. and n. Greenland to sw. Alaska, the Aleutian Isls., s. Mack., ne. Man., n. Hudson Bay and n. Lab., also on Arctic isls. of Siberia, and n. Europe s. to Scotland; winters from s. Calif. to Argentina, occasionally to the Straits of Magellan, and from Fla. to the e. coast of S. A., also from Europe to Cape of Good Hope and the Persian Gulf and occasionally to Australia and N. Z.; casual in the interior of Can. and the U. S. to the Great Lakes, Mo., Kans. and Colo.; accidental in Mass. and Me. in winter and occasional on the Atlantic Coast in summer.

Long Island, rare S. V., tolerably common T. V. in fall, Apr. 30–June 3; July 25–Nov. 15. Bronx region, very rare T. V.; perhaps A. V.; July 26–Sept. 29. Boston, common T. V., especially in fall; June–Oct. N. Ohio, casual on Lake Erie.

Nest, on the moors or tundras, a slight depression in the ground scantily lined with grasses, etc., or on rocks by the sea. *Eggs*, 2–4, light olive-brown, with frequently a strong greenish tinge and chocolate markings, more numerous and sometimes confluent at the larger end, 2·25 × 1·65. *Date*, Iceland, May 23; Bering Isl., Kamchatka, May 29.

"The Jaeger singles out some Tern that has just caught a fish, perhaps, and darts after it, following every twist and turn of its victim, menacing it with hooked beak and clutching at it with strong, curved claws until the Tern either drops or disgorges the fish, when the dashing robber catches his ill-gotten booty in the air" (Forbush).

234. LONG-TAILED JAEGER. Stercorarius longicaudus *Vieillot.*

[38.] *Ads., light phase.*—Back, wings and tail slaty fuscous; top of head and lores nearly black; sides of head, back and sides of neck straw-yellow; throat sometimes washed with same color; underparts white; sides, lower belly, and crissum slaty fuscous; central tail-feathers extending about 7·00 beyond the others, the projecting ends narrow and pointed. (No dark phase of this species has been described.) *Im.*—Similar in plumage to im. of *S. parasiticus,* but differing otherwise as pointed out under that species. L., 21·00; W., 12·50; T., Ad., 12·00; Im., 5·50; B., 1·08.

Range.—Breeds on the Arctic coasts and isls. of Europe and Asia, the n. and nw. coasts of Alaska, n. Mack., Ellesmere Isl. and n. Greenland s. to n. Lab. Winters s. to Gibraltar and Japan and recorded in winter on the coasts of S. C. and Fla. and in migration off the Atlantic Coast and in Chile and Argentina, and in the interior from B. C., Man., Mo., Ia., Ind. and Ills. Casual on the Pacific Coast of N. A. s. to Calif.

Long Island, casual, Aug., Sept. Boston, rare T. V., mainly Aug. and Sept.

Nest, a slight depression in the ground, sometimes scantily lined with grasses. *Eggs*, 2–3, similar in color to those of the preceding, 2·10 × 1·50. *Date*, S. Greenland, June 1.

The rarest of our Jaegers.

PLATE XVI

GULLS AND PETRELS
Herring Gull.

Bonaparte's Gull.   Wilson's Petrel.

235. NORTHERN SKUA. Catharacta skua *Brünnich.* [35.] *Ads.*—
Upperparts, tail and wings dark, dirty brown; shafts of the wing and tail-feathers white, except at the tip; outer wing-feathers with inner vanes white at the base; underparts somewhat lighter; neck more or less streaked with whitish. *Im.*—"Similar to adult, but more distinctly streaked with yellowish, especially on the head and neck." L., 22·00; W., 15·91; Tar., 2·63; B., 2·06 (Ridgway).

Range.—Reported to breed near Lady Franklin Isl., and on se. Baffin Land: breeds in Iceland, and on the Faroe, Shetland, and Orkney isls. Winters on fishing-banks off N. F., N. S., and Mass. Casually s. to L. I. and in the interior; in Europe from the British Isles and Norway s. to Gibraltar and casually to Madeira and the Mediterranean Sea.

Long Island, two records, Jan. and Aug.

Nest, of grass, on the ground. *Eggs,* 2, pale olive-brown or greenish gray spotted with chocolate, 2·80 × 1·90. *Date,* Greenland, May 5.

A heavy-bodied, dark-colored, hawklike robber of the tundra and high seas.

FAMILY LARIDÆ. GULLS AND TERNS.

This family contains about 100 species, divided equally between subfamily *Larinæ* (Gulls) and subfamily *Sterninæ* (Terns). They are distributed throughout the world. Some forty species inhabit North America. With few exceptions, they agree in possessing the marked characters of their respective subfamilies, under which they may be more conveniently treated.

Subfamily Larinæ. Gulls.

The fifty-odd members of this subfamily are distributed throughout the world; twenty-three of them have been recorded from North America, where the greater number nest north of the United States; in Eastern North America, the Laughing Gull being the only species which nests south of latitude 41°.

Franklin's Gull is a bird of the Mississippi Valley, and many of the maritime species nest on the islands of inland lakes, where, indeed, they may be represented throughout the year; but, as a family, Gulls are true birds of the sea and its bays. They throng our harbors from early fall to late spring, and during this season are ever in attendance on coast-wise craft, and are not wanting in mid-ocean.

Gulls average larger and stockier than Terns, and have less pointed, broader wings, and, as a rule, square tails. They procure their food largely by picking it from the surface of the water with their strong, hooked bills, not by plunging or darting, as do the Terns. They are among nature's scavengers of the water, and perform a service of great value to man by devouring various forms of aquatic animals which, in dying, come to the surface. They also aid in freeing the waters of our harbors from the garbage which inevitably finds its way there. Although feeding thus on offal, many Gulls are highly predacious and feed upon the eggs and young of the other birds among which they nest, rarely, however, preying on their own species.

Gulls are buoyant swimmers, and unlike Terns, roost on the water, often gathering in close-massed 'beds.' They usually nest in colonies on islands. The young are born covered with down of mottled pattern, and though they may leave the nest in their natal dress, are dependent on their parents until they acquire the power of flight. The voices of Gulls possess a certain indescribable human quality which adds in no small degree to the impression created when storms rule and their wild cries are heard above the tumult of wind and wave.

1915. COOKE, W. W., Distribution and Migration of North American Gulls and Their Allies, Bull. 292, U. S. Dept. Agric., 70 pp.—1923. MILLER, R. C., Flight of Sea Gulls, Condor, 5–15, illus.—1925. DWIGHT, J., Gulls of the World, Bull. Amer. Mus. Nat. Hist., XLII, 63–401, illus.—1929. GRISCOM, L., Field Identification of Massachusetts Gulls, Bull. Essex Inst. (Salem), 13–26.

KEY TO THE SPECIES

I. Wing over 15·00.
  1. Back dark slaty black . . . . 238. GREAT BLACK-BACKED GULL.
  2. Back not dark slaty black.
    A. Back pearl-gray.
      a. Outer primaries marked with black . . . 241. HERRING GULL.
      b. No black on primaries.
        b^1. Bill under 2·00.
          b^2. Primaries light pearl-gray, fading gradually into white at their tips . . . . 237. ICELAND GULL.
          b^3. Primaries pearl-gray, tipped with white, and with well-defined gray spaces on the outer webs of the outer two primaries and on both webs of the third and fourth primaries . . . . 237 + 241a. KUMLIEN'S GULL.
        c^1. Bill over 2·00 . . . . 236. GLAUCOUS GULL.
    B. Back grayish, whitish, or brownish, or mottled or spotted with grayish or brownish.
      a. Tail black or blackish, with or without irregular white markings.
        a^1. Wing over 17·50; depth of bill at nostril over ·70.
                                238. GREAT BLACK-BACKED GULL., im.
        a^2. Wing under 17·50; depth of bill at nostril under ·70.
                                241. HERRING GULL, im.
      b. Tail white or whitish or grayish brown, with or without black markings.
        b^1. Bill under 2·00 . . . . 237. ICELAND GULL, im.
        b^2. Bill over 2·00 . . . . 236. GLAUCOUS GULL, im.
II. Wing under 15·00.
  1. Tail white.
    A. Head and throat slaty black.
      a. Outer primary black or mostly black.
        a^1. Outer primary entirely black . . . . 245. LAUGHING GULL.
        a^2. Inner half of inner web of first primary white.
                                252. SABINE'S GULL.
      b. Outer primary mostly white.
        b^1. Tip of first primary white . . . . . 246. FRANKLIN'S GULL.
        b^2. Tip of first primary black . . . . 247. BONAPARTE'S GULL.
    B. Head white, sometimes washed with pearl-gray.
      a. Wings white . . . . 249. IVORY GULL.
      b. Primaries with more or less black.
        b^1. Wing over 11·00.
          b^2. Hind toe very small, without a nail. 250. ATLANTIC KITTIWAKE.

b^3. Hind toe normal, with a nail . . 242. Ring-billed Gull.
c^1. Wing under 11·00 . . . . 251. Ross's Gull.
2. Tail marked with black.
 A. Wing over 13·25.
   a. Primaries mostly white . . . . 249. Ivory Gull, im.
   b. Primaries black or mostly black . 242. Ring-billed Gull, im.
 B. Wing under 13·25.
   a. Hind toe very small, without a nail.
                                      250. Atlantic Kittiwake, im.
   b. Hind toe normal, with a nail.
     b^1. Tarsus 1·50 or over . . . . . . 245. Laughing Gull, im.
     c^1. Tarsus under 1·50.
       c^2. Secondaries pearl-color, tail square.
                                      247. Bonaparte's Gull, im.
       c^3. Secondaries mostly white, tail rounded.
                                      251. Ross's Gull, im.

236. GLAUCOUS GULL. Larus hyperboreus *Gunnerus.* [42.] With no black markings. *Ads. in summer.*—Back and wings pale pearl-gray; primaries lightly tinted with pearl, inner half of their inner webs and tips fading gradually into white; rest of plumage pure white. *Ads. in winter.*—Similar, but with head and neck lightly streaked with grayish. *Im.*—Upperparts varying from ashy gray to white, feathers widely barred, mottled, or streaked with buffy or ashy gray; primaries varying from pale smoky gray to pure white; tail ashy or brownish gray; underparts varying from dirty whitish to ashy gray, generally darker on belly, sometimes mottled with buffy or grayish. (Birds of the second year are said to be pure white) L., 28·00; W., 17·10; B., 2·35; depth of B. at projection on the lower mandible ·75 to 1·00; Tar., 2·60.

Range.—Breeds on Arctic coasts and isls. from nw. Alaska, Melville Isl., and n. Greenland s. to the Pribilof Isls., n. Mack., James Bay, e. Lab., and N. F. and on Arctic isls. of the E. Hemisphere. Winters from the Aleutians and Greenland s. to Calif., the Great Lakes, and L. I., and casually to Bermuda, N. C., Tex., Mo., and Hawaiian Isls.; in Europe and Asia s. to Red Sea and Japan.

Washington, casual W. V., Feb. and Apr. Long Island, uncommon W. V., (July 24) Nov. 2–June 6. Bronx region, rather rare W. V.; Oct. 13–Apr. 25. Boston, uncommon W. V., Nov.–Apr.

Nest, of grasses, moss, etc., on the ground. *Eggs,* 2–3, varying from pale olive-brown to grayish white, spotted or speckled with shades of chocolate, 3·10 × 2·20. *Date,* Cumberland Sound, June 8.

Mr. Chamberlain remarks that this species combines "with some gull-like traits many of the coarse characteristics of both Falcon and Vulture.

"Some observers have reported that flocks are at times very noisy, particularly when settling for the night; but those I have met with in winter have been rather silent. Their cry is harsh and at times very loud; it sounds something like the syllables *kuk-lak.* I have seen it written *cut-leek.*"

237. ICELAND GULL. Larus leucopterus *Vieillot.* [43.] Resembles the preceding but is much smaller; specimens in juvenal plumage more frequently have white or brownish shafts untinged with yellow, as in *hyperboreus;* others are mottled with black rather than brownish (Dwight, *The Auk,* 1906, 34). W., 15·40–16·50; B., 1·65–1·90; depth of B. at projection on the lower mandible, ·60–·70; Tar., 2·05–2·20 (B., B., and R.).

Range.—Arctic regions. Breeds from Victoria Land and Boothia Peninsula to cent. Greenland and e. to Jan Mayen Isl. Winters from s. Greenland and the coast of France s. to L. I.; and casually to Cape Hatteras and on the Great Lakes; in Europe s. to the British Isles, Scandinavia, and the Baltic Sea. Accidental in Nebr. and Md.

Long Island, uncommon W. V., Nov. 2–June 3. Bronx region, rare but regular W. V., Nov. 22–May 15; casual July 31. Boston, not uncommon W. V., Nov.–Apr. N. Ohio, casual on Lake Erie in winter.

Nest, of grasses, moss, etc., on the ground. *Eggs,* 2–3, clay-color with numerous chocolate markings, 2·79 × 1·89. *Date,* Julianshaab, Greenland, June 1.

"It is not particularly difficult for the trained observer to distinguish the white-winged Gulls in the field from the Herring Gull; but as between *L. hyperboreus* and *L. leucopterus* a positive identification is not so easy. . . . One soon gets to recognize the white-winged species flying, even at a considerable distance, and the smaller size of the Iceland Gull is seen perhaps more distinctly on the wing than when the bird is sitting. The bill, when it can be seen, is an excellent field-mark, the Iceland Gull's like that of Kumlien's Gull, being much smaller in proportion. . . ." (F. H. Allen, *The Auk*, 1908, p. 300, status near Boston).

Fig. 83. Two outer primaries of Adult Iceland Gull.

238. GREAT BLACK-BACKED GULL. Larus marinus *Linnæus.* [47.]

Ads. in summer.—Back and wings *slaty black;* wing-feathers tipped with white; rest of plumage white; tail sometimes mottled with dusky. *Ads. in winter.*—Similar, but with head and neck streaked with grayish. *Im.*—Head and nape whitish, streaked with grayish; back and wings, except primaries, brownish, the feathers margined and irregularly marked with pale buffy; primaries dark brownish black, inner ones with small white tips; tail mottled with black and white; underparts whitish, more or less streaked or barred with grayish. L., 29·00; W., 18·50; T., 8·00; B., 2·50.

Range.—Breeds from Iceland and cent. Greenland s. to N. S. and Me., n. British Isles, Scandinavia and n. Russia. Winters from s. Greenland s. to the Great Lakes and Del. Bay (casually to Fla.), also to Canaries and Caspian Sea. Accidental in Nebr. and in Bermuda.

Long Island, common W. V., Sept. 2–May 30; rare in summer. Bronx region, fairly common W. V., Sept. 15–Apr. 27. Boston, common W. V., July–May. N. Ohio, four records.

Nest, of grasses, seaweed, etc., on the ground. *Eggs,* 2–3, clay-color, brownish ashy or buffy, rather evenly spotted with chocolate, 3·00 × 2·15. *Date,* Kings Co., N. S., May 23.

A larger and more northern species than the Herring Gull. Mr. Brewster, who observed it in numbers in the island of Anticosti in July, writes:

"The Black-backs are exceedingly noisy birds, especially when their young are in danger, as well as toward

Fig. 84. Two outer primaries of Adult Great Black-backed Gull.

evening. . . . I identified four distinct cries: a braying *ha-ha-ha*, a deep *keow, keow*, a short barking note, and a long-drawn groan, very loud and decidedly impressive. . . At all times of the year, during the breeding season as well as in winter, it is by far the wariest bird that I have ever met."

239. WYMAN'S GULL, *Larus occidentalis wymani* Dickey and Van Rossem, [49*b*], of the Pacific Coast is recorded as accidental at Chicago, Ills.

240. The LESSER BLACK-BACKED GULL, *Larus fuscus grællsi* Brehm, an Old-World species, is recorded as accidental in Greenland.

241. HERRING GULL. LARUS ARGENTATUS SMITHSONIANUS *Coues.* [51, 51*a.*] (Pl. XVI.) *Ads. in summer.*—Bill yellow, a red spot near tip of lower mandible; feet pink; back and wings deep pearl-gray; first primary tipped with white, then crossed by a small black mark, then a much larger white one; this is followed by a black space; the black runs down the outer web of the feather to near its base and the shaft part of the inner web nearly as far, leaving the inner two-thirds of the web below the black mark white (Fig. 85); second primary similar, but second white mark is a round spot on inner web and black occupies a greater space near tip, but does not continue so far down on feather; third to sixth primaries tipped with white, which is succeeded by a gradually diminishing black band which extends farther down on the outer web of the feather than on the inner; rest of plumage pure white. *Ads. in winter.*—Similar, but with head and neck streaked and spotted with grayish. *Im.*—Upperparts ashy fuscous; head and nape more or less streaked with pale buffy; back and wings margined or irregularly marked with same color; primaries brownish black; tail the same, sometimes tipped or margined with buffy; underparts ashy fuscous, sometimes lightly barred or streaked; bill and feet flesh-color, former darker at end. L., 24·00; W., 17·50; T., 7·50; B., 2·30.

Range.—Breeds from s. cent. Alaska and s. Baffin Isl. s. to s. B. C., s. Alberta, n. N. Dak., cent. Wisc., s. Ont., n. N. Y., and Me., and casually Mass. Winters from s. Alaska s. to L. Calif. and w. Mex., and from Gulf of St. Lawrence and the Great Lakes s. to the Bahamas, Cuba, Yucatan, and coast of Tex.

FIG. 85. Two outer primaries of adult Herring Gull.

Washington, common W. V., Oct. 16–June 13. Long Island, abundant W. V., arrives Sept., common in summer. Bronx region, abundant W. V.; a few usually summer; Aug. 2–June 15. Boston, abundant W. V., less common S. V., not breeding. N. Ohio, common P. R. on Lake Erie. Glen Ellyn, T. V. chiefly spring, occasional W. V., Dec. 4–Apr. 24. SE. Minn., common T. V., Mch. 16–June 2; Sept. 4–Nov. 29.

Nest, of grasses, moss, seaweed, etc., on the ground, but, where the birds have been persistently robbed, it is more compactly built and placed in trees sometimes 50 feet or more from the ground. *Eggs*, 2–3, grayish olive-brown, rarely whitish, spotted, blotched, and scrawled with distinct and obscure chocolate markings, 2·85 × 1·90. *Date*, Midriff Lake, N. Y., May 3; Isle Royal, Mich., May 20.

This species is by far the most abundant winter Gull along the coasts of the middle and southern states. Unlike the more pelagic species, it frequents our rivers and harbors, feeding about piers and wharves, and near the cities where as a scavenger it is of the highest value. Sometimes one may see them 'bedded' in flocks on the water where they alight to rest. It is generally this species which follows in the wake of our coast-wise vessels, sailing astern, when the wind is from ahead, without the slightest perceptible movement of the wings.

1900. CHAPMAN, F. M., Bird-Lore, 10, 11 (value as scavengers).— 1902. MACKAY, G. H., Auk, 221–228.—1903. DUTCHER, W. and BAILY, W. L., Auk, 417–431 (nesting).—1914, 1923. STRONG, R. M., Habits and Behavior. Auk, 22–49, 178–199; 1923. 609–621, illus. (also WOLFE, L. R., *Ibid.*, 621–626).—1928. LINCOLN, F., Auk, 49–59 (migration).—1930. ALLEN, A. A., Bird-Lore, 71–83, illus. (autobiography).

KUMLIEN'S GULL. LARUS KUMLIENI *Brewster.* [45.] Very similar in general color to the two preceding species, but differs from them in color of the primaries. These, instead of being uniformly pure white or but lightly tinted with gray, are marked with sharply defined spaces of ashy gray. The first primary is tipped with white and marked with ashy gray on the outer web and shaft part of the inner web; the second primary is ashy gray on only part of the outer web; the third and fourth primaries have smaller white tips and are marked with ashy gray near their ends on both webs. W., 15·50–17·00; B., 1·65–1·88; depth of B., at projection on the lower mandible, ·60–·66; Tar., 2·10–2·35 (Brewster).

Remarks.—For a plate and detailed discussion of the status of this and related species see Dwight, Auk, 1906, 26–43; Bull. Amer. Mus. Nat. Hist., 1925, 52, 197.

Range.—N. Atlantic Coast of N. A., breeding in Cumberland Sound. S. in winter to the Gulf of St. Lawrence, rarely to Conn. and L. I., N. Y.

Long Island, casual, Mch. 8–Apr. 1. Bronx region, two sight records, Feb. 21, Apr. 12. Boston, rare W. V., Oct.–Mch.

The opinion of Dwight that 'Kumlien's Gull' is a hybrid between *L. argentatus thayeri* and *L. leucopterus* has been accepted by the A. O. U. Committee.]

241a. THAYER'S GULL, *Larus argentatus thayeri* Brooks, [51b], breeds in Arctic North America west of Greenland, winters regularly on the Pacific Coast to British Columbia, and casually to Illinois and Quebec and New Jersey. It resembles *La. argentatus* but the bill is not quite so deep, and there is a tendency to slaty or grayish rather than black primaries at all ages and a maximum of white rather than gray in the wing-pattern of the adult. In juvenal and first-year, as well as second- and probably third-year plumages, *thayeri* is not much different from other Herring Gulls. Depth of B. at angle, ·70 (Dwight).

242. RING-BILLED GULL. LARUS DELAWARENSIS *Ord.* [54.] *Ads. in summer.*—Back and wings pearl-gray; first primary black, with a white spot near tip, base of inner half of inner web pearl-gray (Fig. 86); second primary black, basal half of inner web pearl-gray; on the third to sixth primaries the black decreases rapidly, and each one is tipped with white; rest of plumage pure white; bill greenish yellow with a black band in front of the nostril. *Ads. in winter.*—Similar to above, but head and nape streaked with grayish. *Im.*—Upperparts varying from ashy fuscous, the feathers margined with whitish, to pearl-gray, the feathers more or less mottled, spotted, or, on head and neck, streaked with ashy fuscous; outer primaries black, tail varying from pearl-gray, more or less mottled with blackish, to white, and *crossed near end by a wide band of black;* basal half of bill yellowish, end black; feet greenish. L., 18·50; W., 14·00; T., 6·00; B., 1·60.

Range.—Breeds mainly on interior lakes of Can. and the U. S., from s. Alaska, cent. B. C., Great Slave Lake, n. Man., James Bay s. to s. Ore., s. Colo., n. Utah, Idaho, N. Dak., s. Ont., n. N. Y. (casually) and se. Que.

and formerly in Minn., Wisc. and n. Mich. Winters from B. C., Colo., Idaho, Mont., the Great Lakes and on both coasts from Me. and cent. Calif. to the Gulf Coast, Cuba, and s. Mex. Accidental in Bermuda and Hawaiian Isls.

Washington, very common T. V., Feb.–June 15; Sept. 14–Dec. 22; rare in winter. Long Isl..nd, common T. V., uncommon W. V., casual S. V., July 21–May 29; Sept. 5–Nov. 12; Mch. 27–May 15. Bronx region, fairly common T. V., occasionally winters; July 29–May 15 (June 2). Boston, T. V., not uncommon in fall; rare W. V. N. Ohio, common all the year. Glen Ellyn, rare W. V. SE. Minn., common T. V., Mch. 18–June 4; Sept. 2–Nov. 28.

Nest, of grasses, etc., on the ground. *Eggs,* 2–3, clay-color, buffy, or whitish, rather evenly spotted with chocolate, 2·30 × 1·65. *Date,* Stump Lake, N. Dak., May 31.

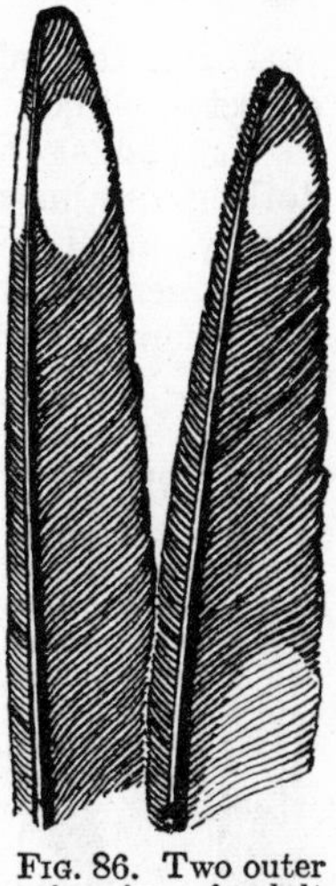

The coast-inhabiting individuals of this species resemble the Herring Gull in habits, but when the two are seen together, the smaller size of the Ring-bill and its differently colored bill and feet are noticeable. In the interior, where the species is locally common, it feeds in part on insects, which it catches both on the ground and in the air.

243. The SHORT-BILLED GULL, *Larus canus brachy-rhynchus* Richardson, [55], of western North America is accidental in Quebec (?).

FIG. 86. Two outer primaries of adult Ring-billed Gull.

244. The BLACK-HEADED GULL, *Larus ridibundus ridibundus* Linnæus, [55.1], an Old-World species, is accidental in Greenland and at Newburyport, Mass. (Jan 27, 1930, Emilio and Griscom, Auk, 1930, 243).

FIG. 87. Two outer primaries of adult Laughing Gull.

245. LAUGHING GULL. LARUS ATRICILLA *Linnæus.* [58.] (Fig. 42.) *Ads. in summer.*—Back and wings dark pearl-gray; *primaries black,* inner ones with small white tips (Fig. 87); whole head and throat deep slate-color; rest of plumage, including nape, pure white, breast sometimes suffused by a delicate peach-blossom tint; bill dark reddish, brighter at the tip. *Ads. in winter.*—Resemble above, but have the head and throat white, crown and sides of head and sometimes nape spotted or streaked with grayish. *Im.*—Upperparts light ashy fuscous, the feathers margined with whitish; *primaries black;* forehead and underparts white, sometimes washed in places with dusky; tail dark pearl-gray, broadly tipped with black. L., 16·50; W., 12·50; T., 4·90; B., 1·65.

Range.—Breeds from Me. and Mass. (formerly N. S.) s. on the coast to Tex., the Lesser Antilles and Venezuela. Winters from S. C. to Chile and Brazil. Casual in Colo., Nebr., Wisc., Ont., Ia., and Que.; accidental in L. Calif., Bermuda, and Europe.

Washington, irregular in Apr., May; Aug.–Oct. Long Island, common T. V., rare S. R., Apr. 26–June 2; June 30–Nov. 23 (Jan. 13). Bronx region, formerly rare; at present a common spring and abundant fall T. V., Apr. 21–June 20; July 12–Nov. 26 (Dec. 15). Boston, common S. V., rare in winter.

Nest, of grasses, seaweed, etc., on sandy islets and in grassy marshes. *Eggs*, 3–4, varying from grayish olive-brown to greenish gray, spotted, blotched, and scrawled with chocolate, 2·15 × 1·55. *Date*, Corpus Christi, Tex., Apr. 8; Cobb's Isl., Va., May 26; Muskeget Isl., Mass., June 7.

This is the only Gull nesting on our Atlantic Coast south of Massachusetts. When nesting on Cobb's Island, Va., the sitting birds were so conspicuous that from a distance they looked like white flowers dotting the marsh. The downy young, however, were much darker than young Terns, the general tone of their plumage resembling that of the reeds of which the nest was made. The resemblance of its call to wild, maniacal laughter has won for this species its common name.

1895. MACKAY, G. H., Auk, 332–336 (habits in Mass.).

246. FRANKLIN'S GULL. LARUS PIPIXCAN *Wagler.* [59.] *Ads. in summer.*—Whole head and throat sooty black, nape, sides of neck, and underparts, except throat, white, generally suffused (in fresh specimens) with an exquisite peach-blossom tint; tail white; back and wings pearl-gray; first primary white, outer web black, except at the tip, shaft part of the inner web grayish on basal half; second primary white, with a black mark on inner web and a black stripe on outer web near the tip, rest of outer web and shaft part of inner web pearl-gray; third to sixth primaries tipped with white, then banded with gradually diminishing bars of black, which are succeeded by a whitish space, while the rest of the feather is pearl-gray; bill dark coral-red. *Ads. in winter.*—"Similar, but head and neck white, the occiput, with orbital and auricular regions, grayish dusky; bill and feet dusky, the former tipped with orange reddish." *Young, first plumage.*—"Top and sides of the head (except forehead and lores), back and scapulars grayish brown, the longer scapulars bordered terminally with pale grayish buff; wing-coverts bluish gray tinged with grayish brown; secondaries dusky, edged with pale grayish blue and broadly tipped with white; primaries dusky, the inner more plumbeous, all broadly tipped with white. Central portion of the rump uniform light bluish gray; lateral and posterior portions

FIG. 88. Two outer primaries of adult Franklin's Gull.

of the rump, upper tail-coverts, entire lower parts, forehead, lores, and eyelids white. Bill brownish, dusky terminally; feet brown (in skin)." L., 14·25; W., 11·25; B., 1·30; depth through nostrils, ·35; Tar., 1·60 (B., B., and R.).

Range.—Breeds in prairie regions of interior N. A. from s. Alberta, cent. Sask., and s. cent. Man., to S. Dak., Ia. (formerly), Utah, and s. Minn. Winters from the coast of La. to Chile. Accidental in Colo., Ont., O., Ills., Mich., Mass., N. B., Calif., Lesser Antilles, and Hawaii.

Nest, of grasses, etc., in reedy marshes. *Eggs*, 2–3, varying from dark chocolate to creamy brown and sooty white, irregularly marked with small spots or large blotches of umber, and with obsolete lilac shell markings, 2·12 × 1·40 (Preston). *Date*, Heron Lake, Minn., May 8.

Many Gulls nest in the interior, but of them all Franklin's has rarely been found on either our Atlantic or Pacific coasts, though it reaches the Pacific Coast of South America in winter.

Pausing in its billowy flight over the prairies to circle about one curiously; hovering over the plowman, or exploring the furrow in his

GULLS

wake; eagerly chasing grasshoppers, like a flock of pearl-plumaged hens; gathered in thousands in the reeds where it nests or in vast flocks prior to its fall migration, Franklin's Gull is one of the most interesting, as it is unexpected, forms of bird-life of our interior.

1886. PRESTON, J. W., Orn. and Oöl., 54, 55.—1900. ROBERTS, T. S., Auk, 272–283 (one of the first as well as one of the best of American bird studies with a camera).—1902. JOB, H. K., Among the Water-Fowl, 159–165.—1910. Bird-Lore, 124–127.

247. BONAPARTE'S GULL. LARUS PHILADELPHIA (*Ord*). [60.] Smallest of our Gulls. (Pl. XVI.) *Ads. in summer.*—Whole head and throat dark, sooty slate-color; nape and sides of the neck, underparts, except throat, and tail white; back and wings pearl-gray; first primary, seen from above, white, outer web and tip black; second and third primaries white, tipped with black; third to sixth primaries with small whitish tips, then large black spaces, the rest of feather white or pearl-gray; bill black. *Ads. in winter.*—Similar, but head and throat white, back and sides of head washed with grayish. *Im.*—Top of the head and nape and a spot on the auriculars more or less washed with grayish; back varying from brownish gray to pearl-gray; lesser wing-coverts grayish brown, secondaries mostly pearl-gray; first primary with outer web, tip, and most of shaft part of inner web black; inner margin of inner web at end of feather narrowly bordered with black; second and third primaries much the same, but with slightly more black at ends; tail white, banded with black and narrowly tipped with white; underparts white. L., 14·00; W., 10·30; T., 4·00; B., 1·15.

Range.—Breeds from nw. Alaska and n. Mack. s. to B. C. and cent. Alberta. Winters from Mass. (Me. rarely) to Fla. and on the Gulf Coast to Yucatan, and on the Pacific Coast from se. Alaska s. to L. Calif. and w. Mex.; in migration w. to Kotzebue Sound and e. to Que. (Ungava). Casual in Peru, Bermuda, and the Bahamas.

Washington, common T. V., Mch.–May 30; Oct. 23–Jan. 1. Long Island, common T. V., rare W. V., casual S. V., Aug. 6–Jan. 21; Mch. 30–May 24. Bronx region, fairly common T. V., Mch. 9 and Apr. 14–June 13; Aug. 17–Dec. 27 (Feb. 9). Boston, common T. V., Mch.–May; Aug.–Dec.; variable W. V., casual S. V. N. Ohio, common T. V., Apr. 10–May 20; Sept. 1–20. Glen Ellyn, rare T. V. SE. Minn., common T. V., Apr. 23–May 16; Aug. 11–Nov. 4.

FIG. 89. Two outer primaries of adult Bonaparte's Gull.

Nest, of sticks lined with grasses, etc., on stumps, in bushes or trees 4 to 20 feet from the ground. *Eggs*, 3–4, grayish olive with a greenish tint and small clove-brown spots, chiefly about the larger end, 1·97 × 1·40 (B., B., and R.). *Date*, Anderson River, June 6.

"This little Gull is more often found in flocks than our other species, and is frequently seen flying over swamps and plowed fields searching for worms and insects; but it is usually met with on the lakes and rivers hunting its food like the Herring Gull. It is far less wary than that species" (Eaton).

It may sometimes be seen in active, fluttering groups feeding in our harbors.

1926. HENDERSON, A. D., Auk, 288–294, illus. (nesting).

248. The LITTLE GULL, *Larus minutus* Pallas, [60.1], an Old-World species, has been recorded twice from Maine (July, Aug.), three times from Long Island (Jan., May, Sept.), once from Staten Island, N. Y. (May), and twice from New Jersey (May, Aug.).

249. IVORY GULL. PAGOPHILA ALBA *(Gunnerus).* [39.] *Ads.*—Entire plumage pure white; bill yellow, feet black. *Im.*—Similar to ad., but wing and tail-feathers, and sometimes wing-coverts, with a black spot at their tips. L., 17·00; W., 13·25; T., 5·50; B., 1·35.

Range.—Breeds in high Arctic latitudes from Prince Patrick's Isl. and n. Baffin Land to n. Greenland, and on Arctic isls. of E. Hemisphere. Winters in the Arctic regions and casually s. to Man., Lake Ontario, and L. I.; in Europe s. casually to France.

Long Island, A. V., one record, Jan.

Nest, of grass, moss, and feathers on rocky cliffs. *Eggs,* light yellowish olive, marked with small blotches of brown and larger cloudings of lilac, 2·45 × 1·70 (Brewer). *Date,* Prince Patrick's Isl., Arctic Ocean, June 18.

"The Ivory Gulls appear to spend most of the time amid the pack-ice, often at a long distance from land" (Chamberlain).

250. ATLANTIC KITTIWAKE. RISSA TRIDACTYLA TRIDACTYLA *(Linnæus).* [40.] *Ads. in summer.*—Head, neck, tail and underparts pure white; back and wings pearl-gray; outer web of first primary and 3·00 of the ends of the first and second primaries black; third to fifth primaries black at ends and with white tips; hind toe very small, *a mere knob without a nail;* bill yellowish, *feet black. Ads. in winter.*— Similar to above, but top of head and back of neck washed with pearl-gray, and a dark spot about eye. *Im.*—Similar to winter adults, but with the *back of the neck, lesser wing-coverts, and part of the tertials black;* tail, except outer pair of feathers, with a black band at its tip; four outer primaries black, except the inner half or more of their inner webs; fifth and sixth tipped with black and white; bill black, feet yellowish. L., 16·00; W., 12·00; T., 4·50; B., 1·30.

Remarks.—This species can always be distinguished by the small size of the hind toe.

Range.—Breeds from the e. Arctic isls. w., probably, to Somerset Isl., and on the e. coast of Baffin Isl. s. to Gulf of St. Lawrence, and from the Arctic isls. of Europe and w. Siberia to n. France. Winters from the Gulf of St. Lawrence s. to N. J. and casually to Va., Fla., Bermuda, and also to the Canaries, Azores, and the Mediterranean, Black, and Caspian seas. Accidental in Mich., O., Wisc., Mo., Colo., and Wyo.

Long Island, common W. V., (Aug. 14) Nov. 4–Apr. 8. Bronx region, two records, Nov. 26 and Dec. 8. Boston, common W. V., Sept.–Apr. N. Ohio, casual.

FIG. 90. Two outer primaries of adult Kittiwake.

Nest, of grass, moss, and seaweed in colonies on the ledges of rocky cliffs. *Eggs,* 3–5, varying from shades of buffy to grayish brown, distinctly and obscurely marked with chocolate, 2·25 × 1·60. *Date,* Bird Rock, Que., May 23.

"Our bird differs but little in its habits from other oceanic Gulls. Feeding chiefly on fish, but accepting any diet that drifts within range of its keen sight; drinking salt-water in preference to fresh; breasting a gale with ease and grace—soaring in midair, skimming close above the crested waves, or swooping into the trough for a coveted morsel; resting upon the rolling billows, and sleeping serenely as they roll, with head tucked snugly under a wing; wandering in loose flocks, and making comrades of other wanderers; devoted to mate and young, and attached to all its kin—wherever seen or however employed, the Kittiwake is revealed as a typical gleaner of the sea.

"The name is derived from the bird's singular cry, which resembles the syllables *kitti-aa, kitti-aa*" (Chamberlain).

251. ROSS'S GULL. RHODOSTETHIA ROSEA (*Macgillivray*). [61.] Middle tail-feathers longest. *Ads. in summer.*—Head, neck and underparts exquisite rosy shell-pink; a black ring around the neck; back and wings pearl-gray, outer margin of outer primary black above except at tip; tail white, pink tinged. *Ads. in winter.*—Similar but without black collar and with less pink (Saunders). *Im.*—No collar, no pink tint; central tail-feathers tipped with blackish; crown and back pearl-gray; rump barred; ear-coverts dusky, region around eye streaked with dusky; below white; outer primaries blackish, white on the inner webs, increasing to nearly white inner primaries and white secondaries; tertials and coverts, blackish, white tipped. In a succeeding plumage the tail is white and the collar evident. L., 13·50; W., 10·50; T., 5·25; B., ·75.

Range.—Arctic regions, erratic and irregular. Breeds in delta of Kolyma River, ne. Siberia, and Indigirka River, from its mouth to 300 miles inland. Recorded in summer from Spitzbergen, Franz Josef Land, Bennett and Wrangle Isls., Siberia and Melville Peninsula. Migrates to Kamchatka, n. coast of Alaska, w. coast of Greenland. Casual in England, Faroe Isls., Helgoland, France, and Italy.

Nest, on the ground of dry grass and *Carices*, sometimes with a few *Betula* or *Salix* leaves, or of reindeer moss. *Eggs*, 2–3, "beautiful deep rich olive-green without any of the grayish or sandy shade, spotted, especially near the large end, with chocolate-brown, 1·65 × 1·22." *Date*, June 13. (See Buturlin, Ibis, 1906, 131–139, 333–337.)

In 1905, Ross's Gull was discovered by Buturlin breeding in numbers in the delta of the Kolyma River, northeast Siberia. His observations are given in *The Ibis* as above. (See also a review of his paper in *The Auk*, 1906, p. 348.)

252. SABINE'S GULL. XEMA SABINI (*Sabine*). [62.] *Ads. in summer.*—Whole head and throat slate-color, bordered posteriorly by black; back and sides of neck, underparts, except throat, and *slightly forked tail* pure white; back and wings dark pearl-gray; secondaries tipped with white; first primary black, inner half of inner web, except at end, white; second to fourth primaries similar, but tipped with white; bill black, end yellow. *Ads. in winter.*—"Similar to the summer plumage, but the head and neck white, except occiput, nape, and auricular region, which are dull, dusky plumbeous" (B., B., and R.). *Im.*—Forehead and lores white, rest of upperparts ashy brown, feathers slightly tipped with whitish; tail white, broadly tipped with blackish; underparts white. L., 14·00; W., 10·50; T., 4·50; B., ·95.

Range.—Breeds on the coast of Alaska from Kuskokwim River to Norton Sound, and in n. Mack., n. Keewatin, and n. Greenland, and on Arctic isls. and coasts of Europe and Asia (Taimyr Peninsula and Spitzbergen). Winters on the coast of Peru and migrates along the Pacific coasts of B. C. and Calif., the main flight apparently some miles from shore; casual on the Atlantic Coast and in the interior (Me., Mass., Ills., Mo., Kans., Mont., Sask., N. Y., O., Ia., Nebr., and Utah). Accidental in Bermuda.

Long Island, A. V., two records, July, Oct. Boston, A. V. N. Ohio, two records.

Nest, of grasses, etc., on the ground. *Eggs*, 2–3, deep olive (varying in intensity, however), rather indistinctly spotted or blotched with brown, 1·78 × 1·26 (Ridgway). *Date*, Alaska, May 28.

This boreal species is of rare occurrence in the northern United States.

Subfamily Sterninæ. Terns.

The Terns number some fifty species, distributed throughout the world, fourteen inhabiting North America. They are more southern than the Gulls, only two species nesting north of Maine, in eastern North America. They are also more migratory, none wintering on our coasts north of the Carolinas.

Terns are littoral, not pelagic, and, although characteristic of our seacoasts, like the Gulls, several species nest in the interior, the Black Tern breeding only on bodies of fresh water. Beautiful as pearls, graceful and active as Swallows, Terns are a constant delight to the eye. They capture their prey of small fish by darting toward it like a living arrow, plunging recklessly into the water, and, in some cases, swimming a few feet beneath the surface. When looking for food they usually fly with the bill pointed downward, a habit which will aid in distinguishing them from the Gulls, whose bill is carried more nearly in a line with the body.

Terns nest in colonies on islands and when disturbed are much bolder than most Gulls, hovering close overhead and swooping toward one fearlessly. The young are born covered with down, mottled in pattern like that of Gulls. This plumage is both countershaded and obliteratively marked; further proof of its protective value being furnished by the birds themselves, which, in obedience to the warning note of their parent, squat flat and become almost invisible as long as they remain motionless. Like the young of Gulls, young Terns are dependent on their parents until they acquire the power of flight. During this period, the young of some, possibly of all, species, enter the water of their own volition and swim freely, a habit in which the adult indulges only on occasion.

1912. BICKERTON, W., Home-Life of the Terns or Sea Swallows, 88 pp., illus. (Witherby & Co., London).

KEY TO THE SPECIES

I. Wing under 13·00.
  1. Entire top of the head jet-black.
    A. Bill black, or mostly black.
      a. Feet black or blackish.
        a^1. Underparts black or blackish . . . . . 265. BLACK TERN.
        a^2. Underparts white; bill black . . 253. GULL-BILLED TERN.
        a^3. Underparts white; bill black, broadly tipped with yellow.
                                          263. CABOT'S TERN.
      b. Feet yellowish or orange.
        b^1. Outer tail-feathers pure white; outer web of first primary black.
                                          258. ROSEATE TERN.

PLATE XVII

TERNS AND SKIMMERS

Common Terns   Black Skimmers.

Least Terns.

From the Habitat Group of Cobb's Island in the American Museum of Natural History

b^2. Inner web of outer tail-feather gray; outer web of first primary
  gray . . . . 255. FORSTER'S TERN.
B. Bill mostly or entirely yellowish, reddish, brownish, or orange.
  a. Underparts tinged with grayish; outer web of outer tail-feather
    gray; inner web white.
    a^1. Bill broadly tipped with blackish; tarsus generally over ·70.
        256. COMMON TERN.
    a^2. Bill without a distinct black tip; tarsus generally under ·70.
        257. ARCTIC TERN.
  b. Underparts pure white; inner web of outer tail-feather gray;
    outer web white . . . . 255. FORSTER'S TERN.
2. Entire top of head not jet-black.
  A. Forehead white; lores black; crown jet-black or silvery.
    a. Wing under 8·00; back pearl-gray . . . . 261. LEAST TERN.
    b. Wing over 8·00; back grayish brown or blackish.
      b^1. Back grayish brown; a white stripe from the forehead to behind
        the eye . . . . 260. BRIDLED TERN.
      b^2. Back blackish; white of forehead not reaching to behind the
        eye . . . . 259. SOOTY TERN.
      b^3. Crown silvery, rest of plumage sooty . . . . . 267. NODDY.
  B. Forehead or crown white or grayish, sometimes speckled with black;
    lores not entirely black.
    a. Wing pearl-gray.
      a^1. Outer tail-feather entirely pure white.
        a^2. Bill over 1·75, tipped with yellowish . 263. CABOT'S TERN.
        a^3 Bill under 1·75, without a yellow tip.
            258. ROSEATE TERN, im.
      b^1. Outer tail-feather not pure white.
        b^2. Inner web of outer tail-feather darker than outer web; outer
          web mostly or entirely white; a black space generally on
          the side of the head inclosing the eye.
              255. FORSTER'S TERN, im.
        b^3. Outer web of outer tail-feather darker than inner web;
          tarsus over ·70 . . . . . 256. COMMON TERN, im.
        b^4. Outer web of outer tail-feather darker than inner web; tarsus
          under ·70 . . . . 257. ARCTIC TERN, im.
        b^5. Tail wholly gray, not deeply forked, wing under 9·00; belly
          white or mottled with black . . 265. BLACK TERN, im.
    b. Wing blackish.
      b^1. Underparts blackish . . . . 259. SOOTY TERN, im.
      b^2. Underparts white . . . . 260. BRIDLED TERN, im.
II. Wing over 13·00.
  A. Wing 15·00 or over; outer primary mostly gray. 264. CASPIAN TERN.
  B. Wing under 15·00; inner half of inner web of first primary white.
        262. ROYAL TERN.

253. GULL-BILLED TERN. GELOCHELIDON NILOTICA ARANEA *Wilson.*
[63.] *Ads. in summer.*—Top of head and nape black; back and wings pale
pearl-gray; outer web of outer primaries silvery; tip and shaft part of inner
web darker; inner part of inner web, except for a narrow margin at end of
feather, white; tail white, slightly forked, the middle feathers grayish; underparts white; bill and feet black, the former rather short and stout. *Ads. in
winter.*—Similar to the above, but top of the head white, auriculars grayish,
and a space in front of the eye blackish. L., 14·50; W., 12·00; T., 5·50;
B., 1·40; depth of B. at base, ·50.
  Range.—Breeds on the Atlantic and Gulf coasts from Va. (formerly N. J.),
to Ga. and Tex., and in the Bahamas, Cuba, and at the mouth of the Amazon;
a large breeding colony recently established on Salton Sea, s. Calif. Casual
on the Fla. coast and n. to Me., N. B., O., and Ills. Winters from Tex. (La.),
to w. Panama and from Brazil to Patagonia and Chile.

Washington, casual in autumn, no recent records. Long Island, A. V., July.

Nest, of shells and pebbles, on beaches. *Eggs*, 3–5, rather uniform buffy white, with numerous distinct and obscure chocolate markings, 1·80 × 1·30. *Date*, Corpus Christi, Tex., Apr. 30; Cobb's Isl., Va., May 30.

The Gull-billed Tern has greatly decreased in numbers during recent years, and it now breeds only locally and in small numbers from Cobb's Island, Va., southward. It is a less excitable bird than the Common Tern, from which and its near allies it may be known by

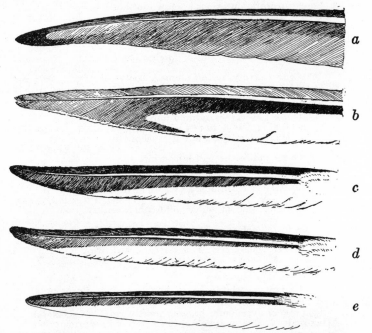

FIG. 91. First primaries of adult Terns, seen from below: (*a*) Caspian Tern; (*b*) Royal Tern; (*c*) Common Tern; (*d*) Arctic Tern; (*e*) Roseate Tern.

its short, comparatively heavy, black bill and short, less-forked tail. Its notes are a high, reedy *tee-tee-tee*, sometimes suggesting those of a weak-voiced katydid. It is said to feed only on insects.

254. TRUDEAU'S TERN, *Sterna trudeaui* Audubon, [68], a species of southern South America, has been taken once at Egg Harbor, N. J.

255. **FORSTER'S TERN.** STERNA FORSTERI *Nuttall.* [69.] *Ads. in summer.*—Whole top of head black; back and wings pearl-gray; inner border of inner web of outer primaries white, except at the tip; rump and *entire underparts white;* tail light pearl-gray, the outer feather darker toward the end, where *the inner web is always darker* than the outer; bill dull orange, the end

third blackish; feet orange. *Ads. in winter.*—Similar to the above, but head white, more c. less washed with grayish or spotted with black, a large black spot on the side of the head inclosing the eye; bill mostly black; feet brownish. *Im.*—Similar to the preceding, but the back and wings more or less mottled or washed with light brownish, and the tail much shorter. L., 15·00; W., 10·25; T., 7·00; Tar., ·90; B., 1·50.

Range.—Breeds interiorly in Calif. s. Ore., Utah, and Nev., and from Man. s. to n. Colo., n. Nebr., Minn., ne. Ills., and on coasts of Tex., La., and Va. Winters from cent. Calif., Gulf of Mex., and S. C. to s. Guat.; in migration occurs as far n. as Mass.

Washington, casual T. V. Long Island, irregular T. V. in fall (July 16) July 31–Oct. 16 (Dec. 26). Bronx region, rare S. V. or fall T. V.; Aug. 17–Sept. 23 (Oct. 14). N. Ohio, casual T. V. Glen Ellyn, rare T. V., May 18. SE. Minn., uncommon T. V., Apr. 25–May 17; Aug. 13–Oct. 1.

Nest, of seaweed, flags, or weeds on a slight elevation in grassy marshes. *Eggs*, 3, very variable, olive-gray, or olive brownish ashy, more rarely whitish or buff, heavily marked with chocolate, 1·80 × 1·30. *Date*, Corpus Christi, Tex., Apr. 29; Cobb's Isl., Va., June 1; Swan Lake, Minn., June 13.

Forster's Tern, although so like the Common Tern in appearance, differs materially from it in habits. It is not dependent on sandy beaches for a nest-site, but is a marsh inhabitant, laying on a platform nest in the grasses. I have never found it in large colonies, but in scattered pairs. Its notes are a long-drawn, reedy cackle and a *tweet-tweet-tweet-tweet.*

256. COMMON TERN. STERNA HIRUNDO HIRUNDO *Linnæus.* [70.] (Figs. 43, 91c; Pl. XVII.) *Ads. in summer.*—Whole top of head black; back and wings pearl-gray; inner border of inner web of outer primaries white, except at tip; throat white; *breast and belly pale pearl-gray;* tail white, the *outer* webs of the outer feathers gray or pearl-gray; bill red at the base, the end third *black;* feet orange-red. *Ads. in winter.*—Similar, but front part of head and underparts white; bill mostly black. *Im.*—Similar, but back more or less washed or mottled with light brownish; lesser wing-coverts slaty gray, and tail much shorter. L., 15·00; W., 10·25; T., 5·50; Tar., ·75; B., 1·40.

Range.—Breeds from Great Slave Lake, n. Man., cent. Ont. s. to n. N. Dak., s. Wisc., n. O., nw. Pa. and N. C. Breeds in the Bahamas, Venezuela, the Fla. Keys, Dutch W. I., and the Gulf Coast, Ala., La., and Tex., also in Europe, Asia, and n. Africa, Azores, Canaries, and Madeira. Winters from Fla. to the Straits of Magellan, also in s. Asia and Africa; in migration on Pacific Coast from B. C. to s. L. Calif.

Washington, irregular T. V., Apr.; May; Oct.–Dec.; sometimes common. Long Island, common T. V., local S. R. (Apr. 15) May 1–Nov. 11 (Nov. 26). Bronx region, fairly common T. V., chiefly fall; May 7–June 10; July 9–Oct. 30. Boston, abundant T. V., May–June; July–Nov. N. Ohio, S. R. in large colonies on islands in Lake Erie. May 5–Sept. 10. Glen Ellyn, irregular, uncommon T. V.; May 15–24; Sept. 9. SE. Minn., common T. V., Apr. 29–June 1; Sept. 28–?.

Remarks.—The Common Tern is closely related to Forster's Tern and also to the Arctic Tern. From the former it is to be distinguished by the color of the long outer tail-feathers. In the Common Tern the outer web of these feathers is always darker than the inner web; in Forster's Tern the inner web is always darker than the outer one. Adult Common Terns have the breast and belly washed with *pearl-gray*, while in Forster's Tern these parts are pure *white.*

The Common Tern differs from the Arctic Tern in having the bill tipped with black instead of being entirely red; in having longer tarsi, and in the color of the primaries.

Nest, a slight depression in the sand, scantily lined with seaweed or grasses. *Eggs*, 3–4, not distinguishable with certainty from those of the preceding, but averaging paler and greener, and less heavily marked, 1·60 × 1·20 (Pl. III). *Date*, Cobb's Isl., Va., May 28; Muskeget Isl., Mass., May 28; Mille Lacs, Minn., June 22.

It is many years since I visited my first breeding colony of Common Terns (on Gull Island, L. I.), but I can close my eyes and still feel the air vibrate with the harsh, half-threatening, half-pleading chorus of nearly two thousand excited voices. There is a dull, heavy, hopeless monotone, broken only by the scream of some half-maddened bird who fearlessly darts downward to protect its nest at my feet. A shot is fired; there is a moment of awe-struck silence, then, with renewed violence, the screaming is resumed. Pandemonium reigns: *tearr, tearrr, swish!* the air is full of darting, diving, crying Terns. It was useless to attempt to secrete myself. At no time during my stay did the outcry cease or hovering flock disperse.

It was only after I had exchanged a gun for a camera that I learned how quickly Terns will go back to their nest if one will conceal oneself in a blind, which in itself may be conspicuous enough, if it be motionless. Then one learns that the *tearrr* note of alarm and protest gives way to a great variety of calls incident to the activities of the birds when not disturbed; for example, a sharp *chirp* not unlike that of a White-throated Sparrow, and a *tue, tue, tue*, uttered by a bird in pursuit of another. The young are fed on fish which they take from the bill of the parent. They promptly and instinctively squat at the parent's warning-note and remain motionless until touched. They enter the water of their own volition and swim freely, while the parents stand on the shore and watch them, webbed feet apparently being more functional in the young than in the adult.

Thanks to the movement for the protection of our birds, Terns, which thirty years ago seemed to be doomed to extinction, are now abundant and our shores are again enlivened by these beautiful, graceful creatures.

1879. BREWSTER, WM., Bull. Nutt. Orn. Club., 13–22 (habits).—1895–99. MACKAY, G. H., Auk, 32–48, 178; 21, 22, 278–284, 383–390; 168–172; 259–266 (on Muskeget and Penikese Isls., Mass.).—1900. CHAPMAN, F. M., Bird Studies with a Camera, 106–127.—1902. JONES, L., Wilson Bull., 94–100; 1906, 35–47 (on Weepeckets).—1927. LINCOLN, F. C., Bull. Northeastern Bird-Banding Assoc., 23–28, map (migration of young).—1928. FLOYD, C. B., Bull. Northeastern Bird-Banding Assoc., 125–132; 1929, 43–46; map, 144–148 (banding).—1929. AUSTIN, O. L., JR. Contribution to Our Knowledge of the Cape Cod Sterninæ, Bull. Northeastern Bird-Banding Assoc., 123–140.

257. ARCTIC TERN. STERNA PARADISÆA *Brünnich*. [71.] Very similar in color to the Common Tern, from which it differs in having less gray on the shaft part of the inner web of the outer primaries (Fig. 91*d*); in having the tail somewhat longer, the tarsi and bill shorter, while the latter, in the adult, is generally without a black tip. L., 15·50; W., 10·25; T., 7·50; Tar., ·65; B., 1·30.

Range.—Breeds from n. Alaska and n. Greenland, s. to Commander and Aleutian Isls., se. Alaska, n. B. C., Lower Slave River, n. Man., Me., and Mass., and in entire Arctic regions of Europe and Asia. Winters in the Antarctic Ocean, s. to lat. 74°; in migration, Pacific Coast s. to s. Calif., and Atlantic Coast s. to L. I. and coasts of Brazil, Peru, Chile, s. Africa. Accidental in interior of the U. S. and in Hawaii.

Long Island, rare or casual in summer. Boston, not uncommon T. V.

Nest, as in the preceding. *Eggs,* 3–4, not distinguishable with certainty from those of the preceding, 1·62 × 1·15. *Date,* Seal Isl., Me., June 17, 1875.

Comparing the notes of this bird with those of the Common Tern, Mr. Brewster writes: "Their notes are similar, but several of them can be distinguished. The usual cry of *S. macrura* [= *paradisæa*] corresponds to the *tearr* of *S. hirundo,* but is shriller, ending in a rising inflection, and sounding very like the squeal of a pig. The bird also has a short, harsh note similar to that of Forster's Tern. At any distance within fair gun-range I could usually separate it from Wilson's [= Common] Tern by its longer tail, and by the uniform and deeper color of the bill. In flight and habits the two seemed to me identical" (*Proc. Bost. Soc. Nat. Hist.,* 1883, p. 402).

1928. AUSTIN, O. L., JR., Bull. Northeastern Bird-Banding Assoc., 121–124 (migration routes).

258. ROSEATE TERN. STERNA DOUGALLI DOUGALLI *Montagu.* [72.] *Ads. in summer.*—Top of head black; back and wings pearl-gray; outer web of outer primaries and shaft part of the inner web slaty black (Fig. 91*e*); underparts white, generally delicately tinted with pinkish; tail *pure white;* bill black, the base reddish; feet red. *Ads. in winter.*—Similar to the above, but front of the head white, more or less streaked or spotted with black; underparts pure white. *Im., first plumage.*—"Pileum and nape pale buffy grayish finely mottled or sprinkled with darker, and streaked, especially on the crown, with dusky; orbital and auricular regions dusky blackish; remainder of the head, extreme lower part of the nape, and entire lowerparts white, the nape and sometimes the breast finely mottled with buffy gray; back, scapulars, wing-coverts, rump, upper tail-coverts, and tail pale pearl-blue, the back and scapulars overlaid with pale buff irregularly mottled with dusky, each feather with a submarginal dusky V-shaped mark; primary coverts and primaries dark bluish gray edged with paler, the inner webs of the latter broadly edged with white; tail-feathers, marked near their ends much like the longer scapulars, their outer webs rather dark grayish; bill brownish dusky; feet dusky." L., 15·50; W , 9·50; T., 7·50; B., 1·50 (B., B., and R.).

Range.—Breeds locally from Sable Isl., N. S., to Va.; in Bermuda, the Bahamas, Lesser Antilles and Dry Tortugas to Venezuela and British Honduras; also in Europe from 57° N. to the Mediterranean Sea, and the coasts of Africa, Ceylon and s. China. Winters from La. (occasionally) and the Bahamas to Brazil and Chile. Accidental in O., Ind., and w. N. Y.

Long Island, uncommon T. V. and local S. R.; May 20–Sept. 15. Bronx region, one record, Aug. 24. Boston, common T. V., July–Sept. N. Ohio, casual T. V.

Nest, as in Common Tern. *Eggs,* 3, not distinguishable with certainty from those of *S. forsteri* or *S. hirundo,* but averaging paler and less heavily marked, 1·65 × 1·20. *Date,* Cobb's Isl., Va., May 13, 1871; Muskeget Isl., Mass., June 7.

This species is found associated with colonies of Common Terns, often making its nest among theirs. It is a less excitable bird than *hirundo*, and its harsh *cack* may be distinctly heard above the uproar of Common Terns, as it hovers somewhat in the background. Its white breast and long outer tail-feathers also aid in distinguishing it.

259. SOOTY TERN. STERNA FUSCATA FUSCATA *Linnæus.* [75.] *Ads.*— Forehead and a line reaching to the eye white, lores and rest of the head black; nape, back, and wings nearly as dark as the head; outer tail-feathers white, brownish on the end half of the inner web; rest of tail-feathers of the same color as the back; underparts white; bill and feet black. *Im., first plumage.*—Sooty slate-color; linings of the wings and under tail-coverts whitish; wing-coverts, scapulars, upper tail-coverts, and tail-feathers more or less tipped with white. L., 17·00; W., 11·50; T., 7·25; B., 1·75.

Range.—Breeds in America from Fla. Keys (Dry Tortugas) and Bahamas to Venezuela and w. to British Honduras, formerly to Tex.; wanders n. rarely to N. S. Winters from La. to the Falkland Isls. Casual in Bermuda.

Long Island, casual after hurricanes in the S.; Sept. 13–23.

Nest, a slight hollow in the sand. *Egg,* 1, whitish or buff, speckled or spotted with chocolate, 2·00 × 1·45. *Date,* Tortugas, Fla., May 7.

So far as I am aware the Sooty Tern breeds in the Atlantic States only in the Dry Tortugas of Florida, where about 19,000 nested when Watson made his important studies of their habits in 1907. They reach the island the last week in April and remain until about September 1. The period of incubation is twenty-six days. The warning note is a shrill *e-e-e-e;* they also utter a squeaky *quack* and a nasal *ker-wacky-wak,* and other calls, being very noisy birds.

Flocks of Terns seen darting actively and repeatedly into schools of small fish in West Indian waters are very apt to be of this species.

1903. THOMPSON, J., Bird-Lore, V, 77–84.—1905. JOB, H. K., Wild Wings, 83–99.—1908. WATSON, J. B., Tortugas Lab. of Carnegie Inst., 189–255.—1908. CHAPMAN, F. M., Camps and Cruises, 192–199.

260. The BRIDLED TERN, *Sterna anæthetus melanoptera* Swainson, [76], breeds in the Bahamas and West Indies. It is recorded as accidental in Florida, Georgia, and South Carolina, but may prove to be of more or less regular occurrence in southern Florida. It resembles the Sooty Tern but is smaller (W. 10·50), has the back dark gray instead of black, and the white line from the forehead reaches to *behind* the eye.

261. LEAST TERN. STERNA ANTILLARUM ANTILLARUM *(Lesson).* [74.] (Pl. XVII.) *Ads. in summer.*—Forehead white, *lores* and crown black; back, tail and wings pearl-gray; outer web of outer primaries and shaft part of inner web slaty black; underparts white; bill yellow, generally tipped with black; feet orange. *Ads. in winter.*—Top of head white, more or less spotted with black; back of head black; bill blackish. *Im.*—Upperparts and tail at end mottled with blackish and buffy, primaries as in adult, underparts white, bill blackish. L., 9·00; W., 6·90; T., 3·50; B., 1·10.

Range.—Breeds on the Atlantic and Gulf coasts from Mass. to the Fla. Keys and Tex. and on isls. in the Miss. and Mo. rivers, formerly, at least, to S. Dak. and Ia. and w. to sw. Kans. and n. Nebr., also in the Bahamas and W. I. to the coasts of Venezuela and British Honduras. Winters from the coast of La. to Argentina and the e. coast of Africa. Casual in Minn., Ont. and N. S.

Washington, casual T. V. Long Island, tolerably common local S. R., May 18–Sept. 27. Bronx region, occasional in summer, July 31 and Aug. 28. Boston, rare S. V. N. Ohio, casual.

Nest, a slight depression in the sand. *Eggs,* 3–4, buffy white, speckled or spotted with chocolate, 1·25 × ·90. *Date*, Matanzas Inlet, Fla., May 18, 1894; Cobb's Isl., Va., May 28, 1886.

The Least Tern was brought so near the verge of extinction by milliners' collectors that in spite of protection it has never recovered from the attack. Small size is always a good character in identifying this species, and in breeding plumage its white forehead and largely yellow bill are distinctive. Its call, as described by Job, is "a shrill, staccato *yip, yip, yip*."

262. ROYAL TERN. THALASSEUS MAXIMUS MAXIMUS (*Boddaert*). [65.] Tail more deeply forked than in the Caspian Tern. *Ads. in spring.*—Top and back of head shining black, feathers lengthened to form a crest; back of neck, underparts, and tail white; back and wings pearl-gray; inner web of primaries. except at tip, white; outer web, and shaft part of inner web dark, silvery slate-color (Fig. 91*b*). *Ads. after the breeding season and in winter.*—Similar but top of head streaked with black and white. *Im.*—Resembling young of *H. caspia*, but smaller and with the inner half of the inner web of the primaries white. L., 19·00; W., 14·00; T., 7·00; B., 2·50.

Range.—Breeds in the Bahamas, W. I., and on s. Atlantic and Gulf coasts from Va. to Tex.; and the Pacific Coast of L. Calif. and Mex.; wanders casually to Mass.; not rare in summer from San Francisco Bay s. to w. Mex. Winters from Fla., La., the Bahamas and Calif., s. to Argentina.

Long Island, one record, Aug. 27.

Eggs, 2–4, more pointed than those of *H. c. imperator*, grayish white, with rather small, distinct, and obscure chocolate markings, 2·65 × 1·75. *Date*, Corpus Christi, Tex., Apr. 8, 1885; near Charleston, S. C., May 15.

A common species on our southern coasts. During the winter it is about the only Tern one sees in Florida waters. It is a strong, active bird on the wing, and a reckless, dashing diver, frequently disappearing beneath the surface in catching its prey. The slow-flying Pelicans are at its mercy, and it sometimes deftly robs them of their food.

263. CABOT'S TERN. THALASSEUS SANDVICENSIS ACUFLAVIDA (*Cabot*). [67.] *Ads. in spring.*—Whole top of head and crest black; back and wings light pearl-gray; primaries silvery gray; the shaft part of the inner web white except at the tip; rest of the plumage white; feet and bill black, the latter with a *conspicuous yellowish tip*. *Ads. after breeding season and in winter.*—Similar, but crown white, sometimes spotted with black; back of head and crest more or less streaked with white. *Im.*—Similar, but back spotted with blackish; tail slaty gray and much shorter; bill slightly if at all tipped with yellow. L., 16·00; W., 10·50; T., 5·50; B., 2·05.

Range.—Breeds on the Atlantic and Gulf coasts from Va. and N. C. to Fla., Tex., British Honduras, the Bahamas and W. I. Winters from Fla., the Bahamas, and W. I. to Colombia and Brazil and on the Pacific coasts of Oaxaca and Guat. Accidental in Ont., Mass., and N. J.

Eggs, 2–3, buffy white, spotted, speckled, and scrawled with distinct and obscure chocolate markings, 2·05 × 1·40. *Date*, Tampa, Fla., Apr. 10; coast of S. C., second week in June.

Cabot's Tern was formerly abundant along the coasts of Florida, but it now breeds only locally. There is a small breeding colony in Pamlico Sound, North Carolina (Pearson), and in Bull's Bay, South Carolina (Wayne). The bird winters from the Florida Keys southward. Its black, yellow-tipped bill is a good field-mark.

264. AMERICAN CASPIAN TERN. HYDROPROGNE CASPIA IMPERATOR *(Coues).* [64.] (Fig. 91a.) *Ads. in spring.*—Top and back of head shining black, the feathers lengthened to form a crest; back of neck, underparts, and tail white; back and wings pearl-gray; primaries dark slaty, silvery on the outer web; bill coral-red, darker near tip; feet black. *Ads. after the breeding season and in winter.*—Similar to the above, but top of the head streaked with black. *Im.*—Top of head streaked with black and white; back of neck and underparts white; back, wing-coverts, and tertials pearl-gray, spotted or barred with brownish black; primaries dark slaty, silvery on the outer web; tail pearl-gray, more or less barred with brownish black; bill orange-red; feet blackish brown. L., 21·00; W., 16·20; T., 6·00; B., 2·80.

Range.—Breeds at Great Slave Lake, Lake Winnipeg, Lake Winnepegosis, Klamath Lake, Ore., Sutler Basin, Calif., on isls. in lakes Michigan, Huron, and Ontario; on the coast of se. Que. and also on the coasts of Tex., La., Miss., S. C., and Va. Winters from the coast of cent. Calif. to L. Calif. and w. Mex. (Colima), and on the Atlantic and Gulf coasts from S. C. to Mex. Casual in migration n. to Wash., mouth of the Mack. River and N. F.

Washington, casual, Apr.–June; Sept., Oct. Long Island, uncommon T. V., rare in spring, Apr. 29–May 30 (July 21); Aug. 10–Oct. 5. Bronx region, two records, Aug. 24, June 3. Boston, T. V., rare in spring; not uncommon in fall. N. Ohio, tolerably common T. V. SE. Minn., uncommon T. V., May 12–June 7; Sept. 18–Oct. 15.

Eggs, 2–3, grayish white or buffy white, with rather small, distinct, and obscure chocolate markings, 2·70 × 1·83. *Date,* Corpus Christi, Tex., Apr. 8, 1885; Gravel Isl., Wisc., June 10.

The singularly interrupted distribution of this, the largest of our Terns, indicates that it was once a far more abundant bird. It resembles the smaller red-billed Terns in general habits, but its large size prevents it from being confused with any other species except the Royal Tern. From Gulls it may be known by its red, pointed bill and forked tail.

265. BLACK TERN. CHLIDONIAS NIGRA SURINAMENSIS *(Gmelin).* [77.] *Ads. in summer.*—Whole head and underparts, except under tail-coverts, black; back, wings, and tail slate-color; bill and feet black. *Ads. in winter.*— Forehead, nape, and underparts white; back of the head black mixed with white; back, wings, and tail deep pearl-gray. *Im.*—Similar to the preceding, but upperparts more or less washed and tipped with brownish; sides washed with grayish. L., 10·00; W., 8·30; T., 3·30; B., 1·00.

Range.—Breeds in interior N. A. from cent. e. Alaska, s. to inland lakes of Calif., Nev., Colo., Kans., n. Mo., and Tenn.; also on lake-shores of n. O., nw. Pa. and w. N. Y. Winters from Surinam to Chile; migrating n. through interior, along the e. coast of the U. S. in autumn but rarely in spring. Accidental in Prince Edward Isl., Magdalens, N. S., and N. B.; casual in Bermuda, the W. I. and the Bahamas.

Washington, irregular T. V., May 3–July 22; Aug. 11–Sept. 22. Long Island, T. V., rare in spring, irregularly common in fall, May 16–June 27; July 12–Oct. 16 (Oct. 27). Bronx region, uncommon fall T. V., July 31–Oct. 15. Boston, T. V., rare in spring, not uncommon in fall; May–June; July–Sept. N. Ohio, common S. R. Glen Ellyn, occasional T. V., May 13–18; Aug. 23–Sept. 5. SE. Minn., common S. R., May 1–Sept. 2.

Nest, of reeds, grasses, etc., an islet in marsh or slough. *Eggs,* 2–3, grayish olive-brown, rarely whitish, heavily spotted and blotched with chocolate markings, frequently confluent about the larger end, 1·35 × ·98. *Date,* Dodge Co., Wisc., May 28; se. Minn., May 26.

To one who associates all Terns with sandy beaches, it is a novel experience, when driving over the prairies, to be surrounded by an active flock of these birds, darting eagerly here and there in pursuit of the insects flushed by one's team from the grass. When on their nesting-grounds in the interior, Black Terns, indeed, appear to feed largely on insects, but when migrating southward along our coasts in late summer and autumn, in habits, and doubtless in food also, they more nearly resemble the coast-breeding members of their family.

It is difficult to recognize in the silent bird of this season the excitable, noisy Tern of June, which with its frequently repeated, sharp *peek* protests loudly against trespass on its haunts whether or not it has a nest there.

H. K. Job found "scores and scores" of Black Terns in full breeding plumage on an island at the mouth of Chesapeake Bay in late June, but there appears to be no record of their breeding on the Atlantic Coast, where they are rarely seen before the fall migration.

1908. CHAPMAN, F. M., Camps and Cruises, 324–329 (nesting).

266. The WHITE-WINGED BLACK TERN, *Chlidonias leucoptera* (Temminck), [78], an Old-World species, has been taken at Lake Koshkonong, Wisc., July 5, 1873 (Kumlien and Hollister, Bull., Wisc. Nat. Soc., III, 14), and in the Barbados.

267. NODDY. ANOUS STOLIDUS STOLIDUS (*Linnæus*). [79.] *Ads.*—Top of head silvery whitish, lores black; rest of plumage dark sooty brown; tail rounded, the *central* tail-feathers longest. *Im.*—Similar, but top of head like rest of plumage, silvery whitish appears as a line from bill to above eye. L., 15·00; W., 10·25; T., 5·90; B., 1·70.

Range.—Breeds in Fla. Keys (Dry Tortugas), the Bahamas, and W. I., and from British Honduras to Margarita Isl., Venezuela, and on St. Helena, Tristan da Cunha and Ascension Isls. Casual in Bermuda and e. Fla.

Nest, of sticks, grasses, etc., on a bush, or low tree, sometimes on the ground or in crevices of rocks. *Egg*, 1, pale buffy white, sparingly marked with rufous, 2·05 × 1·35. *Date*, Tortugas, Fla., May 4.

In our Atlantic States the Noddy is known to nest only on Bird Key in the Tortugas of Florida, where, in 1907, Watson found about seven hundred pairs.

According to this author, whose exceptionally important paper on the habits of the Noddy and Sooty Terns should be read by everyone interested in bird psychology, it arrives late in April and remains until September. The period of incubation is from thirty-two to thirty-five days, and the young, according to Thompson, are dependent upon their parents "until they are over three months old."

The Noddy's exceptional tameness is apparently temperamental rather than the result of ignorance of man, since the Sooty and Bridled Terns, with which it often breeds, are far more shy.

As the only Tern with a rounded tail, the Noddy, as might be expected, differs widely in flight from other members of its subfamily. In the air it suggests a light-bodied Pigeon with long wings and tail. It flies rapidly and does not hover over its nesting-ground, as do the Sooty, Common, and other fork-tailed Terns. Its note is a low, reedy *cack*, at times increased to a rolling guttural *k-r-r-r-r*.

References to papers on the habits of this species will be found under the Sooty Tern.

FAMILY RYNCHOPIDÆ. SKIMMERS.

The five closely allied species constituting this small but distinct group are found in the warmer parts of the earth. Three species inhabit the Western Hemisphere, of which one reaches North America. Skimmers nest in colonies on beaches. The black adults are conspicuous when incubating and correspondingly wary; but the sand-colored down of the young is obviously intended to picture their background, and, like young Terns and Gulls, they squat close and are then exceedingly difficult to discover. Skimmers are unique both in the form of the bill and in their manner of feeding. Opening the mouth, the bladelike lower mandible is dropped just beneath the surface of the water; then, flying rapidly, they may be said literally to "plow the main" in search of their food of small aquatic animals.

268. BLACK SKIMMER. RYNCHOPS NIGRA NIGRA *Linnæus.* [80.] (Fig. 45; Pls. IX, XVII.) *Ads.*—Forehead, sides of the head, underparts and tips of the secondaries white; upperparts and wings black; outer tail-feathers white, inner ones more or less brownish; base of bill red, end black. L., 18·00; W., 14·50; T., 4·75; B., 2·60.

Range.—Breeds from N. J. and Mass. (formerly) to Fla., the Gulf Coast and Tex.; wanders casually n. to Bay of Fundy and Lake Ontario. Winters from the Gulf Coast to n. and e. coasts of S. A. Casual in the W. I.; accidental inland, in N. Y., S. C., Tenn. and in Bermuda.

Washington, A. V., Sept., 1858. Long Island, casual, May 22–25; July 22–Sept. 18 (Oct. 16). Bronx region, A. V.; two records, July 17, Sept. 14. Boston, A. V., late summer.

Nest, a slight hollow in the sand or shells of a beach. *Eggs*, 3–5, white or buffy white, heavily blotched with chocolate, 1·80 × 1·35. *Date*, Nueces Co., Tex., May 15; Cobb's Isl., Va., June 6.

The Black Skimmer breeds in colonies from New Jersey southward. They make their nest-hollow by squatting on the sand and turning slowly around, boring with their bodies. They are exceedingly noisy when one invades their haunts, and calling loudly, charge one repeatedly. They are evidently more or less nocturnal, and while feeding at this time utter their sharp *yap, yap*, like a pack of hounds on the trail.

1905. JOB, H. K., Wild Wings, 120.—1908. CHAPMAN, F. M., Camps and Cruises, 64–75 (nesting in Va.).—1921. ARTHUR, S. C., Auk, 566–574, illus.; also STONE, W., *Ibid.*, 595 (feeding habits).—1931. GILLESPIE, J. A., Bird-Banding, 52–58 (study by banding).

SUBORDER ALCÆ. AUKS, MURRES, PUFFINS
(1 family)

FAMILY ALCIDÆ. AUKS, MURRES, PUFFINS.

Twenty of the twenty-three species contained in this family are North American, and all are confined to the northern parts of the Northern Hemisphere. Only six species are found in the north Atlantic,

PLATE XVIII

GANNET (flying over), MURRES, PUFFINS, AND RAZOR-BILLED AUKS
From a photograph made on Bird Rock, Gulf of St. Lawrence, July 24, 1898.

where none nests south of Maine. They are, without exception, maritime birds, visiting our bays and harbors at certain seasons, but passing much of their lives on the open sea. They nest in communities, often in vast numbers, on islets or rocky shore-fronts difficult of access. Puffins stand on the toes and run about freely, but the other species rest on the whole foot and tail, and their progress is more awkward. Unlike the Grebes and Loons, they use their wings rather than their feet when swimming under water. In the air their flight is direct and rapid, suggesting, in some instances, that of a Duck, but the shorter neck should prevent confusion here. The young are born covered with down but spend some time in or near the nesting-place.

The *Alcidæ* feed on fish, crustacea, sand-eels, and other forms of sea-life.

1900. CHAPMAN, F. M., Bird Studies with a Camera, 152–190 (Appleton).—1902. JOB, H. K., Among the Water-Fowl, 50–96 (Doubleday).—1905. Wild Wings, 153–170 (Houghton, Mifflin & Co.).

KEY TO THE SPECIES

I. Bill under ·75 . . . . 273. DOVEKIE.
II. Bill over ·75.
  1. Depth of bill at nostril over ·60
    A. Bill yellowish, depth at nostril over 1·00.
               276. PUFFIN. 276a. LARGE-BILLED PUFFIN.
    B. Bill black, depth at nostril under 1·00 . 270. RAZOR-BILLED AUK.
  2. Depth of bill at nostril under ·60.
    A. Wing-coverts white or tipped with white.
      a. Greater wing-coverts entirely white. 274a. MANDT'S GUILLEMOT.
      b. Basal half of greater wing-coverts black . 274. BLACK GUILLEMOT.
    B. No white on wing-coverts.
      a. Bill over 1·60 . . . . 271. ATLANTIC MURRE.
      b. Bill under 1·60 . . . . 272. BRÜNNICH'S MURRE.

269. GREAT AUK. PLAUTUS IMPENNIS (*Linnæus*). [33.] Upperparts fuscous-black, a large white spot before the eye; secondaries tipped with white; sides of the neck and throat seal-brown, rest of the underparts silvery white. L., 28·00–30·00; W., 5·75; B., 3·15–3·50; greatest depth of B., 1·50 (Ridgway).
Range.—Now extinct. Former known breeding-places, Funk Isl., N. F., the Faroes and isls. off the sw. coast of Iceland and probably on the coast of Sweden. In winter s. to Me. and Mass., casually to S. C. and Fla., also to Norway, Denmark, France, n. Spain and the Mediterranean.
Egg, 1, pyriform-ovate, pale olive buffy, variously marked with brown and black, 4·67 × 2·91 (Ridgway).

The Great Auk was flightless. Like other birds of this family, it frequented certain localities in large numbers each year to breed. Early voyagers and fishermen visited its nesting-grounds, killing the helpless birds in enormous numbers for their flesh, feathers, and oil. The result was extinction, and no Great Auk has been taken since 1844 (Elderry Island, Iceland). About seventy specimens are known to be preserved in collections.

In 1902, two humeri of the Great Auk, both from the left side, were found in a shell-mound at Ormond, Fla. (Hay, *The Auk*, XIX, p. 255), where their discovery gives new meaning to Catesby's statements that the "Penguin" was a winter visitant to South Carolina.

1888. Lucas, F. A., Auk, V, 278–283.—1887–8. Rep. U. S. Nat. Mus., 493–529.—1891. *Ibid.*, 709–728 (history).—1893. Newton, A., Dictionary of Birds (history, bibliography).

270. RAZOR-BILLED AUK. Alca torda *Linnæus.* [32.] (Fig. 46d; Pl. XVIII.) *Ads. in summer.*—Upperparts, wings and tail sooty black; foreneck somewhat browner; tips of secondaries, a line from eye to bill, breast, and belly white; bill black, crossed by a white band. *Ads. in winter.*—Similar, but with sides and front of neck white. *Im.*—Similar to ad. in winter, but with bill smaller and without white bar. L., 16·50; W., 7·90; Tar., 1·35; B., 1·25.

Range.—Breeds from s. Greenland to N. F. and N. B.: formerly to Me.; and from Iceland to the British Isles e. to Norway and Lapland. Winters from s. Lab. to L. I. and casually s. to N. C.

Long Island, rare W. V., Nov. 2–Mch. 14 (May 18). Bronx region, one record, Dec. 11. Boston, not uncommon W. V., Nov.–Apr.

Nest, in the crevices and fissures of cliffs and rocky places. *Eggs*, 1–2, pale bluish white or buffy, thickly spotted and speckled with chocolate markings most numerous and sometimes confluent at the larger end, 3·00 × 1·90. *Date*, Bird Rock, Que., May 24.

"When brooding, it crouches along, not across, the egg, its mate often standing near; and both sexes incubate, though the male may be seen bringing food to the sitting female. ... The young flutter from the rocks to the sea, or are

Fig. 92. Great Auk. Note the short wings of a flightless bird. (Much reduced.)

taken by the neck and carried down by the parents. They are at first very loath to follow the old bird in diving, and remain crying plaintively on the surface of the water. The Razor-bill utters a peculiar grunting or groaning, especially when sitting. On the water it may be distinguished from the Guillemot, [= Murre] at a distance, by its upturned tail" (Saunders).

271. ATLANTIC MURRE. Uria aalge aalge (*Pontoppidan*). [30.] (Fig. 46b; Pl. XVIII.) *Ads. in summer.*—Upperparts, wings, tail and neck all around, dark sooty brown, blacker on back, wings and tail; tips of secondaries, breast and belly white, sides more or less streaked with blackish. *Ads. in winter and Im.*—Upperparts, wings, and tail much as in summer; underparts white, throat more or less washed with sooty brown, flanks sometimes streaked with brownish, and feathers of belly more or less lightly margined with blackish. L., 16·00; W., 8·00; Tar., 1·40; B., 1·75; depth of B. at nostril, ·50.

Remarks.—Some specimens have a white ring around the eye and a white stripe behind it. They have been named *U. ringvia* (Brünnich), but represent merely an individual variation or mutation.

Range.—Coasts and isls. of the n. Atlantic. Breeds from s. Greenland to N. S.; in nw. Europe. Winters s. to Me.; casually to Mass.

Nests, in communities, side by side, on the bare ledges of rocky cliffs. *Egg*, 1, pyriform, pale blue or greenish blue to whitish or buffy, singularly spotted, scrawled, or streaked with shades of chocolate, rarely unmarked, 3·25 × 2·00. *Date*, Bird Rock, Que., May 15.

When on the water, Murres bear a general resemblance to Ducks, but may be distinguished by their short, thick necks and pointed bill. Unlike the Razor-bill, they do not swim with upturned tail. When nesting, probably no other birds are more closely associated than Murres. They often gather on favorable ledges of rocky islets in such numbers that a newcomer finds an alighting place with difficulty, while the place vacated by a departing bird is immediately filled by pressure from all sides. Nevertheless the birds lay their single egg on the bare rock, and under these apparently unfavorable conditions rear their young. Long-continued studies of Murres on the coast of Yorkshire warrant the belief that, although the eggs of no two Murres (or Guillemot as it is termed in England) are alike, those of the same individual more or less closely agree, and that the same bird lays year after year on the same ledge.

Murres perch on the entire foot or tarsus, and when undisturbed usually turn their back to the sea and hold their egg between their legs with its point outward. When alarmed they face about, bob and bow and utter their bass-voiced *murre*.

272. BRÜNNICH'S MURRE. Uria lomvia lomvia (*Linnæus*). [31.] *Ads. in summer.*—Upperparts, wings and tail sooty black; foreneck somewhat browner; tips of secondaries, breast and belly white; base of upper mandible greenish, rounded outward beyond edge of lower mandible. L., 16·50; W., 8·40; Tar., 1·30; B., 1·25; depth of B. at nostril, ·47.

Remarks.—Adults are to be distinguished from adults of *U. a. aalge* by the darker color of the head, which in *lomvia* is darker than the throat, by the size of the bill and thickening of its cutting edge at the base. Winter and immature birds can be distinguished from those of *U. a. aalge* only by the size of the bill, which, as the measurements show, is longer in that species.

Range.—Breeds on the Eastern Arctic isls. and n. Greenland to the Gulf of St. Lawrence; also the Arctic coasts of Europe and Siberia. Winters from s. Greenland and Hudson Bay to L. I., and casually to S. C., also to Great Britain and the North Sea. Occasional through the Great Lakes to Ia., Ills., Ind., and O.

Washington, A. V., several, Dec., 1896. Long Island, irregular W. V., Nov. 13–Mch. 30. Bronx region, very rare W. V., six records; Dec. 11–Feb. 12. Boston, not uncommon W. V., Nov.–Apr. N. Ohio, casual on Lake Erie in winter.

Nests in communities, side by side, on the bare ledges of rocky cliffs. *Egg*, 1, not distinguishable from that of *U. a. aalge*. *Date*, Bird Rock, Que., June 17.

Brunnich's Murre often nests in the same colonies with the Common Murre, which it resembles in habits, and from which, at close range, it may be distinguished by its shorter, heavier bill and swollen, whitish margin of the base of the mandible. The downy young of the two species can be distinguished by the somewhat hairy, gray-streaked back of *aalge* as compared with the more downy, brown mottled back of *lomvia*. Both utter the characteristic *screech* of young Murres while young Razorbills whistle. This species sometimes invades the interior in numbers.

1905. FLEMING, J. H., Proc. Fourth Int. Orn. Cong., 528–543.—1910. EATON, E. H., Birds of New York, 108, 109.

273. DOVEKIE. ALLE ALLE (*Linnæus*). [34.] *Ads. in summer.*—Upperparts, wings and tail sooty black; sides and front of neck and upper breast somewhat browner; secondaries tipped and scapulars streaked with white; lower breast and belly white. *Ads. in winter and Im.*—Similar, but throat whiter or washed with dusky, and sometimes a gray collar on nape. L., 8·00; W., 4·50; Tar., ·70; B., ·50.

Range.—Breeds on the n. coasts and isls. of Greenland, Iceland, Spitzbergen, and Novaya Zemlya. Winters from s. Greenland to L. I. and casually to Del. Bay and rarely to S. C.; also from the North Sea and the British Isles to the Azores, Canaries, and Madeira. Accidental near Melville Isl., and in Wisc., Mich., Ont., and Bermuda.

Long Island, irregular W. V., Oct. 31–Mch. 24; casual in summer. Bronx region, two records, Dec. 5, Feb. 6. Boston, W. V., sometimes common, Nov.–Apr.

Nest, on the ledges and in the crevices of rocky cliffs. *Egg*, 1, pale, bluish white, 1·85 × 1·27. *Date*, Disco Bay, Greenland, June 28.

"On the approach of a vessel this bird has a peculiar way of splashing along the surface of the water, as if unable to fly, and then diving through the crest of an advancing wave; it swims rather deep and very much 'by the stern.' . . ." (Saunders).

"Its wings are small, but they are moved almost as rapidly as a Hummingbird's, and propel the bird through the air with great rapidity. This bird is an expert diver too, and, though awkward on land, swims with ease and grace. . . ." (Chamberlain).

1900–02. FIGGINS, J. D., Abst. Proc. Linn. Soc., 61–63 (use of, for food).

274. BLACK GUILLEMOT. CEPPHUS GRYLLE GRYLLE (*Linnæus*). [27.] (Fig. 46c.) *Ads. in summer.*—Sooty black, lighter below and with slight greenish reflections above; lesser wing-coverts and terminal half of the greater wing-coverts white, *the basal half of the greater coverts black;* linings of the wings white. *Ads. in winter.*—Upperparts gray or black, the feathers all more or less tipped with white; wings as in summer; underparts white. *Im.*—Upperparts as in winter adults; underparts white, mottled with black; wing-coverts tipped with black. L., 13·00; W., 6·25; Tar., 1·25; B., 1·20.

Range.—Breeds from cent. Lab. s. to N. S. and Me., and in Europe from Iceland and Scandinavia to n. Scotland. Winters from Cumberland Sound s. to Cape Cod and casually to N. J.

Long Island, casual W. V., Nov. 5–Mch. 12. Boston, rather common W. V., Sept.–Apr.

Nest, in the crevices and fissures of cliffs and rocky places. *Eggs*, 2–3, dull white, sometimes with a greenish tinge, more or less heavily spotted with clear and obscure dark chocolate markings, more numerous, and sometimes confluent at the larger end, 2·18 × 1·40. *Date*, Grand Manan, N. B., June 14.

Whether in black summer, or grayish winter plumage, the Guillemot's white wing-coverts on a black wing are a conspicuous and un-

mistakable identification mark, whether the bird is swimming or
flying.

Guillemots (in England this name is applied to the Murre, *Lomvia*)
are not usually found in the great colonies of Murres and Puffins, but
nest apart by themselves. They stand on the whole foot or tarsus and
often sit or lie comfortably on their lower parts. When approached they
emit a high, squealing whistle, opening wide their coral-lined mouths.
They feed their young largely on sand-eels, and it is a common sight
to see them with a number of these fish hanging from the sides of their
bill, flying low over the water to the base of the breeding-cliff, then
rising abruptly to the nest in the rocks above.

274a. MANDT'S GUILLEMOT. CEPPHUS GRYLLE MANDTI (*Mandt*).
[28.] Resembles the preceding, but the bases of the greater wing-coverts are
white instead of black.

Range.—Breeds on Arctic coasts and isls. s. to n. Hudson Bay, James
Bay, and mainland of Siberia. Winters in the Arctic Ocean and casually
s. to Norton Sound, s. Que. and Lake Ontario. Accidental in N. B.

Nest, in crevices and fissures of cliffs and rocky places. *Eggs*, 2–3, not
distinguishable from those of *C. g. grylle*, 2·34 × 1·15.

A northern form of the preceding, which it doubtless resembles in
habits.

275. The ANCIENT MURRELET, *Synthliboramphus antiquus* (Gmelin),
[21], of the north Pacific is accidental in Minnesota, Wisconsin, southern
Quebec, Ontario, and on Lake Erie.

276. ATLANTIC PUFFIN. FRATERCULA ARCTICA ARCTICA (*Linnæus*).
[13.] (Fig. 46*a*; Pl. XVIII.) *Ads.*—Upperparts, wings, tail and foreneck
blackish, browner on the head and foreneck; nape with a narrow grayish
collar; sides of the head and throat white, sometimes washed with grayish;
breast and belly white. (Breeding birds have the bill larger and brighter,
and a horny spine over the eye.) L., 13·00; W., 6·10; Tar., 1·05; B., 1·85;
depth of B. at base (in winter), 1·50.

Range.—Breeds from s. Greenland and Ungava Bay, s. to N. S., Bay of
Fundy and Me.; also from Norway and the British Isles to Portugal. Winters
s. to Mass., casually to L. I. and N. J.; also to Morocco and casually to the
Azores. Accidental in Ont. (Ottawa).

Long Island, casual W. V., Dec. 15–Mch. 30. Boston, rare W. V.

Nest, in a burrow in the ground or in crevices among rocks. *Egg*, 1,
dull white, sometimes with obscure markings, 2·49 × 1·68. *Date*, Bird Rock,
Que., May 26; Cape Whittle, Lab., June 11.

One has only to see a Puffin to realize why it is commonly known as
'Sea Parrot'; and when the bird on outstretched, short, rounded wings
hovers for a moment before alighting, it bears the strongest resemblance
to a Japanese bird-kite. In flight the Puffins' wings move more rapidly
than those of the Murre and Razorbill, and unlike those birds it stands
only on its toes, and can run about easily and rapidly.

While Murres and Razorbills usually resort to rocky islets whose
ledges and crannies afford nesting-sites, Puffins may use low-lying, flat
islands in the turf of which they excavate their burrows. It was a
surprising experience, in crossing an apparently deserted bit of ground

on the Farne Islands, to have at nearly every step dozens of Puffins burst from the earth at my feet. The only note I have heard from a Puffin is a hoarse grunt or groan, but C. W. Townsend records "a low purring note, *purr-la-la-la.*" Puffins can inflict serious wounds with their powerful bill, which they use ferociously.

1883. BREWSTER, W., Proc. Bost. Soc. Nat. Hist., 407 (habits).

276a. LARGE-BILLED PUFFIN. FRATERCULA ARCTICA NAUMANNI *Norton.* [13*a.*] Similar to the preceding, but larger. W., 6·80–7·40; B., 2·00–2·30 (B., B., and R.).
Range.—Coasts and isls. of the Arctic Ocean, from cent. w. Greenland to Novaya Zemlya and Spitzbergen; mainly resident.

277. The TUFTED PUFFIN, *Lunda cirrhata* (Pallas), [12], inhabits the north Pacific from California to Alaska. The specimen figured by Audubon was said by him to have been procured at the mouth of the Kennebec River, Maine. It has also been recorded from Greenland.

XI. ORDER COLUMBIFORMES. PIGEONS, SAND GROUSE, ETC.

SUBORDER COLUMBÆ. PIGEONS AND DOVES
(2 families, 1 North American)

FAMILY COLUMBIDÆ. PIGEONS AND DOVES.

The 450-odd species and subspecies recognized by Salvadori in his Monograph of this suborder (Cat. Bds. Brit. Mus., XXI, 1893) were placed by him in five families as follows: (1) *Treronidæ* or Fruit Pigeons, restricted largely to Malayan and Polynesian regions, 199 species; (2) *Columbidæ*, the true Pigeons, distributed throughout the world, 99 species; (3) *Peristeridæ* or Doves, distributed throughout the world but more numerous in the tropics, 155 species; (4) *Gouridæ* or Crown Pigeons of New Guinea, 6 species, and (5) *Didunculidæ*, containing only the Toothed Pigeon of Samoa. The total number of forms now recognized is doubtless over 600.

The Family *Columbidæ* of the A. O. U. 'Check-List' contains representatives of both the *Columbidæ* and *Peristeridæ* as grouped by Salvadori, which, in North America, number twelve species. The birds of this order differ widely in their choice of haunts. Some are strictly arboreal, others as strictly terrestrial. Some seek the forests and others prefer fields and clearings. The former feed chiefly on fruit; the latter, on seeds. Some nest in colonies, others in isolated pairs, but most species are found in flocks of greater or less size after the breeding season. When drinking, they do not raise the head as most birds do to swallow, but keep the bill immersed until the draught is finished. The eggs number two, rarely one, and are white or creamy in color. Both sexes incubate, the male's daily period, so far as known, being from about 10 A.M. to 4 P.M. The young are born naked, and are fed by regur-

gitation on predigested food, or 'Pigeons' milk,' from the crop of
the parent.

1898. WHITMAN, C. O., Animal Behavior, Biol. Lecture M. B. L., 314 *et
seq.* (Ginn & Co.).—1908. CRAIG, W., The Voices of Pigeons Regarded as a
Means of Social Control, Am. Journ. Soc., XIV, 86–100.

KEY TO THE SPECIES

A. Tail widely tipped with white or gray.
  a. Tail pointed.
    a^1. Back or rump bluish slate-color . . . . 283. PASSENGER PIGEON.
    a^2. Back olive grayish brown . . . . 282. MOURNING DOVE.
  b. Tail square or slightly rounded.
    b^1. Belly vinaceous . . . . 281. ZENAIDA DOVE.
    b^2. Belly pearl-gray . . . . 284. WHITE-WINGED DOVE.
B. Tail not tipped with white.
  a. Upperparts dark slate-color . . . . . 278. WHITE-CROWNED PIGEON.
  b. Upperparts not slate-color.
    b^1. Upperparts rufous with purplish reflections.
      b^2. Line below the eye and belly white or whitish.
            286. KEY WEST QUAIL DOVE.
      b^3. Line under the eye and belly buffy ochraceous.
            287. RUDDY QUAIL DOVE.
    c^1. Upperparts grayish olive-brown.
    c^2. Crown pinkish or like the back . . . 285, 285a. GROUND DOVES.

278. WHITE-CROWNED PIGEON. COLUMBA LEUCOCEPHALA *Linnæus.*
[314.] *Ad.* ♂.—Rich slate-color; crown white; back of head purplish chest-
nut; back of neck with greenish reflections, each feather with a black border.
Ad. ♀.—Similar, but paler; crown ashy, less purplish chestnut; back and
sides of neck brownish ash with metallic reflections and black margins.
L., 13·50; W., 7·50; T., 5·10; B., ·70.
  Range.—S. Fla. Keys, the Bahamas, Greater Antilles, some of the Lesser
Antilles, Swan Isl., Cozumel Isl., and isls. off the coast of Cent. A. from
British Honduras to w. Panama. Casual in winter in Monroe and Dade
counties, Fla. (About twelve Fla. records.)
  Nest, in low trees and bushes. *Eggs,* 2, glossy white, 1·41 × 1·02. *Date.*—
Andros Isl., Bahamas, June 15.

This Pigeon occurs in the keys off southern Florida, and has been
found on the mainland. According to J. W. Atkins (*The Auk,* VI,
1889, p. 246), it arrives at Key West early in May and remains until
November.

279. The SCALED PIGEON, *Columba squamosa* Bonnaterre, [314.1], has
been taken at Key West, Fla., Oct. 24, 1898 (Atkins, Auk, 1899, 272), and
May 6, 1929 (Chapman, Auk, 1931, 116).

280. DOMESTIC PIGEON; ROCK DOVE. COLUMBA LIVIA *Linnæus.*
Ads.—Slate-color, the head and neck and breast darker, the two latter with
greenish and purplish reflections; back and wings much paler; belly, upper
tail-coverts and tail between head and back in color; wings crossed with two
black bands; a broad black terminal tail-band; rump white. L., 13·00; W.,
8·70; T., 5·00. Described from a Morocco specimen of *Columba livia livia.*

The Domestic Pigeon is now naturalized and self-supporting throughout its American range and may, therefore, like the Starling and House
Sparrow, be considered as a member of our fauna. The introduced

individuals of the two latter, however, were feral, but the Pigeon has descended from the domesticated variety of the Rock Dove. While many of our Pigeons more or less resemble the Rock Dove from which they have descended, others, in their varied colors show their relation to the numerous varieties which have been produced by artificial selection under the guidance of the 'fancier.'

281. ZENAIDA DOVE. Zenaida zenaida zenaida (*Bonaparte*). [317.] *Ad.*—Bears a general resemblance to *Z. macroura*, but the tail is square and tipped with ashy, and the underparts are deep, rich vinaceous. L., 10˙00; W., 6˙10; T., 3˙50; B., ˙66.

Range.—Fla. Keys, the Bahamas, Greater and Lesser Antilles.

Nest, on or near the ground. *Eggs*, 2, glossy white, 1˙22 × ˙92. *Date*, Bahamas, May 27.

This is a common West Indian species. Audubon found it in numbers in the keys off southern Florida, where he records it as a summer resident, arriving in April and departing in October. The few naturalists who have visited these keys since Audubon's time have not been there in the summer, and we do not therefore know whether this species still occurs there at that season. It is more terrestrial in habits than the Mourning Dove, and its notes are deeper, louder, and more solemn than the notes of that species.

282. EASTERN MOURNING DOVE. Zenaidura macroura carolinensis (*Linnæus*). [316.] *Ad.* ♂.—Upperparts olive grayish brown; forehead vinaceous; crown bluish slate-color; sides of neck with metallic reflections, *a small black mark below the ear*; middle tail-feathers like back, the others, seen from above, slaty gray for the basal half, then banded with black and broadly tipped with ashy and white; tertials with large black spots; breast vinaceous; belly cream-buff. *Ad.* ♀.—Similar, but with less iridescence; breast and forehead washed with grayish brown. *Im.*—Much like ♀, but the feathers tipped with whitish. L., 11˙85; W., 5˙72; T., 5˙50; B., ˙53.

Remarks.—The Dove is sometimes mistaken for the Wild Pigeon, but, aside from the differences in size, may always be distinguished by its olive grayish brown instead of bluish slate-color rump, the black mark below the ear, and other characters.

Range.—Breeds in Austral and Lower Transition zones from N. B., N. S., s. Me., Ont., Mich., Wisc., w. to e. Kans. and Ia. and s. to the Gulf Coast and the Bahamas, straggling to Que., Lab. and Bermuda; winters from Ia., s. Mich., and Mass. s. throughout its range, and casually along the e. coast of Mex. and Cent. A. to Panama.

Washington, P. R., common, except in midwinter. Bronx region, common S. R., occasionally wintering, Mch. 3–Dec. 11; Jan. 12. Boston, uncommon S. R., Mch.–Oct. N. Ohio, common S. R., not common P. R. Glen Ellyn, tolerably common S. R., formerly common, Mch. 12–Dec. 27. SE. Minn., common S. R., Mch. 15–Oct. 28; rare W. R.

Nest, a flat structure of small twigs rather loosely put together, on the lower branches of a tree, generally within 10 feet of the ground; rarely on the ground in the eastern states. *Eggs*, 2, white, 1˙07 × ˙83. *Date*, D. C., Apr. 18; Nazareth, Pa., Apr. 15; Ossining, N. Y., Apr. 17; Boston, May 8; se. Minn., May 12. Later broods follow, sometimes to Sept.

Doves resemble Wild Pigeons, but are much smaller, and their rapid flight is accompanied by the whistling sound of wings, while the flight of the Wild Pigeon is said to have been noiseless.

PLATE XIX

PASSENGER PIGEON

During the nesting season they may be found in pairs, generally in open woodlands or tree-bordered fields. They also visit roads and lanes to dust themselves. The sweet, sad call of the male has won for this species its common name; it consists of several soft *coos*, which may be written: *Coo-o-o, ah-coo-o-o—coo-o-o—coo-o-o.* Under favorable circumstances these notes may be heard at a distance of at least two hundred and fifty 'yards; they are uttered slowly and tenderly, and with such apparent depth of feeling that one might easily imagine the bird was mourning the loss of his mate, instead of singing a lovesong to her.

At this season one or both birds may be seen performing a peculiar aërial evolution. Ascending to a height of about 30 feet, they fly for some distance in an unnatural manner, and then, after a short sail, return to their perch. When engaged in this performance they very closely resemble a Sharp-shinned Hawk.

After the nesting season Doves gather in flocks of varying size and frequent grain and cornfields. During the day they visit the nearest supply of fine gravel, which they eat in large quantities as an aid to digestion. In some localities, soon after sunset, they regularly repair in numbers to some favorite place to drink, and then retire to their roosts.

1911. CRAIG, W., Auk, 398–407 (expression of emotion).—1922. NICE, M. M., Auk, 457–474; 1923, 37–58, illus. (nesting).—1930. TABER, W. B., JR., Wilson Bull., 17–28 (fall migration).

283. PASSENGER PIGEON. ECTOPISTES MIGRATORIUS (*Linnæus*). [315.] (Fig. 47.) *Ad.* ♂.—Upperparts rich bluish slate-color; back and sides of neck with metallic reflections; middle of back and scapulars more or less washed with olive-brown; middle tail-feathers fuscous, outer ones black at the base, then slaty blue, fading into a broad, white tip; underparts deep, rich vinaceous; lower belly white; throat bluish slate-color. *Ad.* ♀.—Similar, but upperparts with less iridescence and more olive-brown; breast pale grayish brown; belly whitish. *Im.*—Generally similar to the ♀, but the feathers of the upperparts and breast tipped with whitish, the primaries edged and tipped with rufous. L., 16·29; W., 7·82; T., 7·53; B., ·71.

Range.—Now extinct; bred formerly from middle w. Mack., cent. Keewatin, cent. Ont., and N. S. s. to Kans., Miss., Ky., Pa., and N. Y.; wintered principally from Ark. and N. C. s. to cent. Tex., La., and Fla.; casual w. to Ore., Nev., Wash. and e. Mex.; accidental in Bermuda, Cuba, the British Isles, and Europe.

Washington, formerly T. V. or W. V. Bronx region, formerly common T. V. and rare S. R., Apr. 15–May 17; Aug. 21–Oct. 11 (A. K. Fisher); last seen Oct. 11, 1888 (G. H. Thayer). Boston, formerly abundant, now extinct. Glen Ellyn, extinct; last seen Sept. 4, 1892. SE. Minn., formerly abundant, no recent record.

Nest, a platform of sticks, in a tree. *Eggs,* 1, very rarely 2, white, 1·45 × 1·09. *Date,* Upton, Me., June 15, 1872; Wisc., first week in Apr.; se. Minn., May 9, 1879.

Wilson, writing about 1808, estimated that a flock of Wild Pigeons observed by him near Frankfort, Ky., contained at least 2,230,272,000 individuals. Bendire, writing in 1892, says: ". . . It looks now as if their total extermination might be accomplished within the present century. The only thing which retards their complete extinction is that it no longer pays to net these birds, they being too scarce for this now, at least in the more settled portions of the country, and also, perhaps, that from constant and unremitting persecution on their breeding-grounds they have changed their habits somewhat, the majority no longer breeding in colonies, but scattering over the country and breeding in isolated pairs" ('Life Histories of North American Birds,' p. 133).

An article by William Brewster on 'The Present Status of the Wild Pigeon as a Bird of the United States, with some Notes on its Habits' (*The Auk*, 1889, pp. 285–291), gives much information concerning the history of the bird in Michigan, one of its last strongholds. According to an informant of Mr. Brewster's, the last nesting in Michigan of any importance was in 1881. "It was of only moderate size—perhaps 8 miles long." The largest known Michigan nesting occurred in 1876 or 1877. It was 28 miles long and averaged 3 to 4 miles in width.

The report that countless Passenger Pigeons were destroyed by falling to the water while migrating over the Gulf of Mexico is false. They did not migrate over the Gulf of Mexico. Equally groundless are the rumors of their existence in the western United States, or the Bahamas, Mexico, and even South America. Such reports, when made in good faith, are based on some other species of wild Pigeon. Similarly, current statements of the occurrence of the Passenger Pigeon in its former haunts are invariably found, when investigated, to result from misidentification of the Mourning Dove. The Passenger Pigeon has gone. There is no unquestionable record of its existence in nature since August, 1906, when a bird was shot in Fairfield County, Connecticut.

Man, and man alone, is responsible for the Passenger Pigeon's extermination. From his first contact with it in the Atlantic States to the date of its disappearance he was its merciless destroyer. The story is clearly told in Forbush's fine biography cited beyond.

1907. MERSHON, W. B., The Passenger Pigeon, 225. A Monograph (Outing Co.).—1910. WRIGHT, A. H., Auk, 428–443; see also 1911, 49–66, 111, 346–366, 427–449.—1910. DILLIN, J. G., Cassinia, 33–36 (early records).—1911. HODGE, C. F., Auk, 49 (present status); 1912, 169–175 (last word).—1911. CRAIG, W., Auk, 408–427 (expression of emotion).—1913. BIRD-LORE, 77–103: Articles on Passenger Pigeon by M. FISCHER, A. H. WRIGHT, W. CRAIG, and E. H. FORBUSH, with photographs from life by J. G. HUBBARD.—1914. Auk, 566 (last one died in Cincinnati Zoo, Sept. 1, 1914).—1915. SHUFELDT, R. W., Auk, 29–41, illus. (anatomy).—1917. BISHOP AND WRIGHT, Auk, 208 (last one).—1919. FRENCH, J. C., The Passenger Pigeon in Pennsylvania (Altoona, Pa.), 257 pp., illus.—1921. BOND, FRANK, Auk, 523–527, illus. (later flights).—1927. FORBUSH, E. H., Birds of Mass., 54–82 (biography).

284. The EASTERN WHITE-WINGED DOVE, *Melopelia asiatica asiatica* (Linnæus), [319], is of general distribution from the Mexican border of the United States south to Costa Rica, and it has been recorded from Cuba, Jamaica, and San Domingo. It is of accidental occurrence in Georgia, at Key West and Kissimmee, Fla. (Ridgway, Auk, 1897, 88). It may be known by its gray belly and the broad white margins to the wing-coverts, giving the appearance of a white wing-patch, which is conspicuous in life.

285. EASTERN GROUND DOVE. COLUMBIGALLINA PASSERINA PAS-
SERINA *Linnæus*. [320.] *Ad. ♂.*—Forehead and underparts vinaceous,
centers of breast-feathers blackish; top and back of head bluish slate-color;
back brownish gray; tail blackish, the outer feathers with small white tips;
inner vane of primaries rufous, showing in flight; base of bill coral-red, tip
black. *Ad. ♀.*—Similar, but forehead and underparts pale brownish gray.
Im.—Resembles ♀, but the feathers are tipped with whitish. L., 6·75;
W., 3·50; T., 2·50; B., ·50.

Range.—Lower Austral Zone of the South Atlantic and Gulf States from
S. C. to se. Tex. Accidental farther n. (Tenn., N. C., Va., Md., Pa., N. J.
and N. Y.).

Washington, accidental; several records, Sept.; Oct.; Dec.; Feb.

Nest, on the ground or in low trees or bushes. *Eggs*, 2, white, ·85 × ·67.
Date, San Mateo, Fla., Mch. 12.

This diminutive Pigeon frequents pines and 'hammocks,' lake-
shores, and old fields, and in some southern towns is a familiar bird of
the quieter streets. It is by no means shy, and runs before one with
quick, short steps and a graceful movement of the head. Occasionally
it holds its tail upright, giving it a peculiar bantamlike appearance.
Its flight is short, and when on the wing it bears an odd resemblance
to a short-tailed Japanese kite.

A favorite roosting-place is densely foliaged orange trees, and frequently when the bird is hidden in their depths one may hear its mellow,
crooning *coos* uttered so softly that they float on the air as though
born of the wind.

285a. BAHAMAN GROUND DOVE. COLUMBIGALLINA PASSERINA
BAHAMENSIS (*Maynard*), [320b]. Resembles the preceding but averages
somewhat paler below and grayer above; the bill usually black. W., 3·40.

Range.—Bahamas and Bermuda.

286. KEY WEST QUAIL-DOVE. OREOPELEIA CHRYSIA *Bonaparte*.
[322.] Upperparts rufous, with brilliant metallic reflections; wings rufous;
a white line beneath the eye; breast vinaceous; belly white. L., 11·00; W.,
6·20; T., 5·00; B., ·50.

Range.—Key West (formerly: Sept. 15, 1889; Oct. 20 and Nov. 12, 1897),
the Bahamas, Cuba, Isle of Pines, and Haiti.

Nest, in trees. *Eggs*, 2, ochraceous-white, 1·22 × ·94 (Bendire). *Date*,
Cuba, Feb.

A West Indian species which occurs during the summer in the
Florida Keys.

The Quail-Doves inhabit wooded districts where they live on the
ground. Their flight is low and noiseless, and they are difficult birds
to observe unless one can find some tree on the fallen fruits of which
they are feeding.

287. The RUDDY QUAIL-DOVE, *Oreopeleia montana* (Linnæus), [322.1],
is a Tropical American species, which has been twice recorded from Key
West. It bears a general resemblance to *O. chrysia*, but the back is more
rufous and the belly is deep cream-buff.

[The BLUE-HEADED QUAIL-DOVE, *Starnænas cyanocephala* (Linnæus),
[323], a Cuban species, was recorded by Audubon from the Florida Keys,
but there do not appear to be any later records. The back is olive-brown,
the crown and sides of the throat are deep grayish blue, throat black, line
beneath eye white.]

XII. ORDER PSITTACIFORMES. PARROTS, MACAWS, ETC.

(2 families, 1 North American)

FAMILY PSITTACIDÆ. PARROTS AND PAROQUETS.

The approximately 800 species and subspecies currently recognized in the Order *Psittaciformes* are commonly placed in three families. Of this number, about 275, all members of the family *Psittacidæ*, inhabit the Western Hemisphere. Only two species have been recorded from the United States: the Thick-billed Parrot, which barely enters Arizona from Mexico, and the once-abundant Carolina Paroquet, unknown from beyond our boundaries. Parrots and Paroquets—the dividing-line between the two can not be sharply drawn—are forest-inhabiting, fruit- and seed-eating birds. They are poor walkers, good climbers, and strong fliers, making extended flights in search of food. Their voices in nature are harsh and discordant; nevertheless, almost all the species possess the power of speech. Some, however, rarely learn to talk, while others invariably do. The red-tailed, gray African Parrot (*Psittacus erythacus*) takes first rank for ability in this direction, while the Mexican Double Yellow-head (*Amazona oratrix*) is usually accorded second place. Parrots are believed to mate for life. They nest in holes, usually in trees, and lay white eggs. The young are hatched with a covering of white down and are reared in the nest.

288. CAROLINA PAROQUET. CONUROPSIS CAROLINENSIS CARO- LINENSIS (*Linnæus*). [382.] (Fig. 49.) *Ads.*—Head and neck all around yel- low; forehead and cheeks deep orange; bend of the wing and tibiæ orange; rest of the plumage bright green; the inner vanes of the wing-feathers fuscous; the under surface of the tail yellowish. *Im.*—Similar, but the head and neck green like the back; forehead and region in front of the eye orange; tibiæ and bend of the wing without orange. L., 12·50; W., 7·40; T., 6·50.

Range.—Now apparently extinct (last specimen 1904). Formerly ranged throughout Fla. n. along the Atlantic Coast to s. Va. and w. to Ga. and Ala.; casually farther n. to the D. of C., Pa., and N. Y.

Washington, extinct, known only from specimens shot in Sept., 1865.

Nest, said to be in a hollow cypress or sycamore tree, but no authentic account of the nidification of this species has been published. *Eggs* (laid in captivity), white, 1·44 × 1·12. *Date*, probably lay in June.

The extermination of the Paroquet is due chiefly to four causes: first, it was destructive to fruit orchards, and for this reason was killed by agriculturists; second, it has been trapped and bagged in enormous numbers by professional bird-catchers; third, it has been killed in myriads for its plumage; and, fourth, it has been wantonly slaughtered by so-called sportsmen. In short, the Paroquet has always disappeared soon after its haunts were settled by civilized man. Reports of the continued existence of the Paroquet have proved, when investigated, to be based on other species of this family which have escaped or been released from captivity. So far as I know, the Carolina Paroquet was last taken near Taylor Creek, northeast of Lake Okeechobee, where, in April, 1904, I saw thirteen and shot four.

1891. Hasbrouck, E. M., Auk, 369–379; Butler, A., *Ibid.*, 1892, 49–56 (range).—1912. Wright, A. H., Auk, 343–363 (early records).

288a. LOUISIANA PAROQUET. Conuropsis carolinensis ludovicianus (*Gmelin*). [382a.]—Resembles the preceding but the upperparts are more or less washed with light blue-green.

Range.—Now extinct. Formerly ranged from La. and Miss. n. to Tenn., Ky., O., w. N. Y. (shore of Lake Erie), Ind., Wisc., Mo., Nebr., Colo., Kans., Ark., and Indian Territory.

The fact that Paroquets from the Mississippi Valley are slightly different from those of the Atlantic Coast was not discovered until long after the more western form had become extinct. Comparatively few specimens of it exist, but the Carolina Paroquet is well represented in collections.

XIII. ORDER CUCULIFORMES. CUCKOOS, AND ALLIES

SUBORDER CUCULI. CUCKOOS, ANIS, ETC.

(1 family)

Family Cuculidæ. Cuckoos, Anis, Etc.

Cuckoos are distributed throughout the greater part of the world but are more abundant in the tropical regions. Of the more than 250 species and subspecies, 80 are American and 8, representing 6 species, reach the United States.

Cuckoos, as a rule, are rather solitary birds, inhabiting wooded areas. The Anis, however, are always gregarious and live in open places. Their flight is weak, generally from tree to tree, and their feet are largely used as a means of progression. Some species hop, others walk, and one is celebrated for its speed as a runner. They are possessed of peculiar vocal powers, and their strange calls are frequently the origin of their popular names. Many species are remarkable for the irregularity of their breeding habits. The Old-World Cuckoo (*Cuculus canorus*), like our Cowbird, lays its eggs in the nests of other birds, and leaves to them the duties of incubation and rearing of the young. The Anis are communistic and build but one nest, in which several females lay and, probably with the males, share the task of incubation. The smaller species are insectivorous, but the larger ones add small reptiles and batrachians to their fare. The eggs of all North American species are white or bluish white, and are sometimes laid at such widely separated intervals that the same nest may contain fresh eggs and young birds. The young are hatched naked and the feathers of the juvenal plumage, which is the first to be acquired, remain in their sheaths until they are well grown.

1928. Friedmann, H., Parasitic Habits in Cuculidæ, Auk, 33–38.

289. MAYNARD'S CUCKOO. COCCYZUS MINOR MAYNARDI *Ridgway.* [386 +386*a.*] *Ads.*—Upperparts brownish gray with glossy reflections, crown grayer, ear-coverts *black;* wings and middle pair of tail-feathers like back; remaining rectrices black broadly tipped with white; underparts white washed with ochraceous-buff; bill black, lower mandible basally yellow. L., 12·50; W., 5·40; T., 6·00; B. from N., ·80.

Range.—Bahama Isls., Cuba, Fla. Keys and s. coast of Fla., n. to Anclote Keys.

A regular summer resident in southern Florida.

1930. BIRD-LORE, 251, 255 (dist., pl.).

290. YELLOW-BILLED CUCKOO. COCCYZUS AMERICANUS AMERICANUS (*Linnæus*). [387.] (Fig. 48.) *Ads.*—Upperparts brownish gray with slight greenish gloss; the wing-feathers *rufous*, except at the tip; outer tail-feathers *black*, conspicuously tipped with white, which extends down the outer vane of the outer feather; underparts dull whitish; bill black, the lower mandible *yellow* except at the tip. L., 12·20; W., 5·70; T., 6·20; B. from N., ·76.

FIG. 93.   Tail-feathers of Yellow-billed Cuckoo.

Remarks.—This species bears a general resemblance to the Black-billed Cuckoo, but may always be known from that species by its yellow lower mandible, rufous wing-feathers, and black, white-tipped tail-feathers.

Range.—Breeds mainly in the Austral zones from N. Dak., Minn., s. Ont., Que., and N. B. s. to Nuevo Leon, Tamaulipas, La., and the Fla. Keys and w. to S. Dak., Nebr., e. Colo., and Okla.; migrates through Mex., W. I. and Cent. A., casually Bermuda, and winters s. to Brazil. (Said to breed in Jamaica, Porto Rico and Cuba.) Accidental in Greenland, Great Britain, Italy, and Belgium.

Washington, common S. R., May 3–Oct. 13. Bronx region, common S. R., May 3–Oct. 31. Boston, uncommon S. R., May 12–Sept. 15. N. Ohio, common S. R., Apr. 20–Sept. 25. Glen Ellyn, quite common S. R., May 15– Sept. 29. SE. Minn., common S. R., May 10–Oct. 1.

Nest, a platform of small sticks, with a few grasses or catkins, generally in low trees or vine-covered bushes, 4–10 feet up. *Eggs*, 3–5, pale greenish blue, 1·22 × ·92. *Date*, Gainesville, Fla., Apr. 9, laying; Buckingham Co., Va., May 13; Boston, May 25; Mt. Carmel, Ills., May 20.

A long, slim, dovelike bird slips noiselessly by and disappears in the depths of a neighboring tree. If you can mark his position you will find him perched motionless, and apparently slightly dazed. After a moment he recovers and begins to hop about the tree in an active search of his favorite fare of caterpillars. He is especially fond of the kind which make nests in trees, commonly known as 'tent caterpillars,' and if you examine the conspicuous homes of these pests you will frequently find them punctured with many holes made by the Cuckoo's bill. A Cuckoo I shot at 6 o'clock one September morning had the partially digested remains of forty-three of these caterpillars in his stomach.

The notes of the Cuckoo are strikingly characteristic, and while subject to much variation may be fairly represented by the syllables *tut-tut, tut-tut, tut-tut, tut-tut, cl-uck-cl-uck-cl-uck, cl-uck-cl-uck, cl-uck, cow, cow, cow, cow, cow, cow.* It is not usual, however, to hear the whole song given at once.

1930. BIRD-LORE, 249, 254 (mig., pl.).

291. BLACK-BILLED CUCKOO. COCCYZUS ERYTHROPHTHALMUS (*Wilson*). [388.] *Ads.*—Upperparts grayish brown with a slight green gloss; wings and tail the same, the latter narrowly tipped with white, underparts dull white; bill black, the mandible sometimes yellow basally. L., 11·83; W., 5·50; T., 6·26; B. from N., ·74.

Remarks.—This species is to be distinguished from the Yellow-billed Cuckoo chiefly by the absence of rufous in the wings, of conspicuous black and white in the tail, and by its wholly or nearly black bill.

Range.—Breeds mainly in the Transition Zone from se. Alberta, s. Man., s. Que., s. to Kans., Ark., N. C., and mountains of Ga.; occasionally to S. C. and n. Fla. Winters in S. A. from Colombia to Peru. Accidental in the Azores, Italy, and Ireland.

Washington, rather rare S. R., May 2–Oct. 28. Bronx region, common S. R., May 2–Oct. 19. Boston, common S. R., May 12– Sept. 20. N. Ohio, tolerably common S. R., May 1–

FIG. 94. Tail-feathers of Black-billed Cuckoo.

Sept. 25. Glen Ellyn, S. R., May 5–Oct. 21. SE. Minn., common S. R., May 8–Oct. 2.

Nest, similar to that of the preceding, but more compactly built; location the same. *Eggs*, 2–5, greenish blue, of a deeper shade than those of the preceding species, 1·14 × ·85. *Date*, Ossining, N. Y., May 28; Boston, May 20; Mt. Carmel, Ills., May 7; se. Minn., May 16.

This species resembles the preceding in habits. The two birds may be distinguished in life by the differences in the color of their bills and tails. William Brewster has called my attention to an easily recognizable difference in their calls. The present species has a much softer voice, and the *cow, cow* notes are connected.

1911. HERRICK, F. H., Journ. Ex. Zoöl., IX, 171–223 (behavior).—1930. BIRD-LORE, 252–254 (mig., pl.).

292. SMOOTH-BILLED ANI. CROTOPHAGA ANI Linnæus. [383.] *Ads.*—Bill much compressed vertically, nearly as high as long; maxilla smooth without grooves. Black; feathers of foreparts of the body with iridescent margins; wings and tail with bluish reflections; tail much rounded. L., 12·50; T., 7·75; W., 5·75; B., ·95; depth, ·85.

Range.—W. I., Yucatan, Cent. and S. A.; rare or casual in La., and s. Fla.; accidental near Philadelphia, and Edenton, N. C., and se. Minn.

Nest, in trees usually densely foliaged or in vine-grown thickets; of twigs lined with leaves, occupied by from two to a dozen birds composing a family group. *Eggs*, 4 to over 20, bluish white overlaid by a chalky covering, 1·35 × 1·00.

I have observed this species at Miami in April, and in view of its numbers in the Bahamas it may be expected to occur in southern Florida with more or less frequency. Its long tail, short wings, singularly shaped bill, and long-drawn, whining, whistled call are distinctive.

1892. TAYLOR, C. B., Auk, 369–371 (nesting).

293. The GROOVE-BILLED ANI, *Crotophaga sulcirostris sulcirostris* Swainson, [384], of the lower Rio Grande valley and southward has occurred in Arizona, Kansas, Louisiana, and Florida (Lake Worth, Jan., 1891.—Auk, 1891, 313). It is slightly smaller than *C. ani*, has the maxilla grooved from base to tip, and the nape is margined with silver rather than with bronze.

XIV. ORDER STRIGIFORMES. OWLS
(2 families)
SYNOPSIS OF FAMILIES

Middle toe with a comb-like edge; primaries not notched or emarginate.
　　　　　　　　　　Family Tytonidæ. BARN OWLS. P. 334.
Middle toe without a comb-like edge; one or more primaries notched or
　emarginate . . . . *Family Strigidæ.* OWLS. P. 335.

FAMILY TYTONIDÆ. BARN OWLS.

The Barn Owls, numbering some twenty-five species and subspecies, are found nearly throughout the temperate and tropical regions. They differ from other Owls in structure, but share with them the characteristic habits of the *Strigidæ*, the other of the two Owl families.

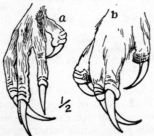

FIG. 95. *a.* Barn Owl. *b.* Barred Owl.

294. BARN OWL. TYTO ALBA PRATINCOLA (*Bonaparte*). [365.] (Figs. 50. 95*a;* Pl. XX.) *Ads.*—Upperparts mixed with gray and ochraceous-buff, finely speckled with black and white; tail varying from white to ochraceous-buff, generally mottled with black, and sometimes with three or four narrow black bars; underparts and facial disk varying from pure white to deep ochraceous-buff, the former generally with numerous small, black, round spots, the facial disk narrowly margined by ochraceous-buff or rufous; eyes black. L., 18·00; W., 13·25; T., 5·50; B., 1·30.

Range.—Breeds in Upper and Lower Austral zones from n. Calif., Colo., Nebr., Ills., s. Wisc., s. Mich., O., w. N. Y., and Conn., s. to the Gulf States and s. Mex., and casually to Ore., B. C., Minn., Ont., Vt., and Mass.; in winter at least to Nicaragua.

Washington, uncommon P. R. Bronx region, rare P. R., numerous records at all seasons; several breeding. Boston, A. V. N. Ohio, not common P. R. Glen Ellyn, rare, Jan. 5, 1928. SE. Minn., uncommon P. R.

Nest, in a tower or steeple, a hole in a tree or bank. *Eggs,* 5–9, white, 1·72 × 1·30. *Date,* D. C., Apr. 16; Delaware Co., Pa., Apr. 24.

The Barn Owl conceals itself so well during the day that, in my experience, it is a difficult bird to observe, even in localities where it is

PLATE XX

HEADS OF OWLS

Long-eared Owl.	Hawk Owl.	Short-eared Owl.
Barn Owl.	Great Horned Owl.	Barred Owl.
Saw-whet Owl.	Snowy Owl.	Richardson's Owl.
	Screech Owl.	

common. For this reason the capture of one of these odd-visaged birds is frequently the cause of much excitement over the supposed discovery of an animal entirely new to science, and which, by the local press, is generally considered half bird, half monkey!

The only notes I have ever heard from the Barn Owl are a sudden wild, startling scream, a high, rapidly repeated *cr-r-ree, cr-r-ree, cr-r-ree*, and, in captive birds, a hissing sound; but Bendire mentions "a feeble querulous note like *quäek-quäek*, or *äek-äek*, sounding somewhat like the call of the Night Hawk (*Chordeiles m. minor*), frequently repeated, only not so loud."

"Of 29 stomachs examined, 1 contained poultry; 3, other birds; 17, mice; 17, other mammals; 4, insects; and 7 were empty" (Fisher).

1925. POTTER, J. K., and GILLESPIE, J. A., Auk, 177–192, illus. (habits).

FAMILY STRIGIDÆ. HORNED OWLS, HOOT OWLS, ETC.

The over 500 species and subspecies of the Family *Strigidæ* are distributed throughout the world, about 175 being known from the Western Hemisphere. Many species respond readily to the influences of their environment and, when wide-ranging, are hence represented by numbers of geographical races. In North America, for example, we have 17 species, but 55 subspecies, of which no less than 15 are races of the Screech Owl (*Otus asio*). With few exceptions, Owls are woodland birds, but some species live in grassy marshes or dry plains, while others make their home in towers, steeples, or outbuildings. Owls are nocturnal birds of prey, and for this reason feed more largely on small mammals—most of which are nocturnal—than do the diurnal birds of prey. They are therefore of even greater value to the agriculturist than Hawks. Their prey is captured with their talons, and, unless too large, is swallowed entire. The bones and hair are afterward ejected at the mouth in matted pellets.

Owls' eyes are so fixed in their sockets that they can not look from one point to another by simply 'rolling' the eyeball, but are obliged to turn their head. Their unusually large ear aperture is accompanied by an exceptionally keen sense of hearing. The weird, almost human, voices of Owls add not a little to the superstitious fear with which they are frequently regarded. The eggs of Owls are uniformly white, unmarked. Their young are thickly covered with white down.

KEY TO THE SPECIES

I. Wing over 10·00.
   A. Belly without bars, striped longitudinally.
      a. Upperparts with cross-bars.
         a^1. Toes feathered . . . . 300. BARRED OWL.
         a^2. Toes nearly bare . . . . 300a. FLORIDA BARRED OWL.
      b. Upperparts striped longitudinally . . . . 303. SHORT-EARED OWL.
   B. Belly with cross-bars.

a. With conspicuous 'horns' or 'ears.'
   a[1]. Wing over 13·00 . . . 296*a–c*. GREAT HORNED OWL and races.
   a[2]. Wing under 13·00 . . . . 302. LONG-EARED OWL.
b. Without 'horns' or 'ears.'
   b[1]. Plumage white, more or less barred with black. 297. SNOWY OWL.
   b[2]. Plumage fuscous, mottled and barred with whitish.
                                    301. GREAT GRAY OWL.
II. Wing under 10·00.
  A. Toes heavily feathered.
    a. Wing more than 6·00.
      a[1]. Tail more than 6·00 . . . . 298. HAWK OWL.
      a[2]. Tail less than 6·00 . . . . 304. RICHARDSON'S OWL.
    b. Wing less than 6·00 . . . . 305. SAW-WHET OWL.
  B. Toes thinly, if at all feathered.
    a. Tarsi heavily feathered; with conspicuous 'horns.'
                 295, 295*a, b.* SCREECH OWL and races.
    b. Tarsi partly bare; no 'horns' . . 299*a.* FLORIDA BURROWING OWL.

295. EASTERN SCREECH OWL. OTUS ASIO NÆVIUS (*Gmelin*). [373.] (Pl. XX, XXI.) Size small; ear-tufts conspicuous, about an inch in length. *Ads., rufous phase.*—Upperparts bright rufous, finely streaked with black; underparts white, the feathers centrally streaked with black and irregularly barred with rufous; toes rather scantily feathered; eyes yellow. *Gray phase.*— Upperparts generally brownish gray, streaked with black and finely mottled with ochraceous-buff; underparts white, finely streaked and more finely and irregularly barred with black, more or less bordered by rufous. *Nestling.*— Entire plumage regularly barred with grayish or rufous and white. ♂ L., 9·40; W., 6·40; T., 3·10; B., ·63. ♀ L., 10·00; W., 6·75; T., 3·35; B., ·64.
    Remarks.—The Screech Owl may be known by its small size and ear-tufts. Its color phases are not dependent upon age, sex, or season, and both phases are sometimes represented in the same brood. Between the two there is a complete intergradation.
    Range.—N. B., Me., n. N. Y., Ont., Wisc., Minn., and s. Man., s. to the uplands of Ga., Ala., Tenn., e. Okla. and n. Ark. Accidental in Prince Edward Isl.
    Washington, uncommon P. R. Bronx region, common P. R. Boston, common P. R. N. Ohio, common P. R. Glen Ellyn, common P. R. SE. Minn., common P. R.
    Nest, generally in a hollow tree. *Eggs,* 4–6, white, 1·55 × 1·22. *Date,* Chevy Chase, Md., Apr. 6; Ossining, N. Y., Apr. 6; Boston, Apr. 15; Milton, Mass., Apr. 9; Poweshiek Co., Ia., Apr. 9.

The Screech Owl frequently makes its home near our dwellings, and sometimes selects a convenient nook in them in which to lay its eggs. But its favorite retreat is an old apple orchard, where the hollow limbs offer it a secure refuge from the mobs of small birds which are ever ready to attack it. A search in the trees of an orchard of this kind rarely fails to result in the discovery of one or more of these feathered inhabitants who may have resided there for years. They attempt to escape capture by a show of resistance and a castanetlike cracking of the bill, but when brought from their hiding-place sit quietly, dazzled for a moment by the sudden light. They then elongate themselves and almost close their eyes, thus rendering themselves as inconspicuous as possible. How differently they appear when the western sky fades and *their* day begins! Is any bird more thoroughly awake than a hungry Screech Owl? With ear-tufts erected, and his great, round eyes opened to the utmost, he is the picture of alertness.

PLATE XXI

SCREECH OWL
Gray and rufous phases of plumage

When night comes, one may hear the Screech Owl's tremulous, wailing whistle. It is a weird, melancholy call, welcomed only by those who love Nature's voice whatever be the medium through which she speaks.

"Of 255 stomachs examined, 1 contained poultry; 38, other birds; 91, mice; 11, other mammals; 2, lizards; 4, batrachians; 1, fish; 100, insects; 5, spiders; 9, crawfish; 7, miscellaneous; 2, scorpions; 2, earthworms; and 43 were empty" (Fisher).

1893. HASBROUCK, E. M., Am. Nat., 521–533, 638–649; ALLEN, J. A., Auk, 347–351.—1896. CHADBOURNE, A. P., Auk, 321–325; 33–39 (dichromatism).—1911. SHERMAN, A., Auk, 155–168 (home-life).—1924. ALLEN, A. A., Auk, 1–16, illus. (habits and economic status).

295a. SOUTHERN SCREECH OWL. OTUS ASIO ASIO (*Linnæus*). [373 part.] Resembles the Eastern Screech Owl in color and markings but is smaller. ♂ W., 6·00. ♀ W., 6·40.

Range.—Lower Austral Zone from Va. to Ga. and the Gulf States w. to La., n. in the Miss. Valley to w. Tenn., s. Ills., se. Kans., Okla., and Ark.

This is an intermediate form connecting the northern Screech Owl with the Florida Screech Owl. The colors of Screech Owls appear to be exceptionally responsive to environmental influences, and this fact, in connection with their non-migratory habits, has evidently resulted in the development of many geographic races, fifteen being known from North America.

295b. FLORIDA SCREECH OWL. OTUS ASIO FLORIDANUS (*Ridgway*). [373a.] Much like *O. a. asio* but smaller, with the colors deeper and markings of the underparts heavier. The rufous phase is comparatively rare in this subspecies. ♂ W., 5·50. ♀ W., 5·75.

Range.—Peninsular Fla.

Nesting-date, Archer, Fla., Mch. 31.

The call of the Florida Screech Owl is not so loud and usually lacks the musical, whistled quality of that of the northern bird. It is, indeed, more like a crooning refrain of the northern bird's call.

296. ARCTIC HORNED OWL. BUBO VIRGINIANUS SUBARCTICUS *Hoy*. [375b.] Similar to *B. v. virginianus*, but much lighter in color, the ochraceous-buff markings largely replaced by gray or white.

Range.—Breeds from Hudson Bay and the tree-limit in valley of the Mack. s. to n. Alberta, cent. Man., sw. Sask. and n. Ont., and in winter to the n. U. S. from Idaho to Nebr., Wisc. and casually N. Y. and Mass.

Bronx region, A. V., one record, Feb. 15. Boston, A. V. SE. Minn., uncommon W. V.

296a. LABRADOR HORNED OWL. BUBO VIRGINIANUS HETEROCNEMIS (*Oberholser*). [375f.] Similar to *B. v. virginianus*, but much darker, the prevailing color fuscous or dusky.

Range.—N. Ungava and Lab., N. F. and N. S.; migrating in winter to Ont., and casually to Conn.

296b. GREAT HORNED OWL. BUBO VIRGINIANUS VIRGINIANUS (*Gmelin*). [375.] (Pl. XX.) *Ads.*—Size large; ear-tufts conspicuous, nearly two inches in length; upperparts mottled with varying shades of ochraceous-buff and black; facial disk ochraceous-buff; ear-tufts black and ochraceous-buff; a white patch on the throat, rest of the underparts ochraceous-buff, barred with black; legs and feet feathered; eyes yellow. ♂ L., 22·00; W., 15·00; T., 8·50; B., 1·60.

Range.—Ont., Que. and N. B., s. to the Gulf Coast and Fla., w. to Wisc., e. Minn., Ia., se. S. Dak., Kans., Okla., and e. Tex.

Washington, rare P. R. Bronx region, decidedly uncommon W. V., rare P. R., Nov. 20–Apr. 23 (June 12). Boston, rare P. R. N. Ohio, not common P. R. SE. Minn., common P. R.

Nest, generally in an old Crow's, Hawk's, or squirrel's nest. *Eggs*, 2–3, white, 2·20 × 1·80. *Date*, Merritt's Isl., Fla., Dec. 17; Chester Co., Pa., Feb. 15; Boston, Feb. 22; Black Hawk Co., Ia., Feb. 14; se. Minn., Feb. 21.

This "tiger among birds" is an inhabitant of heavily forested regions, and is common therefore only in the wilder, less settled portions of our country. It is the only one of our resident Owls which destroys poultry and birds in any numbers, but, in spite of its frequent visits to the farmyard, Dr. Fisher considers that in many localities it is a "beneficial species" because of its great fondness for rabbits.

Its usual call is a loud, deep-toned *whōō, hoo-hoo-hoo, whōōō, whōōō.* The syllables are all on the same note, and bear some resemblance to a bass-voiced dog barking in the distance.

A much rarer call is a loud, piercing scream, one of the most blood-curdling sounds I have ever heard in the woods.

"Of 127 stomachs examined, 31 contained poultry or game-birds; 8, other birds; 13, mice; 65, other mammals; 1, a scorpion; 1, fish; 10, insects, and 17 were empty" (Fisher).

1925. REED, B. P., Auk, 14–31, illus. (growth and reactions of young).—1929. GARDNER, L. L., Auk, 58–69 (nesting of).

296c. WESTERN HORNED OWL. BUBO VIRGINIANUS OCCIDENTALIS *Stone.* "Much paler than *B. v. virginianus*, with grayish and buffy predominating on upperparts, the underparts more extensively white, with black bars narrower; legs and toes buffy to nearly white, usually immaculate, or nearly so; size larger." ♂ W., 13·75; T. 8·40. ♀ W., 14·80; T., 9·10 (Ridgway).

Range.—Minn., S. Dak., Nebr., and Kans. w. to Nev., se. Ore., nw. Calif., Wyo. and Mont., n. to cent. Alberta; s. in winter to Ia.

297. SNOWY OWL. NYCTEA NYCTEA (*Linnæus*). [376.] (Pl. XX.) *Ad.* ♂.—Size large; no ear-tufts; white, more or less barred with dark grayish brown or fuscous; legs and feet heavily feathered; eyes yellow. *Ad.* ♀.—Similar, but more heavily barred. L., 25·00; W., 17·00; T., 9·50; B., 1·50.

Range.—N. parts of N. Hemisphere. In N. A. breeds on Barren Grounds from the isls. of Bering Sea and the Yukon delta to Melville Isl. and n. Greenland s. to cent. Mack., cent. Keewatin, and n. Ungava and n. B. C.; winters from the Arctic Coast s. to the s. Canadian Provinces and Mont., and irregularly to the Middle States and Ohio Valley, straggling to Calif., Tex., La., S. C., and Bermuda.

Washington, casual W. V. Bronx region, rare and irregular W. V., Nov. 4 –Apr. 5. Boston, rare and irregular W. V. N. Ohio, rare W. V. Glen Ellyn, very rare W. V. SE. Minn., common W. V., Oct.–Apr.

Nest, on the ground. *Eggs*, 3–10, white, 2·24 × 1·76. *Date*, Pt. Barrow, Alaska, June 7.

"The Snowy Owl is diurnal in its habits, but like most birds is more active in search of prey during the early morning and again toward dusk. Like many of the Hawks, it occupies a commanding perch for hours, watching what is going on about it, occasionally varying the monotony by dropping on a mouse or launching out over the broad country, soon to return to its perch. During its southern wanderings it is very partial to localities in the vicinity of water, especially the barren sand wastes along the seashore or extensive marshy flats bordering the bays and rivers. . . .

"The flight is firm, smooth, and noiseless, and may be long protracted. It is capable of rapid flight, and, according to Audubon, is able to capture Ducks, Pigeons, and even Grouse on the wing, striking them down after the manner of the Duck Hawk.

"Of 38 stomachs examined, 2 contained game-birds; 9, other birds; 18, mice; 2, other mammals; and 12 were empty" (Fisher).

1906. DEANE, R., Auk, 283–298 (flight of).—1927. GROSS, A. O., Auk, 479–493, illus. (flight of); see also SUTTON, G. M., The Cardinal, II, 2 (Carnegie Mus., Pittsburgh, Pa.).

298. AMERICAN HAWK OWL. SURNIA ULULA CAPAROCH (*Müller*). [377*a*.] (Pl. XX.) *Ads.*—Size medium; no ear-tufts; upperparts dark grayish brown or fuscous; head and hindneck spotted with white; back, and especially tertials, barred with white; tail with broken whitish bars, *long and rounded*, the outer feathers more than an inch shorter than the middle ones; middle of the throat with a fuscous spot, and below it a white one; sides of the neck and upper breast streaked with fuscous, rest of the underparts barred with fuscous and white; legs and feet fully feathered. L., 15·00; W., 8·75; T., 7·25.

Range.—Breeds from nw. Alaska, nw. Mack., and Hudson Strait to s. B. C., cent. Alberta (casually Mont.), and Ungava; winters s. to the s. Canadian Provinces, casually to Wash., Nebr., Minn., Mo., Ind., O., N. Y., N. J., R. I., Mass., and Me.; accidental in England and Bermuda.

Boston, very rare W. V. N. Ohio, rare W. V. SE. Minn., uncommon W. V., Oct.–Mch.

Nest, in coniferous trees or in the holes of dead trees or stubs. *Eggs*, 3–7, white, 1·50 × 1·23. *Date*, Red Deer, Alberta, Apr. 16.

"The Hawk Owl is strictly diurnal, as much so as any of the Hawks, and like some of them often selects a tall stub or dead-topped tree in a comparatively open place for a perch, where it sits in the bright sunlight watching for its prey.

"Although the flight is swift and hawklike, it has nevertheless the soft, noiseless character common to the other Owls; when starting from any high place, such as the top of a tree, it usually pitches down nearly to the ground, and flies off rapidly above the tops of the bushes or high grass, abruptly arising again as it seeks another perch.

"The note is a shrill cry, which is uttered generally while the bird is on the wing" (Fisher).

299. The BURROWING OWL, *Speotyto cunicularia hypugæa* (Bonaparte), [378], is well known in the western United States from the Pacific Coast to Minnesota and Louisiana, and from British Columbia and Manitoba south to Panama; it is migratory north of Oregon and northern Kansas, and accidental in New York and Massachusetts.

299a. FLORIDA BURROWING OWL. Speotyto cunicularia flori-dana *Ridgway.* [378a.] *Ads.*—Size small; no ear-tufts; *legs and feet nearly naked;* upperparts grayish brown, spotted and barred with white; throat white, rest of the underparts barred with grayish brown and white in about equal amounts. L., 9·00; W., 6·50; T., 3·00; Tar., 1·75.

Range.—S. Fla., chiefly in the Kissimmee 'prairie' region of Osceola, Polk, and DeSoto counties, and also Manatee Co.

Nest, in a hole in the ground excavated by the bird. *Eggs,* 5–7, white, 1·23 × 1·03. *Date,* Ft. Thompson, Fla., Mch. 26.

This diurnal Owl is locally abundant in its restricted range. Excellent accounts of its habits will be found under the following references: Rhoads, *The Auk,* 1892, pp. 1–8; Scott, *Ibid.* 216–218; Palmer, *Ibid.,* 1896, 100–108; Pennock, *Wilson Bull.,* 1922, pp. 21–28.

300. NORTHERN BARRED OWL. Strix varia varia *Barton.* [368.] (Figs. 51, 95b; Pl. XX.) *Ads.*—No ear-tufts; upperparts grayish brown, each feather with two or three white or buffy white bars; tail with six to eight similar bars; facial disk gray, finely barred or mottled with fuscous; underparts white, more or less tinged with buffy, the breast *barred,* the sides and belly broadly *streaked* with fuscous; bill yellow; legs and feet feathered to or near the bases of the nails; eyes brownish black. L., 20·00; W., 13·50; T., 9·50; B., 1·50.

Range.—Breeds from n. Ont., Man., Sask., s. Que. and N. F., s. to Ark., Tenn., Ky., n. Ga. and nw. S. C. and w. to e. Wyo., cent. Mont., and e. Colo. Washington, not common P. R. Bronx region, fairly common P. R. Boston, P. R., sometimes common in Nov. and Dec. N. Ohio, common P. R. Glen Ellyn, rare and local P. R. SE. Minn., common P. R.

Nest, in a hollow tree; sometimes in an old Crow's or Hawk's nest. *Eggs,* 2–4, white, 2·00 × 1·65. *Date,* New London, Conn., Mch. 22; Black Hawk Co., Ia., Mch. 1; se. Minn., Mch. 7.

The deep-toned, questioning voice, the absence of 'horns,' and the dark brown, nearly black eyes, combine to make Barred Owls appear among the most human of these strangely human birds. They inhabit large tracts of woodland, and are generally resident in certain localities. Their notes are uttered more or less throughout the year, but are more frequently heard during the nesting season. As a rule they call only during the first part of the night and again before sunrise, but on moonlight nights they call throughout the night, and occasionally they may be heard during the day. They readily respond to an imitation of their cries, and even at midday I have drawn them from their resting-place to meet a supposed intruder on their domain. Under favorable circumstances they may be heard at a distance of at least half a mile.

Their usual call is a sonorous *whŏŏ-whŏŏ-whŏŏ whŏ-whŏŏ, tŏ-whŏŏ-äh.* This is varied, both as to relative position and length of the syllables, by the same individuals, and is apparently the cry of question and response. When two birds, perhaps rival males, come together, there ensues a striking medley of *whă-whăs* mingled with rolling *whōō-ăhs,* the whole reminding one of deep-voiced, mirthless laughter. Sometimes two birds give a concerted performance. One utters about ten rapid hoots, while the other, in a slightly higher tone, hoots half as fast.

both performers ending together with a *whōō-ăh*. At times they utter a single, prolonged *whōō-ăh*, and more rarely a weird, gasping shriek, emphasized at its conclusion like a cry of distress.

"Of 109 stomachs examined, 5 contained poultry or game; 13, other birds; 46, mice; 18, other mammals; 4, frogs; 1, a lizard; 2, fish; 14, insects; 2, spiders; 9, crawfish; and 20 were empty" (Fisher).

300a. FLORIDA BARRED OWL. STRIX VARIA ALLENI *Ridgway.* [368a.] Similar to the preceding, but averaging somewhat darker, and with the toes nearly naked. W., 12·50; T., 8·50.

Range.—South Atlantic and Gulf States from cent. N. C. to e. Tex., n. Ala. and Ark.

Nesting-date, San Mateo, Fla., Jan. 5.

301. GREAT GRAY OWL. SCOTIAPTEX NEBULOSA NEBULOSA (*J. R. Forster*). [370.] *Ads.*—No ear-tufts, size very large; upperparts fuscous, everywhere mottled with white, and with little or no buffy; facial disk gray, barred with black; underparts white, the breast broadly streaked, and belly and sides irregularly barred and streaked with fuscous; legs and feet heavily feathered; bill and eyes yellow. L., 27·00; W., 17·50; T., 12·00.

Range.—Breeds in Hudsonian and Upper Canadian zones from tree-limit in n. cent. Alaska and nw. Mack. s. to the cent. Sierra Nevada of Calif.; n. Idaho, n. Mont. and Ont.; s. in winter through the s. Canadian Provinces, Wyo., Nebr., Minn., Ind., O., n. N. J., N. Y., and N. E.

Boston, very rare and irregular W. V. SE. Minn., rare W. V.

Nest, in trees. *Eggs*, 2–4, white, 2·16 × 1·71. *Date*, Buffalo Lake, Alberta, Apr. 10 (Norris).

"Dr. Dall considers it a stupid bird, and states that sometimes it may be caught in the hands. Its great predilection for thick woods, in which it dwells doubtless to the very limit of trees, prevents it from being an inhabitant of the barren grounds or other open country in the north. . . . The note of this Owl is said to be a tremulous, vibrating sound, somewhat resembling that of the Screech Owl. . . .

"Of 9 stomachs examined, 1 contained a small bird; 7, mice; and 4, other mammals" (Fisher).

302. LONG-EARED OWL. ASIO WILSONIANUS (*Lesson*). [366.] (Pl. XX.) *Ads.*—Ear-tufts conspicuous, an inch or more in length, black bordered by white and buffy; upperparts fuscous-brown mottled with white, the bases of the feathers ochraceous-buff; tail with six to eight fuscous cross-bars; facial disk buffy bordered by black; underparts mixed white and ochraceous-buff, the breast broadly streaked, the sides and belly irregularly *barred* with fuscous; eyes yellow. L., 14·80; W., 11·90; T., 6·00; B., 1·06.

Range.—Breeds from cent. B. C., s. Que., and N. F. s. to s. Calif., Ark. and Va.; winters from s. Can. to s. Fla. and cent. Mex. Casual in se. Alaska.

Washington, rare P. R. Bronx region, fairly common W. V., rare P. R., Oct. 11–Apr. 24. Boston, rare P. R., but sometimes common in fall and winter. N. Ohio, uncommon P. R. Glen Ellyn, rare, fall and winter records only, Nov. 7–Dec. 27. SE. Minn., P. R.

Nest, generally in an old Crow's, Hawk's, or squirrel's nest. *Eggs*, 3–6, white, 1·65 × 1·30. *Date*, Ossining, N. Y., Mch. 31; Boston, Apr. 1; se. Minn., Apr. 16.

"This species, like the Screech Owl, is nocturnal in its habits, and differs from the Short-eared Owl in never hunting during the daytime. It usually spends the day in some evergreen woods, thick willow copse, or alder swamp, although rarely it may be found in open places. . . .

"The bird is not wild, and will allow itself to be closely approached. When conscious that its presence is recognized, it sits upright, draws the feathers close to the body, and erects the ear-tufts, resembling in appearance a piece of weather-beaten bark more than a bird. . . .

"Like the other Owls, its flight is slow and wavering, but in common with them it is buoyant and devoid of any appearance of heaviness. The note of this Owl is said by some to resemble the noise made by kittens, while others state it is like the barking of small dogs.

"Of 107 stomachs examined, 1 contained a game-bird; 15, other birds; 84, mice; 5, other mammals; 1, insects; and 15 were empty" (Fisher).

303. SHORT-EARED OWL. ASIO FLAMMEUS FLAMMEUS (*Pontoppidan*). [367.] (Pl. XX.) *Ad. ♂.*—Ear-tufts very short, difficult to distinguish in a dried skin; upperparts fuscous, the feathers margined with cream-buff or ochraceous-buff, not mottled with white; tail with ochraceous-buff and fuscous bands of about equal width; underparts whitish, the breast broadly and the belly more finely *streaked* with fuscous; eyes yellow. *Ad. ♀.*—Similar, but underparts rich ochraceous-buff. L., 15·50; W., 12·75; T., 6·05; B., 1·20.

Range.—Breeds irregularly and locally from n. Alaska and Aleutian isls., n. Mack., n. Que. (Ungava) and Greenland s. to Calif., Colo., s. Kans., Mo., n. O., n. Ind., and the coast of N. J.; winters from B. C., Wyo., Minn., Ind., O., and Mass. s. to La., Cuba, and Guat.; also breeds in Europe and n. Asia.

Washington, common W. V. Bronx region, fairly common T. V. and W. V., probably no longer breeds; Aug. 1–Apr. 26. Boston, T. V., Mch. 15–Apr. 15, rare; Oct.–Nov., uncommon. N. Ohio, uncommon P. R. Glen Ellyn, rare S. R., more common W. R., chiefly T. V., Apr. 19–Dec. 10. SE. Minn., uncommon P. R.

Nest, on the ground, in grassy marshes. *Eggs,* 4–7, white, 1·60 × 1·25. *Date,* St. Clair Flats, Mich., Apr. 20.

This species might well be named Marsh Owl, for, unlike most of our Owls, it does not frequent the woods, but lives in grassy marshes. It is not shy and does not take wing until almost stepped upon, when it arises noiselessly and flies low over the marsh. Sometimes it alights on a knoll or slight elevation, and watches the intruder in the intent, half-human manner of Owls.

During the migrations and in the winter this bird is occasionally found in flocks or colonies containing one or two hundred individuals.

"Of 101 stomachs examined, 11 contained small birds; 77, mice; 7, other mammals; 7, insects; and 14 were empty" (Fisher).

1923. DuBois, A. D., The Short-eared Owl as a Foster-Mother, Auk, 383–393, illus.—1923. Urner, C. A., Auk, 30–36; 1925, 31–37 (habits and nesting).

304. RICHARDSON'S OWL. CRYPTOGLAUX FUNEREA RICHARDSONI (*Bonaparte*). [371.] (Pl. XX.) *Ads.*—Upperparts grayish brown, both the head and back *spotted* with white; tail with four or five imperfect white bars; underparts white, heavily streaked with grayish brown; legs and feet heavily feathered, whitish, barred with grayish brown; eyes yellow. *Im.*—Upper-

parts dark cinnamon-brown, with a few more or less concealed white spots;
tail as in the ad.; breast like the back; belly ochraceous-buff. L., 10'00;
W., 6'75; T., 4'40.

Range.—Breeds in Hudsonian and Upper Canadian zones from limit of
trees in cent. Alaska and n. Yukon and Mack. s. to n. B. C., n. Alberta, Man.,
N. S., and Magdalen Isls.; s. in winter to s. Can. but rare e.; casual s. to Ore.,
Colo., Nebr., Ia., Ills., w. Pa., and N. E.

Boston, very rare W. V.

Nest, in holes in trees (and in old nests of other birds?). *Eggs*, 3–7,
white, 1'35 × 1'14. *Date*, Ft. Simpson, Mack., May 7.

"Richardson's Owl is nocturnal in its habits, remaining quiet during
the day in the thick foliage of the trees or bushes. In fact, its vision is
apparently so affected by bright light that many specimens have been
captured alive by persons walking up and taking them in their hands.
On this account the Eskimos in Alaska have given it the name of 'blind
one.' "The song of this Owl, according to Dr. Merriam (*Bull. Nutt.
Orn. Club*, VII, 1882, p. 237), is a low liquid note that resembles the
sound produced by water slowly dropping from a height" (Fisher).

305. COMMON SAW-WHET OWL. CRYPTOGLAUX ACADICA ACADICA
(*Gmelin*). [372.] (Pl. XX.) *Ads.*—Upperparts dark cinnamon-brown, the
head finely *streaked*, the back *spotted* with white; tail with three or four imperfect white bars; underparts white, heavily streaked with cinnamon-brown
or dark rufous; legs and feet feathered, buffy white, unbarred; eyes yellow.
Im.—Upperparts as in the ad., but head and back with little or no white;
breast like the back; belly ochraceous-buff. L., 8'00; W., 5'40; T., 2'80; B., '60.

Remarks.—Its small size and absence of 'ears' at once distinguish this
species from any Owl of eastern North America except *C. f. richardsoni*, from
which it may be known by its lighter color, streaked instead of spotted head,
and unbarred legs and feet.

Range.—Breeds from s. Alaska, cent. B. C., Que., N. B., and N. S. s. to
the Sierra Nevada of Calif., cent. Ariz., N. Mex., Okla., and the mountains
of Mex. to Vera Cruz; also in s. Nebr., n. Ind., n. Ills., and in the mountains
of Pa. and Md. Winters s. to s. Calif., La., Va., and casually to the Carolinas and Ga.

Washington, rare W. V., Oct.–Mch. Bronx region, regular but uncommon
W. V., Oct. 11–Apr. 18. Boston, rare P. R., not uncommon W. V., Nov.–
Mch. N. Ohio, rare P. R. SE. Minn., uncommon P. R.

Nest, in a hole in a tree; frequently a Woodpecker's, sometimes a squirrel's
deserted nest. *Eggs*, 3–5, white, 1'19 × 1'00. *Date*, Trenton Falls, N. Y.,
Mch. 31; Farmington, Me., May 21; se. Minn., May 9 (hatching).

"This species is not migratory, but is more or less of an irregular
wanderer in its search for food during the fall and winter. It may be
quite common in a locality and then not be seen again for several years.
It is nocturnal, seldom moving about in the daytime, but passing the
time in sleeping in some dark retreat. So soundly does it sleep that
oftentimes it may be captured alive. . . .

"During the day it frequents the thick evergreen woods, though
sometimes it is found in comparatively open groves, but always in
dense trees. . . . The note of this species is peculiar and has a rasping
character, resembling the sound made when a large-toothed saw is
being filed; hence the name. It is more often heard during March and
early April, though occasionally it is heard at other times of the year.

"The flight resembles that of the Woodcock very closely—so much so, in fact, that the writer once killed a specimen as it was flying over the alders, and not until the dog pointed the dead bird was he aware of his mistake. . . .

"Of 22 stomachs examined, 17 contained mice; 1, a bird; 1, an insect; and 3 were empty" (Fisher).

1911. TAVERNER, P. A., and SWALES, B. H., Auk, 329–334 (migration).

XV. ORDER CAPRIMULGIFORMES. GOATSUCKERS AND OILBIRDS

SUBORDER CAPRIMULGI. WHIP-POOR-WILLS, NIGHTHAWKS, ETC.

(4 families, 1 North American)

FAMILY CAPRIMULGIDÆ. NIGHTHAWKS, WHIP-POOR-WILLS, ETC.

Goatsuckers are found in most parts of the world, but are more numerously represented in the tropics. Over 200 species and subspecies are known, of which about one-half are American, of which seventeen, representing six species, are found, chiefly as summer residents, in North America. Most of the American species are forest-inhabiting, passing the day upon the leaves or perched lengthwise upon the branches of trees, where their dull, blended colors harmonize with their surroundings. The Nighthawks, however, are equally at home in treeless countries. Nighthawks feed high in the air, like Swifts, while other species frequent the borders of forests or clearings, where they feed nearer the ground. All the species capture their food of insects on the wing, their enormous mouths and the long, stiffened bristles, which in some species beset its base, especially adapting them to this mode of feeding. Many of the species are possessed of remarkable vocal powers, and their cries are among the most striking of bird-notes. They make no nest but lay their two mottled or marbled eggs on the ground. The young are hatched covered with down.

KEY TO THE SPECIES

A. A white spot in the wing. . . . . 308. NIGHTHAWK AND RACES.
B. No white spot in the wing; primaries spotted with rufous.
    a. Wing under 7·50 . . . . 307. WHIP-POOR-WILL.
    b. Wing over 7·50 . . . . 306. CHUCK-WILL'S-WIDOW.

306. CHUCK-WILL'S-WIDOW. ANTROSTOMUS CAROLINENSIS (*Gmelin*). [416.] *Ad.* ♂.—Upperparts streaked with black and finely mottled with ochraceous-buff and black; primaries black, with broken rufous bars; tail mottled with black and ochraceous-buff, the end half of all but the two middle feathers white, more or less washed with buffy on the *inner vane;* underparts mottled with black, ochraceous, and cream-buff; an imperfect whitish band across the upper breast; base of the bill beset with long, stiffened bristles, the basal half of these bristles grown with *hairlike branches. Ad.* ♀.—

Similar, but with no white patches in the tail, the upper breast with an ochraceous-buff instead of white band. L., 12·00; W., 8·50; T., 6·00; B., ·40.

Range.—Breeds in Lower Austral Zone from s. Mo., s. Ind., se. Kans., and s. Md., s. to cent. Tex. and Gulf States; casual in W. Va. and Md.; accidental in Mass., Conn., N. S., and Ont.; migrates through e. Mex.; winters from Fla. to Greater Antilles, Cent. A., and Colombia.

Washington, two records. Boston, A. V.

Eggs, 2, laid on the ground or leaves, in woods or thickets, dull white, with delicate, obscure pale lilac markings, and a few distinct brownish gray spots, 1·40 × ·98. *Date*, San Mateo, Fla., Apr. 14.

Generally speaking, this species resembles the Whip-poor-will in habits. Its notes are quite similar to those of that species, but are louder, less rapidly uttered, and each call has an additional syllable. Its gape is enormous, the wide-open mouth of an adult measuring about 2 inches from corner to corner. For this reason it can swallow large objects with ease, and both Hummingbirds and Sparrows have been found in the Chuck-will's-widow's stomach. Possibly they were mistaken for large moths, but Gerald Thayer records a Chuck-will's-widow which, following a steamer off the Carolina coast, was seen to pursue and catch Warblers on the wing. (*The Auk*, 1899, pp. 273–276.)

1926. BIRD-LORE, 117, 121 (mig.; pl.).

307. EASTERN WHIP-POOR-WILL. ANTROSTOMUS VOCIFERUS VOCIFERUS (*Wilson*). [417.] *Ad.* ♂.—Upperparts streaked with black, the *head* finely mottled with black and white, the back mottled with ochraceous-buff and black; primaries black, with broken rufous bars; tail irregularly barred with black and mottled with whitish or cream-buff; end half of three outer feathers *white;* black on the outer vane of the outer feather extending farther

FIG. 96. Whip-poor-will

down than on the others; throat and breast blackish, finely mottled with cream-buff or ochraceous-buff; a narrow white band across the upper breast; belly cream-buff, irregularly barred with blackish; base of the bill beset with long, stiffened bristles, which are *without* hairlike branches. *Ad.* ♀.—Similar, but outer three tail-feathers narrowly tipped with ochraceous-buff; band on the throat cream-buff instead of white. L , 9·75; W., 6·08; T., 4·65; B., ·37.

Range.—Breeds from Man. and N. B., s. to n. parts of La., Miss., Ala., Ga., nw. S. C. and from e. N. Dak., Nebr., and Kans. eastward; winters from the lowlands of S. C. and the Gulf States to Costa Rica.

Washington, common S. R., Apr. 1–Nov. 21. Bronx region, uncommon T. V. and local S. R., Apr. 16–Oct. 18. Boston, formerly S. R., now chiefly T. V., Apr. 30–Sept. 20. N. Ohio, locally common S. R., Apr. 29–Sept. 15. Glen Ellyn, uncommon T. V., Apr. 19–May 23; Aug. 7–? SE. Minn., common S. R., Apr. 17–Sept. 28.

Eggs, 2, laid on the ground or leaves, in woods or thickets; dull white, with delicate, obscure lilac markings and a few distinct brownish gray spots, 1·18 × ·84. *Date,* Raleigh, N. C., May 2; Boston, May 26; Lake City, Minn., May 20; se. Minn., May 26.

In walking through rather densely grown woods I have sometimes been surprised by having a Whip-poor-will fly up from beneath my feet and disappear in the surrounding growth. I say surprised, because the bird's flight is as noiseless as a moth's, and this unusual ghostly silence is almost as startling as the *whir* of a Grouse.

The Whip-poor-will's day begins when the sun goes down. Then he passes out into bushy fields near his home, and, flying low, catches his supper on the wing. Between courses he rests on some low perch, and gives utterance to the notes familiar to many who have never seen their author. *Whip'-poor-will', whip'-poor-will'* he calls, rapidly and with unexpected snap and vigor. If one is quite near the singer, a preliminary *chuck* may be heard before each call. These notes are given for about two hours after sunset and for a short time before sunrise.

It is a singular fact that, in spite of the marked difference in their habits and notes, the Nighthawk and Whip-poor-will are frequently considered to be the same species. It is not the only case, however, where the notes of some species difficult of observation have been attributed to a species whose habits render it conspicuous.

1926. BIRD-LORE, 118, 121 (mig.; pl.).

308. EASTERN NIGHTHAWK. CHORDEILES MINOR MINOR (*J. R. Forster*). [420.] (Fig. 52.) *Ad.* ♂.—Upperparts black, irregularly marked with whitish, cream-buff, or ochraceous-buff; primaries fuscous, crossed in the middle by a conspicuous white bar which rarely reaches the outer vane of the first primary; tail fuscous or black, with broken bars of cream-buff and a white band near the end on all but the middle feathers; throat with a broad white band; chin and upper breast black, the feathers tipped with ochraceous-buff, cream-buff, or white; the rest of the underparts barred with black and white, sometimes tinged with buff. *Ad.* ♀.—Similar, but with no white on the tail, throat-patch ochraceous-buff, underparts more or less washed with ochraceous-buff. L., 10·00; W., 7·85; T., 4·60; B., ·25.

Range.—Breeds from s. Yukon and s. Que., s. to nw. Wash., s. cent. Ills., n. Ark., se. Tenn., n. Ga. and s. Va. and w. to edge of Plains from Minn. to ne. Okla.; migrates through the Greater Antilles and Cent. A.; winters in S. A. from Colombia to Argentina. Accidental on Melville Isl., Arctic Ocean, and Scilly Isles, Great Britain.

Washington, not common S. R.; common T. V., Apr. 18–Oct. 11. Bronx region, fairly common S. R.; occasionally abundant T. V., May 1–Oct. 24. Boston, rather common S. R., nesting on city roofs; common T. V., May 15–Sept. 25. N. Ohio, locally common S. R., May 1–Sept. 20. Glen Ellyn, not common S. R.; common T. V., May 1–Oct. 14. SE. Minn., common S. R., Apr. 10–Oct. 9.

Eggs, 2, laid on the bare ground or a flat rock in open fields, rarely on the roof of a house, dull white, evenly marked with small, irregularly shaped blotches or fine specklings of grayish brown or brownish gray, 1·20 × ·86. *Date*, Beaufort, S. C., May 7; Chester Co., Pa., May 24; New London, Conn., June 1; Boston, June 5; se. Minn., June 7.

In wooded regions the Nighthawk passes the day perched lengthwise on a limb, but on the plains he roosts upon the ground, where his colors harmonize with his surroundings. Soon after sunset he mounts high in the air to course for insects. Batlike he flies erratically about, and at more or less regular intervals utters a loud nasal *peent*, this call being followed by two or three unusually quick, flitting wing-beats. Long after the light has faded from the western horizon we may hear this voice from the starlit heavens, for the Nighthawk is one of our few truly nocturnal birds. Occasionally the

FIG. 97. Primaries of *a*. Whip-poor-will. *b*. Nighthawk.

peents are given more rapidly, and, after calling several times in close succession, the bird on half-closed wings dives earthward with such speed that one fears for his safety; but when near the ground, or while still high above it, he checks his rapid descent by an abrupt turn, and on leisurely wing again mounts upward to repeat this game of sky-coasting. At the moment the turn is made one may hear a rushing, booming sound, which, as writers have remarked, can be imitated in tone by blowing across the bung-hole of an empty barrel. It is made by the passage of the air through the bird's primaries.

In late summer Nighthawks gather in large flocks and begin their southward migrations. When flying the white mark on their primaries is a conspicuous character, and has the appearance of being a hole in the bird's wing.

1905. HERRICK, F. H., Home-Life of Wild Birds, 129–135.—1926. BIRD-LORE, 255, 261 (mig.; pl.).

308a. FLORIDA NIGHTHAWK. CHORDEILES MINOR CHAPMANI *Coues*. [420*b*.] Similar to the preceding, but smaller, and with the white and cream-buff markings of the upperparts more numerous. L., 8·60; W., 7·10; T., 4·10.

Range.—South Atlantic and Gulf States from cent. N. C. to e. Tex.; n. to cent. Ala., s. Ills. and s. cent. Ark. Winters in S. A. from Colombia to Argentina.

Nesting-date, Volusia Co., Fla., May 8.

308b. SENNETT'S NIGHTHAWK. CHORDEILES MINOR SENNETTI *Coues.* [420c.] Palest of our Nighthawks; whitish prevailing in wing-coverts and scapulars; less rufous than in *C. m. henryi;* less heavily barred below than *C. m. minor.* W., 7·10.

Range.—N. portion of the Great Plains; breeds in n. N. Dak. and ne. Mont., s. to e. Wyo., nw. Ia. and n. Nebr.; migrating s. through Okla., and Tex. probably to S. A.

XVI. ORDER MICROPODIFORMES. SWIFTS, HUMMINGBIRDS, ETC.

SUBORDER MICROPODII. SWIFTS

(2 families, 1 North American)

FAMILY MICROPODIDÆ. SWIFTS.

The approximately 150 species and subspecies of Swifts are distributed throughout the greater part of the world but are most abundant in the tropics. About one-third this number are American but only five advance north of Mexico. Some Swifts nest in colonies and most species are associated in companies, at other times of the year. Hollow trees and caves are the natural nesting- and roosting-places of many species, while others fasten their nests to the under surface of palm leaves, and the East Indian Tree Swifts attach their nest to a limb. Most Swifts appear to employ the glutinous secretion of the salivary glands in nest-construction and the edible nests of the Swifts of the genus *Collocalia* are composed entirely of this substance.

Swifts lay white eggs and the young are naked when hatched. They feed entirely while flying, and with their unusually long wings and small, compactly feathered bodies possess unrivaled powers of flight. Swifts are popularly confused with Swallows, but the resemblance is only superficial and exists chiefly in the similarity of flight and feeding habits, while the structural differences between the two are numerous and important.

309. CHIMNEY SWIFT. CHÆTURA PELAGICA *(Linnæus).* [423.] (Fig. 53.) *Ads.*—Entire plumage fuscous, more grayish on the throat; a sooty black spot before the eye; shafts of the tail-feathers extending beyond the vanes. L., 5·43; W., 4·94; T., 1·90; B. from N., ·15.

Range.—Breeds from cent. Alberta, se. Sask., s. Que., and N. F., s. to Fla. and the Gulf Coast, and w. to e. cent. Mont. and e. Tex. Winters s. of the U. S., probably in Amazonas, Brazil; common spring transient in Haiti and reported from Mex. and Cent. A. Accidental in N. Mex., Greenland, and Bermuda.

Washington, abundant S. R., Apr. 5–Nov. 19. Bronx region, common S. R., Apr. 12–Oct. 26. Boston, common S. R., Apr. 25–Sept. 20. N. Ohio, abundant S. R., Apr. 10–Oct. 20. Glen Ellyn, common S. R., Apr. 16–Oct. 17. SE. Minn., common S. R., Apr. 17–Oct. 26.

Nest, a bracketlike basket of dead twigs glued together with saliva; attached to the wall of a chimney, generally about 10 feet from the top, by the gummy secretion of the bird's salivary glands. *Eggs,* 4–6, white, ·80

X ·50. *Date*, Chester Co., Pa., June 3; Ossining, N. Y., June 8; Boston, June 10; Petersburg, Mich., June 7.

It is unnecessary to give any aids to the identification of a bird as well known as the Chimney Swift, or, as it is more frequently called, 'Chimney Swallow.' It is not, however, a Swallow, but a Swift, and its structural relations are with the Hummingbirds and not with the Passerine Swallows.

Few sights in the bird-world are more familiar than the bow-and-arrow-like forms of these rapidly flying birds silhouetted against the sky. They are most active early in the morning and late in the afternoon, when one may hear their rolling twitter as they course about overhead. Sometimes they sail with wings held aloft over their backs, and sometimes, it is said, they use their wings alternately. It is a common thing to see a trio of birds flying together, but it has never been ascertained that the Chimney Swift is polygamous.

When migrating, Chimney Swifts congregate in large flocks, making their temporary headquarters in a disused chimney which morning and evening they leave and return to in a body. In perching they cling to the side of the chimney, using the spine-pointed tail, as Woodpeckers do, for a support. The habit of frequenting chimneys is, of course, a recent one, and the substitution of this modern, artificial home for hollow trees, illustrates the readiness with which a bird may take advantage of a favoring change in its environment.

1926. BIRD-LORE, 9, 14 (mig.; pl.).—1930. GREEN, W. R., Bird-Banding, 110–118; illus. (banding).—1931. CHAPMAN, F. M., Auk, 119, (winter range).

SUBORDER TROCHILI. HUMMINGBIRDS
(1 family)

FAMILY TROCHILIDÆ. HUMMINGBIRDS.

Hummingbirds are found only in the New World. About 750 species and subspecies are known. They range from Alaska to Patagonia, but are most numerous in the Andean regions of Colombia and Ecuador. Eighteen species have been found in the United States; only 8 of these advance beyond our Mexican border states, and but one species occurs east of the Mississippi.

Several species inhabit the depths of dark tropical forests, but, as a rule, they are found with the flowers which bloom in the clearings, or far overhead in the sunlight. They are not gregarious, but an abundance of food sometimes brings large numbers of them together, when the air becomes animated with their rapidly moving forms. The smaller species fly so swiftly that their wings are lost in hazy circles, and it is difficult for the human eye to follow their course. The flight of the larger species is less insectlike, and each wing-beat can be detected. As a rule their voice is a weak squeak or excited chippering, but some of the tropical species have songs of decided character which they sing with much energy.

Hummingbirds feed largely on insects, which they generally capture in flowers, but many species catch insects on the wing or pick them from beneath leaves. They also feed on the juices of flowers. The nest is usually composed of plant-down, bound about with spiders' webs and covered with lichens skilfully attached to a limb or leaf, and is as exquisitely dainty in appearance as its maker. All the species whose nesting habits are known lay two white eggs. The period of incubation with our Ruby-throat is fourteen days. The young are naked when hatched, but a mere breath of down precedes the growth of the juvenal plumage.

Strangely enough, these beautiful little creatures are possessed of a most unfortunate disposition, which frequently leads them to attack any bird they fancy is trespassing on their domain. They know no fear, and with equal courage rush at one of their kind or a passing Hawk.

1892. RIDGWAY, R., Rep. U. S. N. M., for 1890, 253–383 (monograph).

310. RUBY-THROATED HUMMINGBIRD. ARCHILOCHUS COLUBRIS (*Linnæus*). [428.] (Fig. 54.) *Ad.* ♂.—Upperparts bright, shining green; wings and tail fuscous, with purplish reflections; throat beautiful metallic ruby-red, bordered on the breast by whitish; rest of the underparts dusky, washed with greenish on the sides; tail forked. *Ad.* ♀.—No ruby throat-patch; bronzy green above, whitish below; tail nearly even, outer three feathers tipped with white. *Im.* ♂.—Similar to ♀, but throat with dusky streaks, and, in older birds, with ruby-colored feathers. L., 3·74; W., 1·54; T., 1·15; B., ·67.

Range.—Breeds from cent. Sask., Alberta, Man., and Cape Breton Isl. s. to Gulf Coast and Fla., w. to N. Dak., Nebr., Kans., and cent. Tex.; winters from middle and s. Fla. and La. through s. Mex. and Cent. A. to Panama; casual in Cuba and Bermuda in migration. Accidental near St. Michael, Alaska.

Washington, common S. R., Apr. 16–Oct. 20. Bronx region, common T. V. and fairly common S. R., Apr. 30–Oct. 19. Boston, common T. V., uncommon S. R., May 10–Sept. 20. N. Ohio, common S. R., May 1–Sept. 15. Glen Ellyn, rare S. R., May 1–Oct. 9. SE. Minn., common S. R., Apr. 30–Oct. 8.

Nest, of plant-down, covered externally with lichens and firmly wound with almost invisible plant-fibers; generally 15–25 feet up, saddled on a limb. *Eggs*, 2, white, ·50 × ·35. *Date*, Lafayette Co., Miss., May 6; Iredell Co., N. C., May 11; Ossining, N. Y., May 20; Boston, May 24.

The Ruby-throat needs no song. Its beauty gives it distinction, and its wings make music. Its only note, so far as I know, is a squeak, expressive of distrust or excitement. It has no rival in eastern North America, and is to be confounded with nothing but sphinx (humming-bird) moths. One hears of 'Hummingbirds' seen in the evening about flower-beds. The mistake is not unnatural, and a correction is sometimes received with incredulity. The birds spend but a comparatively small part of the time upon the wing. Whoever watches a female busy about her nest will see her constantly perching here and there in certain branches of the tree, preening her plumage and looking about her.

The male, at the same season, forgetful, to all appearance, of his conjugal and parental duties, may be found at home day after day on a dead twig in some tall tree, where he sits so constantly as to make the observer wonder what he can be about, and when, if ever, he takes his food. Further investigation, however, will show that he makes frequent and regular rounds of favorite feeding-places. A tall blueberry bush, for example, will be visited at short intervals as long as the observer has patience to stand beside it. The Hummingbird is curiously fearless. Sometimes one will probe a flower held in the hand, and when they fly into houses, as they pretty often do, they manifest but the smallest degree of suspicion, and will feed almost at once upon sugar held between the lips. The old bird feeds the young by regurgitation—a frightful-looking act—the food consisting largely of minute insects. The young remain in the nest for some three weeks, and on leaving it are at once at home on the wing. BRADFORD TORREY.

1924. BIRD-LORE, 108, 112 (mig.; pl.).—1930. ALLEN, A. A., Bird-Lore, 223–231, illus. (autobiography).

310.1. THE RUFOUS HUMMINGBIRD, *Selasphorus rufus* (Gmelin), of Western North America, is accidental at Charleston, South Carolina (Dec. 18, 1909. See Sprunt, A. Jr., Auk, 1929, 237).

XVII. ORDER CORACIIFORMES. KINGFISHERS, ROLLERS, HORNBILLS, ETC.

SUBORDER ALCEDINES. KINGFISHERS
(3 families, 1 North American)

FAMILY ALCEDINIDÆ. KINGFISHERS.

The majority of the more than 250 species and subspecies of Kingfishers inhabit the Malayan region and islands of the Pacific. Of the 6 American species (14 species and subspecies) 2 are contained in the genus *Megaceryle* and 4 in the genus *Chloroceryle*. Kingfishers are solitary birds of somewhat local habit. All the American species are fish-eaters and are rarely found far from the water. Some of the Old-World species, however, are forest-inhabiting and feed on small insects, mollusks, etc. Kingfishers nest in holes, usually made by themselves in a bank, and lay white eggs. The young are hatched naked, and the juvenal plumage is the first to be acquired.

311. EASTERN BELTED KINGFISHER. MEGACERYLE ALCYON ALCYON (*Linnæus*). [390.] (Fig. 55.) *Ad.* ♂.—Upperparts bluish gray; wings with small white spots, most of the feathers tipped with white, the inner webs of the primaries white at the base; tail-feathers with numerous spots and broken bands of white; a white spot before the eye; throat white, this color passing on to the sides of the neck and nearly meeting on the back of the neck; a band across the breast, and the sides bluish gray—in immature specimens tinged with rufous—lower breast and belly white. *Ad.* ♀.—Similar to the male, but the sides and a band on the belly rufous. L., 13·02; W., 6·17; T., 3·60; B., 2·00.

Range.—Breeds from Mack. and s. Lab., s. to the s. border of U. S. and w. to the base of the Rocky Mts.; winters from B. C., O., and Va. s. to the W. I., Colombia, and British Guiana, and irregularly as far n. as Mass., N. H., and Ont.; accidental in Holland, Ireland, and the Azores.

Washington, common P. R., except in midwinter. Bronx region, common S. R., frequent W. R., Feb. 24–Jan. 16. Boston, common S. R., Apr. 10–Nov. 1; rare W. V. N. Ohio, common S. R., Mch. 20–Nov. 1; rare W. V. Glen Ellyn, isolated pairs, Apr. 1–Nov. 19. SE. Minn., common S. R., Mch. 21–Dec. 12; uncommon W. R.

Nest, in a hole in a bank, about 6 feet from the entrance. *Eggs*, 5–8, white, 1·34 × 1·05. *Date*, Shelter Isl., N. Y., May 4; Boston, May 15; se. Minn., May 9.

The shores of wooded streams or ponds are the chosen haunts of the Kingfisher. Silently he perches on some limb overhanging the water, ever on the alert for food or foe. Paddle toward him as quietly as you please, just as you reach his danger-line he drops from his perch and with a loud, rattling call flies on ahead. This may be repeated several times, until finally the limits of his territory are reached, when he makes a wide detour and returns to the starting-point.

The Kingfisher hunts after the manner of the Fish Hawk. In passing over the water it needs only the glint of a shining fin or scale just beneath the surface to catch his watchful eye. On quickly moving wings he hovers over the place, waiting only a fair chance to plunge on the unsuspecting fish below. Emerging from the water with his prey in his bill, he shakes the spray from his plumage, and, with an exultant rattle, flies away to some favorite perch.

1905. HERRICK, F. H., Home-Life of Wild Birds, 136–145.—1907. FINLEY, W. L., American Birds, 139–147.—1929. ALLEN, A. A., Bird-Lore, 214–221, illus. (autobiography). 1930. Bird-Lore, 414–417 (mig.; pl.).

XVIII. ORDER PICIFORMES. WOODPECKERS, JACAMARS, TOUCANS, ETC.

SUBORDER PICI. WOODPECKERS AND PICULETS
(1 family)

FAMILY PICIDÆ. WOODPECKERS.

Woodpeckers are found throughout the forested parts of the world, except in Madagascar and the Australian region. Approximately 700 species are recognized, of which one-half is found in the Western Hemisphere. Of this number 64 (22 species) occur in North America. Woodpeckers are rather solitary birds, but are sometimes found associated in scattered companies during their migrations. Above all other birds they are especially adapted to creep or climb. The peculiar structure of the foot, with its two toes directed forward and two backward (except, in North America, in one genus), assists them in clinging to an upright surface, while the pointed, stiffened tail-feathers serve as a prop. The stout, chisel-like bill of the more typical species is used to cut away wood and expose the hiding-places of grubs, etc.; then the long, extensile tongue, with its horny, spearlike tip, is thrust forward, the food impaled and drawn out. The vocal powers of Woodpeckers are supplemented by the bill which is used to beat the long, rolling call forming their love-song. The eggs of Woodpeckers are uniformly white, and are placed in a hole, generally in a dead tree or limb, hollowed out by the bird.

1901. ECKSTORM, F. H., The Woodpeckers (Houghton, Mifflin & Co.).— 1911. MCATEE, W. L., Woodpeckers in Relation to Trees, Bull. 39, Biol. Surv.—1930. BURT, W. H., Adaptive Modifications of Woodpeckers. Univ. Calif. Pub. in Zoöl. Vol. 32, 455–524.

KEY TO THE SPECIES

I. No red on the head or nape.
  1. Underparts not streaked or spotted.
    A. Entire underparts black.
      a. Wing about 10·00, bill ivory-white.
                    323. IVORY-BILLED WOODPECKER, ♀.
    B. Underparts white, without black spots or streaks.
      a. Wing under 4·00; outer tail-feathers barred with black.
            319, 319a, b. DOWNY WOODPECKER and races, ♀.
      b. Wing over 4·00; outer tail-feathers white, without black bars.
            318, 318a–c. HAIRY WOODPECKER and races, ♀.
  2. Underparts with black spots, bars, or streaks.
    a. Back entirely black . . 321. ARCTIC THREE-TOED WOODPECKER.
    b. Back black and white.
      b¹. Outer tail-feathers entirely white, crown yellow or spotted with white . . . . 322. AMERICAN THREE-TOED WOODPECKER.
      b². Outer tail-feathers barred with black, no black patch on the breast, ear-coverts white.
            320. RED-COCKADED WOODPECKER, ♀.
      b³. Outer tail-feathers black, with generally a narrow white margin; rump white . . . . 315. RED-HEADED WOODPECKER, Im.
      b⁴. Outer tail-feathers black and white, a large black patch on the breast . . . . . . 317. YELLOW-BELLIED SAPSUCKER, ♀.
II. With red on the head or nape.
  1. Whole top of head red.
    A. Throat red.
      a. Primaries spotted with white, belly yellowish.
            317. YELLOW-BELLIED SAPSUCKER, ♂.
      b. Primaries black, rump and belly white.
            315. RED-HEADED WOODPECKER, ♂.
    B. Throat white.
      a. Breast and belly black.
          313, 313a, b. PILEATED WOODPECKER and races, ♂.
      b. Breast black or blackish, sides streaked, belly yellowish white.
            317. YELLOW-BELLIED SAPSUCKER, ♀.
      c. Underparts tinged with red, without streaks or spots.
            314. RED-BELLIED WOODPECKER, ♂.
  2. Crown black, brown or gray, a red band across the nape, a red crest on the back of the head, or small patches of red on either side of the nape.
    A. Underparts largely or wholly black; wing over 8·00.
      a. Bill ivory-white . . . . . 323. IVORY-BILLED WOODPECKER, ♂.
      b. Bill blackish . . . . . 313, 313a. PILEATED WOODPECKER, ♀.
    B. Underparts not largely black; wing under 8·00.
      a. Underparts more or less spotted or streaked with black.

a^1. A black patch on the breast, throat brown, rump white.

312, 312a. FLICKERS.

a^2. Head black, ear-coverts white, a few red feathers on either side of the nape . . . 320. RED-COCKADED WOODPECKER, ♂.

b. Underparts white, or whitish, without black streaks or spots.

b^1. Crown gray, a reddish tinge on the belly.

314. RED-BELLIED WOODPECKER, ♀.

c^1. Crown black.

c^2. Outer tail-feathers barred with black.

319a. DOWNY WOODPECKER and races, ♂.

c^3. Outer tail-feathers white.

318b. HAIRY WOODPECKER and races, ♂.

312. NORTHERN FLICKER. COLAPTES AURATUS LUTEUS *Bangs.* [412a.] *Ad.* ♂.—Top of the head ashy gray, a bright scarlet band across the back of the neck; back, wing-coverts, and exposed part of secondaries brownish gray, barred with black; rump white; primaries black externally, the inner surface of the wing and the shafts of the feathers yellow; upper tail-coverts barred or streaked with black and white; tail black above, yellow tipped with black below, the outer edges of the feathers slightly margined or barred with white; sides of the head, throat, and upper breast vinaceous; a broad black stripe on each side of the throat from the base of the bill, and a broad black crescent across the breast; rest of the underparts white, more or less tinged with vinaceous, and thickly spotted with black. *Ad.* ♀.—Similar, but without the black streaks on the side of the throat. L., 12·00; W., 6·00; T., 4·00; B., 1·40.

Remarks.—Exceptional specimens have a few red feathers in the throat-stripes. A male from Louisiana has this mark entirely red and the head grayish brown, while another specimen from Toronto has half the tail orange-red. These unusual markings are supposed to be due to hybridization of our Flicker with the western or Red-shafted Flicker, which resembles the eastern species in pattern of coloration, but has the crown brownish gray or grayish brown, the throat stripes scarlet, the throat and breast gray, the under surface of the wings and tail dull red, and lacks the red nuchal band. (See an important paper on the relationships of these birds by Dr. J. A. Allen, in the *Bull. Am. Mus. Nat. Hist.* IV, 1892, 21–44).

Range.—Breeds from Can. e. of the Rocky Mts. and n. to the limit of trees in Alaska and throughout the n. and cent. U. S. s. to the n. edge of the Lower Austral Zone; more or less regularly resident except in the extreme n. parts of its range. S. in winter to the Gulf Coast and s. Tex. Accidental in Greenland and on the Pribilof Isls., Alaska.

Washington, common S. R., rare W. V. Bronx region, common S. R., frequently wintering; Feb. 25–Dec. 28 (Jan. and Feb.). Boston, very common S. R., common W. V. N. Ohio, common S. R., tolerably common P. R., Mch. 10–Nov. 15; a few winter. Glen Ellyn, common S. R., Mch. 7–Dec. 24; a few winter. SE. Minn., common S. R., Mch. 19–Nov. 11; rare W. V.

Nest, in trees, at varying heights from the ground, frequently in orchards. *Eggs*, 5–9, 1·10 × ·86. *Date*, Chester Co., Pa., May 13; D. C., May 4; Boston, May 10; se. Minn., Apr. 28.

The habits, notes, and colors of this well-known bird are reflected in the popular names which have been applied to it throughout its wide range. No less than 124 of these aliases have been recorded, and many have doubtless escaped the compiler.

The Flicker is a bird of character. Although a Woodpecker, he is too original to follow in the footsteps of others of his tribe. They do not frequent the ground, but that is no reason why he should not humor his own terrestrial propensities and a fondness for ants, and we may therefore frequently flush him from the earth, when, with a low chuckle, he goes bounding off through the air, his white rump showing conspicuously as he flies.

The Flicker, like other Woodpeckers, beats a rolling tattoo in the spring, but his vocal song proper is a rapidly repeated, mellow *cŭh-cŭh-cŭh-cŭh-cŭh*, etc., as springlike a sound as the peeping of frogs. His usual note is a vigorous, nasal *kèe-yer*. It recalls frosty fall mornings when the High-holes are gathering to feed on the woodbine and pepperidge berries. Approaching their feeding-grounds, one may hear the 'Flicker' note. It can be closely imitated by the swishing of a willow wand: *weèchew, weèchew, weèchew*. I do not remember hearing a bird utter this note when alone. It is accompanied by the oddest gestures, as with tails stiffly spread the birds bob and bow to each other.

1892. ALLEN, J. A., Bull. Am. Mus. Nat. Hist., 21–44 (hybridism).— 1900. BURNS, F. L., Wilson Bull., 1–82 (monograph).—1910. SHERMAN, A. R., Wilson Bull., 135–171 (home-life).—1917. BALES, B. R., Wilson Bull., 188–191 (egg-laying).—1927. BIRD-LORE, 110, 114 (mig.; pl.).

312a. SOUTHERN FLICKER. COLAPTES AURATUS AURATUS (*Linnæus*).
[412.] Smaller, darker, black dorsal bars wider than in the following form. W., 5·70; T., 3·60; B., 1·35 (cf. Bangs, Auk, XV. 1898, 177).
Range.—Lower Austral Zone of S. Atlantic and Gulf States from N. C. and s. Ills. to s. Fla. and cent. Tex., n. to extreme s. Ills. and Ind. and se. Mo. and se. Kans.
Nesting-date, San Mateo, Fla., Apr. 10.

313. NORTHERN PILEATED WOODPECKER. CEOPHLŒUS PILEATUS ABIETICOLA *Bangs*. [405a.] Larger, bill longer, white markings more extensive. W., 9·10; T., 6·30; B., 2·00 (cf. Bangs, Auk XV, 1898, 176).
Range.—Transition and Canadian zones from Mack. and N. B., s. to Minn., Ills., Ind., O., Pa. and s. in the Alleghanies.
Washington, rare P. R. N. Ohio, rare P. R. SE. Minn., P. R., increasing of late.
Nest, 12 to 80 feet up. *Eggs*, 3–5, white, 1·30 × ·94. *Date*, Me., May 11; se. Minn., May 12.

This large northern form of the Pileated Woodpecker resembles the southern race in habits. Its presence in a region is more often revealed by the large cavities it excavates in dead stumps and trunks than by actual observation of the bird itself.

1901. MORRELL, C. H., Journ. Me. Orn. Soc., 32–35 (in Me.).—1928. BIRD-LORE, 112, 113 (dist.; pl.).

313a. PILEATED WOODPECKER. CEOPHLŒUS PILEATUS PILEATUS (*Linnæus*). [405.] *Ad.* ♂.—Upperparts blackish fuscous; whole top of the head scarlet, the feathers lengthened to form a crest; a narrow white stripe bordering this crest separates it from the fuscous ear-coverts; a stripe beginning at the nostril and passing down the sides of the neck to the shoulders is tinged with yellow before the eye and is white back of the eye; it is separated from the white throat by a scarlet stripe at the base of the lower mandible; basal half of the wing-feathers white; underparts fuscous, the feathers sometimes lightly margined with white; bill horn-color. *Ad.* ♀.— Similar, but without red on the forepart of the crown or at the base of the lower mandible. L., 17·00; W., 8·90; T., 6·20; B., 1·85.
Range.—Lower Austral forests of s. U. S. from se. Pa., Ills., and Okla., s. to n. Fla. and the Gulf Coast, w. to cent. Tex.
Nesting-date, San Mateo, Fla., Apr. 14.

This species is common only in the wilder parts of its range. In the hammocks and cypress swamps of Florida it occurs in numbers. There, contrary to the experience of Audubon, I found it by no means a wild bird. Indeed, Flickers were more difficult to approach. On the Suwanee River, in March, and in Maine, in June, I have called these birds to me by simply clapping my slightly closed palms, making a sound in imitation of their tapping on a resonant limb.

The flight of this species is rather slow, usually direct, sometimes undulating. When under way, the white markings of the wings show

FIG. 98. Tip of tongue of Pileated Woodpecker, showing barbed horny tip. (Much enlarged.)

conspicuously. Their usual call-note is a "loud, high-pitched, nasal *kuk-kuk, kuk-kuk,* etc.; a distinctly faster, more excited sort of call than the Flicker's" (Harper). Like the Flicker, they have also a *wichew* note uttered when two birds come together.

313b. FLORIDA PILEATED WOODPECKER. CEOPHLŒUS PILEATUS FLORIDANUS (*Ridgway*). [405*b*.] "Similar to *C. p. pileatus,* but decidedly blacker (that is, the general black color less slaty or sooty, and average size less, with bill usually relatively shorter and broader" (Ridgway).
Range.—Cent. and s. Fla., n. to Orange Co.

314. RED-BELLIED WOODPECKER. CENTURUS CAROLINUS (*Linnæus*). [409.] *Ad.* ♂.—Whole top of head and back of the neck bright scarlet; back regularly barred with black and white; primaries black at the end, white, irregularly barred with black, at the base; secondaries black, regularly spotted and barred with white; upper tail-coverts white, with streaks or arrowheads of black; outer tail-feathers and inner vanes of the middle ones irregularly marked with broken black and white bars; cheeks and underparts dull ashy white, the region about the base of the bill, the middle of the belly, and sometimes the breast, more or less tinged with red. *Ad.* ♀.—Similar, but with the crown grayish ashy, the scarlet confined to the nape and nostrils. *Im.*—Similar, but with the belly sometimes tinged with buffy instead of red. L., 9·50; W., 5·00; T., 3·40; B., 1·10.
Range.—Upper and Lower Austral zones of e. U. S. from se. S. Dak., se. Minn., sw. Ont., w. N. Y., sw. Pa., and Del. s. to cent. Tex., the Gulf Coast, and Fla. Keys; casual n. to Colo., Mass. and N. Y. Accidental in Ariz. and nw. Nebr.
Washington, locally common P. R. Bronx region, A. V., one recent record, May 13. Boston, A. V. N. Ohio, tolerably common P. R. SE. Minn., uncommon P. R., increasing.
Nest, in dead or living trees, from 20 feet up. *Eggs,* 4–6, white, 1·05 × ·75. *Date,* Charleston, S. C., last of Apr.; Black Hawk Co., Ia., May 5; se. Minn., May 16.

This is a common bird in our southern states. It inhabits alike coniferous and deciduous growths, but prefers the latter. It ascends a tree in a curious, jerky fashion, accompanying each upward move by a hoarse *chŭh-chŭh*. It also utters a *k-r-r-r-ring* roll and, when mating, a *whicker* call like that of the Flicker.

1927. BIRD-LORE, 260, 261 (mig.; pl.).

315. RED-HEADED WOODPECKER. MELANERPES ERYTHROCEPHA-LUS (*Linnæus*). [406.] *Ads.*—Head, neck, throat, and upper breast deep red; upper back, primaries, bases of the secondaries, and wing-coverts bluish black; end half of the secondaries, rump, and upper tail-coverts white; tail black, the feathers more or less tipped or margined with white; lower breast and belly white, the middle of the latter generally tinged with reddish. *Im.*—Red head and neck of the adult replaced by mixed grayish brown and fuscous; upper back bluish black, barred with ashy; primaries and wing-coverts black; end half of the secondaries irregularly barred with black; tail black, generally tipped with white; lower breast and belly white, more or less streaked or spotted with fuscous. L., 9·75; W., 5·52; T., 3·30; B., 1·17.

Range.—Transition and Austral zones from se. B. C., cent. Alberta, Man., and se. Ont. s. to the Gulf Coast and s. Fla., and from cent. Wyo., cent. Colo., N. Mex. and cent. Tex. e. to valleys of the Hudson and Delaware; irregular and local in N. E.; casual in Ariz., Utah, N. S., s. Que., and N. B.; irregularly migratory in the n. parts of its range.

Washington, rather common S. R., rare W. V. Bronx region, uncommon and local P. R., occasionally abundant T. V. Boston, rare S. R. and T. V., casual in winter. N. Ohio, common S. R., Apr. 20–Sept. 25; occasionally winters. Glen Ellyn, common S. R., quite regular W. R., Mch. 7–Nov. 6. SE. Minn., common S. R., frequent in winter.

Nest, generally in a dead tree. *Eggs*, 4–6, white, 1·00 × ·75. *Date*, San Mateo, Fla., May 5; Chester Co., Pa., June 8; Jay Co., Ind., May 21, inc. adv.; se. Minn., Apr. 17.

Give some birds an abundance of their favorite food, and their movements no longer seem to be governed by the calendar. Red-headed Woodpeckers were supposed to migrate southward in the fall and pass the winter south of Maryland, until Dr. Merriam, in his interesting account of the habits of this species (*Bull. Nutt. Orn. Club*, III, 1878, pp. 123–128), told us that in Lewis County, northern New York, their abundance in winter was in no way affected by the severity of the weather, but was entirely dependent upon the success of the crop of beechnuts which constitute their food.

Indeed, few birds seem better able to adapt themselves to their surroundings. They change their fare and habits with the season, and to the accomplishments of Woodpeckers add those of Flycatchers and fruit-eaters. We should expect, therefore, to find them very generally distributed, but in the northern states they show an evident choice for certain localities, and may be wanting over wide stretches of inter-vening territory.

They are noisy, active birds, and their loud, rolling, tree-toadlike call, *ker-r-ruck*, *ker-r-ruck*, and bright colors combine to render them conspicuous. When on the wing the white secondaries of both adult and immature birds make a striking field mark.

1927. BIRD-LORE, 323, 411, 414 (migr.; pl.).

316. LEWIS'S WOODPECKER, *Asyndesmus lewis* (Gray), of the western United States, is accidental in Rhode Island.

317. YELLOW-BELLIED SAPSUCKER. SPHYRAPICUS VARIUS VARIUS

(*Linnæus*). [402.] *Ad.* ♂.—Crown deep scarlet, back irregularly barred with black and yellowish white; wing-feathers spotted with white, their coverts *mostly white;* tail black, the middle feathers with broken black bars, the outer ones with white margins; a white line from the bill passes below the eye; throat cardinal; breast black; sides streaked with black; belly pale yellow. *Ad.* ♀.—Similar, but throat white; crown sometimes black; outer tail-feathers with broken white bars. *Im.*—Similar to ads., but with the crown dull blackish, the breast brownish gray barred with black, the throat whitish. L., 8·56; W., 4·87; T., 3·20; B., ·92.

Range.—Breeds in Canadian and upper part of Transition Zone from cent. Mack., s. Que., and Cape Breton Isl. s. to cent. Mo., n. O., N. C. (mts.), and Mass. (mts. of n. Berkshire Co.); casually Conn. Winters from Ia., Mich. and Mass. to the Gulf Coast, Bahamas, Cuba, w. Mex. (Jalisco), and w. Panama; casual in Wyo. and e. Colo.; accidental in Greenland and Bermuda.

Washington, common T. V., Mch.–May; Sept. and Oct., occasional in winter. Bronx region, common T. V., occasional in winter; Apr. 1–May 20; Sept. 14–Dec. 13 (Jan. 25, Feb. 13). Boston, not uncommon T. V., Apr. and Sept. 15–Nov. 1; occasional W. V. N. Ohio, common T. V., Apr. 1–May 20; Sept. 15–Oct. 20. Glen Ellyn, common T. V., Mch. 31–May 12; Sept. 14–Oct. 13. SE. Minn., common S. R., Mch. 25–Oct. 30.

Nest, about 40 feet up. *Eggs*, 5–7, ·87 × ·67. *Date*, Trenton Falls, N. Y., May 26; Goodrich, Mich., May 20; se. Minn., May 13.

As migrants, Sapsuckers are rather inconspicuous. They frequent living trees, where they are concealed by the foliage and their weak call-note is not likely to attract attention.

On reaching their summer homes in the spring their character changes, and Merriam speaks of them as "noisy, rollicking fellows; they are always chasing one another among the trees, screaming meanwhile at the tops of their voices" (*Bull. Nutt. Orn. Club*, IV, 1879, p. 2). Brewster describes the note of the adults at this season as "a clear, ringing *cleur*, repeated five or six times in succession"; while young and old utter "a low, snarling cry that bears no very distant resemblance to the mew of the Catbird" (*Bull. Nutt. Orn. Club*, 1876, p. 69).

The Sapsucker feeds largely on the juices of trees, which it obtains by perforating the bark (Bolles, *The Auk*, 1891, p. 256; 1892, p. 110), a habit which, Forbush remarks, may impair the value of the tree for lumber without actually causing its destruction.

1928. BIRD-LORE, 253–258 (mig.; pl.).

318. NORTHERN HAIRY WOODPECKER. DRYOBATES VILLOSUS

SEPTENTRIONALIS *Nuttall.* [393*h*.] Similar to *D. v. villosus* but larger and whiter. L., 10·00; W., 5·20.

Range.—Canadian Zone of n. N. A. from cent. s. Alaska, n. Man., and se. Que. s. to cent. Ont., n. N. Dak., Mont., and s. cent. B. C.; s. in winter to Nebr.

318a. NEWFOUNDLAND WOODPECKER. DRYOBATES VILLOSUS

TERRÆNOVÆ *Batchelder.* [393*g*.] Similar to *D. v. villosus,* "but slightly larger, the black areas of the upperparts increased, the white areas reduced both in number and size, especially in the remiges and wing-coverts. W., 4·90" (Batchelder).

Range.—N. F.

318b. EASTERN HAIRY WOODPECKER. Dryobates villosus villosus (*Linnæus*). [393.] (Fig. 56a.) *Ad. ♂.*—Upperparts black; scarlet band on the nape; middle of the back white; wing-feathers and their coverts spotted with white; middle tail-feathers black, the outer ones *white;* a white stripe above and another below the eye; underparts white. *Ad. ♀.*—Similar, but without scarlet on the back of the neck. L., 9·40; W., 4·78; T., 3·30; B., 1·22.

Range.—Transition and Upper Austral zones of ne. U. S. and s. Can., from Man., cent. N. Dak., s. cent. Ont., cent. s. Que., and Magdalen Isls., to w. N. C., n. Ala. and cent. Tex. w. to e. Colo.

Washington, uncommon P. R. Bronx region, uncommon P. R. Boston, P. R., uncommon summer; rather common winter. N. Ohio, common P. R. Glen Ellyn, fairly common P. R. SE. Minn., common P. R.

Nest, generally in a dead tree. *Eggs,* 4–6, white, ·95 × ·75. *Date,* Nazareth, Pa., Apr. 25; Boston, Apr. 22; Wheatland, Ind., Apr. 30.

This species resembles the Downy Woodpecker in habits, but is less frequently observed out of the woods. Its notes are noticeably louder than the Downy's, and when one is familiar with both there is no difficulty in distinguishing the two by their voices.

In speaking of the difference which exists between the rolling tattoo of some Woodpeckers, Mr. Brewster says: "Thus, *D. pubescens* has a long, unbroken roll; *D. villosus* a shorter and louder one with a greater interval between each stroke; while *S. varius,* commencing with a short roll, ends very emphatically with five or six distinct disconnected taps. In this latter species I am convinced it is literally a call of recognition, as I have repeatedly seen the bird, after producing it, listen a moment when it would be answered from a distance, and its mate would shortly appear and join it" (*Ann. Lyc. Nat. Hist.,* 1875, p. 144).

1930. Bird-Lore, 120–123 (mig.; pl.).

318c. SOUTHERN HAIRY WOODPECKER. Dryobates villosus auduboni (*Swainson*). [393b.] Similar to *D. v. villosus,* but smaller, and with somewhat less white in the plumage. L., 8·10; W., 4·50; T., 2·80; B., 1·15.

Range.—Lower Austral Zone of S. Atlantic and Gulf States from se. Mo., s. Ills., and se. Va. to se. Tex. and s. Fla.

Nesting-date, San Mateo, Fla., Apr. 24; Weaverville, N. C., May 3.

This is simply a small southern race of the preceding species. It resembles the northern forms in habits, but is much more common, being nearly as numerous as the Downy Woodpecker.

319. NORTHERN DOWNY WOODPECKER. Dryobates pubescens medianus (*Swainson*). [394c.] (Fig. 18.) *Ad. ♂.*—Upperparts black, a scarlet band on the nape; middle of the back white; wing-feathers and their coverts spotted with white; middle tail-feathers black, the outer ones white, *barred with black;* a white stripe above and another below the eye; underparts white. *Ad. ♀.*—Similar, but without scarlet on the nape. L., 6·83; W., 3·70; T., 2·53; B., ·68.

Remarks.—The Downy and Hairy Woodpeckers differ in coloration only in the markings of the outer tail-feathers, which are white, barred with black in the former, and white *without* bars in the latter; the difference in size between the two, however, is always diagnostic.

Range.—Canadian and Transition zones of cent. parts of e. N. A. from se. Alberta, Man., and s. Ungava s. to e. Nebr., Kans., Tenn. and Va. Casual w. to e. Colo.

Washington, common P. R. Bronx region, common P. R. Boston, common P. R. N. Ohio, common P. R. Glen Ellyn, common P. R. SE. Minn., common P. R.

Nest, generally in a dead tree. *Eggs*, 4–6, white, ·75 × ·60. *Date*, Nazareth, Pa., May 9; Boston, May 22; Mt. Carmel, Ills., May 7.

Woodland, orchards, and the shade trees of lawns are alike frequented by this, the smallest and most familiar of our Woodpeckers. Sometimes he tells of his presence by an industrious *tap, tap*—tapping as he patiently digs out the grubs and larvæ which form his bill-of-fare. Again he hails us with a businesslike *peek, peek*—a note closely resembling the sound produced by a marble-quarrier's chisel, and which sometimes is prolonged into a rattling call. Like other Woodpeckers, in the spring he beats a rolling tattoo on a resonant limb, sounding a reveille which is a credit to so small a drummer.

The Downy is a sociable Woodpecker, and when the gay summer visitors have returned to their southern homes and the wind whistles drearily through the leafless trees, he joins the Chickadees and Nuthatches, and during the winter they are inseparable companions.

1928. ALLEN, A. A., Bird-Lore, 415–424, illus. (autobiography).

319a. SOUTHERN DOWNY WOODPECKER. DRYOBATES PUBESCENS PUBESCENS (*Linnæus*). [394.] Similar to *D. p. medianus* but smaller, browner below and with the white markings more restricted. L., 6·00; W., 3·50.

Range.—Lower Austral Zone of S. Atlantic and Gulf States from Fla. to e. Tex., n. to Okla. and N. C,

Nesting-date, St. Simons, Ga., Apr. 12.

319b. NELSON'S DOWNY WOODPECKER. DRYOBATES PUBESCENS NELSONI *Oberholser.* "Similar to *D. p. medianus*, but decidedly larger, white of underparts, etc., purer, and black bars on lateral rectrices usually narrower or less numerous, sometimes nearly obsolete." W., 3·80; T., 2·50 (Ridgway).

Range.—Canadian Zone from nw. Alaska and sw. Mack. to s. Alaska, extreme n. B. C., and cent. Alberta; casually farther e., probably to n. N. E.

Ridgway (Bull. 50, VI, 235) states that "many winter specimens from eastern Massachusetts closely approach this form in size and agree exactly in coloration. . . ."

320. RED-COCKADED WOODPECKER. DRYOBATES BOREALIS (*Vieillot*). [395.] Ad. ♂.—Crown black, *a small tuft of scarlet feathers on each side of the back of the head;* back barred with black and white; wings spotted with black and white; middle tail-feathers black, outer ones with broken black bars; ear region white, separated from the white throat by a black stripe running from the bill to the shoulder; sides and under tail-coverts spotted and streaked with black; rest of the underparts white. *Ad.* ♀.—Similar, but without scarlet on the head. L., 8·40; W., 4·65; T., 3·10; B., ·80.

Range.—Lower Austral Zone of S. Atlantic and Gulf States n. to se. Va., Tenn., w. Ky., and s. Mo., and casually to N. J. and se. Pa.

Nest, usually well up in a living pine. *Eggs*, 2–5, white, ·91 × ·68. *Date*, San Mateo, Fla., Apr. 29.

This species is a common inhabitant of the 'piny woods.' It prefers the higher branches of the trees, and frequently hangs head downward while feeding at the extremity of a branch. Its call-note suggests the *yank, yank,* of the White-bellied Nuthatch, but is louder, hoarser, and not so distinctly enunciated.

1929. BIRD-LORE, 255 (dist.; pl.).

321. ARCTIC THREE-TOED WOODPECKER. PICOIDES ARCTICUS (*Swainson*). [400.] (Fig. 56*b*.) *Ad.* ♂.—Toes three, two in front; middle of the crown with a bright orange-yellow patch; rest of the upperparts *shining black,* unmarked; wing-feathers spotted with white; middle tail-feathers black, outer ones white, except at the base; a white line from the nostril passes below the eye; sides barred with black and white; rest of the underparts white. *Ad.* ♀.—Similar, but without orange-yellow on the crown. L., 9·50; W., 5·10; T., 3·40; B. from N., ·98.

Range.—Canadian Zone, from cent. Alaska, and n. Que. s. to Ore., the Sierra Nevada of Calif. (Mariposa Co.), Mont., Wyo. (Black Hills), n. Minn., Mich., n. Ont., n. N. Y., Vt., N. H., and Me.; casual in winter to Nebr., Wisc., Ills., O., Mass., Conn., s. N. Y., Pa., and n. N. J.

Bronx region, rare W. V., about ten recent records from Oct. 10–Feb. 6. Boston, uncommon to rare W. V. N. Ohio, rare W. V. SE. Minn., rare.

Nest, in a tree usually not over 15 feet up. *Eggs,* 4–6, white, 1·05 × ·78. *Date,* Seventh Lake, Fulton Chain, N. Y., May 27.

"It is a restless, active bird, spending its time generally on the topmost branches of the tallest trees, without, however, confining itself to pines. Although it cannot be called shy, its habitual restlessness renders it difficult of approach. Its movements resemble those of the Red-cockaded Woodpecker, but it is still more petulant than that bird. . . . Its cries also somewhat resemble those of the species above mentioned, but are louder and more shrill, like those of some small quadruped suffering great pain. . . .

"Its flight is rapid, gliding, and deeply undulating. . . . Now and then it will fly from a detached tree of a field to a considerable distance before it alights, emitting at every glide a loud, shrill note" (Audubon).

While preferring pines that have been killed by fire, it is not at this season necessarily restricted to them. Its calls are variously described as "a sharp, shrill, *chirk, chirk*"; a loud single *click, click,* and a low, single *pert, week* or *tup*—(see Forbush).

1926. VAN TYNE, J., Auk, 469–474 (unusual flight of).—1929. BIRD-LORE, 110, 111 (dist.; pl.).

322. AMERICAN THREE-TOED WOODPECKER. PICOIDES TRIDAC-TYLUS BACATUS *Bangs.* [401.] *Ad.* ♂.—Toes three, two in front; head spotted with white and with an orange-yellow patch on the crown; *back barred with black and white;* wing-feathers spotted with black and white; middle tail-feathers black; outer ones black and white; region below the eye mixed black and white; sides more or less barred with black and white; rest of the underparts white. *Ad.* ♀.—Similar, but crown spotted with black and white, and without yellow. L., 8·75; W., 4·55; T., 3·10; B. from N., ·95.

Range.—Hudsonian and Canadian zones from Lab. and n. Que., s. Mack. and n. Man. to n. Minn., cent. Ont., n. N. Y., Me., and N. H.; casual in winter to Mass., s. Ont., s. Wisc. and s. B. C.

Nest, in a tree usually not over 12 feet up. *Eggs,* white, ·92 × ·70 (Merriam, Bull. Nutt. Orn. Club, 1878, 200). *Date,* Herkimer Co., N. Y., June 4.

"It is said to greatly resemble *P.* [= *D.*] *villosus* in habits, except that it seeks its food principally upon decaying trees of the pine tribe, in which it frequently makes holes large enough to bury itself. It is not migratory" (B., B., and R.).

1929. BIRD-LORE, 110, 111 (dist.; pl.).

323. IVORY-BILLED WOODPECKER. CAMPEPHILUS PRINCIPALIS (*Linnæus*). [392.] *Ad.* ♂.—Upperparts shining black, a large scarlet crest; a white stripe begins below the eye and, passing down the side of the neck, meets its fellow in the middle of the back; ends of the inner primaries and the end half or two-thirds of the secondaries white; outer tail-feathers very short, the central ones elongated and much stiffened; bristles over the nostrils white; bill ivory-white; underparts shining black. *Ad.* ♀.—Similar, but with the crest black. L., 20·00; W., 10·00; T., 6·50; B., 2·75.

Range.—Formerly S. Atlantic and Gulf States from Tex. to N. C., n. in Miss. Valley to Okla., Mo., s. Ills., and s. Ind.; now occurs locally in small numbers in cent. Fla.; possibly in s. Miss. and La.

Nest, usually in a cypress over 40 feet up; entrance oval. *Eggs*, 3–5, white, "1·37 × ·99" (Bendire). *Date*, Tarpon Springs, Fla., Mch. 17, one-third grown; Lafayette Co., Fla., Apr. 19.

The home of this magnificent Woodpecker is in the almost limitless cypress forests of our southern coasts and river valleys. Even there it exists in but few localities.

The Ivory-bill is a wild, shy bird and has never long survived contact with civilization. It does not remain long in one place, and during the day ranges over an extended territory. Its call is a high, rather nasal, *yap, yap-yap,* sounding in the distance like the note of a penny trumpet.

1891. HASBROUCK, E. M., Auk, 174–186 (dist.).—1900. BEYER, G. G., Auk, 97–99 (nesting).—1915. KENNARD, F. H., Auk, 1–14, illus. (on the trail of).—1930. BIRD-LORE, 265–267 (pl., dist.).

XIX. ORDER PASSERIFORMES. PERCHING BIRDS

Doubtless every Order of birds has had its day when, if it were not a dominant type, it was at least sufficiently near it to be considered modern; and as we review what is known to us of that great series of feathered forms, from the Archæopteryx to the Finches, we can realize how varied has been the characteristic avifauna of each succeeding epoch from the Jurassic period to the present.

Now has come the day of the Order Passeres, the Perching Birds; here belong our Flycatchers, Larks, Swallows, Wrens, Thrushes, Vireos, Warblers, Tanagers, Finches, and many others. A recent authority classifies existing birds in 21 Orders, but more than one-half of the approximately 28,000 living species and subspecies are included in the single Order Passeres.

All our Passerine birds are born in an almost naked condition, having only a mere trace of down on the feather-tracts of the upperparts of the body. At its full development this natal down presents a soft, fluffy appearance over the cowering nestlings. It is pushed outward

FLYCATCHERS

1. Wood Pewee.
2. Acadian Flycatcher.
3. Yellow-bellied Flycatcher.
4. Alder Flycatcher.
5. Least Flycatcher.

PLATE XXII

by the feathers of the juvenal plumage, to the tips of which portions of it may be seen adhering when the young bird leaves the nest. With some Passerine birds (*e. g.*, Song Sparrow) this is at the end of only seven days (Owen, *The Auk*, 1899, p. 222). Compare this surprisingly rapid development with that of a Noddy Tern, for instance, which does not venture to leave its home until it is two months old, and is dependent on its parents for a month more (Thompson, *Bird-Lore*, 1903, p. 81).

In most cases the nestling or juvenal plumage is soon followed by the first winter plumage, but some few birds (*e. g.* Seaside and Sharp-tailed Sparrows) wear it for two months or more, and Swallows do not undergo a postjuvenal molt until they have reached their winter quarters. As a rule, at the postjuvenal molt, the feathers of the body and small wing-feathers are molted, while the primaries and secondaries with their coverts and the tail are retained, and it is often only by the color and appearance of these feathers that the bird of the year can be distinguished from the adult in winter, and during the former's first breeding season.

The spring molt is rarely complete; more frequently it is restricted to the body feathers, more frequently still it affects only the region about the head and throat, while some species undergo no feather renewal at that season. The post-breeding molt of the bird a year old, as well as of those older, is complete.

1900. DWIGHT, J., JR., Sequence of Plumages and Moults of the Passerine Birds of New York, Ann. N. Y. Acad. Sci., 173–360.

SUBORDER TYRANNI. SONGLESS PERCHING BIRDS

(13 families, 2 North American, 1 eastern North American)

FAMILY TYRANNIDÆ. TYRANT FLYCATCHERS.

From the systematist's standpoint, Flycatchers are songless perching birds. It does not follow that they are voiceless, or even truly songless, but that, having the voice-organ, or syrinx, less highly developed than other Passeres, they are possessed of comparatively limited vocal powers. This family is peculiar to America. The Old-World Flycatchers belong to the family *Muscicapidæ* and are true *Oscines*. Flycatchers are among the most numerous birds of the American tropics. Hellmayr's recently published 'Check-List' of this family includes 750 species and subspecies (358 species), and of this number only 39 (30 species) inhabit the United States.

Flycatchers are found wherever there are trees. As a rule they are of sedentary and solitary disposition. Their manner of feeding is characteristic. From a favorable perch, hawklike, they await passing insects, and with an aim that rarely misses, launch forth into the air; there is a sharp, suggestive *click* of the broad bill, and completing their aërial circle, they return to their perch and are again *en garde*.

Both the nature of their food and tropical origin induce in Flycatchers highly migratory habits, the Phœbe being the only eastern species to winter in the United States north of southern Florida.

KEY TO THE SPECIES

I. Wing over 3·00.
  1. Outer web of outer tail-feather white.
    A. Tail, 9·00, deeply forked, sides of breast scarlet, flanks salmon.
                             329. SCISSOR-TAILED FLYCATCHER.
    B. Tail black, not forked, outer web of outer feather, white, belly yellow, back gray . . . . 327. ARKANSAS KINGBIRD.
  2. Outer web of outer tail-feather not white at base.
    A. Tail black or blackish, sometimes tipped with white, adults with a concealed orange-red crown-patch.
      a. Under wing-coverts yellowish, no white tip on the tail.
                           325. GRAY KINGBIRD.
      b. Under wing-coverts blackish, tail tipped with white . 324. KINGBIRD.
    B. Tail not tipped with white, no crown-patch.
      a. Inner vane of tail-feathers pale rufous; throat and breast grayish; belly sulphur-yellow . . . 330, 330*a*. CRESTED FLYCATCHERS.
      b. Tail fuscous.
        *b*¹. Entire bill black; wing rarely more than ·50 longer than tail; tarsus decidedly longer than bill; under tail-coverts always pale, yellowish white . . . . 331. PHŒBE
       *c*¹. Under mandible generally in whole or part pale brownish; wing always more than ·50 longer than tail; tarsus about equal to bill; some of under tail-coverts frequently with darker centers.
       *c*². Wing over 3·50; sides and breast, except a narrow whitish line through its center, of the same color as the back.
                    338. OLIVE-SIDED FLYCATCHER.
       *c*³. Wing under 3·50; breast and sides washed with olive-gray.
                        337. WOOD PEWEE.
II. Wing under 3·00.
  A. Upperparts between olive-brown and dark olive-green, but with an evident brownish tinge, or *lower mandible brownish.*
    a. Wing over 2·60; lower mandible flesh-color or whitish; underparts with only a very slight tinge of yellow. . . . 335. ALDER FLYCATCHER.
    b. Wing under 2·60; lower mandible rarely clear flesh-color, generally strongly tinged with brownish . . . 336. LEAST FLYCATCHER.
  B. Upperparts olive-green *without* a brownish tinge; lower mandible straw-color.
    a. First primary about equal to fifth; underparts white, slightly washed with yellowish on the breast and belly; *throat white.*
                      334. ACADIAN FLYCATCHER.
    b. First primary shorter than fifth; underparts sulphur-yellow; the *throat* and breast more or less washed with olive-green.
                     333. YELLOW-BELLIED FLYCATCHER.

324. KINGBIRD. TYRANNUS TYRANNUS (*Linnæus*). [444.] *Ads.*—Upperparts grayish slate-color, darker on the head and upper tail-coverts; head with a concealed orange-red crest; tail black, tipped with white; underparts white, washed with grayish on the breast. *Im.*—Similar, but without the crown-patch, and with the plumage more or less tinged with ochraceous-buff. The male has two outer primaries deeply emarginate at the tip, the female usually only one, the immature bird, none. L., 8·51; W., 4·64; T., 3·55; B. from N., ·55.

Range.—Breeds from s. B. C., s. Que., and N. S. s. to cent. Nev., se. Tex., and s. Fla. Winters from s. Mex. to Bolivia. Casual in Cuba in migration; accidental in sw. Greenland.

Washington, common S. R., Apr. 18–Sept. 23. Bronx region, common S. R., Apr. 28–Oct. 14. Boston, common S. R., May 5–Sept. 1. N. Ohio, common S. R., Apr. 20–Sept. 15. Glen Ellyn, fairly common S. R., Apr. 16–Sept. 6. SE. Minn., common S. R., Apr. 26–Sept. 23.

Nest, compact and symmetrical, of weed-stalks, grasses, and moss, lined with plant-down, fine grasses, and rootlets, generally at the extremity of a branch 15–25 feet up. *Eggs*, 3–5, white, spotted with umber, 1·00 × ·73. *Date*, White Sulphur Springs, Va., May 17; Boston, May 30; St. Louis, Mo., May 14, inc. adv.; se. Minn., May 14.

The Kingbird is most frequently seen on a fence or dead twig on a tree, where leaves do not come in the way of his sight. He stands very upright, like a Hawk or an Owl, and, though as quiet as if he had nothing to do, he is keenly awake to every movement about him, and every few minutes he dashes into the air, seizes a passing insect, and returns to the spot from which he started. While his mate is sitting, he usually establishes himself near the nesting tree, and spends hour after hour in this apparently monotonous way, varying it only to relieve her by watching the nest, and thus give her an opportunity to seek food for herself. I never saw a Kingbird either assist in brooding, or carry food to his mate, but his manners to her are most affectionate and he is untiring in his labors in the feeding of the young.

This bird is accused of being quarrelsome and aggressive to other birds, and his scientific name means Tyrant Flycatcher, but in my study of his ways I have found him less aggressive than are most birds in the neighborhood of their nest. With the exception of the Crow, against whom he seems to have a special grudge, I have never seen a Kingbird take notice of any bird unless he alighted near his nest, and the meekest creature that wears feathers will try to drive away strangers who approach that sacred spot.

The calls and cries of the Kingbird are generally loud and attractive, if not particularly musical, but while his mate is sitting—and possibly at other times—he indulges in a soft and very pleasing song, which I have heard only in the very early morning.

OLIVE THORNE MILLER.

1905. HERRICK, F. H., Home-Life of Wild Birds, 49–55.—1908. BIRD-LORE, 166 (pl.).

325. GRAY KINGBIRD. TYRANNUS DOMINICENSIS DOMINICENSIS *(Gmelin).* [445.] *Ads.*—Above ashy gray; an orange-red crown-patch; wings and tail fuscous; under wing-coverts pale sulphur-yellow; underparts white, tinged with grayish on the breast. L., 9·00; W., 6·60; T., 3·50; B. from N., ·80.

Range.—Breeds from the coast of se. S. C. (rarely), Ga., and Fla., to the Bahamas, Porto Rico, Haiti, and Jamaica. Migrates along the coast of middle America from Cozumel Isl. to Panama and winters in n. S. A. (Venezuela and Colombia). Accidental in B. C., Mass., L. I., and s. N. J.

Nest, of grass and weeds, lined with fine grass and rootlets, in trees. *Eggs*, 4, deep salmon, irregularly spotted and blotched with umber and lilac. 1·00 × ·75 (Maynard). *Date*, Little Sarasota, Fla., May 15.

The Gray Kingbird is a common summer resident of parts of our South Atlantic States, arriving early in May. It resembles the Kingbird in appearance, but lacks the white band at the end of the tail, and has quite different notes. Its usual call is a vigorous *pitirri, pitirri*, which, in Cuba, gives it its common name.

1913. THURSTON, H. T., Bird-Lore, 165–168, illus. (at home).

326. LICHTENSTEIN'S KINGBIRD, *Tyrannus melancholicus chloronotus* Berlepsch, of southern Mexico and southward, is accidental in Maine (Scarborough, Oct. 31, 1915; Norton, Auk, 1916, 382).

327. ARKANSAS KINGBIRD. TYRANNUS VERTICALIS *Say.* [447.] *Ads.* —Crown gray with a more or less concealed scarlet patch; back greenish washed with gray; upper tail-coverts and tail black, outer web of outer pair of tail-feathers yellowish white; chin whitish; breast gray; belly yellow. Tips of outer primaries incised, more so in male. L., 8·25; W., 5·00; T., 3·50; B. from N., ·60.

Remarks.—Distinguished from Cassin's Flycatcher by its paler breast and outer white vanes on outer rectrices.

Range.—Breeds mainly in Austral Zones, from s. B. C. and s. Man. s. to n. L. Calif. and Chihuahua, e. to w. Minn., w. Ia., cent. Kans., Okla., and w. Tex. Winters from w. Mex. to Nicaragua. Accidental in Mo., Wisc., Ills., Me., Mass., N. Y., N. J., Del., Md., and Fla.

Washington, one record, Sept. 30. Bronx region, A. V., two records, Aug. 14; Oct. 19. Boston, A. V. SE. Minn., extending eastward, first seen, 1923.

328. The FORK-TAILED FLYCATCHER, *Muscivora tyrannus* (Linnæus), [442], a South American species rarely found north of southern Mexico and the southern Lesser Antilles, has been recorded from Mississippi, Kentucky, New Jersey, Massachusetts, Maine, and Bermuda.

329. The SCISSOR-TAILED FLYCATCHER, *Muscivora forficata* (Gmelin), [443], is found in the summer as far north as southern Kansas and western Louisiana. It has occurred accidentally near Hudson Bay, in Manitoba, Ontario, New Brunswick, Connecticut, New Jersey, Virginia, and Florida. There are two records for the Washington, D. C., region. It may be known by its long, deeply forked tail and scarlet sides.

330. SOUTHERN CRESTED FLYCATCHER. MYIARCHUS CRINITUS CRINITUS (*Linnæus*). [452 part.] Similar to *M. c. boreus* but averaging slightly smaller and with a larger bill.

Range.—Peninsular Fla., n. along Atlantic Coast to s. S. C.

Nesting-date, San Mateo, Fla., May 10.

A summer resident, possibly wintering in the southern part of its range. Doubtless at any season the Crested Flycatchers occurring in Peninsular Florida may be referred to this slightly differentiated race.

330a. NORTHERN CRESTED FLYCATCHER. MYIARCHUS CRINITUS BOREUS *Bangs.* [452.] *Ads.*—Upperparts grayish brown, washed with olive-green; outer vane of primaries margined with pale rufous; *inner vane* of all but the middle tail-feathers *pale rufous;* throat and breast pearl-gray; belly sulphur-yellow. L., 9·01; W., 4·14; T., 3·75; B. from N., ·62.

Range.—Breeds from the upper edge of the Transition Zone in s. Man., s. Ont., s. Que., and N. B. s. to s. Tex. and S. C. Winters from e. and s. Mex. to Panama and Colombia. Accidental in Wyo. and Cuba.

Washington, very common S. R., Apr. 19–Sept. 29. Bronx region, common S. R., Apr. 24, and 30–Oct. 1. Boston, rather common S. R., May 8–Sept. 10. N. Ohio, common S. R., Apr. 25–Sept. 15. Glen Ellyn, not common S. R., May 1–Sept. 18. SE. Minn., common S. R., Apr. 25–Oct. 10.

Nest, of grasses, twigs, and rootlets, with generally a piece of a cast snakeskin, in a hole in a tree, generally less than 20 feet up. *Eggs*, 3–6, creamy white, streaked *longitudinally* with chocolate, ·90 × ·68. *Date*, Weaverville, N. C., May 20; Madison, Conn., June 2; Boston, June 9.

During the spring migration each day brings its own surprise and pleasure. The bare, silent woods where I walked alone before are now astir with flitting wings and ringing with glad music. Each morning I hurry out, full of eager anticipation, to be thrilled by the greeting of some old friend come home again.

FIG. 99. Crested Flycatcher. (Natural size.)

There are red-letter days, however, even in this calendar. Hark! from the woods a loud whistle pierces far through the clearing. The Great-crest has come!

I break away from the confusing chorus of small voices and hurry off to the woods for the first sight of the distinguished bird. Full of life and vigor, he flies about in the green tree-tops, chattering to himself or calling loudly as he goes.

Not many days pass, however, before he is so taken up with domestic matters that his voice is rarely heard outside the woods. Is he engaged in his famous pursuit—hunting snake-skins to line his nest? Absorbed in my daily round of nest calls, I cherish the memory of each passing glimpse of him. Now I see him launch from a basswood top, with wings and tail spread, to sail down through the air, his tail glowing red against the light. Again, when looking for a rare Warbler, his calls arrest me. In the dead top of the highest tree in sight I find him with his mate. With crests raised, the handsome birds chase each other about the bare branches. Tired of that, they explore the old Woodpecker's holes in the trunk, and one of them walks out of sight down a hollow limb. A Blackbird lights in the tree, and the Great-crest above becomes so agitated that I am convinced his mate has gone to her nest, when lo! both Flycatchers are off and away to another of the great trees that overtop the forest. FLORENCE MERRIAM BAILEY.

1909. BIRD-LORE, 12 (mig.; pl.).—1915. GABRIELSON, I. N., Wilson Bull., 421–434, illus. (home-life).—1924. GILLESPIE, J. A., Auk, 41–44, illus. (nesting).

331. EASTERN PHŒBE. SAYORNIS PHŒBE (*Latham*). [456.] (Fig. 58.)
Ads.—Upperparts grayish brown with an olive-green cast; crown distinctly darker, *fuscous;* wings and tail fuscous, wing-bars not conspicuous; outer vane of outer tail-feather white or yellowish white, except at the tip; underparts white, more or less washed with yellowish, and tinged with brownish

gray on the breast and sides; bill *black*. *Im. and Ads. in winter.*—Similar, but upperparts more olive, underparts more yellow, and wing-bars more distinct. L., 6·99; W., 3·38; T., 2·95; B. from N., ·41.

Remarks.—The Phœbe's principal distinguishing characters are its fuscous crown-cap, white outer vane of the outer tail-feather, and blackish lower mandible.

Range.—Breeds from cent. w. Mack., s. Que., and N. B. s. to ne. N. Mex., cent. Tex., n. Miss., and the highlands of Ga. Winters in the U. S. chiefly s. of latitude 37° s. to Vera Cruz and Oaxaca; in migration casual w. to e. Colo. and Wyo. Accidental in Calif., L. Calif., and Cuba.

Washington, common S. R., Feb. 25–Oct.; occasionally winters. Bronx region, common S. R., Mar. 5, and 10–Nov. 26 (Jan. 4). Boston, common T. V., and not uncommon S. R., Mch. 25–Oct. 10. N. Ohio, common S. R., Mch. 14–Oct. 15. Glen Ellyn, S. R., Mch. 13–Oct. 6. SE. Minn., common S. R., Mch. 8–Nov. 3.

Nest, bulky, largely moss and mud lined with grasses and long hairs, on a beam or rafter, under a bridge or bank. *Eggs*, 4–6, white, rarely with a few cinnamon-brown spots, ·78 × ·59. *Date*, Delaware Co., Pa., Apr. 18; Boston, Apr. 28; Galesburg, Ills., Apr. 22; se. Minn., Apr. 19.

There is something familiar, trustful, and homelike in the Phœbe's ways which has won him an undisputed place in our affections. With an assurance born of many welcomes he returns each year to his perch on the bridge-rail, barnyard gate, or piazza, and contentedly sings his humble, monotonous *pewit phœbe, pewit phœbe*—a hopelessly tuneless performance, but who that has heard it in early spring, when the 'pussy willow' seems almost to *purr* with soft blossoms, will not affirm that Phœbe touches chords dumb to more ambitious songsters!

Sometimes Phœbe is inspired to greater effort, and, springing into the air on fluttering wings, he utters more *phœbes* in a few seconds than he would sing ordinarily in an hour.

Phœbe is a devoted parent, and is rarely found far from home. His nest seems to be the favorite abode of an innumerable swarm of parasites which sometimes cause the death of his offspring, and when rearing a second family he changes his quarters.

Aside from a few Great-crests, no other Flycatcher winters in numbers in our southern states, and Phœbe's notes heard in January in the heart of a Florida 'hammock' seem strangely out of place.

1908. BIRD-LORE, 210 (mig.; pl.).

332. SAY'S PHŒBE, *Sayornis saya saya* (Bonaparte), [457], a western species, is of accidental occurrence east of the Mississippi. It has been found in northern Illinois, Missouri, Wisconsin, and on Cape Cod, Massachusetts (Miller, Auk, 1890, 228).

333. YELLOW-BELLIED FLYCATCHER. EMPIDONAX FLAVIVENTRIS (*W. M.* and *S. F. Baird*). [463.] (Pl. XXII.) *Ads.*—Upperparts rather dark olive-green; wings and tail fuscous; greater and lesser wing-coverts tipped with white or yellowish white; underparts sulphur-yellow, the belly pure, the throat, breast, and sides more or less washed with olive-green; upper mandible black, lower mandible whitish or flesh-color; second to fourth primaries of equal length, the first shorter than the fifth. *Im.*—Yellow of the underparts brighter, wing-bars more yellow, and sometimes tinged with pale ochraceous-buff. L., 5·63; W., 2·65; T., 2·16; B. from N., ·33.

Remarks.—This is the most yellow of our small Flycatchers. In any plumage the entire underparts, including the *throat*, are sulphur-yellow or dusky yellowish. In the other eastern species of this genus the throat is white.

Range.—Breeds in Canadian Zone from n. B. C., cent. Que., and N. F. s. to cent. Alberta, n. Minn., n. Mich., N. Y., n. Pa., and s. N. H. W. in migration to the e. border of the plains, e. Tex., and e. Mex. Winters from s. Mex. to Panama. Occasional in w. Fla. Accidental in Greenland.

Washington, rather common T. V., May 9–June 1; July 28–Oct. 6. Bronx region, fairly common T. V., May 11–June 17; Aug. 8–Sept. 27 (Oct. 6). Boston, uncommon T. V., May 25–June 3; Aug. 28–Sept. 8. N. Ohio, rare T. V., May 10. Glen Ellyn, rather rare T. V., May 20–June 5; Sept. 3–12. SE. Minn., common T. V., May 4–May 29; Aug. 12–Sept. 16.

Nest, of moss, lined with grasses, on the ground, beneath the roots of a tree or imbedded in moss. *Eggs*, 4, creamy white, with numerous pale cinnamon-brown markings, chiefly about the larger end, ·68 × ·54. *Date*, Wilmurt, N. Y., June 10; Grand Manan, N. B., June 16, inc. adv.

To see this little Flycatcher at his best, one must seek the northern evergreen forest, where, far from human habitation, its mournful notes blend with the murmur of some icy brook tumbling over mossy stones or gushing beneath the still mossier decayed logs that threaten to bar its way. Where all is green and dark and cool, in some glen overarched by crowding spruces and firs, birches and maples, there it is we find him, and in the beds of damp moss he skilfully conceals his nest. He sits erect on some low twig, and, like other Flycatchers, the snap of his bill tells of a sally after his winged prey. He glides quietly away when approached, and his occasional note of complaint may be heard as long as one remains in his vicinity. During the migration this species is silent, and its several distinctive notes are not available for its identification, and the same thing may be said of our other small Flycatchers. Great similarity in plumage exists between them all, and without the bird in hand, identifications are at best questionable.

The song is more suggestive of a sneeze on the bird's part than of any other sound with which it may be compared. It is an abrupt *psĕ-ĕk′*, almost in one explosive syllable, harsh like the deeper tones of a House Wren, and less musical than the similar but longer songs of the Alder or the Acadian Flycatcher. It is hardly surprising that the birds sing very little when we see with what a convulsive jerk of the head the notes are produced. Its plaintive call is far more melodious —a soft, mournful whistle consisting of two notes, the second higher pitched and prolonged, with rising inflection, resembling in a measure *chū-ē-ē′-p*. J. DWIGHT, JR.

1908. BIRD-LORE, 114 (mig.; pl.).

334. ACADIAN FLYCATCHER. EMPIDONAX VIRESCENS (*Vieillot*). [465.] (Pl. XXII.) *Ads.*—Upperparts between olive-green and dark olive-green; wings and tail fuscous; greater and lesser wing-coverts yellowish white, forming two conspicuous wing-bars; underparts white, washed with pale yellowish and *slightly* tinged with greenish on the breast; the throat, and frequently the middle of the belly, pure white; upper mandible black, lower mandible whitish or flesh-color; second to fourth primaries of about equal length, the first and fifth shorter and also of equal length. *Im.*—Upperparts greener;

underparts more tinged with yellow; wing-bars and outer edges of the *tips of the secondaries* ochraceous-buff. L., 5·75; W., 2·85; T., 2·35; B. from N., ·36.

Remarks.—This species has the upperparts fully as olive-green as the Yellow-bellied Flycatcher, but the underparts are never entirely yellow, and the throat is always white.

Range.—Breeds from the n. upper limit of upper Austral Zone in ne. Nebr., cent. Ia., s. Mich., se. Ont., N. Y., s. Vt. (casually), and Mass. (casually) s. to s. Tex., the Gulf States, and cent. Fla. Migrates through Yucatan and Cent. A., casually to the Bahamas and Cuba. Winters in Colombia and Ecuador.

Washington, common S. R., Apr. 29–Sept. 15. Bronx region, formerly common, now decidedly rare S. R., May 15–Sept. 19. Boston, casual S. R. N. Ohio, common S. R., May 4–Sept. 15. Glen Ellyn, not common S. R., May 6–Aug. 27, and probably later.

Nest, shallow, of plant-stems, grasses, and blossoms, generally on a fork of a beech about 8 feet up. *Eggs*, 2–3, creamy white, with a few cinnamon-brown spots about the larger end, ·74 × ·56. *Date*, Gainesville, Fla., May 12; Chatham Co., Ga., May 13; Chester Co., Pa., May 31; Ossining, N. Y., June 5.

Look for the Acadian Flycatcher in woodlands watered by small streams. It selects a low rather than a high perch, and is rarely seen more than twenty feet from the ground. The frequently uttered calls of this bird are characteristic and will enable you to identify it with more ease in the field than in the study. The most common is a single *spee* or *peet*, repeated at short intervals and accompanied by a rapid twitching of the tail. A more peculiar note is a louder *pee-e-yúk*. The bird seems to articulate this note with difficulty, with bill pointed upward and wings trembling like a fledgling begging for food.

Sometimes you may hear only the first call, sometimes only the second, while on other occasions the two may be uttered alternately. A rarer note may be heard when the bird makes a short, fluttering flight. It resembles the soft murmuring of whistling wings.

1908. Bird-Lore, 114 (mig.; pl.).

335. ALDER FLYCATCHER. Empidonax trailli trailli (*Audubon*). [466a.] (Pl. XXII.) Upperparts between olive-green and olive or *olive-brown;* wings and tail fuscous; greater and lesser wing-coverts tipped with brownish ashy; underparts whitish, washed with dusky grayish on the breast and sides and pale yellowish on the belly; throat pure white; upper mandible black, lower mandible whitish or flesh-color. *Im.*—Similar, but wing-bars ochraceous-buff and underparts slightly yellower. L., 6·09; W., 2·87; T., 2·33; B. from N., ·35.

Remarks.—This is the *brownest* of our small Flycatchers. The upperparts have an evident tinge of brown or olive-brown, a color entirely wanting in the Acadian and Yellow-bellied Flycatchers. In this respect it resembles the much smaller Least Flycatcher, from which, indeed, some specimens can be distinguished only by size.

Range.—Breeds mainly in the Hudsonian and Canadian zones from cent. Alaska, cent. Que., and N. F. s. to s. B. C., ne. Colo., cent. Ark., Ky. and in the mts. of W. Va., w. Md. and Pa.; and in n. N. J. Winters from Yucatan to Ecuador.

Washington, irregularly common T. V., May 7–June 1; Aug. 16–Sept. 17. Bronx region, fairly common but local S. R., May 15–Aug. 20; (Sept. 17 ?). Boston, S. R. and T. V., May 28–June 6; Aug. N. Ohio, common S. R.,

May 7–Sept. 10. Glen Ellyn, quite common S. R., May 8–Oct. 17. SE. Minn., S. R., May 1–Sept. 5.

Nest, of coarse grasses, plant-down, and plant-fibers, lined with fine grasses, in the crotch of a small bush or sapling near the ground. *Eggs*, 3–4, creamy white, with cinnamon-brown markings about the larger end, ·73 × ·54. *Date*, Boston, June 15; Columbus, O., June 12.

While the Yellow-bellied Flycatcher is distinctively a bird of the deep woods, this more abundant Flycatcher in its summer home resorts to the alder patches of the open country and is seldom found far from their protecting shade. It flits restlessly about, keeping well out of sight below the waving tops of the bushes, and its presence is betrayed only by a single *pēp* of alarm that in no way resembles the mournful wail of the Yellow-bellied Flycatcher. It, too, is silent when migrating, and on its breeding-grounds sings but little, so that if it did not take pains to call out to everyone who passes it would not be noticed among the rustling alders. The song most resembles that of the Acadian Flycatcher, an *ēē-zēē-ē-ŭp*, with stress on the rasping *zēē*, the latter part more musical. The performer jerks out the notes rapidly, doubling himself up and fairly vibrating with the explosive effort.

J. DWIGHT, JR.

1901. FARLEY, J. A., Auk, 347–355 (in Mass.).—1902. ALLEN, F. H., *Ibid.*, 84 (song).—1908. BIRD-LORE, 115 (mig.; pl.).—1910. STANWOOD, C. J., Journ. Me. Orn. Soc., 3–5 (nesting in Maine).

336. LEAST FLYCATCHER. EMPIDONAX MINIMUS (*W. M.* and *S. F. Baird*). [467.] (Pl. XXII.) *Ads.*—Upperparts between olive-green and olive or olive-brown; wings and tail fuscous; greater and lesser wing-coverts tinged with ashy white; underparts whitish, washed with dusky grayish on the breast and sides and generally with a slight tinge of yellowish on the belly; lower mandible generally *horn-color*. *Im.*—Underparts slightly more yellow; wing-bars more buffy. L., 5·41; W., 2·51; T., 2·21; B. from N., ·31.

Remarks.—This is the smallest of our Flycatchers. Its size, the comparative absence of yellow on the underparts, and the generally horn-colored or brown lower mandible are its chief distinguishing characters.

Range.—Breeds in the Canadian and Transition zones from w. cent. Mack., s. Que., and Cape Breton Isl. s. to cent. Mont., Ia., Ind., n. Pa., n. N. J., and in the Alleghanies to N. C. In migration w. to e. Colo. and cent. Tex. Winters from ne. Mex. and Yucatan to Panama. Accidental in Peru and W. I.

Washington, common T. V., Apr. 20–May 27; Aug. 13–Oct. 1. Bronx region, common S. R., Apr. 21–Sept. 23 (Oct. 4). Boston, common S. R., May 1–Aug. 25. N. Ohio, common T. V., Apr. 15–May 25; Aug. 25–Oct. 1; rare in summer. Glen Ellyn, not common S. R., chiefly T. V., May 4–Sept. 24. SE. Minn., common S. R., Apr. 30–Oct. 2.

Nest, of plant-down, plant-fibers, rootlets, fine strips of bark, and long hairs, generally in a crotch 5–15 feet up. *Eggs*, 3–5, white, unmarked, ·63 × ·51. *Date*, New York City, May 30; Boston, May 20; se. Minn., May 24.

When music was distributed, I believe most of our Flycatchers had back seats. It was an unfortunate circumstance, for their sedentary habits and apparently thoughtful, serious, even poetic dispositions make one believe that with proper training they might have taken high rank as musicians.

Instead of the simple melody we might expect to hear from the modest Least Flycatcher, he salutes us with a singularly inappropriate, business-like *chebéc, chebéc,* varying the performance by murderous sallies after passing insects. In crescendo passages he literally rises to the occasion, and on trembling wings sings an absurd *chebéc, tooralooral, chebéc, tooral-ooral,* with an earnestness deserving better results.

The Chebec, however, possesses originality; we cannot confuse his voice with that of any other bird, and young ornithologists should give him a vote of thanks for his clear enunciation.

He prefers fruit and shade trees to those of forest growth, and is therefore an inhabitant of our lawns and orchards.

1908. BIRD-LORE, 116 (mig.; pl.).

337. EASTERN WOOD PEWEE. MYIOCHANES VIRENS (*Linnæus*). [461.] (Pl. XXII.) *Ads.*—Upperparts very dark, between olive and fuscous; with sometimes a tinge of dark olive-green, wings and tail fuscous; wing-coverts tipped with whitish, forming two more or less distinct wing-bars; underparts white or yellowish white, washed with olive-gray on sides of throat and breast, and, to a less extent, on center of breast; upper mandible black; lower mandible yellowish or brownish, the tip frequently darker. *Im.*—Similar, but yellower below, wing-coverts edged with cream-buff. L., 6·53; W., 3·34; T., 2·62; B. from N., ·42.

Remarks.—The Wood Pewee and the Olive-sided Flycatcher differ from our other Flycatchers in having the wings decidedly longer than the tail, and in their short tarsi. From the species of the genus *Empidonax* they may be known by these characters and their darker, more fuscous coloration.

Range.—Breeds from s. Man. and s. Que. to s. Tex. and cent. Fla., w. to cent. Nebr. and w. cent. Tex. Winters from Nicaragua to Peru. Casual in Colo.; accidental in Cuba.

Washington, common S. R., Apr. 29–Oct. 12. Bronx region, common S. R., May 3–Oct. 11 (Dec. 13). Boston, common T. V., not uncommon S. R., May 18–Sept. 15. N. Ohio, abundant S. R., May 2–Sept. 27. Glen Ellyn, fairly common S. R., May 9–Sept. 29. SE. Minn., common S. R., May 5–Oct. 6.

Nest, compact and symmetrical, of fine grasses, rootlets, moss, etc., thickly covered with lichens, saddled on a limb, 20–40 feet up. *Eggs,* 3–4, white, with a wreath of distinct and obscure umber markings about the larger end, ·68 × ·54. *Date,* Gainesville, Fla., May 9; Fairfax Co., Va., May 25; Ossining, N. Y., June 8; Boston, June 10; Mt. Carmel, Ills., May 20; se. Minn., June 7.

Pee-a-wee

Thoroughly to appreciate how well the Pewee's disposition is suited to his haunts and notes, we have only to imagine him taking the Phœbe's place and singing the Phœbe's song. He was not intended to adorn a bridge or barn, but in the darkened woods, high up in the trees, he finds a congenial home.

His pensive, gentle ways are voiced by his sad, sweet call: The notes are as musical and restful, as much a part of Nature's hymn, as the soft humming of a brook. All day long the Pewee sings; even when the heat of summer silences more vigorous birds, and the midday sun sends light-shafts to the ferns, the clear, sympathetic notes of the retiring songster come from the green canopy overhead, in perfect harmony with the peace and stillness of the hour.

1908. BIRD-LORE, 168 (mig.; pl.).

338. OLIVE-SIDED FLYCATCHER. NUTTALLORNIS MESOLEUCUS (*Lichtenstein*). [459.] *Ads.*—Upperparts between fuscous and dark olive; wings and tail fuscous; throat, middle of the belly, and generally a narrow line on the center of the breast white or yellowish white; rest of the underparts of nearly the same color as the back; under tail-coverts marked with dusky; *a tuft of fluffy, yellowish white feathers* on either flank; upper mandible black, lower mandible yellowish or pale grayish brown, the tip darker. *Im. and Ads. in winter.*—Similar, but with rather more olive above, more yellow below, and with the wing-coverts edged with ochraceous-buff. L., 7·39; W., 4·05; T., 2·70; B. from N., ·54.

Range.—Breeds in Canadian and Transition zones from cent. Alaska, s. Que., and Cape Breton Isl. s. in coniferous forests of the w. U. S. to n. L. Calif., and w. Tex., n. Mich., N. Y., and Mass. and s. in mts. to N. C. Migrates through Mex. and Cent. A. and winters in n. S. A. from Colombia to Peru. Accidental in Greenland.

Washington, irregular T. V., May; Aug.; Sept. Bronx region, uncommon but regular T. V., May 12–June 11; Aug. 6–Sept. 24. Boston, rare T. V., May 20–June 6; Sept.; formerly bred. N. Ohio, tolerably common T. V. Glen Ellyn, not common T. V., May 13–June 11; Aug. 11–Sept. 23. SE. Minn., common T. V., Apr. 30–June 9; Aug. 4–Sept. 26.

Nest, of twigs and moss, in coniferous trees, about 25 feet up, near the extremity of a limb. *Eggs*, 3–5, vinaceous-white, spotted, chiefly about the larger end, with distinct and obscure rufous markings, ·85 × ·62. *Date*, Wareham, Mass., June 8; Kentville, N. S., June 15.

Both the Olive-side's habits and notes make it conspicuous. It perches on the topmost limb of some high tree, where, even at a distance, its stocky body and large head are evident, and calls its loud, strongly accented "come right *here*, come right *here*," in a voice that commands attention.

1908. BIRD-LORE, 258 (mig.; pl.).

339. The VERMILION FLYCATCHER, *Pyrocephalus rubinus mexicanus* Sclater, [471], of our Mexican boundary and southward, has been taken once in Florida (Tallahassee, Mch. 25, 1901; Williams, Auk, 1901, 273).

SUBORDER OSCINES. LARKS, SWALLOWS, CROWS AND JAYS, TITMICE, NUTHATCHES, WRENS, THRASHERS, THRUSHES, WAXWINGS, VIREOS, WARBLERS, TANAGERS, SPARROWS, ETC.

(51 families, 22 North American, 20 eastern North American)

SYNOPSIS OF FAMILIES

For the same reasons given in connection with the Synopsis to Orders and Suborders, I give here, as in earlier editions of the Handbook, a Synopsis rather than a Key to Families. While a Key is simpler, its use will not give one that knowledge of classification and structure which will result from familiarity with a Synopsis that follows the accepted order of arrangement and presents the more salient characters by which families may be distinguished. Study of the Synopsis as a whole, and not merely as a means of identification in specific instances, will soon give the student that grasp of fundamentals which will make its further use unnecessary. We should know the distinguishing characters of families as well as those of species.

Walking birds with claw of hind toe longer than middle toe without claw; front of tarsus with transverse scales, its back rounded instead of ridged (as in all our other Oscines); bill rather short, not slender but pointed; the nostrils with bristly tufts; head subcrested or 'horned.'

FIG. 100. Horned Lark.

Family Alaudidæ. LARKS. P. 378.

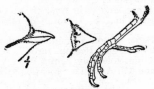

FIG. 101. Cliff Swallow.

Long-winged, weak-footed birds of the air; obvious primaries nine, "the longest more than twice as long as the longest secondaries" (Ridgway); bill short and flattened, much wider than high at the base; tip of maxilla slightly hooked; gape wide, reaching to below the eye, a flying insect catcher's mouth but without evident bristles at its base; outer tail-feathers usually the longest; tarsus short, feet small, unfit for walking.

Family Hirundinidæ. SWALLOWS and MARTINS. P. 381.

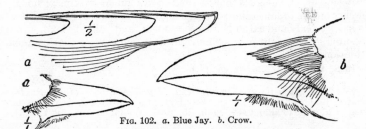

FIG. 102. *a.* Blue Jay. *b.* Crow.

Large birds, 10·00–20·00 long, bill stout, the nostrils concealed by bristly feathers; ten primaries, fourth to fifth the longest, the first about half as long; outer tail-feathers shortest; feet and claws heavy.

Family Corvidæ. CROWS and JAYS. P. 387.

FIG. 103.
Chickadee.

Length 4·50–6·50; bill comparatively short, stout and rounded, maxilla unnotched, less than ·50 long; nostrils concealed by bristly feathers; wings rounded, primaries ten, fourth or fifth longest, first not more than one-third as long; tail well developed, more than three-fourths as long as wing; feet strong.

Family Paridæ. TITMICE. P. 393.

Small creeping birds 4·50–6·10 long, with gray upper-parts; bill rather long, straight, and slender, without notch or hook; outline of lower mandible deflected upward terminally; nostrils more or less covered with bristles; wings rather long and pointed, primaries ten, the first less than an inch long, the third or fourth longest; tail short and square, less than three-fourths length of wing; feet and claws notably large. *Family Sittidæ.* NUTHATCHES. P. 397.

Fig. 104.
White-breasted
Nuthatch.

Fig. 105. Brown Creeper.

A small, brownish, climbing bird about 5·50 long; bill slender and markedly decurved; primaries ten, the first about one-third as long as the second; tail-feathers sharply pointed and slightly stiffened; claws well developed. *Family Certhiidæ.* CREEPERS. P. 400.

Small brownish birds 4·00–6·00 long, with in-distinctly barred wings and tail; bill slender, more or less decurved terminally, no rictal bristles; wings rounded, primaries ten, third to fifth longest and but little longer than the longest secondaries, the first (outer) about half as long as the longest; tail usually short, rounded, the outer feather shortest.
Family Troglodytidæ. WRENS. P. 401.

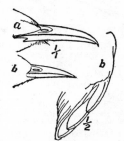

Fig. 106. *a.* Carolina Wren.
b. House Wren.

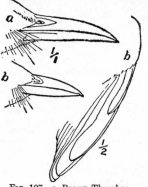

Length 8·00–12·00; bill long, maxilla notched and more or less decurved terminally, rictal bristles evident; wing rather rounded, primaries ten, third to fifth the longest, first about half as long; tail well developed, graduated, the outer feathers at least half an inch shorter than middle ones; tarsus obviously longer than middle toe with claw, scutellate, its front with trans-verse scales.
Family Mimidæ. THRASHERS, CAT-BIRDS, and MOCKINGBIRDS. P. 407.

Fig. 107. *a.* Brown Thrasher.
b. Catbird.

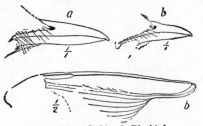

Fig. 108. *a*. Robin. *b*. Bluebird.

Length usually from 6·00–10·00;
bill well developed; maxilla
notched; nostrils exposed;
rictal bristles evident; wings
long and pointed, primaries
ten, third the longest, the
first less than an inch long;
tail square; feet strong, the
tarsus smooth (booted), the
scales, if any, fused and indistinct; nestling plumage
spotted both above and below.
Family Turdidæ. THRUSHES,
   BLUEBIRDS, ETC. P. 411.

Length 3·50–5·00; bill as small and slender
as that of the smallest Warbler bill,
but with maxilla notched and the
nostrils more or less covered with
bristly feathers; primaries ten, fourth
and fifth longest, the first about one-
third as long; tail medium (Kinglets)
or long (Gnatcatchers); feet slender.
   Family Sylviidæ. KINGLETS and
      GNATCATCHERS. P. 420.

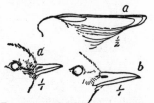

Fig. 109. *a*. Golden-crowned Kinglet. *b*. Blue-gray Gnatcatcher.

Fig. 110. Pipit.

Walking birds, our two species (Pipits)
about 6·30 long, brownish with outer
tail-feathers largely white; bill slender,
nostrils not covered by bristles; maxilla
notched; wings with nine obvious primaries, the first three of about equal
length; the tertials much elongated; claw of hind toe much lengthened,
as long as its toe . . *Family Motacillidæ.* WAGTAILS and PIPITS. P. 423.

Length 7·00–8·00; plumage soft,
brownish; chin, and a narrow
band across the forehead and
through the eyes to the back of
the head, black; tail tipped with
yellow; lower tail-coverts elongated; bill small, gape wide; wings
pointed, primaries ten, the first
rudimentary, the second longest.
   Family Bombycillidæ.
      WAXWINGS. P. 425.

Fig. 112. Migrant Shrike.

Fig. 111. Cedar Waxwing.

Grayish birds, 8·00–9·00 in length; a
black band from the bill through
the eyes; tail with white-tipped
feathers; bill strongly hooked; nostrils fringed with bristly feathers;
wings rather short, primaries ten;
tail graduated, the outer feathers
shortest; feet normal, the claws
not paralleling the 'hawklike' bill
in development.
   Family Laniidæ. SHRIKES. P. 427.

Walking birds, adults chiefly, black with metallic reflections; bill long, flattened, especially toward end, where wider than high; wings long and pointed; primaries ten, the first (outer) less than half an inch long, the second longest; tail short, about half the length of the wing, nearly square; feathers of neck and breast long, narrow.

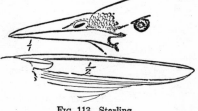

FIG. 113. Starling.

Family *Sturnidæ*.
STARLINGS. P. 429.

FIG. 114. Blueheaded Vireo.

Small birds 5·00–7·00 in length; with generally olive-green backs and with no white spots or patches in the tail-feathers; bill rather stout, higher than broad at base, not sharply pointed, the tip of the maxilla notched, decurved and hooked; bristles at base of bill barely evident; primaries ten, the first rudimentary and in some species not evident, when the bird falls into the 'nine-primary' group . . . Family *Vireonidæ*. VIREOS. P. 430.

Small birds, length generally under 6·00 (but in four species 6·50–7·50) with, usually, brightly colored plumage, olive-green and yellow prevailing; bill usually rounded, straight and pointed, its base without conspicuous bristles, the end of the maxilla without notch or hook (except in *Icteria* where it is stout and decurved, and *Sylvania* and *Setophaga* where it is broader than high at the base and has well-developed bristles, thus resembling that of a true Flycatcher, but the back of the tarsus is always thin and narrow, never rounded as in front); wing with nine obvious primaries, second or third longest, the first little if any shorter; tail-feathers generally of about equal length, the outer ones often with white areas.

Family *Compsothlypidæ*.
WOOD WARBLERS. P. 437.

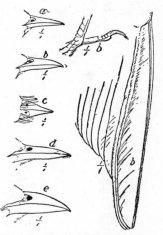

FIG. 115. *a*. Tennessee Warbler. *b*. Pine Warbler. *c*. Redstart. *d*. Water-Thrush. *e*. Chat.

FIG. 116.
House Sparrow.

In external structure not distinguishable from the Fringillidæ. Postjuvenal molt complete; nest domed; voice harsh. Our species the introduced House Sparrow.

Family *Ploceidæ*.
WEAVER FINCHES. P. 479.

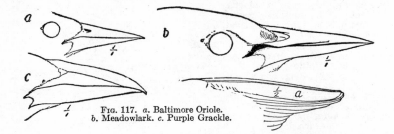

Fig. 117. *a*. Baltimore Oriole.
b. Meadowlark. *c*. Purple Grackle.

Length 7·00–17·00; base of the culmen, between the nostrils extending backward and dividing the feathers of the forehead; end of maxilla not hooked or notched; nostrils not concealed by bristles; nine obvious primaries, the first three of about equal length; outer tail-feathers generally shortest.

Family Icteridæ. ORIOLES, BLACKBIRDS, MEADOWLARKS, ETC. P. 481.

Length 7·00–7·50; the males of our species wholly or largely red; bill finch-like but less conical, somewhat swollen, the culmen more or less rounded; the commissure not basally angled; cutting edge (tomium) of maxilla usually 'toothed' near middle (not always evident in our species); obvious primaries nine; tail-feathers of equal length.

FIG. 118.
Scarlet Tanager.

Family Thraupidæ. TANAGERS. P. 494.

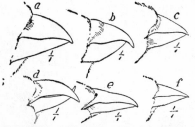

FIG. 119. *a*. Cardinal. *b*. Pine Grosbeak.
c. Purple Finch. *d*. Red Crossbill. *e*. Seaside
Finch. *f*. Goldfinch.

Length 4·75–9·10, generally under 8·00; bill short, stout and conical; line of juncture of maxilla and mandible (commissure) not straight, but basally angled; obvious primaries nine, the third and fourth usually of about the same length, the first never more than half an inch shorter than the longest.

Family Fringillidæ.
SPARROWS, FINCHES,
GROSBEAKS, ETC. P. 496.

FAMILY ALAUDIDÆ. LARKS.

Over 250 species and subspecies of Larks are known, the proportion of the latter to the former being exceptionally large, the Horned Lark, the only American species, being represented in North America by no less than 16 subspecies.

They are eminently terrestrial birds, always nest on the ground, rarely alight in trees, usually run instead of hop, 'dust' instead of bathe, and sing while on the wing. They are generally colored in harmony with their haunts, and, except during the nesting season, are usually found in flocks.

340. SKYLARK. ALAUDA ARVENSIS ARVENSIS *Linnæus.* [473.] (Fig. 101.) Hind toe-nail as long as or longer than toe. *Ads.*—Above brownish ochraceous streaked with black; tail blackish, central feather margined with ochraceous-buff; outer feathers more or less white; below whitish more or less washed with ochraceous-buff, especially on breast, which is distinctly streaked with black. L., 7·50; W., 4·10; T., 2·60; B., ·45. Bears a superficial resemblance to a Vesper Sparrow, but, aside from structural differences, is larger and more buffy.

Range.—Breeds in Europe (except se. portion and s. Italy) and the British Isles. Winters as far n. as Germany. Accidental in Greenland and Bermuda. Introduced and resident on Vancouver Isl., B. C., also introduced but not permanently established in various localities in the U. S.

The Skylark has been introduced several times in this country. In 1887 a small colony had become established near Flatbush, Long Island, where a nest with young was found. (See Dutcher, *The Auk*, 1888, p. 180.) After a supposed extinction a singing bird and nest were observed in July, 1895. (See Proctor, *The Auk*, 1895, p. 390.) According to Braislin (*Abst. Proc. Linn. Soc.* 17, 1907, p. 76) the bird was still present at Flatbush where it could be heard singing from March to October, but Griscom states that the haunts of this colony were destroyed by building and the species has not been observed since 1913.

341. HOYT'S HORNED LARK. OTOCORIS ALPESTRIS HOYTI *Bishop.* [474k.] "Similar to *O. a. alpestris* but with the upperparts generally paler and more gray, the posterior auriculars gray rather than brown, and the yellow of the head and neck replaced by white, excepting the forehead, which is dirty greenish white, and the throat, which is distinctly yellow, most pronounced toward the center. . . . The adult female in spring plumage differs in a similar manner from the female of *alpestris*, but in the female of *hoyti* the yellow on the throat is much paler than in the male." W., 4·35 (Bishop).

Range.—Breeds from the mouth of the Mack. to the w. shore of Hudson Bay, s. to n. Alberta and n. Man. Winters s. to Nev., Utah, Kans., Mich., O., N. Y., and Conn.

341a. NORTHERN HORNED LARK. OTOCORIS ALPESTRIS ALPESTRIS (*Linnæus*). (Fig. 100.) [474.] *Ad. ♂.*—Forehead, line over the eye, ear region, and throat sulphur-yellow; fore part of crown, a tuft of elongated feathers on either side of head, a mark from bill below eye and then downward to side of throat, and a patch on breast black; back of head and neck and rump vinaceous, more or less washed with grayish brown; back grayish brown, edged with brownish ash and tinged with vinaceous; wing-coverts deep vinaceous; tail black, outer vanes of outer feathers margined with white, middle feathers broadly margined with brownish and vinaceous; lower breast and belly white, the former more or less soiled with dusky spots; sides vinaceous. *Ad. ♀.*—Similar, but the markings, especially those of the head, less sharply defined, neck less vinaceous, etc. *Im. and Ad. in winter.*—Similar, but with the black markings veiled by yellowish or whitish tips to the feathers. L., 7·75; "W., 4·27; T., 2·84; B. from N., ·40" (Dwight).

Range.—Breeds in Can. from Hudson Strait s. to head of James Bay, Lab., se. Que. and N. F. Winters s. to the O. Valley and Ga. and w. to Man. Casual in La. and Bermuda; accidental in Greenland.

Washington, common but irregular W. V., Oct.–Apr. Bronx region, common T. V. and W. V., Oct. 7–Apr. 13. Boston, common T. V. and rather common W. V., Oct.–Apr. N. Ohio, common W. V., Nov. 1–Apr. 1.

Nest, of grasses, on the ground. *Eggs*, 3–4, pale, bluish or greenish white, minutely and evenly speckled with pale grayish brown, ·84 × ·60. *Date*, Hebron, Lab., May 30.

These hardy birds visit us in flocks in the winter. They frequent the vicinity of the seacoast or large, flat, open tracts in the interior, and are rarely found in well-wooded regions. They are terrestrial, and may be seen running over the snow or barren ground in scattered companies. They take wing with a sharp, whistled note, and seek fresh fields, or, hesitating, finally swing about and return to near the spot from which they were flushed. They are sometimes found associated with Snow-Buntings, and flocks may contain numbers of our resident Shore Lark, *O. a. praticola*.

341b. PRAIRIE HORNED LARK. Otocoris alpestris praticola *Henshaw*. [474b.] (Fig. 100.) Similar to the preceding, but smaller and somewhat paler, with the forehead and line over the eye *white* instead of yellow, the throat but slightly tinged with yellow, and sometimes entirely white. L., 7·25; "W., 4·08; T., 2·86; B. from N., ·37" (Dwight).

Range.—Breeds from s. Man. and s. cent. Que. to e. Kans., cent. Mo., O., W. Va., and Conn. Winters s. to Tex., Tenn., Ga. and Fla. (rarely) and casually to Ariz. and Colo.

Washington, common but irregular W. V., Aug. 11–Apr.; casual S. R. Bronx region, probably rare T. V., Nov. 2–May 2 (July 29). Boston, rare S. R., fairly common T. V., Feb.–Dec. N. Ohio, common P. R. Glen Ellyn, common P. R., less so in winter. SE. Minn., S. R., Mch.–Nov., a few in mild winters.

Fig. 120. Prairie Horned Lark.
(Natural size.)

Nesting-date, Buffalo, N. Y., Mch. 9; se. Minn., Mch. 10.

This is one of the birds that has changed its range since the settlement of America. It is properly a species of the prairies and open barrens, but since the once-continuous forest of the older states and provinces has been broken up, it has made its appearance in the East, wherever the country is suited to its requirements.

It is strictly a ground-bird, never perching on trees, though it commonly alights on the top of a fence-post or other low, level surface. When encountered on a pathway it often runs before the pedestrian after the manner of the Vesper Sparrow, from which bird, however, it may be distinguished by the black feathers in its tail, by its brown back, and by the black marks on its face; also by the fact that it *runs*, but does not *hop*, and when it flies it usually utters a whistle, whereas the Vesper Sparrow invariably flies off in silence.

Its chief song is poured forth in the air as it soars aloft, like a Skylark; but it often utters this same song while perched on some clod or stone, especially just before dawn and after sunset, as well as in the springtime, while the snow is yet on the ground.

ERNEST THOMPSON SETON.

1916. MOUSLEY, H., Auk, 281–286 (breeding in Quebec).—1918. BIRD-LORE, 344, 350 (mig.; pl.).—1927. SUTTON, G. M., Wilson Bull., 131–141, illus. (habits).

FAMILY HIRUNDINIDÆ. SWALLOWS.

The nearly 200 known species and subspecies of Swallows are distributed throughout the world, but are most poorly represented in the Australian region, where only 4 species occur. About 40 species (60 species and subspecies) are American, and 9 of these are found north of Mexico. In their long, powerful wings and small, weak feet, Swallows present an excellent illustration of the effects of use and disuse. The

FIG. 121. Barn Swallow.   Cliff Swallow.   Tree Swallow.
Bank Swallow.

greater part of their day is passed on the wing, and in alighting they select a perch which they can grasp with ease. Swallows live almost exclusively upon insects, which they capture on the wing, their large mouths, as in the case of the Swifts and Goatsuckers, being especially adapted to this mode of feeding.

They nest both in pairs and colonies, and during their migrations, associate, in countless numbers, at regularly frequented roosting-places or migration stations. These are sometimes in trees, but more often in marshes, and to them the Swallows regularly return each night. They migrate, as far as known, entirely by day, their wonderful power of flight enabling them to escape the dangers which beset less rapid fliers, and to make journeys of great extent. Swallows' nests are remarkable for their wide diversity of architecture, as well as for the skill shown by these small-billed, weak-footed birds in their construction, and comparison of the mud dwelling of the Cliff Swallow with the tunnelled home of the Bank Swallow, illustrates how small the relation may be between the structure of the bird and the character of its nest. Swallows are not distinguished as vocalists but their twittering, chirpy notes have a cheerful, homelike quality.

KEY TO THE SPECIES

1. Upperparts with metallic reflections.
    A. Underparts steel-blue.
        a. Feathers on the belly fuscous at the base. 351. PURPLE MARTIN, ♂.
        b. Feathers on the belly white at the base . 352. CUBAN MARTIN, ♂.
    B. Underparts not steel-blue.
        a. Throat chestnut, rufous, or brownish.
            a^1. Upper tail-coverts the same as the back; tail with white spots.
                                    347. BARN SWALLOW.
            a^2. Upper tail-coverts rufous or buffy; no white in the tail.
                                    349. CLIFF SWALLOW.
        b. Throat gray or white.
            b^1. Entire underparts white . . . . 343. TREE SWALLOW.
            b^2. Throat and breast brownish gray . . 351. PURPLE MARTIN, ♀.
            b^3. Throat, breast, and sides sooty brownish gray.
                                    352. CUBAN MARTIN, ♀.
2. Upperparts without metallic reflections.
    a. Underparts entirely white . . . . 343. TREE SWALLOW.
    b. Throat and breast brownish gray . 345. ROUGH-WINGED SWALLOW.
    c. Throat and belly white; a brownish gray band across the breast.
                                    344. BANK SWALLOW.

342. The BAHAMA SWALLOW, *Callichelidon cyaneoviridis* (H. Bryant), [615.1], has been once recorded from the Dry Tortugas and Tarpon Springs, Fla., and may occur more or less regularly in the Keys off southeastern Florida (Scott, Auk, 1890, 265). It is satiny white below, dull bottle-green above; wings and tail bluer, the outer tail-feathers an inch longer than the middle ones.

343. **TREE SWALLOW.** IRIDOPROCNE BICOLOR (*Vieillot*). [614.] (Figs. 14, 121.) *Ads.*—Upperparts steel-blue or steel-green; underparts pure white; outer tail-feathers somewhat longer than the middle ones. *Nestling.*—Upperparts dull brownish gray; underparts pure white, with sometimes a dusky breast-band. L., 5·90; W., 4·70; T., 2·35; B. from N., ·22.
    Range.—Breeds from nw. Alaska,, s. and w. Mack., n. Man., and n. Que. to s. Calif., Colo., Kans., ne. Ark., and Va. Winters from cent. Calif., s. Tex., s. parts of the Gulf States, and e. N. C. (often N. J.) s. over the greater part of Mex. to Guatemala and Cuba. Occasional in Bermuda in migration.
    Washington, common T. V., Mch. 4–May 26; July 3–Oct. 14. Bronx region, common, occasionally abundant T. V., rare S. R., Mch. 20–June 13; July 1–Oct. 31 (Dec. 6). Boston, rather common S. R., Apr. 5–Oct. 8; common T. V. N. Ohio, common S. R., Apr. 10–Sept. 20. Glen Ellyn, fairly common T. V., rare S. R., Apr. 3–Sept. 8. SE. Minn., common S. R., Mch. 21–Oct. 4.
    Nest, of coarse grasses and feathers, in a hollow tree or bird-box. *Eggs,*

4–7, white, ·74 × ·55. *Date*, Saybrook, Conn., May 13; Boston, May 20; Jackson Co., Mich., May 15; se. Minn., May 5.

While our eastern Barn and Cliff Swallows have abandoned their primitive methods of nesting in caves or beneath cliffs, and the Bank Swallows still adhere to the customs of their ancestors, Tree Swallows are passing through a transition period in their history. Some accept the houses or boxes erected by man as substitutes for the holes in trees or stumps which others still use.

Near New York City they are the first migrants to flock after the nesting season, and they begin to gather in our marshes as early as July 1. Their numbers rapidly increase, and the maximum of abundance is reached about August 15, when they outnumber all other Swallows together by at least three to one. They return to their roosts in the reeds with great regularity every night, and early in the morning fly out over the country to feed. Their flight in the evening is comparatively low, at an average height of 30 to 40 feet. They sail about in circles more than other Swallows, and many pause to rest on telegraph wires, where their pure white breasts easily distinguish them from the Swallows which may be associated with them. In the morning their flight is much higher and more direct. They migrate by day, leaving their roosting-ground in flocks, which sometimes contain myriads, and, after attaining a great height, pursue their journey to the south. When migrating along the coast they sometimes collect in large numbers in bayberry bushes (*Myrica*) and feed on their fruit.

1900. CHAPMAN, F. M , Bird Studies with a Camera, 89–105 (roosting).— 1917. BIRD-LORE, 322, 331 (mig.; pl.).

344. BANK SWALLOW. RIPARIA RIPARIA RIPARIA (*Linnæus*). [616.] (Fig. 121.) *Ads.*—Upperparts brownish gray; throat white; a brownish gray *band on the breast;* outer vane of first primary *without* recurved hooklets; a small tuft of feathers above the hind toe. L., 5·20; W., 3·95; T., 2·00; B. from N., ·18.

Range.—Breeds from n. Alaska and n. Que. s. to s. Calif., Ariz., Tex., cent. Ala. and Va.; also in Europe and the British Isles, e. to Siberia and from 70° n. lat. s. to Tunisia and Algeria. Migrates through Mex. and Cent. A. to Brazil and Argentina.

Washington, common S. R., more common T. V., Apr. 4–Sept. 21. Bronx region, fairly common but local S. R., Apr. 12–Sept. 20 (Oct. 11). Boston, rather common S. R., locally, Apr. 28–Sept. 1. N. Ohio, common S. R., Apr. 6–Sept. 20. Glen Ellyn, fairly common T. V.; a few S. R., Apr. 22–Sept. 3. SE. Minn., common S. R., Apr. 10–Sept. 28.

Nest, of grasses and feathers, in a hole in a sand-bank, 2–3 feet from the entrance. *Eggs*, 4–6, white, ·68 × ·48. *Date*, Chester Co., Pa., May 10; Ossining, N. Y., May 20; Boston, May 28; se. Minn., May 1.

This is a locally distributed species, breeding in colonies only where sand-banks offer it a favorable nesting-site. Probably for the reason that such banks are more frequently found bordering streams than inland, the birds are more numerous in the vicinity of water.

Bank Swallows may be readily known from other Swallows, excepting the Rough-winged, by their nesting habits, small size, and absence of metallic coloring. From the Rough-wing they differ in having the underparts white, with a conspicuous band across the breast, and in their somewhat quicker movements.

1917. BIRD-LORE, 326, 331 (mig.; pl.).—1925. STONER, D., Auk, 86–94, illus.—1926. 198–213.—1928. 41–45; 310–320 (banding).

345. ROUGH-WINGED SWALLOW. STELGIDOPTERYX RUFICOLLIS SERRIPENNIS (*Audubon*). [617.] *Ads.*—Upperparts brownish gray; throat and breast pale brownish gray; belly white; outer web of first primary with a series of *recurved hooklets* (sometimes absent in ♀); no tuft of feathers above the hind toe. *Im.*—Similar, but without recurved hooklets on the first primary; throat and breast more or less washed and wing-coverts edged with rufous. L., 5·75; W., 4·35; T., 2·10; B. from N., ·19.

Range.—Breeds from s. B. C., Mont., N. Dak., Minn., cent. Wisc., se. Ont., s. N. Y., w. Mass., and Conn. s. to s. U. S. from s. Calif. to cent. Fla., and to Vera Cruz and Jalisco. Winters from s. Ariz. s. to Costa Rica. Casual in Man.

Washington, common S. R., Mch. 27–Sept. 11. Bronx region, fairly common S. R., Apr. 10–Sept. 9. Boston, casual T. V. N. Ohio, common S. R., Apr. 15–Sept. 20. SE. Minn., common S. R., Apr. 14–Aug. 26.

FIG. 122. Section of outer primary of adult Rough-winged Swallow. (Enlarged.)

Nest, of coarse grasses and feathers, under bridges, in stone walls, or in a hole in a bank. *Eggs*, 4–8, white, ·72 × ·51. *Date*, D. C., May 17; se. Minn., May 2.

Rough-winged Swallows resemble Bank Swallows both in habits and appearance. They do not, however, always nest in holes in banks, but are sometimes found nesting about bridges, railway trestles and their abutments.

With the Bank Swallow this bird differs from our other Swallows in the absence of metallic colors, while from the Bank Swallow it is to be distinguished by its plain, pale brownish gray, uniformly colored throat and breast, and somewhat slower, less erratic flight.

1917. BIRD-LORE, 328, 331 (mig. pl.).

346. The EUROPEAN MARTIN, *Chelidonaria urbica urbica* Linnæus, [615.2], is of accidental occurrence in Greenland.

347. BARN SWALLOW. HIRUNDO ERYTHROGASTER *Boddaert*. [613.] (Fig. 121.) *Ad.* ♂.—Forehead, throat, and upper breast chestnut-rufous; rest of the underparts washed with the same color; upperparts steel-blue; tail *deeply forked*, all but the middle feathers with white spots on their inner webs. *Ad.* ♀.—Similar, but underparts usually paler and outer tail-feathers shorter. *Im.*—Upperparts mixed with dusky, forehead and throat paler; outer tail-feathers shorter. L., 6·95; W., 4·67; T., 3·30; B. from N., ·24.

Range.—Breeds from nw. Alaska, n. Mack. (Great Bear Lake), s. Man., and cent. Que. s. to s. Calif., s. Tex. (w. of long. 97°), n. Ark., n. Ala. and N. C. and in Mex. s. to Jalisco and Tepic. Migrates through the Bahamas and the W. I. and winters from Mex. to Argentina. Accidental in the Galapagos, and Bermuda.

Washington, common S. R., more abundant T. V., Mch. 30–Sept. 23. Bronx region, common S. R., Apr. 5–Oct. 21 (Nov. 17). Boston, rather common S. R., Apr. 20–Sept. 10. N. Ohio, abundant S. R., Mch. 30–Sept. 22. Glen Ellyn, S. R., fairly common, Apr. 7–Sept. 1. SE. Minn., common S. R., Apr. 24–Sept. 27.

Nest, of mud and grasses, lined with grasses and feathers, generally on the rafter of a barn or other building. *Eggs,* 4–6, white, with numerous spots of cinnamon-, olive-, or rufous-brown, generally smaller than those on the eggs of *P. albifrons,* ·77 × ·54. *Date,* Chester Co., Pa., May 19; Portsmouth, R. I., May 18; Boston, May 25; se. Minn., May 17.

Barn Swallows nest both in pairs and colonies, and during the breeding season are more generally distributed than any other of our Swallows. Almost every old-fashioned barn with its great doors hospitably opened is cheered by their sweet call-notes and happy twittering song as they dart in and out on their errands of love.

Barn Swallows take first rank among a family of birds famous for their power of flight. While their relatives are circling about feeding on insects in the air above, they capture their prey nearer the ground, skimming low over the fields, turning quickly to right or left, up or down, and pursuing their erratic course with marvelous ease and grace.

1917. BIRD-LORE, 262 (pl.).—1918, 150 (mig.).—1929. ROBINSON, H. J., Bull. Northeastern Bird-Banding Assoc., 108–113 (colony studies).

348. The EUROPEAN SWALLOW, *Hirundo rustica rustica* Linnæus [613.1], is of accidental occurrence in Greenland.

349. NORTHERN CLIFF SWALLOW. PETROCHELIDON ALBIFRONS ALBIFRONS *Rafinesque.* [612.] (Fig. 121.) *Ads.*—Forehead whitish, crown steel-blue, throat and sides of the head chestnut; a brownish gray ring around the neck; breast brownish gray, tinged with rufous and with a steel-blue patch in its center; belly white; back steel-blue, lightly streaked with white; shorter upper tail-coverts *pale rufous;* tail fuscous, the feathers of nearly equal length. *Im.*—Similar, but upperparts duller; throat black, sometimes mottled with white. L., 6·01; W., 4·34; T., 2·01; B. from N., ·20.
Remarks.—The Cliff Swallow may be known from our other Swallows by its rufous upper tail-coverts.
Range.—Breeds from cent. Alaska, the upper Yukon Valley, n. cent. Mack., n. Ont., s. Que., Anticosti Isl., and Cape Breton Isl. s. over nearly all of the U. S. except Fla. and the Rio Grande Valley (casual as a breeder s. of lat. 38° and e. of long. 97°); also along the coast district of w. Mex. Migrates through Fla. and Cent. A. and probably winters in Brazil and Argentina.
Washington, rare S. R., Apr. 10–Sept. 23. Bronx region, fairly common T. V., apparently no longer breeds; Apr. 19–June 4; July 2–Oct. 6. Boston, uncommon T. V., Apr. 20–May; Aug.–Sept. 15; formerly S. R. N. Ohio, tolerably common S. R., Apr. 6–Sept. 25. Glen Ellyn, formerly local S. R., now apparently T. V., not common, Apr. 15–25; Sept. 16. SE. Minn., once common, now rare S. R., Apr. 13–Oct. 7.
Nest, of mud, generally retort- or pocket-shaped, beneath cliffs or the eaves of a barn or other building. *Eggs,* 4–5, white, with numerous spots of cinnamon-, olive-, or rufous-brown, ·81 × ·55. *Date,* Shelter Isl., N. Y., May 29; se. Minn., May 19.

During the nesting season these Swallows are of very local distribution. They will return year after year to their rows of mud tenements beneath the eaves of some barn or outbuilding, and, although familiar birds to residents of the immediate vicinity, they may be entire strangers to those who have never had a colony of these birds settled near them. Like Barn Swallows, they are masons, and they may be seen on muddy shores rolling the little pellets of clay which enter into the construction of their nest. In the fall they are found in flocks with other Swallows, but at all times they may be readily identified by their pale rufous upper tail-coverts, which make a conspicuous field-mark.

1917. Bird-Lore, 320, 330 (mig.; pl.).

350. The Cuban Cliff Swallow, *Petrochelidon fulva cavicola* Barbour and Brooks, [612.1], has been once recorded from the Dry Tortugas, Fla. (Scott, Auk, 1890, 265). It resembles *albifrons* but has the forehead and rump chestnut and no black on the throat.

351. PURPLE MARTIN. Progne subis subis (*Linnæus*). [611.] *Ad.* ♂.
—Shining blue-black; wings and tail duller. *Im.* ♂ *in winter.*—Resembles the ♀. *Im.* ♂ *in summer.*—Similar to ♀, but bluer above and with a number of adult blue feathers scattered through underparts. The ad. ♂ plumage is acquired at the first postnuptial molt. *Ad.* ♀.—Upperparts glossy bluish black, duller than in the ♂; wings and tail black; throat, breast, and sides brownish gray, more or less tipped with white; belly white. L., 8·00; W., 5·80; T., 2·90; B. from N. ·32.

Range.—Breeds from w. cent. Alberta, cent. Sask., s. Man., nw. Ont., N. B., and N. S., w. to Vancouver Isl., B. C., and s. to the Mex. boundary, the Gulf Coast, Fla., Vera Cruz, and Jalisco. Occurs in migration in Cent. A., Venezuela and Guiana and winters in Brazil. Accidental in Bermuda and the British Isles.

Washington, rather common S. R., Mch. 9–Sept. 23. Bronx region, uncommon T. V., local S. R., Apr. 5–Sept. 24. Boston, formerly locally common S. R., Apr. 20–Aug. 25; now an uncommon T. V. N. Ohio, common S. R., Apr. 1–Sept. 5. Glen Ellyn, local S. R., less common than formerly, Mch. 23–Sept. 12. SE. Minn., common S. R., Apr. 1–Oct. 21.

Nest, of straws, twigs, etc., in houses or gourds erected for the purpose. *Eggs,* 4–5, white, 1·00 × ·73. *Date,* Tarboro, N. C., May 19; Boston, May 30; St. Louis, Mo., May 21.

The Purple Martin is very common throughout the South, and breeds wherever gourds or boxes are erected for its occupation. In the northern states it is a comparatively rare bird of local distribution.

In *Forest and Stream*, Vol. XXII, 1884, p. 484, Mr. Otto Widmann, of Old Orchard, Mo., presents an interesting table showing how often young Martins are fed. He watched a colony of sixteen pairs of birds from 4 A.M. to 8 P.M., during which time the parents visited their offspring 3,277 times, or an average of 205 times for each pair. The males made 1,454, the females 1,823 visits.

1903. Jacobs, J. W. (Waynesburg, Pa.), The Story of a Martin Colony (methods of attracting, etc.).—1906. Taverner, P. A., Wilson Bull., 87–92 (roost).—1917. Bird-Lore, 262 (pl.); 1918. 147 (mig.).—1918. [Notes on Martin Colonies and Roosts.] A Symposium. Bird-Lore, 125–132. 1919. 92–99.

352. CUBAN MARTIN. Progne cryptoleuca *Baird.* [611.1.] *Ad.* ♂.— "Similar to *P. subis,* but feathers of ventral region marked beneath surface, with a broad spot or bar of white." *Ad.* ♀ *and Im.* ♂.—Similar to those of *P. subis,* but "whole under portion and sides of head and neck, chest, sides and flanks uniform sooty grayish brown, in marked contrast with pure white of belly, anal region, and under tail-coverts. L., 7·60; W., 5·50; T., 3·10" (Ridgway).
Range.—Cuba; occasional or accidental in s. Fla.

FAMILY CORVIDÆ. CROWS, JAYS, ETC.

The *Corvidæ* are found throughout the world except in New Zealand. They number over 400 species and subspecies of which about one-fourth inhabit the Western Hemisphere. Of this number 39 (17 species) occur in North America. Our Crows and Jays inhabit wooded regions, and are resident throughout the year, except at the northern limits of their range. They are omnivorous feeders, taking fruits, seeds, insects, eggs, nestlings, and refuse.

Crows and Jays exhibit marked traits of character and are possessed of unusual intelligence. Some systematists place them at the top of the avian tree, and, if their mental development be taken into consideration, they have undoubted claims to this high rank. Although possessed of extended vocabularies by means of which they can apparently give expression to a wide range of feelings, they cannot vocally be classed as songsters.

KEY TO THE SPECIES

A. Plumage black.
  a. Wing about 15·00; bill over 2·50 . . . . 357. RAVEN.
  b. Wing about 13·00; bill about 2·00 . . . . . 358, 358*a*, *b*. CROWS.
  c. Wing about 11·00; bill about 1·50 . . . . 359. FISH CROW.
B. Plumage bluish or grayish.
  a. Back blue; tail tipped with white; a black breast-patch.
354, 354*a*, *b*. BLUE JAYS.
  b. Back bluish gray; tail not tipped with white; throat and breast indistinctly streaked with whitish . . . . 355. FLORIDA JAY.
  c. Back gray; back of head and nape blackish; forehead whitish.
353, 353*a*, *b*, *c*. CANADA JAYS.

353. CANADA JAY. PERISOREUS CANADENSIS CANADENSIS (*Linnæus*). [484.] *Ads.*—Forepart of the head white, back of the head and nape sooty black, back gray; wings and tail gray, most of the feathers narrowly tipped with white; throat and sides of the neck white, rest of the underparts ashy gray. *Im.*—Nearly uniform sooty gray. L., 12·00; W., 5·85; T., 5·80; B., ·82.
Range.—Breeds in Boreal zones from the limit of conifers in n. Mack., n. Man., and cent. Que. to s. cent. B. C., n. Minn., Mich., the Adirondack Mts. of N. Y., n. Me., N. H., and N. B. Casual in Nebr., Pa., and Mass. Boston, A. V.
Nest, of coarse twigs and strips of bark, in coniferous trees. *Eggs*, 4–5, white, distinctly and obscurely spotted with light olive-brown, 1·12 × ·81. *Date*, Stewiacke, N. S., Apr. 17, inc. adv.; Mahoning, Mich., Mch. 18.

While studying the habits of birds in the great coniferous forest of the North, I soon found that I was very safe in attributing any new strange shrieks or wails, whose origin I was otherwise unable to trace, to the Canada Jay. Many of the notes resemble those of the Blue Jay, but it has a number that are distinctly its own. Some of these are musical, but most of them are harsh and discordant.

In its habits it is much like its blue cousin, but it is less shy, and becomes almost tame if allowed to come unmolested about the camp for a few days in succession. In form it is like a magnified Chickadee, clad in singularly furlike, thick, puffy gray feathers; on its forehead is a white spot, the size of a dime, and its wings and tail are of a much darker gray than the other parts. This description, remembered in conjunction with the habits, will at once identify the species.

It nests early in March—that is, while deep snow still covers the ground and hard frost reigns supreme; and no satisfactory explanation of this strange habit has yet been brought forward. No doubt one or other of the parents always remains with the eggs, but still it is difficult to see how they can keep them from freezing when the surrounding air is chilled to 30° below zero.

It is a non-migratory species, and it is said that in autumn it provides against the annual famine of winter by laying up a store of nuts and other food.   ERNEST THOMPSON SETON.

1899. WARREN, O. B., Auk, 12–19 (nesting).—1919. BIRD-LORE, 354, 356 (mig.; pl.).

353a. LABRADOR JAY. PERISOREUS CANADENSIS NIGRICAPILLUS *Ridgway*. [484c.] Similar to the preceding, but darker, the black of the head and neck extending forward and surrounding the eye.
Range.—N. and e. Ungava, and Lab.
Nesting-date, Lab., Apr. 16.

This race, and the two following races of the Canada Jay, are not formally recognized in the A.O.U. Check-List, but referred to without comment in a foot-note (p. 220).

353b. ANTICOSTI JAY. PERISOREUS CANADENSIS BARBOURI *Brooks*. "Size about as in *P. c. nigricapillus* Ridgway of Labrador. In color this Jay differs at a glance from *P. c. nigricapillus*, or *P. c. canadensis* in that the upperparts, including lesser wing-coverts and upper tail-coverts, are plain slate-color (instead of mouse-gray), the black of the crown and occiput slate-black (instead of brownish black), and the underparts deep gray, less brownish or smoky" (Brooks).
Range.—Anticosti Isl., Que.

353c. NEWFOUNDLAND JAY. PERISOREUS CANADENSIS SANFORDI *Oberholser*. "Similar to *P. c. nigricapillus* but even smaller; the lower surface much paler, the crissum whitish." W., 5·30; T., 5·50 (Oberholser).
Range.—N. F. and N. S.

354. BLUE JAY. CYANOCITTA CRISTATA CRISTATA (*Linnæus*). [477.] (Fig. 102a.) *Ads.*—Upperparts grayish blue; underparts dusky whitish, whiter on the belly; forehead, and a band passing across the back of the head down the sides of the neck and across the breast, black; head crested; exposed surface of wings blue, the greater wing-coverts and secondaries barred with black and tipped with white; tail blue barred with black, and all but the middle pair broadly tipped with white, this white tip rarely less than 1·00 in width on the outer feather. L., 11·74; W., 5·14; T., 5·19; B., 1·04.
Range.—Breeds from s. Alberta, n. Man., Que., N. B., N. S., and N. F. s. to cent. Ills., Tenn. and Va., and w. to w. Nebr., e. Colo., and cent. Tex. Ranges farther s. in winter. Casual in N. Mex.
Washington, common P. R. Bronx region, common P. R. Boston, common P. R. N. Ohio, common P. R. Glen Ellyn, common P. R., less so in winter. SE. Minn., common P. R.
Nest, of twigs, compactly interwoven, lined with rootlets generally in a

tree crotch 10–20 feet up. *Eggs*, 4–6, pale olive-green or brownish ashy, rather thickly marked with distinct or obscure spots of varying shades of cinnamon-brown, 1·10 × ·85. *Date*, Boston, Apr. 28; se. Minn., May 2.

The Blue Jay, I fear, is a reprobate, but, notwithstanding his fondness for eggs and nestlings, and his evident joy in worrying other birds, there is a dashing, reckless air about him which makes us pardon his faults and like him in spite of ourselves. Like many men, he needs the inspiration of congenial company to bring out the social side of his disposition. Household duties may perhaps absorb him, but certain it is that when at home he is very different from the noisy fellow who, with equally noisy comrades, roams the woods in the fall. How his *jay, jay* rings out on the frosty morning air! It is a signal to his companions, breakfasting in a near-by oak or chestnut, "Here, here, here's some fun!" and the poor, blinking Owl he has discovered looks helplessly at the blue-coated mob, whose uproar alone is terrifying. Suddenly there is absolute silence; every Jay has disappeared. One of them has seen you, and not until your silence reassures the band will they return to the sport of teasing their victim.

The Blue Jay is both a mimic and a ventriloquist. Besides an inexhaustible stock of whistles and calls of his own, he imitates the notes of other species, notably those of the Red-shouldered, Redtail, and Sparrow Hawks.

1908. CHAPMAN, F. M., Camps and Cruises, 5–14 (nesting).—1919. BIRD-LORE, 170, 172 (mig.; pl.).

354a. FLORIDA BLUE JAY. CYANOCITTA CRISTATA FLORINCOLA *Coues.* [477*a*.] Similar to the preceding species, but smaller, the upperparts somewhat grayer, the white tips to the feathers narrower, those on the outer pair of tail-feathers generally *less* than 1·00 in length. L., 10·75; W., 5·15; T., 4·80; B., ·96.

Range.—S. Atlantic and Gulf States from N. C. to Fla., n. of the Everglades, w. to La.

Nesting-date, Archer, Fla., Apr. 4.

Blue Jays in Florida are common inhabitants of towns with live-oaks, and hop about the fences and gardens with all the domesticity of the Robins on our lawns. It has always seemed to me that the Florida birds were possessed of greater vocabularies than their northern brethren.

354b. SEMPLE'S BLUE JAY. CYANOCITTA CRISTATA SEMPLEI *Todd.* Similar to *C. c. cristata*, but general coloration paler, the underparts white, with less grayish suffusion, the lower throat with less bluish wash, and the upperparts paler and duller blue, with less purplish tone (Todd).

Range.—Extreme s. Fla., s. of the Everglades.

355. FLORIDA JAY. APHELOCOMA CŒRULESCENS (*Bosc*). [479.] *Ads.*— Top and sides of the head and neck, wings and tail, grayish blue; back pale brownish gray; underparts dirty white, obscurely streaked on the throat and breast; sides of the breast and faint breast-band grayish blue. L., 11·50; W., 4·45; T., 5·40; B., ·98.

Range.—Fla., local, chiefly along coasts, between lat. 27° and 30°.

Nest, of sticks and roots lined with weeds and rootlets, in trees and bushes. *Eggs*, 4, olive-green spotted and blotched with black, 1·17 × ·75 (Maynard). *Date*, Lantana, Fla., Apr. 6.

"The Florida Jays are noisy birds at all times, and the first intimation which one receives of their presence is a harsh scream which is given as a note of alarm. As they usually move in flocks, this cry is taken up by others, and soon the scrub for many rods around will be resounding with these peculiar sounds. When undisturbed they feed on the ground or in bushes, but, upon the approach of an intruder, they will mount the highest point available, where they remain until driven away. They are not usually shy, and will allow one to approach them quite closely, but when one or two are shot the survivors usually disappear. . . . They will glide through the bushes with remarkable rapidity, never once showing themselves, or, if they have an open space to cross, dart over it, not in flocks, but singly, and, plunging into the next thicket, they will at once be lost to view" (Maynard).

1920. BIRD-LORE, 90, 91 (mig.; pl.).

356. AMERICAN MAGPIE. PICA PICA HUDSONIA (*Sabine*). [475.] *Ads.* —Belly, scapulars, inner vanes of primaries, except at end, and rump-band white; rest of plumage glossy black; wings and tail with iridescent reflections. L., 17·50; W., 8·00; T., 10·25; B., 1·40.

Range.—Principally Boreal and Transition zones from the Alaska Peninsula, middle Yukon, cent. Alberta, cent. Sask., and s. Man., s. to n. Ariz. and N. Mex., and from e. Wash. and the e. slope of the Sierra Nevada to w. N. Dak. and N. Mex. Casual in Ia., Wisc., Ills., Mich., Minn., Ont., and the Hudson Bay region; accidental in Que.

A representative of the European Magpie from which it differs but slightly.

357. NORTHERN RAVEN. CORVUS CORAX PRINCIPALIS *Ridgway*. [486a.] *Ads.*—Entire plumage black with steel-blue reflections; feathers on the throat narrow, lengthened, and pointed. "L., about 22·00–26·50; W., 16·99; T., 9·86; B., 3·03; depth of B. at N., 1·04" (Ridgway).

Remarks.—The Raven differs from the Crow in its much greater size and in having long, pointed, instead of the usual short, rounded feathers on the throat.

Range.—NW. Alaska, Melville Isl., n. Ellesmere Land, and n. Greenland s. to Wash., cent. Minn., Mich., coast region of N. J. and Va., and the higher Alleghanies to Ga.

Boston, A. V. SE. Minn., formerly casual W. V., Nov. 4, 1876; Oct. 23, 1892.

Nest, compact and symmetrical, of sticks lined with grasses, wool, etc., added to from year to year, in trees or on cliffs. "*Eggs*, 2–7, pale bluish green, pale olive, or olive spotted or dashed (or both) with olive-brown (sometimes nearly uniform olive from density of markings), 2·02 × 1·38" (Ridgway). *Date*, Grand Manan, Apr. 9.

"The usual note of the Raven is a hoarse, rolling *cr-r-r-cruck*, but he has other cries. . . .

"Despite their difference in size and habits, I must confess that I often had difficulty in distinguishing Ravens from Crows. Everyone must have noticed how the apparent size of a Crow will vary under different conditions of the atmosphere; it is the same with the Raven. At times he looks as big as an Eagle; at others scarcely larger than a Fish Crow. But when actually in company with Crows he can not be possibly mistaken, for he then appears, as he is, nearly double the size of any of them. His flight did not seem to me as characteristic as it has been described. True, he sails more than does the Crow, and there is something peculiar in his wing-strokes, but the difference is not always appreciable unless there is an opportunity for direct comparison" (Brewster, *Proc. Bost. Soc. Nat. Hist.*, 1883, p. 378).

1910. HARLAN, R. C., Cassinia, 11–18 (nesting in Pa.).—1922. Auk, 399–410 (nesting).—1919, BIRD-LORE, 23, 24 (mig.; pl.).

357a. AMERICAN RAVEN. CORVUS CORAX SINUATUS *Wagler.* [486.] Similar to *C. c. principalis* but with a "smaller or slenderer bill, the tarsus more slender, with less of upper portion concealed by feathering of lower part of thighs." W., 16·87; T., 9·86; B., 2·80; depth of B. at N., ·94 (Ridgway).

Range.—SE. B. C., Ore., Mont., and N. Dak. s. to Nicaragua, and e. probably to Mo., Ills., and Ind.

358. EASTERN CROW. CORVUS BRACHYRHYNCHOS BRACHYRHYNCHOS *Brehm.* [488.] (Fig. 102b.) *Ads.*—Entire plumage black, with steel-blue or deep purplish reflections; the underparts duller than the upperparts; feathers on the neck normal, short, and rounded. L., 19·30; W., 12·18; T., 7·52; B., 2·00.

Range.—Breeds from sw. Mack., n. Man., s. Que. and N. F. s. to Md., the n. part of the Gulf States and n. Tex. Winters from near the n. boundary of the U. S. s.

Washington, abundant P. R. Bronx region, common P. R. Boston, common P. R., abundant T. V. N. Ohio, common P. R. Glen Ellyn, common P. R. SE. Minn., common S. R., Mch.–Nov., rather common W. R.

Nest, bulky, of sticks lined with strips of grape-vine bark, grasses, moss, etc., in trees, averaging about 30 feet up. *Eggs*, 4–6, generally bluish green, thickly marked with shades of brown, but sometimes light blue or even white with almost no markings, 1·65 × 1·19. *Date*, Washington, D. C., Mch. 27; Delaware Co., Pa., Apr. 11; Ossining, N. Y., Apr. 14; Boston, Apr. 15; se. Minn., Apr. 12.

Throughout his wide range the size, color, voice, habits, and abundance of the Crow combine to make him the most conspicuous and consequently the best known of our birds. But in spite of his great circle of acquaintances he has few friends. An unfortunate fondness for corn has placed him under the ban of the agriculturist; there is a price on his head; every man's hand is against him. Apparently he does not mind this in the least; in fact, he seems to rejoice in being an outlaw. As for fear, I doubt if he knows what it means; he has far too much confidence in his undoubted ability to escape his human persecutors. He laughs at their attempts to entrap him; his insolent assurance is admirable. For several centuries man has been his sworn enemy, nevertheless he appears to have held his own, accepting and adjusting himself to every new condition.

Afraid of no one, he migrates boldly by day, and in March and October we may see him with his comrades high in the air, returning to or leaving their summer homes. In winter the Crows are exceedingly abundant along our seacoasts, where they congregate to feed on mollusks, fish, and other sea food. At this season they roost in colonies. It has been estimated that some roosts contain upward of three hundred thousand birds. Early in the morning, with regularly executed maneuvers, they start on the day's foraging, flying low, on the lookout for food. Late in the afternoon they return at a much greater height— "as the Crow flies"—and, alighting at some point near the roost, wait the coming of the last stragglers. Then, at a given signal, they all rise and retire for the night. No one who has listened to Crows will doubt that they have a language. But who can translate it?

1886. RHOADS, S. N., Am. Nat., 691–700; 777–786 (roosts).—1895. BARROWS and SCHWARZ, Bull. 6, Biol. Surv., 1–98 (food).—1895. BURNS, F. L., Wilson Bull. No. 5, 1–41 (monograph).—1897. BUTLER, A. W., Proc. Ind. Acad. Sci., 175–178 (roosts).—1918. KALMBACH, E. R., Bull. 621, U. S. Dept. Agric., 92 pp. (relations to man).—1918. TOWNSEND, C. W., Auk, 405–416 (winter roost).—1919. BIRD-LORE, 100, 102 (mig.; pl.).—1928. ALLEN, A. A., Bird-Lore, 73–83, illus. (autobiography).

358a. SOUTHERN CROW. CORVUS BRACHYRHYNCHOS PAULUS *Howell*. Similar to *C. b. brachyrhynchos* but smaller and with a more slender bill. ♂, W., 11·50; T., 6·75; B., 1·80; depth of B., 1·00 (Howell).
    Range.—Lower Potomac and O. s. to e. Tex., s. Ga. and the Gulf Coast (except Fla.).

358b. FLORIDA CROW. CORVUS BRACHYRHYNCHOS PASCUUS *Coues*. [488a.] Similar to the preceding, but wings and tail somewhat shorter, and bill and feet slightly larger. L., 20·00; W., 11·50–12·30; T., 7·00–7·70; B., 2·00–2·20; depth of B. at base, ·75–·85; Tar., 2·40–2·50 (Ridgway).
    Range.—Peninsula of Fla.
    Nesting-date, San Mateo, Fla., Mch. 3.

359. FISH CROW. CORVUS OSSIFRAGUS *Wilson*. [490.] *Ads.*—Entire plumage black, with steel-blue or deep purplish reflections, generally more greenish on the underparts. L., 16·00; W., 11·00; T., 6·40; B., 1·50.
    Remarks.—The Fish Crow may be distinguished from the common Crow (1) by its much smaller size. (2) By the uniform and somewhat richer color of the back. In *brachyrhynchos* the feathers of the back have dull tips; when the freshly plumaged bird is held between the observer and the light these tips give the back a ringed or slightly *scaled* appearance. In *ossifragus* these tips are wanting, and the back is uniformly colored. (3) By the brighter color of the underparts. In *brachyrhynchos* the underparts are generally much duller than the upperparts; in *ossifragus* they are nearly as bright.
    Range.—Atlantic and Gulf coasts from the lower Delaware and Hudson River valleys and s. Mass. to La., Fla., and e. Tex.
    Washington, rather common P. R. Bronx region, fairly common P. R., less common in winter, Feb. 19–Jan. 1. Boston, A. V.
    Nest, of sticks, lined with strips of grape-vine bark, moss, grasses, etc., generally in pines or cedars, 20–50 feet up. *Eggs*, 4–6, similar in color to those of the preceding species, 1·52 × 1·06. *Date*, Lake Kissimmee, Fla., Apr. 30; D. C., May 5; Seven-Mile Beach, N. J., May 15.

The Fish Crow can be distinguished from the common Crow in life only by its call. Its voice is cracked and reedy, and its notes resemble those of a young common Crow. Instead of the loud, clear, open *caw* of adults of that species, it utters a hoarser *car*, as if it talked through its nose!. The difference is perhaps not appreciable upon paper, but one who is familiar with their calls need never confuse these two birds in the field. The Fish Crow, while not confined to the coast or even the vicinity of water, is not found far inland.

1919. BIRD-LORE, 102 (mig.; pl.).

360. The EUROPEAN ROOK, *Corvus frugilegus frugilegus* Linnæus, [490.1], and 361, the EUROPEAN HOODED CROW, *Corvus cornix cornix* Linnæus, [490.2], are both of accidental occurrence in Greenland.

362. CLARKE'S NUTCRACKER, *Nucifraga columbiana* (Wilson), [491], of western North America is of casual occurrence in Iowa, Wisconsin, and Minnesota.

FAMILY PARIDÆ. TITMICE.

Like the Nuthatches, with which, after the nesting season, they are often associated, the Titmice are largely restricted to the more northern, or more elevated parts of Eurasia. Of the approximately 300 known species and subspecies only 42 (16 species) are North American, where they range to the southern border of the Mexican tableland. They inhabit wooded countries, where their destructiveness to insects, their eggs and larvæ, is of incalculable value. Their nests vary widely in character. The true Titmice (*Penthestes*) excavate holes in dead trees; *Ægithalus* builds a felted, purse-shaped structure of plant-down with the entrance near the top; *Auriparus* a not dissimilar but more globular home which is covered with thorny twigs, and *Psaltriparus* a long, loosely woven bag of plant-down, covered with lichens. They are migratory at the northern limit of their range and, except when nesting, are usually found in small troops.

KEY TO THE SPECIES

A. Crown black.
    a. Wing over 2·50, greater wing-coverts with white margins.
                    363. BLACK-CAPPED CHICKADEE and race.
    b. Wing under 2·50, wing-coverts without white margins.
                364, 364a. CAROLINA CHICKADEE and race.
B. Crown not black.
    a. Crown brown . . . . . . 365, 365a. ACADIAN CHICKADEE and race.
    b. Crown gray; crested . . . . 366. TUFTED TITMOUSE.

363. BLACK-CAPPED CHICKADEE. PENTHESTES ATRICAPILLUS ATRICAPILLUS (*Linnæus*). [735.] (Fig. 103.) *Ads.*—Top of the head, nape, and throat shining black; sides of the head and neck white; back ashy; outer vanes of greater wing-coverts distinctly margined with white; wing and tail-feathers margined with whitish; breast white; belly and sides washed with cream-buff. L., 5·27; W., 2·53; T., 2·43; B., ·37.

Range.—Canadian and Transition zones from n. Ont., cent. Que., and N. F. s. to s. Mo., Ills., n. Ind., O., Pa., n. N. J., and in the Alleghanies s. to N. C. Irregularly somewhat farther s. in winter.

Washington, rare and irregular W. V., Oct. 19–Apr. 19. Bronx region, common P. R. Boston, common P. R., more numerous in fall and winter.

N. Ohio, common P. R. Glen Ellyn, fairly common P. R. SE. Minn., common P. R.

Nest, of moss, grasses, feathers, and plant-down, in old stumps; holes in trees, etc., not more than 15 feet up. *Eggs*, 5–9, white, spotted and speckled, chiefly at the larger end, with cinnamon- or rufous-brown, ·60 × ·48. *Date*, Saybrook, Conn., May 6; Boston, May 10; Holland Patent, N. Y., May 15; Brookville, Ind., Apr. 22; se. Minn., Apr. 13.

When most birds were strangers to me, I remember thinking what a blessing it would be if everyone spoke his name as plainly as does this animated bunch of black and white feathers. No need of a text-book to discover his name; with winning confidence he introduced himself, and probably for this reason he has always been my best friend among birds. 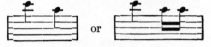 I never hear his voice in the woods without answering him: This is the so-called 'Phœbe' note, which, it may be added, is uttered by both sexes. Soon he comes to me, mildly inquisitive at first, looking about for the friend or foe whose call has attracted him. In an unconcerned way he hops from limb to limb, whistling softly the while, picking an insect's egg from beneath a leaf here or larva from a crevice in the bark there, all the time performing acrobatic feats of which an accomplished gymnast might be proud. Finally his curiosity becomes aroused, he ceases feeding, and gives his entire attention to the discovery of the bird who so regularly replies to him. Hopping down to a limb within three feet of my head, he regards me with puzzled intentness; his little black eyes twinkle with intelligence, he changes his call, and questions me with a series of *chick-ă-dēēs*, liquid gurgles, and odd chuckling notes which it is beyond my power to answer, and finally, becoming discouraged, he refuses to renew our whistled conversation and retreats to the woods.

On several occasions Chickadees have flown down and perched upon my hand. During the few seconds they remained there I became rigid with the emotion of this novel experience. It was a mark of confidence which seemed to initiate me into the ranks of woodland dwellers.

1900. CHAPMAN, F. M., Bird Studies with a Camera, 147–161 (nesting).— 1911. STANWOOD, C. J., Journ. Me. Orn. Soc., 25–32 (nesting).—1916. BIRD-LORE, 14, 16, (mig.; pl.).—1929. ALLEN, A. A., Bird-Lore, 69–77, illus. (autobiography).—1931. BUTTS, W. K., Bird-Banding, 1–26 (banding study).

363a. The LONG-TAILED CHICKADEE, *Penthestes atricapillus septentrionalis* (Harris), of western North America is found eastward to western Minnesota and western Iowa. It is similar to *P. a. atricapillus* but larger and paler, the white margins of wings and tail wider. W., 2·70; T., 2·60.

364. CAROLINA CHICKADEE. PENTHESTES CAROLINENSIS CAROLINENSIS (*Audubon*). [736.] Similar to the preceding species, but smaller; greater wing-coverts *not* margined with whitish; wing and tail-feathers with less white on their outer vanes. L., 4·06–4·75; W., 2·20–2·48; T., 1·88–2·12; B., ·30–·32.

Range.—Breeds in Upper and Lower Austral zones from cent. Mo., Ind., cent. O., se. and sw. Pa., and cent. N. J., s. to se. La. and the Gulf Coast. Washington, very common P. R. N. Ohio, two spring records.

Nest, of grasses, fine strips of bark, feathers, hair, etc., in holes in trees, stumps, etc. *Eggs*, 5–8, similar in color to those of *P. atricapillus. Date*, Mt. Pleasant, S. C., Mch. 23; Iredell Co., N. C., Apr. 13; D. C., Apr. 24.

My experience with this southern Chickadee has been confined largely to Florida. There I found it a comparatively shy bird, with notes quite unlike those of *P. atricapillus*. Instead of the two clear whistles which *atricapillus* in New Jersey utters, the Florida bird repeats *four* rather tremulous notes, and there is also a substantial difference in its other calls, one of which resembles the words *my watcher key, my watcher key*.

Dr. C. W. Richmond writes me that at Washington the *chick-ă-dēē* call of *carolinensis* is higher pitched and more hurriedly given than that of *atricapillus*, and that the whistle consists of three notes, but in New Jersey, according to W. DeW. Miller, it consists of four.

Writing from the mountains of North Carolina, where both species occur together, Mr. Brewster says: "In one place a male of each species was singing in the same tree the low, plaintive, *tswee-dee-twsee-dee* of the *P. carolinensis*, contrasting sharply with the ringing *te-derry* of its more northern cousin" (*The Auk*, 1886, p. 177).

1916. BIRD-LORE, 14, 16 (mig.; pl.).

364a. FLORIDA CHICKADEE. PENTHESTES CAROLINENSIS IMPIGER (*Bangs*). [736*b*.] Similar to *P. c. carolinensis*, but smaller (except bill) and darker above.
Range.—Peninsula of Fla.

365. HUDSONIAN CHICKADEE. PENTHESTES HUDSONICUS HUD-SONICUS (*J. R. Forster*). [740.] Similar to *P. h. littoralis* but more rufescent; crown averaging lighter; difference between color of back and crown more pronounced; flanks averaging brighter rufous; size somewhat larger, bill averaging slightly heavier. W., 2·60; T., 2·50.
Range.—Breeds in Hudsonian and Canadian zones from Kowak Valley, Alaska, and tree-limit in cent. Mack. and n. Man. s. to cent. Man. and cent. Ont. In winter casually to n. Ills.

365a. ACADIAN CHICKADEE. PENTHESTES HUDSONICUS LITTORALIS (*Bryant*). [740*a*.] *Ads.*—Crown and nape dull light grayish brown; back somewhat brighter, with a slight rufous tint; flanks pale rufous; wings and tail gray; sides of the head, breast, and belly white; throat black. L., 4·80; W., 2·50; T., 2·40; B., ·38.
Range.—Breeds in Boreal zones from Lab., cent. Que., and N. F. s. to N. S., Me., the mountains of n. Vt. and cent. N. H. and the Adirondacks of N. Y. In winter casually to Mass., R. I., Conn., s. N. Y., n. Pa., and n. N. J. Boston, rare, perhaps only casual, W. V., Nov. 1–Apr. 1.
Nest, of moss and felted fur, in holes in trees and stumps. *Eggs*, 6–7, not distinguishable from those of *P. a. atricapillus*, ·61 × ·50. *Date*, Stewiacke, N. S., May 25.

The general habits of this northern Chickadee resemble those of *atricapillus* but its notes are recognizably different. Wright (*The Auk*, 1890, p. 407) speaks of its "sweet, warbling song," and Clark (*Journ. Me. Orn. Soc.*, 1906, p. 27) writes of "a sweet, little song of three or four notes," but Brewster ('Birds of the Cambridge Region,' p. 379) says "besides low, chattering, conversational sounds—difficult of description but far from musical in character—which the birds occasionally make while feeding, I have heard them utter only a low *chip* much like that of the common Chickadee, but rather feebler, an abrupt, explosive *tch-tchip*, and a nasal drawling *tchick, chee-day-day*. In the call last mentioned the intervals between the doubled middle note and the single notes which precede and follow it are very pronounced, and the accented notes are very strongly emphasized—characteristics which serve at once to distinguish these sounds from any that the Black-capped Chickadee ever produces."

1910. ALLEN, F. H., The Auk, 86 (song).—1914. WRIGHT, H. W., Auk, 236–242 (in Boston and vicinity).—1916. BIRD-LORE, 15, 16 (mig.; pl.).—1917. TOWNSEND, C. W., Labrador Chickadee in Southward Migration, Auk, 160–163 (also WRIGHT, H. W., 164–170; The Labrador Chickadee was subsequently shown by Banks to be *P. h. littoralis* in first winter plumage).

366. TUFTED TITMOUSE. BÆOLOPHUS BICOLOR (*Linnæus*). [731.] *Ads.*—Head crested. Forehead black; rest of upperparts, wings, and tail gray; back in winter tinged with olive-brown; underparts whitish; sides washed with rufous. L., 6·00; W., 3·10; T., 2·70; B., ·45.

Range.—Upper and Lower Austral zones from Nebr., Ia., Ills., Ind., O., Pa., and N. J. s. to cent. Tex., the Gulf Coast, and s. Fla.; casual in s. parts of Wisc., Mich., N. Y., Me. and in Conn.

Washington, very common P. R. Bronx region, formerly a rare P. R., now only occasional T. V., Nov. 6–May 20. N. Ohio, common P. R. Glen Ellyn, rare visitant, Mch. 21–Apr. 4; Aug. 23–Nov. 19. SE. Minn., 15 records, Sept. 13–Apr. 3.

Nest, of leaves, moss, strips of bark, feathers, etc., in Woodpeckers' deserted holes, stumps, etc. *Eggs*, 5–8, white or creamy white, rather coarsely and evenly marked with rufous-brown, ·71 × ·55. *Date*, Mt. Pleasant, S. C., Apr. 21; Weaverville, N. C., Apr. 8; Brookville, Ind., Apr. 22.

The Tufted Titmouse is a bird of very general distribution in woodlands, where its presence is always made known by its notes. Its common call is a loud, clearly whistled *peto, peto, peto, peto*, which may be repeated by the same individual for hours at a time. Occasionally the key is changed, and at first the notes are decidedly pleasing, but the bird finally wearies one by its monotonous repetition. It utters also other whistled calls, and a *de-de-de-de*, much like the notes of the Chickadee, though somewhat louder and hoarser. The Tufted Tit is not a shy bird and may be approached with ease. Its conspicuous crest is an excellent field-mark.

FIG. 123. Tufted Titmouse. (Natural size.)

1915. BIRD-LORE, 378, 379 (dist.; pl.).—1930. GILLESPIE, M., Bird-Banding, 113–127, map (habits).

FAMILY SITTIDÆ. NUTHATCHES.

The Nuthatches, numbering about 80 species and subspecies, are mainly restricted to the northern parts of the Northern Hemisphere, 4 species occurring in the New World. Although expert creepers, they receive no support from the tail while climbing, nor does their foot conform to the usual Woodpecker type of two toes in front and two behind. Both their toes and toe-nails are, however, well developed, and the birds run up or down a tree trunk with equal ease. Their notes are pronounced, characteristic, and freely uttered, but their singing powers are limited. They nest in holes in trees, but, contrary to the rule that birds which nest in such situations lay white unmarked eggs, their eggs are spotted. Their name is derived from the habit of wedging a nut in a crevice of the bark and then attempting to 'hatch' or 'hack' it by repeated strokes with the bill.

KEY TO THE SPECIES

A. Underparts more or less washed with rufous; a black or gray streak through the eye . . . . 368. RED-BREASTED NUTHATCH.
B. Underparts white or whitish; under tail-coverts more or less rufous; tail with white spots.
     367*a, b.* NORTHERN WHITE-BREASTED NUTHATCH AND RACES.
C. Whole top of the head brown . . . 369. BROWN-HEADED NUTHATCH.

367. FLORIDA WHITE-BREASTED NUTHATCH. SITTA CAROLINENSIS ATKINSI *Scott.* [727*b.*] (Fig. 104.) Similar to the preceding, but somewhat smaller, the wing-coverts and quills but slightly or not at all tipped with whitish, the female with the top of the head and nape black, as in the male. W., 3·32; T., 1·80; B., ·70.
Range.—Breeds in the Lower Austral Zone of Ga. and Fla., and along the Gulf Coast, n. in the Miss. Valley to Ky., s. Ills., and se. Mo.
Nesting-date, San Mateo, Fla., Mch. 16.

367a. NORTHERN WHITE-BREASTED NUTHATCH. SITTA CAROLINENSIS CAROLINENSIS *Latham.* [727.] (Fig. 000.) *Ad.* ♂.—Top of head shining black; rest of upperparts bluish gray; inner secondaries bluish gray, marked with black; wing-coverts and quills tipped with whitish; outer tail-feathers black, with white patches near their tips; middle ones bluish gray; sides of head and underparts white; lower belly and under tail-coverts mixed with rufous. *Ad.* ♀.—Similar, but black of head veiled by bluish gray. L., 6·07; W., 3·60, T., 1·92; B., ·70.
Range.—Breeds in Canadian, Transition, and Upper Austral zones from s. Man., n. Minn., cent. Ont., s. Que. s. to n. Tex., cent. Ills., and S. C. Casual in ne. Man.
Washington, common P. R. Bronx region, fairly common P. R. Boston, P. R., uncommon summer, rather common winter; most numerous in Oct. and Nov. N. Ohio, common P. R. Glen Ellyn, fairly common P. R. SE. Minn., common P. R.
Nest, of feathers, leaves, etc., in a hole in a tree or stump. *Eggs*, 5–8, white or creamy white, thickly and rather evenly spotted and speckled with rufous and lavender, ·75 × ·57. *Date*, Boston, Apr. 19; se. Minn., Apr. 7.

When the cares of a family devolve upon him, the Nuthatch eschews all society and rarely ventures far from his forest home. But in the winter I believe even the birds are affected by the oppressive loneliness; the strangers of summer become for a time boon companions, and we find Downy Woodpeckers, Chickadees, and Nuthatches wandering about the woods or visiting the orchards on apparently the best of terms.

Few birds are easier to identify: the Woodpecker pecks, the Chickadee calls *chickadee*, while the Nuthatch, running up and down the tree trunks, assumes attitudes no bird outside his family would think of attempting. His powers of speech are in nowise disturbed by his often inverted position, and he accompanies his erratic clamberings by a conversational twitter or occasionally a loud, nasal *yank, yank*, which frequently tells us of his presence before we see him.

He is not too absorbed in his business to have a mild interest in yours, and he may pause a moment to look you over in a calm kind of way, which somehow makes one feel that perhaps, after all, Nuthatches are of as much importance as we are. But his curiosity is soon satisfied; affairs are evidently pressing, and with a *yank, yank*, he resumes his search for certain tidbits in the shape of grubs or insects' eggs hidden in the bark.

There is such a lack of sentiment in the Nuthatch's character, he seems so matter-of-fact in all his ways, that it is difficult to imagine him indulging in anything like song. But even he cannot withstand the all-conquering influences of spring, and at that season he raises his voice in a peculiar monotone—a tenor *hah-hah-hah-hah-hah*—sounding strangely like mirthless laughter.

1915. BIRD-LORE, 443, 445 (mig.; pl.).—1916. TYLER, W. M., Wilson Bull., 18–25 (habits).—1929. ALLEN, A. A., Bird-Lore, 423–431, illus. (autobiography).—1931. BUTTS, W. K., Bird Banding, 59–76 (study by banding).

368. RED-BREASTED NUTHATCH. SITTA CANADENSIS *Linnæus.* [728.] *Ad.* ♂.—Top of head and a wide stripe *through eye to nape* shining black; a white line over eye; upperparts bluish gray, no black marks on

secondaries, or tips to wing-coverts; outer tail-feathers black, with white patches near their tips; middle ones bluish gray; throat white; rest of underparts *ochraceous-buff. Ad.* ♀.— Similar, but top of head and stripe through the eye bluish gray, like the back; underparts paler. L., 4·62; W., 2·66; T., 1·58; B., ·50.

FIG. 124. Red-breasted Nuthatch. (Natural size.)

Range.—Breeds in the Canadian Zone from the upper Yukon Valley, s. Que., and N. F. s. to n. Minn., Mich., Mass., and Ind. (casually); s. in the Sierra Nevada and Rocky mts. to Calif., Ariz., and N. Mex., and in the Alleghanies to N. C.; also on Guadalupe Isl., L. Calif. Winters from s. Can. s. to s. Calif., N. Mex., the Gulf Coast, and n. Fla.; migrates periodically and irregularly s. in autumn, but never common in spring.

Washington, irregularly abundant W. V., sometimes rare, Aug. 22–May 20. Bronx region, irregular T. V.; occasionally winters; Aug. 8–May 24 (July 10). Boston, irregular T. V. and W. V., commonest in fall; Aug. 15–Nov. 25; Nov. 25–Apr. 15; has bred. N. Ohio, tolerably common W. V., Sept. 4–May 22. Glen Ellyn, irregular T. V., rare W. V., Apr. 24–June 7;

Aug. 19–Dec. 18. SE. Minn., common T. V., uncommon W. V., Apr. 12–
May 29; Aug. 16–Nov. 11.
Nest, of grasses, in a hole in a tree or stump. *Eggs,* 4–7, white or creamy
white, speckled with cinnamon-, rufous-brown, and lavender, ·60 × ·47.
Date, Calais, Me., May 7.

While resembling the White-breasted Nuthatch, this more northern
species differs from it sufficiently both in notes and appearance to be
easily distinguished. Its black face-stripe is a noticeable character,
while to the trained ear its higher, finer, more nasal, slightly drawled,
penny-trumpet-like *yna, yna* is quite unlike the White-breast's vigorous
yank, yank. The Redbreast has an evident partiality for pine trees,
and may be seen hovering about the cones while looking for a foothold
from which to extract their seeds.

1915. BIRD-LORE, 443, 446 (mig.; pl.).

369. BROWN-HEADED NUTHATCH. SITTA PUSILLA PUSILLA *Latham.*
[729.] *Ads.*—Top and back of head grayish brown, sometimes tipped with
pale ashy; a whitish patch on nape; no white over eye; rest of upperparts
bluish gray; outer tail-feathers black, tipped with *grayish,* middle ones bluish
gray; underparts grayish white; the breast, particularly in the fall, with a
tinge of buff; sides gray. L., 4·50; W., 2·60; T., 1·25; B., ·52.
Range.—Lower Austral Zone from s. Mo. and s. Del. s. to e. Tex. Casual
in O. and N. Y.
Nest, of feathers, grasses, etc., generally near the ground, in a hole in a
tree or stump. *Eggs,* 5–6, white or creamy white, heavily spotted or blotched
with cinnamon- or olive-brown, ·56 × ·46. *Date,* Charleston, S. C., Mch. 12;
Edgecombe Co., N. C., Mch. 28.

This little Nuthatch, the Red-cockaded Woodpecker, and Pine
Warbler, are characteristic birds of the great pineries in our southern
states. Frequently they are found associated. The Woodpeckers
generally keep to the tree-tops, the Warblers live on or near the ground,
while the Nuthatches scramble about from the base of the trunk to the
terminal twigs, but feed chiefly among the smaller branches, actively
and spirally, getting food which they take to the main trunk to wedge
behind the large bark scales. They are talkative sprites, and, like a
group of school children, each one chatters away without paying the
slightest attention to what his companions are saying. When feeding
they utter a liquid, conversational *pit-pit,* a note which is accelerated
and emphasized as the birds take wing. At intervals, even when the
individuals of a troop are quite widely separated, they all suddenly
break out into a thin, metallic *dee-dee-dee* or *tnee-tnee-tnee.*

1915. BIRD-LORE, 445, 446 (mig.; pl.).

369a. GRAY-HEADED NUTHATCH. SITTA PUSILLA CANICEPS *Bangs.*
[729 part.] Similar to *S. p. pusilla* but back slightly, and head distinctly
paler; wing shorter. W., 2·45 (Howell, Auk, 1930, 43).
Range.—Peninsula of Fla.
Nesting-date, San Mateo, Fla., Mch. 4.

A form occurs in Great Bahama.

FAMILY CERTHIIDÆ. CREEPERS.

This is an Old-World family; numbering about 12 species, of which only one is found in America where, represented by 6 subspecies, it ranges as far south as the southern extremity of the Mexican tableland. It is a true tree-creeper, and, like a Woodpecker, uses its tail as a prop in climbing.

370. BROWN CREEPER. CERTHIA FAMILIARIS AMERICANA *Bonaparte.* [726.] (Figs. 18, 105.) *Ads.*—Upperparts mixed with white, fuscous, and ochraceous-buff; *rump pale rufous;* tail pale grayish brown; a band of cream-buff through all but outer wing-feathers; bill curved; tail feathers stiffened and sharply pointed; underparts white. L., 5·66; W., 2·56; T., 2·65; B., ·63.

Range.—Breeds mainly in Canadian and Transition zones from s. Man., s. Que., s. to e. Nebr., n. Ind., N. Y., and Mass., and s. along the Alleghanies to N. C., and casually in se. Mo. Winters over a large part of its breeding-range and s. to cent. Tex. and s. Fla.

Washington, common W. V., Sept. 22–May 3. Bronx region, common T. V. and W. V., several recent breeding records; Sept. 3–May 15 (27). Boston, common T. V., rather common W. V., Sept. 23–May 1; breeds locally in small numbers. N. Ohio, common W. V., Oct. 1–May 9. Glen Ellyn, tolerably common W. V., Sept. 15–May 19. SE. Minn., common T. V., Mch. 2–May 22; Sept. 14–Nov. 29; frequent in winter.

Nest, of twigs, strips of bark, bits of dead wood, moss, etc., placed behind the loose bark of a tree. *Eggs,* 5–8, white, spotted and speckled with cinnamon- or rufous-brown and lavender, chiefly in a wreath at the larger end, ·62 × ·47 (Brewster, Bull. Nutt. Orn. Club., 1879, 199). *Date,* Holland Patent, N. Y., May 20.

The facts in the case will doubtless show that the patient, plodding Brown Creeper is searching for the insects, eggs, and larvæ which are hidden in crevices in the bark; but after watching him for several minutes one becomes impressed with the thought that he has lost the only thing in the world he ever cared for, and that his one object in life is to find it. Ignoring you completely, with scarcely a pause, he winds his way in a preoccupied, near-sighted manner up a tree-trunk. Having finally reached the top of his spiral staircase, one might suppose he would rest long enough to survey his surroundings, but like a bit of loosened bark, he drops off to the base of the nearest tree and resumes his never-ending task.

He has no time to waste in words, but occasionally, without stopping in his rounds, he utters a few *screeping,* squeaky notes, which are about as likely to attract attention as he is himself. As for song, one would say it was quite out of the question; but Mr. Brewster, in his biography of this bird, tells us that in its summer home, amid the northern spruces and firs, it has an exquisitely pure, tender song of four notes, "the first of moderate pitch, the second lower and less emphatic, the third rising again, and the last abruptly falling, but dying away in an indescribably plaintive cadence, like the soft sigh of the wind among the pine boughs."

1879. BREWSTER, W., Bull. Nutt. Orn. Club, 199–209 (biography).— 1895. WIDMANN, O., Auk, 350–355 (nesting in Mo.).—1905. CHADBOURNE,

A. P., Auk, 179–183; KENNARD, F. H. and McKECHNIE, F. B., 183–193
(nesting in Mass.).—1914. TYLER, W. M., Auk, 50–62 (home-life in Mass.).
—1915. BIRD-LORE, 199, 126 (mig.; pl.).

FAMILY TROGLODYTIDÆ. WRENS.

The Wrens are one of the few families of birds represented in both
hemispheres, in which there is a larger number in the New World than
in the Old; only 30-odd of the over 350 known forms occur in the
Old World, while the remainder are American. In this country they
are most abundant in the tropics, only 10 species (46 species and subspecies) occurring within our limits. Wrens, as a rule, are haunters of
the undergrowth in well-thicketed places, but some species are marsh-
inhabiting and others live among rocks. They are active, nervous little
creatures, whose usually up-cocked tail is an index to their excitable
dispositions. Their notes of alarm or displeasure are loud, harsh and
insistent, but the songs of most species are marked by rare sweetness
and brilliancy of execution. Their irrepressible energy finds expression
in nests of great size or complex structure as well as in exceptionally
large sets of eggs.

KEY TO THE SPECIES

A. Upperparts bright rufous, a long, conspicuous whitish line over the eye;
    underparts cream-buff or ochraceous-buff; wing 2·25 or over.
                 374. CAROLINA WREN. 374a. FLORIDA WREN.
B. Upperparts not bright rufous.
  a. Upperparts uniform dark, reddish olive-brown; back without white
    streaks.
    a¹. Underparts whitish; primaries finely barred; no white line over the
        eye . . . 371. HOUSE WREN. 371a. WESTERN HOUSE WREN.
    a². Underparts whitish; primaries not barred; a white line over the eye.
                 373. BEWICK'S WREN.
    a³. Underparts brownish, finely barred with black. 372. WINTER WREN.
  b. Back with white streaks.
    b¹. White streaks confined to the center of the back; a white line over
       the eye . 375, 375a–d. LONG-BILLED MARSH WREN and races.
    b². Crown, back, and wing-coverts streaked with white.
                 376. SHORT-BILLED MARSH WREN.

371. HOUSE WREN. TROGLODYTES AËDON AËDON *Vieillot.* [721.]
(Fig. 106*b*.) *Ads.*—Above cinnamon olive-brown, *more rufous on the rump
and tail;* back generally with indistinct bars; feathers of the rump with concealed, downy white spots; wings and tail finely barred; below *grayish white,*
flanks rusty, sides and flanks usually, breast rarely, under tail-coverts always
barred with blackish. L., 5·00; W., 1·97; T., 1·71; B., ·50.
  Range.—Breeds chiefly in Transition and Upper Austral zones from Mich.,
s. Ont., s. Que., and N. B. s. to Ky. and Va. Winters in e. Tex. and Tamaulipas, and in the S. Atlantic and Gulf states, rarely to s. N. J.
  Washington, common S. R., Mch. 26–Nov. 26. Bronx region, common
S. R., Apr. 12–Oct. 23. Boston, locally common Apr. 28–Sept. 25. N. Ohio,
common S. R., Apr. 17–Oct. 5. Glen Ellyn, S. R., in isolated pairs, Apr. 26–
Nov. 7. SE. Minn., common S. R., Apr. 3–Oct. 12.
  Nest, of twigs lined with grasses, feathers, etc., generally filling the hole
in a tree, bird-box, crevice, etc., in which it is placed. *Eggs,* 6–8, vinaceous,

uniform, or minutely speckled, with generally a wreath of a deeper shade at the larger end, ·65 × ·51. *Date,* White Sulphur Springs, Va., Apr. 27; D. C., May 1; Boston, May 25; se. Minn., May 6.

No native bird more quickly accepts an invitation to make our home his than the House Wren. Offer him a bird-box at the right time and place and the chances are in favor of his investigating it before the sun has set. When the opening to this dwelling is small enough to prevent the entrance of competing species, he is provided with quarters in which he is exempt from many of the dangers that beset nesting birds.

To what extent the general abundance of the House Wren is due to the innumerable houses with which of recent years he has been provided, I have no means of determining, but, beyond question, his numbers have been increased by the creation of a favorable environment during the season of reproduction. An aggressive species, he at times makes a bad neighbor.

But the Wren population may be locally regulated by control of his nesting-sites. We may, therefore, be a host to House Wrens, enjoy their companionship, marvel at their tireless energy, and be cheered by their songs without having to part with other bird neighbors.

Through the efforts of the Baldwin Bird Laboratory, near Cleveland, Ohio, the nesting habits of the House Wren have doubtless been more intensively studied than those of any other bird. Some of the results obtained are included in the publications mentioned below.

1905. HERRICK, F. H., Home Life of Wild Birds, 38–44.—1917. BIRD-LORE, 86 (pl.).—1921. BALDWIN, S. P., Auk, 237–244 (marriage relations). —1925. BIRD-LORE, 1925–26. A series of papers for and against.—1926. MCATEE, W. L., Bird-Lore, 181–183 (judgment on).—1927. ALLEN, A. A., Bird-Lore, 290–301, illus. (autobiography).—1927. BALDWIN, S. P. and KENDEIGH, S. C., Auk, 207–216, illus. (nesting behavior).—1927. BOULTON, R., Auk, 387–414 (ptilosis).—1928. BALDWIN, S. P. and BOWEN, W. W, Auk, 186–199 (nesting and local distribution).—1928. KENDEIGH, S. C. and BALDWIN, S. P., Am. Nat., 249–278 (temperature control in nestling).

371a. WESTERN HOUSE WREN. TROGLODYTES AËDON PARKMANI *Audubon.* [721a.] Similar to *T. a. aedon* but grayer, bars above usually more distinct; black bars of tail usually more or less margined posteriorly with grayish or buffy; flanks less rusty.
Range.—Breeds from s. B. C., cent. Alberta, cent. Sask., s. Man., and n. Wisc. s. to L. Calif., w. Tex., s. Mo., and sw. Ky. Winters from Calif. and Tex. s. to Mex.; also casually in n. and cent. Fla.

372. EASTERN WINTER WREN. NANNUS HIEMALIS HIEMALIS *(Vieillot).*
[722.] *Ads.*—Tail very short; a cinnamon-buff line over eye; upperparts dark, nearly uniform cinnamon-brown; back indistinctly barred; feathers of the rump with concealed, downy white spots; wings and tail barred; underparts *cinnamon-buff;* flanks and belly heavily barred with black. L., 4·06; W., 1·89; T., 1·24; B., ·35.
Range.—Breeds in Canadian Zone from s. Alberta, s. Man., n. Ont., cent. Que., and N. F. s. to cent. Minn., n. Wisc., cent. Mich., Mass., R. I. and through the Alleghanies to n. Ga. Winters from about its s. breeding limit to Tex. and cent. Fla.
Washington, rather common W. V., Aug. 10–May 1. Bronx region, fairly common T. V., frequently winters; Sept. 17–May 13. Boston, T. V., un-

common, Sept. 20–Nov. 25; rare, Apr. 10–25; a very few winter. N. Ohio, tolerably common W. V., Sept. 14–May 17. Glen Ellyn, fairly common T. V., Mch. 25–May 10; Sept. 9–Nov. 23. SE. Minn., uncommon T. V., Mch. 23–May 11; Sept. 11–Nov. 14.

Nest, of small twigs and moss, lined with feathers, in the roots of a tree, brush-heap, or similar place. "*Eggs*, 5–7, white or creamy white, finely but rather sparingly speckled with reddish brown, sometimes nearly immaculate, ·69 × ·50" (Ridgway). *Date*, Upton, Me., June 11.

When looking for a Winter Wren during the fall migration I go to an old raspberry patch, and in the woods watch the stumps and fallen trees. In the shadow of the woods it is easy to overlook the small dark bird creeping under a log or clambering over an old stump. But often, when sitting alone in the deserted patch, my heart has been warmed by the sudden apparition of the plump little Wren atilt of a dry golden-rod stalk close beside me, his tail standing straight over his back and his head cocked on one side. He would bow to me with a droll bobbing motion, but his hearty *quip-quap* and the frank look of interest in his bright eyes showed that he was quite ready to make friends. Many a dull morning has been gladdened by such an encounter.

Perhaps my choicest memories, however, are of a Wren who left his usual home in the dark coniferous forest for our brighter woodlands of maple and beech. He built his nest in an upturned root on the edge of a bit of marshy land, helping himself to some feathers the Scarlet Tanager had left at his bath in the swamp behind.

I had never before had a chance to listen to his famous song, and it was the event of the summer in the woods. Full of trills, runs, and grace notes, it was a tinkling, rippling roundelay. It made me think of the song of the Ruby-crowned Kinglet, the volume and ringing quality of both being startling from birds of their size. But while the King-let's may be less hampered by considerations of tune, the Wren's song has a more appealing human character. It is like the bird himself. The dark swamps are made glad by the joyous, wonderful song.

FLORENCE MERRIAM BAILEY

1917. BIRD-LORE, 87 (pl.).

373. BEWICK'S WREN. THRYOMANES BEWICKI BEWICKI (*Audubon*). [719.] *Ads.*—Above dark *cinnamon-brown without* bars or streaks; feathers of rump with concealed, downy white spots; outer vane of primaries little if at all barred; central tail-feathers grayish brown, barred, at least on sides, with black; outer ones black, tipped with grayish; the outer one or two with more or less bars on the outer vane; a white or buffy line over eye, underparts grayish white; flanks brownish. L., 5·00; W., 2·30; T., 2·10; B., ·50.

Range.—Breeds chiefly in the Upper Austral Zone from se. Nebr., n. Ills., s. Mich., and cent. Pa. s. to cent. Ark., n. Miss., cent. Ala., cent. Ga., and highlands of S. C. Winters from near the n. limit of its range s. to the Gulf Coast and cent. Fla. Casual east to N. J.; accidental in N. Y., Ont. and N. H.

Washington, rare and local T. V., Mch. 26–July; may winter, Nov. 24–Dec. 22, and

FIG. 125. Bewick's Wren.
(Natural size.)

Feb. 8. N. Ohio, several summer records. SE. Minn., casual, [Redwing, Apr. 28, 1924.

Nest, resembles that of *T. a. aëdon;* location the same. *Eggs*, 4–6, white, speckled with cinnamon-, rufous-brown, or lavender, evenly, or in a wreath at the larger end, ·66 × ·50. *Date*, Buncombe Co., N. C., Apr. 14; Old Orchard, Mo., Apr. 20.

"No bird more deserves the protection of man than Bewick's Wren. He does not need man's encouragement, for he comes of his own accord and installs himself as a member of the community wherever it suits his taste. He is found about the cow-shed and barn along with the Pewee and Barn Swallow; he investigates the pig-sty, then explores the garden fence, and finally mounts to the roof and pours forth one of the sweetest songs that ever was heard. Not . . . like the House Wren's merry roundelay, but a fine, clear, bold song, uttered as the singer sits with head thrown back and long tail pendent—a song which may be heard a quarter of a mile or more, and in comparison with which the faint chant of the Song Sparrow sinks into insignificance. The ordinary note is a soft, low *plit*, uttered as the bird hops about, its long tail carried erect or even leaning forward, and jerked to one side at short intervals. In its movements it is altogether more deliberate than either *T. ludovicianus* or *T. aëdon*, but nothing can excel it in quickness when it is pursued" (Ridgway).

1917. BIRD-LORE, 86 (pl.).

374. CAROLINA WREN. THRYOTHORUS LUDOVICIANUS LUDOVICIANUS (*Latham*). [718.] (Fig. 106a.) *Ads.*—Above *bright rufous* or *rufous-brown* without bars or streaks; feathers of rump with concealed downy white spots; a long, conspicuous whitish or buffy line over eye; wings and tail rufous-brown, finely barred with black; underparts ochraceous-buff or cream-buff, whiter on the throat; flanks sometimes with a few blackish bars. Worn breeding plumage is dingier above and whiter below. The largest of our Wrens. L., 5·50; W., 2·30; T., 2·00; B., ·60.

Range.—Upper and Lower Austral zones from se. Nebr., s. Ia., O., s. Pa., and lower Hudson and Conn. valleys s. to cent. Tex., Gulf States, and n. Fla. Casual n. to Wisc., Mich., Ont., Mass., N. H., and Me.

Washington, common P. R. Bronx region, occasional T. V., rare P. R. Boston, rare or casual at any season; has bred. N. Ohio, tolerably common P. R. Glen Ellyn, occasional at all seasons; possibly rare S. R. SE. Minn., Apr. 12–June 6, 1926.

Nest, bulky, of grasses, feathers, leaves, etc., lined with finer grasses, long hairs, etc., in holes in trees or stumps, nooks and crevices about buildings, etc. *Eggs*, 4–6, white or creamy white, with numerous cinnamon-, rufous-brown, and lavender markings, sometimes wreathed about the larger end, ·75 × ·58. *Date*, Weaverville, N. C., Apr. 20.

The cozy nooks and corners about the home of man which prove so attractive to the House Wren are less commonly chosen by this bird. His wild nature more often demands the freedom of the forests, and he shows no disposition to adapt himself to new conditions. Undergrowths near water, fallen tree-tops, brush heaps, and rocky places in the woods where he can dodge in and out and in a twinkling appear or disappear like a feathered Jack-in-the-box, are the resorts he chooses.

The nervous activity so characteristic of all Wrens reaches in him a high development. Whatever he may be when alone, he is never at rest so long as he imagines himself observed. Now he is on this side of us, now on that; a moment later, on a stump before us, bobbing up and down and gesticulating with his expressive tail; but as a rule he is seldom in sight more than a second at a time. Of course, so excitable a nature must find other than bodily outlet for its irrepressible energy, and the bird accompanies his movements by more or less appropriate notes: scolding *cacks*, clinking, metallic rattles, musical trills, tree-toadlike *krrrings*—in fact, he possesses an almost endless vocabulary. He is sometimes called Mocking Wren, but the hundreds of birds I have heard were all too original to borrow from others. In addition to his peculiar calls he possesses a variety of loud, ringing whistles, somewhat similar in tone to those of the Tufted Titmouse or Cardinal, and fully as loud as, if not louder than, the notes of the latter. The more common ones resemble the syllables *whee-udel, whee-udel, whee-udel*, and *tea-kettle, tea-kettle, tea-kettle*.

1909. Townsend, C. W., Auk, 263–269 (in N. E.).—1916. Bird-Lore, 362 (pl.).

374a. FLORIDA WREN. Thryothorus ludovicianus miamensis *Ridgway*. [718a.] Similar to the preceding, but larger; above darker; below more deeply colored. W., 2·46; T., 2·19; B., ·70.
Range.—Fla. s. of Levy and Putnam counties.
Nesting-date, San Mateo, Fla., Apr. 6.

375. LONG-BILLED MARSH WREN. Telmatodytes palustris palustris (*Wilson*). [725.] Crown *unstreaked*, its sides black, its center olive-brown, a white line over eye; middle of back black broadly streaked with white; rest of back cinnamon-brown; middle tail-feathers narrowly, outer tail-feathers broadly barred; below white, the sides and flanks pale cinnamon-brown sometimes extending to breast; under tail-coverts rarely barred. Worn breeding plumage is grayer. L., 5·20; W., 1·95; T., 1·68.
Range.—Breeds in Transition and Upper Austral zones from s. Ont. and s. Que. s. to the Potomac Valley and coast of Va. Winters from s. N. J. to S. C. and sparingly to Fla.; casual in N. B.

Fig. 126. Long-billed Marsh Wren. (Natural size.)

Washington, very numerous S. R., Apl. 15–Nov. 1. Bronx region, common T. V. and S. R., occasional in winter (Mch. 18), Apl. 15–Nov. 14 (Jan. 11). Boston, locally abundant S. R., May 15–Oct. 1; sometimes a few winter. N. Ohio, common S. R., Apl. 21–Sept. 20. Glen Ellyn, fairly common S. R., less plentiful than formerly, May 10–Oct. 10.

Nest, globular, the entrance at one side, of coarse grasses, reed-stalks, etc., lined with fine grasses, attached to reeds or bushes. *Eggs*, 5–9, uniform chocolate or minutely speckled or thickly marked with cinnamon- or olive-brown, ·65 × ·49. *Date*, D. C., June 4; Boston, June 12.

If you would make the acquaintance of this Marsh Wren, you have only to visit his home in the cattails and tall, reedy grasses bordering rivers, creeks, and sloughs. It will be unnecessary to announce yourself;

he will know of your presence long before you know of his, and from the inner chambers of his dwelling will proceed certain scolding, *cacking* notes before this nervous, excitable bit of feathered life appears on his threshold. With many flourishes of the tail and much bobbing and attitudinizing, he inquires your business, but before you have had time enough to inspect him he has darted back into his damp retreats, and you can tell of his frequently changing position only by his scolding, grumbling notes.

All this time his neighbors—and he generally has numbers of them— have doubtless been charming you with their rippling, bubbling, gurgling song. They seem filled to overflowing with an inexhaustible supply of music. Sometimes, like a mine of melody, it explodes within them and lifts them from the dark recesses of the flags up into the air above.

1917. BIRD-LORE, 87 (pl.).

375a. WORTHINGTON'S MARSH WREN. TELMATODYTES PALUSTRIS GRISEUS (*Brewster*). [725*b*.] Grayest of the Marsh Wrens. *Ads.*—Above olive-gray; sides of crown narrowly blackish, black of back much reduced in extent, white streaks less conspicuous than in other races; below white, the sides grayish, bars, if present, indistinct; *under tail-coverts barred*, in this respect resembling *T. p. marianæ* from which it may be readily distinguished by its much grayer color. W., 1·80; T., 1·52; B., ·53.
Range.—Lower Austral Zone in the S. Atlantic Coast region from S. C. to n. Fla.
Nesting-date, Matanzas Inlet, Fla., May 24.

375b. MARIAN'S MARSH WREN. TELMATODYTES PALUSTRIS MARIANÆ (*Scott*). [725*e*.] Similar to *T. p. palustris*, but smaller, with the upperparts darker, the sides and flanks more heavily washed and of about the same color as rump; the *under tail-coverts*, and sometimes sides and breast barred or spotted with black. W., 1·80; T., 1·50; B., ·52.
Remarks.—The amount of black above is variable and the general tone of color in some specimens closely approaches that of *T. p. palustris*, from which, however, the heavily barred under tail-coverts separate this race.
Range.—Gulf Coast from Charlotte Harbor, Fla., to Miss.

375c. LOUISIANA MARSH WREN. TELMATODYTES PALUSTRIS THRYOPHILUS *Oberholser*. "Similar to *T. p. marianæ* but much paler, more grayish brown above, the pileum with much less black, often with almost none, the upper tail-coverts absolutely or not at all barred; chest not spotted" (Oberholser).
Range.—Coast district of La. and Tex.

375d. PRAIRIE MARSH WREN. TELMATODYTES PALUSTRIS DISSAËPTUS (*Bangs*). [725*d*.] "Similar to *T. p. palustris*, but slightly larger and with the coloration much more rufescent, the brown of the upperparts russet-brown to cinnamon-brown or russet, the flanks conspicuously deep cinnamon-buff or cinnamon" (Ridgway).
Range.—Breeds in Transition and Upper Austral zones from the Canadian boundary s. to cent. Miss. Valley and e. to Ind. Winters s. over Mex. to Jalisco, Zacatecas, the Vera Cruz, and along the Gulf Coast to s. Fla. SE. Minn., S. R., Apl. 14–Oct. 21.
Nesting-date, se. Minn., June 10.

376. SHORT-BILLED MARSH WREN. CISTOTHORUS STELLARIS (*Naumann*). [724.] *Ads.*—Entire upperparts *streaked* with white, black, and ochraceous-buff; wings and tail barred; underparts *unbarred*, white; under tail-coverts, flanks, and a more or less broken band across breast ochraceous-buff. L., 4·00; W., 1·75; T., 1·41.

Range.—Breeds in Transition and Upper Austral zones from se. Sask., cent. Man., s. Ont., and s. Me. s. to e. Kans., cent. Mo., cent. Ind., and n. Del. Winters from s. Ills. and s. N. J. to s. Tex., La., and s. Fla. Accidental in Colo. and Wyo.

Washington, vary rare T. V., three instances, May. Bronx region, rather rare S. R., Apr. 22–Oct. 23 (Dec. 13, 21). Boston, locally common S. R., May 12–Sept. 25. N. Ohio, not common S. R., May 12 and 19. Glen Ellyn, fairly common S. R., May 8–Oct. 17. SE. Minn., common S. R., Apr. 14–Oct. 26.

Nest, globular, the entrance on one side, of grasses, lined with plant-down, on or near the ground, in a tussock of tall grass. *Eggs*, 6–8, pure white, rarely with a few lavender spots, ·62 × ·47. *Date*, Boston, May 25.

FIG. 127. Short-billed Marsh Wren. (Natural size.)

This bustling, energetic little creature will much more often be heard than seen. Its ordinary call-note, like the sound of two pebbles struck together, may be heard in a dozen directions for a quarter of an hour before one of the birds comes in view, so careful are they to keep concealed among the protecting sedge. The ordinary song of the species has much the same *timbre* as the call-note; it resembles the syllables *chap——chap—chap–chap, chap chap-chap-chap-p-p-rrrr;* but during the height of the love season it vents its feelings in a much more ambitious refrain, one which, while it is everywhere varied and in parts very musical, is still conspicuous for the amount of· *chappering* that enters into its composition. While singing, it is usually seen clinging to the side of some tall swaying reed with its tail bent forward so far as almost to touch the head, thus exhibiting in an exaggerated manner a characteristic attitude of all the Wrens.

This is less a species of the deep-water marshes than is the long-billed member of the genus, and often it will be found in places that are little more than damp meadows. It is remarkably mouselike in its habits and movements, and can be flushed only with extreme difficulty.

ERNEST THOMPSON SETON

1917. BIRD-LORE, 87 (pl.).

FAMILY MIMIDÆ. THRASHERS, MOCKINGBIRDS, ETC.

Most of the 60-odd species contained in this distinctively American family are restricted to the tropics, only 11 being found north of Mexico. Generally speaking, they frequent scrubby growths and bushy borders of wooded land. When singing they take a more or less exposed perch and devote themselves seriously and exclusively to the delivery of their musical message. As a rule they are possessed of exceptional vocal ability, and the Mockingbirds, of which there are some 20 species, some quite as talented as ours, are conceded first rank among American song-birds, so far as variety of expression and execution are concerned.

KEY TO THE SPECIES

A. Back slate-color; cap black; under tail-coverts rufous-brown.
378. CATBIRD.
B. Back and crown grayish; underparts whitish; outer tail-feathers white.
377. MOCKINGBIRD.
C. Back rufous; underparts streaked with black . 379. BROWN THRASHER.

377. MOCKINGBIRD. MIMUS POLYGLOTTOS POLYGLOTTOS (*Linnæus*). [703.] *Ads.*—Above ashy; wings and tail fuscous; primary coverts white, centrally, black at end, primaries basally white, showing conspicuously in flight; outer tail-feather white, next two or three with a decreasing amount; below soiled white. L., 10·50; W., 4·50; T., 4·90; B., ·70.

Remarks.—The sexes can not be certainly distinguished in color, but in the female the white areas average slightly smaller. Nestlings are grayish brown above, white, spotted with fuscous below.

Range.—Chiefly in Austral zones, from e. Nebr., s. Ia., Ills., Ind., O., and Md. s. to e. Tex., s. Fla., and the Bahamas, and sparingly to Mass. and Me. Accidental in Wisc., Ont., and N. S.; introduced in Bermuda.

Washington, not uncommon P. R. Bronx region, rare T. V., Apr. 6–July 23; Sept. 30–Nov. 21 (Feb. 17). Boston, rare P. R., less rare Nov.–Apr. N. Ohio, occasional in spring, locally P. R. Glen Ellyn, one record, June 5, 1927.

Nest, of coarse twigs, weed-stalks, etc., lined with rootlets, cotton, etc., in thickets, orange trees, etc. *Eggs,* 4–6, pale greenish blue or bluish white, sometimes with a brownish tinge, rather heavily spotted and blotched, chiefly at the larger end, with cinnamon- or rufous-brown, 1·00 × ·72. *Date,* Gainesville, Fla., Apr. 1; Raleigh, N. C., May 9; Boston, May 20.

The Mockingbird might be called our national song-bird; his remarkable vocal powers have made him famous the world over, while our more retiring Thrushes are scarcely to be found mentioned outside the literature of ornithology. He is a good citizen, and courting rather than shunning public life, shows an evident interest in the affairs of the day. He lives in our gardens, parks, and squares, and even in the streets of the town, and is always alert and on the *qui vive;* a self-appointed guardian, whose sharp alarm-note is passed from bird to bird like the signals of watchmen.

In Florida, Mockingbirds begin to sing in February, and by March 1 the air rings with music. The heat of midday is insufficient to quell their ardor, and on moonlight nights many birds sing throughout the night. It is customary to consider the Mockingbird a musician possessed of marvelous technique but with comparatively little depth of feeling. He is said to create intense admiration without reaching the soul. But listen to him when the world is hushed, when the air is heavy with the rich fragrance of orange blossoms and the dewy leaves glisten in the moonlight, and if his song does not thrill you then confess yourself deaf to Nature's voices.

It must not be supposed that every Mockingbird is a mocker; there is much variation in their imitative gifts. Mr. L. M. Loomis tells me of a Mockingbird he once heard singing in South Carolina which imitated the notes of no less than thirty-two different species of birds found in the same locality, and this during ten minutes' continuous singing! This was a phenomenal performance, one I have never heard approached, for in my experience many Mockingbirds have no notes besides their own, and good mockers are exceptional.

1902. DANIELS, J. W., Wilson Bull., 68–71 (nesting).—1916. BIRD-LORE, 172 (pl.).—1921. WRIGHT, H. W., Auk, 382–432 (in New England).—1922. WHITTLE, C. L., Auk, 496–506 (in Arnold Arboretum).—1928. VISSCHER, J. P., Wilson Bull., 207–216 (habits and song).

378. CATBIRD. DUMETELLA CAROLINENSIS (*Linnæus*). [704.] (Fig. 107*b*.) *Ads.*—Crown and tail black; *under tail-coverts chestnut*, sometimes spotted with slaty, and rarely largely slaty; rest of the plumage slaty gray. L., 8·94; W., 3·54; T., 3·65; B., ·60.

Range.—Breeds mainly in Transition and Austral zones from cent. B. C., s. Que., and N. S. s. to ne. Ore., Utah, ne. N. Mex., se. Tex., and n. Fla.; resident in Bermuda; winters from southern states to the Bahamas and Cuba and through Mex. to Panama; casual in winter n. to the Middle States; accidental on the Farallon Isls. and in Europe.

Washington, abundant S. R., Apr. 24–Oct. 11; occasionally winters. Bronx region, common S. R., occasional in winter; Apr. 16–Dec. 25. Boston, abundant S. R., May 6–Oct. 1; occasional in winter. N. Ohio, common S. R., Apr. 21–Oct. 5. Glen Ellyn, common S. R., Apr. 29–Oct. 14. SE. Minn., common S. R., Apr. 30–Oct. 6.

Nest, of twigs, grasses, and leaves, lined with rootlets, in thickets or densely foliaged trees. *Eggs*, 3–5, rich greenish blue, ·94 × ·67. *Date*, D. C., May 17; Cambridge, May 22; Utica, N. Y., May 21; se. Minn., May 18.

The name by which this bird is called and, worse luck, will probably ever be known, was doubtless given it by a casual listener who only gave ear to the short, grating alarm-note and passed on. Even then it is a misnomer and suggests only a falsetto imitation.

The angler out at dawn, whipping a stream, hears a low, hushed, introspective warble, broken suddenly and then taken up in a higher key. It dies away. He pauses and listens when, from a bush overhanging the water, comes a flood of notes expressing every mood from reverie to astonishment, and even anger, which quickly turns to mockery and ceases suddenly as the bird is convinced that the angler means no harm.

No bird so thoroughly responds to the security of protection or seemingly recognizes the efforts of gardeners to bribe him to overlook their produce in favor of synthetic delicacies. Three pairs of the birds nesting in the vicinity of the house have this year eaten more than two dozen boxes of raisins scattered nightly upon shelves convenient to the two bathing-pools, while in return we have had the most bewitching melody from a little after sun-up until after dusk with only a negligible number of *zay-zay-ay-aya*; which those with defective ears insist upon calling *miou-s*.

Trim, with a glistening coat of slate and black, a pert black cap to match his sidewise rapid glance, he and his mate are good parents and tireless providers, in spite of the fact that they *appear* never to be at home. For, friendly as they are, their nest is usually so well concealed that some detective work is needed to locate it and they will slip out by a roundabout way, the male singing as unconsciously as if he had no cares, but watching all the while for the slightest unfriendly move. During the molt they are very furtive, slipping through the underbrush to the bathing-pools as if ashamed to be seen in shabby plumage. Their period of song is all too short, and, like the Brown Thrasher, only an occasional note is heard after the first of July.

MABEL OSGOOD WRIGHT.

1905. HERRICK, F. H., Home-Life of Wild Birds, 122–128.—1913. GABRIELSON, I. N., Wilson Bull., 166–187 (nest-life).—1916. BIRD-LORE, 172 (pl.).—1923. WHITTLE, H. G., Auk, 603–606 (nesting).

379. BROWN THRASHER. TOXOSTOMA RUFUM (*Linnæus*). [705.] (Fig. 107a.) *Ads.*—Upperparts, wings, and tail rufous; wing-coverts tipped with whitish, underparts white (buffy in fall), heavily streaked with black or cinnamon, except on throat and middle of belly. L., 11·42; W., 4·06; T., 5·03; B., ·96.

Range.—Breeds mainly in Transition and Austral zones from s. Alberta, n. Mich., sw. Que., and n. Me. s. to e. La., Miss., Ala., and cent. Fla., and from base of the Rocky Mts. in Mont., Wyo., and Colo. e.; winters from se. Mo. and N. C. to cent. s. Tex., s. Fla., and casually farther n.; accidental in Ariz. and Europe.

Washington, very common S. R., Mch. 4–Nov. 13; occasionally winters. Bronx region, common S. R., occasional in winter; Apr. 10–Nov. 22. Boston, common S. R., Apr. 26–Oct. 20. N. Ohio, common S. R., Apr. 6–Oct. 15. Glen Ellyn, common S. R., Apr. 2–Oct. 11. SE. Minn., common S. R., Apr. 14–Oct. 18.

Nest, of twigs, coarse rootlets, and leaves, lined with finer rootlets, in bushes, thickets, or on the ground. *Eggs,* 3–6, bluish white or grayish white, thickly, evenly, and minutely speckled with cinnamon- or rufous-brown, 1·08 × ·80. *Date,* D. C., May 7; Montgomery Co., Pa., May 15; Boston, May 21; Wheatland, Ind., May 7; se. Minn., May 4.

Hedgerows, shrubbery about the borders of woods, scrubby growth, or thickets in dry fields, are alike frequented by the Thrasher. Generally speaking he is an inhabitant of the undergrowth, where he passes much time on the ground foraging among the fallen leaves. He is an active, suspicious bird, who does not like to be watched, and expresses his annoyance with an unpleasant kissing note or sharply whistled *wheèu*.

Like many thicket-haunting birds, who ordinarily shun observation, he seeks an exposed position when singing. Morning and evening he mounts to a favorite perch—generally in the upper branches of a tree—and deliberately gives his entire attention to his song. This is repeated many times, the bird singing almost continuously for an extended interval. He is a finished musician, and, although his repertoire is limited to one air, he rivals the Mockingbird in the richness of his tones and execution. I never listen to the Thrasher's song without involuntarily exclaiming, "What a magnificent performance!" Nevertheless, there is a certain consciousness and lack of spontaneity about it which makes it appeal to the mind rather than to the heart.

1912. GABRIELSON, I. N., Wilson Bull., 65–94, illus. (home-life).—1916. BIRD-LORE, 172 (pl.).

FAMILY TURDIDÆ. THRUSHES, BLUEBIRDS, ETC.

Over 700 species and subspecies are included in this large family of which about 200 (100 species) are found in the Western Hemisphere. Of this number, 31 (14 species) inhabit North America. Thrushes inhabit wooded regions; our species are migratory, and gregarious or sociable to a greater or less extent during their migrations and in winter. As songsters, they are inferior to some of our birds in power of execution, but their voices are possessed of greater sweetness and expression, and they are conceded first rank among song-birds by all true lovers of bird music.

1915. BEAL, F. E. L., Food Habits of Thrushes of U. S., Bull. 280, U. S. Dept. Agric.

KEY TO THE SPECIES

I. Tail blue, back blue or bluish . . . . 389. BLUEBIRD.
II. Tail not blue.
  1. Tail with white.
    A. Tail black, outer feathers tipped with white . . 381, 381a. ROBIN.
    B. Tail white tipped with black . . . 390. GREENLAND WHEATEAR.
  2. No white in tail; which is olive-brown or rufous.
    A. Tail not brighter than back.
      a. Upperparts cinnamon-rufous.
        a^1. Entire underparts, including *sides*, more or less heavily marked with round, blackish spots; back *brighter* than tail.
                        384. WOOD THRUSH.
        a^2. Throat and upper breast pale buffy, with small, cinnamon-brown, wedge-shaped spots; belly pure white; sides with a barely perceptible grayish wash . . . . . . 388. VEERY.
      b. Upperparts olive.
        b^1. Throat, breast, cheeks, eye-ring, and lores deep cream-buff.
                  386. OLIVE-BACKED THRUSH.
        b^2. Throat and breast, white, with only a *very slight* buffy tinge; eye-ring whitish, lores grayish.
        387. GRAY-CHEEKED THRUSH. 387a. BICKNELL'S THRUSH.
    B. Tail brighter than back.
      a. Upperparts olive-brown, sometimes inclining to cinnamon; upper tail-coverts and *tail* rufous . . . . . . 385. HERMIT THRUSH.

380. The RED-WINGED THRUSH, *Arceuthornis musicus* (Linnæus), of Eurasia, is accidental in Greenland.

381. **EASTERN ROBIN.** TURDUS MIGRATORIUS MIGRATORIUS *Linnæus.* [761.] (Figs. 57, 108a.) *Ads.*—Top and sides of the head black, a white spot above and below the eye; rest of the upperparts grayish slate-color; margins of wings slightly lighter; tail blackish, the outer feathers with white spots at their tips; throat white, streaked with black; rest of the underparts rufous (tipped with white in the fall), becoming white on the middle of the lower belly; bill yellow, brownish in fall. Im. females *average* paler below and with less black on the head, but fully adult birds are as richly colored as the brightest males. *Nestling.*—Back and underparts spotted with black. L., 10·00; W., 4·96; T., 3·87; B., ·84.

Range.—Breeds in Boreal, Transition, and Upper Austral zones from limit of trees in nw. Alaska, n. Mack., n. Man., n. Que., and N. F. s. to Cook Inlet, Alaska, cent. Alberta, Kans., Ills., Ind., O., Pa., N. J.; winters from cent. Kans., O. Valley, and Mass. (irregular farther n.) to the Gulf Coast and s. Fla., and to Nuevo Leon, Mex.; accidental in Bermuda and Cuba.

Washington, abundant T. V., from Feb.–Apr.; irregularly common W. V. Bronx region, common S. R., usually winters; Feb. 4–Dec. 28. Boston, very abundant S. R., common but irregular W. V. N. Ohio, abundant S. R., Feb. 26–Nov. 30; a few winter. Glen Ellyn, very common S. R., rare W. V., Jan. 25–Dec. 31; usually Mch. 7–Nov. 19. SE. Minn., common S. R., rare W. V., Mch. 1–Nov. 3; a few in winter.

Nest, of coarse grasses, leaves, rootlets, etc., with an inner wall of mud and lining of fine grasses, most frequently in fruit or shade trees, 5–30 feet up. *Eggs,* 3–5, greenish blue, very rarely with brownish markings, 1·14 × ·80. *Date,* New York City, Apr. 20; Boston, Apr. 25; se. Minn., Apr. 28.

While the few Robins that have the courage to winter with us are seeking protection from chilling winds in the depths of friendly evergreens, their comrades who extended their journey to the south are holding carnival under sunny skies. In Florida, during the winter, Robins may be found in enormous flocks, feeding on the berries of the China tree, holly, palmetto and mistletoe. Occasionally they give voice to a half-suppressed chorus, as though rehearsing for the approaching season of song.

Robins migrate in flocks, and the arrival of the advance guard makes the dreariest March day seem bright. It is a question whether these pioneers are summer residents or transients *en route* to a more northern summer home, but in my experience they make the sunny side of some woods their headquarters and remain there until paired. They are then in full song, and we see them in their accustomed haunts about our lawns and orchards.

Toward the last of June the young of the first brood, with the old males, resort in numbers nightly to a roosting-place. These roosts are generally in deciduous second growths, usually in low, but sometimes on high ground. The females are now occupied with the cares of a second family, and the males are said to return each day to assist them in their duties.

Early in September, when the nesting season is over, Robins gather in large flocks, and from this time until their departure for the south, roam about the country in search of food, taking in turn wild cherries, dogwood and cedar berries.

The songs and call-notes of the Robin, while well known to every one, are in reality understood by no one, and offer excellent subjects for the student of bird language. Its notes express interrogation, suspicion, alarm, caution, and it signals to its companions to take wing; indeed, few of our birds have a more extended vocabulary.

1890. Brewster, W., Auk, 360–373 (summer roosts).—1892. Torrey, B., Foot-path Way, 153–175 (summer roosts).—1895. Widmann, O., Auk, 1–11, also 274 (winter roosts).—1898. Howe, R. H., Jr., Auk, 162–167 (nesting).—1905. Herrick, F. H., Home-Life of Wild Birds, 72–85.—1907. Bird-Lore, 76 (mig.; pl.).—1928. Allen, A. A., Bird-Lore, 142–152, illus. (autobiography).

381a. SOUTHERN ROBIN. Turdus migratorius achrusterus (*Batchelder*). [761b.] Smaller than *T. m. migratorius*, colors in general much lighter and duller. W., 4·80; T., 3·60.

Range.—Breeds in s. part of Upper Austral Zone from s. Ills. and Md. to n. Miss., cent. Ala., n. Ga., and upper S. C.

Washington, common S. R.; some may winter.

382. The EUROPEAN BLACKBIRD, *Turdus merula merula* Linnæus is of accidental occurrence in Greenland.

383. The NORTHERN VARIED THRUSH, *Ixoreus nævius meruloides* (Swainson), of western North America is accidental in Kansas, New Jersey, New York, Massachusetts, and Quebec.

384. **WOOD THRUSH.** HYLOCICHLA MUSTELINA *(Gmelin).* [755.] (Pl. XXIII.) *Ads.*—Upperparts bright cinnamon-brown, *brightest on the head,* and changing gradually to pale olive-brown on the upper tail-coverts and tail; underparts white, thickly marked with *large, round blackish* spots except on the throat and middle of the belly. L., 8·29; W., 4·44; T., 2·92; B., ·65.

Remarks.—The Wood Thrush may be distinguished from our other Thrushes (1) by its larger size; (2) by its brighter, more rufous color above; and (3) especially by the numerous large, round blackish spots on its underparts. These cover not only the breast, but are equally numerous on the sides, where they extend well up under the wings.

Range.—Breeds in Transition and Austral zones from s. S. Dak., cent. Minn., cent. Wisc., se. Ont., and s. N. H. and s. Me. (casually) s. to e. Tex., La., and n. Fla.; winters from s. Mex. to Canal Zone, rarely in Fla.; casual in migration in the Bahamas, Cuba, and Jamaica; accidental in Colo., Me., and Bermuda.

Washington, common S. R., Apr. 13–Oct. 30. Bronx region, common S. R., Apr. 23–Oct. 23. Boston, locally common S. R., May 10–Sept. 15. N. Ohio, common S. R., Apr. 20–Oct. 1. Glen Ellyn, fairly common local S. R., Apr. 30–Sept. 30. SE. Minn., common S. R., May 1–Oct. 15.

Nest, of leaves, rootlets, fine twigs, and weed-stalks, firmly interwoven, with an inner wall of mud and lining of fine rootlets, generally in saplings, about 8 feet up. *Eggs,* 3–5, greenish blue, lighter and with less green than those of the Catbird, *averaging* lighter, but not certainly distinguishable in color from those of the Robin, 1·05 × ·76. *Date,* Yemassee, S. C., May 12; D. C., May 1; Chester Co., Pa., May 17; Boston, May 26; se. Minn., May 22.

The Wood Thrush is not so distinctively a bird of the woods as the Veery. Well-shaded lawns are sometimes graced by its presence, and at all times it is more familiar and easier to observe than its retiring relative. Large size, bright cinnamon upperparts, and especially a conspicuously spotted breast and *sides,* are its most striking field characters.

The Wood Thrush's call-notes are a liquid *quirt* and a sharp *pit-pit.* The latter is the more characteristic and is often heard after nightfall. When the bird is alarmed or imagines its young in danger, its loud and rapid utterance of this call, resembling the sound produced by striking large pebbles together, gives painful evidence of its fear and anxiety.

The songs of the Wood and Hermit Thrushes are of the same character, but, while the Hermit is the more gifted performer, the Wood Thrush does not suffer by the comparison. His calm, restful song rings through the woods like a hymn of praise rising pure and clear from a thankful heart. It is a message of hope and good cheer in the morning, a benediction at the close of day:

Come to me.

The flutelike opening notes are an invitation to his haunts; a call from Nature to yield ourselves to the ennobling influences of the forest.

1907. BIRD-LORE, 32 (mig.; pl.).—1910. WEYGANDT, C., Cassinia, 21–27 (biography).

385. EASTERN HERMIT THRUSH. HYLOCICHLA GUTTATA FAXONI *Bangs and Penard.* [759*b.*] (Pl. XXIII.) *Ads.*—Upperparts olive-brown, sometimes cinnamon-brown; *tail pale rufous,* of a distinctly different color from the back; throat and breast with a slight buffy tinge; feathers of the sides of the throat with wedge-shaped black spots at their tips; those of the breast with large, rounded spots; middle of the belly white; sides brownish gray or brownish ashy. L., 7·17; W., 3·56; T., 2·74; B., ·51.

Remarks.—The Hermit Thrush may always be easily identified by its rufous tail. It is the only one of our Thrushes which has the tail brighter than the back.

Range.—Breeds in Canadian and Transition zones from Yukon, sw. Mack., n. Man., and s. Que. s. to cent. Alberta, cent. Sask., cent. Minn., n. Mich., Ont., Mass., Conn., L. I. (locally), and mountains of Pa. and Md.; winters from Mass. (locally) and the lower Del. and O. valleys to Tex., Fla., and Cuba; occasional in Bermuda; accidental in Greenland and Europe.

Washington, very common T. V., sometimes not uncommon W. V., Mch. 8–May 17; Sept. 18–Nov. 20. Bronx region, common T. V., very rare or casual S. R.; Mch. 23–May 17; Sept. 23–Dec. 28; casual in winter. Boston, common T. V., Apr. 15–May 5; Oct. 5–Nov. 15; rather common S. R., rare in winter. N. Ohio, common T. V., Mch. 21–May 10; Oct. 2–28. Glen Ellyn, common T. V., Mch 18–May 15; Sept. 14–Nov. 7. SE. Minn., common T. V., Mch. 26–May 17; Sept. 13–Nov. 3.

Nest, of moss, coarse grasses, and leaves, lined with rootlets and pine needles, on the ground. *Eggs,* 3–4, greenish blue, of a slightly lighter tint than those of the Wood Thrush, ·88 × ·69. *Date,* Holland Patent, N. Y., May 23; Grand Menan, N. B., May 26.

This Thrush comes to us in the spring, when the woods are still bare, and lingers in the autumn until they are again leafless—the earliest as it is the latest of our Thrushes. It is common on its migrations, but attracts little notice, for, though not really a shy bird, its disposition is retiring, and it is most at home in secluded woodland and thickety retreats. Still, it often finds seclusion enough along shrubby roadsides, and may so far doff its hermit traits as to approach dwellings, where its attractive lightness of motion and ease of manner may be observed from indoors. It frequently descends to the ground, but is soon back again in the branches, making short flights from perch to perch, often with long, quiet pauses in the intervals. It may be known at sight by its habit of lifting its tail slightly, especially after alighting. This action is usually accompanied by the bird's customary note—a low *chuck*, which sounds scarcely thrushlike.

The Hermit Thrush bears high distinction among our song-birds. Its notes are not remarkable for variety or volume, but in purity and sweetness of tone and exquisite modulation they are unequaled. Some, indeed, have deemed the Wood Thrush not inferior; but though the Wood Thrush at its best seems sometimes to touch the very highest chords of bird music, the strains of its wilder cousin, in tranquil clearness

PLATE XXIII

THRUSHES OF THE GENUS HYLOCICHLA
1. Wood Thrush.   3. Olive-backed Thrush.
2. Veery.   4. Gray-cheeked Thrush.
                    5. Hermit Thrush.

A

of tone and exalted serenity of expression, go beyond any woods music we ever hear.

While traveling, the Hermit Thrush is not in full voice, and he who would know its song must follow it to the mossy forests, which are its summer home.   EUGENE P. BICKNELL.

1907. BIRD-LORE, 123 (mig.; pl.).—1910. MCCLINTOCK, N., Auk, 409–418 (nesting).—1918. PERRY, E. M., and W. A., Auk, 316–321 (home-life).

386. OLIVE-BACKED THRUSH. HYLOCICHLA USTULATA SWAINSONI (*Tschudi*). [758a.] (Pl. XXIII.) *Ads.*—Upperparts uniform *olive;* back and tail practically the same color; eye-ring deep *cream-buff*, lores *the same;* whole throat and breast with a *strong* tinge of deep cream-buff or even ochraceous-buff; the feathers of the sides of the throat with wedge-shaped black spots at their tips, those of the breast with rounded black spots at their tips; middle of the belly white; sides brownish gray or brownish ashy. L., 7·17; W., 3·93; T., 2·76; B., ·50.

Remarks.—This bird will be confused only with the Gray-cheeked and Bicknell's Thrushes, from which it differs in the much stronger suffusion of buff on the throat and breast, its buff eye-ring and lores.

Range.—Breeds mainly in lower Hudsonian and Canadian zones from nw. Alaska, nw. Mack., n. Man., cent. Que., and N. F. s. to Kenai Peninsula, Alaska, e. Ore., n. Calif., Nev., Utah, Colo., n. Mich., N. Y., and in mts. from Mass. to Pa. and W. Va.; winters from s. Mex. to Argentina; casual in L. Calif., Cuba and Bermuda.

Washington, common T. V., Apr. 19–June 2; Sept. 2–Nov. 1. Bronx region, common T. V., Apr. 28–June 5; Sept. 3–Oct. 18 (Nov. 3). Boston, common T. V., May 12–28; Sept. 15–Oct. 5. N. Ohio, common T. V., Apr. 22–June 13; Sept. 2–Oct. 24. Glen Ellyn, common T. V., Apr. 23–June 7; Aug. 16–Oct. 24. SE. Minn., common T. V., May 1–June 1; Sept. 3–Oct. 10.

Nest, of coarse grasses, moss, rootlets, leaves and bark, lined with rootlets and grasses, in bushes or small trees, about 4 feet up. *Eggs*, 3–4, greenish blue, more or less spotted and speckled with cinnamon-brown or rufous, ·90 × ·64. *Date*, Upton, Me., June 4.

Passing northward in the spring, in small, silent bands, scattered through the woodland undergrowth, whence they quietly slip away, if disturbed, often to the higher branches of the trees, these birds easily escape observation. In late September or early October their loud, metallic call-notes may be recognized overhead at night, and during the day the birds themselves may be found on the edges of the woods or along tangled hedgerows, associated with Sparrows and other migrants. Their summer home is in the coniferous forest of the North, although they do not confine themselves strictly to the evergreen woods, and, avoiding its depths, seek rather the vicinity of clearings well grown up with firs and spruces. Here, day after day, the same musician may be seen pouring forth his ringing song from some commanding elevation—preferably a dead tree-top. If approached, he promptly dives down into the underbrush, where he is very likely joined by his mate, and both proceed to scold, in a mild way, the chance intruder. Little is ever seen of these shy birds, but fortunately their notes are quite characteristic, and the sole obstacle in distinguishing them from those of the Hermit Thrush, a bird frequenting the same localities, lies in the difficulty of tracing them to their source.

The effect of its loud and beautiful song is much enhanced by the evening hush in which it is most often heard. It lacks the leisurely sweetness of the Hermit Thrush's outpourings, nor is there pause, but in lower key and with greater energy it bubbles on rapidly to a close rather than fading out with the soft melody of its renowned rival. There are also a variety of other notes, the most frequent being a *pŭk* of alarm, pitched higher than a corresponding *cluck* of the Hermit Thrush.　　　　　　　　　　　　　　　　　　　　　　J. DWIGHT, JR.

1907. BIRD-LORE, 122 (mig.; pl.).—1913. STANWOOD, C. J., Wilson Bull., 118–137, illus. (home-life).

387. GRAY-CHEEKED THRUSH. HYLOCICHLA MINIMA ALICIÆ (*Baird*). [757.] (Pl. XXIII.) *Ads.*—Upperparts uniform *olive*, practically no difference between the colors of the back and tail; eye-ring *whitish*, lores *grayish;* middle of the throat and middle of the belly white; sides of the throat and breast with a *very faint* tinge of cream-buff (richer in the fall); the feathers of the sides of the throat spotted with wedge-shaped marks, those of the breast with half-rounded black marks; sides brownish gray or brownish ashy. L., 7·58; W., 4·09; T., 2·96; B., ·55.

Remarks.—The uniform olive of the upperparts of this species at once separates it from our other eastern Thrushes except its subspecies *bicknelli* and the Olive-backed Thrush. From the latter it may be known by the comparative absence of buff on the breast and sides of the throat, by its whitish eye-ring and grayish lores.

Range.—Breeds in Hudsonian Zone in a narrow belt just s. of tree-limit from ne. Siberia, through nw. Alaska, nw. Mack., and n. Man., to cent. Que., and in N. F.; migrates through e. N. A. and along the e. coast of Cent. A. and winters in Colombia, Ecuador, Peru, Venezuela, and British Guiana; w. in migration to Mont., Kans., and Tex.; accidental in Cuba, Greenland, and Helgoland.

Washington, rather common T. V., May 7–June 4; Sept. 1–Oct. 20. Bronx region, common T. V., May 5–June 6; Sept. 9–Oct. 21. Boston, uncommon T. V., May 18–28; Sept. 15–Oct. 9. N. Ohio, not common T. V., Apr. 29–May 23. Glen Ellyn, common T. V., May 1–June 4; Aug. 26–Oct. 14. SE. Minn., common T. V., May 1–June 4; Aug. 22–Sept. 24.

Nest, of grasses, leaves, strips of fine bark, etc., lined with fine grasses, in low trees or bushes. *Eggs*, 4, greenish blue, spotted with rusty brown, ·92 × ·67. *Date*, Ft. Yukon, Alaska, June 9.

The Gray-cheeked and Bicknell's Thrushes differ more widely in name than in anything else. As a matter of fact, they are representatives of one and the same species which, in the northern parts of its range, is somewhat larger than it is in the southern parts of its range. But here the difference stops: the northern bird (*aliciæ*) resembling the southern bird (*minima*) in notes and habits; while the difference between them in size is so slight that during their migrations, where both might be expected to occur together, it would be impossible to say which bird was under observation. During the nesting season, however, it will be safe to call any olive-backed, gray-cheeked Thrush found south of the St. Lawrence, Bicknell's and all to the north of that river the Gray-cheeked.

The Olive-backed Thrush (*swainsoni*) may be distinguished in life from the gray-cheeked bird (*aliciæ* and *minima*) by its buff cheeks and eye-ring; but the identification should be made under favorable conditions and by one familiar with specimens of the birds.

1907. BIRD-LORE, 121 (mig.; pl.).

387a. BICKNELL'S THRUSH. HYLOCICHLA MINIMA MINIMA (*Lafresnaye*). [757*a*.] Similar to the preceding, but smaller. L., 6·25–7·25; W., 3·40–3·80; T., 2·60–2·70; B., ·50–·52 (Ridgway).

Range.—Breeds in Hudsonian and Upper Canadian zones in N. S., mts. of n. N. E., the Catskills and Adirondacks of N. Y., and probably mts. of w. Mass.; migrates through se. U. S. and the Bahamas; winters in Haiti and n. S. A.

Washington, apparently rare T. V., May 14–24; Oct. 3. Bronx region, rare T. V., May 12–24; Sept. 20. Boston, rather common T. V., May 2–30; Sept. 25–Oct. 5.

Nest, essentially like that of *H. u. swainsoni,* both in construction and position. *Eggs,* greener and more finely spotted than those of *swainsoni* (Brewster, Minot's Land Birds and Game Birds, 2d ed., appendix, 468). *Date,* Seal Isl., N. S., June 13 (Thayer Coll.).

"In northern New England Bicknell's Thrush breeds from an altitude of about 3000 feet (scattered pairs may be found lower than this) to the extreme upper limits of tree growth, but most abundantly among the dwarfed, densely matted spruces and balsams which cover such extensive areas on the upper slopes and ridges of our higher mountains. Here, in an atmosphere always cool and ordinarily saturated with moisture from passing clouds, it spends the summer in company with such birds as Swainson's Thrushes, Winter Wrens, Yellow-rumped and Black-poll Warblers, Juncos, White-throated Sparrows, and Yellow-bellied Flycatchers. In many places it is quite as numerous as any of these species, and in certain favored localities it probably outnumbers them all put together. Nevertheless one may spend hours in its chosen haunts without getting a fair view of a single individual, for, despite (or perhaps really because of) the fact that these solitudes are rarely invaded by man, Bicknell's Thrush is, while breeding, one of the very shyest of our smaller birds. . . .

"The song is exceedingly like that of the Veery, having the same ringing, flutelike quality; but it is more interrupted, and it ends differently—the next to the last note dropping a half tone, and the final one rising abruptly and having a sharp emphasis. The ordinary calls are a whistled *pheu* practically identical with that of *H. fuscescens,* a harsh note which recalls the cry of the Night Hawk, a low cluck much like that of the Hermit Thrush, and a *pip* or *peenk* similar to that of Swainson's [=Olive-backed] Thrush. The last is rarely heard" (Brewster, 'Minot's Land and Game Birds,' p. 467).

1882. BICKNELL, E. P., Bull. Nutt. Orn. Club, 152–159.—1883. BREWSTER, W., *Ibid.,* 12–17 (biographical).

388. VEERY. HYLOCICHLA FUSCESCENS FUSCESCENS (*Stephens*). [756.] (Pl. XXIII.) *Ads.*—Upperparts, wings, and tail nearly uniform cinnamon-brown, not so bright as in the Wood Thrush; center of the throat white; sides of the throat and breast with a delicate tinge of cream-buff, spotted with small *wedge-shaped spots of nearly the same color as the back;* belly white; sides white, with *only a faint* tinge of grayish. L., 7·52; W., 3·84; T., 2·87; B., ·53.

Remarks.—The Veery's distinguishing characters are (1) its uniform cinnamon-brown upperparts; (2) its delicately marked breast; and (3) particularly its almost white sides. The Wood Thrush has the sides heavily spotted, and the other Thrushes have this part more or less strongly washed with grayish or brownish.

Range.—Breeds in Lower Canadian and Transition zones from Mich., s. Ont., s. Que., Anticosti, s. to n. Ind., n. O., and N. J., and in the Alleghanies to N. C. and n. Ga.; migrates through Yucatan and Cent. A.; winters in Colombia, British Guiana, and Brazil.

Washington, common T. V., Apr. 9–June 2; Aug. 18–Oct. 1. Bronx region, common S. R., Apr. 27 (12)–Sept. 28. Boston, locally abundant S. R., May 8–Sept. 5. N. Ohio, tolerably common S. R., Apr. 20–Oct. 1. Glen Ellyn, regular but not common T. V., Apr. 24–May 29; Aug. 26–Sept. 11.

Nest, of strips of bark, rootlets, and leaves, wrapped with leaves and lined with rootlets, on or near the ground. *Eggs,* 3–5, greenish blue, of the same shade as those of the Wood Thrush, ·88 × ·65. *Date,* Ossining, N. Y., May 26; Boston, May 28; Farmington, Me., June 2.

The Veery's home is in low, wet, rather densely undergrown woodlands. He is a more retiring bird than the Wood Thrush; he lives nearer the ground and is less likely to leave the cover of his haunts. For this reason, even in localities where both are equally common, the Wood Thrush is more frequently observed.

The Veery's call-notes are a clearly whistled *whèe-o* or *whèe-you,* the first note the higher, and a somewhat softer *too-whee* or *tewèu,* with the first note lower, all of which can be closely imitated. His song is a weird, ringing monotone of blended alto and soprano tones. Neither notes nor letters can tell one of its peculiar quality; it has neither break nor pause, and seems to emanate from no one place. If you can imagine the syllables *vee-r-r-hu* repeated eight or nine times around a series of intertwining circles, the description may enable you to recognize the Veery's song.

The Veery has a double personality, or he may repeat the notes of some less vocally developed ancestor, for on occasions he gives utterance to an entirely uncharacteristic series of *cacking* notes, and even mounts high in the tree to sing a hesitating medley of the same unmusical *cacks,* broken whistled calls, and attempted trills. Fortunately, this performance is comparatively uncommon, and to most of us the Veery is known only by his own strange, unearthly song. His notes touch chords which no other bird's song reaches. The Water-Thrush is inspiring, the Wood and Hermit Thrushes "serenely exalt the spirit," but the Veery appeals to even higher feelings; all the wondrous mysteries of the woods find a voice in his song; he thrills us with emotions we can not express.

1907. BIRD-LORE, 33 (mig.; pl.).

388a. WILLOW THRUSH. HYLOCICHLA FUSCESCENS SALICICOLA *Ridgway.* [756a.] Similar to the preceding, but with the upperparts slightly darker.

Range.—Breeds in Lower Canadian and Transition zones from s. B. C.,

cent. Alberta, cent. Sask., s. Man., and Wisc., apparently also N. F., s. to
cent. Ore., Nev., Utah, n. N. Mex., and cent. Ia.; winters in S. A. to Brazil,
in migration to Ind., Miss., and e. U. S.

Washington, casual T. V., May 7; Sept. 2. Boston, apparently very rare
T. V. Glen Ellyn, tolerably common T. V., May 3–June 4; Aug. 26–Sept. 25.
SE. Minn., common S. R., May 4–Sept. 29.

Nesting-date, se. Minn., May 24.

389. EASTERN BLUEBIRD. SIALIA SIALIS SIALIS (*Linnæus*). [766.]
(Figs. 59, 108*b*.) *Ad.* ♂.—Upperparts, wings, and tail bright blue, tipped
with rusty in the fall; throat, breast, and sides dull cinnamon-rufous; belly
white. *Ad.* ♀.—Upperparts with a grayish tinge; throat, breast, and sides
paler. *Nestling.*—Back spotted with whitish; the breast feathers margined
with fuscous. L., 7·01; W., 3·93; T., 2·58; B., ·47.

Range.—Breeds from Lower Canadian to Lower Austral zones from s.
Man., n. Ont., s. Que., and N. F. s. to cent. and se. Tex., the Gulf Coast, and
s. Fla.; casually w. to base of the Rocky Mts. in Mont., Wyo., and Colo.;
winters most commonly s. of the O. Valley and the Middle States; resident
in Bermuda; accidental in Cuba.

Washington, common P. R. Bronx region, common S. R., frequently
winters; Feb. 6–Dec. 29. Boston, common S. R., Mch. 6–Nov. 1; more
numerous during migrations in Mch. and Nov. N. Ohio, common S. R.,
Feb. 17–Nov. 18; a few winter. Glen Ellyn, not common S. R., Feb. 19–
Nov. 18. SE. Minn., common S. R., Mch. 3–Nov. 10; occasional in winter.

Nest, of grasses, in hollow trees or bird-houses. *Eggs*, 4–6, bluish white,
sometimes plain white, ·85 × ·65. *Date*, Ft. Pierce, Fla., Mch. 17; Mt.
Pleasant, S. C., Mch. 26, small embryos; Boston, Apr. 15; se. Minn., Apr. 10.

A bird so familiar as the Bluebird needs no introduction; in fact,
he seems so at home in our orchards and gardens or about our dwellings
that one wonders what he did for a home before the white man came.

In the winter, it is true, Bluebirds are greater rovers, and one may
see them in the southern states whirling through the woods in large
flocks or feeding on the berries of the mistletoe. But the warmth of
returning spring reminds them of cozy bird-boxes or hospitable pear
or apple trees, and soon we see them inspecting last summer's home,
evidently planning repairs and alterations.

The Bluebird's disposition is typical of all that is sweet and amiable.
His song breathes of love; even his fall call-note—*tùr-wee, tùr-wee*—
is soft and gentle. So associated is his voice with the birth and death
of the seasons that to me his song is freighted with all the gladness of
springtime, while the sad notes of the birds passing southward tell me
more plainly than the falling leaves that the year is dying.

1905. HERRICK, F. H., Home-Life of Wild Birds, 115–121.—1930.
ALLEN, A. A., Bird-Lore, 151–159, illus. (autobiography).

390. GREENLAND WHEATEAR. ŒNANTHE ŒNANTHE LEUCORHOA
(*Gmelin*). [765*a*.] *Ad.* ♂.—Upperparts light gray; forehead and upper tail-
coverts white; cheeks and wings black; the basal two-thirds of the tail white,
the end black; underparts whitish, more or less washed with buffy. *Ad.* ♀.—
Similar, but duller, the black grayer, the white parts more buffy. *Ad. in
winter and Im.*—Upperparts cinnamon-brown, wings edged with lighter;
upper tail-coverts and base of the tail white; end of the tail black, tipped with
buffy; underparts ochraceous-buff. L., 6·25; W., 4·00; T., 2·20; B., ·50.

Range.—Breeds in Arctic Zone from Ellesmere Land and Boothia Peninsula e. to Greenland and Iceland, and s. to n. Que.; winters in W. Africa,

migrating through the British Isles and France; casual in migration to
Keewatin, Ont., N. B., Que., N. Y., Pa., Bermuda, La., and Cuba.
Boston, A. V.

Nest, of moss and grasses, usually in crevices among rocks. *Eggs*, 4–7,
bluish white, ·81 × ·59. *Date*, Holsteinborg, Greenland, June 8.

This European species is a common summer resident in Greenland.
It has been found nesting in Labrador, and there is evidence of its
having bred at Godbout, Province of Quebec (Merriam, *The Auk*, 1885,
p. 305; Comeau, *Ibid.*, 1890, p. 294). South of these points it is of accidental occurrence.

Mr. Saunders writes: "From early spring onward the Wheatear is
to be seen, jerking its white tail as it flits along, uttering its sharp *chack,
chack*, on open downs, warrens, and the poorer land; ascending the
mountains almost to the highest summits. . . .

"The song of the male is rather pretty, and the bird also displays
considerable powers of imitating other species."

391. TOWNSEND'S SOLITAIRE, *Myadestes townsendi* (Audubon), [754],
of western North America, is of accidental occurrence in Illinois and
New York.

FAMILY SYLVIIDÆ. OLD-WORLD WARBLERS, KINGLETS, AND GNATCATCHERS.

No generally accepted classification of the birds of this family has as
yet been proposed, but for our present purposes they may be divided
into three subfamilies: (1) The *Sylviinæ*, or Old-World Warblers, numbering over 500 species and subspecies, confined exclusively to the
Old World, with the exception of one species found in Alaska; (2) the
Regulinæ, or Kinglets, of which 2 of the 7 known species are found in
the New World; (3) the *Polioptilinæ*, or Gnatcatchers, an American
group containing about 15 species and subspecies 7 of which are found
in the United States.

The Old-World Warblers are generally dull, olivaceous birds with
ten, instead of the nine, primaries of our Warblers, with which, indeed,
they have no close relationship. Many of the species are highly musical,
whence the origin of the family name, a misfit when applied to the New-
World Warblers, to which it was given because of their superficial
resemblance to the Old-World forms, rather than for their musical en-
dowments. The Kinglets and Gnatcatchers are typically represented
by the species described below.

KEY TO THE SPECIES

A. With a bright-colored crest.
　　a. Crest ruby, without black　.　.　394. RUBY-CROWNED KINGLET, ♂ ad.
　　b. Crest yellow, or orange and yellow, bordered by black.
　　　　　　　　　　　　　　　393. GOLDEN-CROWNED KINGLET.
B. Without a colored crest.
　　a. Back ashy blue; outer tail-feathers white. 392. BLUE-GRAY GNATCATCHER.
　　b. Back olive-green; no white in tail. 394. RUBY-CROWNED KINGLET, ♀ and im.

392. BLUE-GRAY GNATCATCHER. Polioptila cærulea cærulea (*Linnæus*). [751.] (Fig. 109b.) *Ad.* ♂.—Upperparts bluish gray; forehead and front of the head narrowly bordered by black; wings edged with grayish, the secondaries bordered with whitish; outer tail-feathers white, changing gradually until the middle ones are black; underparts dull grayish white. *Ad.* ♀.— Similar, but without the black on the head. L., 4·50; W., 2·05; T., 2·00; B., ·40.

Range.—Breeds in Lower and Upper Austral zones from e. Nebr. and s. parts of Wisc., Mich., and Ont., and sw. Pa., Md., and s. N. J. s. to s. Tex. and cent. Fla.; winters from s. Tex., Gulf States, and S. C. (rarely Va.) to the Bahamas and Cuba and through e. Mex. to Yucatan and Guatemala; casual n. to se. Minn., N. E., and N. Y.

Washington, rather common S. R., Mch. 6–Nov. 23. Bronx region, rare visitant between Apr. 15–Oct. 11. Boston, A. V. N. Ohio, common S. R., Apr. 20–Sept. 15. Glen Ellyn, rare S. R., Apr. 22–Aug. 20; possibly later. SE. Minn., rare S. R., Apr. 18–Aug. 23.

Nest, of tendrils, fine strips of bark, and fine grasses firmly interwoven and covered externally with lichens, on a horizontal branch or in a crotch, 10–60, usually 30 feet up. *Eggs*, 4–5, bluish white, thickly spotted and speckled with cinnamon-, rufous-brown, or umber, ·56 × ·46. *Date*, Mt. Pleasant, S. C., Apr. 17; Iredell Co., N. C., May 6.

The Blue-gray Gnatcatcher frequents rather densely foliaged trees, generally in the woods, showing a preference for the upper branches. He is a bird of strong character, and always seems to me like a miniature Mockingbird with some of the habits of Kinglets. His exquisitely finished song is quite as remarkable as the ordinary performance of his large prototype, but is possessed of so little volume as to be inaudible unless one is quite near the singer. His characteristic call-note—a rather sudden *ting*, like the twang of a banjo-string—can be heard at a greater distance.

1915. Bird-Lore, 201, 203 (mig.; pl.).

393. GOLDEN-CROWNED KINGLET. Regulus satrapa satrapa *Lichtenstein.* [748.] (Fig. 128.) *Ad.* ♂.—Center of crown bright reddish orange, bordered by yellow and black; a whitish line over the eye; rest of upperparts olive-green; wings and tail fuscous, margined with olive-green; tail slightly forked; underparts soiled .whitish. *Ad.* ♀.—Similar, but crown without orange, its center bright yellow, bordered on each side by black. L., 4·07; W., 2·14; T., 1·75; B., ·28.

Range.—Breeds in Boreal zones from cent. Alberta, s. Que., and Cape Breton Isl. s. to Mich., N. Y., and mts. of Mass., and in the higher Alleghanies s. to N. C.; winters from Ia. (casually Minn.), Ont., and N. B. to n. Fla. and Tamaulipas, ne. Mex.

Fig. 128. Golden-crowned Kinglet. (Natural size.)

Washington, abundant W. V., Sept. 20–Apr. 27. Bronx region, common T. V. and fairly common in winter; Sept. 10–May 15. Boston, very common T. V., not uncommon W. V., Sept. 25–Apr. 20; very rare S. R. N. Ohio, common W. V., Sept. 26–May 4. Glen Ellyn, common T. V., irregular W. V., Sept. 19–May 8. SE. Minn., common T. V., Mch. 19–May 16; Sept. 21–Nov. 29; rare W. V.

Nest, generally pensile, of green mosses, lined with fine strips of soft inner bark, fine black rootlets, and feathers, in coniferous trees, 6–60 feet from the ground. *Eggs*, 9–10, creamy white to muddy cream-color, speckled and blotched with pale wood-brown, and rarely, faint lavender, ·55 × ·44. (See Brewster, Auk, 1888, 337.) *Date*, Grand Menan, N. B., May 24.

This Kinglet resembles in habits its ruby-crowned cousin, with which during the migrations it is frequently associated. Its notes, however, are quite unlike those of that species, its usual call-note being a fine, high *ti-ti*, audible only to practiced ears. In his extended account of the nesting habits of this species, as observed by him in Worcester County, Mass. (*The Auk*. l. c.), Mr. Brewster writes that its song "begins with a succession of five or six fine, shrill, high-pitched,somewhat faltering notes, and ends with a short, rapid, rather explosive warble. The opening notes are given in a rising key, but the song falls rapidly at the end. The whole may be expressed as follows: *tzee, tzee, tzee, tzee, ti, ti, ter, ti-ti-ti-ti*."

Muffled in its thick coat of feathers, the diminutive Goldcrest braves our severest winters, living evidence that, given an abundance of food, temperature is a secondary factor in a bird's existence.

1915. BIRD-LORE, 118, 126 (mig.; pl.).

394. EASTERN RUBY-CROWNED KINGLET. CORTHYLIO CALENDULA CALENDULA (*Linnæus*). [749.] (Fig. 109a.) *Ad.* ♂.—Crown with a partly concealed crest of bright red; rest of upperparts grayish olive-green, brighter on the rump; wings and tail fuscous, edged with olive-green; two whitish wing-bars; tail slightly forked, the middle feathers shortest; underparts soiled whitish, more or less tinged with buffy. *Ad.* ♀ *and Im.*—Similar, but without the red crown-patch. L., 4·41; W., 2·24; T., 1·73; B., ·29.

Remarks.—Females and young are warblerlike in general appearance, but note the short first primary, barely one inch in length.

Range.—Breeds in Boreal zones from nw. Alaska, nw. Mack., n. Man. and w. cent. Que., to s. Ariz., cent. N. Mex., n. Ont., N. B., and N. S. (casually Me.). Winters from s. B. C., Ia., and Va. (casually farther n.) s. over the U. S. and the Mex. tableland to Guatemala and in L. Calif.; accidental in Greenland.

Washington, abundant T. V., Mch. 20–May 17; Sept. 17–Nov. 9; occasionally winters. Bronx region, common T. V., occasional in winter; Mch. 20–May 21; Sept. 14–Dec. Boston, rather common T. V., Apr. 12–May 5; Oct. 10–30. N. Ohio, common T. V., Apr. 1–May 23; Sept. 9–Nov. 3. Glen Ellyn, fairly common T. V., Mch. 22–June 8; Sept. 9–Nov. 21. SE. Minn., T. V., Mch. 12–May 27; Sept. 8–Nov. 1; rare W. V.

Nest, usually semipensile, of moss and fine strips of bark, neatly interwoven, lined with feathers, in coniferous trees, 12–30 feet from the ground. *Eggs*, 5–9, dull whitish or pale buffy, faintly speckled or spotted with pale brown, chiefly at the larger end, ·55 × ·43 (Davie). *Date*, Boulder Co., Colo., June 3.

When the leaves begin to turn you will notice numerous very small, olive-green birds flitting about the terminal twigs of the trees and lower growth, in the woods, orchards, or hedgerows. They resemble Warblers, but are much tamer—you can almost touch them—and have a habit of nervously flitting their wings every few seconds, perhaps accompanying the action by a wrenlike, scolding note. You will not often hear them sing at this season, and there is little in their voice or appearance to tell you that they are among the most famous of feathered songsters.

The May morning when first I heard this Kinglet's song is among the most memorable of my early ornithological experiences. The bird was in the tree-tops in the most impassable bit of woods near my home. The longer and more eagerly I followed the unseen singer the greater the mystery became. It seemed impossible that a bird which I supposed was at least as large as a Bluebird could escape observation in the partly leaved trees. The song was mellow and flutelike, and loud enough to be heard several hundred yards; an intricate warble past imitation or description, and rendered so admirably that I never hear it now without feeling an impulse to applaud. The bird is so small, the song so rich and full, that one is reminded of a chorister with the voice of an adult soprano. To extend the comparison, one watches this gifted but unconscious musician flitting about the trees with somewhat the feeling that one observes the choir-boy doffing his surplice and joining his comrades for a game of tag.

1915. BIRD-LORE, 121, 126 (mig.; pl.).

FAMILY MOTACILLIDÆ. WAGTAILS AND PIPITS.

Of the over 125 species and subspecies included in this family, only about 15 are American, the remainder being distributed throughout the Old World. A single Wagtail (*Motacilla flava alascensis*) breeds in Alaska, and two species of Pipits (*Anthus*) inhabit North America, the remaining American members of this genus being scattered from Panama to Patagonia.

Wagtails are found about the borders of streams and where there is more or less vegetation, while the Pipits are more larklike and usually inhabit an open, treeless country. Both Wagtails and Pipits are eminently terrestrial. They walk or run, instead of hop, rarely (with one or two exceptions) if ever alight in trees, sing on the wing, the Pipits ascending much the higher, and nest on the ground, and both have a pronounced habit of tail-wagging.

395. The EUROPEAN WHITE WAGTAIL, *Motacilla alba alba* Linnæus, [694], is accidental in Greenland and Ungava.

396. AMERICAN PIPIT. ANTHUS SPINOLETTA RUBESCENS (*Turnstall*). [697.] (Fig. 110.) *Ads. in winter.*—Outer tail-feather largely white, next one or two white-tipped. Above warm grayish brown; wing-coverts tipped with whitish or buffy; longest tertial longer than fifth primary; a whitish or buffy line over eye; below buffy (whitish just before spring molt) breast and sides streaked with fuscous; *hind toe-nail longest, as long as or longer than its toe.* After spring molt upperparts grayer, underparts more pinkish buff, but these colors fade as breeding season advances. L., 6·38; W., 3·50; T., 2·69; B., ·47.

Range.—Breeds in Arctic Zone from ne. Siberia, n. Alaska to Greenland s. to Great Slave Lake, n. Man., cent. Que., and N. F., and from the Aleutian Isls. to Prince William Sound, and on high mts. s. to Ore. and N. Mex.; winters from n. Calif. and the O. and lower Del. valleys to the Gulf Coast, L. Calif. and Guatemala; casual in Bermuda; accidental in Helgoland.

Washington, W. V., sometimes abundant, Oct. 1–May 14. Bronx region, common T. V., Feb. 22–May 15; Sept. 18–Jan. 30. Boston, T. V., common, Sept. 20–Nov. 10; rare Apr. 10–May 20. N. Ohio, common T. V., Apr. 6–May 26; Oct. 19. Glen Ellyn, not common T. V., Apr. 15–?; Sept. 19–Oct. 18. SE. Minn., uncommon T. V., Apr. 16–May 15; Sept. 19–Oct. 31.

Nest, of grasses, on the ground. *Eggs*, 4–6, bluish white or grayish white, thickly and evenly speckled with cinnamon- or vinaceous-brown, ·78 × ·57. *Date*, Whale River, Lab., June 20.

Large, open tracts in the vicinity of the coast are the localities in which Pipits are most common, but they are also found in numbers in old fields, meadows, and pastures inland. A recently burned or newly plowed field is a good place in which to look for them. Once seen, there is little difficulty in identifying these graceful *walkers*, as they run on before you, or with constantly wagging tail await your approach. The individuals of a flock are generally scattered over a varying space while feeding, but when flushed they rise together and, with a soft *dee-dee, dee-dee,* mount high in the air as though bound for parts unknown, but often, after hovering above you for several seconds in an undecided way, they will return to or near the place from which they rose. Their flight is light and airy, and in loose companies they undulate gently through the air without apparent effort, uttering their faint *dee-dee* as they fly.

The Pipit's song is delivered in the air both as he mounts to and descends from a height of as much as two hundred feet. To me it sounds like the ringing of a little bell. Townsend ('Along the Labrador Coast,' p. 52) describes it as *"che-whèe, che-whèe,"* with a vibratory resonance on the *whee.*"

1916. BIRD-LORE, 240 (pl.).

397. The MEADOW PIPIT, *Anthus pratensis* (Linnæus), [698], of Europe is accidental in Greenland.

398. **SPRAGUE'S PIPIT.** ANTHUS SPRAGUEI (*Audubon*). [700.] Hind toe-nail longer than its toe. *Ads.*—Above grayish brown *widely margined with buffy or ashy;* tail fuscous, two outer feathers largely white, wings browner with two indistinct bars; below white, buff-tinged, a band of streaks across the breast. L., 6·25; W., 3·30; T., 2·40; B., ·50.

Range.—Interior plains. Breeds in Transition Zone from w. cent. Sask. and s. Man. s. to w. Mont. and N. Dak.; winters from Tex., s. La., and s. Miss. through e. and cent. Mex. to Vera Cruz, Puebla, and Michoacan; casual in Ga., S. C., and Fla.

Nest, of grasses on the ground. *Eggs*, 3–5, grayish white, thickly and finely speckled with blackish and purplish.

This species appears to be of rare but more or less regular occurrence on the coast of South Carolina and Georgia. In general habits it resembles the Pipit, but its song appears to be far more noteworthy than the vocal effort of that species. Seton ('Birds of Manitoba') writes that the song, which is delivered from a height of 500 feet or more, is loud and ventriloquial. "At the beginning it is much like that of the English Skylark, and the notes are uttered deliberately but continuously, and soon increase in rapidity and force till in a few seconds the climax is reached, after which they fade away in a veerylike strain, and then suddenly stop."

FAMILY BOMBYCILLIDÆ. WAXWINGS.

Of the three known species of Waxwings, one (*Bombycilla garrula*) is common to the northern parts of both the Old and New Worlds; one (*B. cedrorum*) is found only in America, and one (*B. japonica*) is restricted to eastern Asia. Our Waxwings are notable for the irregularity of their migrations or wanderings, and *B. cedrorum* for the lateness of its nesting season. Their voice is doubtless the least developed in the group of our so-called singing birds.

399. BOHEMIAN WAXWING. BOMBYCILLA GARRULA PALLIDICEPS *Reichenow.* [618.] *Ads.*—Forehead, chin, and line through the eye velvety black; a conspicuous crest; front of crown chestnut-rufous; upperparts rich grayish brown; upper tail-coverts, wings, and tail grayish; primary coverts and secondaries *tipped with white*, the latter with small, red, seed-shaped sealing-wax-like tips; all but the outer primaries tipped with *yellow* or *white* on the outer web; end of tail with a yellow band; breast like the back, grayer on the belly; under tail-coverts *chestnut-rufous.* L., 8·00; W., 4·60; T., 2·60; B. from N., ·29.

Range.—Breeds from w. Alaska to n. Mack. and ne. Man., s. to s. B. C. and s. Alberta; winters e. to N. S. and s. irregularly to Pa., O., Ind., Ills., Kans., Colo. and Calif.; casual in Ariz.

Bronx region, very rare W. V., Feb. 1924 (collected); several recent sight records. Boston, very rare and irregular W. V., Sept.–Mch. N. Ohio, occasional W. V. Glen Ellyn, one record, Jan. 22, 1908. SE. Minn., irregular W. V., Oct. 9–Apr. 26.

FIG. 129. Bohemian Waxwing.

Nest, of twigs, roots, moss, etc., in trees. *Eggs,* similar in color to those of *B. cedrorum,* ·92 × ·65. *Date,* Cariboo, B. C., June 15.

The distribution of this bird in the United States is not unlike that of the Evening Grosbeak. It is exceedingly rare and irregular in the Atlantic States, but occurs with some frequency in the northern Mississippi Valley. In habits, it is said to resemble its small cousin, the Cedar Waxwing. Its voice is described as a "chatter" and a "wooden, unmusical trill."

1909. ANDERSON, R. M., Auk, 10–12 (nesting).—1918. BIRD-LORE, 219, 223 (mig.; pl.).—1921. WRIGHT, H. W., Auk, 59–78 (in New England).

400. CEDAR WAXWING. BOMBYCILLA CEDRORUM *Vieillot.* [619.] (Fig. 111.) *Ads.*—Forehead, chin, and a line through the eye velvety black; a conspicuous crest; upperparts rich grayish brown; upper tail-coverts, wings, and tail gray; secondaries often, tail rarely, with small, red, seed-shaped, sealing-wax-like tips; tail with a yellow band at its end; breast like the back, changing gradually into yellowish on the belly; under tail-coverts *white.* The absence of the red tips is doubtless an indication of immaturity. The nestling is streaked below. L., 7·19; W., 3·70; T., 2·37; B. from N., ·26.

Range.—Breeds from cent. B. C., n. Ont., and Cape Breton Isl. s. to nw.

Calif., Kans., n. Ark., N. C. and n. Ga.; winters throughout nearly all of the U. S. and s. to Cuba, Mex., L. Calif., and Panama; accidental in the Bahamas, Bermuda, Jamaica, and British Isles.

Washington, common P. R., less so in winter. Bronx region, common T. V., uncommon S. R., occasional in winter; Apr. 27–Dec. 28. Boston, not common P. R., common S. R., abundant T. V. in spring, Feb. 1–Apr. 25. N. Ohio, common P. R. Glen Ellyn, S. R., Jan. 21–Sept. 24; occasional W. V. SE. Minn., common S. R., Feb. 25–Sept. 28; frequent W. R.

Nest, bulky, of strips of bark, leaves, grasses, twigs, rootlets, moss and sometimes mud, lined with finer materials of the same nature, often in fruit or shade trees, 5–20 feet up. *Eggs*, 3–5, pale bluish gray or putty color, distinctly and obscurely spotted with black or umber, ·88 × ·62. *Date*, Weaverville, N. C., May 30; Boston, June 6; se. Minn., June 10.

When the spring migration is over and the home-birds have gone to nest-building, small flocks of Goldfinches and Waxwings—two peculiarly gentle, attractive birds—may still be seen wandering about the country. The squads of Cedar-birds fly evenly, on a level with the tree-tops, in close ranks, often of five, seven, or nine. Frequently, when under full headway, they suddenly wheel and dive down to an apple tree for a meal of canker-worms.

In following the beautiful Waxwings about, one listens in vain for a song, but soon comes to relish their two peculiar calls—a hushed whistle and the subdued call Thoreau describes as their "beady note," a succession of short notes strung together—for they both seem to harmonize with the quiet reserve of the delicately tinted birds.

In July, when the wandering flocks are no longer seen, a walk through the neighboring orchards may show where both tardy builders have at last gone to nesting, and few bird homes afford pictures of such human tenderness and devotion. If there is an evergreen in the vicinity, the Cedar-bird mounts guard upon its tip, but occasionally relieves the monotony of his watch by flying up in the air for light luncheons of passing insects.

The strong individuality of the Waxwings makes them interesting birds to the field student. The use of their crests in expressing emotion, and the protective attitudes they assume when watched at their nests, throw much light upon bird psychology.

To the bird-lover, however, the Cedar-birds have their own attraction; their proverbially gentle, refined ways make them seem superior creatures of the air to whom he can but yield his affection.

I shall never forget a pair that I once found by a clear mountain lake. They were perched upon two evergreen spires that guarded a silent bay, whose dark water was gilded by the lingering light of the setting sun. FLORENCE MERRIAM BAILEY.

1905. HERRICK, F. H., Home Life of Wild Birds, 36–38, 86–102.—1911. SAUNDERS, A. A., Auk, 323–329 (nesting).—1916. POST, K. C., Wilson Bull., 175–193 (during July and August).—1918. BIRD-LORE, 220, 223 (mig.; pl.). —1930. ALLEN, A. A., Bird-Lore, 298–307; illus. (autobiography).

FAMILY LANIIDÆ. SHRIKES.

The number of species ascribed to this family by different authors varies widely, few agreeing as to exactly what subfamilies should be admitted. The true Shrikes, however, of the subfamily *Laniinæ*, numbering over 90 species and subspecies, are a well-defined group, of which 8 (2 species) occur in the New World. Their habits, in the main, conform to those of our species.

401. NORTHERN SHRIKE. LANIUS BOREALIS BOREALIS *Vieillot.*
[621.] *Ads.*—Upperparts gray; wings and tail black; primaries white at the base, secondaries tipped with white or grayish; outer, sometimes all, the tail-feathers tipped with white, the outer feather mostly white; forehead *whitish;* lores *grayish* black; ear-coverts black; underparts white, generally finely barred with black; bill hooked and hawklike. *Im.*—Similar, but entire plumage more or less heavily barred or washed with grayish brown. L., 10·32; W., 4·55; T., 4·00; B. from N., ·55.
Range.—Breeds in the Hudsonian Zone and locally in the Canadian from n. Ungava to s. Ont., and s. Que., w. at least to the e. side of Hudson Bay. Winters s. to Ky., Va., and N. C. (casually).
Washington, rare and irregular W. V., Oct.–Feb. Bronx region, irregular W. V., Oct. 26–Apr. 22. Boston, irregular W. V., sometimes rather common, Oct. 15–Apr. 15. N. Ohio, not common W. V., Nov. 6–Apr. 3. Glen Ellyn, rare W. V., Oct. 24–June 5. SE. Minn., common W. V., Oct. 17–Apr. 14.
Nest, of twigs, grasses, etc., in low trees or bushes. *Eggs,* similar in color to those of *L. ludovicianus,* 1·05 × ·76. *Date,* Ft. Anderson, Mack., June 11.

This bird may be known at once by his colors—gray, black, and white,—by the consternation his appearance causes among the Sparrows, and by his peculiar flight, which is steady and straightforward, with much flapping, and close to the ground till he nears his intended perch, which is reached at the last moment by a sudden upward turn.

He is so well known as a bird of hawklike, sanguinary character that most students are astonished when they find out that toward springtime he develops into a vocalist of no mean powers. Often in the warm days of March he may be heard singing on the top of some tall tree, a song that would do credit to a Catbird—indeed, it recalls strongly that loquacious songster. He is, I think, a better singer than his southern cousin, but resembles him in habitually impaling his prey on a thorn, a fence barb, or a forked twig. His food consists chiefly of mice, noxious insects, and the equally noxious English Sparrow, so that the Shrike is a bird worthy of all protection.

ERNEST THOMPSON SETON.

1918. BIRD-LORE, 286, 290 (mig.; pl.).—1928. FLOYD, C. B., Bull. Northeastern Bird-Banding Assoc., 43–49 (winter habits).

402. LOGGERHEAD SHRIKE. LANIUS LUDOVICIANUS LUDOVICIANUS *Linnæus.* [622.] *Ads.*—Upperparts gray, wings and tail black, primaries white at the base, secondaries tipped with white; outer, sometimes all, the tail-feathers tipped with white; the outer feather mostly white; lores *black,* connected by a narrow *black* line on the forehead at the base of the bill; ear-coverts black; underparts white, sometimes tinged with gray.

L., 9·00; W., 3·82; T., 3·87; B. from N., ·48; depth of B. at N., ·35 (average of nine Florida specimens).

Range.—Lower Austral Zone of the Atlantic and Gulf States from s. N. C. to s. Fla. and w. to cent. La.

Nest, of strips of bark, small twigs, and vegetable fibers, lined with grasses, in thorny hedges or low trees, about 7 feet up. *Eggs*, 3–5, dull white or creamy white, thickly marked with cinnamon-brown and lavender, ·98 × ·78. *Date*, Archer, Fla., Mch. 10.

Like some of the Hawks and Flycatchers, the Loggerhead does not search for his prey, but waits for it to come within striking distance. It is of importance, therefore, that his perch should command an uninterrupted view of his surroundings. For this reason one rarely or never sees a Shrike *in* a tree, but always on its outermost or highest branches. He will fly directly toward its center, but just as he reaches it swing up and light on its top. He also selects telegraph wires, peaks of houses, and especially the apex of a lightning-rod or weather-vane.

From his point of vantage he maintains a constant outlook for any unsuspecting grasshopper, small snake, or lizard which may appear below. The distance at which he can detect these gives evidence of his power of sight. I have seen Shrikes fly 50 yards with the evident object of capturing a grasshopper which they undoubtedly saw before starting.

Like the Butcher-bird, the Loggerhead frequently impales its prey on a convenient thorn or spike. Doubtless this habit aids him in dissecting his food, but I do not think that he does it for this reason alone. The bird's vigilance, like that of the waiting Hawk, is probably attended by varying results. One hour may yield excellent returns, the next may be fruitless. But under any circumstances he cannot resist taking advantage of an opportunity to secure food. Sometimes the opportunities exceed the demands of his stomach, and then, after capturing his unfortunate victim, he simply impales and leaves it.

If perseverance deserved success, the Loggerhead would take high rank as a songster. But his notes are harsh and unmusical. They consist of a series of guttural gurgles, squeaky whistles, and shrill pipes, some of which might be attributed to the creaking weather-vanes he so often chooses as a perch.

1918. BIRD-LORE, 288, 290 (mig.; pl.).

402a. MIGRANT SHRIKE. LANIUS LUDOVICIANUS MIGRANS *W. Palmer.* [622e.] (Fig. 112.) Similar to *L. l. ludovicianus* but paler above and somewhat grayer below; the bill smaller, the wing longer, 3·90.

Range.—Breeds chiefly in Transition and Upper Austral zones from se. Man., Wisc., Mich., s. Ont., s. Que., Me., and N. B. s. to ne. Tex., e. Okla., Ark., s. Ills., Ky., w. N. C., and Miss., and interior of Va. (locally in the e.); winters chiefly in the Miss. Valley and Tex., irregularly n. to s. N. E.

Washington, not rare P. R. Bronx region, irregular T. V., mostly in fall; one probable breeding record; Aug. 4–Nov. 12 (Dec. 16; Apr. 21 and 24). Boston, rare T. V., Apr.; Sept.–Nov. N. Ohio, tolerably common S. R. Mch. 10–Nov. 1. Glen Ellyn, formerly fairly common S. R., now only isolated pairs., Mch. 2–Sept. 29. SE. Minn., common S. R., Mch. 15–Oct. 29.

Nesting-date, Auburn, N. Y., May 11; se. Minn., Apr. 7.

FAMILY STURNIDÆ. STARLINGS.

The over 70 species and subspecies of true Starlings are distributed throughout the Old World except in Australia and New Guinea. The only American representative of the group was introduced into this country in 1890.

403. STARLING. STURNUS VULGARIS VULGARIS *Linnæus.* [493.] (Fig. 113.) *Ads. in summer.*—Metallic purplish or greenish; feathers of the upperparts all tipped with cream-buff spots, feathers of the underparts marked only on the sides; lower belly and under tail-coverts, wings, and tail dark brownish gray, edged with cream-buff; *bill yellow. Ads. and Im. in winter.*—Similar, but the upperparts heavily spotted with brownish cream-buff; the entire underparts heavily spotted with white; *bill blackish brown.* L., 8·50; W., 5·10; T., 2·50.

Range.—W. and cent. Europe; winters s. to Africa; accidental in Greenland; introduced in 1890 in N. Y. C. and thence has spread as far n. as N. B., sw. Que., se. Ont., w. to Kans. and Okla., and s. to Tex. and Fla.

Washington, abundant P. R. Bronx region, abundant P. R., first noted May 9, 1891. Boston, abundant P. R. N. Ohio, common P. R. Glen Ellyn, possibly P. R.

FIG. 130. Starling; Summer Plumage. (Reduced.)

Nest, of grasses, twigs, etc., in a crevice in a building or hollow tree. *Eggs,* 4–6, pale bluish, 1·20 × ·86. *Date,* Englewood, N. J., May 15, young on wing.

Starlings are walkers, not hoppers, and, aside from their color, may be known by their long, pointed wings, rather long and (as compared with our other black birds) slender bill, and short, square tail. They were introduced into this country by Eugene Schieffelin, who also imported one of the early shipments of House or 'English' Sparrows. Sixty Starlings were released in Central Park, New York City, in 1890, and 40 more in 1891. From these 100 birds (other introductions having failed) have descended the innumerable Starlings now occupying the greater part of the United States east of the plains. While they are to be classed as permanent residents, there are pronounced seasonal fluctuations in their numbers. About New York City the Starling is one of the earliest Passerine birds to nest, and the harsh, grating food-call of the young may be heard by May 15. A second brood may be raised, but in the latter part of May the young of the first brood begin to form the flocks which in late summer number thousands of individuals. Their striking aërial evolutions are now one of the features of the season and admirably illustrate that unity of spirit which controls the movements of large bodies of birds of the same species.

The call of the male Starling is a high, clear, rather long-drawn whistle which may be easily imitated. This appears in its song which, usually delivered from a high perch and with flittings of the half-open wings, is a choking, gasping, guttural soliloquy, with imitations of the notes of other birds interspersed. The flocking chorus is an indescribable chattering.

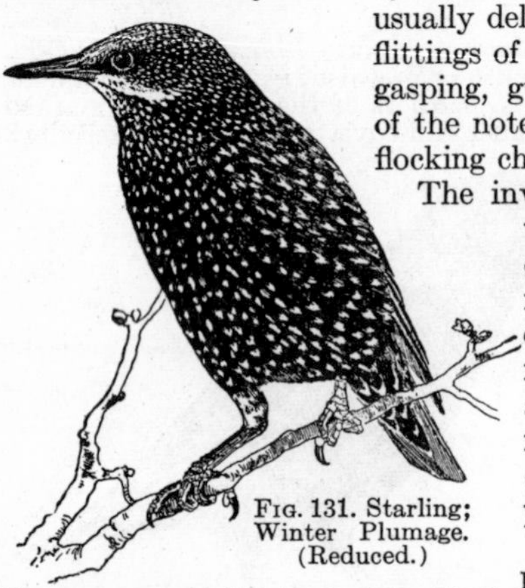

The investigations of the Biological Survey show that, so far as its food is concerned, the Starling is a beneficial species. But aside from its occupation of the nesting-sites of native species, every one to whom a bird is an expression of Nature must resent the presence of a species, which, as an alien, is out of place in our fauna.

Fig. 131. Starling; Winter Plumage. (Reduced.)

1920. BIRD-LORE, 213, 216 (mig.; pl.).—1921. KALMBACH, E. R. and GABRIELSON, I. N., Bull. 868, U. S. Dept. Agric., 66 pp., illus. (economic value).—1922. KALMBACH, E. R., Auk, 189–195, A Comparison of the Food Habits of British and American Starlings.—1925.—CHAPMAN, F M., Nat. Hist., 480–485 (as an American citizen).—1927. LEWIS, H. F., Biol. Bull. 30, Univ. of Toronto, 57 pp. (economic value).—1928. COOKE, M. T., U. S. Dept. Agric. Circular No. 40, 1–9, illus. (spread in North America).

FAMILY VIREONIDÆ. VIREOS.

The Vireos, numbering about 150 species and subspecies (75 species), are peculiar to America. Most of them are confined to tropical America, only 12 species reaching the United States where, except along our southern boundaries, they are migratory.

Vireos are for the most part arboreal, though several species haunt the lower, rather than the higher growth. For small, insect-eating birds they are rather slow in their movements. We do not see them darting out after insects as do the Flycatchers, nor do they flit through the foliage after the manner of many Warblers, but patiently glean their food from the under surfaces of leaves, crevices in the bark, etc., often singing as they work. They are more musical than the small Warblers; all our species have pleasing songs, and some of them are especially gifted. Their nests are neatly constructed cups suspended from the arms of a forked branch.

1925. CHAPIN, E. A., Food Habits, Bull. 1355, U. S. Dept. Agric.

A. With distinct white or yellowish white wing-bars.
  a. Eye-ring or line from eye to bill yellow.
    a¹. Throat and breast bright yellow; rump gray.
           406. YELLOW-THROATED VIREO.
    a². Underparts white or whitish; sides and sometimes breast washed
      with greenish yellow; rump olive-green.
          404, 404*a, b.* WHITE-EYED VIREOS.
  b. Eye-ring and line from eye to bill white.
    b¹. Head lead-blue; wing over 2·50.
        407. BLUE-HEADED VIREO. 407*a.* MOUNTAIN VIREO.
    b². Head grayish, nearly like back; wing under 2·50.
          405. BELL'S VIREO (Illinois).
B. Without white wing-bars.
  a. Underparts yellowish; first primary as long as fifth.
          411. PHILADELPHIA VIREO.
  b. Underparts white; *sides* washed with yellowish; first primary ·75 long.
          412. WARBLING VIREO.
  c. Underparts white, with little if any yellowish on sides; head with a
    lead-gray cap, bordered by narrow black lines over the eye.
      410. RED-EYED VIREO. 408. BLACK-WHISKERED VIREO.

404. WHITE-EYED VIREO. VIREO GRISEUS GRISEUS (*Boddaert*).
[631.] *Ads.*—Upperparts, including upper *tail-coverts*, bright olive-green,
more or less washed with grayish; greater and middle wing-coverts tipped
with yellowish white, forming two distinct wing-bars; outer web of tertials
edged with whitish; *lores* and eye-ring yellow; throat white or whitish; belly
white; breast and sides washed with greenish yellow; iris white, hazel in the
young. L., 5·27; W., 2·37; T., 1·95; B. from N., ·29.
    Range.—Breeds chiefly in Austral zones from se. Nebr., s. Wisc., N. Y.,
and Mass. to cent. Tex. and s. Fla.; winters from Tex. and S. C. through
e. Mex. to Yucatan and Guat.; casual n. to Vt., Ont., N. B., and in Cuba.
    Washington, common S. R., Apr. 10–Oct. 28. Bronx region, fairly com-
mon S. R., Apr. 29–Oct. 3. Boston, formerly rather common local S. R.,
May 8–Sept. 20, now rare. N. Ohio, casual in spring. Glen Ellyn, rare,
spring only, May 11–June 1.
    Nest, generally similar to that of *V. olivaceus*, suspended from a forked
branch in thickets. *Eggs*, 3–4, white, with a few specks of black, umber, or
rufous-brown at the larger end, ·75 × ·55. *Date*, Chatham Co., Ga., Apr. 22;
Ossining, N. Y., May 27; Boston, June 1; Mt. Carmel, Ills., May 11.

    If birds are ever impertinent, I believe this term might with truth
be applied to that most original, independent dweller in thickety undergrowths, the White-eyed Vireo. Both his voice and manner say that
he doesn't in the least care what you think of him; and if, attracted
by his peculiar notes or actions, you pause near his haunts, he jerks
out an abrupt "Who are you, eh?" in a way which plainly indicates
that your presence can be dispensed with. If this hint is insufficient,
he follows it by a harsh scolding, and one can fancy that in his singular
white eye there is an unmistakable gleam of disapproval.

    I have always regretted that the manners of this Vireo have been a
bar to our better acquaintance, for he is a bird of marked character and
with unusual vocal talents. He is a capital mimic, and in the retire-
ment of his home sometimes amuses himself by combining the songs
of other birds in an intricate potpourri.

    1909. BIRD-LORE, 118 (mig.; pl.).

404a. KEY WEST VIREO. VIREO GRISEUS MAYNARDI *Brewster.* [631a.]
Scarcely distinguishable in color from the preceding, but averaging somewhat
paler and less yellow below, and with a larger bill. L., 5·12; W., 2·40; T.,
2·12; B. from N., ·35.
Range.—Fla. Keys.

404b. BERMUDA VIREO. VIREO GRISEUS BERMUDIANUS (*Bangs and
Bradlee*). [631b.] Similar to *V. g. griseus* but wing averaging shorter, tarsus
longer, general coloration grayer, less yellow and olivaceous. (Auk, 1901, 252.)
Range.—Bermuda.

405. BELL'S VIREO. VIREO BELLI BELLI *Audubon.* [633.] *Ads.*—
Crown ashy gray, changing to olive-green on the rump; greater and middle
wing-coverts narrowly tipped with white; lores and eye-ring whitish; underparts white, breast and sides washed with greenish yellow. L., 4·75; W.,
2·20; T., 1·80; B. from. N., ·28.
Range.—Breeds in Austral zones from ne. Colo., s. S. Dak., n. Ills., and
nw. Ind. to e. Tex. and Tamaulipas; winters from Mex. to Nicaragua; accidental in N. H. and Mich.
SE. Minn.; nesting Minneapolis May 27, 1922; one record.
Nest, pensile, of strips of bark and plant-fibers firmly and smoothly interwoven, lined with finer grasses, etc., in bushes or low trees. *Eggs,* 4–6, white
with a few specks of black, umber, or rufous-brown at the larger end,
·66 × ·50. *Date,* Corpus Christi, Tex., Apr. 24; Mercer Co., Ills., May 25.

This is a common bird in its range, and is locally not uncommon
as far east as Illinois. "In their food, habits, and actions they are very
similar to the White-eyed. Their call- and alarm-notes are not quite
so harsh, and their song is delivered in a less emphatic manner; an
indescribable sputtering, that does not rank it high in the musical
scale" (Goss).

1901. CARY, M., Proc. Nebr. Orn. Un., 46–48 (habits).—1909. BIRD-
LORE, 119 (mig.; pl.).

406. YELLOW-THROATED VIREO. VIREO FLAVIFRONS *Vieillot.*
[628.] *Ads.*—Upperparts *bright* olive-green, changing to gray on the rump
and upper tail-coverts; greater and middle wing-coverts tipped with white,
forming two distinct wing-bars; outer web of tertials edged with white; eye-
ring, throat and breast *bright* yellow; belly white. L., 5·95; W., 3·05; T.,
2·10; B. from N., ·36.
Range.—Breeds in Transition and Austral zones from e. cent. Sask.,
s. Man., se. Ont., sw. Que., and Me. s. to cent. Tex., s. cent. La., and n.
Fla.; winters from Yucatan and s. Mex. through Cent. A. to Venezuela;
casual in winter in Cuba and the Bahamas.
Washington, common S. R., Apr. 16–Sept. 29. Bronx region, fairly
common S. R., Apr. 26–Oct. 1. Boston, rare S. R. (formerly common),
May 6–Sept. 10. N. Ohio, common S. R., Apr. 25–Sept. 25. Glen Ellyn, not
common S. R., May 2–Sept. 26. SE. Minn., common S. R., Apr. 27–Sept. 23.
Nest, pensile, of strips of bark, plant-fibers, etc., interwoven, lined with
fine grasses and covered externally with lichens, suspended from a forked
branch 10–30 feet up. *Eggs,* 3–4, white, with a few specks or spots of black,
umber, or rufous-brown, chiefly about the larger ends, ·80 × ·60. *Date,*
New London, Conn., May 21; Boston, May 26; Holland Patent, N. Y.,
May 24; se. Minn., June 1.

The Yellow-throated Vireo is a dweller in tree-tops, and whether
in woodland, orchard, or lawn, he seldom comes below the upper story

of his home. But even at a distance his bright yellow breast is a conspicuous mark, at once distinguishing him from other members of his family.

If the Red-eyed Vireo is a soprano, the Yellow-throat is a contralto. He sings much the same tune, but his notes are deeper and richer, while they are uttered more deliberately and with greater expression than those of his somewhat too voluble cousin. "See me; I'm here; where are you?" he calls, and at intervals repeats his question in varying forms. Sometimes he astonishes us by an intricate liquid trill which suggests the wonderful song of the Ruby Kinglet, but which unfortunately is sometimes marred by the scolding notes that precede or follow it.

1909. BIRD-LORE, 165 (mig.; pl.).

407. BLUE-HEADED VIREO. VIREO SOLITARIUS SOLITARIUS (*Wilson*). [629.] (Fig. 114.) *Ads.*—Top and *sides* of the head *bluish gray;* eye-ring and lores *white;* back olive-green; greater and middle wing-coverts tipped with white, forming two distinct wing-bars; outer web of tertials edged with whitish; underparts white; sides washed with greenish yellow. L., 5˙61; W., 2˙96; T., 2˙15; B. from N., ˙28.

Remarks.—This species may be known by its white lores and eye-ring, and bluish gray *cheeks* and crown.

Range.—Breeds in Canadian and Transition zones from s. Mack., cent. Man., s. Que., and Cape Breton Isl., s. to cent. Alberta, n. N. Dak., cent. Minn., Mich., mts. of s. Pa., and R. I.; winters in the Gulf States from Tex. to Fla. and from e. Mex. to Guat.; accidental in Cuba.

Washington, common T. V., Apr. 6–May 25; Sept. 6–Nov. 3. Bronx region, fairly common T. V., Apr. 14–May 29; Sept. 8–Oct. 27 (Nov. 24). Boston, common T. V., uncommon S. R., Apr. 20–May 8; Sept. 15–Oct. 5. N. Ohio, common T. V., Apr. 17–May 20; Sept. 1–30. Glen Ellyn, not common T. V., May 7–June 4; Aug. 11–Oct. 9. SE. Minn., common T. V., May 1–June 4; Aug. 27–Oct. 6.

Nest, pensile, of pine needles, plant-down, etc., firmly interwoven, suspended from a forked branch 5–10 feet up. *Eggs*, 3–4, white, with a few specks or spots of black, umber, or rufous-brown, chiefly at the larger end, ˙80 × ˙53. *Date*, Taunton, Mass., May 21; Boston, May 28; Webster, N. H., May 29.

This large and handsome Vireo—a bird of the woods—is the first of its family to reach the northern states in the spring and the last to depart in the autumn. Like its congeners, but unlike birds in general, it sings at its work. In form its music resembles the Red-eye's, the Philadelphia's, and the Yellow-throat's; but to me it is more varied and beautiful than any of these, though some listeners may prefer the Yellow-throat for the richness and fullness of its 'organ tone.' The Solitary's song is matchless for the tenderness of its cadence, while in peculiarly happy moments the bird indulges in a continuous warble that is really enchanting. It has, too, in common with the Yellow-throat, a musical chatter—suggestive of the Baltimore Oriole's—and a pretty trilled whistle. Its most winning trait is its tameness. Wood bird as it is, it will sometimes permit the greatest familiarities. Two birds I have seen which allowed themselves to be stroked in the freest manner while sitting on the eggs, and which ate from my hand as readily as any pet canary; but I have seen others that complained loudly whenever I approached their tree. Perhaps they had had sad experiences.　　　　　　　　　　　　　　　　　　BRADFORD TORREY.

1909. BIRD-LORE, 166 (mig.; pl.).

407a. MOUNTAIN VIREO. VIREO SOLITARIUS ALTICOLA *Brewster.*
[629c.] Similar to the preceding, but with a much larger bill, and the back generally with more or less slaty blue. W., 3·15; T., 2·25; B. from N., ·35; depth of B. at N., ·20.
Range.—Breeds in Canadian and Transition zones in the Alleghanies from w. Md. to e. Tenn. and n. Ga.; winters in lowlands from S. C. to Fla.
Nesting-date, Iredell Co., N. C., Apr. 9.

This race of the Blue-headed Vireo is a common summer resident in the southern Alleghanies (see Loomis, *The Auk*, 1891, p. 329).

A single specimen of the PLUMBEOUS VIREO, *V. s. plumbeus*, a western species, has been taken at Peterboro, N. Y. (Miller, Auk, 1894, 79).

408. BLACK-WHISKERED VIREO. VIREO CALIDRIS BARBATULUS (*Cabanis*). [623.] *Ads.*—Similar to the next species, but somewhat duller above and with a fuscous streak on either side of the throat.
Range.—W. coast of s. Fla. (as far n. as Anclote Keys), Key West, Dry Tortugas, Cuba, Haiti, Little Cayman, and the Bahamas.
Nest, pensile, of dry grasses, shreds of bark, cotton, lichens, and spiders' webs, lined with soft, cottonlike fibers, suspended from a forked branch, 5–20 feet up. *Eggs*, 3–4, white, with a pinkish hue, speckled and spotted, chiefly at the larger end, with reddish brown, ·78 × ·55.

This is a not uncommon summer resident in southern Florida, arriving from its winter home in the West Indies early in May. Its song resembles that of the Red-eyed Vireo, but is somewhat more hesitating and emphatic.

409. The YELLOW-GREEN VIREO, *Vireo flavoviridis flavoviridis* (Cassin), [625], a Mexican and Central American species, has been once recorded from Godbout, Quebec.

410. RED-EYED VIREO. VIREO OLIVACEUS (*Linnæus*). [624.] *Ads.*—
Crown slaty gray, *bordered on either side by blackish;* a conspicuous white line over the eye; rest of the upperparts, wings, and tail light olive-green; no wing-bars; underparts pure white. Iris red in ad., brown in im. L., 6·23; W., 3·20; T., 2·20; B. from N., ·40.
Remarks.—The well-defined slaty gray cap, bordered by narrow black lines, is the best distinguishing mark of this species.

FIG. 132. Red-eyed Vireo. (Natural size.)

Range.—Breeds from cent. B. C., Anticosti Isl., and Cape Breton Isl. s. to se. Wash., e. Colo., w. Tex., n. Coahuila, and cent. Fla.; migrates through e. Mex. and Cent. A. (casually Cuba and the Bahamas); winters in Colombia and s. to s. Brazil; accidental in Nev., Calif., Greenland, and England.

Washington, very common S. R., Apr. 21–Nov. 11. Bronx region, common S. R., Apr. 24–Oct. 27 (Nov. 14). Boston, common S. R., May 10–Sept. 10. N. Ohio, abundant S. R., Apr. 27–Oct. 1. Glen Ellyn, common S. R., May 5–Oct. 13. SE. Minn., common S. R., May 4–Oct. 2.

Nest, pensile, of strips of bark, bits of dead wood, paper, and plant-down, firmly and smoothly interwoven, lined with finer strips of bark and vine tendrils, suspended from a forked branch, 5–40 feet up. *Eggs*, 3–4, white, with a few black or umber specks or spots about the larger end, ·85 × ·55. *Date*, D. C., May 26; Boston, May 28; Mt. Carmel, Ills., May 23; se. Minn., May 29.

This, the most common and generally distributed of our Vireos, is found alike in the shade trees of our lawns, in orchards, or woodlands. The conspicuous white line over the eye, with its black border, and the bird's red eye, and its frequently uttered, complaining note, a nasal *whang*, are good characters by which to distinguish it from its relatives.

Wilson Flagg's description of the Redeye to my mind exactly reflects the character of the bird and its song: "The Preacher is more generally known by his note, because he is incessant in his song, and particularly vocal during the heat of our long summer days, when only a few birds are singing. His style of preaching is not declamation. Though constantly talking, he takes the part of a deliberative orator, who explains his subject in a few words and then makes a pause for his hearers to reflect upon it. We might suppose him to be repeating moderately, with a pause between each sentence, 'You see it—you know it—do you hear me?—do you believe it?' All these strains are delivered with a rising inflection at the close, and with a pause, as if waiting for an answer."

1905. HERRICK, F. H., Home-Life of Wild Birds, 103–114.—1909. BIRD-LORE, 81 (mig.; pl.).

411. PHILADELPHIA VIREO. VIREO PHILADELPHICUS (*Cassin*). [626.] *Ads.*—Upperparts light olive-green; the crown sometimes grayish; a whitish line over the eye; wings and tail edged with olive-green; no wing-bars; first primary nearly as long as second; entire underparts nearly uniform pale, greenish yellow. L., 4·75; W., 2·60; T., 1·95; B. from N., ·26.

Remarks.—The pale, greenish yellow color spread almost uniformly over the entire underparts distinguishes this bird from our other Vireos.

Range.—Breeds in Canadian Zone from n. and cent. Alberta, s. Man., n. Ont., N. B., and Me. to n. N. Dak., Mich. and N. H.; winters from Cozumel Isl. and Guat. to Veragua.

Washington, rare T. V., May 6; Oct. 5. Bronx region, rare T. V., Sept. 17–Oct. 20; May 7–21. Boston, rare T. V. N. Ohio, not common T. V. Glen Ellyn, rather rare T. V., May 14, June 4; Aug. 21–Sept. 30. SE. Minn., uncommon T. V., May 9–June 2; Aug. 18–Sept. 16.

Nest, pensile, of fine grass and birch bark, suspended from a forked branch about 8 feet from the ground. *Eggs*, 4, similar in color to those of *V. olivaceus* (Seton). *Date*, Duck Mt., Man., June 4.

This species resembles the Red-eyed Vireo in habits, and Mr. Brewster writes that its song is so nearly identical with the song of that species "that the most critical ear will, in many cases, find great difficulty in distinguishing between the two. The notes of *philadelphicus* are generally pitched a little higher in the scale, while many of the utterances are feebler and the whole strain is a trifle more disconnected.

But these differences are of a very subtile character, and, like most comparative ones, they are not to be depended upon unless the two species can be heard together. The Philadelphia Vireo has, however, one note which seems to be peculiarly its own, a very abrupt, double-syllabled utterance with a rising inflection, which comes in with the general song at irregular but not infrequent intervals. I have also on one or two occasions heard the male when in pursuit of his mate utter a soft *pseuo*, similar to that sometimes used by *V. olivaceus*, and both sexes when excited or angry have a harsh, petulant note exactly like that of *V. gilvus*" (*Bull. Nutt. Orn. Club.*, 1880, p. 5).

1897. DWIGHT, J. D., JR., Auk, 259–272 (biography).—1909. BIRD-LORE, 78 (mig.; pl.).—1914. MILLER, E. F., Bird-Lore, 93–95 (song).—1921. LEWIS, H. F., Auk, 26–44, 185–202 (nesting).

412. EASTERN WARBLING VIREO. VIREO GILVUS GILVUS (*Vieillot*). [627.] *Ads.*—Upperparts ashy olive-green; a whitish line over the eye; no wing-bars; wings and tail edged with the color of the back; first primary *very short*, not more than 1·00 in length; underparts white *slightly* washed with yellowish. L., 5·80; W., 2·85; T., 2·14; B. from N., ·30.

Range.—Breeds in Transition and Austral zones from Sask., s. Man., cent. Ont., and N. S. s. to nw. Tex., s. La., e. Ky., N. C., and Va. w. to N. Dak.; winter home unknown, but s. of the U. S.

FIG. 133. Wing of Warbling Vireo, to show short first primary.

Washington, rather common S. R., Apr. 21–Sept. 12. Bronx region, fairly common S. R., Apr. 28–Sept. 20 (Oct. 12). Boston, uncommon and local S. R., May 5–Sept. 15. N. Ohio, abundant S. R., Apr. 17–Oct. 10. Glen Ellyn local, not common S. R., May 1–Sept. 15. SE. Minn. common, S. R.,, May 2–Sept. 15.

Nest, pensile, of grasses and plant-fibers, firmly and smoothly interwoven, lined with fine grasses, suspended from a forked branch 8–40 feet up. *Eggs*, 3–4, white, with a few specks or spots of black, umber, or rufous-brown, chiefly about the larger end, ·76 × ·55. *Date*, Boston, May 30; Holland Patent, N. Y., May 27; se. Minn., May 18.

Unlike its cousin, the Preacher, the Warbling Vireo is not generally distributed, but shows a decided preference for rows of shade trees, particularly rows of elms. It passes the greater part of its time in the upper branches, and is more often heard than seen.

Although resembling the Redeye in general appearance, its song is so different that singing birds need never be mistaken for that species. Instead of the Redeye's broken, rambling recitative, the song of the Warbling Vireo is a firm, rich, continuous warble with a singular alto undertone.

1909. BIRD-LORE, 79 (mig.; pl.).

413. The BAHAMA HONEY CREEPER, *Cœreba bahamensis* (Reichenbach), [635], of the family Cœrebidæ, was found by Dr. Würdemann in January, 1858, on Indian Key, southeastern Florida, and by J. T. Nichols in February, 1921, at Miami Beach. It is a common Bahaman bird and might be expected to occur more frequently in Florida. The upperparts are sooty black, the rump and middle of the underparts yellow, and a line over the eye, the throat, and the lower belly are white or whitish; length about 4·50.

FAMILY COMPSOTHLYPIDÆ. WOOD WARBLERS.

The Wood Warblers are found only in America. About 160 species are known, of which 44 visit the United States, there being nearly twice as many in the eastern as in the western states. With three or four exceptions, they are inhabitants of woodland, but, during their migrations, may be found in the trees of lawns or orchards. They feed almost exclusively upon insects, and are thus highly migratory, thousands of miles frequently separating their summer and winter homes.

The majority are among the last of the spring arrivals; their coming caps the climax of the migration, and the first severe frost leaves but few with us. They migrate by night, and are chief among the victims of lighthouses and electric-light towers. When migrating, they are generally found in straggling companies composed of a number of species, which during the day travel slowly through the woods from tree to tree.

They capture their insect food in a variety of ways. Some species flit actively from branch to branch, taking their prey from the more exposed parts of the twigs and leaves; others are gleaners, and carefully explore the under surfaces of leaves or crevices in the bark; while several, like Flycatchers, capture a large part of their food on the wing. As a rule, they are arboreal, but many are thicket-haunting, and some are terrestrial.

Several species have remarkable vocal ability, but, generally speaking, they have rather weak voices, and take low rank as songsters.

Warblers are at once the delight and the despair of field students. To the uninitiated, their existence is unknown, and when search reveals the before unsuspected fact that our woods are thronged with birds as exquisitely colored as the daintiest tropical forms, we feel as though a new world were opened to us. Entering an apparently deserted bit of woods, we hear faint voices, lisping *tseeps*, and soon discover that the tree-tops are animated with flitting forms. What limitless possibilities there are in a flock of Warblers! Who can say what rare species may be among them?—perhaps the bird we have long vainly looked for; perhaps a stranger from another clime!

1903–06. BIRD-LORE, Dec. 1903–Dec. 1906 (mig.; pl.); also in following: 1907. CHAPMAN, F. M., and others, The Warblers of North America, 8vo., 306 pp., 24 col. pls.—1917. HENSHAW, H. W., Friends of Our Forests, Nat. Geog. Mag., April, 297–321; 32 col. pls. of Warblers by Fuertes.

KEY TO THE SPECIES

First Group.—Throat yellow, yellowish, or orange.

I. Underparts *without* streaks or spots.

II. *With* black or brown streaks on the breast or sides, or (in one species) a blackish brown band across the throat, or (in one species) a black patch on the breast.

Second Group.— Throat black, gray, ashy, white, whitish, brown, or buffy.

   I. Throat and upper *breast* one color, black, gray, ashy, or brown, *very* different from the white or yellow belly.

  II. Throat white or whitish, with or without streaks or spots; rest of underparts *streaked* or *spotted* with black, bluish, chestnut, or yellow.

 III. Underparts white, whitish, or buffy, *without* streaks, spots, or patches.

FIRST GROUP

I. Underparts without streaks or spots.

  1. Tail with conspicuous white spots or patches.

    A. Wings with white wing-bars.

      a. Underparts entirely pure yellow.

        a^1. Forehead yellow; a black line through the eye; rump same as back . . . . 419. BLUE-WINGED WARBLER.

        a^2. Crown ashy; rump yellow . . 426. MAGNOLIA WARBLER, im.

      b. Underparts not entirely pure yellow.

        b^1. Throat bright yellow; belly white or whitish.

          b^2. Back olive greenish . . . . 440, 440a. PINE WARBLERS.

          b^3. Back bluish, with a yellowish patch in the middle.

                      424, 424a. PARULA WARBLERS, im.

        c^1. Underparts pale yellowish white or buffy; throat not brighter than belly.

          c^2. Back olive green, slightly streaked with black.

            c^3. Underparts pale cream-buff, stronger on the flanks.

               438. BAY-BREASTED WARBLER, im.

            c^4. Underparts pale yellowish white.

               439. BLACK-POLL WARBLER, im.

        d^2. Back not streaked.

          d^3. Back olive-green, without streaks.

               440, 440a. PINE WARBLERS, ♀.

          d^4. Back with a bluish tinge and without streaks.

               434. CERULEAN WARBLER, im.

    B. Without white wing-bars.

      a. Underparts bright orange or orange-yellow; wings, tail-coverts, and tail bluish gray . . . . 415. PROTHONOTARY WARBLER.

      b. Underparts pure yellow; wings, rump, and tail greenish; head sometimes blackish; inner web of outer tail-feathers white.

            453. HOODED WARBLER, ♀ and im.

      c. Underparts pale yellowish; head ashy; rump olive-green; small white tail-spots, not reaching to ends of feathers.

           420. BACHMAN'S WARBLER, ♀ and im.

      d. Underparts pale yellowish; entire upperparts olive-green; a white spot at the base of the primaries.

        428, 428a. BLACK-THROATED BLUE WARBLER, ♀ and race.

  2. Tail without white spots or patches; wings without white wing-bars.

    A. Cap, or forehead, or cheeks black or blackish.

      a. Cap black; forehead and cheeks yellow.

                454. WILSON'S WARBLER.

      b. Band on the forehead and cheeks black or blackish; no yellow line over the eye.   451a, b. MARYLAND YELLOW-THROATS, ♂.

      c. Forehead or crown and cheeks black or blackish; a clear yellow line over the eye . . . . . . 447. KENTUCKY WARBLER.

    B. No black on forehead.

      a. Crown ashy, of a very different color from the olive-green back, or with the bases of the crown feathers rufous-brown or chocolate.

        a^1. Crown plain ashy; under tail-coverts white.

                 420. BACHMAN'S WARBLER.

a^2. Crown ashy; bases of feathers chestnut; eye-ring distinctly white; most of underparts and under tail-coverts bright yellow . . . . 423. NASHVILLE WARBLER.

a^3. Crown of nearly the same color as the back; the feathers with rufous-brown bases; underparts dull greenish yellow.
422. ORANGE-CROWNED WARBLER.

b. Crown of the same color as the back; forehead the same, or yellowish, or brownish.

  b^1. Underparts uniform yellow or yellowish.

    b^2. Underparts bright yellow.

      b^3. Upperparts bright olive-green; forehead yellowish; short bristles at base of bill; tail greenish brown.
454. WILSON'S WARBLER, im.

      b^4. Upperparts bright greenish yellow; inner web of tail-feathers yellow . . . . . 425. YELLOW WARBLER, ♀.

      b^5. Upperparts ashy greenish; eye-ring white.
423. NASHVILLE WARBLER, im.

  c^2. Underparts dull yellow or yellowish.

    c^3. Underparts dull greenish yellow, obscurely streaked with dusky; back ashy greenish.
422. ORANGE-CROWNED WARBLER, im.

    c^4. Underparts yellowish or buffy yellowish; outer tail-feathers decidedly shortest; legs flesh-color.
451a, b. MARYLAND YELLOW-THROATS, ♀.

    c^5. Breast somewhat yellower than rest of underparts; flanks brownish; legs blackish; tail-feathers of same length.
423. NASHVILLE WARBLER, im.

    c^6. Inner margins of tail-feathers yellow.
425. YELLOW WARBLER, ♀.

    c^7. Back bright olive-green; under tail-coverts white.
421. TENNESSEE WARBLER, im.

    c^8. A small white spot at the base of the primaries.
428, 428a. BLACK-THROATED BLUE WARBLER, ♀ and race.

  c^1. Throat and breast yellow; belly white or whitish.

    c^2. A black spot before the eye and a white line over it; wing 3·00.
452. YELLOW-BREASTED CHAT.

    c^3. Legs flesh-color; outer tail-feathers shortest; forehead sometimes brownish.
451a, b. MARYLAND YELLOW-THROATS, ♀.

    c^4. Legs blackish; tail-feathers even; wing under 3·00.
423. NASHVILLE WARBLER, im.

II. With black or brown streaks on the breast or sides, or (in one species) a blackish brown band across the throat, or (in one species) a black patch on the breast.

I. Underparts streaked or spotted.

  1. Underparts streaked with rufous-brown.

    A. Crown chestnut.

      a. Entire underparts rich yellow. 443a. YELLOW PALM WARBLER.

      b. Throat and breast bright yellow; belly yellowish white.
443. PALM WARBLER.

    B. No chestnut crown-cap.

      a. Underparts yellowish white; eye-ring yellowish.
443. PALM WARBLER, im.

      b. Underparts yellow, washed with brownish; eye-ring yellowish.
443a. YELLOW PALM WARBLER, im.

      c. Underparts bright yellow; forehead yellow; inner webs of tail-feathers yellow . . . . . . 425. YELLOW WARBLER, ad.

2. Underparts streaked or spotted with black.
   a. Back unspotted, the same as the head, olive-green or olive-browr.
     a[1]. Underparts pale sulphur-yellow, streaked with black; no wing-bars; wing 3·00 or over.
         445. WATER-THRUSH. 445*a*. GRINNELL'S WATER-THRUSH.
     a[2]. Underparts bright yellow; no black streaks on the flanks; wing nearly 3·00 . . . . 440, 440*a*. PINE WARBLERS.
     a[3]. Underparts bright yellow; sides streaked with black; wing about 2·00 . . . 442, 442*a*. PRAIRIE WARBLERS, ♀ and im.
     a[4]. Throat pale yellow, indistinctly spotted or streaked; belly whitish; cheeks bright yellow; outer web of outer tail-feather white at the base.
         433, 433*a*. BLACK-THROATED GREEN WARBLERS, im.
     a[5]. Throat and breast yellow, distinctly spotted; median wing-coverts white . . . 427. CAPE MAY WARBLER, ♀ and im.
   b. Head not olive-green or olive-brown.
     b[1]. Back black or streaked with black, or center of crown orange.
       b[2]. Underparts pale yellow; black spots confined to sides; no white wing-bars . . . . . 441. KIRTLAND'S WARBLER.
       b[3]. Underparts pale yellow, indistinctly streaked with blackish; two white or whitish wing-bars.
            439. BLACK-POLL WARBLER, im.
       b[4]. Throat orange or yellow, without streaks; ear-coverts gray or black; center of crown yellowish or orange.
             575. BLACKBURNIAN WARBLER.
       b[5]. Underparts streaked with black; ear-coverts rufous; cap black.
             427. CAPE MAY WARBLER.
       b[6]. Crown bluish gray or ashy; rump bright yellow; eye-ring white; white tail-spots not reaching to ends of feathers.
             426. MAGNOLIA WARBLER.
     c[1]. Back not black.
       c[2]. Back ashy gray.
        c[3]. Throat yellow; belly white; wing-bars and tail-spots white.
         c[4]. A yellow line from the bill to the eye.
           436. YELLOW-THROATED WARBLER.
         c[5]. A white line from the bill to and over the eye.
           436*a*. SYCAMORE WARBLER.
       d[3]. Entire underparts yellow; breast with a necklace of black spots; no wing-bars or tail-spots . 455. CANADA WARBLER.
       d[2]. Center of back brick-red; underparts yellow; sides streaked with black . . . . 442, 442*a*. PRAIRIE WARBLERS.
II. Underparts not streaked.
   A. Throat yellow; breast with a band of copper or blackish chestnut; upperparts blue; center of back greenish yellow.
            424, 424*a*. PARULA WARBLERS.
   B. Throat and forehead yellow; breast and crown-cap black.
            420. BACHMAN'S WARBLER.

SECOND GROUP

I. **Throat and upper breast one color, black, gray, ashy, or brown, very different from the white or yellow belly.**

  A. Belly white or whitish.
    a. Back gray or greenish gray, crown yellow, cheeks black or gray, wing-bars yellow . . . . . 418. GOLDEN-WINGED WARBLER.
    b. Back and crown bright olive-green, cheeks yellow, wing-bars white.
       433, 433*a*. BLACK-THROATED GREEN WARBLER, and race.
    c. Back and crown dark blue, a white spot at the base of the primaries.
       428, 428*a*. BLACK-THROATED BLUE WARBLER, ♂ and race.

d. Back streaked with gray and black; cap, throat, and sides chestnut.
438. BAY-BREASTED WARBLER, ♂.
e. Back streaked with black and white, a white line through the center of the crown . . . . . 414. BLACK AND WHITE WARBLER, ♂.
f. Back black; sides, center of wings, and base of tail salmon-red.
456. REDSTART, ♂.
B. Belly yellow.
   a. Throat black.
      a¹. Cheeks bright yellow, black crown-cap connected with black throat by a black line, end half of inner web of outer tail-feathers white . . . . 453. HOODED WARBLER.
      a². Cheeks dull greenish yellow, black crown-cap not connected with black throat, white tail-spots not reaching to the ends of feathers . . . . 420. BACHMAN'S WARBLER.
      a³. A black streak through the eye, wing-bars white.
418 +419. LAWRENCE'S WARBLER.
   b. Throat bluish gray, ashy, or brownish.
      b¹. A white eye-ring, wing 2·90 . . . 448. CONNECTICUT WARBLER.
      b². A yellowish eye-ring, wing 2·56 . 449. MOURNING WARBLER, im.
      b³. No white eye-ring, wing 2·56 . . 449. MOURNING WARBLER, ad.

II. Throat white or whitish, with or without streaks or spots; rest of the underparts spotted or streaked with black, bluish, chestnut or yellow.

A. Back streaked with black.
   a. With chestnut streaks on the sides, under tail-coverts white.
      a¹. Wing over 2·50, head with chestnut or black streaks or spots, wing-bars white . . . . 438. BAY-BREASTED WARBLER, ♀.
      a². Wing under 2·50, crown and wing-bars yellow or yellowish.
437. CHESTNUT-SIDED WARBLER.
   b. With black or bluish streaks on the sides or entire underparts.
      b¹. Cap solid black . . . . . . 439. BLACK-POLL WARBLER, ♂.
      b². Crown, rump, and sides of the breast with a yellow patch or spot.
429. MYRTLE WARBLER.
      b³. Cap black, with a white streak through the center.
414. BLACK AND WHITE WARBLER, ♀.
      b⁴. Crown olive-green, with small black streaks.
439. BLACK-POLL WARBLER, ♀.
      b⁵. Crown blue, a bluish black band across the breast.
434. CERULEAN WARBLER, ♂.
      b⁶. Crown brownish, under tail-coverts yellow.
443. PALM WARBLER, im.
B. Back without streaks or spots.
   a. With white or yellow spots in the tail.
      a¹. Wing-bars white, cheeks yellow, back greenish.
433, 433*a.* BLACK-THROATED GREEN WARBLER, im. and race.
      a². Wing-bars, cheeks, and back grayish, under tail-coverts white.
427. CAPE MAY WARBLER, ♀ and im.
      a³. Back brownish, under tail-coverts yellow.
443. PALM WARBLER, im.
      a⁴. Sides of breast, band in wings, and base of tail yellow.
456. REDSTART, ♀ and im.
   b. Without white or yellow spots in the tail.
      b¹. A pale rufous streak bordered by black through the center of the crown . . . . 444. OVENBIRD.
      b². A white line over the eye, throat generally without spots, wing over 3·00, bill over ·50 . . 446. LOUISIANA WATER-THRUSH.
      b³. A buffy line over the eye, throat with small black spots, wing under 3·00, bill under ·50 . . . . . . 445. WATER-THRUSH.
445*a.* GRINNELL'S WATER-THRUSH.

III. Underparts white, whitish, or buffy, without streaks, spots, or patches.
   A. Tail with white or yellow spots or patches.
     a. Wing-bars white or grayish.
       a^1. Underparts pure white, back greenish yellow, cheeks gray, wing
           under 2·50 . . . . . .   437. CHESTNUT-SIDED WARBLER, im.
       a^2. Underparts tinged with buffy, back and cheeks olive-green, with
           generally distinct black streaks, wing over 2·50.
                       438. BAY-BREASTED WARBLER, im.
       a^3. Underparts soiled whitish, back brownish or grayish green, eye-
           ring white, wing-bars grayish, wing over 2·50.
             440, 440*a*. PINE WARBLER, and race, ♀ and im.
       a^4. Underparts white, back streaked with pure black and white.
                414. BLACK AND WHITE WARBLER, ♀.
     b. Wing-bars yellowish, greenish, or absent.
       b^1. Back and head bright greenish yellow, cheeks gray, underparts
           pure white . . . . . .   437. CHESTNUT-SIDED WARBLER, im.
       b^2. Back, head, and cheeks yellowish green, underparts yellowish,
           inner margins of tail-feathers yellow.
                        425. YELLOW WARBLER, im.
       b^3. Back gray or grayish, a black line through the eye.
                   418+419. BREWSTER'S WARBLER.
       b^4. Back and head brownish, wings and base of tail with a yellow
           band . . . .   456. REDSTART, ♀ and im.
       b^5. Back bright green, head and cheeks grayish, a small black spot
           in front of the eye . . . .   421. TENNESSEE WARBLER, ♂.
   B. Tail without white or yellow spots or patches.
     a. Under tail-coverts yellow.
       a^1. Back olive-green, outer tail-feathers shortest, legs flesh-color.
           451, 451*a*, *b*. MARYLAND YELLOW-THROAT, and races, ♀ and im.
       a^2. Back grayish olive-green, tail-feathers of equal length, legs
           blackish . . . .   422. ORANGE-CROWNED WARBLER.
     b. Under tail-coverts white or whitish.
       b^1. Head plain brown, a whitish line from the bill over the eye.
                   416. SWAINSON'S WARBLER.
       b^2. Center of crown and line from the bill over the eye buffy, bor-
           dered by black stripes . . . .   417. WORM-EATING WARBLER.
       b^3. Crown greenish, a small white spot at the base of the primaries
           almost concealed by wing-coverts.
           428, 428*a*.
           BLACK-THROATED BLUE WARBLER, and ♀ race, and im.
       b^4. Crown grayish, bend of the wing yellow.
                  420. BACHMAN'S WARBLER, ♀.

A FIELD KEY TO THE
ADULT MALE WARBLERS OF EASTERN NORTH AMERICA IN
SPRING AND SUMMER PLUMAGE

   I. Throat yellow, white, or whitish; underparts *without* streaks or patches.
  II. Throat black, brown, or slate-color.
 III. Throat yellow or orange, underparts *with* streaks. (In one species a
     blackish brown band across the breast.)
 IV. Throat white or whitish, *with* streaks or spots on the underparts. (In
     two species a yellow patch on the sides of the breast.)

I. Throat yellow, white, or whitish; underparts without streaks or patches.
   1. Throat yellow.
     A. Length over 6·00, the largest of the Warblers; haunts dense thickets
        in second growth; song, a peculiar mixture of whistles, *chucks*,
        and crow-calls, delivered from the undergrowth, from the trees

above, or on the wing, when the bird resembles a bunch of falling
leaves . . . . 452. YELLOW-BREASTED CHAT.
B. Length under 6·00.
  a. Head and neck bright golden yellow like the breast; tail-feathers
     white, except at the tip; haunts near the water; especially low
     bushes and willows hanging over streams and ponds; call, a
     sharp *peek;* range, from Virginia and s. Minnesota southward.
                              415. PROTHONOTARY WARBLER.
  b. Forehead and cheeks black, a yellow line over the eye; song, a
     loud whistled call of five to seven notes; haunts near the ground;
     range from lower Hudson valley southward.
                              447. KENTUCKY WARBLER.
  c. Forehead and cheeks black, bordered by grayish; no line over the
     eye; haunts undergrowth; call, a frequently repeated *chack;*
     song, a loud, rapid *I beseech you, I beseech you, I beseech you,* or
     witch-e-weè-o, witch-e-weè-o, witch-e-weè-o; movements restless;
     abundant.
           451, 451a, b. MARYLAND YELLOW-THROAT and races.
  d. Head and back olive-green; wings with two white bars; outer
     tail-feathers with white; haunts pine woods; song, a musical trill.
                     440, 440a. PINE WARBLER, and race.
  e. Crown bluish ash, eye-ring white; call-note sometimes like the
     sound produced by striking two pebbles together.
                              423. NASHVILLE WARBLER.
  f. Forehead yellow, a small black mark in front of the eye; wings
     with two white bars; outer tail-feathers with white; song, *swēē-
     chee,* the first note higher, and also *wēē, chĭ-chĭ-chĭ-chĭ, chŭr,
     chēē-chŭr* . . . . 419. BLUE-WINGED WARBLER.
  g. Forehead yellow; crown-cap black; cheeks yellow; wings and
     tail unmarked; rather rare . . . . 454. WILSON'S WARBLER.
2. Throat white or whitish.
A. Length 5·00; crown brown or with blackish and buffy stripes.
  a. A conspicuous whitish line through the center of the crown, bor-
     dered by black lines; not common.
                              417. WORM-EATING WARBLER.
  b. Crown plain brown; range, Virginia and southward.
                              416. SWAINSON'S WARBLER.
B. Length 4·50; crown ashy or forehead yellow.
  a. Forehead yellow.
    a¹. Breast white, with a barely perceptible tinge of yellow; wing-
        bars white or yellow, a black mark in front of the eye; rare.
                              418+419. BREWSTER'S WARBLER.
  b. Forehead not yellow.
    b¹. Breast white, crown plain bluish ashy, clearly defined from the
        bright olive-green back . . . 421. TENNESSEE WARBLER.
    b². Breast whitish, tinged with yellow and indistinctly streaked
        with dusky; crown dull ashy, not clearly defined from the
        back and with a partly concealed patch of rufous-brown;
        rare in the Atlantic States north of South Carolina.
                              422. ORANGE-CROWNED WARBLER.

II. Throat black, brown or slate-color.

1. Belly white.
  a. Back blue, a white spot near the outer edge of the wing; common.
           428, 428a. BLACK-THROATED BLUE WARBLER, and race.
  b. Back green, cheeks yellow; song, a buzzlike *zee* repeated five or six
     times, the next to last note the lowest; common.
           433, 433a. BLACK-THROATED GREEN WARBLER, and race.

    c. Back grayish, forehead yellow, a black mark through the eye and a white line below it; a large patch of yellow on the wings; song, *zee-zee-zee-zee*, all on the same note; not common.

            418. GOLDEN-WINGED WARBLER.

    d. Back black; sides of the breast, middle of the wing, and base of the tail-feathers reddish orange; movements active, tail frequently spread, the reddish color showing conspicuously; abundant.

            456. REDSTART.

    e. Back streaked with black and white; song fine and wiry; movements like those of a Creeper; common.

            414. BLACK AND WHITE WARBLER.

    f. Back streaked with buffy and black; forehead and cheeks black; crown-cap, throat, upper part of the breast, and sides chestnut; rather rare . . . . 438. BAY-BREASTED WARBLER.

  2. Belly yellow.
    A. Throat slate-color; haunts near the ground.
      a. Breast showing traces of black, no white eye-ring; rare in most places . . . . 449. MOURNING WARBLER.
      b. Breast with no traces of black, a white eye-ring; call a sharp *peek;* very rare in the spring . . . . 448. CONNECTICUT WARBLER.
    B. Throat black.
      a. Forehead and crown yellow, wings with white bars, a black line through the eye; very rare. 418+419. LAWRENCE'S WARBLER.
      b. Forehead and cheeks yellow, rest of the head and sides of the neck black; outer tail-feathers almost entirely white; haunts near the ground, generally in wet woods; movements active, the white tail-feathers showing conspicuously in flight; lower Hudson valley southward; common . . . . . 453. HOODED WARBLER.
      c. Forehead yellow, a small black patch on the crown, white patches on the tail not reaching to the ends of the feathers; range, South Carolina southward . . . . . . 420. BACHMAN'S WARBLER.

III. Throat yellow or orange, underparts with streaks. (In one species a blackish brown band across the breast.)

  1. Belly white, with or without black streaks.
    a. Throat rich orange; back black, streaked with white; tolerably common . . . . 435. BLACKBURNIAN WARBLER.
    b. Throat bright yellow, back grayish; range, Virginia and southern Wisconsin southward; abundant.

            436. YELLOW-THROATED WARBLER.
            436*a.* SYCAMORE WARBLER.

    c. Throat yellow, with a blackish band crossing the upperpart of the breast; abundant . . . . . 424, 424*a.* PARULA WARBLERS.

  2. Belly yellow, with streaks or spots on the breast or sides.
    A. With *black* streaks or spots on the underparts.
      a. Back grayish, unstreaked; a necklace of black spots on the breast, no streaks on the sides nor white on the wings or tail; common.

            455. CANADA WARBLER.

      b. Back black, crown grayish, a black stripe through the eye; breast and sides streaked with black; end of tail black, a white band across its middle; common . . . 426. MAGNOLIA WARBLER.
      c. Back streaked with white, center of the crown and line over the eye orange . . . . 435. BLACKBURNIAN WARBLER.
      d. Back greenish, streaked with black; crown black, a rufous ear-patch, a white patch on the wings, rump yellow; rather rare.

            427. CAPE MAY WARBLER.

      e. Back greenish, with a patch of rufous-brown; haunts second growths and old bush-grown pastures; common in some places.

            442, 442*a.* PRAIRIE WARBLER, and race.

f. Back grayish, streaked with black; crown bluish; no conspicuous white marking on the wings; very rare.
441. KIRTLAND'S WARBLER.

B. Underparts with *rufous-brown* streaks.

   a. Crown yellow, back greenish, inner border of tail-feathers yellow; general appearance that of a yellow bird; haunts lawns, orchards, and second growths; rarely seen in deep woods; abundant.
425. YELLOW WARBLER.

   b. Crown chestnut, back brownish, outer tail-feathers tipped with white; haunts near the ground, frequently seen along roadsides and in old fields; movements leisurely, constantly wags its tail; common.
443. PALM WARBLER.   443a. YELLOW PALM WARBLER.

IV. Throat white or whitish, with streaks or spots on the underparts. (In two species a yellow patch on the sides of the breast.)

1. A patch of yellow on the sides of the breast.
   a. Back grayish, streaked with black; rump and a partly concealed crown-patch yellow; note, a loud *tchip*, generally uttered during flight; abundant . . . . 429. MYRTLE WARBLER.
   b. Back brown, breast more or less spotted with black; a yellow band across the middle of wings and tail; movements active, tail frequently spread, the yellow band showing conspicuously; abundant.
456. REDSTART, im.

2. No yellow patch on the sides of the breast.
   A. With wing-bars; back streaked with black; haunts in trees.
     a. Back bright blue; very rare near the Atlantic Coast.
434. CERULEAN WARBLER.

     b. Back grayish, crown black; movements slow; abundant.
439. BLACK-POLL WARBLER.

     c. Back greenish yellow, crown bright yellow, sides chestnut; common . . . . 437. CHESTNUT-SIDED WARBLER.
   B. Without wing-bars; back not streaked; haunts on or near the ground; *walkers,* not *hoppers.*
     a. Crown pale rufous, bordered by black streaks; song, a loud *teacher,* repeated eight or nine times and increasing in volume; common.
444. OVENBIRD.

     b. Crown like the back, breast with a tinge of sulphur-yellow, an inconspicuous buffy line over the eye; bill less than ·50 in length; common . . . . 445. WATER-THRUSH.
     c. Crown like the back, breast and particularly flanks tinged with buffy, a conspicuous white line over the eye; bill nearly ·75 in length; a far shyer bird than the preceding; song loud and ringing . . . . 446. LOUISIANA WATER-THRUSH.

414. BLACK AND WHITE WARBLER. MNIOTILTA VARIA (*Linnæus*). [636.] (Fig. 134.) *Ad.* ♂.—No yellow anywhere; upperparts streaked with black and white; ear-coverts black; inner webs of outer tail-feathers with white patches; wing-coverts black, tipped with white; throat and upper breast black or black and white; sides streaked with black and white; middle of the belly white. *Ad.* ♀.—Similar, but the underparts with fewer black streaks; sides washed with brownish. *Im.* ♂.—Similar to the ♀, but with more streaks on the underparts. L., 5·30; W., 2·73; T., 2·02; B. from N., ·37.

Range.—Breeds from cent. w. Mack., n. Ont., N. F., and N. S. to e. Tex., cent. Ala., and n. Ga., w. to S. Dak. and casually to Wyo., Mont., and Colo. Winters from Colima and Nuevo Leon to Ecuador and Venezuela, and in Fla., the Bahamas, and W. I. to Guadeloupe; casually in s. Tex., cent. and s. Calif. Accidental in Wash. and Bermuda.

Washington, abundant T. V., less common S. R., Mch. 30–Oct. 18. Bronx region, common S. R., Apr. 18–Oct. 23 (Nov. 1). Boston, very common S. R., Apr. 25–Sept. 5. N. Ohio, common T. V., a few S. R., Apr. 17–Sept. 26. Glen Ellyn, common T. V., Apr. 28–June 1; Aug. 11–Sept. 27. SE. Minn., common T. V., uncommon S. R., Apr. 17–Oct. 12.

Nest, of strips of bark, grasses, etc., lined with rootlets or long hairs, on the ground at the base of a stump, log, or rock. *Eggs*, 4–5, white, spotted and speckled with cinnamon-brown to umber, chiefly in a wreath at the larger end, ·66 × ·54. *Date*, Iredell Co., N. C., Apr. 18; New York City, May 18; Boston, May 18.

None of our Warblers can be more readily identified than this conspicuously marked *creeper*. It is generally distributed throughout woodland, and climbs with even more agility than a true Creeper, hanging from the under surface of branches and twigs, and flitting actively from tree to tree after apparently the most superficial examination. Its alarm-note is a sharp *pit*, sometimes rapidly repeated. The usual song is a thin, wiry, *see-see-see-see*.

1910. STANWOOD, C. J., Journ. Me. Orn. Soc., 61–66 (nesting).

415. PROTHONOTARY WARBLER. PROTONOTARIA CITREA (*Boddaert*). [637.] *Ad.* ♂.—Whole head, neck and underparts rich orange, lighter on the belly; back greenish yellow, changing to bluish gray on the rump; wings and tail ashy; inner webs of all but middle tail-feathers white, except at tip; no wing-bars. *Ad.* ♀.—Similar, but yellow paler, belly with more white. L., 5·50; W., 2·90; T., 1·85; B. from N., ·42.

Range.—Breeds in the Lower Austral Zone and along river-bottoms of the Upper Austral Zone from ne. Nebr., se. Minn., s. Wisc., s. Mich., O., cent. Del., and e. Md. (once in n. N. J.) s. to e. Tex., s. Ala., and n. Fla. Winters from Nicaragua to Colombia and casually in Venezuela and s. Mex.; but apparently crosses the Gulf in migration and is not found in Mex. n. of Campeche. Accidental in the W. I., casual n. to N. Y., N. E., Mich., Ont., and N. B., and in Ariz.

Washington, rare, Apr.–June. Bronx region, A. V., about four recent records from Apr. 28–June 6. Boston, A. V. N. Ohio, not common S. R. Glen Ellyn, uncommon T. V., May 4–15; Aug. 18–Sept. 21. SE. Minn., common S. R. of Mississippi bottoms, May 2–Aug. 17.

Nest, of rootlets, fine twigs, and moss, plant-down or feathers, in a hole in a stub or stump, generally of a willow, black gum, or cypress. *Eggs*, 5–7, white, thickly and rather coarsely marked distinctly and obscurely with cinnamon-brown, chestnut, or rufous-brown, ·69 × ·56. *Date*, Charleston, S. C., May 3; Lewis Co., Mo., May 20; Mt. Carmel, Ills., May 8; Pierce Co., Wisc., May 31; se. Minn., June 1.

This exquisite Warbler frequents bushes and low trees—particularly willow trees—hanging over the water. Its call-note so closely resembles that of a Water-Thrush (*Seiurus*), I have sometimes mistaken it for that species. Its usual song, as Mr. Brewster remarks in his admirable biography of this species, "sounds at a distance like the call of the Solitary Sandpiper, with a syllable or two added—a simple *peet, tweet, tweet, tweet*, given on the same key throughout. . . . Nearer at hand, however, the resemblance is lost, and a ringing, penetrating quality becomes apparent in the Warbler's song." (*Bull. Nutt. Orn. Club*, 1878, pp. 153–162.)

Thoroughly to appreciate the Prothonotary's radiant beauty, one

PLATE XXIV

1, 2, 3. BACHMAN'S WARBLER
5. SWAINSON'S WARBLER   4. WORM-EATING WARBLER
(From "Warblers of North America.")

should float quietly in a canoe past its haunts. Its color shows to best
advantage against the dark background of its home and its every
movement is a delight to the eye.

416. SWAINSON'S WARBLER. LIMNOTHLYPIS SWAINSONI (*Audubon*).
[638.] (Pl. XXIV.) *Ads.*—Crown cinnamon-brown; a whitish line over the
eye; back, rump, wings and tail olive grayish brown without white; underparts soiled yellowish white, grayer on the sides. L., 5·00; W., 2·75; T., 1·90;
B. from N., ·46.
Range.—Breeds in the Lower Austral Zone from ne. Okla., se. Mo., s. Ills.,
s. Ind., and se. Va. (Warwick Co.) s. to La. and n. Fla. Winters in Jamaica
and s. Yucatan; migrates through Cuba and the Bahamas. Casual in Nebr.,
Tex., and Vera Cruz.
Nest, externally of leaves, lined with pine needles and rootlets, in bushes,
canes, palmettos, and clumps of vines, from 3–10 feet above the ground or
surface of the water. *Eggs*, 3–4, white, with a faint bluish tinge, ·75 × ·54.
Date, Charleston, S. C., May 7.

The history of Swainson's Warbler is very similar to that of Bachman's Warbler. It was discovered by Dr. Bachman near Charleston,
S. C., in 1832, and for somewhat over fifty years was practically a lost
species, but proves now to be a common bird in some parts of its range.
Its rediscovery near Charleston by Mr. A. T. Wayne and Mr. Brewster
is recounted by the latter in an article which adequately portrays the
bird, its habits and haunts. It lives on and near the ground, and,
according to Mr. Brewster's experience, four things seem indispensable
to its existence—"water, tangled thickets, patches of cane, and a rank
growth of semi-aquatic plants." Its song, which is highly ventriloquial,
is described by the same author as "a series of clear, ringing whistles,
the first four uttered rather slowly, and in the same key, the remaining
five or six given more rapidly, and in an evenly descending scale. . . .
In general effect it recalls the song of the Water-Thrush (*Seiurus
noveboracensis*). It is very loud, very rich, very beautiful, while it has
an indescribable tender quality that thrills the senses after the sound
has ceased." *The Auk*, 1885, pp. 65–80; see also *Ibid.*, pp. 346–348, and
also Perry, *Orn. and Oöl.*, 1886, p. 188; 1887, p. 141.

417. WORM-EATING WARBLER. HELMITHEROS VERMIVORUS
(*Gmelin*). [639.] (Fig. 135; Fl. XXIV.) *Ads.*—A black line from the eye to
the nape, and two on the crown from either nostril; an olive-buffy line over
either eye, and a third through the center of the crown; back, wings, and
tail olive-green without white; underparts whitish cream-buff, whiter on the
throat and belly. L., 5·51; W., 2·78; T., 2·05; B. from N., ·39.
Range.—Breeds mainly in the Upper Austral Zone from s. Ia., n. Ills.,
w. N. Y., se. and sw. Pa., and the Hudson and Conn. river valleys s. to s. Mo.,
n. Ala., n. Ga., Tenn., Va., and the mts. of S. C. (casually farther s.). Winters
from Chiapas to Panama, in Cuba and the Bahamas, and rarely in Fla.
Casual in Mass., Vt., s. Ont., and s. Wisc.
Washington, quite common S. R., Apr. 25–Sept. 13. Bronx region, fairly
common S. R., Apr. 29–Sept. 20 (Oct. 2). Boston, A. V. N. Ohio, occasional
in spring.
Nest, of rootlets, leaves, and bark, on the ground. *Eggs*, 4–6, white,
speckled, spotted, or blotched with cinnamon- or rufous-brown, ·68 × ·54.

Date, Iredell Co., N. C., May 10; Waynesburg, Pa., May 16; New Haven, Conn., May 25.

This comparatively rare, retiring Warbler may be found on dry wooded slopes, hillsides, and ravines, generally where there is a rather dense undergrowth, but occasionally where the ground is quite clear and open. It lives on or near the ground, and in its slow, deliberate actions resembles a Vireo more than the usually active Warblers. Its call-note is a sharp *chip,* while its song, as all observers agree, closely resembles that of the Chipping Sparrow, but is somewhat weaker.

418. GOLDEN-WINGED WARBLER. VERMIVORA CHRYSOPTERA (*Linnæus*). [642.] (Fig. 137.) *Ad. ♂.*—Crown bright yellow; rest of the upperparts bluish gray, sometimes washed with greenish; a *large* black patch about the eye, separated from another on the throat by a white stripe; a white line over the eye; wings and tail bluish gray; tips of middle wing-coverts and outer webs of greater ones bright yellow, forming a large yellow patch on the wing; outer three tail-feathers with large white patches on their inner webs at the tip, fourth feather with a smaller patch; lower breast and belly white; sides grayish. *Ad. ♀.*—Similar, but the crown and upperparts duller, the patch on the sides of the head and throat grayish instead of black. L.,5·10; W., 2·46; T., 1·94; B. from N., ·34.

Range.—Breeds in the Transition Zone from cent. Minn., se. Ont., and Mass. s. to s. Ia., s. Ills., n. Ind., n. N. J., and in the mts. to n. Ga. Winters from Guat. to Colombia and Venezuela, and casually in s. Mex. Very rare in Fla. and s. Ga. (crossing the Gulf of Mex. in migration); casual in Kans., accidental in Man. and Cuba.

Washington, uncommon T. V., Apr. 24–May 20; Aug. 8–Sept. 14. Bronx region, uncommon T. V., rare S. R., May 4–Sept. 15. Boston, rather common S. R., May 10–Aug. 25. N. Ohio, rare T. V. Glen Ellyn, irregular, not common T. V., May 4–22; Aug. 16–Oct. 7. SE. Minn., fairly common T. V., uncommon S. R., May 3–Sept. 30.

Nest, much like that of *V. pinus,* on or near the ground, in second growths or bushy fields. *Eggs,* 4–5, white, speckled and spotted, chiefly about the larger end, with cinnamon-brown, chestnut, or umber, ·62 × ·50. *Date,* Buncombe Co., N. C., May 16; Bethel, Conn., May 29; Monroe Co., Mich., May 17.

In their actions and choice of haunts the Golden-winged resemble the Blue-winged Warblers. Their song is of much the same quality, but the notes are all of the same kind and length, and the bird utters a rather lazy *zee-zee-zee-zee,* at once distinguishable from the song of *pinus.*

419. BLUE-WINGED WARBLER. VERMIVORA PINUS (*Linnæus*). [641.] (Fig. 136.) *Ad. ♂.*—Crown and entire underparts bright yellow, *a black line through the eye;* back and rump *bright* olive-green; wings and tail bluish gray; greater and middle wing-coverts tipped with white or yellowish white; outer three tail-feathers with large white patches on their inner webs, fourth feather with a much smaller patch. *Ad. ♀.*—Similar, but yellow on the head confined to the forehead; underparts duller. L., 4·80; W., 2·40; T., 1·80; B. from N., ·33.

Remarks.—The only variation of note in the plumage of otherwise typical specimens of this species occurs in the color of the wing-bars, which in some specimens are tinged with yellow. A specimen in Mr. Brewster's collection (No. 25,511, Seymour, Conn., June 11, 1889, E. A. Eames) shows this variation carried to an extreme, and has the wing-bars as broadly yellow as in *V. chrysoptera,* though in every other respect it is typical *pinus.* Between this species and *V. chrysoptera* there exists a complete set of hybrids which are variously called *V. leucobronchialis* and *V. lawrencei.*

Range.—Breeds from se. Minn., s. Mich., w. N. Y., s. Mass. (rarely), R. I. (occasionally), and s. Conn., s. to ne. Kans., cent. Mo., n. Ala., n. Ga., Ky., Md., and Del. Winters from s. Mex. to Guat. and casually to Colombia; very rare migrant across the Gulf of Mexico and in se. U. S. s. of Va. Occasional in s. Ont.; accidental in the Bahamas.

Washington, rather uncommon T. V., Apr. 23–May 22; Aug. 13–Sept. 5; a few breed. Bronx region, common S. R., Apr. 26–Sept. 25; one winter record, Jan. 6. Boston, very rare S. R. N. Ohio, common S. R., Apr. 27–Sept. 15. Glen Ellyn, not common T. V., very rare S. R., May 1–Sept. 15. SE. Minn., uncommon S. R., Apr. 30–Sept. 1 (Fillmore Co.).

Nest, of bark and leaves, lined with fine strips of bark and tendrils, and firmly wrapped with numerous leaves, whose stems point upward, on the ground, generally in or at the border of second growth. *Eggs*, 4-6, white, thinly speckled with rufous, cinnamon-brown, or rufous-brown, ·62 × ·50. *Date*, Chester Co., Pa., May 22; New Haven, Conn., May 20; Oberlin, O., May 10; se. Minn., May 16 (nest finished).

This species may be found in scrubby second growths, woodland borders, or even the lower trees of dense woods. Its movements are rather slow and leisurely, and, like a Chickadee, it may sometimes be seen hanging head downward while searching for food.

It is at times a rather persistent songster, and its peculiar song is not likely to be mistaken for that of any other Warbler. As a rule, it consists of the two drawled, wheezy notes *swēē-chee;* the first inhaled, the second exhaled. A less common song, uttered later in the season, is *wēē, chĭ-chĭ-chĭ-chī, chūr, chēē-chūr*, and is sometimes accompanied by peculiar *kik* notes.

1909. WRIGHT, H. W., Auk, 337–345 (nesting in Mass.).

418+419. BREWSTER'S WARBLER. VERMIVORA LEUCOBRONCHIALIS (*Brewster*). *Ad.* ♂.—Forehead and forepart of the crown yellow, a black line from the bill through the eye; rest of the upperparts bluish gray; wing-bars broadly yellow; tail like the back, three to four outer feathers marked with white; underparts pure white, *faintly* washed with yellow on the breast. Fall specimens are more heavily washed with yellow, and the upperparts are margined with olive-green. *Ad.* ♀.—Similar, but wing-bars white, and crown not so bright.

Remarks.—The descriptions are from typical specimens of the bird known as *V. leucobronchialis.* Between it and *V. pinus* there are specimens showing every degree of intergradation. Typical examples are comparatively rare, and the most common form has the breast heavily washed with yellow, the back tinged with olive-green, and the white wing-bars washed with yellow; in other words, about intermediate between typical *leucobronchialis* and typical *pinus.*

Washington, 2 records, May. Bronx region, rare T. V. and S. R., May 9–25; several recent breeding records. Boston, rare S. R. N. Ohio, occasional in summer.

This hybrid between *pinus* and *chrysoptera* has been found in Louisiana, from Virginia northward to Connecticut, and as far west as Michigan. Its breeding-range apparently coincides with the northern portion of that of *pinus.* In the Connecticut River Valley the bird is stated to be more frequent than *chrysoptera.* In general habits it resembles both *pinus* and *chrysoptera.* Some individuals sing like the former, some like the latter, while others have notes of their own. The significant facts in the bird's interesting and puzzling history are admirably presented by Maurice Brown in Forbush's 'Birds of Massachusetts' (pp. 212–218), but see especially J. T. Nichols' application of Mendel's Law to this case (*The Auk*, 1908, p. 86) and the results of Walter Faxon's conclusive field observations (Memoirs Mus. Comp. Zoöl., 1910, pp. 57–78; 1911, p. 68; 1913, pp. 311–316. *The Auk*, 1917, pp. 481, 482).

1923. CARTER, T. D., and HOWLAND, R. H., Auk, 423–430, illus., A Brewster's Warbler and His Brood.

418+419. LAWRENCE'S WARBLER. VERMIVORA LAWRENCEI (*Herrick*). *Ad.* ♂.—Forehead and forepart of the crown yellow, rest of the upperparts bright olive-green; wing-bars white; tail bluish gray, the three to four outer feathers marked with white; a black patch on the cheek divided by a yellow line from the black patch on the throat and upper breast; lower breast and belly yellow, under tail-coverts white. *Ad.* ♀.—Forehead dingy yellow, rest of the upperparts bright olive-green; wing-bars white, tinged with yellow; tail as in the ♂, black patches of the ♂ replaced by dusky olive-green.

Remarks.—This bird combines the characters of *pinus* and *chrysoptera;* it has the black cheek-patches and breast-patch of the latter, but in other respects resembles the former. Its history and a discussion of its relationships will be found under the references given above. It is a much rarer bird than Brewster's Warbler.

Washington, 1 record, May. Bronx region, rare T. V. and S. R., May 7–Sept. 10; about five recent breeding records. Boston, casual S. V.; not known to breed.

This hybrid between Blue-winged and Golden-winged Warblers resembles those birds in habits. Its song may contain parts of both parents', or may be like that of either.

420. BACHMAN'S WARBLER. VERMIVORA BACHMANI (*Audubon*). [640.] (Pl. XXIV.) *Ad.* ♂.—Forehead yellow, bordered by a black patch on the crown; back of the head bluish gray; back and rump bright olive-green; lesser wing-coverts yellow; tail grayish, all but the middle feathers with white patches on their inner web near the tip; throat and belly yellow, a large black patch on the breast. *Im.* ♂.—Throat-patch smaller than in ad. ♂; less black or none on head. *Ad.* ♀.—Crown grayish; forehead yellowish; back, wings, and tail as in the ♂; underparts whitish, washed with yellow on the throat and breast; bend of the wing yellow. *Im.* ♀.—Similar, but with less yellow; back grayer. L., 4·25; W., 2·40; T., 1·80; B. from N., ·32.

Range.—Breeds in the Lower Austral Zone in se. Mo., ne. Ark., w. Ky., n. Ala., and near Charleston, S. C., and probably in s. Ind. and e. N. C. Winters in Cuba; in migration occurs in La., Miss., Ala., and Fla. Casual in Va. and the Bahamas.

Nest, chiefly of fine grasses, cane leaves, skeletonized leaves and occasionally *Tillandsia* (Wayne); in low bushes, 1–3 feet up. *Eggs*, 3–4, pure, glossy white, ·63 × ·49. *Date*, Charleston, S. C., Apr. 17; Dunklin Co., Mo., May 13; Logan Co., Ky., May 14.

Bachman's Warbler was described by Audubon from a pair of birds taken by Dr. Bachman at Charleston, S. C., in July, 1833. Several specimens were subsequently taken in the West Indies during the winter, but over fifty years passed before the species was again found in the United States. It proves now to be a common bird in parts of its range, and has been found in large numbers near New Orleans, and on the Suwannee River in Florida in March and April, and at Key West in late July and August. The nest remained undiscovered until 1897, when it was found by Widmann in Missouri, and it has since been found by Embody in Kentucky and Wayne in South Carolina.

Mr. Brewster and I had excellent opportunities to study its habits on the Suwannee River, and in *The Auk* for 1891, pp. 149–157, will be found a detailed account of our observations written by Mr. Brewster. It was migrating with other Warblers, and kept to the tops of the highest trees, but in its breeding haunts it proves to be a low-ranging bird like most of the members of this genus. Its movements are rather leisurely, and resemble those of *V. pinus* or *V. celata*. Its song is described by Brewster as resembling that of the Parula Warbler.

421. TENNESSEE WARBLER. VERMIVORA PEREGRINA (*Wilson*). [647.] (Fig. 115a.) *Ad. ♂.*—Top and sides of the head bluish gray, sharply defined from the *bright* olive-green back and rump; wings and tail edged with olive-green; no white wing-bars; inner margin of inner vane of outer tail-feathers generally white at the tip; underparts white, sometimes tinged with yellow. *Ad. ♀.*—Similar, but crown tinged with greenish and underparts washed with yellowish. *Im.*—Upperparts uniform olive-green; underparts washed with yellowish; under tail-coverts *white*. L., 5·00; W., 2·63; T., 1·69; B. from N., ·32.

Remarks.—The adults of this and the two following species may be distinguished with ease; immature birds, however, are frequently confused. The Nashville is distinctly *yellow* on the breast and under tail-coverts; the Orange-crowned is pale greenish yellow, with dusky streaks and yellow under tail-coverts; the Tennessee is pale greenish yellow, *without* streaks, and with the under tail-coverts *white*.

Range.—Breeds in the Canadian Zone from the upper Yukon Valley, s. Mack., n. Man., cent. Que., and Anticosti Isl. s. to s. B. C., s. Alberta, s. Man., n. Minn., n. Mich., Ont., N. Y. (Adirondacks), n. Me., and N. H. Winters from Oaxaca to Colombia and Venezuela; in migration occurs mainly in the Miss. Valley, usually rare in spring on the Atlantic slope. Occasional in Fla. and Cuba; accidental in Calif.

Washington, T. V., May 4–June 3; occasionally common, Aug. 31–Nov. 30. Bronx region, fairly common spring, occasionally abundant fall T. V., May 3–30; Aug. 9–Oct. 17. Boston, T. V., May 10–31; Aug.–Sept., formerly rare, later common, now less so. N. Ohio, common T. V., May 4–25; Sept. 10–Oct. 10. Glen Ellyn, common T. V., Apr. 30–June 9; July 29–Oct. 12. SE. Minn., common T. V., Apr. 25–June 1; Aug. 8–Oct. 3.

Nest, of fine hempen fibers, grasses, and moss, lined with hair, on the ground in moss or grass. *Eggs*, pearly white, with a circle of brown and purplish spots about the larger end, ·60 X ·50 (B., B., and R.). *Date*, S. Lewiston, Me., June 4.

"The Tennessee is easily discovered and identified by its peculiar song—a twittering, semi-trilled, rather prolonged utterance of three parts, not very unlike the weaker and buzzier strains of the American Goldfinch's song" (Thayer in 'Warblers of North America'). Bradford Torrey says the Tennessee's song "is more suggestive of the Nashville's than of any other, but so decidedly different as never for a moment to be confounded with it," and adds a detailed description ('The Footpath Way,' p. 8).

1916. BOWDISH, B. S., and PHILIPP, P. B., Auk, 1–8 (in N. B.).

FIG. 134. Black and White Warbler.

FIG. 135. Worm-eating Warbler.

FIG. 136. Blue-winged Warbler.

FIG. 137. Golden-winged Warbler.

FIG. 138. Parula Warbler.

FIG. 139. Myrtle Warbler.

FIG. 140. Magnolia Warbler.

FIG. 141. Chestnut-sided Warbler.

422. ORANGE-CROWNED WARBLER. VERMIVORA CELATA CELATA *(Say).* [646.] *Ads.*—Upperparts rather ashy olive-green; feathers of the crown *orange-rufous* at the base; wings and tail edged with olive-green and without white; eye-ring yellow; underparts greenish yellow, obscurely streaked with dusky on the breast. *Im.*—Similar, but without orange-rufous in the crown; upperparts more ashy; underparts duller; eye-ring white. L., 5·00; W., 2·50; T., 1·95; B. from N., ·31.

Range.—Breeds in the Lower Hudsonian and Canadian zones from Kowak River, Alaska, se. to n. Man. Winters in the Gulf and S. Atlantic States n. to S. C., casually to O. and Mass.; also on the Pacific Coast from s. Calif. s. through L. Calif., and in Mex. to Mt. Orizaba; in migration mainly in the Miss. Valley; rare along the Atlantic slope from N. H.

Washington, casual T. V., two records, Oct. Bronx region, rare T. V., May 11–22; Oct. 9 (Jan. 20). Boston, rare T. V., in fall, Oct. 5–Nov. 15; casual in winter. N. Ohio, not common T. V., Apr. 27–May 21. Glen Ellyn, not common T. V., May 1–21; July 28–Oct. 7. SE. Minn., common T. V., Apr. 22–May 25; Aug. 18–Oct. 17.

Nest, of leaves and fine grasses, on or near the ground. *Eggs,* 4–5, white, with specks or spots of cinnamon-brown or rufous, more numerous at the larger end, ·63 × ·49.

Orange-crowned Warblers are rare in the Atlantic States north of South Carolina. In Florida, where they are common in the winter, they evidently prefer the densely foliaged live and water oaks. Their sharp *chip* is sufficiently characteristic to be recognized after one has become thoroughly familiar with it. Their song, which I have never heard, is described by Colonel Goss as consisting of "a few sweet trills uttered in a spirited manner, and abruptly ending on a rising scale."

423. NASHVILLE WARBLER. VERMIVORA RUFICAPILLA RUFICAPILLA *(Wilson).* [645.] *Ads.*—Top and sides of the head bluish gray, a partially concealed *chestnut patch* in the center of the crown; back and rump bright olive-green; wings and tail edged with the same and *without* white; underparts bright yellow, whiter on the belly. *Im.*—Upperparts dull olive-green, more or less washed with brownish; crown-patch often absent; rump brighter; wings and tail as in the ad.; sides of the head brownish ashy, eye-ring white; underparts yellowish, brighter on the breast; sides brownish. L., 4·77; W., 2·33; T., 1·81; B. from N., ·28.

Range.—Breeds mainly in the Canadian Zone from cent. Sask., cent. Ont., s. Que., and Cape Breton Isl. s. to Nebr., n. Ills., n. Pa., n. N. J., and Conn. Winters from Vera Cruz and Chiapas to Guat. and casually in Fla. and s. Tex.; migrates across the Gulf of Mex. and is very rare on the Atlantic slopes s. of Chesapeake Bay.

Washington, uncommon T. V., Apr. 20–May 20; Sept. 5–Oct. 13. Bronx region, common T. V., probably breeds, Apr. 26–May 30 (June 10); Aug. 11–Oct. 20; casual Dec. 16–Jan. 9. Boston, rather common S. R., May 5–Sept. 15; abundant T. V. N. Ohio, common T. V., Apr. 28–May 27; Sept. 1–Oct. 16. Glen Ellyn, regular T. V., Apr. 26–May 30; Aug. 18–Oct. 19. SE. Minn., common T. V., uncommon S. R., Apr. 29–Oct. 25.

Nest, of grasses and moss, lined with finer grasses and fine, hairlike rootlets, on the ground, in partial clearings or tree-grown pastures. *Eggs,* 4–5, white, thickly speckled, chiefly at the larger end, with rufous or cinnamon-brown, ·61 × ·48. *Date,* Boston, May 25; Lancaster, N. H., May 25; Bangor, Me., June 3.

This Warbler is an inhabitant of rather open woodland, young second growth, or tree-bordered fields. In addition to the usual *chip,* it has a sharp, characteristic call-note, while its song is about as likely to attract attention as that of the Chestnut-sided Warbler. Thayer ('Warblers of North America') writes: "The Nashville has at least two perch-songs and a flight-song, all subject to a good deal of variation. . . . Its commoner perch-song consists of a string of six or eight or more, lively, rapid notes suddenly congested into a pleasant, rolling twitter. . . . In the other perch-song, the notes of what correspond to the rolling twitter are separate and richer, and the second part of the song is longer and more noticeable than the first whose notes are few and slurred, while the whole is more languidly delivered. . . . The flight-song, a fairly common performance in late summer, is sung from the height of 5 to 40 feet above the (usually low) tree-tops. It is like the commoner perch-songs, but more hurried, and slightly elaborated, —often with a few chippings added at both ends."

1910. Stanwood, C. J., Journ. Me. Orn. Soc., 28–33 (nesting).

424. NORTHERN PARULA WARBLER. Compsothlypis americana pusilla *(Wilson)*. [648a.] (Fig. 138.) *Ad.* ♂.—Upperparts grayish blue; a *greenish yellow patch in the middle of the back;* greater and lesser wing-coverts tipped with white; outer tail-feathers with a white patch near the end; throat and breast yellow, more or less marked with pale rufous, *a black or bluish black, or rufous band across the breast;* belly white; sides sometimes marked with rufous. *Ad.* ♀.—Similar, but the rufous color and band on the breast sometimes absent. *Im.*—Resembling the ♀. L., 4·73; W., 2·40; T., 1·76; B. from N., ·32.

Range.—Breeds mainly in the Transition and Austral zones from e. Nebr., n. Minn., cent. Ont., Anticosti Isl., and Cape Breton Isl. s. to Tex., La., and Md. Winters in the Bahamas and the W. I. to Barbados, and from Vera Cruz and Oaxaca to Nicaragua. Casual in Wyo. and Colo.; accidental in Greenland.

Washington, T. V., but dates not distinguishable from those of *americana.* Bronx region, common T. V., rare S. R., Apr. 23–June 8; Aug. 14–Oct. 28. Boston, common T. V., May 1–28; Sept. 10–30. N. Ohio, not common T. V., May 1–18. Glen Ellyn, not common T. V., Apr. 30–May 31; Aug. 25–Oct. 1. SE. Minn., uncommon T. V., May 5–June 5; Sept. 4–21.

Nest, in a bunch of Usnea 'moss.' *Eggs,* similar to those of the following. *Date,* New Haven, May 18; Lancaster, N. H., May 31; Ann Arbor, Mich., May 12.

This slightly differentiated form of the Parula Warbler resembles the southern race in song and habits. During its migrations it is generally distributed, but when nesting it selects only localities where the Usnea moss in which it builds is found.

1924. Mousley, H., Auk, 263–288; 1926. 184–187 (home-life).

424a. PARULA WARBLER. Compsothlypis americana americana *(Linnæus).* [648.] Similar to *C. a. usneæ* but with less black about the lores, throat in ♂ with more yellow, the blackish throat band very narrow or poorly defined. ♀ not distinguishable from ♀ of *usneæ.* Smaller than specimens of *usneæ* from the northern Atlantic States; larger than specimens of *usneæ* from the lower Mississippi Valley. W., 2·25; T., 1·60; B., ·38 ('Warblers of North America').

Range.—Breeds in Austral zones from D. C. s. to Ala. and Fla. Winters in Fla. and the Bahamas (Great Inagua).

Washington, T. V., and a few breed, Apr. 17–Oct. 17.

Nest, generally in bunches of Tillandsia. *Eggs*, 4–5, white, with rufous markings, chiefly in a wreath about the larger end, ·66 × ·47. *Date*, Mt. Pleasant, S. C., Apr. 15; Iredell Co., N. C., May 11.

In Florida the Parula's notes mark the beginning of a new ornithological year, and its song is associated in my mind with the beauties of a southern spring when the cypresses are enveloped in a haze of lace-like blossoms, and the woods are fragrant with the delicious odor of yellow jasmine. Then the dreamy softness of the air is voiced by the Parula's quaint, drowsy, little gurgling sizzle, *chip-er, chip-er, chip-er, chee-ee-ee-ee.* The abundance of the Tillandsia 'moss' furnishes the Parula with unlimited nesting-sites, and the bird is proportionately common.

425. EASTERN YELLOW WARBLER. DENDROICA ÆSTIVA ÆSTIVA (*Gmelin*). [652.] *Ad. ♂.*—Upperparts bright greenish yellow, brighter on the crown; wings edged with yellow; tail fuscous, the *inner vanes of the feathers yellow;* underparts bright yellow, streaked with rufous. *Ad. ♀.*—Upperparts uniform yellowish olive-green; *tail as in the ♂*; wings fuscous, edged with yellow; underparts bright yellow, slightly, if at all, streaked with rufous on the breast and sides. *Im. ♂.*—Similar to the *♀. Im. ♀.*—Upperparts light olive-green; tail fuscous, the inner margins of the *inner vanes of the tail-feathers yellow;* underparts uniform dusky yellowish. L., 5·10; W., 2·40; T., 1·89; B. from N., ·33.

Remarks.—In any plumage this bird may be known by the yellow on the inner vanes of the tail-feathers.

Range.—Breeds through N. A. e. of Alaska and the Pacific slope from tree-limit s. to Nev., n. N. Mex., s. Mo., n. Ala., n. Ga., and n. S. C. Winters from Yucatan to Guiana, Brazil, and Peru.

Washington, common S. R., abundant T. V., Apr. 2–Oct. 31. Bronx region, common S. R., Apr. 27–Sept. 25 (Oct. 5). Boston, common S. R., May 1–Sept. 15. N. Ohio, abundant S. R., Apr. 14–Sept. 10. Glen Ellyn, not common S. R., Apr. 30–Sept. 12. SE. Minn., common S. R., Apr. 28–Sept. 28.

Nest, of fine grasses and hempen fibers, with a conspicuous amount of plant-down, lined with plant-down, fine grasses, and sometimes long hairs, in the shrubs or trees of lawns or orchards, about water, etc. *Eggs*, 4–5, bluish white, thickly marked with cinnamon- and olive-brown, with frequently a wreath about the larger end, ·70 × ·50. *Date*, Waynesburg, Pa., May 14; New Haven, Conn., May 20; Boston, May 23; Lancaster, N. H., June 7; Black Hawk Co., Ia., May 19; se. Minn., May 14.

When anyone tells me he has seen a 'Wild Canary,' I feel reasonably sure he refers to the Yellow Warbler, for the casual observer at once betrays his inexperience by entirely overlooking the bird's streaked breast and slender bill. It has, it is true, the general appearance of a yellow bird, and its bright colors and preference for gardens, orchards, the shrubbery of our lawns or bushy brooksides, instead of the woods, frequently bring it to the attention of those to whom most birds are strangers. It is an active bird, and its song—*wee-chee, chee, chee, cher-wee*—though simple, has a pleasing, happy ring.

1913. BIGGLESTONE, H. C., Wilson Bull., 49–67 (nesting).—1926. MOUSLEY, H., Auk, 187–190 (home-life).

426. MAGNOLIA WARBLER. DENDROICA MAGNOLIA (*Wilson*). [657.] (Fig. 140.) *Ad. ♂.*—Crown bluish gray, cheeks and forehead black, a white line behind the eye; back black, bordered with olive-green, a large white patch on the wing-coverts; rump yellow, tail black, inner vanes of all but the central feathers with white patches on *their middle,* the end third of the feather being entirely *black;* throat yellow, breast and sides heavily streaked with black. *Ad. ♀.*—Similar, but with the colors duller and less sharply defined; back greener. *Ads. fall and im. ♂.*—Top and sides of the head ashy; back olive-green, with nearly concealed black spots; two narrow wing-bars; rump yellow, *tail as in the adults;* underparts yellow; whiter on the belly; sides with black streaks. *Im. ♀.*—Similar, but no black streaks above, those on sides barely evident. L., 5·12; W., 2·30; T., 2·00; B. from N., ·30.

Remarks.—In any plumage this bird may be known by the white patches on the tail being near the middle instead of at the tip of the feathers.

Range.—Breeds in the Canadian and Upper Transition zones from sw. Mack. (casually Great Bear Lake), cent. B. C., cent. Man., cent. Que., and N. F. s. to cent. Alberta, s. Sask., Minn., n. Mich., and n. Mass., and in the mts. of N. Y., W. Va., Md., and winters from s. Mex. to Panama, and also rarely in Haiti and Porto Rico; in migration w. to base of the Rocky Mts.; accidental in Calif., B. C., the Bahamas, and Cuba.

Washington, common T. V., Apr. 22–June 4; Aug. 15–Oct. 28. Bronx region, common T. V., May 1–June 12; Aug. 15–Oct. 19. Boston, T. V., rather common, May 12–25; not uncommon, Sept. 10–25; has bred. N. Ohio, common T. V., Apr. 28–May 27; Sept. 1–Oct. 10. Glen Ellyn, common T. V., Apr. 27–June 5; Aug. 12–Oct. 9. SE. Minn., common T. V., May 6–June 7; Aug. 12–Sept. 30.

Nest, of fine twigs, leaf-stems, etc., lined with hairlike rootlets, in coniferous trees, usually 3–6 feet up. *Eggs,* 3–5, white, marked with cinnamon- and olive-brown, chiefly in a wreath about the larger end, ·66 × ·48. *Date,* Branchport, N. Y., June 2; Lancaster, N. H., May 24.

Adult Magnolia Warblers are so distinctly marked that ordinarily they may be identified at sight. Immature birds are less strikingly colored, but in any plumage the species may be known by having the white tail-spots nearer the middle than the ends of the feathers. Seen from below, the birds thus appear to have a white tail broadly tipped with black.

The Magnolia's summer home is among the spruces and hemlocks. Its typical song, which is of somewhat the same character as that of the Yellow Warbler, is described by Thayer (in 'Warblers of North America') as a "peculiar and easily remembered: *weeto weeto weeeétee-eet,*— or *witchi, witchi, whichi tit,*—the first four notes deliberate and even and comparatively low in tone, the last three hurried and higher pitched, with decided emphasis on the antepenult *weet* or *witch.*"

1910. STANWOOD, C. J., Auk, 384–389 (nesting).—1926. NICE, M. M., Wilson Bull., 185–199; 1927, 236 (nesting).

427. CAPE MAY WARBLER. DENDROICA TIGRINA (*Gmelin*). [650.] (Fig. 4.) *Ad. ♂.*—Crown black, slightly tipped with greenish; *ear-coverts rufous,* bounded behind by a large yellow patch on the side of the neck; back olive-green, broadly streaked with black; rump yellow or greenish yellow; *a large white patch on the wing-coverts;* outer tail-feathers with a large white patch on their inner webs, near the tip; underparts yellow, heavily streaked with black; lower belly and under tail-coverts whitish. *Ad. ♀.*—Upperparts grayish olive-green; crown with more or less concealed black; *rump yellowish;* a yellow line over the eye; middle wing-coverts with narrow white tips;

outer tail-feathers with a white patch on their inner webs near the tip; underparts yellow, streaked with black; belly and under tail-coverts whiter.
Im. ♂.—Resembles the ♀, but the wing-coverts have more white. *Im. ♀.*—
Similar to ad. ♀, but with little or no yellow on the underparts; upperparts
duller, and more uniform in color. L., 5·00; W., 2·61; T., 1·88; B. from N.,
·30.

Range.—Breeds in the Canadian Zone from s. Mack., n. Ont., N. B., and
N. S. s. to s. Man., Me., and N. H., w. in migration to Kans. and N. Dak.
Winters in the Bahamas and the W. I. to Tobago. Accidental in Yucatan.

Washington, sometimes very common, usually uncommon T. V., Apr.
19–May 30; Aug. 4–Oct. 18; two winter records (Dec. 16). Bronx region,
fairly common T. V., May 6–June 5; Aug. 22–Oct. 16. Boston, uncommon
T. V., May 15–25; Aug. 25. N. Ohio, not common T. V., May 4–18. Glen
Ellyn, irregular T. V., Apr. 30–June 3; Sept. 8–15. SE. Minn., uncommon
T. V., May 4–31; Aug. 26–Sept. 28.

Nest, partially pensile, of twigs and grass fastened with spiders' webbing,
lined with horsehair, on a low branch of a small tree in pasture or open
woodland. *Eggs,* 3–4, dull white or buffy, slightly speckled, and wreathed
around the larger end with spots of brown and lilac, ·70 × ·50 (Chamberlain).
Date, St. John's, N. B., June 16.

During its migrations this generally rare Warbler may be found
associated with its wood-inhabiting congeners and it also frequents the
coniferous trees of our lawns. In the summer it haunts the higher
branches of coniferous trees. Gerald Thayer (in 'Warblers of North
America') writes of its song: "The whole utterance, in tone phrasing
and accentuation, strongly suggests the Black and White Warbler's
shorter song. . . . On the other hand, the Cape May's singing is near
akin to the Blackpoll's."

428. BLACK-THROATED BLUE WARBLER. DENDROICA CÆRULES-
CENS CÆRULESCENS (*Gmelin*). [654.] *Ad. ♂.*—Upperparts grayish blue,
back sometimes blackish; wings and tail edged with blue; *base of the primaries white,* forming a white spot on the wing at the end of the primary coverts;
inner vanes of outer tail-feathers with a white patch near their tips; sides
of the head and throat black; sides mixed black and white; breast and belly
white. *Ad. ♀.*—Upperparts uniform olive-green; tail generally with a faint
bluish tinge, the white patch on the outer feathers scarcely distinguishable;
white at the base of the primaries much reduced and sometimes concealed
by the primary coverts; ear-coverts dusky gray; underparts soiled buffy
yellowish. *Im. ♂.*—Similar to ad. ♂, but the upperparts washed with
greenish, the throat tipped with white, and less black on the sides. *Im. ♀.*—
Similar to ad. ♀, but somewhat yellower. L., 5·28; W., 2·52; T., 2·06; B.
from N., ·29.

Remarks.—The white spot at the base of the primaries is the distinguishing mark of this species.

Range.—Breeds in the Canadian and Transition zones from n. Minn.,
cent. Ont., and s. Que. s. to cent. Minn., n. Mich., s. Ont., Pa. (mts.), and
n. Conn. Winters from Key West, Fla., to the Bahamas, Greater Antilles,
and Cozumel Isl., and casually to Guat. and Colombia; in migration casually
to N. Dak., Nebr., Kans., Colo., and N. Mex. Accidental on the Farallon
Isls., Calif.

Washington, very common T. V., Apr. 19–May 30; Aug. 4–Oct. 29.
Bronx region, common T. V., Apr. 25–May 28; Aug. 16–Oct. 29 (Dec. 9).
Boston, rather common T. V., May 10–25; Sept. 20–Oct. 10. N. Ohio,
common T. V., Apr. 27–May 29; Sept. 5–Oct. 16. Glen Ellyn, common T.
V., Apr. 29–June 3; Aug. 23–Oct. 10. SE. Minn., uncommon T. V., May
10–28; Aug. 6–Sept. 30.

Nest, of strips of bark, fine grasses, and pine needles, lined with hairlike black rootlets, in the heavier undergrowth of dense woods, usually within 2 feet of the ground. *Eggs*, 3–5, grayish white, with distinct and obscure olive-brown markings, chiefly about the larger ends, ·68 × ·50. *Date*, Litchfield, Conn., June 8; Lancaster, N. H., June 19; Kalamazoo Co., Mich., May 29.

Where the range of this species reaches the Canadian Zone, it nests in coniferous forests, but southward its summer home is in deciduous

FIG. 142. Black-throated Blue Warbler. (Reduced.)

woods, always, however, with a dense undergrowth. Its call-note is a sharp, recognizable *chip*, its common song may be written *zwee-zwee-zwee*, but it is subject to much variation, indeed Thayer (in 'Warblers of North America') describes three additional songs.

The male Black-throated Blue Warbler can be identified at sight, but the female's obscure colors call for closer observation; the white patch at the base of the primaries will distinguish the adult, but in the bird of the year even this mark may be wanting.

428a. CAIRNS'S WARBLER. DENDROICA CÆRULESCENS CAIRNSI *Coues.* [654*a*.] Similar to *D. c. cærulescens* but ♂ with the back always more or less spotted with black, sometimes the center of the back being entirely black. *Ad.* ♀ generally darker than ♀ of *cærulescens*. While specimens of true *cærulescens* not infrequently show more or less black in the back, *cairnsi* is very rarely without this character.

Range.—Breeds in Canadian and Transition zones in the s. Alleghanies from Md. to Ga.; winters in the W. I.

429. MYRTLE WARBLER. DENDROICA CORONATA (*Linnæus*). [655.] (Fig. 139.) *Ad.* ♂.—A yellow patch on the *crown, rump, and each side of the breast;* upperparts bluish gray, streaked with black; two white wing-bars; outer tail-feathers with white spots on their inner vanes near the tip; throat white; breast and upper belly heavily marked with black; lower belly white. *Ad.* ♀.—Similar, but with less black below; breast simply streaked with black; upperparts browner. *Im. and ads. in winter.*—Yellow crown-patch more or less concealed by brownish tips to the feathers; rump bright yellow; yellow on the sides of the breast much reduced; upperparts grayish brown, streaked with black; wing-bars grayish; tail with white patches; underparts soiled white, streaked with black. L., 5·65; W., 2·85; T., 2·25; B. from N., ·29.

Remarks.—The yellow patches on the crown, rump, and sides of the breast are characteristic of this species.

Range.—Breeds in the Hudsonian and Canadian zones from tree-limit in nw. Alaska, n. Mack., n. Man., and cent. Que. s. to n. B. C., n. Minn., n. Mich., cent. Ont., N. H., and Me., and in the mts. of N. Y., Vt., and Mass. Winters from Kans., the O. Valley, and N. J. (locally s. N. E.) s. to the Greater Antilles and Panama, and on the Pacific Coast from cent. Ore. to n. L. Calif. Accidental in Greenland and e. Siberia.

Washington, abundant W. V., Aug. 7–May 30. Bronx region, abundant T. V., usually winters; Apr. 5–June 12; Aug. 16–Dec. 26. Boston, abundant T. V., Apr. 12–May 20; Sept. 1–Nov. 1; a few winter. N. Ohio, common T. V., Apr. 12–May 20; Sept. 15–Nov. 3. Glen Ellyn, common T. V., Apr. 7–May 28; Sept. 24–Dec. 29. SE. Minn., common T. V., Apr. 3–May 28; Sept. 6–Nov. 5.

Nest, of vegetable fibers lined with grasses, in coniferous trees 5–10 feet up. *Eggs*, 4–5, white or grayish white, distinctly and obscurely spotted and speckled or blotched with olive-brown or rufous-brown, ·70 × ·52. *Date*, Bangor, Me., May 30; Kentville, N. S., May 29.

These strong, hardy Warblers leave their cousins of the woods and in loose companies forage in old fields and scrubby growths among the bayberry or myrtle (*Myrica*) bushes, which bear their favorite food. So fond are they of these berries that their movements are largely governed by the success or failure of the bayberry crop. Near my home at Englewood, N. J., Myrtle Warblers are always common during the winter if there is an abundance of bayberries and always absent when the berries are wanting.

No Warbler is more easily identified than this bird with its *four* distinct patches of yellow. The yellow rump is conspicuous in life, and, in connection with the bird's characteristic *tchep*, forms an excellent field-mark. It begins to sing on its spring migrations a bright, cheery trill suggesting the song of the Junco.

430. AUDUBON'S WARBLER, *Dendroica auduboni auduboni* (Townsend), [656], of the western states, has been recorded from Minnesota, Massachusetts (Boston), and Pennsylvania.

431. The BLACK-THROATED GRAY WARBLER, *Dendroica nigrescens* (Townsend), of the western United States, has been three times recorded from Massachusetts.

432. TOWNSEND'S WARBLER, *Dendroica townsendi* (Townsend), [668], of western North America, has been once recorded from Pennsylvania.

433. BLACK-THROATED GREEN WARBLER. DENDROICA VIRENS VIRENS (*Gmelin*). [667.] *Ad.* ♂.—Upperparts bright olive-green, back sometimes spotted with black; line over the eye and cheeks bright yellow, ear-coverts dusky; two white wing-bars; inner vanes of outer tail-feathers entirely white, *outer* web white at the base; throat and breast black; belly white, sometimes tinged with yellow; sides streaked with black. *Ad.* ♀.— Similar, but the black of throat and breast more or less mixed with yellow-ish. *Ad.* ♂ *in fall and im.* ♂.—Similar to the ♀, but with more yellow on the chest, the black sometimes being almost entirely hidden or wanting. *Im.* ♀.—Similar to ad. ♀, but duller above, black on chest sometimes en-tirely absent. L., 5·10; W., 2·46; T., 1·99; B. from N., ·25.

Remarks.—The bright yellow cheeks of this species, in connection with the large amount of white in the tail, will serve to distinguish it in any plumage.

Range.—Breeds in the Lower Canadian and Transition zones from cent. Alberta, s. Man., cent. Ont., cent. Que., and N. F. s. to s. Minn., s. Wisc., n. O., n. N. J., Conn., and L. I., and in the Alleghanies s. to n. S. C., n. Ga. and n. Ala. In migration w. to e. Tex.; winters from Mex. to Panama. Oc-casional in the W. I. and the Fla. Keys; accidental in Colo., Calif., Ariz., Greenland, Porto Rico, and Europe; recorded in Va. (Dismal Swamp) in summer (possibly *D. v. waynei*).

Washington, very common T. V., Apr. 18–June 10; Aug. 26–Oct. 21, Bronx region, fairly common S. R., common T. V., Apr. 21–June 9; Aug. 21–Nov. 20. Boston, abundant S. R., May 1–Oct. 15. N. Ohio, common T. V., Apr. 25–May 24; Sept. 1–Oct. 16; a few breed. Glen Ellyn, common T. V., Apr. 28–June 8; Aug. 22–Oct. 12. SE. Minn., common T. V., un-common S. R., Apr. 29–Sept. 26.

Nest, of small twigs and moss, lined with rootlets, fine grasses, and ten-drils, in coniferous trees, 15–50 feet from the ground. *Eggs,* 4, white, dis-tinctly and obscurely spotted and speckled with olive-brown or umber, chiefly at the larger end, ·65 × ·46. *Date,* New Haven, Conn., May 21; Boston, June 5; Grand Manan, N. B., June 14.

When migrating, this species joins the ranks of the Warbler army and visits wooded land of almost any kind. When nesting it prefers coniferous forests, where it is a dweller among the tree-tops.

While resembling its congeners in general habits, the song of the Black-throated Green is so unlike their generally humble ditties that the bird seems possessed of more character than they impress us with having. Mr. Burroughs graphically represents its notes by straight lines: ———— V ——; a novel method of musical annotation, but which nevertheless will aid one in recognizing the bird's song. There is a quality about it like the droning of bees; it seems to voice the restfulness of a midsummer day.

1910. Stanwood, C. J., Auk, 289–294 (nesting).

433a. WAYNE'S WARBLER. Dendroica virens waynei *Bangs.* Similar to *D. v. virens* but black area of throat and sides of the breast averag-ing smaller; yellow of sides of the head slightly paler; bill more slender.

Range.—Resident in the coastal district of S. C.

1919. Wayne, A. T., Auk, 489–492 (nesting).

434. CERULEAN WARBLER. Dendroica cerulea (*Wilson*). [658.] *Ad.* ♂.—Upperparts bright cerulean blue, the sides of head and back streaked with black; wings and tail edged with blue; two white wing-bars; inner vanes of all but the central tail-feathers with white patches at their tips; underparts white, a bluish black band across the breast; sides streaked with bluish black. *Ad.* ♀.—Upperparts bluish olive-green; wings and tail much as in the ♂; underparts white, generally more or less tinged with pale yellow. *Im.*—Similar to ad. ♀, but yellower. L., 4·50; W., 2·65; B. from N., ·31.

Range.—Breeds mainly in Austral zones from se. Nebr., se. Minn., s. Mich., s. Ont., w. N. Y. (and usually in Dutchess Co.), w. Pa., and W. Va. s. to ne. Tex. and n. Ga., and locally in the Hudson Valley, w. N. C., w. Va., e. Md., and cent. Del. Winters from Venezuela to e. Peru; in migration through Cent. A. Casual in L. Calif., N. Mex., Colo., N. H., R. I., Conn., N. J., e. Pa., Man., Cuba, and the Bahamas.

Washington, several records in May. Bronx region, rare T. V., May 4–27. N. Ohio, common S. R., Apr. 29–Sept. 20. Glen Ellyn, not common, local S. R., May 8–Aug. 19. SE. Minn., rare S. R., May 5–(July 16).

Nest, of fine grasses bound with spiders' silk, lined with strips of bark and fine grasses and with a few lichens attached to its outer surface, in a tree, 25–50 feet from the ground. *Eggs*, 3–4, creamy white, thickly covered with rather heavy blotches of reddish brown, ·60 × ·47 (Allen, Bull. Nutt. Orn. Club, 1879, 26). *Date*, Oberlin, O., May 15; Ann Arbor, Mich., May 20.

In writing of this species as observed by him in Ritchie County, West Virginia, Mr. Brewster says:

"Decidedly the most abundant of the genus here. The first specimen taken May 5. They inhabit exclusively the tops of the highest forest trees, in this respect showing an affinity with *D. blackburniæ*. In actions they most resemble *D. pensylvanica*, carrying the tail rather high and having the same 'smart bantamlike appearance.' Were it not for these prominent characteristics they would be very difficult to distinguish in the tree-tops from *Parula* [= *Compsothlypis*] *americana*, the songs are so precisely alike. That of the latter bird has, however, at least two regular variations: in one, beginning low down, he rolls his guttural little trill quickly and evenly up the scale, ending apparently only when he can get no higher; in the other the commencement of this trill is broken or divided into syllables, like *zee, zee, zee, ze-ee-ee-eep*. This latter variation is the one used by *D. cærulea*, and I could detect little or no difference in the songs of dozens of individuals. At best it is a modest little strain and far from deserving the encomium bestowed upon it by Audubon, who describes it as 'extremely sweet and mellow'; decidedly it is neither of these, and he must have confounded with it some other species. In addition to the song they utter the almost universal Dendroicine lisp and also the characteristic *tchep* of *D. coronata*, which I had previously supposed entirely peculiar to that bird."

1924. Gray, G. W., Auk, 161, 162 (in Dutchess Co., N. Y.).

435. BLACKBURNIAN WARBLER. Dendroica fusca (*Müller*). [662.]

Ad. ♂.—Center of the black crown, a line over the eye, patch behind the black ear-coverts, throat, and breast beautiful *rich orange;* back black, streaked with whitish; wing-coverts white, forming a large white patch on the wing; inner vane of most of the tail-feathers almost *entirely* white, except at the tip; the outer vane of the outer feather white at the base; belly tinged with orange, sides streaked with black. *Ad.* ♀.—Resembles the ♂, but the orange markings are paler, the upperparts are ashy olive-green streaked with black and whitish; the white on the wings and tail is less extensive. *Im.* ♂.—Resembles the ♀, but has the orange markings dull yellow, the crown-patch nearly absent. *Im.* ♀.—Similar to the im. ♂, but the yellow markings much paler, nearly buffy, the back browner. L., 5·25; W., 2·71; T., 1·96; B. from N., ·31.

Remarks.—In connection with other markings, the large amount of white in the tail, appearing on even the *outer* vane of the outer feather, is characteristic of this species.

Range.—Breeds in the Lower Canadian and Upper Transition zones from cent. Man., Que., and Cape Breton Isl. to cent. Minn., n. Mich., Mass., and Conn., and in the Alleghanies from Pa. to Ga. Winters from Venezuela to cent. Peru and less commonly n. to Yucatan; in migration to Nebr., Tex., and Kans., straggling to Mont., N. Mex., and the Bahamas.

Washington, common T. V., Apr. 23–June 3; Aug. 2–Oct. 10. Bronx region, common T. V., May 1–June 6; Aug. 12–Oct. 4 (Oct. 15). Boston, T. V., uncommon, May 12–22; rare, Sept. 15–30. N. Ohio, common T. V., Apr. 27–May 25; Sept. 1–25. Glen Ellyn, fairly common T. V., May 4–June 8; Aug. 12–Sept. 22. SE. Minn., common T. V., May 1–31; Aug. 22–Sept. 8.

Nest, of fine twigs and grasses, lined with grasses and tendrils, in coniferous trees, 10–40 feet up. *Eggs*, 4, grayish white or bluish white, distinctly and obscurely spotted, speckled, and blotched with cinnamon-brown or olive-brown, ·68 × ·50. *Date*, Branchport, N. Y., May 24; Lancaster, N. H., June 4; Kalamazoo Co., Mich., June 2.

The Blackburnian is uncommon enough to make us appreciate his unusual beauty. Coming in May, before the woods are fully clad, he seems like some bright-plumaged tropical bird who has lost his way and wandered to northern climes. The summer is passed among the higher branches in coniferous forests, and in the early fall the bird returns to surroundings which seem more in keeping with its attire.

Mr. Minot describes its summer song as resembling the syllables *wee-seé-wee-seé-wee-seé* (*wee-seé-ick*), while in the spring its notes may be likened to *wee-see-wee-see, tsee-tsee, tsee, tsee, tsee-tsee, tsee, tsee,* the latter syllables being on ascending scale, the very last shrill and fine.

436. YELLOW-THROATED WARBLER. DENDROICA DOMINICA DOMINICA (*Linnæus*). [663.] *Ad. ♂.*—A *yellow* line in front of the eye and a white line over it; upperparts *gray*, forehead blackish; wings and tail edged with grayish, two white wing-bars; outer tail-feathers with white patches near their tips; cheeks and sides of the throat black; a white patch on the side of the neck; throat and breast yellow, belly white, sides streaked with black. *Ad. ♀.*—Similar, but with less black on the head, throat and neck. L., 5·25; W., 2·60; T., 2·01; B., ·49.

Range.—Breeds mainly in the Lower Austral Zone from s. Md., Dela., and s. N. J. to middle Fla. Winters in s. Fla., the Bahamas, and Greater Antilles, and also casually north to Ga. and S. C. and in the Lesser Antilles Casual in N. Y., Mass., and Conn.

Washington, rare S. R., rather common in late July and Aug.; Mch. 30–Oct. 10. Bronx region, A. V.; one recent record, May 18. Boston, A. V.

Nest, of twigs, strips of bark, and Tillandsia 'moss,' lined with vegetable down, 30–40 feet from the ground, in pines or live oaks, sometimes in a bunch of Tillandsia 'moss.' *Eggs*, 4–5, white or grayish white, with numerous distinct and obscure cinnamon- or olive-brown markings, sometimes evenly distributed, sometimes in a wreath at the larger end, ·74 × ·52. *Date*, Charleston, S. C., Apr. 2; Raleigh, N. C., Apr. 22.

Some birds are so characteristic of certain places that wherever heard or seen they recall their accustomed haunts. I have only to remember the song of the Yellow-throated Warbler to give form to a mental picture of some tree-bordered stream or bayou in the South.

The song bears some resemblance to that of the Indigo Bunting, but has a wilder, more ringing quality. In this respect it suggests the song of *Seiurus motacilla.* It may be written *ching-ching-ching, chicker, cher-wee.* It is to some extent ventriloquial, and this in connection with the rather deliberate movements of the birds, and the fact that they resort to the upper branches, makes it sometimes difficult to locate the singer.

436a. SYCAMORE WARBLER. DENDROICA DOMINICA ALBILORA *Ridgway.* [663a.] Similar to the preceding, but with a smaller bill and the line in front of the eye white instead of yellow. W., 2·60; T., 2·00; B., ·45.

Range.—Breeds in Upper and Lower Austral zones of Miss. Valley from se. Nebr., s. Wisc., s. Mich., O., W. Va., and w. N. C. s. to cent. Tex. and La.; winters from Puebla, Tepic, and Colima, Mex., to Nicaragua and Costa Rica and casually in the Lower Rio Grande Valley. Acc. in S. C. and Conn.

"The Sycamore Warbler is a common summer resident in the bottom-lands [of Illinois], where, according to the writer's experience, it lives chiefly in the large sycamore trees along or near the water-courses. On this account it is a difficult bird to obtain during the breeding season, the male usually keeping in the topmost branches of the tallest trees, out of gunshot and often, practically, out of sight, although its presence is betrayed by its loud, very unwarblerlike song" (Ridgway).

437. CHESTNUT-SIDED WARBLER. DENDROICA PENSYLVANICA (*Linnæus*). [659.] (Fig. 121.) *Ad.* ♂.—Crown bright yellow, a black line behind the eye; front part of the cheeks black; ear-coverts white; back streaked with black and margined with bright olive-green; wing-bars yellowish white; tail black, the outer feathers with white patches on their inner vanes at the tip; underparts white, the *sides chestnut. Ad.* ♀.—Similar, but somewhat duller in color. *Ad. in fall and Im.*—Very different; upperparts bright yellowish olive-green, back sometimes streaked with black; wing-bars yellowish white; underparts pure, silky white, the sides in ads. with spots or patches of chestnut. L., 5·14; W., 2·45; T., 2·00; B. from N., ·29.

Range.—Breeds mainly in the Transition Zone from cent. Sask., s. Que., and N. F. s. to e. Nebr., Ills., Ind., n. O., n. N. J., and R. I., and in the Alleghanies and outlying ridges and foothills to Tenn. and S. C.; also casually in s. Mo. and the Wabash Valley. Winters from Guat. to Panama. Casual in Fla., and accidental in Calif., the Bahamas, and s. Mex.

Washington, abundant T. V., Apr. 19–June 2; Aug. 10–Oct. 14. Bronx region, common T. V., fairly common S. R., Apr. 26–Sept. 23 (Oct. 9). Boston, abundant S. R., May 5–Sept. 10. N. Ohio, T. V., May 2–25. Glen Ellyn, rare S. R., common T. V., May 1–Oct. 8. SE. Minn., common S. R., May 2–Sept. 26.

Nest, of strips of bark, leaf-stems, etc., lined with tendrils and rootlets, in bushes, about 3 feet up. *Eggs,* 4–5, white, with numerous distinct and obscure cinnamon- and olive-brown markings, chiefly in a wreath about the larger end, ·69 × ·50. *Date,* New Haven, Conn., May 23; Boston, May 26; Ann Arbor, Mich., May 20; se. Minn., May 27.

When settled for the summer, Chestnut-sided Warblers may be found in second growths, scrubby clearings, or the bushy borders of woodlands. There is a suggestion in their movements of the restless activity of the Redstart, as with drooped wings and slightly raised tail they flit among the lower growth. They have two songs, both of which closely resemble those of the Yellow Warbler, though a practiced ear can at once recognize the song of either.

Adults of this species are too conspicuously marked to be mistaken for any other Warbler, but in the fall have a care in identifying the very differently colored young.

438. BAY-BREASTED WARBLER. DENDROICA CASTANEA (*Wilson*). [660.] *Ad.* ♂.—Forehead and cheeks black, a cream-buff patch on the sides of the neck; *crown chestnut; throat, upper breast, and sides chestnut-rufous;* back brownish ashy, streaked with black; two white wing-bars, inner vanes of outer tail-feathers with white patches at their tips; lower breast and belly buffy white. *Ad.* ♀.—Crown olive-green, streaked with black and with generally some chestnut; rest of upperparts as in the ♂; underparts *buffy* white; breast and sides more or less stained with rufous. *Ad. in fall and Im.*—Upperparts bright olive-green, indistinctly streaked with black; wings and tail much as in the ads.; underparts white, tinged with *cream-buff*, especially on the flanks; ads. usually have some concealed chestnut in crown and traces of chestnut on sides. L., 5·63; W., 2·95; T., 2·12; B. from N., ·30.

Range.—Breeds in the Canadian Zone from e. cent. Alberta and N. F. s. to s. Man., n. Me., the mts. of Vt. and N. H. and the Adirondacks of N. Y. Winters in Panama and Colombia; irregular in migration in the Atlantic slope and rare s. of Va.; but a regular migrant across the Gulf of Mex. and through Guat. to Panama. Casual in Mont., S. Dak., and Tex.

Washington, sometimes abundant, usually uncommon T. V., May 2–June 5; Aug. 17–Nov. 6. Bronx region, common T. V., May 4–June 6; Aug. 16–Oct. 4 (Oct. 13). Boston, rather rare T. V., May 15–25; Sept. 12–28. N. Ohio, common T. V., May 4–23; Sept. 7–Oct. 10. Glen Ellyn, tolerably common T. V., May 8–June 5; Aug. 13–Oct. 11. SE. Minn., uncommon T. V., May 11–June 4; Aug. 13–Sept. 23.

Nest, of grasses and plant-fibers, lined with plant-down and long hairs, in coniferous trees, 15–20 feet up. *Eggs*, 4–5, white, finely marked, chiefly at the larger end, distinctly and obscurely with cinnamon-, olive-, or rufous-brown, ·72 × ·52. *Date*, Bangor, Me., June 15.

During its migrations this tastefully marked Warbler is generally uncommon enough to be considered somewhat of a prize, though at irregular intervals it becomes comparatively common. It is said to be much rarer in fall than in spring, but at this season Bay-breasts so closely resemble Black-polls, that it is sometimes difficult to determine specimens, while, in immature plumage, many birds cannot possibly be distinguished in nature.

In the summer the Bay-breasts inhabit the northern coniferous forests, living, it is said, in the tree-tops. "In a grouping based on songs, the Bay-breast should stand in a quintette with the Blackburnian, the Black-poll, the Black and White, and the Cape May. . . . The Bay-breast's singing, in the spring at least, is the most liquid and inarticulate of the lot and sometimes the loudest" (Thayer in 'Warblers of North America').

1909. STANWOOD, C. J., Journ. Me. Orn. Soc., 103–110 (nesting).

439. BLACK-POLL WARBLER. DENDROICA STRIATA (*J. R. Forster*). [661.] (Fig. 143.) *Ad.* ♂.—Crown black; ear-coverts white; nape streaked, black and white; back and rump ashy, streaked with black; two white wing-bars; inner vanes of outer tail-feathers with white patches at their tips;

underparts white, streaked with black, the streaks most numerous on the sides, and wanting on the middle of the breast and belly. *Ad.* ♀.—Upperparts olive-green, distinctly streaked with black; wings and tail as in the ♂; underparts white, tinged with *yellow*, the breast and sides distinctly streaked with black. *Ads. fall and Im.*—Similar to ♀, but the upperparts are brighter and not distinctly streaked, the underparts yellower and not distinctly streaked. L., 5·56; W., 2·92; T., 2·05; B. from N., ·30.

Remarks.—No two of our Warblers more closely resemble each other than do immature and fall examples of this and the preceding species. There is no difference in the color of the upperparts, but *castanea* has the underparts tinged with delicate *cream-buff*, strongest on the flanks, while *striata* is distinctly *yellowish* below.

Range.—Breeds in the Hudsonian and Canadian zones from the limit of trees in nw. Alaska, n. Mack., and N. F. s. to n. B. C., Mich., n. Me., and the mts. of N. Y., Vt., and N. H. Winters from Guiana and Venezuela to Brazil; migrates through the Bahamas and W. I. Casual in N. Mex., Colo., Mex., Chile, and Ecuador. Accidental in Greenland. (Fig. 6.)

Washington, abundant T. V., Apr. 21–June 16; Aug. 17–Nov. 14. Bronx region, abundant T. V., May 3–June 17; Aug. 30–Oct. 29. Boston, abundant T. V., May 12–June 5; Sept. 8–Oct. 20. N. Ohio, common T. V., May 6–June 2; Sept. 1–Oct. 16. Glen Ellyn, common T. V., May 2–June 8; Aug. 23–Sept. 27. SE. Minn., common T. V., May 5–June 4; Aug. 24–Sept. 29.

Nest, of twigs, moss, rootlets, etc., lined with fine grasses and tendrils, generally in spruce trees, about 6 feet up. *Eggs*, 4–5, white, more or less speckled and spotted, and generally heavily blotched at the larger end with cinnamon-, olive-, or rufous-brown, ·70 × ·54. *Date*, Grand Manan, N. B., June 11.

The Black-poll is not the last Warbler to reach us in the spring, but it is usually the last of the transients to leave us, the length of its stay and its abundance making its passage one of the features of the spring migration. In the fall it is even more abundant. Adults and young are now alike in plumage, but they are to be confused only with the much rarer Bay-breasts.

Gerald Thayer (in 'Warblers of North America') describes the Black-poll's main song, from which there are many variations, as "a string of six to twelve or more, short, equal and equally divided sibilant notes, cobweb-thin and glassy-clear,—uttered rather fast; the whole song smoothly swelling in volume to the middle, or the second third, and then smoothly falling off."

440. NORTHERN PINE WARBLER. DENDROICA PINUS PINUS (*Wilson*). [671.] (Fig. 115.) *Ad.* ♂.—Upperparts bright olive-green, sometimes washed with ashy; two whitish wing-bars; outer tail-feathers with white patches on their inner vanes near the tip; underparts bright yellow, more or less washed with ashy, turning to white on the lower belly and under tail-coverts; sides sometimes with a few black streaks. *Ad.* ♀.—Similar, but upperparts brownish olive-green; underparts soiled whitish; breast tinged with yellow. L., 5·52; W., 2·81; T., 2·25; B., ·47.

Range.—Breeds in the Transition and Austral zones from n. Man., s. Que., and N. B., s. to e. Tex. and the Gulf States. Winters from s. Ills. and the coast of Va. to Fla., e. Tex., and Tamaulipas, and casually n. to Mass. Occasional in Bermuda and Prince Edward Isl.

Washington, quite common S. R., Mch. 5–Oct. 4; abundant in fall. Bronx region, uncommon T. V.; no recent breeding records; Mch. 24–May 15; Sept. 23–Nov. 7, and occasionally in Dec. Boston, locally common S. R., Apr. 10–Oct. 20; occasional W. V. N. Ohio, not common T. V., Apr. 29–

May 15; a few breed. Glen Ellyn, not common T. V., spring records only,
Apr. 17–June 3. SE. Minn., common T. V., Apr. 26–May 26; Aug. 23–
Oct. 15.

Nest, of strips of bark, leaves, plant-fibers, etc., in pines 10–80 feet up.
Eggs, 4–5, white or grayish white, with numerous distinct and obscure
cinnamon-brown to umber markings, chiefly in a wreath or band at the
larger end, ·70 × ·52. *Date*, Raleigh, N. C., Mch. 24; Boston, May 20.

True to its name, the Pine Warbler is rarely found outside of pine
woods. In the South, where pineries may extend over half a state, it
is an abundant and generally distributed bird; in the more northern
part of its range it is, from force of circumstances, a local species,
occurring only with the pines.

In the winter it is found in small flocks, which may contain a few
Myrtle or Palm Warblers, and at this season it lives on or near the
ground. In the summer it is more arboreal. Its habit of clinging to
the trunk of a tree, or hopping along a limb while searching for insects
in crevices in the bark, has given it the misnomer of Pine Creeping
Warbler. Its song which, in Florida, is often heard in the winter, is a
clear, sweet, even trill.

440a. FLORIDA PINE WARBLER. DENDROICA PINUS FLORIDA (*Maynard*). Similar to *D. p. pinus* but bill longer, head and back more yellowish,
less greenish. B., ·55 (Howell, Auk, 1930, 42).

Range.—Fla. s. of Volusia, Lake, and Citrus counties.

441. KIRTLAND'S WARBLER. DENDROICA KIRTLANDI (*Baird*). [670.]
Ad. ♂.—Head bluish gray, sometimes spotted with black; lores and sides
of the throat black; back brownish ashy, spotted with black; no white wing-
bars; outer tail-feathers with white patches on their inner webs at the tips;
underparts pale yellow; sides streaked and spotted with black. *Ad.* ♀.—
Similar, but lores and cheeks grayish, black streaks less pronounced. Fall
specimens of both sexes are much browner. L., 5·75; W., 2·75; T., 2·30;
B. from N., ·32.

Range.—Breeds in Transition Zone in Oscoda, Crawford, and Roscommon
counties, Mich.; winters in the Bahamas as far s. at least as the Caicos Isls.;
in migration recorded from Minn., Wisc., Ont., O., Ills., Ind., Mo., Va.,
S. C., Ga., and Fla.

Washington, one record, Sept. 25, 1887. N. Ohio, rare T. V., May 9
and 11. Glen Ellyn, one record, May 7, 1894. SE. Minn., one record, Minneapolis, May 13.

Nest, on the ground at the foot of a pine or oak, of soft bark, strips of
vegetable fiber, grass, etc., lined with fine grass, pine needles, and hair.
Eggs, 3–5, white, speckled with umber, wreathed at the larger end, ·71 × ·54.
Date. Oscoda Co., Mich., June 6. (See Wood, Warblers of N. A., 206–209.)

During the summer this, the rarest of North American Warblers,
is known only from north-central Michigan, while during the winter it
appears to be restricted to the Bahamas. It reaches Florida about
April 20 and Michigan about May 15. The return journey is made
between August and November.

Aside from its size and color, Kirtland's Warbler may be known by
its habit of tail-wagging in which it rivals the Palm Warbler. When
migrating it frequents the lower growth and when nesting lives only

in high, sandy jack-pine plains. According to Wood (in 'Warblers of North America') this Warbler has several distinct songs, "all of which belong to the whistling type and have the clear, ringing quality of the Oriole's."

1924. LEOPOLD, N. F., Auk, 44–58, illus. (nesting).

442. PRAIRIE WARBLER. DENDROICA DISCOLOR DISCOLOR (*Vieillot*). [673.] (Fig. 144.) *Ad. ♂*.—Upperparts bright olive-green; *back spotted with chestnut-rufous;* wing-bars yellowish; outer tail-feathers with large white patches at their tips, the *outer* vane of the outer feather white at the base; a yellow line over the eye; lores and a crescent below the eye black; under-parts bright yellow; sides heavily streaked with black. *Ad. ♀*.—Similar, but with less, and sometimes no chestnut-rufous in the back. *Im. ♀*.—Upperparts uniform ashy olive-green; no apparent wing-bars; outer tail-feathers with white on their inner webs at the tips; ear-coverts ashy; under-parts yellow; sides indistinctly streaked with blackish. L., 4·75; W., 2·20; T., 1·95; B. from N., ·28.

Remarks.—The chestnut-rufous patch in the back at once identifies the adults; but the young females are puzzling birds to be known chiefly by their small size, absence of wing-bars and streaks on the sides.

Range.—Breeds chiefly in the Upper and Lower Austral zones from e. Nebr., e. Kans., s. O., sw. Pa., s. N. J., Mass. (along the coast) and casually in Dutchess Co., N. Y., s. to Ark., sw. Mo., n. Miss., s. Ala., cent. Ga., and the Bahamas, and n. locally to cent. Mich., s. Ont., and N. H.; rarely and locally in the Gulf States. Winters from cent. Fla. through the Bahamas and the W. I. and casually on isls. off the coast of Cent. A.

Washington, very common S. R., Apr. 12–Oct. 3. Bronx region, fairly common T. V., uncommon S. R., Apr. 26–June 5; Aug. 16–Oct. 3. Boston, locally common S. R., May 8–Sept. 15. N. Ohio, not common in spring, Apr. 29, May 9 and 14.

Nest, of plant-fibers and plant-down, lined with rootlets and long hairs, in briary bushes. *Eggs*, 4–5, white, spotted distinctly and obscurely with cinnamon- or olive-brown, or chestnut, chiefly in a wreath at the larger end, ·64 × ·48. *Date*, Savannah, Ga., Apr. 25; Raleigh, N. C., May 14; Boston, May 28; Ottawa Co., Mich., May 26.

The Yellow, Palm, and Prairie Warblers are the three 'Wood War-blers' that are rarely found in the woods. The latter, however, differs decidedly in habits from either of the former. It is a rather retiring inhabitant of scrubby clearings, bushy fields, and pastures, or thickets of young pines and cedars. But while the Prairie, if silent, might readily escape observation, no one with an ear for bird-music will pass within sound of a singing bird without at least trying to solve the mystery of its peculiar notes, a series of six or seven quickly repeated *zees*, the next to the last one the highest.

442a. FLORIDA PRAIRIE WARBLER. DENDROICA DISCOLOR COLLINSI *Bailey*. Female "has a much lighter breast, and throat almost white at base of lower mandible; with less reddish on back; which is decidedly grayish. The males lack the heavy wide black markings on sides, the heavy orange on throats, and the heavy reddish backs, all so pronounced on the northern breeding birds" (Bailey).

Range.—Mangrove swamps on the coast of Fla. from New Smyrna and Anclote Key s. (Also in myrtle bushes in sloughs of interior—Howell, Auk, 1930, 42.)

443. PALM WARBLER. DENDROICA PALMARUM PALMARUM (*Gmelin*).
[672.] *Ads.*—Crown chestnut; back olive grayish brown, indistinctly streaked;
rump olive-green; no wing-bars; tail black, the outer feathers with white
patches on their inner vanes at the tips; a yellow line over the eye; throat
and breast bright yellow; belly soiled whitish, tinged with yellow; sides of the
throat, the breast, and sides streaked with chestnut-rufous; under tail-
coverts yellow. *Ad. in winter and Im.*—Crown-cap partly concealed by
brownish tips to the feathers and sometimes wanting; line over the eye and
eye-ring *white;* underparts soiled whitish, more or less tinged with yellow;
breast streaked with dusky. L., 5·25; W., 2·64; T., 2·10; B. from N., ·32.
Range.—Breeds in the Canadian Zone from s. Mack. and n. Man. s.
to n. Minn. Winters from s. Fla. and the Bahamas to the Greater Antilles
and Yucatan; occurs casually in migration on the Atlantic slope mainly in
autumn. Accidental in Calif., Mont., and Colo.
Washington, rare T. V., Apr. 22–May 20; Sept. 18–Oct. 11. Bronx
region, uncommon T. V., chiefly fall; Apr. 20–May 15; Sept. 5–Nov. 13.
Boston, uncommon T. V., in fall, Sept. 15–Oct. 10. N. Ohio, tolerably common T. V., Apr. 24–May 20; Sept. 10–Oct. 16. Glen Ellyn, common T. V.,
Apr. 22–May 19; Sept. 4–Oct. 18. SE. Minn., common T. V., Apr. 11–May
31; Sept. 6–Oct. 23.
Nesting-date, Ft. Resolution, Mack., June 18.

This interior race of the Yellow Palm Warbler is occasionally met with
in the North Atlantic States, while in Florida it is much more common
than the eastern form. Sometimes the two birds may be seen in the same
flock, when the brighter colors of *hypochrysea* are usually apparent.

443a. YELLOW PALM WARBLER. DENDROICA PALMARUM HYPO-
CHRYSEA *Ridgway*. [672a.] *Ads.*—Crown chestnut; back brownish olive-
green; rump olive-green; no white wing-bars; secondaries sometimes tinged
with chestnut; tail edged with olive-green, the outer feathers with white
spots on their inner vanes near the tips; line over the eye and eye-ring yellow; underparts *entirely* bright yellow; sides of the throat, the breast, and
sides streaked with chestnut-rufous. *Ad. in winter and Im.*—Crown-cap
partly concealed by the brownish tips to the feathers and sometimes wanting;
line over the eye and eye-ring *yellowish; entire* underparts uniform yellow,
washed with ashy; the sides of the throat, the breast, and sides streaked
with chestnut-rufous or dusky. L., 5·43; W., 2·61; T., 2·10; B. from N., ·31.
Remarks.—In any plumage this bird may be distinguished from the
preceding by its uniform yellow underparts.
Range.—Breeds in the Canadian Zone from Ont., cent. Que., and N. F.
s. to s. N. S., N. B., and Me. Winters from La. to Fla., casually to W. Va.,
Pa. and Mass. Accidental in O, Cuba, Jamaica, and Bermuda.
Washington, common, T. V., Mch. 31–May 13; Sept. 4–Nov. 18. Bronx
region, common T. V., Apr. 3–May 13; Sept. 16–Nov. 27. Boston, usually
common, sometimes abundant, T. V., Apr. 15–May 5; Oct. 1–15.
Nest, of rather coarse grasses lined with finer grasses, on or near the
ground. *Eggs*, 4–5, white or buffy white, with some distinct and obscure
cinnamon- or olive-brown markings, chiefly at the larger end, ·65 × ·51.
Date, Dartmouth, N. S., May 26.

This species is a renegade *Dendroica*. He has no liking for the
woods, and even trees in the open do not seem to attract him. His
tastes bring him to fields and roadsides, where he lives on or near the
ground, but is ever active and much on the move. During the winter,
in the south, he is a common bird in the streets and gardens of towns,
and like a Chippy hops familiarly about piazzas.

He has the same nervous peculiarity, which, irrespective of family, seems to affect some birds, and, as though life were a matter of beating time, never ceases to wag his tail. His fine *chip* is recognizable after one has become familiar with it, while his two songs are described by Gerald Thayer (in 'Warblers of North America') as "chiefly trills, one slower and fuller-toned, the other much quicker and thinner."

444. OVEN-BIRD. Seiurus aurocapillus (*Linnæus*). [674.] (Fig. 145.) *Ads.*—Center of the crown pale rufous or ochraceous-buff, bordered on either side by black lines; rest of the upperparts, wings, and tail brownish olive-green; no wing-bars or tail-patches, underparts white; the sides of the throat, the breast, and sides streaked with black. L., 6·17; W., 3·00; T., 2·15; B. from N., ·35.

Range.—Breeds from sw. Mack., cent. Que., and N. F. s. to s. Alberta, Colo., Kans., Ark., s. Mo., n. Ala., n. Ga., and e. N. C. Winters from n. Fla. (casually S. C.) and isls. on the La. coast through the Bahamas and W. I. to St. Thomas, and from Mex. (Nuevo Leon) to Colombia. Casual in migration in Calif. and at Mazatlan.

Washington, very common S. R., Apr. 10–Nov. 13. Bronx region, common S. R., Apr. 26–Oct. 22 (Nov. 6). Boston, very common S. R., May 6–Sept. 15. N. Ohio, abundant S. R., Apr. 22–Oct. 1. Glen Ellyn, fairly common S. R., common T. V., Apr. 28–Oct. 10. SE. Minn., common S. R., Apr. 27–Sept. 30.

Nest, bulky, covered, the entrance at one side, of coarse grasses, weed-stalks, leaves, and rootlets, on the ground. *Eggs*, 4–5, white, speckled or spotted with cinnamon- or rufous-brown markings, sometimes finely distributed, sometimes confluent about the larger end, ·80 × ·60. *Date*, Weaverville, N. C., May 7; Chester Co., Pa., May 22; Boston, May 25; se. Minn., May 19.

During the nesting season Oven-birds are among our commonest woodland birds. We hear them everywhere; one singer scarcely ceases before another begins. But when the song period has passed how comparatively rare they become! The reason is not hard to find. At most times the Oven-bird is somewhat of a recluse. He passes much of his time on or near the ground, generally where the woods are more or less undergrown. Only the practised ear will detect his sharp, weak *cheep*.

If there be such a thing as inspiration, I believe the Oven-bird sings under its influence. Not that his usual song is in the least remarkable, but because the bird is so obviously moved by a spirit which demands utterance. Watch him now as he is about to sing. Flying up from the ground, how cautiously he hops from branch to branch, and, with crest slightly erect, *walks* carefully along a limb, when, suddenly overcome by the music in his soul, he throws fear to the winds and lifts up his voice in a crescendo chant which vibrates through the woods. Teacher, *teacher*, ᴛᴇᴀᴄʜᴇʀ, TEACHER, *TEACHER*, Mr. Burroughs writes it, and the description is difficult to improve upon. The bird fairly quivers with the violence of his effort. The result seems inadequate; we feel that he is striving for something better, and, in truth, as Mr. Bicknell says, he sometimes breaks the bonds that ordinarily beset his expression, and "bursts forth with a wild outpouring of intricate

Fig. 143. Black-poll Warbler.

Fig. 144.   Prairie Warbler.

Fig. 145.   Oven-bird.

Fig. 146. Kentucky Warbler.

Fig. 147. Maryland Yellow-throat.

Fig. 148. Wilson's Warbler.

Fig. 149. Hooded Warbler.

Fig. 150. Canadian Warbler.

and melodious song," the very force of which carries him up into the air among the tree-tops.

1911. STANWOOD, C. J., Journ. Me. Orn. Soc., XIII, 18–20 (nesting).—1926. MOUSLEY, H., Auk, 190–196 (home-life).—1918. ROBERTS, T. S., Bird-Lore, 329–334, illus. (habits).—1931. NICE, M. M., Auk, 215–218 (nesting).

445. NORTHERN WATER-THRUSH. SEIURUS NOVEBORACENSIS NOVEBORACENSIS (*Gmelin*). [675.] (Fig. 115*d*.) *Ads.*—Upperparts, wings, and tail uniform olive; no wing-bars or tail-patches; a buffy line over the eye; underparts white, tinged with pale sulphur-yellow (richer in fall), and everywhere—*including throat*—streaked with black. L., 6·04; W., 2·99; T., 2·11; B. from N., ·36.

Range.—Breeds chiefly in Canadian Zone from n. Ont., n. Que., and N. F. s. to s. Ont., nw. N. Y., and n. N. E. (casually s. N. E.), and in the mts. s. to Pa. and W. Va. Winters from the Valley of Mex. to Colombia and British Guiana, and from Fla. and the Bahamas throughout the W. I.; in migration w. to Minn., Ia. and Mo.

Washington, common T. V., Apr. 16–June 2; July 21–Oct. 16. Bronx region, common T. V., Apr. 23–June 8; July 28–Oct. 9 (Oct. 20). Boston, common T. V., May 8–June 1; Aug. 10–Oct. 10; rare local S. R. N. Ohio, common T. V., Apr. 26–May 25; Sept. 1–15. Glen Ellyn, Apr. 25–May 23, spring only.

Nest, of moss, lined with tendrils and fine rootlets, in a mossy bank or under the roots of a fallen tree. *Eggs*, 4–5, white, or buffy white, with numerous cinnamon-brown markings, chiefly about the larger end, ·76 × ·59. *Date*, Branchport, N. Y., May 18; Pittsfield, Me., May 28.

In general habits this bird resembles its southern relative, the Louisiana Water-Thrush, but during its migrations it is frequently found some distance from water, and I have known birds to spend several days beneath evergreen trees on a lawn a quarter of a mile from the woods. It is, too, much less shy than *motacilla*, and one can generally approach closely enough to take note of the characters which distinguish it from that species—a smaller bill, more sharply defined and darker streaks, and yellower underparts.

The sharp, steely alarm-note, *clink*, is not so penetrating as that of *motacilla*, and the loud, ringing song, while lacking in the wild quality which so characterizes the notes of that species, is nevertheless more musical.

445a. GRINNELL'S WATER-THRUSH. SEIURUS NOVEBORACENSIS NOTABILIS *Ridgway*. [675*a*.] Similar to the preceding, but slightly larger, upperparts darker, underparts and line over the eye whiter. W., 3·10; T., 2·20; B. from N., ·37.

Range.—Breeds chiefly in Boreal zones from the limit of trees in n. Man. s. to s. B. C., cent. Mont., n. Nebr., n. Minn., and nw. Mich. Winters in Cuba, Haiti, Porto Rico, and the Bahamas, and from L. Calif. and Mex. to n. S. A.; migrates throughout the Miss. Valley and along the Atlantic Coast from S. C. southward. Accidental at East Cape, Siberia, and in Calif. and N. J.

Washington, casual, three instances, May and Aug. Glen Ellyn, fairly common T. V., Apr. 14–June 5; Aug. 17–Oct. 6. SE. Minn., common T. V., Apr. 22–June 4; Aug. 13–Oct. 15.

446. LOUISIANA WATER-THRUSH. SEIURUS MOTACILLA (*Vieillot*). [676.] (Fig. 115*d*.) *Ads.*—A conspicuous *white* line over the eye; upperparts, wings, and tail olive; no wing-bars or tail-patches; underparts white, tinged with cream-buff, especially on the flanks, and streaked with blackish, *except on the throat and middle of the belly.* L., 6·28; W., 3·23; T., 2·14; B. from N., ·40.

Remarks.—Aside from its larger size, this bird may be known from the preceding species by the whiter, more conspicuous line over the eye, buffy instead of yellowish tinge on the underparts, and absence of spots on the throat.

Range.—Breeds mainly in the Upper Austral Zone from e. Nebr., se. Minn., and the s. parts of Mich., Ont., N. Y., and N. E. s. to ne. Tex., s. Ala., n. Ga., and cent. S. C. Winters from n. Mex. to Colombia, the Greater Antilles, Antigua, and the Bahamas. Accidental in Calif.

Washington, rare S. R., Mch. 31–Sept. 30. Bronx region, fairly common S. R., Mch. 31–Oct. 4. Boston, very rare S. R. N. Ohio, tolerably common S. R., Mch. 28–Sept. 15. SE. Minn., common S. R., Apr. 17–Oct. 8.

Nest, of leaves, twigs, and rootlets, under a bank or the upturned roots of a fallen tree. *Eggs,* 4–6, white, evenly speckled or spotted, distinctly and obscurely, with cinnamon- or rufous-brown, ·75 × ·60. *Date,* Iredell Co., N. C., Apr. 21; Waynesburg, Pa., May 5, hatching; New Haven, Conn., May 6; Petersburg, Mich., May 5; se. Minn., June 6.

Few birds are more particular in their choice of homes than this Water-Thrush. He lives where dashing brooks leap down wooded hillsides, or where quieter streams flow through the lowland forests. He is a wild, shy bird, and his never-ceasing alertness suggests the watchfulness of the savage. Approach as quietly as you will, the Water-Thrush knows of your coming. With a tilting motion he *walks* on ahead, springs from rock to rock, or with a sharp, metallic *clink* of alarm takes wing and darts through the woods so low you scarcely get a glimpse of him. From a distant limb near the ground he watches you, constantly teetering his body as though even when resting he must find some outlet for his surplus nervous energy.

As a songster the Water-Thrush is without a rival. His song is not to be compared with the clear-voiced carol of the Rose-breasted Grosbeak, the plaintive chant of the Field Sparrow, or the hymnlike melody of the true Thrushes; it is of a different kind. It is the untamable spirit of the bird rendered in music. There is an almost fierce wildness in its ringing notes. On rare occasions he is inspired to voice his passion in a flight-song, which so far exceeds his usual performance that even the memory of it is thrilling.

447. KENTUCKY WARBLER. OPORORNIS FORMOSUS (*Wilson*). [677.] (Fig. 146.) *Ad.* ♂.—A yellow line from the bill passes over and around the back of the eye; crown, region below the eye, and the side of the throat black, the crown tipped with gray; rest of the upperparts, wings, and tail olive-green; no wing-bars or tail-patches; underparts bright yellow. *Ad.* ♀. –Similar, but the black areas more grayish and less clearly defined. L., 5·40; W., 2·60; T., 1·90; B. from N., ·32.

Range.—Breeds in the Upper and Lower Austral zones from se. Nebr., s. Wisc., n. O., cent. w. Pa., and the Hudson Valley s. to e. Tex., s. Ala., and n. Ga. Winters from Mex. to Colombia. Accidental in Vt., Mich., and Cuba.

Washington, not very uncommon S. R., Apr. 26–Sept. 5. Bronx region, uncommon and local S. R., May 2–11; Sept. 11. Boston, A. V. N. Ohio, rare, Apr. 27 and May 12.

Nest, bulky, of twigs and rootlets, firmly wrapped with several thicknesses of leaves, lined with fine rootlets, on or near the ground. *Eggs*, 4–5, white or grayish white, finely and evenly speckled or coarsely blotched with rufous to umber, ·72 × ·58. *Date*, Buncombe, N. C., May 23; West Chester, Pa., May 27; Dunklin Co., Mo., May 15.

The Kentucky Warbler frequents rather densely grown, well-watered woods. Here he may be found, on or near the ground, hopping from limb to limb or *walking* about searching for food. When singing, he generally mounts to the lower branches of the higher trees. His song is entirely unlike that of any other Warbler. It is a loud, clearly whistled performance of five, six, or seven notes—*tur-dle, tur-dle, tur-dle*—resembling in tone some of the calls of the Carolina Wren. Even in the woods it may be heard at a distance of about one hundred and fifty yards.

In the height of the breeding season this Warbler is a most persistent singer. On one occasion, at Englewood, N. J., I watched a male for three hours. During this period, with the exception of five interruptions of less than forty-five seconds each, he sang with the greatest regularity once every twelve seconds. Thus, allowing for the brief intervals of silence, he sang about 875 times, or some 5,250 notes. I found him singing, and when I departed he showed no signs of ceasing.

448. CONNECTICUT WARBLER. Oporornis agilis (*Wilson*). [678.] *Ad.* ♂.—Head, neck, and breast bluish gray, lighter on the throat; crown in fall tipped with olive-green; eye-ring *white;* rest of upperparts, wings, and tail olive-green; no wing-bars or tail-patches; belly yellow; sides washed with olive-green. *Ad.* ♀ *and Im.*—Similar to the ♂, but upperparts uniform olive-green; throat and breast pale grayish brown; belly pale yellow. L., 5·40; W., 2·90; T., 1·90; B. from N., ·32.

Range.—Breeds in the Canadian Zone from Alberta and Man. to cent. Minn., and possibly n. Mich. Winters from Colombia, Venezuela, to n. Brazil, migrating through S. C., Fla., and the Bahamas; rare in spring e. of the Alleghanies but common in the Miss. Valley; in autumn rare in the Miss. Valley but common e. of the Alleghanies. Casual ne. of Mass. and in Ont.; accidental in Colo.

Washington, T. V., very rare in spring, Apr. 30–May 30; common from Aug. 28–Oct. 24. Bronx region, irregular fall T. V., Aug. 20–Oct. 23. Boston, fall T. V., sometimes locally abundant, Sept. 10–30. N. Ohio, tolerably common T. V., May 7–24. Glen Ellyn, fairly common T. V., May 12–June 28; Aug. 14–Sept. 27. SE. Minn., uncommon spring migrant, May 18–June 3.

Nest, of dry grasses, on the ground. *Eggs*, 4, white, with a few spots of lilac-purple, brown, and black about the larger end, ·75 × ·60. (Seton, Auk, 1884, 192.) *Date*, Carberry, Man., June 21.

'Connecticut Warbler' is an unfortunate misnomer for this species. 'Swamp' or 'Tamarack Warbler,' or 'Bog Black-throat,' would have been much more truly descriptive.

In the cold, boggy tamarack swamps of Manitoba, where I found it breeding, it was the only one of the family, and almost the only bird whose voice broke the silence of those gray wastes. Its loud song was much like the *teacher, teacher* chant of the Oven-bird, but it also uttered another, which I can recall to mind by the aid of the syllables *free-chapple, free-chapple, free-chapple,* WHOIT.

The nest was placed on the ground, or, rather, in the moss which everywhere covered the ground to a depth of a foot or two, and was composed of fine vegetable fibers.

This species has somewhat the manners of the Vireos, but is much more active and sprightly in its movements. During the migrations it is generally found on or near the ground, in the undergrowth of low, damp woods, and also in bordering, weedy fields, where it sometimes announces its presence by a sharp *peek*. ERNEST THOMPSON SETON.

1929. HUFF, N. L., Auk, 455–465, illus.; 551 (nesting).

449. MOURNING WARBLER. OPORORNIS PHILADELPHIA (*Wilson*). [679.] *Ad. ♂*.—Head, neck, and throat bluish gray, *changing to black on the breast;* no white eye-ring; rest of upperparts, wings, and tail olive-green; no wing-bars or tail-patches; belly yellow. *Ad. ♀*.—Similar, but upperparts olive-green, slightly grayer on the head; breast grayish, throat whiter. *Im.*—Similar to ♀ but throat paler and with a yellowish eye-ring. L., 5·63; W., 2·56; T., 2·13; B. from N., ·32.

Remarks.—This species bears a general resemblance to the preceding, but is smaller. Adults may be distinguished from it by the absence of a white eye-ring, immature birds by their paler throat.

Range.—Breeds in the Lower Canadian Zone from e. cent. Alberta, cent. Sask., and N. F., s. to cent. Minn., Mich., cent. Ont., and in the mts. of N. Y., Pa., Mass., and W. Va. Winters from Nicaragua to Venezuela and Ecuador; in migration mainly w. of the Alleghanies and to e. Tex. but rare in the lowlands of the Gulf States apparently making a continuous flight across the Gulf of Mex. Accidental in Porto Rico. (Fig. 7.)

Washington, very rare T. V., May 6–June 7; Aug. 17–Oct. 1. Bronx region, rare but regular T. V., May 18–June 5; Aug. 5–Oct. 1. Boston, rare T. V., May 22–June 5; Sept. 12–25. N. Ohio, tolerably common T. V., May 5–28. Glen Ellyn, rather rare T. V., May 18–June 8; Aug. 17–?. SE. Minn., uncommon T. V., May 9–June 7; Aug. 1–Sept. 25.

Nest, of strips of bark and other fibrous materials, lined with hair, on or near the ground. *Eggs*, 4, white, sprinkled with reddish dots near the larger end, ·71 × ·54. *Date*, Orleans Co., N. Y., May 31; Listowel, Ont., June 3; Kalkuska Co., Mich., June 7.

The Mourning Warbler inhabits the undergrowth, choosing situations not unlike those selected by the Maryland Yellow-throat.

"Its common song consists of a simple, clear, warbling whistle, resembling the syllables *'trúē, 'trúē, 'trúē, 'trú, 'toó*, the voice rising on the first three syllables and falling on the last two.

"Sometimes, when otherwise occupied, the first, or first two, syllables are omitted. All through the breeding season, and till late in July, they have a very characteristic habit of perching, at frequent intervals during the day, on some branch, generally a dead one, and commonly 10 to 15 feet from the ground, and singing for half an hour at a time" (Merriam, 'Birds of Connecticut,' 24).

450. MACGILLIVRAY'S WARBLER, *Oporornis tolmiei* (Townsend), of western North America, is a casual migrant in Nebraska, Illinois, and Indiana. Adults resemble the Mourning Warbler but have the eye-ring, above and below the eye, white.

451. NORTHERN YELLOW-THROAT. GEOTHLYPIS TRICHAS BRACHIDACTYLA (*Swainson*). [681*d*.] (Fig. 147.) *Ad. ♂*.—A broad band across the forehead, and on the cheeks and ear-coverts black, bordered behind by grayish; rest of the upperparts, wings, and tail olive-green, sometimes tinged with brownish; no wing-bars or tail-patches; throat and breast bright yellow, changing to whitish on the belly; sides washed with brownish; under tail-coverts yellow. *Ad. ♂ in fall.*—Similar, but browner above; black mask tipped with grayish; belly more yellow; sides browner. *Im. ♂.*—Similar, but the black mask more concealed, sometimes merely indicated by a dusky area. *Ad. ♀.*—No black mask; upperparts, wings and tail olive-green, the forehead sometimes tinged with rufous; throat and breast yellowish, changing to whitish on the belly; under tail-coverts yellow; sides brownish. L., 5·33; W., 2·20; T., 2·04; B., ·42.

Range.—Breeds from N. F., s. Lab., and Que., s. to n. Pa., s. N. Y., and n. N. J., and w. to N. Dak. Winters in the Bahamas, W. I., and through e. Mex. to Costa Rica; and rarely in O.

Bronx region, common S. R., Apr. 26–Oct. 24 (Nov. 15); casual in winter. Boston, abundant S. R., May 5–Oct. 20; occasional in winter. N. Ohio, abundant S. R., Apr. 25–Sept. 25. Glen Ellyn, common S. R., May 2–Oct. 3. SE. Minn., common S. R., Apr. 30–Oct. 6.

Nest, bulky, of strips of bark, coarse grasses, and dead leaves, lined with fine grasses, tendrils, and rootlets, on or near the ground. *Eggs*, 3–5, white, rather thinly speckled and spotted with rufous to umber, chiefly—some, times entirely—at the larger end, ·70 × ·53. *Date*, Chester Co., Pa., May 19; Boston, May 25; Lancaster, N. H., June 2; Melbourne, Ia., May 24.

Doubtless one of the first acquaintances you will make, among the Warblers, will be this black-masked inhabitant of thickets and bushes. Indeed, you have only to pause near his home, when he will meet you halfway. He announces his coming by an impatient, quickly repeated *chack*, varying to *chit, pit, quit*, as, hopping from twig to twig, he finally appears for a moment and then darts back into the cover of his haunts.

His song is characteristic of his active, nervous nature, and is delivered with much force and energy. It varies greatly with locality, a fact which may account for the quite different descriptions given of it by authors. Sometimes it is written *wichity, wichity, wichity, wichity;* again, *rapity, rapity*, etc.; but the birds near New York City seem to me to say *I beseech you, I beseech you, I beseech you, I beseech you;* though, to be sure, the tone is far from pleading.

They sing throughout the summer, and include a flight-song in their repertoire. This is usually uttered toward evening, when the bird springs several feet into the air, hovers for a second, and then drops back to the bushes.

451a. MARYLAND YELLOW-THROAT. Geothlypis trichas trichas (*Linnæus*). [681.] Similar to *G. t. brachidactyla* but averaging smaller and paler, with yellow of underparts usually confined to throat, chest, breast, and under tail-coverts, the back, etc., more grayish. W., 2·10; T., 1·95 (Ridgway).

Range.—Breeds from s. Pa. s. to e. Tex. and n. parts of Ga. and Ala. Winters from N. C. and La. to Fla., the Bahamas, and Haiti; casually Pa. and N. J.

Washington, abundant S. R., Apr. 13–Nov. 2.

451b. FLORIDA YELLOW-THROAT. Geothlypis trichas ignota *Chapman*. [681*b*.] Similar to the preceding, but with longer tarsus, tail, and bill; yellow of underparts of a deeper shade and of greater extent; flanks of a much darker color; upperparts browner; black mask wider, its ashy border (in summer specimens) slightly paler and of greater extent; first primary shorter, equaling the eighth instead of the sixth. W., 2·17; T., 2·18; B., ·47.

Range.—Breeds in the Lower Austral Zone from the Dismal Swamp, Va., cent. Ala., and cent. Ga. s. to Fla. and along the Gulf Coast to La. Winters from the coast of S. C. and s. Ala.

Nesting-date, Charleston, S. C., May 9.

In Florida this southern representative of the Maryland Yellow-throat is usually found in dense growths of scrub palmetto. Its song differs recognizably from that of the northern bird.

452. YELLOW-BREASTED CHAT. ICTERIA VIRENS VIRENS (*Linnæus*). [683.] (Fig. 115*e*.) *Ads.*—Largest of the Warblers; upperparts, wings and tail olive-green; line from the eye to the bill, one on the side of the throat, and eye-ring white; throat, breast, and upper belly bright yellow; lower belly white; sides grayish. L., 7·44; W., 3·00; T., 3·07; B. from N., ·41.

Range.—Breeds mainly in Upper and Lower Austral zones from s. Minn., Wisc., Mich., Ont., cent. N. Y. to s. Fla. Winters in Mex. and Cent. A. Casual in s. Sask., N. H., and Me.

Washington, common S. R., Apr. 14–Sept. 29. Bronx region, fairly common S. R., Apr. 28–Oct. 3. Boston, rare and irregular S. R., May 15–Sept. N. Ohio, common S. R., May 1–Sept. 15. Glen Ellyn, very rare S. R., occasional T. V., May 10–Aug. 16. SE. Minn., very rare S. R., Houston Co., June 30, 1920.

FIG. 151. Yellow-breasted Chat. (Natural size.)

Nest, rather bulky, of coarse grasses, leaves, and strips of bark well interwoven, lined with finer grasses, in a crotch, near the ground. *Eggs*, 3–5, white, rather evenly speckled and spotted with rufous-brown, ·90 × ·66. *Date*, Chatham Co., Ga., May 7; Waynesburg, Pa., May 10; New Haven, Conn., May 22; Oberlin, O., May 15.

Bushy undergrowths or thickets in partial clearings form the home of the Chat. After an acquaintance of many years I frankly confess that his true character is a mystery to me. While listening to his strange medley and watching his peculiar actions, we are certainly justified in calling him eccentric, but that there is method in his madness no one who studies him closely can doubt.

Is the odd jumble of whistles, *chucks*, and caws uttered by one bird in that copse yonder, or by half a dozen different birds in as many places? Approach cautiously, and perhaps you may see him in the air—a bunch of feathers twitched downward by the queer, jerky notes which animate it. One might suppose so peculiar a performance would occupy his entire attention, but nevertheless he has seen you; in an instant his manner changes, and the happy-go-lucky clown, who a moment before was turning aërial somersaults, has become a shy, suspicious haunter of the depths of the thicket, whence will come his querulous *chŭt, chŭt* as long as your presence annoys him.

453. HOODED WARBLER. WILSONIA CITRINA (*Boddaert*). [684.] (Fig. 149.) *Ad. ♂.*—Forehead and cheeks bright yellow; crown black, connected behind with the black throat; upperparts, wings, and tail olive-green; outer tail-feathers with inner vane mostly white; breast and belly yellow; bill with evident bristles at its base. *Ad. ♀.*—Similar, but with the black hood usually developed as a narrow line on the nape and crown, and a blackish wash on the throat or chest. *Im. ♂.*—Similar to ad. ♂, but the black feathers with yellow tips. *Im. ♀.*—Similar to ad. ♀, but with no black on the head or breast. L., 5·67; W., 2·58; T., 2·30; B. from N., ·31.

Range.—Breeds in the Upper Austral and Lower Austral zones from se. Nebr., n. Ia., s. Mich., cent. N. Y., and the lower Conn. Valley s. to the coast of La., Ala., and in n. Fla. Winters from Vera Cruz and Yucatan to Panama. Occasional in the Bahamas, Cuba, and Jamaica and casually n. to Wisc., Mich., Ont., and Mass.

Washington, locally common S. R., Apr. 3–Oct. 1. Bronx region, fairly common S. R., Apr. 28–Sept. 26 (Oct. 1). Boston, casual T. V. N. Ohio, not common S. R.

Nest, of leaves, strips of bark, and rootlets, lined with fine grasses and rootlets, in the crotch of a bush or sapling, about four feet up. *Eggs*, 4–5, white or creamy white, rather thinly speckled or spotted with rufous or rufous-brown, generally in a wreath at the larger end, ·71 × ·53. *Date*, Charleston, S. C., Apr. 30, inc. adv.; Saybrook, Conn., May 26; Kalamazoo Co., Mich., June 10.

This beautiful bird is a lover of well-watered, rather densely grown woods. It is a bird of the lower growth rather than the trees, but is not a thicket-haunter, and its habit of flitting restlessly from bush to bush renders it easily observed. When on the wing its white outer tail-feathers are conspicuously displayed, and, with the striking markings of the head, make an excellent field-mark.

The song of the Hooded Warbler is sweet and graceful. It is subject to much variation, but as a rule consists of eight or nine notes. To my ear the bird seems to say, "You must come to the woods, or you won't see me." Its call-note is a sharp, characteristic *cheep*, frequently uttered when the bird is anxious for the safety of its nest or young, and accompanied by a flit of the tail, which reveals the white outer tail-feathers.

454. WILSON'S WARBLER. WILSONIA PUSILLA PUSILLA (*Wilson*). [685.] (Fig. 148.) *Ad. ♂.*—Forehead yellow, crown black, back olive-green, wings and tail edged with olive-green; no wing-bars or tail-patches; underparts bright yellow; bill with bristles at its base. *Ad. ♀.*—Similar, but generally without the black cap. *Im. ♀.*—Similar, but without black cap. L., 5·00; W., 2·21; T., 2·03; B. from N., ·25.

Range.—Breeds in Boreal zones from tree-limit in nw. and cent. Mack., cent. Que., and N. F. s. to s. Sask., n. Minn., and N. S. Winters in e. Cent. A., occasionally n. to Mex.; migrates mainly along the Alleghanies; practically unknown in the Lower Austral Zone from N. C. to La., apparently crossing this region and the Gulf of Mex. in a continuous migratory flight. Casual in B. C., Wash., and Colo.

Washington, rather common T. V., May 1–31; Aug. 2–Oct. 13. Bronx region, fairly common T. V., May 1–June 6; Aug. 10–Oct. 9 (Nov. 22). Boston, uncommon T. V., May 12–25; Sept. 5–20. N. Ohio, tolerably common T. V., May 5–June 2; Sept. 5–15. Glen Ellyn, not very common T. V., May 5–June 26; Aug. 16–Sept. 21. SE. Minn., common T. V., May 2–June 7; Aug. 19–Sept. 30.

Nest, on the ground, almost wholly of fine, dry grass, lined with a few hairs, deeply cupped and quite substantial for a Warbler. *Eggs,* 4, white, with or without light brown splashes and with a small wreath of dark specks at the larger end, ·59 × ·48. *Date,* Bangor, Me., June 1. (See 'Warblers of North America,' 277.)

The Black-cap frequents the lower woodland or bushy growths. Like other members of this genus, it has decided talents as a fly-catcher and captures much of its prey on the wing, darting out into the air. but does not, like a true Flycatcher, return to the same perch. It is an alert little bird and its motions of wings, tail or crest suggest a certain pertness of manner.

"The song has much of the ringing clarity of the Canada's and Hooded's songs. The commonest form of it, a rapid bubbling warble of two nearly equal parts, the second lower-toned and sometimes diminuendo, has always reminded me of a Northern Water-Thrush's song" (Thayer in 'Warblers of North America').

454a. The NORTHERN PILEOLATED WARBLER, *Wilsonia pusilla pileolata* (Pallas) of western North America is recorded by the A. O. U. 'Check-List' as casual in Minnesota and Missouri.

455. CANADA WARBLER. WILSONIA CANADENSIS (*Linnæus*). [686.] (Fig. 150.) *Ad.* ♂.—Upperparts, wings, and tail gray; no wing-bars or tailpatches; crown spotted with black; line from the bill to the eye and underparts yellow; sides of the neck black; *a necklace of black spots across the breast;* under tail-coverts white; bill with evident bristle at its base. *Ad.* ♀ *and Im.* ♂.—Similar, but with no black on the head or sides of the throat; necklace indicated by dusky spots. *Im.* ♀.—Similar, but with breast spots fainter or wanting. L., 5·61; W., 2·53; T., 2·23; B. from N., ·31.

Range.—Breeds in the Canadian Zone and casually in the Transition from s. Alberta, cent. Que., and N. F. s. to cent. Minn., s. Ont., cent. N. Y., and Conn., and along the Alleghanies to n. Ga. and Tenn. Winters in Ecuador and Peru and casually in Guat. and Costa Rica; in migration to e. Mex. Casual in Colo.

Washington, very common T. V., May 3–June 2; July 31–Oct. 23. Bronx region, common T. V., rare in summer, May 2–June 11; Aug. 9–Oct. 11 (Oct. 29). Boston, T. V., rather common, May 12–30; rare Sept. 1–15; uncommon local S. R. N. Ohio, common T. V., Apr. 28–May 27; Sept. 1–18. Glen Ellyn, common T. V., May 5–June 7; Aug. 15–Sept. 22. SE. Minn., common T. V., May 5–June 6; Aug. 17–Sept. 20.

Nest, of strips of bark, bits of dead wood, and moss wrapped in leaves, and lined with fine rootlets, in mossy banks or under roots. *Eggs,* 4–5, white, speckled and spotted, chiefly at the larger end, with rufous or rufousbrown, ·66 × ·51. *Date,* Lancaster, N. H., June 9; Bay City, Mich., June 2.

Although when associated with other migrating Warblers this bird may be found in woodland of varied character, it prefers low, wet woods, in which, like Wilson's Warbler, it frequents the lower growth. Like that bird also it is an expert fly-catcher.

Its song is sweet, loud, and spirited. Fuertes writes "It suggests to me the unfinished song of a Goldfinch more than that of a Warbler. It is very broken and energetic and also possesses a large quality" ('Warblers of North America').

456. AMERICAN REDSTART. Setophaga ruticilla (*Linnæus*). [687.] (Fig. 115c.) *Ad.* ♂.—Upperparts, throat, and breast shining black; basal half of the wing-feathers salmon, end half and wing-coverts black; basal two-thirds of all but the middle tail-feathers salmon, end third and middle feathers black; sides of the breast and flanks deep reddish salmon; belly white, tinged with salmon; bill with prominent bristles at its base. *Ad.* ♀.—Salmon of the ♂ replaced by dull yellow; head grayish; back ashy, with a greenish tinge; underparts, except where marked with yellow, white. *Im.*—Resemble the ♀; the ♂ acquires his full plumage at the end of his first breeding season during which he resembles the ♀, but is more or less mottled with black. L., 5·41; W., 2·57; T., 2·27; B. from N., ·27.

Range.—Breeds mainly in the Canadian and Transition zones from n. B. C., cent. w. Mack., cent. Man., s. Que., and N. F. to Ore., cent. Okla., s. Ala., n. Ga., and N. C. Winters in the W. I. and from cent. Mex. ,s. L. Calif. (casually), to Ecuador and British Guiana. Casual in Ore., Calif., Ariz., and n. Ungava. (Fig. 9.)

Washington, very abundant T. V., and less common S. R., Apr. 15–Oct. 8. Bronx region, abundant T. V., common S. R., Apr. 24–Oct. 16 (Nov. 16). Boston, common S. R., May 5–Sept. 20. N. Ohio, common S. R., Apr. 27–Sept. 20. Glen Ellyn, not common S. R., common T. V., May 2–Oct. 5. SE. Minn., common S. R., May 2–Oct. 6.

Nest, of fine strips of bark, leaf-stalks, and plant-down, firmly interwoven, lined with tendrils and fine rootlets, in the crotch of a sapling, 5–20 feet up. *Eggs,* 4–5, grayish white or bluish white, spotted and blotched, chiefly at the larger end, with cinnamon- or olive-brown, ·68 × ·50. *Date,* Raleigh, N. C., May 12; Waynesburg, Pa., May 19; New Haven, Conn., May 20; Boston, June 2; se. Minn., May 18.

If this active, brilliantly colored inhabitant of woodlands were as rare as he is beautiful, we would consider a meeting with him an event demanding at least a page in our journals. In Cuba most of our Wood Warblers are known simply as '*Mariposas*'—butterflies; but the Redstart's bright plumage has won for him the name '*Candelita*'—the little torch that flashes in the gloomy depths of tropical forests.

Ching, ching, chee; ser-wee, swee, swe-e-e he sings, and with wings and tail outspread whirls about, dancing from limb to limb, darting upward, floating downward, blown hither and thither like a leaf in the breeze. But the gnats dancing in the sunlight and the caterpillars feeding in the shade of the leaves know to their sorrow that his erratic course is guided by a purpose.

Family Ploceidæ. Weaver Finches.

The true Weaver Birds are Finches having the outermost primary "in plain view on the underside of the wing" (Chapin). The entire group numbers about 250 species and is found from Europe and Africa to Australia. As a family they are remarkable for their woven nests and communal habits. Many are familiar to us as cage-birds under the names Java Sparrow, Waxbill, Strawberry Finch, etc. Systematists have reached widely different conclusions concerning the birds which should be included in this group, but the contention of Dr. Peter P. Sushkin that the genus *Passer*, and some other Old-World genera, should be placed in a subfamily (*Passerinæ*) between the true Finches and Weaver Birds, but nearer the latter, has been generally accepted. The House Sparrow, therefore, is now classified with the Weaver Birds rather than with the true Finches. Its position between these two groups is indicated by having the outer primary concealed, as in the Finches, and its more obvious characters as a 'Weaver Bird' are found in the structure of its horny palate combined with a *complete* postjuvenal molt (including wings and tail) and the habit of building a domed nest with a side entrance.

The classification of these birds and their allies is still far from settled. It is discussed in the papers below mentioned.

1917. CHAPIN, J. P., Bull. Amer. Mus. Nat. Hist., XXXVII, 243–280 (classification of Weaver Birds).—1924–2. SUSHKIN, P. P., Bull. Brit. Orn. Club, XLV, 36.—1925. Auk, 256–260.—1926. Ibis, 831.—1927. Bull. Amer. Mus. Nat. Hist., 57, 1–32 (classification of *Ploceidæ* and *Fringillidæ*).

457. HOUSE OR ENGLISH SPARROW. PASSER DOMESTICUS DOMESTICUS (*Linnæus*). (Fig. 116.) *Ad.* ♂.—Crown gray, bordered from the eye backward and on the nape by chestnut; lesser wing-coverts chestnut, middle coverts tipped with white; back streaked with black and chestnut; rump ashy; middle of the throat and breast black; sides of the throat white; belly whitish. *Ad.* ♀.—Head and rump grayish brown; back streaked with black and deep ochraceous-buff; underparts dirty whitish, the breast and sides washed with pale grayish brown. L., 6·33; W., 3·01; T., 2·30; B., ·48.

Range.—Throughout Europe and the British Isles, except Italy where a different species is found, e. to Siberia. Introduced into the U. S. at Brooklyn, N. Y., in 1850 and during the next twenty-five years in various other cities including Quebec, Can., and Halifax, N. S.; now thoroughly naturalized throughout N. A. as far as settlements extend.

Bronx region, common P. R., first noted Apr. 11, 1879. Boston, abundant P. R.

Nest, of any available material in any available place. *Eggs,* 4–7, varying from plain white to almost uniform olive-brown, generally white, finely and evenly marked with olive, ·86 × ·62. *Date,* D. C., Mch. 1; Boston, Apr.–Aug.

This pest was first introduced into the United States at Brooklyn, New York, in 1850 and 1852. As late as 1870 it was largely confined to the cities of the Atlantic States, but since that date, partly through man's agency and partly through the bird's rapid increase in numbers and its adaptability, it spread over most of the United States and Canada; and its harsh, insistent *chirp* became the dominant bird-voice about our homes, where it seemed as though we might never again hope to hear a chorus of native bird-music unmarred by the discordant chatter of this alien. But relief has come from a wholly unexpected quarter. As automobiles displaced horses, there has been a diminution in the Sparrow's food-supply, followed, in towns and cities, at least, by a marked decrease in their numbers.

1889. BARROWS, W. B., Bull. No. 1, Biological Survey, 1–405 (economic status).—1909. TOWNSEND, C. W., Auk, 13–19 (habits).—1924. EATON, W. F., Auk, 604–606 (decrease of in e. Mass.).—1931. ALLEN, A. A., Bird-Lore, 144–154, illus. (autobiography).

458. The EUROPEAN TREE SPARROW, *Passer montanus montanus* (Linnæus), of Europe, was introduced at St. Louis, Mo., in 1870 and has become

established there. Unlike the House Sparrow, the sexes are alike. Both have a black throat-patch, which does not extend to the breast, a black spot on the ear-coverts, and a brown instead of gray head and nape. In juvenal plumage both throat and ear-coverts are blackish. The juvenal plumage in both sexes resembles that of the female, but at the postjuvenal molt the male acquires a black throat which is heavily veiled with gray.

FAMILY ICTERIDÆ. MEADOWLARKS, BLACKBIRDS, AND ORIOLES.

This distinctively American family is most abundantly represented in the tropics, where the majority of the 150-odd known species (about 240 species and subspecies) are found, only 18 (42 species and subspecies) advancing north of Mexico. With the exception of the Orioles, they are gregarious after the nesting season, while some of the species nest in colonies and are found in flocks throughout the year. They differ markedly in habits, and are found living in country of every nature, from dry plains and wet marshes to the densest forest growth. Some species possess marked vocal ability, while the voices of others are harsh and unmusical. They feed on fruit, seeds, grain and insects.

KEY TO THE SPECIES

I. With yellow or orange in the underparts.
II. Underparts black, with or without metallic reflections.
III. Underparts grayish, slate-color, chestnut, or buffy.
IV. Underparts black and white, or black tipped or margined with rusty.

I. With yellow or orange in the underparts.

1. Throat or breast-crescent black.
   a. Back black . . . . 465. BALTIMORE ORIOLE.
   b. Back greenish . . . . 464. ORCHARD ORIOLE, ♂ im.
   c. A black or blackish crescent on the breast; outer tail-feathers white.
       460, 460*a.* MEADOWLARKS. 461. WESTERN MEADOWLARK.
2. Throat not black, no breast-crescent.
   A. Entire underparts yellow, yellowish, or orange.
      a. Rump and tail orange . 465. BALTIMORE ORIOLE, ♀ and im.
      b. Underparts yellowish green . 464. ORCHARD ORIOLE, ♀ and im.
      c. Upperparts brownish, streaked and spotted with black; tail-feathers pointed . . . 459. BOBOLINK, ♀ ad. ♂, fall and im.
   B. Throat and breast yellow or yellowish; belly black or dark grayish brown . . . . 462. YELLOW-HEADED BLACKBIRD.

U. Underparts black, with or without metallic reflections.

A. Outer tail-feathers ·75 or more shorter than middle ones; bill 1·00 or more in length.
   a. Tail over 6·00 . . . . 469. BOAT-TAILED GRACKLE, ♂.
   b. Tail under 6·00.
      b¹. Back bronzy purple or shining, brassy bluish green, the feathers with *iridescent bars* . . . 470. PURPLE GRACKLE, ♂.
      b². Back bronze, *without* iridescent bars.
                              470*b.* BRONZED GRACKLE, ♂.
      b³. Back bottle-green, the feathers more purple at their base, and with a narrow iridescent bar near the middle.
                              470*a.* FLORIDA GRACKLE, ♂.
      b⁴. Back bluish black, with or without iridescent bars.
          470. PURPLE GRACKLE, ♀. 470*a.* FLORIDA GRACKLE, ♀.

B. Outer tail-feathers little if any shorter than middle ones; bill less than 1·00 in length.

    a. Entire plumage bluish black, the feathers sometimes tipped with buffy or rufous . . . . 467. Rusty Blackbird, ♂.

    b. Body greenish black, head deep blue-black.

                            468. Brewer's Blackbird, ♂.

    c. A red and buff shoulder-patch.

                 463, 463*a–d.* Red-winged Blackbirds, ♂.

    d. Head and neck all around seal-brown . . . 495. Cowbird, ♂.

    e. Nape buffy, rump whitish . . . . 459. Bobolink, ♂.

III. Underparts grayish, slate-color, chestnut, or buffy.

    A. Underparts grayish or slate-color.

        a. Underparts grayish; bill finchlike; wing under 4·00.

                            471. Cowbird, ♀.

        b. Underparts slate-color, sometimes tipped with brownish, bill more thrushlike; wing over 4·00.

    467. Rusty Blackbird, ♀. 468. Brewer's Blackbird, ♀.

    B. Underparts buffy or chestnut.

        a. Underparts buffy, generally with a few black streaks.

                         459. Bobolink, ♀.

        b. Underparts buffy, without black streaks; tail about 5·00.

                   469. Boat-tailed Grackle, ♀.

        c. Underparts chestnut; throat black. 464. Orchard Oriole, ♂ ad.

IV. Underparts black and white, or black tipped or margined with rusty.

    a. Underparts streaked black and white, or black tipped with white; shoulder generally red or reddish.

        463, 463*a–d.* Red-winged Blackbirds, ♀ and im.

    b. Upperparts and underparts tipped with rusty.

                     467. Rusty Blackbird, im.

    c. Nape buffy, rump whitish . . . . 459. Bobolink, ♂.

459. BOBOLINK. Dolichonyx oryzivorus (*Linnæus*). [494.] (Pl. XXV.) *Ad.* ♂, *breeding plumage.*—Top and sides of the head and underparts black, the feathers more or less tipped with a narrow whitish or cream-buff fringe, which wears off as the season advances; back of the neck with a large yellowish cream-buff patch; middle of back generally streaked with cream-buff; scapulars, lower back, and upper tail-coverts soiled grayish white; wings and tail black; tail-feathers with *pointed tips;* bill blue-black. *Ad.* ♀.—Upperparts olive-buff, streaked with black; crown blackish, with a central stripe of olive-buff; nape finely spotted and back broadly streaked with black; wings and tail brownish fuscous; tail-feathers with *pointed tips;* underparts yellowish or buffy white. *Ads. in fall and Im.*—Similar to female, but buffier and more olivaceous throughout. L., 7·25; W., 3·76; T., 2·73; B., ·55.

Remarks.—The young and adults in fall plumage are known as Reedbirds. Adults acquire this plumage by a complete molt after the breeding season. The breeding plumage is regained by a complete molt in the spring, and not, as has been supposed, by a change in the color of the feathers without molting. Freshly plumaged males have the black veiled by yellow tips to the feathers; these gradually wear off, and by June have almost entirely disappeared (cf. Chapman, Auk, 1893, 309).

Range.—Breeds mainly in Transition Zone from se. B. C., cent. Alberta, cent. Sask., s. Man., s. Ont., s. Que., and Cape Breton Isl. s. to ne. Calif., n. Nev., Colo., Utah, n. Mo., Ills., Ind., cent. O., W. Va., Pa., and N. J. Winters in s. Brazil, Bolivia, Paraguay, and n. Argentina; in migration to the W. I. and e. coast of Cent. A.; casual in Bermuda and the Galapagos. (Fig. 8.)

PLATE XXV

PLUMAGES OF THE BOBOLINK

1. Adult male, summer. 2. Adult male in post-nuptial (fall) molt. 3. Adult male and adult female after postnuptial molt, and young in first winter. (This is the Reedbird plumage.) 4. Adult female, summer. 5. Adult male after complete prenuptial (spring) molt. Plumage No. 1 is then acquired by wear and fading.

Washington, T. V., common in spring, abundant in fall; Apr. 26–June 12; July 23–Nov. 14. Bronx region, fairly common S. R., Apr. 19 and 28, to Oct. 30. Boston, fairly common S. R., May 8–Sept. 10. N. Ohio, common S. R., Apr. 16–Oct. 10. Glen Ellyn, common S. R., Apr. 27–Oct. 9. SE. Minn., common S. R., May 2–Oct. 6.

Nest, of grasses, on the ground. *Eggs*, 4–7, grayish white, frequently tinged with the color of the numerous irregular spots and blotches of olive-brown or umber, ·85 × ·62. *Date*, Ossining, N. Y., May 29; Boston, June 1; Erie Co., N. Y., May 15; Austin, Ills., May 20.

In June our fields and meadows echo with the Bobolink's 'mad music' as, on quivering wing, he sings in ecstasy to his mate on her nest in the grasses below. What a wonderful song it is! An irrepressible outburst; a flood of melody from a heart overflowing with the joy of early summer.

But this glad season is soon over. Even before the tide of the year is full, the Bobolink begins to prepare for the long journey to his winter resorts. Doffing his jaunty costume of black, white, and buff, he dons the less conspicuous dress of his mate, and travels in disguise under the assumed name of Reedbird or Ricebird. His voice is hushed, save for a single call-note—a metallic *chink*. He travels both by day and night, and from the sky we hear his watchword as he signals his companions.

The wild-rice marshes of our coasts and rivers are the rendezvous of the countless flocks of Bobolinks, which later will invade South America, stopping *en route* to visit the rice fields of South Carolina and Georgia. They pass the winter south of the Amazon, and in March or April begin their northward journey. The males, in flocks of two or three hundred, precede the females by several days. They reach Florida about April 25, and are then in full song. Only one who has heard the Bobolink sing can form an idea of the effect produced by a flock of three hundred or more singing in chorus.

1920. BIRD-LORE, 213, 216 (mig.; pl.).

460. EASTERN MEADOWLARK. STURNELLA MAGNA MAGNA (*Linnæus*). [501.] (Fig. 117*b*.) *Ads. in summer.*—Prevailing color of upperparts black, crown with a buffy line through center, back bordered and tipped with rufous and buffy; outer tail-feathers mostly white, middle ones with imperfect, connected bars, *not* reaching the outer edge of the feather; line from bill over eye yellow; sides of the throat and ear-coverts whitish; throat, between the lower branch of the under mandible, breast, and middle of the upper belly bright yellow; a black crescent on breast; sides and lower belly whitish, spotted or streaked with black. *Ads. and Im. in winter.*—Feathers all much more widely margined, the prevailing color of the upperparts rufous-brown; black breast crescent veiled with buffy; yellow of underparts duller. L., 10·75; W., 4·76; T., 3·16; B., 1·30.

Remarks.—This bird is to be distinguished from the western species by its much darker upperparts, by the imperfect, confluent tail-bars, and, especially, by the absence of yellow on the *sides* of the throat.

Range.—Breeds in Transition and Upper Austral zones from e. Minn., s. Ont., s. Que., and N. B. s. to n. Tex., Mo., and N. C., and w. to w. Nebr., Kans., and nw. Tex.; winters regularly from the Potomac and O. valleys s. to the Gulf States, and n. locally to the Great Lakes and s. Me.

Washington, common P. R., less common in winter. Bronx region, common P. R.; more numerous in migration; less common in winter. Boston, rather common S. R., not common W. V. N. Ohio, abundant S. R., Mch. 5–Nov. 15; a few winter. Glen Ellyn, common S. R., Jan. 24–Nov. 15; irregular W. R. SE. Minn., common S. R., Mch. 14–Nov. 19; rare W. R.

Nest, of grasses, usually arched, on the ground. *Eggs*, 4–6, white, spotted or speckled with cinnamon or reddish brown, 1·15 × ·80 (Pl. III). *Date*, Beech Haven, N. J., May 7; Chester Co., Pa., May 9; Boston, May 28; Tampico, Ills., May 5; se. Minn., May 16.

In walking through grassy fields, meadows, or marshes, we sometimes flush rather large, brownish birds, which, alternately flapping and sailing, scale away with a flight that suggests a Quail's. Their white outer tail-feathers show conspicuously, and, if, instead of returning to the ground, they alight on a fence or the outer branch of a tree, as they utter a *dzit* or *yert* and metallic twitter, they will nervously flit their tails, displaying the same white feathers. When in an exposed position they are wary and difficult to approach, but when walking about on the ground they trust to the long grasses for protection, and sometimes do not take wing until one is within a few feet of them.

In Cuba I noticed that a Meadowlark, closely related to ours, was very careful to conceal its brightly colored breast, with its distinctly marked crescent, and, although even perching birds were not shy, they would invariably turn their backs upon me as I drew near.

The Meadowlark's song is a clear, plaintive whistle of unusual sweetness. It is subject to much variation, both individually and geographically. The birds near my home at Englewood, N. J., generally

sing: But the songs of

Florida birds are so different, I hardly recognized them by their notes.

In the fall, Meadowlarks at the north gather in flocks and resort to large marshes.

1908. CHAPMAN, F. M., Camps and Cruises, 15 (nesting).—1921. BIRD-LORE, 79, 83 (mig.; pl.).

460a. SOUTHERN MEADOWLARK. STURNELLA MAGNA ARGUTULA *Bangs.* [501*c*.] Similar to *S. m. magna* but smaller and darker. W., 4·40.

Range.—Lower Austral Zone from s. Ills., sw. Ind., and S. C. s. to Fla. and the coast of La. and se. Tex.

Nesting-date, San Mateo, Fla., Apr. 22.

461. WESTERN MEADOWLARK. STURNELLA NEGLECTA *Audubon.* [501.1.] *Ads.*—Prevailing color of upperparts grayish brown, crown with a central buffy stripe; back black, feathers widely margined with grayish brown; rump and upper tail-coverts with narrow black bars; outer tail-feathers mostly white; middle ones brownish gray, barred with black, the bars generally *not* connected, and as a rule reaching the margins of the feathers; line from the bill over the eye yellow; ear-coverts grayish white; throat yellow, this color reaching up on the *sides* of the throat and touching ear-coverts; breast and upper belly yellow, a black crescent on breast; sides and lower belly whitish, spotted or streaked with black. *Ads. and Im. in winter.*—Upperparts more widely margined with grayish brown, these grayish brown tips with small, broken black bars; yellow of underparts duller, the black crescent veiled with whitish. W., 4·60; T., 3·00; B., 1·25.

Range.—Breeds from s. B. C., cent. Alberta, and s. Man. s. to nw. L. Calif., n. Mex., and cent. Tex.; winters from s. B. C. and Ia. s. to s. L. Calif., Jalisco, and Guanajuato; e. casually to Wisc., s. Mich., and n. Ills.; accidental in s. Mack.

N. Ohio, casual S. R. SE. Minn., common S. R., Mch. 4–Nov. 19.

The Western Meadowlark resembles the eastern bird in habits, but its markedly different song and the fact that at the junction of their ranges in the Mississippi Valley both birds may be found nesting without evidence of geographical intergradation, have finally won for the western bird the rank of a species. Just what the relations of the two forms may be in the Rio Grande Valley, and what part *S. magna hoopesi*, of that region, plays in the problem has not yet been determined.

The call-note of *neglecta* is a *chuck, chuck* followed by a wooden rolling *b-r-r-r-r*, analogous to but very unlike the *dzit* or *yert* and metallic twitter of *magna*. The song of *magna* is a clean-cut fifing without grace notes; that of *neglecta* is of mellow bubbling flute-notes. The flight-songs of the two birds are much alike, but, in my experience, *neglecta* sings much more frequently on the wing, and, in the height of the mating season, sings as often in the air as from a perch.

Fig. 152. Upper tail-coverts of *a*. Eastern Meadowlark. *b*. Western Meadowlark.

1890. Seton, E. T., Proc. U. S. N. M., 373–379 (biography).—1896. Belding, L., Auk, 29, 30 (songs).—1906. Chapman, F. M., Bull. Amer. Mus. Nat. Hist., XXII, 297–320 (relationships).—1921. Bird-Lore, 79, 83 (mig.; pl.).

462. YELLOW-HEADED BLACKBIRD. Xanthocephalus xanthocephalus *(Bonaparte).* [497.] *Ad.* ♂.—Head, neck, throat, and breast orange-yellow; region before the eye and chin black; outer wing-coverts white, rest of the plumage black. *Ad.* ♀.—Forehead, line over the eye, sides of the head, throat, and upper breast pale, dirty yellow, more or less mixed with white; lower breast generally more or less marked with white; rest of the plumage grayish brown. L., 10·00; W., 5·50; T., 4·05; B., ·85.

Range.—Breeds from s. B. C., s. Mack., cent. Man. and n. Minn. s. to n. L. Calif., Ariz., and Valley of Toluca, Mex., and e. to s. Wisc., cent. Ia., n. Ills., and Ind.; winters from sw. Calif. and sw. La. s. to Cape San Lucas, and Puebla; accidental in Greenland and in various e. localities from Ont. and Que. to S. C., Fla. and Cuba.

Washington, A. V., one instance, Aug. Boston, A. V. N. Ohio, casual T. V. Glen Ellyn, A. V., May 21, 1898. SE. Minn., common S. R., Apr. 10–Nov. 8.

Nest, bulky, of coarse reeds, grasses, etc., in marshes. *Eggs,* 4–5, grayish white, evenly and rather obscurely speckled with pale cinnamon-brown, 1·00 × ·72. *Date,* se. Minn., May 18 (first egg).

When nesting, the Yellow-head is one of the characters of the quill-reed or tule marshes. Later, he joins others of his kind, forming vast flocks which frequent corn and grain fields or wherever food can be found.

"If result were commensurate with effort, the Yellow-head would be a world-famed songster; but something besides unbounded ambition and limitless muscular exertion is required to produce music. In vain the Yellow-head expands his lungs and throws out his chest, his wide-spread tail testifying to the earnestness of his endeavor; sound he produces in volume, but surely such a series of strained, harsh calls, whistles like escaping steam, grunts, groans and pig-like squeals never before did duty as a song. In his youth he does far better, the note of the young bird being a wooden rolling call as different from the voice of the parent as is that of the young Baltimore Oriole." (Chapman, F. M., 'Camps and Cruises.')

1909. ROBERTS, T. S., Auk, 371–389 (home-life).—1921. BIRD-LORE, 78, 84 (mig.; pl.).

463. EASTERN RED-WINGED BLACKBIRD. AGELAIUS PHŒNICEUS PHŒNICEUS (*Linnæus*). [498.] (Pl. VI.) *Ad. ♂.*—Lesser wing-coverts— 'shoulders'—bright scarlet; middle wing-coverts varying from ochraceous-buff to buffy white; rest of the plumage black. *Ad. ♂ in winter.*—Similar, but upperparts margined with rusty. *Im. ♂ in winter.*—Upperparts margined with rusty and buffy; underparts tipped with whitish; lesser wing-coverts dull orange-red mixed with black. *Ad. ♀.*—Head and back black-ish, streaked with rusty and buffy; rump and upper tail-coverts fuscous, more or less edged with ashy; wings fuscous, edged with buffy, the lesser coverts sometimes tinged with reddish; underparts conspicuously streaked with black and white; the throat tinged with orange or yellow. ♂ L., 9·51; W., 4·72; T., 3·77; B., ·88, depth at base ·50.

Range.—Breeds from Ont., N. S., and Que. s. to the n. parts of the Gulf States; winters mainly s. of the O. and Del. valleys. Locally n. to Mass.

Washington, common S. R., abundant in migration; rare in winter. Bronx region, common S. R., uncommon in winter; Feb. 16–Jan 1. Boston, abundant S. R., Mch. 10–Nov.; a few winter. N. Ohio, abundant S. R., Mch. 1–Nov. 15. Glen Ellyn, common S. R., Mch. 5–Dec. 2. SE. Minn., common S. R., Mch. 3–Nov. 23; flocks frequently winter.

Nest, of coarse grasses, weed-stalks, etc., lined with finer grasses and root-lets, attached to low bushes or reeds (Pl. II). *Eggs*, 3–5, pale blue, singularly streaked, spotted or scrawled with dark purple or black, chiefly at the larger end, 1·04 × ·72. *Date*, Chester Co., Pa., May 16; Boston, May 16; se. Minn., May 8.

A swiftly moving, compact band of silent birds, passing low through the brown orchard, suddenly wheels, and, alighting among the bare branches, with the precision of a trained choir breaks into a wild, tink-ling glee. It is quite possible that in the summer this rude chorus might fail to awaken enthusiasm, but in the spring it is as welcome and inspiring a promise of the new year as the peeping of frogs or blooming of the first wild flower.

Plain, streaked Mrs. Redwing, who has been spending the winter in flocks composed only of others of her sex, soon appears, but mating is delayed until late April or early May. Then we find the old homes in the wet meadows and marshes occupied by apparently the same birds which have dwelt there for years.

Mounting the topmost branch of a tree not far from the nest, the male becomes an ever-vigilant sentinel. His rich *kong-quĕr-rēē*, which by association is so strongly suggestive of reedy marshes, is a signal

BLACKBIRDS, ORIOLES, ETC. 487

that "all's well." He challenges all males of his kind by an inquiring *chŭt, chuck,* and with a long, shrill alarm-note, *chee-e-e-e-e,* circles out on fluttering wings, his gorgeous crimson epaulets showing conspicuously.

The nesting season is a short one, and in July young and old begin to gather in flocks in the marshes, where later they will be found, in countless numbers, feeding on the wild rice.

1905. HERRICK, F. H., Home-Life of Wild Birds, 45–48.—1914. ALLEN, A. A., The Red-winged Blackbird, A Study in the Ecology of a Cattail Marsh. (Important.) Abst. Proc. Linn. Soc. N. Y., Nos. 24, 25; 43–128, illus.—1922. BIRD-LORE, 85, 89 (mig.; pl.).

463a. FLORIDA RED-WING. AGELAIUS PHŒNICEUS MEARNSI *Howell and Van Rossem.* [498c. part.]—Smaller than *A. p. phœniceus,* bill longer and more slender; upperparts in females more brownish (less blackish); underparts more buffy (less whitish), the dark streaks more brownish. ♂ W., 4·50; T., 3·40; B., 1·00; depth of B., ·45 (H. and Van R.).

Range.—Greater part of the Fla. peninsula, s. to the lower Kissimmee Valley and the Caloosahatchee River, n. to Putnam Co. and Anastasia Isl. w. on the Gulf Coast to Apalachicola.

463b. MAYNARD'S RED-WING. AGELAIUS PHŒNICEUS FLORIDANUS *Maynard.* [498b.] Intermediate between *A. p. mearnsi* and *A. p. bryanti* of the Bahamas. Similar to *mearnsi* in size but upperparts in female paler, less brownish, more whitish; superciliary averaging broader and more whitish (less buffy); underparts more whitish (less buffy) (H. and Van R.).

Range.—Fla. Keys and the s. portion of the Fla. peninsula, n. to Lake Worth and Everglade, Collier Co.

463c. GULF COAST RED-WING. AGELAIUS PHŒNICEUS LITTORALIS *Howell and Van Rossem.* [498c part.] Darkest of eastern races; female darker than that of *A. p. phœniceus,* particularly on rump; general tone of upperparts in breeding female fuscous black, with median crown-stripe and buffy edgings on nape and interscapular region nearly obsolete; ground-color of underparts less buffy (more whitish) the dark streaks broader and averaging more blackish; wings and tail slightly shorter; bill slightly more slender in profile. ♂ W., 4·50; T., 3·40; B., ·95; depth of B., ·45 (H. and Van R.).

Range.—Gulf Coast region from Choctawhatchee Bay w. at least to Galveston, Tex.

463d. GIANT RED-WING. AGELAIUS PHŒNICEUS ARCTOLEGUS *Oberholser.* Resembling *A. p. phœniceus* in color but larger and with a bigger bill. Similar to *A. p. fortis* but female decidedly darker below, the streaks more blackish and extensive, about as broad as the white interspaces; above more blackish. Male with wings and tail averaging shorter; bill larger; and buff wing-coverts somewhat paler. ♂ W., 4·90; T., 3·65; B., ·95; depth of B., ·50 (Oberholser).

Range.—Breeds in Mack. and Keewatin s. to Mont., N. Dak., Minn. and n. Mich.; in winter to Ark., La., Ala., Tex., and Ills. Accidental in Conn. SE. Minn., common T. V., frequent W. V.

463e. THICK-BILLED RED-WING. AGELAIUS PHŒNICEUS FORTIS *Ridgway.* [498d.] Similar to *A. p. phœniceus* but larger (largest of the genus), bill shorter and proportionately thicker, ♀ somewhat paler and browner. ♂ W., 5·00; B., ·80; depth at base ·50.

Range.—Breeds from Idaho, Wyo., and S. Dak., to Colo. and n. Tex.; winters principally in the s. part of its breeding range, wandering to La. and Ark.

464. ORCHARD ORIOLE. ICTERUS SPURIUS (*Linnæus*). [506.] (Pl. XXVI.) *Ad.* ♂.—Head, neck, throat, and upper back black; breast, belly, lower back, and lesser wing-coverts chestnut; wings and tail fuscous, more or less edged or tipped with whitish. *Ad.* ♀.—Upperparts grayish olive-green, brighter on the head and rump; wings fuscous, middle and greater coverts tipped with whitish; tail bright olive-green; underparts dull yellow. *Im.* ♂, *first winter plumage.*—Similar to the ad. ♀, but with the back browner. *Im.* ♂, *first nuptial plumage.*—Similar to the ad. ♀, but with the throat black and occasionally patches of chestnut on the underparts. L., 7·32; W., 3·18; T., 2·92; B., ·65.

Remarks.—The interesting changes of plumage which the Orchard Oriole undergoes are well illustrated by the accompanying plate (pl. xxvi). The juvenal or nestling plumage (not shown) resembles, but is browner above and paler below than the first winter plumage (Fig. 6), which is acquired by molt of the body feathers and wing-coverts in July. The male in first winter plumage is indistinguishable from the female in first winter plumage; and differs only slightly from the adult female in summer plumage (Fig. 5). In first nuptial plumage, acquired by partial molt in spring, the male has the throat black, but, as a rule, is otherwise like the female (Fig. 4). The amount of black in the throat varies. Sometimes it is restricted to a few feathers, again it spreads somewhat down the breast, and such highly developed birds usually have traces of chestnut in the underparts (Fig. 3).

The postnuptial (fall) molt apparently does not occur until after the bird has left us for the South, when it passes into winter plumage (Fig. 2) which, as Dwight has said, resembles that of the adult. There is no spring molt and the adult chestnut and black breeding plumage (Fig. 1) is acquired by a wearing off of the buffy tips which fringe the winter plumage.

Range.—Breeds from N. Dak., nw. Minn., Wisc., Mich., se. Ont., cent. N. Y., and Mass. s. to s. Fla. and the Gulf Coast to s. Tex., and in Mex. to Oaxaca and Jalisco, and w. to cent. Nebr., ne. Colo., and w. Kans.; winters from s. Mex. to n. Colombia; casual n. to Vt., N. H., Me., and N. B., and w. to Colo.

Washington, common S. R., Apr. 25–Sept. 14. Bronx region, fairly common but local S. R., Apr. 28–Aug. 28. Boston, rare and irregular S. R., May 15–Sept. N. Ohio, common S. R., Apr. 28–Sept. 5. Glen Ellyn, rare S. R., Apr. 28. SE. Minn., uncommon S. R., May 7–Sept. 3.

Nest, pensile, of grasses interwoven, near the extremity of a limb, 10–15 feet up. *Eggs,* 3–5, bluish white, distinctly and obscurely spotted, blotched, and scrawled with fuscous or black, ·79 × ·58. *Date,* Ossining, N. Y., May 29; St. Louis, Mo., May 14; se. Minn., June 3.

Although the Orchard Oriole generally frequents apple orchards, he is entirely at home among the shade trees of our lawns.

There is an air of refinement about this bird which seems to pervade his whole life history. He dresses quietly but with excellent taste, his nest is of the choicest materials, while his song suggests the finished effort of a perfectly trained performer. His voice is indeed unusually rich and flexible, and he uses it with rare skill and expression. Words can not describe his song, but no lover of bird-music will be long in the vicinity of a singing Orchard Oriole without learning the distinguished songster's name.

1923. BIRD-LORE, 119, 128 (mig.; pl.).

465. BALTIMORE ORIOLE. ICTERUS GALBULA (*Linnæus*). [507.] (Fig. 117a.) *Ad.* ♂.—Head, neck, throat, and upper back black; breast, belly, lower back, and lesser wing-coverts deep, rich, reddish orange; wings black, the outer margin of the greater coverts and quills edged with white;

PLATE XXVI

PLUMAGES OF THE ORCHARD ORIOLE

1. Adult male, summer.
2. Adult male, winter.
3. Male, first nuptial plumage.

4. Male, first nuptial plumage.
5. Adult female.
6. Male, first winter.

end half of middle tail-feathers black, base orange; all the others orange, crossed by a black band in the middle. *Ad.* ♀.—Upperparts brownish or grayish orange, brighter on the rump; head and back mottled with black; wings fuscous, greater and middle coverts tipped with white; tail like the rump, the middle feathers stained with black; underparts dull orange, throat sometimes spotted with black. L., 7·53; W., 3·52; T., 2·84; B., ·70.

Range.—Breeds mainly in Transition and Upper Austral zones from cent. Alberta, Ont., and N. B. s. to s. Tex. and n. Ga., and w. to e. Mont., Wyo., and Colo. e. of the Rocky Mts.; migrates through e. Mex.; winters from s. Mex. to Colombia; accidental at York Factory, Hudson Bay, and in Cuba.

Washington, rather common S. R., Apr. 24–Sept. 14. Bronx region, common S. R., Apr. 27–Oct. 23 (late November). Boston, common S. R., May 8 through Aug. N. Ohio, common S. R., Apr. 15–Sept. 10. Glen Ellyn, common S. R., Apr. 26–Sept. 4. SE. Minn., common S. R., May 1–Sept. 1.

Nest, pensile, of grasses, bark, plant-fibers, hair, strings, etc., firmly interwoven, in fruit or shade trees, near the extremity of a limb 20–40 feet up. *Eggs,* 4–6, white, singularly scrawled with fine, distinct or obscure black or fuscous lines, and with a few spots or blotches, ·94 × ·63. *Date,* D. C., May 27; Boston, June 1; Martin's Ferry, Ohio, May 20; se. Minn., May 22.

Sometimes Nature, as if to remind us of the richness of her stores, sends from the tropics a gayly attired bird which seems quite out of place among the more soberly clad inhabitants of northern climes. The genus *Icterus* contains nearly forty species, all more or less brightly dressed in orange, yellow, and black, but not one is more beautiful than our Baltimore Oriole. There is reason to believe that he is not unaware of his own charms; indeed, we may almost suspect him of intentionally displaying them. His splendor is not to be lost in the forest, and, whistling loudly, he flashes through our fruit and shade trees.

He leaves to the female the task of constructing their wonderfully made nest, but he seems quite as deeply interested in the performance as if he were a skilled weaver himself; indeed, he would probably assist if he were permitted.

Young Orioles have been well named by Mrs. Olive Thorne Miller the cry-babies of the bird world. Their ceaseless call for food is almost as much a midsummer voice as the song of cicadas. Long after they have left the nest we may find them in the different trees about our lawn calling out monotonously and persistently *dee-dee-dee-dee*, until one of the parents arrives and momentarily fills their mouths.

1922. BIRD-LORE, 339, 341 (mig.; pl.).—1928. ALLEN, A. A., Bird-Lore, 214–221, illus. (autobiography).

466. BULLOCK'S ORIOLE, *Icterus bullocki* (Swainson), [508], a species of our western states, has been taken in New York and in Maine.

467. RUSTY BLACKBIRD. EUPHAGUS CAROLINUS (*Müller*). [509.]

Ad. ♂, *breeding plumage.*—Entire plumage *uniform* glossy bluish black; tail-feathers of nearly equal length. *Ad.* ♂ *and Im.* ♂ *in winter.*—Similar, but the upperparts widely tipped with rufous or rusty, the underparts similarly tipped with ochraceous- or cream-buff; a buffy line over the eye. *Ad.* ♀ *in breeding plumage.*—Slate-color, glossy above, duller below; wings and tail darker and more glossy. *Ad.* ♀ *and Im.* ♀ *in winter.*—Similar, but somewhat lighter, the upperparts widely tipped with rufous or rusty, the underparts similarly tipped with ochraceous- or cream-buff. L., 9·55; W., 4·61; T., 3·52; B., ·80.

Range.—Breeds in Boreal Zone from the Kowak River, Alaska, n. Mack., and n. Que., s. to s. Alaska, cent. Alberta, cent. Ont., N. Y., Vt., N. H., n. Me., N. B., and N. F.; winters mainly s. of the O. and Del. valleys to the Gulf Coast; w. in migration to the plains; casual in B. C., Mont., and Colo.; accidental in Calif., L. Calif., and Greenland.

Washington, common W. V., Sept. 13–May 14. Bronx region, common T. V., fairly frequent in winter; Feb. 12–May 13; Sept. 18–Dec. 27. Boston, very common T. V., Mch. 10–May 8; Sept. 15–Oct. 31. N. Ohio, common T. V., Mch. 5–May 10; Sept. 10–Nov. 15. Glen Ellyn, common T. V., Mch. 3–May 11; Sept. 12–Nov. 21. SE. Minn., common T. V., Mch. 16–May 12; Sept. 8–Nov. 29; a few winter records.

Nest, of twigs and coarse grasses lined with finer grasses, in coniferous trees or on the ground. *Eggs,* 4–7, grayish green to pale green, thickly blotched with light and dark brown and purple, 1·00 × ·76 (Chamberlain). *Date,* Wilmurt, N. Y., May 7; Kings Co., N. S., May 11.

This bird is found during the migrations in small flocks on fresh-water meadows or about open, bushy swamps, feeding on the ground in alder thickets or along the edges of swampy woods. It resembles, more or less, the Red-winged Blackbird in size, flight, and notes, but unlike this species, with which it sometimes associates, it is compara-tively quiet and retiring. Only at times, in the spring, do we find the flocks musical centers, whence issues a confused medley of whistles, sweeter and higher-pitched than the best efforts of the Redwings. Little is known of this Blackbird in its northern home. It gathers into flocks early in the summer, and the most frequently heard note is a *cluck,* not in the least characteristic. Its quiet demeanor, pale yellow eye, and uniform color are its chief distinguishing characters in the field, where it may be mistaken for the Bronzed or Purple Grackle. The gray female is unlike the streaked female Redwing.   J. DWIGHT, JR.

1920. KENNARD, F. H., Auk, 412–422, illus. (breeding habits in northern N. E.).—1921. BIRD-LORE, 295, 299 (mig.; pl.).

468. BREWER'S BLACKBIRD. EUPHAGUS CYANOCEPHALUS (*Wagler*). [510.] *Ad.* ♂.—Head, neck, and throat shining bluish purple, rest of the plumage shining greenish black. Young males in winter plumage have the head and anterior parts more or less tipped with grayish brown. *Ad.* ♀.— Resembling female of *E. carolinus* but plumage always without rusty margins. L., 9·65; W., 5·00; T., 3·70.

Remarks.—Male to be distinguished from that of the Rusty Blackbird by its greenish, instead of bluish body and fewer brownish tips to winter plumage. The female lacks these tips at all seasons and therefore resembles female *carolinus* in worn breeding plumage but is larger, and has the head, throat and breast browner, the rump and upper tail-coverts glossy greenish instead of dull gray.

Range.—Breeds from cent. B. C., Athabaska Landing, and cent. Man., to n. L. Calif., N. Mex., and w. Tex., and from the Pacific to nw. Minn., w. Nebr., and Kans.; winters from s. B. C. and Kans. s. to Guat.; in migration e. casually to Wisc., Ills., Mo., La., S. C., and Fla.

SE. Minn., common S. R., Mch. 26–Nov. 4; nest, Minn., May 21, half-fledged young.

469. BOAT-TAILED GRACKLE. CASSIDIX MEXICANUS (*Vieillot*). [513.] *Ad.* ♂.—Glossy bluish black; head, throat, and breast more purplish, wings and tail more blackish. *Ad.* ♀.—Much smaller, upperparts blackish brown, underparts soiled ochraceous-buff. ♂ L., 16·00; W., 7·50; T., 7·00; B., 1·55.

Range.—Lower Austral Zone of the S. Atlantic and Gulf States from Chesapeake Bay to Fla. Keys and w. to the e. coast of Tex.

Nest, bulky and compact, of grasses, seaweed, etc., with a median layer of mud or partially decayed vegetation, in colonies in bushes. *Eggs,* 3–5, pale bluish white, frequently tinged with vinaceous-brown, singularly spotted, blotched, and scrawled with purplish or blackish, 1·32 × ·90. *Date,* Ft. Pierce, Fla., Mch. 20; Ft. Macon, N. C., Apr. 26; Accomac Co., Va., Apr. 28.

Boat-tailed Grackles are rarely if ever found far from water. Shallow lakes or marshy lagoons grown with aquatic plants are their favorite resorts. Here they may be seen in small groups, which usually contain more males than females, *walking* or jumping from plant to plant, sometimes springing into the air to catch a passing insect, or wading along the shore in search of food. Their usual notes are hoarse, rather forced whistles; more rarely they utter a singular rolling call, which bears a close resemblance to the sound produced by a Coot in pattering over the water. The Great-tailed Grackle, the larger southern form of this species, is unquestionably polygamous, but it is unknown whether the Boat-tail has more than one mate.

1920. HARPER, F., Auk, 295–297 (song).—1922. BIRD-LORE, 204 (mig.; pl.).

470. PURPLE GRACKLE. QUISCALUS QUISCULA QUISCULA (*Linnæus*). [511.] (Fig. 117c.) *Ad. ♂.*—Head, neck, throat, and upper breast all around varying from brilliant metallic purple to bluish green or steel-blue; back and rump varying from bottle-green to metallic purple or shining brassy green, *the feathers with iridescent bars;* wings and tail externally metallic purple or bluish black; lower breast and belly resembling the back but duller. *Ad. ♀.*— Much duller than the male, but the feathers of the back generally showing at least traces of iridescence. ♂ L., 12·00–13·50; W., 5·66; T., 5·18; B., 1·18.

Remarks.—Intermediates between this and the Bronzed Grackle are found where their ranges adjoin, but typical *quiscula* always has iridescent bars on the feathers of the back, rump, and belly, while in *æneus* these bars are wanting. (On relationships of this group see Chapman, Bull. Am. Mus. Nat. Hist., IV, 1892, 1–20.)

Range.—Middle Atlantic Coast region of the U. S. Breeds in the Carolinian fauna from the n. shore of L. I. Sound and the lower Hudson Valley w. to the Alleghanies and s. to the uplands of Ga., Ala., and e. Tenn.; winters mainly s. of the Del. Valley.

Washington, common T. V. and S. R., Feb. 20; a few winter. Bronx region, common S. R., Feb. 15–Nov. 8. Boston, rare S. R.

Nest, bulky and compact, of mud and coarse grasses lined with finer grasses, in colonies, generally in coniferous trees about 30 feet up, sometimes in bushes or holes in trees. *Eggs,* 3–7, very variable, generally pale bluish or bluish green, singularly spotted, blotched, or scrawled with cinnamon-brown, umber, or black, but sometimes evenly speckled with brownish, and rarely almost solid cinnamon- or rufous-brown, 1·15 × ·82. *Date,* D. C., Apr. 17; Del. Co., Pa., Apr. 25.

When winter gives signs of retreating, there comes from the south in sable array the tried advance guard of the feathered army which is impatiently awaiting the order to march. In close rank they come, phalanx after phalanx, to retake the land which winter—once conquering, now defeated—yields to them. The air resounds with martial music; their harsh voices, united, rise in an inspiring chorus.

The campaign over, they settle in colonies on their recently acquired possessions, and these careless rovers become so attached to their homes and families that they are rarely seen far from their vicinity. Sometimes we may see them walking sedately over the lawns near their home, their glossy plumage gleaming in the light, and their yellow eyes giving them a peculiar, unbirdlike expression. But when their young are old enough to care for themselves, the old habits return, and, leading their offspring into the world, they teach them the ways of wanderers. Meeting others of their kind, they join forces, and in the fall we find them in hordes ravaging the country.

The Grackle's disposition is as gloomy as his plumage is dark. Life with him is a serious affair. He seems utterly to lack the Blue Jay's sense of humor. As a parent he is beyond reproach, and every moment is devoted to the care of his young, but it is all done in a joyless way. Eggs and nestlings form part of his fare, and I can imagine bird-mothers frightening their young into obedience by threatened visits from that ogre, the Grackle.

1892. CHAPMAN, F. M., Bull. Am. Mus. Nat. Hist., 1–20 (relationships). —1897. JONES, L., Wilson Bull. No. 15, 39–56 (roosts).–1921, BIRD-LORE, 192, 195 (mig.; pl.).

470a. FLORIDA GRACKLE. QUISCALUS QUISCULA AGLÆUS *Baird.*

[511a.] *Ad.* ♂.—Head, neck, throat and upper breast all around metallic violet-purple; back and rump rich bottle green, the feathers with more or less concealed *iridescent bars;* wings and tail externally metallic purple or bluish black; the wing-coverts generally with iridescent tips; lower breast and belly similar to the back but duller. *Ad.* ♀.—Not distinguishable in color from the ♀ of *Q. q. quiscula,* but differing in size. W., 5·38; T., 4·90; B., 1·25.

Range.—S. Atlantic Coast from S. C. to Fla., and w. in the s. part of the Gulf States to se. Tex.

Nesting-date, San Mateo, Fla., Mch. 30.

This is a locally abundant bird, and is found in flocks throughout the year. In Florida it sometimes lives in the towns in which live-oaks grow, and it also makes its headquarters in cypress 'bays,' but its favorite resort is among the cabbage palmettos, upon the berries of which it feeds.

470b. BRONZED GRACKLE. QUISCALUS QUISCULA ÆNEUS *Ridgway.*

[511b.] *Ad.* ♂.—Head, neck, throat, and upper breast all around varying from brilliant metallic purple to bluish green or steel-blue; back metallic seal-bronze, the feathers *without iridescent bars;* wings and tail metallic purplish or bluish black; lower breast and belly similar to the back but duller. *Ad.* ♀.—Much duller, the back and belly brownish, sometimes without metallic reflections and never with iridescent bars. W., 5·62; T., 5·04; B., 1·21.

Range.—Breeds from Great Slave Lake, n. Man., and N. F. s. to Colo. (e. of the Rocky Mts.) and Tex. and se. to the n. parts of the Gulf States, w. Pa., N. Y., and Conn. (s. of N. Y. breeds only w. of the Alleghanies); winters mainly from the O. Valley s. to s. Tex.; in migration and winter occurs e. of Alleghanies.

Washington, rare T. V., between Feb. 14 and Apr. 17. Bronx region, T. V., fairly frequent in winter; Mch. 8–Apr. 18; Oct. 12–Dec. 28 (Jan. 19).

Boston, abundant S. R., Mch. 10–Nov. 1; occasional in winter. N. Ohio, abundant S. R., Mch. 1–Nov. 15; rarely winters. Glen Ellyn, common S. R., Mch. 5–Nov. 15. SE. Minn., common S. R., Mch. 11–Nov. 14; rare in winter.

Nesting-date, Boston, May 2; Grinnell, Ia., May 2; se. Minn., Apr. 6.

"The general habits of the Bronzed Grackle are in all respects identical with those of the Purple Grackle. . . .

"From an almost equal familiarity with the two birds we are able to say that their notes differ decidedly, especially those of the male during the breeding season, the 'song' of the western bird being very much louder and more musical or metallic than that of its eastern relative" (Ridgway).

1921. BIRD-LORE, 192, 195 (mig.; pl.).

471. COWBIRD. MOLOTHRUS ATER ATER (*Boddaert*). [495.] *Ad.* ♂.— Head, neck, and breast coffee-brown; rest of the plumage glossy black, with metallic bluish and greenish reflections. *Ad.* ♀.—Dark brownish gray, lighter below, especially on the throat. *Juvenal plumage.*—Similar to the female, but whiter below, all the feathers edged with buffy. This plumage is worn but a short time, and is then changed for that of the adult. ♂ L., 7·92; W., 4·24; T., 3·03; B., ·67.

Range.—Breeds from s. Ont., s. Que., N. S. and N. B., s. to cent. Va., se. Ky., cent. Tenn., s. cent. Ark., La. and cent. Tex., and w. to Minn., ne. Ia., se. Nebr., sw. Kans. and N. Mex. Winters from the O. and Potomac valleys, casually to N. Y. and Mich., and s. to Fla. and the Gulf Coast.

Washington, rather rare P. R., common T. V. Bronx region, common S. R., occasional in winter; Mch. 8–Dec. 28 (Feb. 6). Boston, common S. R., Mch. 25–Nov. 1; occasional in winter. N. Ohio, abundant S. R., Mch. 10– Nov. 15. Glen Ellyn, common S. R., Mch. 15–Oct. 1. SE. Minn., common S. R., Mch. 21–Oct. 5.

Nest, none, the eggs being laid in the nests of other species. *Eggs*, white, evenly and distinctly speckled with cinnamon-brown or umber, ·86 × ·65. *Date*, Montgomery Co., Pa., May 10; Boston, May 15.

The long-drawn *kluck-tse-e-e* of the male Cowbird announces his arrival some late March morning, and we readily see him silhouetted against the sky in the upper part of a still, leafless tree. He accompanies his glassy call with watery, gurgling notes uttered with apparently nauseous effort as, raising his wings, he leans forward in his courtship display.

The Cowbird has long been held in disrepute as an immoral parasite, but Dr. Herbert Friedmann's studies have forced us to revise our beliefs concerning its sexual relationships. The fact that the males out-number the females about three to two gives some ground for the suspicion that it may occasionally be polyandrous, but in Friedmann's opinion if the Cowbird is "not strictly monogamous at least the tendency toward monogamy is very strong." In the breeding season the female has a definite territory and the male a favorite song-perch. During the

FIG. 153. Cowbird. (Natural size.)

laying period only one pair of Cowbirds is resident in such areas, and the further fact that all the Cowbird eggs found within these restricted districts are very similar to each other indicates that they were laid by but one female. Dr. Friedmann's studies resulted in the acquisition of much additional information concerning the Cowbird's habit of laying its eggs in the nests of other birds. This is done during the absence of the owner, and usually in nests containing eggs in which incubation is not yet well started. Cowbird eggs hatch in ten days, about the shortest period of any of our passerine birds.

While some birds are specifically parasitic, that is, lay in the nest of but one species, the Cowbird, as is well known, shows its versatility by laying in the nests of many species. In this and a succeeding publication, Dr. Friedmann ('29) presents the names of 209 of its victims. These are mostly Flycatchers, Finches, Vireos, and Warblers. As a rule, the species imposed upon accept the strange egg, but Robins and Catbirds eject it, and a number of species, notably the Yellow Warbler, cover the parasitic egg if, when it was laid in their nest, they had no eggs of their own.

Dr. Friedmann finds his clue to the parasitic habits of our Cowbird in his study of the older South American species of this group. He presents his theory at length in the monograph listed below, to which interested students are referred, not alone for the information it contains, but as a representative piece of modern ornithological research.

1920. BIRD-LORE, 343, 347 (mig.; pl.).—1928. ALLEN, A. A., Bird-Lore, 352–365, illus. (autobiography).—1929. FRIEDMANN, H., The Cowbirds: A Study in the Biology of Social Parasitism, 8vo., 421 pp. (Chas. G. Thomas, Springfield, Ills.). (See also The Auk, 1931, 52–65.)

FAMILY THRAUPIDÆ. TANAGERS.

Although a distinctively American family, the Tanagers are so closely related to the Finches that it is not clear to which family certain genera should be referred. About 550 species and subspecies are known, most of them being confined to the tropics, only 5, all migratory, reaching the United States. They are remarkable, as a whole, for the brilliancy of their plumage, as well as for their marked sexual differences in color, and our Scarlet Tanager is, therefore, no exception to the rule.

They are arboreal and for the most part forest-inhabiting birds, feeding on flowers, fruit, and insects. The tropical species are of a roving disposition, and wander through the forests in search of certain trees bearing ripe fruit, near which they may always be found in numbers. As a rule, they are not musical. A few species, including ours, have more or less pleasing songs, but the voices of the majority are weak and squeaky.

A. With red in the plumage.
  a. Wings and tail black . . . . 473. SCARLET TANAGER, ♂.
  b. Wings and tail like the body . . . . . 474. SUMMER TANAGER, ♂.
B. Without red in the plumage.
  a. Underparts, including under wing-coverts, dull buffy yellow.
                                              474. SUMMER TANAGER, ♀.
  b. Underparts greenish yellow, under wing-coverts white.
                                              473. SCARLET TANAGER, ♀.

472. The WESTERN TANAGER, *Piranga ludoviciana* (Wilson), [607], a species of our western states, has been recorded from Maine, Massachusetts, Connecticut, New York, Louisiana, Wisconsin and Minnesota. The male has the back, wings, and tail black, the rump and belly yellow, the head and throat dipped in red. The female resembles the female of *P. erythromelas* but has yellow or white wing-bars and is usually yellower, particularly on the crown.

473. SCARLET TANAGER. PIRANGA ERYTHROMELAS *Vieillot.* [608.] (Fig. 118; Pl. IV.) *Ad. ♂ in summer.*—Bright scarlet, wings and tail black, under wing-coverts white. *Ad. ♂ in winter.*—Similar to the ♀, but wings and tail black. *Im. ♂ in winter.*—Similar to ♀, but wing-coverts black. *Im. ♂ in summer.*—Similar to ad. ♂ in summer, but primaries and secondaries as in winter. The adult summer plumage is acquired at the second spring (prenuptial) molt. *Ad. ♀.*—Upperparts light olive-green; wings and tail *fuscous,* lightly margined with olive-green; underparts greenish yellow. L., 7·25; W., 3·75; T., 2·09; B. from N., ·46.
Range.—Breeds mainly in Transition and Upper Austral zones from s. Sask., s. Que., and N. S. s. to s. Kans., n. Ark., n. Ala., n. Ga., and mts. of Va. and S. C.; winters from Colombia to Bolivia; migrates through Cuba, Jamaica, and Yucatan, and along the e. coast of Cent. A.; casual in migration in Wyo., Colo., the Bahamas, and Lesser Antilles.
Washington, common T. V., less common S. R., Apr. 17–Nov. 13. Bronx region, fairly common S. R., May 3–Oct. 30. Boston, rather common S. R., May 12–Oct. 1. N. Ohio, common S. R., Apr. 28–Oct. 2. Glen Ellyn, fairly common local S. R., Apr. 30–Oct. 2. SE. Minn., common S. R., Apr. 29–Oct. 6.
Nest, of fine twigs and weed-stalks, lined with vine tendrils and blossom stems, generally near the end of a horizontal limb, 7–20 feet up. *Eggs,* 3–4, pale bluish white or greenish blue, with numerous rufous or rufous-brown markings, ·88 × ·68. *Date,* Del. Co., Pa., May 28; New London, Conn., May 31; Cambridge, June 7; Black Hawk Co., Ia., May 23; se. Minn., May 21.

In watching birds, there are certain sights and sounds that make a day memorable much as a beautiful sunset does. I say to myself, "I have seen a Scarlet Tanager today!" or, "I have listened to a Hermit Thrush this evening."

High among the tree-tops of the cool green woods the Tanager sings through the summer days. Hidden by the network of leaves above us, we often pass him by; but once discovered he seems to illuminate the forest. We marvel at his color. He is like a Bird of Paradise in our northern landscape.

We are first guided to him by his call and song. They are peculiar, and both have a rare woods flavor. The call is a distinctly uttered *chip-chirr.* The song is a loud, cheery, rhythmical carol, suggesting the song of the Robin.

Inside the green woods the Tanager spends the summer, flying down to visit his nest in the fresh young undergrowth or to bathe in the still forest pools, and hunting and singing in the tree-tops high overhead.

FLORENCE MERRIAM BAILEY.

1918. BIRD-LORE, 16, 19 (mig.; pl.).

474. SUMMER TANAGER. PIRANGA RUBRA RUBRA (*Linnæus*). [610.]
Ad. ♂.—Rose-red, brighter below; wings fuscous, margined with rose-red. *Im.* ♂ *in winter.*—Similar to the ♀, but with more or less of a reddish tinge throughout the plumage. *Im.* ♂ *in summer.*—Variable; sometimes a mixture of ad. ♂ and ♀ plumages, at others like the ad. ♂, but wing-quills as in ♀. The ad. ♂ plumage is acquired at the first postnuptial molt and retained thereafter at all seasons. *Ad.* ♀.—Upperparts orange olive-green; underparts yellowish orange. L., 7·50; W., 3·75; T., 2·90; B. from N., ·55.
Range.—Breeds in Upper and Lower Austral zones from se. Nebr., s. Ia., se. Wisc., cent. Ind., cent. O., Md. (formerly N. J.), and Del. s. to ne. Mex. and s. Fla.; winters from cent. Mex. to Peru and Guiana; straggles n. to N. B., Que., N. S., Me., and Ont., migrant in w. Cuba; accidental in s. Calif., L. Calif., and in the Bahamas.
Washington, uncommon S. R., Apr. 18–Sept. 19. Bronx region, A. V.; one recent record; June 12. Boston, one record. N. Ohio, several summer records.
Nest, of leaves, strips of bark, etc., generally near the extremity of a limb, about 20 feet up. *Eggs*, 3–4, bluish white or greenish blue, with numerous cinnamon- or olive-brown markings, ·96 × ·68. *Date*, San Mateo, Fla., May 9; Mt. Pleasant, S. C., May 12; Mt. Carmel, Ills., May 28.

This is a common summer resident of our southern states, arriving in Florida early in April. It frequents open, rather than dense woods, and is particularly numerous in pineries having an undergrowth of oaks. It may be easily identified, not alone by its color but by its unique call-note—a clearly enunciated *chicky-tucky-tuck*. Its song bears a general resemblance to that of the Scarlet Tanager, but to my ear is much sweeter and less forced.

1918. BIRD-LORE, 145, 153 (mig.; pl.).

FAMILY FRINGILLIDÆ. GROSBEAKS, FINCHES, SPARROWS, AND BUNTINGS.

This, the largest family of birds, is distributed throughout the world, except in the Australian region. The number of species allotted to it depends upon one's views in regard to the relationships of allied forms, but in the Western Hemisphere about 800 species and subspecies are currently recognized. Sparrows are plastic birds, responding so readily to environmental influences that probably not more than half the forms recognized in this family deserve standing as species, while the remaining half are climatic or geographic races. They present wide diversity of form and habit, but generally agree in possessing stout, conical bills, which are admirably adapted to crush seeds. They are thus chief among seed-eaters, and for this reason are not so migratory as insect-eating species. It is only of late years that their great economic value as the destroyers of weed-seeds has been recognized.

The brown, streaked Sparrows are, to a large extent, field- or plain-inhabiting, and their neutral colors are therefore a means of protection in the exposed situations they inhabit. The brighter Grosbeaks and Finches are more arboreal. Many species take high rank as songsters, and some of our favorite cage-birds belong to this family.

The birds of this family are now generally considered to represent the most highly developed type of the Class *Aves,* and the structural reasons on which this claim is based are supported by their numerical abundance; thus the Order *Passeres,* beyond question the highest of avian groups, contains the greatest number of species, a distinction in turn shared by this, its 'highest' family.

KEY TO THE SPECIES

I. Underparts with red.
II. Underparts with no red and without distinct streaks; throat or breast sometimes with a patch or spot.
III. Underparts without red and with numerous streaks.

I. Underparts with red.

1. Wing-coverts plainly tipped with white or whitish, or with a white or yellow band in the wing.
  A. No red in the upperparts.
    a. Back black, rump whitish, throat black, breast and under wing-coverts rosy red . . . 476. ROSE-BREASTED GROSBEAK, ♂ ad.
    b. Back and underparts streaked with black; under wing-coverts rosy red . . . . . 476. ROSE-BREASTED GROSBEAK, ♂ im.
  B. With red in the upperparts.
    a. Red on upperparts confined to crown or forehead, and sometimes a tinge on the rump; wing under 3·25.
      a^1. Rump and flanks generally without blackish streaks; feathers of back generally with whitish borders.
        489. HORNEMANN'S REDPOLL. 489a. HOARY REDPOLL.
      a^2. Rump and flanks always streaked; feathers of back with little white, if any, and generally with brownish borders.
        490, 490a, b. REDPOLL and races.
      a^3. Back cinnamon-brown, unstreaked; crown, nape, and sides of neck black; a yellow band in the wing.
        488. BRITISH GOLDFINCH.
    b. Red or pink spread more or less over entire upperparts; wing over 3·25.
      b^1. Tips of mandibles crossed.
        494. WHITE-WINGED CROSSBILL, ♂ ad.
      b^2. Bill stout; mandibles not crossed.
        486, 486a. PINE GROSBEAKS, ♂ ad.
2. Wing-coverts not tipped with white.
  a. Throat black or blackish; wings and tail red; body red or olive.
        475, 475a, b. CARDINALS.
  b. Throat and more or less of underparts red or greenish red.
    b^1. Plumage blood-red, brownish red, or greenish red; tips of the mandibles crossed . . . . 493, 493a. RED CROSSBILLS, ♂.
    b^2. Plumage dull reddish; belly whitish; back indistinctly streaked, with bristly feathers over the nostrils.
        485. PURPLE FINCH, ♂ ad.
    b^3. Head blue; back green; rump red.
        480. PAINTED BUNTING, ♂ ad.

II. **Underparts with no red and without** distinct streaks; throat or breast
   sometimes with a patch or spot.

1. Tail with white spots, bars, or patches.
   A. Back plain, without streaks.
      a. Throat and breast black, brown, or slate-color, sharply defined
         from the white belly.
         a^1. Breast black or brown; sides rufous . . . . . 496. TOWHEE.
         a^2. Breast slate-color; sides the same, or brownish.
                        513. JUNCO. 513a. CAROLINA JUNCO.
      b. Throat and breast not black or brown.
         b^1. Throat and belly more or less yellow or ashy.
         b^2. Wing over 4·00; bill stout, greenish yellow.
                              484. EVENING GROSBEAK.
            b^3. Bill small and sharp; back brown; throat yellowish.
                              492. GOLDFINCH, ♀ and im.
            b^4. Body bright yellow, cap black . . 492. GOLDFINCH, ♂ ad.
         c^1. Underparts pure white, middle of back black.
                                   532. SNOWFLAKE.
   B. Back streaked with black, brown, or white.
      a. Underparts with a black spot or patch.
         a^1. Crown black.
            a^2. Throat black . . . . 529. LAPLAND LONGSPUR, ♂.
            a^3. Throat buffy, belly black.
                         531. CHESTNUT-COLLARED LONGSPUR, ♂.
            a^4. Throat and belly white . . 528. McCOWN'S LONGSPUR, ♂.
            a^5. Entire underparts black . . . . . 498. LARK BUNTING, ♂.
         b^1. Crown not black.
            b^2. Second tail-feather from without white, its outer web black
                  at tip . . . 531. CHESTNUT-COLLARED LONGSPUR, ♂ im.
            b^3. Second tail-feather broadly tipped with black.
                           528. McCOWN'S LONGSPUR, ♂ im.
            b^4. Tail-feathers black tipped with white . 510. LARK SPARROW.
      b. Underparts without a black spot or patch.
         b^1. Only two outer tail-feathers with white.
            b^2. Bend of wing yellow; length under 5·00.
                              501. GRASSHOPPER SPARROW.
            b^3. No yellow on bend of wing; length over 5·00.
                              530. SMITH'S LONGSPUR.
         c^1. More than two outer tail-feathers with white.
            c^2. Wing over 4·00; secondaries largely white 532. SNOW BUNTING.
            c^3. Wing under 4·00; secondaries not white; entire tip of second
                  tail-feather from without black.
                              528. McCOWN'S LONGSPUR, ♀.
            c^4. Wing under 4·00; secondaries not white; entire tip of second
                  tail-feather from without not black.
                        531. CHESTNUT-COLLARED LONGSPUR, ♀.

2. Tail without large white spots or patches.
   A. Back plain, without distinct streaks.
      a. Back blue, bluish or brownish blue.
         a^1. Wing over 3·00; lesser wing-coverts chestnut or with broad
                chestnut tips . . . . 477. BLUE GROSBEAK.
         a^2. Wing under 3·00; lesser wing-coverts blue or bluish, tipped with
                light brown . . . . 478. INDIGO BUNTING.
      b. Back not blue.
         b^1. Back green or greenish, or rump yellow or greenish yellow.
         b^2. Mandibles not crossed.
            b^3. Back greenish . . . . . . 480. PAINTED BUNTING, ♀.
            b^4. Back and underparts slaty gray; bill black.
                        486, 486a. PINE GROSBEAKS, ♀ and im.

b^5. Forehead, rump, underparts, and scapulars yellow or brownish yellow; secondaries white; bill yellow.

484. Evening Grosbeak, ♂.

c^2. Mandibles crossed.

c^3. Wing-bars white . . 494. White-winged Crossbill.

c^4. Without white wing-bars 493, 493a. Red Crossbills.

c^1. Back brown or brownish, ashy, or slate-color.

c^2. Head and rump yellowish or reddish; wing-bars white; wing over 4·00 . . . 486, 486a. Pine Grosbeaks, ♀ and im.

c^3. Underparts brownish cream-buff; wing-coverts with broad chestnut tips; wing over 3·00 . 477. Blue Grosbeak, ♀.

c^4. Underparts whitish; wing without yellow and under 3·00.

478. Indigo Bunting, ♀.

c^5. Back ashy; spot before the eye and on bend of wing yellow.

506, 506a–e. Seaside Sparrow and races.

B. Back distinctly streaked.

  a. Bend of the wing yellow.

    a^1. Tail over 2·20.

      a^2. A white throat-patch; breast gray; a yellowish line over the eye . . . . 523. White-throated Sparrow.

      a^3. A black spot on the throat; breast yellow, or both.

483. Dickcissel.

      a^4. No yellow over the eye; breast ashy or buffy; outer tail-feathers much the shortest.

511a. Pine-woods Sparrow. 511. Bachman's Sparrow.

    b^1. Tail under 2·20, the feathers narrow and sharply pointed.

      b^2. Crown olive-brown, a blue-gray line through its center; cheeks and breast ochraceous-buff.

505b. Nelson's Sparrow.

      b^3. Crown blackish, a cream-buff line through its center.

501, 501a. Grasshopper Sparrows.

  b. Bend of the wing not yellow.

    b^1. Crown bright reddish brown, the feathers sometimes tipped with ashy or brownish, but *without black streaks.*

    b^2. No white or whitish wing-bars; outer tail-feathers much shorter than middle one; lesser wing-coverts, upper tail-coverts, and margins of most of the tail-feathers rufous; wing under 2·50 . . . . . . 526. Swamp Sparrow.

    b^3. Cheeks and throat ashy, a narrow reddish brown line from back of the eye to the nape, an indistinct black spot in the center of the breast . . . . 515. Tree Sparrow.

    b^4. Eye-ring whitish, entire bill brownish flesh-color.

519. Field Sparrow.

    b^5. Rump slaty gray; underparts generally all grayish white; forehead black, with a narrow grayish line in its middle, a narrow black line from back of the eye to the nape.

516. Chipping Sparrow.

    c^1. Crown not bright reddish brown.

      c^2. Crown with black or blackish streaks or stripes.

      c^3. Lower tail-coverts buffy; crown with chestnut.

526. Swamp Sparrow.

      c^4. Lower tail-coverts buffy; crown black and white.

521. White-crowned Sparrow.

      c^5. Lower tail-coverts streaked; mandibles crossed.

494. White-winged Crossbill.

      c^6. Lower tail-coverts white, unstreaked; rump gray.

516. Chipping Sparrow, im.

      c^7. Lower tail-coverts white, unstreaked; rump brownish ashy.

517. Clay-colored Sparrow.

d^2. Crown mixed grayish brown and rufous, ashy, or slate-color, *without black streaks.*

d^3. Wing 2·50; bill brownish flesh-color; back rufous, streaked with black . . . . 519. FIELD SPARROW.

d^4. Wing 3·00; center of crown grayish brown, bordered by chestnut-rufous; back grayish brown, spotted with olive-brown . . . . 521. WHITE-CROWNED SPARROW.

III. Underparts without red and with streaks.

1. Tail-feathers without white or yellow spots or patches.

A. Outer tail-feathers little if any shorter than the middle pair.

  a. Head of the same general color as the back.

    a^1. No yellow over the eye or on the bend of the wing or under wing-coverts.

    a^2. Rump yellowish or yellowish green; mandibles crossed.

     a^3. Wing-coverts tipped with white.

      494. WHITE-WINGED CROSSBILL, ♀.

     a^4. Wing-coverts not tipped with white.

      493. RED CROSSBILL, ♀.

    b^2. Rump brownish or sandy or rufous; mandibles not crossed.

     b^3. Back pale brownish ashy, streaked with brownish; a whitish streak over the eye; legs flesh-color; first primary as long as or longer than the second . 499. IPSWICH SPARROW.

     b^4. Back and most of underparts streaked with black and reddish brown; upper and under tail-coverts streaked; first primary shorter than second; outer tail-feathers shorter than middle ones . . . 527, 527a, b. SONG SPARROWS.

     b^5. Back distinctly streaked; a cream-buff band across the breast . . . . 525. LINCOLN'S SPARROW.

     b^6. Back grayish brown, the feathers with or without distinct streaks; first primary nearly as long as or longer than second; outer tail-feathers longer than middle pair; legs and feet blackish; with bristly feathers over the nostrils. 485. PURPLE FINCH, ♀.

     b^7. Back without streaks; no bristly feathers over the nostrils. 478. INDIGO BUNTING, ♀.

     b^8. Upper tail-feathers and tail bright reddish brown, without black streaks; rump brighter; wing about 3·50. 524. FOX SPARROW.

     b^9. Cheeks buffy, bill pinkish; breast with a band of blackish blotches . . . . 520. HARRIS'S SPARROW, im.

    b^1. A yellow mark before the eye, or on the bend of the wing, or under wing-coverts yellow.

    b^2. Wing about 4·00; under wing-coverts deep yellow. 476. ROSE-BREASTED GROSBEAK, ♀.

    b^3. Wing generally under 2·90; feathers of the crown black, bordered by chestnut-brown; a buffy line through the center of crown . . . . . . 500, 500a. SAVANNAH SPARROWS.

    b^4. Wing generally over 2·90; feathers of crown with small black centers bordered with cinnamon-brown and pale brownish gray . . . . 499. IPSWICH SPARROW.

    b^5. Wing about 3·00; breast washed with yellow. 483. DICKCISSEL.

    b^6. Wing about 3·00; sides brownish; throat white, quite different from the grayish breast. 523. WHITE-THROATED SPARROW.

  b. Head not the same color as the back.

    b^1. A bright red crown-cap.

    b^2. Rump and flanks always heavily streaked with blackish 490. REDPOLL and races.

b^3. Rump white, generally without streaks; flanks lightly streaked; more or less white in the feathers of the back.

489. HORNEMANN'S REDPOLL. 489a. HOARY REDPOLL.

c^1. Crown-cap black . . . . . . 520. HARRIS'S SPARROW, ad.

B. Tail-feathers narrow and generally sharply pointed, the outer ones always much shorter than the middle pair.

  a. Crown of a different color from the back, or a buffy line over the eye.

    a^1. Center of crown with a more or less distinct brownish or buffy line.

    a^2. Nape dull, pale olive-green, of the same color as the line over the eye, but finely streaked with black; back rufous-brown, streaked with black . . 504, 504a. HENSLOW'S SPARROWS.

    a^3. Nape bright rufous-brown, the feathers bordered by gray; the feathers of the back black, bordered by buffy whitish.

503. LECONTE'S SPARROW.

    b^1. Center of crown with a more or less distinct stripe of ashy blue.

    b^2. Breast and sides distinctly streaked with black or blackish.

505a. SHARP-TAILED SPARROW.

    b^3. Breast and sides buffy or brownish, the former generally without distinct black streaks.

505b. NELSON'S SPARROW.

505. ACADIAN SHARP-TAILED SPARROW.

  b. Crown of the same color as the back; no buffy line over the eye.

    a. A yellow spot before the eye and on the bend of wing.

      a^1. Upperparts very dark brown or black; the feathers edged with olive-gray or ashy, breast generally with black streaks. (Florida.) . 506a–e. SCOTT'S SEASIDE SPARROW and allies.

507. DUSKY SEASIDE SPARROW.

      a^2. Back olive-gray; breast with grayish brown streaks.

506, 508. SEASIDE SPARROWS.

    b. No yellow before the eye.

      b^1. Bend of wing yellow.

511a. PINE-WOODS SPARROW. 511. BACHMAN'S SPARROW.

      b^2. A broad cream-buff band across the breast.

525. LINCOLN'S SPARROW.

      b^3. No cream-buff band on the breast; streaks on the breast tending to form a spot in its middle. 581. SONG SPARROW.

2. Tail with white patches or base of tail yellow.

  A. Base of the tail yellow . . . . 491. PINE SISKIN.

  B. Outer tail-feathers with white patches.

    a. Hind toe-nail shorter than the bill from the nostril.

      a^1. Lesser wing-coverts rufous; breast streaked with black.

509. VESPER SPARROW.

      a^2. Sides of crown and ear-coverts chestnut; a black spot on the center of the breast . . . . 510. LARK SPARROW.

      a^3. Wing-coverts broadly tipped with cream-buff.

498. LARK BUNTING, ♀.

    b. Hind toe-nail longer than bill from nostril.

      b^1. Underparts cream-buff; two outer tail-feathers mostly white.

530. SMITH'S LONGSPUR.

      b^2. Underparts whitish; breast streaked or spotted with black or entirely black; second outer tail-feather with but little white.

529. LAPLAND LONGSPUR.

A FIELD KEY TO THE
ADULT MALE FINCHES AND SPARROWS OF THE MIDDLE STATES
(VIRGINIA TO MASSACHUSETTS) IN BREEDING PLUMAGE

I. Breast with more or less yellow.
II. Breast blue.
III. Breast or throat red.
IV. Breast without either yellow, blue, or red.

I. Breast with more or less yellow.
    A. Chin white, throat black; haunts grassy fields; song an unmusical effort of six or seven notes delivered with great earnestness from a low perch (rare east of the Alleghanies) . . . . 483. DICKCISSEL.
    B. Underparts and breast pure yellow, crown and wings black; song a sweet canarylike warble; flight undulating, frequently accompanied by the notes *chic-o-ree, per-chic-o-ree* . . . . . . 492. GOLDFINCH.

II. Breast blue.
    A. Length over 6·00; plumage deep blue, a chestnut bar across the wings (not found north of Virginia) . . . . 477. BLUE GROSBEAK.
    B. Length under 6·00; plumage indigo-blue; haunts woody fields, scrub or second growth; song clear and musical, generally delivered from a tree-top . . . . 478. INDIGO BUNTING.

III. Breast or throat red.
    1. Length over 7·00.
        A. Length 8·00; throat and region about the base of the bill black, rest of the plumage bright vermilion-red; head with a conspicuous crest; song a rich, musical whistle; call-note an insignificant *cheep;* haunts thickets and bushy woodland (rare north of New York City) . . . . 475. CARDINAL.
        B. Length 7·50; breast rose-red; belly, tip of the tail, rump, and a band in the wings white; rest of the plumage black; haunts wooded growths; song loud, clear, and highly musical; call-note a metallic *peek* . . . . 476. ROSE-BREASTED GROSBEAK.
    2. Length under 7·00.
        A. Length under 6·50; plumage more or less heavily washed with dull reddish; haunts orchards and wooded growths; song a liquid warble; call-note a metallic *chink,* frequently uttered while on the wing . . . . 485. PURPLE FINCH.
        B. Length about 6·00; plumage dull blood-red; mandibles crossed at the tips; generally found in small flocks in coniferous woods; utters a clicking or whistled note when on the wing (rarely found south of New England after May 1) . . . 493, 493*a.* RED CROSSBILLS.
        C. Breast white, tinged with brown; region about the bill red, a yellow band in the wings. 488. BRITISH GOLDFINCH.

IV. Breast without either yellow, blue, or red.
    1. Underparts distinctly streaked or spotted.
        A. Outer tail-feathers white, showing conspicuously when the bird flies; haunts dry fields and roadsides; song loud and musical.
                              509. VESPER SPARROW.
        B. Outer tail-feathers not white.
            a. Song loud and musical; an abundant and familiar bird of general distribution; spots on the breast tending to form one larger spot in the center; crown umber, a whitish line over the eye.
                              527. SONG SPARROW.

b. Song not loud and musical; short and generally unattractive; haunts wet meadows or marshes; passes most of the time on the ground, rarely perching far from it, and when flushed generally returning to it.

   b¹. A buffy line over the eye and at the side of the throat, breast generally washed with buffy; haunts only salt marshes (rarely found far from the vicinity of the seashore).

                505*a.* SHARP-TAILED SPARROW.

   b². No buff on the sides of the head or breast; upperparts blackish; song *tsĭp-tsĭp-tsĭp'sē-ē-ē-s'r-r-r;* rarely breeds south of New York City; haunts both salt- and fresh-water marshes.

               500, 505*a.* SAVANNAH SPARROWS.

   b³. Back reddish, head and neck buffy olive; haunts generally wet pastures; song an inconspicuous *see-wick* (rather rare, living in small colonies of local distribution).

              504, 504*a.* HENSLOW'S SPARROWS.

2. Underparts not distinctly streaked or spotted.

 A. Underparts not white or whitish, or all one color.

   a. Throat pure white, sharply defined from the grayish breast, a yellow spot over the eye; crown black, with a central stripe of white; haunts thickets or bushy woodlands; song a high, clear, musical whistle; call-note a sharp *chink.*

          523. WHITE-THROATED SPARROW.

   b. Throat not white.

     a. Throat and breast black.

      a¹. Length 8·00; sides of the body light rufous, outer tail-feathers tipped with white; haunts thickets and bushy woodlands; call-note a vigorous *towhee* or *chee-wink.*

         496, 496*a, b.* TOWHEES.

     b. Throat and breast slate-color, like the back; belly and outer tail-feathers white; bill flesh-color (nests, in the Middle States, only on the higher parts of the Alleghanies) . 513, 513*a.* JUNCOS.

 B. Underparts white or whitish, practically all one color.

   a. Haunts wet marshes.

     a¹. Haunts always salt marshes, generally near the sea; back grayish . . . . 506, 506*a–e.* SEASIDE SPARROWS.

     a². Haunts both salt- and fresh-water marshes; back brown, streaked with black; cap and wings chestnut; song a loud, sharp, rapidly repeated *weet-weet-weet,* etc.

         526. SWAMP SPARROW.

   b. Haunts dry fields, pastures, roadsides, lawns, thickets, etc.

     b¹. Outer tail-feathers white, middle of the breast with a small black spot (accidental east of the Alleghanies).

         510. LARK SPARROW.

     c¹. Outer tail-feathers not white.

      c². Upperparts reddish brown, bill pinkish flesh-color; haunts bushy fields and pastures; song a musical, plaintive, *cher-wee, cher-wee, cher-wee, cheeo-dee-dee-dee-dee-dee.*

         519. FIELD SPARROW.

      c³. Bill dark brown, a buffy line through the center of the crown; song an insect-like *pit-tŭk, zee-zee-zee-zee-zee.*

         501, 501*a.* GRASSHOPPER SPARROWS.

      c⁴. Back streaked with black, cap chestnut, a white line over the eye, bill black; song a monotonous *chippy-chippy-chippy,* etc.

         516. CHIPPING SPARROW.

      c⁵. Larger, length about 7·00; crown black, with a white central stripe; throat not noticeably different from the breast; no yellow over the eye (rare; nests north of New England).

         521. WHITE-CROWNED SPARROW.

475. EASTERN CARDINAL. Richmondena cardinalis cardinalis (*Linnæus*). [593.] (Fig. 119*a*.) *Ad.* ♂.—Throat and regions about the base of the bill black; rest of the plumage bright rosy red, the upperparts tipped with grayish; a conspicuous crest; bill red. *Ad.* ♀.—Throat and region about the base of bill grayish black; crest, wings, and tail dull red; upperparts olive brownish ash; underparts buffy ochraceous, lighter on the belly, and sometimes tinged with red on the breast. L., 8·25; W., 3·75; T., 4·00; B., ·64.

Range.—Upper and Lower Austral zones e. of the Great Plains from se. S. Dak., s. Ia., n. Ind., n. O., se. Minn., se. Ont. (locally), se. and sw. Pa., and the s. Hudson Valley, s. to the n. part of Gulf States; casual in Colo., Wisc., Mich., N. B., Mass., and Conn., resident in Bermuda and introduced in s. Calif. (vicinity of Los Angeles).

Washington, common P. R. Bronx region, at present rather rare T. V. and P. R., formerly more numerous. Boston, casual. N. Ohio, common P. R. Glen Ellyn, fairly common local P. R. SE. Minn., common P. R. s. of Redwing; nests at Minneapolis.

Nest, of twigs, rootlets, and strips of bark, lined with grasses and rootlets, in bushes. *Eggs,* 3–4, white or bluish white, speckled or spotted with grayish brown, cinnamon-brown, or umber, 1·00 × ·70. *Date,* D. C., Apr. 15; Chester Co., Pa., Apr. 30; Central Park, N. Y. C., May 5.

The Cardinal is a famous singer, his song being a loud, clear whistle, into which usually enters quite frequently the sound of *q! q! q!* and a peculiar long-drawn-out *e-ē!* sometimes syllabled as "three cheers!" He is a favorite cage-bird. The female Cardinal is herself a charming singer, more pleasing to many than her mate, her music being softer in tone and otherwise different from his. The common call-note of both is a sharp, abrupt *tsip!* easily recognized after being once heard.

As the head of a family the Cardinal is admirable, not only in his attentions to his lovely dove-colored mate, but in singing to her by the hour, and in protecting her from intrusion or danger. To the young in the nest he is an untiring provider of worms and grubs, and thus most useful in a garden. Nothing can be more comical than his behavior when he first conducts his young family out into the world while his mate is engaged with her second sitting. He is as fussy as any young mother, hopping about in great excitement, and appearing to think the whole world thirsting for the life of his pretty little ones.

The Cardinal mother shows the restless manners and anxious spirit of her mate, taking one's intrusion upon her domestic affairs greatly to heart, and being so much disturbed that there is more pain than pleasure in making acquaintance with her nestlings.

OLIVE THORNE MILLER.

1913. Bird-Lore, 171, 172 (dist.; pl.).

475a. FLORIDA CARDINAL. Richmondena cardinalis floridanus (*Ridgway*). [593*d*.] Similar to *R. c. cardinalis* but smaller, male averaging deeper red; female darker and richer in color, particularly on breast. W., 3·40.

Range.—Peninsular Fla.
Nesting-date, San Mateo, Fla., Apr. 12.

475b. LOUISIANA CARDINAL. Richmondena cardinalis magnirostris (*Bangs*). Bill larger and heavier than in any of the other races of the *cardinalis* group, otherwise, most like *cardinalis floridanus*, but wing slightly longer, tail shorter, and foot and tarsus larger. In color the male has the same olivaceous edging to the feathers of the back, but the red of head and underparts is not so dark as in the Florida bird, though decidedly more intense than is usual in *cardinalis cardinalis*. The female is colored as in *cardinalis floridanus*, the back being olivaceous and the underparts strongly buffy; the middle of the belly, however, is rather paler—more whitish. ♂ W., 3·60; T., 3·80; B., ·40 (Bangs).

Range.—E. Tex. and s. La.

476. ROSE-BREASTED GROSBEAK. HEDYMELES LUDOVICIANUS (*Linnæus*). [595.] *Ad. ♂ in summer.*—Head, throat, and back black; breast and under wing-coverts bright rose-red, this color sometimes extending down the center of the white belly; rump white tipped with black; wings black; primaries white at the base; tail black, the outer feathers tipped with white on the inner web. *Ad. ♂ in winter.*—Similar but upperparts and breast margined with brown; throat rose; superciliary whitish, sides with black spots. *Im. ♂ in winter.*—Resembles the ♀, but under wing-coverts rose-red; breast tinged with rose. *Im. ♂ in summer.*—Similar to ad. ♂ in summer but wing-quills and some tail-feathers brownish as in ♀. The ad. winter plumage is acquired at the next (first postnuptial) molt, and the ad. summer the following spring. *Ad. ♀.*—Upperparts grayish brown, margined with cream-buff and pale grayish brown; a buffy line through the center of the crown, and a conspicuous whitish line over the eye; wings and tail dark grayish brown; wing-coverts tipped with white; under wing-coverts *orange;* underparts buffy, streaked with dark grayish brown. L., 8·12; W., 4·02; T., 2·99; B., ·69.

Range.—Breeds in lower Canadian and Transition zones from s. cent. Mack., s. Que., and Cape Breton Isl., s. to cent. Kans., s. Mo., cent. O., cent. N. J., and in the mts. to n. Ga. Winters from s. Mex. and Yucatan to Venezuela and Ecuador. Casual in migration in Cuba, Jamaica, Haiti and the Bahamas. Accidental in Ariz., Colo., and Calif.

Washington, rather common T. V., Apr. 17–June 3; Aug. 29–Oct. 16. Bronx region, fairly common S. R., Apr. 28–Oct. 21. Boston, very common S. R., May 10–Sept. 10. N. Ohio, common S. R., Apr. 27–Sept. 15. Glen Ellyn, fairly common S. R., common T. V., Apr. 27–Sept. 28. SE. Minn., common S. R., Apr. 27–Oct. 27.

Nest, of fine twigs, weed-stalks, and rootlets, in bushes or trees, 5–20 feet up. *Eggs,* 4–5, pale blue, with numerous olive-brown or rufous-brown markings, ·90 × ·69. *Date,* Carmel, N. J., May 20; Boston, May 25; se. Minn., May 11.

Sometimes in passing through young second growths, and more rarely densely undergrown woodland, I hear a singular kind of questioning call-note, not loud, but distinct—a steely *peek, peek*. It is a signal to me to pause and look for its author; even a glimpse of him is worth several minutes' waiting and watching. There is no mistaking his black, white, and rose costume; but the identity of his more modestly attired mate may long remain an open question. So little does she resemble him that she might pass for an overgrown Sparrow with a rather conspicuous whitish stripe over her eye.

The song of the Rose-breasted Grosbeak is generally compared to that of the Robin, and musical annotation would doubtless show that the comparison is not misleading. But the similarity is largely one of form; in expression there is no more resemblance in their voices than there is between the birds themselves. There is an exquisite purity in

the joyous carol of the Grosbeak; his song tells of all the gladness of a
May morning; I have heard few happier strains of bird-music. With
those who are deaf to its message of good cheer I can only sympathize,
pitying the man whose heart does not leap with enthusiasm at the sight
of rival males dashing through the woods like winged meteors, leaving
in their wake a train of sparkling notes.

1912. Bird-Lore, 158, 162 (mig.; pl.).—1915. Gabrielson, I. N.,
Wilson Bull., 357–368, illus. (habits).—1916. Allen, F. H., Auk, 53–56
(nesting).

477. EASTERN BLUE GROSBEAK. Guiraca cærulea cærulea (Linnæus). [597.] Ad. ♂.—Deep purplish blue; lores and chin black; back
blackish; wings and tail black, slightly edged with blue; middle wing-coverts
widely, and greater coverts narrowly tipped with chestnut-rufous. Ad. ♂
in winter.—Similar, but widely margined with rusty brown, particularly on
back. Im. ♂ in winter.—Resembles the ♀. Im. ♂ in summer.—Plumage
mottled brown and blue. The ad. winter plumage is acquired at the next
(first postnuptial) molt, and the ad. summer by wearing off of brown margins
the following spring. Ad. ♀.—Upperparts grayish brown; in some specimens
more or less blue about the head and rump and lesser wing-coverts; rump
inclined to ashy; wings fuscous, the greater and middle coverts tipped with
ochraceous-buff; tail fuscous, slightly margined with bluish gray; underparts
brownish cream-buff, the feathers of the breast sometimes blue at the base.
L., 7·00; W., 3·50; T., 2·75; B., ·65.

Range.—Breeds in Upper and Lower Austral zones from e. Nebr., Mo.,
s. Ills., and Md., s. to e. Tex. and cent. Fla. Winters from s. Mex. to Costa
Rica. Casual in s. Ind. and s. Pa.; accidental in Wisc., N. E., the Maritime
Provinces, and Cuba.

Washington, very uncommon and local S. R., May 1–Sept. 20. Boston,
A. V. N. Ohio, several summer records.

Nest, of grasses, in bushes or high weedy growths. Eggs, 3–4, pale bluish
white, ·84 × ·65. Date, Chatham Co., Ga., May 14; Raleigh, N. C., June 8.

"Unless seen under the most favorable circumstances the adult
male does not appear to be blue, but of an ill-defined, dusky color, and
may easily be mistaken for a Cow Blackbird (Molothrus ater), unless
most carefully watched; besides, they usually sit motionless, in a
watchful attitude, for a considerable length of time, and thus easily
escape observation.

"The Blue Grosbeak frequents much the same localities as those
selected by the Indigo Bird and Field Sparrow, viz., the thickets of
shrubs, briers, and tall weeds lining a stream flowing across a meadow
or bordering a field, or the similar growth which has sprung up in an
old clearing. The usual note is a strong, harsh ptchick, and the song
of the male is a very beautiful, though rather feeble, warble, somewhat
like that of the Purple Finch, but bearing a slight resemblance also to
that of the Rose-breasted Grosbeak" (Ridgway).

1911. Bird-Lore, 198, 202 (mig.; pl.).

478. INDIGO BUNTING. Passerina cyanea (Linnæus). [598.] Ad.
♂ in summer.—Rich blue, deeper on the head, brighter on the back; lores
blackish; wings and tail black, margined with blue. Ad. ♂ in winter.—
Resembles the ♀, but has more or less blue in the plumage. Ad. ♀.—Upperparts uniform grayish brown without streaks; wings and tail fuscous, some-

times lightly margined with bluish; wing-coverts margined with grayish brown; underparts whitish, washed with grayish brown and indistinctly streaked with darker; belly whiter. *Im.*—Resembles the ♀, but is darker. L., 5·59; W., 2·58; T., 2·11; B., ·41.

Remarks.—The female of this species is rather a puzzling bird, and may be mistaken for a Sparrow. Its unstreaked back and the slight tinge of blue generally present on the outer web of the wing- and tail-feathers should serve to distinguish it.

Range.—Breeds chiefly in the Transition and Austral zones from cent. e. N. Dak., s. Que., and s. N. B., s. to cent. Tex. and cent. Ga. Winters from Morelos, Yucatan, and Cuba through Cent. A. to Panama. Occasional in the Bahamas in migration; casual in e. Colo., s. Sask., and s. Man.

Washington, common S. R., Apr. 18–Dec. 13. Bronx region, common S. R., Apr. 26–Oct. 16. Boston, common S. R., May 15–Oct. 1. N. Ohio, common S. R., Apr. 26–Oct. 10. Glen Ellyn, fairly common S. R., May 1– Sept 22. SE. Minn., common S. R., Apr. 28–Oct. 6.

Nest, of grasses, bits of dead leaves, and strips of bark, lined with fine grasses, rootlets, and long hairs, generally in the crotch of a bush. *Eggs*, 3–4, pale bluish white, ·73 × ·57. *Date*, Richmond, Va., May 28; Chester Co., Pa., May 26; Boston, June 4; Brooklyn, Ind., May 21; se. Minn., June 9.

In walking among clumps of bushes in clearings or old pastures, look sharp if a small brown bird flies before you, especially if she calls *cheep* and twitches her tail nervously from side to side. Though she be a sparrowy-looking bird, look well to her shoulders and tail. If you discover a glint of blue and her cries call her mate, you will ever after be a more trustworthy observer—for his brilliant coat is unmistakable.

Having made sure of your birds, watch them to their nest—a compactly made cup—too cleverly hidden in the dense green thicket to be easily discovered. The color of the eggs will again test your accuracy of observation; in varying lights they look green, blue, and white.

The female Indigo is so suspicious that it is not hard to be vexed with her, but the primary virtues of an observer are conscientiousness and patience; so take your hard cases as a means of grace.

However distrustful the poor mother bird is, her mate's cheery song makes up for it all. After most birds have stopped singing for the year, his merry voice still gladdens the long August days.

I well remember watching one Indigo-bird, who, day after day, used to fly to the lowest limb of a high tree and sing his way up from branch to branch, bursting into jubilant song when he reached the topmost bough. I watched him climb as high into the air as he could, when, against a background of blue sky and rolling white clouds, the blessed little songster broke out into the blithest round that ever bubbled up from a glad heart. FLORENCE MERRIAM BAILEY.

1911. BIRD-LORE, 199, 202 (mig.; pl.).

479. The VARIED BUNTING, *Passerina versicolor versicolor* (Bonaparte), [600], of our Mexican border, has been once recorded from Michigan.

480. PAINTED BUNTING. PASSERINA CIRIS (*Linnæus*). [601.] *Ad.* ♂.—Head and sides of the neck indigo-blue; back golden green; rump dull red; underparts bright red; wings and tail tinged with dull red; greater wing-coverts green. *Im.* ♂.—Resembles the ♀. *Ad.* ♀.—Upperparts bright olive-green; underparts white, washed with greenish yellow; wings and tail fuscous, margined with olive-green. L., 5·25; W., 2·70; T., 2·15; B., ·42.

Range.—Breeds in the Lower Austral Zone from s. Kans., cent. Ark., n. Miss., and se. N. C. s. to s. La., n. Fla., se. N. Mex., and Tex. Casual in s. Ariz. and s. Ills. (reported occasionally farther north but doubtless on basis of escaped cage birds). Winters in the Bahamas and Cuba (rarely), and from cent. Fla., cent. Mex., and Yucatan to Panama; occasional in winter in s. La.

Nest, similar to that of *P. cyanea,* in bushes or low trees. *Eggs,* 3–4, white or bluish white, with numerous chestnut or rufous-brown markings, ·78 × ·56. *Date,* Chatham Co., Ga., May 16.

Mr. Maynard found this species in southern Florida in January, but it does not migrate northward until about May 1. He writes that it "is always shy and retiring, seldom appearing in the open, but remaining in the dense, thorny undergrowth which covers all waste places in Florida, especially if the soil has been cultivated. Whenever the birds perceive an intruder they retire into the depths of these fastnesses, and it requires considerable beating to drive them out, when they at once dart into the nearest cover. The adult males are especially shy, and seldom show themselves. Even while singing they remained concealed, and, although we were thus furnished with a clew to their whereabouts, it was with the utmost difficulty that we caught sight of the authors of the harmonious strains which nearly always greeted our ears when we were in the vicinity of their homes" ('Birds of Eastern North America').

"Their notes very much resemble those of the Indigo-bird, but lack their energy and are more feeble and concise" (B., B., and R.).

1911. Bird-Lore, 248, 250 (mig.; pl.).

481. The Grassquit, *Tiaris bicolor bicolor* (Linnæus), [603], of the Bahamas has been once recorded from Miami, Fla.

482. The Melodious Grassquit, *Tiaris canora* (Gmelin), [603.1], of Cuba, has been once recorded from Sombrero Key, Fla.

483. DICKCISSEL. Spiza americana *(Gmelin).* [604.] *Ad.* ♂ *in summer.*—Head and sides of the neck ashy gray; forehead tinged with yellow; a yellow line over the eye and one on the side of the throat; a black patch on the throat; chin white; breast yellow, spreading down on to the white belly; back streaked with black and pale grayish brown; rump brownish ash; lesser wing-coverts rufous; wings and tail fuscous. *Ad.* ♂ *in winter.*—Has less yellow and a more or less concealed throat-patch. *Im.* ♂.—Resembles ♀. *Ad.* ♀.—Similar, but the head grayish brown, streaked with blackish, and with no black patch on the throat and less yellow on the breast, which is sometimes lightly streaked with black. L., 6·00; W., 3·20; T., 2·35; B., ·55.

Fig. 154. Dickcissel. (Natural size.)

Range.—Breeds chiefly in Austral zones from ne. Wyo., nw. N. Dak., nw. Minn., s. Mich., cent. Ala., n. Ga., and se. Ont., s. to s. Tex. and s. Miss.; formerly bred on the Atlantic coastal plain from Mass. (casually wandering to Me.) to S. C., but now extremely rare e. of the Alleghanies, Winters from Cent. A. to Trinidad, migrating through Mex. and Cent. A. Accidental in L. Calif., Ariz., Man., N. S., and Jamaica.

Washington, formerly "very abundant," now casual; May–Aug. Boston, A. V., has bred (see Bull. Nutt. Orn. Club, III, 1878, 45, 190). N. Ohio, common S. R., west, rare east, May 1. Glen Ellyn, fairly common S. R., May 3–Sept. 5. SE. Minn., irregular S. R., May 11–Aug. 20.

Nest, bulky, of coarse grasses and leaves, lined with finer grasses and sometimes long hairs, on the ground or in low trees or bushes. *Eggs*, 4–5, pale blue, ·80 × ·60. *Date*, St. Louis, Mo., May 23; Avondale, Ohio, May 14; Poweshiek Co., Iowa, May 28; se. Minn., June 15.

Prior to 1880 these birds were more or less common in the Middle Atlantic States, but they are now of rare occurrence east of the Alleghanies. In Texas I have seen them migrating in closely massed flocks of several hundred individuals, all silent, except for an occasional *cack*. They alight on the prairie to feed; birds in the rear are constantly arising and passing to the front; there is ceaseless motion.

In the summer Dickcissel makes his home in grassy fields and pastures, and from a weed stalk or bordering fence, with uplifted head, he announces his presence as though life itself depended on his vocal exertions. It is a poor song from a musical standpoint, but pleasing because of the singer's earnestness.

1903. RHOADS, S. N., Cassinia, 17–28 (historical).—1904. MILLER, W. DE W., Auk, 487 (nesting in N. J.).—1911. BIRD-LORE, 83, 89 (mig.; pl.).—1921. GROSS, A. O., Auk, 1–26, 163–184; illus. (monograph).

484. EASTERN EVENING GROSBEAK. HESPERIPHONA VESPERTINA VESPERTINA (*W. Cooper*). [514.] *Ad. ♂.*—Forehead yellow, crown black; upperparts olive-brown, becoming dull yellow on rump; belly and scapulars yellow, wings and tail black; end half of the secondaries and their coverts white. *Ad. ♀.*—Brownish gray, lighter on the underparts, more or less tinged with yellow, especially on the nape; wings black, inner primaries white at the base, secondaries edged with white; tail black, the feathers tipped with white on the inner web; upper tail-coverts black tipped with white. *Ads. and Im. in winter.*—Similar to ads. in summer. L., 8·00; W., 4·50; T., 3·50; B., ·72.

Range.—Breeds in w. Alberta e. to n. Mich. and once at Woodstock, Vt. (Auk, 1926, 549). Winters in the interior of N. A., s. of the Sask. and e. of the Rocky Mts., and more or less irregularly to Que., N. E., N. Y., and Pa., and s. sporadically to Mo., Ky., O., D. C., Del., and N. J.

Washington, casual W. V., Apr. 3–May 26, 1922. Bronx region, irregular W. V., Nov. 13–May 6. Boston, rare and irregular W. V. N. Ohio, casual W. V. Glen Ellyn, one record, Dec. 11, 1889. SE. Minn., common W. V., Sept. 6–May 24.

"*Nest*, body of hard, clean sticks, lined with black and brown hair-like rootlets, with a sprinkling of moss between outer body and the lining"; in pines 25–50 feet up (Ligon). *Eggs*, 3–4, greenish, blotched with pale brown (see Davie).

FIG. 155. Evening Grosbeak. Ad. Male. (Natural size).

Date, Whitefish Point, Lake Superior, Mich., July 28, young on wing (Ligon).

Prior to 1910, the Evening Grosbeak was only a casual wanderer to the eastern United States; now it is a more or less regular winter visitant in flocks of from six or eight to as many as a hundred birds. Individuals banded in Michigan have been taken in Massachusetts and Connecticut, showing that they come to us from the West. They feed largely on the buds and seeds of trees, particularly of box-elder. They are not shy and an offer of sunflower seeds will usually bring them to our feeding-shelves. Their notes are described by different observers as a shrill *"cheepy-teet,"* and a *"frog-like peep,"* while one writer remarks that "the males have a single metallic cry like the note of a trumpet, and the females a loud chattering like the large Cherry Birds (*Ampelis garrulus*)." Their song is given as a wandering, jerky warble, beginning low, suddenly increasing in power, and as suddenly ceasing, as though the singer were out of breath.

1901. BIRTWELL, F. J., Auk, 388–391 (nesting).—1910. ROBERTS, T. S., Bull. Minn. Acad. Sci., 406–414 (habits in Minn.).—1911. BIRD-LORE, 298, 300 (mig.; pl.).—1914. ALLEN, A. A., Bird-Lore, 429–437, illus. (on the trail of).—1923. LIGON, J. S., Auk, 314–316, illus. (nesting in n. Mich.).—1929. MAGEE, M. J., Bull. Northeastern Bird-Banding Assoc., 157; Bird-Banding, 1930, 43–45.—1930. MAGEE, M. J., Bird-Banding, 40, 41, 145; also, 1928, Bull. Northeastern Bird-Banding Assoc., 56–59 (banding studies).

485. EASTERN PURPLE FINCH. CARPODACUS PURPUREUS PURPUREUS (*Gmelin*). [517.] (Fig. 119c.) *Ad.* ♂.—Body streaked, suffused with rose-red, strongest on the head, rump, and breast, more brownish on the back; whiter, generally white, on the belly; wings and tail brownish fuscous, the outer webs of the feathers finely edged with rose-red; a small tuft of bristly feathers over the nostrils; *outer* tail-feathers longest. This plumage is acquired at the first postnuptial molt. *Ad.* ♀.—Very different, sparrowlike in appearance; upperparts dark grayish brown, finely streaked with black; wings and tail dark grayish brown; underparts white, streaked, or with wedge-shaped spots of fuscous. A whitish superciliary line. *Im.* ♂.—Similar to adult female. L., 6·22; W., 3·24; T., 2·29; B., ·45.

Remarks.—Females and young males bear a decided resemblance to some Sparrows, but the rounded bill, tufts of feathers over the nostrils, and forked tail are distinguishing characters.

Range.—Breeds in the Canadian and Transition zones from nw. B. C. to N. F. s. to N. Dak., cent. Minn., n. Ills., Md. (mts.), n. N. J., and L. I., N. Y. Winters from considerably n. of the s. boundary of its breeding-range to the Gulf Coast from Tex. to Fla. Accidental in Colo.

Washington, common W. V., Aug. 31–May 29, largely a migrant. Bronx region, common T. V. and W. V., rare S. R., Sept. 14–May 26 (June 9). Boston, common P. R. N. Ohio, common W. V., Sept. 1–May 20. Glen Ellyn, fairly common T. V., Mch. 2–May 26; Aug. 25–Nov. 24; rare W. R. SE. Minn., common T. V., Mch. 7–May 14; Aug. 20–Nov. 30; frequent all winter.

FIG. 156. Purple Finch
(Natural size.)

Nest, of twigs, grasses, and rootlets, thickly lined with long hairs, in coniferous trees, 5–30

feet up. *Eggs*, 4–6, blue, spotted about the larger end with fuscous, ·79 ×
·56. *Date*, Boston, May 25; Holland Patent, N. Y., May 15.

During the nesting season the Purple Finch frequently takes up
its abode in private grounds, even becoming a familiar garden bird,
while others of its race find a congenial home in wild mountain forests,
far away from the society of man. The rosy plumage of the males
makes it attractively noticeable as a garden bird; but a serious offense
must be charged against it—it has far too ready a taste for the blossoms of fruit trees, and is, perhaps, the most confirmed bud-eater of
all our birds. It has naturally a roving disposition, and, in the autumn
especially, seems ever to be impelled by some restless impulse. At this
season it may often be seen descending with airy, sweeping flight into
some leafless tree-top, as if from a far aërial journey, its identity made
known by its very characteristic utterance, a short, rather dull-sounding
note, scarcely metallic—the metal pressed the instant the bell is struck.

Although the Purple Finch often essays to sing in the autumn and
earliest spring, its full powers of voice belong alone to the nuptial
season. Then it easily takes its place among our noteworthy song-
birds. Its full song is a sweet-toned, carelessly flowing warble—not
too brief to miss definite character as a song, and positive enough in
modulation and delivery to find ready place in the memory. At times,
indeed, its singing is of a character not to be easily forgotten. The
song bursts forth as if from some uncontrollable stress of gladness,
and is repeated uninterruptedly over and over again, while the ecstatic
bird rises high into the air, and, still singing, descends into the trees.

EU GENE P. BICKNELL.

1914. BIRD-LORE, 21, 24 (mig.; pl.).—1920. WELLMAN, G. B., Auk,
584, 585 (dance).—1927. WHITTLE, C. L. and H. G., Bull. Northeastern
Bird-Banding Assoc., 62–68; MAGEE, M. J., 101–104; 1928, WHITTLE, C. L.,
25–27; WHITTLE, H. G., 102–104. See also MAGEE, M. J., Bird-Banding,
1930, 136–139 (plumage changes).

486. PINE GROSBEAK. PINICOLA ENUCLEATOR LEUCURA (*Müller*).
[515.] (Fig. 119*b*.) *Ad.* ♂.—Slaty gray, more or less strongly washed with
rose-red, strongest on the crown, rump, upper tail-coverts, and breast;
wings fuscous, their coverts edged with white; tail fuscous. This plumage is
acquired at the first postnuptial molt. *Ad.* ♀.—Slaty gray, crown, upper
tail-coverts, and breast more or less strongly washed with olive-yellow;
wings and tail as in the ♂. *Im.*—Resembles the ♀, but is somewhat brighter.
♂ L., 9·50; W., 4·65; T., 3·80; B., ·54. ♀ W., 4·40; T., 3·60.

Range.—Breeds in Boreal forests from nw. Mack. (Great Bear Lake),
n. Man., n. Que. and Lab., to the White Mts. of N. H., Me., cent. N. B.,
s. N. S., and Cape Breton Isl. Winters s. to Ia., Ind., Pa., n. N. J., and s.
N. E., and casually to Ky.; w. to Man., Minn., and e. Kans.

Washington, casual in winter. Bronx region, rare and irregular W. V.,
Nov. 7–Apr. 12. Boston, irregular W. V., frequently common, sometimes
abundant, Nov. 1–Mch. 25. N. Ohio, occasional W. V. Glen Ellyn, uncommon and irregular W. V. SE. Minn., uncommon W. V., Oct. 20–Mch. 19.

Nest, of twigs and rootlets lined with finer materials, in coniferous trees a
few feet up. *Eggs*, "pale greenish blue, spotted and blotched with dark
brown surface markings and lilac shell-spots, 1·05 × ·74." *Date*, Bangor,
Me., June 5.

The Pine Grosbeak, like the Spruce Partridge and Canada Jay, may be said to find its true home in the coniferous forest or Canadian belt, which crosses the continent diagonally from Maine to Alaska.

Like many of its congeners in this inhospitable region, it nests so early in the springtime that the winter's frost and snow are still dominant among the evergreens when the eggs come to claim the attention of the pair.

Its habits at this season are but little known; but in midwinter, when it comes southward in search of food, it is a well-known frequenter, in flocks, of plantations of mountain-ash trees, or groups of sumach bushes, whose unfallen berries provide it with a bountiful supply of nourishing diet.

Its form has a general resemblance to that of the common Robin, but its very short, thick beak and its forked tail are striking differences. It is rather slow and inactive when in a tree, and when on the wing it has a loud whistle which is very characteristic and during the springtime has a prolonged and melodious song. At all times its colors, as above described, should distinguish the bird at a very considerable distance.   ERNEST THOMPSON SETON.

1895. BREWSTER, WM., Auk, 245–256 (remarkable flight of).—1911. BIRD-LORE, 345, 346 (mig.; pl.).

486a. NEWFOUNDLAND PINE GROSBEAK. PINICOLA ENUCLEATOR ESCHATOSUS *Oberholser.* Resembling *P. e. enucleator* but smaller; male darker and duller above and below in both red and gray areas; female darker on upper and lowerparts, the yellowish areas more purely yellow, less tinged with orange. ♂W., 4·40; T., 3·50. ♀ W., 4·15; T., 3·45 (Oberholser).
Range.—N. F., s. to Mass. in winter.
Boston, casual W. V.

The A. O. U. 'Check-List' mentions this race in a foot-note without comment.

487. HEPBURN'S ROSY FINCH, *Leucosticte tephrocotis littoralis* Baird, [524a.], of the Northwest, is accidental in Minnesota.

488. BRITISH GOLDFINCH. CARDUELIS CARDUELIS BRITANNICA (*Hartert*). [526.1.] *Ads.*—Region about the base of the bill *bright red;* crown, and a stripe extending from it on to the sides of the neck, black; back cinnamon-brown; wings black, crossed by a broad yellow band; tail black, inner webs of the feathers tipped with white; underparts white, sides tinged with the color of back. L., 5·50; W., 3·00; T., 2·95; B., ·50.
Nest, externally, of grasses and plant-down, lined with plant-down, in coniferous trees. *Eggs,* 4–5, white, with purplish spots, ·72 × ·50. *Date,* Central Park, N. Y. C., Apr. 26.

This European species was introduced into this country at Hoboken, N. J., in 1878, and probably descendants of the original birds existed at Englewood, N. J., as late as 1915. In 1879 it appeared in Central Park, New York City, where it was probably introduced, but it has not been observed there since 1920. C. L. Whittle (Bird-Banding, 1931, 85) records an individual which visited a feeding-stand at West-

field, Mass., between January 29 and March 11, 1930, and January 6
and February 13, 1931. Acting on the probability that the birds introduced into this country came from England, the A. O. U. Committee
has used the name of the British race for the birds recorded from this
country. The species has also been introduced in Bermuda. The
Bermuda bird has been described as *Carduelis carduelis bermudiana*
Kennedy, but Dr. Percy R. Lowe writes me that specimens from that
island agree with the race from Madeira, the Azores, and Canary
Islands, *Carduelis carduelis parva* Tchusi.

489. HORNEMANN'S REDPOLL. Acanthis hornemanni horne-
manni (*Holbœll*). [527.] Similar to the next, but "larger (length about 5·50
–6·50), with proportionally thicker and less acute bill. ♂ W., 3·37; T., 2·75;
exposed culmen, ·35; depth of B. at base, ·31."
  Range.—Breeds in Greenland, n. to 70° and in Iceland. Winters in its
breeding area and s. to Ungava. Casual at Ft. Churchill, Hudson Bay, and
Galt, Ont.; accidental in England and France.

489a. HOARY REDPOLL. Acanthis hornemanni exilipes (*Coues*).
[527a.] *Ad.* ♂.—Bill very sharply pointed, a small tuft of bristly feathers
over the nostrils; crown-cap bright red; back dark grayish brown, the feathers
more or less margined with white; rump white, generally unstreaked, and
tinged with pink; wings and tail brownish fuscous, the feathers all more or
less edged with white; middle of the throat blackish, breast tinged with pink,
belly white, a few streaks on the side. *Ad.* ♀.—Similar, but with no pink
on the rump or breast. *Im.*—Similar to the ♀, but without the red crown-
cap. L., 5·00; W., 3·00; T., 2·30; B., ·30.
  Remarks.—This species is to be distinguished from *Acanthis linaria* and
its races by the greater amount of white in its plumage, its unstreaked rump,
and comparatively unstreaked underparts.
  Range.—Breeds from w. Alaska to Ungava, and on the Chukchi Peninsula, ne. Asia. Winters occasionally s. to B. C., Mont., n. Minn., Mich.,
Ills., Ont., Me., Mass., Conn., and s. N. Y., and in Asia to the Commander
Isls. and n. Japan.
  Bronx region, A. V., one record, Mch. 24. Boston, rare W. V. SE. Minn.,
W. V., Nov. 28–Jan. 15.
  Nest, of grass and twigs lined with feathers, in a low tree or on the ground.
Eggs, 3–5, white, tinged with blue or green, spotted with reddish brown,
·65 × ·50 (Chamberlain). *Date*, Ft. Chimo, Lab., May 19.
  1914. Bird-Lore, 21, 24 (mig.; pl.).

490. COMMON REDPOLL. Acanthis linaria linaria (*Linnæus*).
[528.] (Pl. XXVII.) *Ad.* ♂.—Bill very sharply pointed, a small tuft of
bristly feathers over the nostrils; crown-cap bright
red; back fuscous grayish brown, the feathers
margined with ochraceous-buff; rump tinged with
pink; wings and tail fuscous, the feathers more
or less edged with whitish; chin and upper throat
blackish, breast suffused with pink, belly white,
sides streaked with fuscous. This plumage is acquired at the first postnuptial molt. *Ad.* ♀.—
Similar, but without pink on the rump or breast,
the sides more heavily streaked. *Im.*—Similar to
the ♀, but without a red crown-cap. L., 5·32; W.,
2·80; T., 2·32; B., ·36; depth of B. at base, ·22.
  Range.—Breeds in Boreal zones from nw. Alaska
and n. Que. s. to n. Alberta, n. Man., and isls. in

Fig. 157. Redpoll.
(Natural size.)

the Gulf of St. Lawrence; also through n. Europe and Asia; has occurred in Mich. and w. Pa. in summer. Winters in the n. parts of the U. S., irregularly s. to se. Ore., ne. Calif., Colo., Kans., Ind., O., Ala., and S. C.; also over the greater part of Europe and s. to cent. Asia. Accidental in Bermuda.

Washington, very rare and irregular W. V. Bronx region, irregular W. V., Nov. 13–May 4. Boston, irregular W. V., often abundant, Oct. 25–Apr. 10. N. Ohio, rare W. V. Glen Ellyn, irregular W. V., Nov. 6–May 6. SE. Minn., common W. V., Oct. 24–Apr. 30.

Nest, of dry grass and moss lined with hair, feathers, or plant-down, in a low tree or tuft of grass. *Eggs*, 4–6, white, tinged with green or blue, spotted with reddish brown, ·65 × ·50 (Chamberlain). *Date*, St. Michael's, Alaska, June 6.

The little Redpoll is one of those birds that are best known as winter visitors. Sometimes it comes from the north in flocks when driven from home by the annual failure of the food-supply, and speedily attracts attention by frequenting the gardens and orchards, even when these are within the limits of a town. In general habits it resembles a Goldfinch, and while with us it finds its wants supplied chiefly by the various grasses and herbs which project through the snow and still retain their seed in spite of wind and weather. It is noted for its affectionate and confiding disposition, and although it is not known to breed in captivity it has always proved an easily tamed and interesting pet.

ERNEST THOMPSON SETON.

1914. BIRD-LORE, 19, 24 (mig.; pl.).

490a. HOLBŒLL'S REDPOLL. ACANTHIS LINARIA HOLBŒLLI (*Brehm*). [528a.] Similar to *A. l. linaria*, but larger, the bill longer. W., 3·20; T., 2·35; B., ·38; depth of B. at base, ·22.

Range.—Breeds on Herschel Isl. S. in winter to Germany, Japan and se. Siberia. Occasional in winter or migration to nw. Alaska and se. to Keewatin, B. C., Mont., Ia., Ills., Mass., Me., and Que.

Boston, very rare W. V.

This is an intermediate between *A. l. linaria* and *A. l. rostrata*, most closely approaching the former, from which it sometimes can with difficulty be distinguished. It is an exceedingly rare bird in eastern North America, where there are but few records of its occurrence.

490b. GREATER REDPOLL. ACANTHIS LINARIA ROSTRATA (*Coues*). [528b.] Similar to *A. l. linaria*, but larger, the margins to the feathers of the upperparts averaging darker, the bill shorter and stouter. L., 5·50; W., 3·20; T., 2·55; B., ·35; depth of B. at base, ·28.

Range.—Resident in Greenland. In winter s. through Man., Ont., and Ungava to Colo., n. Ills., Mich., n. Ind., s. N. Y., Mass. and Conn.

Bronx region, Feb. 12 and 13, 1883 (A. K. Fisher). Boston, irregular W. V., never common, Nov.–Feb. SE. Minn., uncommon W. V., Mch. 3.

"The Greater Redpoll is often rather common, and in February, 1883, it occurred along the seacoast near Boston in positive abundance. As one sees them in winter in New England, the forms just mentioned, with *A. hornemannii exilipes*, do not differ appreciably in notes, habits, or general appearance. It is true that *A. l. rostrata* may be often recognized by its superior size, but the birds as a rule are so nervous and rest-

PLATE XXVII

PINE SISKIN

REDPOLL

TREE SPARROW

SNOW BUNTING

less, and when in large flocks so constantly in motion and so likely to depart altogether at any moment, that a free use of the gun is ordinarily indispensable to positive identification" (Brewster, Minot's 'Land Birds and Game Birds,' 2d ed., App., p. 472).

491. PINE SISKIN. Spinus pinus pinus (*Wilson*). [533.] (Pl. XXVII.)
Ads.—Bill sharply pointed, a small tuft of bristly feathers over the nostrils; upperparts streaked with black, the feathers margined with buffy; wings fuscous, most of the feathers margined with yellow, and *yellow at the base;* tail fuscous, all but the middle feathers *yellow at the base;* underparts white, tinged with buffy and heavily streaked with black. L., 5·00; W., 2·76; T., 1·90; B., ·40.

Remarks.—The yellow markings in the wings and tail of this species will always serve to distinguish it.

Range.—Breeds mainly in Canadian Zone from cent. Alaska, s. Mack., cent. Man., and cent. Que., s. through the higher mts. of w. U. S. to s. Calif., s. N. Mex., and to se. Nebr., n. Minn., n. Mich., N. B., N. S., and the mts. of N. C.; casually in the lower Hudson Valley and Mass. Occurs in winter over most of the U. S., s. to s. Fla. and n. Mex.

Washington, irregularly abundant W. V., Oct. 15–May 22. Bronx region, common but somewhat irregular T. V. and W. V., one breeding record; Sept. 27–May 15 (June 10). Boston, irregular W. V., Oct. 15–May 10; sometimes abundant; has bred occasionally. N. Ohio, tolerably common W. V., Sept. 20–May 15. Glen Ellyn, irregular T. V. and W. V., Apr. 8–June 3; Sept. 8–Nov. 29. SE. Minn., uncommon W. V., Sept. 30–May 29.

Nest, of twigs and rootlets, lined with plant-down and long hairs, in coniferous trees. *Eggs*, 4, pale bluish white, thinly spotted with reddish brown, ·67 × ·46. *Date*, Ossining, N. Y., May 25; Lyons Falls, N. Y., Apr. 25; Farmington, Me., June 14.

Like some other winter birds whose movements are governed by the food-supply, the Siskin is more or less irregular in its occurrence south of its breeding range, being abundant some years and rare or absent others.

During the summer it is an inhabitant of coniferous growths and its habits now resemble those of the Goldfinch. It has a flight-song, but this with its perch-song is less musical than that of its more brightly plumaged relative.

During its post-breeding wandering, it is found in closely massed flocks which move as one bird and which feed much upon the ground where they may be closely approached.

1887. Allen, J. A., Auk, 284–286 (nesting).—1910. Bird-Lore, 139, 142 (mig.; pl.).—1929. Swenk, M. H., Wilson Bull., 77–92, illus. (distribution and nesting in Nebr.).

492. EASTERN GOLDFINCH. Spinus tristis tristis (*Linnæus*). [529.] (Fig. 119*f*.) *Ad. ♂ in summer.*—Bright canary-yellow; crown, wings and tail black; wing-bars and inner vanes of tail-feathers white; longer upper tail-coverts gray; *lesser wing-coverts yellow.* This plumage is acquired at the second prenuptial molt. *Ad. ♂ in winter.*—Wings and tail as in summer but white edgings wider, *lesser wing-coverts still yellow;* back grayish brown, olive-tinged; throat and chest dull yellow, belly whitish, sides brownish buff. *Im. ♂ in winter.*—Similar to ad. ♂ in winter but lesser wing-coverts olive-green or olive-gray. *Im. ♂ in summer.*—Similar to ad. ♂ in summer but lesser wing-coverts as in winter. *Ad. ♀ in summer.*—No black crown-cap;

upperparts yellowish brown; below dull yellow; wings and tail less black than in ad. ♂; lesser wing-coverts olive-green. *Ad.* ♀ *and Im.* ♀ *in winter.*—Similar to im. ♂ in winter, but wings and tail less black. L., 5·10; W., 2·82; T., 1·95; B., ·40.

Range.—Breeds from s. Man., s. Que., and N. F., s. to e. Colo., s. Okla., cent. Ark., n. Ala., and n. Ga. Winters over most of its breeding area and s. to the Gulf Coast.

Washington, common P. R. Bronx region, common P. R. Boston, common P. R. N. Ohio, common P. R. Glen Ellyn, common P. R. SE. Minn., P. R., common May–Nov., less so in winter.

Nest, externally of fine grasses, strips of bark, and moss, thickly lined with thistledown, in trees or bushes, 5–30 feet up. *Eggs,* 3–6, pale bluish white, ·65 × ·48. *Date,* D. C., July 5; Newport, R. I., June 20; Boston, July 21; Ogle Co., Ills., June 30; se. Minn., June 4.

Except when nesting, Goldfinches are generally found in small flocks. Few birds seem to enjoy life more than these merry rovers. Every month brings them a change of fare, and in pursuit of fresh dainties the nesting-time is delayed almost until summer begins to wane.

Seed-bearing plants, whether in field or garden, form their larder; the old sunflowers rattle before their vigorous attack; the thistles spring into sudden blossom of black and gold as they swing from the nodding heads.

Their flight is expressive of their joyous nature, and as they bound through the air they hum a gay

"PER-CHIC-O-REE"   "PER-CHIC-O-REE"

Their love-song is delivered with an ecstasy and abandon which carries them off their feet, and they circle over the fields sowing the air with music. The song has a canarylike character, and while it is less varied it possesses a wild, ringing quality wanting in the cage-bound bird's best efforts.

1898. BRUCE, M. E., Auk, 239–243 (home-life).—1910. BIRD-LORE, 140, 142 (mig.; pl.).—1928. ALLEN, A. A., Bird-Lore, 287–292, illus. (autobiography).—1930. MOUSLEY, H., Can. Field Nat., 177–179, 204–207 (home-life).

493. RED CROSSBILL. LOXIA CURVIROSTRA PUSILLA *Gloger.* [521.] (Fig. 119d.) *Ad.* ♂.—Tips of the mandibles *crossed;* body dull red, brighter on the rump, browner on the back; wings and tail fuscous. This plumage is acquired at the first postnuptial molt. *Ad.* ♀.—Dull olive-green, yellow on the rump, indistinctly mottled with blackish on the head and back, mixed with whitish on the underparts. *Im.* ♂.—Similar to the ♀, but mixed with red and green. ♂ W., 3·45; T., 2·00; B., ·63. ♀ W., 3·40; T., 1·98; B., ·62.

Range.—Breeds from cent. Alaska, n. Mack., cent. Que., n. Minn., s. to Mich., and in the Alleghanies to n. Ga. (casually in Mass., Md., and Va.); winters irregularly s. to n. Tex., La., and Fla.; casual in Bermuda.

Washington, irregular W. V., sometimes abundant. Bronx region, irregular T. V. and W. V.; one breeding record; Nov. 3–May 28. Boston, of common but irregular occurrence at all seasons except midsummer, when rare. N. Ohio, irregular, often common, sometimes breeds. Glen Ellyn, uncommon and irregular, Oct. 20–June 11. SE. Minn., W. V., Sept. 27–Apr. 28.

Nest, of twigs and grasses, lined with bits of moss and rootlets, in coniferous trees, 15–30 feet up. *Eggs*, 3–4, "pale greenish, spotted and dotted about the larger end with various shades of brown and lavender shell-markings, 1·75 × ·57." *Date*, Morehouseville, N. Y., Mch. 30.

These parrotlike Finches are famous for their erratic wanderings. They seem to have no regard for the laws of migration which regulate the journeys of most birds, and, having no home ties, may linger in regions which offer them abundant fare without much regard to season. They nest early in the spring, sometimes when they are far south of their breeding range, but they seem quite unconcerned by their unusual surroundings, and their young are born and raised in a foreign land. Coniferous forests form their natural surroundings, and their bills are especially adapted to aid them in forcing off the scales from the cones of these trees to obtain the seed within.

They live in flocks, and when in the trees climb about like Parrots, sometimes exhibiting as little fear of man as Polly on her pedestal. When feeding, they have a short, whistled call-note; they take wing in a body, and their undulating flight is accompanied by a sharp clicking or whistled note. Their song is described as "varied and pleasing, but not powerful or in any respect remarkable."

1912. Bird-Lore, 45, 47 (mig.; pl.).

493a. NEWFOUNDLAND CROSSBILL. Loxia curvirostra percna *Bent.* [521*b*.] Similar to *L. c. pusilla* but larger, especially the bill; darker than any of the American races of *L. curvirostra*, reds deeper, richer and more brilliant, greenish yellow shades richer and brighter than in other forms. ♂ W., 3·70; T., 2·20; B., ·70. ♀ W., 3·50; T., 2·10; B., ·70 (Bent).
Range.—N. F. and N. S.; s. in winter as far as n. Va.
Boston, casual W. V.

494. WHITE-WINGED CROSSBILL. Loxia leucoptera *Gmelin.* [522.] *Ad.* ♂.—Tips of the mandibles *crossed;* body dull pink, brighter on the rump, more or less marked with black on the back; belly whitish; wings and tail black, the greater and middle wing-coverts, and sometimes tertials, *tipped with white.* This plumage is assumed at the first postnuptial molt. *Ad.* ♀.—Dull olive-green, yellow on the rump, grayer on the underparts, mottled with blackish on the head and back; wings and tail as in the ♂. *Im.* ♂.—Similar to ♀, but plumage often with more or less pink. L., 6·05; W., 3·27; T., 2·41; B., ·62.
Range.—Breeds in Boreal zones from the limit of trees in n. Alaska, n. Mack., n. Man., and n. Que. s. to B. C., s. Alberta, cent. Ont., N. Y. (Adirondacks), N. H. (White Mts.), s. Me., and s. N. S. Winters in much of its breeding area and s. irregularly to n. Ore. (Cascades), Nev., Colo., Kans., s. Ills., s. O., and N. C.; more or less frequently to Greenland, British Isles, and Helgoland.
Washington, irregular W. V. Bronx region, rare and irregular W. V., Oct. 29–Apr. 7 (May 10). Boston, irregular W. V. N. Ohio, rare W. V.

Glen Ellyn, rare, fall records only, Oct. 22, 1916. SE. Minn., W. V., Oct. 16–Mch. 4.

Nest, of twigs and strips of birch bark, covered exteriorly with moss (*Usnea*), and lined with soft moss and hair, on the fork of an evergreen in deep forests. *Eggs*, 3 (?), pale blue, spotted and streaked near larger end with reddish brown and lilac, ·80 × ·55 (Chamberlain). *Date*, Wolfeville, N. S., Feb. 6 (Thayer Coll.).

Goss writes that in general habits these birds resemble the American Crossbill. Their flight is swift and undulating. While feeding and moving about they are quite noisy, almost constantly uttering a plaintive *wheep* or *cheeping* note. Their song is low, soft, and sweet, much like that of the American Goldfinch.

1912. Bird-Lore, 46, 48 (mig.; pl.).

495. The Green-tailed Towhee, *Oberholseria chlorura* (Audubon), [592.1], of the western United States, is accidental in Virginia and South Carolina.

496. RED-EYED TOWHEE. Pipilo erythrophthalmus erythrophthalmus (*Linnæus*). [587.] *Ad.* ♂.—Upperparts black, sometimes margined with rufous; throat and breast black, belly white, sides rufous; outer web of primaries with white; tail black, the three outer feathers tipped with white; outer web of the outer feather entirely white; *iris red. Ad.* ♀.—Upperparts, wings, throat, and breast bright grayish brown; tail fuscous-brown, the three outer feathers tipped with white; sides rufous, middle of the belly white. *Nestlings* have the back and underparts streaked with black. L., 8·35; W., 3·34; T., 3·68; B., ·55.

Range.—Breeds in the Transition and Upper Austral zones, e. of the Great Plains from se. Sask., s. Man., s. Ont., and s. Me., s. to cent. Kans. and n. Ga. Winters from se. Nebr., the O. and Potomac valleys (casually N. E.) to cent. Tex., the Gulf Coast, and cent. Fla.

Washington, common S. R., very common T. V., Mch.–Oct. 30; a few winter. Bronx region, common S. R., occasional in winter; Apr. 10–Dec. 28. Boston, common S. R., Apr. 25–Oct. 15. N. Ohio, common S. R., Mch. 10–Oct. 25. Glen Ellyn, fairly common S. R., Mch. 15–Nov. 18. SE. Minn., common S. R., Apr. 11–Nov. 15.

Nest, externally of dead leaves and strips of bark, lined with fine grasses, on or near the ground. *Eggs*, 4–5, white, finely and evenly speckled with shades of rufous, sometimes blotched at the larger end, ·96 × ·71. *Date*, Fairfax Co., Va., May 8; Montgomery Co., Pa., May 17; Boston, May 20; Rosetta, Ills., May 2; Wheatland, Ind., May 6.

There is a vigorousness about the Towhee's notes and actions which suggests both a bustling, energetic disposition and a good constitution. He entirely dominates the thicket or bushy undergrowth in which he makes his home. The dead leaves fly before his attack; his white-tipped tail-feathers flash in the gloom of his haunts. He greets all passers with a brisk, inquiring *chewink, towhee*, and if you pause to reply, with a *fluff-fluff* of his short, rounded wings he flies to a near-by limb better to inspect you.

It is only when singing that the Towhee is fully at rest. Then a change comes over him; he is in love, and, mounting a low branch, he repeatedly utters his *sweet bird s-i-n-n-g* with convincing earnestness.

1912. Bird-Lore, 287, 290 (mig.; pl.).

496a. ALABAMA TOWHEE. PIPILO ERYTHROPHTHALMUS CANASTER *Howell.* [587*b*.] Similar to *P. e. erythrophthalmus* but with a larger bill and slightly longer tail; white markings on tail-feathers less extensive, sides and flanks averaging paler; female with head, neck, chest and upperparts more grayish; iris red. W., 3·50; T., 3·80; B., ·60.

Range.—Ala. and cent. Ga.

496b. WHITE-EYED TOWHEE. PIPILO ERYTHROPHTHALMUS ALLENI *Coues.* [587*a*.] Similar to the preceding, but with less white in the wings and tail; rufous areas paler; *iris yellowish or white.* L., 8·00; W., 3·20; T., 3·60; B., ·52.

Range.—Coast region from about Charleston, S. C., s. including Fla. *Nesting-date,* San Mateo, Fla., Apr. 18.

This southern race of the Towhee does not associate with the northern bird, which is abundant in the south in the winter. The latter selects haunts of much the same nature as those in which it passes the summer, while the southern bird lives in heavy growths of scrub palmetto. The notes of *alleni* differ from those of *erythrophthalmus; its towhee* is much higher, and its song, as Dr. Allen pointed out years ago, is shorter. It is also a shyer bird than its northern cousin.

497. The ARCTIC TOWHEE, *Pipilo maculatus arcticus* (Swainson), [588], of the Great Plains and Rocky Mt. region, is of casual occurrence in Illinois and Wisconsin. It bears a general resemblance to *P. e. erythrophthalmus,* but has more white in the tail and the scapulars and back are marked with white.

498. The LARK BUNTING, *Calamospiza melanocorys* Stejneger, [605], of the western United States, is accidental in Massachusetts (Boston), Long Island, and South Carolina. The adult male is black with a large white patch in the wing and the tips of the inner webs of the tail-feathers white. The female is streaked above and below but has the tail tipped much as in the male and the wing-coverts broadly tipped with cream-buff. Immature males wear an intermediate plumage. L., 6·40; W., 3·40; T., 2·50.

499. IPSWICH SPARROW. PASSERCULUS PRINCEPS *Maynard.* [541.] *Ads.*—Generally with a spot of sulphur-yellow before the eye and on the bend of the wing; upperparts pale brownish ashy, streaked on the head, back, and upper tail-coverts with black and cinnamon-brown; the nape and rump with few or no streaks; a white line over the eye; wings grayish brown, outer webs of greater coverts and tertials margined with pale ochraceous-buff; tail grayish brown, the outer webs of the feathers margined with brownish ashy; underparts white; breast and sides lightly streaked with blackish and ochraceous-buff. L., 6·25; W., 3·00; T., 2·25; B., ·40.

Range.—Breeds on Sable Isl., N. S. Winters from Sable Isl. s. along the sand-dunes of the Atlantic Coast to Ga.

Bronx region, occasional T. V. and W. V.; Oct. 29–Mch. 28. Boston, uncommon T. V., probably also winters.

Nest, on the ground, in a cup-shaped hollow scratched by the birds, of weed-stalks and coarse grasses, lined with finer grasses. *Eggs,* 4–5, indistinguishable from those of the Savannah Sparrow but averaging a little larger (Dwight). *Date,* Sable Isl., N. S., June 4.

Those who care to visit in winter the bleak, wind-swept sand hillocks of our Atlantic Coast will find this bird much less rare than it was once supposed to be. It never strays far from the waving tufts of coarse beach-grass that scantily cover the sand-drifts, and single individuals may be found skulking among such surroundings. They seldom allow a near approach, but fly wildly away to considerable distances, and on alighting run off so rapidly that they are difficult to find a second time. The flight is rapid and irregular, and the birds may easily be mistaken for Savannah Sparrows, with which, during the migrations, they are sometimes associated. On rare occasions a sharp chirp is heard, but as a rule they are silent.

It is an interesting species, discovered in 1868, and at first mistaken for Baird's Sparrow of the Far West, a species, by the way, that it resembles very little. For many years nothing was known of its breeding-range. In 1884 some large eggs from Sable Island, N. S., supposed to be of the Savannah Sparrow, were unearthed at the National Museum, Washington, and later a summer specimen of the Ipswich Sparrow was obtained from this island. Ten years later I had the pleasure of visiting Sable Island and solving all the conjectures that had become current regarding the Ipswich Sparrow's summer home. The bird proved to much resemble the Savannah Sparrow in breeding habits, song, nest, and eggs.   J. DWIGHT, JR.

1895. DWIGHT, J. H., JR., Mem. No. II, Nutt. Orn. Club, 1–56 (monograph).—1902. SAUNDERS, W. E., Auk, 267–271 (nesting).—1911. BIRD-LORE, 144, 148 (mig.; pl.).

500. EASTERN SAVANNAH SPARROW. PASSERCULUS SANDWICHENSIS SAVANNA (*Wilson*). [542a.] *Ads.*—A pale yellow mark over the eye and on the bend of the wing; general tone of the upperparts brownish black, the centers of the feathers black, margined first by rufous or ochraceous-buff, then by ashy; wings fuscous, the outer webs of the feathers margined with ochraceous-buff; tail fuscous, the outer web of the feathers margined with whitish; underparts white, heavily streaked, except on belly, with blackish and rufous, the breast feathers tipped with wedge-shaped marks. *Ads. and Im. in winter.*—Similar, but color deeper, more suffused with ochraceous. L., 5·68; W., 2·62; T., 2·09; B., ·40.

Range.—Breeds mainly in the Boreal and Transition zones from n. Man. and n. Que., s. to n. Ia. (casually Mo.), n. Ind., mts. of Pa., Conn., and L. I., and casually on the coast of s. N. J. Winters from s. Ind. and s. N. J., s. to ne. Mex., the Gulf Coast, Bahamas, and Cuba. Casual in Bermuda.

Washington, abundant T. V., Feb. 14–May 14; Sept. 21–Nov. 22; a few winter. Bronx region, common T. V., occasionally winters; several breeding records; Mch. 6–June 9; Aug. 22–Dec. 8. Boston, abundant T. V., Apr.; Oct.; breeds sparingly. N. Ohio, common T. V., Mch. 20–May 12; occasional S. R. Glen Ellyn, fairly plentiful S. R., Apr. 8–Oct. 20. SE. Minn., common S. R., Apr. 13–Oct. 26.

Nest, of grasses and sometimes moss, lined with finer grasses or hair, on the ground. *Eggs*, 4–5, bluish white, thickly marked, sometimes heavily washed, with reddish brown or cinnamon, ·78 × ·56. *Date*, Bolton, Mass., May 9; Boston, May 21; Utica, N. Y., May 19.

This is essentially a bird of the fields, and one of the most abundant species of the Maritime Provinces of Canada—in fact, characteristic of them. The roadsides abound with the birds bobbing up and down on the fence-posts and *chipping* vigorously at every passerby. Their boldness is tempered with a certain timidity that becomes apparent when they are followed, for, dropping into the grass, they will slip away with surprising rapidity. They have a startling way, sometimes,

of springing up with a whirr of wings almost from under your very feet
as you cross the fields where they have been feeding. At the southern
limits of their breeding range they gather into irregularly distributed,
isolated colonies frequenting wet, boggy meadows, and exhibit a shyness that is not shared by their northern brethren. In the fall, young
and old gather into bands, and, joining with other species, form an
important part of the large flocks of migrating Sparrows that fill the
fields and hedgerows.

The song is insignificant—a weak, musical little trill following a grass-
hopperlike introduction, and is of such small volume that it can be heard
but a few rods. It usually resembles *tsĭp-tsĭp-tsĭp' sē'-ē-ē-s'r-r-r*. More
singing is heard toward sunset, when of a quiet evening the trills are
audible at greater distances. Each male seems to have a number of
favorite perches, weeds or fence-posts, which are visited as inclination
dictates, but he is of too restless a disposition to remain long on any of
them. The most familiar note is a sharp *tsĭp* of alarm or expostulation
heard during migration, but so constantly employed by both sexes in
the breeding season, even on slight provocation, that one gets to think
of them as veritable scolds.

They are more likely to be mistaken for the Vesper Sparrow, which
they resemble even in flight, than for any other except perhaps the
Ipswich and Sharp-tailed Sparrows.   J. Dwight, Jr.

1911. Bird-Lore, 144, 147 (mig.; pl.).

500a. LABRADOR SAVANNAH SPARROW. Passerculus sandwichensis labradorius (*Howe*). [542a., part]. Similar to *P. s. savanna*
but wings and tarsi longer; bill shorter and thicker. W., 2·90.

Range.—Breeds in Lab., winters s. along Atlantic Coast.

501. EASTERN GRASSHOPPER SPARROW. Ammodramus savannarum australis *Maynard.* [546.] (Pl. XXVIII.) *Ads.*—Upperparts
mixed black, rufous-brown, ashy, and cream-buff; crown blackish, a cream-
buff line through its center; nape rufous-brown, each feather with a small
black central spot and bordered by ashy; back black, the feathers bordered
by cream-buff and with a small central tip of rufous-brown; rump rufous-
brown and ashy; an orange mark before the eye; bend of the wing yellow;
lesser wing-coverts yellowish olive-green; greater coverts tipped with whitish;
tail-feathers pointed, of about equal length, dark grayish brown, the centers
of the feathers darker, the end half of the outer feather generally dusky
whitish; underparts generally not streaked; breast and sides buffy; belly
white. *Nestlings* have the breast spotted with blackish. L., 5·38; W., 2·38;
T., 1·79; B., ·43.

Remarks.—The yellow on the wing, unstreaked underparts, even, pointed
tail-feathers, and grayish mark on the outer tail-feather are the principal
characters of this species.

Range.—Breeds in Austral zones (sporadically in Transition), e. of the Great Plains from
s. Wisc., s. Ont., and s. N. H., s. to s. La., cent.
Ala., n. Ga., and n. S. C. Winters from s. Ills.
and N. C., s. to the Bahamas, Cuba, Cozumel
Isl., Yucatan, and the Gulf Coast of Mex.
Casual in Me.

Fig. 158. Tail of Grasshopper
Sparrow.

Washington, very common S. R., Mch. 30–
Nov. 20. Bronx region, fairly common S. R.,

Apr. 17–Oct. 29. Boston, rare S. R., May 16–Sept. 1. N. Ohio, common S. R., Apr. 20–Sept. 20. Glen Ellyn, not common S. R., Apr. 28–Sept. 26. SE. Minn., common S. R., Apr. 25–Sept. 28.

Nest, of grasses, sometimes lined with hairs, arched, on the ground. *Eggs*, 4–5, white, distinctly spotted and speckled with rufous, ·73 × ·54. *Date*, Hall Co., Ala., May 11; Richmond, Va., May 25: Chester Co., Pa., May 27; se. Minn., June 6.

Few common birds may be more easily overlooked than this Sparrow. Its terrestrial habits and weak notes place it among the birds that you are not likely to find unless you know how and where to look for them. I remember once introducing this bird and its song to a visiting ornithological friend. On returning to his home, greatly to his surprise, he found it a common resident of the fields about his house, where, owing to his unfamiliarity with its notes and habits, its presence had been before unsuspected.

In the North you will generally find it in old, dry daisy or sorrel fields; in the South it inhabits the broom sedge. It will not take wing until almost stepped upon; then, if bushes are near, it takes refuge in or under them, but out in the open field it flies rapidly some distance and drops to the ground.

Its usual perch, when singing, is a fence-rail; and it does not often seek a more elevated position. Its fine, insectlike notes give it the name of Grasshopper Sparrow. They may be written *pit-tuck, zee-e-e-e-e-e-e-e.* Under favorable circumstances they can be heard by an attentive listener at a distance of two hundred and fifty feet, but the casual observer would pass within ten feet of a singing bird and be none the wiser.

1910. BIRD-LORE, 12, 18 (mig.; pl.).

501a. FLORIDA GRASSHOPPER SPARROW. AMMODRAMUS SAVANNARUM FLORIDANUS (*Mearns*). [546*b*.] Similar to *A. s. australis* "but smaller, with larger bill, longer tarsus, and much darker coloration above, paler below; chestnut of upper surfaces much reduced in amount and replaced by black; lateral dark areas of crown almost black, interscapular region much blacker." (Mearns, Proc. U. S. Nat. Mus., XXIV, 1902, 915.)

Range.—Cent. Fla. (Kissimmee prairie region).

502. BAIRD'S SPARROW, *Ammodramus bairdi* (Audubon), [545], (Pl. XXVIII), a bird of the Great Plains region, has been once recorded from east of the Mississippi—Montauk Point, L. I., Nov. 13, 1899 (Helme, Auk, 1900, 296).

503. LECONTE'S SPARROW. PASSERHERBULUS CAUDACUTUS (*Latham*). [548.] (Pl. XXVIII.) *Ads.*—No yellow before the eye or on the bend of the wing; a broad ochraceous-buff line over the eye, and a cream-buff line through the center of the blackish crown; nape *rufous-brown*, each feather with a small black central spot and an ashy border; back black, the feathers margined first by rufous, then cream-buff and whitish; tail grayish brown, with a slight rufous tinge, darker along the shaft; the feathers narrow and sharply pointed, the *outer* ones much the shortest; breast and sides tinged with buffy, and more or less streaked with black; belly white. L., 5·00; W., 2·00; T., 2·05; B., ·35.

Range.—Breeds in Canadian and Transition zones from Great Slave Lake,

PLATE XXVIII

1. Grasshopper Sparrow
2. Henslow's Sparrow, ad.
3. Henslow's Sparrow, im.
4. Baird's Sparrow
5. Leconte's Sparrow, ad.
6. Leconte's Sparrow, im.

Mack., s. Sask., and Man.. s. to N. Dak. and s. Minn. Winters from s. Kans. and s. Mo. to Tex., Fla., and the coast of S. C., and occasionally to N. C. Casual in Ont. and N. Y.; accidental in Idaho and Colo.

Glen Ellyn, not common T. V., Mch. 28–?; Sept. 8–Oct. 6. SE. Minn., uncommon S. R., Apr. 8–Oct. 17.

Nest, of fine grasses, on the ground. *Eggs*, 3–5, delicate pink, lightly spotted with brownish and black near the larger end, ·75 × ·50 (Seton). *Date*, Raeburn, Man., June 6.

My experience on the coast of Texas with this elusive little Sparrow conforms with that of most observers, and the few specimens I found were in wet marshes. Mr. L. M. Loomis, however, tells us that at Chester, S. C., where Leconte's Sparrow is a locally common winter visitant, it shows a marked preference for dry 'old fields of broom sedge' (*The Auk*, II, 1885, p. 190).

Few birds are more difficult to flush. It exhibits a rail-like disinclination to take wing, and flying low and feebly, makes for the nearest cover. Ernest Thompson Seton records it as an abundant summer resident in the willow sloughs and grassy flats of Manitoba, and describes its call-notes as a thin, sharp, ventriloquial *tweet*, and a single, long-drawn *bizz;* while its song, which is delivered from some low perch a little above the grass, is a tiny, husky, double-noted *reese, reese*, "so thin a sound and so creaky, that I believe it is usually attributed to a grasshopper."

1901. Peabody, P. B., Auk, 129–134 (nesting).—1910. Bird-Lore, 14, 18 (mig.; pl.).

504. EASTERN HENSLOW'S SPARROW. Passerherbulus henslowi susurrans *Brewster*. [547.] (Pl. XXVIII.) *Ads.*—Top and sides of head and nape dull, pale *olive-green*, more buffy in the fall; sides of crown black; nape finely streaked with black; back rufous-brown, the feathers with narrow, central, wedge-shaped black streaks, and narrow ashy margins; bend of wing pale yellow; wing-coverts much like back; tail-feathers very narrow and sharply pointed; middle feathers rufous-brown; the outer ones much the shortest; underparts white, more or less washed with buffy and *streaked with black* on the breast and sides. *Nestlings* have no spots on the breast. L., 5·00; W., 2·20; T., 2·00; B., ·42.

Remarks.—The peculiar olivaceous color of the head and nape, and the bright rufous-brown color of the back, wing-coverts, and middle tail-feathers are the best distinguishing marks of this species.

Range.—Breeds in the Transition and Upper Austral zones from N. Y. and s. N. H., s. to n. Va. Winters in the se. states to Fla.

Washington, locally common S. R., Apr. 11–Oct. 21. Bronx region, rather rare T. V. and S. R., Apr. 4–Oct. 28; casually later. Boston, rare S. R., May–Oct. N. Ohio, S. R. Glen Ellyn, fairly common S. R., Apr. 28–Sept. 26. SE. Minn., uncommon S. R., Apr. 25.

Nest, of grasses, sometimes lined with hairs, on the ground. *Eggs*, 4–5, grayish white, thickly and evenly speckled with pale rufous-brown, ·75 × ·57. *Date*, Cape May Co., N. J., May 25; Richland Co., Ills., May 23.

During the summer this species seems to prefer wet meadows, but in the winter it inhabits the dry 'old fields' grown with broom sedge, which are so common in the South. It has the secretive habits of the Grasshopper and Leconte's Sparrows, and takes wing only when forced to.

Mr. P. L. Jouy writes of its song: "Besides the characteristic notes of *tee-wick*, they have quite a song which may be fairly represented by the syllables *sis-r-r-rit-srit-srit*, with the accent on the first and last parts. This song is often uttered while the bird takes a short flight upward; it then drops down again into the tangled weeds and grasses, where it is almost impossible to follow it" (*Bull. Nutt. Orn. Club*, 1881, p. 57).

1910. Bird-Lore, 14, 18 (mig.; pl.).

504a. WESTERN HENSLOW'S SPARROW. Passerherbulus henslowi henslowi *Audubon*. [547a.] Similar to *P. h. susurrans*, but margins to the feathers above more terminal than lateral; in breeding plumage general color of the upperparts duller, black areas larger, chestnut areas smaller.

Range.—Breeds from S. Dak. and Ont. to n. Tex. and O. Winters from se. Tex. to nw. Fla.

505. ACADIAN SHARP-TAILED SPARROW. Ammospiza caudacuta subvirgata (*Dwight*). [549.1a.] Similar to *A. c. caudacuta*, but paler above and with the throat, breast, and sides washed with cream-buff and indistinctly streaked with ashy. "L., 5·55; W., 2·30; T., 2·00; B., ·46" (Dwight).

Range.—Breeds in salt marshes of the Atlantic coast from se. Que., Prince Edward Isl., and Cape Breton Isl. to Me. Winters on coasts of S. C., Ga., and nw. Fla.

Bronx region, rare T. V., May 30 and June 3; Sept. 29–Nov. 18. Boston, probably rather common in Sept. and Oct.

Nest, "on ground in grass; built of and lined with grass. *Eggs*, 4 or 5, .71 to .80 × .58 to .60 in.; pale greenish-blue, marked with 'cinnamon-brown, umber, and blue-gray'" (Forbush).

Since this race was separated by me in 1887 few new facts have been developed regarding it, except that, as I anticipated, it has been found in other parts of the Maritime Provinces, and never far from salt water. While frequenting brackish or fresh-water marshes, where the grasses grow more luxuriantly than in the haunts of its southern relative, it prefers the more open spots or those where damp ditches make highways of escape for it afoot. It is locally abundant, particularly in the great marshes that border the Bay of Fundy, but so retiring that, save for its little song, its presence might be easily overlooked. Swaying on a tall stalk of meadow rue or squatting on a convenient fence, the males may be found at all hours of the day repeating their song a few times and then flying to some new perch or burying themselves in the grass. Occasionally toward nightfall one will mount into the air and with set wings float down, fairly gushing with song, a habit shared by the ordinary Sharp-tail and by the Seaside Sparrow as well.

With these birds they associate in autumn, and may be flushed one or two at a time from the strips of grass or reeds that are left on the salt marshes along the ditches after the hay has been cut.

The song is a husky, gasping effort, not very loud, and executed with a nod of the head. It is sung in less than a second, and resembles *ksh-sh-sh-ōōlp*, the last syllable occupying one-fifth of the time and rather musical compared with the harsh lisp that precedes it. They also have a *tchĕp* of alarm, but it is the exception for them to show much anxiety about their nests or young. **J. DWIGHT, JR.**

1910. BIRD-LORE, 112, 113 (mig.; pl.).—1922. NORTON, A. H., Auk, 568 (nesting).

505a. SHARP-TAILED SPARROW. AMMOSPIZA CAUDACUTA CAUDACUTA (*Gmelin*). [549.] *Ads.*—General color of the upperparts a brownish olive-green; crown olive-brown, with a blue-gray line through its center; gray ear-coverts, inclosed by ochraceous-buff lines, one of which passes over the eye and one down the side of the throat; feathers of the back margined with grayish and sometimes whitish; bend of the wing yellow; tail-feathers narrow and sharply pointed, the outer feathers much the shortest; breast and sides washed with buffy, paler in summer, and *distinctly* streaked with black; middle of the throat and belly white or whitish. "L., 5·85; W., 2·30; T., 1·90; B., ·50" (Dwight).

Remarks.—The chief points of difference between this and the two associated races are found in the markings of the breast and sides. In the present race these parts are pale ochraceous-buff; distinctly streaked with *blackish;* in *nelsoni* they are deep ochraceous-buff, lightly if at all streaked; in *subvirgata* they are cream-buff, indistinctly streaked with *grayish.*

Range.—Breeds in salt marshes of the Atlantic Coast from Mass. to Va. Winters on salt marshes from N. J. (casually from Mass.) to Fla.

Bronx region, fairly common but local S. R., Apr. 10–Dec. 26. Boston, not uncommon S. R.

Nest, of grasses and seaweed, lined with fine grasses, on the ground. *Eggs,* 3–4, white or grayish white, finely speckled with cinnamon-brown, especially at the larger end, ·78 × ·57. *Date,* Amityville, N. Y., May 31; Lynn, Mass., June 6.

This species is confined exclusively to the salt-water marshes of our coast, where it may be found in large numbers. It runs about among the reeds and grasses with the celerity of a mouse, and is not apt to take wing unless closely pressed. Mixed flocks of the several varieties of the Sharp-tail, together with the Seaside Sparrow, gather in the fall among the sedges, and may be observed hiding in the grass or clinging to the tall stalks of the cattails. In the breeding season it is usually associated with the Seaside Sparrow on the same marsh, but it prefers the drier parts, and builds its nest in the tussocks on the bank of a ditch or in the drift left by the tide, rather than in the grassier sites chosen by its neighbor.

From some bit of driftwood or a convenient stake, its infrequent song may be heard morning and evening. It is short and gasping, and only less husky than the somewhat similar performance of the Seaside Sparrow. **J. DWIGHT, JR.**

1910. BIRD-LORE, 111, 113 (mig.; pl.).

505b. NELSON'S SPARROW. AMMOSPIZA CAUDACUTA NELSONI (*Allen*). [549.1.] Similar to *A. c. caudacuta*, but smaller, the upperparts darker, the feathers of the back more olive-brown and more broadly *margined with whitish;* the throat, breast, and sides deeper ochraceous-buff, very slightly if at all streaked with blackish. "L., 5·50; W., 2·25; T., 1·90; B., ·43" (Dwight).

Range.—Breeds in the Canadian and Upper Transition zones from Great Slave Lake and w. cent. Alberta to sw. Man., Minn., and ne. S. Dak. Winters on the Atlantic and Gulf coasts from N. C. to Fla. and Tex.; n. on the Atlantic Coast during migration to Me. Accidental in Calif.

Washington, rare T. V., May; Sept. Bronx region, rare T. V., Sept. 28–
Nov. 13; no spring records. Boston, rare T. V. in fall. N. Ohio, several
records. Glen Ellyn, two records; Oct. 2, 1893; Sept. 16, 1911. SE. Minn.,
uncommon S. R., May 18–Sept.

Nest, on the ground, of fine grasses. *Eggs*, 5, grayish white ground,
thickly sprinkled and clouded all over with markings of brown, thickening
on the extreme butt into a dark brown zone, ·65 × ·50. *Date*, found by E.
S. Rolfe, at Devil's Lake, N. Dak., June 14, 1899 (Auk, 1899, 356).

This interior representative of the Sharp-tailed Sparrow occurs on
the Atlantic Coast only as a migrant and winter visitant when it is
associated with the Sharp-tail and Acadian Sharp-tail.

1910. BIRD-LORE, 111, 113 (mig.; pl.).

506. NORTHERN SEASIDE SPARROW. AMMOSPIZA MARITIMA MARI-
TIMA (*Wilson*). [550.] (Fig. 119*e*.) *Ads.*—A line from bill to eye and bend
of wing yellow; upperparts grayish olive-green; tail grayish brown, the outer
webs of the feathers margined with olive-greenish; a dusky line from the
base of the lower mandible passes down the sides of the throat; breast more

or less suffused with buffy (wanting in
summer specimens), and indistinctly
streaked with grayish; throat and middle of the belly grayish white; sides
grayish. L., 6·00; W., 2·50; T., 2·20;
B., ·60.

Range.—Breeds in salt marshes of the
Atlantic Coast from s. Mass. to Va.
Winters from Va. to n. Fla., rarely n.
to Mass.

Bronx region, uncommon and local
S. R., Apr. 4–Dec. 27.

Nest, of coarse grasses and reed-stalks,
lined with grasses, on the ground.

FIG. 159. Seaside Sparrow.
(Natural size.)

Eggs, 3–4, white or bluish white, clouded or finely speckled with cinnamon-
brown, especially at the larger end, ·80 × ·63. *Date*, Northampton Co., Va.,
May 18; Oyster Bay, N. Y., May 24.

Like most marsh-loving birds, Seaside Sparrows are so consistent
in their choice of a home that it would be quite useless to look for them
anywhere but in a marsh, and that a salt one, generally within sound
or at least sight of the sea. The baymen call them 'Meadow Chippies,'
and often when Snipe and Plover shooting, I have drawn numbers to me
by simply *squeaking*. They tipped all the reeds about my blind, chirping
excitedly at the peculiar sound which aroused their curiosity. They pass
much of their time on the ground among the reeds and grasses, but
mount a stalk to sing their short, unattractive song of four or five notes.
Sometimes they flutter into the air a few feet above the reeds and deliver
their song while on the wing.

The absence of distinct streaks on the breast and lack of rufous
in their olivaceous or grayish plumage will distinguish them from the
Sharp-tailed, Swamp, Savannah, or Song Sparrows, the only ones which
are likely to be found in their haunts.

1910. BIRD-LORE, 112, 113 (mig.; pl.).

506a. MACGILLIVRAY'S SEASIDE SPARROW. Ammospiza maritima
macgillivraii (*Audubon*). [550*d.*] Similar to *A. m. fisheri* but above grayer,
less black; breast and flanks but faintly washed with buff and streaked with
dusky grayish. Grayer above than *A. m. peninsulæ* and less heavily streaked
below.
Range.—Salt marshes from N. C. to n. Fla.
Nesting-date, Matanzas Inlet, Fla., Apr. 20.

506b. SCOTT'S SEASIDE SPARROW. Ammospiza maritima penin-
sulæ (*Allen*). [550*a.*] Similar to the preceding, but much darker; prevailing
color of the upperparts brownish black, the feathers margined with grayish
olive-green; underparts more heavily streaked, the breast and sides streaked
with black or blackish. W., 2·30; T., 2·00; B., ·52.
Range.—Salt marshes of the w. coast of Fla., from Tampa Bay to Lafayette Co.

506c. WAKULLA SEASIDE SPARROW. Ammospiza maritima junci-
cola (*Griscom and Nichols*). [550*e.*] The darkest and blackest race of *maritima,* our single female in fresh plumage a decided approach to *nigrescens.*
Never with a brownish tinge as in *peninsulæ,* the crown almost unmarked
(never sharply streaked), and the markings of the underparts diffuse and
vaguely defined, except in fresh plumage when they are much broader and
blacker. Only the faintest suggestion of buff on the breast in any plumage,
an additional character separating it from *fisheri* (Griscom and Nichols).
Range.—Gulf Coast of Fla., from St. Andrews Bay to s. Taylor Co. and
probably farther.

506d. HOWELL'S SEASIDE SPARROW. Ammospiza maritima howelli
(*Griscom and Nichols*). [550*f.*] "Close to *maritima* and *macgillivraii,* the tone
of the upperparts most like *maritima,* paler than *macgillivraii,* slightly more
olive, less grayish than either. The crown streaked like *macgillivraii,* though
less conspicuously so; the nape immaculate like *maritima.* The back with
broad ill-defined markings. The underparts darker, more extensively washed
with gray than in either, and in fresh specimens the breast is deep ochraceous-
buff, deeper than in any other race, except *fisheri*" (Griscom and Nichols).
Range.—Coast of Ala. and Miss., spreading to the coasts of n. Fla. and
Tex. in winter.

506e. LOUISIANA SEASIDE SPARROW. Ammospiza maritima fisheri
(*Chapman*). [550*c.*] Similar to *A. m. peninsulæ* but darker above, breast
and sides *heavily washed with rusty buff* and streaked with gray.
Range.—Breeds in salt marshes on Gulf Coast from Grand Isle, La., to
High Isl., Tex.; winters s. to Corpus Christi, Tex.

507. DUSKY SEASIDE SPARROW. Ammospiza nigrescens (*Ridgway*).
[551.] *Ads.*—Upperparts *black,* narrowly margined with grayish and grayish
olive-green; underparts *sharply* streaked with black and white in about
equal proportions. "L., 5·95; W., 2·25–2·40; T., 2·10–2·50; B., ·50–·60"
(Ridgway).
Range.—Marshes at n. end of Indian River, e. coast of Fla.
Nest, of grasses about 1 foot above the ground in *Salicornia,* switch-grass,
or *Juncus. Eggs,* 3–4, "more richly marked than those of Macgillivray's,
with bolder markings of rich chestnut and often capped at the larger end.
Specimens of both species are, as a rule, finely sprinkled with light browns,
grays, and lavender, and some sets are indistinguishable" (Nicholson).
Date, Apr.–Aug.

This Sparrow has been recorded from Salt Lake, near Titusville,
Fla., and a small breeding colony has been discovered west of Indian

River City (Nicholson, *The Auk*, 1929, 391), but with these exceptions it appears to be confined to the western side of Merritt's Island on the opposite shore of Indian River. In March, 1898, I found it to be abundant near the mouth of Dummitt's Creek where it inhabited the sedge (*Borrichia*) bordering the water and the adjoining grassy marshes. Savannah and Swamp Sparrows were also common in these marshes. The paler color and darting, more extended flight of the former at once distinguished it from *nigrescens*, which, while more like the Swamp Sparrow, was soon recognized by its darker colors and shorter, more hesitating flight. The birds were not in song.

In view of the fact that this species is abundant and that the region it inhabits is in no sense isolated, but that both to the north and south there are marshes apparently similar to those it occupies, makes noteworthy the restriction of its range to an area only a few square miles in extent.

1910. BIRD-LORE, 114 (pl.).—1928. NICHOLSON, D. J., Wilson Bull., 225–237 (nesting habits of Fla. species).

508. CAPE SABLE SEASIDE SPARROW. AMMOSPIZA MIRABILIS (*Howell*). General color of upperparts ashy greenish (greener than in our other Seaside Finches), sides of crown broadly and distinctly striped with black; center of back and scapulars broadly marked with blackish widely margined with greenish white; underparts white (grayish in *maritima*) without buffy suffusion; the breast and sides definitely streaked with fuscous; line from bill to eye and bend of wing yellow. W., 2˙25; T., 2˙00.

Range.—Coastal marshes in the vicinity of Cape Sable, Fla.

Nest, of grasses in switch-grass or salt-grass "several" to 16 inches from the ground. *Eggs*, 3–4, "like those of other Seasides" (Nicholson). *Date*, about Mch. 15.

This representative of *Ammospiza maritima* is apparently completely isolated from other members of the group from which it is sufficiently distinct to be ranked as a full species. It was discovered by Arthur H. Howell in February, 1918, and is not only the latest but probably the last new species of bird to be found in eastern North America.

509. EASTERN VESPER SPARROW. POOECETES GRAMINEUS GRAMINEUS (*Gmelin*). [540.] *Ads.*—Upperparts brownish gray, streaked with black and a little ochraceous-buff; wings fuscous, greater and middle coverts tipped with white, lesser coverts *bright rufous;* tail fuscous, the outer feather mostly *white*, the next one with much less white; underparts white; the breast and sides streaked with black and ochraceous-buff. L., 6˙12; W., 3˙06; T., 2˙38; B., ˙41.

Remarks.—The white tail-feathers and rufous lesser wing-coverts will always distinguish this species from any other of our Sparrows.

Range.—Breeds from w. cent. Man., cent. Ont., s. Que., and Cape Breton Isl., s. to e. Nebr., cent. Mo., Ky., Va., and N. C., w. to w. Minn. Winters from the s. part of its breeding-range to the Gulf Coast, s. Fla., and cent. Tex. Casual in Bermuda and Yucatan.

Washington, P. R., common T. V., less so in summer and winter. Bronx region, fairly common T. V. and S. R., rarely winters; Mch. 13–Dec. 9. Boston, rather common S. R., Apr. 5–Oct. 25. N. Ohio, abundant

S. R., Mch. 20–Nov. 7. Glen Ellyn, fairly common S. R., Mch. 21–Oct. 25. SE. Minn., common S. R., Mch. 23–Nov. 3.

Nest, of rather coarse grass, lined with finer grasses, rootlets, and long hairs, on the ground. *Eggs*, 4–5, bluish white or pinkish white, speckled and spotted with rufous-brown or umber, 1·83 × ·61. *Date*, Chester Co., Pa., May 5; Norwich, Conn., May 8; Boston, May 10; se. Minn., Apr. 30.

In walking through dry upland fields or along dusty roadsides a rather pale, streaked Sparrow will sometimes run rapidly ahead of you, wait for you to catch up, then run ahead again. It is best to be content with what measure of his confidence and society he

Fig. 160. Outer tail-feathers of Vesper Sparrow.

voluntarily grants you, for, if you quicken your steps and try to overtake him, he will rise and bound on before you or swing off to one side, showing, as he flies, the white feathers on each side of his tail.

Frequently he will alight on a fence-rail or even the higher branch of a tree, for, although a field Sparrow, he is by no means a purely terrestrial one. When singing, he generally selects an elevated perch and gives himself entirely to his musical devotions. Early morning and late afternoon are his favorite hours, but he can be heard at other times. His song, which is loud, clear, and ringing, may be heard at a distance of several hundred yards. It resembles that of the Song Sparrow, but is sweeter and more plaintive. When heard in the evening it is a truly inspired and inspiring melody.

1911. BIRD-LORE, 86, 89 (mig.; pl.).—1918. PERRY, E. M. and W. A., Auk, 310–316 (home-life).

510. EASTERN LARK SPARROW. CHONDESTES GRAMMACUS GRAMMACUS (*Say*). [552.] *Ads.*—Sides of the crown and ear-coverts *chestnut*, a whitish line over the eye and through the center of the crown; a black streak on the sides of the throat; upperparts brownish ash; back streaked with blackish; tail fuscous or black, the outer feathers tipped with white; underparts white, a small black spot in the middle of the breast. L., 6·25; W., 3·50; T., 2·75; B., ·45.

Range.—Breeds mainly in Austral zones from e. Nebr., nw. Minn., cent. Wisc., and s. Ont., s. to s. La. and cent. Ala., e. to w. Pa. and nw. W. Va. Winters from s. Miss. to e. Mex. Casual in N. S., N. B., Me., N. Y., Mass., N. J., e. Md., D. C., N. C., and Fla.

Washington, A. V., Aug., three records. Boston, A. V. N. Ohio, rare S. R., Apr. 28. Glen Ellyn, local and rare S. R. SE. Minn., common S. R., Apr. 18–Aug. 18.

Fig. 161. Lark Sparrow. (Natural size.)

Nest, of grasses, lined with rootlets, fine grasses, and long hairs, on the ground or in low trees or bushes. *Eggs*, 3–5, white or pinkish white, spotted, blotched, or scrawled with purplish or black, chiefly at the larger end, ·78 × ·60. *Date*, se. Minn., May 13.

This is a common bird in the West. It frequents localities of much the same nature as those selected by the Vesper Sparrow, and in its general habits reminds one of that species. The song is described by Ridgway ('Birds of Illinois,' I, p. 262) as "composed of a series of chants, each syllable rich, loud, and clear, interspersed with emotional trills. At the beginning the song reminds one somewhat of that of the Indigo Bird (*Passerina 'cyanea*), but the notes are louder and more metallic, and their delivery more vigorous. Though seemingly hurried, it is one continued gush of sprightly music; now gay, now melodious, and then tender beyond description—the very expression of emotion. At intervals the singer falters, as if exhausted by exertion, and his voice becomes scarcely audible; but suddenly reviving in his joy it is resumed in all its vigor until he appears to be really overcome by the effort."

1911. BIRD-LORE, 84, 89 (mig.; pl.).

511. BACHMAN'S SPARROW. AIMOPHILA ÆSTIVALIS BACHMANI (*Audubon*). [575a.] Similar to the preceding subspecies, but the upperparts rufous, black streaks generally confined to the back, or absent; line over the eye buffy; breast and sides brownish cream-buff without streaks.

Range.—Breeds in Upper and Lower Austral zones in cent. Ills. (locally to se. Ia.), s. Ind., s. O., and cent. Va., s. to cent. Tex. and extreme nw. Fla. Winters from s. N. C. s. into Fla. Casual near Washington, D. C.

Washington, irregular S. V., Apr.–June, or later. N. Ohio, two summer records.

Nest, of grasses, domed and cylindrical, on the ground. *Eggs*, 3–4, pure white, ·74 × ·60 (Bendire, Auk, 1888, 356). *Date*, Weaverville, N. C., May 6; Greensboro, Ala., May 8.

In Florida, where this bird is not uncommon during the winter, I have found it in pine woods undergrown with turkey oats, and not in localities frequented by *æstivalis*. In South Carolina it was observed in essentially similar localities, and its song did not differ materially from that of *æstivalis*. Mr. Ridgway writes that in Illinois this is "emphatically a bird of open oak woods, where large white and post oaks prevail, with grass land immediately adjoining, or where the intervals between the trees consist of sward rather than undergrowth; but neglected fields, grown up to weeds, and in which dead trees are left standing, are also its favorite haunts."

He speaks of its song as reminding one somewhat of the plaintive chant of the Field Sparrow, but as far sweeter and louder; "the modulation, as nearly as can be expressed in words, resembling the syllables *théééééé-thut, lut, lut, lut*, the first being a rich, silvery trill, pitched in a high musical key, the other syllables also metallic, but abrupt, and lower in tone."

1888. BENDIRE, C. E., Auk, 351–356 (nesting).—1914. BIRD-LORE, 176, 179 (mig.; pl.).

511a. PINE-WOODS SPARROW. AIMOPHILA ÆSTIVALIS ÆSTIVALIS (*Lichtenstein*). [575.] *Ads.*—Upperparts light *chestnut*, more or less streaked with black and margined with *gray;* a grayish line over the eye; bend of the wing yellow; tail-feathers narrow, grayish fuscous, the outer ones much the shortest; breast and sides washed with pale brownish ash; breast sometimes with a few black spots; middle of the belly white. L., 5·80; W., 2·50; T., 2·50; B., ·45.

Range.—Breeds in Lower Austral Zone from se. Ga., s. to cent. Fla. Winters in cent. and s. Fla.

Nest, of fine grasses, on the ground, beneath scrub palmetto. *Eggs*, 3–5, pure white, ·72 × ·61. *Date*, Lake Okeechobee, Fla., Apr. 14; San Mateo, Fla., Apr. 23.

This is a common bird in Florida. It winters in the southern part of the state and migrates northward in March. It is found only in pine woods having an undergrowth of scrub palmetto. Here it passes most of its time on the ground, and is difficult to flush.

When singing, it seeks an elevated perch. In my opinion its song is more beautiful than that of any other American Sparrow. It is very simple—I write it, *che-e-e-e—de, de, de; che-e—chee-o, chee-o, chee-o, chee-o*—but it possesses all the exquisite tenderness and pathos of the melody of the Hermit Thrush; indeed, in purity of tone and in execution I should consider the Sparrow the superior songster. It sings most freely very early in the morning and late in the afternoon, when the world is hushed and the pine trees breathe a soft accompaniment to its divine music.

1914. BIRD-LORE, 176, 179 (dist.; pl.).

512. The WHITE-WINGED JUNCO, *Junco aikeni* Ridgway, has been reported as "seen" on four occasions in New England, but Forbush very properly refuses to give this species an unquestioned place in his 'Birds of Massachusetts' on the basis of a sight record. Single individuals have also been reported trapped by bird-banders in New York, and in Pennsylvania (Auk, 1926, p. 245). This species resembles *J. hyemalis* but is slightly larger (W., 3·50), has two white wing-bars and the *three* outer tail-feathers are wholly or largely white.

513. SLATE-COLORED JUNCO. JUNCO HYEMALIS HYEMALIS (*Linnæus*). [567.] *Ad. ♂.*—Upperparts, throat, and breast grayish slate-color; upperparts more or less washed with grayish brown; belly white, sides grayish; no wing-bars; tail fuscous, the two outer feathers and part of the third white; bill flesh-color. *Ad. ♀.*—Similar, but the upperparts browner, throat and breast paler. *Ads. in winter.*—Resemble ads. in summer but are more richly washed with brownish or rusty. *Nestlings*, resemble the adults, but have the upperparts, throat, and breast streaked with black. L., 6·27; W., 3·03; T., 2·71; B., ·41.

Range.—Breeds in the Hudsonian and Canadian zones in nw. Alaska, n. Mack. (tree-limit), n. Man., and cent. Que., s. to the base of the Alaska peninsula, s. Yukon, cent. Alberta, n. Minn., cent. Mich., Ont., and mts. of N. Y., Pa., and Mass. Winters throughout the e. U. S. and s. Ont., s. to Gulf Coast. Casual in Calif., Ariz., N. Mex., and L. Calif.; straggles to Siberia.

Washington, abundant W. V., Sept. 14–May 7. Bronx region, common T. V. and W. V., Sept. 10–May 27 (June 2). Boston, rather common W. V., abundant T. V., Sept. 20–Nov. 25; Mch. 20–Apr. 20; occasionally breeds. N. Ohio, abundant W. V., Oct. 2–May 5. Glen Ellyn, W. V., abundant T. V., less common W. R., Aug. 30–May 13. SE. Minn., common T. V., Mch. 4–May 24; Sept. 16–Nov. 28; many winter.

Nest, of grasses, moss and rootlets, lined with fine grasses and long hairs, on or near the ground. *Eggs*, 4–5, white or bluish white; finely and evenly speckled or spotted, sometimes heavily blotched at the larger end with rufous-brown, ·76 X ·58. *Date,* Wilmurt, N. Y., May 27; Grand Manan, N. B., May 25.

When the snow begins to fly, you will look out some gray morning to find a flock of small, plump, slate-colored birds hopping about the dooryard, picking up what they can find, or sitting in the bushes with an air of contentment that it is pleasant to see.

Coming, as they do, when most of the home birds have left for the South, they bring their own welcome, and soon seem like old friends. But if you would really know your gentle winter visitors, you must go back into the woods when summer comes and find them in their own homes.

Look for them in a tangle of fallen tree-tops, logs, and upturned roots. A pair I once surprised in such a place at first sat and chirped at me—with bills full of food—but soon they were flying freely back and forth to the upturned root where they had hidden their nest.

I noticed with surprise that their gray plumage toned in so well with the dark earth that they were hard to see. The sharp horizontal line across the breast where the gray turns abruptly to white added to the disguise, the straight line breaking the round form of the bird.

The *'tsip* of the Junco is unmistakable and more often heard than his song, but he has both a trill and a low, sweet song as unpretentious and cheery as the friendly bird himself.   FLORENCE MERRIAM BAILEY.

1914. BIRD-LORE, 438, 442 (mig.; pl.).

513a. CAROLINA JUNCO. JUNCO HYEMALIS CAROLINENSIS *Brewster.* [567*e.*] Similar to the preceding, but slightly larger, the upperparts, throat, and breast uniform grayish slate-color *without* a brownish wash, bill horn-color. W., 3·26; T., 2·85; B., ·43.

Range.—Breeds mainly in the Canadian Zone of the mts. from w. Md., Va., and W. Va., s. to n. Ga. Winters in adjacent lowlands.

Nesting-date, Cold Knob, W. Va., May 21.

This is a common bird in the higher parts of the Alleghanies, from Maryland to Georgia.

1924. SPRUNT, A., JR., Auk, 610–612 (nesting).

514. The OREGON JUNCO, *Junco oreganus oreganus* Townsend, [567*a*], of the north Pacific Coast, has been once recorded from Massachusetts (Wellesley, Jan. 28, 1919). See Forbush, Birds of Mass., III, p. 90.

514*a.* SHUFELDT'S JUNCO, *Junco oreganus shufeldti* Coale, of British Columbia and southward, is recorded as casual in Illinois (A. O. U. 'Check-List').

514b. MONTANA JUNCO. JUNCO OREGANUS MONTANUS (*Ridgway*). [567*f*]. Similar to *J. h. hyemalis,* but head and breast blacker, the former sharply defined from the brownish black, the sides strongly washed with brownish pink. W., 3·15; T., 2·60.

Range.—N. Rocky Mts. Breeds in Canadian Zone from s. Alberta s. to n. Idaho and nw. Mont.; winters s. to Ariz., N. Mex., Chihuahua, and Tex., and e. casually to Kans., Ills., Ind., Mass., and Md.

Washington, one record. Boston, A. V. (Mch. 25, 1874). (See Forbush, Birds of Mass., III, p. 90.)

515. EASTERN TREE SPARROW. Spizella arborea arborea (*Wilson*). [559.] (Pls. XXVII, XXIX.) *Ads.*—No black on the forehead; an indistinct *black spot on the center of the breast;* top of the head rufous-brown sometimes edged with ashy; a grayish line over the eye and a rufous-brown line behind it; back streaked with rufous-brown, black, and pale ochraceous-buff; rump pale grayish brown; greater and middle wing-coverts tipped with white; outer web of the outer tail-feather whitish; breast grayish white; middle of the belly white; sides tinged with pale grayish brown; upper mandible black; lower, yellow at the base, the tip black. L., 6·36; W., 2·99; T., 2·82; B., ·41.

Range.—Breeds in the Hudsonian Zone from cent. Mack. (Great Bear Lake) to Great Slave Lake, n. Man., n. Que., and N. F. Winters from s. Minn., Ont., and the Maritime Provinces, s. to e. Okla., cent. Ark., S. C., and Ga. (rarely).

Washington, abundant W. V., Oct. 3–Apr. 24. Bronx region, abundant W. V., Oct. 10–Apr. 29. Boston, common W. V., abundant T. V., Oct. 25–Nov. 25; Mch. 20–Apr. 20. N. Ohio, abundant W. V., Oct. 24–May 3. Glen Ellyn, common W. V., Oct. 4–Apr. 28. SE. Minn., common T. V., Mch. 4–May 15; Sept. 21–Nov. 30; many winter.

Nest, of grasses, rootlets, and hair, on or near the ground. "*Eggs,* 4–5, pale green or greenish blue, spotted with reddish brown, ·75 × ·60" (Chamberlain). *Date,* Ft. Chimo, Lab., June 16.

Tree Sparrows wear a small black dot on the center of their otherwise unmarked breasts, a badge which will aid in their identification. They come in flocks when the fields are beginning to look brown and dreary, but seem contented with the surroundings from which other birds have fled. They feed on the seeds of weeds and grasses, and even when the snow is deepest always find an abundance of food. I like to see them feasting on the seed-stalks above the crust, and to hear their chorus of merry, tinkling notes, like sparkling frost crystals turned to music.

Winter Chippies they are sometimes called, but at this season there is little of the Chippy's nature about them. In February or March they begin to sing a song which has been compared to that of a Canary, but is "finer, sweeter, and not so loud."

1909. Bird-Lore, 254 (mig.); 1910, 16 (pl.).

516. EASTERN CHIPPING SPARROW. Spizella passerina passerina (*Bechstein*). [560.] (Pl. XXIX.) *Ads.*—Forehead black, a short grayish line in its middle; top of the head rufous; the nape generally with a few black streaks; a grayish line over the eye and a black line behind it; back of the neck grayish, separating the rufous crown from the back; back streaked with black, a little rufous, and more pale buffy ochraceous; rump *slaty gray;* wing-bars not conspicuous; underparts grayish white, whiter on the throat and belly; bill entirely *black. Ads. in winter and Im.*—Similar, but crown streaked with black and with a median buffy line (grayer in adult); line over eye, cheeks, and underparts buffier; bill brownish. *Juv.*—Similar to winter but underparts distinctly streaked with black; breast is streaked with black. L., 5·37; W., 2·74; T., 2·29; B., ·36.

Remarks.—In adults the rufous crown, black forehead, gray rump, and black bill are characteristic; in winter the gray rump is a good distinguishing mark.

Fig. 162. Chipping Sparrow. (Natural size.)

Range.—Breeds from Yukon, n. B. C., Sask., cent. Man., n. Ont., s. Que., and Cape Breton Isl. to cent. Tex., s. Miss., and cent. Ga. Winters chiefly in the s. states, occasionally as far n. as Okla. and s. N. J. Casual in Cuba and ne. Mex.

Washington, common S. R., abundant T. V., Feb. 9–Dec. 17; occasionally winters. Bronx region, common S. R., occasional in winter; Mch. 21–Nov. 15. Boston, abundant S. R., Apr. 12–Oct. 25. N. Ohio, abundant S. R., Mch. 23–Oct. 10. Glen Ellyn, not very common S. R., Apr. 3–Nov. 5. SE. Minn., common S. R., Mch. 15–Nov. 2.

Nest, of grasses, fine twigs, or rootlets, thickly lined with long hairs, in trees or bushes, 5–20 feet up. *Eggs,* 4–5, blue or greenish blue, with cinnamon-brown or blackish markings, chiefly at the larger end, ·72 × ·51. *Date,* Montgomery Co., Pa., May 8; Cambridge, May 12; se. Minn., May 10.

The Chippy is among Sparrows what the Phœbe is among Flycatchers—the humblest, most unassuming member of its family. Both show trustfulness, which, in spite of their unattractive appearance and far from pleasing voices, wins our affection. Chippy makes his nest in the vines on our piazza, and feeds on the crumbs at our doorstep, quite as though he were a member of the family; and he needs only a little encouragement to give evidence of his entire confidence in our good will by feeding from our hands. His song is a monotonous *chippy-chippy-chippy-chippy,* rather high and wiry and frequently running into an insectlike trill—by no means a musical performance.

In the fall, Chippy changes his dress, dons a streaked cap for the one of bright bay, and, with others of his kind, goes to the fields to feast on the year's harvest of seeds. He is generally found near trees and hedgerows, into which, when alarmed, he flies with his companions.

1909. BIRD-LORE, 256 (mig.); 1910, 16 (pl.).—1929. ALLEN, A. A., Bird-Lore, 138–147, illus. (autobiography).

517. CLAY-COLORED SPARROW. SPIZELLA PALLIDA *(Swainson).* [561.] (Pl. XXIX.) *Ads.*—With a general resemblance to immature *S. passerina,* but much less rufous above, whiter below; auriculars brownish, the line over the eye white, and the rump pale grayish brown instead of slaty gray. The juvenal plumage is streaked below. W., 2·40; T., 2·35; B., ·34.

Range.—Breeds in Canadian and Transition zones from s. Mack. (Great Slave Lake), cent. Man., and Mich. (Isle Royale), to w. Mont., se. Colo., n. Nebr., and nw. Ills. Winters from s. N. Mex. and s. Tex., to Cape San Lucas, Guanajuato, Puebla, Oaxaca, and Chiapas, Mex. Casual in Ont., Ind., Mass., and S. C.

Nest, of grasses, lined with hairs, on the ground or in bushes. *Eggs,* 3–5, similar to those of the preceding. *Date,* se. Minn., May 23.

"This pale Sparrow of the plains is very similar in actions to the Chipping Sparrow, but less familiar and confiding in habits" (Goss). Dr. Roberts describes its song as a fine, high-pitched monotone—*zee-zee-zee.*

518. BREWER'S SPARROW, *Spizella breweri breweri* Cassin, [562], (Pl. XXIX), a western species, has been recorded once from Massachusetts (Watertown, Dec. 15, 1873—Brewster, Am. Nat., 1874, 366).

PLATE XXIX

1. Chipping Sparrow, ad.
2. Chipping Sparrow, im.
3. Tree Sparrow

4. Field Sparrow
5. Clay-colored Sparrow
6. Brewer's Sparrow

519. FIELD SPARROW. SPIZELLA PUSILLA PUSILLA (*Wilson*). Bill reddish brown. *Ads.*—Top of head rufous, a gray line over the eye; nape slightly gray; back like the crown, but finely streaked with black and narrowly edged with brownish ashy; rump brownish ashy; middle and greater wing-coverts tipped with white; underparts whitish, tinged with ochraceous-buff on the breast and sides. *Ads. in winter and Im.*—Similar, but the colors duller, the crown edged with grayish and sometimes a faint grayish line through its center. *Nestlings* have the breast streaked with black. L., 5·68; W., 2·50; T., 2·55; B., ·36.

Remarks.—This bird may be known by its brightly colored back, buffy breast, and especially by its reddish bill.

Range.—Breeds in the Transition and Austral zones from s. Minn., s. Mich., s. Que., and s. Me. to cent. Tex., cent. La., and n. Fla. Winters from Mo., Ills., s. Pa., and N. J. to the Gulf Coast, casually farther n.

Washington, very common P. R.; less numerous in winter. Bronx region, common S. R., winters regularly; Mch. 5–Dec. 21. Boston, common S. R., Apr. 12–Nov. 1; casual in winter. N. Ohio, abundant in summer, Mch. 6–Oct. 25. Glen Ellyn, common S. R., Mch. 27–Oct. 11. SE. Minn., common S. R., Apr. 1–Oct. 28.

Nest, of rather coarse grasses, weed-stalks, rootlets, etc., lined with fine grasses and long hairs, on the ground or in low bushes. *Eggs*, 3–5, white or bluish white, with numerous rufous markings, chiefly about the larger end, ·70 × ·52. *Date*, Raleigh, N. C., May 4; Montgomery Co., Pa., May 5; New London, Conn., May 21; Boston, May 25; Wheatland, Ind., Apr. 30; se. Minn., May 17.

Its bright rufous color, the absence of spots on its breast, and especially its flesh-colored bill, are the best field-marks of this misnamed Sparrow, for he is not a true Field Sparrow, but prefers old pastures dotted with clumps of bushes or young cedars. There is something winning in his appearance; he seems such a gentle, innocent, dove-like little bird. His song is in keeping with his character, being an unusually clear, plaintive whistle, sweeter to the lover of birds' songs than the voice of the most gifted songstress. It is subject to much variation. Not only do the same individuals sing several different songs, but two individuals in the same locality rarely sing alike. There is also much variation in the songs of birds from different regions. For this reason it is quite impossible to give a description of the song which will apply throughout the bird's range. However, an average song consists of the syllables *chĕr-wēē, chĕr-wēē, chĕr-wēē, chĕr-wēē, chēē-o, de-de-de-de-de*, the last notes joined in a trill.

This gives, of course, no idea of the quality of the Field Sparrow's song, but to be convinced of its rare beauty one need only hear it as the sun goes down and the hush of early evening is quieting the earth.

1909. BIRD-LORE, 258 (mig.); 1910, 16 (pl.).—1922. SAUNDERS, A. A., Auk, 386–399 (song).

519a. The WESTERN FIELD SPARROW, *Spizella pusilla arenacea* Chadbourne, [563a], a pale form, has been recorded from the vicinity of New Orleans.

520. HARRIS'S SPARROW. ZONOTRICHIA QUERULA (*Nuttall*). [553.] Bill pinkish; crown and throat or breast more or less black. *Ads.*—Crown, throat, breast and lores glossy black, cheeks gray; above brownish gray streaked with black; rump brownish ashy, tail fuscous-gray; two white wing-bars; belly white, sides with blackish streaks. *Im.*—Similar, but crown tipped with brownish; breast, and sometimes throat, with black streaks or blotches; cheeks, flanks and under tail-coverts buffy. L., 7·50; W., 3·50; T., 3·25; B., ·50.

Range.—Breeds in the Hudsonian Zone at Fort Churchill, Hudson Bay, Artillery Lake, Mack., and probably to Great Bear Lake and the district just s. of the Barren Grounds. In migration, ranges e. to w. Ont. and e. Ills., and w. to cent. Mont. and e. Colo.; winters from n. Kans. and w. Mo. to s. Tex. Casual in B. C.; accidental in Calif., Ore., Wash., O., and Mass.

Boston, A. V. Glen Ellyn, two records, May 19, 1897; Mch. 14, 1914. SE. Minn., common T. V., May 2–25; Sept. 15–Nov. 9.

Nest (found Aug. 5, 1907, by E. T. Seton, at Last Wood, Great Slave Lake, and the first one known), "was on the ground under a dwarf birch, was made of grass and resembled the nest of a White-throated Sparrow. It contained three young nearly ready to fly" (Auk, 1908, 72).

This handsome Sparrow barely enters the western limits of the region covered by the 'Handbook.' It there inhabits brushy undergrowths and much the same localities which White-throats frequent. Its pink or reddish bill and buff cheeks are excellent field characters. Its call-note is a sharp, metallic *clink*, louder than the White-throat's call, and, like that species, it utters low, chuckling, contented musical notes. Goss describes its song as composed of "pleasing, plaintive, whistling notes, in musical tone much like the White-throated Sparrow's, but delivered in a widely different song."

1913. BIRD-LORE, 301, 304 (mig.; pl.).—1929. NICE, M. M., Condor, 57–61 (in Oklahoma).—1929. SWENK, M. H. and STEVENS, O. A., Wilson Bull., 129–176, illus. (monograph).

521. WHITE-CROWNED SPARROW. ZONOTRICHIA LEUCOPHRYS LEU-COPHRYS (*Forster*). [554.] *Ads.*—No yellow before the eye or on the bend of the wing; center of crown white bordered on either side by black stripes, no *white* before the eye; a white line from *over* the eye passes backward along the side of the head; nape gray; back dark grayish brown, margined with gray; rump dark brownish ash; greater and middle wing-coverts tipped with white; tail fuscous; underparts grayish, white on the belly, flanks and under tail-coverts cream-buff. *Im.*—Similar, but much browner, sides of the crown rufous-brown, center of the crown pale grayish brown; nape brownish ash; back margined with the same color. L., 6·88; W., 3·03; T., 2·88; B., ·43.

Range.—Breeds in the Hudsonian and Canadian zones of high mts. from s. Ore. to cent. Calif., and e. to Wyo. and s. N. Mex., and from limit of trees in n. Man. and n. Que. to cent. Man., s. Que., and s. Greenland. Winters from s. L. Calif., s. Ariz., s. Kans., and the O. Valley (casually from the Potomac Valley), s. to La. and Miss. and over the Mexican plateau.

Washington, irregularly common T. V. and W. V., Apr. 11–May 19; Oct. 1–Nov. 8. Bronx region, uncommon spring, fairly common fall T. V., Apr. 28–May 27; Sept. 28–Nov. 14 (Jan. 31). Boston, uncommon T. V., May 12–22; Oct. 1–20. N. Ohio, common T. V., Apr. 22–May 20; Sept. 5–Oct. 16. Glen Ellyn, not common T. V.; chiefly spring, Apr. 24–May 31; Oct. 2–21. SE. Minn., common T. V., Apr. 17–May 21; Sept. 26–Nov. 2.

Nest, of grasses, on the ground or in bushes. *Eggs*, 4–5, pale greenish blue, speckled and spotted with bay, especially at the larger end, ·90 × ·62 (Davie). *Date*, Ft. Chimo, Lab., June 3.

FIG. 163. White-crowned Sparrow. (Natural size.)

This is one of the aristocrats of the family. Its size and its handsome markings at once distinguish it from its congeners, and are sure to attract attention. Though its season of love and music is spent in the far north, it often favors us with selections of its melodies as it rests in thickets and hedgerows while slowly passing through our country on its northward pilgrimage. Its usual song is like the latter half of the White-throat's familiar refrain, repeated a number of times with a peculiar sad cadence and in a clear, soft whistle that is characteristic of the group. It resembles its relatives also in singing its sweetest songs in the woods, sometimes during the darkest hours of the night.

ERNEST THOMPSON SETON.

1912. BIRD-LORE, 98, 106 (mig.; pl.).

521a. GAMBEL'S SPARROW. ZONOTRICHIA LEUCOPHRYS GAMBELI (*Nuttall*). [554a.] Similar to *Z. l. leucophrys* but the lores wholly gray or whitish, the white superciliary therefore reaching the bill.

Range.—Breeds in Boreal zones from limit of trees in nw. Alaska and n. Mack. (rarely outside the mts. s. of Great Slave Lake), s. to cent. Mont., w. to coast mts. of sw. Alaska and B. C. Winters from n. Calif. and Utah, s. to San Luis Potosi, Mazatlan, L. Calif., and outlying isls. Casual e. in migration to Minn., Ills., Mich., Wisc., Ia., Kans., and e. Tex.

522. The GOLDEN-CROWNED SPARROW, *Zonotrichia coronata* (Pallas), [557], of the Pacific Coast region is of accidental occurrence in Wisconsin (Nelson, Bull. Essex. Inst., 1876, 108), and Massachusetts (Boston).

523. WHITE-THROATED SPARROW. ZONOTRICHIA ALBICOLLIS (*Gmelin*). [558.] *Ads.*—A yellow line before the eye; bend of the wing yellow; center of the crown with a white stripe bounded on either side by much wider black stripes; a white stripe from the eye passes backward along the side of the head; back rufous or rufous-brown, streaked with black and slightly margined with whitish; rump grayish brown; greater and middle wing-coverts tipped with white; tail grayish brown; underparts grayish, more so on the breast; throat with a square white patch; belly whitish; flanks and under tail-coverts tinged with grayish brown. *Im. and Ads. in winter.*—Yellow before the eye, and on the bend of the wing duller; crown streaks brownish ashy and mixed chestnut and black, instead of white and black; throat-patch less sharply defined and in some (Im.) specimens practically obsolete when the breast is obscurely streaked with blackish. L., 6·74; W., 2·89; T., 2·86; B., ·44.

Range.—E. N. A. Breeds in Canadian and Lower Hudsonian zones from n. Mack. (Ft. Good Hope), and cent. Que. to cent. Alberta, s. Mont., cent. Minn., cent. Wisc., s. Ont., and the mts. of ne. Pa., N. Y., and Mass. Winters from Mo., the O. Valley, s. Pa., Conn., and Mass. (casually Me.), s. to ne. Mex. and Fla. Casual in Ore., Calif., and Colo. and on Guadalupe Isl., L. Calif.

Washington, very common W. V., abundant T. V., Mch. 18–June 14; Sept. 14–Dec. 16. Bronx region, common T. V. and W. V., Sept. 12–May 28 (June 10). Boston, very common T. V., Apr. 25–May 15; Oct. 1–Nov. 10; a few winter; occasionally breeds. N. Ohio, common T. V., Apr. 1–May 21; Sept. 10–Nov. 7, occasional S. R. Glen Ellyn, common T. V., Apr. 9–May 26; Sept. 9–Nov. 7. SE. Minn., common T. V., occasional S. R., Mch. 20–June 1; Sept. 2–Nov. 13; a few winter records.

Nest, of coarse grasses, rootlets, moss, strips of bark, etc., lined with finer grasses, on the ground or in bushes. *Eggs*, 4–5, bluish white, finely and evenly speckled or heavily and irregularly blotched with pale rufous-brown,

·82 × ·60. *Date*, Wilmurt, N. Y., May 28; Lancaster, N. H., June 5; Charlotte Co., N. B., June 5.

In September, when the hedgerows and woodland undergrowths
begin to rustle with Sparrows, Juncos, and Towhees, I watch eagerly
for the arrival of these wel-
come fall songsters. There
are a few sweet, tremulous
trials before their plaintive,
sympathetic whistle brings
cheer to the browning woods:
Few birds are more socia-
ble than the White-throats.

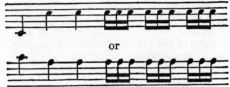

At this season they are always in little companies, and they frequently
roost together in large numbers in the depths of dense thickets or clumps
of evergreens. After they have retired one may hear the sharp *chink* of
their 'quarrier' chorus, and when darkness comes, with low, brooding
notes of cozy companionship they are hushed for the night.

1912. BIRD-LORE, 101, 105 (mig.; pl.).

524. FOX SPARROW. PASSERELLA ILIACA ILIACA (*Merrem*). [585.]
Ads.—Upperparts rufous-brown, the feathers margined by cinnamon-
brown and without black; upper tail-coverts and tail *bright rufous;* wings
margined with rufous; underparts *heavily* streaked and spotted with rufous-
brown and blackish; middle of the belly white; lower mandible yellowish.
L., 7·26; W., 3·39; T., 2·85; B., ·50.

Range.—Breeds in Boreal zones from tree-limit in nw. Alaska and n.
Que., s. to n. Man. and N. F. Winters from lower O. and Potomac
valleys (occasionally farther n.) to cent. Tex. and n. Fla. Casual on the
coast of s. Alaska and in Ariz. and Calif.

Washington, abundant T. V., Mch. 4–
May 11; Oct. 3–Jan. 1; a few winter.
Bronx region, common T. V., frequently
winters; Feb. 13–Apr. 30; Sept. 30–Jan.
19. Boston, abundant T. V., Mch. 15–
Apr. 12; Oct. 20–Nov. 15; occasional in
winter. N. Ohio, common T. V., Mch.
12–Apr. 23; Oct. 1–Nov. 16. Glen Ellyn,
fairly common T. V., Mch. 11–Apr. 28;
Sept. 22–Dec. 15. SE. Minn., common
T. V., Mch. 11–May 19; Sept. 17–Nov. 12;
rare in winter.

FIG. 164. Fox Sparrow. (Natural size.)

Nest, of coarse grasses, lined with
finer grasses, hair, moss, and feathers,
on the ground, and in low trees and bushes. *Eggs,* 4–5, pale bluish, evenly
speckled or heavily blotched with umber or vinaceous-brown, ·80 × ·63 (see
Bendire, Auk, 1889, 108). *Date*, Ft. Resolution, Mack., June 1.

In the early spring the Fox Sparrow is seen mostly about damp
thickets and roadside shrubbery; later it takes more to woodsides,
foraging on leaf-strewn slopes where there is little or no undergrowth,
often associated with small parties of Juncos. On its return in the
autumn it again becomes a common denizen of hedgerows and thickets,
and also invades the weedy grainfields, rarely, however, straying far

from some thickety cover. Sometimes large numbers congregate among withered growths of tall weeds, whence they emerge with a loud whirring of wings as their retreat is invaded, and hie away in tawny clouds, flock after flock. It is a great scratcher among dead leaves, and can make the wood rubbish fly in a way which, in proportion to its size, a barnyard fowl could scarcely excel.

The usual note of the Fox Sparrow is a feeble *tseep*. A note of excitement is louder and sharper in tone. Its song is not surpassed by that of any of our Sparrows. It is a revelation to hear it at sundown on some vernally softened evening of early springtime; little swarms of gnats hover in the balmy air; from the twilight meadows comes the welcome, half-doubtful piping of the first hylas—no other sound. Then perhaps from some dusky thicket a bird's song! An emotional outburst rising full-toned and clear, and passing all too quickly to a closing cadence, which seems to linger in the silent air. It is the song of the Fox Sparrow with that fuller power and richness of tone which come into it, or seem to, at the sunset hour. It breaks forth as if inspired from pure joy in the awakened season, though with some vague undertone, scarcely of sadness, rather of some lower tone of joy.

EUGENE P. BICKNELL.

1889. BENDIRE, C. E., Auk, 107–116 (nesting).—1913. MOORE, R. T., Auk, 177–187 (song).—1913. BIRD-LORE, 104, 108 (mig.; pl.).

525. LINCOLN'S SPARROW. MELOSPIZA LINCOLNI LINCOLNI (*Audubon*). [583.] *Ads.*—Upperparts streaked with black, brownish gray, and grayish brown; tail-feathers narrow and rather pointed, the outer ones shortest; underparts white, rather finely streaked with black, *a broad cream-buff band across the breast*, a cream-buff stripe on either side of the throat; sides tinged with cream-buff. L., 5·75; W., 2·50; T., 2·40; B., ·41.

Remarks.—The cream-buff band on the breast is distinctive of this species.

Range.—Breeds in Boreal zones from the Kowak and Yukon valleys, Alaska, s. to N. F., s. to n. Minn., cent. Ont., n. N. Y., and N. S., and s. in the mts. to s. Calif. and n. N. Mex. Winters from cent. Calif. and n. Miss. (occasionally n. Ills. and e. Pa.) to s. L. Calif. and cent. Guat. Casual s. of Washington, D. C., e. of the Alleghany Mts.; accidental in Panama.

Washington, rare T. V., Apr. 21–May 30; Sept. 30–Oct. 2. Bronx region, uncommon but regular T. V., Apr. 25–May 26; Sept. 12–Oct. 22. Boston, not uncommon T. V., May 15–25; Sept. 14–Oct. 10. N. Ohio, tolerably common T. V., Apr. 25–May 25. Glen Ellyn, not common T. V., May 17–; Sept. 11–Oct. 9. SE. Minn., common T. V., Apr. 17–May 22; Aug. 26–Oct. 30.

Nest, generally similar to that of the Song Sparrow, on the ground. "*Eggs*, 4–5, pale green or buffish, sometimes almost white, thickly spotted and blotched with reddish brown and lilac, ·80 × ·60" (Chamberlain). *Date*, Wilmurt, N. Y., June 10; Racine, Wisc., June 6.

The most striking characteristic about the Lincoln's Sparrow is its shyness, whether migrating in the lavish abundance of the West, straying casually through the states of the Atlantic seaboard, or settled for the summer in a chosen spot of the northern evergreen woods. Scampering like a mouse along some tumble-down stone wall half buried in poison ivy, sumach, and all the tangled growth that goes to make up an old hedgerow, or peering out from a clump of low-spreading bushes, this little bird may sometimes be detected; but as he hurries northward late in the migration, when all the woods and fields are ringing with bird-music, our attention is seldom directed toward the silent straggler, while in the autumn he is lost in the waves of Sparrows that flood the country.

If we follow him northward, we find him irregularly distributed in small colonies or single pairs in damp clearings, perhaps along brooks or ponds, but avoiding almost entirely the wetter, more open localities, where the Swamp Sparrow is at home. Attracted by a sharp chirp which, at times reduplicated, resembles that of a young Chipping Sparrow, we may succeed in catching a glimpse of him as he lurks beneath a little spruce perhaps no bigger than an umbrella.

Sometimes venturing timidly to the outer boughs of a spruce, he surprises the hearer with a most unsparrowlike song. It is not loud, and suggests the bubbling, guttural notes of the House Wren, combined with the sweet rippling music of the Purple Finch, and when you think the song is done there is an unexpected aftermath. The birds sing very little and at long intervals, and are seldom heard during the later hours of the day, ceasing at once if anybody approaches.   J. DWIGHT, JR.

1913. BIRD-LORE, 236, 241 (mig.; pl.).

526. SWAMP SPARROW. MELOSPIZA GEORGIANA (*Latham*). [584.] *Ads. in summer.*—Crown chestnut-rufous; forehead black; a grayish line over the eye; a blackish line behind the eye; nape slaty gray with a few black streaks; feathers of the back broadly streaked with black and margined with rufous and cream-buff or ashy buff; wing-coverts rufous, the greater ones with black spots at their tips; rump rufous grayish brown, sometimes streaked with black; tail rufous grayish brown, the middle feathers darker along their shafts; throat and middle of the belly white, breast grayish, sides washed with pale grayish brown. *Ads. in winter and Im.*—Similar, but the top of the head streaked with black, rufous-brown, and grayish; nape less gray; breast washed with brownish. L., 5·89; W., 2·34; T., 2·32; B., ·46.

Remarks.—The underparts resemble those of some immature White-throated Sparrows, but the wing-bars and the yellow bend of the wing will always distinguish the latter.

Range.—Breeds in the Canadian, Transition, and part of Upper Austral zones from w. cent. Alberta, s. Que., and N. F., s. to n. Nebr., n. Mo., n. Ills., W. Va. (mts.), s. Pa. and N. J. Winters from Nebr., O. Valley, and N. J. (Mass. rarely), s. to the Gulf Coast from s. Fla. to s. Tex. and Jalisco, Mex. Accidental in Utah, Colo. and Calif.; casual in Bermuda.

Washington, very common T. V., Mch.–May 27; Sept. 28–Dec. 3; a few winter. Bronx region, common P. R.; somewhat scarcer in winter. Boston, abundant S. R., Apr. 12–Nov. 10; a few winter. N. Ohio, common T. V., Mch. 23–May 20; breeds locally. Glen Ellyn, tolerably common T. V., Apr. 2–May 26; Sept. 2–Oct. 25; possibly S. R. SE. Minn., common S. R., Apr. 2–Oct. 31; rarely Nov.

Nest, generally similar to that of the Song Sparrow, on the ground. *Eggs*, 4–5, similar in color to those of the Song Sparrow, but the markings generally more confluent, ·76 × ·57. *Date*, Boston, May 13; New Canada, N. S., May 19; Pewaukee, Wisc., May 23; se. Minn., May 25.

While wintering in the South, Swamp Sparrows frequently belie their name, and I have often found numbers of them in dry 'old fields' of broom sedge; but at the north they are more consistent, and one rarely sees them beyond the confines of a wet meadow, or, more preferably, a large grassy marsh with reed-bordered streams.

Swamp Sparrows may be distinguished from their cousins, the Song Sparrows, by their unstreaked breast, much darker upperparts, and totally different notes. Their usual call-note is a sharp *cheep*, not unlike that of the White-throated Sparrow, and quite different from the rather nasal *chimp* of the Song Sparrow. Their song is a simple, sweet, but somewhat monotonous *tweet-tweet-tweet*, repeated many times, all on one note, and sometimes running into a trill.

1913. BIRD-LORE, 239, 241 (mig.; pl.).

527. EASTERN SONG SPARROW. MELOSPIZA MELODIA MELODIA (*Wilson*). [581.] (Pl. VII.) *Ads.*—Crown rufous-brown, with a grayish line through its center; a grayish line over the eye; a rufous-brown line from behind the eye to the nape; feathers of the back streaked with black and margined with rufous-brown and grayish; greater wing-coverts with black spots at their tips; no white wing-bars or yellow on the wing; tail rufous grayish brown, the middle feathers darker along their shafts; outer feathers shortest; sides of the throat with black or blackish streaks; breast with wedge-shaped streaks of black and rufous-brown which tend to form one *larger blotch* on the center; sides washed with brownish and streaked with black and rufous-brown; middle of the belly white. L., 6·30; W., 2·52; T., 2·62; B., ·49.

Range.—Breeds in the Canadian, Transition, and Upper Austral zones from s. Mack. (Great Slave Lake), n. Man., n. Ont., s. Que., and Cape Breton Isl. s. to s. Va., s. N. C. (mts.), and n. Ga. Winters from Mass. (locally) and N. J. s. to s. Fla. and the Gulf Coast, and sporadically n. to Lab. (Pl. VIII.)

Washington, common P. R., abundant T. V., Mch. and Oct. Bronx region, common P. R. Boston, very abundant S. R., Mch. 10–Nov. 1; locally common W. V. N. Ohio, P. R., abundant in summer, common in winter. Glen Ellyn, common S. R., quite regular W. R., Feb. 12–Nov. 5. SE. Minn., common S. R., Mch. 16–Nov. 11; a few winter records.

Nest, of coarse grasses, rootlets, dead leaves, strips of bark, etc., lined with finer grasses and sometimes long hairs, on the ground, sometimes in bushes. *Eggs*, 4–5, white or bluish white, with numerous rufous-brown markings which sometimes nearly conceal the ground-color, ·76 × ·60. *Date*, Montgomery Co., Pa., Apr. 27; Boston, Apr. 30; se. Minn., Apr. 27.

The Song Sparrow's vast range in a dozen varying climates, its readiness to adapt itself to the different conditions in each of the regions it inhabits, its numerical abundance and steady increase while some of its family are dying out, its freedom from disease and vermin, and its perennial cheerfulness, evidenced by its never-failing music—all proclaim that it is indeed one of Nature's successes.

Its irrepressible vivacity and good spirits in spite of all circumstances are aptly illustrated by the fact that its song may be heard in every month of the year and in all weathers; also by night as well as by day—for nothing is more common in the darkest nights than to hear its sweet chant in half-conscious answer to the hooting of the Owl or even the report of a gun.

It is never seen far from water, and when it is alarmed it flies downward or along—never upward—into some low thicket, pumping its tail as it flies.

Its alarm-note is a simple metallic *chip*, which is very distinctive when once learned. But its merry chant—which has won for it the name of "Song Sparrow"—is its best-known note. It is a voluble and uninterrupted but short refrain, and is, perhaps, the sweetest of the familiar voices of the meadow lands. The song that it occasionally utters while on the wing is of quite a different character, being more prolonged and varied.

Though so abundant, it can not be styled a sociable species. Even during the migrations it is never seen in compact flocks like the Redpoll or Snowflake; at most it will be found forming a part of a long, scattered migrating train that usually includes a number of different but nearly related species. ERNEST THOMPSON SETON.

1899. OWEN, D. E., Auk, 221-225 (growth of young).—1910. BIRD-LORE, 67, 71 (mig.; pl.).—1924. WHEELER, W. C., and NICHOLS, J. T., Auk, 444-451 (song).—1931. ALLEN, A. A., Bird-Lore, 211-219 (autobiography).

527a. ATLANTIC SONG SPARROW. MELOSPIZA MELODIA ATLANTICA *Todd.* [581t.] Similar to *M. m. melodia* of the Atlantic slope region, but much grayer above, with the blackish streaking more distinct and the reddish brown feather-edging reduced to a minimum. More nearly resembling *M. m. juddi*, but more grayish above even than that form (Todd).

Range.—Coastal Isls. and edge of the mainland from L. I. to N. C., apparently resident.

527b. MISSISSIPPI SONG SPARROW. MELOSPIZA MELODIA BEATA *Bangs.* [581u.] Similar to *M. m. melodia* but bill very much larger and rather differently shaped, the maxilla much swollen basally, therefore less evenly conical in outline; commissural tooth much larger and more pronounced; general color darker and grayer, with little admixture of rusty in the upperparts; black striping of back heavy and pronounced; lateral crown-stripes very dark brown (Bangs).

Range.—Miss. Valley region. Casual e. to Fla. in winter and migration.

1931. NICE, M. M., Bird-Banding, 89-98 (banding studies).—1931. HALDEMAN, D. W., Auk, 385-406 (monograph).

527c. DAKOTA SONG SPARROW. MELOSPIZA MELODIA JUDDI *Bishop.* [581j.] Similar to *M. m. melodia* "but with the ground-color of the upperparts paler, especially the superciliary streak and sides of the neck, and the white of the lower parts clearer; the interscapulars with the black center broader, the reddish brown portions narrower, and the gray edgings paler; the dark markings on the breast restricted, and more sharply defined against the ground-color" (Bishop).

Range.—Breeds from sw. Sask. and e. Mont. to the Turtle Mts., N. Dak. In winter s. to Tex. and N. Mex. ("Keweenaw Point and Isle Royale, Mich., Iron Co., Wisc," L. E. Wing.)

528. McCOWN'S LONGSPUR. RHYNCHOPHANES MCCOWNI (*Lawrence*). [539.] *Ad. ♂ in summer.*—No rufous on nape; crown, short stripe from base of bill, and breast-patch black; rest of underparts, lores and line over eye white; back brownish gray streaked with black; lesser wing-coverts rufous; all but central pair of tail-feathers white; outer pair slightly tipped with

black on outer web, rest with a broad terminal band on both webs. *Ad.* ♀
in summer.—Upperparts grayish brown streaked with black; a whitish line
over the eye; underparts whitish; tail much as in the male; a trace of rufous
in the wing-coverts. ♂ *in winter.*—Crown streaked much like back; breast-
patch more or less hidden (more in im.) by buffy tips; cheeks and throat
buffy, black stripe from bill absent.

Range.—Breeds mainly in the Transition Zone from cent. Alberta and
s. Sask. to se. Wyo., ne. Colo., and se. Minn. Winters from Colo. and Kans.,
s. through Ariz. and Tex. to n. Sonora and Durango. Casual in migration
to e. B. C., Idaho, and Ills.

529. LAPLAND LONGSPUR. Calcarius lapponicus lapponicus
(*Linnæus*). [536.] Hind toe-nail as long as or longer than toe. *Ad.* ♂ *in
summer.*—Head, neck, throat, and breast black; a buffy line behind the eye;
nape rufous; back streaked with black and ochraceous- and cream-buff; tail
fuscous, the two outer feathers with more or less white; belly white; sides
streaked with black. *Ad.* ♀ *in summer.*—Upperparts streaked with black,
rufous, ochraceous- and cream-buff; nape ochraceous-buff; the color sometimes concealed by the tips of the feathers; tail fuscous, the outer one or two
feathers marked with white; underparts white, the breast and sides streaked
with black and ochraceous-buff. ♂ *in winter.*—Similar

to ♀ in summer, but upperparts blacker, nape more
rufous, breast more heavily marked with black, most
of the feathers black at the base. ♀ *in winter.*—
Similar to ♀ in summer, but upperparts duller, nape
with little or no ochraceous. L., 6·25; W., 3·75; T.,
2·55; B., ·40.

Remarks.—In some plumages this bird bears a
general resemblance to certain Sparrows, but differs
from them in having the hind toe-nail as long as or
longer than the toe.

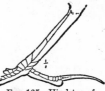

Fig. 165. Hind toe of
Lapland Longspur.

Range.—In N. A. breeds from about lat. 73° on
Arctic isls. s. to the limit of trees in Mack. (at least as far w. as long. 120°),
n. Man., and in n. Que. Winters from s. Que. and n. cent. U. S. irregularly
s. to the Middle States and Tex., rarely to Ky. and S. C.

Washington, W. V., one instance, Dec. Bronx region, rare and irregular
W. V., Oct. 22–Mch. 13. Boston, T. V. and W. V., uncommon winter;
commoner fall; rare spring. N. Ohio, tolerably common W. V., Nov. 15–
Apr. 25. Glen Ellyn, not very common W. V., formerly common, Oct. 16–
May 16. SE. Minn., common W. V., Oct. 5–May 3.

Nest, of grasses and moss, lined with grasses, on the ground. *Eggs*, 4–6,
bluish white, almost obscured by a uniform grayish brown, ·82 × ·60. *Date*,
Pt. Barrow, Alaska, June 6.

In the east, Lapland Longspurs are generally found among flocks
of Shorelarks or Snowflakes, but on the western plains they occur in
great numbers. "High in the air they fly in long, straggling flocks, all
singing together; a thousand voices, a tornado of whistling. . . . When
in the fields they have a curious habit of squatting just behind some
clod, and, as their colors are nearly matched to the soil, they are not
easily observed, nor will they move until you are within a few feet; they
then run a few feet and squat again. . . ." (Seton).

One of the most remarkable bird tragedies of which we have any
knowledge is recorded by Dr. T. S. Roberts (*The Auk*, 1907, pp. 369–377)
as occurring in southwestern Minnesota on March 13, 1904, when at
least several *million* Lapland Longspurs were killed in a single night as

the result of a storm in which they became exhausted and fell, or were confused and struck various obstacles.

1910. BIRD-LORE, 241, 243 (mig.; pl.).

530. SMITH'S LONGSPUR. CALCARIUS PICTUS (*Swainson*). [537.] *Ad. ♂ in summer.*—Top and sides of the head black, a line over the eye and the ear-coverts white; back and rump streaked with black and ochraceous-buff; lesser wing-coverts black, broadly tipped with white; tail fuscous, the two outer feathers mostly white; nape and underparts ochraceous-buff. *Ad. ♀ in summer.*—Upperparts black, the feathers margined and tipped with pale cream-buff; *two* outer tail-feathers mostly white; underparts pale cream-buff; breast and sides sometimes lightly streaked with blackish. *♂ in winter.*—Similar to ♀ in summer, but with the lesser wing-coverts black, tipped with white. L., 6·60; W., 3·75; T., 2·50; B., ·42.

Range.—Breeds in the Arctic Zone on the Barren Grounds from Ft. Anderson, Mack., e. to Hudson Bay (Ft. Churchill); has been taken w. to Ft. Yukon. Winters from Kans. to cent. Tex.; e. in migration to the prairies of Ills. and sw. Ind. Casual in S. C. and B. C. N. Ohio, one record. Glen Ellyn, two records (Apr. 20; May 1).

Nesting, similar to that of the preceding. *Date,* Ft. Anderson, Mack., June 12.

FIG. 166. Tip of second tail-feather from without of *a.* McCown's Longspur. *b.* Lapland Longspur. *c.* Smith's Longspur. *d.* Chestnut-collared Longspur.

"Their habits are quite similar to those of *C. lapponicus* while upon the ground. . . When flushed they invariably uttered a sharp, clicking note, rapidly repeated several times. When driven from their feeding-place by my approach they would rise in a loose flock, and, after wheeling about a few times, start off in a direct line, gradually rising higher until they disappeared. After a short time their peculiar note would be heard, and, darting down from a considerable height, they would alight near the place from which they were driven" (Nelson).

1911. BIRD-LORE, 15, 17 (mig.; pl.).

531. CHESTNUT-COLLARED LONGSPUR. CALCARIUS ORNATUS (*J. K. Townsend*). [538.] *Ad. ♂ in summer.*—Nape rufous; underparts black, only throat and ventral region white, the former often buffy; crown and stripes from eye and ear black; line over eye white; back brownish gray and black; outer tail-feathers white, outer pair with black on outer web near tip; lesser wing-coverts black. *Ad. ♀.*—Entire upperparts grayish brown, streaked with black; nape rarely with a trace of rufous; underparts buffy white, the breast deeper, sometimes basally black; outer pair of tail-feathers white, with terminal blackish margin on the outer vane, the second from without often with a blackish margin on the *inner* vane. *♂ winter.*—Rufous nape and black of crown and underparts heavily veiled with brownish.

Remarks.—The female bears a general resemblance to that of *R. mccowni* but is more buffy throughout and has a different tail-pattern.

Range.—Breeds in the Transition and Upper Austral zones from Mont.,

se. Alberta, s. Sask., and Man., s. to e. cent. Wyo., cent. Kans., e. Nebr.,
and w. Minn. Winters from Colo., Nebr., and Ia. to Ariz, Sonora, and the
s. end of the Mexican tableland. Accidental in Me., Mass., N. Y. (L. I.),
Md., Calif., and B. C.

Glen Ellyn, Apr. 20, 1915, five.

532. SNOW BUNTING. PLECTROPHENAX NIVALIS NIVALIS (*Linnæus*).
[534.] (Fig. 11; Pl. XXVII.) *Ad. ♂ in summer.*—Whole head and neck,
rump, and underparts white; back and scapulars black; outer primaries
black, white basally, secondaries wholly white; outer tail-feathers white,
inner ones black. *Ad. ♀ in summer.*—Similar, but entire upperparts streaked
with black; outer primaries all fuscous; secondaries more or less tipped with
fuscous. *♂ in winter.*—Upperparts a kind of rusty brown, almost umber on
the center of the crown; back streaked with black, caused by the black
bases of the feathers showing through their rusty tips; wings and tail much
as in summer, but more or less edged with rusty; underparts white, the
breast and sides washed with rusty. *♀ in winter.*—Similar to ♂, but wings
as in summer ♀. L., 6·88; W., 4·07; T., 2·70; B., ·42.

Range.—In N. A. breeds in the Arctic Zone from at least lat. 83° n. (in-
cluding Greenland) to the n. parts of the mainland from Alaska to n. Que.
Winters from Unalaska, s. Alberta, cent. Man. and cent. Que., s. to then.
U. S. and irregularly to Colo., Kans., s. Ind., s. O., e. Ore., and Fla.
Casual in Bermuda.

Washington, W. V., irregular. Bronx region, fairly common T. V. and
W. V., Oct. 16–Apr. 1; casual in Sept. and early Oct. Boston, common
W. V., Nov. 1–Mch. 15; abundant in migrations. N. Ohio, tolerably common W. V., Dec. 10–Mch. 15. Glen Ellyn, rare W. V., Jan.. 1928. SE. Minn.,
common W. V., Oct. 9–Apr. 7; a pair taken May 5, 1876.

Nest, of grasses, rootlets, and moss, lined with finer grasses and feathers,
on the ground. *Eggs*, 4–7, pale bluish white, thinly marked with umber
or heavily spotted or washed with rufous-brown, ·85 × ·64. *Date*, Pt.
Barrow, Alaska, June 12.

The Snowflake may readily be known by the fact that it is the only
one of our sparrowlike birds that has *white* predominating on its wings
and tail, as well as on its body. It feeds exclusively on seeds, and is so
much like the Horned Lark in habits that the two species occasionally
associate. The Snowflake is also strictly a ground bird, rarely perching
on a tree, though it often does so on a house or fence. It always progresses by walking, not by hopping.

Throughout Canada and the northern tier of states this is the familiar
little white bird of winter. As soon as the chill season comes on in icy
rigors, the merry Snowflakes appear in great flocks, and come foraging
about the barnyards when there is no bare ground left in the adjacent
fields. Apparently they get but little to eat, but in reality they always
find enough to keep them in health and spirits, and are as fat as butter
balls. In midwinter, in the far north, when the thermometer showed
thirty degrees below zero, and the chill blizzard was blowing on the
plains, I have seen this brave little bird gleefully chasing his fellows,
and pouring out as he flew his sweet, voluble song with as much spirit
as ever Skylark has in the sunniest days of June. As long as the snow
lasts the Snowflake stays, and as soon as the ground grows bare and
there is promise of better days, this bird of winter betakes himself

again to the north as far as the most northern habitation of man, and
there builds his nest.   ERNEST THOMPSON SETON.

1913. BIRD-LORE, 16, 18 (mig.; pl.).—1919. EKBLAW, W. E., Wilson
Bull., 41–45 (home-life).—1931. SALMONSEN, F., Ibis, 57–70, illus. (geographical variation).

SUMMARY

Species 532
Subspecies 143
                                         ―――
Total number of forms 675
Of casual or accidental occurrence 111
Extinct   6
                                         ―――
                                         117
                                         ―――
Of regular occurrence 558

Geographic Analysis of Casuals and Accidentals

From the east 33
Recorded only from Greenland 16
From the west 40
From the south 22
                                          ―――
                                          111

BIBLIOGRAPHICAL APPENDIX

The appended titles of general and local ornithological publications have been selected from the great mass of literature relating to American birds, in part with regard to their historic importance, but mainly on the basis of their present working value. They include chiefly systematic and faunal works, references to special books and papers being given in their proper connection in the body of the book.

It is hoped that the section devoted to 'local lists,' as they are commonly termed, will be of much assistance to the faunal naturalist and particularly to students of the bird-life of the regions to which, respectively, they refer. Unfortunately many of these papers are now out of print, but the Librarian of the American Museum of Natural History may be consulted with a view to securing, at cost, type-written copies of those not otherwise available, and which are of sufficient importance to warrant the expense involved.

THE WORLD

1875-95. SHARPE, R. B., and others, Catalogue of Birds in the British Museum, 27 vols., with descriptions of the birds of the world, illus.—1885. STEJNEGER, L., and others, Riverside Natural History, Vol. IV, Birds, 4to., 558 pp., illus. (Houghton, Mifflin & Co.), Classification, structure, habits, distribution.—1893-96. NEWTON, A., and others, A Dictionary of Birds. Pop. Ed., 8vo., 1088 pp., illus. (Macmillan).—1894-95. LYDEKKER, R., and others, Royal Nat. Hist., Birds, 4to., Vol. III, 584 pp., and IV, 576 pp., illus., General account.—1899. EVANS, A. H., Birds, Vol. IX, Cambridge Natural History, 8vo., 635 pp., illus. (Macmillan), Classification, habits, distribution.—1899-1909. SHARPE, B., A Hand-List of the Genera and Species of Birds, 8vo., 5 vols., (British Museum), Names and Ranges.—1909. KNOWLTON, F. H., and others, Birds of the World, sm. 4to., 873 pp., illus. (Holt), Habits, distribution.—1928. ALEXANDER, W. B., Birds of the Ocean: A Handbook for Voyagers, 16mo., xxiii+428 pp., illus. (Putnam's).—1931-19—). PETERS, J. L., Check-List of Birds of the World, 8vo., Vol. I, xviii+345 pp. (Harvard Univ. Press, Cambridge).

WESTERN HEMISPHERE

1918-19. Catalogue of Birds of the Americas, Zoöl. Ser., Vol. XIII, Field Mus. Nat. Hist.—1918. CORY, C. B., Pt. II, No. 1, Owls, Parrots, Oil-Birds, Kingfishers, Toddies, Motmots, Goatsuckers, Swifts, Hummingbirds.—1919. CORY, C. B., Pt. II, No. II, Trogons, Cuckoos, Capitos, Toucans, Jacamars, Puff-birds, Woodpeckers.—1924. HELLMAYR, C. E., Pt. III, Tapacolas, Gnat Eaters, Antbirds.—1925. HELLMAYR, C. E., Pt. IV, Ovenbirds, Woodhewers.—1927. HELLMAYR, C. E., Pt. V, Flycatchers.—1929. HELLMAYR, C. E., Pt. VI, Sharp-bills, Manakins, Chatterers, Cocks-of-the-Rock, Plant-cutters.

NORTH AMERICA

1808-14. WILSON, A., American Ornithology, 9 vols., 4to., Many subsequent editions, the last, in one volume, by Porter & Coates, Philadelphia, is crude, but at least places Wilson's text within reach of everyone.—1831-39. AUDUBON, J. J., Ornithological Biography, 5 vols., 8vo. of text to accompany the 4 elephant folios of plates (1827–38). Republished in 8 vols., 8vo., 1840–44 and later editions. The elephant folios with the 5 volumes of text sell for $2500–$3000; the text can sometimes be purchased at $5 per volume; the first 8vo. edition brings about $350.—**1832-34.** NUTTALL, T., Manual of the Ornithology of the United States and Canada, 2 vols. Several later editions, the last revised by Montague Chamberlain (Little, Brown & Co.), 1903, 2 vols. in one, 473 and 431 pp.—**1872.** COUES, E., Key to North American Birds, 1903, 5th and last ed., 2 vols., roy. 8vo., 1152 pp. The introduction, of 233 pages, treats of general ornithology and the anatomy of birds.—**1874-84.** BAIRD, S. F., BREWER, T. M., and RIDGWAY, R., History of North American Birds: Land-birds, 3 vols.; water-birds, 2 vols., 4to. The volumes on land-birds republished in 8vo. size but from same plates, 1905, 596, 590, 560 pp. (Little, Brown & Co.).—**1886.** American Ornithologists' Union Check-List of North American Birds, rev. ed., 1910, 8vo., 430 pp. (New York).—**1887.** RIDGWAY, R., A Manual of North American Birds, 2d ed., 1896, 653 pp. (Lippincott).—**1892-95.** BENDIRE, C., Life Histories of North American Birds, I, 414 pp., Gallinaceous birds, Pigeons, Hawks, and Owls; II, 1895, 508 pp., Parrots, Cuckoos, Trogons, Kingfishers, Woodpeckers, Goatsuckers, Swifts, Hummingbirds, Cotingas, Flycatchers, Larks, Crows and Jays, Blackbirds and Orioles. (U. S. Nat. Mus.)—**1893.** NEHRLING, H., Our Native Birds of Song and Beauty, Vol. I, 371 pp.; Vol. II, 1896, 452 pp., Biographical.—**1898.** DAVIE, O., Nests and Eggs of North American Birds, 5th ed., 8vo., 509 pp. (Columbus, Ohio).—**1901-19.** RIDGWAY, R., The Birds of North and Middle America, Bull. 50, U. S. Nat. Mus., Part I, 1901, Fringillidæ; Part II, 1902, Tanagridæ, Icteridæ, Cœrebidæ, Mniotiltidæ; Part III, 1904, Motacillidæ, Hirundinidæ, Ampelidæ, Ptilogonatidæ, Dulidæ, Vireonidæ, Laniidæ, Corvidæ, Paridæ, Sittidæ, Certhiidæ, Troglodytidæ, Cinclidæ, Chameidæ, Sylviidæ; Part IV, 1907, Turdidæ, Zeledoniidæ, Mimidæ, Sturnidæ, Ploceidæ, Alaudidæ, Oxyruncidæ, Tyrannidæ, Pipridæ, Cotingidæ; Part V, 1911, Pteroptochidæ, Forimicariidæ, Furnariidæ, Dendrocolaptidæ, Trochilidæ, Micropodidæ, Trogonidæ; Part VI, 1914, Picidæ, Capitonidæ, Ramphastidæ, Bucconidæ, Galbulidæ, Alcedinidæ, Todidæ, Momotidæ, Caprimulgidæ, Nyctibiidæ, Tytonidæ, Bubonidæ; Part VII, 1916, Cuculidæ, Psittacidæ, Columbidæ; Part VIII, 1919, Jacanidæ, Œdicnemidæ, Haematopodidæ, Arenariidæ, Aphrizidæ, Charadriidæ, Scolopacidæ, Phalaropodidæ, Recurvirostridæ, Rhynchopidæ, Sternidæ, Laridæ, Stercorariidæ, Alcidæ. Other volumes to follow. The standard work.—**1903.** CHAPMAN, F. M., Color Key to North American Birds, 312 pp., upward 800 col. illus.—**1904.** REED, C. S., North American Birds' Eggs, 356 pp., many illus.—**1910.** American Ornithologists' Union Abridged Check-List of North American Birds, Pocket ed., 77 printed +77 blank pp. (New York.)—**1917.** PEARSON, T. G., Editor-in-Chief, Birds of America, 4to., 3 vols., (University Soc., New York); the colored plates by Fuertes are from Eaton's Birds of New York.—**1919-.** BENT, A. C., Life Histories of North American Birds, Bulls. U. S. Nat. Mus.: No. 107, 1919, Diving Birds; No. 113, 1921, Gulls and Terns; No. 121, 1922, Petrels, Pelicans and their Allies; No. 126, 1923, Wild Fowl; I, No. 130, 1925, Wild Fowl; II, 1926, Marsh Birds [Herons, Rails, etc.]; No. 142, 1927, Shore Birds; I, No. 146, 1929, Shore Birds, II.—**1931.** Check-List of North American Birds, 4th ed. (rev.), Witmer Stone, Editor; American Ornithologists' Union, 8vo.

EASTERN NORTH AMERICA

1872-81. MAYNARD, C. J., Birds of Eastern North America, 1896, rev. ed., 4to., 721 pp., illus. (West Newton, Mass.).—**1884.** LANGILLE, J. H., Our Birds in Their Haunts, 12mo., 624 pp. (Cassino).—**1889.** MERRIAM, F. A., Birds Through an Opera-glass, 12mo., 223 pp. (Houghton, Mifflin & Co.).—**1895.** WRIGHT, M. O., Birdcraft, 12mo., 317 pp., illus. (Macmillan). —**1895.** CHAPMAN, F. M., Handbook of the Birds of Eastern North America, 421 pp., illus., 1912, rev. ed. (Appleton).—**1897.** CHAPMAN, F. M.,

Bird-Life: A Guide to the Study of our Common Birds, 12mo., 269 pp., 75 pls., 1901, rev. ed., with col. pls. (Appleton's).—1897. WRIGHT, M. O., and COUES, E., Citizen Bird, 12mo., 430 pp., illus. (Macmillan).—1898. BLANCHAN, N., Bird Neighbors, 234 pp., col. pls. (Doubleday).—1898. MERRIAM, F. A., Birds of Village and Field, 12mo., 406 pp., illus. (Houghton, Mifflin & Co.).—1898. SCOTT, W. E. D., Bird Studies, an Account of the Land Birds of Eastern North America, 4to., 363 pp. Many half-tones (Putnam's).—1898. APGAR, A. C., Birds of the United States East of the Rockies, 12mo., 415 pp., illus. (Am. Book Co.).—1899. CORY, C. B., The Birds of Eastern North America, 8vo., 387 pp., illus. (Field Museum).— 1905-6. REED, C. A., Bird-Guide, Oblong, 32mo., Part I, 254 pp.; Part II, 197 pp.; many illus. (Doubleday).

GREENLAND

1861. REINHARDT, J., List of Birds Hitherto Observed in Greenland, Ibis, III, pp. 1–19, 118 species.—1875. NEWTON, A., Notes on Birds Which Have Been Found in Greenland, . . . London, 8vo. pamphlet, pp. 94–115 (author's extra from Man. Nat. Hist. Greenland), 63 +62 species, bibliography.—1889. HAGERUP, A., Some Account of the Birds of Southern Greenland, from the MSS. of A. Hagerup, edited by Montague Chamberlain. Auk, VI, pp. 211–218, 291–297, 39 species.—1891. HAGERUP, A. T., The Birds of Greenland, translated from the Danish by Fremann B. Arngrimson, edited by Montague Chamberlain, 8vo., 62 pp., 139 species (Little, Brown & Co., Boston).—1892. STONE, W., Birds Collected by the West Greenland Expedition, Proc. Acad. Nat. Sci., Phila., 1892, pp. 145–152, 147 species.— 1895. STONE, W., List of Birds Collected by the Peary Expedition, Proc. Acad. Nat. Sci., Phila., 1895, pp. 502–505, 28 species.—1895. SCHALOW, H. VON., Ueber eine Vogelsammlung aus Westgrönland, Jour. für Orn., 1895, pp. 457–481, 35 species.—1899. CHAPMAN, F. M., Report on Birds Received Through the Peary Expeditions to Greenland, Bull. Am. Mus. Nat. Hist., XII, pp. 219–244, 48 species.—1904. SCHALOW, H., Die Vögel der Arktis. Band IV, Leiferung, I, pp. 81–288 (Gustav Fischer, Jena), a detailed synopsis of Arctic bird-life.—1922. GIBSON, L., Bird Notes from North Greenland, Auk, pp. 350–363.—1925. SHIOLER, E. L., Danmarks Fugle med Henblik paa de i Gronland, paa Faeroerne og i Kongeriget Iceland—Forekommende Arter (Gyldendalske Boghandel, Nordisk Forlag, Kobenhavn), large 4to., Vol. I, pp. 1–552, pls. 1–98 (Anseriformes); Vol. II, 1926, pp. 1–338, pls. 1–86 (Anseriformes); Vol. III, 1931, pp. 1–413, pls. 1–91 (Falconiformes). The second volume treats especially of Greenland birds of which 168 species and subspecies are enumerated. (See ALLEN, G. M., The Auk, 1926, pp. 218–227; 1931, pp. 457, 458.)

BRITISH POSSESSIONS

BERMUDA

1859. JONES, J. M., WEDDERBURN, J. W., and HURDIS, J. L., The Naturalist in Bermuda, Birds, pp. 23–97.—1884. REID, S. G., List of the Birds of Bermuda, Bull. U. S. Nat. Mus., No. 25, pp. 165–279, 186 species. (See also, MERRIAM, C. H., Ibid., 283, 284.)—1901. BANGS, O., and BRADLEE, T. S., The Resident Land Birds of Bermuda, Auk, pp. 249–257, 10 species.

CANADA

1908. PREBLE, E. A., A Biological Investigation of the Athabaska-Mackenzie Region, N. A. Fauna, No. 27, 574 pp., Birds, pp. 251–500, 296 species, bibliography.—1909. MACOUN, J. and J. M., Catalogue of Canadian Birds, 8vo., xviii+761 pp. (Government Printing Bureau, Ottawa), distribution and nesting (important).—**1915.** TAVERNER, P. A., Suggestions for Ornithological Work in Canada, Ottawa Field-Nat., XXIX, pp. 14–18, 21–28.—**1919.** TAVERNER, P. A., Birds of Eastern Canada, Can. Geol. Surv., Ottawa, 297 pp., 50 col. pls., 2nd ed., 1922.—**1928.** SOPER, J. D., Faunal Investigation of Baffin Island, Bull. 53, Nat. Mus. Can., 143 pp., 85 species.

KEEWATIN

1902. PREBLE, E. A., Birds of Keewatin. N. A. Fauna, No. 22, pp. 75–131, 260 species.

LABRADOR

1861. COUES, E., Notes on the Ornithology of Labrador, Proc. Acad. Nat. Sci., Phila., XIII, pp. 215–257, 82 species.—**1885.** TURNER, L. M., List of the Birds of Labrador, including Ungava, East Main, Moose, and Gulf Districts of the Hudson's Bay Company, together with the Island of Anticosti, Proc. U. S. Nat. Mus., VIII, pp. 233–254, 207 species. (See also PACKARD, A. S., The Labrador Coast, 1891).—**1887.** FRAZAR, M. A., An Ornithologist's Summer in Labrador, Orn. and Oöl., XII, pp. 1–3, 17–20, 33–35, 62 species.—**1902.** BIGELOW, H. B., Birds of the Northeastern Coast of Labrador, Auk, pp. 24–31, 85 species.—**1907.** TOWNSEND, C. W., and ALLEN, G. M., Birds of Labrador, Proc. Bost. Soc. Nat. Hist., XXXIII, pp. 277–428, map, 213 species. (See also TOWNSEND, C. W., and BENT, A. C., The Auk, 1910, pp. 1–18, 93 species.)—**1913.** TOWNSEND, C. W., Some More Labrador Notes, Auk, pp. 1–10.—**1917.** TOWNSEND, C. W., In Audubon's Labrador, Auk, pp. 133–146.—**1918.** TOWNSEND, C. W., In Audubon's Labrador, 12mo., 354 pp. (Houghton, Mifflin & Co.)—**1925.** LEWIS, H. F., Notes on Birds of the Labrador Peninsula in 1923, Auk, pp. 74–86, 29 species, illus.; pp. 278–281, 9 species.—**1927.** LEWIS, H. F., Birds of Labrador Peninsula in 1925 and 1926, Auk, pp. 59–66.—**1928-29.** HANTSCH, B., Avifauna of Northeastern Labrador, Can. Field-Nat. XLII, pp. 2–9, 33–40, 87–94, 123–125, 172–177, 201–207, 221–227; XLIII, pp. 11–18, 31–34, 52–59.

MANITOBA

1886. SETON, E. T., The Birds of Western Manitoba, Auk, pp. 145–156, 320–329, 453, 258 species.—**1891.** SETON, E. T., The Birds of Manitoba, Proc. U. S. Nat. Mus., XIII, pp. 457–643, 1 pl., 266 species. (See also 14 additions, Auk, 1893, p. 49.)—**1909.** SETON, E. T., Fauna of Manitoba, British Assoc. Handbook, Winnipeg, pp. 1–47, 273 species.

NEW BRUNSWICK

1857. BRYANT, H., A List of Birds Observed at Grand Menan and at Yarmouth, N. S., from June 16 to July 8, Proc. Bost. Soc. Nat. Hist., VI, pp. 114–123, 55 species.—**1873.** HERRICK, H., A Partial Catalogue of the Birds of Grand Menan, N. B., Bull. Essex. Inst., V, pp. 28–41, 194 species.—**1879.** PEARSALL, R. F., Grand Menan Notes, Summers of 1877 and 1878, Forest and Stream, XIII, p. 524, 43 species.—**1882.** BATCHELDER, C. F., Notes on the Summer Birds of the Upper St. John, Bull. N. O. C. V. I, pp. 106–111, 147–152, 105 species.—**1882.** CHAMBERLAIN, M., A Catalogue of the Birds of New Brunswick, Bull. Nat. Hist. Soc. New Brunswick, No. 1, pp. 23–68, 269 species.—**1912.** TOWNSEND, C. W., Notes on the Summer Birds of the St. John Valley, N. B., Auk, pp. 16–23.—**1917.** PHILIPP, P. B., and BOWDISH, B. S., Some Summer Birds of Northern New Brunswick, Auk, pp. 265–275; also, *Ibid.*, 1919, pp. 36–45.

NEWFOUNDLAND

1869. REEKS, H., Notes on the Zoölogy of Newfoundland, Zoölogist, 2nd ser., IV, pp. 1609–1614, 1689–1695, 1741–1759, 1849–1858, 212 species. See also Canad. Nat. and Quart. Journ. Sci., V, 1870–71, pp. 38–47, 151–159, 289–304, 406–416; and HARVEY, M., Forest and Stream, III, pp. 53, 196, 341.—**1900.** PORTER, L. H., Newfoundland Notes, Auk, pp. 71–73, 50 species summer birds.—**1912.** ARNOLD, E., A Short Summer Outing in Newfoundland, Auk, pp. 72–79, 68 species.—**1919.** NOBLE, G. K., Notes on Avifauna of Newfoundland, Bull. Mus. Comp. Zoöl., LXII, pp. 543–568, 61 species.—**1926.** GRISCOM, L., Notes on Summer Birds of the West Coast of Newfoundland, Ibis, pp. 656–683, 87 species.

NOVA SCOTIA

1857. BRYANT, H. (See New Brunswick.)—**1858.** BLAKISTON, R. A., BLAND, R. E., and WILLIS, J. R., List of Birds of Nova Scotia, Thirteenth Ann. Rep. Smiths. Inst., pp. 280–286, 206 species.—**1879.** JONES, J. MATTHEW, List of the Birds of Nova Scotia—Land Birds, Forest and Stream, XII, pp. 65, 66, 105, 106, 205, 245, 128 species.—**1887.** DWIGHT, J., JR., Summer Birds of the Bras d'Or Region of Cape Breton Island, Nova Scotia. Auk, pp. 13–16; 59 species. (See also ALLEN, F. H., Ibid., 1891.)—**1888.** DOWNS, A., Birds of Nova Scotia, edited by Harry Piers, Proc. and Trans. Nova Scotia Inst. Nat. Sci., VII, ii, pp. 142–178, 240 species.—**1923.** LEWIS, H. F., Spring Migration of 1914 at Antigonish, N. S., Trans. N. S. Inst., XV, pp. 2, 119–128, 91 species.

ONTARIO

1860. McILWRAITH, T., List of Birds Observed in the Vicinity of Hamilton, Canad. Journ. V, pp. 387–396 (see also Proc. Essex. Inst., V, 1866 pp. 79–96), 241 species.—**1882.** MORDEN, J. A., and SAUNDERS, W. E., List of the Birds of Western Ontario, Canad. Sportsm. and Nat., II, pp. 183–187, 192–194, also III, pp. 218, 219, 243, 236 species.—**1891.** FARLEY, F. L., A List of the Birds of Elgin County, Ontario, Oölogist, VIII, pp. 81–87, 190 species.—**1891.** Ottawa Field Nat. Club, The Birds of Ottawa, Ottawa Nat., V, pp. 31–47, 224 species.—**1894.** McILWRAITH, T., The Birds of Ontario, 8vo., x+426 pp. (Wm. Briggs, Toronto), 317 species.—**1897-98.** NASH, C. W., Birds of Ontario in Relation to Agriculture, Rep. Farmers' Inst. of Ont., 8vo., 32 pp.—**1900.** NASH, C. W., Check-List of the Birds of Ontario, 8vo., 58 pp. (Warwick Bros. and Rutter, Toronto), 302 species.—**1901.** FLEMING, J. H., A List of the Birds of the Districts of Parry Sound and Muskoka, Ont., Auk, pp. 33–45, 196 species. (See also Ibid., XIX, p. 403.)—**1905.** NASH, C. W., Check List of the Birds of Ontario, 82 pp., 324 species (L. K. Cameron, Printer, Toronto, Ont.).—**1906.** SWALES, B. H., and TAVERNER, P. A., Remarks on the Summer Birds of Lake Muskoka, Ont., Wilson Bull., XVIII, pp. 60–68, 59 species.—**1906-7.** FLEMING, J. H., Birds of Toronto, Ont., Auk, XXIII, pp. 437–453; XXIV, pp. 71–89, 290 species. —**1907.** HUBEL, F. C., Preliminary List of the Summer Birds of the Cobalt Mining Region, Nipissing District, Ont., Auk, pp. 48–52, 76 species.—**1907-8.** TAVERNER, P. A., and SWALES, B. H., The Birds of Point Pelee, Wilson Bull., XIX, pp. 37–53, 82–99, 133–153; XX, pp. 79–96, 107–129, 209 species. See also WOOD, N. A., Ibid., 1910, pp. 63–78.—**1910.** EIFRIG, G., A Winter of Rare Birds at Ottawa, Auk, pp. 53–59.—**1910.** EIFRIG, C. W. G., Birds of Ottawa, Ottawa Field-Nat., XXIV, pp. 152–163, 116–144, 222–227, 246 species.—**1913.** FLEMING, J. H., Birds of Toronto, Nat. Hist. Toronto Region, Canadian Inst., pp. 212–237.—**1920.** FLEMING, J. H., and LLOYD, H., Ontario Bird Notes, Auk, pp. 429–439, 71 species.—**1920-21.** WOOD, A. A., Birds of Coldstream, Ont., Can. Field-Nat., XXXIV, pp.

47–53; XXXV, 1, 199 species.—**1923.** SOPER, J. D., The Birds of Wellington and Waterloo Counties, Ontario, Auk, pp. 489–513, 206 species.—**1925.** CALVERT, E. W., Birds of the Lindsay District, Ontario, Can. Field-Nat., XXXIX, pp. 47–51, 72–74, 177 species.

QUEBEC

1878. CORY, C. B., A Naturalist in the Magdalen Islands (Boston), Part II, pp. 33–83, list of birds, 109 species.—**1882.** WINTLE, E. D., Ornithology of the Island of Montreal, Canad. Sportsm. and Nat. II, pp. 108–110, 116, 117, 168 species.—**1882-85.** MERRIAM, C. H., List of Birds Ascertained to Occur within Ten Miles of Point des Monts, Province of Quebec, Canada (based chiefly upon the notes of Napoleon A. Comeau), Bull. N. O. C., VII, pp. 233–242, and Addenda; VIII, pp. 244, 245; Auk, I, 1884, p. 295; II, 1885, pp. 113, 315, 180 species.—**1884.** BREWSTER, W., Notes on the Birds Observed During a Summer Cruise on the Gulf of St. Lawrence, Proc. Bost. Soc. Nat. Hist., XXII, pp. 364–412, 92 species.—**1889.** BISHOP, L. B., Notes on the Birds of the Magdalen Islands, Auk, pp. 144–150, 66 species.—**1889.** DIONNE, C. E., Catalogue des Oiseaux de la Province de Quebec avec des Notes sur leur Distribution Géographique. . . . (Quebec des Presses à Vapeur de J. Dussault, Port Dauphin), 8vo., 119 pp., 273 species.—**1891.** PALMER, WILLIAM, Notes on the Birds Observed During the Cruise of the United States Fish Commission Schooner Grampus in the Summer of 1887, Proc. U. S. Nat. Mus., XIII, 1890, pp. 249–265, 78 species.—**1893.** DWIGHT, J., JR., Summer Birds of Prince Edward Island, Auk, pp. 1–15, 81 species.—**1896.** WINTLE, E. D., The Birds of Montreal, W. Drysdale & Co., Montreal, 8vo., xiv+181 pp., 254 species.—**1908.** MACSWAIN, J. A., Catalogue of the Birds of Prince Edward Island, Proc. and Trans. Nova Scotia Inst. of Science, XI, pp. 570–592, 220 species.—**1916-27.** MOUSLEY, H., Notes on the Birds of Hatley, Stanstead County, Quebec, Auk, pp. 57–73, 168–185, 122 species; 1918, pp. 289–306; 1919, pp. 472–487; 1921, pp. 51–59, total now 175 species, 108, 126; 1924, pp. 572–589; 1927, pp. 520–523.—**1920.** LEWIS, H. F., Changes in Status of Certain Birds Near Quebec, Can. Field-Nat., XXXIV, pp. 132–136.—**1920-23.** TOWNSEND, C. W., Summer Birds Gaspé Peninsula, Quebec, Can. Field-Nat., XXXIV, pp. 78–80, 87–95; XXXVII, pp. 6–11, illus. 143 species.—**1923-24.** LLOYD, H., The Birds of Ottawa, Can. Field-Nat., XXXVII, pp. 101–105, 125–127, 151–156; XXXVIII, pp. 10–16, 242 species.—**1924.** LEWIS, H. F., Birds from the Island of Anticosti, Quebec, Can. Field-Nat., XXXVIII, pp. 43–46, 72–75, 88–90, 125–155, 146, 147, 171 species; also XL, pp. 179–181.—**1925.** PHILIPP, P. B., Some Summer Birds of the Magdalen Islands, Can. Field-Nat., Apr.—**1926.** DEMILLE, J. B., Birds of Gaspé County, Quebec, Auk, pp. 508–527, 165 species.

UNITED STATES

MISSISSIPPI VALLEY

1888. COOKE, W. W., Report on Bird Migration in the Mississippi Valley in the years 1884 and 1885, edited and revised by C. Hart Merriam, Bull. No. 2, Div. Economic Ornithology [=Biological Survey], 313 pp., 1 map.

NEW ENGLAND

1877. MINOT, H. D., The Land and Game Birds of New England, 2d ed., edited by Wm. Brewster, 1895, 492 pp. (Houghton, Mifflin & Co.).—**1881-83.** STEARNS, W. A., and COUES, E., New England Bird-Life, 2 vols., pp. 324–409.—**1904.** HOFFMANN, R. A., Guide to the Birds of New England

and Eastern New York, 350 pp. (Houghton, Mifflin & Co.).—**1909.** ALLEN,
G. M., Birds of New England, occasional papers Bost. Soc. Nat. Hist.,
VII, pp. 1–230, annotated list of 402 species.—**1925–29.** FORBUSH, E. H.,
Birds of Massachusetts and other New England States, with colored pls.
by Louis Agassiz Fuertes and Allan Brooks: Part I, 1925, Water Birds,
Marsh Birds and Shore Birds; Part II, 1927, Land Birds from Bob-Whites to
Grackles; Part III, 1929, Land Birds from Sparrows to Thrushes.

ALABAMA

1878-79. BROWN, N. C., A List of Birds Observed at Coosada, Central
Alabama, Bull. N. O. C., III, pp. 168–174; IV, pp. 7–13, 119 species.—
1890-91. AVERY, W. C., Birds Observed in Alabama, Am. Field, XXXIV,
pp. 584, 607, 608; XXXV, 1891, pp. 8, 32, 55, 184 species.—**1908.** SAUNDERS,
A. A., Some Birds of Central Alabama, Auk, pp. 413–424, 129 species.—
1914. GOLSAN, L. S., and HOLT, E. G., Birds of Autauga and Montgomery
Counties, Alabama, Auk, pp. 212–235, 184 species.—**1921.** HOLT, E. G.,
Annotated List of the Avery Bird Collection in the Alabama Museum of
Natural History, Mus. Paper No. 4, 142 pp., 216 species.—**1924.** HOWELL,
A. H., Birds of Alabama (Brown Ptg. Co., Montgomery, Ala.), pp. 384,
illus. (see also N. A. Fauna, No. 25).

CONNECTICUT

1843. LINSLEY, J. H., A Catalogue of the Birds of Connecticut, Am.
Journ. Sci. and Arts, XLIV, pp. 249–274, 302 species; see also *Ibid.*, XLVI,
1844, pp. 50, 51.—**1877.** MERRIAM, C. H., A Review of the Birds of Connecticut, with Remarks on their Habits, Trans. of the Conn. Acad., IV, pp.
1–165, 292 species.—**1887.** PLATT, F., A List of the Birds of Meriden, Conn.,
Trans. Meriden Scientific Assoc., II, 1885–86, pp. 30–53; III, p. 41, 116
species.—**1892.** AVERILL, C. K., JR., List of Birds Found in the Vicinity of
Bridgeport, Conn., Bridgeport Scientific Soc., 8vo., pp. 1–19, 246 species.—
1906. CHAPMAN, F. M., (see New York).—**1908.** COMMITTEE, A List of the
Birds of the New Haven Region, Bull. No. 1, New Haven Bird Club, pp.
1–32, 217 species.—**1913.** SAGE, J. H., and BISHOP, L. B., The Birds of
Connecticut, 8vo., 370 pp., Bull. 20, State Geol. Surv., 329 species.—**1921.**
BISHOP, L. B., Notes from Connecticut, Auk, pp. 582–589, 66 species.—
1923. BAGG, A. C., Connecticut Valley—A Highway for Migration, Auk,
pp. 256–275, illus.—**1923.** GRISCOM, L. (See New York.)

DELAWARE

1897-1929. STONE, W., Editor, Numerous Notes on Delaware Birds,
Proc. Del. Valley Orn. Club, Phila.—**1905.** RHOADS, S. N., and PENNOCK,
C. J., Birds of Delaware: A Preliminary List, Auk, pp. 194–205, 211 spe-
cies. (See also Auk, 1908, pp. 282–288.)

DISTRICT OF COLUMBIA

1883. COUES, E., and PRENTISS, D. W., Avifauna Columbiana, 2d ed.
Bull. U. S. Nat. Mus. No. 26, 8vo., pp. 1–133, many woodcuts, 4 maps,
248 species.—**1888.** RICHMOND, C. W., An Annotated List of Birds Breed-
ing in the District of Columbia, Auk, pp. 18–25, 100 species.—**1888.** SMITH,
HUGH M., and PALMER, WILLIAM, Additions to the Avifauna of Washington,
D. C., and Vicinity, Auk, pp. 147, 148, adds 12 species to Coues' and
Prentiss' list of 1883.—**1929.** COOKE, MAY T., Birds of Washington, D. C.
Region, Proc. Biol. Soc. Wash., Vol. 42, 80 pp., 301 species.

FLORIDA

1871. ALLEN, J. A., On the Mammals and Winter Birds of East Florida, Bull. Mus. Comp. Zoöl., II, pp. 161–450, pls. ix–xiii, 181 species.—**1888.** CHAPMAN, F. M., A List of Birds Observed at Gainesville, Florida, Auk, pp. 267–277, 149 species.—**1888-90.** SCOTT, W. E. D., A Summary of Observations on the Birds of the Gulf Coast of Florida, Auk, pp. 373–379; VI, pp. 13–18, 152–160, 245–252, 318–326; VII, pp. 14–22, 114–120, 262 species.— **1890.** SCOTT, W. E. D., On Birds Observed at the Dry Tortugas, Florida, during parts of March and April, 1890, Auk, pp. 301–314, 80 species.— **1891.** BREWSTER, W., and CHAPMAN, F. M., Notes on the Birds of the Lower Suwannee River, Auk, pp. 125–138, 116 species. (See also Brewster, *Ibid.*, pp. 149–157.)—**1892.** SCOTT, W. E. D., Notes on the Birds of the Caloosahatchie Region of Florida, Auk, pp. 209–218, 259 species.—**1895.** WAYNE, A. T., Notes on the Birds of the Wacissa and Aucilla River Regions of Florida, Auk, pp. 362–367, 161 species.—**1896.** CORY, C. B., Hunting and Fishing in Florida, with a Key to the Water Birds of the State.—**1904.** WILLIAMS, R. W., JR., A Preliminary List of the Birds of Leon County, Florida, Auk, pp. 449–462, 156 species. (See also *Ibid.*, XXIII, pp. 153–161; XXIV, pp. 158, 159.)—**1906.** FOWLER, H. W., Birds Observed in June in the Florida Keys, Auk, pp. 396–400, 33 species.—**1913.** BAYNARD, O. E., Breeding Birds of Alachua County, Florida, Auk, pp. 240–247, 98 species.—**1914.** PHELPS, F. M., Resident Bird Life of the Big Cypress Swamp Region (Florida), Wilson Bull., pp. 86–101, 65 species.—**1914.** WILLIAMS, R. W., Notes on the Birds of Leon County, Auk, pp. 494–498; 1928, pp. 164–169; 1929, p. 122, total, 223 species.—**1919.** PANGBURN, C. H., Birds of Pinellas County, Florida, Auk, pp. 393–405, 135 species.—**1919.** WILLIAMS, J. [= PENNOCK, C. J.], Birds of Wakulla County, Florida, Wilson Bull., pp. 109–117; 1920, pp. 5–12, 48–58, 238 species.—**1921.** HOWELL, A. H., A List of the Birds of the Royal Palm Hammock, Florida, Auk, pp. 250–263, 128 species.—**1925.** BAILEY, H. H., The Birds of Florida, 4to., 146 pp., 76 col. pls. by G. M. Sutton.—**1926.** HOLT, E. G., and SUTTON, G. M., Birds Observed in Southern Florida, Ann. Carnegie Mus., pp. 16, 409–439, illus.—**1926.** FARGO, W. G., Birds of Pinellas and Paco Counties, Florida, Wilson Bull., pp. 140–155, 187 species.—**1926.** WORTHINGTON, W. W., and TODD, W. E. C., Birds of the Choctawhatchee Bay Region, Florida, Wilson Bull., pp. 204–229, 160 species.—**1927.** BENT, A. C., and COPELAND, M., Notes on Florida Birds, Auk, pp. 371–386, 165 species.—**1932.** Howell, A. H., Florida Bird Life, 4to. 37 col. pls. by F. L. Jaques, Dept. Game and Fresh Water Fish, Tallahassee, Fla.

GEORGIA

1883. BAILEY, H. B., Memoranda of a Collection of Eggs from Georgia, Bull. N. O. C., VIII, pp. 37–43, 104 species.—**1903.** SMITH, R. S., Birds of Kirkwood, De Kalb County, Georgia, Wilson Bull., XV, pp. 49–59, 125 species.—**1909.** HOWELL, A. H., Notes on the Summer Birds of Northern Georgia, Auk, pp. 129–137, 76 species.—**1913.** WRIGHT, A. H., and HARPER, F., A Biological Reconnaissance of Okefinokee Swamp: The Birds, Auk, pp. 477–505, 94 species.—**1919.** ERICHSEN, W. J., Some Summer Birds of Liberty County, Georgia, Auk, pp. 380–392, 37 species; also, pp. 590, 591, 4 species.—**1921.** ERICHSEN, W. J., Breeding Water Birds of Chatham County, Georgia, Wilson Bull., pp. 16–28, 69–82.—**1922.** PEARSON, T. G., Birds of Cumberland Island, Georgia, Wilson Bull., pp. 84–90, 97 species.—**1927.** BUREIGH, T. D., Birds of Campus Georgia State College, Athens, The Cypress Knee, pp. 29–45.—**1927.** BURLEIGH, T. D., Breeding Birds of Northeastern Georgia, Auk, pp. 229–234.

ILLINOIS

1855. KENNICOTT, R., Catalogue of Animals Observed in Cook County, Illinois, Trans. Ills. State Agric. Soc. for 1853–54, I, Birds, pp. 580–589, 187 species.—**1868.** ALLEN, J. A. (See Iowa.)—**1874.** RIDGWAY, R., Catalogue of

the Birds Ascertained to Occur in Illinois, Ann. Lyc. Nat. Hist. N. Y., X, pp.
364–394, 311 species.—1876. NELSON, E. W., Birds of Northeastern
Illinois, Bull. Essex Inst., VIII, pp. 90–155, 316 species.—1877. NELSON,
E. W., Notes upon Birds Observed in Southern Illinois, between July 17
and September 4, 1875, Bull. Essex Inst., IX, pp. 32–65, 133 species.—
1881. RIDGWAY, R., A Revised Catalogue of the Birds Ascertained to Occur
in Illinois, Ills. State Lab. Nat. Hist., Bull. No. 4, pp. 161–208, 352 species.
—1884. COOKE, W. W., Bird Migration in the Mississippi Valley, Southern
Illinois, Forest and Stream, XXIII, pp. 444, 445, 463, 464, 144 species based
on Ridgway's list of 1881 and observations of Cyrus W. Butler in the vicinity
of Anna, Ills., during December, 1882, and January, 1883.—1887. RIDGWAY,
R., List of the Birds Found Breeding within the Corporate Limits of Mt.
Carmel, Illinois, Bull. No. 2, Ridgway Orn. Club, pp. 26–35, 85 species.—
1890-95. RIDGWAY, R., The Ornithology of Illinois, roy. 8vo., Vol. I,
1890, 520 pp., 32 pls., Land-birds to Gallinæ; Vol. II, 1895, 282 pp., 33 pls.,
Gallinæ and Water-birds, 363 species.—1891. LOUCKS, W. E., List of Birds
Found Breeding in the Vicinity of Peoria, Illinois, The Oölogist, VIII,
pp. 224–226, 80 species.—1904. WALTER, H. E., and A. W., Wild Birds in
City Parks, rev. ed., Chicago, 16mo., 66 pp., 145 species.—1907. WOOD-
RUFF, F. M., The Birds of the Chicago Area, Chicago Acad. Sci. Bull. VI,
Nat. Hist. Surv., 221 pp., 12 pls., 318 species.—1909. CORY, C. B., Birds of
Illinois and Wisconsin, Field Mus., Zoöl. Ser. IX, 8vo., 764 pp., many
illus., 398 species.—1910. HESS, I. E., One Hundred Breeding Birds of an
Illinois Ten-Mile Radius, Auk, XXVII, pp. 19–32.—1914-15. RIDGWAY,
R., Bird-Life in Southern Illinois, Bird-Lore, pp. 409–420; 1915, pp. 1–7, 91–
103, 191–198, illus.—1922. GAULT, B. T., Check-List of the Birds of Illinois,
80 pp., illus. (Audubon Soc., Chicago).—1923. FORBES, S. A., and GROSS,
A. O., Numbers and Local Distribution of Illinois Birds of Open Country
in Winter, Spring, and Fall, illus., Nat. Hist. Surv. 14, pp. 397–453.—1928.
SCHANTZ, O. M., Birds of Illinois, Pub. No. 6, Dept. Conservation.

INDIANA

1869. HAYMOND, R., Birds of Franklin County, Indiana, Cox's Geol.
Surv., Indiana, Rep. for 1869, pp. 209–235, 163 species.—1888-89. EVER-
MANN, B. W., Birds of Carroll County, Indiana, Auk, V, pp. 344–351; VI,
pp. 22–30, 203 species.—1891. BUTLER, A. W., The Birds of Indiana, with
Illustrations of Many of the Species; prepared for the Indiana Horticul-
tural Society and originally published in its Transactions for 1890; 8vo.,
135 pp., 305 species.—1905. McATEE, W. L., Ecological Notes on the Birds
Occurring within a Radius of Five Miles of the Indiana University Campus,
Proc. Ind. Acad. Sci., pp. 65–202, 32 illus., 225 species.

IOWA

1868. ALLEN, J. A., Notes on Birds Observed in Western Iowa, in the
Months of July, August, and September; also on Birds Observed in Northern
Illinois, in May and June, and at Richmond, Wayne County, Indiana, be-
tween June 3 and 10, Mem. Bost. Soc. Nat. Hist., I, pt. IV, pp. 488–526:
Ogle County, Ills., 84 species; Cook County, Ills., 94 species; Richmond,
Ind., 72 species; Western Iowa, 108 species.—1873. TRIPPE, F. M., Notes
on the Birds of Southern Iowa, Proc. Bost. Soc. Nat. Hist., XV, pp. 229–
242, 162 species.—1888. KEYES, CHARLES R., and WILLIAMS, H. S., A Pre-
liminary Annotated Catalogue of the Birds of Iowa, Proc. Davenport Acad.
Nat. Sci., V, 8vo., 49 pp., 260 species.—1890. COONE, JOHN V., Summer
Residents of Buena Vista County, Iowa, The Oölogist, VII, pp. 45–47,
52 species.—1895. JONES, LYNDS, Bird Migration at Grinnell, Iowa, Auk,
pp. 117–134, 231–237.—1897. ANDERSON, R. M., An Annotated List of the
Birds of Winnebago and Hancock Counties, Iowa (Author, Forest City,
Iowa), 16mo., 19 pp., 218 species.—1906. WILSON, B. H., Birds of Scott

County, Iowa, Wilson Bull., XVIII, pp. 1–11; 166 species.—1907. ANDER-
SON, R. M., The Birds of Iowa, Proc. Davenport Acad. Sci., XI, pp. 125–
417, 355 species.—1916. FENTON, C. L., Preliminary List Birds of Floyd
County, Iowa, Wilson Bull., pp. 130–138.—1917. GABRIELSON, I. N., Birds
Observed in Clay and O'Brien Counties, Iowa, Proc. Iowa Acad. Sci.,
XXIV, pp. 259–272, 136 species.—1919. BAILEY, B. H., Raptorial Birds of
Iowa, Iowa Geol. Surv., 238 pp., illus.—1925. PRAEGER, W. E., Birds of Des
Moines Rapids, Auk, pp. 563–577.—1930. PIERCE, F. J., Birds of Buchanan
County, Iowa, Wilson Bull., pp. 253–285, 215 species.

KANSAS

1875. SNOW, F. H., A Catalogue of the Birds of Kansas, contributed to
the Kansas Academy of Science, 8vo., 14 pp., 3d ed., 295 species.—1886.
GOSS, N. S., A Revised Catalogue of the Birds of Kansas, with Descriptive
Notes of the Nests and Eggs of the Birds Known to Breed in the State
(Topeka), 8vo., vi+76 pp., 335 species. (See also review in Auk, III, 1886,
p. 399.)—1891. GOSS, N. S., History of the Birds of Kansas, illustrating
529 birds. Geo. W. Crane & Co., Topeka, Kans., royal 8vo., 692 pp., 35
photogravure pls., 343 species. —1899. LANTZ, D. E., A Review of Kansas
Ornithology, Trans. Kans. Acad. Sci., 1896–97, pp. 224–276, 351 species.—
1903. SNOW, F. H., A Catalogue of the Birds of Kansas, 5th ed., Trans.
Kans. Acad. Sci., XVIII, 23 pp., 342 species.—1912. ISELEY, D., A List of
the Birds of Sedgwick County, Kansas, Auk, pp. 25–44, 208 species.—
1918-19. DOUTHITT, B. P., Migration Records for Kansas Birds, Wilson
Bull., pp. 100–111; 1919, pp. 6–20, 45–52; see also 1920, PEABODY, P. B.,
pp. 139–149.—1919. HARRIS, H., Birds of the Kansas City Region, Trans.
Acad. Sci., St. Louis, Vol. 23, No. 8, 159 pp., 311 species.—1927. LINSDALE,
J., Summer Birds Southwestern Kansas, Auk, pp. 47–58, 88 species.

KENTUCKY

1883. BECKHAM, C. W., A List of the Birds of Bardstown, Nelson
County, Kentucky, Journ. Cinc. Soc. Nat. Hist., VI, pp. 136–147, 167
species.—1885. BECKHAM, C. W., List of the Birds of Nelson County,
Kentucky, Geol. Surv., (John R. Proctor, Director), Author's Edition, 4to.,
pp. 1–58, 171 species.—1887. PINDAR, L. O., List of the Birds of Fulton
County, Kentucky, Orn. and Oöl., XII, pp. 54, 55, 84, 85, 122 species.—
1889. PINDAR, L. O., List of the Birds of Fulton County, Kentucky, Auk,
VI, pp. 310–316, 183 species.—1910. HOWELL, A. H., Notes on the Summer
Birds of Kentucky and Tennessee, Auk, pp. 295–304; Kentucky, 80 species.—
1921. STONE, W., Some Birds Observed at Pine Mountain, Kentucky (add
to Howell, 1910), Auk, p. 464.—1922. WILSON, G., Birds of Bowling Green,
Kentucky, Auk, pp. 233–243, 179 species.—1922-27. HORSEY, R. E., Bird
Distribution in Eastern Kentucky, Auk, XXXIX, 79–84; 1923, 143, 144;
1927, 119, 120.—1925. BLINCOE, B. J., Birds of Bardstown, Kentucky,
Auk, pp. 404–420, 158 species.—1925. PINDAR, L. O., Birds of Fulton
County, Kentucky, Wilson Bull., pp. 77–88, 163–169.

LOUISIANA

1900. BEYER, G. E., The Avifauna of Louisiana, Proc. La. Soc. Nat.,
45 pp., 323 species.—1904. ALLISON, A., The Birds of West Baton Rouge
Parish, Louisiana, Auk, pp. 472–484, 130 species.—1906. BEYER, G. E.,
ALLISON, A., KOPMAN, H. H., List of the Birds of Louisiana, Auk, pp. 1–15,
275–282; XXIV, pp. 314–321; XXV, pp. 173–180, 339–448, 128 species to
Pici.—1908. HOWELL, A. H., Notes on the Winter Birds of Northern
Louisiana, Proc. Biol. Soc. Washington, XXI, 119–124 pp., 70 species.—
1915. KOPMAN, H. H., List of Birds of Louisiana, Auk, pp. 15–29, 183–194,
323 species.—1918. ARTHUR, S. C., The Birds of Louisiana, Bull. 5, Dept.
Conserv., 80 pp., 368 species and subspecies.

BIBLIOGRAPHICAL APPENDIX 557

MAINE

1862. BOARDMAN, G. A., Catalogue of the Birds Found in the Vicinity of Calais, Maine, and about the Islands at the Mouth of the Bay of Fundy, edited by A. E. Verrill, Proc. Bost. Soc. Nat. Hist., IX, pp. 122–132, 236 + 4 species. (For 12 additions, see Verrill, *Ibid.*, pp. 233, 234.)—**1862.** VERRILL, A. E., Catalogue of the Birds Found at Norway, Oxford County, Maine, Proc. Essex. Inst., III, pp. 136–160, 159 species.—**1872.** MAYNARD, C. J., A Catalogue of the Birds of Coos County, New Hampshire and Oxford County, Maine, with notes by Wm. Brewster, Proc. Bost. Soc. Nat. Hist., XIV, 1871, pp. 356–385, 164 species.—**1882.** BROWN, N. C., A Catalogue of the Birds Known to Occur in Portland, Maine, Proc. Portl. Soc. Nat. Hist., Dec. 14, 1882, pp. 1–37, 250 species. (See also Proc. Portl. Soc. Nat. Hist., 1889, pp. 37–40.)—**1900.** HOWE, R. H., JR., Summer Birds Near Isleboro and the Fox Islands, Journ. Maine Orn. Soc., II, pp. 28–32; III, pp. 14, 15; IV, p. 18, 100 species.—**1908.** KNIGHT, O. W., The Birds of Maine (pub. by Author, Bangor), 8vo., 693 pp., 30 illus., 327 species.—**1916.** NORTON, A. H., Notes on Some Maine Birds, Auk, pp. 376–383.—**1918.** MILLER, CARRIE E., Birds of Lewiston-Auburn, Maine and Vicinity.—**1924.** BREWSTER, W., Birds Lake Umbagog Region of Maine, Bull. LXVI, Mus. Comp. Zoöl. (Cambridge, Mass.), 209 pp.—**1925.** BREWSTER, W., Birds of Umbagog Region, Bull. Mus. Comp. Zoöl., LXVI, pp. 213–402.

MARYLAND

1895. KIRKWOOD, F. C., A List of the Birds of Maryland, Trans. Md. Acad. Sci., 1895, pp. 241–382, 290 species.—**1900.** MERRIAM, C. H., and PREBLE, E. A., The Summer Birds of Western Maryland, Maryland Geol. Surv., pp. 291–307, 100 species.—**1904.** EIFRIG, G., Birds of Alleghany and Garrett Counties, Western Maryland, Auk, pp. 234–250, 180 species.—**1920.** EIFRIG, G., Six adds. to Birds Alleghany and Garrett Counties, Maryland, Auk, pp. 598–600.

MASSACHUSETTS

1870. MAYNARD, C. J., Catalogue of the Birds of Eastern Massachusetts, The Naturalist's Guide, Part II, pp. 81–170, 299 species.—**1886.** ALLEN, J. A., A Revised List of the Birds of Massachusetts, Bull. Am. Mus. Nat. Hist., I, pp. 221–271. 349 species.—**1887.** CLARK, H. L., The Birds of Amherst and Vicinity, Including Nearly the Whole of Hampshire County, Massachusetts, 8vo., 55 pp., 177 species.—**1888.** BREWSTER, W., Notes on the Birds of Winchendon, Worcester County, Auk, V, pp. 386–393, 82 species.—**1889.** FAXON, W., On the Summer Birds of Berkshire County, Mass., Auk, pp. 39–46, 99–107: Southern Berkshire, 76 species; Graylock Mountain, 80 species.—**1889.** INGALLS, C. E., Birds of Templeton and the Adjoining Towns, Gardner News, XX, June, 155 species. Not seen; title from Howe and Allen.—**1891.** COLBURN, W. W., and MORRIS, R. O., The Birds of the Connecticut Valley in Massachusetts, 16mo., 24 pp. (published by the Authors, Springfield), 212 species.—**1891.** WAKEFIELD, J. R., A List of the Birds of Dedham, Dedham Hist. Reg., II, pp. 70–74, 181 species. Not seen; title from Howe and Allen.—**1897.** MORSE, A. P., Birds of Wellesley (published by Author, Wellesley), 16mo., 56 pp., 224 species.—**1900.** FAXON, W., and HOFFMANN, R., The Birds of Berkshire County, Coll. Berkshire Hist. and Sci. Soc., III, pp. 109–166, 200 species.—**1901.** HOWE, R. H., JR., and ALLEN, G. M., The Birds of Massachusetts (published by the Authors), 8vo., 154 pp., 362 species.—**1901.** MORRIS, R. O., The Birds of Springfield, Mass., and Vicinity (H. R. Johnson, Springfield), 8vo., 54 pp., 255 species.—**1905.** TOWNSEND, C.. W., The Birds of Essex County, Massachusetts, Memoirs Nutt. Orn. Club, III, 4to., 352 pp., frontispiece and map, 319 species.—**1906.** BREWSTER, W., The Birds of the Cambridge Region of Massachusetts,

Memoirs Nutt. Orn. Club, IV, 426 pp., pls. 7, 429 species.—1909. WRIGHT, H. W., Birds of the Boston Public Garden. (Houghton, Mifflin & Co.), 16mo., 238 pp., 116 species.—1912. FORBUSH, E. H., Gamebirds, Wildfowl, and Shorebirds of Massachusetts, 8vo., pp. 622, illus. (State House, Boston). —1912. MORSE, A. P., A Pocket List of the Birds of Eastern Massachusetts, with Special Reference to Essex County (Peabody Museum, Salem), 92 pp.—1920. TOWNSEND, C. W., Supplement to Birds of Essex County, Mem. No. 7, Nuttall Orn. Club, Cambridge, Mass., 4to., 196 pp.—1922. FAXON and HOFFMANN, Supplementary Notes on Berkshire County Birds, Auk, pp. 65–72.—1925-27. FORBUSH, E. H. (See New England.)

MICHIGAN

1857. KNEELAND, S., On the Birds of Keeweenan Point, Lake Superior, Proc. Bost. Soc. Nat. Hist., VI, 231–241 pp., 147 species.—1875. BOIES, A. H., Catalogue of the Birds Ascertained to Occur in Southern Michigan, 8vo., 12 pp., 211 species.—1876. COVERT, A. B., Birds of Lower Michigan, Forest and Stream, VI, pp. 99, 132, 163, 214, 266, 318, 354, 402; VII, pp. 147, 164, 276 (see also VI, p. 197), 213 species.—1879. GIBBS, M., Annotated List of the Birds of Michigan, Bull. U. S. Geol. and Geograph. Survey of the Territories, V. 3, pp. 481–497, 310 species.—1880. STEERE, J. B., A List of the Mammals and Birds of Ann Arbor and Vicinity, 8vo., 8 pp., 111 species of birds.—1884. ATKINS, H. A., Summer Birds of Locke, Michigan, Orn. and Oöl., IX, pp. 43–45, 80 species.—1884. ATKINS, H. A., Winter Birds of Locke, Michigan, Orn. and Oöl., IX, pp. 31, 32, 31 species.—1885. ATKINS, H. A., Summer Birds of Locke, Michigan, Orn. and Oöl., X, p. 3, 82 species.—1885. GIBBS, M., A Catalogue of the Birds of Kalamazoo County, Michigan, Orn. and Oöl., X, pp. 6, 7, 38, 39, 54, 55, 68–70, 86, 87, 118, 119, 133–135, 149–151, 166, 167, 189, 190, 230 species.—1885-87. GIBBS, M., The Birds of Michigan, Forest and Stream, XXIII, pp. 483, 484; XXIV, pp. 5, 6, 26, 27, 44, 45, 65, 84, 104, 105, 124, 125, 144, 145, 184, 224, 267, 268, 288, 289, 307, 347, 387, 388, 427; XXV, pp. 4, 5, 304, 305, 365, 366; XXVI, pp. 305, 306; XXVII, pp. 123, 124, 223, 224, 68 species.—1890. WHITE, T. G., Birds of Mackinac Island, Michigan, The Oölogist, VII, pp. 48, 49, 101 species.—1893. COOK, A. J., Birds of Michigan, Bull. 94, State Agricultural College, 8vo., 148 pp., 332 species.—1893. WHITE, S. E., Birds Observed on Mackinac Island, Michigan, During the Summers of 1889, 1890, and 1891, Auk, pp. 221–230, 143 species.—1897. BOIES, A. H., Birds of Neebish Island, St. Mary's River, Michigan, Bull. Mich. Orn. Club, I, pp. 17–20, 27–29, 149 species.—1903. SWALES, B. H., Notes on the Winter Birds of Wayne Co., Michigan, Wilson Bull., XIV, pp. 20–24; XV, 1904, p. 82, 71 species.—1903. SWALES, B. H., A List of the Land Birds of Southeastern Michigan, Bull. Mich. Orn. Club., IV, pp. 14–17, 35–40; V, pp. 37–43, 165 species (see also Wilson Bull. XVII, 1905, pp. 108–114; 1912, 126–130); Auk, XXV, pp. 230–232.—1905. WOOD, N. A., and FROTHINGHAM, E. H., Notes on the Birds of the Au Sable Valley, Michigan, Auk, XXII, 1905, pp. 39–54, 103 species.—1906. WOOD, N. A., PEET, M. M., and McCREARY, O., Annotated List of the Birds of Porcupine Mountains [89 species] and Isle Royale [81 species], Mich., Rep. Geol. Surv. Mich., 1905, pp. 113–127; see also McCreary, *Ibid.*, pp. 56–67.—1909. BLACKWELDER, E., Summer Birds of Iron County, Auk, pp. 363–370, 80 species.—1910. WOOD, J. CLAIRE, Some Winter Birds of the Season 1908–9 in Wayne County, Auk, pp. 36–41.—1910. WOOD, N. A., and TINKER, A. D., Notes on Some of the Rarer Birds of Washtenaw County, Auk, pp. 129–141, 34 species.—1910. CHANEY, R. W., Summer and Fall Birds of the Hamlin Lake Region, Mason County, Auk, pp. 271–279, 119 species.—1911. WOOD, N. A., Expedition to Charity Islands, Lake Huron, Wilson Bull., XXIII, pp. 78–112, 162 species.—1911. WOOD, N. A., and GAIGE, F., Birds Sand Dune Region, South Shore Saginaw Bay, Mich., Mich. Geol. and Biol. Surv., Pub. 4, 128 species.—1912. BARROWS, W. B., Michigan

Bird Life, 8vo., 822 pp., illus., 326 species.—1918. WOOD, N. A., Notes on the Birds of Alger County, Michigan, Occ. Papers, Mus. Zoöl., Univ. Mich., No. 50, 15 pp., 120 species.—1923. WOOD, N. A., Birds Berrien County, Michigan, Occ. Papers, Univ. Mich. 119 pp., 35 species.—1923. VAN TYNE, J., Summer Birds of Les Chenaux Islands, Mich., Wilson Bull., pp. 21–26, 94 species.

MINNESOTA

1871. TRIPPE, T. M., Notes on the Birds of Minnesota, Proc. Essex Inst., VI, pp. 113–119, 138 species.—1874. HATCH, P. L., Report on the Birds of Minnesota, Bull. Minn. Acad. Nat. Sci., pp. 43–68, 230 species.—1876. ROBERTS, T. S., A List of Some Birds Observed in the Vicinity of Minneapolis, Minn., not Enumerated in Dr. Hatch's List (The Scientific Monthly, Toledo, Ohio), I, 5, p. 231.—1880. ROBERTS, T. S., and BENNER, F., A Contribution to the Ornithology of Minnesota, Bull. N. O. C., V, pp. 11–20, 86 species.—1881. HATCH, P. L., A List of the Birds of Minnesota, 9th Ann. Rep. Geol. and Nat. Hist. Surv. Minn., for 1880–1881, pp. 361–372, 281 species.—1881. ROBERTS, T. S., The Winter Birds of Minnesota, 9th Ann. Rep. Geol. and Nat. Hist. Surv. Minn., for 1880–1881, pp. 373–383, 52 species.—1883. BRACKETT, F. H., Ornithological Notes from Minnesota, Quart. Journ. Bost. Zoöl. Soc., II, pp. 47–49; III, pp. 7–16, 134 species.—1890. CANTWELL, G. C., A List of the Birds of Minnesota, Orn. and Oöl., XV, pp. 129–139 (see also p. 156 and XVI, p. 157), 295 species.—1892. HATCH, P. L., Notes on the Birds of Minnesota, Geol. and Nat. Hist. Surv. Minn., 8vo., 487 pp., 302 species.—1904. CURRIER, E. S., Summer Birds of the Leech Lake Region, Minn., Auk, pp. 29–44, 117 species.—1907. ROBERTS, T. S., List of Birds of Becker Co., Minn., Pioneer Hist. of Becker Co. (Pioneer Press, St. Paul), pp. 159–190, 262 species.—1916. ROBERTS, T. S., Winter Bird Life of Minnesota, Occ. Papers, No. 1, Geol. and Nat. Hist. Surv. Minn., 20 pp., illus.—1919. ROBERTS, T. S., Water Birds of Minnesota: Past and Present, Rep. Forest, Fish, and Game Com. ending July, 1918, pp. 56–91, illus.—1919. ROBERTS, T. S., A Review of the Ornithology of Minnesota, Univ. of Minn., 102 pp., illus.—1920. JOHNSON, C. E., Summer Bird Records from Lake County, Minnesota, Auk, pp. 541–551, 89 species; Ibid., XXXVIII, pp. 124–126, 17 species.— —. ROBERTS, T. S., The Birds of Minnesota (Univ. Minn. Press, Minneapolis), 2 vols., 4to., 92 col. pls., 500 text cuts. (In press.)

MISSISSIPPI

1905. STOCKARD, C. R., Nesting Habits of Birds in Mississippi, Auk, pp. 146–158, 273–285, 83 species.—1906. ALLISON, A., Notes on the Winter Birds of Hancock County, Mississippi, Auk, pp. 44–47, 61 species; also, Ibid., p. 232.—1907. ALLISON, A., Notes on the Spring Birds of Tishomingo County, Mississippi, Auk, pp. 12–25.—1922. CARRINGTON, J. D., Winter Birds of Biloxi, Mississippi Region, Auk, pp. 530–556, 112 species.

MISSOURI

1879. SCOTT, W. E. D., Notes on Birds Observed During the Spring Migration in Western Missouri, Bull. N. O. C., IV, pp. 139–147, 148 species.—1884. HURTER, J., List of Birds Collected in the Neighborhood of St. Louis, Mo., Orn. and Oöl., IX, pp. 85–87, 95–97 (see also p. 128), 265 species.—1896. WIDMANN, O., The Peninsula of Missouri as a Winter Home for Birds, Auk, pp. 216–222.—1907. WIDMANN, O. Preliminary Catalogue of the Birds of Missouri, Trans. Acad. Sci., St. Louis, XVIII, pp. 1–288, 383 species.—1908. WOODRUFF, E. S., Birds of Shannon and Carter Counties, Missouri, Auk, pp. 191–213, 172 species.

NEBRASKA

1878. AUGHEY, S., Notes on the Nature of the Food of the Birds of Nebraska, First Ann. Rep. U. S. Ent. Com. for the year 1877, Appendix II, pp. 13–62, 252 species.—**1883.** HALL, A., Spring Birds of Nebraska, Forest and Stream, XX, pp. 265, 266, 284, 114 species.—**1888.** TAYLOR, W. EDGAR, A Catalogue of Nebraska Birds, . . . Ann. Rep. Nebr. State Board of Agric. for the year 1887, pp. 111–118, 314 species.—**1888-89.** TAYLOR, E. W., and VAN VLEET, A. H., Notes on Nebraska Birds, Orn. and Oöl., XIII, pp. 49–51, 169–172; XIV, pp. 163–165, 137 species.—**1896.** BRUNER, L., Notes on Nebraska Birds, Rep. Nebr. State Hort. Soc., pp. 48–178, 415 species.—**1901.** BRUNER, L., Birds that Nest in Nebraska, Proc. Nebr. Orn. Union, pp. 48–61, 212 species.—**1904.** BRUNER, L., WALCOTT, R. H., and SWENK, M. H., A Preliminary Review of the Birds of Nebraska, 1–116+5 pp. (Klopp and Bartlett, Omaha, Nebr.), 406 species.—**1909.** WALCOTT, R. H., An Analysis of Nebraska's Bird Fauna, Proc. Nebr. Orn. Union, IV, pp. 25–55.—**1913.** ZIMMER, J. T., Birds of Thomas County, Nebraska, Forest Reserve, Proc. Nebr. Orn. Union, pp. 51–104, 142 species. —**1915.** SWENK, M. H., Birds of Nebraska, Nebraska Blue Book, 418 species. (See Revisory Notes, Wilson Bull., 1919, pp. 112–117.)—**1921.** SWENK, M. H., and DAWSON, R. W., Distribution and Migration of Nebraska Birds, Wilson Bull., pp. 132–141.

NEW HAMPSHIRE

1872. MAYNARD, C. J. (See Maine.)—**1877.** GOODHUE, C. F., The Birds of Webster and Adjoining Towns, Forest and Stream, VIII, pp. 33, 49, 96, 113, 146, 151 species.—**1882.** KNOWLTON, F. H., A Revised List of the Birds of Brandon, Vt., The Brandon Union, Feb. 10, 1882, 149 species.— **1887.** CHADBOURNE, A. P., A List of the Summer Birds of the Presidential Range of the White Mountains, N. H., Auk, pp. 100–108, 47 species.— **1888.** FAXON, W., and ALLEN, J. A., Notes on the Summer Birds of Holderness [65 species], Bethlehem [50 species], and Franconia, N. H. [87 species], Auk, pp. 149–155.—**1889.** ALLEN, F. H., Summer Birds at Bridgewater, N. H., Auk, pp. 76–79.—**1898.** DEARBORN, N., Preliminary List of the Birds of Belknap and Merrimack Counties, N. H., New Hampshire College, Durham, 8vo., 34 pp., 175 species.—**1900.** BATCHELDER, F. W., and FOGG, E. H., Preliminary List of Birds . . . . of Manchester, N. H., Proc. Manchester Inst. Arts and Sci., I, pp. 123–138, 132 species. (See also Proc. for 1901, 1902.)—**1900.** DEARBORN, N., The Birds of Durham and Vicinity, Cont. Zoöl. Lab. N. H. College Agric. and Mech. Arts, VI, 121 pp., map.— **1904.** ALLEN, G. M., The Birds of New Hampshire, Proc. Manchester Inst. Arts and Sci., IV, pp. 23–222, 283 species.—**1904.** COMEY, A. C., A Partial List of the Summer Birds of Holderness, N. H., Wilson Bull., XVI, 5–9 pp., 94 species.—**1911.** WRIGHT, H. W., The Birds of the Jefferson Region in the White Mountains, N. H., Manchester Inst. Arts and Sci., 126 pp., 188 species.—**1922.** WHITE, F. B., Check-List of the Birds of New Hampshire (Concord, N. H.), 120 pp., 292 species.—**1924.** WHITE, F. B., Birds of Concord, N. H. (E. C. Eastman Co., Concord), pp. 153.

NEW JERSEY

1885. BARRELL, H. F., Birds of the Upper Passaic Valley, New Jersey, Orn. and Oöl., X, pp. 21–23, 42, 43, 149 species.—**1887.** THURBER, E., A List of Birds of Morris County, N. J. (True Democratic Banner [newspaper], Morristown, N. J., Nov. 10, 17, 24), 205 species.—**1894.** STONE, W., The Birds of Eastern Pennsylvania and New Jersey, 8vo., 185 pp., Del. Valley Orn. Club, Phila., 346 species.—**1894.** STONE, W., Summer Birds of the Pine Barrens of New Jersey, Auk, pp. 133–140, 90 species.—**1897-1929.** STONE, W., Editor, Numerous Notes on Birds of Chiefly Southern New

Jersey, Proc. Del. Valley Orn. Club, Phila.—**1901. BABSON, W. A.**, The Birds of Princeton, N. J., Bull. Bird Club, Princeton Univ., I, pp. 7–82, 230 species.—**1906. CHAPMAN, F. M.** (See New York.)—**1907. HOLMES, L. K.**, Birds Found within a Radius of 12 Miles of Summit, N. J., Wilson Bull., XIX, pp. 21–27, 201 species (see also list of Summer Birds); *Ibid.*, XVII, pp. 8–12, and Hann, List of Summit Birds, *Ibid.*, pp. 117–122.— **1909. STONE, W.**, The Birds of New Jersey, Ann. Rep. N. J. State Museum for 1908, pp. 11–347, 409–419, pls. 1–84.—**1909. BAILY, W. L.**, Breeding Birds of Passaic and Sussex Counties, Cassinia, pp. 29–36, 94 species.— **1920. MILLER, W. DEW.**, The Summer Resident Warblers of Northern New Jersey, Auk, pp. 592, 593.

NEW YORK

1844. GIRAUD, J. P., JR., The Birds of Long Island . . . New York, 1 vol., 8vo., 397 pp., 286 species.—**1844. DEKAY, JAMES E.**, Zoölogy of New York, Part II, Birds (Albany), 1 vol., 4to., xii+380 pp., 141 col. pls.—**1876. FOWLER, H. G.**, Birds of Central New York, Forest and Stream, VI, pp. 180, 233, 284, 337, 402; VII, pp. 36, 52, 84, 230; also Additions *Ibid.*, p. 180, 170 species.—**1877. ROOSEVELT, T., JR.**, and **MINOT, H. D.**, The Summer Birds of the Adirondacks in Franklin County, N. Y., 8vo., 4 pp., 97 species.— **1879. RATHBUN, FRANK R.**, A Revised List of Birds of Central New York, (Cayuga, Onondaga, Seneca, Wayne, and Yates Counties, Auburn, N. Y.), 47 pp.; see also Orn. and Oöl., VII, 1882, pp. 132, 133, 14 additions.–**1879-80. MEARNS, E. A.**, A List of the Birds of the Hudson Highlands, Bull. Essex Inst., X, pp. 166–179; XI, pp. 43–52, 154–168, 189–204; XII, pp. 11–25, 109–128; XIII, pp. 75–93. (See also Auk, VII, 1890, pp. 55, 56), 214 species.—**1880. GREGG, W. H.**, Revised Catalogue of the Birds of Chemung County, New York (O. H. Wheeler, Elmira, N. Y.), 217 species.— **1881-84. MERRIAM, C. H.**, Preliminary List of Birds Ascertained to Occur in the Adirondack Region, Northeastern New York, Bull. N. O. C., VI, pp. 225–235; and Addenda VII, 1882, pp. 128, 256, 257. Auk, I, 1884, pp. 58, 59, 211 species.—**1882. BICKNELL, E. P.**, A Review of the Summer Birds of a part of the Catskill Mountains, with prefatory remarks on the faunal and floral features of the region, Trans. of the Linn. Soc. of New York, I, pp. 115–168, 90 species.—**1885. HOLLICK, A.**, Preliminary List of the Birds Known to Breed on Staten Island, Proc. Nat. Sci. Assoc. Staten Island, Extra No. 4, December, 67 species.—**1886. BARNUM, M. K.**, A Preliminary List of the Birds of Onondaga County, N. Y., Bull. of the Biol. Lab. of Syracuse University, 8vo., pp. 1–34, 204 species.—**1886. RALPH, W. L.**, and **BAGG, E.**, An Annotated List of the Birds of Oneida County, N. Y., and Its Immediate Vicinity, Trans. Oneida Hist. Soc., III, pp. 101–147, 224 species (see also *Ibid.*, VII, 1890, pp. 229–232); Orn. and Oöl. XIII, 1888, pp. 58, 59; Auk, XI, 1894, pp. 162–164.—**1886. WOODRUFF, L. B.**, and **PAINE, A. G., JR.**, Birds of Central Park, New York City: A Preliminary List, Forest and Stream, XXVI, pp. 386, 387, 487, 121 species.—**1889. BERGTOLD, W. H.**, A List of the Birds of Buffalo and Vicinity, Bull. Buffalo Nat. Field Club, I, 7, pp. 1–21, 237 species.—**1889. DAVISON, J. L.**, Birds of Niagara County, New York, Forest and Stream, XXXIII, pp. 164, 183, 303, 190 species.—**1892. CLUTE, W. N.**, The Avifauna of Broome Co., N. Y., Wilson Quart., pp. 59–64, 106 species.—**1896. SHORT, E. H.**, Birds of Western New York (F. H. Lattin, Albion, N. Y.), 20 pp., 229 species.—**1901. EATON, E. H.**, Birds of Western New York, Proc. Roch. Acad. IV, 64 pp., 299 species.—**1901. EMBODY, G. C.**, Birds of Madison County, N. Y., Bull. Dept. Geol. and Nat. Hist., Colgate University, Hamilton, N. Y., 8vo., 36 pp., 191 species. (See also Maxon, Auk, XX, p. 263.)—**1904. CHAPMAN, F. M.**, An Annotated List of the Birds Known to Breed within 50 Miles of New York City, Guide Leaflet, No. 14, Am. Mus. Nat. Hist., 31 pp., 13 illus.—**1906. CHAPMAN, F. M.**, The Birds of the Vicinity of New York City, Am. Mus. Nat. Hist., Guide Leaflet, No. 22, rev. ed., 96 pp., numerous illus., 353 species.—1907. BRAISLIN, W. C., A List of the Birds of Long Island, N. Y., Abst. Proc. Linn. Soc., N. Y., 1907, pp. 31–123, 364 species. (See also Auk, 1909, pp. 314–316.)—1910. REED, H. D., and WRIGHT, A. H., Vertebrates of the Cayuga Lake Basin, Proc. Am. Philos. Soc., XLVIII, pp. 370–459, 257 species.—1910. WRIGHT, A. H., and ALLEN, A. A., The Increase of Austral Birds at Ithaca, Auk, XXVII, pp. 63–66.— 1910. EATON, E. H., Birds of New York, I, Water and Game Birds, 4to., pp. 1–501, col. pls. [by Fuertes] 42.—1912. MURPHY, R. C., The Birds of Prospect Park, Brooklyn, Mus. News, Brooklyn Inst. Arts and Sci., VII, No. 8, 147 species.—1914. EATON, E. H., Birds of New York, Vol. II, 719 pp., illus., Land Birds.—1916. NICHOLS, J. T., and HARPER, F., Field Notes on Long Island Shore Birds, Auk, pp. 237–255, illus.—1920. SILLOWAY, P. M., Guide to the Summer Birds of the Bear Mountain Region, Bull. II, No. 21, N. Y. College Forestry, Syracuse, 105 pp., illus.—1922. DALEY, M. W., Birds of Frost Valley, Slide Mountain Region, southern Catskills, Auk, pp. 176–188, 90 species.—1923. GRISCOM, L., Birds of New York City Region, Am. Mus. Nat. Hist., 400 pp., 377 species and subspecies, illus.— 1923.—CROSBY, M. S., Supplementary Notes on the Birds of Dutchess Co., Auk, pp. 94–105, 106 species.—1923. SAUNDERS, A. A., Summer Birds of Alleghany State Park, Roosevelt Wild Life Bull., I, illus. (Univ. Syracuse, N. Y.).—1923. SILLOWAY, P. M., Summer Birds of the Adirondack Forest, Roosevelt Wild Life Bull., I, 4, pp. 387–526, 101 species, illus.—1925. CROSBY, M. S., Ten All-Day Censuses from Dutchess Co., N. Y., Wilson Bull., pp. 150–157, 220, from 102 to 129 species in mid-May.—1926. WALSH, L. L., Birds in Prospect Park, N. Y., Abst. Proc. Linn. Soc.—1926. SAUNDERS, A. A., Summer Birds in Central New York Marshes, Roosevelt Wild Life Bull., III, pp. 329–479, illus. (Univ. Syracuse, N. Y.).—1926. BICKNELL, E. P., Notes on Birds of Riverdale, N. Y., 1872–1901, edited by L. Griscom, Abst. Proc. Linn. Soc.—1926. KUERZI, J. F., Bird-Life of Greater Bronx Region, Abst. Proc. Linn. Soc., 274 species.—1928. CAHALANE, V. H., Wild Life of Southwestern Cattaraugus County, N. Y., Roosevelt Wild Life Bull., V, pp. 9–144.—1929. GRISCOM, L., Changes in Status of New York City Birds, Auk, pp. 45–57.—1929. Saunders, A. A., Summer Birds of the Northern Adirondack Mts., Roosevelt Wild Life Bull., V, 3, pp. 328–499. —1931. SPIKER, C. J., Biological Reconnaissance of the Peterboro Swamp and Labrador Pond Areas, Roosevelt Wild Life Bull., VI, pp. 1–151, illus.

NORTH CAROLINA

1871. COUES, E., Notes on the Natural History of Fort Macon, N. C., and Vicinity, Proc. Acad. Nat. Sci. Phila., XXIII, Birds, pp. 18–47; also *Ibid.*, 1878, pp. 22–24, 133 species.—1885. BRIMLEY, H. H. and C. S., Summer Birds of Raleigh, N. C., Orn. and Oöl., X, pp. 143, 144, 82 species.— 1885. BRIMLEY, H. H. and C. S., Winter Birds of Raleigh, N. C., Orn. and Oöl., X, p. 128, 72 species.—1886. BREWSTER, W., An Ornithological Reconnaissance in Western North Carolina, Auk, pp. 94–112, 173–179, 102 species.—1886. BATCHELDER, C. F., The North Carolina Mountains in Winter, Auk, pp. 307–314, 40 species.—1887. ATKINSON, G. F., Preliminary Catalogue of the Birds of North Carolina, Journ. Elisha Mitchell Sci. Soc., Part 2, pp. 44–87, 255 species: A compilation with some errors.— 1887. CAIRNS, J. S., A List of Birds of Buncombe County, N. C., Orn. and Oöl., XII, pp. 3–6, 169 species.—1887. SENNETT, G. B., Observations in Western North Carolina Mountains in 1886, Auk, pp. 240–245, 29 species.— 1888. BRIMLEY, C. S., A List of Birds Known to Breed at Raleigh, N. C., Orn. and Oöl., XIII, pp. 42, 43, 54 species; see also *Ibid.*, p. 187, Auk, XIV, p. 165.—1889. CAIRNS, J. S., The Summer Birds of Buncombe County, N. C., Orn. and Oöl., XIV, pp. 17–22, 123 species.—1893. BRIMLEY, C. S., Some Additions to the Avifauna of North Carolina, with Notes on Some Other Species, Auk, pp. 241–244, 48 species.—1897. SMITHWICK, J. W. P., Ornithology of North Carolina, Bull. 144, N. C. Agric. Exp. Sta., pp. 193–

228, 303 species.—**1899. Pearson, T. G.**, Preliminary List of Birds of Chapel Hill, N. C., Journ. Elisha Mitchell Sci. Soc., XVI, pp. 33–51, 132 species.—**1901. Bishop, L. B.**, The Winter Birds of Pea Island, N. C., Auk, pp. 260–268, 42 species.—**1905. Oberholser, H. C.**, Notes on the Mammals and Summer Birds of Western North Carolina (published by Biltmore Forest School), Birds, pp. 11–24, 136 species.—**1910. Philipp, P. B.**, (see S. C.).—**1917. Brimley, C. S.**, Thirty-two Years of Bird Migration at Raleigh, N. C., Auk, pp. 296–308.—**1919. Pearson, T. G.**, and **Brimley, C. S.** and **H. H.**, Birds of North Carolina, IV, Geol. and Econ. Surv., Raleigh, 380 pp., 24 col. pls., 275 text-figs.—**1928. Skinner, M. P.**, A Guide to the Winter Birds of the North Carolina Sandhills, 301 pp., illus. (Science Press, N. Y.).

Ohio

1877. Langdon, F. W., A Catalogue of the Birds of the Vicinity of Cincinnati, 8vo., 18 pp. (Salem, Mass.), 279 species.—**1879. Langdon, F. W.**, A Revised List of Cincinnati Birds, Journ. Cin. Soc. Nat. Hist., I, 4, pp. 167–193; see also *Ibid.*, III, pp. 121–127; V, 1882, p. 186; VI, 1883, pp. 12–31, 256 species.—**1882. Wheaton, J. M.**, Report on the Birds of Ohio, Rep. Geol. Surv. of Ohio, IV, I, pp. 188–628, 298 species.—**1891. Smith, R. W.**, A List of the Birds of Warren County, Ohio, Journ. Cin. Soc. Nat. Hist., XIV, pp. 105–133, 189 species.—**1896. Oberholser, H. C.**, A Preliminary List of the Birds of Wayne County, Bull. Ohio Agric. Exp. Sta., I, 4, pp. 243–354, 183 species.—**1902. Heninger, W. F.**, A Preliminary List of the Birds of Middle Southern Ohio, Wilson Bull., IX, pp. 77–93, 209 species; see also *Ibid.*, pp. 130–132; XII, 1905, pp. 89–93.—**1902. Jones, L.**, Bird Studies in Lorain County, Ohio, Wilson Bull., IX, pp. 37–58; also pp. 94–100.—**1903. Dawson, W. L.**, The Birds of Ohio, 4to., xlv+671 pp., many illus. (Wheaton Pub. Co., Columbus).—**1903. Field, A. I.**, Birds of Lecking County, Ohio, Bull. Sci. Lab. Denison Univ., XV, 203 species.—**1903. Jones, L.**, The Birds of Ohio, A Revised Catalogue, Ohio State Acad. of Sci., Special Papers, No. 6, 141 pp., 1 map, 318 species.—**1906. Heninger, W. F.**, A Preliminary List of Birds of Seneca County, Ohio, Wilson Bull., XVIII, pp. 47–60, 205 species.—**1909-10. Jones, L.**, The Birds of Cedar Point and Vicinity, Wilson Bull., XXI, pp. 55–76, 115–131, 187–202; XXII, pp. 25–41, 97–115, 172–182.—**1912. Jones, L.**, Avifauna of Lake Erie Islands, Wilson Bull., pp. 6–18, 95–108, 142–153, 171–186.—**1914. Jones, L.**, Nineteen Years of Bird Migration at Oberlin, Wilson Bull., pp. 198–205.

Pennsylvania

1844. Baird, W. M. and **S. F.**, List of Birds Found in the Vicinity of Carlisle, Cumberland County, Pa., Am. Journ. Sci. and Arts, XLVI, pp. 261–273, 201 species.—**1845. Baird, S. F.**, Catalogue of Birds Found in the Neighborhood of Carlisle, Cumberland County, Pa., Lit. Rec. and Journ. Linn. Assoc. of Penna. College, I, pp. 249–257, 203 species.—**1861. Barnard, V. A.**, A Catalogue of the Birds of Chester County, Pa.: Times of Arrival in Spring, Ann. Rep. Smiths. Inst., 1860, pp. 434–438, 191 species.—**1869. Turnbull, W. P.**, The Birds of East Pennsylvania and New Jersey. . . . 1 vol., roy. 8vo., and also 4to., xii+62 pp., 342 species.—**1880. Warren, H. B.**, The Birds of Chester County, Pa., Forest and Stream, XIII, pp. 1024, 1025; XIV, pp. 6, 25, 218 species.—**1886. Parker, H. G.**, List of Birds Near Philadelphia with the Dates That Sets of Eggs Were Taken, Orn. and Oöl., XI, pp. 70, 71, 76 species.—**1887. Pennock, C. J.**, Birds of Chester County, Pa., The Oölogist, IV, pp. 1–10, 234 species.—**1889. Ressel, C. B.**, Birds of Chester County, Pa., Orn. and Oöl., XIV, pp. 97–101, 112–116, 129, 130, 199 species.—**1890. Warren, B. H.**, Report on the Birds of Pennsylvania, with Special Reference to the Food Habits, 2d ed., Harrisburg, 8vo., xiv+434 pp., 100 col. pls.—**1891. Stone, W.**, The Summer Birds of Harvey's Lake, Luzerne County, Pa., with Remarks on the Faunal Position of the

Region, Proc. Acad. Nat. Sci., Phila., 1891, pp. 431–438, 54 species.—1892.
DWIGHT, J., JR., Summer Birds of the Crest of the Pennsylvania Alleghanies,
Auk, pp. 129–141, 84 species.—1893. JACOBS, J. W., Summer Birds of
Greene County, Pa., 8vo., 15 pp., 90 species (published by Author, Waynes-
burg, Pa.).—1893. TODD, W. E. C., Summer Birds of Indiana [65 species]
and Clearfield [55 species] Counties, Pa., Auk, pp. 35–46.—1894. STONE, W.,
The Birds of Eastern Pennsylvania and New Jersey, 8vo., vii+185 pp.,
(Del. Valley Orn. Club, Philadelphia), 346 species.—1895. ROTZELL, W. E.,
Birds of Narbeth, Pa., and Vicinity, The Citizen, June 22 and 29, and re-
printed in pamphlet, 8 pp., 108 species.—1896. BAILY, W. L., Summer Birds
of Northern Elk Co., Auk, pp. 289–297, 69 species.—1896. YOUNG, R. T.,
Summer Birds of Anthracite Coal Regions of Pennsylvania, Auk, pp. 278–
285, 69 species.—1897. MONTGOMERY, T. H., JR., A List of the Birds of the
Vicinity of West Chester, Chester County, Pa., Am. Nat., pp. 622–628,
812–814, 907–911, 145 species.—1897-1929. STONE, W., Editor Numerous
Notes on and Short Lists of Eastern Pennsylvania Birds, Proc. Del. Valley
Orn. Club, Phila.—1899. RHOADS, S. N., Notes on Some of the Rarer Birds
of Western Pennsylvania, Auk, pp. 308–313, 65 species.—1901. BURNS,
F. L., A Sectional Bird Census, at Berwyn, Pa., Wilson Bull. No. 36, pp.
84–103, 62 species.—1904. TODD, W. E. C., The Birds of Erie and Presque
Isle, Erie County, Pa., Annals Carnegie Mus., II, pp. 481–596, 4 pls.,
237 species.—1904. TODD, W. E. C., The Mammal and Bird Fauna of
Beaver County, Pa., Bausman's History of Beaver County, II, pp. 1195–
1202, 178 species.—1913. [BARTRAM, W., Migration at Kingsessing,
Philadelphia.] See STONE, W., Auk, pp. 325–358.—1919. BURNS, F. L.,
Ornithology of Chester County, Pa., 122 pp., illus. (Gorham Press, Boston),
247 species.—1923. BURLEIGH, T. D., Birds of Alleghany County, Pa.,
Wilson Bull., pp. 79–99, 138–147.—1924. BECK, R. H., Ornithology of
Lancaster County, Pa., p. 39 (Franklin and Marshall College).—1924.
BURLEIGH, T. D., Migration Notes from State College, Center County,
Pa., Wilson Bull., pp. 68–77, 128–131, 79 species.—1928. SUTTON, G. M.,
Birds of Pymatuning Swamp and Conneat Lake, Crawford County, Annals
Carnegie Museum XVIII, pp. 19–39.—1928. SUTTON, G. M., Introduction
to Birds of Pennsylvania; for beginners, with many line-cuts (J. H. McFar-
land Co., Harrisburg).—1930. POOLE, E. L., Bird-Life of Berks County,
Pa., Bull. No. 12, Reading Pub. Mus. and Art Gallery, pp. 1–70.

RHODE ISLAND

1899. HOWE, R. H., JR., and STURTEVANT, E., The Birds of Rhode
Island (published by Authors), 8vo., 111 pp., 291 species.—1908. Commis-
sioners of Birds, A Check-List of Rhode Island Nesting Birds, pp. 1–26,
104 species.—1913. HATHAWAY, H. S., Notes on the Occurrence and Nesting
of Certain Birds in Rhode Island, Auk, pp. 545–558, 65 species.

SOUTH CAROLINA

1868. COUES, E., Synopsis of the Birds of South Carolina, Proc. Boston
Soc. Nat. Hist., XII, pp. 104–127, 294 species.—1879. LOOMIS, L. M., A
Partial List of the Birds of Chester County, S. C., Bull. N. O. C., IV, pp.
209–218, 140 species; see also additions and notes, Auk, 1885, pp. 188–193;
1891, pp. 49–59, 167–173; 1892, pp. 28–39; 1894, pp. 26–39, 94–117.—1885.
HOXIE, W., Notes on the Birds of the Sea Islands, Orn. and Oöl., X, pp.
13–27, 29, 44–46, 62, 63; also Corrections and Additions, *Ibid.*, XI, 1886,
pp. 33, 34, 238 species.—1890. LOOMIS, L. M., Observations on Some of the
Summer Birds of the Mountain Portions of Pickens County, Auk, pp. 30–
39, 124–130, 76 species.—1891. LOOMIS, L. M., June Birds of Cæsar's Head,
S. C., Auk, pp. 323–333, 52 species.—1910. PHILIPP, P. B., List of Birds
Observed [in the Carolinas], Auk, pp. 312–322; see also Wayne, *Ibid.*, p.
464.—1910. WAYNE, A. T., Birds of South Carolina, Cont. from Charleston

Mus., I, 8vo., xxi+254, pp. 337 species.—1912. BRAGG, L. M., Birds of South Carolina, Suppl. to Wayne. Bull. Charleston Mus., VIII, Nos. 2, 3, 96 species.—1925. SPRUNT, A., JR., Avian City of the South Carolina Coast, Auk, pp. 311–319, illus.—1928. PICKENS, A. L., Birds of Upper South Carolina, Wilson Bull., pp. 182–191, 238–246, 220 species.

TENNESSEE

1886. FOX, W. H., List of Birds Found in Roane County, Tenn., During April, 1884, and March and April, 1885, Auk, pp. 315–320, 114 species.— 1895. RHOADS, S. N., Cont. Zoöl. Tenn., Proc. Acad. Nat. Sci., Phila., 1895, pp. 463–501; also Auk, 1896, p. 181, 223 species.—1910. HOWELL, A. H., Notes on the Birds of Kentucky and Tennessee, Auk, pp. 295–304, 162 species.—1917. TENNESSEE ORNITHOLOGICAL SOCIETY, Preliminary List of the Birds of Tennessee, 8vo., 28 pp., 270 species (Dept. Fish and Game, Nashville).

VERMONT

1901. HOWELL, A. H., Preliminary List of Summer Birds of Mt. Mansfield, Vt., Auk, pp. 337–347, 86 species.—1902. PERKINS, G. H., A Preliminary List of the Birds Found in Vermont, 21st Ann. Rep. Vt. State Bd. Agric., pp. 85–118, 261 species; see also HOWE, R. H., JR., Cont. N. A. Orn. II, pp. 5–22.—1903. DAVENPORT, E. B., Birds Observed on Mt. Mansfield and the West End of Stowe Valley at the Base of the Mountain, in the Summer of 1902, Wilson Bull., XV, pp. 77–86, 74 species.—1907. DAVENPORT, E. B., Birds of Windham and Bennington Counties, Bull. No. 2, Vermont Bird Club (Burlington, Vt.), pp. 5–14, 176 species.—1908. ALLEN, F. H., Summer Birds of Southern Vermont, Auk, pp. 56–64, 86 species.—1926. EATON, W. F., and CURRY, H. B., Summer Birds of Vermont, Joint Bull. No. 11, Vt. Bot. and Bird Clubs, 102 species.

VIRGINIA

1890. RIVES, WM. C., M. D., A Catalogue of the Birds of the Virginias, Proc. Newport Nat. Hist. Soc., Document VII, Newport, R. I., 8vo., 100 pp., 305 species.—1902. DANIELS, J. W., Summer Birds of the Great Dismal Swamp, Auk, pp. 15–18, 41 species.—1910. EMBODY, G. C., A List of Birds Observed at Ashland, Va., Auk, pp. 169–177, 114 species.—1911. HOWELL, A. B., A Comparative Study at Cobb's Island, Va., Auk, pp. 449–453; see also PEARSON, T. G., Oölogist, IX, No. 8, and CHAPMAN, F. M., Camps and Cruises.—1912. SMYTH, E. A., JR., Birds Observed in Montgomery County, Va., Auk, pp. 508–527, 195 species.—1913. BAILEY, H. H., The Birds of Virginia (J. P. Bell Co., Lynchburg), 8vo., 362 pp., illus.; see Auk, XXX, p. 594.—1927. SMYTH, E. A., JR., Add. Notes on Birds Montgomery Co., Va., Auk, XLIV, 44–46, 13 species; total, 208.

WEST VIRGINIA

1873. SCOTT, W. E. D., Partial List of the Summer Birds of Kanawha County, W. Va., with Annotations, Proc. Boston Soc. Hist., XV, pp. 219–227, 86 species.—1875. BREWSTER, W., Some Observations on the Birds of Ritchie County, W. Va., Annals of the Lyc. Nat. Hist., N. Y., XI, pp. 129–146, 100 species.—1888. DOAN, W. D., Birds of West Virginia, Bull. 3, Agric. Exp. Sta., Morgantown, 200 species.—1889. SURBER, T., Birds of Greenbriar County, W. Va., The Hawkeye Orn. and Oöl. (E. B. Webster, Cresco, Iowa), II, pp. 2–4, 13–15, 29–32, 121 species.—1890. RIVES, W. C. (See Virginia.)—1898. RIVES, W. C., Summer Birds of the West Virginia Spruce Belt, Auk, pp. 131–137, 46 species.—1909. BROOKS, E. A., West Virginia Birds in State Board of Agriculture, Report W. Va. State Board

Agric. for 1908, pp. 3–62, 193 species.—1913. BROOKS, E. A., Birds of West Virginia, Second Biennial Rep. Forest Game and Fish Warden, pp. 87–106, 246 species.—1924. JOHNSON, J. H., Birds of West Virginia, 138 pp., illus. (Dept. Agric., Charleston).

WISCONSIN

1853. HOY, P. R., Notes on the Ornithology of Wisconsin, Proc. Acad. Nat. Sci., Phila., VI, pp. 304–313, 381–385, 423–429, 283 species; revised with additions in the Trans. Wisc. State Agric. Soc., 1852, II, pp. 341–364.— 1854. BARRY, A. C., On the Ornithological Fauna of Wisconsin, Proc. Boston Soc. Nat. Hist., V, 1854, pp. 1–13, 218 species.—1882. KING, F. H., Economic Relations of Wisconsin Birds, Wisc. Geol. Survey, I, pp. 441– 610; figs. 103–144, 295 species.—1883. WILLARD, S. W., Migration and Distribution of North American Birds in Brown and Outgamie Counties, Trans. Wisc. Acad. Sci. Arts and Letters, VI, pp. 177–196, 210 species.— 1894. GRUNDTVIG, F. L., The Birds of Shiocton in Bovina, Outgamie County, Wisc., Trans. Wisc. Acad. Sci., X, pp. 73–158, 183 species.—1903. KUMLIEN, L., and HOLLISTER, N., The Birds of Wisconsin, Bull. Wisc. Nat. Hist. Soc., III (N. S.), pp. 1–143, 8 half-tones, 357 species.—1909. CORY, C. B., (see Illinois).—1913. CAHN, A. R., Birds of Waukeshaw County, Wisc., Wisc. Nat. Hist. Soc., XI, pp. 113–149, 202 species.—1915. LOWE, J. N., Birds of Green Lake County, Wisc., Bull. Wisc. Nat. Hist. Soc., XXXI, p. 2, 211 species.—1923. JACKSON, H. H. T., Notes on the Summer Birds of the Mamie Lake Region, Wisc., Auk, pp. 478–489, illus., 89 species.—1925. SCHORGER, A. W., Summer Birds of Lake Owen, Wisc., Auk, pp. 64–70, 75 species.—1927. SCHORGER, A. W., Distribution of Some Wisconsin Birds, Auk, pp. 235–240, 17 species.—1929. SCHORGER, A. W., Birds of Dane County, Wisc., Wisc. Acad. Sci. Arts and Letters, XXIV, pp. 457– 499.

INDEX

CATALOGUE OF DOVER BOOKS

Books Explaining Science and Mathematics

WHAT IS SCIENCE?, N. Campbell. The role of experiment and measurement, the function of mathematics, the nature of scientific laws, the difference between laws and theories, the limitations of science, and many similarly provocative topics are treated clearly and without technicalities by an eminent scientist. "Still an excellent introduction to scientific philosophy," H. Margenau in PHYSICS TODAY. "A first-rate primer . . . deserves a wide audience," SCIENTIFIC AMERICAN. 192pp. 5⅜ x 8.   S43 Paperbound **$1.25**

THE NATURE OF PHYSICAL THEORY, P. W. Bridgman. A Nobel Laureate's clear, non-technical lectures on difficulties and paradoxes connected with frontier research on the physical sciences. Concerned with such central concepts as thought, logic, mathematics, relativity, probability, wave mechanics, etc. he analyzes the contributions of such men as Newton, Einstein, Bohr, Heisenberg, and many others. "Lucid and entertaining . . . recommended to anyone who wants to get some insight into current philosophies of science," THE NEW PHILOSOPHY. Index. xi + 138pp. 5⅜ x 8.   S33 Paperbound **$1.25**

EXPERIMENT AND THEORY IN PHYSICS, Max Born. A Nobel Laureate examines the nature of experiment and theory in theoretical physics and analyzes the advances made by the great physicists of our day: Heisenberg, Einstein, Bohr, Planck, Dirac, and others. The actual process of creation is detailed step-by-step by one who participated. A fine examination of the scientific method at work. 44pp. 5⅜ x 8.   S308 Paperbound **75¢**

THE PSYCHOLOGY OF INVENTION IN THE MATHEMATICAL FIELD, J. Hadamard. The reports of such men as Descartes, Pascal, Einstein, Poincaré, and others are considered in this investigation of the method of idea-creation in mathematics and other sciences and the thinking process in general. How do ideas originate? What is the role of the unconscious? What is Poincaré's forgetting hypothesis? are some of the fascinating questions treated. A penetrating analysis of Einstein's thought processes concludes the book. xiii + 145pp. 5⅜ x 8.   T107 Paperbound **$1.25**

THE NATURE OF LIGHT AND COLOUR IN THE OPEN AIR, M. Minnaert. Why are shadows sometimes blue, sometimes green, or other colors depending on the light and surroundings? What causes mirages? Why do multiple suns and moons appear in the sky? Professor Minnaert explains these unusual phenomena and hundreds of others in simple, easy-to-understand terms based on optical laws and the properties of light and color. No mathematics is required but artists, scientists, students, and everyone fascinated by these "tricks" of nature will find thousands of useful and amazing pieces of information. Hundreds of observational experiments are suggested which require no special equipment. 200 illustrations; 42 photos. xvi + 362pp. 5⅜ x 8.   T196 Paperbound **$2.00**

THE UNIVERSE OF LIGHT, W. Bragg. Sir William Bragg, Nobel Laureate and great modern physicist, is also well known for his powers of clear exposition. Here he analyzes all aspects of light for the layman: lenses, reflection, refraction, the optics of vision, x-rays, the photoelectric effect, etc. He tells you what causes the color of spectra, rainbows, and soap bubbles, how magic mirrors work, and much more. Dozens of simple experiments are described. Preface. Index. 199 line drawings and photographs, including 2 full-page color plates. x + 283pp. 5⅜ x 8.   T538 Paperbound **$1.85**

SOAP-BUBBLES: THEIR COLOURS AND THE FORCES THAT MOULD THEM, C. V. Boys. For continuing popularity and validity as scientific primer, few books can match this volume of easily-followed experiments, explanations. Lucid exposition of complexities of liquid films, surface tension and related phenomena, bubbles' reaction to heat, motion, music, magnetic fields. Experiments with capillary attraction, soap bubbles on frames, composite bubbles, liquid cylinders and jets, bubbles other than soap, etc. Wonderful introduction to scientific method, natural laws that have many ramifications in areas of modern physics. Only complete edition in print. New Introduction by S. Z. Lewin, New York University. 83 illustrations; 1 full-page color plate. xii + 190pp. 5⅜ x 8½.   T542 Paperbound **95¢**

CATALOGUE OF DOVER BOOKS

THE STORY OF X-RAYS FROM RONTGEN TO ISOTOPES, A. R. Bleich, M.D. This book, by a member of the American College of Radiology, gives the scientific explanation of x-rays, their applications in medicine, industry and art, and their danger (and that of atmospheric radiation) to the individual and the species. You learn how radiation therapy is applied against cancer, how x-rays diagnose heart disease and other ailments, how they are used to examine mummies for information on diseases of early societies, and industrial materials for hidden weaknesses. 54 illustrations show x-rays of flowers, bones, stomach, gears with flaws, etc. 1st publication. Index. xix + 186pp. 5⅜ x 8.   T622 Paperbound **$1.35**

SPINNING TOPS AND GYROSCOPIC MOTION, John Perry. A classic elementary text of the dynamics of rotation — the behavior and use of rotating bodies such as gyroscopes and tops. In simple, everyday English you are shown how quasi-rigidity is induced in discs of paper, smoke rings, chains, etc., by rapid motions; why a gyrostat falls and why a top rises; precession; how the earth's motion affects climate; and many other phenomena. Appendix on practical use of gyroscopes. 62 figures. 128pp. 5⅜ x 8.   T416 Paperbound **$1.00**

SNOW CRYSTALS, W. A. Bentley, M. J. Humphreys. For almost 50 years W. A. Bentley photographed snow flakes in his laboratory in Jericho, Vermont; in 1931 the American Meteorological Society gathered together the best of his work, some 2400 photographs of snow flakes, plus a few ice flowers, windowpane frosts, dew, frozen rain, and other ice formations. Pictures were selected for beauty and scientific value. A very valuable work to anyone in meteorology, cryology; most interesting to layman; extremely useful for artist who wants beautiful, crystalline designs. All copyright free. Unabridged reprint of 1931 edition. 2453 illustrations. 227pp. 8 x 10½.   T287 Paperbound **$3.00**

A DOVER SCIENCE SAMPLER, edited by George Barkin. A collection of brief, non-technical passages from 44 Dover Books Explaining Science for the enjoyment of the science-minded browser. Includes work of Bertrand Russell, Poincaré, Laplace, Max Born, Galileo, Newton; material on physics, mathematics, metallurgy, anatomy, astronomy, chemistry, etc. You will be fascinated by Martin Gardner's analysis of the sincere pseudo-scientist, Moritz's account of Newton's absentmindedness, Bernard's examples of human vivisection, etc. Illustrations from the Diderot Pictorial Encyclopedia and De Re Metallica. 64 pages.   **FREE**

THE STORY OF ATOMIC THEORY AND ATOMIC ENERGY, J. G. Feinberg. A broader approach to subject of nuclear energy and its cultural implications than any other similar source. Very readable, informal, completely non-technical text. Begins with first atomic theory, 600 B.C. and carries you through the work of Mendelejeff, Röntgen, Madame Curie, to Einstein's equation and the A-bomb. New chapter goes through thermonuclear fission, binding energy, other events up to 1959. Radioactive decay and radiation hazards, future benefits, work of Bohr, moderns, hundreds more topics. "Deserves special mention . . . not only authoritative but thoroughly popular in the best sense of the word," Saturday Review. Formerly, "The Atom Story." Expanded with new chapter. Three appendixes. Index. 34 illustrations. vii + 243pp. 5⅜ x 8.   T625 Paperbound **$1.60**

THE STRANGE STORY OF THE QUANTUM, AN ACCOUNT FOR THE GENERAL READER OF THE GROWTH OF IDEAS UNDERLYING OUR PRESENT ATOMIC KNOWLEDGE, B. Hoffmann. Presents lucidly and expertly, with barest amount of mathematics, the problems and theories which led to modern quantum physics. Dr. Hoffmann begins with the closing years of the 19th century, when certain trifling discrepancies were noticed, and with illuminating analogies and examples takes you through the brilliant concepts of Planck, Einstein, Pauli, Broglie, Bohr, Schroedinger, Heisenberg, Dirac, Sommerfeld, Feynman, etc. This edition includes a new, long postscript carrying the story through 1958. "Of the books attempting an account of the history and contents of our modern atomic physics which have come to my attention, this is the best," H. Margenau, Yale University, in "American Journal of Physics." 32 tables and line illustrations. Index. 275pp. 5⅜ x 8.   T518 Paperbound **$1.50**

SPACE AND TIME, E. Borel. Written by a versatile mathematician of world renown with his customary lucidity and precision, this introduction to relativity for the layman presents scores of examples, analogies, and illustrations that open up new ways of thinking about space and time. It covers abstract geometry and geographical maps, continuity and topology, the propagation of light, the special theory of relativity, the general theory of relativity, theoretical researches, and much more. Mathematical notes. 2 Indexes. 4 Appendices. 15 figures. xvi + 243pp. 5⅜ x 8.   T592 Paperbound **$1.45**

FROM EUCLID TO EDDINGTON: A STUDY OF THE CONCEPTIONS OF THE EXTERNAL WORLD, Sir Edmund Whittaker. A foremost British scientist traces the development of theories of natural philosophy from the western rediscovery of Euclid to Eddington, Einstein, Dirac, etc. The inadequacy of classical physics is contrasted with present day attempts to understand the physical world through relativity, non-Euclidean geometry, space curvature, wave mechanics, etc. 5 major divisions of examination: Space; Time and Movement; the Concepts of Classical Physics; the Concepts of Quantum Mechanics; the Eddington Universe. 212pp. 5⅜ x 8.   T491 Paperbound **$1.35**

CATALOGUE OF DOVER BOOKS

Nature, Biology

NATURE RECREATION: Group Guidance for the Out-of-doors, William Gould Vinal. Intended for both the uninitiated nature instructor and the education student on the college level, this complete "how-to" program surveys the entire area of nature education for the young. Philosophy of nature recreation; requirements, responsibilities, important information for group leaders; nature games; suggested group projects; conducting meetings and getting discussions started; etc. Scores of immediately applicable teaching aids, plus completely updated sources of information, pamphlets, field guides, recordings, etc. Bibliography. 74 photographs. + 310pp. 5⅜ x 8½.   T1015 Paperbound **$1.75**

HOW TO KNOW THE WILD FLOWERS, Mrs. William Starr Dana. Classic nature book that has introduced thousands to wonders of American wild flowers. Color-season principle of organization is easy to use, even by those with no botanical training, and the genial, refreshing discussions of history, folklore, uses of over 1,000 native and escape flowers, foliage plants are informative as well as fun to read. Over 170 full-page plates, collected from several editions, may be colored in to make permanent records of finds. Revised to conform with 1950 edition of Gray's Manual of Botany. xlii + 438pp. 5⅜ x 8½.   T332 Paperbound **$2.00**

HOW TO KNOW THE FERNS, F. T. Parsons. Ferns, among our most lovely native plants, are all too little known. This classic of nature lore will enable the layman to identify almost any American fern he may come across. After an introduction on the structure and life of ferns, the 57 most important ferns are fully pictured and described (arranged upon a simple identification key). Index of Latin and English names. 61 illustrations and 42 full-page plates. xiv + 215pp. 5⅜ x 8.   T740 Paperbound **$1.35**

MANUAL OF THE TREES OF NORTH AMERICA, Charles Sprague Sargent. Still unsurpassed as most comprehensive, reliable study of North American tree characteristics, precise locations and distribution. By dean of American dendrologists. Every tree native to U.S., Canada, Alaska, 185 genera, 717 species, described in detail—leaves, flowers, fruit, winterbuds, bark, wood, growth habits etc. plus discussion of varieties and local variants, immaturity variations. Over 100 keys, including unusual 11-page analytical key to genera, aid in identification. 783 clear illustrations of flowers, fruit, leaves. An unmatched permanent reference work for all nature lovers. Second enlarged (1926) edition. Synopsis of families. Analytical key to genera. Glossary of technical terms. Index. 783 illustrations, 1 map. Two volumes. Total of 982pp. 5⅜ x 8.   T277 Vol. I Paperbound **$2.25**
                                                                  T278 Vol. II Paperbound **$2.25**
                                                                  The set **$4.50**

TREES OF THE EASTERN AND CENTRAL UNITED STATES AND CANADA, W. M. Harlow. A revised edition of a standard middle-level guide to native trees and important escapes. More than 140 trees are described in detail, and illustrated with more than 600 drawings and photographs. Supplementary keys will enable the careful reader to identify almost any tree he might encounter. xiii + 288pp. 5⅜ x 8.   T395 Paperbound **$1.35**

GUIDE TO SOUTHERN TREES, Ellwood S. Harrar and J. George Harrar. All the essential information about trees indigenous to the South, in an extremely handy format. Introductory essay on methods of tree classification and study, nomenclature, chief divisions of Southern trees, etc. Approximately 100 keys and synopses allow for swift, accurate identification of trees. Numerous excellent illustrations, non-technical text make this a useful book for teachers of biology or natural science, nature lovers, amateur naturalists. Revised 1962 edition. Index. Bibliography. Glossary of technical terms. 920 illustrations; 201 full-page plates. ix + 709pp. 4⅝ x 6⅜.   T945 Paperbound **$2.35**

FRUIT KEY AND TWIG KEY TO TREES AND SHRUBS, W. M. Harlow. Bound together in one volume for the first time, these handy and accurate keys to fruit and twig identification are the only guides of their sort with photographs (up to 3 times natural size). "Fruit Key": Key to over 120 different deciduous and evergreen fruits. 139 photographs and 11 line drawings. Synoptic summary of fruit types. Bibliography. 2 Indexes (common and scientific names). "Twig Key": Key to over 160 different twigs and buds. 173 photographs. Glossary of technical terms. Bibliography. 2 Indexes (common and scientific names). Two volumes bound as one. Total of xvii + 126pp. 5⅝ x 8⅜.   T511 Paperbound **$1.25**

INSECT LIFE AND INSECT NATURAL HISTORY, S. W. Frost. A work emphasizing habits, social life, and ecological relations of insects, rather than more academic aspects of classification and morphology. Prof. Frost's enthusiasm and knowledge are everywhere evident as he discusses insect associations and specialized habits like leaf-rolling, leaf-mining, and case-making, the gall insects, the boring insects, aquatic insects, etc. He examines all sorts of matters not usually covered in general works, such as: insects as human food, insect music and musicians, insect response to electric and radio waves, use of insects in art and literature. The admirably executed purpose of this book, which covers the middle ground between elementary treatment and scholarly monographs, is to excite the reader to observe for himself. Over 700 illustrations. Extensive bibliography. x + 524pp. 5⅜ x 8.   T517 Paperbound **$2.45**

COMMON SPIDERS OF THE UNITED STATES, J. H. Emerton. Here is a nature hobby you can pursue right in your own cellar! Only non-technical, but thorough, reliable guide to spiders for the layman. Over 200 spiders from all parts of the country, arranged by scientific classification, are identified by shape and color, number of eyes, habitat and range, habits, etc. Full text, 501 line drawings and photographs, and valuable introduction explain webs, poisons, threads, capturing and preserving spiders, etc. Index. New synoptic key by S. W. Frost. xxiv + 225pp. 5⅜ x 8. T223 Paperbound **$1.45**

THE LIFE STORY OF THE FISH: HIS MANNERS AND MORALS, Brian Curtis. A comprehensive, non-technical survey of just about everything worth knowing about fish. Written for the aquarist, the angler, and the layman with an inquisitive mind, the text covers such topics as evolution, external covering and protective coloration, physics and physiology of vision, maintenance of equilibrium, function of the lateral line canal for auditory and temperature senses, nervous system, function of the air bladder, reproductive system and methods—courtship, mating, spawning, care of young—and many more. Also sections on game fish, the problems of conservation and a fascinating chapter on fish curiosities. "Clear, simple language . . . excellent judgment in choice of subjects . . . delightful sense of humor," New York Times. Revised (1949) edition. Index. Bibliography of 72 items. 6 full-page photographic plates. xii + 284pp. 5⅜ x 8. T929 Paperbound **$1.65**

BATS, Glover Morrill Allen. The most comprehensive study of bats as a life-form by the world's foremost authority. A thorough summary of just about everything known about this fascinating and mysterious flying mammal, including its unique location sense, hibernation and cycles, its habitats and distribution, its wing structure and flying habits, and its relationship to man in the long history of folklore and superstition. Written on a middle-level, the book can be profitably studied by a trained zoologist and thoroughly enjoyed by the layman. "An absorbing text with excellent illustrations. Bats should have more friends and fewer thoughtless detractors as a result of the publication of this volume," William Beebe, Books. Extensive bibliography. 57 photographs and illustrations. x + 368pp. 5⅜ x 8½. T984 Paperbound **$2.00**

BIRDS AND THEIR ATTRIBUTES, Glover Morrill Allen. A fine general introduction to birds as living organisms, especially valuable because of emphasis on structure, physiology, habits, behavior. Discusses relationship of bird to man, early attempts at scientific ornithology, feathers and coloration, skeletal structure including bills, legs and feet, wings. Also food habits, evolution and present distribution, feeding and nest-building, still unsolved questions of migrations and location sense, many more similar topics. Final chapter on classification, nomenclature. A good popular-level summary for the biologist; a first-rate introduction for the layman. Reprint of 1925 edition. References and index. 51 illustrations. viii + 338pp. 5⅜ x 8½. T957 Paperbound **$1.85**

LIFE HISTORIES OF NORTH AMERICAN BIRDS, Arthur Cleveland Bent. Bent's monumental series of books on North American birds, prepared and published under auspices of Smithsonian Institute, is the definitive coverage of the subject, the most-used single source of information. Now the entire set is to be made available by Dover in inexpensive editions. This encyclopedic collection of detailed, specific observations utilizes reports of hundreds of contemporary observers, writings of such naturalists as Audubon, Burroughs, William Brewster, as well as author's own extensive investigations. Contains literally everything known about life history of each bird considered: nesting, eggs, plumage, distribution and migration, voice, enemies, courtship, etc. These not over-technical works are musts for ornithologists, conservationists, amateur naturalists, anyone seriously interested in American birds.

BIRDS OF PREY. More than 100 subspecies of hawks, falcons, eagles, buzzards, condors and owls, from the common barn owl to the extinct caracara of Guadaloupe Island. 400 photographs. Two volume set. Index for each volume. Bibliographies of 403, 520 items. 197 full-page plates. Total of 907pp. 5⅜ x 8½.
Vol. I T931 Paperbound **$2.50**
Vol. II T932 Paperbound **$2.50**

WILD FOWL. Ducks, geese, swans, and tree ducks—73 different subspecies. Two volume set. Index for each volume. Bibliographies of 124, 144 items. 106 full-page plates. Total of 685pp. 5⅜ x 8½.
Vol. I T285 Paperbound **$2.50**
Vol. II T286 Paperbound **$2.50**

SHORE BIRDS. 81 varieties (sandpipers, woodcocks, plovers, snipes, phalaropes, curlews, oyster catchers, etc.). More than 200 photographs of eggs, nesting sites, adult and young of important species. Two volume set. Index for each volume. Bibliographies of 261, 188 items. 121 full-page plates. Total of 860pp. 5⅜ x 8½.
Vol. I T933 Paperbound **$2.35**
Vol. II T934 Paperbound **$2.35**

THE LIFE OF PASTEUR, R. Vallery-Radot. 13th edition of this definitive biography, cited in Encyclopaedia Britannica. Authoritative, scholarly, well-documented with contemporary quotes, observations; gives complete picture of Pasteur's personal life; especially thorough presentation of scientific activities with silkworms, fermentation, hydrophobia, inoculation, etc. Introduction by Sir William Osler. Index. 505pp. 5⅜ x 8. T632 Paperbound **$2.00**

Puzzles, Mathematical Recreations

SYMBOLIC LOGIC and THE GAME OF LOGIC, Lewis Carroll. "Symbolic Logic" is not concerned with modern symbolic logic, but is instead a collection of over 380 problems posed with charm and imagination, using the syllogism, and a fascinating diagrammatic method of drawing conclusions. In "The Game of Logic" Carroll's whimsical imagination devises a logical game played with 2 diagrams and counters (included) to manipulate hundreds of tricky syllogisms. The final section, "Hit or Miss" is a lagniappe of 101 additional puzzles in the delightful Carroll manner. Until this reprint edition, both of these books were rarities costing up to $15 each. Symbolic Logic: Index. xxxi + 199pp. The Game of Logic: 96pp. 2 vols. bound as one. 5⅜ x 8. **T492 Paperbound $1.50**

PILLOW PROBLEMS and A TANGLED TALE, Lewis Carroll. One of the rarest of all Carroll's works, "Pillow Problems" contains 72 original math puzzles, all typically ingenious. Particularly fascinating are Carroll's answers which remain exactly as he thought them out, reflecting his actual mental process. The problems in "A Tangled Tale" are in story form, originally appearing as a monthly magazine serial. Carroll not only gives the solutions, but uses answers sent in by readers to discuss wrong approaches and misleading paths, and grades them for insight. Both of these books were rarities until this edition, "Pillow Problems" costing up to $25, and "A Tangled Tale" $15. Pillow Problems: Preface and Introduction by Lewis Carroll. xx + 109pp. A Tangled Tale: 6 illustrations. 152pp. Two vols. bound as one. 5⅜ x 8. **T493 Paperbound $1.50**

AMUSEMENTS IN MATHEMATICS, Henry Ernest Dudeney. The foremost British originator of mathematical puzzles is always intriguing, witty, and paradoxical in this classic, one of the largest collections of mathematical amusements. More than 430 puzzles, problems, and paradoxes. Mazes and games, problems on number manipulation, unicursal and other route problems, puzzles on measuring, weighing, packing, age, kinship, chessboards, joiners', crossing river, plane figure dissection, and many others. Solutions. More than 450 illustrations. vii + 258pp. 5⅜ x 8. **T473 Paperbound $1.25**

THE CANTERBURY PUZZLES, Henry Dudeney. Chaucer's pilgrims set one another problems in story form. Also Adventures of the Puzzle Club, the Strange Escape of the King's Jester, the Monks of Riddlewell, the Squire's Christmas Puzzle Party, and others. All puzzles are original, based on dissecting plane figures, arithmetic, algebra, elementary calculus and other branches of mathematics, and purely logical ingenuity. "The limit of ingenuity and intricacy," The Observer. Over 110 puzzles. Full Solutions. 150 illustrations. vii + 225pp. 5⅜ x 8. **T474 Paperbound $1.25**

MATHEMATICAL EXCURSIONS, H. A. Merrill. Even if you hardly remember your high school math, you'll enjoy the 90 stimulating problems contained in this book and you will come to understand a great many mathematical principles with surprisingly little effort. Many useful shortcuts and diversions not generally known are included: division by inspection, Russian peasant multiplication, memory systems for pi, building odd and even magic squares, square roots by geometry, dyadic systems, and many more. Solutions to difficult problems. 50 illustrations. 145pp. 5⅜ x 8. **T350 Paperbound $1.00**

MAGIC SQUARES AND CUBES, W. S. Andrews. Only book-length treatment in English, a thorough non-technical description and analysis. Here are nasik, overlapping, pandiagonal, serrated squares; magic circles, cubes, spheres, rhombuses. Try your hand at 4-dimensional magical figures! Much unusual folklore and tradition included. High school algebra is sufficient. 754 diagrams and illustrations. viii + 419pp. 5⅜ x 8. **T658 Paperbound $1.85**

CALIBAN'S PROBLEM BOOK: MATHEMATICAL, INFERENTIAL AND CRYPTOGRAPHIC PUZZLES, H. Phillips (Caliban), S. T. Shovelton, G. S. Marshall. 105 ingenious problems by the greatest living creator of puzzles based on logic and inference. Rigorous, modern, piquant; reflecting their author's unusual personality, these intermediate and advanced puzzles all involve the ability to reason clearly through complex situations; some call for mathematical knowledge, ranging from algebra to number theory. Solutions. xi + 180pp. 5⅜ x 8.
T736 Paperbound $1.25

MATHEMATICAL PUZZLES FOR BEGINNERS AND ENTHUSIASTS, G. Mott-Smith. 188 mathematical puzzles based on algebra, dissection of plane figures, permutations, and probability, that will test and improve your powers of inference and interpretation. The Odic Force, The Spider's Cousin, Ellipse Drawing, theory and strategy of card and board games like tit-tat-toe, go moku, salvo, and many others. 100 pages of detailed mathematical explanations. Appendix of primes, square roots, etc. 135 illustrations. 2nd revised edition. 248pp. 5⅜ x 8.
T198 Paperbound $1.00

MATHEMAGIC, MAGIC PUZZLES, AND GAMES WITH NUMBERS, R. V. Heath. More than 60 new puzzles and stunts based on the properties of numbers. Easy techniques for multiplying large numbers mentally, revealing hidden numbers magically, finding the date of any day in any year, and dozens more. Over 30 pages devoted to magic squares, triangles, cubes, circles, etc. Edited by J. S. Meyer. 76 illustrations. 128pp. 5⅜ x 8. **T110 Paperbound $1.00**

THE BOOK OF MODERN PUZZLES, G. L. Kaufman. A completely new series of puzzles as fascinating as crossword and deduction puzzles but based upon different principles and techniques. Simple 2-minute teasers, word labyrinths, design and pattern puzzles, logic and observation puzzles — over 150 braincrackers. Answers to all problems. 116 illustrations. 192pp. 5⅜ x 8.
T143 Paperbound **$1.00**

NEW WORD PUZZLES, G. L. Kaufman. 100 ENTIRELY NEW puzzles based on words and their combinations that will delight crossword puzzle, Scrabble and Jotto fans. Chess words, based on the moves of the chess king; design-onyms, symmetrical designs made of synonyms; rhymed double-crostics; syllable sentences; addle letter anagrams; alphagrams; linkograms; and many others all brand new. Full solutions. Space to work problems. 196 figures. vi + 122pp. 5⅜ x 8.
T344 Paperbound **$1.00**

MAZES AND LABYRINTHS: A BOOK OF PUZZLES, W. Shepherd. Mazes, formerly associated with mystery and ritual, are still among the most intriguing of intellectual puzzles. This is a novel and different collection of 50 amusements that embody the principle of the maze: mazes in the classical tradition; 3-dimensional, ribbon, and Möbius-strip mazes; hidden messages; spatial arrangements; etc.—almost all built on amusing story situations. 84 illustrations. Essay on maze psychology. Solutions. xv + 122pp. 5⅜ x 8.
T731 Paperbound **$1.00**

MAGIC TRICKS & CARD TRICKS, W. Jonson. Two books bound as one. 52 tricks with cards, 37 tricks with coins, bills, eggs, smoke, ribbons, slates, etc. Details on presentation, misdirection, and routining will help you master such famous tricks as the Changing Card, Card in the Pocket, Four Aces, Coin Through the Hand, Bill in the Egg, Afghan Bands, and over 75 others. If you follow the lucid exposition and key diagrams carefully, you will finish these two books with an astonishing mastery of magic. 106 figures. 224pp. 5⅜ x 8. T909 Paperbound **$1.00**

PANORAMA OF MAGIC, Milbourne Christopher. A profusely illustrated history of stage magic, a unique selection of prints and engravings from the author's private collection of magic memorabilia, the largest of its kind. Apparatus, stage settings and costumes; ingenious ads distributed by the performers and satiric broadsides passed around in the streets ridiculing pompous showmen; programs; decorative souvenirs. The lively text, by one of America's foremost professional magicians, is full of anecdotes about almost legendary wizards: Dede, the Egyptian; Philadelphia, the wonder-worker; Robert-Houdin, "the father of modern magic;" Harry Houdini; scores more. Altogether a pleasure package for anyone interested in magic, stage setting and design, ethnology, psychology, or simply in unusual people. A Dover original. 295 illustrations; 8 in full color. Index. viii + 216pp. 8⅜ x 11¼.
T774 Paperbound **$2.25**

HOUDINI ON MAGIC, Harry Houdini. One of the greatest magicians of modern times explains his most prized secrets. How locks are picked, with illustrated picks and skeleton keys; how a girl is sawed into twins; how to walk through a brick wall — Houdini's explanations of 44 stage tricks with many diagrams. Also included is a fascinating discussion of great magicians of the past and the story of his fight against fraudulent mediums and spiritualists. Edited by W.B. Gibson and M.N. Young. Bibliography. 155 figures, photos. xv + 280pp. 5⅜ x 8.
T384 Paperbound **$1.35**

MATHEMATICS, MAGIC AND MYSTERY, Martin Gardner. Why do card tricks work? How do magicians perform astonishing mathematical feats? How is stage mind-reading possible? This is the first book length study explaining the application of probability, set theory, theory of numbers, topology, etc., to achieve many startling tricks. Non-technical, accurate, detailed! 115 sections discuss tricks with cards, dice, coins, knots, geometrical vanishing illusions, how a Curry square "demonstrates" that the sum of the parts may be greater than the whole, and dozens of others. No sleight of hand necessary! 135 illustrations. xii + 174pp. 5⅜ x 8.
T335 Paperbound **$1.00**

EASY-TO-DO ENTERTAINMENTS AND DIVERSIONS WITH COINS, CARDS, STRING, PAPER AND MATCHES, R. M. Abraham. Over 300 tricks, games and puzzles will provide young readers with absorbing fun. Sections on card games; paper-folding; tricks with coins, matches and pieces of string; games for the agile; toy-making from common household objects; mathematical recreations; and 50 miscellaneous pastimes. Anyone in charge of groups of youngsters, including hard-pressed parents, and in need of suggestions on how to keep children sensibly amused and quietly content will find this book indispensable. Clear, simple text, copious number of delightful line drawings and illustrative diagrams. Originally titled "Winter Nights Entertainments." Introduction by Lord Baden Powell. 329 illustrations. v + 186pp. 5⅜ x 8½.
T921 Paperbound **$1.00**

STRING FIGURES AND HOW TO MAKE THEM, Caroline Furness Jayne. 107 string figures plus variations selected from the best primitive and modern examples developed by Navajo, Apache, pygmies of Africa, Eskimo, in Europe, Australia, China, etc. The most readily understandable, easy-to-follow book in English on perennially popular recreation. Crystal-clear exposition; step-by-step diagrams. Everyone from kindergarten children to adults looking for unusual diversion will be endlessly amused. Index. Bibliography. Introduction by A. C. Haddon. 17 full-page plates. 960 illustrations. xxiii + 401pp. 5⅜ x 8½.
T152 Paperbound **$2.00**

Entertainments, Humor

ODDITIES AND CURIOSITIES OF WORDS AND LITERATURE, C. Bombaugh, edited by M. Gardner. The largest collection of idiosyncratic prose and poetry techniques in English, a legendary work in the curious and amusing bypaths of literary recreations and the play technique in literature—so important in modern works. Contains alphabetic poetry, acrostics, palindromes, scissors verse, centos, emblematic poetry, famous literary puns, hoaxes, notorious slips of the press, hilarious mistranslations, and much more. Revised and enlarged with modern material by Martin Gardner. 368pp. 5⅜ x 8. T759 Paperbound **$1.50**

A NONSENSE ANTHOLOGY, collected by Carolyn Wells. 245 of the best nonsense verses ever written, including nonsense puns, absurd arguments, mock epics and sagas, nonsense ballads, odes, "sick" verses, dog-Latin verses, French nonsense verses, songs. By Edward Lear, Lewis Carroll, Gelett Burgess, W. S. Gilbert, Hilaire Belloc, Peter Newell, Oliver Herford, etc., 83 writers in all plus over four score anonymous nonsense verses. A special section of limericks, plus famous nonsense such as Carroll's "Jabberwocky" and Lear's "The Jumblies" and much excellent verse virtually impossible to locate elsewhere. For 50 years considered the best anthology available. Index of first lines specially prepared for this edition. Introduction by Carolyn Wells. 3 indexes: Title, Author, First lines. xxxiii + 279pp. T499 Paperbound **$1.35**

THE BAD CHILD'S BOOK OF BEASTS, MORE BEASTS FOR WORSE CHILDREN, and A MORAL ALPHABET, H. Belloc. Hardly an anthology of humorous verse has appeared in the last 50 years without at least a couple of these famous nonsense verses. But one must see the entire volumes—with all the delightful original illustrations by Sir Basil Blackwood—to appreciate fully Belloc's charming and witty verses that play so subacidly on the platitudes of life and morals that beset his day—and ours. A great humor classic. Three books in one. Total of 157pp. 5⅜ x 8. T749 Paperbound **$1.00**

THE DEVIL'S DICTIONARY, Ambrose Bierce. Sardonic and irreverent barbs puncturing the pomposities and absurdities of American politics, business, religion, literature, and arts, by the country's greatest satirist in the classic tradition. Epigrammatic as Shaw, piercing as Swift, American as Mark Twain, Will Rogers, and Fred Allen, Bierce will always remain the favorite of a small coterie of enthusiasts, and of writers and speakers whom he supplies with "some of the most gorgeous witticisms of the English language" (H. L. Mencken). Over 1000 entries in alphabetical order. 144pp. 5⅜ x 8. T487 Paperbound **$1.00**

THE PURPLE COW AND OTHER NONSENSE, Gelett Burgess. The best of Burgess's early nonsense, selected from the first edition of the "Burgess Nonsense Book." Contains many of his most unusual and truly awe-inspiring pieces: 36 nonsense quatrains, the Poems of Patagonia, Alphabet of Famous Goops, and the other hilarious (and rare) adult nonsense that place him in the forefront of American humorists. All pieces are accompanied by the original Burgess illustrations. 123 illustrations. xiii + 113pp. 5⅜ x 8. T772 Paperbound **$1.00**

MY PIOUS FRIENDS AND DRUNKEN COMPANIONS and MORE PIOUS FRIENDS AND DRUNKEN COMPANIONS, Frank Shay. Folksingers, amateur and professional, and everyone who loves singing: here, available for the first time in 30 years, is this valued collection of 132 ballads, blues, vaudeville numbers, drinking songs, sea chanties, comedy songs. Songs of pre-Beatnik Bohemia; songs from all over America, England, France, Australia; the great songs of the Naughty Nineties and early twentieth-century America. Over a third with music. Woodcuts by John Held, Jr. convey perfectly the brash insouciance of an era of rollicking unabashed song. 12 illustrations by John Held, Jr. Two indexes (Titles and First lines and Choruses). Introductions by the author. Two volumes bound as one. Total of xvi + 235pp. 5⅜ x 8½. T946 Paperbound **$1.25**

HOW TO TELL THE BIRDS FROM THE FLOWERS, R. W. Wood. How not to confuse a carrot with a parrot, a grape with an ape, a puffin with nuffin. Delightful drawings, clever puns, absurd little poems point out far-fetched resemblances in nature. The author was a leading physicist. Introduction by Margaret Wood White. 106 illus. 60pp. 5⅜ x 8. T523 Paperbound **75¢**

PECK'S BAD BOY AND HIS PA, George W. Peck. The complete edition, containing both volumes, of one of the most widely read American humor books. The endless ingenious pranks played by bad boy "Hennery" on his pa and the grocery man, the outraged pomposity of Pa, the perpetual ridiculing of middle class institutions, are as entertaining today as they were in 1883. No pale sophistications or subtleties, but rather humor vigorous, raw, earthy, imaginative, and, as folk humor often is, sadistic. This peculiarly fascinating book is also valuable to historians and students of American culture as a portrait of an age. 100 original illustrations by True Williams. Introduction by E. F. Bleiler. 347pp. 5⅜ x 8. T497 Paperbound **$1.35**

THE HUMOROUS VERSE OF LEWIS CARROLL. Almost every poem Carroll ever wrote, the largest collection ever published, including much never published elsewhere: 150 parodies, burlesques, riddles, ballads, acrostics, etc., with 130 original illustrations by Tenniel, Carroll, and others. "Addicts will be grateful . . . there is nothing for the faithful to do but sit down and fall to the banquet," N. Y. Times. Index to first lines. xiv + 446pp. 5⅜ x 8.
T654 Paperbound **$2.00**

DIVERSIONS AND DIGRESSIONS OF LEWIS CARROLL. A major new treasure for Carroll fans! Rare privately published humor, fantasy, puzzles, and games by Carroll at his whimsical best, with a new vein of frank satire. Includes many new mathematical amusements and recreations, among them the fragmentary Part III of "Curiosa Mathematica." Contains "The Rectory Umbrella," "The New Belfry," "The Vision of the Three T's," and much more. New 32-page supplement of rare photographs taken by Carroll. x + 375pp. 5⅜ x 8.
T732 Paperbound **$1.65**

THE COMPLETE NONSENSE OF EDWARD LEAR. This is the only complete edition of this master of gentle madness available at a popular price. A BOOK OF NONSENSE, NONSENSE SONGS, MORE NONSENSE SONGS AND STORIES in their entirety with all the old favorites that have delighted children and adults for years. The Dong With A Luminous Nose, The Jumblies, The Owl and the Pussycat, and hundreds of other bits of wonderful nonsense. 214 limericks, 3 sets of Nonsense Botany, 5 Nonsense Alphabets, 546 drawings by Lear himself, and much more. 320pp. 5⅜ x 8.
T167 Paperbound **$1.00**

THE MELANCHOLY LUTE, The Humorous Verse of Franklin P. Adams ("FPA"). The author's own selection of light verse, drawn from thirty years of FPA's column, "The Conning Tower," syndicated all over the English-speaking world. Witty, perceptive, literate, these ninety-six poems range from parodies of other poets, Millay, Longfellow, Edgar Guest, Kipling, Masefield, etc., and free and hilarious translations of Horace and other Latin poets, to satiric comments on fabled American institutions—the New York Subways, preposterous ads, suburbanites, sensational journalism, etc. They reveal with vigor and clarity the humor, integrity and restraint of a wise and gentle American satirist. Introduction by Robert Hutchinson. vi + 122pp. 5⅜ x 8½.
T108 Paperbound **$1.00**

SINGULAR TRAVELS, CAMPAIGNS, AND ADVENTURES OF BARON MUNCHAUSEN, R. E. Raspe, with 90 illustrations by Gustave Doré. The first edition in over 150 years to reestablish the deeds of the Prince of Liars exactly as Raspe first recorded them in 1785—the genuine Baron Munchausen, one of the most popular personalities in English literature. Included also are the best of the many sequels, written by other hands. Introduction on Raspe by J. Carswell. Bibliography of early editions. xliv + 192pp. 5⅜ x 8.
T698 Paperbound **$1.00**

THE WIT AND HUMOR OF OSCAR WILDE, ed. by Alvin Redman. Wilde at his most brilliant, in 1000 epigrams exposing weaknesses and hypocrisies of "civilized" society. Divided into 49 categories—sin, wealth, women, America, etc.—to aid writers, speakers. Includes excerpts from his trials, books, plays, criticism. Formerly "The Epigrams of Oscar Wilde." Introduction by Vyvyan Holland, Wilde's only living son. Introductory essay by editor. 260pp. 5⅜ x 8.
T602 Paperbound **$1.00**

MAX AND MORITZ, Wilhelm Busch. Busch is one of the great humorists of all time, as well as the father of the modern comic strip. This volume, translated by H. A. Klein and other hands, contains the perennial favorite "Max and Moritz" (translated by C. T. Brooks), Plisch and Plum, Das Rabennest, Eispeter, and seven other whimsical, sardonic, jovial, diabolical cartoon and verse stories. Lively English translations parallel the original German. This work has delighted millions, since it first appeared in the 19th century, and is guaranteed to please almost anyone. Edited by H. A. Klein, with an afterword. x + 205pp. 5⅝ x 8½.
T181 Paperbound **$1.15**

HYPOCRITICAL HELENA, Wilhelm Busch. A companion volume to "Max and Moritz," with the title piece (Die Fromme Helena) and 10 other highly amusing cartoon and verse stories, all newly translated by H. A. Klein and M. C. Klein: Adventure on New Year's Eve (Abenteuer in der Neujahrsnacht), Hangover on the Morning after New Year's Eve (Der Katzenjammer am Neujahrsmorgen), etc. English and German in parallel columns. Hours of pleasure, also a fine language aid. x + 205pp. 5⅝ x 8½.
T184 Paperbound **$1.00**

THE BEAR THAT WASN'T, Frank Tashlin. What does it mean? Is it simply delightful wry humor, or a charming story of a bear who wakes up in the midst of a factory, or a satire on Big Business, or an existential cartoon-story of the human condition, or a symbolization of the struggle between conformity and the individual? New York Herald Tribune said of the first edition: ". . . a fable for grownups that will be fun for children. Sit down with the book and get your own bearings." Long an underground favorite with readers of all ages and opinions. v + 51pp. Illustrated. 5⅜ x 8½.
T939 Paperbound **75¢**

RUTHLESS RHYMES FOR HEARTLESS HOMES and MORE RUTHLESS RHYMES FOR HEARTLESS HOMES, Harry Graham ("Col. D. Streamer"). Two volumes of Little Willy and 48 other poetic disasters. A bright, new reprint of oft-quoted, never forgotten, devastating humor by a precursor of today's "sick" joke school. For connoisseurs of wicked, wacky humor and all who delight in the comedy of manners. Original drawings are a perfect complement. 61 illustrations. Index. vi + 69pp. Two vols. bound as one. 5⅜ x 8½.
T930 Paperbound **75¢**

Say It language phrase books

These handy phrase books (128 to 196 pages each) make grammatical drills unnecessary for an elementary knowledge of a spoken foreign language. Covering most matters of travel and everyday life each volume contains:

Over 1000 phrases and sentences in immediately useful forms — foreign language plus English.

Modern usage designed for Americans. Specific phrases like, "Give me small change," and "Please call a taxi."

Simplified phonetic transcription you will be able to read at sight.

The only completely indexed phrase books on the market.

Covers scores of important situations: — Greetings, restaurants, sightseeing, useful expressions, etc.

These books are prepared by native linguists who are professors at Columbia, N.Y.U., Fordham and other great universities. Use them independently or with any other book or record course. They provide a supplementary living element that most other courses lack. Individual volumes in:

Russian 75¢	Italian 75¢	Spanish 75¢	German 75¢
Hebrew 75¢	Danish 75¢	Japanese 75¢	Swedish 75¢
Dutch 75¢	Esperanto 75¢	Modern Greek 75¢	Portuguese 75¢
Norwegian 75¢	Polish 75¢	French 75¢	Yiddish 75¢
Turkish 75¢		English for German-speaking people 75¢	
English for Italian-speaking people 75¢		English for Spanish-speaking people 75¢	

Large clear type. 128-196 pages each. 3½ x 5¼. Sturdy paper binding.

Listen and Learn language records

LISTEN & LEARN is the only language record course designed especially to meet your travel and everyday needs. It is available in separate sets for FRENCH, SPANISH, GERMAN, JAPANESE, RUSSIAN, MODERN GREEK, PORTUGUESE, ITALIAN and HEBREW, and each set contains three 33⅓ rpm long-playing records—1½ hours of recorded speech by eminent native speakers who are professors at Columbia, New York University, Queens College.

Check the following special features found only in LISTEN & LEARN:

- **Dual-language recording.** 812 selected phrases and sentences, over 3200 words, spoken first in English, then in their foreign language equivalents. A suitable pause follows each foreign phrase, allowing you time to repeat the expression. You learn by unconscious assimilation.
- **128 to 206-page manual** contains everything on the records, plus a simple phonetic pronunciation guide.
- **Indexed for convenience.** The only set on the market that is completely indexed. No more puzzling over where to find the phrase you need. Just look in the rear of the manual.
- **Practical.** No time wasted on material you can find in any grammar. LISTEN & LEARN covers central core material with phrase approach. Ideal for the person with limited learning time.
- **Living, modern expressions,** not found in other courses. Hygienic products, modern equipment, shopping—expressions used every day, like "nylon" and "air-conditioned."
- **Limited objective.** Everything you learn, no matter where you stop, is immediately useful. You have to finish other courses, wade through grammar and vocabulary drill, before they help you.
- **High-fidelity recording.** LISTEN & LEARN records equal in clarity and surface-silence any record on the market costing up to $6.

"Excellent . . . the spoken records . . . impress me as being among the very best on the market," **Prof. Mario Pei,** Dept. of Romance Languages, Columbia University. "Inexpensive and well-done . . . it would make an ideal present," CHICAGO SUNDAY TRIBUNE. "More genuinely helpful than anything of its kind which I have previously encountered," **Sidney Clark,** well-known author of "ALL THE BEST" travel books.

UNCONDITIONAL GUARANTEE. Try LISTEN & LEARN, then return it within 10 days for full refund if you are not satisfied.

Each set contains three twelve-inch 33⅓ records, manual, and album.

SPANISH	the set $5.95	GERMAN	the set $5.95
FRENCH	the set $5.95	ITALIAN	the set $5.95
RUSSIAN	the set $5.95	JAPANESE	the set $5.95
PORTUGUESE	the set $5.95	MODERN GREEK	the set $5.95
MODERN HEBREW	the set $5.95		

Americana

THE EYES OF DISCOVERY, J. Bakeless. A vivid reconstruction of how unspoiled America appeared to the first white men. Authentic and enlightening accounts of Hudson's landing in New York, Coronado's trek through the Southwest; scores of explorers, settlers, trappers, soldiers. America's pristine flora, fauna, and Indians in every region and state in fresh and unusual new aspects. "A fascinating view of what the land was like before the first highway went through," Time. 68 contemporary illustrations, 39 newly added in this edition. Index. Bibliography. x + 500pp. 5⅜ x 8. **T761 Paperbound $2.00**

AUDUBON AND HIS JOURNALS, J. J. Audubon. A collection of fascinating accounts of Europe and America in the early 1800's through Audubon's own eyes. Includes the Missouri River Journals —an eventful trip through America's untouched heartland, the Labrador Journals, the European Journals, the famous "Episodes", and other rare Audubon material, including the descriptive chapters from the original letterpress edition of the "Ornithological Studies", omitted in all later editions. Indispensable for ornithologists, naturalists, and all lovers of Americana and adventure. 70-page biography by Audubon's granddaughter. 38 illustrations. Index. Total of 1106pp. 5⅜ x 8.
T675 Vol I Paperbound **$2.25**
T676 Vol II Paperbound **$2.25**
The set **$4.50**

TRAVELS OF WILLIAM BARTRAM, edited by Mark Van Doren. The first inexpensive illustrated edition of one of the 18th century's most delightful books is an excellent source of first-hand material on American geography, anthropology, and natural history. Many descriptions of early Indian tribes are our only source of information on them prior to the infiltration of the white man. "The mind of a scientist with the soul of a poet," John Livingston Lowes. 13 original illustrations and maps. Edited with an introduction by Mark Van Doren. 448pp. 5⅜ x 8.
T13 Paperbound $2.00

GARRETS AND PRETENDERS: A HISTORY OF BOHEMIANISM IN AMERICA, A. Parry. The colorful and fantastic history of American Bohemianism from Poe to Kerouac. This is the only complete record of hoboes, cranks, starving poets, and suicides. Here are Pfaff, Whitman, Crane, Bierce, Pound, and many others. New chapters by the author and by H. T. Moore bring this thorough and well-documented history down to the Beatniks. "An excellent account," N. Y. Times. Scores of cartoons, drawings, and caricatures. Bibliography. Index. xxviii + 421pp. 5⅝ x 8⅜. **T708 Paperbound $1.95**

THE EXPLORATION OF THE COLORADO RIVER AND ITS CANYONS, J. W. Powell. The thrilling first-hand account of the expedition that filled in the last white space on the map of the United States. Rapids, famine, hostile Indians, and mutiny are among the perils encountered as the unknown Colorado Valley reveals its secrets. This is the only unvaried version of Major Powell's classic of exploration that has been printed in the last 60 years. Includes later reflections and subsequent expedition. 250 illustrations, new map. 400pp. 5⅝ x 8⅜.
T94 Paperbound $2.25

THE JOURNAL OF HENRY D. THOREAU, Edited by Bradford Torrey and Francis H. Allen. Henry Thoreau is not only one of the most important figures in American literature and social thought; his voluminous journals (from which his books emerged as selections and crystallizations) constitute both the longest, most sensitive record of personal internal development and a most penetrating description of a historical moment in American culture. This present set, which was first issued in fourteen volumes, contains Thoreau's entire journals from 1837 to 1862, with the exception of the lost years which were found only recently. We are reissuing it, complete and unabridged, with a new introduction by Walter Harding, Secretary of the Thoreau Society. Fourteen volumes reissued in two volumes. Foreword by Henry Seidel Canby. Total of 1888pp. 8⅜ x 12¼. **T312-3 Two volume set, Clothbound $20.00**

GAMES AND SONGS OF AMERICAN CHILDREN, collected by William Wells Newell. A remarkable collection of 190 games with songs that accompany many of them; cross references to show similarities, differences among them; variations; musical notation for 38 songs. Textual discussions show relations with folk-drama and other aspects of folk tradition. Grouped into categories for ready comparative study: Love-games, histories, playing at work, human life, bird and beast, mythology, guessing-games, etc. New introduction covers relations of songs and dances to timeless heritage of folklore, biographical sketch of Newell, other pertinent data. A good source of inspiration for those in charge of groups of children and a valuable reference for anthropologists, sociologists, psychiatrists. Introduction by Carl Withers. New indexes of first lines, games. 5⅜ x 8½. xii + 242pp. **T354 Paperbound $1.75**

Art, History of Art, Antiques, Graphic Arts, Handcrafts

ART STUDENTS' ANATOMY, E. J. Farris. Outstanding art anatomy that uses chiefly living objects for its illustrations. 71 photos of undraped men, women, children are accompanied by carefully labeled matching sketches to illustrate the skeletal system, articulations and movements, bony landmarks, the muscular system, skin, fasciae, fat, etc. 9 x-ray photos show movement of joints. Undraped models are shown in such actions as serving in tennis, drawing a bow in archery, playing football, dancing, preparing to spring and to dive. Also discussed and illustrated are proportions, age and sex differences, the anatomy of the smile, etc. 8 plates by the great early 18th century anatomic illustrator Siegfried Albinus are also included. Glossary. 158 figures, 7 in color. x + 159pp. 5⅝ x 8⅜. **T744 Paperbound $1.50**

AN ATLAS OF ANATOMY FOR ARTISTS, F Schider. A new 3rd edition of this standard text enlarged by 52 new illustrations of hands, anatomical studies by Cloquet, and expressive life studies of the body by Barcsay. 189 clear, detailed plates offer you precise information of impeccable accuracy. 29 plates show all aspects of the skeleton, with closeups of special areas, while 54 full-page plates, mostly in two colors, give human musculature as seen from four different points of view, with cutaways for important portions of the body. 14 full-page plates provide photographs of hand forms, eyelids, female breasts, and indicate the location of muscles upon models. 59 additional plates show how great artists of the past utilized human anatomy. They reproduce sketches and finished work by such artists as Michelangelo, Leonardo da Vinci, Goya, and 15 others. This is a lifetime reference work which will be one of the most important books in any artist's library. "The standard reference tool," AMERICAN LIBRARY ASSOCIATION. "Excellent," AMERICAN ARTIST. Third enlarged edition. 189 plates, 647 illustrations. xxvi + 192pp. 7⅞ x 10⅝. **T241 Clothbound $6.00**

AN ATLAS OF ANIMAL ANATOMY FOR ARTISTS, W. Ellenberger, H. Baum, H. Dittrich. The largest, richest animal anatomy for artists available in English. 99 detailed anatomical plates of such animals as the horse, dog, cat, lion, deer, seal, kangaroo, flying squirrel, cow, bull, goat, monkey, hare, and bat. Surface features are clearly indicated, while progressive beneath-the-skin pictures show musculature, tendons, and bone structure. Rest and action are exhibited in terms of musculature and skeletal structure and detailed cross-sections are given for heads and important features. The animals chosen are representative of specific families so that a study of these anatomies will provide knowledge of hundreds of related species. "Highly recommended as one of the very few books on the subject worthy of being used as an authoritative guide," DESIGN. "Gives a fundamental knowledge," AMERICAN ARTIST. Second revised, enlarged edition with new plates from Cuvier, Stubbs, etc. 288 illustrations. 153pp. 11⅜ x 9. **T82 Clothbound $6.00**

THE HUMAN FIGURE IN MOTION, Eadweard Muybridge. The largest selection in print of Muybridge's famous high-speed action photos of the human figure in motion. 4789 photographs illustrate 162 different actions: men, women, children—mostly undraped—are shown walking, running, carrying various objects, sitting, lying down, climbing, throwing, arising, and performing over 150 other actions. Some actions are shown in as many as 150 photographs each. All in all there are more than 500 action strips in this enormous volume, series shots taken at shutter speeds of as high as 1/6000th of a second! These are not posed shots, but true stopped motion. They show bone and muscle in situations that the human eye is not fast enough to capture. Earlier, smaller editions of these prints have brought $40 and more on the out-of-print market. "A must for artists," ART IN FOCUS. "An unparalleled dictionary of action for all artists," AMERICAN ARTIST. 390 full-page plates, with 4789 photographs. Printed on heavy glossy stock. Reinforced binding with headbands. xxi + 390pp. 7⅞ x 10⅝. **T204 Clothbound $10.00**

ANIMALS IN MOTION, Eadweard Muybridge. This is the largest collection of animal action photos in print. 34 different animals (horses, mules, oxen, goats, camels, pigs, cats, guanacos, lions, gnus, deer, monkeys, eagles—and 21 others) in 132 characteristic actions. The horse alone is shown in more than 40 different actions. All 3919 photographs are taken in series at speeds up to 1/6000th of a second. The secrets of leg motion, spinal patterns, head movements, strains and contortions shown nowhere else are captured. You will see exactly how a lion sets his foot down; how an elephant's knees are like a human's—and how they differ; the position of a kangaroo's legs in mid-leap; how an ostrich's head bobs; details of the flight of birds—and thousands of facets of motion only the fastest cameras can catch. Photographed from domestic animals and animals in the Philadelphia zoo, it contains neither semiposed artificial shots nor distorted telephoto shots taken under adverse conditions. Artists, biologists, decorators, cartoonists, will find this book indispensable for understanding animals in motion. "A really marvelous series of plates," NATURE (London). "The dry plate's most spectacular early use was by Eadweard Muybridge," LIFE. 3919 photographs; 380 full pages of plates. 440pp. Printed on heavy glossy paper. Deluxe binding with headbands. 7⅞ x 10⅝. **T203 Clothbound $10.00**

CATALOGUE OF DOVER BOOKS

THE AUTOBIOGRAPHY OF AN IDEA, Louis Sullivan. The pioneer architect whom Frank Lloyd Wright called "the master" reveals an acute sensitivity to social forces and values in this passionately honest account. He records the crystallization of his opinions and theories, the growth of his organic theory of architecture that still influences American designers and architects, contemporary ideas, etc. This volume contains the first appearance of 34 full-page plates of his finest architecture. Unabridged reissue of 1924 edition. New introduction by R. M. Line. Index. xiv + 335pp. 5⅜ x 8.   T281 Paperbound **$2.00**

THE DRAWINGS OF HEINRICH KLEY. The first uncut republication of both of Kley's devastating sketchbooks, which first appeared in pre-World War I Germany. One of the greatest cartoonists and social satirists of modern times, his exuberant and iconoclastic fantasy and his extraordinary technique place him in the great tradition of Bosch, Breughel, and Goya, while his subject matter has all the immediacy and tension of our century. 200 drawings. viii + 128pp. 7¾ x 10¾.   T24 Paperbound **$1.85**

MORE DRAWINGS BY HEINRICH KLEY. All the sketches from Leut' Und Viecher (1912) and Sammel-Album (1923) not included in the previous Dover edition of Drawings. More of the bizarre, mercilessly iconoclastic sketches that shocked and amused on their original publication. Nothing was too sacred, no one too eminent for satirization by this imaginative, individual and accomplished master cartoonist. A total of 158 illustrations. lv + 104pp. 7¾ x 10¾.   T41 Paperbound **$1.85**

PINE FURNITURE OF EARLY NEW ENGLAND, R. H. Kettell. A rich understanding of one of America's most original folk arts that collectors of antiques, interior decorators, craftsmen, woodworkers, and everyone interested in American history and art will find fascinating and immensely useful. 413 illustrations of more than 300 chairs, benches, racks, beds, cupboards, mirrors, shelves, tables, and other furniture will show all the simple beauty and character of early New England furniture. 55 detailed drawings carefully analyze outstanding pieces. "With its rich store of illustrations, this book emphasizes the individuality and varied design of early American pine furniture. It should be welcomed," ANTIQUES. 413 illustrations and 55 working drawings. 475. 8 x 10¾.   T145 Clothbound **$10.00**

THE HUMAN FIGURE, J. H. Vanderpoel. Every important artistic element of the human figure is pointed out in minutely detailed word descriptions in this classic text and illustrated as well in 430 pencil and charcoal drawings. Thus the text of this book directs your attention to all the characteristic features and subtle differences of the male and female (adults, children, and aged persons), as though a master artist were telling you what to look for at each stage. 2nd edition, revised and enlarged by George Bridgman. Foreword. 430 illustrations. 143pp. 6⅛ x 9¼.   T432 Paperbound **$1.50**

LETTERING AND ALPHABETS, J. A. Cavanagh. This unabridged reissue of LETTERING offers a full discussion, analysis, illustration of 89 basic hand lettering styles — styles derived from Caslons, Bodonis, Garamonds, Gothic, Black Letter, Oriental, and many others. Upper and lower cases, numerals and common signs pictured. Hundreds of technical hints on make-up, construction, artistic validity, strokes, pens, brushes, white areas, etc. May be reproduced without permission! 89 complete alphabets; 72 lettered specimens. 121pp. 9¾ x 8.   T53 Paperbound **$1.35**

STICKS AND STONES, Lewis Mumford. A survey of the forces that have conditioned American architecture and altered its forms. The author discusses the medieval tradition in early New England villages; the Renaissance influence which developed with the rise of the merchant class; the classical influence of Jefferson's time; the "Mechanicsvilles" of Poe's generation; the Brown Decades; the philosophy of the Imperial facade; and finally the modern machine age. "A truly remarkable book," SAT. REV. OF LITERATURE. 2nd revised edition. 21 illustrations. xvii + 228pp. 5⅜ x 8.   T202 Paperbound **$1.65**

THE STANDARD BOOK OF QUILT MAKING AND COLLECTING, Marguerite Ickis. A complete easy-to-follow guide with all the information you need to make beautiful, useful quilts. How to plan, design, cut, sew, appliqué, avoid sewing problems, use rag bag, make borders, tuft, every other aspect. Over 100 traditional quilts shown, including over 40 full-size patterns. At-home hobby for fun, profit. Index. 483 illus. 1 color plate. 287pp. 6¾ x 9½.   T582 Paperbound **$2.00**

THE BOOK OF SIGNS, Rudolf Koch. Formerly $20 to $25 on the out-of-print market, now only $1.00 in this unabridged new edition! 493 symbols from ancient manuscripts, medieval cathedrals, coins, catacombs, pottery, etc. Crosses, monograms of Roman emperors, astrological, chemical, botanical, runes, housemarks, and 7 other categories. Invaluable for handicraft workers, illustrators, scholars, etc., this material may be reproduced without permission. 493 illustrations by Fritz Kredel. 104pp. 6½ x 9¼.   T162 Paperbound **$1.00**

PRIMITIVE ART, Franz Boas. This authoritative and exhaustive work by a great American anthropologist covers the entire gamut of primitive art. Pottery, leatherwork, metal work, stone work, wood, basketry, are treated in detail. Theories of primitive art, historical depth in art history, technical virtuosity, unconscious levels of patterning, symbolism, styles, literature, music, dance, etc. A must book for the interested layman, the anthropologist, artist, handicrafter (hundreds of unusual motifs), and the historian. Over 900 illustrations (50 ceramic vessels, 12 totem poles, etc.). 376pp. 5⅜ x 8.   T25 Paperbound **$2.00**

Fiction

THE LAND THAT TIME FORGOT and THE MOON MAID, Edgar Rice Burroughs. In the opinion of many, Burroughs' best work. The first concerns a strange island where evolution is individual rather than phylogenetic. Speechless anthropoids develop into intelligent human beings within a single generation. The second projects the reader far into the future and describes the first voyage to the Moon (in the year 2025), the conquest of the Earth by the Moon, and years of violence and adventure as the enslaved Earthmen try to regain possession of their planet. "An imaginative tour de force that keeps the reader keyed up and expectant," NEW YORK TIMES. Complete, unabridged text of the original two novels (three parts in each). 5 illustrations by J. Allen St. John. vi + 552pp. 5⅜ x 8½.

T1020 Clothbound **$3.75**
T358 Paperbound **$2.00**

AT THE EARTH'S CORE, PELLUCIDAR, TANAR OF PELLUCIDAR: THREE SCIENCE FICTION NOVELS BY EDGAR RICE BURROUGHS. Complete, unabridged texts of the first three Pellucidar novels. Tales of derring-do by the famous master of science fiction. The locale for these three related stories is the inner surface of the hollow Earth where we discover the world of Pellucidar, complete with all types of bizarre, menacing creatures, strange peoples, and alluring maidens—guaranteed to delight all Burroughs fans and a wide circle of adventure lovers. Illustrated by J. Allen St. John and P. F. Berdanier. vi + 433pp. 5⅜ x 8½.

T1051 Paperbound **$2.00**

THREE MARTIAN NOVELS, Edgar Rice Burroughs. Contains: Thuvia, Maid of Mars; The Chessmen of Mars; and The Master Mind of Mars. High adventure set in an imaginative and intricate conception of the Red Planet. Mars is peopled with an intelligent, heroic human race which lives in densely populated cities and with fierce barbarians who inhabit dead sea bottoms. Other exciting creatures abound amidst an inventive framework of Martian history and geography. Complete unabridged reprintings of the first edition. 16 illustrations by J. Allen St. John. vi + 499pp. 5⅜ x 8½.

T39 Paperbound **$1.85**

TO THE SUN? and OFF ON A COMET!, Jules Verne. Complete texts of two of the most imaginative flights into fancy in world literature display the high adventure that have kept Verne's novels read for nearly a century. Only unabridged edition of the best translation, by Edward Roth. Large, easily readable type. 50 illustrations selected from first editions. 462pp. 5⅜ x 8.

T634 Paperbound **$1.75**

FROM THE EARTH TO THE MOON and ALL AROUND THE MOON, Jules Verne. Complete editions of two of Verne's most successful novels, in finest Edward Roth translations, now available after many years out of print. Verne's visions of submarines, airplanes, television, rockets, interplanetary travel; of scientific and not-so-scientific beliefs; of peculiarities of Americans; all delight and engross us today as much as when they first appeared. Large, easily readable type. 42 illus. from first French edition. 476pp. 5⅜ x 8.

T633 Paperbound **$1.75**

THREE PROPHETIC NOVELS BY H. G. WELLS, edited by E. F. Bleiler. Complete texts of "When the Sleeper Wakes" (1st book printing in 50 years), "A Story of the Days to Come," "The Time Machine" (1st complete printing in book form). Exciting adventures in the future are as enjoyable today as 50 years ago when first printed. Predict TV, movies, intercontinental airplanes, prefabricated houses, air-conditioned cities, etc. First important author to foresee problems of mind control, technological dictatorships. "Absolute best of imaginative fiction," N. Y. Times. Introduction. 335pp. 5⅜ x 8.

T605 Paperbound **$1.50**

SEVEN SCIENCE FICTION NOVELS, H. G. Wells. Full unabridged texts of 7 science-fiction novels of the master. Ranging from biology, physics, chemistry, astronomy to sociology and other studies, Mr. Wells extrapolates whole worlds of strange and intriguing character. "One will have to go far to match this for entertainment, excitement, and sheer pleasure . . . ," NEW YORK TIMES. Contents: The Time Machine, The Island of Dr. Moreau, First Men in the Moon, The Invisible Man, The War of the Worlds, The Food of the Gods, In the Days of the Comet. 1015pp. 5⅜ x 8.

T264 Clothbound **$4.50**

28 SCIENCE FICTION STORIES OF H. G. WELLS. Two full unabridged novels, MEN LIKE GODS and STAR BEGOTTEN, plus 26 short stories by the master science-fiction writer of all time. Stories of space, time, invention, exploration, future adventure—an indispensable part of the library of everyone interested in science and adventure. PARTIAL CONTENTS: Men Like Gods, The Country of the Blind, In the Abyss, The Crystal Egg, The Man Who Could Work Miracles, A Story of the Days to Come, The Valley of Spiders, and 21 more! 928pp. 5⅜ x 8.

T265 Clothbound **$4.50**

THE WAR IN THE AIR, IN THE DAYS OF THE COMET, THE FOOD OF THE GODS: THREE SCIENCE FICTION NOVELS BY H. G. WELLS. Three exciting Wells offerings bearing on vital social and philosophical issues of his and our own day. Here are tales of air power, strategic bombing, East vs. West, the potential miracles of science, the potential disasters from outer space, the relationship between scientific advancement and moral progress, etc. First reprinting of "War in the Air" in almost 50 years. An excellent sampling of Wells at his storytelling best. Complete, unabridged reprintings. 16 illustrations. 645pp. 5⅜ x 8½.

T1135 Paperbound **$2.00**

Music

A GENERAL HISTORY OF MUSIC, Charles Burney. A detailed coverage of music from the Greeks up to 1789, with full information on all types of music: sacred and secular, vocal and instrumental, operatic and symphonic. Theory, notation, forms, instruments, innovators, composers, performers, typical and important works, and much more in an easy, entertaining style. Burney covered much of Europe and spoke with hundreds of authorities and composers so that this work is more than a compilation of records . . . it is a living work of careful and first-hand scholarship. Its account of thoroughbass (18th century) Italian music is probably still the best introduction on the subject. A recent NEW YORK TIMES review said, "Surprisingly few of Burney's statements have been invalidated by modern research . . . still of great value." Edited and corrected by Frank Mercer. 35 figures. Indices. 1915pp. 5⅜ x 8. 2 volumes. **T36 The Set, Clothbound $12.50**

A DICTIONARY OF HYMNOLOGY, John Julian. This exhaustive and scholarly work has become known as an invaluable source of hundreds of thousands of important and often difficult to obtain facts on the history and use of hymns in the western world. Everyone interested in hymns will be fascinated by the accounts of famous hymns and hymn writers and amazed by the amount of practical information he will find. More than 30,000 entries on individual hymns, giving authorship, date and circumstances of composition, publication, textual variations, translations, denominational and ritual usage, etc. Biographies of more than 9,000 hymn writers, and essays on important topics such as Christmas carols and children's hymns, and much other unusual and valuable information. A 200 page double-columned index of first lines — the largest in print. Total of 1786 pages in two reinforced clothbound volumes. 6¼ x 9¼. The set, **T333 Clothbound $17.50**

MUSIC IN MEDIEVAL BRITAIN, F. Ll. Harrison. The most thorough, up-to-date, and accurate treatment of the subject ever published, beautifully illustrated. Complete account of institutions and choirs; carols, masses, and motets; liturgy and plainsong; and polyphonic music from the Norman Conquest to the Reformation. Discusses the various schools of music and their reciprocal influences; the origin and development of new ritual forms; development and use of instruments; and new evidence on many problems of the period. Reproductions of scores, over 200 excerpts from medieval melodies. Rules of harmony and dissonance; influence of Continental styles; great composers (Dunstable, Cornysh, Fairfax, etc.); and much more. Register and index of more than 400 musicians. Index of titles. General Index. 225-item bibliography. 6 Appendices. xix + 491pp. 5⅝ x 8¾. **T705 Clothbound $10.00**

THE MUSIC OF SPAIN, Gilbert Chase. Only book in English to give concise, comprehensive account of Iberian music; new Chapter covers music since 1941. Victoria, Albéniz, Cabezón, Pedrell, Turina, hundreds of other composers; popular and folk music; the Gypsies; the guitar; dance, theatre, opera, with only extensive discussion in English of the Zarzuela; virtuosi such as Casals; much more. "Distinguished . . . readable," Saturday Review. 400-item bibliography. Index. 27 photos. 383pp. 5⅜ x 8. **T549 Paperbound $2.00**

ON STUDYING SINGING, Sergius Kagen. An intelligent method of voice-training, which leads you around pitfalls that waste your time, money, and effort. Exposes rigid, mechanical systems, baseless theories, deleterious exercises. "Logical, clear, convincing . . . dead right," Virgil Thomson, N.Y. Herald Tribune. "I recommend this volume highly," Maggie Teyte, Saturday Review. 119pp. 5⅜ x 8. **T622 Paperbound $1.25**

Prices subject to change without notice.

Dover publishes books on art, music, philosophy, literature, languages, history, social sciences, psychology, handcrafts, orientalia, puzzles and entertainments, chess, pets and gardens, books explaining science, intermediate and higher mathematics, mathematical physics, engineering, biological sciences, earth sciences, classics of science, etc. Write to:

Dept. catrr.
Dover Publications, Inc.
180 Varick Street, N.Y. 14, N.Y.